Fendall Hall

A True Story Of
Good Times and Bad Times
On The
Chattahoochee River

Edward Young

Hubert Dent

ISBN 1-56837-398-8

To The Memory Of
Caroline Dent McDowell
and
Joy McDowell Crook

Contents

Foreword

PART IV. RECONSTRUCTION AND REDEMPTION

PART V. RENEWAL AND RECOVERY

PART VI. THE TWENTIETH CENTURY

Foreword

In 1824-1825, Edward Brown Young, 24, and his 17-year-old brother, William Henry Young, left the secure home of their parents in New York City to seek their fortunes in the South. Residing briefly in Georgia, they married two of the Beall sisters. Edward and his wife, Ann Fendall Beall, ultimately settled on the Chattahoochee River on lands recently wrested from the Creek Nation, in the new village of Irwinton, Alabama, later renamed "Eufaula." William and his wife, Ellen Beall, also settled on the Chattahoochee, first in Apalachicola, Florida, and later in Columbus, Georgia. Together, Edward and William Young became pioneer entrepreneurs in the commercial development of the Chattahoochee-Apalachicola River Valley cotton economy. Newly-arrived cotton planters were rapidly converting the rich Creek lands from a habitat for whitetail deer into plantations to meet the insatiable worldwide demand for cotton. Edward and William Young helped make these cotton planters successful by identifying and providing for their indispensable need for bankers, warehousemen, suppliers, factors, brokers, and in William's case, manufacturers.

On the crest of the rising tide of cotton wealth of the 1850's, Edward built for Ann in Eufaula a stately home which survives today as "Fendall Hall." Elegantly refurbished during the prosperous 1880's by their daughter, Anna Beall Young, and her husband, Captain Stouten Hubert Dent, Fendall Hall is today exhibited by the Alabama Historical Commission as an example of antebellum Italianate architecture. In Columbus, William built for Ellen an almost identical home, "Beallwood," which has burned.

When the Civil War came, Edward and William loyally cast their lots with the South. They and their families supported the Confederacy in every possible way, including the ultimate sacrifice: both families lost favored sons.

In Eufaula on the eve of the Civil War, Edward and Ann's oldest daughter, Anna, married Stouten Hubert Dent, a young school teacher turned lawyer, recently arrived from Maryland. He commanded Dent's Alabama Battery of artillery in the Army of Tennessee in battles whose names would become household words, from Shiloh to Atlanta and back to Franklin, Nashville, and surrender. Hubert wrote Anna a series of over 80 letters that survive today, providing insights into the daily lives of the Eufaula Youngs and Dents during wartime, both at home and at the battlefront. These letters, many of which have not previously been publicly available, are reproduced *verbatim* here (with minimal editing of punctuation and paragraphing for easier reading), and form a central part of this narrative. It has been suggested that mundane portions of these letters should be abridged for this book. Perhaps so, but the Civil War and Reconstruction, possibly the most important events in the history of America, were certainly the most important events in the lives of the Youngs and Dents. One of the purposes of this work is to preserve Hubert Dent's complete Civil War letters intact, and to view both their mundane and their insightful aspects in historical context. Readers are obviously free to skip portions as desired.

In Columbus, industrialist William Young became one of the South's largest cotton manufacturers. He and his wife, Ellen, sent four sons to fight for the Confederacy: Alfred, who became captain commanding Young's Battery; Lt. George B.; Richard, cited for heroism at Lovejoy Station; and trooper William H., Jr, who was killed fighting with Wheeler's cavalry in the Atlanta campaign.

While enduring with dignity the debacle of defeat and humiliating "reconstruction," the Eufaula and Columbus Young families spearheaded the rebuilding and prospered once again. We find them active in business and politics during the difficult adjustments of reconstruction, and we see them helping to achieve their region's "redemption." In the flush economic conditions of the 1880's, we find the extended Young families, consisting of Youngs, Dents, Weedons, Martins, and Robertses, leading lives of business success and relaxed good times. In the 1890's they confront and survive economic recession and political upheaval. Finally, in the twentieth century, we view them in times of adversity and achievement, providing leadership at the state and national levels.

This work makes no pretense to literary merit. It is merely a modest (if overly long) effort to preserve in one place, in historical context, the true accounts of the lives and times of these Southerners of the Chattahoochee Valley as they experienced American history in good times and bad.

Charles M. Crook

Montgomery, Alabama
Summer 2003

Part I

Prologue

1
Robert,
Involuntary Emigrant

James and Christina Young must have felt considerable dismay in 1824 when their youngest son, 17 year-old William Henry Young, announced that he was leaving their comfortable home in New York City to migrate to the semi-frontier country of southern Georgia. William had accepted a job as clerk to Mr. Ira Peck, a merchant of the small town of Marion, Twiggs County, Georgia, located ten miles from the larger town of Macon. James and Christina's consternation would have only increased when, the following year, their second son, Edward Brown Young, age 23, left home to join his younger brother in the South. Finally, a third son, James, Jr., age, 24, also made the same decision. Thus began the Young boys' grand adventure, which would lead to their becoming successful commercial pioneers of the cotton industry in the Chattahoochee River valley of Alabama and Georgia.

There was little in the Young boys' background or present circumstances to presage their decision to leave the urban security and convenience of New York City to travel a thousand miles to a little-known frontier. The boys' roots in northeastern America were deep, having been planted 140 years earlier. Their first American "Young" forebear was their great-great grandfather, a stubborn Scotsman named Robert Young, whose involuntary migration to the American colonies in 1685 is a strange saga of determined independence and self-reliance.

Born in Scotland about 1663,[1] Robert Young grew to manhood during a dangerous time in Scottish history. Robert was a *Covenanter*,[2] one of the stern breed of John Knox Presbyterians who had "covenanted" never to submit to the authority of the British monarch or the Church of England, which they considered far too "popish." While Robert was a young man, Scottish Presbyterians' refusal to conform resulted in their severe repression by the Royal High Commissioner, James Stuart, Duke of York, who was the Catholic brother of King Charles II and later king himself. The Presbyterians were forced underground to worship in secret "conventicles." During a particularly brutal period known as the "killing time" there was torture, strife, and outright war. The Catholic James II became king upon the death of his brother in February 1685. Soon afterward, the royal authorities rounded up and arrested Robert Young and a group of 167 Scottish Covenanters (45 of whom were women) who refused to take the required oath of allegiance to the Catholic king. Robert and the others were imprisoned from May until July in the dank cellar of Dunnottar Castle, located on the Scottish coast 15 miles south of Aberdeen.[3] When the Covenanters continued to refuse to take the oath of submission, the authorities, "weary of the prisoners," decided to "send good numbers of them to the plantations [i. e., the American colonies] and so rid themselves of any more trouble about them." The prisoners were marched 65 miles to the seaport of Leith, where they were again given another chance to take the required oath. Not only did the obstinate Scots still refuse to take the oath, but Robert Young and 27 others also signed a letter on August 28, 1685 setting out their opinion of the Catholic King and his oath: Taking the oath, they felt, would remove Jesus Christ as head of the church and "deny him any power in his own house," and would "put in his room a man that is a sworn enemy of religion, an avowed papist, whom by our covenants we are bound to withstand, and disown…" As a consequence, most of the prisoners "…were perpetually banished to America, and …were gifted to [George Scot] the Laird of Pitlochy, to be carried thither." Thus, on September 5, 1685, on the ship, *Henry and Francis,* Robert Young involuntarily embarked from Leith, Scotland for the British proprietary colony of New Jersey. The ship carried 200, including prisoners, crew, and Robert Scot, the Laird of Pitlochy, to whom the recalcitrant Covenanters had been "gifted," and his family.[4]

The voyage to New Jersey became a deadly disaster. Many of the captive Covenanters were already sick with "the fever" when they boarded the ship, as a result of their three-month confinement in the dungeon of Dunnottar Castle. After sailing, the fever worsened and spread through the ship. The ship encountered severe storms and developed leaks. The captain and crew treated the prisoners brutally. Much of the meat which the captain provided for the prisoners began to "stink" before the ship sailed, and after a few days out, it was inedible. It became usual to cast three or four bodies overboard each day. Eventually, over 70 persons died at sea, including the captain, and Lord and Lady Pitlochy.[5] After 15 weeks at sea, the *Henry and Francis* limped into Perth Amboy, New Jersey in mid-December 1685. With Pitlochy dead, his son-in-law, one John Johnstone, now found himself responsible for paying the bill for passage. His solution for avoiding financial loss was to try to hold the surviving prisoners (which included Robert Young) on the ship until they signed a "voluntary" declaration binding themselves to four years of indentured servitude. Needless to say, neither Robert Young nor any of the other defiant Scots would think of signing such a document. They left the ship and moved inland until they found a small community of kindly inhabitants who allowed the unfortunate travelers to live with them for the winter. In the spring, Johnstone rounded them up and, based upon the alleged "gift of the prisoners" to his father-in-law, cited them all before the New Jersey provincial court. Probably to Johnstone's surprise, after hearing both sides the Governor impaneled a jury to judge the matter. The jury concluded that since the Covenanters did not board the ship voluntarily, and never bargained with Pitlochy for money or service, they were "assoiled" (acquitted), and could go free. The prisoners scattered among the colonies and made new lives for themselves. Some died in the "plantations" while others returned to Scotland after the ouster of King James II in the "Glorious Revolution" of 1688.[6]

The Chattahoochee Young boys' great, great grandfather, however, had the good judgment to stay in New Jersey. Robert Young made his home in Newark,[7] a village of less than 500 which had been settled 20-odd years earlier. (The town was originally called "New Ark"). It had been settled by three groups of Puritans migrating from the Connecticut communities of Branford, Milford, and Guilford. On May 21, 1666, representatives of the three groups had executed a "Fundamental Agreement," setting out the principles governing the new town.[8]

Apparently, Robert found the principles and outlook of his new Puritan friends to be consistent with his own Covenanter background. Although transported to New Jersey against his will, this was undoubtedly the best thing that ever happened to the "Chattahoochee Youngs'" first American ancestor bearing the Young name. Robert adapted to his new home and prospered. He became a landowner.[9] He acquired a patent to 200 acres from the proprietors (owners) of the colony by paying them, through the governor or his assistants, "quit rent" of one to two shillings per acre per year. He acquired additional tracts which he from time to time sold or traded to other settlers.[10]

Eventually, Robert decided it was time for him to take a wife, and married Sarah Baldwin (sometimes, "Bauldwin" or "Bouldwin").[11] Sarah had been born in Branford, New Haven County, Connecticut, and her family had been among the first settlers of Newark.[12] Her parents were Benjamin Baldwin, the wool weaver, and Hannah Sergeant.[13]

In September 1700, we find Robert being appointed to a special jury to investigate a riot. The jury indicted 36 inhabitants of neighboring "Elizabeth Towne" because they "came to Newark and Riotously assaulted the Sheriff of ye County and forcibly took away the Keyes of the prisson and took away a prisoner out of the prisson."[14]

The raising of sheep was a profitable industry in Newark, and wool was one of its most important products. By March 10, 1704, the flocks had become so numerous in Newark that the town authorities "voted that there shall be a Shepherd hired for to keep the Sheep." Robert Young and three others were chosen as "Sheep Masters."[15]

A Presbyterian Church was organized in Newark, in which Robert was doubtless active. When its minister decided to execute a will, Robert was one of his witnesses.[16] Robert was often called on by friends in the community to witness their wills.[17] When his wife's father, Benjamin Baldwin, made his will on May 16, 1726, he had sufficient confidence in his son-in-law to name Robert as one of the executors of his will.[18] Unfortunately, Robert was unable to serve; he died in that year at the age of 63.[19]

In 1716, a son had been born to Robert and Sarah Baldwin Young, whom they named Stephen.[20] Stephen Young[a] would become the great grandfather and the second American ancestor of the "Young boys" of the Chattahoochee River valley. During his lifetime, Stephen and his sons would see New Jersey converted from a British colony into one of the United States, and would participate in achieving that independence.

---

[a] Robert and Sarah (Baldwin) Young had at least four other sons: Robert, Jr., David, John, and Jonathan. See Seaver, supra

2
Stephen,
Colonists vs. English Proprietors

Arriving at manhood, Stephen, the great grandfather of the Chattahoochee Youngs, took Joanna Crane as his wife. Joanna was the daughter of Daniel and Phoebe (Ward) Crane,[21] whose family had also been among the first settlers of the town.

In 1745, when Stephen was 29, he demonstrated that he had inherited his father's willingness to challenge and resist arbitrary authority. Back in 1701, a Newark town committee had negotiated a purchase of land totaling 13,500 acres from neighboring Indian tribes.[22] The English Proprietors of the colony of New Jersey felt that their royal patent gave them all the land in New Jersey, and strongly objected to this "purchase" from the Indians. The proprietors saw it as a case of the settlers avoiding the payment of "quit rent" to them. In 1702, at the behest of the proprietors, the provincial assembly passed an act nullifying such purchases and imposing a fine of 40 shillings per acre on anyone making such a "purchase." The Newark settlers simply ignored this rule and went on "reaping bountiful crops" from the disputed land.[23] The matter was allowed to drift unresolved for over 40 years (long after Robert was dead), but with the settlers occupying the disputed land.

In 1744, the proprietors again began pressing the colonists to pay for the disputed land they were using, and again they were resisted, this time by Stephen Young and the current generation of colonists, just as in Robert's time. On September 19, 1745, the proprietors' caused the Sheriff of Essex County to arrest of one of the colonists for "trespassing" while he was "sorting saw logs" on land he regarded as his own.[24] It was said that the proprietors, in order to minimize opposition, had carefully timed this arrest while the members of the Newark community were busy harvesting crops and cutting wood for the winter. Chroniclers of the era point out that the proprietors "failed to reckon with the lofty spirit, born of the Puritan regime, and constantly abiding in the community life…they failed also to perceive…the dislike of English aristocracy and its domineering acts…attempted in a most arbitrary manner." As the alleged trespasser was being taken to jail, Stephen Young, his brother, Robert, Jr. and other "well-known citizens" "armed with Clubs, Axes, & Crow Bars, came in a riotous & tumultuous Manner, to the Gaol of the County of Essex, & broke it open and took from thence [the arrested colonist]." Stephen Young, his brother, Robert, Jr., and the "well-known citizens" were later arrested for their roles in this riot.[25] But the arrests did not deter the opposition; to emphasize their defiance, the settlers purchased even more land from the Indians. The dispute continued to fester for another ten years. It eventually reached the courts, and in protracted litigation, the English Proprietors were awarded most of the disputed property.[26]

In the same year in which he was arrested for rioting against the Proprietors (1745), Stephen and Joanna had a son,[b] whom they named Jonas.[27] Jonas would become the

---

[b] Stephen and Joanna had two other sons and a daughter: Aaron, Daniel, and Abigail. See N. J. Gen. Mag., cited supra

grandfather (and the third generation American ancestor) of the "Chattahoochee Young brothers." But first, Jonas would be a patriot and "Minuteman" in the coming Revolution.

3
Jonas,
Newark Minuteman

As Jonas, his brothers and sister were growing into adulthood in Newark, tension and difficulty began to arise between Britain and its American colonies. England viewed its colonies as existing principally for the benefit of the mother country, to send raw materials home to the motherland and to purchase finished manufactured goods from England. After a period of lax enforcement, England was more strictly enforcing restrictions on the colonists' trade. Worse, as Jonas Young was thinking of matrimony and family, England began to attempt to tax the colonists, who had never before paid any significant taxes. The tax that angered the colonists most was the Stamp Act of 1765, to support an English army in America of 10,000 men which the colonists did not want, allegedly to defend against French and Indians. This tax was repealed in 1766 as a result of violent reaction throughout the colonies.

In Newark, Jonas Young may not have been worrying much about English taxation policy. He had his mind on Miss Prudence Riggs, whom he took to be his wife.[28] Prudence was the daughter of Joseph and Abigail Riggs. Prudence's family had been among the original settlers of Newark; Joseph Riggs was a signer of the "Fundamental Agreement"[29] In 1771, Jonas and Prudence had a son, who was named James.[30] James would become the father of the "Chattahoochee" Young brothers, (and their fourth generation American forebear).[c]

Meanwhile, in England a new Chancellor, Charles Townshend, began a new series of blunders, culminating in the Tea Act of 1770, and the Boston Tea Party in 1773. This was the turning point in the colonies' relations with Britain. Events began to slide inexorably toward war. In the early morning of April 19, 1775, near Lexington, Massachusetts, the British Redcoats clashed with a force of colonial "minutemen" and eight colonial volunteers were killed and two wounded. The British proceeded to Concord, destroyed some colonial stores, and began the march back to Boston. However, word of the fighting had spread quickly. Numbers of minutemen hurried to the scene, and as the British attempted to march from Concord back to Boston, the Redcoats received almost continuous fire, leveled at them from behind trees and rock fences. The Revolution had begun. Intense excitement arose throughout the colonies, and war mobilization was accelerated.

The Provincial Congress of New Jersey, in session in Trenton, acted quickly to raise troops. On June 3, 1775, that body noted "the cruel and arbitrary measures adopted and pursued by the British Parliament and present ministry for the purpose of subjugating the American Colonies to the most abject servitude." The Provincial Congress authorized "the immediate raising and equipping of troops of 'Minutemen' to defend the colony against the British and their sympathizers."[31]

Newark answered the call, and a company of "Newark Minutemen" was soon organized. The Young family stepped forward, *en masse*. Jonas and Prudence (Riggs) Young

---

[c] Jonas and Prudence also had three other sons: Joseph, Moses, Stephen, and Paoli. See Seaver, cited supra

by this time had several small children, including three-year-old James. Nevertheless, Jonas, 30, volunteered to fight in the Newark Minutemen.[32] Further, his brothers Aaron and Daniel also enlisted in the unit. Jonas' sister, Abigail had married John Alling, who also joined the company. Remarkably, Jonas' father, Stephen Young, who had rioted against the English colonial proprietors 30 years before, refused to be left out of this fight. Although now in his fifties,[33] (well above 50, the age provided by law), he enlisted as a private soldier. Over one third of the Newark Minutemen were either Youngs or members of families with whom four generations of Youngs had intermarried: Baldwins, Cranes, Wards, and Allings.[34]

Elected captain of the Newark Minutemen was one James Wheeler. The company elected John Alling, Jonas' brother-in-law, to be one of its lieutenants.[d] Apparently, old Stephen Young was unbothered by being under the command of his 29-year old son-in-law.

The new unit began equipping, drilling, and training. Regulations required the "Minutemen" to be

> "held in constant readiness, on the shortest notice, to march to any place where assistance might be required, for the defence of this or any neighboring Colony."[35]

The prescribed uniform for Minutemen was "hunting frocks, as near as may be to the uniform of riflemen in Continental service." Each soldier was directed by regulation to furnish himself with

> "a good musket or firelock and bayonet, sword or tomahawk, a steel ramrod, worm, priming-wire and brush fitted thereto, a cartouch-box to contain twenty-three rounds of cartridges, twelve flints, and a knapsack."[36]

The minutemen were directed to keep "at their respective abodes, one pound of powder and three pounds of bullets." In case of alarm, they were to repair immediately to their captains' residences, and he was to march his company instantly to oppose the enemy.[37]

As the newly established Continental Army grew in strength and organization, the provincial companies of minutemen found that their ranks were being depleted as their members joined the regular army or militia. As a result, New Jersey's Provincial Congress on March 2, 1776 passed an "Ordinance for Incorporating the Minute Men lately Raised in this Colony into the Body of the Militia."[38]

But the "Newark Minutemen" had not lost its men. Jonas Young and his comrades had drilled and trained together, and had achieved a good reputation as a well-disciplined unit of minutemen. They were all eager to avoid having the company dissolved, and wished to stay

---

[d] John Alling was born in Newark April 2, 1746 and died there Dec. 2, 1795. In addition to serving with the Newark Minutemen, he also served as 2nd Lieut. Essex County Militia, and in Baldwin's Artificers, Continental Army. "A monument to his memory is in Mr. Pleasant Cemetery, Newark." N. J. Gen. Mag., Vol. I, p. 35, citing *Alling-Allen*, p 60.

together to enter the regular militia as a unit. Accordingly, in March or April of 1776, Captain Wheeler prepared and presented the following petition on behalf of the "officers and privates" of the Newark Minutemen:[39]

> "*To the honorable the Members of the Provincial Congress or Committee of Safety for the Province of New Jersey—*
> The Petition of Capt. James Wheeler, Officers & Privates of his Company of Minute Men--
> Humbly sheweth—
> That your Petitioners in obedience to the Resolutions of your honorable House, did at a considerable Expence equip themselves as a minute Company being compleatly armed and accourted, and also went to the Expence of putting themselves in a uniform of Dress, and continued as a minute Company for upwards of four Months, and were always ready and willing to do any duty that was imposed on them, and were still desirous of continuing in that Capacity, but being informed that the Minute Companies by a Resolution of the Congress are to be dissolved—do now humbly beg that you will take into Consideration the Service & Expence your Petitioners have been at—and establish them as a Company of Grenadiers to the North Battalion in this Township, and allow the officers to retain the Men that enlisted as minute Men under them & who are still desirous of continuing together-- If you should decline granting this request it would be a means of breaking up a Company who has required Reputation as a well regulated & disciplined Body—Your Petitioners are emboldened to make this Petition from a Sense, that the Integrity and Justice of this House will lead them to deal with honor & equity to every set of Men under their Care and Jurisdiction--
>
> [Signed]
> James Wheeler, Capt…
> John Alling, 3 Lieut…
> Aaron Young…
> Jonas Young…
> Stephen Young…
> Daniel Young…" [And the remaining 55 privates and officers of the company.]

A transcript of this petition is marked, "Read in Committee 17 April 1776 and commissions ordered accordingly." Jonas, his two brothers, his brother-in-law, and his over-aged father, were all later incorporated into the Essex County Militia.[40] Aaron Young was assigned to Captain Josiah Pierson's Company, Second Regiment, Essex.[41] Jonas, Daniel, and their father, Stephen Young, were all assigned to Captain Abraham Lyon's Company, Second Regiment, Essex.[42]

The war for American independence was much in doubt. It dragged on for seven years, during which the Americans won relatively few major battles and suffered grave difficulties. The militia troops from Essex County (Newark) and the other counties of New Jersey were involved in numerous military actions, large and small:[43]

> "The good service performed by the militia of this State is fully recorded in history. At the fights at Quinton's Bridge, Hancock's Bridge, Three Rivers, Connecticut Farms, and Van Neste's Mills they bore an active part; while at the battle of Long Island, Trenton, Assunpink, Princeton, Germantown, Springfield, and Monmouth they performed efficient service in supporting the Continental Line."[44]

Finally, on October 19, 1781, in what would today be called a "surprise upset victory," Gen. Washington with the help of the French fleet trapped the British Army under Lord Cornwallis on the Yorktown peninsula and brought the British to their knees. American independence was later recognized in the Treaty of Paris.

With the Revolution over and independence established, old Stephen, Jonas' father, remained in Newark, as did Jonas,[45] and presumably Stephen's other sons as well. However, Jonas' son, James, (the future father of the Youngs of the Chattahoochee Valley), at some point decided to make a change. Since Robert Young had first landed in New Jersey and served as "Sheep master," the three generations of Youngs had remained in this rural setting. Now, James and his brothers felt drawn to urban pursuits in nearby New York City. All five of Jonas and Prudence's sons made their homes across the Hudson River, where all would become skilled artisans, and James would find his wife, Christina Ridabock.[46]

On May 10, 1790, Jonas' father, Stephen, died in Newark at the age of 74.[47] His will (which he had written on May 10, 1787), was proved on May 10, 1790. To his wife, Joanna (Crane) Young, he left all of his personal property and the use of one half of his real estate. To his son Jonas, he left 6 ½ acres at "Mill Brook Swamp." Stephens' son, Daniel, had died before him, but to Daniel's children, Stephen left his land bounded by Thomas Eagles' land. He left 80 "pounds" (cash) to his daughter Abigail Alling. As executors, Stephen named his wife, Joanna and his son, Aaron. [48]

Eventually, perhaps after his father's death, Jonas himself followed the example of his five sons and moved to New York City, where he settled on Vesey Street. His mother survived her husband's death by only two years; Joanna died in New York City in 1792.[49] Jonas himself lived to age 69, dying in 1814 in his home on Vesey Street. However, as we will presently relate, Jonas had lived long enough to see his son, James, marry Christina Ridabock and produce a large New York family, and to see his sons become successful makers of fine furniture.

18

4
James,
New York Craftsman

Jacob Ridabock, who would become James' father-in-law and the maternal grandfather of the Chattahoochee Youngs, had been born January 2, 1731,[50] in one of the principalities that later became a part of modern Germany.[e] As a young married couple, Jacob and his wife, Maria, came to America and settled in the British colony of New York.[51] Jacob and Maria prospered in the new world; they were able to own a farm, located in the area where Chambers Street is now located in New York City.[52]

1776 was a good year for Jacob, then in his 45th year. The colonies declared their independence from England that year, but equally important, Jacob and Maria became the parents of a baby girl.[53] She was born on Nov. 9, 1776, four months after the signing of the Declaration of Independence, and was named Christina.

Christina Ridabock, wife of James Young of New York City

After independence was won and the new constitution was adopted, New York City became the first capital of the new government. In the spring of 1789, when Christina Ridabock was 13 years old, George Washington arrived in New York to be inaugurated as the first president. He took the oath on the balcony of Federal Hall, which had just been completed and which still stands on Wall Street today. The inauguration was "a festive occasion, and an immense crowd assembled to witness the ceremony." Perhaps Christina and her parents were in the crowd gathered for this celebration. New Yorkers would soon become accustomed to the bustle of officials and diplomats coming and going during the years of George Washington's first administration in the city.

After four years, the capital was moved to Philadelphia, and Christina Ridabock was growing into a young woman. By early 1796, when she was 20, Christina had met James Young, the son of Newark Minuteman, Jonas Young and his wife Prudence (Riggs). James was now 25, and a cabinetmaker of New York. James had probably done an apprenticeship in furniture making, perhaps with one or more of his brothers. On Feb.17, 1796, James and Christina were married in New York,[54] where they settled to raise a family.

---

[e] Some have described the Ridabocks as Dutch, but in an article published during William H. Young's lifetime, which was probably based on an interview with him, he said his mother's parents had "emigrated from Germany at an early time." Biographical Souvenir (cited infra).

By 1801, James had opened his own cabinet shop at 6 Reed Street, in what is now called lower Manhattan. He would conduct his successful furniture-making shop here for many years, and would remain in this business until his death almost 40 years later.[55] All four of James' brothers would pursue the cabinetmaking craft: Stephen, Moses, Paoli, and Joseph.[56] His brothers Stephen and Moses began a partnership in 1804. Their shop was not far from James,' in the heart of the New York cabinetmaking trade at 73 Broad Street, while their home was at 28 Marketfield Street.[57] From 1810 to 1819, their shop was at 79 Broad. In admiring the "excellent craftsmanship" of Stephen and Moses Young, a modern commentator in the *American Collector* magazine found their talent understandable:

> "It is not surprising, for they [Stephen and Moses] came of a family of cabinetmakers. An earlier member, James, was first mentioned in the [Longworth's New York City] Directory of 1801-2. For 20 years he had a shop at 6 Reed Street. There were also Paoli, who was working between 1812 and 1822…and Joseph, who was located at 139 Reed Street from 1821 through 1825."[58]

Modern connoisseurs of antiques are complimentary in their assessments of the quality of work done by the Youngs, especially Stephen and Moses, usually comparing them with their famous contemporary, Duncan Phyfe. *A Dictionary of American Antiques* describes their work:

> "Fine Directoire-styled furniture, custom-made by these artisans at New York City…Sheraton and Regency-styled cabinetwork attributed also to them…their work is as good as Phyfe's." [59]

An example of Stephen and Moses' work is found today in the collection of the United States State Department in Washington. It bears the label, "Stephen and Moses Young's Cabinet & Chair Ware-House, Broad Street, 79, New York." One authority describes the piece as a New York City federal mahogany breakfast or "pillar and claw table," and comments that, without its Young label, the table "might easily be described as having been the work of Duncan Phyfe or cabinetmaker of equal standing."[60] In fact, the similarity with Phyfe's style and quality has led to the suggestion that the Youngs may have apprenticed in the shop of Phyfe himself.[61] Stephen and Moses remained in business together for 20 years, after which Moses retired to operate a mahogany yard, while Stephen continued as a cabinetmaker on Broad Street and later on North Moore Street. [62] James Young, however, would continue his furniture making business until his death in 1840.

**"Pillar and Claw Table" by Stephen and Moses
Young's Cabinet and Chair Warehouse, part of the
U. S. State Department collection, Washington**

The three sons of James and Christina who would migrate to the Chattahoochee valley were born over a seven-year period: the oldest son, James, Jr., was born September 23, 1800; Edward Brown was born August 24, 1802; and William Henry was born January 27, 1807. But James and Christina had a prolific marriage. In addition to these three, they had at least eight other children, all born in New York:[63]

Caroline, born April 5, 1797;
Harriet Prine, born January 12, 1799 (but died at an early age);
Sophia Prine, November 27, 1804;
Harriet, born May 24, 1809;
Amanda Christina, born December 2, 1811
Henry Augustine, born February 24, 1814;
Maria Shaw, born November 14, 1815
Emma Louser Young, born August 2, 1818.

James and Christina's children appear to have enjoyed a normal and happy childhood. As boys, Edward, William, and their siblings skated in the wintertime on a pond then known as the "Meadows," which later became New York City's Canal Street.[64] Edward, and probably all of the boys, worked in their father's furniture shop. There is extant today a small "child's chair," which Edward made in the shop as a boy.[65] In later life, William Young wrote that he had received "a good literary education, and some mercantile education."[66]

James' father-in-law, Jacob Ridabock, died at 85 years of age, on Sept. 7, 1816, in New York,[67] when Jacob's three grandsons, James, Jr., Edward, and William were 16, 14 and 11. Old Jacob had seen the United States defeat the British a second time, in the War of 1812.

If he followed the news closely, he would have known about a special part of that war, in which the Creek Indians, allies of the British, were permanently crushed by Andrew Jackson in 1814 at the Battle of Horseshoe Bend in the future state of Alabama. By opening the way to white settlement of vast new lands in Alabama and Georgia, the Creek defeat would have a significant and favorable effect on the fortunes of Jacob's grandsons.

In the spring of 1824, at the age of 17, William Young reached his life-changing decision to immigrate to the South, to become a clerk for Mr. Ira Peck, a merchant in Marion, Twiggs County, Georgia.[68] Within the year, his older brother Edward joined William in Marion.[69] For these young men to abandon their home in the well-populated area where their family had lived and flourished for over 140 years, to travel to an unknown, sparsely populated wilderness far from home may seem to have been a difficult decision. But the boys could see that, adequate though their father's business was, they wanted more. To satisfy their economic ambitions would require them to seek livelihoods elsewhere. Their decision was entirely consistent with the drive toward economic achievement which would characterize them throughout their lives, and it foreshadowed their characteristic willingness to "pull up stakes" and move to where the commercial opportunities were best.

With the business perception which they would later demonstrate even more fully, Edward and William knew that the Deep South, while still a frontier, was enjoying an economic boom of considerable proportions. Whether they fully understood all the reasons, they could see that the South was "where the action" was. The Northeast had its manufacturing, the Northwest had its grain and meat production, but the South had *cotton*. Eli Whitney's invention of the cotton gin in 1793, together with the development of industrial water-powered looms in England, had made this desirable but hitherto expensive fabric affordable for the public. Growing cotton for export and domestic use had become a highly profitable Southern enterprise. From 1815 to 1860, cotton accounted for over half the value of American exports, no other product even approaching it in importance.[70] By 1860, earnings from cotton would pay for 60% of American imports, and ninety-five percent of this cotton was produced in only eight Southern states.[71] This fiber has been called the "most significant single ingredient in the economic life of the nation before 1860".[72] Opportunities abounded for making money in the South. As we will see, the Youngs' grand adventure in moving South placed them in the right place at the right time, and was a grand success.

Part II

Entrepreneurs On The Chattahoochee

5
Twiggs County, Georgia

"We had a fair degree of success."

William Young

Although Edward and William Young would play pioneering roles in the development of the Chattahoochee valley cotton economy, it should be noted that they never became plantation owners or cotton planters. They were to find that the burgeoning new cotton industry required a new class of entrepreneurs.[73] They were to learn that the cotton trade needed factors, brokers, suppliers, and warehousemen specializing in buying and selling the crop. Middlemen such as commission merchants were necessary to the retail trade; bankers and other financial middlemen were necessary to finance the lengthy process from production to sale; and factories were needed to spin the cotton fiber into cloth. Edward and William Young were to excel in these and other commercial activities, and they would share in the financial rewards of the cotton industry.

Their education into the commercial needs of the frontier began in Twiggs County, Georgia, located on the present outskirts of Macon, about 80 miles from Columbus, (which had not been founded 1825). The town of Marion no longer exists today, but then it was a busy county seat. William had arrived here in 1824 to serve as clerk for Mr. Ira Peck, a local merchant. Upon Edward's arrival in Marion in 1825, William gave up his clerkship with Mr. Peck, and the brothers formed a partnership to operate a mercantile business of their own. William later described their first business venture as having "a fair degree of success."[74]

At some point, Edward and William were joined by their older brother, James Young, Jr. James undoubtedly participated in the business, but because he would die at a relatively early age, unmarried, he did not leave his imprint, and fate did not allow him time to establish a significant role in the commercial successes of his younger brothers.

In 1830, Edward was appointed Justice of the Peace of Marion.[75] As the business continued to prosper, Edward decided to marry. Residing only ten miles away in the fast growing town of Macon, Georgia, was a popular young lawyer, Robert Augustus Beall, Jr. Only 32 years old at this time, Robert Jr. had served in the Georgia Legislature, was a General in the Georgia state militia, and would soon be elected Mayor of Macon.[76] Robert's law practice extended to the nearby town of Marion, and he is listed as a member of the Bar of Marion.[77] It is fair to assume that this active lawyer and a Justice of the Peace of Marion would be known to each other, and would become friends. Now it happened that Robert had a bevy of younger sisters residing with his parents in their home 75 miles across the state in Warrenton, the county seat of Warren County, near Augusta. Two of Robert's attractive younger sisters were Ann, 22, and Ellen, 20. Perhaps during a visit to their popular older brother in Macon, these girls were introduced to the Young boys. Whatever the circumstances, they met, and on June 11, 1832, Edward was married to Ann Fendall Beall, in Warrenton.[78] Edward later noted in his Bible that the wedding service was performed on Monday evening, by the Rev. Joseph Moultry.

The happiness of the newly married couple was marred by the death of Ann's father, Robert, Senior, at the age of 65, in 1832, the same year as Ann's marriage.[79] Ann was to suffer further family losses soon.

Just as Edward and William were partners in business, it seems they were also partners in more domestic matters. Two years later, in 1834,[80] William married Ann's younger sister, Augusta Eleanor Beall, called "Ellen" by her family.[81] As we will see, instances of brothers marrying sisters were not unusual in this time of difficult transportation, sparse population, and limited opportunities for meeting others. In fact, in the next generation two daughters of Edward and Ann married two Dent brothers. (The Dent children liked to call themselves "double first cousins".)

In marrying the Beall girls, Edward and William had chosen well, for several reasons. Of Edward's wife, one of her sisters wrote that Ann was "the sportive, happy spirit of the family and she was so beautiful as well as good."[82] Ann had been born in Warrenton on October 9, 1810, and William's wife, Ellen, had been born there on November 9, 1812.[83] They were the daughters of Robert Augustus Beall, Senior, and his wife Elizabeth Marshall, a family well established not only in the affairs of Warren County but, as we have seen, in the state of Georgia as well. When Georgia had conducted a land lottery as the method for distributing public lands to its citizens, the Governor had chosen Robert, Senior as the Commissioner, with the sensitive duty of supervising the drawings.

Robert, Senior, had been born in Maryland on January 7, 1767, and Elizabeth was born there also in 1774.[84] They had married June 25, 1796,[85] and had settled on a farm on the Potomac River in Montgomery County, Maryland, adjacent to the farm occupied by Robert's brother, Benjamin, and Benjamin's wife, Mary Marshall, who was Elizabeth's sister. (Brothers marrying sisters, again.)[86] Robert, Senior and Elizabeth had themselves made a difficult migration decision when, in about 1809,[87] they had moved from Maryland to Georgia, when they were well into their middle years, and after several of their children had been born.[88] They had been accompanied on the move by his brother and her sister, Benjamin and Mary.[89] In coming to Georgia, the Bealls left behind in Maryland an extensive family with traditions of leadership from early colonial days. The Bealls of Maryland (as well as the Marshals, Bradleys, and Fendalls, who also form important parts of Ann's and Ellen's background) are interesting families in the history of Maryland, and are much written about.

It is time for us to make the acquaintance of the other members of Ann and Ellen's immediate family, because we will encounter them further in our narrative. Robert, Senior and Elizabeth Beall had nine surviving children (two died in childhood), as follows:[90]

Josias Bradley, born May 22, 1797, married Susan B. Butt.
William Marshall, born February 13, 1799, never married.
Robert Augustus, Jr., born November 28, 1800.
Mary Ann, born January 9,1803, married Henry Lockhart.
Susanne Millicent, born December 16, 1804, married John Billups.

A daughter, born April 1807, died the next morning.
Elizabeth Rebecca, born April 9, 1808, married Robert Billups, June 13, 1831.
Ann Fendall Beall, born Oct. 9, 1810, married Edward B. Young, June 11, 1832.
Augusta Eleanor ("Ellen"), born Nov. 9, 1812, married William H. Young., 1834
Jane Louise, born in 1815, married Robert Gunby.

As they each married, Edward and William resumed residence in Marion with their new brides. Although far from their birthplace, throughout their lives Edward and William would stay in contact with James, Christina, and their New York family. In the year following his marriage, Edward took Ann home for a visit to New York. While they were there, their first son was born. Named James William Young (for Edward's father and brother), he would be known as "Will," except by certain boyhood friends, who called him, "Bill." He was born in New York on October 25,1833.[91] Back in Marion a month later, the baby was baptized on Nov 28, 1833 by William J. Park and P. E. Warren.[92]

Two years later, Ann and Edward's second child, also a son, was born in Marion, Ga. on October 22, 1835.[93] Named Henry Augustus Young, Edward noted in his Bible that Henry was born at "15 past 2 o'clock," but we'll have to guess whether A.M. or P.M. He, too, was baptized by William J. Park and P. E. Warren, Sr., on Nov 18, 1835.[94]

In 1835, Edward was appointed postmaster of Marion.[95] He probably maintained the post office in their store, creating additional reasons for potential customers to come in. This would be a short-term position, however, because another major move was about to be made. Sensitive to opportunities, Edward was noting the attractive circumstances developing in the newly-opened lands in Alabama along the Chattahoochee River valley.

In about 1836, after living in Twiggs County, Georgia for approximately 11 years, Edward, then 34, together with Ann, little Will, baby Henry Augustus, and their possessions, moved westward one hundred miles to the recently-settled village of Irwinton, in newly-created Barbour County, Alabama. Edward's older brother, James, Jr., also made the move. William did not move to Alabama. As we will discuss later, William returned to New York to pursue an opening there, but did not remain for long. Lured by commercial opportunity and their preference for the South, William and Ellen would move to Apalachicola, Florida in 1839, where they made their home until commercial advantage beckoned again.[96] Even though after this time Edward and William no longer lived in the same towns, they and their wives nevertheless visited back and forth and maintained their personal closeness. The brothers continued to coordinate their business affairs and to enter into business ventures as partners and associates, much to their mutual advantage.

Before proceeding to Alabama with Edward and Ann, however, we must pause to describe two losses which they suffered in 1836: the deaths of Ann's two older brothers, Josias and Robert, Jr., in two widely separated events of history: the War for Texas Independence, and the Seminole War.

6
Texas Independence; Fannin's Massacre

A wave of sympathy for the "Texicans'" struggle for independence from Mexico was sweeping the South, and troops of volunteers were being raised to go to their aid. In a public meeting in Macon, Ga, on Nov. 12, 1835, prominent citizens, including Ann's brother, Mayor Robert A. Beall, Jr., spoke out in support of aiding Texas' struggle for independence.[97] Robert was appointed to a committee to solicit subscriptions, and over $3000 was raised before the meeting adjourned.[98]

Ironically, among the Georgians who felt called to volunteer to fight in Texas was the older brother of Robert and Ann, Josias Bradley Beall, then 39 years old and married with five children.[99] About 120 men from Georgia formed a battalion commanded by Col. Ward, which reached Texas in early 1836.[100] After several successful engagements against the Mexicans, the Georgia Battalion joined the command of Col. Fannin at Fort Goliad, forming a regiment numbering 500.[101] On March 6, the Alamo fell, and 183 Texans were massacred by Santa Anna. This was not to be Santa Anna's last massacre.

A week later, the Georgia battalion was sent 30 miles from Goliad to relieve Captain King, also in a mission church surrounded by Mexicans. After initially being successfully relieved, in a Mexican counterattack Kings' men were killed, while the Georgians were backed into the church and compelled to surrender. But the Georgians' surrender was specifically conditioned upon the agreement that they were to be returned to the United States.[102] Meanwhile, in a separate fight near Goliad, Col Fannin and the rest of the regiment were also overwhelmed and captured by the Mexicans. The regiment was reunited in captivity with the Georgia Battalion, and in violation of the terms of surrender, Santa Anna ordered the entire regiment butchered. On the pretext of proceeding to American ships for removal, the men were marched past lines of Mexican soldiers, and 350 Texans and Georgians were gunned down.[103] Ann's older brother, Josias, was among them [104]

"Fannin's Massacre" joined "Remember the Alamo!" as a Texas war cry. Satisfaction was not long in coming. Less than one month later, the war ended when Sam Houston routed the Mexican army at San Jacinto and captured Santa Anna himself.[105]

7

Osceola; The Seminole War

Josias' brother, Robert, who in Macon had advocated assistance to the Texans, demonstrated that he too was willing to step forward and fight when his compatriots needed help. The Seminole Indians of Florida, (consisting mainly of Creeks and runaway slaves fleeing from Alabama and Georgia over the years), had signed a treaty in 1833 agreeing to removal to Oklahoma, but thereafter refused to go.[106] Their resistance was led by Osceola, a half-breed Seminole chief born in what is now Macon County, Alabama,[107] who in 1835 carried out a surprise uprising involving the brutal murder of Florida settlers, thereby precipitating the lengthy Seminole War.[108]

Osceola

In February of 1836, five companies of Georgia volunteers assembled in Macon to join the Florida war, and formed themselves into a battalion commanded by Major Cooper.[109] Robert A. Beall, Jr. accompanied these volunteers.[110] This was a well-intentioned, dangerous venture which had tragic results for the Beall family. But it also had its farcical aspects.

On Feb. 5, the Governor of Georgia reviewed the battalion in Macon.[111] Two days later, following an address on the wharf by Robert Beall, Jr., and a response by Major Cooper, the group boarded four boats and proceeded downriver to the stirring strains of "Le Marseillaise," played by the Macon Volunteer Band.[112] A smaller group left the next day with the baggage, but a few miles from Macon, the boat overturned, losing much of the baggage; this group had to proceed overland.[113]

On Feb.18, the main group joined the forces of Gen. Winfield Scott in camp on the St. Johns River, where they were mustered into the United States Army, and then proceeded toward Tampa Bay. Enroute occurred the only fighting during the entire expedition.[114] In a minor encounter with a group of Indians, a militiaman received a flesh wound, a ball shot away part of a Pvt. Dannelly's cap, and another ball went through the coat of one E. D. Williams.

At some time during the expedition, Robert Beall came down with an illness from which he seemed to be slow in recovering. About thirty miles further toward Tampa Bay, Gen. Scott left the Georgia battalion with instructions that they build a fort and await further orders. After three weeks, the men were still awaiting further orders when their food ran out. They were about to kill Major Cooper's horse for food, but the animal was spared when Gen. Scott arrived with supplies.[115]

The Georgia battalion then returned to Macon. When they arrived in Macon on May 25, they were welcomed by the firing of a cannon, and honored with a testimonial dinner.

The casualty list reflects that the unit suffered only 3 men wounded and one death due to sickness. Of the three wounds, the two worst were received during the firing of the cannon that greeted their return.[116] The single death was Robert, who died on June 16, 1836 [117] from unspecified illness contracted while in Florida.[118] He left a wife and a daughter.[119]

When she heard of Robert's death, Ann Young had just received the news of her brother Josias' death in Fannin's Massacre less than three months earlier. She and Edward must have been particularly affected by the untimely death of this accomplished and promising brother and friend. Only 36, Robert had established a high reputation at the Bar. He had helped organize the States Rights Party and had been one of its nominees for Congress. He had served well in the state legislature, served as a General in the militia, been one of the founders of Wesleyan College, been elected Mayor of Macon, been active in his Methodist Church, and contributed to his community and state in a variety of other ways.[120]

Gen. Scott was recalled to Washington in July and court-martialed, based in part on his conduct of the Seminole campaign.[121] Fighting with the Seminoles continued intermittently until 1843, when most of the Seminoles had been destroyed.[122] However, in 1837, the year following Robert's death, Osceola was captured and imprisoned in St Augustine.[123] He had malaria and would soon die.

And here we encounter a strange coincidence indirectly touching the Young family.

Stationed in St Augustine with his wife and two-year old son at the time of Osceola's capture was a U. S. Army surgeon with excellent medical credentials, Dr. Frederick Weedon. When the Seminole War broke out in 1836, Dr. Weedon had organized a company and entered the service as a captain. However, he soon resigned his infantry position to enter the medical corps as a surgeon, stationed at St. Augustine. In 1837, when Osceola was brought in as a captive and confined in Fort Marion, he was treated by Frederick Weedon. It is said that "a friendship, bordering on affection, sprang up between the doctor and the famous captive." As Osceola's health deteriorated, the army authorities decided to transfer him to Fort Moultrie, in Charleston Harbor. At Osceola's own "urgent" request, Dr. Frederick Weedon was detached from the army in Florida and sent with him. Osceola died soon after arriving, and before his death, gave Dr. Weedon his clothes, pipe, earrings, and other trinkets. [124]

It is now generally accepted that, following Osceola's death, but before his coffin was sealed for interment, Dr. Weedon severed Osceola's head, preserved it, and kept it as a souvenir for many years.[125] It was ultimately donated to a New York Medical facility, and probably destroyed when that facility burned.

In 1865, twenty-eight years after Osceola's head was separated from his body by Frederick Weedon, Frederick's then two-year-old son had become a physician himself, Dr. Hamilton Weedon. Hamilton had served as a Confederate surgeon in the campaigns of the western theatre until July, 1864, when he was assigned to the army hospital in Eufaula, Alabama. In the closing days of the Civil War, Dr. Hamilton Weedon would meet and then marry Robert's niece - Edward and Ann's daughter - Mollie Young, and they would ultimately settle happily in Eufaula. We will hear more about this attractive couple in due course.

8
Lands of the Creek Nation

"Among those intruders were some of the most lawless and uncouth men I have ever seen ..."
U. S. Marshal, describing first settlers of Eufaula

The arrival in Irwinton in 1836 of Edward, Ann, and their two boys, Will and Henry, was at a key stage in the brief but turbulent history of this frontier town that they would help to civilize, and the name of which Edward would later cause to be changed to "Eufaula." Irwinton had only recently come into existence, upon land that, at the time, still belonged to the Creek Indian Nation. To understand the context in which Edward and Ann began their lives in Irwinton, it is helpful to briefly summarize important background.

Since the time of the Spanish explorations, most of the area of present southwest Georgia and present central and south Alabama had been controlled by the Creek Indians (often called the Creek Confederacy, because there was a loose confederation of the major Creek towns, or the Creek Nation, or simply "the Nation".) American independence brought increased incursions of white settlers. For a time, Creek control of the area was perpetuated through sophisticated diplomacy by half-breed Creek leaders such as Alexander McGillivray, who manipulated the foreign powers in the area: the U. S., England, and Spain. During the War of 1812, however, the British induced the Creeks into an alliance against the United States. Further inflamed by Tecumseh, a mystical Indian "prophet" from Ohio, the Creeks rose up and massacred a group of settlers at Fort Mims, in the future state of Alabama.

In Nashville, Tennessee, a frontier lawyer and militia leader, infuriated by the attack, resolved that the area should be made safe for white settlers. Although not fully recovered from the wounds suffered in his most recent duel, Andrew Jackson raised a force of "Tennessee Volunteers" (which included David Crockett and Sam Houston), marched south, and defeated the Creek main force at the Battle of Horseshoe Bend on March 24, 1814, killing six hundred warriors and permanently breaking the power of the Creek Nation.[126] In the ensuing Treaty of Ft. Jackson, "Ol' Hickory" imposed draconian terms; he required the Creeks to cede to the United States two thirds of their lands, an area covering almost half of the future state of Alabama.[127]

Infected with "Alabama Fever"[128] which now swept the nation, thousands of white settlers rapidly poured into the rich new lands, and in 1819, Alabama was admitted to the Union as the 22nd state.[129] But there was still a large area on the eastern side of the new state over which it had no jurisdiction, because it was still owned by the Creek Nation. Picture an Alabama-shaped cookie with a big bite out of the middle of the eastern edge.[130] In the bottom corner of the "cookie-bite," on the Creek side of the boundary line as it ran into the Chattahoochee River, were the sites of the future Barbour County and Irwinton.

Settlers in Georgia and Alabama coveted these remaining Creek lands, and there were constant incursions and conflicts with the Indians.[131] This situation festered for 18 years. In 1830, Congress enacted the Indian Removal Act, and federal agents then negotiated the Creek Cession of 1832.[132] This treaty provided incentives for the "voluntary" removal of the Indians to Oklahoma. The treaty conveyed to the United States all of the Creeks' remaining lands, but with certain important conditions which were to cause much trouble. During a five-year period, the land was to be surveyed, and each Indian head of family could select for his personal ownership 320 acres (640 for chiefs), which he could live on, or which he was free to sell if he wished and receive free transportation to Oklahoma.[133] (Of course, he was under pressure to elect the latter.)[134] The United States agreed to keep intruders off the land until this process was completed. But land-hungry settlers were unwilling to wait, and rushed into the area.[135] And in support of the settlers, the

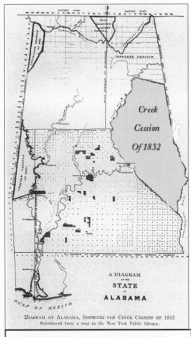

DIAGRAM OF ALABAMA, SHOWING THE CREEK CESSION OF 1832.
Reproduced from a map in the New York Public Library.

The Creek Cession of 1832. The new county of Barbour formed the southern tip.

Alabama Legislature asserted jurisdiction by enacting legislation dividing the new area into nine counties, with Barbour at the southernmost tip,[136] thereby contributing to a developing state-federal confrontation.

The site of the future Irwinton became one of the chief trouble spots. In 1831, even before the Creeks had signed the treaty of cession, a group of white settlers took possession of the Creek town of Ola Ufala, drove off the Creek Eufaulas, burnt their dwellings, and built on the site a "small log town," which the settlers proceeded to incorporate as the town of Irwinton.[137] In response to Creek complaints, the U.S. Marshall felt he had to take drastic action, and in 1832, he caused a detachment of federal troops from Ft. Mitchell to march on Irwinton, expel the settlers, and burn the new log buildings. Reporting to the Secretary of the Army, the U.S. Marshall expressed this view of the future Eufaulians:

> "Among those intruders were some of the most lawless and uncouth
> men I have ever seen ... refugees from the State of Georgia."[138]

But the uncouth settlers ultimately won. Not long after the soldiers departed, they reestablished Irwinton and rebuilt it using methods and materials of permanent construction rather than rough-hewn longs, with the intention of remaining, which they did. [139]

To defuse the tense state-federal conflict that was building, President Jackson sent a mediator to the area, selecting for this assignment an aging government lawyer, Francis Scott Key (yes, he of the bombs bursting in air; but one writer observed that Key found little here to proudly hail.[140]) Key devised a face-saving compromise, which permitted settlers to remain on the land which had not yet been selected as an Indian's allotment.[141]

By 1836, the condition of the Indians who had not yet accepted removal to Oklahoma had deteriorated to a deplorable state.[142] They were being systematically swindled out of their land allotments for whiskey.[143] (Some familiar Eufaula names were allegedly involved,[144] but then, the Indians sometimes sold their allotments two or three times). They had lost their homes; they were no longer farming but had lost the ability to live off the land. Many were addicted to alcohol or were starving.[145] In these desperate straits, the Indians staged one last uprising against the white man. Bands of Indian marauders attacked plantations and killed the settlers; there was burning, plundering, killing, and scalping all across the former Creek country, and terrified white refugees streamed out of the area.[146] Federal troops and state militia were quickly mobilized and went on the counterattack.

We can now return to our narrative of the Youngs, for it was during the Creek War of 1836-1837 that Edward, Ann, and their two small children made their entrance into Irwinton. However, although there was certainly a sufficiency of fighting, maiming, and killing, this was the "last gasp" of the Creeks. As soon as the whites recovered from the initial onslaught, the Indians were overwhelmed and crushed.[147] The last battle was fought in the early spring of 1837, at Hobdy's Bridge on the Pea River in western Barbour County.[148] Within two years, substantially all the Indians were gone, tracked down and moved to Oklahoma[149] leaving nothing, as one historian observed, but arrowheads, shards of pottery, and a legacy of place names.[f]

---

[f] In fact, the Creeks also took their place names with them. Oklahoma is dotted with town names familiar to south Alabamians. There is a Eufaula, as well as a Lake Eufaula; "Tulsa" is a corruption of "Tallassee" (or "Talisi").

9
Eufaula Entrepreneur

"He was a natural born business man...Everything he touched in a business sense seemed to prosper..."

Tom Jackson

Ironically, despite their arrival in the middle of an Indian war, the timing of the Youngs' move to Irwinton could hardly have been better. Although achieved at great cost to those affected, the Indian problem in Alabama had been solved and laid to rest. The permanence and safety of the Irwinton settlement was assured. It was located in and near vast, rich, new lands now available for the taking. Newcomers were daily arriving who were eager to work the new land and make it productive, either as cotton land or otherwise. All of these settlers would have extensive and varied needs: personal, household, and commercial. Edward Young the entrepreneur had the commercial skills and energy to provide for those needs at a reasonable profit, and as we will see, he went to work immediately.

Edward Brown Young, as a young man

Irwinton was situated on a high bluff on the Alabama side of the Chattahoochee River, which forms the border between Georgia and Alabama. When Edward and Ann crossed the Chattahoochee River to reach Irwinton, unless they came by way of Columbus (which is unlikely), they would have had to cross the river by ferryboat. The only bridge across the Chattahoochee was at Columbus, a sturdy wooden bridge constructed in 1832 by John Godwin, and his skilled slave, Horace King, at a cost of $14,000.[150]

With settlers rapidly populating the former Creek lands, Edward Young's enterprising mind immediately recognized the commercial potential of a toll bridge across the Chattahoochee at Irwinton. Not only would it yield profitable tolls, it also would spur the growth of the town by facilitating commerce with the more populated areas of southwest Georgia. Thus, one of Edward's earliest ventures after arriving in the community was to organize such a project. Although it was principally Edward's undertaking, there were other investors. The river flows entirely in Georgia territory, and in 1837, Edward and his friends persuaded the Georgia Legislature to pass an act incorporating the "Irwinton Bridge Company" for the purpose of erecting a bridge across the Chattahoochee River opposite the town of Irwinton. For the abutment on the Georgia side, the act authorized the company to acquire a specific parcel of land under the right of eminent domain and to pay the owner a fair price determined by agreement or appraisal.[151] Land for the Alabama abutment was purchased from Irwinton pioneer, Seth Lore.[152] Edward acquired the Georgia abutment in the manner provided by the Georgia act, but this transaction was to lead to exasperating difficulties in future years.

To construct the bridge, the Irwinton Bridge Company looked to the man who had built the Columbus Bridge six years earlier in 1832: John Godwin. On Nov 10, 1838, the Irwinton Bridge Company, acting through its officers, John M. Moore and William Wellborn entered into a contract with John Godwin and Simon H. Williams, (doing business as Godwin & Williams) for the construction of "a good and substantial bridge…as contemplated in the charter of said company," for the price of $22,500.[153] The flooring of the bridge was to be 30 feet above the high water mark of the Chattahoochee, or "in other words eighty feet from the bed of the river." It was to rest upon "wooden piers and wooden abutments," and would be at least 540 feet long. The height of the "truss" or passageway was to be 17 feet, "covered with a good shingle roof…and painted." The contractors were to receive the first $5000 when "the timber is on the ground and ready for building;" another $5000 would be due when the framing was done; and $5000 "when the bridge is nailed." Upon completion, the builders were to receive a final payment of $5000, along with shares of stock in the Bridge Company in the amount of $2500. The financing appears to have been provided principally by Edward Young. [154]

When Godwin constructed the Columbus Bridge in 1832-83, it was constructed according to a model of "Ithiel Town's patent," [155] a design which apparently also appealed to the owners of the Irwinton Bridge Company, for their contract required Godwin to build their bridge in "a good substantial workman like manner after the Town Patent Lattice form." Godwin was assisted in building the Columbus Bridge by his skilled slave, Horace King, and it is almost certain that King would have also had a significant role in the construction of the Irwinton Bridge. King would later become famous as a well-regarded designer-builder in his own right. Freed by Godwin in 1847, King built dozens of bridges throughout the area, and worked on the Alabama Capitol when that structure was built in 1850-51.[156] He is thought to have designed its graceful "unsupported" curving staircase. His attachment to his former master was such that, when Godwin died in 1859, King used his own funds to install a monument over his grave which referred to the "the love and gratitude he felt for his lost friend and former master."[157] During Reconstruction, King was a member of the Alabama legislature.

Godwin's contract provided for the Irwinton Bridge to be completed in one year, by November 1, 1839. However, it was not declared complete until January 1, 1840.[158] Operated as a toll bridge, the first bridge keeper was Lochlan McLean. The bridge keepers resided in a cottage at the foot of the hill on the Alabama side.[159] In the springtime, when the water sometime reached the high-water mark, steamboats would occasionally have to tie up at the Irwinton wharf and wait, because they couldn't get under the bridge even with their smoke stacks lowered.[160] It is said that the bridge became a popular place for underage couples to get married. The river, and hence the bridge, are in Georgia, so that underage couples without the parental consent required by Alabama law could acquire Georgia licenses and get married on the bridge. [161]

The Irwinton Bridge, completed by Edward Young's company on January 1, 1840, depicted at a later date after the wooden piers had been replaced with brick.

Edward was not long in recognizing Irwinton's need for a bank. A bank would help the local economy by expanding the money supply and extending badly-needed credit to the cotton growers. The Creek lands, which had previously served principally as a habitat for the white-tailed deer, the main basis for the Indian economy, were now being rapidly cleared by the settlers and planted in cotton. In the four years from 1835 to 1839, the new county of Barbour alone went from shipping only a few bales to shipping 5000 bales of cotton to New York and Liverpool.[162] These planters needed financing for their crop expenses; further, after the crop was in, they didn't want to wait several months for the finished product to reach the consumer before being paid.[163] Perhaps Edward fits one historian's description of those who met these needs for local banking facilities in the frontier economy: "aggressive men on the make who seized the opportunities to earn their fortunes in a fast-paced era of development in which the rules of play had not yet been codified."[164] In 1839, Edward organized and opened a bank which was to operate successfully for a number of years.[165] Organized while the Irwinton Bridge was under construction, he named it the "Irwinton Bridge Bank."

The business that was the mainstay of Edward's financial position during the pre-war years was that of cotton factor, warehouseman, and commission merchant. A "cotton factor" was one who *sold* a grower's cotton for him, for which the factor received a commission of 2.5%, while a "commission merchant" was paid a similar commission for *buying* merchandise or commodities that were needed by the planters.[166] The terms came to be used interchangeably because the person hired to sell a planter's cotton crop at harvest time was usually also the one who had bought plantation supplies for the grower throughout the season, and had carried the debt on his books until compensated out of the sale of the crop.[167] This was true of Edward, who operated in both capacities. A historian of Eufaula observed "...the town looked to him not only for credit and the transaction of much of its business in converting its staple, cotton, into money, but commissioned him for buying merchandise..."[168]

In connection with his business of commission merchant, Edward also operated a general merchandise store. This store allowed Edward to also serve the needs of smaller farmers, similar to the services he provided on a larger scale to large plantation owners. As storekeeper, he could extend credit to small farmers in the form of supplies, equipment, or cash, to be paid from the sale of the farmer's cotton.[169]

Selling cotton on commission involved a variety of services. The factor's main job, of course, was to find a buyer and get the cotton sold, but this required him to first evaluate the cotton, repackage it, warehouse it, and arrange financing which would allow the planter to be paid an advance on the purchase price immediately upon delivery, usually one-half to three fourths of the purchase price.[170] Edward built warehouses for storage of the cotton, and provided funds to finance the provisions, supplies, and equipment needed to produce a cotton crop, (probably with financial participation by his brother William, working temporarily in New York, and later a broker himself in Apalachicola).

One of Edward's best customer accounts, both for brokering cotton and the sale of merchandise, came to be that of his friend, John Horry[g] Dent, a successful and wealthy plantation owner in Barbour County for 30 years from 1837 through 1866. Dent had arrived in Barbour County from Charleston, South Carolina about the same time Edward arrived from Twiggs County, Georgia, and they developed a "cordial and trusting" relationship.[171] In time they and their families became fast friends. Dent kept highly detailed records of all aspects of his farming operations that are studied today for their insights into plantation economics. Describing the detailed nature of Dent's plantation journals, Barbour County historian Walker observes[172]:

> "From the day that he [John Horry Dent] acquired the Cowikee land
> and set his slaves to rolling logs in the new ground to the days when
> he was receiving long invoices from the business and banking
> house of Edward and William Young at Irwinton the routine of
> plantation life is mirrored."

To eliminate confusion in names, we point out that this John Horry Dent, the cotton planter, is *not* related to the Stouten Hubert Dent who first came to Eufaula from Maryland in 1854 and became a son-in-law of Edward and Ann in 1859. The identity of the two names has misled one otherwise-careful writer into observing, incorrectly, that, "After years of doing business with each other, the two families were united when Young's daughter married Dent's son."[173] The planter, John Horry Dent did have a son named *Her*bert, but Anna Young's husband was *Hu*bert Dent, and not related to the planter.

Although John Horry Dent had arrived in Barbour County in about 1836, it was not until 1839, that he had cleared enough acres to plant a sizable cotton crop.[174] Dent's journals reflect that almost from the beginning of his relationship with Edward Young, Dent was storing most or all of his cotton at "E. B. Young's Warehouse," and that much of his cotton was being sold to Edward, or through Edward as factor. Dent sold his entire 1839 cotton crop, consisting of 57 bales, through E & W Young.[175] Dent's records reflect that, as his cotton production grew, this trend continued, and by the 1850's, Dent was still consigning his cotton crops primarily to Edward for handling.[176]

The extant journals of John Horry Dent begin with his first "crop year," 1839. The first entry on the first page recites transactions with "E & W Young", such as, "E & W Young account of 1839 as per voucher $227.16 ¾"; and cash remitted to Dent's bank "per E & W Young, $10,022.24".[177] Thereafter, in virtually every month, the journals reflect transactions with Edward or one of his businesses. These entries include every imaginable kind of commercial transaction of the time, including: the shipment of cotton for storage in Young's warehouse; the sale of cotton to or through Young; the deposit of funds with Young or the withdrawal thereof; borrowing funds from Young; lending short term funds to Young; the purchase of supplies and equipment from or through Young; the hiring of slaves to Young; the sale of corn, fodder, molasses, and other farm products to Young; and others. Extracts from Dent's journal entries give the flavor of the journal, and of the times:

> June 21, 1840: "Gave out shirts and shifts to Negroes this day of cotton osnaburgs [h] purchased of E & W Young at 10 cents per good".[178]

> Nov 1, 1840: "Went to Irwinton. Invoice of articles brot from Irwinton by Tom Grey and Wheelers wagon Nov 2nd and recd on the 4th inst.
> 47 bolts bagging--yards 67.71.69.72 @ 34cents   E & W Y
> 3 coils rope, lbs, 90,81, and one unmarked   E & W Y
> 1 hank twine   E & W Y
> ...also
> 1 sack salt, 1 bag coffee 100 pounds, 12 yards homespun, 1 gl lamp oil ($2), 1 pr shoes (1.622) for Mrs. D, 2 pr stockings for Mrs. D, and 2 ½ yards of Marino."[179]

> Dec 2, 1840: "Negroe Shoes
> Bought of E & W Young 31 pr Shoes for Negroes
>   28 pr at $1.37 $38.50
>   3 pr at 125 cts   _3.75_
> $42.25
> And gave them to the Negroes this 3rd of December 1840"

> Feb 25, 1841: "Left with Messrs. E & W Young of Irwinton $1,105.10 to remit to Phil McCloskey of Mobile...Messrs. E & W Young will purchase a check on Mobile if possible otherwise will forward a certificate of deposit on Bank of Columbus, Ga...."

> June 18, 1841: "Day very windy-and cloudy-weather quite unsettled from appearances-showers and thunder-heavy rain.
> Sent to E & W Young of Irwinton for 1 bbl flour, 2 sacks salt..., 2 lbs squirrel shot and 1 Box Caps and 1½ gls Brandy."[180]

---

[h] Clothing made of a heavy, coarse, plain-woven fabric considered suitable for workers.

In 1838, after Edward and Ann had been in Irwinton for about two years, their third child was born, their first little girl. Born on August 12, 1838, she was baptized on June 30, 1839 by John W. Starr.[181] She was named Ellen Louisa Young, in honor of Ann's younger sister-William's wife-Ellen. Sadly, however, this child was to live only one year. During a visit to Ann's family in Warrenton, Georgia, little Ellen died, on August 25, 1839. [182]

In addition to his other ventures, Edward did some dealing in formerly Creek lands. Not being a grower of cotton, he did not usually hold large tracts of land (until later, as we will discuss), but from time to time he would buy and sell smaller parcels of real property. On October 30, 1838, for instance, he bought 320 acres of public land, 80 acres in his sole name, and another 240 acres jointly for himself and his brother William,[183] who was then working in New York but making visits to Eufaula. In 1844, Edward purchased a half acre lot on Randolph Street.[184] The records reflect that he frequently took mortgages on Eufaula lots, other real estate, slaves, or merchants' stocks of good, as security for loans made.[185] Edward also began the operation of a sawmill, to cut lumber for the building boom created by the influx of settlers to the new lands.

10
The Chattahoochee-Apalachicola River Valley Cotton Economy

"They primarily made their fortune in buying plantation supplies for their country clients on credit and selling their cotton on a commission basis when the cotton was harvested... Coastal factors at the seacoast acted as liaisons [with]... 'foreign' markets [of] New York or London."

Willoughby, *"Fair To Middlin' "*

Rather than accompany his two brothers, Edward and James, to Irwinton, William Young had returned to New York City in about 1836 to accept an unusually well paying position as salesman and collector for a large wholesale dealer. He had a five-year contract at $10,000 per year.[186] However, the economic crash of 1836 caused almost universal failure among this and similar wholesale houses. William nevertheless remained with the business for three or four years, and due in part to his collection efforts, the company was able to settle all its outside debt, but was not able to fully pay his own contract.[187]

Even while working in New York, William was visiting his brother in Irwinton/Eufaula and pursuing joint business ventures with him there. There are grounds for speculation that William may have entertained the thought of joining Edward in Eufaula and going into partnership with him. For a number of years, Edward operated his business as "E & W Young." On Oct 30, 1838, Edward bought, in the joint names of himself and William, 240 acres of public lands in Alabama (i. e., formerly Creek lands acquired by the U. S. under treaty.) William and Ellen's first child, Edward Beall Young, died in Eufaula on November 9, 1837, after having lived only one year and three months. He was buried in the Young plot in what is today Eufaula's Fairview Cemetery. Edward Beall's is probably one of the earliest burials in this cemetery.

The failure of the New York company by which William was employed, together with his general preference for the South, prompted William to return permanently to the South in 1839. But if there had ever been a plan to join Edward in Eufaula, it did not materialize. Like Edward, William recognized the potential of the business of cotton broker and commission merchant, but he elected to enter that business in Apalachicola, Florida. Why Apalachicola? This shrewd choice, which would benefit both William and Edward, arose from the way in which the cotton industry was developing.

The Southern cotton industry was actually an assemblage of separate economies, each dependent upon a different river system as its principal commercial highway.[188] There were virtually no roads through the Southern forests, but the South had numerous river systems that connected the sea to the interior. The three rivers that emptied into the Gulf of Mexico were the Mississippi, the Alabama, and the Chattahoochee-Apalachicola system. Charleston and Savannah on the Atlantic were served by similar water routes to the interior. These river valleys saw the development of separate cotton economies, but each having three common characteristics: an ocean port city; small river trading towns along the river; and a major trading center at the further-most navigation point.[189] Thus a mutually beneficial relationship arose between the markets at the opposite ends of the river-system, such as Mobile and Montgomery, Savannah and Augusta, and Apalachicola and Columbus.[190] However, Columbus was not the only important trading center along the Chattahoochee-Apalachicola River. Forty-three miles below Columbus was Eufaula, "another significant regional cotton market, for it often served as the head of navigation during the dry summer months."[191] Like Columbus, Eufaula began as "a raucous frontier town", built on land which white settlers were "so eager to begin cultivating that they had not even paused to purchase it first, precipitating a local war."[192]

In this context, in 1839, the 32-year-old William returned South with his wife Ellen, to settle in Apalachicola, fifteen years after his first migration South at the age of seventeen. There he went into the business of commission merchant and cotton factor. Joining William in the business in Apalachicola was another brother-in-law, Dr. Henry Lockhart, who had married Ellen and Ann's sister, Mary Ann Beall. Their commission business, Lockhart & Young, was to be eminently successful.

In *Fair To Middlin,'* her comprehensive analysis of the cotton economy of the Chattahoochee-Apalachicola river system,

The Chattahoochee-Apalachicola River System

Lynne Willoughby almost seems to have Edward and William Young in mind when she describes the division of labor among the segments of the cotton trade in this system [comments in brackets added]:

> "The various tasks necessary to market the crop were divided among upriver merchants [like Edward in Eufaula] and downstream entrepreneurs [like William in Apalachicola]. Inland cotton factors and commission merchants clustered in the larger communities [like Eufaula and Columbus]. They primarily made their fortune in buying plantation supplies for their country clients on credit and selling their cotton on a commission basis when the cotton was harvested. General storekeepers [which also included Edward] found their niche in the less-populated countryside. They serviced the smaller cotton farmers, who also needed a market for their crop, as well as a source of credit for farm operations throughout the growing season. Coastal factors at the seacoast [like William] acted as liaisons between the inland merchants and the cotton

41

buyers who represented mill owners or speculators in such 'foreign' markets as New York or London."[193]

Willoughby further points out that, because of the necessity of relying on their associates for financial backing and confidential information, many business relationships were based on kinship, and she gives the Young brothers as one of several examples of the success of such relationships: "William H. Young, an entrepreneur of both Apalachicola and [in later years] Columbus, and his brother Edward B. Young at Eufaula, Alabama, assisted one another in their cotton affairs."[194] In fact, for several years after 1839, Edward's mercantile and cotton factoring businesses in Irwinton were conducted under the joint name of "E. & W Young," implying a partnership between "Edward and William." A number of transactions indicate the existence of a partnership, such as a loan to Irwinton merchant, Charles F. Gerke, on February 20, 1842, in which Gerke secured a loan from the Young brothers by giving a mortgage on land and merchandise to "Edward and William Young, merchants trading under the name of E & W Young."[195] On February 25, 1842, William Wellborn sold a lot on Broad Street in Irwinton to Edward and William jointly. [196]

William's firm of Lockhart & Young in Apalachicola was often a participant in Edward's transactions. For example, Edward's Irwinton friend and customer, John Horry Dent, through Edward also became a friend and joint customer of William's. In his journal for April 1841, Dent quotes "Extracts from Letter of E & W Young, 18th April 1841", in which Edward itemizes an invoice of payments made by him on Dent's behalf to Lockhart & Young, for such items as freight, insurance, postage, flour, drayage, wharfage, and 2½ % commissions on these items.[197]

In 1842, Dent had not yet sold his 1841 cotton crop, and he decided to personally transport his cotton to Apalachicola and sell it there himself. His records reflect that steamship passage for Dent and his wife to Apalachicola Bay was booked and paid for through E & Y Young, and that while in Apalachicola, he paid Lockhart & Young for drayage, wharfage, "exchange on draft", and "cash advanced "[198] Dent was not happy with the price he received in Apalachicola, and thereafter, he sold his cotton through one of the Irwinton factors, usually Edward Young.

Another instance of Edward and William's joint business dealings is found in a mortgage on two Randolph Street lots in Eufaula, given to Edward on April 1, 1845 by one Amos Van Epps to secure a note payable from funds Epps is expecting to receive from Lockhart and Young in Apalachicola nine months later, (probably from the expected sale of Epps' cotton crop). [199]

John Horry Dent's plantation journals reveal the large profits being made from cotton by these growers. Historian Ray Mathis has carefully analyzed the journals, and makes these observations:

> "Dent's three cotton crops from 1839 through 1841 earned a combined total of $8800. In 1841, while planning a new indebtedness, he

estimated his annual expenses at $800. He admitted that the estimate was very liberal and that it included the family's living expenses. This means that from 1839 through 1841, Dent netted about $2000 each year on cotton production alone. He also had significant income from short-term loans, the sale of surplus corn and fodder, and for the services of his cotton gin and press, his Negro blacksmith, and his Negro carpenter."[200]

An annual return of $2000 on annual expenses of $800, even if reduced by the capital cost of land and slaves, is still a huge return. The cotton profits being enjoyed by Dent were not unique. Similar financial results were being enjoyed by cotton growers throughout the Chattahoochee valley and indeed, the South. By providing the full array of commercial services needed by these planters, Edward and William tapped into the large profits of cotton. And despite temporary periods of weakness, cotton wealth would only increase during the 1840's and 50's. Edward and William Young would continue to rise financially with this tide.

The year 1840 was a year of mixed sadness and joy for Edward and Ann. Edward's father, James Young, (the Newark Militiaman), died in New York on May 2, 1840.[201] James was 69 when he died, and was buried in the "Marble Cemeteries" in Manhattan.[202] His wife, Christina, would live for many more years. One month later there was a happier event. At "about 8 o'clock," on June 5, 1840, Ann and Edward had their third child, the first surviving girl. She was named to honor Ann herself, Anna Beall Young.[203] Later, this baby girl, her husband, and their children will become central players in the Fendall Hall story.

When the town of Irwinton had been incorporated by the "uncouth intruders" in 1831, while it was still in Creek territory, it was named for a Henry County Indian fighter and political figure, William Irwin. Edward Young came to dislike the name of "Irwinton," principally because its similarity to the name of a town in Georgia (probably Irwinsville) caused confusion in the mails, resulting in important business letters and packages being misdirected between the two towns. Finally, in 1842, when a package of money that Edward was expecting was missent to Georgia, he concluded that the problem had become too serious to ignore. Accordingly, he prepared a petition to change the name back to a version of its old Creek Indian name of "Eufaula." Edward personally carried the petition around to solicit signatures,[204] and was able to obtain the signatures of every man in town but one.[205] He next asked the Barbour County legislative delegation to secure legislative approval of the name change, which was done. The return to "the beautiful Indian name" has traditionally been regarded by Eufaulians as a happy change.

In the same year that Edward got the town's name changed, Ann bore their next child, the second girl. She was named Mary Elizabeth Christina (honoring Edward's mother and others), but soon came to be called simply, "Mollie." She was baptized by Thomas P. C. Scales on August 30, 1842. Now there were four Young children, two boys and two girls: James William (called "Will"), age nine; Henry, age seven; Anna, age two, and baby Mollie.

It will be recalled that, when Edward moved from New York City to Marion, Twiggs County, Georgia in 1825, his younger brother, William, had already arrived the previous year to clerk for Mr. Ira Peck, and that William resigned his position with Peck to go into business with his older brother. It is clear that the Young boys remained on cordial terms with Mr. Peck and earned his confidence in business matters during the ensuing years, even after they moved away from the Marion area. In February, 1844, some years after Edward had arrived in Irwinton, we find Mr. Peck granting to him a wide-sweeping general power of attorney to act on Peck's behalf in business transactions in Barbour County. Reciting "full faith in the ability and integrity" of Edward, Mr. Peck and his wife, Penelope, granted Edward full power to convey lands owned by them, to relinquish Mrs. Peck's dower rights, and to litigate and manage claims in court on their behalf.[206]

Edward's Irwinton Bridge Bank had operated successfully since its inception in 1839. Banks of this era were 'banks of issue', meaning that they created credit by issuing their own bank notes, promising to pay the bearer, on demand, an equivalent amount of specie (that is, gold or silver coin).[207] Notes of this kind were sometimes referred to as "shinplasters," presumably because often that's all they were good for. Knowing that creditors in normal times would not all cash in their banknotes at the same time, the banks customarily issued more notes than the amount of gold or silver actually on hand in the vault,[208] and sometimes overextended themselves. Foreign banks or merchants who lacked confidence in a bank's ability to redeem in specie might not accept its notes at face value, but would impose a discount. The *Columbus Enquirer-Sun* reported on January 8, 1845, and intermittently during that year until October 1845, that the then prevailing discount on notes issued by the Irwinton Bridge Bank was 25%. This compared favorably with notes of the Columbus Bank, discounted 70%, and others. Bills issued by the Columbus City Council at that time were discounted 10%. Edward had exhibited considerable fortitude in commencing his bank in the middle of a national depression that lasted from 1836 to 1842. The fact that the bank survived this depression and was still operating in late 1845 is an achievement in itself. Unfortunately, the success was not to last, and the bank was soon forced to close its doors. Willoughby points out that economic historians have been sympathetic to the difficulties that frontier bankers faced, and have explained the banks' positive effects on the region in creating as much credit for the area's businessmen as possible at a time when it was badly needed for development; observing that without these bankers, a cotton trade in the Chattahoochee/Apalachicola River valley would never have developed.[209]

The closure of the Irwinton Bridge Bank was obviously a serious loss to Edward Young. However, it was not a lasting setback. The fact that his cotton factoring business and other enterprises continued to succeed indicates that Edward's standing in Eufaula and among the Chattahoochee valley business community was not diminished. And in the next decade, Edward would return to the banking business and found a bank that would serve the area for over 40 years.

On August 15, 1844, there arrived in Eufaula a teenaged orphan boy, shoeless and broke, named Thomas J. Jackson. Tom had been leading a vagabond existence in Georgia and Alabama, most recently in the Clayton area, doing odd jobs--plowing, paper carrier, general farmhand -- or anything he might find. An enterprising and likable boy, soon after arriving in Eufaula he landed a job as a "printer's devil" and paper carrier for The *Southern Shield*, a newspaper operated by Benjamin Gardner. Tom thereafter lived in Eufaula for ten years, making his living in various ways. As we will hereafter relate, Tom would become close friends with the two Young boys, Will and Henry, and with the entire Young family. In fact, for a period of two years, he lived in the Youngs' home, and was treated as a member of the family. Tom is particularly important to our narrative because he later became a newspaperman with the Columbus *Enquirer Sun*, and during 1895-1898, he wrote a series of columns consisting in part of his recollections of early Irwinton/Eufaula. The Young family is a frequent subject of his reminiscences. We are indebted to Tom for preserving informative details of the Youngs' daily lives during this period, as well as for his insights into the personalities and characters of the members of the Young family.

This is a convenient point at which to pause and take a brief look at the newly renamed Eufaula, Alabama, as it appeared to Tom in the middle 1840's. First let us establish Tom Jackson's credentials as an observer of the local scene:

> "During my day I knew every man, woman, child,…and dog. They all liked me and I liked them. The place claimed only a population of 1500 or 2000 at that day. They were scattered over a mile square of territory and the town seemed much vaster than it really was. It was an easy job for a newspaper carrier to get acquainted with that many people. I did get acquainted with them and a better, purer, richer, more distinguished set I never met in a town of similar numbers."[210]

Tom observes that, from the brow of what is now known as College Hill, which then had only two residences on it, "looking eastward one could see a lovely little town of 1500 or 2000 situated on an almost level in the valley below."[211] Four-fifths of the buildings were "old style wooden architecture, nearly all of them one story". There was one block of one-story brick stores on the north side of upper Broad Street, and this block, containing fifteen or twenty stores, was called "Brick Row." "Here the monied and toney merchants of old Irwinton and young Eufaula held forth in their glory, and many of them accumulated fortunes; for in those days the town drew a lucrative wagon trade from Stewart, Randolph and Early counties in Georgia, as well as from Macon, Pike, Barbour, Henry, Coffee, and Dale Counties in Alabama," and in addition, Eufaula drew a portion of "the river trade."[212] Eufaula Street, running north and south at the upper end of old "Brick Row", was the western limit of the town. Most of the intervening space between Broad Street and the cemetery, a distance of three-fourths of a mile, was in its "primeval forest state, a vast, level expanse covered by oak and chinquapin growth".[213]

Now Tom takes us for a walk up Eufaula's Broad Street of the mid-1840s, starting at the river wharf and proceeding west. First we see the hardware store of S.S. Wakely. The original town settlement had been clustered close to the river, but during the 1840's, the town moved west up Broad Street, leaving Wakely's hardware store alone near the wharf. Wakely was from Connecticut, and after accumulating a fortune returned to Connecticut in about

1850.[214] Past Wakely's hardware store on the bluff there was a pine barren for about 100 yards called "Hangman's Park," because during the Clay and Polk presidential campaign of 1844, Clay's supporters hung in effigy Zeke Polk, grandfather of James K. Polk, whom the Whigs accused of being a Tory in the Revolutionary War.[215] Next after Hangman's Park came Temperance Hall, a two story wooden tenement where, from 1847 to 1852 the Sons of Temperance held weekly meetings and "scooped in nearly the whole town as members of the Cold Water Army, including every old toper within a radius of five miles." But it didn't last. "In a few years the Bacchanalians rallied and recaptured the fort." Next came the Old Masonic Hall, a two story wooden building with the lodge in the second story. After Masonic Hall was a small wooden store operated by two Frenchmen who were among the town's first settlers, Martin and Couric. Both families became influential and successful in Eufaula.[i] Mr. Martin's initials were J.G.L., but he was universally called "French" Martin, [216] (and J.G.L. Martin's son will later became a part of our story of the Young Family). Next was L.F. Stow, a prominent merchant and cotton factor widely known and respected; and William McLeod, wagon maker and repairer.

In the next block on the north side of Broad, between Orange and Randolph Streets (sometimes referred to as "Rotten Row"), were the following: The post office; Lesterjette and Smith Bakery, selling soda pop and sundries; Charles Snow, druggist; Z.J. Daniel, wood shop and lumberyard; the Eufaula *Democrat*, a newspaper operated by John Black; the *Southern Shield,* a newspaper operated by Benjamin Gardner; the physicians' offices of E. T. and W.P. Shepard; a "Negro Infirmary" operated by Dr. Flake; the shoe shop operated by Dick Stockwell; and the law offices of the Shorter brothers and of Tennent Lomax.

After Rotten Row, we reach the area on the north side of Broad Street between Randolph and Eufaula Streets called "Brick Row" because it was the only continuous block of brick stores in town. It was the extreme western terminus of business activity.[217] First is the store of L.C. Harrison, a Georgian who arrived in Irwinton during the '30s, was educated for the ministry, and who still occasionally delivered sermons at the Methodist Church. Progressing westward, next was R.T. Godwin, dry goods; Charles Delaney, dry goods, who was also a fine singer and for 30 years was chief hymn leader at the Methodist Church; Clayton R. Woods, assorted merchandise (who will later enter into an important business venture with Edward Young); Elias M. and W.D. Kiels, dry goods and groceries. We will later be discussing Elias Kiels in more detail, for after the Civil War, he became the leader of the despised carpetbag/scalawag government of Barbour County, under the protection of the federal troops of occupation.[218] Next is Beauchamp & Beckham Groceries. Green Beauchamp of this firm was an early settler of Barbour County, and one of the Commissioners who located the county seat at Clayton in the 1830's. Next was Kendall and McRae, miscellaneous stock. The McRaes were among the early settlers of the county, and John McRae, a brother of the Eufaula merchant, was the second man elected Sheriff after the Indian War of 1836. The McRaes will also become a part of the story of the Youngs.

---

[i] Couric was the ancestor of Katie Couric who, at the time of this writing, is a popular star of a network television morning show.

Next came the grocery store operated by John Hart and D.C. Scott; and the grocery store operated by L.J. Laird, who also ran a small farm in the neighborhood. Other business houses on upper Brick Row were the Gaston Brothers, Martin H. Joyce, and L.F. Johnson, warehouse and commission merchant.[219] The last business house on the western end of Broad Street was the mercantile store operated by Edward B. Young.

The first hotel in Eufaula had been located on the bluff; known as the Lovelace House, it had enjoyed a good patronage during the 1830s. When the town moved west, three wooden hotels were erected on Broad Street near the center of the city: The Alabama House, kept by W.H. Taylor; The Eufaula House, kept by G.E. Pease; and the Central House by Joe Saulsbury. All three "old styled taverns had up their street signs and sonorous bells, which three times a day summoned hungry boarders and transient visitors to frugal repasts." Good rooms and board could be obtained at from $10 to $12 per month.

There were no railroads serving Eufaula at this time, but

"Old-fashioned stagecoaches, owned by Mott & Mustain of Columbus, and driven by Abe and Jere Gammell, furnished daily mail facilities between Columbus and Eufaula. The memory of the tin bugle, which announced the approach of the old stage is still treasured in fond recollection…We had tri-weekly hack lines to [nearby small towns]."[220]

Old Irwinton had three churches: Baptist, Methodist, and Presbyterian, "all old styled wooden structures, with low steeples."[221] The Baptist Church was located on River Street, for the convenience of wealthy members who, in the original settlement of the town, chose homesteads along the riverfront because the region was well watered and fertile, and the scenery was picturesque. The Presbyterian Church was situated 200 yards from the river, in the extreme southeastern limits of the city, at the edge of a dense forest, which flowed gently toward an old mill near the river. The old Methodist Church was also situated on the south side of town. In these three wooden churches, "the good people met and worshiped for 30 years in the simplicity of the faith as handed down from the fathers, the old gray-haired ministers preaching a gospel of repentance, faith, and regeneration". At that time, the whites and blacks worshiped in the same church buildings, the whites in the forenoon and night, and the blacks at 3:00 p.m. every Sunday.[222] At the Methodist Church it was not an uncommon sight to see the gallery full of servants.

Although the early Youngs in America had been Presbyterians, Edward and William had become Methodists, probably under the influence of their wives, who were strongly Methodist. The Edward Young family was a working, contributing, influential force in the Eufaula Methodist congregation for many years.

During this time, the Youngs were living on North Randolph Street, about 200 yards from Broad, in a comfortable "old style" single story five-room residence, with a double kitchen. They had for neighbors Tom Flournoy, L. C. Harrison, Dr. W. H. Thornton, Alexander McDonald, Mrs. Billing, and others.[223]

On March 26, 1846, Ann and Edward's fifth child, a girl, was born. She was named Ada Louise, and was baptized by Thomas P. C. Scales. Two years later came the sixth child, also a girl, who was named Helen Augusta Young (sometimes called "Ollie"). She was also baptized by Thomas P. C. Scales.

In 1848, when Will Young was 13 years old, and his brother Henry was 11, they made the acquaintance of the aforementioned Tom Jackson, with whom they would share many adventures. Tom, who usually called Will Young, "Bill," describes their first meeting:

> "We met by chance. During the year 1848, they were attending the Eufaula high school, taught by Rev. W. J. Mear. We met one sultry August afternoon at Stepney's ginger-pop shop near the *Shield* office, where we exchanged introductory civilities in a mutual 'set up' to the cooling draught. 'Ginger Pop' is a lost art. It has been superceded by the modern soda fountains…Its effervescing properties were powerful—and the purchaser could hit the bull's eye with the cork at a distance of ten feet…This pop shop was the exact locality where I met and formed the acquaintance of Bill and Henry Young…From that moment until their dying day, Bill, Henry, and Tom were friends of the truest type—inseparable, indivisible. To their influence I was indebted for a two years' residence in the family—the most delightful period of my boyhood history."[224]

The Young's third son (and seventh child) was born at 7 o'clock P. M. on August 14, 1849. He was named Edward Billups Young, and baptized by Thomas P. C. Scales. Named for his father, the reason for "Billups" is not certain. In another example of sisters marrying brothers, Ann's older sister, Susanna Millicent Beall, had married "John Billups of Walton County, Georgia,"[225] while another of Ann's older sisters, Elizabeth Rebecca Beall, had married his brother,[226] "Robert Billups of Alabama" in 1831.[227] Elizabeth and Robert Billups resided in Alabama for 20 years and moved to Texas in 1852.[228] Perhaps Ann wished to honor one or both of these brothers-in-law in naming her third son. Because his initials were the same as his father's, in later life the younger Edward was often referred to as Edward B. Young, Jr. In the family, he was called "Eddie" as a child, and later, "Ed".

When Tom Jackson lived with the Youngs, it was not the only time that Ann and Edward provided a young person with a place to live in their home. James Daniel, age 14, was residing with them in 1850, and was referred to as a "clerk".[229]

Tom Jackson viewed the Youngs as a family "who, by persistent and unwavering kindness through a series of years, made an impression on my life and character which time could not efface."[230] He describes the Young's dealings toward others in this way:

> "I was poor and obscure; the Youngs were wealthy, … prominent. At the same time they were unostentatious, Christian people, who were kind and considerate to everybody deserving of friendly recognition."[231]

Writing many years later, Tom gives this perspective of Edward himself:

"Edward B. Young settled in Irwinton…when quite a young man and grew up with the town. He was a natural born business man—prompt and regular as the town clock; industrious, energetic, methodical, systematic…Everything he touched in a business sense seemed to prosper, yea…was turned into gold…. Physically he was a perfect model of manhood, of the Lee and Washington pattern; possessed an equitable temper and somewhat jovial proclivities. He was not worried by the ordinary trifles which vex and fret humanity and consequently enjoyed the best of health throughout a long life."

We know that Ann had a deep religious faith. Her sister, Elizabeth Billups, writes that, "She was so beautiful as well as good. I have gazed in her face and thought how lovely and innocent she was. In her girlhood she gave her heart to God."[232] Tom Jackson confirms Ann's Christian faith and goodness, but tells of other endearing aspects of her personality. Tom paints an appealing picture of an engaging woman:

"Mrs. E. B. Young, Sr. didn't profess sanctification, but according to my way of thinking, she was as near perfection as any human being can possibly become. She was a true wife, a model mother, a good neighbor, a devout, simple hearted Christian. In physique 'low and chunkey;' in intellect clear and scintillating; in temperament, as bright, genial and hopeful as the spring sunshine and martingale of old time southern early birds….As a conversationalist she held her own with the most gifted people of the South, and during extra emergencies she was delegated to do the talking for the whole family, and it is but just to say she was equal to any intellectual emergency. I have often envied the cheerful and happy nature of this good woman. No human creature ever felt a keener sense of the humorous phases of life, and I have never known a woman who so greatly enjoyed the pleasures of laughter…."

Probably the quality of Ann that most attracted Tom, who had no parents, was that, "This good woman treated me as she did her own boys (Will and Henry)", even to the point that, "When I needed a reprimand she administered it in pellucid vigorous English, not easily misunderstood."[233] As an example of his receiving a good "raking over the coals" from her, Tom relates this expedition with the Young children to see the circus animals:

"In the spring of '52 Robinson & Eldred's combined circus and menagerie gave a performance at Eufaula. Of course the children were crazy to see the show. Mrs. Young had four sweet and lovely daughters—Anna, Mollie, Ada, Ellen, and a little boy, Eddie. At dinner time that day the children excitedly gathered around me and asked me to beg their mother to let them go and see 'the big elephant, the little monkey and hear the band'. The Methodist

Church was then very strict and did not allow members to attend balls, circuses or theatres on the pain and penalty of expulsion. I made an earnest and eloquent appeal in behalf of the little innocents which had the desired effect. Although 45 years have elapsed since that day I can repeat her exact words: 'Tom, (everybody, children and all called me Tom in those days) take the children down to the tent; let them walk through the enclosure and see all the animals from the big elephant to the little monkey. When the band strikes up and the horses rush in, bring the children out and send them home immediately. Do you understand?'

'Yes'm' said I, submissively.

The best of my life has been devoted to the happiness and welfare of children, but I have no recollection of ever having seen a happier little squad than that of which I was captain for a couple of hours on that joyous circus occasion.

I carried them in, trotted them round, explained the nativities, proclivities and ferocious tendencies of the inhabitants of the several cages, dwelling with much show of wisdom upon the monster with two tails (the elephant) and the ancestral progenitor of man who swingeth by the ('narrative') from the high cocoa-nut bough.

The band struck up a lively air. I called the little brood into a bunch and said, 'Less go.'

"Oh, Tom, please let us stay one more minit and see the hosses,' sang out the oldest girl, and all the children joined in the chorus.

In point of fact, I was as anxious to stay as any of them, but knowing the lady's firmness I was afraid to disobey orders.

But I let the children stay 'a minit longer and see the hosses' in the grand entree and the gaily dressed riders.

The band played livelier than ever, and then the children begged to stay just one minute longer to see the ringmaster thresh out the clown with his long whip.

The children kept on begging for 'one more minit' and I kept on yielding; the longer we stayed the happier we all got, until finally discovered that the 'show was closed and the monkey dead'.

My disrespect for orders brought on me a lecture I have never forgotten; I was sorry I saw the elephant, but I do not think those little ones ever spent a happier afternoon than the one spent with me forty four yours ago, when we went out to inspect the 'animals in Robinson & Eldred's Circus."[234]

**Edward Brown Young, from portrait
at Fendall Hall**

**Ann Fendall Beall Young, from
portrait at Fendall Hall**

11
Trouble at the Irwinton Bridge

"[Toll revenues reflect] the importance of securing the bridge in a pecuniary way as well as its great commercial advantage to the town."

Eufaula City Council

The 1837 Act of the Georgia Legislature chartering Edward's Irwinton Bridge Company required the bridge to be commenced within one year and completed within three years. The owners of the property upon which the Georgia abutment was to be built were James and Samuel Harrison and others. Since 1835, the Harrisons (or their predecessors) had owned the land along the Georgia side of the river for about a mile on either side of the proposed bridge site, and were operating a ferry across the river from a point near the site. When Edward was unable to reach agreement with the Harrisons as to the value to be paid for the Georgia abutment site, the Irwinton Bridge Company appointed an appraiser as provided by the act. The Harrisons refused to appoint an appraiser, so upon the petition of the Bridge Company, the Inferior Court of Randolph County, Georgia appointed the required two additional appraisers. The three appraisers rendered a report setting the value at $500. This report and proceedings should have then been recorded with the Inferior Court of Randolph County, Georgia. But the court clerk made the mistake of recording the papers with the *Inferior Court Sitting As a Court of Ordinary,* which was a court composed of the same personnel, but having different jurisdiction. [235] This technical mistake was to have unfortunate and far-reaching repercussions, as we will see.

When the Bridge Company tendered the $500 to the Harrisons, they refused to accept it. They wanted much more. Construction on the bridge commenced anyway, and the Harrisons made no effort to stop it. The bridge was completed on January 1, 1840, and began operations.[236] Soon thereafter, the Harrisons filed suit to eject the Company from their land, alleging that, because of the clerk's mistake, the Company had not complied with the provisions of the act of the Georgia Legislature. But the Irwinton Bridge Company's difficulties were not to be limited to lawsuits. While this litigation was proceeding, an act of nature intervened, with disastrous consequences.

The Columbus newspapers reported that on Tuesday of the week previous to March 11, 1841, rain began falling in torrents and continued with little abatement for forty-eight hours.[237] On Wednesday, the Chattahoochee began to rise rapidly. The town of Columbus appeared as if built on a lake; the falls and rapids on the river disappeared. Whole trunks of trees with their entire root systems were carried away by the current. On Thursday, March 11, at daybreak, one end of Columbus' bridge across the Chattahoochee built by Mr. Godwin dropped off of its pier and the bridge floated away. It was reported that "never was there a more majestic sight than the departure of that noble bridge on its remarkable voyage." [238]

When the surge of water and floating debris reached Irwinton, forty-three miles downriver, it was inevitable that Edward's bridge would be damaged, or worse. Although there is a Young family tradition that the bridge "washed away," other evidence suggests that it was severely damaged but with repairs could be made usable.[239] The disaster to this $20,000 asset made such a permanent imprint upon the folklore of the Young family that five generations later, the tale was still being told that the financial loss caused Edward Young's hair to turn white overnight.[240] Family tradition as well as the Columbus papers refer to this flood as the "Harrison Freshet."[241] It has been assumed that this name probably arose from the election to the presidency the previous November of the Whig candidate, William Henry Harrison, who took office on March 4, 1841, two weeks before the Chattahoochee flooded. However, it is also possible that the name referred to the bitter legal fight that was being waged against the Irwinton Bridge by James and Samuel Harrison.

The destruction or severe damaging of the bridge (which undoubtedly ended the toll revenues) threw the affairs of the Irwinton Bridge Company into disarray. The Company became insolvent, and could not pay its debts. By 1844, we find Edward Young buying out the interests of the other stockholders. In a series of transactions commencing in May 1844, Edward acquired the interests of the other investors and agreed to indemnify them against the debts of the corporation. In exchange for paying its debts, the Company on May 27, 1844 assigned to Edward Young the bridge and the property upon which it was located.[242] But Edward did not allow himself to be saddled with the entire debt. The stockholders were required to at least partially repay Edward for these debts by giving him their promissory notes,[243] in varying amounts, secured by mortgages on Eufaula lots.[j] On April 8, 1845, the sheriff levied execution on a $2,131 judgment against the Irwinton Bridge Company by publicly auctioning the property upon which its Alabama abutment was built. Edward Young bid in the property, thus satisfying the company's debt and further confirming his ownership of the property.[244]

Edward was still faced with the Harrison claims, which he regarded as "vexatious and harassing." In 1847, the bridge, or what was left of it, "fell in," and the Harrisons resumed the operation of their ferry.[245] Later that year, Edward brought his own suit against them,[246] alleging that the Bridge Company had tried in good faith to comply with the legislative act but was thwarted by the Harrisons, who refused to appoint an appraiser and thereafter refused to accept payment of the appraisal amount; that the appraisal report for $500 had been filed with the wrong court merely by clerical mistake; that the Harrisons had allowed the Company to expend great sums building the bridge without making any effort to stop it; that the bridge had now "fallen in"; that he, Edward Young had now purchased the bridge from the Company; that the bridge was "a great public convenience"; that he "was desirous of rebuilding it;" and asking the judge to enjoin further litigation by the Harrisons."

As the litigation wore on, Edward apparently concluded he was not in a position to finance the rebuilding of the bridge. The Irwinton Bridge Bank was also having difficulties at this time which would lead to its closure, and Edward admitted in the litigation that all of these circumstances had left him in "embarrassed circumstances," at least for the moment.[247] However, Eufaula was growing into a regional trade center; the town fathers recognized the

---

[j] We note that one of these mortgages, from John L. Hunter, is witnessed by Edward's oldest brother, James Young, on May 16, 1844, which was three months before James' death on August 14, 1844 at the age of 44.

value of the bridge to the town's economic success and wished to see it rebuilt. Accordingly, on May 10, 1847, the town council authorized a contract for its purchase, under which Edward and Ann agreed to convey to the town council "the lands on which the eastern and western abutments of the old bridge rested, together with all the materials out of which said bridge was built, and also the tollhouse belonging to the same."[248] The purchase price was to be $4000, payable not in cash but in "stock in the bridge which is hereafter to be built across the said River at the same place formerly occupied by the old bridge," to be "reckoned according to the original cost of the said new bridge." Young was to receive "his share of the profits of said new bridge whenever any shall accrue..." In recognition of the pending Harrison claims for title and damages, it was agreed that if the court determined that Edward and the city did not have good title, Edward would not receive the $4000 in stock. If damages were awarded to the Harrisons (which they probably would be, since the Harrisons had not yet accepted any payment for the value of their land) Edward would be responsible for payment of up to $4000, while any damages above that amount would be paid by the town of Eufaula.[249] The contract was signed by Edward and Ann, and on behalf of the town by its "Intendant" (Mayor), John A. Calhoun[k] and by the council: John Hart, Charles W. Snow, and Thomas G. Barnet.

It is unlikely that either of the parties to this agreement foresaw the long and tortuous route that the pending dispute would take, or the difficulties that would be encountered along the way. In fact, the litigation would grind slowly on for a total of sixteen years (1841-1857), and would involve a fight in the Georgia Legislature and at least five appeals to the Georgia Supreme Court. Eufaula historians have sometimes misinterpreted the bridge litigation. It certainly was not a suit by Young against the council to collect a share of the profits. Young and the council had the same interests and were closely allied throughout the dispute. Indeed, after the sale to the city, Young continued to devote time and expense to bridge business and to assisting in the litigation, for which the council routinely granted him reimbursement.[250]

Soon after the city's purchase of the bridge, the Georgia Supreme Court made its first ruling in the case. It rejected the Harrisons' contention that the legislative act was an unconstitutional taking of their private property. But in the maddening way that nineteenth century courts had of exalting procedural form over substance, the court held that the clerks' mistake in recording the appraisal procedure in the wrong court file, thereby providing an excuse for the Harrisons to refuse payment, invalidated the Bridge Company's taking of the property. However, because the Company had acted in good faith to attempt to comply with the law, the Court held that it should be given a reasonable time to comply with the statute, after which the Harrisons would still have their claim for their "damages," and sent the case back to the lower court for these actions.[251] In an effort to comply with this mandate, Edward called on the Harrisons to designate appraisers, which they again refused to do, so he again

---

[k] Intendant John A. Calhoun was the nephew of the famous South Carolina Senator, former Vice-President, and "Great Nullifier," John C. Calhoun. Even while he was entering into the contract with Edward and Ann, Intendant Calhoun was working energetically among Barbour Countians to build support for his uncle's "Southern Rights" faction which advocated early secession. (Mayer, Henry, " 'A Leaven of Disunion', The Growth of the Secessionist Faction in Alabama," *The Alabama Historical Quarterly*, April 1969, Vol XXII, No. 2, p. 104,105)

petitioned the Inferior Court to appoint appraisers, which it now refused to do based on vague technical grounds.

Meanwhile, the city council, as the new bridge owner, moved expeditiously to contract with Eufaula master builder, George W. Whipple to rebuild the structure "on the old site ... to be connected with that portion of the old bridge now standing," for $3,800, with the city to furnish all materials.[252] (Whipple would later build the Union Female College when Edward was president of its board of trustees, and was probably also the builder of Fendall Hall in 1857-59.) To finance the work, a loan of $3000 at 8% was negotiated with Eufaulian, Abner McGhee, guaranteed by the leading businessmen of the community, including E. B. Young & Company, John A. Calhoun, John McNab, L. C. Harrison, John Hart, John N. Copeland, John Gill Shorter, Martin & Couric, Charles W. Snow, and others.

The Irwinton Bridge in a time of flooding. Damage and/or dismantling can be seen. Recognizing the bridge's value in toll revenues and commercial access to southwest Georgia, the Irwinton City Council bought the bridge from Edward, restored it, and operated it for decades.

Next, the Harrisons attempted to use the political arena to improve their litigating posture. In December 1847 they succeeded in inducing the Georgia Legislature to pass two acts: the first act directed the governor to institute legal proceeding to forfeit the charter granted to the Irwinton Bridge Company by the 1837 act. The second act, passed the next day, repealed the 1837 act incorporating the company. Thereafter, in 1848, the Harrisons sued again to enjoin the rebuilding of the bridge by the city, this time including Edward, Intendant Calhoun, and city council of Eufaula as defendants. The council voted to proceed to complete the construction anyway, on the grounds that the bridge was already partially rebuilt; that materials had been ordered and were at hand, the benefit of which would be lost if the bridge were not completed; and that completion of the bridge would not further damage the Harrisons in any way.[253] In this suit, the Harrisons relied on the same grounds as before, and on the additional grounds that the bridge interfered with the operation of their ferry (which they claimed was a very profitable venture), and that the authorizing act had been repealed by the Legislature. When these issues reached the Georgia Supreme Court in January 1849, the Harrisons' contentions were again rejected. The court brushed aside the Georgia Legislature's attempt to withdraw rights previously granted and relied on by Young, remarking that the legislation bore evidence of "haste and inconsideration:" "After having directed the governor to...forfeit the charter, why the very next day attempt to forestall these proceedings by declaring the charter already forfeited?" The Supreme Court then reiterated its earlier ruling that Edward Young had acted in good faith in attempting to comply with the 1837 act, and that he must be allowed to complete the acquisition by the appointment of appraisers to determine the Harrisons' damages, and the case was returned to the lower court for these purposes. However, to protect the rights of all parties pending this further proceeding, the Supreme Court now directed the judge below to appoint a receiver to take possession of the bridge, complete the repairs, open it for public use, and after deducting costs, hold the toll money until the parties' rights were determined. [254]

To represent Edward and the city in these proceedings, Edward had recommended the employment of his Georgia attorney, Hines Holt, which the council authorized at its meeting of October 6, 1848. Holt was given a very unusual contingent fee contract. If the Harrisons received an award of damages not exceeding $1,000, the lawyer's fee would be $1000; for damages not exceeding $2,000, a fee of $750; for damages not exceeding $3000, a fee of $500; for damages over $4,000, no fee at all.

At the town council meeting of November 22, 1848, Intendant John A. Calhoun announced his resignation from the council because of his plans to move from the state. The council immediately elected Edward B. Young to fill the vacancy, and "Mr. Godwin was requested to wait upon him and notify him of his election." Edward's first meeting as a councilman was December 11, 1848, his fellow council members being McNab, Godwin, Barnet, and Snow. John McNab was elected to succeed Calhoun as Intendant.

At a special meeting on Dec 17, Edward and the council adopted a requirement for the cleaning of the town's lots, cellars, allies and privies. The minutes of this meeting appear in Edward's own handwriting, he having been asked to serve as acting clerk. Edward's tenure on the council was not lengthy. The term he was completing for Calhoun expired February 19,

1849, and Edward went off the council.[255] It does not appear that he ever accepted political office again.

As receiver of the bridge during its reconstruction, the Georgia Court appointed one Delaware Morris. For a time, the council enjoyed an acceptable working relationship with him. He appears to have permitted the council to complete the rebuilding of the bridge and thereafter manage its operation, with Morris holding the toll proceeds. With the joint consent of E. B. Young and James Harrison, Morris Generally approved the council's recommendations, such as approving their requests to make payments on the Abner McGhee note of $3000; to contract with the Oglethorpe Stagecoach Line for its coaches to cross the bridge for $200 per year; to the raise the salary of bridge keeper Pournell to $400 per year; and to pay council drafts for purchases of bridge materials.[256]

However, the council later received unexpected notification from Morris that he had decided to "take management of the bridge into his own hands," requesting the Council to dismiss the hands employed by them on the bridge, and stating that he will not pay any more bills drawn by the council. The council protested that this action was unprovoked by anything they had done, that it is unauthorized as well as "dangerous to the stability of the bridge," (especially the eastern abutment which needed repairs), and that they would hold Morris "officially and personally responsible for any and all injury to said bridge which may proceed from his sudden determination."[257] Months later, the Intendant John McNab and Councilman John Hart patched up the relationship with an arrangement by which Morris agreed to pay for any repairs jointly approved by a committee of two "mechanics and judges of the repairs necessary," one appointed by the council (George Whipple), and one appointed by Morris (Jacob Smith).[258] However, Morris continued to sometimes delay ordering materials and other actions desired by the council.[259] Eventually when it came time to build new piers on the Alabama side, Delaware Morris himself submitted a bid to do this work, and the council agreed to contract with him.[260] Later it also contracted with him to build another pier on the Georgia side,[261] and still later contracted with him to build two additional brick piers on the Alabama side.[262] The Bridge Receiver derived substantial amounts of money from his work for the council. While this may have presented an ethical issue, apparently no one objected, and it solved the council's problem of cooperation from Mr. Morris.

Meanwhile, the litigation ground inexorably toward an end. The case went to the Supreme court of Georgia at least three more times,[263] these decisions dealing with technical procedures, or with the standards to be applied in setting the value of the Harrisons' land and their damages. The Harrisons were able to appeal the appraisers' award to a jury trial, and the jury was allowed to hear evidence of the toll profits being enjoyed by the town of Eufaula, and of the ferry profits allegedly lost by the Harrisons. In February 1857 the Georgia Supreme Court approved a jury verdict to the extent of $12,000, and the protracted litigation finally came to an end.[264]

Although they felt some disappointment over the unexpectedly generous damage award, the council was nonetheless relieved to have behind them "the lawsuit so long pending," and quickly set about raising the funds to pay off the judgment promptly.[265]

Because the council's clear title to the disputed property had been upheld, Edward presumably received the $4,000 of stock in the bridge provided by his contract with the council (with the accompanying right to participate in any profits from the bridge). But he would have also been required to pay the first $4,000 of the monetary award. Twenty-five Eufaula citizens stepped forward to lend the council the remaining funds necessary to pay off the judgment and be rid of the Harrisons. The list of lenders is a roll call of Eufaula's pioneer business leaders: Edward B. Young, William H. Thornton, James G. L. Martin, John McNab, Charles M. Couric, Green Beauchamp, A. H. Beauchamp, John Colby, Jacob Ramser, Thomas Cargile, George W. Whipple, Colin Gardner, Lafayette Stow, E. C. Bullock, L.L. Cato, John Gill Shorter, William A. McKenzie, James L. Pugh, B. F. Treadwell, Eli S. Shorter, and others. To secure the loan, the Harrisons' judgment was assigned to the lenders, as well as a pledge of the bridge itself and its toll revenues.[266]

Notwithstanding the litigation and the expense of rebuilding and maintenance, the Eufaula city council considered its acquisition of Edward Young's bridge to be a good civic investment, and viewed the Irwinton Bridge as an important asset to the town. At one meeting when necessary expenditures were authorized, the minutes recite that, despite the cost, "the committee does direct attention to the fact that the bridge toll up to the first of January last amounts to over $14,000, which shows the importance of securing the bridge in a pecuniary way as well as its great commercial advantage to the town."[267] The asset would be successfully operated by the town as a toll bridge for many years to come.

12
Will Young, Chattahoochee Steamboat Captain

"Bill was…a large hearted noble boy, …wild and extravagant"
Tom Jackson

When the oldest of Ann and Edward Young's sons, Will, was about 17 years of age, Edward required him to make a decision about preparing for a "life occupation". Tom Jackson (who usually called him "Bill") reports that Will "was not particularly crazy on book larnin."[268] Will's interest was in mechanical engineering. "Bill hankered after the knowledge that led to the manufacture of railroad engines." Railroad engines were comparatively new in the South at this time, and "this class of mechanics was highly paid." In accordance with his son's inclinations, Edward helped to arrange a mechanical apprenticeship for Will in New York, where Edward still had family and business contacts. Will actually served his apprenticeship in several places: in Newburgh and Mattawan, New York; and in Patterson, Newark, and Rahway, New Jersey.[269] Before he had reached the age of 21, Will had developed the expertise to construct "any kind of engine."

Will's "genial, sunshiny nature won him friends wherever he went." His close friend, Tom Jackson, envied Will's ability to adapt and enjoy life: "What a happy faculty one must have to accommodate himself to time, place and circumstances. Bill would have lived, prospered, and made friends where I would have starved. . . Like his venerated mother, he took a happy, cheerful view of life, and extracted all possible sunshine from surrounding darkness".[270] But even Tom acknowledges a youthful independent streak that at some point apparently caused consternation within the family:

> "Bill was indeed a large hearted noble boy, not exactly a 'black sheep' but a little too wild and extravagant to receive a full share of love and respect from the most sedate and steady-going members of the family. I am sure a merciful creator will condone the foibles of these big hearted unfortunates, who frequently deviate from the straight path of rectitude. . . .Good hearts and good acts are of infinitely more value than … sanctified pretensions…"[271]

There are probably some interesting escapades behind these remarks, which we can never know about.

Will's journey home to Alabama following the completion of his New Jersey apprenticeship included traveling from Columbus to Eufaula by steamboat. At that time Will was involved in an accident which was potentially fatal, but from which he walked away unscathed. Tom Jackson relates the event in his own way:

> "Between Columbus and Eufaula he encountered perils by water. The boiler of the boat on which he was a passenger 'collapsed a flue' and Bill was blown sky high, more or less. He was saved from a watery

grave by the brave colored steward of the boat, who was likewise instrumental in saving three or four other passengers. I have forgotten the brave darkey's name, but his heroic conduct as a rescuer was highly praised and liberally rewarded. Bill lost his trunk and all personal effects, and when he found himself lying out on the river bank to dry, he said he felt right smartly 'collapsed' individually and collectively. It is hard to keep a good man down. So Bill rallied and struck for home through the woods on 'Shanks' mare.' "[272]

In spite of this narrow escape, Will's first employment was that of captain and engineer of a Chattahoochee steamboat, a profession consistent with his adventurous character, which he would follow for two years in the early 1850's.[273] His job was dangerous, but crucially important. It was the steamboat that originally made possible the thriving cotton economy of the Chattahoochee-Apalachicola River valley, and thus the prosperous business that had comfortably supported the Young family. By 1850, Eufaula was receiving and then shipping to Apalachicola 20,000 bales of cotton annually, virtually all of it shipped on steamboats.[274] The first steamboat to navigate from the sea to Columbus was the *Fannie*, and she arrived on January 26, 1828, the year in which Columbus was founded.[275] Others that followed included *Stubenville, Virginia, The Georgian, The Plaquemine, The Andy Jackson,* and *The Siren*.[276] In fact, on *The Siren*, we find E & W Young shipping 20 barrels of supplies, in 1841, for the account of John Horry Dent, for freight cost of 50 cents per barrel, or $10.00 total; with more supplies for J.H. Dent arriving in Eufaula on *The Irwinton*.[277] During the 1830's 51 different ships were making the journey, some carrying up to eighteen hundred bales of cotton and fifty passengers; ultimately there came to be a colorful pageant of over two hundred ships plying the Chattahoochee.[278]

The sternwheeler steamboat, "City of Eufaula," built about 1845.

But each trip was a gamble of life and property. The kind of explosion that threw Will Young "sky high, more or less," because too much pressure was put on thin-walled boilers, was quite common. Cotton is highly combustible, and fires burned ships to the water's edge. Heavy rains or drought led to rapid, accident-causing changes in the river's depth. The wrecks of sunken ships whose hulls had been torn open by rocks or sunken trees were serious hazards. To serve as captain or engineer of such vessels required "swaggering bravado," which Will Young undoubtedly possessed in ample quantity. Historian Mark Fretwell describes the hazards and the rewards:

"The noisy ships at one moment shattered the quiet with their whistles and bells and then around the next bend met an ignominious end, crushed and half sunken against shoals of rock which seemed to have reached up from the river bed to snare them. The rugged masters steered their vessels along the twisting channel with a forthright determination, either the voyage was completed or there was another wreck to mark the passage. The gamble was worth the risk. Thousands of bales of cotton were shipped down the river to be reloaded at Apalachicola for shipment to mills in New England or in the British Isles."[279]

Happily, Will safely survived his two-year career as a steamboat captain and engineer, and he moved on to a less hazardous enterprise. But, although water transportation would continue to have a role for some time to come, even as Will was steering his steamboat through the shoals, the railroad tracks connecting Columbus to the sea at Savannah were under construction, thereby beginning the end of the steamboat era in the Chattahoochee valley.

13
The Youngs and Slavery;
Eufaula and The Secession Movement of 1850

"...I have this day mortgaged to the said *Edward B. Young one Negro*
woman named Charlotte about 36 years of age..."
From a Chattel Mortgage received by Edward Young

"They are warm hearted true people."
Ann Fendall Beall Young writing to Anna

The era we are discussing was one in which the status of black people (or most of them) was legally that of personal property, or "chattels", a legal term embracing all property other than land. Following the transplant of slavery from the Spanish West Indies to the British colonies in the seventeenth century, there were slaves in all the colonies, although more in the South, because its climate and soil favored the agricultural economy in which slavery worked best. Moral debate on the issue of slavery had emerged by the time of the Constitutional Convention of 1787, which recognized the legality of the institution, but postponed the issue by prohibiting any laws limiting the importation of slaves for a period of 20 years.

In 1819, when Edward Young was a teenaged boy in New York, the same year Alabama had been admitted as the 21st state, the first serious controversy over the slave question arose. The territory of Missouri had been carved from the Louisiana Purchase, and there were pending proposals to admit it to the Union as a slave state. A heated discussion arose in Congress that continued for a year and aroused excitement throughout the country, because the debate had several important implications for the future. Most importantly, there were then eleven slave states and eleven free states. At this time, the population of the North was already outstripping that of the South, so the South recognized that if slavery was to continue, it could not permit the North to achieve permanent majority control of the Senate. This central problem would thereafter arise, with increasing intensity, each time new states were admitted, and on each occasion, thoughtful leaders were able to resolve the impasse through a series of grand compromises. In 1820, the Missouri Compromise resolved that year's crisis in this manner: Maine had separated from Massachusetts and was admitted to the Union as a free state: Missouri was admitted as a slave state; and it was provided that thereafter, slavery would be excluded from all remaining lands of the Louisiana Purchase lying north of the latitude of 36 degrees 30 minutes. The settlement resulted in a temporary lull in the agitation over slavery, but the latter provision laid the groundwork for bitter controversy in the future.

Edward Young might have had little familiarity with the South's "peculiar institution" when he left New York in 1825, but when he arrived in Twiggs County, Georgia, he would have quickly become familiar with slavery. In 1830, his prosperous friend and future brother-in-law, Robert A. Beall, Jr., owned 12 slaves.[280] When Ann and Edward later moved to Alabama, Edward, because he was not a cotton planter, had no need to incur the expense connected with owning large numbers of slaves. However, the Youngs would have owned some slaves for use as household servants. In 1840, the Youngs had five slaves: two females between ten and twenty years of age; one male of that age; and two children under ten.[281] In 1860, the Youngs owned nine slaves: four males and five females.[282] In business transactions, Edward also accepted mortgages of slaves as security for loans or credit. Recorded in the Barbour County deed records we find an example of such a "chattel mortgage," executed on June 16, 1845:

"I, John M. Moore, of Barbour County, state of Alabama, for and in consideration that I am indebted by three notes…for the sum of $3000…and for the purpose of securing payment of the said notes…I have this day mortgaged to the said Edward B. Young one Negro woman named Charlotte about 36 years of age, one Negro woman named Milly about 18 years of age, and her child one Negro girl named Caroline about 14 years of age, and one Negro by name Moses boy about 10 years of age. I do hereby sell transfer and convey to the said Edward B. Young, to him and his heirs and assigns in fee simple and warrant and defend the above described Negroes, upon the condition, however, that if I shall pay to the said Edward B. Young the foregoing notes set forth in this mortgage, then this to be void or else to remain in full force and effect."[283]

This 1845 Barbour County document is witnessed by Edward's brother, William, who was living in Apalachicola at that time, suggesting that William was continuing his practice of making periodic visits to the Eufaula Youngs.

It was also common for owners of slaves to hire them out for pay, which was particularly profitable for the owner of a slave skilled in a craft. John Horry Dent owned two slaves, Alfred and "Hard Times", who were skilled carpenters, and a slave named John, who was a skilled blacksmith, all of whom Dent hired out. He had inherited Hard Times from his mother upon her death in 1856. During 1857, Edward Young frequently hired Hard Times, probably to do carpentry on the new Young home later called "Fendall Hall," which was under construction at about this time. Dent's journal for January, 1857 notes, "Hard Times hired to E. B. Young at $25 per month".[284] The going rate for hiring Hard Times seems to have fluctuated. On July 12, 1857 he was "sent to Mr. Young to work by the month at $20 per month."[285] Dent collected seventy to eighty five percent of the slaves' pay and they kept the rest. These skilled slaves were allowed some privileges in the system. Dent permitted them to locate their own employment, complete it, drift back home in their own good time, and then settle accounts with him.[286]

Insight into Edward and Ann's treatment of their slaves is provided by an episode related by Tom Jackson:

"…I will mention a case in point that came under my personal observation…Uncle Amos was one of the good old time darkies whose name deserves mention and perpetuation. He had grown old in the family service and for several years had nothing to do but sit in the kitchen, smoke his pipe, sing and pray, and daily devote the passing hours to the amusement of the children (black and white) in the back yard.

One morning in glorious springtime…when I went home for breakfast I was notified of a sorrowful event in the family. Anna, age 12, and Mollie, aged 10, rushed into the dining room and with tearful eyes and sad hearts startled me with the doleful tidings: "Oh, Tom, Uncle Amos died last night, and we're all feeling very sad this morning!" I tried to comfort then by saying—'The old must die; the young may die'. They refused to be comforted, and they, with the other children of the household, gave vent to sincere demonstrations of grief. The body of Uncle Amos lay in state that day, and the neighbors, both white and black, from the adjoining blocks called to view the remains of the good, faithful old servant. Next morning at nine o'clock we buried the old man in a corner of the old cemetery allotted to colored people. He was put away in good style with the usual Christian ceremonials. Every member of the family, white and black, young and old, attended the funeral; also quite a number of persons from the surrounding neighborhood. That is the way good masters looked after the welfare of faithful servants…"

But other views of slavery were being voiced in New England with increasing stridency. Eufaula, Alabama actively entered the fray when Congress acted upon the admission of California and the other territories won in the 1848 war with Mexico. In the years leading up to this debate, sectional feelings had intensified. The radical New England abolitionist movement had emerged, led by the Rev. William Lloyd Garrison, who was so extreme that he publicly burned the United States constitution because it recognized and permitted slavery, condemning it as a "covenant with death and an agreement with hell." These abolitionists distributed aggressive pamphlets portraying Southern slaveholders in the most extreme possible terms, as brutal tyrants guilty of the most cruel barbarities, systematically starving slaves, and worse. Of course, the South counterattacked, using equally strong language.

When the 1849 Congress assembled, sectional bitterness had reached new heights, and Henry Clay offered a set of resolutions designed to compromise the issues concerning the recently-acquired Mexican lands. Following one of the last great debates among the senatorial giants of that era, including Henry Clay, Daniel Webster, John C. Calhoun, Stephen Douglas, Jefferson Davis and others, the Compromise of 1850 was adopted, containing concessions to both sides. California was admitted as a free state, but the South was given a new fugitive slave law, allegedly to provide more effective return of slaves escaping to free states.

The Compromise of 1850 greatly antagonized the more strongly committed Southern Rights advocates, and stimulated in Alabama an early active movement toward secession. Alabama's two senators had supported the compromise. But at home, William L. Yancey attacked the Compromise as a "great fraud upon the South", which presented the clear choice of "submission or secession", and he called for "action, not talking". Yancey was the leader of a Montgomery faction that included followers of Calhoun who had South Carolina connections. Most had served in the Alabama Legislature, owned land and slaves, and had thriving law practices. "These were men who had gained prominence in the fluid Alabama of the 1830's and 40's; they now worked to preserve the social institutions of the world in which they had prospered."[287]

There emerged in Eufaula, Alabama, a group of lawyers and political leaders who rallied behind Yancey's pro-secession stance, and stepped to the forefront in providing leadership for it. This group of leaders came to be described by the newspapers as the "Eufaula Regency." These Eufaula leaders were in 1850 "Generally young, usually disaffected Whigs, whose party loyalty was outweighed by the demands of the emerging sectional crisis. They had come of political age in the late 1830's during the first excitement over abolitionism, and they were zealous 'Southrons' for the experience." Like others, they were sometimes even stronger in their defense of the south and its institutions than the older Calhoun men who led the Southern Rights movement.[288]

The Eufaula Regency included the following leaders, all friends, neighbors, or business associates of Edward Young:

John Gill Shorter, a lawyer who would become Governor of Alabama during the war.

Eli Sims Shorter, brother of John Gill, also a lawyer, and one of the editors of the Eufaula newspaper, "Spirit of the South", the press organ of the Eufaula Regency. He later served in U. S. and Confederate congresses.

John Cochran, lawyer, judge, and the Southern Rights faction's candidate for U. S. Congress in 1851. Called the "Danton of the secession movement."

Jere N. Williams, lawyer, later a Confederate officer; during Reconstruction, elected to the "dual legislature" with Hubert Dent (hereafter discussed). He was elected U. S. Congressman in the elections of 1874, in which Carpetbag rule was overthrown, defeating the black incumbent, Rapier.[289]

Jefferson Buford, a lawyer who would use his own funds to lead a group of settlers to Kansas to support its admission as a slave state.

Alpheus Baker, a lawyer and state legislator who, when war came, would serve as captain of the "Eufaula Rifles" (with Hubert Dent as his first lieutenant) and would later become a Confederate General; after the war, he would succeed Elias Kiels as Eufaula judge when carpetbag rule was overthrown.[290]

Edward Courtney Bullock, Harvard graduate, brilliant lawyer and state senator from Barbour County, whose promising career would be cut short by his death early in the war. Bullock County was named in his honor.

Lewis Lewellen Cato, lawyer and state senator; he built an elegant home on College Hill next to the Youngs, which later became the residence of Ann and Edward's youngest son, Edward Billups Young and his family.[291]

Sterling G. Cato, lawyer and brother of L. L. Cato. He went to Kansas with the pro-slavery group, was appointed a territorial judge there, and later practiced law in St. Louis, Missouri.

Henry Delamar Clayton, a lawyer of Eufaula and Clayton, who would also lead settlers to Kansas, would become a major General in the Confederate army, and after the war would become a circuit judge and later president of the University of Alabama.

James L. Pugh, lawyer and U. S. Congressman who would serve in the Confederate Senate, and after the war, in the United States Senate.

In *"Party Politics in Alabama 1850-1860,"* Historian Lewy Dorman observes:

> "The most advanced step toward secession came from the 'fire eaters' of southeast Alabama under the leadership of the "Eufaula Regency". A group of prominent business men, planters and lawyers met at Eufaula on October 22, 1850, and drew up a petition to Governor Collier in which it was stated that the crisis demanded that the legislature be called into a special session to take steps to protect Alabama from the aggressions of acts of Congress"[292]

It is interesting to note that, although this call for action was signed by 150 of the leading citizens of Eufaula, Edward B. Young's name is not among them. Perhaps he simply could not attend the meeting due to illness or other reason, or perhaps he felt that the Compromise was the better solution for the time. In any event, it became clear that the people of Alabama were not yet ready for secession in 1850. Gov. Collier did not call a special session of the Legislature, and in the elections of 1851, the secessionist candidates did not prevail at the polls. One of the most hotly contested races was for congressman for the "Montgomery District," which included Barbour County. The Eufaula Regency put forward Eufaula lawyer, John Cochran, who has been described as "the Danton of the Secession Movement."[293] Campaigning vigorously for him was William L. Yancey. Cochran was opposed by James Abercrombie, said to be one of the wealthiest men in south Alabama, who favored the more conciliatory position of reluctant acceptance of the 1850 Compromise. Observers said this race produced the finest display of oratory in Alabama political history. Abercrombie won by a comfortable margin. The area was enjoying too much prosperity to be interested in secession at this time. The press organ of the Eufaula Regency, *Spirit of the South*, lamented this:

> "The present apparent prosperity of the South is one of the causes of whatever there may be of reluctance among her people to advocate resistance, because there is plenty to live on, because we are out of debt, and cotton brings a good price, many are in so good a humor and so well satisfied with themselves and things around them as to shut their eyes to the future in the consoling reflection that the future cannot hurt them."[294]

Historian Lewy Dorman gives this analysis:

"It was a victory for planter conservatism, represented by Abercrombie, who was a large planter, against the aggressive lawyer group, represented by Cochran, who was a lawyer of Eufaula. There could be no doubt of the desire of the people of this district, the home of Yancey and the other important political leaders of Montgomery and Eufaula, to accept the compromise position."[295]

The Eufaula Regency would continue to be "the most consistent secessionists in the State," until it occurred, but the Compromise of 1850 had resulted in the postponement of secession for ten years. These would be ten happy and productive years for the Young family.

14
The Youngs At The 1853 New York World Fair

"Bill trotted the Southern investigators through...our four weeks stay in the big city. He showed us many of the hidden secrets..."

Tom Jackson

In 1853, Edward and his brother William (still living in Apalachicola, but soon to move to Columbus) decided to take their families to the "New York Crystal Palace Exhibition". It was not unusual for Edward to travel to New York. Most southern merchants visited the eastern markets twice a year."[296] However, for the two families to travel to New York to see the first world's fair ever held in the United States was high adventure.

Also called The Exhibition of the Industries of All Nations, the exposition was promoted by a group of New York businessmen including Horace Greeley. It was an effort to recreate, and surpass, the British Crystal Palace exhibition of 1851. The fair was located on thirteen acres of Reservoir Square, (which today is the site of Bryant Park, behind the New York Public Library).[297] The fair's main feature, modeled on the London structure, was a glass and iron, octagonal building with "Greek cross superstructure abutting a round dome at the center and tall minarets at the outer angles."[298] Erected by a private group, the Association for the Exhibition of the Industries of All Nations, it held 4854 exhibits from 23 nations. A companion building was the 350-foot high Latting Building, one block north, built of wood and iron. The fair did not live up to all of its promoters' expectations, but it gave impetus to U. S. manufacturing by stimulating competition with foreign producers.[299]

The Youngs and their relations making the excursion to New York were:[300]
Ann and Edward, and their two oldest sons, Will and Henry. Will had only recently returned from the area, where he had been serving his apprenticeship in mechanics;
William and Ellen, then living in Apalachicola, and their two oldest sons, Alfred (called "Alf"), and George B. (sometimes called "G. B.");
Brother-in-law Robert M. Gunby, a Columbus merchant, and his wife, Jane Louise Beall, the youngest sister of Ann and Ellen;
Nephew Bob Lockhart, the son of another Beall sister, Mary Ann Beall, and her husband, Dr. Henry Lockhart. Until recently, the Lockharts had lived in Apalachicola, where Dr. Lockhart had been a partner of William in their commission merchant firm of Lockhart & Young.

Also making the trip, at the invitation of Edward and Ann, was their young friend, Tom Jackson. Because it is Tom's presence that today permits us to have information about this journey by the Youngs, or to even know that it occurred, before beginning we will digress briefly to relate the circumstances under which the Youngs came to include Tom in the trip:

Tom had become the Postmaster of Eufaula, a job he considered highly desirable, which paid about $800 a year. The incumbent had resigned in 1852, during the last year of

President Fillmore's administration. Tom's friend Ben Gardner, who had given Tom his first job in Eufaula at the *Southern Shield,* was a political ally of Congressman Hilliard (they were both "Union men" in the crisis of the early 1850's), and Gardner procured Tom's appointment to the vacancy. Unfortunately, Fillmore was defeated by Franklin Pierce in 1852, and Tom knew that the days of his political appointment were numbered. Henry Young was helping Tom with his duties at the post office on the evening the unwelcome news arrived. Tom states:

> "Franklin Pierce was inaugurated President March 4th, '53, and I had been expecting to 'hear sumthin' drap' for a month past…. The Democrats were becoming very hungry for spoils…. The fact of the Presidential sword having swiped off the head of an humble Eufaula official in the short space of two months after inauguration shows the celerity of the decapitation movement.
>
> On the early June night…referred to above, I performed my usual functions in the office, then located under the Chewalla Hotel, near the center of the city, and the most popular resort on Broad street. My dear friend Henry Young came down from supper with me that night and assisted me in making up the mails for northern and western post offices.
>
> During my two years as clerk and P. M., I handled a great deal of money--say from $10,000 to $20,000 during cotton season. There were no railroads, no expresses, no telegraphs, and all money for commercial purposes was sent in Uncle Sam's mail bags [by stagecoach]….I think the final memoranda of cash sent from Columbus to Eufaula during the last week of May '53 might have been summed up thusly: Bank of Columbus to Edward B. Young, $5000, and several similar sums sent…to Eufaula for the purchase of cotton during the winter season. The warehouse cotton men who received those mammoth cash packages in those exciting steamboat days were John McNab, E. B. Young, H. P. Adams, L. F. Stow, L. F. Johnson, Colin Gardner, and others….Verily during those two winters I handled enough Georgia, Alabama, and South Carolina bank bills to burn up a 'sure 'nuff wet mule'….
>
> As that dear boy, Henry Young, and myself, sat there that ever memorable evening, conversing freely on general topics, and especially about our sweethearts, who had left the previous day for the Methodist College at Summerfield, Ala., (nine miles west of Selma) we heard the old familiar sound of the Columbus stage trumpet….
>
> In a few minutes the old stage 'Mustain' hove to, and threw out three mail pouches….Henry staid with me till 11 o'clock p. m. and helped to open and distribute the unusually large mail. The department allowed no assistant and I was very glad of his help. He was a splendid scribe, and his directions on the packages gave credit to the office.
>
> …But what interested me most was a long white envelope, containing a suspicious-looking document….I found out the next day the meaning of the suspicious and dubious epistle. It was the commission of Mr. Wellborn as my successor, with the signature of Franklin Pierce at the bottom.[301]

...I found myself 'flat as a flounder,' and this term expresses very much flatness according to fishology...My excellent friends, the Youngs, asked me not to leave Eufaula, at least until the following fall, by which time, perhaps, a favorable opportunity for the future might be presented; they told me that several of the family expected to visit the Crystal Palace at New York in August, and that if I would remain in town until then and go on the party my board bill of the next three months should not cost me one cent; they thought my good company was a fair equivalent for the hash likely to be consumed in the meantime. I think this was a case of misplaced confidence on their part, but an opportunity not to be sneezed at on my part.

So I stayed and had a delightful rest and vacation. Verily, during all of my wearisome sojourn on earth I have never met with truer, more sympathetic, or consistent friends than the Eufaula Youngs."[302]

And so, three months later, the excursion began, with Tom aboard. The group would take four days to reach New York, traveling by stagecoach, train, and steamboat. The best narrator of the trip is, of course, Tom himself:[303]

"About half a dozen of the Eufaula excursionist...left Eufaula about the 10th of August '53, with a view toward tarrying a few days at Columbus, where they expected to be joined by a number of congenial friends and relatives. That good and worthy business man, E. B. Young, myself, and Lucy, a little colored waiting maid of Mrs. E. B. Young, brought up the rear guard on Saturday night, August 14, 1853. We left town at 7 p. m. on the Columbus bound stage....

In bad weather this stage line was very disagreeable, and sometimes it required 14 hours at night between the towns....

After crossing the Chewalla, Mr. Young, who was a constant traveler, and capable of sleeping under almost any condition, soon lost consciousness, and was heard nevermore until the stage ran over a stump and bruised his larboard temple in the 'rhubarbs' of Glennville. As to the little...Lucy, she was hypnotized at Dallin's corner near 'Maiden Lane', and never gained consciousness until eight o'clock next morning. While descending the Girard heights [now Phenix City], she suddenly opened her eyes and exclaimed:

'Mars Ed., whar is we at?'

I alone was sleepless on that dark and dismal night....On and on, through the dark Cowikee swamps we rolled. Every other tree we passed appeared to me as a highway robber....At 11 p. m. we reached the beautiful little town of Glennville, which at that day was considered the Paradise of Barbour—a vast woodland park, two miles long, interspersed with handsome residences and enchanting flower gardens...The stage...arrived at Columbus at 8 a. m.....If it takes thirteen hours to traverse the distance between Eufaula and Columbus, how long will it take me to reach the Crystal Palace in New York?

After services at St. Luke Methodist Church in Columbus on Sunday morning,[304] in the afternoon the group boarded the recently completed Muscogee Railroad for Savannah by way of Macon.[305] In Savannah the party boarded an ocean-going steamboat for the trip to Wilmington, North Carolina, at 4:30 a.m. on August 17, 1853.[306] Tom had never seen any water other than "the rivers, creeks, and branches of Georgia and Alabama". After the boat had gotten a league from the shore, Tom was taken seasick and went to bed. When the boat touched at Charleston, seasick as he was, Tom crept out of his bunk long enough for a quick glance at Fort Sumter and other points of interest around the historic harbor. After leaving Charleston, he was enjoying a beautiful sunset when Tom realized that the boat was completely out of sight of land, and he promised his Maker that if he "could set foot on *terra firma* again he would leave to others the joy and comforts of life on the ocean way", a pledge which he thereafter adhered to. After 28 hours at sea, they reached Wilmington, North Carolina at 8:00 a.m., and boarded the train for Richmond.

In Richmond, the Young party enjoyed a good fresh fish dinner "a veritable feast for the gods,"[307] after which they boarded the train for Washington. But the train only went to "Acquia Creek," 40 or 50 miles below Washington, D.C. There the excursionists disembarked (at 2:00 a.m., Aug. 19, 1853, the fourth day out) and immediately boarded a Potomac steamer bound for Washington. They were assigned berths, but got no sleep because the night watchman would ring the bell and sing out "Mount Vernon" and other ports. At sunrise the travelers reached the Washington and Baltimore Depot to board the morning train for New York.

Tom commented that on the trip from Washington to New York he "saw more sights and more people in that day than in all of his previous or subsequent life added together," including five big cities in one day, three of them among the most populous cities in the United States.[308] Every foot of the route "was replete with interest, and well calculated to overwhelm with surprise a Southern backwoods boy." From the terminus of the railroad, the party took a steamer for Castle Garden at the Battery in Manhattan. Tom wondered how they could make a landing through the "vast and intricate forest of ships and masts" in New York harbor, "And about the first realization I had of the true inwardness of the situation, was conveyed by a gentle tap on the left shoulder by my true and tried friend E. B. Young, who, in addition to the gentle tap articulated in audible tones:

"Tom, this is New York!"[309]

It was 6:30 p.m. on August 19; the Young party had arrived at New York after four days and nights of continuous travel by sea and land.

Because Tom had "heard much of the vast army of cut-throats and pickpockets who infest the highways and byways of New York… with the fear of being garroted I had turned all my money (except $5) over to Mr. E. B. Young, for safe keeping. I thought perhaps I might trust myself with that little sum. So I divided the $5 up into small change, which I secreted in divers inside and outside pockets."[310] After spending the first night in the Astor

House, which cost $3.50, Tom concluded that, "Yea, verily; a night's lodging at the Astor…was glory enough for any one human life."

The Young party included six young men: Edward's sons, Will and Henry; William's boys, Alf and G.B.; Bob Lockhart; and Tom. After the first night, these six boys lodged with Edward's sister, Maria Shaw Young Peniston, then 38 years of age. She had married Anthony J. Peniston on December 12, 1838, and they resided in a house at Number 14 West Eleventh Street, a little north of Grace Church.[311] Tom quotes her as saying "if us boys' (six) are willing to occupy two beds in the garret, she will accommodate the whole 'shebang'". Tom noted that "three in a bed is pretty thick in hot weather", but they were glad to have the accommodations. Other New York Youngs lived with the Penistons, and Tom describes meeting them:

> "On the evening of August 20, 1853, I accompanied my boyhood friends to our headquarters. I shall never forget the cordial greeting of that night. The family consisted of Mr. and Mrs. . . . Peniston and 2 daughters, Misses Carrie, age 17, and Lula, age 12, also, Miss Carrie Young, (an elderly maiden lady of 50). [The latter was Edward's sister, Caroline, born April 5, 1797, and thus actually 56 at this time]."

Tom went on to describe Edward Young's New York relatives in his usual generous way:

> "This family was a model family. Mr. Peniston was an old-time dry-goods merchant, and a brother-in-law of W. H. Young of Columbus, and E. B. Young of Eufaula. They were plain, simple, God-fearing people, hospitable, unpretentious. Miss Carrie Young was a model old maid, ever ready and willing to sacrifice self for others. Possibly no good woman ever added more to the comfort and happiness of those with whom she came in contact. Miss Carrie died at the commencement of the late Civil War, and no doubt many new arrivals at the 'beautiful gate' daily welcomed by her good soul - so self sacrificing and devoted to her fellow creatures while in the flesh."

> My second night in New York was spent at the hospitable home, then far uptown."

While the six young men of the party lodged at the Penistons, the older members, Edward, William and their wives, probably lodged with Edward and William's mother, Christina. Their father, James, had died in 1840.

That night, the boys "devoted the evening to amusement, as is the custom of visitors from the South", and went to see Christie's Minstrels. Christie's made annual trips through the South, and were well known there. Tom observed, "Negro minstrelsy was in its glory then".

After that, "every day for a month our Southern boys had a new program, and a continuous round of pleasure seeking. . . I had made E. B. Young my banker, and knowing my verdant tendency, he would never trust me with more than $5 a day, and told me if I got swindled out of that, I could go to Guinea or Jericho."

As described by Tom 50 years later, the Crystal Palace and the 1853 Fair suffer from comparison with later developments:

"The New York Crystal Palace covered about four acres of ground, and was located on 42nd Street, then the eastern limits of the great city. It was in the shape of a great cross, built of glass, three stories high, with roomy apartments for the several nations represented. It was but an infant in swaddling clothes, when compared to the modern world's fair at Chicago a few years since, but all things considered was a most wonderful event in the history of America and created as much of a furore then as the great fair at Chicago did nearly a half century later on.

Our Columbus and Eufaula colony devoted two days to visiting the great fair, and were not much wiser at the end of our visit than we were at the beginning. It would have taken at least a week to have formed a proper and just opinion of the important exhibition. Some half dozen of the great countries of Christendom were represented . . . The show was dull and uninteresting as compared to the grand strides of modern progress…There were of course a great many things to interest and attract immense crowds, which flocked in from our own and other countries; for the daily attendance was so large that it was almost impossible to gain admission or pass through the various halls with any degree of pleasure or comfort…About all I can recall at this late date was the grand display of machinery, stationery, fine arts, and elegant manufactures from the continent of Europe."

This was the last comment that Tom Jackson had to offer about the 1853 World's Fair. The remainder of the month in New York was spent exploring the area with one or more of the Young boys, usually under the guidance of Will Young (whom he persists in calling "Bill"):

"Bill had been learning the machinist and engineering trade in that vicinity for four years, and was therefore well posted as to dead falls, places of amusements, etc., not only in New York, but also in adjacent neighboring cities and towns. Consequently he was chosen leader and guide of the unsophisticated backwoods youngsters who had never been initiated into the sublime mysteries of city life, especially in that feature of it, which, treats of underground systems . . ..

Bill trotted the Southern investigators through during our four weeks stay in the big city. He showed us many of the hidden secrets, but always warned us by a 'distress signal' in times of danger."

Their first exploration was to Harlem, nine miles out of town, to which half hour excursions were run between the city and the village daily. "Many people took a morning excursion train to inhale pure air and revive a failing appetite. These were delightful excursions and all Southerners avail themselves of them….My friend Bill accompanied me to Harlem several mornings. His genial, sunshiny nature won friends for him wherever he went, and he was as much at home in Harlem as in New York." [312]

Central Park did not then exist. Tom and the Young boys visited Trinity Church, the highest building in Manhattan, and attempted to ascend its church steeple, said to be "365 feet high and probably not excelled in loftiness except by the Washington Monument". Tom observes that "I reckon it was never intended for me to get up in the world (even at the end of a rope) for after ascending 200 feet by winding stair-cases within the steeple I grew dizzy and faint hearted, and had to pause for a rest." He looked through the steeple windows and "far as the eye could scan in every direction, was a grand panorama of a great city's animated existence." At his request, the Young boys took Tom down to the churchyard below, where they contemplated graves dating to the early settlement of New York, including the gravestone of Alexander Hamilton, who was killed by Aaron Burr in a duel in 1804.

Being interested in the newspaper business, and having met someone who worked for the New York Tribune, Tom visited the offices of that newspaper, and much to his delight, "then and there, I was introduced to the eccentric genius and big hearted and big headed editor, Horace Greeley."[313]

Will Young wanted to revisit some of the towns in New Jersey and New York where he had spent his apprenticeship learning to make locomotives, and he insisted on Tom's accompanying him on these visits, which Tom was, of course, happy to do. They first visited Newark, where Will had lived for two years.[314] On this excursion, Tom met the girl who would later become Will's wife.

Newark then had a population of 50,000. It was nine miles from Jersey City to Newark over a flat marsh, and it took just nine minutes to make the trip. Tom continues:

"In the midst of that quiet country town (for it was as quiet as a country churchyard compared to New York) there was a neat little cottage occupied by a family by the name of Hewlett. With this nice, unsophisticated family Bill had boarded for a couple of years and was the same as one of 'em. To that cottage we at once resorted and greeted with a right royal welcome. The family consisted of a widow lady, one son, Sam, and two sweet Jersey lilies - - Misses Annie and Amelia. . . . It was not difficult to guess that Bill was a 'goner' on the queenly little Annie. As to Amelia, the younger, just 16, she seemed to fall in love on sight with this itinerant tramp, and never were two days more greatly enjoyed than while under this hospitable roof. The afternoon was spent in visiting the several shops…and in sightseeing Generally. Miss Annie was a charming pianist, and idle moments were spent in admiring her fine vocal and instrumental efforts."

74

"Bill," Tom, and sometimes other members of the Young group spent several days visiting principal towns in New Jersey, including Patterson, Rahway (where Will had worked for the first year of his apprenticeship), Trenton, Princeton, and several of the Revolutionary battle grounds. In their last day in Newark, the group took an excursion boat to Coney Island. Still conscious of his last unpleasant experience on a boat, Tom is wary:

"About 3:00 p.m. Sept. 4, 1853, two large boats, containing at least 1,000 excursionists, 'irrespective of age, sex, or previous condition,' left the wharf at Newark and steamed down the Passaic River to the celebrated 'Wash Hole' at Coney Island. Among that gay and giddy throng were half a dozen of the Columbus and Eufaula boys and their fair dulcinas, including Bill and his fiancee Queen Annie, and myself and my new found treasure Miss Amelia. All signs were favorable; not an intervening cloud nor threatening gale nor rising tide nor impending disaster cast ominous shadows athwart the happy dreams of the light hearted merry throng, and I am happy to record that hopeful expectations were fully realized. The trip was made in perfect safety. At the island we met perhaps 10,000 pleasure seekers from Gotham, and soon the whole surf for hundreds of yards around was live and working with human bathers, male and female, old and young. Such a scene was an eye opener to a green, piney woods boy who had never dreamed of the co-education of the sexes in the art of swimming. But progress is the law of nature . . . It was certainly an interesting and inspiring sight, even to an 'old fogy' bobbing up and down in the ocean shallows . . .

After due reflection I am in favor of learning girls to swim.[315] Private bathing places for this purpose should be established in every city and hamlet where water can be found for floaters."

Returning to Newark, Tom observed, "That was the last night I ever spent under the hospitable roof of the Hewlitts in that pleasant democratic town. Next morning, under the leadership of Bill, I left for Gotham, with a view toward further excursions and explorations. I shook the parting hand of sweet little Amelia with great regret."

Will Young and Tom Jackson visited Newburgh, New York, about 70 miles above New York City, to see old friends of Will's, and Matawan, a village across the Hudson from Newburgh. Tom says, "The principal industry of Newburgh and Matawan at the date of our visit was the manufacture of locomotives".[316] They returned to New York by steamer down the Hudson. The boat was "magnificently equipped with all the necessary comforts and conveniences for the traveling public, "in short, a regular floating palace crowded with passengers." Tom was impressed with how many boats were plying the Hudson: "Our boat all day long was impeded by every imaginable sort of craft, from the magnificent passenger steamer to the common fishing smack. So jammed was the grand old stream with boats of all sorts that it seemed that constant collisions must inevitably result."

Returning to their lodging at 14 West 11th Street, four miles up Broadway, and within a stone's throw of Grace Church, Tom observed, "This splendid temple of worship was then . . . located in a beautiful park…its lofty steeple served as a guidepost by which strangers wandering far up town were enabled to find their way back to Broadway. Old Trinity served the same purpose in the downtown district."[317]

After further sightseeing in New York, on September 15, 1853, Tom and the Young boys left New York. The returning party consisted of Will and Henry Young and Tom Jackson of Eufaula, and Alf Young and Bob Lockhart of Columbus. The older Youngs, Edward and William and their wives, decided to remain in New York until October 1, because they had not yet completed purchasing their fall stocks. Tom describes the departure:

"We bade an affectionate farewell to our hospitable and clever entertainers, the Penistons and Youngs located at 14 West 11th Street, who for four weeks had exhibited so much interest and solicitude in their efforts to make our visit pleasant. I never saw but two of that good family afterwards - - that was during the year 1858, when they visited relatives at Beallwood, near Columbus."[318]

After crossing the Jersey City Ferry, the group boarded a New Jersey Central train, bound for Philadelphia by way of Newark. At Newark, the train paused for five minutes. "The Misses Hewlett, having been apprized of our departure for the South were in readiness at the depot to extend the parting hand . . . We rushed down on the General passenger platform where we talked thick, fast, and somewhat incoherently. Bill's intended, 'Queen Annie' exhibited symptoms of poignant sorrow, and tears were plainly visible on her fair, pallid cheeks." Annie would soon be Will's wife. Tom describes her family situation:

" . . . The Hewlett Family of Newark, with whom Bill and myself spent four delightful days during our World's Fair visit, . . . were in humble circumstances in life at that time, but had known and seen better days . . . In short, they stood several ranks in advance of the common herd who are generally classified as 'poor but respectable'".

Reaching Washington, the boys stayed at the National Hotel, which Tom describes as "a tony and fashionable hostelry. Many distinguished Americans and foreign officials, including several ministers plenipotentiary, dined at this hotel…. At dinner there were nine courses or changes of dishes. Etiquette required one hour to exhaust the bill of faire. If one did not wish to take a 'full course' he was expected to wait patiently til others went through the motion…To me the whole confab was as incomprehensible as…hieroglyphics…" Tom took this occasion to compare this elegance with the more typical southern meal to which he was accustomed at Fendall Hall:

"Everything was so different from our backwoods style of living, where our daily bill of fair [sic] consisted of oblong corn pones which the cook patted several minutes to get it in proper shape so as to get four into the oven at once; bacon and collards, pot-licker, and pot-dodgers, vegetables and buttermilk. In addition, we had biscuits every Sunday morning, and if it happened to be the preacher's Sunday to call, the menu was enlarged by the addition of chicken served in all styles, and pies 'n things. Then in winter came the happy season of pork and turnips, pumkin pies, and all finally culminating in the grand jubilee of corn-shucking and hog-killing, the most joyous period of the swiftly passing old year. Yea, verily, southern backwoods life was once a great institution."[319]

That night in Washington, the "Southern party" went to the National Theater where they saw a production of Harriett Beecher Stowe's "Uncle Tom's Cabin", which contributed to the intensification of feeling later leading to the Civil War. The next morning, Sunday, the boys visited the White House. As they were looking through the fence, they decided they should visit President Pierce. The following scene ensued:

"A private policeman was on the alert continuously to keep off intruders. As our little squad passed the big iron gate, we asked the watchman if we could see his Excellency, the President of the great United States. He replied, 'no; it's 'ginst the rules.' We importuned: told him we were from the remotest region of the far southwest, and that we never could have another chance to see a sure 'nuff real live president. He responded: 'Can't help it; you can'i see him. Mr. Pierce is partaking of his morning hash, and does not wish to be bothered.' Ah, thought we, even presidents have human appetites and affiliations . . ."[320]

After the "snubbing," the boys went down to the riverbank to watch the boats, but Will Young soon had a bright idea:

"Our guide Bill, not easily discouraged, full of resources, ever on the alert for opportunities, spoke out boldly in meeting and says he: 'Boys, I will tell you how we can see the president. He attends the old Presbyterian Church on D Street. Let's go there and take our stand at 10:30, and we will be sure to see him, 10 or 15 minutes later. We took the hint and followed our guide."

The boys took up station in front of the church, and "probably lingered 10 minutes at the church portals when Bill whispered rather audibly: 'There he comes!'"

"Casting a hurried glance we saw a handsome coach and four, with a liveried white man on the box halt in the street, 20 feet from the church, and perhaps five feet west of the entrance to the church. It was a ludicrous spectacle to see that obsequious sycophant driver dismount and let down the steps, as if preparing for the descent of an angel of mercy. When the fool killer completes his job there will be no liveried coachmen left. Then followed the descent from the coach of President Pierce and wife. The President appeared to be 50 years of age; was handsomely dressed in conventional black; tall, slender, 5-10 or 6, weighed perhaps 145. I did not like him much, because he allowed his partisans to have me turned out of the Eufaula Post Office; and yet I couldn't help feeling fascinated and charmed at the idea of being in the same church with the President. I think we had a very fine sermon, though I couldn't swear to it; it required all my time to look at the President and his wife.... The Washington people did not seem very crazy about presidents, for the church was by no means crowded, and among the attendants were many Southerns."[321]

The boys continued sightseeing at the capitol building, where they walked through the House and Senate Chambers, and visited the Congressional Cemetery, a quarter mile east of the capitol, which prompted Tom's comment that, "the soil, from its prairie-like texture, reminded an Alabamian more of a Cowikee swamp farm than of a national cemetery." Back in their hotel room that night, the boys made a startling discovery:

"In the privacy of our own chamber we held a sort of secret session to compare notes and devise plans for future operations. The result of our deliberations was the discovery that, we each, individually, severally, and collectively, were past becoming financially embarrassed, with scarcely enough money in sight to reach home on. All of my young friends decided to return home via Wilmington and steamer from that city to Savannah. I kicked; told them I had had enough of the briny deep; did not like the idea of being sandbagged down a plank to furnish a square meal for sharks; that I would prefer to stage or tramp 50 miles through South Carolina . . . than to take chances again on the grand though terrible Atlantic. . ."

Accordingly, the boys returned to Columbus and Eufaula by way of steamship and rail, while Tom proceeded at a more leisurely pace by land, after seeing Mount Vernon, and after stopping at several cities on the way home. All of the travelers eventually arrived home safe and in good order.

Ironically, only a few days after Edward and Ann arrived home in Eufaula, they received news from New York that his mother, Christina, had died on October 8, 1853, almost 77 years of age.[322] She died in the home of her daughter, Maria Shaw Young Peniston, at 14 West 11th Street, and was buried in the cemetery of Trinity Church (in private plot 260, Eastern Division), [323] the church which survives today nestled amid the skyscrapers at Wall and Broad Streets. The daughter of German immigrants, born the same year the Declaration of Independence was signed, Christina Ridabock Young had lived to see her Southern sons prosper. Shortly before her death she had enjoyed a month-long visit with them and with some of her Southern grandchildren. And she died surrounded by her other living children, including Caroline Young and Maria Peniston.

15
The Affluent 'Fifties:
A New Home and New Business Ventures

"...aggressive men on the make who seized the opportunities to earn their fortunes in a fast-paced era of development in which the rules of play had not yet been codified."
Willoughby, *Fair To Middlin'*

We have seen from John Horry Dent's journals the ample profits being enjoyed by Southern cotton growers in the 1840's, which were being shared by the cotton financiers, middlemen, and merchants like Edward and William Young. These profits continued to increase to even higher levels in the 1850's. Cotton prices, though they always fluctuated, rose from the range of 6 to 8 cents per pound in the early 1840's to 13.5 cents in 1857.[324] From 1855 through 1860, John Horry Dent would annually net at least $6000 per year above all expenses.[325] To place the currency values in perspective, this was at a time when $1000 per year was regarded as a good salary; when a night at the Astor House, one of New York's best hotels, cost $3.50; when $3.75 would buy a gallon and a half of John Horry's good quality brandy; when a pair of ladies shoes of a quality suitable for Mrs. Dent cost $1.60. With annual living expenses of Dent's growing family of about $3500, his $6,000 annual cotton profits (plus income from other ventures) would result in John Horry Dent's having a net worth of $200,000 by the time of secession. [326]

Serving the commercial needs of numerous planters like J. H. Dent, the 1850's were good times for Edward and William Young and their families. The rumble of the war drums was still distant. The Southern cotton economy was the envy of the nation. The Young families went about enjoying the comfortable lives that industriousness and enterprise had made possible. And Edward and William Young continued to successfully pursue ways in which to participate in the cotton wealth with new business ventures.

With his eyes on matrimony, Edward's son Will Young put his mechanical training into practice in a way that was probably more pleasing to the Young family than that of steamboat captain. He began his own business, Eufaula's first and only iron and brass foundry, called the "Eufaula Iron Works." Will would operate this business for many years, until 1872.[327] Will's shift toward maturity and responsibility was probably motivated by his next major step; he returned to New Jersey for his bride. On October 12, 1854, Will and Anna Maria Hewlett, daughter of Samuel and Maria Hewlett, were married in Newark, New Jersey, by Dr. Eddy.[328] Returning to Eufaula, they took up residence in the "old McGee place" on College Hill, which, when originally built, had been only the second residence on College Hill. There, Will and Anna led a contented and happy life for many years.[329]

The Youngs' friendship with the John Horry Dents continued to be a close one. John noted in his journal for Tuesday, May 21, 1852, that, "Mr. Young and family made us a visit." It is Friday, three days later, before the journal reports, "Mr. Young and family left for Eufaula."[330] There is no indication of just how many Youngs arrived for this impromptu three-day call. The families assisted each other whenever needed. In May of 1853, Mrs. Dent had come into Eufaula to meet her husband upon his return from a trip to Savannah, when she was taken very ill. Ann Young took her into the Young home for several days while she was being treated by Dr. Thornton, who at that time was a neighbor of the Youngs on Randolph Street. As Mrs. Dent began to recover, John made a bed for her in his carriage and drove her home to the plantation.[331]

Later that year, Mrs. Dent was again stricken with illness, but this time much more seriously. After an illness of only nine days, Mrs. Dent died on September 16, 1853, of "typhoid malarial fever". John was devastated with grief; he blamed himself for settling his family in what he came to regard as a "sickly" fever-prone area. He rented a house in Clayton and moved his children there to prevent a recurrence. Dent had eight children to care for, one of whom was less than a year old, and extensive farming interests to attend to. He needed a wife. On July 26, 1854, in Clayton, John Horry Dent married Miss Fanny Whipple, a practical and educated transplanted Yankee from Vermont, who had been teaching in Clayton. The Young family was close by during these events. Dent's journals for 1854 reflect a payment on his account with E. B. Young of $150 "for Mrs. Dent's tomb."[332] His entry for July 3, 1854, three weeks before his marriage to Fanny Whipple, reflects payment of $500 to Henry Young for a ring. The same year, Dent bought the Johnson plantation on Chewalla Creek, to which he moved with his children and his new wife. A memorandum of this purchase, dated September 4, 1854, reflects that at the time of purchase, Alpheus Baker released a mortgage that he had held on the property. The mortgage release is witnessed by Henry A. Young.[333]

On November 5, 1854, Dent was scheduled to go into town the next day to close a major, complicated, three-way financial transaction with Alpheus Baker and William Varner, but found that, because his little daughter was very sick, he would be unable to go to the closing. Accordingly, he wrote Edward Young, entrusted him with two promissory notes totaling $10,400 signed by Dent, described the complex terms of the transaction, and asked Edward to carry out the transaction on his behalf, protecting his interests.

The following year, John H. Dent was the plaintiff in two lawsuits. His lawyer, E. C. Bullock, effected settlements with the two defendants, requiring them to pay the necessary sums "with interest from date, payable at E. B. Young's counting room, Eufaula Alabama."[334] Apparently Edward's "counting room" was enough like a neutral bank to satisfy the litigants.

John Horry Dent was a thinker and a close observer of both domestic and world affairs. At a time when many citizens of Barbour County were discussing little other than the politics of the slavery question, Dent wrote to E. B. Young to give Edward the benefit of his thoughts on the Crimean War, and his admiring view of Britain's commercial character:

"Nov 1ˢᵗ, 1855

"Mr. E. B. Young

Much is now being said in relation to the heavy expenditures of England and France to maintain their armies and carry on the war against Russia. In business relations they talk of panics and disasters. England has ever since her grand struggle with the great Napoleon been considered bankrupt if her debts were paid. Her wisdom though, has been and ever will be, to be a debtor to her commerce instead of another power. As such, her expenditures what they might [be] in this war, so soon as it is terminated, she will draw in to her treasury again by commerce, what has been so freely given to sustain her honor. They are a commercial people, and understand too well business, to ruin themselves by a year or two fighting.

John H. Dent"

In December of 1854,[335] there arrived in Eufaula another Dent, a 21 year-old schoolteacher who was destined to play an important role in the story of the Young family: Stouten Hubert Dent (who was not related to John Horry Dent, the plantation owner). Hubert had been born on Oct 30, 1833, in Charles County, Maryland, to Dr. Stouten Warren Dent and his second wife, Mary Catherine Smoot Dent. Dr. Dent was a well-known physician in Charles County.[336] Hubert was the oldest of three boys and ten girls, and we will come to know his family better later. Hubert had received a good education at Charlotte Hall Academy in St. Mary's, Maryland.[337] His ambition now was to "read law" and become a lawyer, but in the meantime needed employment. He had a cousin in Eufaula (who later moved to Columbus) who assisted Hubert in obtaining a teaching position in Eufaula. The thriving cotton economy of the area, in which an ambitious young lawyer might expect to prosper, together with the availability of a teaching position in the meantime, were sufficient inducements for Hubert to leave Maryland and migrate South.

The Eufaula school in which Hubert Dent first taught is described by Tom Jackson:

One little academy, situated in a beautiful oak grove, was the only house that could be seen west of Brick Row on the old Clayton road. At this charming rural academy the young Irwintonians and Eufaulians received the groundwork of an education [during the '40s and '50s]. The school grounds were beautiful, the teachers kind and efficient; terms ranged from $2 to $5 per month according to grade...[338] It was taught in the olden days by Professors A. B. Steele, J. T. Patterson, S. H. Dent and others, and was the scene of many social and educational assemblages."[339]

Later, Hubert conducted "a popular private school for boys", on Broad Street, in the house that later became the L. A. Sparks home.[340] We will return to Hubert's private school again presently.

Ann and Edward Young's last child was born on January 13, 1855. It was a girl, named Caroline for Edward's sister still living in New York. Caroline was baptized on November 4, 1855 by James L. Cotten.[341] So, as finally constituted, Ann and Edward's family had eight surviving children--three boys: Will, Henry and Ed; and five girls: Anna, Mollie, Ada, Helen, and Caroline. Another child, Ellen Louisa, had lived one year.

81

Only one year after Ann and Edward had their last child, they were presented with their first grandchild, by their oldest and first-married son, Will. On January 15, 1856, Annie Hewlett bore a son, whom they named Charles Augustus,[342] who came to be called "Charlie." He was baptized by William M. Motley.

Edward Young was one of those concerned about the limited educational opportunities for girls of the Eufaula area. In an era when higher education for women did not enjoy a high priority, in a locality just emerging from the frontier, Edward (the father of four daughters) was one of the leaders championing the cause of a college for women in Eufaula. Three Eufaula fraternal organizations joined together to sponsor the college and erect the building: the Masons, the Oddfellows, and the Good Templars, and representatives of each formed the Board of Trustees.[343] This joint sponsorship was the reason for the name chosen: the Union Female College. Edward Young was the first president of the Board of Trustees; the vice president was the respected lawyer, E. C. Bullock; and the treasurer was Edward's able business competitor, John McNab.

Constructed by the builder, George Whipple, at a cost of $12,000, the College was located on the heights that thereafter came to be known as "College Hill." It was located not far from the site of the Youngs' future new home, which would be called "Fendall Hall." The College tuition and board cost $15 per month, or $250 for the term. Under Dr. McIntosh, the first president of the College, French, German, Latin and Greek were required. "A good deal of the cultural and moral outlook was supplied by the literary masterpieces and their emphasis upon moral precepts which were found in the books of William Holmes McGuffey."[344] The students wore uniforms, "for winter, brown marino for best dresses and calico for school, with brown hats, trimmed with crimson".[345] Boarding students were prohibited from spending the night outside the building. Young men were not allowed to visit. The first commencement was held in 1858, and among the seven young women receiving diplomas was Edward and Ann's second oldest daughter, 16-year-old Mollie Young.[346] The institution that Edward assisted in founding, together with its successor, Alabama Brenau, would educate Eufaula area girls (including several generations of Young descendants) for over half a century.[347]

While the Union Female College was being built, as sometimes happens with construction schedules, it became apparent that the work would not be completed in time to begin the school term at the announced time. But Hubert Dent came to the rescue:

> "The college not being completed in time for the opening of school, S. H. Dent, who was then conducting his private school on Broad Street, very magnanimously arranged to meet the emergency by surrendering his school building, while he used the Odd Fellows rooms." [348]

Without detracting in any way from Hubert's magnanimity, we will mention in passing that the young schoolteacher-law student possibly had his eye upon Anna Young, the eldest daughter of the President of the Board of Trustees of the College, and it would not have hurt Hubert's objectives at all to help relieve the College's embarrassment and permit it to open at the announced time.

The Union Female College: Edward Young was the first president of its board of trustees; Mollie Young was in its first graduating class in 1858; and three generations of Young and Dent girls received their educations here.

Will's younger brother, Henry Young, was also preparing for a "life's occupation". Henry was quite different from Will, and his interests took a different direction. Tom Jackson, who knew them both well, assesses Henry in this manner:

> "Henry Augustus Young was one of the purest and best 'Young' men I ever knew—not sinless and faultless, but nearly so. He was three years younger than Bill, but did not resemble him in any respect—physically, mentally or otherwise. Henry was five feet, eight inches in height, weighed 140 pounds, dark complexion, eyes and hair. He was reserved, dignified, scholarly, warm and sincere in his friendships, though somewhat unsocial in his attitude toward society.... He attended several of the best schools in Alabama. Then followed two years of foreign travel.... When he returned from Europe he was looked upon as being a "gentleman and a scholar"--the pride of his family, and worthy of the esteem of the community. His friends predicted that he would develop into a college professor or Methodist minister..."[349]

But Henry did neither. Much to Edward's satisfaction, Henry went into the mercantile and cotton factoring business with his father. In 1858, the name of the business became "E. B. Young & Son". The plantation accounts of John Horry Dent began to reflect transactions with "H. A. Young", and the J. H. Dent cotton was being sold through "E. B. Young & Son".[350] Henry assumed his place in the community.

Edward continued to make periodic business trips to New York. In his journal for Monday, August 17, 1857, John Horry Dent notes, "Fair and very hot. Went to Eufaula. Mr. Young started for New York."[351] The following year, in August of 1858, John Horry Dent himself decided to visit New York with his wife. While there, Mrs. Dent bought a "cooking slave" and had him shipped home, in hopes of learning "Yankee cooking." They shopped and had their daguerreotype taken. On August 27, John was glad to soon be leaving the dirty and noisy city, when they were surprised to receive a visit at their hotel from E. B. Young, along with three of his sisters who resided in New York. Edward and his sisters spent about an hour visiting with the Dents. Mr. and Mrs. Dent later packed their trunks and prepared to start for the South the following morning.[352]

Although the Youngs' house on the east side of Randolph Street in Eufaula had served them well for many years, Edward decided that it was time for him to provide Ann with an elegant and spacious new home. Taking his time, Edward assembled materials over a period of three years. He cut timber from his own land, converted it to lumber at his own sawmill, and allowed it to season and dry in the sun for three years.[353] On February 16, 1856, Edward bought Lot Number 25 "according to the Plan of the city Eufaula (formerly Irwinton)", consisting of four acres on Barbour Street in the College Hill area, upon which the new house would be sited. However, he later added Lot 40, four acres, and the north half of Lot 43, two acres, so that the house was located on a total of ten acres.[354] Said to be one of Eufaula's earliest suburbs, "the Hill" escaped the heat of the town and avoided what the nineteenth century perceived as "noxious airs" from the river. The heights provided cool temperatures and gentle breezes.

Architects as we know them were not involved in residential construction at this period. Edward would have hired an experienced builder to oversee the construction. It has been suggested that Edward probably contracted with master builder, George Whipple,[355] a well-known builder in the area who had reconstructed the Irwinton bridge for the city, and had also built the nearby Union Female College when Edward was president of its board of trustees. Edward and Ann would have had discussions with Whipple and looked through books of architectural styles with him, to reach agreement on doors, windows, columns and details like eves, shutters, and ornaments. The General style selected by Ann was an "Italianate country villa style, popular between 1850 and 1860, and considered well suited to hot, humid climates."[356]

The builder or Edward himself would have hired workers wherever available, and probably hired the services of skilled slaves from their masters, who would sometimes share the pay with the slave. We know from John Horry Dent's farm journals that during 1857, Edward Young frequently hired J. H. Dent's skilled carpenter slave, "Hard Times," probably to do carpentry on the new Young home, which was under construction at about this time. Hard Times' wages seemed to fluctuate. J. H. Dent's journal for January, 1857 notes, "Hard Times hired to E. B. Young at $25 per month".[357] On July 12, 1857 he was "sent to Mr. Young to work by the month at $20 per month."[358]

The Italianate style as implemented in the Young home is characterized by wide overhanging eaves; ornate brackets; one-story porches; twin porch columns; and a large railed belvedere at the top[359] (which in Eufaula has traditionally been called a "cupola"). The porches have no rails; they were lined with planters. There are arched openings over windows and doors. The foundation consists of brick piers, which were stuccoed, scored, and painted to simulate stone building blocks. The window shutters were usually kept closed to avoid heat and fabric fading. The exterior of the house was painted with "buttermilk whitewash," a type of calcimine paint.[360]

Expensive, imported materials were employed, including black-and-white marble squares for the entrance hall floor, Bohemian etched glass for the double doors separating the double parlors, and white marble mantels. The Alabama Historical Commission today describes the final result as follows:

> "The two story frame structure has both an attic and cupola. The house faces north with a one story porch on three sides carried by a series of slender trellis-like supports. The four chimneys are constructed of brick and are stuccoed to simulate coursed ashlar. The high supporting piers that raise the house over an open basement area are of brick and are stuccoed in a similar manner. Latticework connects the supporting piers. Inside, the first floor has a large central hall with four rooms, two on each side. The hallway has a black and white square marble floor. At the end of the hallway is an attached room which was originally a solarium. This solarium was built so that Mrs. Young could bask in the sun year round as treatment for her arthritis. The room was later converted to a breakfast room. The home originally had two stairways. Only one of these remains today… Upstairs are four additional rooms and a smaller room at the front center linked by a pocket door to the bisecting hallway. A service stairway leads from the second story to the attic and from there to the cupola. The cupola is surrounded by a balustrade walk and the cornices of both the hipped main roof and the cupola are supported by brackets. A separate brick kitchen was connected to the southeast corner of the house by a covered breezeway…South of the kitchen was a two room house which was weatherboarded on the exterior and plastered inside. This house is believed to be the one lived in by the Youngs until Fendall Hall was completed. It was later used as a storehouse. West of this structure (southeast of the home) stood a feed house and a barn which had stalls for horses, a carriage house, and a buggy house." [361]

In an ingenious nineteenth century version of "air conditioning," the ceiling of the second floor central hallway has an ornamentally designed medallion grille, permitting airflow to the attic, with another grille in the attic ceiling permitting airflow to the cupola. When the cupola windows are opened, convection (rising warm air) causes air circulation through the house, and even a light breeze passing outside the cupola creates a strong updraft of cooling air throughout the first and second floors.

Fendall Hall in the 1970's

Ann and Edward Young did not give a name to their new home. The Youngs and their descendants often referred to it as simply, "the house on the hill." The name "Fendall Hall" was probably first adopted in the 1940s by the then owner-occupant, Louise Dent Hurt, one of Ann and Edward's granddaughters, and that is the name by which it is known today. Of course, it derives from Ann's middle name. Ann's maternal grandmother, Millicent Bradley, was the daughter of Ann Fendall, and was the granddaughter of Josias Fendall, a controversial early governor of colonial Maryland.

The former schoolteacher, Hubert Dent, was now a lawyer. After teaching school for one year, in 1856 he had studied law in the offices of Pugh & Bullock, two of the most outstanding lawyers of the area. After three months study, Hubert was admitted to the Bar, and immediately formed a partnership with another leading statesman, Judge John Cochran.[362] Pugh, Bullock, and Cochran had formed part of the leadership of the "Eufaula Regency" during the secession debate of 1850, and would continue to be strong leaders of the secession movement. (Pugh would later serve in the U. S. and Confederate Congresses, and then in the U. S. Senate.) After a year in partnership with Judge Cochran, Hubert was ready to practice alone, and opened his own office,[363] located at the "third door north of Bray Brothers."[364]

During or shortly after Hubert's period of association with the firm of Pugh & Bullock, another ambitious young schoolteacher became associated with that group; a future leader destined to become governor of Alabama. In the winter of 1858-1859, William Calvin Oates, a twenty-four year old schoolteacher from Abbeville, county seat of adjacent Henry County, came to Eufaula to read law under these outstanding lawyers.[365] He was thereafter

86

admitted to the bar and returned to Abbeville to begin his law practice. The friendship that Hubert and Oates began in Eufaula continued over many years in several different settings, and would lead to their becoming law partners and close political allies, as we will later discuss.

As Hubert was improving his station in life and pursuing his ambition to become a lawyer, he also had thoughts of matrimony. In surveying the possibilities, he did not aim low. Hubert set his sights on winning the hand of perhaps the most marriageable of Eufaula's young ladies, Anna Beall Young, the eldest daughter of one of Eufaula's most prosperous leaders. While the Youngs' new home on College Hill was under construction and the family was occupying temporary quarters on the premises, Hubert Dent came "courting." He and Anna visited in the completed kitchen building, which was being used as a "parlor."[366] Apparently Edward Young had a sufficiently good opinion of the young lawyer to allow the courtship to proceed. Hubert was no longer an impecunious schoolteacher. His prospects had improved to the point that he was now eligible to press his suit for the hand of a beautiful daughter of Ann and Edward Young.

However, while Anna and Hubert were courting, Anna's older brother, Henry, reached the altar first. On Jan 5, 1860, Henry Augustus Young and Maria Marshall McRae were married, by the Rev. Phil. C. Neely.[367] Maria was the daughter of John McRae and his wife Jane. The McRaes were among the early settlers of the county, having migrated from South Carolina, first to the Louisville area of Barbour County, and later moving to the White Oak community near Eufaula.[368] John McRae served as county sheriff in the 1830's.[369] His brother was a merchant on "Brick Row" on Broad Street in Eufaula.

Henry and Maria's wedding ceremony a few days after the New Year of 1860 was held at the home of Maria's sister and her husband, Mr. and Mrs. J. T. Kendall. But the ensuing celebration was held at the Youngs' elegant new home, and may have been one of the first major family events held there. The festivities were attended by many guests, including not only Henry's Columbus aunts, uncles, and cousins, but also his old friend Tom Jackson. Tom had moved to Columbus in 1854,[370] but had no intention of missing this important occasion of the Youngs, whatever the expense. He describes the event:

"Miss Maria McRae was the worthy lady chosen [by Henry], and it is safe to say no happier match ever occurred in the town. The ceremonies were celebrated at the residence of Mr. J. T. Kendall on North Randolph Street. [The minister] pronounced the presto words by which the two became one. The wedding party adjourned immediately, but not *sine die*. They reassembled in 30 minutes at the palatial residence of the Youngs on College Hill, where an old time Southern wedding feast was spread. [Over a hundred guests attended].... I was at the wedding, but it cost me $25 to procure the necessary wedding garments and appear in presentable shape. I left Columbus at noon on the wedding day on the steamer *Chewalla*, and we made the through trip in five hours, with only one stop.... A number of relatives of the groom from Columbus went down on the same boat to attend the marriage. These are fast times, but I think it is very doubtful as to whether this record has ever been lowered by any boat plying between Columbus and Eufaula."[371]

The couple took up residence in a new house that Henry built for his bride in a secluded location 400 yards north of Chewalla Creek.[372] Here they would have two children. But the war drums could now be faintly heard, and their happiness would soon be shattered.

As though their children were marrying in the order of their births, Edward and Ann celebrated a second wedding in 1860, that of their oldest daughter. Anna had yielded to Hubert Dent's entreaties, and Fendall Hall now saw another wedding. On Anna's birthday, June 5, Rev. Phil. C. Neely married Anna and Hubert [373] in the Young's new home. She was 20, he was 27.

Following the wedding, Hubert and Anna enjoyed a wedding trip to Maryland,[374] where they visited with Hubert's parents at their home, "Oakton Grove" in Charles County, so that Hubert's family and Anna could become acquainted. To briefly anticipate the coming cataclysm, four years later on June 7th, 1864, Captain Hubert Dent would write Anna from the battlefront on the outskirts of Atlanta, wistfully remembering this happy wedding trip, while reflecting on the enormous changes that had occurred in the interim: "…what important events have been crowded together in these four years. How many homes have been made desolate? How many hearts saddened?"[375] At the time of their 1860 wedding trip to Maryland, a history-changing Democratic Convention was meeting in Baltimore, in which occurred the final split of the Democratic Party, facilitating Lincoln's election as President and precipitating the Civil War. Hubert's letter would note that now (1864), Lincoln's Republicans were holding their convention in federally-occupied Baltimore, and "from the common newspaper statements there will be very much such another scene as there was there four years ago when we were there."[376]

Following their return to Eufaula, Anna's father provided the young couple with a house in which to begin their married life.[377] Soon, letters were flying between Anna and Oakton Grove in Maryland. On September 18, 1860, Hubert's sister, Mary Sophia (sometimes called "Mollie", not to be confused with Anna's own sister, Mary Elizabeth, also nicknamed "Mollie"), replied to an earlier letter from Anna. Mary reports to "Annie" items of household news as well as local gossip. Her brother George Dent is now teaching school (he's only 17), with 26 pupils that he likes, although thinks he will tire of it. There have been a number of lively parties and weddings in the neighborhood and a few young men have gone to Baltimore, some say "to get their wedding suits." There is news of individuals (whom Anna perhaps met during her visit). Mary wishes she could accept the invitation of Anna's friends to visit Eufaula this winter, but cannot. "All of the family joins me in love to you and Brother…" A postscript reports "the servants all send love to Miss Annie and Marster Bert."

Since the closing of Edward's Irwinton Bridge Bank in the mid-1840's, Eufaula, although it was a regional cotton-marketing town, had been without a bank.[378] In his business of cotton factoring and commission merchant, Edward had performed for his customers many of the services of a bank. He extended credit, and he kept his customers' funds on deposit for future use when they wished. Like most professional bankers, he did not pay interest on these deposits. Willoughby points out that, "John Horry Dent routinely left a portion of his 'cotton funds' with his factor E. B. Young."[379] But Eufaula needed a bank. The northern end of the Chattahoochee River valley was thriving, and banks were necessary for its continued economic growth. In good economic times such as these, bankers helped the local economy by expanding the money supply and extending credit to those in need of it. Those who met this need for local banking facilities have been referred to as "aggressive men on the make who seized the opportunities to earn their fortunes in a fast-paced era of development in which the rules of play had not yet been codified."[380] Edward and his brother, William, were such men. William, who had recently relocated to Columbus, Georgia had led the organization of a bank for that rapidly expanding commercial center. John McNab and Edward Young, would found two new banks in Eufaula.

In 1858, McNab, one of Edward's principal business competitors, led the organization of the "Eastern Bank of Alabama."[381] It was a stockholder-owned company, and its list of stockholders included many of Edward's friends and business associates, such as E. C. Bullock, J.G.L. Martin, John Gill Shorter, and John Horry Dent.[382] In September, J. H. Dent "sold ten bales of cotton to raise money to pay 10% on stock taken in the Eastern Bank of Alabama." He sold the cotton through E. B. Young & Son, and received the excellent price of $11.45 cents per pound.[383] Later, J. H. Dent withdrew other funds he had on deposit with Edward in order to pay for the remainder of his investment in McNab's bank[384] Indeed, there is evidence that Edward himself may have been one of the founding directors of the Eastern Bank.[385]

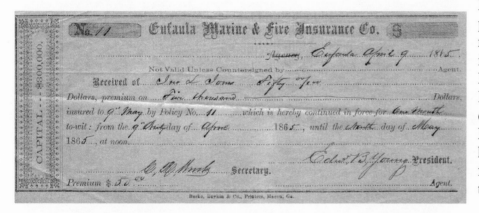

However, Edward was unwilling to leave the banking field solely to McNab, and he correctly concluded that the energetic economy of the Eufaula area needed, and would support, *two* banks. Accordingly, in 1859,[386] Edward formed a partnership with longtime Eufaula merchants, Clayton R. Woods and Colin Gardner. Woods had previously conducted a mercantile business with Gardner under the name, "Woods' & Gardner's Store."[387] Now, in partnership with Edward Young, they commenced a new bank under the name of "Young, Woods and Gardner Bank."[388] This bank would flourish, survive the Civil War, and, through its successor organization, continue to operate into the twentieth century.

A service that had become increasingly essential to the cotton trade was the need for insurance to cover the likely risk of fire or other casualty while the cotton was being transported and stored. As already noted, cotton was an extremely combustible material, and fires in warehouses and on steamboats were a common occurrence.[389] For example, in 1852, the steamer *Mary*, valued at $10,000, sank twelve miles south of Ft. Gaines. One source has compiled a partial list of 19 boats that were sunk or burned on the Chattahoochee between 1834 and 1856.[390] Edward was not to be left out of this niche of the cotton trade. His friend, state Senator E. C. Bullock, obtained the passage in the legislature of a bill authorizing the incorporation of The Eufaula Marine and Fire Insurance Co.[391] Accordingly, that corporation was formed, with capital of $300,000, to act as an insurance agent and to write casualty insurance on warehoused cotton. Edward B. Young was president, and his banking partner, Clayton R. Woods, was secretary. Edward himself also acted as an agent for insurance companies such as the Central Georgia Insurance Company of Macon, Georgia.[392]

16
Columbus Entrepreneur

"...[William Henry Young] would make this place his home, and enter into the business of cotton manufacturing. It became the dream and fixed object of his life, and was never lost sight of."

Worsley, *Columbus on the Chattahoochee*

It will be recalled that, when Edward and Ann left Marion, Georgia, to move to Irwinton, Alabama, William and Ellen returned briefly to New York, but then settled in Apalachicola, Florida, in 1839, where William went into the commission merchant business. As already noted, he operated in partnership with his brother-in-law, Dr. Henry Lockhart, who was married to Ellen and Ann's sister, Mary Ann Beall.

Lockhart and Young had been in the right place at the right time to grow with the Chattahoochee-Apalachicola River system cotton economy, and it had been quite successful. The firm had brokered cotton through Edward in the regional cotton-marketing center of Eufaula, it had handled cotton and merchandise through agents at smaller market centers such as Albany, Ga. at the head of the Flint River,[393] and it had worked through other associates at the head of the Chattahoochee in Columbus. In about 1849, Dr Lockhart withdrew from the partnership; and he and Mary resettled in Columbus, Georgia. William remained in Apalachicola and continued the business. William had joint customers with Edward in Eufaula, so in 1850, William advertised the change of name of his business in the Eufaula newspaper, *Spirit of the South*:

> "Co-partnership Notice: The subscriber having associated himself with John D. Atkins will continue the COMMISSION and FORWARDING business at Apalachicola, under the name and style of W. H. Young and Company. Wm. H. Young"[394]

By 1855, William had correctly concluded that the best opportunities in the cotton industry were shifting away from Apalachicola. "The 1840's were Apalachicola's heyday, but just as this star was burning its brightest, it began to dim."[395] There were several handicaps that contributed to its decline. Apalachicola Bay was shallow and obstructed, requiring smaller, shallow-draft boats. The Chattahoochee-Apalachicola River system was not really boatable in dry summer months. But the principal factor in Apalachicola's decline was the coming of the railroad, a much more satisfactory and reliable means of transport than the river. Savannah was the driving force behind the Georgia railroad movement. Savannah leaders wanted badly to tap the rich cotton lands lying between the Flint and Chattahoochee rivers. Savannah supported the Central of Georgia line, which reached Macon from Savannah in 1843. Savannah then supported the Southwestern Railroad, which planned two lines; Macon to Columbus on the Chattahoochee; and Macon to Albany on the Flint.

Columbus leaders were initially unenthusiastic about a railroad coming to their town. They felt it would take away their "wagon trade" hauling cotton from the east into Columbus.

However, Columbus businessmen soon realized that if the railroad weren't built to Columbus, it would go elsewhere, such as Eufaula. The Columbus Times warned, "Either Eufaula or Macon becomes the grocery mart and depot…and every pull of the Locomotive will remind Columbus of her folly, and echo the laugh of our sister city of Macon, at our simple-minded gullibility."[396] So Columbus sponsored the Muscogee Railroad in 1845, which started building line eastward to meet the Southwestern line.

The tracks connecting Columbus and Savannah did not meet until 1853. "On that day the economic structure of the Apalachicola-Chattahoochee River system was forever altered."[397] It was the completion of this line that permitted the two Young families, later that year, to travel by train from Columbus to Savannah to catch a steamer enroute to the 1853 New York World's fair. By securing a rail linkage to the sea, Columbus insured its future prosperity.[398] Apalachicola's cotton receipts showed a dramatic decline compared to those before the advent of the railroad. There was a 41% drop between 1853 and 1855.[399] The railroad brought many changes, including opening up new cotton lands, and thus dramatically increased production of the staple. "But the old economic order that had focused on the river system was changed. Columbus now looked east and west, where it has previously looked only south."[400]

Thus, in 1855, after having accumulated a substantial fortune in Apalachicola, William and Ellen were once again drawn by economic opportunity, and relocated to Columbus, Georgia, where he would achieve even higher pinnacles of business success. There is a tradition, apparently originating with William himself, that as a young man newly arrived in Georgia, he had viewed the Chattahoochee site upon which Columbus was later built, and recognized its potential for water-powered manufacturing. This tradition, which has been accepted by Columbus historians, states that in about 1827, when William was 20 years old, three years after his arrival in Marion, Georgia, William

"…made a prospective tour in the western part of Georgia, where the whites had recently supplanted the Indians…He pursued his journey to the place now occupied by the city of Columbus. Here surveys had also been made for a city, but at the time of his visit it was in the original forest, the Indians occupying the opposite side of the Chattahoochee river. To reach this place he crossed the river at a point where Florence, Ga, now stands, and rode up the government road in Alabama, stopped at Col. Crowel's house (he was the Indian agent), took dinner with him, proceeded up that road until opposite the proposed site of Columbus, and crossed in a flatboat to the Georgia side. He was charmed with the situation, this place being at the head of navigation. He stood on the bank of the river…both sides of which were high, bold bluffs (no swamp or low lands); the river dashing in falls over the granite rocks, with the spray thrown high and reflected by the sun, showed all the colors of the rainbow. The Indians in their bateaux, and on the Rock Islands, and on the banks of the river were employed in fishing. At least one thousand might be seen. All that would have been necessary to make this a fairyland was to fancy the Indians to be the fairies. But it had other charms for Mr. Young. Here was immense waterpower, easily to be controlled, and a country well adapted by soil and climate to produce cotton in perfection, and he here concluded would be (in the future) a great manufacturing city. Here Mr. Young's prospective tour ended. He returned to Marion, mentally deciding that if ever he became pecuniarily able, or could get others to join him, he would make this place his home, and enter into the business of cotton manufacturing. It became the dream and fixed object of his life, and was never lost sight of." [401]

Even while residing in Apalachicola, William had business interests in Columbus, and was thus well known there.[402] At the time of his relocation to Columbus, a group of businessmen were organizing the "Bank of Columbus." In 1856, soon after his arrival, William was asked to become its first president.[403] William invested in the bank, using capital he had accumulated as a commission merchant in Apalachicola,[404] and he would successfully lead this Bank for many years, until his other interests fully consumed his time. Serving with him on the first board of directors of the Bank of Columbus was his and Edward's brother-in-law, Robert M. Gunby, a Columbus merchant who had married Ann and Ellen's sister, Jane Louise Beall.[405]

In the midst of the economic optimism of the 1850's, there occurred the Panic of 1857. This crisis was not caused by the cotton trade; cotton prices remained firm due to a short crop. It was related to over-expansion of railroads, but the Cotton South was drawn into it when New York banks suspended payments in specie (i.e., redemption of paper in gold or silver coin).[406] The Bank of Columbus, having been organized the year before with William as its president, was the only locally owned bank operating in Columbus at the time. Its financial statement in the spring of 1857 demonstrates its sound position going into the recession, and this bank never suspended paying specie for its notes, as did most other banks in the country.[407] Fortunately, the recession was short-lived.[408]

William Henry Young, President of the Bank of Columbus and founder of Eagle Mills

But William's principal objective upon arriving in Columbus was to operate a factory, powered by the falling waters of the Chattahoochee River at Columbus, to spin cotton into cloth. For the past thirty years, William and Edward had virtually grown up as a part of the Southern cotton economy, and had become wealthy by pioneering almost every commercial facet of that industry in the Chattahoochee-Apalachicola River valley. Now, still only 48, William wanted to own and operate the last process in cotton's commercial chain, converting the fiber into cloth.

Setting to work, William found that the best waterfront locations were already owned by "The Water Lot Company," and were occupied by other enterprises of various kinds. There was a flourmill and a woodenware factory. About a year before William arrived, a cotton mill, Howard Manufacturing Company, had been commenced, as well as the Coweta Falls Company, a small factory devoted to cotton and wool making. Both eventually failed and the stockholders lost their entire investment.[409] William was able to purchase a waterfront lot from The Water Lot Company. He then organized and obtained a charter for the Eagle Mill, in which he owned half the capital stock, the other half being owned by eleven other investors.[410] William served as president.[411] The name of the company later became the "Eagle Manufacturing Company."

Under William's leadership, the Eagle Mill quickly became successful, paying its stockholders a substantial dividend, said to be 25 percent, while also accumulating funds for future expansion.[412] Expansion came rapidly. By April 1860, Eagle had acquired from the creditors of Howard Manufacturing Co. all of its mills, property, and privileges. This significant business event was reported in the April 10, 1860 Columbus Enquirer,[413] which reported that the Eagle Manufacturing Company had purchased the Howard Factory, and would run both establishments, adding:

> "We understand that these united Factories run 10,000 cotton and 1300 woolen spindles; that they have 282 looms weaving cotton and woolen goods; that they consume nine bales of cotton and 1000 pounds of wool per day, and employ 500 hands, at an expense of $240 per day for their labor. The capital employed is $375,000."

Eagle also acquired the sites and privileges of the flourmill, the woodenware company, and all the other waterfront industrial sites except those of the Coweta Falls Company, (which later failed and was reorganized into the Muscogee Manufacturing Co.).[414]

William's factory was now one of the largest textile manufacturing enterprises in the South. Principally as a result of William's Eagle Mill, by 1860 Columbus was being referred to as "the largest manufacturing center south of Richmond, Va".[415] The 1860 U. S. Census ranked Muscogee County, of which Columbus is the seat, second only to Richmond in textile production.[416]

In 1859, William Young and a group of Columbus businessmen organized "a stock fire insurance company in Georgia." Its first Board of Directors included William Young and his brother-in-law, Robert M. Gunby.[417] Georgia Home would become a successful, nationally known company. With leadership from William, Georgia Home began the construction of an elegant home office building. Not completed until after the war, the building featured white-painted ironwork fabricated in Pittsburgh. Designed by Robert Hatcher, it was considered one of the most architecturally beautiful buildings in Columbus for many decades, into the mid-twentieth century. It was later occupied by the First National Bank, called the "White Bank," due to its appearance.[418] In 1928 Georgia Home would merge with the Home Insurance Company of New York, and its headquarters would move to New York in 1948.[419] That company continues to flourish today.

After establishing their place in the Columbus business and social community, William and Ellen undertook the construction of a handsome, stately new home. The Italianate structure that they built bore a strong resemblance to the new Eufaula home of

Edward and Ann, which was being constructed at approximately the same time. The similarity of the two houses suggests that there was coordination between the two brothers and sisters in the selection of styles and plans. William and Ellen's house, which they would call "Beallwood," consisted of three stories, including basement rooms, and stood in the midst of extensive gardens and grounds. A Columbus historian gives this description (sparing no detail, including cost):

> "Wm. H. Young's home in the suburbs cost between $18,000 and $20,000 at a time when that was a lot of money. Beallwood was surrounded by many acres of beautiful grounds, facing South on the Hamilton Road, where two roads come together....
>
> Big gates marked the entrance of the lovely old Young place, which had two long lines of trees leading up to the house. The estate had two irrigated gardens for vegetables and flowers, its own private gas-works and water-works, and even a race track, everything that wealth could provide. On top of the house was a cupola where Mr. Young's oldest son, Alfred I. Young, later Secretary and Treasurer of the Eagle and Phenix Mills, used to observe the stars and study astronomy...."[420]

Also residing nearby in the same suburban neighborhood with William and Ellen were two of Ellen's sisters and their husbands: Mr. and Mrs. Robert M. Gunby (Jane Louise Beall); and Dr. and Mrs. Robert H. Lockhart (Mary Beall). In honor of this congregation of Beall sisters, the entire neighborhood area came to be known as "Beallwood."[421] Counting Ann in Eufaula, four of the six Beall sisters of Warrenton, Georgia resided on the Chattahoochee River within fifty miles of each other.

"Beallwood," Columbus Home of William Henry and Ellen Beall Young

William and Ellen had always remained in close contact with their brother and sister and their family in Eufaula, and the move to Columbus permitted easier and more frequent visits. On July 5, 1858, we find Ellen in Eufaula, where she and her niece (her sister, Anna's daughter), Mollie, now 15, spent a day visiting Mrs. John Horry Dent, whom Ellen and William had known since the 1840's, when the Dents visited in Apalachicola to ship cotton. Also calling on Mrs. Dent with Ellen and Mollie was Mrs. McNab.[422] Ten days later, John Horry Dent accompanied Mrs. Dent to Columbus, where she would take the train to Savannah, enroute to visiting her family in the North. While in Columbus they obtained through William Young a $400 check on the Columbus Bank. A month later, when Dent returned to Columbus to meet his wife upon her return, he called on William and Ellen at Beallwood, where he was invited to spend the night. After a rough night on the stagecoach, he "found it very pleasant and agreeable."[423]

Part III

Cataclysm

17
Prelude to War

"Our people of the South, enthusiastic and full of joyous hope, looking for a bright day coming, felt little fear."

Ada Young reflections

The Compromise of 1850 had avoided secession at that time, but a series of subsequent crises and events kept the slavery controversy at a white-hot pitch for the next decade. In 1854, in order to organize the Great Plains and make that rich farming soil available to settlers, Illinois Senator Stephen Douglas proposed, and Congress enacted, the Kansas-Nebraska Act. Based on the principle of "popular sovereignty," the act provided that these two states would be admitted as slave or free, depending upon the outcome of a vote of their residents. The Southern congressmen fully supported the act, and it is easy to see why: The Missouri Compromise of 1820 had provided that slavery would never be permitted north of latitude 36 degrees, 30 minutes; since both Kansas and Nebraska were north of that line, the act repealed the Missouri Compromise. The North, which had viewed that line as sacrosanct, was infuriated by the act. Further, at the time of the act's adoption, there were virtually no residents in the two territories to vote on the slavery issue. The New England Emigrant Aid Company was formed to finance and encourage emigration of anti-slavery voters into the area. The South responded in kind. The South did not contest Nebraska, so the "colonization" efforts of both sides focused on Kansas. Groups of settlers from the South poured into Kansas.

Members of the "Eufaula Regency" were at the forefront of the Kansas settlement movement. In 1855, Eufaula lawyer, Jefferson Buford, led a group of settlers to Kansas, using his personal funds for the support of his group. Among the group was Alpheus Baker, later captain of the Eufaula Rifles and Confederate General. Baker canvassed the territory of Kansas in support of the proslavery faction. Sterling Cato, Eufaula lawyer and brother of Lewis Cato, also moved to Kansas, and eventually became a territorial judge there. The Alabama Legislature appropriated funds to support an expedition to Kansas that was led by Eufaula lawyer, Henry D. Clayton. Clayton was accompanied by his wife, who described the hardships of the trip. As a result of these and similar efforts, Kansas elected a proslavery territorial legislature. But the antislavery party alleged election irregularities, and set up a competing government. Open war broke out in which both sides committed atrocities, resulting in "Bleeding Kansas." The Puritan minister, Rev. Henry Ward Beecher of New England, helped raise money to send arms to the antislavery men, opining that rifles were a "greater moral " than the Bible. So the Sharp's Rifles used to kill Southerners in Kansas were called "Beecher's Bibles." At Pottawatomie Creek, the Puritan fanatic John Brown and his sons captured five proslavery men, killed them, and mutilated their bodies, all in the name of the Lord. We will see more of Brown's devotion to Christian principles later.

The Republican Party was founded in 1854 on a platform of opposing the further extension of slavery, and within a few years, it quickly became one of the two dominant national parties. Its candidate for president in 1856, the adventurer John C. Fremont, was defeated by the Democrat, John Buchanan, who was acceptable to the South.

In 1857, speaking through Chief Justice Taney, the United Supreme Court handed down its long awaited opinion in the case of Dred Scott, a slave. It was a Pro-Southern decision, holding that rights and privileges under the constitution as then written applied only to whites. It held that Congress lacked the power to prohibit slavery in any of the territories carved out of the Louisiana Purchase, so that the Missouri Compromise had been unconstitutional. The latter holding struck at the very reason for the Republican Party's existence, and aroused a storm of opposition greater than that encountered by any Supreme Court decision, before or since. Horace Greeley of the *New York Tribune* said the opinion was entitled to the same moral weight "as the judgment of a majority of those congregated in any Washington barroom."

In 1858, John Brown made his second appearance on the national stage in support of God's will. He and eighteen followers captured the U. S. Arsenal at Harper's Ferry Virginia, called upon the slaves to revolt against their masters, and placed pikes in the hands of slaves brought in from surrounding plantations to use against their masters. Ironically, Brown had selected for his revolution an area that had very few slaves. No slaves revolted, and a federal troop detachment from Washington quickly put down the raid. Brown was tried and executed for treason, but he was warmly supported by the abolitionists. Ralph Waldo Emerson in an address was loudly cheered when he spoke of Brown as "the new saint, awaiting his martyrdom…will make the gallows glorious like the cross." Southerners were stunned by this confirmation that they were so hated in the North that prominent fellow countrymen wanted them murdered in their beds by revolting slaves. Southerners had a deep-seated fear of slave insurrection; to find it being encouraged and approved by their fellow Americans raised in their minds once again the question of whether there was a place for the South in the Union.

All sectional trust and comity had been destroyed and all the compromises had run out. In the fateful presidential election of 1860, Lincoln's Republican platform did not seek the abolition of slavery in the states where it presently existed. Rather, it sought to stop its further extension, and denied the authority of Congress or any territorial legislature to give legal existence to slavery in any territory in the United States. Yancey had succeeded in splitting the Democratic Party. The Northern wing nominated Stephen Douglas of Illinois; the southern wing nominated John C. Breckenridge of Kentucky. The election was further complicated by a new party, the remnants of the disintegrated Whigs, seeking to save the Union by calling a halt to slavery agitation. It called itself the Constitutional Union party and nominated John Bell of Tennessee. Alabama and Barbour County voted strongly for Breckenridge. But on November 8, 1860, Lincoln was elected. He received only 40% of the popular vote, but a majority of the electoral vote.

On Election Day, Edward and Ann's new lawyer son-in-law, Hubert Dent, was attending a term of court at the Barbour County seat in Clayton. Immediately upon hearing the news of Lincoln's election, Hubert sat down and wrote to Anna, declaring his intent to join the army and fight. At this time, Hubert and Anna would have known or suspected that

Anna was pregnant with their first child (although in this Victorian time, not a hint of this fact would ever appear in writing.) In his letter, Hubert is careful to invite Anna to express her feelings about his joining the army, but he made clear where he felt his duty lay. Hubert addresses her as "Nan," "Nannie," and a variety of other pet names:

"Clayton, Ala
Nov 8, 1860

My own Nan
    I have just concluded trying a case and am now in the courthouse surrounded by people. I was much pleased to receive your note. I was dreaming of my darling last night and as for thinking of you Nan, I always think of my Nan. I have heard the election news but Nannie I am not surprised. I did sometimes hope that something would turn up to defeat Lincoln but I always felt that it was hoping against hope. Some of us have been talking with Judge [soon to be governor, John Gill] Shorter about the propriety of adjourning court, but he says that he will go on and hold it.
    Everyone here looks serious but most every one I hope is determined. I shall rejoin the "Rifles" when I return or get up some other company. I feel like the South now expects every man to do his duty and in such an emergency I know my darling will not want her "old dear" to fail. What say you?
    As long as Lincoln is elected I am glad that every northern state has gone for him by large majorities. No man can now have an excuse. The question comes up in a shape that admits of [no] palliation or evasion. It is absolute submission to Black Republican rule or absolute resistance. If the South does submit, then I shall either emigrate or shut up about Southern Rights and Southern equality. There are not a great many here at court and will not be I think. I will be home on Saturday evening as soon as I can, likely not until after night. I only regret that Breckinridge did not carry the entire South but if the South will secede I am satisfied. Don't be uneasy Darling. Recollect that there is someone willing and able to take care of you. God sees the sparrow when five are sold for a farthing and you are of more value than many sparrows. My love much love to all and for yourself all that I can bestow. May heaven protect you—your own—Hubert"

In early December, Anna and her sister Mollie traveled to Columbus for a visit with the Columbus Youngs. In her absence, Hubert stayed with the Young family at Fendall Hall, which he refers to as the "house on the hill." Hubert writes Anna that the entire family is very kind to him, and the sisters try to "mother" him. Hubert writes that Julia McRae [sister of Henry's wife, Maria] is visiting with Ada; and that six-year old Carrie "said she was going to make me write to you tonight. You can't imagine what a patronizing air she uses towards me since you left and says 'Sissy' [a family nickname for Anna] told her she must take care of 'Bud.'" Despite their kindness, without Anna, Hubert does not feel entirely comfortable in the Youngs' house, and is glad when he must leave for Clayton for a term of court.

100

From Clayton, he writes again to her in Columbus, describing the rising tide of war fever:

"Clayton, Ala
Dec 5, 1860

My own Dearest

I have just received yours of the 1st and may heaven bless you for it, Darling. You will not think me unmanly I know when I tell you that my eyes filled with tears when I read your letter—tears of affection and joy to think that my own Darling thought so much of me and so tenderly. Yes, Darling, I did miss you and I miss you more. Oh, Nannie, I do wish so much that I could always be with my Darling. I am almost afraid that I love you too tenderly and too dearly. But Darling, I never want to love you less. You have become as it were a part of myself—a part of my very being.

You have received before this no doubt my other letters to you. I sent the stamps in my first letter. I think now there is some prospect of court adjourning on Saturday. If it does I want to go for you immediately. I have business here before the probate court on next Monday but I am satisfied that I can get some one to attend to it for me. I will be here until Saturday. Will go home Saturday evening whether court adjourns or not. So if you write to me after you receive this direct it to Eufaula.

Henry Shorter [brother of John Gill and Eli] brought your letter out to me today. He and Chambers and Jim Buford came out today. [Alpheus] Baker and Cary went over to Cuthbert—are getting very patriotic.

It seems to me that the chances at present are that there will be a fight in South Carolina in sixty days. The President is against secession and says he feels bound to execute the Federal laws in the collection of revenue. Such a course on his part will I think bring on a fight. I do not know but that it will unite the South better than anything else. Whenever blood is shed it will put a truce to all negotiations and render the formation of a Southern Confederacy almost certain as I might say as certain as any human affairs. I regret that the President thinks proper to pursue the course he does but it can't be helped. I sometimes think we are going to have troublesome times and then again I think we will not.

Nannie there is an overruling providence in all human affairs and every thing is in his hands. This thought makes me feel much more calm than I would otherwise.

Old Jeff Buford has called a bar meeting for tomorrow to refuse to receive northern claims for collection. It is all a flourish and

_____ and don't amount to any thing at all. If Alabama secedes Northern men can't use our courts to collect their debts. If she does not secede why it makes no difference whenever the North acknowledges our independence. Treaties will be made to regulate commercial intercourse, which will provide for all such things. So such things as Jeff Buford proposes is all stuff and just to create a sensation and if I get a chance I will tell meeting so tomorrow. While I have no objection to signing such resolutions, I hate all such <u>clap-trap</u>.

Well, Darling, my fingers are a little cold. I am writing to you in one part of the courthouse away from any fire and it is a cold _____ day and I will close. Give my love to all friends. Tell Mollie I have sent her a message or messages to her if that is what she means. Give my love to her and tell her to take care of herself. Good by, Darling, may the time soon come when I will take my Dearest in my arms and give her kisses and receive sweet kisses from her in return. Oh, Darling, how I would like to have my sweet Darling's own arms around me. We will be separated longer this time than ever before, but good by Dearest. Your own loving and devoted – Hubert"

On December 19, South Carolina seceded, setting off happy and excited celebrations in Eufaula, Alabama. Lincoln's election also triggered resolutions of the Alabama Legislature requiring the Governor to call an election of delegates to a convention to consider secession. The Convention was to assemble on Jan. 7, 1861. There was little doubt that Alabama would secede. On New Years Day in Barbour County, John Horry Dent, generally regarded as a conservative on secession, recorded these despondent thoughts in his journal:

"The year opens full of troubles to these once United States. Discord reigns supreme. The house is divided, and a breakup is inevitable. How it will terminate God alone can foresee. The South secedes from the Union, owing to northern aggression, and determinations to interfere with our Negro property, a southern confederacy is our only honorable and safe course."[424]

Two days later, on Thursday, January 3, John Horry Dent, his wife, and daughter, Liz, attended a New Year party at the home of Mr. and Mrs. Cato, ardent secessionists, where the guests undoubtedly included the Cato's next-door neighbors, the Edward Youngs. It can be imagined that questions about secession, and about what the future might hold, were the principal topics of talk for that evening. After the party, the J. H. Dents spent the night next door at the Youngs', and returned to the plantation the next day.[425]

In the election of the state convention, the principal debate was between the "cooperationists," i. e. those who wanted to secede only after consultation and cooperation with other Southern states; and the "secessionists," i. e. those who favored immediate, outright secession. A majority of the latter was elected to the convention. Representing

Barbour County were John Cochran, Alpheus Baker, J. C. B. Mitchell, and J. W. L. Daniel, all staunch secessionists. Hubert's former law mentor, now U. S. Congressman James L. Pugh of Eufaula, resigned from his seat in Congress. Arriving in Montgomery the day before the convention voted, he counseled secession, stating there could be no compromise short of accepting Lincoln's election.[426] On January 9, the Ordinance of Secession was adopted and Alabama became a "free, sovereign and independent state."

Next door to the Edward Youngs', at the Cato house, there was a joyous celebration to greet the news that Alabama was out of the Union. In Eufaula "…the cannons fired, the bells rang forth many peals, the military companies were out, much of the city was illuminated…fireworks and shouting filled the air."

Edward and Ann's third daughter, Ada, was at this time an impressionable fifteen year old. Like most Eufaulians, it was not John Horry Dent's grim foreboding that she felt. Writing years later, she remembered the happy optimism of the time:

> "Our people of the South, enthusiastic and full of joyous hope, looking for a bright day coming, felt little fear."[427]

18
Eufaula Rifles; The President's Military Escort

"But the Capt. and Privates Pugh and Cochran are working with the governor to keep us here until the inauguration of Jeff Davis."

Hubert Dent to Anna

"The man and the hour have met."

William L. Yancey

Pursuant to an invitation of the Alabama secession convention, six of the seven states of the lower South assembled in Montgomery. (Texas had not yet completed its secession process). On February 9, 1861, the delegates unanimously adopted a provisional constitution for the Confederate States of America, and unanimously elected Jefferson Davis as provisional president.

In Eufaula, also on February 9, the same day the Confederacy came into being, Hubert Dent enlisted in the Eufaula Rifles, being mustered in by Capt. Reuben Thorne. Pursuant to prevailing practice, the company elected its officers. Alpheus Baker, age 35, was elected Captain, the commanding officer. Hubert Dent, age 28, was elected First Lieutenant, or second in command. This infantry company enrolled over 125 members. The second lieutenant was Horace W. Smith; a "brevet" (temporary) second lieutenant was William ("Bill") A. McTyer.

In addition to Hubert, the Rifles included other Young connections: John McRae, age 21, brother of Henry Young's wife, Maria McRae; and it included the 16-year-old future son-in-law of the Youngs, James ("Jim") H. G. Martin, who would marry Ada Young after the war, become a leader in the Democratic Party and practice law in Washington.

The Rifles also included, as privates, some influential and well-known political leaders from the "Eufaula Regency" days: former state senator E. C. Bullock; former U. S. Congressman James L. Pugh (who would become a Confederate Congressman and later, United States Senator); and former States Rights congressional candidate, Judge John Cochran, under all of whom Hubert Dent had studied or practiced law; and Henry R. Shorter, (brother of John Gill and Eli), who would after the war become a noted lawyer and chairman of the Alabama Railroad Commission. These would not remain privates long.

As Jefferson Davis traveled to Montgomery to be inaugurated as President of the Confederacy, his train entered Alabama from the east at West Point, Georgia on February 16. There he was greeted by a large committee of distinguished Alabamians, chaired by E. C. Bullock, of Eufaula, who gave a welcoming address.[428] Davis arrived in Montgomery at 10 o'clock that night, and was escorted by a large crowd to the Exchange Hotel, where he spoke briefly from the balcony. Also speaking briefly was William L. Yancey, who honored Davis with these words, which would become famous: "...fortunate are the people of the South. They have found the man as well as the principles...the man and the hour have met!"[429]

Also in Montgomery that night were the Eufaula Rifles. Some of the prominent members were probably present for Davis' remarks at the Exchange Hotel, but the company was camped at "the fairgrounds." The Rifles had been ordered by Governor Moore to Fort Barrancas, at Pensacola, Florida, but were first detained in Montgomery to participate in Davis' inauguration. They had left Eufaula on February 12 and traveled by way of Columbus, where Hubert visited briefly with Anna's uncle and aunt, William and Ellen Young, at Beallwood. The Company arrived in Montgomery on February 14, two days before Davis, and were waiting in camp, somewhat impatiently, until they could proceed to Fort Barrancas.

While waiting in Montgomery, Hubert wrote to Anna. Hubert tries to accustom both himself and Anna to the fact that he is marching off to *war*, in which men sometimes get killed. But reflecting the prevailing mood of optimism, Hubert thinks he will be home in two months.

"Camp of the Eufaula Rifles
Near Montgomery, Feb. 14, 1861

My own Sweet Darling
Here am I in camp at the fair grounds. All the commissioned officers except myself have left and about three fourths of the men. I mean they have gone over to Montgomery. The rest of us are here. But as Bill McTyer [the company second lieutenant] said in his lines on the death of a favorite hound, "every dog must have his day," and so I will have mine tomorrow. I preferred remaining here today and sleeping all night so that tomorrow I will be fresh and walk over to Montgomery will remain all day.

Judge [John Gill] Shorter and John T. Morgan have visited us and all the men who came over with us from Eufaula excepting Chambers.

I forgot to say that we reached here about 12 o'clock. It is now nearly 8. I am writing on the tray of my trunk, up in a circus wagon, and my bed is up here too. I went out to Beallwood. Saw everybody out there, stayed a short time. Went back, slept at books and got up at 3 o'clock this morning. Marched to the depot in the rain... I wrote you from Columbus.

It is said that we are to leave here for Pensacola Saturday morning. But the Capt. [Alpheus Baker] and privates Pugh and Cochran are working with the governor [A. B. Moore] to keep us here until the inauguration of Jeff Davis. I would like to see the inauguration very much but I am not satisfied that it would be best for us to remain. It is impossible to have strict discipline while here and drills and the men need both very much. While therefore as a man I would like to remain. As a soldier I don't wish to remain so long. I am impatient to get to Pensacola and get settled at least for the time that I have to stay there. I have been in a state of suspense and uncertainty long enough.

The governor I learn does not favor the idea of our remaining and it is uncertain whether we will have any collision at all or not. Men of information are divided. Judge Shorter thinks we will be releaved in six weeks. I would be content with that.

Nannie, my Darling, this is no idle sport that your old Dear has gone into and he knows it. But he has made up his mind to bear it all like a soldier without a murmur. I think it was the only time I ever saw Hutch Cook in tears, the morning he met us on the boat. He could not keep them back; they would come. He is outraged at the governor calling us out. This of course you will not mention.

But thank God and the Company I am lifted above the most exposed and arduous duties and I intend to take care of myself. I have stood every thing thus far... Never felt better in health and were it not that I am parted from my Darling, Nannie, whom I love better than every thing else on earth I would have nothing to regret. I am in good health, strong, patient, able to undergo fatigue and exposure and if it comes to fighting I am not afraid but what I will win my way to glory with my strong right arm and well tempered sword. The thought that my Nannie will look upon me with a broader and fonder gaze and that she will think of me as one who stands higher with men than he does now will nerve my arm and fire my heart. But I must stop this sort of talk Nannie. I sometimes think that even you have not sounded the depths of my soul and I believe that you have looked deeper into it than any one else. I will stop that.

I will have to make some arrangements with Judge [John Gill] Shorter about getting your letters to me at Pensacola. I will make them and write you. I cannot be deprived of that pleasure. Well my Darling good night. I will finish this in the morning. I hope you will have pleasant dreams of your Dear. Good night my Angel.

Good morning Darling. I hope you are well. I slept well and feel first rate. I expect to leave here tomorrow for Pensacola. I am getting on well. It is a bright and beautiful day and I am going up town to see what is to be seen.

I think we will be back in two months. Our company excites much comment and has quite a reputation. The governor will not consent for us to be the guard of honor to Jeff Davis. The men are all well except McLeod and have behaved well here.

I do not know that I will have an opportunity of writing again here. Good by. My love to all the family from Carrie up also to Will and Henry and families. May heaven's choicest blessings rest upon and guard and protect and cheer you in the prayer of your own devoted --

Hubert

P.S. We remain until Tuesday morning. Are appointed the escort of Jeff Davis. Bill McTyre is well. Tell his wife he will write tomorrow."

Four days later, February 18, 1861, Inauguration Day dawned bright and clear. At 10 o'clock, Dexter Avenue was lined from Court Square fountain to the Capitol with observers, the ladies dressed in finery and carrying silken parasols. Thousands watched from sidewalks, windows, and rooftops. The procession formed beside the Exchange Hotel at the intersection of Commerce and Dexter. The cavalcade led off with Herman Arnold's Band, followed by the military escort, consisting of the Eufaula Rifles and three other units. Then came President Davis and Vice President Alexander Stephens, riding in Tennant Lomax's elegant open carriage drawn by six iron-gray horses. There followed carriages of various congressional, state and city dignitaries, and other citizens on foot.[430]

As Captain Alpheus Baker and First Lieutenant Hubert Dent marched their troop of Eufaula Rifles up Dexter Avenue ahead of President Davis' carriage on this historic occasion, Arnold's band suddenly burst forth with an electrifying, emotion-stirring arrangement that galvanized ten thousand spectators with excitement and patriotism. This was the unveiling of "Dixie." It had been written for a New York minstrel show two years earlier by Dan Emmet, a northerner who penciled it on the stage wall of the Montgomery Theatre. But before this Inaugural parade, it had never been heard set to band music. Almost overnight, this spine-tingling, inspirational music became the unofficial national anthem of the Confederacy, described by one writer as the "Southern 'Marseillaise'"[431]

In the Capitol, after being presented to the Confederate Congress, Davis returned to the portico, took the oath of office administered by Howell Cobb of Georgia, and addressed his inaugural to the Congress and assembled crowd, expressing these themes:

> "...The right solemnly proclaimed at the birth of the States, and which has been affirmed and reaffirmed in the bills of rights of States subsequently admitted into the Union of 1789, undeniably recognize in the people the power to resume the authority delegated for purposes of government. Thus the sovereign States here represented proceeded to form this Confederacy, and it is by abuse of language that their act has been denominated a revolution....
>
> "...Doubly justified by the absence of wrong on our part, and by wanton aggression on the part of others, there can be no cause to doubt that the courage and patriotism of the people of the Confederate States will be found equal to any measures of defense which honor and security may require.... [W]e must prepare to meet the emergency and to maintain, by the final arbitrament of the sword, the position which we have assumed among the nations of the earth....
>
> "...[W]e have vainly endeavored to secure tranquility, and to obtain respect for the rights to which we were entitled. As a necessity, not a choice, we have resorted to the remedy of separation; and henceforth our energies must be directed to the conduct of our own affairs, and the perpetuity of the Confederacy which we have formed..."

Soon after the conclusion of the inauguration, Hubert and the Eufaula Rifles resumed their journey to Fort Barrancas, at Pensacola. At this time, Anna Dent was five months pregnant with their first child.

19
A Year At Fort Barrancas

"Dear Sir, I am happy to inform you that Anna had a fine boy last night."
Edward Young to "Mr. Hubert Dent"

In February of 1861, the two most troublesome strongpoints still held by the federal forces within Confederate coastal defenses were Ft. Sumter at Charleston and Ft. Pickens at Pensacola. Earlier, in January, Alabama Gov. A. B. Moore had the foresight to order Alabama state troops to seize the federal military installations in Alabama: Fort Morgan, Fort Gaines, and the Mount Vernon Arsenal.[432] The Florida government had not been as alert or effective. Florida had taken control of Fort Barrancas at the former U. S. Navy Yard on Pensacola Bay, as well as Fort McRee, across the Bay. However, the federals still held control of Fort Pickens, a well-fortified

Pensacola Bay in 1861, showing Confederate-held Forts Barrancas and McRee, and Federally-held Ft. Pickens

installation at the western tip of Santa Rosa Island, dominating the entrance to Pensacola Bay. The Florida commander had been slow to act, had lost an early opportunity to seize control of the fort, and had thereafter been unable to obtain the fort. Gov. Moore felt that "the safety of the seceding states of the Gulf" was not secure while Fort Pickens remained in federal control.[433] He therefore decided to send Alabama troops to assist in taking Fort Pickens.

The Alabama state troops ordered to Pensacola included the Eufaula Rifles, the Eufaula Pioneers, the Wilcox True Blues, the Tallapoosa Rifles, the Rough and Ready Pioneers, the Red Eagles, and others. These units rendezvoused at Pensacola in February and March, and then reorganized themselves into the First Alabama Infantry Regiment, the very first regiment organized under the act of the Alabama Legislature authorizing the enlistment of troops for twelve months. The Eufaula Rifles became "Company B" of the First Alabama Infantry Regiment.

Shortly after the Eufaula Rifles arrived at Fort Barrancas, Lt. Hubert Dent was detached and put in command of a steam tug, "The Kneaphy" (sometimes spelled "Neaffie"). The duty of this boat was to patrol Pensacola Bay, usually at night, to prevent any communication between Pensacola or Warrington and the federal fleet anchored just outside Pensacola Bay. The Kneaphy had three crewmembers to run the tug, and a command of twenty soldiers armed with muskets, (one of which was the lawyer, Private E. C. Bullock). It was also equipped with a 12-pounder howitzer.[434]

Some time after the First Alabama Infantry Regiment was organized, it was transferred from control of the State of Alabama to the Confederate government. This was done under Confederate Major General Jere Clemens. During this time, Gen. Clemens resided in Pensacola, and one of Lt. Dent's duties on the Kneaphy was to pick up Gen. Clemens each morning, boat him to Fort Barrancas, and to boat him back to Pensacola each evening. Under these circumstances, Hubert saw a good deal of Gen. Clemens. Hubert says that, "In his conversations with me, he early predicted a long and bloody war. This was contrary to the general opinions entertained at that time."[435]

As will be seen, Hubert and Anna, who were separated after only eight months of marriage, corresponded frequently throughout his four years of army service, sometimes several times a week in the early years. Only a few of her letters to him in the field survived, but she meticulously preserved virtually all of his letters to her. As a result, there are extant today over seventy five letters from Hubert to Anna, reporting news from the front, describing his feelings about events, and expressing his love for Anna. He also had correspondence with her sisters, some of which survives, and with her brothers and father, none of which is now available.

During the first weeks at Ft. Barrancas, when no military action had occurred anywhere, Hubert's letters home have a light and festive tone. He describes unusual flowers and shrubs around the officers' quarters of the naval station, and discusses ways to send cuttings to Anna or her mother for planting in Eufaula. He admits that, "So far my experience here is more like visiting a watering place than being on a military campaign…" Some of the Eufaula volunteers began a handwritten camp newsletter, called the "Pioneer Banner," to send back to family and sweethearts in Eufaula. It contained poetry, news, and descriptions of camp life. It spoke of future victories, reflecting the romantic view of the coming war that prevailed at this period.

Since his election in November, Abraham Lincoln, the immediate impetus for all that was happening, had remained ominously silent about his intentions toward the Confederacy. However, his inaugural address on March 4, 1861 shattered all hope that the South would be allowed to leave the Union peacefully. He pledged his administration to "hold, occupy, and possess federal property and places." "Physically speaking," he said, "we cannot separate," and he expressed his intention to carry out his oath to "preserve, protect and defend," the Union.

The men at Fort Barrancas began to acknowledge that there would be heavy work ahead. On March 7, Gen. Braxton Bragg was given overall command of all Confederate forces in the Pensacola area. On the same day, Hubert wrote Anna:

"Barrancas Barracks, Fla.
March 7, 1861

"My own Sweet Pet
I received yesterday yours mailed the 1st inst…. It is early this morning and the mail closes at 9 o'clock and I must hurry. Breakfast is not ready I got up early to write to you.

I was up last night hauling cannon until half past 12 o'clock. We moved three cannon yesterday to a sand Battery--one from Barrancas and two from the navy yard. Instead of moving them on skids as I wrote we would be compelled to do, we got them on truck wheels and pulled them through the sand. One of them weighed 9000 lbs and the wheels buried some 12 or 18 inches in the sand in some places-- so you may well imagine what sort of heavy pulling it was. Our men work well and cheerfully.

The news from Washington is considered warlike and excites considerable commotion. Forney did not go to Montgomery after all - he stopped in Pensacola and went to work getting up sand bags and flannel for cartridges. Baker also turned back and is now here. Boatwright left here yesterday morning. I sent a letter to you – his wife is sick is the reason he got a furlough.

There is considerable variety of opinion here in reference the Presidents message. Some think it means war others think differently. For my own part I think if we want to get possession of Pickens that we will have to fight for it and that is my chief concern just now – and further I would not be surprised if Lincoln should attempt to reoccupy the public property here. If he does and waits ten days or two weeks we will give him a respectable fight and with anything like equality we will whip his army and hold the property.

Nannie my Darling I am beginning to think that our time here is very uncertain. We may remain here for the whole twelve months. I have made up my mind to any thing and will try and be prepared for it. I have plenty of work Nannie plenty of it and when you do not receive letters from me just think of my being up pulling cannon until 12 ½ o'clock at night and being so busy during the day as not to have time for anything that would occupy me an hour.

Give my love to all the family. I must hasten to close. I have had breakfast and it is getting time for me to go to my work. I am not my own man now Darling. I have to obey the orders of superior officers - and just here permit me to say that take out Forney and I would not give a dried apple for three-fourths of the balance. But Forney conducts the whole affair and I depend on him for everything. Well My Dearest I must go, good by god bless you my Darling Love …The weather is fine, goodby my love to all as ever your own devoted and loving Hubert"

Although Lincoln had signaled his intentions, the lack of any actual combat permitted a sense of calm to continue in camp and at home. A number of Eufaula wives chose this time to pay visits to their husbands at Pensacola. Although Anna was three months away from delivering the baby, she made the trip to Pensacola to visit Hubert. She was probably accompanied by a servant, and by one or more other Eufaula wives of men stationed at Fort Barrancas. Under the best of circumstances it would not have been an easy trip for a pregnant lady: stagecoach or steamboat to Columbus, train to Montgomery, and another train to Pensacola. But Anna and Hubert had separated after only eight months of marriage, and it was difficult for her to foresee when she could see him again after the baby was born. Anna arrived in Pensacola early in the second week of March 1861. Hubert was able to arrange suitable quarters in the house in which his regimental offices were located, at the Navy Yard near Fort Barrancas. Anna would remain with Hubert for about two months.

While Anna was in Pensacola, an important family event took place back in Eufaula. On March 19, 1861, her brother Henry and his wife Maria had their first child, a boy. This was Edward and Ann's second grandchild, both boys. When Ada, Anna's fifteen year-old sister, wrote about the baby, a name had not yet been selected. It is a compliment to Hubert's standing in the family that one of the names allegedly being considered was "Hubert McRae." When Ada mentions Hubert's being a "captain," she is referring to his command of the patrol boat. He is still an army first lieutenant:

"Eufaula, March 28
Thursday morning 1861

"My dear Sis:
        You cannot imagine how delighted, Sis, I was to receive a letter from you. I had been looking for one sometime.
        You must not expect an interesting letter for there is no news at all to write. Mollie & Helen received their letters a few moments ago, sent by Mr. Simpson, I expect that you are enjoying yourself finely, I should like very much to come down myself and spend a month or two. I suppose that you do not like house keeping down there anyway. Have you many flowers in the yard around the house that you are in? And what kind are they. I believe all of your cuttings that brother Hubert sent are living. I have not heard Ma say any were dead.
        Oh! Sis the little baby (he has no name yet) is the sweetest little creature that you ever saw, he laughs the prettiest, I have been to see him every day since he was born but one & then I had such a bad headache that I could not go. Mollie spent the night down there last night & the night before, he does not cry hardly any. They say that they have not thought of a name yet. I do wish that you and brother Hubert could see him. Mollie has come & says that brother spoke of two names last night, Willie Augustus & Hubert McRae.
        Ask brother Hubert if he don't think that the "Pioneers" or "Clayton Generals" ought to have been selected to carry the flag.

I expect you enjoy the sailing very much with <u>Captain Dent,</u> how does he like being Captain

...Some of the men of the companies are coming home all the time, several are here now. Julian McKenzie will leave Monday. Ma says she will send brother Hubert's clothes by the first ones that goes. Is it much warmer at Pensacola than here? We have very pleasant weather now. Night before last it rained quite hard & lightened and thundered a great deal.

It is about three weeks since you left but it seems a great deal longer. I suppose more of the ladies will return in sometime.

Sis, I have learned to <u>crochet</u>--since you left & have made several pairs of mats. I like it very much it is very nice work. Do you sew or do not you have time? Have you drawn any flowers since you have been gone? You must try and draw some of all kinds, so that we can see what sort they have. Ma has a good many flowers in bloom in the conservatory, but it does not look as pretty as it has been, her roses are beginning to bloom & look beautiful, but Sis you ought to see the mound all of the Valerias are in bloom and that large bunch of Candy Tuft, soon the yard will be a perfect beauty. Ma is busy in her yard.

Janie and Carrie Toney staid to dinner with us yesterday. Miss Ret is still in Columbus & will not return in five or six weeks, she is enjoying herself very much.

That is all the news, you must excuse the very uninteresting letter as positively I had no news to write, but felt like writing to you, I am going to write oftener hereafter. All send love to you both. Give my love to brother Hubert and tell him he must write to me soon & you also.

Your affectionate sister, Ada"

The baby was given his father's name, Henry Augustus Young.[436] Perhaps because of wartime absences, the Young practice of prompt baptism of babies was suspended, and the baptism of Henry, Jr. was postponed. A number of his important relatives were all in Pensacola: his Aunt Anna and her husband Hubert; his uncle (Maria's brother) John McRae; as well other family friends and connections that the family would wish to be present for the baptism. The Rev. Joseph Cotten would baptize him two years later, under circumstances of great sadness, as we will see.

An even more crucial event occurred during Anna's visit to Pensacola. Hubert's prediction that Lincoln would take a hard line was correct. Negotiations had taken place between Union and Confederate authorities on a possible peaceful transfer of Fort Sumter and Fort Pickens to the Confederacy. Some of his cabinet were advising him to evacuate Fort Sumter, where tension had built up, but hold Fort Pickens. Indeed, the Confederate representatives later said that Secretary of State Seward had in fact agreed to relinquish Fort Sumter. But here Lincoln displayed his political genius. He was not at all sure that his war plans would be supported by the public. The abolitionists were saying, "Good riddance," and many ordinary people would not have yet been ready to support Lincoln's intention to start killing people to coerce the South to stay in a Union it had voluntarily entered. Having been informed that any effort to provision the forts would precipitate war, Lincoln adroitly maneuvered the South into firing the first shot—into "starting" the war. He ordered the supply ship to proceed, and notification of this order sent to the Confederate authorities.

The Confederate cabinet, meeting in the Exchange Hotel in Montgomery, was then faced with a decision. Secretary of State Robert Toombs counseled against firing the first shot, but with the knowledge that the South Carolina authorities might attack regardless of the cabinet's position, the cabinet decided to act. Using the commercial facilities of the Southern Telegraph Company in the Winter Building, across Court Square from the Exchange Hotel, a series of telegrams passed between Secretary of War Leroy Pope Walker and Gen. P. G. T. Beaureard, the Confederate commander in Charleston, culminating in this operative message on April 11, 1861:

> "Do not desire needlessly to bombard Fort Sumter. If Major Anderson [the federal commander] will state the time at which, as indicated by him, he will evacuate, and agree that, in the mean time, he will not use his guns against us, unless ours should be employed against Fort Sumter, you are thus to avoid the effusion of blood. If this or its equivalent be refused, reduce the fort as your judgment decides to be most practicable."

The Confederate batteries opened fire and "reduced the fort," thereby commencing the bloodiest war in American history, before or since. The resulting surge of indignation in the North over the attack on the United States flag and troops provided political cover for Lincoln's action four days later in calling for seventy five thousand volunteer militiamen to "cause the law to be duly executed". But he obscured the seriousness of the future by unrealistically enlisting the volunteers for only three months. On April 19, Lincoln declared a blockade of all Southern ports. Although it was only a "paper" blockade then, it would later have a significant effect on Eufaula, Columbus, and the Chattahoochee valley.

A few days after Sumter fell, Anna, still in Pensacola, received a letter from another sister, Mollie. Mollie reports that their six year old sister, Carrie, is also writing a letter to Anna. The wedding Mollie refers to is that of their Columbus first cousin, Alfred Irwinton Young, oldest son of William and Ellen. He married Clara Wildman on April 1, 1861.[437] As we will later see, eight months after his wedding, Alfred would depart Columbus enroute to Savannah as First Lieutenant and second-in-command of Croft's Battery of artillery, which, before the war's end, would become "Young's Battery".

"Eufaula, April 16, 1861

My dear Sister,
        I received your letter of the 11th last week and Pa's [i.e. the letter to Pa] received Sunday.

Mrs. Clark and Mrs. Boatwright have returned and we got the bundle you sent by them. Carrie was delighted with the sacque and says she is much obliged to you. She said this morning that "Sissy did not do any thing but work for her." She is writing to you now but I doubt if she sends it. Dr. Black leaves for Pensacola today. Mr. McNair left today and <u>Mr. Brown</u> goes tomorrow. I know you will be astonished to hear that he is going.

I suppose you have heard by this time the good news from Fort Sumter. Not one of our men killed or wounded. There was a Dispatch received today saying that Virginia would secede today and that 5 of the Federal officers resigned.

I wonder what Lincoln thinks now. The next thing I expect to hear is that he has disappeared. But enough of old Lincoln.

The family are all well. Marian was coming up to spend two or three days with us but it is so damp & cool that I do no know now when she will be able to do so. I have not seen her since Friday.

There are about 100 men here that wish to go to Pensacola and remain until Pickens is taken. <u>William</u> [her oldest brother] among them he said he would go last night if he could. They only wish to have their expenses paid there and back and stay until the fight is over should there be one.

The "Columbus Guards" (150 men) leave for Tybee this evening. Julius was with them. He is the only one I believe that we know.

We are all very anxious indeed to see you but I would not like to say come home for I would not wish to do so if I were in your place.

I saw Mr. Lilly last Sunday and if all of the men improved as much as he has I think we had better send some more down there.

I have not decided whether I will go to the wedding [of Alfred Young and Clara Wildman, in Columbus] or not. It will depend entirely upon what is going on at Pensacola for if they should have a fight of course I would not like to go for I could not enjoy myself.

Ma had a letter from Aunt Ellen giving a description of Clara Wildman. She has been staying in Beallwood about a week now and they are all perfectly delighted with her.

Lou Dunn said that Lizzie Dent [daughter of John Horry Dent, no relation to Hubert Dent] invited her out to her house the 2nd of May to the wedding. She said she expected it was Mr. Clark though Lizzie would not say any thing more about it.

Come as soon as you can. My love to Brother and take time to write whenever he can to me. I should be glad to hear from you everyday.

Write soon and often to
Your Sister Mollie Young"

Excuse bad writing and mistakes I am in a great hurry"

Unfortunately, "old Lincoln" did not "disappear." The excitement over the fall of Fort Sumter that inspired Will Young to talk of going immediately to Pensacola to fight until the war is over, soon cooled. As we will see in a later chapter, Will's contribution to the Confederacy, though valuable, would take a different form.

Anna and Hubert's next letter from home is written by her sister, Helen. At this time, Helen is fourteen years old and a student at the Union Female College. To get slightly ahead of our story, eight years later, when Helen is 22, she will marry Hubert's younger brother, George Hatch Dent, who is presently living with his parents in Maryland but will soon be fighting in Virginia. In this 1861 letter, the only surviving writing of Helen's, we see characteristics of young teenagers of all centuries. Within two weeks of the nation's rupture at Fort Sumter, when families are broken and the men are leaving to fight the Civil War, Helen makes the teenager's age-old complaint that, "the times are very dull at present in Eufaula."

Eufaula Ala
April 28th/61

My dear brother & Sister,
It is now Sunday evening, and as I have nothing to do I will employ this time on doing that pleasant task which is writing to you.
I received your letters sometime ago, & I do not know exactly the reason why I did not answer them sooner I was perfectly delighted when I received them.
Now I have commenced this letter I know I cannot write an interesting letter for the times are very dull at present in Eufaula.
Mollie received Sissie's [another family nickname for Anna] letter this morning, and we were very sorry to hear that Brother H. [Hubert] was sick, I hope he will soon be well.
Brother Henry, Sister Maria & the baby spent the day with us yesterday, it rained nearly all day such was not very pleasant, you ought to see the baby it is surely the sweetest baby that ever was yesterday was the first day he had on a dress and bonnet, Mrs. Fendell made it a little pink silk bonnet and he does look so cunning and sweet with it on, they waided [weighed] him yesterday and he waided 12 pouns, he is fat as a butterball.
Friday evening was Public [recitations at the Union Female College] there were a good many present, most of the girls had good compositions, There was a piece played on two pianos, Mr. Van Houten [the College music teacher for many years] and Johnny Huff played on the violins, & Mr.Boden on the cornet it sound very prettie, Mr. Cotton [the Methodist minister] made the address.
I am getting a long very well in music and drawing of the two I believe I like music the best, Mr. Van Houten says he is going to give a grand concert, this Summer, so you & both must be home by then, We are going to have a private examination, which I am very sorry.
We have been having strawberries six days this week, yesterday there was 9 quarts, that is a great many for this time of the year,

116

Mollie sends her love to you both and says she will write soon, Ed says he should like for Sissie to answer his letter, all the family send love to you both,

You cannot imagine how much we want to see you.

I must now close with the wish to see you both soon, Please excuse all mistakes and bad writeing as it is written in a hurry, Write soon,

Believe me as ever your affectionate

Sister Helen

Enclosed with Helen's letter to Hubert and Anna was a letter from her mother, Ann, in which she discusses plans to come to Pensacola and accompany Anna home. It is likely that, from the very beginning of Anna's visit to Pensacola, Ann Young had concerns about her daughter's being in a distant, primitive, military installation in an advanced state of pregnancy. The attack on Fort Sumter two weeks before this letter could only have increased her concern and led to the conviction that it was time to bring Anna home. This letter is the only surviving writing of Ann Fendall Beall. In addition to giving notice of her plans to come for Anna, she discusses some of the everyday happenings of the household, the family, and of Eufaula. She also reveals her warm respect for her household slave.

[Enclosed with Helen's letter of April 28, 1861 to Anna and Hubert]

My dear Children

Mollie received yours (Annas) letter this morning. I hope Hubert you are quite well again. It would be so bad to be sick down there away from home.

I am still ready and intend going down to see you and to bring Sissie back with me. As everyone seemed to be of the opinion there would not be an engagement very soon, I have put off going to let her stay as long as she can, knowing it would make you both happier. It will depend on how things go and what I hear from you as to what time I go. If nothing happens I expect it will be about two weeks.

All are well at home. I don't hear of any sickness at all from Ala…I expect they are having hot times in Maryland and Virginia. I hope it will turn out that you will not fight at Pensacola.

Mr Young, Mollie and I are invited to see Lizzie Dent and Whit Clark marry at 11 o'clock thursday. I expect we will go if nothing happens. I don't believe any of the family will get off to Alfs wedding. He and his wife, Mary Jane, and Gussie leave for Norfolk that evening. And Alf is talking of joining the company there.

Sissie you did not say whether you received every thing in that box. I was so glad to hear you had received it. I hope Hubert's clothes went safe. I was quite worried at the idea of their being lost.

Miss Medows spoke of returning soon in a week or two. I reckon I'll go with her. She and the Treadwells have compromised their case. By they (the Treadwells) give her ten thousand dollars. She came home to sue for more of his property. Cato was her Lawyer. Don't mention this, as I should not like her to know I said any thing about it. She says, "Tell Addie not to play in the grass and get <u>snake bit</u>."

Oh I am so crazy to see you both. How I love to have you home again, Willis brought your letter. Goodby my dear children until I see you.

[Name unclear, undoubtedly a black servant] kissed your note and said you had his prayers and best wishes all the while. They are warm hearted true people.

Write often to your affectionate, Mother.

I wish you were here to eat strawberries. We gathered 9 quarts yesterday."

Ann's mention of the wedding of Lizzie Dent refers, not to a relative of Hubert's, but to the daughter of the Youngs' close friends, the John Horry Dents. The wedding of "Alf" is not Ann's nephew, Alfred Young of Columbus; he had married Clara Wildman on April 1. The lawyer, Cato, is the Youngs' next-door neighbor; and the Treadwells, whom he sued, are also friends and neighbors of the Youngs on College Hill. Their daughter, Adriana "Addie" Keitt Treadwell, to whom the cryptic message was sent, was a close companion of Mollie Young. In a few years, we will see Addie as Mollie's co-conspirator in girlish flirting with Mollie's husband-to-be.

While Ann was in Pensacola with her daughter and son-in-law, the question of how long to remain was settled when General Bragg concluded that a fight might be imminent, and ordered that all the ladies be sent home. (In fact, no fight occurred at Pensacola for another six months.) After a two-month visit, Anna started home in early May with her mother. While Ann and Anna were enroute to Eufaula, Hubert received another letter from his sister-in-law, Ada, written from Edward's mercantile store:

"Eufaula May 1861

My dear Brother
I am down to the store and Pa told me that Dr. Wingate was going to Pensacola and I concluded to write a few lines. We heard yesterday that all the ladies would start for home Monday, & expected to reach here last night, we looked for Ma & Sis & were very much disappointed that they did not come. We heard that Bragg had ordered them home in anticipation of a fight. We have only had one letter from Ma since she left. Mollies wrote yesterday but did not send the letter because we looked for them.

Do you expect a fight I believe every one there has written home lately looks for one but if you do take Pickens I suppose you will have to go somewhere else. We hear very little news here now. All are well at home I had a severe sick headache yesterday evening, but it is entirely well this morning. I cannot think of any thing to write so will have to close. Helen says she will write soon. Excuse all mistakes and bad writing as I am in a great hurry. Write soon. Your affectionate sister Ada I will write again in a few days

When the First Alabama Regiment elected its officers, Eufaula lawyer Henry D. Clayton had been elected Colonel and commanding officer. On May 13, 1861, Col. Clayton appointed Lt. Hubert Dent as his regimental adjutant.[438] The adjutant is the chief administrative officer of the regiment; he is the principal point of contact between the commander and his subordinate officers. It is through the adjutant that the commander's orders are issued, sometimes over the signature of the adjutant, acting "for the commander." If this responsible position imposed detailed administrative burdens on Hubert, it also relieved him of some of the everyday drudgery of encampment soldiering. It also permitted him to draw supplemental salary of $10 per month in addition to his first lieutenant's pay of $90 per month.[439] Later, when Col. Clayton transferred to another command, Hubert continued as adjutant under the new post commander, Brigadier General John H. Forney, so that Hubert held the position throughout most the time he was a member of the First Alabama Regiment.

Near the Pensacola Navy Yard was a "million dollar dry dock", which had been taken over from the U. S. Navy when the Confederates occupied the Navy Yard. At first, it had been thought that the dry dock would be a valuable asset, but it soon became apparent that, while Fort Pickens was held by the Federals, Confederate ships could not enter the bay for repairs, nor could the dock be floated out to be used elsewhere. Gen. Bragg decided to sink it in the middle of the channel between Fort Pickens and Fort McRee, thereby blocking the channel. Hubert writes Anna about the efforts to sink the dry dock. Also, as the Confederate government continued to temporize on attempting to take Fort Pickens, Hubert became restive in his position at Fort Barrancas, which he now doubted (correctly) would be the scene of much action, and writes of conspiring with the politically powerful privates of the Eufaula Rifles to get the regiment transferred to Virginia. For Anna's benefit, he writes disarmingly of the mountains and springs of "fashionable" Virginia, but he can't bring off the deception. Hubert goes on to admit his real motive: he expects that Virginia is where most of the fighting will be, and he is anxious to "thrash abolitionists." He may be worried that his brother, George, in Maryland, will see action before he does.

"Barrancas, Florida
May 19, 1861

"My Own Sweet Darling,

I did not write yesterday…I will try and write you as long a letter as I can.

I waited in part to let you know about the sinking of the dry dock. They expected to sink it last night, but failed to get ready and I do not think they will sink it under two or three days.

The idea somehow is gaining ground that we will not fight here for some days or months. I am inclined as I wrote before to think the same way.

We have been crowded to-day with visitors from Georgia and

119

Alabama. It is becoming a great source of annoyance. I suppose from what I have seen to-day that there have been hundreds of outsiders here to–day. Among them such distinguished men as Tom Cobb, Judge Walker R M of Ala. several members of the Southern Congress etc. There is a crowd here now in my room talking …I have moved my office into the large room you occupied when you were here, and keep my own office only as a bed room. This suits me much better. It would be quite monotonous here were it not for the large number of visitors. They are troublesome enough to disturb the monotony of any place.

I am going to tell you something now that you must not tell. I have started a plan to have our regiment or our company (I suppose the company alone would not be ordered however) ordered to Virginia. I have got Bullock, Cochran and Pugh interested in it and they will petition the Secretary of War to have it done. I do not know that it will be done, but we will make the effort. I would be perfectly delighted to succeed. This fact is I think we will have to remain here for the summer and I believe I would rather spend the summer in Virginia. It is more fashionable and nearer the mountains and springs you know.

I received a letter from my Father [Dr. Stoughton Warren Dent in Maryland] to-day written the 9th inst. The people down around him are forming companies but they have no arms. My Father is Captain of the home guards and George [Hubert's younger brother] is a member of a Company also. The people were preparing to leave for Virginia if Md. did nothing. Unless they leave soon they will not have an opportunity of doing it.

I would be perfectly delighted to go to Virginia. I believe Darling that the most of the fighting will be done there and I do want to be in it. I want a chance to thrash these--abolitionists. I like to have said something strong. It seems to me that being the first troops in the field we ought to have some say as to where we ought to go. Bullock is very much interested with me in making the change in fact every one that I have spoken to on the subject is anxious for the change. Although I write this way I have very little idea that we will go

Col. Chambers is here said he saw you and Ma on your way home. Also John Treutlen.

Well Darling I must close my love to all the family. Don't forget to tell Nellie [Anna's sister, Helen Augusta] that if I have not written to her that I will write soon. My love to Henry & Will [Anna's older brothers] and families. I will answer Henry's letter soon as I can. I will keep you posted my darling so you must pay no attention to rumors, write often I know you will on that good by God bless & preserve you. Your old dear. Hubert"

Later, in a letter of May 31, Hubert reports to Anna that a number of troops have been transferred out of Barrancas to Virginia, and some extra hands at the Navy Yard foundry have been discharged, all of which he sees as evidence that Fort Barrancas is not to have a fight anytime soon. Hubert has been looking for a horse to buy, and has received a letter from "Hatch" saying he had a horse that he would soon be sending down to Hubert. [Hatch is undoubtedly a cousin of Hubert's, probably residing in the Eufaula or Columbus area]. Hubert is hoping to get a furlough home in July, which is probably the expected date of Anna's delivery.

By the end of May, the Army of Pensacola numbered over 5000. The Confederate officers, some of whom had seen service in Mexico, were busy shaping these militia into a disciplined army. There was daily instruction in military tactics, army regulations, and the use of arms. The troops were also kept busy preparing gun emplacements and defensive positions.

There are a few surviving letters from Anna to Hubert. In this one, Anna has her mind on economics. She has discovered the wonder of investment interest, and with this knowledge offers Hubert some unsolicited business advice. Also, she threatens to reduce the frequency of her letters because the cost of postage has increased. At this time, Anna is still living alone in the house that Edward had made available for the couple:

"June 3, 1861

My Own Dear Love,
    I would have written you yesterday, but it was Sunday and I had no envelope ready - this morning I sent a pack down and had them all stamped so they would be ready when I wanted them - I did not attend church yesterday and I thought it would be so lonely here by myself that Cal and I went down to Mama's and stayed until church was out - we got home about half an hour before the rest and I set here on a rocking chair and sang to amuse myself… I think of how I used to watch for you and how glad I would be to see you coming in and giving me a kiss as you always do – you mustn't think me foolish Dearest.
    All of us keep very well – I never felt better in my life except very lazy – and I think that if you were here I wouldn't feel so – Are you very busy? I know that you are.
    What is the reason that you could not get the horses from Mr. Cooke and why does Col. Clayton wish to sell his horse? You will of course do what you think best – Write me everything that you do and think.
    Oh: let me tell you something - I don't believe that I told you that Pa put out $75 – of my money – and I get six dollars from now until the first of January – that is doing very well isn't it? The other $25 is loaned out too – Instead of giving $100 of your money for a monument for Jackson – you had better send it to me and let me make something, they are going to be rich any way and I don't know certain whether you will or not – Ma says that I am getting to be so very stingy that she don't know what is to become of me –

Well you see - I must do something while you are away.

Well Love – I don't know why you don't receive my letters regularly – I have written you nearly everyday since I got back – for I thought that you would be anxious to hear often – Now that I have to pay <u>five cents</u> for letters, I will only write every other day-

Dearest I haven't time to write more as it is very late – I am so sorry to hear that Col. Forney is going away - I hope he will get through the War safely – Alf and Clara are expected home shortly Uncle William will return and Aunt Ellen go with him – All the family and cousin Anna send a great deal of love – Mary says that she will write you on the anniversary of our marriage.

Good bye my own dear Love – a hundred kisses and lots of love from

Your Darling Anna"

Hubert and Anna Dent

June 5th is Anna and Hubert's first anniversary, and Hubert does not fail to send an anniversary letter effusively reconfirming his love for her. He is concerned about whether he can get a furlough in July. Hubert's tentmate, Macon, is his regimental sergeant major and assistant. They are moving from the quarters in the Navy Yard to a tent. Hubert also reports a new brigade commander, whom he does not expect to like very much:

"Barrancas, Fl.
June 5, 1861

My Darling wife:

Well Dearest twelve months ago today we were married. Twelve months with their change, trials and vicissitudes have elapsed since we united our destinies for weal or for woe. How great and how numerous have been the changes and yet I expect as great a change in our own feelings as in any thing else. And yet I do not like to call it a change. I know I loved you when we were married. I know that my heart prized you above all others even then. But oh! Dearest, how much stronger my feelings now. How much less restrained. What perfect confidence I have in my own love for you and in yours for myself. The idea of either one of us getting tired loving the other never for an instant is entertained in my mind. I just feel as if I would go on loving you better and better every day. Darling you have no idea how proud I feel when I think of the trust and confidence you have in me. Oh my Darling, I would not have it otherwise for any thing on earth. If my wife was a suspicious exacting doubting kind of woman I would soon have only a certain kind of respect for her because she was my wife and nothing more. There would not and could not be that perfect confidence without which there is but little happiness. Well Dearest, do you feel that you can regret having married me. Have your expectations been realized? …

We have moved back to our old quarters where we first were and I am in a tent under the China tree in the yard. Macon is with me. You ought to have seen us today fixing up. I hope we will soon be comfortably arranged. We cannot of course be as well fixed up as we were in our house, but then you know we can't have everything we desire at home and the reasons are much greater why we can't while we are in the army.

Dearest I hope I will be able to get a leave of absence in July but I am by no means certain. A great many have applied since the troops left here for Virginia under the impression that there would be no fighting and that Gen. Bragg would be more disposed to grant them. I have been quite attentive to my business since I have been here and they are Generally more disposed to favor those that do and I hope I shall succeed.

Col. Forney has left us. From what I can learn of Gen. Walker I do not think I shall like him much. He has not yet taken command of the Brigade but will do so I hope tomorrow. I am tired of doing extra work for nothing.

I have drawn my pay up to the first of June and am waiting to see about getting a horse, and if I can make the arrangement I expect to make, I shall send you some. I want you to try your business qualities.

Well my own sweet Darling, good by. May heaven bless you and preserve you. A great deal of love to all the family. I will write as often as I can. Again good by. Your own devoted old Dear, Hubert"

In a long letter two days later, after much grumbling about the mail, Hubert gives an interesting analysis of his new brigade commander. He suggests that Anna get assistance in a business matter from her brother Henry. Hubert likes living in the tent, and Hatch has finally found him a horse. He has received a drawing from "Charlie," his five-year-old nephew (Will and Annie Young's son). There are veiled references to the impending birth. Hubert hints about a move to Tennessee.

"Barrancas, FL
June 7, 1861

My own Sweet Darling

I received yesterday your letter written June 3rd and most welcome I found it. I do not know what has become of your letters. Perhaps they may come to hand yet. In the last ten days I have only received three letters, one written 25th one 31st and one June 3rd. However as you were in good spirits and had such a fine appetite I feel better satisfied, but I began to be really uneasy and restless. I wrote you on the 4th of June and I might have written yesterday but from the fact that you said you would only write every other day, so I thought I would practice economy myself. I will however try and make up for it by writing a long letter and so must you. Now remember this, I will expect a long letter every time. It seems that it takes letters a day longer than it ought to come here any way. They are generally three days on the way when they ought to get here the 2nd. I shall look with a great deal of interest for your letter written on the 5th. I want to see what you have written.

Oh! Darling, your love and confidence make me feel so happy. I do wish I was with you, I do want so much to take you in my arms and give and receive sweet kisses of affection. Would I not feel so happy so very happy. Do you not enter into and appreciate my feelings, and would you not like to come and sit down in your old Dear's lap and put your arms around his old neck and give him some of your sweet kisses, and such ones they are too. But Dearest I must not pursue this picture. It only makes me feel more keenly the loss of your company and the comforts and pleasure of home. I do wish this war was over, we do enjoy each others company so much. Well Darling we must look forward to the time when we shall happily meet. Oh may it come speedily. Darling if I seem sometimes not to feel as much as others, you understand me don't you? You have sounded the depths of your old Dears heart, have you not? You know that your image is graven there never to be effaced. But I must, I must stop this.

I am sitting down in my office writing this morning. Macon is making out my morning report. I have been laughing at his mistakes, he takes it all in good part however and works away. When he gets so he understands the business I shall have very little to do and will have a good easy time unless Gen. Walker takes some new notion in his head and moves us again or something of that sort. If I have not written before Gen. Walker is from Georgia—Augusta or near there. He was in the old U.S. Service, a Colonel, is full of fight, considered rather rash, has been in several [battles]. Manages to stop all the balls that pass near him. Has five or six in his body now but manages to escape some way. He swears like a trooper, is as bad as the army in Flanders, and is rather communicative, not particular as to the crowd he gets into, but talks away Generally…with many strange oaths. Consequently does not preserve his dignity or rather the dignity of his position. Take him all in all. I should select him as a suitable man for leading a forlorn hope but not the man to manage and control a great movement of a large body of men. Gen. Bragg however is in command as heretofore and Walker only fills the position that Clayton has occupied.

I will now close for the present and finish this either this evening or tonight.

Well Darling it is now late after supper and I am seated at my table to finish this letter. I received today your letter written the 4th. It was so kind in you to write. I will try and not feel so badly if I should not receive them regularly hereafter. More especially as Ma promises to write if any thing occurs.

In reference to [Junius] Jordan I held a note for five hundred dollars on him, which I left with Henry, he talked something of exchanging it for a note on John Bloodworth. See Henry about it and if he has not exchanged it you can give Jordan credit on the note for the cost of the sewing machine and let him receipt the account. Any thing I can do in that way I will gladly do so for it will be an accommodation to me. Tell Henry to jog Jordan's memory about the note if he still has it.

I get a horse after all from Hatch. I received a telegram from today telling me to go to Pensacola tomorrow after him. I shall accordingly go over tomorrow after him. I will write you again in a few days and let you know something about him and what arrangements I have made.

I like living in a tent pretty well. I have my office in the house and keep my clothes in there. I only do my sleeping in my tent and it is glorious. I expect by the time I get home that I will feel like I was smothering in a house. The weather is quite warm here and the dust is intolerable. We have a drill every morning about 5 ½ or 6 o'clock and even the dust and heat are very severe.

From every thing I can learn there is no prospect of a fight here unless we are attacked, and I do not think that at all likely. It is said that there is a good deal of sickness on Santa Rosa and in the fleet. They do not work as hard over at Pickens as they did when you were here.

Tell Charlie I received his picture and that he must keep on drawing. Give my love to all the family. Tell them to write and do you, Darling, write as often as you can.

I have something of interest about Tennessee that is going on here, but I can not write about it now. One thing however I can say is that our friends there are badly frightened. Well my pet good by. Many kisses from your old Dear. Hubert

On June 16, Hubert describes adjustments on troop positions made by the new brigade commander. A Yankee deserter from Fort Pickens is in custody. Though not explicitly stated, the baby is expected in early July, and Hubert plans to be present. Hubert has received a letter from his father, Dr. S. W. Dent, brought by a friend from behind federal lines in Maryland and mailed from Richmond:

"Barrancas, Fla
June 16, 1861

My Sweet Darling
    Your long sweet and interesting letter of the 13th came to hand today and as Capt. Baker has leave of absence and is going home this evening I avail myself of this opportunity of answering it immediately. I can not promise you an interesting letter. Things are going on here quietly. Not quite so many details for fatigue duty as when you were here.

Gen. Walker has made several changes in the Brigade. He is going to concentrate the 1st Regt west of Ft. Barrancas. I think Baker's company will remain where they are. The 7th Regt will be concentrated north of the barracks proper. Two of the independent...companies have been ordered off on Monday and they do not know where they are going. I think from what I can learn that they are going over towards the East…to build batteries. Three other companies are going with them. Not from this Brigade.

The man that came over from Pickens is still in custody. He is a little more communicative than at first. He is a very determined looking man. I place no reliance in what he says, in fact he does not say a great deal. He said there are nine companies in the fort. Some not full, good many sick. Says they have four batteries and a great many eight and ten-inch Columbiads. Any one can take it for what it is worth. You will recollect the restrictions about what is written from here.

Well Darling I hope I shall see you in a month or less time from what you write. I shall apply for leave of absence about the 8th of July. I do hope I shall get it. I do not know what I shall do if I do not. Pretty near go crazy I reckon.

Darling you do not know how well I appreciate your letter. How I enter into all your feelings and how much pleasure it gives me to send such things in your letter. Dearest you must not feel badly over my absence. I want you to be a real soldier's wife and bear up with the absence of your old Dear well and cheerfully.

In reference to the vegetables I do not know what they cost. Hatch paid the express charges on them and hence I had nothing to pay. We are getting vegetables from Mobile and Montgomery tolerably regularly now and I get them fresher than from home. But I do love so much to get such things from home. It makes me think so much of all of you. I wish I was there to get some of the grapes. I could eat your share and mine too I reckon. Be particular and take good care of yourself Darling and don't get sick. …

I hope you have had rain. We have had a fine one and it is so much pleasanter now than before the rain. John [McRae, brother of Henry Young's wife, Maria] has not got any furlough yet and I think it doubtful about his getting one.

Mr. McNair [Presbyterian minister from Eufaula] is getting along here very well. He does not have large congregations and occasionally has none at all. I hope it will be better when the Regt is concentrated.

I received today a letter from my Father written the 27th May mailed in Richmond by a friend. He is very low-spirited and despairs of Maryland for the present. He hopes for the future and that is all he can do. All were well bodily. I wish I could get a letter to him. They would be so glad to hear from me.

Well Darling I must close. My love to all everyone. I will write as often as I can well. I wrote Henry yesterday. Well Dearest good by my love again to all. Many kisses of love from your old Dear. Hubert"

Hubert writes on June 19 that his last letter from home was from Mollie, brought by Tom Flournoy. He went into Pensacola the previous day to try to find out about his saddle, which is still missing. He has been quite sick with an upset stomach. He and his staff are completing the move out of the building they had occupied at the Navy Yard, and into tents.

Hubert observes, "The time is drawing near when I shall apply for leave of absence to see you," having now been away from home for six months.

Writing again the very next day, Lt. Dent banters with his teenage sisters-in-law, Helen, 14, and Ada, 15. He is becoming apprehensive about the coming birth. He regards a battle as unlikely, but needlessly agonizes over the possibility of missing a battle if one should develop while he is at home. It is not as crucial for Hubert to send money home as frequently as some soldiers must, but he nevertheless sends Anna money from time to time:

"Barrancas, Florida
June 20, 1861

My Sugar Plum
      Yours of the 16th came to hand today. … We have been moving all day and are not through yet. We will be a fine mark for Pickens when the fight commences. We are near the ____ Battery, between the fort and it. I shall be altogether in a tent. I do not think I shall like it very well but will have to be content.
      I wrote you…about the vegetables. I hope you received it. You need not give yourself any trouble about sending them down at present. We are getting a good many from Montgomery and Mobile fresher than I could get them from Eufaula. We had today beets, potatoes, cabbage, tomatoes, onions, and occasionally we have green corn. I am now perfectly secured from the attack I had day before yesterday and feel as well as ever.
      I wrote Ada by John McRae and you by Capt. Baker and ____. Tell Ada I shall expect her to do what I told her in my letter. As soon as I get fired up I will write to Mollie and some of the others to whom I owe letters. Darling you must excuse this letter for there are a half a dozen men talking and going on around me. I would not mind that much for you know I get very much absorbed sometimes, but occasionally they address me in person and then I have to reply. Tell Helen she had better write me what that secret is. I am very curious to know. I should like very much to be at the _____ of the girls but I do not know whether they would admit me or not.
      Darling you must not feel badly if I do not write regularly. I will write as often as I can. Well Mr. Johnston (Lt.) will I expect bring his wife down here also. Col. Clayton and probably Will McTyer.
      Darling affairs here now are very different from what they were when you were here. Then a fight was considered imminent, now it is looked upon as quite remote. I have no idea there will be any fight here until after the 4th July... The trouble with me is that just about the time I wish to go home the congresses will be meeting and there is no telling what may happen. It would be most unfortunate if just at the time that I am at home I should miss the fight. But Dearest I would miss three fights to see you if I could not see you without while I might consider it unfortunate but Dearest I should not regret it.
      As I wrote before my Sugar Plum I am getting impatient as the time

approaches and I can't help feeling a good deal about it. Give my love to Ma and tell her to take good care of you. I will not feel half as well satisfied about you if you were anywhere else.

The weather is quite warm here now and it is nearly as dusty now as before the rain. I am sorry to hear that it is so dry in Eufaula. I hope it is not enough so to injure the crops. From what I can hear the prospect for both corn and cotton is very good and I am much pleased to hear it.

I sent you one hundred dollars by John McRae. At least I gave him sixty dollars in gold and a hundred dollar bill and told him to give you the gold and forty dollars and bring me back the remains for I may not be paid off the 1ˢᵗ July and I don't want to be troubled.

Oh, Darling, you let me catch you going barefooted and if I don't well I don't know what I will do. Good by. Give love to all the family every one. Many kisses of love from your old Dear. Hubert."

Three days later, Hubert is again concerned about being able to get a furlough at the important time. He gives a description of their "picturesque" camp, and reports some misconduct by Eufaula soldiers. A postscript is written at the beginning:

"Darling, please hand the enclosed memorandum to Capt. Baker or Lt. Johnston.

Camp Alabama
June 23, 1861

My Darling Nannie:
… Dearest you have no idea of how warm, how very warm it is here now. …last night it was very warm. Very little if any breeze. I went to the beach and bathed. It cooled me off some and I went to sleep. But this morning it is equally warm and sultry.

In regard to going home Darling I hope I will be able to get off. There are more absentees from the 1ˢᵗ Regt now than has been since it came here. I hope most of them will return before I apply. I know if I were to apply now that it would prejudice my application very much, so many being absent. Well Dearest you must not have your expectations too high. You might be disappointed you know I will see you if I can and that I will leave no effort untried to see you.

You ought Darling to see our camp. Tents from one hundred and fifty to two hundred all covered over with bush arbors and various devices to keep out the sun. The men about in groups or engaged in cleaning up their grounds or arranging their tents. Take it all together it is quite a picturesque scene. We are a fine mark for Pickens if it should take a notion to throw some shells amongst us. They have been changing their sandbags since we came here, and I expect they are preparing to move their guns so as to bear upon us. What a scattering there would be if 'Brown' [the Yankee commander at Fort Pickens] should turn loose on us—half a dozen shells would do the thing completely.

Well Darling it is nearly 10 o'clock and I must close and go and hear Bro. McNair [the Presbyterian minister from Eufaula] preach. I wish it was Mr. Cotton [the Methodist minister from Eufaula]. That will be another great pleasure in visiting home to hear some of his fine sermons. …

Well I have found out that there will be no preaching and therefore I will go ahead and finish my letter. So you received the $100 did you. Well I don't know when you will receive any more so you had better take good care of it. The breeze has been blowing for some time and now it is quite pleasant in the shade but still very warm in the sun.

Oh! you little flatterer talking that way to Capt. Baker. Well I expect you will not think that way long, at least after you see me for I am burned pretty tolerably black, both hands and face and by time I get home will be blacker than ever.

Jim McNab took it into his head last night that he was field officer of the day and after visiting some of the guard himself sent Tom Brannon to represent him. The result was both were arrested this morning. Brannon in consideration of his ignorance and inexperience has been discharged. McNab is still under arrest. He is nearly dead from drinking. Clark was detailed and being absent, McNab without any orders undertook and really thought he had to supply his place. Joe Butt and the entire crew have been ordered off the _____. Their places being supplied by Lieut. Ramsy and twelve marines. Joe hated to go back to his company.

Well Darling good by. Give my love to all the family. Take good care of yourself. You little pet you. Many kisses of love from your old Dear Hubert"

Hubert and Anna's first child, a son, is born in Eufaula on June 25, 1861, but Hubert writes Anna on that date, unaware that the birth has occurred. He expresses concern about the approaching time, which he believes will be in July, but is preparing Anna for the possibility that he might not be there.

Camp "Alabama"
June 25, 1861

My Own Dear Nannie

I expect before you get this letter that you will feel as if I had neglected My Darling-but it will not be so. Our Post Master or the man who attended to getting our mail is sick and no mail was sent off yesterday and if any was received I got none. I expect Mr. M. Chais or Dr. Black will be going home today or to-morrow and I will send this letter by them-one of them.

I have nothing particularly new or interesting to write. War vessels are congregating here. I do not know whether it is accident or design nor whether any thing like an attack is meditated or not. One arrived a day or so ago and yesterday a large Steamer supposed to be the *Brooklyn* was seen steaming up. There are now about as many as ever were here.

The climate and hard work is telling on our Regiment now, there has been three deaths in it lately. After all, I do not know for some out of eight hundred men would most likely have died if all had remained at home.

To-day Darling is the 25th June--July will soon be here. You write me when I must come as near as you can and I will do my very best to get off. It makes me slightly nervous to think of it. But My Dearest I know you are in good earthly hands, and besides and above all you are in the hands of God in whom we must all put our trust. You do not know Dearest how much and how constantly I have thought of you lately. I am satisfied you have not been out of my thoughts for a long time. No matter how busily I might be engaged, my thoughts were and still are constantly recurring to my Precious Darling. But I must not write in this strain for I am afraid I will make you sad which I do not wish to do.

Our Regiment officers and all are in tents together except the 'Rifles' and I expect they will move up soon. I hope in a few days to have a floor to our tent (Macon and myself) and then we shall be quite comfortably fixed.

Nannie I like the horse I bought very much, but do you think I never received the saddle. I am afraid I have lost it altogether. From this circumstance my horse has not been of much use to me.

We will eat at our last quarters and find it very inconvenient. I hope we will move our kitchen soon. So you see we are far from being comfortable fixed yet.

We are expecting every day to hear something important from Virginia. We were very much exercised about the evacuation of Harper's Ferry, but it turns out to be an advance instead of a retreat. I wish Lincoln and his Cabinet could be driven from Washington and Maryland relived from the galling yoke to which she is subjected. I would give a good deal to be able to go there and learn for myself exactly what is going on.

Things here now look a little more warlike than a few weeks ago. Bit it fails to excite me as I have been stirred up so often by the same sort of things. Our men have been practicing at guns and Mortars for some days. The 'Rifles' with Mortars. There has been some fine shooting--at least so said Generals Bragg and Walker. The company at guns are still practicing. The Mortar Companies in our Regiment have left off practicing. I have never been able to get down there yet. I am going to try and go this evening. I have been and still am quite busy and will be until this business of moving is completely settled-and I expect about the time we get comfortably fixed we will move some where else.

Well Darling give my love to all the family every one. I sent a memorandum in my letter before this for Capts. Baker or Johnson. You need not trouble yourself with it as I will get Mr. M. Chais to do all I wish in reference to it. You must not be too confident in expecting me home and you will not be so much disappointed if I can't get off. Goodbye again my love to all. Many kisses of love from your old Dear. May Heaven bless and preserve you as ever yours. Hubert"

What follows is the only surviving letter between Edward Young and his son-in-law, written the same day Hubert was writing the letter above. Edward's formal beginning quickly gives way to the fun he is having conveying this happy news to Hubert:

"Eufaula June 25 1861

"Mr. S. H. Dent

Dear Sir,

I am happy to inform you that Anna had a fine boy last night. He was born 5 minutes after 10 o'clock and they are both doing will. Doct Baker said he was as large as his mother. He is very large child and a half hour after he was born was looking around him with his fist in his mouth. Anna says that you must come as soon as you can get off. Carry and the children nearly has a fit over him.

I found the telegraph wires was down in half dozen places between this and Howards and from the words that we have had for two days I expect that you will get this before you could get a dispatch [telegram Ed.]. We have had fine rains about here and it will make most of the corn. They have extended around the country. we are all well. I have no news that can be relied upon. Wiley came from N. Y. he says they say that they are going to pick up every Cotton Stalk from the Potomac to Texas. They have not done much yet. Only to talk.

Yours respectfully

Edw. B. Young"

The baby was named Edward Young Dent, for his grandfather, and was called "Eddie" during his childhood. The effect of wartime conditions is reflected by the fact that, in this Methodist family that had always had its babies baptized soon after birth, it is not until Dec. 29, 1865, after the end of the war, that Eddie is baptized by the Rev. William Shapard.[440]

In his letter to Anna written the next day from Fort Barrancas, Hubert is still unaware of his son's birth

"Barrancas, Florida
June 26, 1861

My Precious Darling
I received your long and interesting letter today marked to be sent by John McRae but brought by Capt. Clark. There has been some disagreement in our mails here and Darling I have not written to you as often as I would.

131

But Dearest you need not feel any uneasiness about me. If any thing happens you will know it.

There has been a great commotion and stir here for the last twenty-four hours. I do not know what will happen yet. It may be something or nothing.

I have a sad piece of news. Alex Neal of our company died today of congestion of the brain. He was taken sick last Friday. Poor fellow. He was insensible and has been so for some days. I did not know he was sick until yesterday. I went to see him this morning and never saw a more pitiable sight.

This hot sun is telling on our men. There have been five deaths in the regiment and the first occurred not more than two weeks ago. I am very particular with myself I tell you and go about in the sun as little as possible.

We had something like an alarm this morning about 10 or 11 o'clock. Gen. Walker has issued an order requiring all companies to repair to their Batteries immediately upon the firing of any guns at Pickens. This morning a salute was fired there and you never saw such running. There has been a salute fired there three days in succession but the other two were fired on the ships and the order did not apply. Bragg has an idea that the fight is going to come off. It makes very little impression on me because I have heard it so often. So Darling you need not be disappointed if I do not get off home between this and the 11th of July or a little later. You know your old Dear will go home as soon as he can of that you may be assured.

Well Darling Mr. McNair will tell all about affairs down here and can not think of any thing interesting to write now. How kind of you my precious Darling to go down and arrange my office. You make me love you too well Darling and think too much of you. I hope this war will end some of these days and that I will get home and repay you for all your kindness and affection.

I received a letter from home [Maryland] today written the 15th inst mailed in Virginia. All were well in body but there was a great deal of excitement there. Dr. Smoot you remember him was raising a company to go to Virginia. George was going with him. They were going over a few at a time and rendezvous at some given place in Virginia. George expected to leave in a few days and I suppose is there by this time. How I should like to be there after seeing you my Darling. It is reported here that Maryland has seceded. I do not know yet whether it is really so or not. I hope Maryland will be relieved by the Confederate troops soon and I think it will be done. There seems to have been no fight (great one) in Virginia yet. I was expecting it.

Darling you must not be troubled about my absence if I should not get there. I will come if possible. But you must be cheerful and think your old Dear is doing his duty. We must all make sacrifices and Darling you and I will have to make ours. Ma will take good care of you I know and I feel so much better satisfied that you are with her.

Tell Ada I received her letter and will reply. But she would please me very much if she would not be formal with me and write whenever she feels like it. Does not Helen owe me a letter? Well Dearest I must close—give my love to all the family. Give yourself no trouble about your old Dear. God bless you and preserve your many kisses of love from your old Dear. Hubert"

Dr. Smoot, referred to by Hubert in the foregoing letter is his kinsman in Maryland, through his mother, Mary Catherine Smoot Dent. "George" is Hubert's younger brother, George Hatch Dent, who will later become an important player in our narrative.

When he received word of the birth of his son, Hubert exerted all of his efforts and used all of his connections to obtain a furlough. He succeeded, and was granted fifteen days leave commencing July 10, so that he arrived in Eufaula and saw his son scarcely two weeks after his birth. [441]

By the time of his next letter, Hubert has visited Eufaula and is back in camp, he is pleased to have helped his regimental sergeant-major obtain an officer's commission, but he thereby loses a good assistant:

"Barrancas Florida
August 14, 1861

My Precious Darling
        As I have promised myself not to let two days pass over without writing to you I have seated myself for that purpose. It has been clear all day the first for some days. A few moments ago however it commenced raining and storming. How long it will last I am unable to tell.
        First of all I must tell you about Macon's promotion. He has been appointed a Lieutenant in Capt Meadows company from Tallapoosa. I think he will be a 1st Lieut though that is not settled. I got him the appointment myself. I thought he deserved it and would appreciate such an act from a friend and I went to work for him and got him the position. I could have done it for any other friend as well. I was sorry to lose him as Sergeant Major, but waived all selfish considerations and went to work for him. He dislikes the idea of leaving me himself and I think we will still mess together. He abandoned the idea of leaving here at my instance in order to see what I could do for him.
        About Joe Butt I am surprised that he should permit his own paper to publish such a falsehood as that he was A A A Gen.l [adjutant General] in place of Wood. It is all a no such a thing. As Cochran would express it he is in the <u>meat business</u>. He has been detailed on special duty in the Commissary's department and instead of being A A A Gen.l he is engaged in weighing out pork, flour, beans &c &c for the different Regiments. I wonder if he will not correct it.
        Bullock is in Bragg's staff and is Judge Advocate of the army. Braggs legal military adviser, in reference to questions which are constantly arising. It is a good position plenty of work. You must not Dearest [be] too much

prejudiced against Bullock about the way he acted in relation to the things sent him. Give him credit for what he is entitled to while you may condemn him for that part of his conduct. I must say that it was a piece of carelessness of which I did not think Bullock would be guilty.

Things are looking a little like a fight. Companies at Batteries are ordered to resume their cannon and Mortar drilling and to fix up their Batteries Magazines &c &c. Col Wood said there were good reasons for all this. That was as definite as he would express it. We have been deceived so often that I have almost ceased to put any confidence in any thing of that sort.

I believe this is all the news here. Darling I had a long talk with Capt Dawson this evening, his wife is in Pensacola. We were talking about our families. Do you know that I love to talk about <u>mine</u> when I meet with a man who seems to think and feel a good deal like myself. Dawson said his wife talked of remaining through the war. He thinks however that that will not do.

I am very much in hopes that the sickness in our regiment will soon get better. A great many men have gone home on sick furlough. Clayton has gone-went yesterday. I did not see him off. Could not leave the Camp. Oh! Me what a life a military life is.

I am sorry for Mrs. Mitchell but expect like you that it is for the best. They have made a bold start if they hold out that way. Will have plenty of <u>responsibilities</u>. I am very glad that nothing of that kind happened with you. Sometimes such things are very hard to get over. I expect leaves of absence are very hard to get in Virginia.

Some effort is being made here to make Pugh a Brigadier General. I do not know how it will succeed. This is private and confidential.

Well Dearest I must close. Give my love to all the family. Write me as often as you can I will write to some of the girls in a few days. I must get a Sergeant Major in place of Macon. I am very busy now. Kiss the boy for his PaPa. Tell him to grow fast. And be a good boy and love his MaMa   Well Darling I am in my tent very warm and the fleas are troublesome. So goodby. Oh, you are such a sweet wife. You never told me that dream. I was dreaming of having you in my arms last night. And oh! How satisfied I felt. Just as I have often felt when I did in fact have you in my arms. I do not believe any one has as sweet and Dear a wife as [I] have. I wish this war would end. I want to go home and be at home for your sake and my own. Well I must close. Again my Dearest sweetest Love goodby. Kiss the boy and take much love and many kisses from your old Dear   Hubert"

A few letters from Anna to Hubert survive, one of which she wrote the day after Hubert's letter above. We often see in Hubert's letters an appeal for more correspondence from her; he craves the kind of detailed news of the baby, the family and the happenings at the home front which Anna provides in this letter. She also apologetically gives what she regards as sufficient reasons for not being more regular in her writing. Parts of the letter are illegible, but it appears there has been some incident downtown involving some drunk boys and northern visitors. It also appears that her brothers, Will and Henry, are wrestling with their feelings about the need to join the army and fight. Henry has heard from his Columbus first cousin, Bob Lockhart, and has been asked to join a company being organized by two other Columbus first cousins, Alf and George Young. Henry declines, but in a later chapter we will learn more about this unit, which came to be named "Young's Battery."

"Eufaula, Aug 15th 1861

My Own Precious Dear,
"You mustn't think that your Nannie loves you any less because she hasn't written for two or three days, will you Dearest. No love, you must not and you will not when I tell you that I have a good excuse - we have had company since Monday until to day and I couldn't write. I thought of you often Dearest and how disappointed you would be not to get a letter for two or three days. I have had three letters from you this week and Dearest I was so sorry to hear that you were not well. If you think you will be sick much you must come home right away if you can. I couldn't bear for you to be sick down there, you could be so much better attended to at home and we all would be better satisfied to have you with us.

We all keep well - and the dear little Baby gets sweeter every day - we went down town yesterday, and weighed the boys Willie and the Baby - Willie weighed <u>17 pounds</u> and the Baby <u>13 pounds</u>. Don't he grow fast, he is a great big busy man - smiles a good deal and laughs too - he is right good, now that he is getting to notice he keeps…quiet and he rarely even has the colic… While I am writing he is laying in his cradle, Carrie [Anna's six-year old sister] and Helen [Anna's fourteen- year old sister] playing with him and he laughing. Every body that sees him says that he is the <u>image</u> of <u>you</u> and he does grow more like you every day - Ma says that he has even your expressions.

The weather has been so bad that he has not been out visiting much - but as soon as it clears we both are going [visiting]. Oh: Dearest I am so anxious for the time to come when we can go down to see you I want to be with you and want you to see the Baby.

We haven't heard a word from Pa since he left which is very strange for it is over a week since he left and Ma feels quite uneasy; I hope we will hear to-night.

Oh! Let me tell you something. Monday morning when Henry and Maria came up, Maria told us there was a card up down town … Will and Henry and spoke of the "City Guards" going off - said there would be a meeting in the evening at which would be present <u>two</u> Yankee Teachers (Mr. Chambers' and Eli Shorter's) and they would address them, also a man <u>just from the North</u> - to tell which Southern Man was _____, it seems that on the day of the election Dr. Plant said that he would not vote for Tompkins for he didn't think him sound and this was a hit at him. William and Henry would go to War if they could go for twelve months - and the Editor of the Express if he could get an office. The Boys were scratching around for all the strong drink to be got after five o'clock and which they would drink to their Northern friends - all such stuff as this. At first I was right mad but when I saw them at dinner he spoke so indifferently about it and said he thought it was several half grown boys and that it wasn't worth nothing I got over my mad fit - I do think such things are contemptible.

I believe I told you of the letter Henry got from Bob Lockhart and what he said about Alf's making a company and he and George going and wanted Henry to wait until that was organized. Henry will wait until fall now it is so late in the summer.

I wish there was some arrangements made about your getting fruits and vegetables there, if were sure that you would get them in short time after they were sent we might keep you supplied. We have some elegant peaches - had one a day or so ago which measured ¼ yd around and weighed 6 oz - and that was not the largest one….

Mrs. Treadwell left to-day for Richmond where she will open a hospital for the sick and wounded, she carried a great many things with her - Henry Shorter has been to the Springs for the last two or three weeks but I believe was expected home last night, I heard that his furlough was extended until October. Andrew _____ looks as well as ever but I don't know whether he will go back or not.

Did you get your shirt - if you don't want to wear it out it will nice and warm this winter.

[Postscript across the top of page one] The Baby has just smiled and given me a kiss to send to Papa he is so much company Dearest - Dr. Pope had a child Monday, his _____. There is nothing new, it looks dull down town. I was sorry that the grapes were so badly bruised - I was thinking how much you would enjoy them, Ma will send you peaches the first opportunity we have…Good bye Dearest, a great deal of love and many kisses from

Your Nannie

Take good care of yourself and you must not sleep on the damp floor any more, but get you a bed – Nan"

The expected great battle in Virginia that Hubert had referred to, the first major battle of the war, occurred near Manassas, Virginia on July 21, 1861. Dignitaries and sightseers had come out from Washington to see the show. What they saw was a complete rout of the Gen. McDowell's Federal army by the Confederates, led by Gen. P. G. T. Beauregard. Dignitaries, sightseers, and Yankee soldiers all fled, panic-stricken, back to Washington.

At Fort Pickens, Col. Harvey Brown, the federal commander, had been observing the Confederates' preparations to sink the dry dock in the channel, and decided to make a preemptive strike. On the night of Sept 2, 1861, he sent a boat with twelve regulars and a lieutenant, who met no resistance as they boarded the dock, placed live shells and combustibles on its floor, applied the torch, and destroyed the dock without firing a shot. Hubert writes Anna of this episode, along with reports of more troops being transferred from Barrancas to Virginia to face the new federal commander, Gen. George B. McClellan, who is slowly building his forces. Talk of Anna's again coming to stay in Pensacola would not materialize.

Barrancas Florida
Sept 9th, 1861

My Dear Darling

Your's of the 6th came to hand today. You will have learned before this why you did not receive my letters as regularly as before. I wrote to you on the 3rd and sent it 4th. I wrote also the 5th & 7th and am writing again to night. I wrote you of the burning of the dry dock on the 3rd which was as soon as I could have written. The letter had not reached you when you wrote. You have received it before this I hope. The telegraph I suppose carried the news you heard.

Things are moving on here pretty much as usual. Gen. Ruggles has assumed command in obedience to an order from Genl Bragg. I suppose Anderson has done the same though, as we have nothing to do with him, I have not seen the order. I learn that artillery company, the Continentals, stationed at Pensacola, also a Louisiana company, Capt St. Paul, has been ordered to Virginia. I do not know how true it may be, but think it likely it is so.

Nine of our marines deserted last night and went to Pickens, at least it is generally believed they went there. It is supposed they went under the idea that they would be better paid over there.

We have had some flying telegraph rumors about an attack on and the capture of Arlington Heights. It turns out to be untrue although it is stated that our forces are advancing and have driven the enemy from Shooter's Hill in the vicinity of Alexandria. I look for some stirring news from there soon.

I still have not heard from George. I can't imagine why does not write. I received, as I wrote you, a letter from my Father and have answered it. I suppose his letter to you contains nothing not in mine and it is therefore useless to send it to me. I feel great uneasiness about his situation and that of my relations there.

I wish Darling you had a fortune. I know you would do a great deal of good with it. It often seems as if the favors of this world were very unequally distributed but it is best to be content with our lot and do our duty in the sphere in which we are placed. The widow that threw her mite in the treasury gave more than all the others. So said our Saviour.

Sickness is no better in camp. Out of forty officers in the Regiment, only about eighteen are fit for duty of all sorts—some can attend to some little matters but are unable to go onward, particularly when the weather is bad. I heard today that Clayton was worse. He has made an application for an extension of his furlough or leave of absence for thirty days. I have not heard whether it is granted. Macon is quite sick. He has chills & fever and I am afraid will be some time getting rid of them. Baker was complaining very much yesterday. I have not seen him today. Clark went home on account of health. Any sick man can get a furlough. Well ones have more trouble and in many cases are refused. In the present condition of the Regiment I do not think it would be right for me to ask a leave of absence and if I were to ask it I have no idea I could get it and I do not wish to be mortified by a refusal.

Why Darling are you so despondent about coming down here. You can come as soon as it is settled that we are not to move, which will be known now in a short time I think. I could get a house near the old Barracks, but you would be troubled with house keeping and I think it will be better for you to board. Mrs. Baker [wife of Captain Alpheus Baker, commander of the Eufaula Rifles], has promised to get a room for you in Pensacola & she told me in a week or two from the time I was there that I could get a room. She sent me word yesterday that in about ten days I could get the room. I think then in about two weeks you can come. I do not know how I am to manage to bring you down. You can't come alone and I am very much afraid I can't go after you. Perhaps some one will be coming down about that time with whom you could come.

Give my love to all the family. Kiss the boy for me and tell him not to trouble his Mama. I am quite anxious to see him. I hope I will see you both soon. Do not get so low spirited when you do not receive my letters. It sounds singular to me for you to charge me with neglect. I never mean Darling to neglect you and I thought you knew that should never think I did. Well goodby—Good bless you Darling. Love & kisses from your old Dear Hubert"

Hubert's next letter describes a review requiring long hours in the sun. Although he criticizes it, he later admits it was an impressive sight. Talk of Anna and the baby living in Pensacola continues, but not very convincingly. Anna's mother is opposed to it. Hubert makes clear that when his twelve-month enlistment is up, he will remain in the army in some capacity, for the duration of the war.

"Barrancas, Fla.
Sept. 20th 1861

"My Darling Nannie,
The great review came off yesterday as I wrote in my last it was expected--The day was exceedingly warm and I expect Five hundred men had to leave rank from the effect of the sun and drinking water. It is currently reported that four men died, but so many 'injun reports' are started that I do not know whether it is so or not. The report is that two of the Florida regiments, one of the fifth Georgia, one of the Louisiana and some one said one from one of the Mississippi Regiments died. It certainly was a severe operation. Our regiment was under arms at 8 o'clock & remained so until one o'clock & that was a shorter time than any regiment here was under arms, we being nearer the parade grounds. It was the level field just west of the Light house. Several officers had to leave ranks. It is over and I hope the vanity whatever else it was that caused the display is gratified.

Today is the day set apart for shooting Mullins of the Miss. Reg. I do not know whether he will be shot or not. He is still a prisoner in Ft. Barrancas and if he is shot our regiment will have it to do. I do not like the idea at all.

And so Darling Ma thinks I am crazy for wanting you to come down here-- well perhaps she knows best, for the sun now is very severe. But I do want you down here so much. Mrs. Baker [wife of Captain Alpheus Baker, commander of Eufaula Rifles] abandoned the house over here on account of mosquitoes--she was over here yesterday, went back however last night I did not see her. I am going to see if I can't make an excuse to go home about the 1st Oct and if I get off I can bring you down with me, and that I expect is as soon as you ought to come. I am satisfied I am here for the term of my enlistment, and shall proceed to make my arrangements accordingly. If I could have you and the baby down here some where near me so I could see you both once a week or something like that I would I believe be very well satisfied.

We are going to have a long war and I may as well take it easy for I expect to be into it as long as it lasts in some capacity, as a private if I can't do any better. In common with several others I will be in an awkward situation when my twelve months are out, and I do not know what I will do. However it is not right to be borrowing trouble & and I shall wait until it comes.

The health of our regiment has improved a good deal. Macon is very sick I did not see him yesterday. His Doctors think that being so badly frightened about his condition his recovery is extremely doubtful. I am surprised at the way he takes his sickness, I thought he had more fortitude. I never saw men down on a man than his Drs. are on him about sickness as Macon, and I am satisfied that unless he can be quieted he will not get well. We have not a great many sick. That is very sick men in the Regiment. I hope we will soon be reporting less than we are.

Well darling I am hurried this morning and I was too tired last night to write & I must hasten to close. The baby must be a first rate boy. I wish I could see him and be with him. I know he would know me very soon. I expect I will spoil him., You must not let me, now remember that.

I wish you could have seen the review yesterday. There were Eighty Companies in the field. Three Cavalry - Two Artillery - Two Marines and Seventy-Three of infantry. It made a long line and a fine sight but after all there were not over 4000 men here.

Give my love to all the family. I will write whenever I can but you need not look for a letter except when you see one. I expect Col. Clayton will be here now in a week or two. Maj. Williams is not well yet & is talking of asking for a leave of absence. I get along with Steedman finely--well I must close. Kiss the boy for me & tell him PaPa sent it-and with many kisses and much love to you Darling I close–Your old Dear Hubert"

At two A. M. on September 14, the federals in a surprise raid burned a Confederate vessel moored at the Navy Yard, the *Juda,* but in the accompanying hand-to-hand fighting left three dead and eight wounded. This was the first bloodshed of the war at Pensacola.

Brown, the Yankee commander at Fort Pickens, was expecting a retaliatory bombardment of the fort, but Gen. Bragg acted more drastically. On October 9, the Confederates launched a night attack on the federal troop encampment on Santa Rosa Island. At two A. M., about 1000 troops under Brigadier General Richard H. Anderson were towed by barge to a point on Santa Rosa Island about four miles east of Fort Pickens by two small steamers, (one of which was the *"Neaffie"*, or *"Kneaphy"*, which had been commanded on patrol duty by Hubert Dent early in his tour at Fort Barrancas). Between the Confederates and Fort Pickens was the camp of the Sixth New York Volunteer Infantry, often called "Billy Wilson's Zouaves." Advancing in three columns over three miles of difficult dunes and thickets, the Confederates made a direct assault upon the camp. They put the torch to the tents, storehouses, and sheds. The flames soon covered the entire camp; the Sixth New York broke and ran for the protection of the batteries at the rear of Fort Pickens. Col. Billy Wilson later said his men "did well," but a Confederate in the fight had a different description:

> "The gallant Colonel took to his heels with nothing but a brief skirted nether garment to cover his nakedness, and the race between him and his valiant braves presented a struggle for precedence more closely contested than any ever witnessed on the race course. Bulls Run was nothing in comparison to it."

When daylight was approaching, Anderson ordered the troops back to their boats. A sharp skirmish occurred as the withdrawing Confederates drove off two companies of regulars sent out from Fort Pickens. The night attack destroyed large stores of supplies, equipment and ammunition, but with similar casualties on each side.

Neither Lt. Dent nor any of the Eufaula Rifles were included in this fight. When Anna wrote Hubert, she comments about something that had been very much on his mind. His position as regimental adjutant was an advantageous one, but this fight demonstrated that by leaving his old position as second in command of the Eufaula Rifles, he reduced his opportunities to command men in battle, which is what he very much wanted to do. Anna also wanted to know the truth of Eufaula rumors about who was in the fight. Anna relates that her brother Will is now commuting to Columbus regularly. This is in connection with the contract work which Will's Eufaula Foundry is performing for the Confederate Navy in the construction of ironclad gunboats. In a later chapter, we will examine in detail Will's services to the Confederacy in the construction of ironclads and gunboats.

Oct 14th 1861

My Own Dearest,

    I have been trying for two or three days to write to you but was prevented once by company. Mrs. McDonald and Mr. & Mrs. Cotten spent the day with us.

I received your letter yesterday, telling of the fight. I had heard many rumors about it, but did not feel uneasy as we heard the "Rifles" were not engaged in it, this I suppose was not true however as Johnny McRae [the brother of Maria, Henry Young's wife] wrote that he was among those who participated.

Don't you wish <u>you</u> had been there. Then if you had your old place in the Rifles, you might have been, and commanded them too - and may be you will have a chance soon. I am anxiously looking for your next letter so that I can hear the truth and see the particulars - we have seen a good deal of it in several papers.

Will you be afraid now for us to go down! I don't know Dearest when I shall see you for I see no prospect now of our going down, of course you cant leave - but I do hope that I shall see you before long - and I want you to see the Baby. I believe that makes me <u>more</u> anxious than I should otherwise be but he is getting to be such a good big boy and so old that I think his Papa ought to see him and know him. He was right sick night before last and yesterday with a very bad cold but Ma got some medicine from the doctor for him and we gave him a good greasing last night and to day he is nearly well. We have all taken cold. I suppose it must be the change in the weather - it is quite cold now we have to keep fires most of the time.

Pa went over to Macon this morning as delegate to the Convention. He will be back Thursday I expect. Henry went up with Will Saturday so we have no Gentlemen of the family home but the very young ones…Will is coming regularly now - he leaves Columbus every Tuesday evening after the four o'clock train comes in - he is quite interested and pleased - I don't know how long he will keep it - as long as he likes I think and the way he went on.

Oh: Dearest you say you have some flowers sent and a yellow oleander for me I am glad you got one for I was anxious to have it - but Love I would not give old P_____ his extravagant prices for flowers - he will ask you a great deal too much I am satisfied, for he will think you do not know much about the price of flowers - I would like to have a double white oleander then we will have all the varieties. Ma moved her plants on the conservatory last Saturday. They are working in well - those I brought home are growing finely.

I didn't make the visit to Mrs. Howard as I expected, she sent in for me on Thursday, but <u>black</u> Mary was sick and Ma going to have company the next day - and I did not I think I ought to take Susan away for I didn't see how she could spare her - she insisted on my doing so - but I thought I ought not - I am going some time this week I think.

You ought to see Joe and Pet - they seem to think ever so much of each other - make as much fuss as <u>I</u> do about <u>you</u> …

I am going to tell you something else, it is quite unfortunate your being away - you have lost the opportunity of making your fortune without much trouble - Ma says if you were home she would give you the case –

Burnly rode by our house a day or so ago and claimed one of our hogs - said he lost it six months ago - Today he wrote a note to Pa saying he would come for it tomorrow. Pa wrote him that we had raised the hog, that the value of it was not so great but that he should have it - So Ma went down town this morning & brought Mr. Cunningham up to swear it was a hog that he had at the mill - I couldn't help laughing - Burnly must be a fool - I don't know how it will end - for you see what you have lost.

Well Love it is nearly time for the mail to close and I must stop.

Ma and I had a great mind to write you to telegraph us whenever a fight occurs again so that we could hear the truth, …particularly if you should be engaged in it - I think they do not wish to fight at Pickens or they certainly would have been a grand fight when our men attacked their encampment.

I will make another effort to close - Much love and many kisses from the Baby and your Nannie who loves you with her whole heart - Goodbye Dearest Love,

Your Nannie -

I want to know if H. Smith was in the fight and Bill McTyer.

The fight on Santa Rosa Island led Hubert to a decision about his future in the army. He decided that it was time for him to resign as adjutant of the First Alabama Regiment and resume his position as second-in-command of the Eufaula Rifles (now renamed Company B of the First Alabama Regiment) under Captain Alpheus Baker. He had gained valuable experience as the chief administrative offer of the regiment, but what Hubert really wanted above all else was an opportunity to lead men in battle, and he correctly concluded that the best strategy for achieving that was to return to his company. We see from his revealing next letter to Anna that Hubert realized that Alpheus Baker might not be well enough to command at this time, and that if there were more "warm work", i.e. fighting, Hubert would likely be in command of the company. He is also considering other options, such as the artillery branch of service. This letter also reflects that Hubert's martial surroundings do not deter him, like many new fathers, from making a fool of himself over his new son:

"Barrancas Fla
Oct 18th, 1861

"My Dearest Nannie
Your letter written the 14th was received yesterday. Did you receive the letter I sent by Folsom. I sent a letter and flower seed by him and you ought to have received both together. I am anxious to hear from you in relation to it.

I wrote you particularly about the fight and what companies were in it. If John McRae was in it he went with some other company, not the Rifles.

As I wrote you in my last I have resigned my position as Adjutant and as soon as I can move will rejoin my company, Baker's, Smith's, & McTyer's sickness the cause apparent. I have privately some others. I have been Adjutant long enough to learn everything that can be learned in the office and

I want to drill and have a company command. Baker will not be well enough to take charge in some time and I will be in command, and if there is any warm work to be done will try and have a hand in it. There is not the slightest chance for our Regiment to be moved from here and the position of Adjutant here not as good if a fight (bombardment) takes place as to have command of a battery. The next thing is I was prejudiced somewhat in the company by taking the position and I want to try and reinstate myself so that I may keep some position if I want to go next year—and besides I want to be familiar with a command so that if I got one I would not be awkward about it. These are selfish reasons all, but then these are selfish times.

I sold my horse to Capt. Dawson. I have just been talking with him and bragging on <u>my boy</u>. He has one four days older than ours and I tell him I know mine is the finest. I let him see Eddies likeness which he pronounced very fine—said he never saw a better one or indeed one as good and said he must be a fine baby, said he was like you.

There is no communication between Pensacola and the navy yard now except to bring over freight. No passengers are allowed. To get to Pensacola every one must go by land and as there are few horses here. Walking or staying in camp is the order of the day. To stay away from camp at night Genl Braggs permission must be obtained which it is not very easy to do—so you see Darling that your visit to Pensacola would not be pleasant to either of us. Besides no one can leave Pensacola without obtaining a permit from the officer in command over there and the rail road agent has to furnish the army with the names of those who come down on the train. These precautions are taken because of the flight of some persons from Florida to Santa Rosa some time since. I expect you saw an account of it. At least I suppose that is the reason and it is only a supposition.

I shall be sorry if the flower seed are lost and I hope you will get them. I do not know how I am to get my flower from here now. It is a bad chance but I will watch my opportunity and send it if I can.

My Love I think you may as well give up all idea of seeing me until next February. Certainly I will not be able to get away if the times continue as they are now. Well Love I will close for the present and finish tonight or in the morning. You have no idea how much I want to see the baby and yourself and in fact all the family.

Oh, how does the Burnly hog case come on. It will look well on the docket will it not:

'Burnly)

   v.   )

Young)

'Plaintiff claims of the Defendant a certain hog of such a description with such marks and a certain number of curls in his tail etc. etc.'

Well really I am in bad luck…I must put up with it so goodby for the present Darling.

Well my Love it is now a bright morning Saturday. I have not moved yet but will move today somehow. Every body is moving down here and the wagons are so busy I could not get one to move me. The rain and clouds of the last week are gone and it looks as if it may be a bright sun shining day. I hope it may for we need such a one to take the dampness out of our clothes.

Keep cheerful and of good heart. Your old Dear will be pretty apt to be home next <u>February</u>. It is only three months and a little more. Kiss the boy ever so many times and give my love to all the family [including] the junior girls I think it is time they were answering my letters – write me long letters all about yourself and matters and things at home. I wish I could see the boy if it was only for a little while. If you wish to go to Columbus go my Love, and if I can come I will but I am satisfied I cannot – well goodby my love to all and with much of it and many kisses to you & the boy goodby. Your old Dear Hubert"

The Regimental Muster Roll reflects that Hubert's resignation as regimental adjutant became effective on October 29, 1861, and he was thereupon transferred back to Company B (the Eufaula Rifles) in accordance with his request.

In his next letter, Hubert writes that his regiment had to witness another execution, which he disliked intensely. There is a false alarm about Mobile; in fact that city is never actually attacked until 1864, when Farragut "damned the torpedoes." Hubert continues to worry about the lack of communication from his father, Dr. Stouten Warren Dent, in Maryland, but Anna is apparently in correspondence with Hubert's younger brother, George, who is now in the army in Virginia.

"Barrancas Florida
Nov 7th, 1861

"My own sweet Darling
I received your long and interesting letter of the 2nd and 3rd today… Today or rather this morning we heard heavy firing about Mobile which lasted for several hours and every one I saw thought Lincoln's fleet was there making an attack on the place about two o'clock the large Steamer that was here the Colorado got under way and went off in the direction of Mobile and that made us think stronger than ever that the fight was going on. Well this evening I learn that Genl Bragg had received a dispatch saying that the firing was only one of the blockading vessels firing at a target. Excitement died out suddenly at that news and no more conjectures were heard.

Two men are to be shot tomorrow one from the 10th Mississippi Regiment for killing his 1st Sergeant and the other from the Louisiana Infantry for striking his Captain and other acts of very great insubordination. Our Regiment is ordered to be under arms at 9 ½ o'clock and I am very much afraid we will be marched off to witness the execution. I do not wish to see it.

144

Men grow callous enough at best in the army and I do not wish to witness any more of such sights than are absolutely necessary. There is a very great difference between shooting down men enemies (at least to ones feelings) when the blood is warm and we are excited to the highest pitch witnessing the shooting of one of our own men by own our men.

Reub Kolb[1] has a furlough for twenty days and will leave tomorrow. Billy Cargile goes with him as he is too weak to travel alone. His Dr. thinks he has symptoms of typhoid fever. Our company escaped pretty well through the summer but we are suffering now. My own health is as robust as usual and every body says I am fattening up. What do you think of that. I however do not see any difference in myself.

The weather is very pleasant now the nights are charming. I think of my <u>courting days</u>, when I used to get sentimental etc.

Oh! The tale I had heard about enlisting the four companies for the war and discharging the others was all humbug. Genl Bragg had never given any such intimation. Well I hear the drum and must go to roll call.

Well roll call is over and the day's duties are done. There is much speculation as to what the steamer that was here went towards Mobile for. Some think that the fleet is about rendezvousing there to attack the place. You will however have learned if such is the case before this letter reaches you.

Darling I must again thank you for your kindness to George [Hubert's younger brother, with the army in Virginia]. It is so strange I do not hear from any of them. It has been nearly a month since I had a letter and the contents that was any thing but consoling. I would like very much to hear from there and know exactly how they are all situated. I can't understand why my Father does not write. I must make an effort in some way to find out what has become of him but I hardly know how to commence.

It is does seem a long time Darling to wait three months before I can see you and when I see others going home on twenty and thirty days furlough—I feel very much like I would be willing to have a short spell of sickness for the sake of being with you and staying with you for thirty days. Just to think that I will have been with you only twelve days (and in fact I believe it was only eleven) out of twelve months. I tell you my love that I feel like I would hardly be doing justice to you or myself to go again into the service immediately. You need never fear Darling that you will become unnecessary for my happiness. I believe I love you better and that you are dearer to me every day you and I are separated. I count the days when I expect to see you and be with you and I often speculate about how happy the meeting will be. Yes Darling I am getting old and the time is getting short for me to accomplish what I wish. This war has made a great change in my calculations and perhaps some in my feelings about these things. Learning "to wait" is a hard lesson. I am delighted with your accounts of our boy. I

---

[1] Private Reuben Kolb recovered from his typhoid fever, later became the captain of Kolb's Battery of artillery, and in the 1890's was nearly elected governor of Alabama, over strong opposition from Hubert Dent, as will be hereafter related.

wish I could have been with you when you were so lonely and cold thinking of your old Dear. Nothing could have afforded me more pleasure than to have taken you in my arms and warmed you up. Your letter carried me back to last fall and winter. Shall we ever be as happy again. I hope so. I feel we will don't you Darling.

Well my sheet is out and I must say goodby. Give my love to all friends in Columbus if you are there and to all at home if you are there. With much love to you and the baby and many kisses for both. I say goodby my Darling. Your old Dear Hubert

Following the Confederate attack on Santa Rosa Island, Col. Brown held conferences with the federal Navy commander to plan a coordinated bombardment of the Confederate positions on the mainland, Forts McRee and Barrancas. The guns of Fort Pickens, its outlying batteries, and those of the U. S. S. *Richmond* and the U. S. S. *Niagara* opened fire at 10 A. M. on November 22. The Confederates replied in kind, and the artillery duel lasted until nightfall. The federals concentrated on Fort McRee, which suffered heavy damage. However, repairs were made during the night, and by dawn the fort was ready to resume the fight. The federals had suffered only one killed and six wounded. Confederate losses were one killed, twenty-one wounded, and six smothered to death in a magazine cave-in. The barrage resumed at ten o'clock on the morning of the twenty third. The nearby villages of Warrington and Woolsey went up in flames from the federals' "hot shots", and one building in the Navy Yard burned. The action did not resume on the twenty fourth. Over 5000 cannon shots had been fired during the duel of the forts, but only eight lives had been lost. The inconclusive bombardment and the limited Confederate attack on Santa Rosa Island demonstrated that with the forces at hand, neither side could take decisive action.

This bombardment was the principal engagement of the Eufaula Rifles' year at Fort Barrancas. From his next letter, we learn that Hubert's decision to resign as adjutant and return to Company B (the Eufaula Rifles) as its second-in-command paid off. Captain Baker and others had been on leave in Eufaula and did not get back to Barrancas until the bombardment was largely over, and this left the command of the company in Hubert's hands. Hubert felt that the Confederates got the best of the fight, and that the First Alabama Regiment conducted itself well. Alpheus Baker has been offered the colonelcy of a new regiment, and Hubert is still analyzing his opportunities for seeing more action:

"Barrancas Florida
Nov 25, 1861

"My Dear Darling
I wrote you last night and sent it off this morning. I was very tired and wrote hurriedly. I am able now to write more at leisure and to correct some things which were not correct in my last letter.
Capt. Baker, Judge Cochran, Mr. Wellborn, and Jim McNab reached here about day light this morning. Baker has not yet taken command. He is leaving every thing to me. I wrote you last night that the enemy were firing at

146

the Navy Yard. Well they kept it up until about 4 o'clock this morning so the sentinels informed me. They then ceased and have not fired again today. I presume they will open in the morning. The last shot fired from our side was about 12 last night and we have not fired again since. There was no fight at deer point as I wrote. Genl Bragg visited our battery this morning and told me there was no fight there. None of our men were killed in the Navy Yard. Not much damage done in there so far. A few mules were killed.

They lost six men at McRee. Five of them were smothered by the bursting in of a rat hole. They were in there to protect themselves from the shot. A shell struck it and it caved in. One man was killed by cannon there. He is the only man killed in that way—seven are wounded.

Genl Bragg is in the finest humor imaginable and compliments the 1st Regt. highly. They occupy the post of danger and of honor and Bragg says they have sustained themselves well. I do not feel the slightest apprehension about danger personally and I believe we have the best of the fight. I have seen several holes in the walls of Pickens and I believe we can batter them down.

I have two curiosities to send home, one a shell conical and the other the same shape but solid. I will keep them and send them home the first chance I get. They are for Ma as ornaments for her front gate. Tell her that I have not forgotten the promise I made her when I left home I believe to send her a couple fired from Pickens. Both these can be fixed up on the posts. I send them of different kinds for the sake of variety or rather I expect to send them.

Today has not seemed at all like Sunday and I have to stop and think before I can realize it. Well Darling we have waited and worked a long time for this fight and it has come at last. The first day the enemy fired very rapidly—the rest not so fast. We have been shooting very slowly all the time. I think the enemy must be satisfied that it is no easy matter to silence our batteries. We drove the ships from McRee yesterday and our men say one of them is badly damaged. There are now five here in all. I think two of them however are only transports.

We confidently look for the fight to commence early in the morning. Brown has been busy all day piling up sand bags that we have knocked down and I suppose repairing damages generally. I am glad the fight has opened. I did not want to go home and say that I had not fired a gun at the enemy. I think now that I will have plenty to talk of when I go home and that is the best part of it, I expect to go home.

Every one tells me I am looking so well. I feel in fine health and it would be a great shame for one of Brown's shells to knock up such a healthy hardy man. I attribute a great deal to my temperance not only in drinking but in eating.

I have seen a circular from Genl Bragg (which would have been made public but for the fight) appealing in the strongest manner to the 1st Regt. to reenlist. I have not determined exactly what I shall do. I have been spoken to by a prominent man in the Regt. who expects to reenlist who desired me for Major of the Regt. I would like such a position very much. Would prefer it to a captaincy or a higher position. In fact if I could get that position in a good <u>regiment for the war</u> I would be perfectly satisfied But I must have some time to go and stay at home. I can't go in right away without some privilege of that sort.

I write you now Darling because I have a chance. If I do not write regularly you may know that I cannot. When the fight is over and we whip the Yankees I will await developments. I expect I will get so full of military that I will lose some of my taste for civil pursuits. I don't believe I have thought of any case or that there was such a thing since I came here except military law.

Baker has said nothing of his taking the colonelcy of the new Regt. He wrote me before he left home that he would accept it. This fight may postpone the matter longer and perhaps altogether.

Give my love to all and tell them not to be uneasy. I shall be more anxious than ever to see you and our boy when the fight is over but I do not expect to be able to go home especially if Baker leaves the company. Goodby Darling—much love and many kisses for you and our boy. Your old Dear Hubert

Back in Eufaula, Anna wanted some household help, and wrote Hubert about the matter. Immediately following their marriage, Anna and Hubert had no need to incur the expense of owning slaves, but after the birth of Eddie, Anna wanted a house servant. In his next letter, Herbert recognized the need and agreed to acquire a servant. He writes her to ask her father or brother to help with the transaction if he cannot get home for Christmas as hoped. Although Hubert claims that soldiering does not suit his tastes, his actions suggest otherwise. He is actually anxious to get into action, and he makes clear that he will reenlist, not for some limited period, but for the duration of the war. He also writes of the illness of his friend and law mentor E. C. Bullock.

"Barrancas Florida
Dec 7, 1861

"My Dear Nannie
Yours of the 3rd was received today…You are right Darling about wanting a nurse for our boy. I intended to take one of the negroes you spoke of to nurse him, and in fact I have been to blame for not taking one sooner. I intend to take the girl that old man Neal has and shall write him to send her there at Christmas, and if it turns out so that I can't be at home to attend to it I wish you would get Henry or Mr. Young to get her from Mr. Neal. I wish it was so that I could get her now, however in three weeks or less you will have her. I do not know much about her and you had better be strict with her from the first and make her know her place. I hope she will suit you. I will send you some money the first good opportunity I have so you can buy any things

you may need.

I did expect to try and get a leave of absence about the 1st of January, but from my last letter you will see why I think it very doubtful whether I can succeed or not.

The weather is pleasant now and the nights are fine. Every thing is quiet and excepting the destruction of property it looks here very little like a fight had taken place. Genl Bragg is building new batteries about McRee and otherwise preparing for a renewal of the fight. He sent over a flag of truce a few days after the fight but it was not received and there is some suspicion that old Brown was killed. It is all however more suspicion.

I wish I could see in the future for a few months, I am troubled a good deal about what I may be able to do another year. As a matter of calculation if I can get any position I had better reenlist and I shall try. It would be much more pleasant for me to be at home, but what could I do there, I am afraid nothing at all, and I can't bear the idea of being a hanger or doing nothing. My poverty presses on me heavily at times, not for myself Darling, but because I am able to do so little for you and the boy. I hope some day to be able to do better, but it looks very little like it now. The conditions of my family in Md. also trouble me. I know I can do them no good but still I can't help feeling badly. But I must not despond or thrust my troubles on you my love. Let us hope for the best and trust that a wise Providence may make all things work together for our good.

I want to see you comfortably situated, and then my heart will be lighter. This war has made a great change in my calculations and expectations. If peace had continued I was in hopes that I would be able to get an humble house and settle down quietly to my profession. But when that can be done no one can tell. Soldiering does not suit my tastes or inclinations, but unfortunately for me at present it is that or nothing. If I could have you with me even it would be much better and I think if I succeed in getting any position here that I will so arrange that you can be with me. That is my wish and my intention.

Keep up your spirits Darling. Your last letter seemed to me different from the letters you generally write and that you were worried and out of patience. Something must be troubling you, what is it Darling? Open your heart to your old Dear. I suppose you have seen Genl Bragg's circular to the army. I am afraid he will not succeed very well in securing recruits. There seems to be great difficulty in getting men to reenlist. The freshness and first excitement of the war has worn off and men, many of them at least, are tired of the service. It is I think an alarming symptom. Many troops will be entitled to their discharges in the next six months and it will not be easy to supply their places unless the new men reenlist. Some troops can not supply their places. Well enough on that subject.

You need not believe any of the reports you hear about men going home. Clark Mabry will go home 17 Jan. We will be discharged 9th Feb. and I do not think we will be discharged a day sooner. I see Saph is going in for 12

149

mos. I never expect to go in that way again. I do not want to be turned loose in the middle of the war in this way again. Well my love to all. I owe some of them letters. Write me whom it is, for really I have forgotten. I think though that is Ada & Helen. Smith is very anxious to go home, but he has great doubt about being able to get a 'leave'. Baker protests that he does not wish to go but that is all in my eye. Bullock is quite sick, and quite alarmed. He fears for his lungs. The company Generally is quite healthy. Well goodby Darling with much love and many kisses for you and the boy I close. Your old Dear   Hubert

Among the rumors passing through the camp, which Hubert's next letter relates as fact, was the inaccurate report that Southern towns had been burned, which sends Hubert into a vengeful mood.   Hubert's reference to Henry's leaving town probably relates to Henry Young's plans to enlist in the army in the new year. He also mentions the plans of Henry Shorter to resign his position so he can retire from the service and be home for Christmas. We will see from later letters that this galled Hubert. Actually, Shorter did not stay out of the service permanently. He later entered the Army of Northern Virginia as an aid to General C. A. Battle, with the rank of major. Hubert is restive at Barrancas; he continues to consider his own options for military service, but reiterates his intention to stay in the army in some capacity for the duration of the war.

> "Barrancas Florida
> Dec 15th 1861
>
> My Dear Nannie
> I am pretty nearly on my last sheet of paper, but being my usual time I have concluded to write you a few lines.
> Baker left yesterday on a twenty-day leave of absence to go to Memphis to see after his regiment. If it is accepted he resigns the Captaincy and takes it otherwise he returns. He went direct to Eufaula and you will hear all about it before this reaches you. He was escorted out of the lines by three companies the Pioneers, Clayton Guards and Rifles. I do not much expect he will return.
> Somehow I feel very much oppressed and don't feel like myself. I am very anxious for my time to be out here. I want to get home.
> I hear today that Charleston has been burned and that Montgomery and Selma have both been set on fire. Oh the horrors of this war. It is enough to make the blood run cold to think of any civilized and Christian people conducting a war on such principles. I believe I am in favor of raising the black flag and neither giving or taking quarter. I hope the government will see the necessity of invading the north and making them feel some of the evil effects that they have visited on us. Well enough of that. I can't do justice to the subject.
> Henry Shorter has resigned his position to take effect the 22nd Dec. He wants to be at home during Christmas and retire from the service.

There will be a great many changes during the next two months. I believe Matt's regiment will take the place of the 1st Ala. Burnett's company will take our battery. They send over a squad of men every morning to drill on our mortars so as to be efficient when the 9th fleet comes.

How are your Columbus friends? I have heard nothing from them.

I wrote to Mr. Neal, Darling, and I supposed he will send up the girl by the 1st Jan—probably sooner. If he does not you can get Mr. Young to speak to him.

Has Henry built him a house yet? I suppose he leaves town altogether next year.

Has Macon been any where about Eufaula? I would like to know where he is. I expect you will see Smith [Horace Smith, one of the Rifles' lieutenants] while he is home he said he would go to Eufaula.

Baker has offered me the position of Adjutant in his regiment with the rank & pay of captain. If he gets it for me I am going there. I would sooner do that than run the chances of doing nothing or getting no position. At the end of that time something may turn up. I will see a part of the country that is new to me and would be more apt to see active service. I expect about the time my service is out here that the thing will be fixed up. If that fails…I will try something else. I am in the war and expect to remain in it.

I see congress has offered bounty & etc. to men who reenlist. I think it was a very judicious move. Thousands of 12 mos men will be discharged in the next six months and it would be very hard to supply their places and the truth is something of the kind ought to have been done.

Give my Love to all the family and if you can't do any better send me a letter by Smith. Kiss the boy for his PaPa and tell him he hopes to see him in about eight weeks with much love and many kisses for you and the boy. I must close. Goodby. God bless you. Your old Dear   Hubert"

In December, Hubert made his decision. He accepted an invitation by Captain Felix H. Robertson, a member of Gen. Bragg's staff, to assist in organizing a new artillery battery and serving as its First Lieutenant. Robertson was a Texan who had entered West Point in 1857 at the age of eighteen. In January 1861, only three weeks before his graduation, he resigned from West Point, giving as his reason Texas's expected secession. He joined the Confederate army as a second lieutenant, and was first stationed at Charleston. He was present for the bombardment of Fort Sumter, and on April 20, 1861 he was assigned to the staff of Gen. Bragg at Pensacola. During November and December, he undertook to organize the new battery. As a result of Hubert's influence, many of the recruits were Eufaula men. Most of its members were from Eufaula and Pollard, Alabama, and from Pensacola and Quincy, Florida. Over one hundred twenty five officers and enlisted men were mustered in as members of the battery. On Jan 2, 1862, Robertson, then twenty-two, assumed command of the battery, which, pursuant to the custom in the artillery service, was known by the name of its commander, "Robertson's Battery." Felix Robertson would become an eccentric and controversial officer. As a West Pointer and favored protégé of Braxton Bragg, he nevertheless rose in the ranks. Hubert, a solid leader of the battery, would eventually be promoted to command of the unit, which then became "Dent's Alabama Battery". But this was in the future. Hubert wrote Anna of his decision, with the hope that she would approve:

"Barrancas Florida
Dec. 19th, 1861

"My Dear Darling
      I often wonder how you are employed and what are your thoughts. A few moments before I commenced this letter I was wondering just in that way. I expect you are very likely in bed and may be sleeping.
      I have just returned from seeing some men in reference to enlisting for "the war". What do you think Darling of my going in? Well I am in. The temptation of going in with Robertson with his light artillery was so great that I have concluded to go in with him. I am busy trying to raise the company or assisting to do it. I do not know yet whether many of the rifles will go in or not. Cochran says he had rather have my position than be Lt. Col. of a regiment. I do not feel exactly that way about it but I would much prefer it to the Captaincy of an infantry company. Robertson offered me the position of his own accord, and being the kind of service I preferred above all others I went in I concluded to go in. I have this advantage over enlisted men I <u>can</u> <u>resign</u>. I hope my Love that you will not feel that I have done wrong in going in.
      I think it will be a month or more before the battery is equipped and ready for service. In the mean time I want to get as long a leave of absence as I can and stay with you as much as I can and another thing my Love I want you to be with or near me during the time I stay here. I may possibly not be home before February. Keep a cheerful heart. When this war is over <u>we will</u> <u>be happy together</u>. I pray for it and I feel that it will be so. My pay is I think $100 per month. The same I have had this year with better chances for promotion and distinction. I feel that it is a grave responsibility and I have tried to think of it as I ought and I sincerely hope it will meet the approbation of my friends.
      If the news we have heard in reference to Englands demand of the surrender of Mason & Slidell be true and it seems to be confirmed I do not think the war can last over a year longer. It looks very much like Lincoln was trying to get up some decent pretext to end the war. Well enough of war & politics.
      We are all getting along here about as well as usual. McTyre is well and has been entertaining us as usual with swatches of song & etc. Reub is well. Henry Shorter leaves for home on Sunday week. I expect to send a letter by him. We have not much to do. Drilling is light and every one is looking forward to the time when he will be at home. Christmas is nearly here. I wish it was so I could be with you all. I expect all the family and <u>connections</u> (I do not know that that is the right word) will be with you except myself—whom will you have for preacher next year? I hope you will have a good and

acceptable man.

Cochran left us tonight. I miss him a good deal. Now Bullock is not expected to live. I received yesterday a letter from Governor Shorter saying that his case was considered hopeless. He will be a great loss to his family and his country. In many respects he is a wonderful man and I doubt very much whether I shall ever look upon his like again. What a brilliant career was opened before him.

Let me hear from you Darling immediately upon the receipt of this. I feel great anxiety to know how you feel about my going in again so early. Give many kisses to our boy and tell him I expect to entertain him and his MaMa after a few years with stories of my campaign. I will be something like a veteran will I not? Serving through our war of independence and it may be when the history of it is written that he may see his Father's name there. If he should I hope it will be so mentioned that he will not be ashamed to own it.

My love to all. Tell them I am busy and have little time to write. God Bless you my own sweet wife. May heaven's choicest blessings be bestowed upon you. With much love and many kisses for you and the boy. Goodnight . Your old Dear Hubert"

We will look ahead briefly to note that, although the struggle in which Hubert and his comrades fought and in which many died did not turn out to be a "war of independence," Hubert's question about how he might appear in the history books can be favorably answered. He left a record of outstanding service, marked by skill and perseverance against difficult odds. Wounded three times, he would serve for four years, from the day the Confederacy was created, until the last day of the last battle and the last surrender of Confederate troops east of the Mississippi. As the stable "anchor" of Robertson's Battery, he was recognized as one of the authors of its successes, and when he was commander of Dent's Battery, it would be acknowledged by one General as one of the three most effective artillery units in the Army of Tennessee.[442] His place is one that little Eddie would not be "ashamed to own".

In his last extant letter from Fort Barrancas, Hubert is excited over the prospect of going home. He engages in introspective musings about his role in life.

Barrancas Florida
Dec. 20th, 1861

My Love

Well my Darling I expect tomorrow to see Genl Bragg and then get a leave and go home. Unless something interferes to prevent I expect to leave the last of this week. I expect to be home in a week from today and oh! Darling have I long to be there. I do not know yet how long a leave I shall get, not less I think than thirty days and will take the other thirty some other time. It looks like a short time to be at home after twelve months absence. But my Love I think that the best. Then when I get you and the boy down here how well pleased I expect to be.

I wonder how long this war will last? I am anxious for it to end so I can go home and stay with my Darling, my boy, and all my kind friends. That time will come my Love. I feel it will come and that we will enjoy each other's society so much and be I trust contented and happy. I have home longing worse than ever. I do not think somehow that I am very well suited for public life. It is true I am in it and may continue in it but I do not enjoy it. I would much oh! So much prefer a quiet happy home to all the splendors and empty honors of public life. I feel now that if I had enough to live on comfortably that I would prefer to retire from the active busy world and live with my Darling and my boy. But it can not be. I have not the means and if I had would it be right? Each man has his part to perform. We can not live entirely for ourselves in the world. And although mine is and may continue a very humble part yet I must strive to perform it. What has put me in this moralizing humor? I do not know. I expect romance is not all out of me yet. The romance of war may be but not the romance of life. Well enough of this. Must write of other things.

Smith [Horace Smith, one of the two company second lieutenants] is busy making out muster and pay rolls for tomorrow. I have done nothing today since 9 o'clock this morning. It is rather tiresome. Darling nothing is hard any time but it is especially hard when one is thinking of home and friends and a Dear wife and a sweet boy all of whom that one is anxious to see. I could not stand to remain away from you and do nothing. I must have employment.

I expect Baker will return to Eufaula and may be here before he takes command of his regiment. Bill McTyer [the other of the two second lieutenants of the company] is in as fine a humor as ever and very well. I am as hearty as ever. No more dyspepsia since I quit smoking and syrup. Our company is in good health. We have only two new sick and they are not much sick. The men generally are very anxious to get home. I am afraid there will be some disgraceful scenes when they do get home. I have heard not a very good account of some who have gone home.

My time as [First] Lt. will soon be out. I wonder who will be elected in my place. Perhaps I can rent my office to whoever it may be. Hardman must give it up. I have written thus far and will wait until night or tomorrow morning.

It is now 10 o'clock and not feeling sleepy, I have concluded to finish this letter. I have nothing new to add. Perhaps I may write tomorrow if I can find out that I am going home I will write and let you know, otherwise I may not write until the next day.

I will stop a day in Montgomery I think as I want to attend to some business there. I will remember the baby's carriage and if there is one there I will get it if I can get money enough. Well give my love to all the family and tell them I will be home as soon as I can. Kiss the baby for me and with much love to you and the boy and many kisses for my Darling. I must say good by. Your old Dear Hubert"

Hubert was granted a Christmas furlough. However, he was able to enjoy only a small part of it. Three weeks before its expiration, he was recalled to Pensacola. He arrived at Fort Barrancas in time for the last artillery duel between the forts, on January 1, 1862. It lasted only four hours. There were few casualties and little damage.

A drastic change in the nature of Hubert's service was about to occur. In February 1862, Gen. Bragg was ordered to take a corps of ten thousand men from the coastal defenses and report to Corinth, Mississippi, to join the command of Gen. Albert Sidney Johnston. Hubert and Robertson's Battery transferred to Corinth with Gen. Bragg, to be part of what would become known as the Army of Tennessee. Hubert would later write that the year that he and the Rifles had spent in Pensacola would in retrospect seem like "a pastime." The real war was about to begin. Within weeks, Lieutenant Dent would be showing his mettle as an officer of artillery under deadly fire near a Tennessee log meeting house called Shiloh Church.

20
The Eufaula Homefront

"The 'minute men'… took up their march…at 9 o'clock, wagons and a few buggies following, and when the men got fatigued walking, they could ride."
Reminiscences of Green Beauchamp

The beginning of the war had sent a thrill of excitement through the citizens of Eufaula. Many had felt that the Southern states would probably be allowed to leave the Union in peace. When war appeared imminent, the challenge was enthusiastically accepted. As we have seen, Eufaula had long been a center of secessionist sentiment; its political leaders had been instrumental in bringing about the secession of Alabama. Few Eufaulians, if any, seriously considered the possibility that the South could be defeated.

Eufaula was filled with uniforms, marching and drilling, as new companies were being formed. As units departed for Pensacola or other stations, and later as men came and went on furlough, there were demonstrations, sendoffs, welcomes, speeches, and cannon salutes. Flags were presented to the companies; young ladies admired their bravery; and support from the home front was pledged.

The tenor of the period is best conveyed by extracts from the reminiscences from 1861 of Green Beauchamp, one of the earliest settlers of Barbour County:[443]

Jan. 11. Alabama seceded today at 2 p. m. One hundred guns were fired in honor of the occasion, amidst great rejoicings.

Jan. 17. Clayton Guards arrived from Clayton, received by the Eufaula Rifles and escorted to quarters. Great preparations going on for departure for the seat of war.

Jan. 19. Saturday. Streets crowded with people from the country to hear the news. Military drilling in the streets.

Feb 1. Large party given for departing soldiers.

Feb. 2. Pioneer Guards and Clayton Guards leave for Pensacola.

Feb. 9. Eufaula Rifles under Capt Alpheus Baker, mustered into the service of the State of Alabama for twelve months.

Feb. 12. Rifles leave for Pensacola on boat by way of Columbus, Ga, many citizens escorting them as far as Montgomery.

March 9. About 20 men belonging to Rifles unfit for active duty and otherwise disqualified, met and organized as the reserve corps of the Eufaula Rifles, to assist in giving aid and comfort to their comrades at the front, and assist in recruiting men for the command, and home protection.

March 11. Wm. Henry Woods, Sergeant of the Eufaula Rifles, returned to duty.

March 15. Our soldiers at Pensacola duly forwarded a letter of thanks for articles sent them by the community.

April 1. John Black [Editor of the *Spirit of the South*], has returned from a visit to Pensacola and gave an interesting statement of facts in the "Spirit."

April 5. The Louisville Blues, 85 strong rank and file, on their way to Pensacola. A fine looking company.

April 13. Surrender of Fort Sumter to the Confederate forces at 2 o'clock today. Great rejoicing, bonfires, etc.

April 15. News of Lincoln's call for 75,000 men to subjugate the South and crush the rebellion, but that number couldn't crush.

April 18. News received of Virginia seceding. Great demonstration of joy, parade of military. Punch, the old cannon on the bluff, was made to awake the echoes.

May 4. A stranger arrested on suspicion of being a black Republican; no proof, so he was dismissed. ["Black" does not refer to the suspect's color; this word always preceded "Republican"].

May 6. Rev. McNair [Eufaula's Presbyterian minister], left for Pensacola to do duty as chaplain for the soldiers.

May 7. Town meeting to ratify the appointment of a vigilance committee, before whom all reasonable and doubtful persons should be tried and disposed of, as interest and public safety demands.

May 17. John C. McRae returned from Pensacola, with order from Rifles to have tents forwarded immediately. They were duly sent, and several glass packages were carefully sealed and packed with them for the comfort of the boys.

June 5. Stores all closed at 5 o'clock to give the citizens time to drill. An organization was formed under the name of the "Shorter Volunteers," to drill and hold themselves in readiness for any emergency.

June 6. The Barbour Greys leave for the seat of war, amidst great demonstrations of encouragement and sad farewells.

June 10. Business almost suspended. At 5 o'clock the Shorter Volunteers, 47 rank and file, out for drill. These drills were kept up daily.

June 13. A day of fasting and prayer. The Volunteers, 40 strong, attended public worship, Rev. W. N. Reeves officiating.

June 17. Mrs. L. L. Cato and Mrs. A. Baker soliciting contributions for the relief of our boys at the front.

June 18. News received of Sewell's Point fight. Capt. Alpheus Baker home on leave of absence, and warmly met by the citizens.

June 20. Dr. Hugh Black, with recruits for Pioneers, left for Pensacola. The ladies hold a meeting and commence to make clothing for the soldiers.

June 21. Heard of appointment of W. F. Robinson as midshipman in C. S. Navy, to report at New Orleans under Commodore L. Rousseau.

June 25, 26, 27. Union Female College commencement exercises. Well attended and very interesting.

June 29. Capt Baker departs for his command, and is escorted to the boat by the Shorter Volunteers. Van Houten and others go with him. Col. John F. Treutlen passed through with his men, numbering 120. on their way to the front. The town alive with excitement.

July 8. Lincoln calls for 400,000 men to put us down, but nobody believes he can do it, even with that number of men additional. Andrew Veal back from Pensacola with sad recitals of his brother's death, the first death in the Rifles.

July 11. The City Guards ordered into service today.

July 22. News received of the great victory of the battle of Manassas…Hon. Jas. L. Pugh left to join the boys at Pensacola.

July 28. Sunday. Thanksgiving services in the churches on account of the late victories. The City Guards are escorted to the boat by the Shorter Volunteers. Speech by E. S. Shorter, Esq.

July 29. New York Herald of 23inst., received and read; full of villainous lies about the South.

Aug. 10. Reuben Kolb left by railroad for Pensacola, after having been home several days on a furlough.

Aug 29. Henry R. Shorter and F. Fenwick left today for Pensacola. Several of the boys home from the front.

Sept. 16. Governor John Gill Shorter, of Alabama, and Hon. E. S. Shorter in the city. The ladies have so far raised $200 in cash for the soldiers.

Sept. 16. Col E. C. Bullock in the city on leave of absence. Rumors of all kinds fill the city. Hear of skirmishes in all directions.

Oct. 9. Departure of Col. Bullock for his command last night, and on the following day, the 10th, heard of the fight at Fort Pickens [i. e. the landing on Santa Rosa Island. Ed.].

Oct. 19. Cotton today brings only 7.9 cents, and but few care to buy even at that. Business almost completely suspended.

Nov. 8. Price of salt in this city today $10 and $12 a sack, and not anxious to sell.

Nov 11. Billy Cargile and Reuben Kolb home from Pensacola, bringing much interesting news.

Nov 15. Fast Day. Services at Presbyterian Church in the morning and afternoon. Remarks made by Gov. Shorter at prayer meeting.

Nov. 22. At 4 ½ o'clock p. m., hear of fight at Pensacola. [i. e. the first major bombardment. Ed.] Capt. Baker at once left for his command. Intense excitement.

Dec 12. "Blind Tom", the Negro musical prodigy and wonder, gives a concert at the Baptist church to a large attendance. Part of the proceeds to go to the soldiers benefit fund.

Often there were reports of favorable military or diplomatic events which caused excitement, followed by news that the reports were false. There were rumors of enemies being in the county. A Vigilance Committee was created to examine persons suspected of being abolitionists or in sympathy with the North. This was not a completely unfounded concern. Other communities, such as Columbus, had instituted similar committees following John Brown's raid, when it was realized that New England abolitionists provided support for fanatics to go south and incite slaves to murder their masters.[444] One case considered by this Committee concerned Professor Charles Kliffmuller, a German-born teacher of music at the Union Female College. The Committee quickly recognized his loyalty, deserving of "double praise," because, when he went New York to place his wife and her sister on the boat to Germany, he could have gone too, but instead returned to "stand by us". Later Professor Kliffmuller would give the ultimate proof of his loyalty.

The beginning of death reports brought home the hardships of war. The town was particularly moved by the death of the well liked and respected Edward Courtney Bullock, whose remains arrived in Eufaula on Christmas Eve, 1861. Having enlisted as a private in the

Eufaula Rifles, Bullock had been appointed as Judge Advocate by General Bragg. Upon the organization of the Eighteenth Alabama Infantry Regiment, Bullock had been commissioned as its colonel, stationed at Mobile. He had asked Gen. Bragg to allow him to return to Barrancas to be present for the expected bombardment of Pensacola, and while there, he contracted typhoid fever. He was moved to the home of his friend, Dr. W. O. Baldwin in Montgomery, and soon died there. Bullock was a friend of the Youngs, and had mentored Hubert Dent's study of law. His intellect and legal ability, coupled with "an irresistible combination of high spirits and charming manners" presaged an outstanding career, which was cut short at the age of 36.

In February and March of 1862, the twelve-month enlistments of the volunteers from Barbour County began to expire. As individual soldiers or entire units returned to Eufaula, they were welcomed with another round of demonstrations, speeches, and salutes similar to their sendoffs a year earlier. The Confederate government made a concerted effort to encourage reenlistment. Many, if not most, of these men reenlisted and returned to fight, in the same unit or different units. But not all reenlisted; some had had enough of soldiering for now.

The Eufaula Rifles arrived back in Eufaula on the steamboat, *Chewalla*, on Feb 15, amid a welcoming celebration. An effort to reorganize the company "for the war" did not succeed. Its leadership had moved on to other units. Captain Alpheus Baker was now colonel of a regiment. Lt. Dent had helped organize Robertson's Battery; some of the "Rifles" had joined him and were now enroute to Corinth, Mississippi.

However, Captain John W. Clark, previously commander of the Pioneer Guards from Clayton, called for enlistments in a new artillery company, to be known as the "Eufaula Light Artillery". There was an enthusiastic response to this call, and the ranks filled up rapidly. On February 21, Eufaula's business houses closed at eleven o'clock for a meeting to raise money to equip this and other Barbour County units enlisting "for the war".

Among those enlisting in the Eufaula Light Artillery was Henry A. Young. Henry and Maria's son, Henry, Jr., was now one year old; Edward's business activities had changed so that the need for his son's help in the business was lessened; and Henry had decided that it was time for him to join his townsmen and shoulder his share of the burdens of the war. He was enlisted as a private on March 31, 1862, "for three years or the war," by Lt. Oliver.[445] The company consisted of 262 officers and men, many of whom had previously served with the Eufaula Rifles or the Pioneer Guards.

One morning in early April, the new company was formed up before a crowd of well-wishers between Parker's store and the Arlington Hotel on Broad Street, and the roll was called.[446] The muster roll of the Eufaula Light Artillery included most of the familiar Eufaula names, practically every family being represented. Henry's brother-in-law, John McRae, now 22, who had served in the Eufaula Rifles, was among them. James H. G. Martin, now 17, who would marry Henry's sister, Ada, after the war, was a sergeant of the company, having previously served with the Eufaula Rifles. John Herbert Dent, seventeen-year-old son of

Edward's friend, John Horry Dent, was in the ranks. Professor Kliffmuller had enlisted. Following roll call, the company was marched down Broad Street and across the river, with crowds of men, women, and children following, to board the train for Tennessee. At that time, the railroad came only to the foot of the railroad bridge on the Georgia side of the Chattahoochee. Before the troops left Alabama soil, the Rev. Mr. Cotten, the Methodist minister, made an inspiring speech, and commended them to the protection of God. They then departed, to become part of the First Alabama Battalion of Artillery. The company served first with Stevenson's Brigade, in the Department of Tennessee, Maj. Gen. E. Kirby Smith, commanding, with headquarters at Knoxville. Camped near the Departmental Headquarters at Knoxville,[447] the company christened its first camp "Camp Bullock," in honor of their recently-deceased townsman and comrade, E. C. Bullock.

Edward Young himself, at the age of sixty-one, enlisted as a private in the Eufaula Home Reserves. Most of the males left in Eufaula were old men, boys, or others exempt from service. On March 28, 1862, two days after Henry and the other members of the Eufaula Light Artillery departed for Tennessee, a meeting was held at 10:00 A. M. to organize the older men into a company of "minute men".[448] Lewy Dorman provides us with the Muster Roll of the "Eufaula Home Reserves," which, in response to an order of Governor Shorter on December 22, 1862, was later certified by Captain Beeman on August 1, 1863.[449] Private Edward Young, at sixty-one, is one of the oldest on this list. It includes Edward's two banking partners, Private Clayton R. Woods, age 54, and Private Colin Gardner, age 52, as well as his banking competitor, Private John McNab, age, 57. It included Ada's future father-in-law, J. G. L. Martin, age 52, and other familiar Eufaula names. There were two boys, 15 and 16, on the roster, one 30 year old with the explanation, "crippled hand", and a 41-year-old "preacher, crippled hand".[450] In enlisting as a "minute man," Edward was following the same course as his grandfather, Jonas, and his great-grandfather, Stephen Young eighty-five years earlier in Newark. Stephen was in his late 50's when he enlisted as a private in the "Newark Minutemen."

The spirits of these elderly Confederate warriors were willing, even if their marching endurance was limited, as revealed by Green Beauchamp's reminiscence for Dec 13, 1862:

> "The 'minute men'… took up their march for Fort Gaines [ten miles from
> Eufaula] at 9 o'clock, wagons and a few buggies following, and when the
> men got fatigued walking, they could ride."

While life went on very much as before in Fendall Hall, the war brought a significant alteration in Edward's business activities. Apalachicola had been the first Gulf coast port to be blockaded, when the federal screw-steamer *USS Montgomery* arrived off the coast with sixty-six men and five guns, on June 11, 1861. One ship did not make an effective blockade, but as additional ships arrived, better suited to the shallow waters of this area, the blockade became increasingly effective. Finally, on April 3, 1862, a federal force landed at Apalachicola and took control of the town, finding that most of the inhabitants had already abandoned the town and fled.

For all practical purposes, the Chattahoochee-Apalachicola river valley was now denied access to the sea. Eufaula's only other outlet was the railroad that stopped on the Georgia side of the Chattahoochee, but this railroad linked to Savannah, which was also blockaded. Eufaula was commercially landlocked. Some cotton was still needed domestically, and some Southern cotton was still reaching Europe through the blockade, which provided the Confederate government with badly needed exchange with which to purchase war and naval materiel. But these demands for cotton were limited. Apalachicola, an abandoned town, was not a center of blockade running activity, and the lucrative cotton exporting industry was dead in Barbour County. Cotton factors without a reliable cotton market had little interest in purchasing, and this was reflected in the price of cotton. Planters who had difficulty selling did not produce large amounts of cotton. Further, the Confederate government was encouraging farmers to plant corn and other food crops, instead of cotton, with which to feed the population and the troops. Under these circumstances, Edward's cotton factoring business, in which planter's paid him fees to finance, warehouse, grade, and market their cotton, became very limited.

However, Edward did have at least one cotton market left. As we will later discuss in detail, his brother William's cotton mill in Columbus, the Eagle Manufacturing Co., was operating at full capacity to meet the needs of the Confederate government for uniforms and other fabric products. When William needed cotton, he naturally gave Edward the opportunity to participate in supplying this need. Edward was thus one cotton factor whom Barbour County planters still planting cotton could look to to market their cotton. Edward, acting either as a broker for the planters or for his own account, sold their cotton to his brother for use by the Eagle Mills. Extant business records of Edward reflect, for instance, that on August 8, 1863, Edward sold William thirteen bales of cotton for $2762.50, and twenty-five bales for $4906.15.

Edward's mercantile business was also affected by the blockade. As a commission merchant, he was paid a commission to supply planters with needed equipment and materials, and he also sold such merchandise in the operation of his general store. In these businesses, Edward was dependent on the import of manufactured goods from the northern United States, or from abroad. Before the war, he regularly traveled to the North to purchase merchandise for resale. Of course, the war eliminated the North as a source of manufactured goods, and the blockade eliminated Europe as a source. The Confederacy's limited manufacturing facilities were being devoted largely to supplying the military, so that manufactured goods for consumers became difficult or impossible to acquire. In the latter part of 1861, Edward closed his general store, which he had operated on Broad Street's "Brick Row" for more than twenty years.

It should not be supposed that these changes rendered Edward inactive in business. Although his cotton factoring and commission merchant had been the foundation of his business success since the 1830's, he had always had a hand in other ventures, and he continued those now. His business papers indicate continued activity in his insurance business. His principle focus, however, shifted to banking, and this would remain his primary business for the rest of his life. It will be recalled that in 1859, he had organized the banking partnership of Young, Woods, and Gardner. Despite reduced economic activity, the area still had banking needs, and Young, Woods, and Gardner adapted to wartime conditions and continued throughout the war and beyond. Examples of its "shinplasters" or currency notes survive. As reflected by note number B 3446, the promise of the bank's fifty-cent note was as follows:

> "We promise to pay the bearer on demand FIFTY CENTS in current
> Bank or Confederate Treasury Notes, when presented in sums of Five
> Dollars or its multiple,
>
> Young, Woods, and Gardner
>
> Eufaula, Ala. April 15, 1862"

In 1861, Edward made an unusual but prescient investment: He purchased 3200 acres of fertile land in the Platte River valley of the Territory of Nebraska, which would soon lie along the path of the Union Pacific transcontinental railroad. There is no reason to assume Edward doubted the ultimate survival of the Confederacy; indeed, the assets underlying his banking business were Confederate currency and obligations of the Confederate government. However, it would have been natural for him to diversify his financial position so as to hedge against all risks to the extent possible.

Edward's investment in this particular Nebraska land provides fascinating insight into his sensitive antennae for business opportunity. For decades, there had been national agitation for federal support for construction of a railroad to the Pacific Ocean, but there had been an impasse between the northern and southern members of congress over whether the railroad should follow a southern or a northern route. Nebraska had been organized as a territory pursuant to the Kansas-Nebraska act of 1854, but it was never contended over and did not suffer the travails of "Bleeding Kansas." In 1859, future president Abraham Lincoln, who was a strong supporter of a transcontinental railroad, was campaigning in Council Bluffs, Iowa (directly across the Missouri River from Omaha, Nebraska), where he spoke with a young railroad construction engineer named Grenville M. Dodge. Dodge had done extensive surveying of potential routes, and Lincoln asked him what was the best route for a Pacific Railroad from the east. Dodge instantly replied, "From this town out the Platte Valley…because of the uniform grade along the Platte Valley to the Rocky Mountains."[451] During the 1860 presidential campaign, Dodge and his group of promoters continued to lobby Lincoln and to advocate a Pacific railroad proceeding west from Omaha. When Lincoln's election precipitated the departure of the Southern Congressmen in early 1861, their absence cleared the way for the railroad promoters to lobby the Congress for a Pacific Railroad bill, with strong support from President Lincoln. [452]

Meanwhile, a leading Eufaula lawyer-planter-businessman, Eli S. Shorter, had been accumulating large amounts of Nebraska land, under interesting circumstances. Years earlier, Congress had enacted legislation granting public land ("bounty land") to officers and privates who had served in America's wars, including the War of 1812 or in any of the Indian wars since 1790. Throughout the 1850's an advertisement was run in the Eufaula newspaper, the *Spirit of the South* by "Shorter and Brother," i. e., the law firm of John Gill Shorter and his brother Eli, in which these lawyers provided information about this legislation. The firm stated that it had an agent in Washington, and would handle claims for clients under these acts. In this way Eli acquired by purchase (or as fees for services rendered) considerable acreage in the Territory of Nebraska.

In August of 1861, Edward Young bought from Shorter 3200 acres of this land, located in the four counties extending west from Omaha along the north bank of the Platte River: Sarpy, Douglas (of which Omaha is the county seat), Dodge, and Colfax Counties. With the Southern states no longer represented in the U. S. Congress, the 1862 Pacific Railroad Act was soon passed, providing enormous construction subsidies of land and money, and giving Lincoln the authority to select the route. After talking again with Dodge (who was now a general in the Union Army, but also connected with the newly-created Union Pacific Railroad Company) Lincoln selected the Platte River route, *which ran through three of the four counties where Edward Young had just purchased 3200 acres.* The Union Pacific Railroad began construction with a grand groundbreaking celebration in Omaha on December 1, 1863, which caused land speculators to enter the area in droves, and land prices soared. [453]

To evidence Edward's 1861 purchase, Eli delivered to Edward the original federal government patents [i. e. deeds from the government], which are found among Edward's business records today, from the United States to the soldier-claimants. These patents are dated in 1860 and bear what appear to be original signatures of President James Buchanan. The soldier-claimants shown on some of these patents were Indians who had fought on the American side in both the Creek War and the Seminole War, such as these:

Farat-Kar, Warrior Captain, James Island's Company, Creek Volunteers, Creek War;
Ailcey, minor child of Chulla Fixico, Deceased, Captain James Island's Company, Creek Volunteers, Creek War;
Sow war hilo, Minor Child of Talladejo Hariyo, Deceased, Warrior Captain, Ufaulau Micco's Company, Creek Volunteers, Seminole War.

Each patent reflects that the patentee had conveyed his allotted bounty land to Eli S. Shorter; Shorter gave Edward a quitclaim deed dated August 6, 1861. However, due to wartime conditions, Edward's quitclaim deed could not be recorded in the Nebraska land records until after the war, on June 25, 1866.

As we will later discuss, this farsighted investment would be a helpful contributor to Edward's financial position after the war.

21
Gunboats On The Chattahoochee

"The services of Mr. J. W. Young, a conscript, are required to work on machinery of Iron Clad Gun Boats. Mr. Young is the proprietor of a Machine shop in Eufaula which I wish to start on this work..."

J. H. Warner, Chief Eng.
Confederate States Navy

If the war curtailed some business activities of the Young family, it also created new opportunities.

The tendency toward independence and the unorthodox which we have seen in Ann and Edward's oldest son, Will, was no different when war came; he did not march to the same drummer as many others. Unlike some other members of his family, Will did not immediately seek military action. He continued the mundane work at his foundry, supporting Annie and five-year old Charlie. As it turned out, in an unglamorous way, Will would render important services to the Confederacy, services at least as valuable as those of a foot soldier, if not as dangerous.

Not only did the blockade of the South's river systems inflict a high economic cost, those river systems that had been so important to the economic development of the South and of the Chattahoochee-Apalachicola river valley now became inviting avenues of attack by federal vessels. To combat a sizable federal navy, the newly appointed Confederate Secretary of the Navy, Stephen R. Mallory, found that he had a motley collection of only ten ships, and none of the administrative structure needed to build a navy.[454] Starting at the bottom, the Confederacy, in addition to attempting to acquire naval vessels abroad, also began a construction program at home. The facilities that already existed on the coast, such as Norfolk, New Orleans, Charleston, and others were first placed in operation. But despite initial successes, these coastal facilities became increasingly vulnerable to federal attack; some came under Union control. Completed and partially completed ships were destroyed during or under threat of federal attack. Safety dictated that Confederate shipbuilding be based in the interior.[455] From this standpoint, Columbus, Georgia, safely located at the head of navigation of the Chattahoochee River, was perfect. Columbus would be transformed from a small trading town into a major facility for the Confederate navy. It would build ships and supply ships' machinery, equipment, cannon and engineering expertise throughout the Confederacy. This wartime activity would have a significant and favorable effect upon the business affairs of the William Young family of Columbus, and the naval facilities would have an even more direct effect on William's nephew in Eufaula, Will Young.

In June of 1862, the Columbus Iron Works, a privately owned facility, was leased to the Confederate Navy,[456] and became the Columbus Naval Iron Works (or sometimes, the "Confederate Naval Iron Works"; either way, the "CNIW"), under the command of Chief Engineer James H. Warner, CSN. Ship construction was under the direct supervision of the capable Lt. Augustus McLaughlin, CSN. It would be Warner's administrative competence and calm persistence that kept "these Works" progressing toward its objectives despite obstacles of every kind. The demands upon the limited facilities and personnel of the Iron Works were sometimes overwhelming. Its assignments included the construction of several ships, including the ironclad *Jackson,* and the gunboat *Chattahoochee.* To build ships, it had to first build facilities to construct the ships, while at the same time locating and procuring the necessessary equipment, supplies, and parts. An equally important part of its mission was to manufacture steam engines and engine parts for Confederate ships built elsewhere, and to send crews to other points in the Confederacy for construction, fitting out, and repairs on vessels there.

To enable the CNIW to carry out this extensive program, Chief Engineer Warner realized that it was necessary that he identify and make use of other resources in the Chattahoochee valley. Warner early became aware of Will Young, who had been operating his foundry and machine shop in Eufaula since 1854. Will advertised his machine shop in the newspapers, with emphasis on the advantages of steam power.[457] Warner began a business relationship with Will that eventually led to Will's machine shop becoming a major satellite installation of the CNIW. Will first became an important supplier of materials. Scrap iron, wood, charcoal and "a long list of other supplies flowed through him as middle man to the Confederate government". But his involvement in the construction of steam engines for the Confederacy progressively increased. In her well-researched and detailed work, *Navy Gray, Engineering the Confederate Navy on the Chattahoochee and Apalachicola Rivers*, historian Maxine Turner makes this observation about Will Young's Eufaula operation:

> "[Young's] farsighted investment in the advanced technology of the
> day paid large dividends for him and the Columbus Naval Iron Works
> in parts for steam machinery."[458]

Confederate Secretary of the Navy Mallory had observed that in modern warfare a steam engine had become as indispensable to a fighting ship as its battery of guns. With the help of Will Young and others, the CNIW supplied steam engines and parts to most of the ships in the Confederate Navy, and in the latter years of the war became "virtually the power plant of the Confederate Navy". [459]

Among Will Young's most important projects at the Columbus Navel Iron Works was his work on the high-priority ironclad gunboat, *Jackson,* whose objectives included defeating the blockading ships at Apalachicola and lifting the blockade. The craft was temporarily known by its "yard name", the *Muscogee*, to be officially named later, the *Jackson.*[460] It's construction would demonstrate the capabilities of the Columbus Naval Iron Works and the Columbus Navy Yard, for her design was "state of the art" for 1862.[461] It would be an impressive vessel, 200 feet long and 50 feet wide. She would be made invulnerable with iron cladding--a floating fortress. Flat bottomed like a river steamer, she was initially designed for a paddle wheel, but this was later changed to twin screw propellers, to facilitate tighter turns for river and bay maneuvering.[462]

The timetable for the *Jackson* project presented difficulties for CNIW's already stretched facilities. Turner succinctly identifies the central problem: "As the Civil War raged elsewhere, the battle in Columbus was with time and limited resources." And at a most inopportune time, Chief Engineer Warner was faced with the loss of one of his valuable resources, Will Young.

The Confederate Congress had enacted a conscription law requiring mandatory military service by all healthy males between 18 and 35 years. (In the later stages of the war, it would be expanded to include males between 16 and 50). There were a variety of exemptions, however, such as men owning twenty or more slaves (because they were needed to supervise the slaves), physicians, farmers, and mechanics. Will might have been under the impression that he was exempt as a mechanic, and he may have legally been exempt. But nevertheless, his name came up in the conscription bureau; he was drafted into the army and sent to Camp Watts at Notasulga, Alabama, for training. In due course, Chief Engineer Warner at the Columbus Naval Iron Works became aware of these circumstances, and would have none of it. Using the authority of the Navy Department to commandeer personnel, he dispatched this letter to the commander of the training camp:

"Naval Iron Works
Columbus, Geo.
Sep 27th 1862

"Major W. G. Swanson, CSA
Comndg. Camp "Watts"
Notasulga, Ala.

Sir-

The services of Mr. J. W. Young, a conscript, are required to work on machinery of Iron Clad Gun Boats. Mr. Young is the proprietor of a Machine shop in Eufaula which I wish to start on this work in connection with these Works.

I therefore respectfully request his detail for work under my supervision.

I am respectfully
Your obt. Sevt.
J. H. Warner
Chf Eng. CSN"

Will was soon back at work on iron-clad gunboats for the Confederacy. Historian Maxine Turner summarizes the effect of Warner's having Will "detailed" to work for the Columbus Naval Iron Works:

"Warner's successful appeal to have J. W. Young sent home from the
army to Eufaula began to pay dividends. From February 15 through March

167

[1863], Warner kept the Steamer *Indian* occupied with regular trips to deliver and return machinery and supplies. Cargoes of steam pumps and fifteen tons of castings going downriver indicate that Warner had contracted with Young to manufacture parts. The shipment of alloys like white and red lead fill in details of Young's work. Cargoes of machinery hauled to the wharf at Eufaula and shipped back to Columbus indicate that the Eufaula operation became quite important to CNIW operations."[463]

In addition to the contract work that Will and his work force did for CNIW in his Eufaula shop, Will was also called on to reside in Columbus for periods of time. We learned from Anna's letter of October 19, 1861, to Hubert that Will was commuting home from Columbus every Tuesday on the four o'clock train. Will also traveled to the CNIW satellite operations, to perform specialized skilled work on steam engines.[464]

Another important project of the Columbus Naval Iron Works was to construct a gunboat capable of patrolling and defending the river to the Gulf, and of running the blockade. The steam gunboat *Chattahoochee* was designed for this purpose. It was to have a 130-foot length, a 30-foot beam and a 10-foot depth of hold, with twin screw propellers instead of a paddle wheel, and a heavy battery of guns. It was to also have three masts with sails for use on the open sea, but the masts could be lowered into the hold to assume the low profile needed by blockade-runners.

Because of CNIW's multiple assignments, on October 19, 1861 a contract for the construction of the *Chattahoochee* had been entered into with David S. Johnson, of Saffold, Georgia, for a total price of $285,000. Johnson was a strange choice for a contractor. He was a plantation owner who had never built a ship. To perform the contract, he was building a shipyard at his plantation on the Chattahoochee at Saffold, in Early County, Georgia, 175 miles south of Columbus and 140 miles north of the port of Apalachicola. The relationship with him turned out to be highly unsatisfactory.

In July 1862, Johnson was five months behind schedule for completing the *Chattahoochee*, but in anticipation of her completion, the Navy assigned a naval crew to take up residence aboard the boat at Saffold and start installing her guns. It was a prestigious crew: the captain was Lt. Catesby Ap Jones, who had achieved prominence the previous March as the Executive Officer of the Confederacy's first ironclad, *Virginia* (*Merrimac*) in its historic encounter with the *Monitor* at Hampton Roads. Assigned as Assistant Engineer on the *Chattahoochee* was Horry Dent, Jr., oldest son of Edward Young's Barbour County friend, John Horry Dent. Horry had served on Confederate vessels at New Orleans before being captured in the fall of Fort Jackson in April 1862. Following imprisonment, he was exchanged on August 5 and arrived on the *Chattahoochee* a month later.

In November 1862, David S. Johnson's contract was revoked and CNIW took over the completion of the *Chattahoochee*. Lt. Catesby Ap Jones, in his efforts to get the *Chattahoochee* to sea, then encountered an even more formidable impediment than construction delays. The Confederate government, with the support of leaders of Columbus, had become increasingly concerned that the Yankee fleet at Apalachicola would steam upriver and assume control of Columbus and the Chattahoochee-Apalachicola River valley. The decision was made to sink obstructions in the river to prevent an invasion from the sea. But the same obstructions that would keep the Yankees from coming upriver would also keep the *Chattahoochee* from reaching the sea. Installation of the obstructions was completed by March 1863, before the *Chattahoochee* was operational, thereby insuring that, when it did reach completion, this brand new blockade-runner and gunboat would be relegated to permanent river duty, never to reach the sea. Its officers all requested transfers. Lt. Catesby Ap Jones was reassigned to head the Naval Iron Works at Selma, Alabama, a position he would ably discharge until the war's end.

A few riverboats still plied the Chattahoochee as for south as the landing at Chattahoochee, Florida, but in 1861, the Confederate government had taken over most of them for the use of CNIW. The *Indian,* the *Munnerlyn*, and one with a name familiar to us, the *William H. Young*, were kept particularly busy by CNIW hauling supplies, equipment, mail, money, and personnel to Eufaula and its other downriver operations.

CNIW Chief Engineer Warner was a careful administrator, and he insisted that those with whom he conducted business, including Will, follow correct procedures. Over the years, the *Indian*, the *Munnerlyn*, the *Uchee*, the *William H. Young,* and other steamships carried down the Chattahoochee a steady stream of letters to Will, some transmitting payment, some giving orders on substantive matters, and others requiring adherence to the proper administrative practice. Dictated to an assistant who was sometimes careless in punctuation, these terse letters left little doubt about what Chief Engineer Warner wanted done. Samples:

"Jan. 13, '63
J. W. Young
Eufaula Ala
Sirs, We send by the boat one hundred and seventy dollars to pay the enclosed bills in form, which sign and return to these works. There is no overtime allowed... Resp. J. H. Warner, Chf. Eng. CSN

"Feb 19, '63
J. W. Young
Eufaula Ala
Sir, The bill you sent does not specify the quantity nor price of material. have a regular bill made saying how much wood & oil & the price with all material & have sent to these works. Resp. J. H. Warner, Chf. Eng. CSN

"April 21, '63
J. W. Young
Eufaula Ala
Sir, We send by Str *Indian* six hundred thirty nine 22/100 dollars to pay labor of men employed as per pay roll sent these works. We will pay M. Campbell

169

& L. S. Smith, they are on our pay roll & have sent them wages by this boat to 18 April.

	Statement	
Amt Pay Roll Sent to Apr 16th		$566.13
Deduct for M. Campbell	$30.00	
Deduct for L. S. Smith	34.75	54.75
		$511.38
25 per cent		127.84
		$639.25

This amt Sent is to pay the labor of those employed in making up your Pay Roll. omit the ½ cent, instead of 4.12 1/2 make it 4.12 or 4.13. Resp., J. H. Warner, Chf. Eng. CSN"

The foregoing letter and others make clear that the contractual arrangements between the Navy and Will were on a "cost plus" basis, meaning that Will was paid his costs of manufacturing the parts or providing the materials, plus an additional amount equal to 25% of his costs, to provide for overhead and profit. This method of contracting is still sometimes used today among private parties, but the government seeks to avoid it because it provides no incentive for the contractor to find and adopt cost-reducing measures.

In April 1863 Warner made changes in these arrangements that reduced Will's profit to some extent. Previously, Will had been paying his own workers' payrolls, the cost of which was then included in Will's bills to CNIW, plus 25%. Under Warner's new arrangements, Will's employees became employees of CNIW. They were to be paid directly by CNIW, as part of its payroll, twice a month, although the money was transmitted to Will for actual distribution to the workers. With this bookkeeping change, the Navy thereby avoided paying Will an additional 25% of the payroll.[465]

The lack of cost-saving incentives in a "cost plus" contract is illustrated by the pay scale Will was paying his workers. He was content to pay them "top dollar", since the cost was being passed on to the government. Once Will's workers became employees of the Confederate Navy, Warner stepped in to bring their pay more into line with the market:

"May 6, '63
J. W. Young
Eufaula Ala
Sir, We send by the Boat six hundred & fifty dollars. Send receipt of workmen for wages paid to the 1st May. Six Dollars is all we pay Blacksmiths here. Resp., J. H. Warner, Chf. Eng. CSN"

In April 1863, after a number of mishaps, the *Chattahoochee* finally became operational and began cruising the river. Its new commander, Lt. Guthrie, steamed down to the obstruction, which was located at the "Narrows", a point fifty-five miles below Chattahoochee, Florida and thirty-six miles north of Apalachicola. Guthrie wanted to determine whether it might be possible at high water for his ship to cross the obstruction. On

May 26, he had determined that this was not possible, and had given the order to raise steam for the return trip. An argument occurred in the engine room over how much water was in the boilers. Someone turned on the donkey engine, water poured in to boilers, and they exploded. Eighteen men died from scalding or drowning. The steamer *William H. Young* was the first to reach the scene. It made three trips back to Columbus, ferrying wounded, recovering the dead, and salvaging valuable guns. The Chattahoochee rested on the bottom of the Apalachicola River, having never been in the vicinity of an enemy ship.

Hopes for raising the blockade of Appalachicola now focused entirely on the ironclad ram, *Jackson*, and CNIW doggedly continued its work. Administrative detail continued; Warner's stream of brusque letters to Will Young continued:

"May 11, '63
J. W. Young
Eufaula Ala
Sir, We send you by Express two hundred thirty four 35/100 dollars to pay bills in your favor the 23rd please acknowledge receipt. We send forms for the Zinc. Pay master... requiring duplicates. Resp., J. H. Warner, Chf. Eng. CSN"

"June 13, '63
J. W. Young
Eufaula Ala
Sir, We send you by the boat $498 49/100 to pay materials as furnished to these Works, including the bill scrap Iron & Lead...acknowledge receipt of same to these works. Resp., J. H. Warner, Chf. Eng. CSN"

"July 10, '63
J. W. Young
Eufaula Ala
Sir, We send you by the Str Indian six hundred ninety five 18/100 dollars to pay bills of material as furnished to date also to pay the per cent on men as sent from these works. Settled in full as per statement sent you. in future have the bill of materials in detail. no lumping charges as you had in our bill of Lamp Wicks $.15. Say how much in weights &c, and how much per #. Acknowledge receipt of money sent. Resp., J. H. Warner, Chf. Eng. CSN"

David. S. Johnson's contract to build the *Chattahoochee*, had been revoked in November 1862 against a background of delays, questionable financial measures and general unsatisfactory performance. Surprisingly, however, after revoking this contract, CNIW continued to give work of various kinds to Johnson. It even contracted with him to salvage the *Chattahoochee*, to raise the wreck and tow it to Columbus for repairs.[466] It appears that some of the work given Johnson might have taken the form of a sub-contract through Will Young.

Warner was suspicious of Johnson, however. Warner made clear to Will that he was closely monitoring payments to Johnson, and he wanted payments to Johnson separately stated and accounted for:

"July 10, '63
J. W. Young
Eufaula Ala
Sir, We have sent by Express $535.91 to pay labor for statement sent. Hereafter have two Pay Rolls made One for Col. Johnson & one for these works and send Col. Johnson's Pay Roll direct to him – Sign the forms sent for materials and return the same to these works with receipts of labor paid. Resp., J. H. Warner, Chf. Eng. CSN"

"Mar 8th, 1864
J. W. Young
Eufaula Ala
Sir, In your letter to Mr. Warner of Dec. 16th/63 You say you will chg. the full amt of material to Naval Iron Works and when Col. Johnson's work is finished will furnish a statement of his part. This you will please send up. Very Resptfly, Naval Iron Works

A "rolling machine" is a device for rolling out or shaping hot metal to a desired thickness, and is very necessary to the work Will and CNIW were doing. Will had built or acquired two such machines, and Warner wanted them in Columbus:

"Jan 16, 1864
J. W. Young
Eufaula Ala
Sir, You will please send up the two Leather Rolling Machines by the Steamer *Uchee* on her return trip. She will pass Eufaula next Wednesday morning. Resp., J. H. Warner, Chf. Eng. CSN"

By mid-1864, the Confederacy's need for soldiers was critical, and it was searching for every available man subject to the conscription law that could be spared from other essential duties:

"Mar 8th, 1864
J. W. Young
Eufaula Ala
Sir, You will report the names of all employees at your Works, giving their ages, the duty they are performing and whether they are liable to duty in the field under the present law; if not liable the special reason for exemption. Please make this report at your earliest possible convenience. Resp., J. H. Warner, Chf. Eng. CSN"

The "ironworks personnel assigned to Eufaula" were as follows:[467]

[J. W.] Young	Prop. & Sup.	Age 31
Chas. McVay	Fireman	31
Jas. Milton	Machinist	37
Jas. Dunham	Machinist	33
Wm. Scott	Machinist	19
James Lewis	Machinist	19
John Powell	Machinist	38
Wm. Shields	Machinist	20
A. M. Pernell	Machinist	17
W. S. Willis	Blacksmith	29
Victor Bonifay	Blacksmith	47

By July, there is a hint that the Confederacy might be encountering funding difficulties:

"July 13, 1864
J. W. Young
Eufaula Ala
Sir, We have Expressed to you Twenty one hundred & sixty six 25/100 dollars for bill April   1717.00

$$
\begin{array}{rr}
\text{25 per cent} & \underline{429.25} \\
& 2146.25 \\
\text{with Amt short} & \underline{20.00} \\
& 2166.25
\end{array}
$$

there are seven due bills for May 2 & 6 & June 12, which we will send as soon as funds are received. Resp., J. H. Warner, Chf. Eng. CSN"

In August, a further hint of Confederate government funding difficulties:

"Aug 11, 1864
J. W. Young
Eufaula Ala
Sir, Receipt the forms and return the same to these Works, and funds will be sent you as soon as … to pay the same. Resp., J. H. Warner, Chf. Eng. CSN"

By November 1864, Mobile Bay had been taken, and Atlanta had fallen to Sherman, who was moving toward Savannah. Chronic, acute shortages of supplies and labor were bringing the production system to a halt, but the Columbus Naval Iron Works persevered. When Sherman's advance on Savannah required that much of CNIW's personnel report to the army to fight before Savannah, the CNIW closed down, but only temporarily. In anticipation that Columbus itself might be attacked by Sherman, Warner undertook to hide his crucial supplies. He sent copper, sheet iron, and other stores to Will Young in Eufaula, with orders to secure them in scattered caches.[468]

In December 1864, after design changes and other delays, the ironclad ram *Jackson* was completed. The *Columbus Enquirer* reported on December 23 that, "This splendid ram was successfully launched yesterday at about 11 o'clock and now sits as calmly upon the Chattahoochee as a duck upon a pond."[469] The supreme irony was that this advanced "super weapon," having been successfully completed at enormous effort and expense in the face of extreme difficulties during the last days of the Confederacy, would go to the bottom of the Chattahoochee River without ever having fired a shot at the enemy.

On January 14, 1865, Warner wrote Will, "We have sent you by the Str. Munnerlyn thirty two hundred & eighty seven hundred 23/100 dollars to pay Pay Rolls for December 1864…" Written ninety days before Appomattox, this was the last surviving letter that Will Young received from Chief Engineer Warner.

Models of Ships which Will Young helped to construct: Ironclad Ram, *CSS Jackson* (left); *CSS Chattahootchee*

22

The Columbus Homefront

*"In response to the Confederate government's need for fabric, Eagle Mills expanded
its production significantly and... became one of the leading wartime producers ..."*
Telfair, A History of Columbus, Georgia

As in Eufaula, Columbus had festive celebrations during the early part of the war. In
March 1861, the first Columbus unit to depart, Company D of the Southern Guard, was
escorted to the depot by large crowds, and left amid speeches and prayers for their safe return.
In Macon it was incorporated into the First Georgia Regiment. Two weeks later the secession
of South Carolina set off bells, cannon, and drums. By February 1862, Columbus had sent
eighteen military companies, enlisting over 1200 men, to fight for the Confederacy.[470]

The Columbus Young family supported the war effort and the Confederate
government in every possible way. Columbus had organized a vigilance committee after John
Brown's raid. It now instituted a "Committee of Safety," the members of which included
William Young and his brother-in-law Robert M. Gunby.[471] In March 1862, the Committee
obtained instructions from Richmond on how to construct breastworks, and at a cost of $3000,
appropriated by the city council, constructed fortifications on the banks of the Chattahoochee
designed to protect it against attack from the Gulf. An active home guard was organized by a
wounded Confederate veteran. In addition, the "Independent Home Guard" was organized by
men over 45, including William Young, then age 55.

William's Eagle Mills, in June 1861, pledged to make monthly purchases of
Confederate bonds, in the amount of $1000 per month, until the end of the war. In addition,
Eagle contributed to the city's fund for soldiers' families, of $100 per month.[472] It also gave
free cloth to the Ladies Soldiers' Friends Society. As wartime conditions resulted in price
increases, Eagle Mills reserved one third of its fabric production to be sold to consumers at
below market prices. This practice, however, had to be later discontinued when, in order to
meet the needs of the Confederate Army, the State of Georgia obtained a contract for all
textiles produced by Eagle. In 1864, Eagle Mills began the first free school for the poor in
Columbus.[473]

The Bank of Columbus, of which William was founder and president, in 1861
subscribed to over $130,000 in Confederate bonds. It also loaned the State of Georgia $35,000
for military purposes.[474]

Even before the war, Columbus had a manufacturing industry, well advanced in some
fields, such as textiles, and under development in other fields. Wartime conditions and the
needs of the Confederacy spurred a rapid growth of Columbus industries of all kinds.
Wartime contracts were plentiful. Many small enterprises seemed to spring up overnight.
Shopkeepers began making tents; a jeweler became a sword manufacturer; small shops
appeared producing lampblack, wooden buttons, oilcloth, and other items. Brands and
Morton, music store proprietors, began producing Indian rubber cloth; Sappington, a grocer,

became the largest shoe manufacturer in the Confederacy; Rothschild, a dry goods merchant, began making army uniforms.[475] Workers for these industries flowed in from rural areas, raising the city's population to 15,000; however, there were still labor shortages, as well as raw material shortages. When the private businesses could not meet its needs for uniforms, the government established the Confederate Quartermaster Depot, which set up its own sewing machines and was soon producing high volumes of uniforms. When Sappington couldn't meet the orders for shoes because he couldn't procure enough hides, the Confederate Quartermaster set up its own facility in Columbus and began "impressing" hides, making 300,000 pairs of army shoes between 1861 and 1864. The Sword Factory of Louis Haiman and his brother became the largest in the South, producing 250 swords and cutlasses a day. Rifles were manufactured by J. P. Murray.[476]

In addition to being the home of the Columbus Naval Iron Works, with which Will Young of Eufaula worked closely, Columbus was also the site of the Columbus Arsenal. Established in June 1862 after the Iron Works had been leased to the Confederate Navy, the Arsenal produced harnesses, knapsacks, ammunition and cannon. Its production was soon greater than that of the arsenals at Selma, Charleston, and Macon. It became even more important later when Sherman's advance required the removal of the Atlanta Arsenal to Columbus.[477]

By far the most successful and prosperous industry in wartime Columbus was the Eagle Manufacturing Co.[478] Although William Young was the largest stockholder, his brother-in-law, Robert M. Gunby held the title of president during the war; William was treasurer. In March 1861, having absorbed the assets of Howard Manufacturing the year before, Eagle reported a six-month profit of over $30,000, and this was before serious governmental war procurement had gotten underway.[479]

In response to the Confederate government's need for fabric, Eagle expanded its production significantly and with its two mills became one of the leading wartime producers of uniforms, shirts, tents, and knapsacks.[480] Eagle began operating night and day shifts, turning out enough cloth every 24 hours to clothe a regiment.[481] In early 1862, Eagle produced daily over 2000 yards of gray tweed for uniforms, at $2 per yard. It produced over 1500 yards per day of cotton duck for tents, at 22 cents per yard. Its regular production of cotton "stripes" for army shirts, "osnaburgs", sheeting and yarn grossed $1500 per day. In 1862 Eagle doubled its production of India rubber cloth from 500 to 1000 yards per week.[482]

In the operation of his mills, William was sensitive to the effects of wartime inflation on consumers. In addition to setting aside one third of his production for sale to consumers below market prices, on one day each week householders could purchase a quota of thread and cloth at actual mill cost.[483]

William's Bank of Columbus was called on for important services to the Confederate government. On April 29, 1862, Farragut's Yankee gunboats captured New Orleans. The Confederate government had saved over $2,300,000 in gold and silver coin by seizing it from the Bank of Louisiana, and a secure depositary was required for this rare and badly needed

176

specie. A stable bank located well into the interior of the Confederacy fit the requirements perfectly. The arrangements were made between William and Confederate Secretary of the Treasury C. G. Memminger:[484]

Confederate States of America
Treasury Department
Richmond, June 10th, 1862

W. H. Young, Esq.
President, Bank of Columbus
Columbus, Ga.

Sir,

Enclosed I hand you a copy of an agreement between R. M. Davis, Esq., President of the Bank of Louisiana, and myself in relation to the coin of that bank which has been seized by the Government, and is now deposited with you for safe keeping. As prescribed in the terms of the agreement, you will please retain the coin until the Government orders otherwise.

Respectfully,
C. G. Memminger
Secty. Of Treasury

This deposit consisted of 300 kegs and boxes of gold and silver coin totaling $2,323,798.79. It remained in the Bank of Columbus until later ordered transferred to Savannah by Secretary Memminger and Gen. Beauregard.[485]

Confederate States of America,
TREASURY DEPARTMENT.
Richmond, June 10th 1862

W. H. Young Esq.
President Bank of Columbus,
Columbus, Ga.
Sir,

Enclosed I hand you a copy of an agreement between A. M. Davis, Esq. President of the Bank of Louisiana, and myself, in relation to the coin of that bank which has been seized by the Government and is now deposited with you for safe keeping. As prescribed in the terms of the agreement, you will please retain the coin until the Government orders otherwise.

Respectfully
C. G. Memminger,
Secty. of Treasury

Letter to William Young from Confederate Treasury Secretary Memminger regarding safekeeping of 300 kegs of gold and silver coin.

In the spring of 1861, Edward Croft, a Columbus merchant, called on Georgia Governor Joseph Brown in Milledgeville, and was granted authorization to raise a battery of light artillery and serve as its captain.[486] Significant support and much of the leadership of the new artillery unit would be provided by Young family and business associates. In fact, Ed

Croft himself was the business partner of Robert M. Gunby (William's brother-in-law and wartime president of Eagle Mills), in "Gunby and Croft's Store." Croft sought from among his friends and associates a cadre of competent officers to help recruit and train the unit. His efforts received a boost of prestige when Alfred I. Young, William and Ellen's oldest son, signed up as First Lieutenant of the new battery. Alf's younger brother, George B. Young ("G. B."), also joined Croft's battery as Junior First Lieutenant. It will be recalled that we last encountered Alf and G. B. when Ann and Edward, Ellen and William, their oldest boys, and Tom Jackson, made the excursion to the New York Crystal Palace World's Fair eight years earlier in 1853.

William donated to Croft's Battery 110 uniforms and 50 sets of heavy artillery harness.[487] One authority reports that William outfitted the entire battery at an expense of $65,000.[488] Captain Croft recruited men from the surrounding Alabama and Georgia counties as far west as Tallapoosa County, Alabama. A good portion of the company was from Russell County, Alabama.

Recruiting Poster for Croft's-Young's Battery.

179

On Nov. 9, 1861, the *Columbus Daily Sun* reported that "This Company has received their splendid battery, consisting of four brass six-pounders and two twelve pounder howitzers, and from the appearance of the recruits in camp, and the acknowledged qualifications of Captain Croft and Lieutenant Young, it promises to be worked with efficiency." Captain Croft's 23-year-old son, William G. Croft, had earlier enlisted as a private in the Columbus Guards, but now transferred to his father's battery as second lieutenant of artillery.

Company elections were held on November 13, 1861, and those who had recruited and trained the company were recognized in the results:[489]

Captain Alfred Young, C.S.A.

(circa 1880)

Edward Croft, Captain
Alfred I. Young, First Lieutenant
George B. Young, Junior First Lieutenant
William G. Croft, Second Lieutenant

Later in the war, William and Ellen's youngest son, Richard T. Young would join his two older brothers in Croft's Battery. A fourth son, William H. Young Jr. served in Wheelers' Cavalry, and would be killed during the battle of Atlanta. In March 1862, Captain Croft's brother, George Newton Croft, would join the battery as Quartermaster Sergeant, a position he would hold until the end of the war.[490]

A change in the captaincy of the company would occur during the war. At the time of his election, Captain Croft was over forty-six years old, somewhat older than the typical battery commander. The rigorous life of days in the saddle took their toll on Croft's health, and he was often absent sick, leaving Alf in command of the company, which was still called "Croft's Battery", or sometimes the "Columbus Artillery". In mid-1864, after arduous service, Croft would be placed on the Confederate Army's Invalid List. Alf Young would be promoted to captain and become battery commander officially as well as in fact. The Battery would become known as "Young's Battery" for the remainder of the war.[491] But these changes were still in the future.

On December 12, 1861, after weeks of drilling and artillery training, Croft's Battery gave a demonstration of its battle-readiness for the Columbus townspeople. The *Daily Sun* favorably reported the performance:[492] "As it was a novelty to many, a large crowd of both sexes turned out...The company went through a variety of evolutions and the exercises of firing, all of which were very creditable to the officers as well as to the men considering the brief period they have been exercising...the company can not fail to attain a high degree of proficiency, and will render a flattering account of itself in the day of conflict with the enemy."

In December, the new company received its orders. As the Eufaula Rifles had first been ordered to Pensacola to protect the coast, similarly Croft's Battery was ordered to Savannah to protect that port. The troop left Columbus on Christmas Eve, 1861, by special train of the Muscogee Railroad, arriving in Savannah on Christmas Day with 125 men; a battery of four six-pounders; two howitzers; and 65 horses fully caparisoned.[493] Savannah was the headquarters of Brig. Gen. Mercer, commander of the District of Georgia, which was a part of the Department of South Carolina and Georgia, commanded by Maj. Gen. Pemberton. One of the Georgia District's responsibilities was the defense of Savannah, an important port and center of blockade running activity. One of the port's important strong points was a heavily defended promontory above the city called Causten's Bluff. Upon its arrival, Croft's Battery was assigned to this Bluff, where it would remain until August 1862.

The camp settled into a regular routine. As Captain, Croft received pay of $140 per month; First Lieutenant Alf Young and junior First Lieutenant George B. Young were each paid $100 per month. In February 1862, Croft went back to Columbus to seek additional recruits to bring the unit up to its authorized strength of 150 men. In his absence Alf served as commander, with George taking over in the event of Alf's absence. In February, the company received from the Columbus "Soldiers' Friends Society", 100 shirts, 100 pairs of drawers, 50 pairs of socks, 10 pairs of pants, 4 pairs of gloves, and one comforter. The unit was also given $200, the proceeds of a concert given by Columbus music teacher Madame Bailini and her pupils for the benefit of the Columbus Artillery.

In August 1862, Union Maj. Gen. McClellan's Richmond offensive had failed, and Richmond was able to send additional troops to protect against increased federal threats to the Savannah port. In the reorganized defenses, Gen. Mercer moved Croft's Battery to "Miller's Station" on the Little Ogeechee River, ten miles from Savannah.[494] This camp was in a swampy, unhealthy marsh area, and disease quickly took its toll on The Columbus Artillery. At one point, 76 men were hospitalized, of whom ten died. Another seven "died in camp." Sick furloughs home to recuperate or die were frequent. In September, Captain Croft again went to Columbus to recruit men to replace these losses, leaving Lieutenant Alf Young in command of the battery. Alf located a more healthy location at which the battery could still effectively protect its area, and obtained permission to move the battery. On September 17, the company marched three miles to its new camp at Cheves' Landing on Groves' River, and the health of the men started gradually to improve. [495]

In August 1862, Gen. Pemberton had been transferred to command of the Department of Mississippi to defend Vicksburg and the Mississippi. Gen. Beauregard replaced him as new commander of the Department of South Carolina and Georgia. Beauregard's review of the defenses of Savannah led to a number of rearrangements, and on November 17, 1862, Croft's Battery was moved to "Camp Mercer." a fortified position three miles southeast of Savannah on the "shell" road leading to Skidaway Island. The unit would remain here until spring. [496] Lt. George Young was granted leave for a trip to Augusta; while Alf was "sick in camp" with a lingering illness from the marshes. In December Lt. Croft was given leave by his father to visit Columbus, and Alf accompanied him home in an effort to recover his own health. Alf was still too sick to return when his leave expired, and he was granted additional leaves until

March 8, 1863, when he returned to camp still sick. Upon returning to camp, he was immediately hospitalized at Savannah General Hospital. He was released on May 1 to return home for further convalescence.

On April 5, 1863, while Alf Young was hospitalized at Savannah General, a Yankee fleet of eight ships appeared outside Charleston Harbor, and attacked Charleston on April 7. Reinforcements from Savannah were ordered to Charleston, including Croft's Battery. The attack failed, and the federal fleet withdrew and left before the Columbus Artillery arrived on the scene. The battery was back in camp at "Camp Mercer" by April 21. With everything quiet in Savannah, Captain Croft took a twenty-day convalescent furlough, and, with Alf also still convalescing from the fever, command of the battery devolved upon Lt. George B. Young.[497]

During May 1863, the Federals were pressing their offensive against Vicksburg, and the Confederates badly needed reinforcements in the west. When Captain Croft returned to Camp Mercer from convalescent leave on May 15, he learned that troops from Savannah would be sent to Mississippi. He took the opportunity to request that his battery be sent. He found on May 21 that his request had been successful and that the Columbus Artillery had been selected for transfer to Mississippi.[498]

The route to Mississippi took Croft's Battery through its hometown, and the day before its arrival the Mayor of Columbus published this notice:

"Mayor's Office
Columbus, May 23, 1863

It having been ascertained definitely that Captain EDWARD CROFT and his command will pass through the city on Sunday evening [the 24th] on their way to the Army of the West, I therefore invite the ladies of Columbus and vicinity to extend them the same hospitality heretofore extended to other troops. Milk and vegetables, from our fair country ladies, will be very acceptable.
A committee of Gentlemen will be in attendance at the Depot on Sunday evening at 2 o'clock PM to receive and arrange such articles as may be sent.

F. G. Wilkins, Mayor"[499]

For over two years, the Columbus unit had essentially served "guard duty" at Savannah, somewhat as Hubert Dent had done at Pensacola for one year. Like Robertson's Battery however, Croft's Battery was now about to enter the real war. For the next two years it would distinguish itself in the bloody fighting of the western theater.

23

Maryland, My Maryland!

"The number of letters and papers [Dr. Dent] could conceal in his pockets and boot legs was astonishing."

Thomas A. Jones, Confederate Secret Agent

Hubert Dent's letters to Anna often expressed concern over the situation of his family behind enemy lines in federally-occupied Maryland. Life could be difficult for Marylanders with Southern sympathies, and Hubert's father, Dr. Stouten Warren Dent,[m] was a strong Southern loyalist. As we will see however, despite difficulties, Hubert's Maryland family were thriving and were diligently serving the Confederacy in unexpected ways.

Dr. Stouten W. Dent had been born January 15, 1806 on his father's "dwelling-plantation," a part of "Dent's Inheritance" and "Dent's Addition,"[500] which were located in Newport Hundred, near present-day Dentsville in Charles County Maryland, on a waterway known as "Gilbert's Swamp."[n] Stouten was the son of Hatch and Susannah (or Susan) Edwards Dent.[501] When Hatch Dent died in 1816, his will was admitted to probate February 16, having being executed by him only days before on January 19. Under the will, Stouten and his brother, Llewellin Marshall, inherited Dent's Inheritance and Dent's Addition, subject to the use of one third of the property by Elizabeth, their father's then-wife, during her lifetime.[502] Stouten was only 10 when his father died, and his older brother, John Blackman Edwards Dent, served as guardian for him and his minor siblings.

After attending various schools, in 1821 Stouten entered Charlotte Hall Academy,[503] a military school in neighboring St. Mary's County. (Founded in 1774, the school would continue to operate for over 200 years, until 1976). Despite interruptions for health reasons, he completed his course of study there. Under the tutelage of the principal, Philip Briscoe, he excelled in the study of Latin, for which he demonstrated a particular facility.[504] During a severe attack of pneumonia, when his friends had difficulty obtaining proper medical attention for him, he resolved to study medicine.

In 1826, Stouten entered the offices of Doctors Ridgely and Redont in Annapolis, and a year later, became a student in the office of Dr. Calistus Lancaster of Charles County, for one year.[505] He enrolled in the University of Maryland in the fall of 1828, and following a brief interruption graduated in 1831. Stouten had first married Lydia B. Watts, on January 5, 1830, who died without surviving children the following year on January 13, 1831. He later married Mary Catherine Smoot (the daughter of George and Mary Smoot) on June 5, 1832, who would bear him ten children.[506]

---

[m] Newman sometimes spells Dr. Dent's first name "Stoughton," but "Stouten" appears to be the spelling the doctor used. His son, Stouten Hubert, always used the latter spelling.

[n] Charles County is in southern Maryland, on the Potomac River, which forms the border between Maryland and Virginia. Gilbert's Swamp is a wide, boggy creek that runs generally north to south into Newport Run, (formerly "Pile's Fresh,") and then into the Wicomico River, which runs into the Potomac.

Following his graduation from the University of Maryland, Dr. Dent returned to the Gilbert Swamp area, apparently to the property inherited from his father, (his brother Lewellen having died in 1827) and established his medical practice.[507] However, he later acquired property in the Allen's Fresh district, where he and his family lived and actively farmed. This is presumably the "Oakton Grove" which datelined his letters to Hubert, and about which his sons later reminisced.[o] While farming there, he also conducted an extensive medical practice throughout the area. He is described by Newman as "a well-known physician in Southern Maryland."[508]

Dr. Dent served as a magistrate of Charles County for ten years, and for eight years was one of the judges of the Orphans' Court. He was active in educational affairs, and was viewed as having been "largely instrumental" in obtaining the passage of a general education bill for Charles County in 1838. Thereafter, he became one of the School Trustees. Dent was originally a member of Trinity Parish of the Episcopal Church at Newport, "the long-time church of the Gilbert Swamp area Dents," and served as vestryman there in 1831. However, in 1833 he joined the Methodist Episcopal Church, in which he served as a steward.[509] His sons became active Methodists.

Stouten and Mary Catherine Dent had three surviving sons: the oldest, Stouten Hubert, whom we have already met, born October 30, 1833; Hubert's younger brother, George Hatch, born June 21,1843; and the youngest son, Warren Fillmore, not born until March 4, 1855, after Hubert had moved to Eufaula in 1854.[p] All three sons would attend their father's alma mater, Charlotte Hall Academy. All three would migrate to Eufaula, Alabama and have roles in the story of the Youngs. When war came, all three would serve the Confederacy, with little Warren's contribution being the most unusual.

A surviving receipt tells us what Dr. Dent paid for Hubert Dent's tuition at Charlotte Hall:

> "Rec'd Dec.11, 1849 of Dr. Stouten Dent five dollars for one quarters tuition of his son S. H. Dent at Charlotte Hall School commenced 16th Oct 1849. Jas. Mittinson, Treas. Ch. Hall School"

---

[o] In 1915, Hubert Dent described an automobile trip made by himself and George on June 5 from Washington to "our old home" in Charles County, where "my brother George was born threescore and twelve years ago…We lunched on the piazza at the old home, and drank water from the old well…Many of the shade trees were gone, so that the old name of "Oakton Grove" was hardly any longer applicable. We also missed the splendid orchard which in days of yore, afforded so much pleasure to man and beast." They also visited the graves of their parents and two sisters. (*Eufaula Times,* June 24, 1915)

[p] The daughters of S. W. and Mary Catherine Dent were: Lydia Susanna Dent, married Frederick Levi Dent; Mary Sophia Dent (called "Molly"), born Aug, 1840, died June 23, 1890, married James Marion Freeman; Emma Catherine Dent, Born July 20, 1846, died May 19, 1850; Julia Columbia Dent, Born Aug. 10, 1849, died Mar 10, 1910, Married William J. Naylor; Emma Smoot Dent, born July 14, 1852, died Dec. 28, 1924;Ella Dent, born August 25, 1858, died Washington, D. C. April 1940.

184

Also, we know that Hubert fully justified his father's payment of this $5.00 per quarter expense. One of his report cards from Charlotte Hall also survives today, and reveals a very serious and dedicated eighteen-year old youth. Every grade is a perfect score:

"Report of studies and deportment of S. H. Dent for the quarter ending June 20, 1851. N. B. The number 9 indicates the highest merit; 8, indifferent; 7, bad.

"Latin Classics	Primary Branches	Mathematics	Habits
9 Horace	9 Reading	9 Arithmetic	9 Conduct
9 Livy	9 Spelling	9 Trigonometry	9 Diligence
	9 Writing	9 Surveying	1 Days Absent
French Classics	9 English Grammar		4 Days at Church"
9 Manesca's Course	9 Geography		
9 B. L. Grammar	9 Composition		

The year after this report, Hubert completed his studies at Charlotte Hall and, at the age of 19, began teaching school in Maryland. After teaching there from 1852 to 1854, he migrated to Eufaula, Alabama to begin teaching school while studying law.[510]

After moving to Eufaula, Hubert remained in close contact with his Maryland family. A series of extant letters received by Hubert in Eufaula during the late 1850's from his father; his brother, George; his sister, Mollie (not to be confused with Hubert's sister-in-law, Anna's sister, M. E. C. "Mollie" Young); and others, reflects close and regular communication with his family. These letters deal with Maryland crops, the weather, how business is faring, family illnesses, births, deaths, politics, and the myriad of details of daily life. On October 6, 1857, Dr. Dent feels that "… politics is a little Brasher here now - but I think its highly probable that none but Democrats will be elected to any office…" In 1858, Dr. Dent is growing tobacco, wheat, corn and other fodder for livestock. On February 12, Hubert's parents are pleased to hear that Hubert (who is now a practicing lawyer) is "doing a fair business." We learn that Dr. Dent has a "large share of obstetrical practice…which is our best paying practice." Dr. Dent notes, "I have collected & paid over a pretty fair share of money this season & think I shall be able to meet all my liabilities…" In other letters, we find that some of Hubert's relatives refer to him as "Burt," while the farm servants address him as "marster Burt." His brother, 15 year-old George Hatch, is now at Charlotte Hall, and on April 30, reports that the family has received the "likeness" sent by Hubert. George opines that, "I think your beard improves your looks in some degree. You look like a soldier ready for battle." On Oct 2, 1859, the less-scholarly George banters with his serious older brother:

"Dear Brother
…Well, now for letting you know what I am doing, in the first place I am growing very fast now, all my last winters, (and indeed this summers) clothes are too small for me. I am reading Xenaphon in greek, Cicero in latin, in English I have no study except Arithmetic which I am reviewing with a very large class. I do not think, to tell you the truth (which I know you would rather

for me to do) I stand very high in the estimation of Mr. N F D Browne but I think I am increasing a <u>little</u> more than before August…this winds up my scholarly history…

Sister gave birth to a fine daughter about two weeks ago which makes you have two nieces which you have never seen, you have also a very interesting sister which you have never seen [This would be Ella, born two months previously. Ed.] besides a number of other relations which you have never seen. I would like very much to see you here this coming summer, but I suppose you do not intend to come in until you get the madam to bring with you, well I wish you would be in a hurry about it. Everybody that inquires about you asks if you are not married yet, and I reckon after a while that they will say there is no one that will have you.

…all join me in love to you and relations so good bye. Your Brother George.

We have previously seen that Hubert had already found someone who would "have him," and eight months after his impertinent young brother's unsolicited advice, Hubert married Anna Beall Young in Fendall Hall on June 5, 1860.

As sectional conflict drew closer, Maryland was divided. It was a slave state and identified with the South, but it was also a border state, with commercial ties to the North. Perhaps its predominant sentiments were revealed in the crucial election of November 1860. Lincoln got very little support; the state went heavily for the two pro-Southern candidates, Breckenridge and Bell.[511] Dr. Dent had traditionally been a supporter of the conservative Whig Party, which had now collapsed under the slavery issue. An outspoken Southern sympathizer, Dent voted Democratic in 1860,[512] undoubtedly for the Breckenridge wing of that party, rather than for Stephen Douglas.

By the end of February 1861, the cotton states of the Deep South had seceded and created the Confederate States of America, but the "middle South" states held back. Looking to Virginia for leadership, they hoped for a compromise that would save the Union. Maryland's decision was particularly dependent upon Virginia because of its geographic location. If Maryland seceded but Virginia did not, it would be isolated from the Confederacy. Thus, in the spring of 1861, S. W. Dent and the other Maryland secessionists were compelled to await Virginia's actions while various attempts at compromise were being pursued (unsuccessfully). Unfortunately, events soon overtook the Maryland secessionists; and due to aggressive action by the Washington government, and inaction by a weak governor, the option of secession was lost forever.

Following the firing on Fort Sumter on April 12, President Lincoln issued his "Proclamation of Insurrection" on April 15 calling for 75,000 volunteers to put down the rebellion. Lincoln's decision to make war on the seceding states and force them to remain in the Union electrified the country, and it outraged the upper South states. These moderates strongly opposed coercion of their sister Southern states. The upper South now quickly began to secede, led by Virginia, who seceded on April 17. In Maryland, however, where public sentiment was now strongly secessionist, the vacillating Gov. Hicks temporized and put off calling the legislature into session.

April 19, 1861 was a day which would be long remembered by Marylanders. On the previous day, there had been a clash in Baltimore between pro-secession citizens and Pennsylvania Volunteers enroute through the city to defend Washington. On the 19th, a pro-Southern group of prominent citizens met to hear speeches denouncing Lincoln's plans for coercion. At that point, the 6th Massachusetts Volunteer Militia arrived at the station to change trains for Washington. A group of irate citizens gathered and blocked the tracks, forcing some of the militia into the street. "As the soldiers marched westward on Pratt Street under a hail of bricks and paving stones, shots rang out, the troops opened fire, and soldiers and civilians fell in the first real bloodshed of the war."[513] The Baltimore riot further inflamed upper-South Southerners who opposed Lincoln's coercion policy.[q] Maryland state militia units had been drilling and assembling. Pro-Southern in sentiment, they were now called out by Gov. Hicks.[514] In Charles County, Dr. Dent was the captain of a militia company, "the Home Guard," and his son George was also a member of a company. Unfortunately, like most of the militia units, they had no weapons.[515]

The Baltimore riot, and the ensuing preparations to defend Maryland's borders, also dramatized to Lincoln and his cabinet the dangerous position of the federal capital. The District of Columbia was a square, bordered on the south by Virginia, and on *all three other sides* by Maryland. The main routes to Washington ran through Baltimore. If Maryland were allowed to secede, Washington would be cut off and surrounded – landlocked - by Confederate territory, necessitating the removal of the capital to a location further north. Such an evacuation would be disastrous in its effect on the European powers, and was an unacceptable result. Accordingly, Lincoln and his War Department began sending out desperate appeals to the northern states to quickly send troops to defend Washington's open border with Virginia and to occupy Maryland to prevent its joining the enemy.

The northern states responded with stunning rapidity. Within days, large numbers of federal troops were streaming toward Maryland. On April 22, Brig. Gen. Benjamin Butler landed a force at Annapolis, the state capital, and occupied that city. Gov. Hicks, by now so hated that his life was in danger, finally called the legislature in session. Because the state capital was occupied, it convened in Frederick. Thousands of troops were pouring into Maryland, with orders to seize and hold all key points. On April 26, Gen. Butler was ordered

---

[q] James Ryder Randall, a young Marylander teaching school in New Orleans was inspired by the Baltimore riot to write his pro-secession poem, "Maryland, My Maryland!" which was later set to the music of the German tune, "O Tannenbaum." The militaristic words of Randall's poem and this stirring music made it a war anthem of the Confederacy, second in popularity only to "Dixie:"

"The despot's heel is on they shore,	Avenge the patriotic gore,
Maryland, my Maryland!	That flecked the streets of Baltimore,
His torch is at thy temple door,	And be the battle-queen of yore,
Maryland, My Maryland!	Maryland, My Maryland!"

to watch the legislature and if it took action toward arming (i. e. secession), to use "the most prompt and efficient means" to stop it. Butler was also given the power to suspend the right of habeas corpus, thereby allowing him to make indiscriminate arrests of secessionist leaders. As the situation deteriorated further, the Legislature realized it could no longer control events. It had no meaningful military force, the state was in the grip of the federals, efforts to resist would have failed and would have resulted in destruction, and their lives were actually at risk.[516] Under these circumstances the legislature on the 27th decided not to risk attempting secession, and instead adopted a series of strongly pro-Southern resolutions condemning the Lincoln administration for its policy of coercion.

Historians who have analyzed the evidence conclude that, if Marylanders had been free to act, they would have voted to secede.[517] Lincoln prevented secession by treating the state as though it had seceded. Benjamin Butler was rewarded by Lincoln with a promotion to Major General for his role in the efficient takeover of Maryland.[r]

The federals next began to seal the borders of Maryland to prevent volunteers from reaching the Confederate Army. By early fall of 1861, tens of thousands of federal soldiers patrolled all major roads, bridges, railroads, and the Maryland side of the Potomac; while federal gunboats aggressively patrolled the Potomac and the Chesapeake. Orders were issued to arrest men attempting to leave the state.[518]

George Hatch Dent, however, like his older brother, was determined to fight for the Confederacy. On May 9, Dr. Dent wrote Hubert that "the people were preparing to leave for Virginia if Md. did nothing. Unless they leave soon they will not have an opportunity of doing it."[519] In May, as it became apparent that Maryland probably would not secede, Maryland secessionists "voted with their feet" and made their way into the Confederacy to form an all-Maryland Regiment, naturally called the "First Maryland Infantry Regiment."[520] On June 15, a week before his 18th birthday, George Dent was preparing to infiltrate into Virginia with a group of volunteers raised by his kinsman, Dr. Smoot. The group was planning to "go over a few at a time and rendezvous in Virginia."[521] George turned eighteen on June 21, and by July 11, he had infiltrated the border, reached Richmond, and enlisted as a private in Company I of the 1st Maryland Infantry.[522] He would fight with that unit as it participated in numerous engagements, including the First Battle of Manassas and Stonewall Jackson's Valley Campaign. As we will see, Company I of the First Maryland would disband on June 13, 1862,[523] and on September 2, 1862 George would join Lt. Hubert Dent in Robertson's Battery (then camped in the Sequatchie Valley of Tennessee, enroute to invading Kentucky).[524] George would ultimately become First Sergeant of Dent's Alabama Battery.

---

[r]   Butler was later the heavy-handed military governor of occupied New Orleans, earning the sobriquet, "Beast" Butler; and during Reconstruction was one of the Radical Republican managers of the impeachment prosecution of pro-Southern President Andrew Johnson. Butler's infamy in the South made such an impression in the Dent family that, 100 years later in the 1960's, Hubert Dent's son, Henry A. Dent, by then in his 90's, frequently quoted a description he had apparently heard often in childhood: *Some names are beyond pardon or oblivion, and chief among these is Benjamin Butler of Massachusetts! "*

Despite his age of fifty-five, Dr. Dent was also determined to fight for the Confederacy. He would have preferred to serve as a uniformed officer in the surgeon's corps. His son Hubert, now in the Confederate army at Ft. Barrancas, sought to use his Alabama connections to assist his father in obtaining a medical commission. Hubert wrote his old Barbour County Circuit judge, John Gill Shorter, before whom his had practiced law for some years, now Governor of Alabama. Gov. Shorter immediately responded to Hubert's request for help and wrote directly to President Jefferson Davis himself. Davis replied affirmatively to the governor, and favorably referred the request to his Secretary of War:[525]

"His Excellency   Richmond, Dec. 24, 1861
Jn. Gill Shorter
Gov. of Ala.

Dear Sir
          I am instructed by the President to acknowledge the receipt of your letter of the 16th inst in behalf of Dr. S. W. Dent for an appointment as Surgeon and to inform you that the Dr. has his sympathy and he hopes to be able to comply with your request. Your letter has been referred to the *special attention* of the Secretary of War.

                                              Very Respectfully,
                                              Robert Josselyn, P. W.

The hoped-for appointment did not materialize. However, as it turned out, Dr. Dent, as well as his small son, Warren, would serve the Confederacy in another important but unexpected way.

The Richmond government had decided that it was important for the Confederacy to have regular, reliable written communication with friends in the United States and Canada. Accordingly, Mr. Thomas A. Jones, who lived on the Potomac River in Charles County (and had been successful in smuggling Marylanders into the Confederacy), was recruited to serve as Chief Confederate Agent in Maryland, to organize a system for transmitting Confederate mail within and through the state of Maryland to points north. One of Jones' "most active agents" would be Dr. Stouten Warren Dent. In his book written in 1893, Jones describes the origins of this undertaking: [526]

          "[Major William Norris, the Chief of the Confederate Signal Service]…said that it was of the utmost importance to the Confederacy that it should have communication with points north of the Potomac, and that nowhere on the river was there a better location for a signal station than the bluffs near Pope's Creek, or a more suitable place for putting the mail across the river than off my [Thomas Jones'] shore."

It was arranged that each evening, unless a black signal was hung in a dormer window of Jones' neighbors, the Watsons, to warn of unsafe circumstances, a courier would boat across from the Virginia side at dusk. At this time of day, boats were difficult to spot and the federal night pickets had not yet come on duty. The courier would place the northbound mail packet in the fork of a dead tree, and he would pick up the southbound packet to take back. Jones would retrieve the packet from the tree and give routine letters to one of his agents to mail in scattered U. S. post offices outside the immediate area. Important papers were not mailed but relayed personally by a trusted agent.

And this is where Dr. Dent's value arose. As a well-known physician making house calls around southern Maryland, Dr. Dent could come and go without arousing suspicion. He could be frequently seen in the vicinity of Jones' house and he could deliver or pick up mail at locations throughout the area, unquestioned. Jones describes how Dr. Dent did it:[527]

Dr. Stouten Warren Dent of Dentsville, Maryland; father of Hubert, George, and Warren Dent

"Stowten (sic) W. Dent, M. D. and my brother-in-law, Thomas H. Harbin, were two of our most active agents.

"Dr. Dent, who died in 1883 at the advanced age of eighty...was a practicing physician, and used to make his professional rounds on horseback. In winter he invariably wore an overcoat that came down below his knees, provided with numerous and capacious pockets, and high boots; and in summer, a long linen duster also well provided with pockets. The number of letters and papers he could conceal in his pockets and boot legs was astonishing. Some one in the neighborhood of Pope's Creek was always sick. Scarcely a day passed that some member of the Watson family or mine did not need Dr. Dent. He came and went unquestioned and unsuspected. He would take the mail as far as Port Tobacco, ten miles from my home; or Bryantown, a village in the eastern part of the county about fifteen miles from Pope's Creek; or even as far as Charlotte Hall in St Mary's County, fully twenty miles off, and then transfer it to some other agent who would convey it further on toward its destination."

This was not casual duty. Jones points out that it required "great caution and unrelaxing vigilance." Not only was the river filled with gunboats day and night, but also "an armed patrol guarded the shore and the Federal Government had a spy upon nearly every river farm in southern Maryland. There was a detachment of troops at Pope's Creek..." Dangerous and lengthy travel, often at night, was grueling work for a physician in his mid-fifties who also had responsibility for a medical practice. With the approval of Mr. Jones, Dent's youngest son, Warren, not yet ten years old, became his father's trusted helper. Under the exigencies of war, the little boy matured quickly and learned to be a skilled secret Confederate agent. Chief Agent Jones had high praise for Warren: [528]

> "The doctor had a son named Warren, a mere lad of about ten years of age, who, child though he was, was as energetic, discreet and intelligent as any agent in the Confederate service. The most important matter was often intrusted to his care, and always safely intrusted."[s]

There is an historic epilogue to the relationship between Jones and Dr. Dent, which could have had seriously adverse effects on Dr. Dent, but fortunately did not. After Booth shot Lincoln on April 14, 1865, breaking his leg in the process, he and his accomplice, David Herold, fled into Charles County, MD in an effort to reach Virginia. After receiving treatment for his leg from Dr. Mudd (on April 15), they were placed in contact with one Cox, a half-brother of Confederate agent, Thomas Jones. Cox urged Jones to help the two men reach Virginia. Jones had misgivings, but after seeing Booth's pitiful condition, reluctantly agreed to help.[529] He provided the two men with food in a pine thicket for five days (April 15-20) until the way was clear, and then gave them his boat to cross the river. Booth was killed at Garret's farm six days later (April 26). Due to some coincidental suspicious circumstances, Jones was arrested and imprisoned in Washington, but revealed nothing about his encounter with Booth. As Jones was being taken away to Washington, he became concerned about having someone take his horse from the place of his arrest back to his home. He asked his captors to be allowed to write a note to Dr. Dent. Jones relates that his guards readily supplied him with pencil and paper...

> "...in the hope that I might attempt to covey some secret intelligence to Dr Dent, who was well known to be a warm southern sympathizer and a fearless man."[530]

This was a time when Washington was in a frenzy to arrest anyone and everyone perceived to have a possible connection to the assassination plot, and this lapse by the normally careful and savvy agent could have potentially caused great difficulty for Dr. Dent. Of course, Dent had nothing to do with Booth or his plot, but this was a time when even innocent people were being arrested and tried. Fortunately, nothing came of the incident; no attention was ever focused on Dr. Dent, and Jones himself was set free after several weeks.

S. W. Dent's support of the Confederacy was not limited to carrying secret mail. He was also available to help Confederate soldiers returning to the Confederacy after escaping from federal prison. One such incident involved Pvt. William S. Humphries, who with a

---

[s] As an adult, Warren's childhood services rendered him eligible for membership in the United Confederate Veterans, and for the Cross of Honor bestowed by the United Daughters of the Confederacy (Confederate Veteran, Vol XXXIII, No 5, May 1925, p. 188). The appealing story of Dr. Dent and his 10-year old son as secret agents found its way into histories, magazines, newspaper stories, and even a novel. In *House Divided*, a best-selling novel by Ben Ames Williams, (Houghton Mifflin, 1947; reprinted by Eagle Books) at p. 787-788, a fictional character describes the signal station, secret mail arrangements, Jones, Dr. Dent and 10 year-old Warren, in language paralleling that quoted from Jones' book above. See also Thompson's *History of Barbour County*, p. 392 (cited supra); and *The Times-Crescent* (La Plata, MD), August 29, 1902.

friend had managed to escape from Point Lookout, a notorious federal POW prison in neighboring St. Mary's County, Maryland. A fashionable resort hotel before the war, it had now become a deplorable prison where at least 14,000 Confederate prisoners died from neglect. After his escape in September 1864, Humphries fled through federally-occupied Charles County, where he was fed and hidden by a number of southern sympathizers there. Humphries later related that, after staying several days at one house, a Dr. Dent arrived at the house and told him that the escapees had better go now to Dr. Dent's house, "which was some distance on our way…They were exceedingly kind to us, giving us food and clothing. For the first time since leaving prison we felt clean and genteel." After leaving "Dr. Dent's hospitable home," the fugitives were ferried across the river to Virginia, and made their way to Richmond. [531]

24
The Army of Tennessee

"It was led by a changing succession of well-meaning generals with limited military talent."

To follow the wartime careers of Hubert Dent, (and his brother George Hatch) and Henry Young of Eufaula, and of their Columbus Young cousins, Alfred, George B., Richard, and William H., Jr., we must follow the fortunes of that great Confederate army known to history as the Army of Tennessee. Robertson-Dent's Battery, the Eufaula Light Artillery, and Croft-Young's Battery, all became part of the Army of Tennessee, as did most (but not all) of the Confederate soldiers from Eufaula and Columbus. Hence, we will view the Civil War through the eyes of that army.

Most readers with any familiarity with the Civil War are well aware of the heroic accomplishments of the "Army of Northern Virginia" under the leadership of Gen. Robert E. Lee and his great lieutenants like Stonewall Jackson and Jeb Stuart. For much of the four years of the War, Lee made monkeys of the Yankee Generals sent to oppose him. Time and again he and his lieutenants outmaneuvered, outsmarted, and defeated superior federal forces, several times coming close to winning Southern independence.

While Lee's Army of Northern Virginia was thus defending Virginia and threatening Washington, another war, equally important, was being waged in the "west," by the Army of Tennessee. While Lee defended the Confederacy's "front entrance," it was the duty of the Army of Tennessee to protect the "side door," or left flank of the Confederacy. It was necessary to oppose Yankee invasion of the heartland of the South diagonally through Kentucky, Tennessee, north Alabama and Georgia. The Army of Tennessee fought with unexcelled valor against great odds in some of the bloodiest battles of the war, achieving some major victories and partial victories. Unfortunately the quality of its fighting men was not equaled by that of its commanding generals, and the blood of brave men was often squandered ineffectually. As observed in the Foreword to Stanley F. Horn's seminal book, "The Army of Tennessee" (to which the war narrative of this work is heavily indebted), this army "never had a truly first-class commander."[532] It was led by a changing succession of well-meaning Generals with limited military talent. After the early death at Shiloh of the promising (but untested) Albert Sidney Johnson, the army was commanded by Braxton Bragg (whom we first encountered commanding the coastal defenses in Pensacola), then Joseph E. Johnston, and then John Bell Hood. These three commanders, of mixed abilities, were opposed at times by the Federals' best: Grant, Sherman, and Thomas. The fierce Confederate fighters won partial victories that could have been routs under an inspired general, but instead resulted in gradual retreat from Kentucky and across Tennessee into Georgia. Through the eyes of Hubert Dent, we will presently see that, after Bragg was maneuvered out of Tennessee his army won an enormous victory at Chickamauga in north Georgia that could have changed the course of the war but for the vacillating, sluggish Bragg. After disaster at Chattanooga, with its numbers now reduced to inadequacy, the Army of Tennessee, Dent's Battery, and Young's Battery, were inexorably pushed back to Atlanta: first yielding ground without battle under Johnston's Fabian strategy; then fighting and extracting Yankee blood for each step under Hood's aggressive policy, but draining its own lifeblood in the process. Until finally Atlanta fell and Sherman could march unopposed to the sea.

The South's ultimate loss in the western theatre was not the result of any lack of bravery, dedication, and sacrifice by the Youngs, the Dents, their comrades and their families, whose wartime lives we will now review, in the context of the western campaigns.

From its inception, the Confederacy sought to have its left flank's northern border with the United States placed as far north as possible. When Kentucky failed to secede and declared neutrality instead, the Confederates realized that the federals were about to ignore this neutrality and use Kentucky as an invasion route to Tennessee. To meet this threat, the Confederate army in 1861 crossed the Tennessee border and occupied the southern tier of Kentucky, including Bowling Green. But the Tennessee and Cumberland Rivers, which flowed out of Kentucky and into Tennessee on almost parallel routes, still provided an ideal invasion route into Middle Tennessee. In an effort to plug these holes, the Confederates hastily built Fort Henry on the Tennessee and Fort Donelson on the Cumberland, near where those rivers entered Tennessee. But the forts were poorly located and inadequately completed. Back east, the Confederates fortified the Cumberland Gap, to close that route into Tennessee from Kentucky through the Appalachian Mountains into Middle Tennessee. Thus the Confederacy had a defensive frontier that ran hundreds of miles along the Tennessee-Kentucky border, from Cumberland Gap to Bowling Green to Forts Henry and Donelson. Unfortunately, the Confederacy did not have an army of sufficient size to adequately guard such a lengthy frontier.

Even while these defenses were being established, a highly respected officer of the old United States army, Albert Sidney Johnston, was resigning his federal commission and post in California, in order to offer his services to the South. As soon as Johnston reached Richmond on September 5, 1861, Jefferson Davis appointed him general in command of the Tennessee theater, which led to great public confidence. Johnston was dismayed to learn that, to defend his sector from the Tennessee mountains to the Mississippi, he had only 20,000 men, and those poorly trained and equipped.

Despite Johnston's effort to use his limited resources to the best advantage, he was spread too thin. The inadequately manned line began to crumble almost immediately. At the eastern end, a force of Tennessee Confederates under General Zollicoffer sought to advance into Kentucky through the Cumberland Gap, to establish a better defensive position in Kentucky. The Confederates were repulsed and Gen. Zollicoffer killed, in the Battle of Fishing Creek on January 19, 1862.

On the western end of the line, the federal forces were commanded by an obscure Illinois officer who had previously served in the army, had been court-martialed for drinking, and had recently reentered the army: Ulysses S. Grant. On February 4, 1862, Grant's gunboats appeared on the Tennessee River at Fort Henry with an overwhelming force of 14,000 men. The heavily outnumbered Confederate commander evacuated the fort to save his men, and after a token fight, surrendered the fort. Ten days later, Fort Donelson on the Cumberland also fell to Grant, along with 7000 Confederate prisoners.

The fall of Forts Henry and Donelson opened an invasion route to the heart of Tennessee by gunboat down the Cumberland and Tennessee Rivers. It meant the collapse of the whole line, the loss of the Confederacy's narrow foothold in Kentucky, and the loss of Nashville with a large part of middle Tennessee. As soon as Fort Henry fell, opening the Tennessee, Gen. Johnston ordered Gen. Hardee to evacuate Bowling Green, Kentucky and retreat to Nashville, sixty-five miles south. And on February 16, 1862, the Confederate army began the evacuation of Nashville. On February 25, Nashville was occupied by federal General Buell's army.

The South was stunned by this disastrous series of shocks. Grant was now astride the Tennessee River with an army of 30,000 and expecting reinforcements. The time and direction of his next move were not known, but measures to stop his further invasion were imperative. The Confederate leadership decided to select a strategic location from which it could respond to Grant's next move, and to assemble there all of the dispersed Confederate troops not badly needed elsewhere. The assembly point selected was Corinth, in northern Mississippi near the Tennessee border. Corinth was 22 miles south of a place on the west bank of the Tennessee River called Pittsburgh Landing. Later, by coincidence and without knowledge that the Confederates were concentrating at Corinth, Grant decided to concentrate his forces in the bend on the west bank of the Tennessee River at Pittsburgh Landing. The stage was being set for one of the most ferociously fought battles of the Civil War, in which Hubert Dent and Robertson's battery would distinguish themselves.

Gen. Johnston and his second-in-command, Gen. Beauregard, sent out the call for every available Confederate commander to assemble with his troops at Corinth. Aware that 10,000 troops were sitting at Fort Barrancas and Pensacola under Gen. Braxton Bragg, essentially performing guard duty, Gen. Beauregard appealed to Richmond to transfer Gen. Bragg's army to the Army of Tennessee at Corinth. In light of the difficult circumstances in the west, Bragg readily consented to the transfer, and in early March 1862 started moving toward Corinth. Among the troops transferred with Bragg was Robertson's Battery. In this manner Hubert Dent's long-held wish to get into the thick of the action was realized many times over; he would see three years of the bitterest fighting the war had to offer.

When Robertson's Battery left Fort Barrancas it was not fully equipped. It had been issued four 12-pounder Napoleon guns manufactured by Leeds and Company of New Orleans, one caisson, and 231 rounds of ammunition. Enroute through Montgomery, Robertson's Battery was issued a battery wagon and a traveling forge.[533] Such a forge was essential to the Battery's ability to keep its guns and other equipment repaired and in working order. Once in Corinth, Capt. Robertson barraged the ordinance officer with requests for items "absolutely necessary for the full equipage of this company".[534]

As Captain Robertson and Lieutenant Dent proceed with their battery toward Corinth, we will briefly explain some of the workings and jargon of a Confederate artillery battery, to help in following battle accounts to come. The basic unit of artillery can be called a company, but is more often called a battery (although this word is also used to describe the actual group of guns.) An artillery battery was usually commanded by a captain; its size varied in the 100 to 200 men range, depending on the number of guns. Early in the war most batteries, including Robertson's, had four guns. Later, Robertson/Dent's Battery was allowed by Gen. Bragg to have six guns. The battery was subdivided into sections of two guns each, each section being commanded by a lieutenant. Robertson-Dent's battery usually had six smooth bore "Napoleon 12 pounders," with a range of about 1000 yards. It derived its name from its having been originally designed for Napoleon III, and from hurling a ball weighing 12 pounds. The ball could be solid, or it could be "spherical case shot", which exploded overhead, bombarding the troops with small balls, set off by a fuse automatically lighted when the weapon was fired. It also fired canister, a container of many metal particles that scattered when fired at close range, like a shotgun. Canister was devastating to a line of infantry. These smoothbore cannon were often preferred over rifled cannon because the latter, although they had a longer accurate range, could not effectively fire canister, and their longer range was not useful in the thickly wooded terrain of many civil war battles in the western theater.

Transporting a battery of artillery was an arduous undertaking. The cannon and its two-wheeled carriage were towed backwards, attached to another two-wheeled vehicle called a limber, which also carried an ammunition chest. The cannon and limber (totaling four wheels), required six horses. But accompanying each cannon and limber was also a second limber towing a caisson, which is also a two-wheeled vehicle, carrying two more ammunition chests. Each caisson and limber (also 4 wheels) required six horses. A six-gun battery required a minimum of 72 horses just to move its weapons. A driver rode on the right horse of each pair of horses. To spare the horses, the other enlisted men walked. The officers rode, if they provided their own horses. In addition to its guns, limbers, and caissons, the battery also had its traveling forge and its battery wagon, carrying tools and equipment. Its personnel included a farrior (who repaired horseshoes), a blacksmith (who repaired guns and ironwork), and a leatherworker.

A Napoleon cannon tube weighed 1200 pounds, and its wooden carriage and attached ironwork weighed another 1100 pounds, for a total of 2300 pounds per cannon, which tore up dry roads and rendered wet roads almost impassable.

When the battery is getting rigged to travel, it is "limbering up". When it arrives at its firing position, it "unlimbers," and "goes into battery", that is, its guns are unhitched and lined up side by side for firing. For safety, the limber and its ammunition chest are parked at least 30 yards back from the cannon. The caissons and horses are placed even further away, in the safest place available.

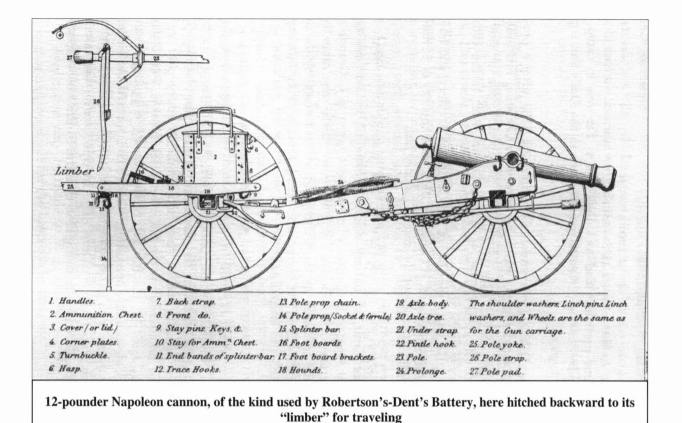

1. Handles.	7. Back strap.	13. Pole prop chain.	19. Axle body.	The shoulder washers, Linch pins, Linch
2. Ammunition Chest.	8. Front do.	14. Pole prop (Socket & ferrule)	20. Axle tree.	washers, and Wheels, are the same as
3. Cover (or lid.)	9. Stay pins, Keys, &.	15. Splinter bar.	21. Under strap.	for the Gun carriage.
4. Corner plates.	10. Stay for Amm". Chest.	16. Foot boards.	22. Pintle hook.	25. Pole yoke.
5. Turnbuckle.	11. End bands of splinter bar.	17. Foot board brackets.	23. Pole.	26. Pole strap.
6. Hasp.	12. Trace Hooks.	18. Hounds.	24. Prolonge.	27. Pole pad.

12-pounder Napoleon cannon, of the kind used by Robertson's-Dent's Battery, here hitched backward to its "limber" for traveling

Firing the cannon involved an elaborate and complicated set of well-rehearsed routines. Each gun has a "gunner," usually a corporal. He shouts back to the two men on the limber chest the type of round he wants to fire, and the distance to the target, such as, "spherical case shot, 500 yards!" The two men on the limber chest, known as Cannoneers Number 6 and 7, pull out the requested round, which consists of a premeasured quantity of black gunpowder in a cloth cartridge bag, attached to the projectile, allowing the round to be handled as a unit. Numbers 6 and 7 then cut the Bormann fuse, which is a strip of paper with powder wrapped inside. It is cut to the number of inches indicated by a table, to explode when the projectile has traveled the number of yards to the target. Cannoneer Number 5, the runner, then carries the round up to the gun and gives it to Number 2, who places it in the muzzle. Number 1 then shoves the round down the bore with a rammer. While Number 1 is ramming, Number 3 is holding his thumb on the vent, a small hole on the top rear of the gun. This was very important, because it cut off the air supply to the inside of the cannon, thereby preventing an accidental spark and premature firing. After the round is rammed home, Number 3 sticks a small wire pick into the vent to perforate the cartridge bag. Number 4 then inserts a friction primer into the vent, so that a yank on the attached lanyard sent a spark down the vent to the powder and the gun fired. Number 1 then rams a wet sponge down the barrel to extinguish any remaining sparks, to get ready for reloading for the next shot. The men in the gun crew soon learned to refer to each other by number. Each crew was supervised by a sergeant known as the "chief of the piece."

Although this procedure sounds complicated, a well-drilled gun crew could load and fire 2 shots per minute. The time-consuming part was re-sighting the cannon after every shot. These cannon had no shock-absorbing mechanism, so that each discharge made the gun leap back in recoil. It had to be rolled back into line and resighted. The gunner was responsible for sighting, which was crude and largely guesswork. A handspike was used to move the cannon left or right. The barrel was moved up and down by an elevating screw.

By March 22, 1862, Robertson's Battery was in Corinth, Mississippi. An unprecedented concentration of Confederate troops, almost 40,000 soldiers, had been amassed. Gen. Johnston's enlarged artillery corps now comprised twenty-three batteries, about 122 guns, and two thousand artillerymen. Hubert writes Anna about his new situation. (At this time, the Army of Tennessee is still being called "the Army of the Mississippi Valley").

"Camp Near Corinth, Miss
March 22nd, 1862

"My own Dear Darling:
It has been more than three weeks since I received a letter from you and it seems to me that it has been more than three months…. I wonder if my letters reach you. I suspect they have been very irregular and that you hardly know yet what has become of me or where I am.
Troops are still concentrating here and field works are being made between this place and the river and the Yankees will have pretty hard work to get here whenever they think proper to try it.
Gen. Polk is here and Earl Van Dorn is expected—so you may judge from that what sort of an army we are collecting here and with determination this place will be defended. Gen. Polk commands the 1st Grand Division of the army of the Mississippi Valley, Gen. Bragg the second and I do not know who may command the third.
Gen. Beauregard is not yet well and being at Jackson Tenn. is coming down here for greater safety as in case he should get unable to travel, the Yankees might take him there alive. Beauregard would be a prize of great value in their eyes.
Since Gen. Bragg came here we have had no more ration orders - before that Gen. Ruggles sent us every day or two orders to cook sometimes five and sometimes three days rations - and occasionally ordering us to harness up and be ready to move or report to him and soon as we were ready. As I was saying however we have not had one such order since Gen. Bragg landed here and everything is going on much more quietly.
Our scouts run against the Yankee pickets every once and a while sometimes having a small skirmish with them. The last news I have of their whereabouts is that they are camped about one and a half miles from the river under cover of their gun boats.

I heard today that the 1st Ala Regt. had a fight with some gun boats of the enemy at Island No. 10 up above Memphis and that they sunk one gun boat and crippled two others driving the enemy off. The Regt. is highly complimented. I do not know what other troops are there.

We are drilling and fixing up and if we only had fifty more men as good as some we have I would not be afraid of any battery that could be sent against us. [Eli] Shorter's regiment is still here and I think now it never left—like our battery it only _____ its camp. I saw Shorter today.

I wonder how much longer we will remain here inactive. I hope our Generals will soon be able to act on the offensive and go and look for the enemy.

We are having wintry weather. Yesterday and last night it sleeted or rather sleet fell but did not lay on the ground. It was [raw] cold and disagreeable. It has been cloudy and disagreeable today but no rain or any thing of that kind. This sort of weather cannot last much longer which is consoling. I stand it finely and except a slight cold am as well as I ever was in my life. Our company too stands it well we having only one or two men sick and they are not much sick.

I would give a good deal to hear from you and if a letter does not reach me in a day or two I will telegraph again and ask for an answer. It has been nearly two weeks since I telegraphed you and no letter. I am afraid some times that you did not receive it. Give my love to all the family. I will try and write to some of them soon, when I get something interesting to write, but you can tell them what is going on as far as I am able to tell. It is surprising how little one knows here of what is going on right around him. Having no business out of camp I seldom leave except to drill and then see no one but come right back with my company. Well Darling good by. This is Saturday night I hope I may have a letter from you tomorrow and not having as much as usual to do I will spend most of the day reading it. May heaven bless and preserve you and our dear boy. Your own old dear-- Hubert

Meanwhile, the Federal army, unaware of Johnston's force at Corinth, was concentrating at Pittsburgh Landing, 22 miles away. With little thought of defense, Grant's divisions were carelessly arrayed in a bend in the Tennessee River where a tributary creek enters that river. The position had been selected by Gen. Sherman, who thought it easy to defend, but it also had aspects of a trap. Sherman established his headquarters at a nearby log cabin meeting house called Shiloh Church, thereby fixing the place and name of one of the bloodiest battles of the war.

25

Shiloh

"...the way the balls whistled past my head was not at all pleasant...we took a position near where the enemy had lost a gun and there lay three or four dead Yankees...in getting into position our wheel ran over a dead man and mashed him into jelly."
Hubert to Anna

" With such batteries...there could be no failure"
Brig. Gen. Jones M. Withers, Official Reports

As noted by Hubert in his letter of March 22, the Confederate scouts did not fail to notice the concentration of federals at their camp near the river. Hubert's hope that "our Generals will soon be able to act on the offensive and go and look for the enemy" was quickly gratified. Gen. Albert Sidney Johnston and his Chief of Staff, Gen. Beauregard, made the decision to attack. Johnston had total effective strength of about 38,700 including the cavalry, while Grant's strength was 39,900.[535] On the morning of April 3, Johnston's army started the 22-mile march to the Yankee position on the Tennessee.

The Confederate attack began at daybreak on Sunday, April 6. Although both Grant and Sherman would indignantly and repeatedly deny it in later years, they were in fact caught completely by surprise. Grant was not even at Pittsburgh Landing, but in another camp nine miles away.

Confederate attack, first morning at Shiloh

Gen. Beauregard had arranged the army's four corps in a somewhat unusual battle order: Hardee's Corps, to which Robertson's Battery was attached, was in a line extending across the entire front, the first to meet the enemy; with Bragg's Corps in a parallel line behind Hardee; with Polk parallel to and behind Bragg on the left; and Breckenridge parallel to and behind Bragg on the right.

At daylight, the Confederates swarmed forward along a three-mile front, screeching the piercing *Rebel Yell* that terrified the startled Yankee soldiers and became legendary as "...the voice that rang through Shiloh's woods, and Chickamauga's solitudes - the fierce South cheering on her sons".

As Gladden's Brigade of Hardee's Corps advanced toward the Union line of Prentiss, Gen. Gladden instructed Capt. Felix Robertson, the commander of the artillery battery attached to the Brigade, to halt the battery and wait for his order to come up to the line. The battery waited in a small valley near a brook. Robertson later wrote that, as rifle bullets from the battle line passed through the trees above the battery, "they cut the half grown leaves which fell on the battery in a continuing shower."[536] After a short time, Capt. Scott, an aide to Gen. Gladden, sent orders for Robertson's Battery to quickly advance. Captain Robertson, an ambitious officer, turned to Lieutenant Dent and, "with a glow on his face" said, *Well, Dent, here goes for a Brigadier General's commission, or a coffin*".[537] The battery then dashed toward the action, Robertson leading the way, closely followed by Hubert Dent, who was in command of the two lead guns.[538] The enemy was 100 to 150 yards away. As the battery galloped toward the battle line, it passed Gen. Gladden being assisted to the rear. "…His eyes were blazing and he was still mounted but the attentions given by the men around him plainly told that he had been wounded." [539]

Command of the Brigade devolved upon Col. Daniel Adams, who found that "the enemy was pouring a most destructive fire upon us…the fire became so very severe that I found the whole brigade began to falter and finally to fall back".[540] As Robertson's battery came up to the line, passing retreating men, Hubert Dent shouted to the men to stand firm, then unlimbered his guns and with his gunners, began blasting away at the Yankees. The battery had fired only about six or eight volleys when the Yankee line broke and started running. With a cheer, the Confederate infantry took up the chase, and drove the enemy out of his own camp and so far in advance of the battery as to make it dangerous to fire the cannon. Col. Daniel reported "…Captain Robertson's battery of artillery, attached to the brigade, opened on the enemy with great power and effect, greatly aiding in accomplishing the enemy's defeat."[541] Without waiting for orders, Robertson's Battery limbered up and moved forward to follow the fleeing Yankees.

The success of Gladden's Brigade and Robertson's Battery was being repeated up and down the line. By eight a. m., Hardee's men were in complete possession of the Union camps of General Prentiss. The completeness of the surprise was proven by the half-eaten breakfasts on the mess tables, the abandoned stores, flags, and ammunition. Captain Felix Robertson later recalled "…as we passed to our position seeing the breakfast table of some of the officers already set, and while I was not used to eating doughnuts for breakfast I particularly enjoyed a taste of them that morning taken from their set but abandoned table."[542]

Seeing Prentiss' Division in full retreat, Union Gen. Hulbert attempted to come to his relief and to plug the hole in the line. Unfortunately for this effort, Prentiss's pursuers included Robertson, Dent, and their battery of Napoleons. The battery had taken up a position at the edge of an open field that became known as "the Peach Orchard Field". Robertson had had his men roll some nearby bales of hay in position to give some protection against rifle fire.[543] In *Cannoneers in Gray*, Historian Larry J. Daniel describes what happened:

> "As Prentiss's shattered division streamed northward, General Stephen H. Hulbert's division attempted to patch the line in a peach orchard west of the Hamburg-Savannah Road. Even before his troops established a position, Rebel artillery opened fire. One of these batteries was [Robertson's Battery], commanded by Captain Felix Robertson…This was his first time in combat,

but he was to leave his mark. His gunners trained their four Leeds & Company 12-pounder Napoleons on the forming Union Line. An early round wounded one of Hulbert's brigadier Generals. Another shell struck a caisson in the 13th Ohio Battery and caused a huge explosion. The panic-stricken Yankee gunners abandoned all six guns without firing a shot. Hulbert was so enraged that he had the battery disbanded and the commanding officer, Captain John Meyers, dismissed from the service. Thus, in a single shot, one artilleryman's career began and another's ended."[544]

Col. Adams later reported that Robertson's Battery "was rapidly placed in position, and returned the enemy's fire with such promptness and great effect, that it drove them from their guns and caused them to abandon their battery..."[545] Robertson's men retrieved the five or six abandoned guns of the Ohio battery and parked them with their own guns. In the fight at this position, battery member Frank Pierce was killed.[546]

General Withers, commanding the Second Division of Hardee's Corps, noted the quality of the artillery, which achieved such accomplishments in the rough terrain upon which they were operating:

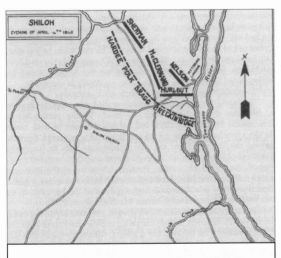

Positions at end of the first day at Shiloh

"The nature of the ground over which we had to pass rendered it most difficult for the artillery to keep up with the eager and rapid movements of the infantry. With such batteries, however, as Robertson's, Girardey's, and Gage's, there could be no failure."[547]

On the Confederate left, Gen. Pat Cleburne crossed a marshy hollow to fight Sherman's men. Cleburne's first assault was thrown back, but with support from the second Confederate line, Cleburne struck again and drove Sherman from his camps. The two armies became entangled in a fury of combat, but the early momentum that the Confederates had seized gave them the advantage. The Yankees fought and rallied whenever favorable terrain gave them some opportunity, but under the repeated battering being administered by the Confederates, the Federals were forced to fall back steadily all along the line.

In midafternoon, however, the Confederates' relentless advance hit a snag. As the Union divisions of Wallace and Hulbert retreated, together with the remaining remnant of Prentiss's Division, they fortuitously stumbled into a strong defensive position. Along the crest of a ridge was the shallow depression of an abandoned roadway, a natural rifle pit protected by bushes, trees, and undergrowth. From this sheltered position, the Yankees could pour out volleys of musket and artillery fire on the successive waves of advancing

Confederates. One of Bragg's division commanders, Brigadier General Daniel Ruggles, realized that this position, which became known as "the hornet's nest", could not be taken with infantry alone, and that massed artillery was the answer. It was the policy at this time to assign one artillery unit to each brigade, so the batteries were scattered around the battlefield. Ruggles started collecting batteries and massing them to fire on the Hornet's Nest. Some 53 guns were assembled, including the Napoleons of Robertson's Battery. The results were spectacular. The barrage sounded like "a mighty hurricane sweeping everything before it".[548] One of the Yankee batteries targeted Robertson's Battery, and a Parrott shell blew to pieces one of Robertson's men, William Campbell. At one point, two of Robertson's guns had to be temporarily abandoned. But the Confederate artillery was too much for the Hornet's Nest.[549] The Union batteries started withdrawing, and Hulbert's men started running for the river. General Wallace was killed and his command was surrounded. Gen. Prentiss surrendered the remaining 2200 Union troops of his division.

Although the Hornet's Nest was overwhelmed, this did not occur until about 5:30, and this delay probably saved Grant's army. It was during the fight for the Hornet's Nest that the Confederates received their worst blow, the death of their commander, Gen. Albert Sidney Johnson. Earlier, Gen. Johnson had been at the front, leading charges and urging his men forward. He had then returned to the rear when a random shot hit him in the right rear thigh, a few inches above the knee, cutting an artery. It was a wound that today would have been easily managed. At that time, however, it did not receive immediate attention, and in a few minutes, at about 2:30, Gen. Johnston was dead from loss of blood. Gen. Beauregard was notified, and assumed command. Fighting continued until six o'clock, when Beauregard gave the order to cease firing. There has been a sharp debate over the contention of many Southerners that Beauregard stopped the battle prematurely, at a time when he could have wiped out Grant's army by fighting a little longer. His defenders dispute this. Night was falling; the troops were too disorganized and too exhausted for further effective fighting.

In any event, there is no question that at the end of the day on Sunday, Grant was badly defeated; his army had disintegrated. His subordinate, Gen. Nelson, later wrote that when he and his division arrived on the west side of the Tennessee about 5 P. M. on Sunday night to reinforce Grant, " I found cowering under the riverbank from seven to ten thousand men, frantic with fright and utterly demoralized, who received my gallant division with cries of 'We are whipped! Cut to pieces!', etc.... Indignant of such poltroonery, I asked permission to fire on the knaves."[550] However, the battle was not yet over.

Grant was saved at Shiloh by two allies: nightfall and the arrival of Buell with reinforcements. During the night, Grant was augmented by Buell's army of 25,000 men and by Gen. Lew Wallace's division of 5000 men. Grant attacked on Monday morning with an army reinvigorated by fresh manpower. The Confederates could field only about 20,000 men on the second day. Beauregard hoped for the arrival of Van Dorn with his 20,000 troops from Arkansas, but to no avail. Nevertheless, the Confederates fought doggedly, Generally holding their line, sometimes being pressed back, then recovering and counterattacking. But the men seemed to share the feeling that yesterday's success could not be repeated against this significantly enlarged army.

As the ferocious fighting wore on into the afternoon, Beauregard concluded that it would be judicious to withdraw his army to fight another day. It was an orderly, well-executed withdrawal. Robertson's Battery and others were ordered to withdraw while continuing to fire. It did this with the use of "prolonges", ropes with hooks attached between the gun carriages and the limbers so that the guns could be withdrawn while firing.[551] Efforts were made to carry away as many of the captured Yankee cannon as possible, but there was a shortage of horses. Some artillery units left their own guns and departed with better Yankee cannon. A section of guns commanded by Hubert Dent joined a force of artillery and infantry posted on a ridge south of Shiloh Church to protect the rear of the withdrawing Confederates. This force kept up a heavy gunfire as the main army fell back. Lieutenant Dent and his section were therefore among the last to leave the field. But the Yankees had no interest in pursuit; they were pleased enough to see the Confederates stop fighting and go. Beauregard's army returned to Corinth without molestation.

The losses on both sides had been enormous. The total Confederate casualties were over 10,000, the Federal's, over 13,000.

Hubert wrote Anna on April 9, as soon as his unit reached Corinth, three days after the battle. This was even before the battle had acquired a name; he refers to it as simply as "the fight near Monterrey". This is one of the best letters of the collection. It contains Hubert's most detailed and vivid description of managing men, cannon, and horses while under scorching fire in pitched battle:

Camp near Corinth, Miss.
April 9, 1862

My own Dear Pet,

I was much disappointed this evening Darling in not being able to send a dispatch to you to relieve the anxiety I know you must have felt when you heard of the fight near Monterrey on Sunday – Monday. Lt. DuBarry who was unable to remain with the Battery, sent you a letter announcing that I was well, being unable to send a dispatch. I shall try again to-morrow as I think it very doubtful whether the mails are running regularly or not.

Well Dearest you will have learned no doubt through the papers of the battle. You will have heard of the death of Gen.l A. S. Johnston and many other officers of less note - and therefore I will leave those things for the newspapers to tell you and endeavor to give you a description of what I saw in the fight.

We left Corinth on Friday - camped that night a few miles from the battle on the hills above the enemy's camp about the middle of the day – We remained there until Sunday morning – when just as the sun rose clear & bright the quiet of that bright Sabbath was broken by the firing between the pickets of the two armies. Gen.l Gladden commanded our Brigade and immediately the whole of his line commenced advancing. We (and I mean our battery) followed slowly in the rear of our Second line of battle. The fight began to wax warmer and warmer as our troops were gradually pressing towards the enemy's camps. A few minutes before 8 o'clock the fight became very warm, the bullets whistled over our heads and sometimes uncomfortably near. Our battery meanwhile was standing idle, sharing only in the danger – at this point the enemy's camp, or rather one of his camps, was reached and there making a desperate stand our troops began to waver.

At this critical moment our battery was ordered forward into battery, that is, into position for firing. I had command of the two leading guns and dashed forward at a gallop through the open field - Robertson leading, I following and my piece bringing up the rear – not the rear of the battery but only my part of it. I could see the enemy not over one hundred and fifty yards - some say not over 100 yards distant, firing away at us. As we galloped up we met our men falling, no not falling, but swarming back. I shouted to them to stand firm. They halted as we went past and one officer pointing at us said as we passed, men do not disgrace yourselves by deserting those brave fellows.

I tell you Darling the way the balls whistled past my head was not at all pleasant. I dismounted, tied my horse, and went to work at my guns. I did not fire over six or eight shots before there was not an enemy in sight and not a bullet could be heard – our men who were falling back rushed past us with a cheer and soon drove the enemy entirely from his own camp and got so far in advance of our own battery as to render it dangerous for us to fire. We lost some horses and had a man wounded.

I thought it miraculous to come off so well. I did feel like death was staring me in the face every minute while going up but as soon as I got to work with my guns, I forgot all about minnie balls and danger and became thoroughly excited and then I could have gone anywhere or faced any danger without the slightest quiver. What made the thing more impressive was the fact that we took a position near where the enemy had lost a gun and there lay three or four dead Yankees with as many horses and in getting into position our wheel ran over a dead man and mashed him into jelly. I had no time then for picking roads. I was surprised to find how indifferent I felt to the suffering and death going on all around me. So Darling while you no doubt were taking your breakfast I was preparing to give the Yankees shell and canister –

Well to go on – our battery then limbered up and galloped through the camp of the enemy and coming to position fired on the retreating column of the enemy. We had not fired more than two or three shots before an officer came riding up saying stop that shooting you are firing on our friends. I ceased firing but could see a column of men with a battery of artillery forming through the woods & soon they opened fire on us and not feeling disposed to stand that I banged away again and soon silenced the battery and soon ran off the infantry – orders then came from Gen.l Hindman to cease firing. We did so and waited a short time.

In the meantime I went up to a tent near and found these two wounded Yankees – I asked them a few questions and about the time I got back to my gun a battery of artillery opened on our battery. We had it there warm for over two hours, at the end of that time the enemy's battery was silenced and we found afterwards had been driven from their guns by our battery alone, not a single musket being fired at it. We went and brought the guns to our position with our own horses, many of their horses having been killed and the balance taken out by cutting the harnesses. This was warm work. We here lost a man killed and had some wounded only slightly, we also had some horses killed.

This brought the middle of the day. We rested for some time and then advanced with our battery to attack another column and camp of the enemy further on. We there got into a very hot place, the bullets whistled and cut bushes all around. We could not see the enemy from this position and were ordered to leave it. We did so and took another place more to our left and just on the edge of an old field. The enemy opened a fire on us with infantry and a battery of 20 lb guns. This was the hottest place I ever got into – a man was shot down within a few feet of me with a cannon ball – a horse, in fact several, were shot – Van Houten's among them. It was so hot that we had to leave two of our guns – one for want of horses and the other because our trail got into a hole and our men could not pull it out. We fired a few more shots after that but not many, on Sunday, and these ended our part of the fight.

We went back and got our guns away – well we retired to the hills and slept. It rained hard and I got sick. The enemy were driven back to the river and a good many prisoners were taken and I thought they were so badly whipped that they would not fight next morning. In this however I was badly mistaken.

I was sitting on a log next morning writing to you when we received orders to harness up and go into the battle. I could hear the firing going on and was much surprised to hear it. I knew our men were wearied and a good many regiments disorganized and I went into the fight with a heavy heart. Darling I felt somehow that I would be killed and that our battery would be cut up. As I went down to the battle field I met many men running away from it – as I was saying I went down with a heavy heart – I got down to the enemy's camp, at least that camp where we fought, and soon after we got there a regiment came running through the camp utterly routed. This was the Crescent Regiment from N. O. I also saw a battery of the Washington Artillery running like very cowards – we unlimbered and came into battery and opened. I could see the enemy running up following our men, at about the second or third discharge I could see them turn and run the other way. The day in that part of the field was saved again and by our battery –

At this place a splinter struck me on the nose and knocked up some skin and drew a little blood. This is the only scratch I have received. I had on a Yankee hat with a feather in it and it (the feather) was cut off and Robertson says it must have been done by a ball, for he said he looked at me and saw the feather and a moment after it was gone and bullets were flying round thick. I knew nothing of it myself until some time after. I do not think there are ten men in the company who did not have some such narrow escape.

Well to continue with the fighting – after our battery went and took the same position we had on Sunday morning after driving the enemy from their camp. We fought there for a long time. Gen.l Hardee ordered us to hold the position at all hazards. At one time our men came running through the woods to the left of our battery. There is a fence down by the side of these woods between it and a field. I suggested to Robertson that a road leading down this fence would be a good place to put a gun and placed it there and opened with it. The enemy were within a short distance of us. I fought the gun very hard and drove them back and some say that I saved the battery with the position. The men who were with me at the gun said it was the hottest place they were ever into – and one said it was the only time he felt like running. In fact he did run a little way but I called him back to his post. The whole battery then formed just in rear of where this gun was and I had that one run back and we fought there for some hours until in the evening – when Gen.l Hardee came back and ordered us to retire slowly firing.

We did so – after retiring for some distance – he sent for a section of our battery to help cover our falling back. I went in charge of it and was about the last to quit the field.

Gen.l Bragg had two horses killed under him. Gen.l Gladden lost his left arm. The two men we lost were named Pierce and Campbell – both very fine soldiers. I think we lost eight horses besides what were wounded only slightly.

The enemy were badly whipped on Sunday and were held in check and driven back some on Monday. If we could only have had 20,000 good fresh troops on Monday I believe we could have taken nearly the whole Yankee army. The Yankees had collected all their troops in one place and we could not drive them from it – occasionally they advanced from it but after a while would be driven back.

Well darling a battle field is a grand sight. I have often expressed a desire to see a great battle – my curiosity is now thoroughly gratified. I have seen the ghastly corpse – heard the groans of the wounded and dying and seen men fall at my side. I have heard the *z-i-p-i-p* of the musket balls – the whine of the cannon balls and the explosion of the shells.

Darling when I read your letter of the 28th March yesterday after returning to camp and found in the conclusion of it your prayer for my protection – I involuntarily felt that I owed my safety during the fight to the prayers of my own Darling – God bless her –

I have a fine ladies handkerchief captured in the Yankee camp for you – I have a splendid overcoat for myself, besides pants. I would not take $75 for the coat – all our men have Yankee things. There must have been women and children in the camp from the clothing found.

My love and much love to all the family. Tell them bombardments are a mere pastime compared to such a fight as we had. Much love and many kisses for you and the boy. Your old Dear Hubert

A contemporary newspaper article contained this account:

"…Robertson's battery performed most effective service. Capt. Robertson is from Texas, though most of his men hail from Alabama and Mississippi, and were enlisted from the twelve months troops at Pensacola. The company lost two killed—Wm. Campbell of Wilcox County, Alabama, and F. Pearce of Natchez, Miss, …

This battery performed the extraordinary feat of completely silencing and capturing another battery, from Minnesota [should be "Ohio". Ed.] Its firing is represented to have been splendid. It took two 12 pounder and three 6 pounder Parrott guns, together with the flag of the Minnesota battery. It had eight horses killed, and as many wounded, and lost one caisson and part of another, for the want of horses to bring them away. The enemy's guns were saved. Among the best officers of the company is Lieut S. H. Dent of Barbour County."[552]

Upon returning to Corinth, Beauregard had his engineers construct a new line of breastworks three miles north of the town and carefully positioned his troops in preparation for a follow up attack by the Federals. However, the Yankees had had enough for now. It would be many weeks, after much reinforcement, before the Union Army would make a movement toward the Confederates, and then very carefully.

Hubert's next letter suggests that the news that he survived Shiloh may have been slow in reaching Anna in Eufaula. He suffers a spell of sickness in the hospital. One of his principal concerns at this time is foraging for a square meal, which he finds. He has heard of the departure from Eufaula of Capt. Clark's Eufaula Light Artillery, which, as we have already seen in an earlier chapter, marched off with Henry Young and other Eufaulians in early April. Hubert sends Henry's wife, Maria, the cheery message that "we will all be back after a while;" sadly, this well-meant message turned out to be incorrect in every respect. Hubert also resolves to write in future letters of something other than Shiloh, which he feels he has "exhausted".

Camp Near Corinth, Mississippi
April 23, 1862

My own dearest wife:
Your letter of the 8th just reached me today. My heart bled Darling while reading it, for I know what must have been your feelings. I have felt all the while a great deal for you, but this letter made me feel if any thing worse than ever before. As I wrote you Dearest I tried frequently and for a week to

send you a dispatch but could not. I hoped that my letters might reach you soon or that you would see something in the papers that would relieve your anxiety. Surely long before this you have heard. [DuBarry] mailed a letter for me to you on the 8th and one on the 9th and mine ought to have yours the 10th or 11th. Your letter has been so long coming that I am afraid you have suffered by the interruption of the mails. Perhaps the Yankees got some of my letters when they took Huntsville. I sometimes think they did. I hope Darling you are well and that you all are well. In your anxiety, my Darling, you even forgot to tell me of our darling boy. This fact is of itself enough to show how great and earnest was your solicitude.

Yes Darling the battle is over and I am safe thank Heaven—and as I wrote in a former letter I feel that your prayers for my safety were answered. Oh! Darling you do not know how much I feel indebted to you. Dearest while sick at the hospital I thought over many things and I felt I had great reason to be thankful and I hope and pray and shall try for the future to be a better man. May God help me to be. Well I will write of other things.

We have had transferred to our company forty men from an artillery company that was broken up for inefficiency of its officers....I am very glad we have them. DuBarry is still sick in Mobile. _____ is still sick and a good many other men—some of whom I fear will never get well.

What do you think I did today? I took two men and started in the country to find something to eat. I rode for several miles—but could find nobody willing to sell me a chicken or any thing at all. At last I met a wagon which had only eggs. I had despaired of finding any thing. I bought from the wagon forty-three dozen eggs and I would have taken all the man had over a hundred dozen—but had no way to take them into camp. I paid 33 ½ cts a dozen for them. I have eaten nearly a dozen today. Of course I divided with the company as well as I could—but I keep about fifteen dozen for my own mess. If I could only have found some butter I would have lived like a lord for a few days. I have a great appetite since I got well.

I suppose from what you write that Clarks Company has gone. Where did it to go? And did Henry go with it? I would like to meet him and think it likely I will. I am glad I was not there I have had too much already of such scenes. I believe I had rather go though a battle.

Our company is getting straight again. The weather is fine now—today fine as you ever saw.

I wish you could have been with me in my ride. My way was through woods and across streams the whole distance. I felt like I would have given any thing for your company. In fact I got to castle building and thought of ever so many fine things we would do when this war was over. Oh! how many are there who like me are forming plans for the future when the war is over. I believe still that it will last a long time through the whole of Lincoln's term perhaps—three years longer. It may not and I hope will not most ardently and sincerely.

Well Darling every one in camp is abed. I alone am up. I intended writing to you yesterday but as I forgot to mail Mollies and the girls letter I concluded to postpone it until today.

Many of our officers are resigning since the fight. I do not like the indication many a man has formed out that he could not stand the service on account of health since the fight who to all appearances at least were perfectly healthy before the fight. I tell you my Love they had enough of battle.

I know very little of what is going on here. I believe part of Van Dorn's and Price's army is here but I know nothing except by mere rumor. Beauregard rode past our battery this morning. The first time I have seen him since the fight. He is very gray.

Well Darling my Love to all. Tell Maria if Henry has gone to cheer up that we will all be back after a while. Kiss our boy for me. Tell Ma I want to write her a long letter but must wait until I get something of news interest to write. I have exhausted Shiloh. Goodby Darling many kisses and much love to you and the boy from your own husband who loves you better and better every day. Hubert

26

Fight At The Bridge

"...skillfully and gallantly handled by Lieutenant Dent, of Robertson's Battery."
Col. Joseph Wheeler, Official Reports

Following Shiloh, Ulysses Grant was temporarily out of favor in Washington. Gen. Halleck, the overall army commander, assumed field command, and started concentrating his forces to move on Beauregard at Corinth. Some indication of Halleck's respect for Confederate fighting ability is suggested by the size of the army he now gathered: 125,000 men, the largest single army assembled in one place during the entire war.[553] Beauregard, even after collecting the forces of Gen. Van Dorn and others, had only 50,000 men. With his overwhelming force, on April 29 Halleck started gingerly inching his way from Shiloh toward Corinth. Having learned from Grant's experience the consequences of surprise, his army stopped after each day's march and entrenched itself for the night. By this deliberate process, Halleck spent the entire month of May moving the 15 miles from Shiloh to the outskirts of Corinth – as one historian noted, the slowest uncontested advance ever recorded of any army.[554]

Beauregard noticed that one of Halleck's more aggressive corps commanders, Gen. Pope, had marched ahead of the main force and was in an isolated position near Farmington, a village only four miles from Corinth. On May 9, 1862, Beauregard sent Confederate forces under Generals Ruggles and Van Dorn with the assignment of defeating Pope before he could be reinforced. Robertson's Battery was present at Farmington and made its presence felt. Unaided, it repulsed multiple charges by a regiment of Wisconsin Cavalry.[555] Gen. Patton Anderson, commanding the Confederate First Brigade, reported that Robertson's Battery "swept the field the full length of our front, dealing death and dismay in the ranks of the enemy's cavalry, a squadron of which had the temerity to attempt a charge upon our line".[556] Ruggles' attack was successful, but unexpected obstacles kept Van Dorn from providing planned support. Pope was driven back to his former position.

As Halleck slowly moved closer, Beauregard made the decision to secretly evacuate Corinth and retire to Tupelo, 52 miles south. Ruses and disinformation were used to disguise the Confederates intentions. The wounded, equipment and heavy baggage were quietly moved out in advance. Trains were frequently run into town amid cheering, as though reinforcements were arriving for an attack. Commanders were carefully instructed on their movements when the order of withdrawal came.

In connection with this withdrawal, Lieutenant Hubert Dent would come to the attention of Col. Joseph Wheeler. Later in the war, General Wheeler would become a legendary commander of cavalry for the Army of Tennessee,[t] but in May of 1862, in Corinth,

---

[t] After the Civil War, Wheeler settled near Tuscumbia, and represented Alabama in the U. S. Congress for a number of years. At the time of the Spanish American War in 1898, to remove any question that the South would fight for America, Wheeler left his seat in Congress to serve as a United States cavalry general against Spain in Cuba. He was the only man to serve as an American general after being a Confederate general.

Mississippi, he was still a colonel of Confederate infantry, temporarily serving as the commander of the former Gladden's Brigade.

On May 28, Halleck finally arrived at the outskirts of the Corinth defenses and began a demonstration and cannonade all along the line, which lasted all day. Beauregard ordered the evacuation to begin on the following night, May 29. During Halleck's demonstration on the 28th, a force of about 200 Confederates, including a two-gun section of Robertson's Battery under the command of Lieutenant Hubert Dent, had been driven back about one half mile from the Confederate outpost on the Monterrey road north of Corinth. That night, Col. Wheeler was ordered to take reinforcements of 300 to 400 men to this point and recapture the outpost. After a heated skirmish involving 8 Confederates killed, the outpost was retaken, and Wheeler held it, as instructed, until the next night, May 29, when the general evacuation of Corinth began at 11 P. M. At midnight, Wheeler silently brought the brigade, including Dent and his two guns, back to Corinth, picked up the infantry pickets remaining in the breastworks, and continued south of Corinth, following as part of the rearguard to the withdrawing main army.

After crossing the bridge over the Tuscumbia River five miles south of Corinth, Wheeler was ordered to hold the bridge until it had been crossed by the Confederate cavalry, which would then burn the bridge. Wheeler deployed lines of skirmishers on both sides of the road near the bridge, and positioned men to   defend any river crossings near the road. On the south side of the bridge, he placed Lieutenant Dent and one of his guns, in battery, with a prolonge attached to the limber, so that, if necessary, it could retire firing. He had details prepared to burn the bridge, with nearby fires made, to permit quick firing of the bridge.

Wheeler then learned that the main Confederate cavalry was crossing by another road instead. Wheeler sent a scouting squad of three cavalry back up the road to scout for any enemy pursuit. Wheeler's men had begun burning the bridge when the three cavalry scouts came galloping back, closely pursued by a force consisting of six companies of Yankee cavalry. The Yankees dismounted, deployed, and began an assault on the Confederates with a rapid and heavy fire. When the Union force had approached to about 40 yards away, the Confederates began returning fire. From his position on the bridge, Hubert's section of artillery began firing volley after volley of canister into the attackers. The Yankees made a valiant effort, but could not withstand this withering barrage. After five of their number had been killed, and nine wounded, they remounted their horses and fled. Col. Wheeler later reported that the artillery "was skillfully and gallantly handled by Lieutenant Dent, of Robertson's Battery".[557]

The destruction of the bridge was then completed. Leaving Dent's guns and some infantry to continue as rearguard, Wheeler proceeded to rejoin the main army. Beauregard's main army had halted not far south of the Tuscumbia River, to give battle if there were pursuit. But other than the fight just described, there was no pursuit, in part because the withdrawal had been so well screened that Halleck had only the vaguest idea of the direction of the retreat of the main body of Beauregard's army.[558]

There was an interesting epilogue to this fight at the bridge. Three or four weeks later, a force of Confederate Cavalry made a raid on the Union-held Memphis and Charleston Railroad, and, among other things, captured a Yankee mail train. In the mail was a Yankee letter describing the fight at the Tuscumbia River. A friend of Hubert's took it to him, and he later sent it to Anna. Hubert said he was sure it related to his section's fight because they were fighting dismounted cavalry, just as the writer reports. Here is the Yankee letter:

"Camp East-Side Tennessee River
 Near Tuscumbia, Alabama
 June 18, 1862

"My Dear Wife:
After the evacuation of Corinth our six companies being joined, Colonel Oakes commanding, we proceeded in pursuit of Beauregard's Army, General Pope taking one road and about 1500 cavalry another. Of course our six companies being in the advance four or five miles from Corinth we came on the rear of the rebel army, they had burned a bridge and we had to dismount and fight on foot. We did not make much of this work for the enemy opened on us with a masked battery in the woods killing 5 and wounding 9 of the 3rd Kentucky Cavalry. Our 6 companies were mounted to charge if an opening offered Captain Crittenden was along and very sick, so sick that he had to be carried away in an ambulance.
Next morning our commanders were not satisfied. So we went down again. This time our fellows took on foot and some sharp skirmishing went on for about half an hour when Colonel Oakes seen the enemy was surrounding us ordered a retreat, which was very well executed, "D" company covering the others 'till they all got mounted. When we broke for our horses and left one man of "G" company was killed and one man of "K" company wounded.

We are attached to General Buells command and don't know where we are going to. Some of the men say Tennessee and some Virginia. This country is very rich large fields of corn and potatoes very little of anything else is planted. I have only seen one field of cotton.

Dear Mary it is now a long time since you have written to me. Do try and write often. I feel very uneasy when I don't hear from you regular and I'm always thinking something is amiss with Katy.

I sent you by Mrs. Gorden $15. I thought it was the best way to send it. We left little Hugh, Smith, and K___ back in the hospital sick. "K & G" companies are the colonels pets ____ would not make a good company.

Give my respects to Mrs. Doyle and all friends. Kiss Katy for me.
                                                    Yours (illegible)
PS: Direct Co. D. 4th Regular Cavalry

213

Army of the Ohio
Sent Buells Command
Tenn. In the field

I forgot to say that we escaped very lucky in the skirmish. We found out afterwards there was 6000 rebels waiting for us. Little Johnny that used to work for Major Hunter is in "K" company and sends you his respects."

Beauregard continued south and reached Tupelo on June 9. It soon became clear that Halleck had no intention of advancing into the interior of Mississippi.

Perhaps because of the recent stress of Shiloh and the fighting retreat from Corinth, Hubert's next letter to Anna is even more heavily sentimental than usual. Hubert has received from her a package that suffered from its long trip from Eufaula. Hubert also reports despondent camp talk about the Confederacy's chances.

"Camp near Tupelo Miss
June 21, 1862

My own Dear Wife:
At last Darling I can announce the reception of the valise. Its true I do it on very dingy paper and with a poor pen and not very good ink – but I know my Darling will excuse these when I assure her it is the very best her old dear can do. I felt like writing you a long letter and after diligent inquiring & search I found this sheet and here I am writing. I sent a letter by Maj Johnston this morning which I expect you will receive before this. It was through him that I got my valise.

Well next about the contents. The bottles were broken & most of the potatoes rotten and consequently the contents were not in a very good fix. Shirts drawers handkerchiefs and socks were mildewed – but will be good enough for a soldier. Your Bible <u>Our</u> Bible was unfortunately in a very bad fix. Some of the leaves are loose and the whole of them are very much disposed to come out. The needle cases were likewise damaged. Robertson [the battery commander] asked for his as soon as he saw the valise – and returns his thanks. For the valise my Dearest I thank you most sincerely. The shirts and drawers are especially welcome. I have them in water now and I hope the stain and mildew will come out.

Dearest you can hardly imagine my feelings when I read your note sent with <u>our</u> Bible. Darling you touched some tender chords in that note and I felt that with you it would be easy for me to be a better man. I will endeavor through Gods help darling to be a better man – For my own sake but most of all for the sake of my darling wife and sweet boy. Yes Dearest when I feel that your prayers are added to mine I feel that I will succeed – May God help me.

Well Darling I have not mentioned one other thing which gave me yet I must write it – more pleasure than all else – that you know Darling was your likeness [picture]. It came through less injured than any thing else – In fact it is not injured at all except slightly on the outside. How long and earnestly I gazed on that loved and familiar face. How I studied each part of the picture and oh! Darling how I longed to see and be with the original – I think I hope I may be before a great while. As I have already written home, I intend asking for a leave in about two weeks or a little more. I hope I may get it.

Darling I shall carry the note that accompanied the Bible in my pocket book. Your picture already occupies a place over my heart. Each will always remain with me. Oh! Darling how I wish I could be with you to-day. I feel some how especially like I wanted to be with you. I could remain by you so contentedly this evening. I could lay my head in my darlings lap (would she let me?) and there let it remain. I feel like I especially wanted it there this evening. When will I have it there? Oh! That I could answer <u>soon</u> with the certainty that it would be so. Darling you want me to write you a long letter just as I feel – well let me tell you how I feel this evening. I feel like I had the dearest Sweetest and best of wives and that I loved her better and better every day and that I am hardly worthy of her - and wish most heartily that I were.

Well I expect I have written enough of my personal feelings and thoughts and I will now write of other things. However I will wait until later – this is immediately after dinner so my darling Pet – goodby for an hour or two you own old Dear   Hubert

Well Darling now I will finish my letter to you.

Terry is out here. He thinks our Lt. Should be sent to a hospital. He will very likely go tomorrow. I do hope I will not get sick. I had a headache a few days ago but feel very well now.

Nothing new this evening. Everything indicated that the army will move from here before a great while. I hope we may accomplish something if we do move. Nearly every body I hear talk is beginning to despair of the Southern Confederacy. How is it about Eufaula? For my own part I have ceased to think about it almost. I feel like I was sort of automaton being moved about for I know not what and carried I know not where. I am like "Micawber" waiting for something to turn up – and I hope something will turn up soon to relieve the [suffering] at the South.

I hear Pugh [Hubert's old law mentor from Eufaula, now a Confederate congressman] says the Southern Confederacy is on rising ground and that Richmond is impregnable – well I have seen so many impregnable places fall during this war that I begin to be suspicious of impregnable places, and as for the rising ground I do not see it. I hope Pugh and Cochran [another of Hubert's Eufaula law mentors] will come up here. I hear that Bragg has invited Pugh to come. I want to hear him talk.

I will not let the idea of subjugation enter my head but a great many people seem to think of these things and talk of them. God only knows what would become of us if we should be subjugated. I do not think I could live in the south. I would be in favor of moving north or at least of getting away from the South. Let us get among the masters and not live among the slaves.

But notwithstanding our prospects look dark and gloomy we are not whipped yet and if we can manage to keep our large armies together for three or four months longer we will not be in such a bad fix It would not surprise me any day to get an order to march somewhere – probably to East Tennessee. As I am an unlucky individual I expect such an order will come just about the time I want to go home. That would be bad would it not. Johnston promised me to go and see you and tell you how I was getting. He can tell you a good deal that I could never write.

You can preserve this letter to show our boy some day what sort of paper his PaPa had to use to write his MaMa on [She did. Ed.] Bless the Dear little fellow. How I would like to see him and he is always calling "Pa". I wish I could hear him. Give my love to all the family and write me a long free letter. I do not know where I am to get an envelope from – but I reckon I will find one. I hope to get some paper tomorrow – Sunday – yes Darling Sunday, and I promise to read my our Bible and think of my Darling Nannie. Goodby my love, may Heaven bless and preserve you – with much love and many kisses for you and the boy I bid you goodby. Old Dear Hubert

The evacuation of Corinth on May 29 had far-reaching consequences in addition to the obvious. It rendered untenable the position of Fort Pillow on the Mississippi north of Memphis; it was evacuated on June 4, thereby opening the Mississippi to Federal gunboats down to Memphis. After a sharp naval battle, Memphis was surrendered on June 6, placing the Mississippi under Federal control down to Vicksburg. Jefferson Davis and the Confederate government were naturally upset, and propounded a series of hostile written questions to Beauregard about his decision to retreat from Corinth. With his army in Tupelo and Halleck not pursuing, Beauregard, who had been complaining of bad health for months, took this occasion to follow earlier advice from his doctor to take a vacation. He departed for Bladon Springs, a well-known mineral springs resort in Alabama on the Tombigbee River north of Mobile. President Davis used this as the basis for relieving Beauregard and appointing Gen. Braxton Bragg as the new commander of the Army of Tennessee. (The following August, when Beauregard's health was recovered and he was partially restored to President Davis' favor, he was given the less prestigious position of Commander of the Department of South Carolina and Georgia. His rearrangement of Savannah's defenses led to the change in location of Croft's Battery we saw in an earlier chapter.)

Bragg was not liked by the men, but Hubert Dent was pleased with the appointment, as he told Anna, when he sent her the Yankee latter we saw earlier:

"Camp near Tupelo
June 22, 1862

"Dear Love

I believe I have sent you nearly everything I could in the way of a Yankee relic except a letter. Well, here is one. Dr. Terry brought this over to me this morning because it contained the Yankee account of our skirmish at Tuscumbia [Mississippi]. I send it to you to let you see what my <u>section</u> did there. I know this was my section because we were fighting dismounted cavalry.

One of our cavalry companies went up on the Memphis and Charleston rail-road a day or so ago and burned a bridge, also three thousand bales of cotton collected by the Yankees, and captured a mail train, and this is one of the letters. Some of the letters captured give terrible accounts of this country and it seems to be pretty certain that Buell with his army has gone to East Tennessee.

Terry told us that we would have orders to march in a few days, perhaps today. But where we are going? No one knows except Bragg, who is now in command of this Department. Beauregard has gone to Bladen Springs. I am glad Bragg is in command. I therefore look for stirring times soon.

If it would serve the interests of the country as well I would like to remain here a week longer. Our men and horses are improving.

Well good by Darling. Love to all. Much love and many kisses for you and the boy from old Dear. Hubert."

In Hubert's next letter, we learn that his father, Dr. Stouten Warren Dent, an outspoken Southern sympathizer, has apparently been forced out of his home in Charles County, Maryland by pressure from the occupying federals, and has temporarily immigrated to Jackson, Mississippi for safety. He has visited with Hubert in camp at Tupelo.

"Camp near Tupelo Miss.
 June 28 1862

My Own Dear Wife,

I had just seated myself to write you when your's of the 22nd was handed me - of course I was glad to get it - for I am always glad to hear from own Dear Darling.

Well by this time Ada has graduated and I am sure she acquitted herself well. I wish I could have been with you but regrets are useless. Congratulate Ada for me and say to her that I hope her future may be a bright and happy one undimmed by sorrow or distress. I believe I have coined a word - but she will understand me.

My Father remained with me until late yesterday evening - also another gentleman named Barry, a refugee from Maryland. The latter showed me a letter written by the notorious Dan Sickles to his (Barry's) wife releasing her from arrest. She lives in Prince George's Co. Md. And was arrested by Sickles for communicating with the rebels. It was the same crowd that ran my Father from home. He (my Father) is in only tolerable health. Both have gone to Jackson Miss and may be there some time.

George [H. Dent, Hubert's younger brother], as I wrote, is in Richmond. He stood the marching and fighting under Stone-wall Jackson finely. His company suffered some and he lost among others his Captain whom he loved very much. I believe I wrote you that his Company had disbanded. George is quite anxious to remain with the 1st Md Reg. Especially as they have been so highly complimented for whipping the famous Bucktail Penn Reg. But it seems uncertain whether he can get into a Company to suit him. He may join my Company. I [decided] however to not persuade him as he will have to be a private for a good while and may never in fact get any higher - while I would like very much to have him yet he might not be very well satisfied and therefore I do not like to persuade him.

My father expressed a good deal of confidence in our ability to hold Richmond. I hope he may be correct but I am very much afraid of the burrowing propensity of McLellan. Things remain quiet there a long time.

I have just heard to-day that four thousand men have been sent from here to Chattanooga - whether more will go and when I know not. I hear also that troops have gone from Mobile up there.

Our Division commanded by Withers has been made a reserve Corps. So we will not be the first in a fight while we remain thus. Although the best troops are Generally held in reserve I cannot say that I would like this very well were it not for the fact that in this way I will stand a better chance to get a leave of absence. I think now my chances are pretty good - but I will not be able to get more than twenty days. If I get it at all I expect to leave here about the 10th July. I will only have a short time to remain - but even that will be gladly accepted.

Well I have given you all the news here personal and otherwise and will now write of something else. That boy of ours must be a great little fellow. And so he wants PaPa's letters and kisses them. How I do want to see him hear him talk and see him walk. I wonder if he will get so he will know me while I am at home. I hope so. I believe I want to see him almost as bad as I do my Darling. Did the poor little fellow ever get a carriage? If you ever wrote me that he did I have forgotten it. How much does he weigh? Well I hope I will soon see him and his dear MaMa too.

I am very sorry to hear such news of Willie Toney - poor boy - and I feel so sorry for his family. I tell you what Darling these surgeons are too fond of cutting off limbs. Should I ever be unfortunate as to be wounded either in the leg or the arm I am not going to let a surgeon cut them off without I think it necessary.

I am much obliged for your suggestions about going to Mr. Hudson's at Columbus - but I hope at the same time that I will keep well. I am very well and if I can miss bullets & all I think I will go through the war all right. I have been living well this week having had potatoes, onions and black berry pies in addition to our usual fare.

218

The weather is still very warm. We had a little rain last night and some little again to-day. It is still cloudy and I hope we will have a good deal shortly.

I do not think I envy your hearing the commencement sermon. I have an idea that I would have been greatly <u>bored</u>.

Well it is after dinner[midday meal] and every body nearly is asleep. I will lay this aside and finish tonight. Goodby God Bless you My Darling wife.

It is now after supper and I propose to finish this letter.

I have heard this evening that there has been another terrible fight before Richmond in which we were the attacking party and that we had been successful, but to what extent could not learn. I shall look anxiously for the particulars. We have so often been successful at first and then lost all the fruits of Victory that I shall wait to hear more before I throw up my hat and shout my hurrah! I hope we have defeated McLellan and that we will gain the fruits of the victory. The whole south would breathe freer and the wavering be strengthened, and I hope the war will be made aggressive and carried into the enemy's country.

Oh, there is one thing about Willie Toney that I do not understand. How come he in our line if the Yankees got hold of him?

We have a pretty good camp here now, plenty of good water & all our men are Generally in fine health and spirits. Our horses are improving and we will soon be in fine condition for a march or a fight. Clayton's regiment is suffering a good deal from sickness and I heard that Mitchell's Company only turned out six men for duty a day or two ago. New men have to go through a certain amount of sickness. We have had very little rain - but that little helped.

I was much amused at your account of the visit to Mrs. Rainey. They must be a powerful loving couple. I wonder how Bill ever managed to tear himself away from her loving embraces.

Tell Maria [the wife of Anna's brother, Henry Young] she must not be getting sad and talking trouble by anticipation. That is much better for her to be cheerful so long as Henry is all right. How does Mrs. Chambers bear the absence of the Co. or is she in Montgomery with him. I am very busy now.

Robertson and myself and the officers with the Battery are the only officers with the battery and are both kept pretty busy. What an immense amount of suffering has been caused by this war - and when will it end? I believe that if McLellan is whipped before Richmond that it will postpone rather than hasten foreign intervention - certainly as far as England is concerned. My idea is that Europe wishes to see a final separation of this country - but that she wants both Countries to be badly used up before peace is made - hence I think England would be more apt to interfere to prevent our subjugation than any thing else - as long as we seem able to hold our own she will "let us alone." The war I think is certain to last some years.

Give my love to all the family. I think I should have Mollie's letter by this time. Keep in good spirits My Darling and try and be cheerful. Tell the boy to be good and kiss him for PaPa. I expect he will be spoiled with so much petting. With much love and many kisses for you and the boy I close. Your own old Dear who loves you better and better every day. Hubert

In Tupelo, Gen.Bragg set about strengthening the organizational structure of his army and restoring the health of his men. About ten days after his bloodless occupation of Corinth, Halleck started dismantling the huge army he had assembled. On June 11, Halleck ordered Buell to take his army back to East Tennessee and occupy that area, but to repair the Memphis and Charleston Railroad as he went. Buell moved very leisurely across northern Alabama toward East Tennessee, not reaching Stevenson, Alabama until mid-July, from which he could occupy Chattanooga, his apparent objective.

Bragg would not turn out to be a very good general, but he made perhaps his best move at this point. Starting July 21, and using rail connections from Tupelo to Mobile, Montgomery, and Atlanta, Bragg rapidly moved his army to Chattanooga and beat Buell there. Hubert had predicted this move in his June 21 letter to Anna. On the trip from Tupelo to East Tennessee, the infantry rode the railroad, but the artillery walked. The infantry boarded the cars and took the train south to Mobile, then east to Atlanta, then north to Chattanooga. The artillery, including Hubert Dent and Robertson's Battery, with its horses pulled its tons of guns and equipment by dirt road overland through Aberdeen and Columbus, Mississippi; through Tuscaloosa, Alabama; through Will's Valley to Gadsden, Alabama; and on to Rome, Georgia, where it finally got to ride the train into the Chattanooga area, arriving in mid-August.[559] It was a very difficult trip, a logistical nightmare, but discipline was good.

The Battle Flag of Robertson-Dent's Battery, made by the ladies of Tuscaloosa in 1862.

Passing through Tuscaloosa, Robertson's Battery stopped for a few days rest. Apparently Hubert had been sent ahead to Chattanooga ahead of the main column, or perhaps he got the ten day furlough he was hoping for in his last letter, for he was not in Tuscaloosa at the time his Battery rested there. During the delay in Tuscaloosa, Capt. Robertson made or renewed the acquaintance of a number of young ladies of that town, who presented the battery with a new Confederate battle flag, hand sewn by them. Those who made the flag included Miss Mary Leland (with whom, as we will presently see, Captain Robertson established special rapport, or thought he did); Miss Stella Searcy, the sister of Dr. James T. Searcy, Director of the Alabama Hospital for the Insane in Tuscaloosa; and Mrs. Van Hoose, the daughter of Bishop Hamner Cobb, the first Episcopal bishop for the diocese of Alabama.[560] This flag was carried by the battery in its battles from that time forward, continuing after it became Dent's Battery, and until the end of the war. When the battery was disbanded following the surrender, Hubert took the flag home to Eufaula with him, and it survives to this day in the hands of his family.

220

By August 6, 1862, Hubert had arrived in camp 10 miles from Chattanooga, ahead of the battery, and wrote Anna. The brigade to which the Battery was attached at this point was being commanded by Hubert's old friend from Eufaula, Col. Henry D. Clayton. Hubert has heard that Maria Young, accompanied by her sister-in-law, Ada, has gone to Knoxville to visit Henry, who is detailed to the headquarters there of Gen. Kirby Smith, commander of the Department of Tennessee. Hubert is ambitious for advancement, and complains about his lack of promotion thus far.

"Camp Near Tinersville, Tenn
August 6th, 1862

"My own Sweet Jewel
    I am in camp once more after a rather long and fatigueing trip of eight days. I am on the Knoxville rail-road and about ten miles from Chattanooga— right in the woods with plenty of good water and a country that does seem to afford a few things more than that portion of Miss in which we have been encamped.

    There are not a great many troops here yet I suppose it will be ten days before all arrive even if they do in that time. I do not expect our horses will be here under ten days and maybe longer time. I have no boy here to cook for me so I am boarding at a house near Camp. Rather common folks, fare quite ordinary. I have had as much fruit as I could eat on this trip and so far have had plenty in camp, but we only reached here yesterday evening.

    I have been quite busy since my arrival and indeed have not got straight yet. A Camp to clear up and my guns to get in Camp. You see I have no horses, and every thing of that kind to do with only half the Company. The weather is very warm—it seems warmer than ever, though it is now August.

    Clayton is in command of the Brigade. He is the only Colonel here and Gardner has not arrived. I wish I had known that I was coming up in this country in time to have let you know it for you could have come along with Maria & Ada—although you would not have seen me unless you had remained in Chattanooga, as I am over one hundred miles from Knoxville. I hope however that we will be going that way soon and in the mean time I might get board for you somewhere here in the country.

    I have been told that there is a man named Dent near here who is pretty sick and I believe I will go out and see what sort of people they are and speak for board for you. What say you Darling? Well, rest assured my love that as soon as I get where I think I will remain for any length of time and where you can be comfortable I will send for you. You do not know how anxious I am to see you. I hope the letter I mailed you in Montgomery reached you safely and if it did you had better take care of it so you can use it in coming to see me. You can bring one of the girls with you if they will come, and I hope soon to be able to have you with me.

I saw Capt. [Reuben] Kolb and a good many Eufaula men at Dalton, Ga. on my way up here. Jim Hunter told me he had seen you and the [boy] recently and that all were well. They were waiting there for transportation to Louden, Tenn. They seemed very glad to see me.

I do not think we will remain idle long. I have just seen an <u>Extra</u> published in Chattanooga in which there is a good deal of stirring news and I think Old Bragg will keep the thing in motion. This is as you know a rough mountainous country and it will be pretty hard on artillery horses but I hope I will be able to get hold of some new ones soon. I am out of boots and am very anxious to get into another Yankee camp and get hold of a pair or pull a good pair off a dead Yankee either will suit me very well. I will save at least $25 by it as that is what boots are selling for all up in this country. I do not expect however to have another such a chance as I had at Shiloh.

<u>Sugar</u> I have not heard from you in a long time. I hope I will get a letter soon. I ought to have one on the way now in answer to my Montgomery letter. I am glad Maria has gone up to see Henry. I know it will do them both so much good. I hope I will get a chance to see them before a great while. I hardly know what to say to you about directing my letters but I expect I will get them as soon by directing them to Chattanooga giving, as I wrote, the Brigade and Division. I will try and get this mailed today or tomorrow. Flewellen has gone home on 20 days [leave]. I wish I could go. Kolb told me that there was some talk of making one of Reeves companies…infantry instead of artillery. I do not expect that he will like that much.

I believe I have lost all hope of promotion and think it is fated for me to go through this war as a 1st Lieut. There is no doubt that <u>fortune is blind</u>— what do you think? I hope the boy will be more fortunate in such things.

Well I must hasten to a close. I am seated out in a large grove which I am having cleaned up all round me. My men are as busy as beavers. It is just about 9 o'clock but warm Oh—the sun is indeed severe. I saw Van Houten [the music teacher from Eufaula] also on my way up. He was hunting up Maj. Johnson.

Well Dearest I believe I have written all the news about camp and myself & will close. I will write again in a day or two as soon as I get things a little better regulated. It will take me three days to get every thing to running smooth. You see our fixing up camp is just like a family moving. Every thing gets into confusion and it takes some time to get things in good fix again. I expect I was the <u>dirtiest</u> fellow when I reached here you ever saw, travelling in a box car or on platform cars. All the dust and cinders from the engine had full play on me.

I am very anxious to hear from you & hope I will soon. My love to all the family & all friends, and with much love & many kisses for you & the boy I close. Your own old Dear   Hubert"

27
Foray Into Kentucky

"I went in the country to-day the first time since I reached this camp. I found more people favorable to our cause than I thought this country contained."

Hubert Dent to Anna

Bragg's plans for Tennessee included his cooperating with Major General Kirby Smith, Commander of the Department of East Tennessee, in which Bragg's army was now located. This was slightly awkward, because, although Bragg outranked Smith, Smith had an independent command. But they worked together to avoid problems as much as possible. Bragg's initial intention had been for their joint forces to proceed against Buell with the goal of retaking Nashville and Middle Tennessee. However, as the operation evolved, it became instead an invasion of Kentucky. Kirby Smith began moving first, leaving Knoxville on August 14 to proceed against Federal Gen. Morgan at the Cumberland Gap (north of Knoxville on the Tennessee-Kentucky border). Bragg waited at Chattanooga for the remainder of his army and equipment to arrive from Tupelo.

In an undated letter written to Anna about his time, before leaving the Chattanooga area, Hubert expresses the hope and expectation that they will be moving on Nashville:

[Near Chattanooga, Fall 1862]

We had a report a day or two ago that Smith had captured Morgan at the [Cumberland Gap] – but it turned out to be untrue. I saw Genl Buckner at Chattanooga the other night. He looked rather thin but very much like he might be a General. He is a medium sized man - hair looked at night rather light – rather a thin beard, he wore mustaches – had a fine grey eye. He will take command of a Division [u]....I expect from what Pugh said that Congress will raise the conscript act so as to embrace men up to 45 yrs. Substitutes will the be higher than ever ....I hope to [get to] Nashville and that I will stop [there long] enough to have you come and see [me]. ... You may soon begin to look out for us either marching or fighting somewhere between here and Nashville..."

Finding a direct assault on Gen. Morgan at the Cumberland Gap to be impracticable, Kirby Smith went around him and proceeded to Richmond, Kentucky, where, on August 30, he routed the union force of General Nelson, capturing 4000 Yankees and all of his supplies, including 10,000 small arms. He moved on to occupy Lexington and Frankfurt, made cavalry raids on Louisville and Covington (across the river from Cincinnati), and controlled central Kentucky throughout September.

---

[u] Hubert would meet Gen. Buckner again in September 1896, when Hubert and other "Sound Money" Democrats in convention in Indianapolis nominated Buckner as their candidate for vice-president.

Bragg had departed Chattanooga headed north on August 28, with his destination still vague and dependent on developments. Buell assumed Bragg was proceeding to attack Nashville and marched his entire army there to defend it. Bragg continued north through middle Tennessee's Sequatchie Valley, through Pikeville and Sparta, and on to Carthage and Gainesboro on the Cumberland River. He could now turn left toward Nashville, or he could continue north into Kentucky.

In Hubert's next letter to Anna, after a grueling march through the mountains, Bragg's army has reached the Cumberland River, but Hubert still believes (or hopes) that the destination will be Nashville. We learn from this letter that Hubert's younger brother, George Hatch Dent, who has been fighting as a private in the First Maryland Infantry until his unit disbanded, has now come south to join Hubert in Robertson's Battery in the Army of Tennessee.

"Camp in Sequatchie Valley
Tenn. Sept 2nd, 1862

Well I am on my way towards Nashville and have travelled this far. The Division crossed Walden's ridge yesterday and pretty severe crossing it was. We went up up up until it looked as if we were on our way to the moon and then after travelling five or six miles over such roads as we ordinarily find we commenced going down down down until it looked like we were on our way to the lower regions. We reached our present camp about half-an-hour before sunset yesterday and will remain here today from present indications.

I received orders about 12 o'clock at night on Wednesday to leave at once for Harrison's landing. I however put it off until day light and then left for the Tenn river—crossed over that day and camped about two miles from the river. From there I sent back a letter which I hope you received.

Well I will give you a short account of our trip. We left our camp on this side the river on Saturday—travelled every day since—on Sunday we reached the foot of the Mountain (Walden's ridge)—and commenced going up. There were so many wagons on the road that only one section went up that evening and only half way that evening. We waited very late when finding there was no chance to get up - I laid down and went to sleep on my saddle blanket and overcoat—no supper—next morning no breakfast except a year of corn - and no dinner. Supper last night went first rate—rained a little yesterday.

I think the road we travelled much worse than the road up look-out [Mountain] - A great many more rocks – and very large flat rocks and the horses would slip down on them. In one place the hill was so steep that the [wagons] would slide down very rapidly although locked. The horses would fall down but fortunately no accident. The people along the road stared at us in silent wonder. In only one place did I see a handkerchief wave. I think, how ever, that handkerchiefs are rather scarce articles among most of these people. They seem to be poor and ignorant.

We are now camped in a very pretty valley [Sequatchie], Walden's ridge on one side and the Cumberland Mts on the other. We are right on a creek bank under some very large and fine shade trees. I expect we will commence crossing the Cumberland this evening or tomorrow. Twenty-two miles across - The Yankees are said to be holding one of the passes through which Genl. Buckner has to pass and some say they are occupying McMinneville and others that they have abandoned it. Gen.l Cheathim's Division is crossing the Mts today.

There is very little for men or horses in this country so far. The Yankees have foraged it pretty thoroughly. I hope we will get some where after a while where we can find something—our horses are suffering as well as the men. I am now very well - much better than while I was in camp at Tyner's.

Well Darling I never received your letters until just before I left my last camp—never knew any thing about your being sick. I hope my Love that you did not have any more chills and that you are very well now. I feel right badly Darling when I read your letters. I know my Love that you are very anxious to see me and I am very anxious to see you but somehow I can never fix it up. Had I received your letters sooner I would have sent for you any how—but I could not get a place that I thought you would be comfortable in and I did not send for you.

I am writing this but do not know when this will be mailed. I will add some as I go along and send it the first chance I have. I have some things to attend to and for the present must close. Many kisses, much love for the boy and yourself—so goodby Your old Dear Hubert

[Additions to the letter, written in pencil]
I have a chance to send this & saved it. George joined me to-day he is very well. We leave here in the morning.

Direct your letters as before except instead of directing to any place [say] "in the Field." And I hope they [will] be forward for me. Good by love to all & much love and many kisses to you and the boy. Your own Dear Hubert

Kirby Smith, already in Kentucky, wrote Bragg to encourage him to come into Kentucky and join forces to draw Buell into Kentucky, so they could fight him together. Bragg accepted the suggestion and started a direct march into Kentucky, where he hoped that a decisive victory would encourage pro-Southern Kentuckians to provide additional manpower by enlisting in his army. It did not take Buell long to see Bragg's intentions. Buell left Nashville and started marching into Kentucky also, his objective being Louisville. By Sept. 14, Buell had reached Bowling Green. Bragg avoided contact with him and proceeded to Munfordville, where he surrounded the 4000 man federal garrison there. Federal Gen. Wilder was in a hopeless position, and on Sept 17, surrendered the Munfordville Fort, the entire garrison, his artillery, stores, and 5000 small arms. The South was jubilant over this success, so soon after Kirby Smith's defeat of Nelson at Richmond, Kentucky.

With Buell at Bowling Green 30 miles south of Munfordville, Bragg's army was now astride Buell's communications and his line of march from Bowling Green to Louisville. Bragg was in a favorable position to turn and fight Buell, which is what he had come into Kentucky to do. He had the momentum of a recent victory, he was not heavily outnumbered, and he had Buell where he wanted him. But incredibly, Bragg failed to give fight. Having created the situation he wanted for a major blow, Bragg inexplicably let the opportunity slip through his fingers. On September 19, he announced his decision to march on to Bardstown, without contesting Buell's advance to Louisville and reinforcements. One military authority observed, "Here was the first exhibition of that vacillation, that fatal irresolution, which was to wither the bright hopes his promises and his previous action had aroused…the strange contrast exhibited by the nerve and purpose of his plan and the timidity and vacillation of his conduct."[561] This was to be the story of Bragg's time as commander of the Army of Tennessee.

Writing Anna, even Hubert, who is normally loyal to Bragg, questioned his strategy. Hubert had received a letter from his brother-in-law, Henry Young, who was detailed to Gen. Kirby Smith's East Tennessee Departmental Headquarters, which may explain why Henry could arrange to send the letter to Hubert by courier. Hubert doesn't know whether Henry is now with Kirby Smith in Lexington, or still at the headquarters in Knoxville. Mr. Cotten is the Methodist minister in Eufaula.

"Camp near Bardstown Ky
Sept. 27th, 1862

"My own Dear Wife:
    I am writing late at night by a short piece of borrowed candle having just learned that a mail would be sent tomorrow.
    First Darling I am very well. I went in the country to-day the first time since I reached this camp. I found more people favorable to our cause than I thought this country contained. I made some purchases for our mess - prices more reasonable than I ever found them before. A young Lady gave me a secession flag. Don't you feel jealous—especially as she singled me out of three Gentlemen the other two being single ones. But that is not all—she knew I was married—another promised to come and see me at our camp. But I have just learned that we are to move camp tomorrow so I think it doubtful whether she will find us or not.
    It seems to me that we are going to hunt a good camp and remain here for this winter—that seems to me rather strange. I thought we would certainly take Louisville but I suppose Gen.l. Bragg knows best.
    The weather so far quite pleasant. We had some rain today not much. Water is getting scarce. George has about recovered. We have a man very sick and I am afraid he will die – one of the Rifles named Thompson – you never knew him.

I have sent you three letters since I left Tyner's. I hope you received them all. I expect we will have some regular means of communicating, at least I hope so.

I feel very curious to know what we are doing to-day. I think however that we are going to hold the principal portion of Ky and give the people a chance to do something for themselves and if we increase our army much by Kentuckians joining us that we will try and get possession of the entire state.

I would like very much to hear all the particulars of the fights in Md but we hear nothing except through northern sources and that we cannot depend on.

I received a letter to-day from Henry [Young, Hubert's brother-in-law], a courier brought it. He also sent me two newspapers and hoped we would soon meet on the banks of the Ohio. In this I am afraid we will be disappointed. He was very well but long before this reaches you you will have later dates from him.

I feel Darling a long way from home and a <u>very very</u> long way from my own Precious Darling. May God preserve and protect us and bring us together again in his own good time. We are in his hands my Love and let us try as far as we can and be cheerful and contented. I would give almost any thing to see you and our dear boy and indeed the whole family. When I will I have no idea.

If we are to remain here long I will try and get home if the communications are opened on the line of rail roads. And Darling if you find you can come and see me and feel willing to suffer some privations & come! God knows how my heart yearns to see you of late. I have dreamed of you every night, dreamed all sorts of things of our courting days of our married days. I have been right melancholy lately but I know this will not do and I try to shake it off. This evening when I returned I was told there was a letter for me and I thought of course it was from home and my Dearest my heart leaped for joy and I must confess I was disappointed when I found it was not from you. Now Dearest this is not saying I was not glad to hear from Henry for I was. I hope soon to get a letter or letters from you.

Henry was at Knoxville when he wrote. Kirby Smith is in Lexington. I do not know whether he is with him or not. I will answer his letter any how and send it to him the first opportunity. My candle is nearly gone. I will write as long as I can and finish in the morning. A good many of our men are sick, I mean in our army. They suffered a good deal on our march. I still preserve my usual health.

Remember me to all friends. I heard through Henry of [Mrs.] Cotton's death. Poor Mr. Cotton [the Methodist minister] I know he must have suffered a great deal. Give lots of love to all the family and tell them how anxious I am to see them. Oh! it has been such a long time since I saw you and that is not the worst, it may yet be so long before I do see you. May Heavens blessings rest on you Dearest with much much love - light went out – to you and our Dear boy with many kisses to you both. I must close. It is

227

now Sunday morning & we are busy moving so good by my love. May God bless you all. Your own old Dear who loves you better & better every day. Hubert"

Buell arrived in Louisville on Sept 27. Meanwhile, Bragg ordered Kirby Smith to Frankfurt, where Bragg staged an inaugural ceremony to induct Richard Haws as governor of Kentucky under a Confederate government. Kentucky had been officially accepted as one of the Confederate States of America; it had representatives in the Confederate Congress, and it had a star in the Confederate flag. Bragg sought to cultivate public opinion for the Southern cause by establishing a *de facto* Confederate government in Frankfurt.

On October 1, Buell moved out of Louisville toward Bardstown to give battle, but as a feint, he sent a division under Gen. Sill toward Frankfurt. Sill's approach broke up the Frankfurt inauguration. Bragg fell for the feint, thinking Buell's main attack would be against Kirby Smith at Frankfurt. Bragg moved 36,000 of his men toward Frankfurt, leaving Gen. Polk with only 16,000 at Bardstown. Despite competent advice from his experienced commanders, Bragg insisted on leaving his forces divided in this manner. As planned, Buell did not proceed to Frankfurt, but concentrated his main army of 58,000 near Bardstown, at the nearby village of Perryville, Kentucky, and that is where the battle occurred on October 8.

Despite being badly outnumbered due to Bragg's misjudgment, the Battle of Perryville was a complete victory for the Confederates. Gen. Polk drove the Federals back over a mile, broken and disorganized. Two Union Generals were killed, and large numbers of officers were wounded. The Confederate infantry was skillfully supported by the artillery, but unfortunately, neither Hubert and George Dent nor Robertson's Battery got to participate in this victory. They were off with the troops Bragg took to oppose the Federal feint; Robertson's Battery was in a skirmish with Gen. Sill's Division, miles away.

At Perryville, the Confederate soldiers thought they would renew the fight the next morning, but instead, Bragg belatedly decided it was now time to concentrate his forces. Kirby Smith's forces were now at Harrodsburg, and Bragg ordered his army to Harrodsburg to join Kirby Smith there. Thus, on October 10, Bragg was now able to seek battle with his greatest available force. The next day, Buell arrived at Harrodsburg with his entire army, once again setting the stage for the decisive battle Bragg had come to Kentucky for. Kirby Smith, as soon as he joined Bragg, urged a drive on the enemy: "for God's sake, General, let us fight Buell here". After first indicating that he would do that, Bragg's resolution failed him again, and he did not fight. Military historians view this as a loss of a great opportunity.[562] Instead, Bragg starting moving south. Buell could not believe his adversary was retreating. On October 13, Bragg began his withdrawal from Kentucky entirely. When they arrived back in Tennessee, Bragg's men had marched a thousand miles, fought and won a bloody battle while outnumbered, and were back where they started two months before. The results were exactly nothing, except for the further deterioration of Bragg's reputation.

Back in Tennessee, Hubert wrote Anna from near Knoxville. He had seen her brother Henry in Knoxville, as well as Eufaula resident Charles Kliffmuller, who, like Henry, was also detailed to Kirby Smith's headquarters there. Early in the war Hubert wrote of unpleasant details to Anna only infrequently, but here he tells her of hanging "sixteen Yankee bushwhackers". He badly wants a furlough, and jokes about taking one without leave. He will later get a furlough, but at an inopportune time.

"Camp Eight Miles from Knoxville, Tenn
Oct 25th, 1862

"My own Dear Wife:
       I wrote a few lines and sent them by Mr. Kliffmuller three days ago. I hope they will reach you safely. I have some idea that our winter destination or other destination for the winter is Corinth or that vicinity. I am going to try very hard to get home before I go there. I have been put off & put off until I feel somewhat reckless and if I do not get home one way I will another.
       I don't know how long we will remain here but several days I expect. Man and horses are very much fatigued and worn down. The men are actually emaciated from long marching and hard living - for four days our men had for bread—corn. The officers among the number. A Supper of parched corn and pork does not go so badly after all.
       Our Division is greatly reduced in numbers since we entered Ky and I think the men will not be fit for duty under a months recruiting.
       About the only thing I have to show for my Ky campaign is a good looking bay horse which I got up there and which I want to send as a present to Mr. Young [Hubert's father-in-law, Edward B. Young] when I get nearer Eufaula. You need not tell him as some accident might happen to him, But I will certainly send him. If he needs him he can keep him if he does not he can sell him. I was offered $250 for him yesterday – cash but I refused to sell him because I want to send him to Mr. Young. He would be worth a good deal more than $250 in Eufaula.
       Horse stealing is quite common in the army and I had my horse stolen from me one night but found him next morning. I saw Pat Powers yesterday going to Knoxville hunting his horse which some one had stolen from him at the Gap. He was well and said his company would be at the Gap this winter. I heard that the whole of Hilliards legion would be there.
       I went into Ky thinking I would get every thing I needed but I came out not a single bit better than I went in. My shirts are wearing out – my boots in the same fix and hat utterly gone. Unless I get some clothes soon I do not know what I will do. If I had got into a fight as I expected I would have supplied myself abundantly.
       Well Darling it has been now nearly nine months since I was at home. It seems to me it has been at the least two years. It seems hard that the best part of my life should be spent in the army. I hope I will get a letter or letters from you soon.
       The weather is warm and pleasant for October much more so than one would expect. Henry was looking very well and expects to go home soon.

229

If I can't get a regular leave and we go to Chattanooga and all around to Corinth I am going home by getting off the cars and go – and run the risk of being Court martialed. What do you say to that? I hope I will get a regular leave however and be saved all that trouble.

Dearest I have not written for so long that I do not know how to write. Oh! Darling if you can send my coat (overcoat) to me I wish you would but I hope to get home and then I can get it myself.

I am so tired so very tired of this horrible war. What think you Darling of sixteen men being hung in one pile? Well sixteen Yankee bushwhackers were hung at the Cumberland river on our retreat. They were taken by our cavalry and it is said they had been following up our army on this whole march. This is certainly the most horrible war the world has ever seen. What a horrible condition society will be left in when it closes.

Well Love I will leave a short space to add a few lines more my Love to all much love and many kisses for you & the boy. Your own old Dear Hubert

Darling: It is now Sunday morning Oct 26th, 1862 and the ground is covered with snow. What do you think of that? I am in Knoxville with Henry Reeves & Bob Hunter. I do not feel so very well this morning. Don't forget Darling to send my overcoat if you can find it to me. You will find out where we will go. I don't know yet where we will go. It is snowing some yet & pretty cold. Well goodby Darling. I will write soon again as I can – my love to all much love & many kisses to for you & the boy.   Hubert"

For its winter quarters, Bragg's army was centered in Murphreesboro, 30 miles southeast of Yankee-occupied Nashville, with the army fanned out in a wide semicircle facing Nashville, permitting Bragg to watch the enemy and concentrate if necessary. Murphreesboro provided the army with some social life, but Lt. Hubert Dent wanted leave to go to Eufaula. On October 29, 1862, he submitted this request through channels:[563]

"Sir:
"I have the honor to ask for a leave of absence for twenty-five days or as near that time as the good of the service will allow.

S. H. Dent
Robertson's Battery"

Captain Robertson duly forwarded the request with this recommendation that it be granted:

"Respectfully forwarded. All the Company officers are present and for duty. This officer has had one leave since the organization of the Company but was recalled three weeks before its expiration.
F. W. Robertson, Capt Cmdg Co."

Despite Robertson's favorable recommendation, the request is marked "Not Approved", by Major General B. F. Cheatham.

If the leave had been granted, Hubert would have been present with Anna in Eufaula for another happy family event. A baby daughter was born to Henry and Maria Young on November 13, 1862, their second child.[564] Named "Julia", she was Edward and Ann's fourth grandchild (after Henry, Jr.; Will's son, Charlie; and Anna's Eddie). Henry was granted leave from Gen. Kirby Smith's Knoxville headquarters to come home for the occasion, (although we don't know whether he arrived in time for the birth or not.) Henry remained in Eufaula until November 23 before returning to Knoxville.[565] Perhaps because of wartime conditions and the brevity of Henry's furlough, the normal Young practice of prompt baptism was suspended, and Julia's baptism was postponed, as that of her brother Henry, Jr. had been. Unfortunately, sad circumstances would accompany the baptism of the two children four months later.

In Murfreesboro, a visit from President Jefferson Davis was the occasion for receptions and a military review. Confederate cavalry commander, Gen. John Hunt Morgan, married a Murphreesboro lady, the service being performed by Gen. Polk, who was also an Episcopal bishop. Morgan was fresh from his dramatic cavalry raid on a Federal brigade behind enemy lines at Hartsville, Tennessee, 50 miles north of Nashville. On December 7, with only 1300 men, Morgan captured 1,834 Yankees, wounded 204, and killed 58, receiving total casualties himself of only 139.

We learn from Hubert's next letter to Anna that Gen. Morgan was not the only soldier with matrimonial designs. Hubert's captain, Felix Robertson, has gone to Tuscaloosa to get married. Apparently, when Captain Robertson and the battery stopped to rest in Tuscaloosa enroute from Tupelo five months earlier, Felix fell under the spell of Miss Mary Leland, as she and her friends were sewing the new Confederate flag for the battery. But alas, Hubert reports that Felix has returned to camp wifeless, amid unanswered questions. The mystery goes unresolved. Further, we find Hubert's brother, George, in correspondence with Ada, Hubert's seventeen-year-old sister-in-law. Is Cupid at work here? Maybe, but some years from now when Cupid fires his arrow for George, it will not hit Ada, but will strike nearby at Ada's sister, Helen. Hubert is exultant over Morgan's exploits, but depressed over conditions in Mississippi, which we will return to later. Much of Hubert's letter relates to his eagerness for a 30-day furlough, and his plans to obtain one within the next eight or ten days. His report of the "general impression" that there will be no fight soon is, unfortunately, dead wrong.

> "Camp near Murfreesboro Tenn
> December 11th, 1862
>
> "My own Darling Nannie
>   As Thom Hardman will leave for home to-day I write. It is a bright beautiful morning the sun shines brightly and joyously and the ground is covered with frost and hard frozen. I wrote by Col Clayton day before yesterday....

231

Robertson reached home this morning. Not married. This is a singular story. I will tell you when I see you if you do not hear it sooner. However I know you will not hear all the inside particulars. He went to Tuscaloosa Ala. The Lady Miss Leland married a Lieut Haine. Robertson retired from the Contest so he says. He has not finished his story yet.

George wrote to Ada yesterday. I hope my letters go better and quicker than yours come. Well Darling Robertson has returned and I shall ask for a leave as soon as I can get one forwarded. Whether I shall succeed in getting one or not I can't tell. I am very very anxious to get home and am getting more anxious every day.

I have no news to write. Morgan's affair at Hartsville was brilliant. He took more prisoners than he had men Twenty-one hundred and ten. The Yankee prisoners were in Murfreesboro Tenn yesterday being paroled. They were a dirty rough looking set of men. I thought some of our soldiers looked hard and rough. But these prisoners looked as rough as I ever saw any of our men look. They were rather better clothed than most of our men.

This is very fine weather, as fine as one could wish. The Company is very healthy. Only one man sick and his is a chronic case. I have not been very well for some days, have taken cold and it has fallen on my bowels. I do not apprehend any thing serious. I feel much better this morning.

Well Darling I shall make out my application to-day for a leave of thirty days whether I get it or not, and I am going to give a Chapter of reasons as long as my arm. I am going also to see Col Garner, Bragg's Adgt. Gen.l. Gen.l.

[Confederate General] Joe Johnston hear left this morning for Miss. I hear it rumored that we are going there. But I can't say any thing about it. From what I hear it looks as if some one ought to go there and stop the headway of the Yankees. They will soon have all the State.

Bruton [one of the battery lieutenants] has just received a box and I have got molasses candy all over this side of the paper. None of their boxes come up to mine. The rice and potatoes are heartily enjoyed, by all hands. Well Darling I am so full of my leave that I can hardly write. I hope I may get a letter from you to-day.

The rail road between here and Bridgeport [Alabama] is in a horrible fix The cars are full of lice and no seats. A gentleman who brought his wife over the road said that as his wife is now here he is glad of it. But that he would not take her over it again for any thing. Said if we had to leave here that he would sooner leave his wife behind and run the risk of the Yankees getting her than send her over the road.

I will finish this letter at my leisure as Hardman will not leave before this evening. I tell you a secret. He asked for permission to go home to fulfill a promise of marriage. His lady lives in Montgomery. Every body to their taste.

I am sorry Darling that I have no nice uniform coat and pants and vest to wear home. I think I shall order a suit in Augusta. It will cost me one hundred and thirty dollars. Rather heavy and I hardly know whether I can stand it or not. I expect you will have the same opinion of my appearance that Bill McTyer had when you see me. I am rough looking and hard looking and I am not certain that my friends will know me when I get home. My hands are black and rough looking and inclined to be chapped. My beard is haggard and rough. And my clothes are about on a par with the rest. I have set around a log fire and been smoked so much that I am in a fine state of preservation however and look as if I would keep for a long time.

I am glad Robertson has returned but sorry he is not married. If I remain in the Company I want him to marry.

Every thing has quieted down here about a fight and the General impression now is that we will not fight. Cheathim made a reconnaissance some days ago but found the enemy too well posted and too strong to effect any thing and therefore fell back to his original position.

Well I will finish this later in the day, I must attend to some other matters now. Love and kisses to you and the boy, old Dear.

Well Darling it is now after dinner and I will finish my letter. The day continues fine. The finest we have had lately. Hardman is flying round trying to get money enough to get off before to-morrow.

I heard to-day that President Davis was in Chattanooga and that he had dispatched for General Johnston. But I hear so much that turns out to be untrue that I don't know whether to believe it or not. The department of the west is certainly in a very bad fix. Pemberton's army seems not to be worth any thing or rather the army of Van Dorn and Price. The fight at Corinth turns out to be a very serious disaster. I see foreign intervention is again talked of. If it is coming I wish it would hasten I should be delighted to be able to spend the winter at home. At least the balance of it.

Robertson is blowing round about his trip – evading the many questions asked him about it. Well Darling I must close. No letter from you again to-day. "What can the matter be." I am very anxious to hear from you. Give my love to all the family. If I have good luck I will be at home about eight or ten days after you receive this. Much love and many kisses for the boy and my own Darling wife. Your own old Dear   Hubert"

Hubert's "chapter of reasons as long as his arm" worked. Not having had leave for a year, i. e. since Christmas of 1861, Hubert succeeded in obtaining a furlough during the season of Christmas, 1862, and departed for Eufaula. On December 25, the Confederates in Murfreesboro observed traditional Christmas festivities. But the Yankees in Nashville did not.

28
Capt. Felix Robertson; A Controversial Artillery Officer

"Robertson has been soundly criticized by modern writers, who describe him as an overly ambitious Bragg crony who was not beyond lying."

Larry J. Daniel, *Cannoneers in Gray*

In Nashville, Gen. Buell had been replaced by Gen. Rosecrans as the Federal commander. On December 26, 1862, Rosecrans' troops began moving toward Murfreesboro. Immediately informed by his scouts, Bragg quickly assembled his force, and by December 30, the two armies were lined up outside Murfreesboro across Stones River, ready to fight. At daybreak on the 31st, the Confederates launched their attack.

Since his days at Fort Barrancas, Hubert Dent had entertained the fear that he would miss an important battle by being absent on furlough at the wrong time. Now it happened. Neither Hubert nor anyone else had anticipated that Rosecrans would provoke a fight in mid-winter. Later Hubert would record that he had been present and participated in every battle that his battery participated in, except for Murphreesboro, when he was in Eufaula on leave. Although his ambition caused him be chagrined at missing the battle, it may have been in Hubert's best interests not to be present, for it was here that his captain, Felix Robertson, became embroiled in a controversy involving the battery and the highest leaders of the Army of Tennessee.

The Battle of Murfreesboro, or Stones River, was in effect two battles, consisting of two engagements separated by a day of inaction. On the first day, December 31, 1862, the Confederates badly whipped Rosecrans. The Yankees were driven back 4 or 5 miles, and the Confederates held the field at the end of the day.

Robertson's Battery saw extensive action on the 31st. At 4:00 P. M. the Battery was firing on enemy skirmishers in its front when the 2nd Minnesota and 8th Wisconsin counterattacked. One of Robertson's caissons was struck, causing a large explosion. An Illinois regiment made a dash for Robertson's guns. Ironically, who should arrive to support Robertson's Battery at this time of need but the Eufaula Light Artillery, led by Lieutenant W. A. McDuffie. The Eufaula battery immediately succeeded in disabling one of the guns of the Wisconsin Battery, and with help from the 154th Tennessee, the Yankee charge was repulsed.[566] It is safe to conclude that the Eufaulians in Robertson's Battery were never happier to see their neighbors from home. Fourteen men of Robertson's Battery were killed or wounded.

Bragg thought it likely that the Federals would retreat during the night. In fact, Rosecrans did come close to retreating, but was informed, erroneously, that his retreat route was cut off, so he stayed in place that night. Neither side made any effort to resume the contest the next day, New Years Day. Bragg did nothing until the afternoon of January 2, 1863, when he ordered Breckenridge's Corps to assault and take a ridge on the Federal left which he considered important. Breckenridge protested, pointing out that the Federals held the high ground behind the ridge he was supposed to take, and his men would be raked by fire. Bragg was adamant, so at 4:00 Breckenridge advanced.

Bragg had assembled 53 guns, half his artillery, including Robertson's Battery, to support Breckenridge's assault. Felix Robertson had command, not only of his own battery, but additional guns as well, totaling 10 pieces in all. Just as the time arrived for the assault to begin, Captain Robertson and Gen. Breckenridge got into a sharp dispute over the intended role of the artillery. In a later report, Robertson quotes Breckenridge as ordering that the artillery advance in combination with the infantry, positioned between two lines of infantry. Robertson refused to advance in this manner, contending that his instructions from Gen. Bragg were "to wait until the infantry had crowned the crest, and then to rush up and occupy it." Robertson quoted himself as arguing that the arrangement ordered by Breckenridge would cause crowding of the field and misdirection of fire, and that in the event of a reversal, every gun might be lost. While the views that Robertson attributes to himself had merit, later circumstances have caused some writers to question the accuracy of his version of this argument, or even whether it occurred at all. In any event, two things are fairly clear: first, when Breckenridge's infantry and artillery advanced, Felix Robertson and the ten guns under his command stayed behind; secondly, Robertson had explicit orders that when the ridge had been taken, his guns were to take certain specified positions on the ridge in order to support the infantry. [567]

At first the charge succeeded, and the Yankees on the ridge fled down the other side. But as the Confederates pursued over the ridge, they came within range of massed Federal artillery on the high ground beyond, which started blasting the Confederates with devastating effect, somewhat as Breckenridge has predicted. Confederate artillery support on the ridge was now crucial, and it was imperative that Robertson bring his guns forward and attempt to neutralize the Federal guns. But Robertson could not be found. A staff officer vainly searched the field for him. [568]

The Southerners streamed back up the slope in disorder, receiving some protection from the Confederate artillery that remained on the slope firing at the Yankee guns. As the survivors headed back to the starting point of the assault, Robertson placed his guns there and assisted in protecting the fleeing infantry and deterring the Yankees from pursuing. Both sides bivouacked where they had begun, except that Breckenridge now had 1700 more casualties.

On the night of January 3, Bragg retreated. The men marched away, cold and dispirited. It was the old Bragg story that the soldiers could never understand: fight, win, and fall back. Bragg established a new headquarters 30 miles away at Tullahoma. On the morning of the January 4, Rosecrans was surprised and delighted to find Bragg gone, and made no effort to follow.

Hubert returned from his furlough in late January, after having stopped in Columbus to visit Anna's Uncle William, Aunt Ellen, and their family. Back in camp, Hubert wrote Anna about the battle as related to him by Robertson. Either Hubert decided not to write about Robertson's controversy with Gen. Breckenridge, or Robertson omitted mentioning this to Hubert, or as some historians have speculated, it never occurred and was manufactured later in amended after-action reports. Controversy over Bragg's performance at Murfreesboro would result in Robertson's becoming involved in intrigue at the highest levels. There is no indication that he confided in Hubert about these circumstances. Also, Robertson may have overstated to Hubert the "credit" that the battery received at Murfreesboro.

Camp Near Shelbyville, Tenn
Jan. 28, 1863

My Own Darling,

I arrived in Camp last night safe and sound. Left Columbus on Friday morning and came directly through. I saw Alfred and Bob Lockhart [Columbus cousins] after writing to you there. Both well - Alfred looking rather thin - he reported his Mother and Sister much better - all the rest well.

I made the connection at every point. In Chattanooga I met up with McOliver Couric and_____ I found an officer in charge of the peace on the train whom I knew and he very kindly gave us all seats in the Ladies car. He was Lieut Tanner, a brother of Bragg's Adj. Genl.

About twenty miles this side of Chattanooga the rear car of our train ran off the track and turned a complete somersault down a bank about thirty feet high. It was full of soldiers - no one in the car seriously hurt. One man who was on the platform of the car in front of it, seeing the car going and thinking his own would go, attempted to get off by jumping. He fell and before he could get out of the way the car fell on him and mashed him so badly that it was thought he would die - Fortunately I was on the front car. Notwithstanding this we reached the junction of the Shelbyville road about one hour after the usual time.

I saw Mrs. Pope and Mrs. Clayton, the old Lady, in Tullahoma. [They] went inside the Yankee lines but Rosenkranz refused them permission to visit the hospital to see Joe Clayton and ordered them out of the lines. They were waiting to see if they could not get a letter from him or about him.

Did Mr. Cottrell succeed in finding his step-son and did he get in the Yankee lines?

I found the company camped in a mud hole - we have Corinth No 2 here except we have good water. Robertson is not with the Company. he would have returned but Genl Polk went off on leave to see his family - Bragg has never been to Richmond and is at Tullahoma.

The Company lost in the fight four men killed and seventeen wounded, the slightest wound being a shot through the arm. There were five others with some slight scratches. All the wounded are off at hospitals and some home. John Gillespie, a son of Mrs._____, was wounded. I expect he will go to Eufaula – Joe Watson who formerly clerked for Kendall was also wounded. These are the only ones from that section.

I have not seen Robertson yet. I expect he will be down this evening. He stays right in Shelbyville.

It was raining last night when I arrived and very dark - consequently I could not see what sort of a place Shelbyville is - we are twenty-five miles from Murphreesboro and our pickets are eighteen miles from here, consequently the Yankees are twenty seven miles from Murfreesboro so far - I hear that Bragg has only twenty-five thousand effective men and if that is so, and I don't see where he can get more from, I expect we will fall back as soon as the Yankees advance, but when they will advance seems doubtful. We have a good many supplies at Tullahoma but only one day's rations up there - So you see we are certainly not going to try and hold this country. We are in advance of Duck River which was said to be our line of defense –

I have seen no one out of the Company yet. This [is] Sunday and I shall remain close in camp – I owe a good many letters at home and will try and write them all up in a while - You may stir McKenna up about my uniform. I believe I cannot do better than take it - I must have some thing in the shape of a uniform or I will be taken for a conscript - you can pay him. I will send you five hundred dollars as soon as I draw my pay and think I can send it safely – I expect you can get [Thom] Brannon to bring my uniform. He can box it up and get transportation for the box from Lee Johnston having it marked "soldier's clothes" and then he will have no trouble with it –

I left Thom Brannon in Columbus. I was right sick there Thursday evening and thought something of getting an extension - but feeling so much better next morning that I came on.

The sun is out now finely but hope it will dry up the mud and water some.

Well Darling I must hurry up, but as I can't mail this letter until in the morning, will finish this evening.

Well Darling it is now Monday morning and I am about to finish this letter. I am feeling very well.

I had a long talk with Robertson yesterday evening in reference to the fight & a good many other things. He says the battery did not near as much service at the Murfreesboro fight as it did at Shiloh, but gets a good deal more credit for it. Says it was a very hard fought battle - our loss in every thing about ten thousand - Genl Bragg does not ____ his real force unknown but he had only Twenty-nine thousand infantry and artillery in the fight. The enemy about Seventy thousand. Bragg's army now is nearly as strong as before the fight.

A good many of the officers are down on Bragg - and yet a council of war advised the retreat twenty-four hours before Bragg began it. I am afraid some trouble will grow up yet out of this thing. I will write you more particulars some future time.

My love to all the family. I will write Ada and Mr. Young soon. Tell Mollie her letter is delivered. Goodby Darling - much love and many kisses for you and the boy and tell him to be good and love MaMa and not forget PaPa. God bless and take care of you all Darling - your own old Dear Hubert

Hubert's prediction that "some trouble will grow out of this thing" turned out to be an understatement. Bragg's withdrawal from Murfreesboro, and his overall performance there, caused widespread public dissatisfaction. The criticism prompted Bragg to send a circular letter to his corps commanders, asking for their support and offering to resign if he had lost their confidence. Invited to be "candid", every one of them stated, in the most tactful terms possible, that they and their brigadiers lacked confidence in him and felt a change of commanders should occur. This was the view of Hardee, Cleburne, and Breckenridge. Polk wrote the same view directly to President Davis. Bragg did not resign, and Davis appointed General Joseph E. Johnston to investigate the disaffection with Bragg. Johnston's investigation took three weeks. Johnston felt that this assignment placed him in a difficult position. He was sensitive to the possibility that if he recommended Bragg's removal, he might appear to be seeking the command for himself. He eventually recommended retaining Bragg.

Among Bragg's unattractive traits was his tendency to look for scapegoats and to carry out vendettas. It has been suggested that by late 1862, Bragg, sensing growing hostility to himself, had begun to surround himself with a group of hardcore supporters who had served under him in the early months at Pensacola, and that the list of Bragg protégés included Felix Robertson.[569] Historians have concluded that, in the aftermath of Murfreesboro, Bragg sought to purge certain "enemies," including Gen. Breckenridge, and that Hubert's captain, Felix Robertson, was called upon to assist in this effort. It is suggested that Robertson supplemented his after-action report on Murfreesboro to add strong criticism of Gen. Breckenridge. Robertson's second report did in fact make criticisms not mentioned in the original, and Robertson was soon after given a promotion and new responsibilities in spite of questionable battlefield conduct. In *Cannoneers in Gray*, Daniel reaches these conclusions:

> "After Murphreesboro, Bragg became involved in an obsessive vendetta to purge the army of those Generals whom he disliked. The artillery was not unaffected by this high-level power struggle. In an attempt to obtain evidence against General John C. Breckenridge, Bragg turned to his old crony, Captain Robertson. Because the Captain's Murphreesboro report had not been particularly critical of Breckinridge, Bragg requested that he prepare a revised report to 'do justice' that would skip regular channels and be sent directly to his headquarters. Robertson understood what was wanted. He now wrote a scathing denunciation of Breckinridge's conduct during the January 2 assault. Shortly thereafter, the captain was allowed a brief tour in Richmond…during which he lobbied on Bragg's behalf. Upon his return, he was greeted with a major's commission (Bragg's attempt to obtain him a lieutenant colonelcy had been unsuccessful) and command of the newly organized artillery reserve, an organization that was to report direct to army headquarters. All of this came on the heels of Robertson's own miserable performance during the Battle of Murphreesboro."[570]

Daniel reports, "Robertson has been soundly criticized by modern writers, who describe him as an overly ambitious Bragg crony who was not beyond lying".[571] Daniel portrays Robertson as "an odd looking fellow" who was disliked by his men because of actions such as this:

> "Robertson was a harsh disciplinarian who was intensely disliked by his men. Because of his dark complexion and slanted eyes, rumors spread that he was of Indian descent. His name around the campfire became 'Comanche Robertson.' A drunken artilleryman who called him 'half Injin' one night paid dearly. The next day, the captain had him strung up by his thumbs with his feet barely touching the ground. This cruel punishment incurred so much animosity among the men that some of them expected the young Texan to be murdered."

Daniel reports that, when Gen. Bragg organized an artillery reserve battalion and made Robertson its commander, there was much chagrin among those men who were transferred to Robertson's new command because his harsh disciplinary measures had made him the most unpopular officer in the artillery. One Georgia Battery, learning that it had been transferred out of Robertson's reserve, marched past his headquarters imprudently shouting, "Goodbye Comanche". Robertson was heard to mutter, "Never mind, I'll have you again". Sure enough, Bragg granted Robertson's request to return the unit to his control, and "it was a mournful set of men as we took the line of march back to Robertson..." a Georgia artilleryman lamented.[572]

Although we have seen that Robertson was capable of performing ably, as at Shiloh and Farmington, some writers have no doubt that his promotion to chief of Braggs' artillery reserve was the result of his close ties with Gen. Bragg.[573] Eventually, he attained the rank of Brigadier General, a rank also held by his father, Jerome Robertson, in the Army of Northern Virginia.[574]

It is important to state that in none of his letters home nor in any other writings did Hubert Dent ever express a word of criticism of Felix Robertson. These conclusions relating to the controversies surrounding Robertson come from professional historians' interpretations of the historical record, not from Hubert Dent. On rare occasions, in the privacy of his letters to Anna, Hubert did make critical comments about a fellow officer, but Felix Robertson was never one of them. As far as is known today, Robertson and Dent had a cooperative and mutually respectful relationship. Even after Robertson was promoted out of the battery, Hubert's letters home reflect continued social contacts with him. At one point, Hubert gave consideration to going with Robertson into his new assignment, although he ultimately decided not to do so. To look briefly ahead of our narrative, we note that, following the war, Dent and Robertson continued in contact through correspondence and conventions of the United Confederate Veterans, and they always exhibited warm regard for each other. In fact, in a letter of April 25, 1909, Robertson wrote this generous statement to Hubert:

> " ... I have known many men and of those, I have known a considerable number under circumstances well calculated to sho clearly the real qualities of

the individual, and I want to say to you and to each one of your children that you are the best man I have ever known."

Upon the death of Robertson in 1925, (nine years after Dent's death in 1917), Hubert's oldest son, Ed, wrote to Robertson's son in Dallas, recalling being present when their fathers were together at Confederate reunions, and observing that "...your father and mine were not only personal friends with the warmest of attachments, but each had the most high regard for the merits of the other."[575]

In 1863, the controversy following Murfreesboro indirectly helped Hubert Dent realize his ambition to hold his own command. Captain Robertson's promotion to major would take several months, until June, to make its way through the bureaucracy, but his reassignment as chief of Bragg's reserve artillery battalion soon removed him from Robertson's Battery, and left Hubert Dent in command of the unit. From now until the end of the war, the battery would be Hubert's unit. Hubert had been yearning for the responsibility of his own command. He had been eager for the opportunity of leading men in battle, and now it was his. Hubert would soon be promoted to Captain, the rank normally associated with a battery commander, and the battery would become officially known as "Dent's Battery", or sometimes, "Dent's Alabama Battery".

These changes had not yet been completed when Hubert next wrote Anna. He discusses camp conditions, child discipline, and war developments. Anna has been visiting the Columbus Youngs, who have apparently had illness and death in the family.

"Camp near Shelbyville Tenn
February 6th, 1863

"My own Dear wife
    I received yours of 30th Jan yesterday. It should have arrived sooner. I of course was very glad to receive it, but I am afraid you will be uneasy when you begin to receive my letters. Feel no uneasiness now My Darling for I am entirely well.
    Yesterday morning I found it snowing very fast. It then hailed and snowed alternately all day. The ground was hard frozen this morning and for a short time at least we were rid of the mud and <u>sloppiness</u> of our Camp. To-day is clear bright and cold and I hope we may have several days of just such weather.
    The picture you draw Darling of the desolation and sorrow of your Uncle's family is very saddening and they have no consolation but that they may all meet her who has gone before in Heaven. I sometimes wonder whether I would be much missed and mourned should death remove me. I know there are some hearts that would sorrow for my departure. But I do not know that I would care much for others grief. However as I do not like to dwell on such themes I will not now. I am very glad to hear that Aunt Ellen is out of danger.

I thought from the way in which you wrote from Columbus that you had left Eddie at home, but I see by your last that you took him with you. I am sorry to hear he is getting so bad. The idea of his fighting his Grand Ma all the way to Columbus and while there is bad against him. You will be compelled to commence whipping him I see you will or have a ruined boy. And so he calls for Pa Pa does he, and kisses Ma Ma for Pa Pa bless his little heart I wish I was there to get his kisses and give Ma Ma some in the place of them.

I have not heard a word from Joe Clayton, nor any thing from Mrs. Pope or his Mother since I saw them at Tullahoma.

As I have already written, I expect Sissie M. does make a terrible <u>fuss</u> over her baby and her Mother I expect is about as bad. But you can tell Mrs. A. Young (Clara) [the wife of Anna's Columbus first cousin, Alfred Young] that I am sure she is a Lady of the most decided good taste and that I am prepared to like her amazingly well and that I am sure I could not please her better than by wishing that all her babies may be just what she thinks of ours. You can tell her the last or not as you please.

Well Darling now for the strange story, if it be true it is indeed a strange story and certainly of all other stories in the Bible none could have been more encouraging. I hope some of our officers and men especially those who get behind Clay Roots will take courage from this and not be frightened at the whistling of the musket balls or the rushing and bursting of shells. I have always believed that God was with us. If I had not my arm would long since have palsied. And I now as firmly believe that when the end does come it will give independence and peace to our Country as I ever believed any thing. But I differ with those who think there [will] be peace in the spring. I can see no signs of it. The enemy struck us a severe blow by the capture of Arkansas Post. I am afraid the silence from about Vicksburg is ominous. I fear the enemy will do us some great injury there. I had rather lose the whole state of Tennessee than be cut off in our communications with the trans-Miss dept.

The bread question is an important one. Our army here is eating corn bread and it is making them sick. Unless they could sift it and have it ground finer it will continue to make them sick. We are however carrying flour from this country and I suppose are storing it somewhere. I heard yesterday that troops were being sent from here to Port Hudson but I do not think it can be true. Braggs army has certainly been reduced enough before.

I have heard nothing more of any further movements around here. We had a picket fight two or three days ago. Did not amount to much.

I have a copy of a very singular and well written letter picked upon the field of Murfreesboro as soon as I get time to copy it legibly, it is only in pencil now, I will send it to you. It is an old letter but so well written that it attracted my attention. It was written by a Lady to a gentleman, at least purports to be.

241

Bibb Gardner came to see me yesterday and to-day. He lost his left eye in the fight at Murfreesboro. It is not entirely out but it is thought he will lose it. He fought in the 22nd Ala regt. in our Brigade. He was in the 1st Ala cavalry but did not go into Ky and was dropped from the rolls. He was a 1st Lt. He is endeavoring to be reinstated. I hardly think he will succeed. He succeeded in borrowing $20 from me however.

Well I must close Give my love to all the family and I hope Ma has returned by this time. I know how much you all miss her when she is gone. Tell Eddie he must be a better boy or Pa Pa will not love him much. God bless and take care of you all Darling and may we soon meet. February is fast going. It is one fourth gone already. I shall be glad when winter is over not so much on account of cold as wind. Again my love to all, and much love and many kisses for my Darling and my boy. As ever Your own old Dear who loves you better every day. Hubert"

(P S. on top of page 1)
We are to be reviewed to day by Gen.l Joe Johnston. It bids fair to be a fine day. Feby 7th/63. The letter I spoke of in this letter turns out to be a plagiarism from "The Rivals" a novel written by Jere Clemons of Alabama."

29
Death Visits the Youngs

"Henry Was The Idol Of The Family"

Tom Jackson

On February 19, 1863, the Eufaula Youngs suffered the ultimate consequence of war. Henry Augustus Young was killed in a railroad accident enroute to a new duty assignment.

In early April 1862, Henry had marched down Broad Street with the Eufaula Light Artillery, amid throngs of adoring well-wishers, to board the cars for Knoxville, Tennessee. Arriving at Knoxville, the company named their camp, "Camp Bullock" in honor of their recently-deceased friend. Gen. Kirby Smith, commander of the Department of East Tennessee maintained his Departmental Headquarters in Knoxville.

Henry was well educated and had always had a "scholarly" inclination. It was apparently recognized that Private Young had talents that would be valuable in administrative duties at the headquarters level. On April 9, 1862, pursuant to Special Order No. 79,[576] Henry was "detailed to Department Headquarters as clerk." He would remain attached to Gen. Kirby's headquarters throughout the short time remaining for him to live. Later, another Eufaula Light Artillery private was also recognized as qualified for headquarters duty by virtue of education and ability: Charles Kliffmuller. Before the war, Kliffmuller had served as a professor of music at the Union Female College in Eufaula. By Special Orders No. 98, he was detailed to Gen. Smith's Department Headquarters on June 23, 1863, and he would also remain in this position until his death.[577]

Young and Kliffmuller were probably present with Gen. Smith's staff during portions of Gen. Kirby Smith's invasion of Kentucky in cooperation with Bragg during August and September 1862, but the available records do not permit confirmation of this.

As we have already seen, in November 1862, Henry was granted a furlough to visit Eufaula on the occasion of the birth of his second child, Julia. He returned to Knoxville on November 23. [578]

In early January 1863, Gen. Kirby Smith was called to Richmond to discuss a change in commands. In the first year of the war, Smith had received recognition for his performance at Manassas, Virginia; and his victories during the recent invasion of Kentucky had added popularity to his name. President Davis now wished to use him in another capacity, and after several positions were discussed, on February 9, 1863, he was appointed commander of the Trans-Mississippi Department. This placed him in command of all Confederate troops and military operations west of the Mississippi River. Gen. Smith took with him to his new command all his old trusted staff members, physician, and servants. Privates Young and Kliffmuller continued to be detailed to Gen. Smith and were also making the move to the new command. The Headquarters for the Trans-Mississippi Department was in Alexandria, Louisiana, which was west of the Mississippi, on the Red River. With federal gunboats operating on the Mississippi, Alexandria was not easy to reach. Kirby Smith, his wife, baby, and principal entourage left Knoxville for Louisiana in late January. Henry Young and Charles Kliffmuller were among those remaining in Knoxville to finish last details of the move and to follow soon thereafter.

By February 15, the Kirby Smith party was in Mobile waiting for transportation of horses and baggage.[579] Difficulty was expected in crossing the Mississippi River because two federal gunboats were reported between Vicksburg and Port Hudson, (a strong Confederate river fort between New Orleans and Vicksburg). From Mobile, Gen. Smith and his party traveled to the Mississippi River, crossed the River at Port Hudson, and were taken by boat up the Red River to his new headquarters at Alexandria.

On February 19, four days after Gen. Smith's main party had left Mobile, Privates Young and Kliffmuller were traveling by train enroute from Knoxville, and had reached the Chunkey River, not far west of Meridian, Mississippi. The train was apparently crossing a bridge at a point known only as "Chunkey Bridge," Mississippi, when there was a serious railroad accident, resulting in the death of Henry Young, as well as the death of Charles Kliffmuller.

Henry was twenty-eight years old, and left in Eufaula Maria, his wife of three years, and their infant children, Henry, Jr, and Julia. In fact, he died four months to the day after his daughter, Julia, was born. Chunkey Bridge was close enough to Eufaula that, when notified of Henry's death, Edward was able to arrange to have his son's remains brought back to Eufaula for burial. Edward also had Charles Kliffmuller's remains brought to Eufaula, and gave him a burial in the Young family cemetery plot.

Henry's boyhood friend, Tom Jackson, who had attended Henry and Maria's wedding only three years previously, traveled 200 miles to be present for the funeral, and "was one among the many sincere mourners present on that solemn occasion." Tom reports, "Henry was the idol of the family"[580], and every member of the family was devastated by his death. Henry was the son who had pleased his parents in every way. He had attended college, he had traveled widely, he had married a fine girl from a local family, and he commanded the respect of the community. He had made his father happy by entering the family business; he was the second half of "E. B. Young & Son". He had shown talent as a businessman, and had a promising future.

That Charles Kliffmuller died in the service of the South is particularly ironic. When war approached he had sent his wife and her sister back to their native Germany. The Eufaula Vigilance Committee had considered his loyalty, correctly concluding that he was doubly loyal for staying and sharing in a fight that was not his own, when he could just as easily have left. He had little personal stake in the outcome of the war, but stayed to fight beside his friends.

We have seen that when Henry and Maria's son, Henry, Jr. was born March 19, 1861, (while Ann and Anna were visiting Hubert at Fort Barrancas), and their daughter, Julia, was born on November 19, 1862, their baptisms had been postponed, perhaps because of wartime circumstances. Now, a month after their father's death, Henry and Julia were baptized in Eufaula by the Youngs' longtime minister, the Rev. James L. Cotten, on March 14, 1863.

Hubert Dent, writing from Tennessee a month after the tragedy, still found it difficult to find words to write to Anna about her brother's death, and could not yet write his father-in-law about this loss. He expresses the strange fear that the death of Henry, who was adored by the whole family, might cause Anna and her family not to love Hubert as well as before. He resolves not to continue to write about Henry in future letters, but this resolution was not kept.

"On Picket Eagleville Pike
7 Miles from Shelbyville Tenn
March 18, 1863

"My own Darling Nannie
        I was disappointed in not receiving a letter from you today. Well I will look all the more anxiously for one tomorrow.
        I am still on picket. The weather continues fine. I have heard nothing more of the rumor about the evacuation of Murfreesboro by the Yankees. It is only another sensational rumor I expect. We are having a very quiet time out here and as the weather is so fine I am as well satisfied here, as I would be in camp. I have been thinking a good deal since I come out here about myself the future and the past and perhaps in some of my letters I may give you some of my reflections but not now.
        We have pretty good news from Port Hudson and I only hope the good news will continue. But it has been a little remarkable that in nearly all our fights we had the best at first – such things make one suspicious – we will hear more soon I expect.
        The weather is so pleasant that I went to the creek near our camp this morning and took a bath. The water was rather cold at first, but as you know I do not mind that much so I went in and took a fine bath and felt much better from the operation. Twelve more days after to-day and April will be upon us.
        I wonder if we will celebrate the anniversary of the battle of Shiloh with another big fight. It would not surprise me for one to come off about that time or sooner. I do not think Gen.l. Bragg will give up this country without a fight and when it comes off I expect it to be a severe one. I heard that our cavalry in front were organizing a reconnoitering expedition to find out the truth about the evacuation of M. or what movements the Yankees were making. If the expedition went I presume we will hear something tomorrow. We have Gen.l. Wharton on this road.
        I am very anxious to hear from you my Darling and from all at home. I am anxious to learn all that can be learned about that unfortunate affair that has brought such grief upon us all. The ways of Providence are mysterious. I was reading in the Bible a day or so ago and was struck with the number of passages there that looked like they promised long life to such men as I know

Henry was. Write me Darling and how you are all getting along and every thing about the family. Somehow I feel sometimes that you all will not love me as well now as before. I do not know either that I should complain if it is so. For I know Darling how great is the void this loss occasions and I do not wonder that your hearts and feelings are so absorbed and taken up with it that you do not and cannot think of others as you could before. But my Love do not forget that I love you and all better than ever that you feel nearer to me and there is no sacrifice however great that I would not have made sooner than this should have come upon you. I must stop writing this way it may only grieve my Darling worse.

I hope I may get a letter from you tomorrow and as soon as Ada and Mollie feel that they can write tell them to write. I would write to Mr. Young but really Darling I hardly feel competent to do it. After awhile I may but not just now. I think that in every letter I will make my last allusion to Henry's death and yet I find myself writing of it again every time I write. Excuse this Darling I do not think I ought to do it. Give my love to all and say I am very anxious to hear from them.

Has any thing been heard of Kliffmuller? I will send this to town tomorrow morning. I hope the next time I write I will have one of yours to answer till then goodby. Much love and many kisses for Darling and Baby from your devoted dear   Hubert"

30
Passive Interlude At Shelbyville, Tennessee

"...we have been here longer than at any one place since we have been in the service. And the indications are that we will remain here sometime longer."

Hubert Dent to Anna

Following the Battle of Murfreesboro, Capt. Robertson was often away from the battery intriguing with Gen. Bragg. For a while, Robertson was off on leave in Richmond. According to Historian Daniel, he was there lobbying in support of Bragg's version of events during the Battle of Murfreesboro.[581] Hubert was left to run the battery. Also, Robertson was in process of being promoted to major, and preparing to assume command of the new Artillery Reserve Battalion which Bragg was creating. This would lead to Hubert's promotion to captain in command of the battery, but we will see complaints in Hubert's letters about the long administrative delays in implementing both of these promotions. In the meantime, Robertson was "floating around," and effective command of the Battery devolved upon Hubert.

In early 1863, Hubert Dent was undoubtedly ready for action, and he would get all the action he wanted, but first, he would have to wait. The army now entered a long period of passivity. No other Confederate army during the war had such a protracted period of inaction as the Army of Tennessee during the first half of 1863. For six months, it remained encamped with its left wing under Polk at Shelbyville (which included Dent's Battery), and its right under Hardee at Wartrace, Tennessee. Bragg maintained his headquarters behind Wartrace at Tullahoma. Rosecrans was equally passive in Murfreesboro. During this time, Rosecrans made no movement against Bragg, and Bragg reciprocated the policy.

The lack of pressure is reflected in the lighter tone of Hubert's next letter to Anna. Hubert may be laughing at himself (or if not, he should be), about injuring his horse while playing cavalry swordsman, ineptly. Robertson had apparently not informed Hubert of his whereabouts during his leave to Richmond in support of Gen. Bragg's interests.

"Camp near Shelbyville Tenn
March 24th, 1863

My own Nannie
I returned from picket yesterday evening late. It commenced raining yesterday morning and drizzled all day last night it came down in earnest and has continued with only a slight interruption ever since. While I write it is pattering down noisily on the tent and beating through so badly that I can scarcely write. So if this sheet looks dirty and soiled you may charge it to that. I have not received that letter that you were to write the day after Ada's – no mail today. I hope I will get it tomorrow. It seems a very long time since I had a letter from you – more than a week.

I am very well Darling. While I was out on picket I had some symptoms of dyspepsia [indigestion]. It annoyed me a good deal – so much meat and bread and syrup has given it to me I suppose. I laid up in camp out there and did nothing. I am going to exercise a good deal if it ever clears up.

I rode out this morning and took some cavalry exercise but it came on to rain again and I left. I managed to cut my horse a little on the hind leg. I was cutting at what was supposed to be a Yankee's head while he (the Yankee) was lying down. It is the first time I ever exercised and I was rather awkward and my horse ran shy. I am going to practice some and see how I can do. It will exercise me and that is what I need.

Well Darling after two weeks of clear weather we're having another rainy spell. This will make the roads that were beginning to be tolerable as bad as ever. If Rosenkranz had any idea of advancing which I doubt, this will delay him.

I see the newspapers are full of the news of the evacuation of Murfreesboro. That may turn out like the report of the evacuation of Nashville shortly before the battle of Murfreesboro. In fact I can't believe a word of it.

I have not heard a word from Robertson and can't imagine what has become of him. He has been gone four weeks tomorrow. I am getting along very well with the company – have very little trouble and I must own that I have a very hard set of men or at least some very hard cases. But of one thing I feel certain I can rely on them in a fight.

Well Darling I must go and look after my horses now. In a battery a horse is a great thing and I must have mine well looked after. Goodby my Love I will finish this tonight or in the morning.

Well Darling it is Wednesday morning, a bright cool morning. Every thing is very wet but it is clear. How long it may remain so I can't tell.

I have no news of interest. I heard the other day that Gen.l. Bragg had been relieved from command here and would go to Mobile or Vicksburg. I have not seen any one that knew any thing about it. I hope it is not so for no matter how much others may abuse him I like him as a general and I hope he will remain with this army. I would go into a fight under him with greater confidence than any other general however able and distinguished he might be. There are a great many men who want to see him relieved and I expect it is some of them who have started the report. You see I still stand up for my old general.

Genl. Withers returned last week. He has been absent since the battle of Murfreesboro and Genl. Anderson has been commanding the Division. I like Genl. A. very much and think him a fine soldier.

March is passing away very fast and we will soon have summer upon us. The Yankees are certainly moving very slowly. Rosenkranz has been seen reinforced with twenty thousand men but he does not seem to think these sufficient for his purposes. If we can hold this country three months longer I think we can hold it the balance of the year. In fact if we can stay here until the 1st June I think we will not only hold this country but drive the Yankees back.

The Yankees are working very energetically at Vicksburg. They work like beavers. The Yankees had rather work six months with picks and spades than fight one battle while our soldiers had rather fight six battles than work one month. We have not worked enough with the spade. I wish our Gen.ls would work more with them.

Well Darling I must close now. Give my love to all the family. I will write Ada soon. With much love and many kisses for my Darling Nannie and our baby I must say goodby. Your own devoted and affectionate husband Hubert

In his next letter Hubert reports that his family in Maryland are well. Apparently Dr. Dent has returned from Jackson. Anna and the family are still in grief over Henry. Hubert learns where Robertson has been. Unlike many others, Hubert still has confidence in Gen. Bragg, who has been his commander since Fort Barrancas.

"Camp near Shelbysville, Tenn.
March 27th 1863

"My Dearest Nannie,
I received your's and Mr. Young's letters by W.[illiam] H. Woods [an officer of the Eufaula Light Artillery, Henry Young's old unit] yesterday. I did not see him. He sent them to my camp by one of the company. I was very glad to get them.

I am very well Darling and I believe I have got over my dyspepsia. To day you know is the day appointed by the President as a day of fasting, humiliation and prayer. I gave the company freedom for the day and went in town to church. I heard a very good discourse, but poorly delivered.

I had a letter from home today written on the 18th of March. I mean from Md. All were well. They had not received any letters from us since the battle of Murfreesboro. They had heard that our letters had reached Richmond but had not received any of them. They sent and always do a great deal of love to you and Eddie.

Robertson has returned from Richmond. He will go to Atlanta and Columbus to get some ordnance and he says he may go to Eufaula. He expects his commission in a few weeks.

Things are pretty quiet just around here. I heard this morning that Van Dorn had captured eight hundred prisoners near or in Franklin. He must worry old Rosy a good deal.

Our surgeon who was left at Murfreesboro in charge of our wounded arrived last night. He was sent home by way of Louisville, Cincinnati, Baltimore and Fortress Munroe. He says he was treated very well by the Yankees. One of the men of our Co. left there died. The others got well and is now in Camp Chase. He says he met a great many persons in Ohio who sympathized with the South but in Baltimore nearly every one sympathized with us especially the ladies.

The enemy acknowledged that they were whipped at Murfreesboro but Rosecrans in his official report only acknowledged a loss of thirteen guns when we carried 33, I think it was, to Chattanooga, and they show three guns in Murfreesboro which they say they captured from Robertson's Battery. I can show them six here and I did not know before that we had nine guns.

He gives horrid accounts of the manner in which they treated our people in and around Murfreesboro. They turned women and children out of their houses in that cold January weather and robbed the farmers of nearly every thing they had to eat, taking also their horses, mules and cattle.

The spring is passing and so far we have held our own remarkably well. But I feel that this is an important crisis in our affairs. The Yankees are working so very silently and persistently at Vicksburg that I have some fears of what they may accomplish there. If we can hold them in check there and here I have great hopes that something favorable for us will turn up in the summer. But if we are defeated at either point it will postpone any movement for peace.

I am uneasy about another thing - Subsistence for our troops. I do hope that our people at home will raise all the bread stuff they can and everything that will do for men to live on. It will all be needed. There is so much suspense now that somehow I feel oppressed by it. Flour here now is worth 20 cents per lb. It could be bought for ten when I first came here. The mens portions have been reduced and every thing looks like commissary supplies were becoming scarce.

Darling, I have been thinking about you a great deal today and wished I could have been with you to join in your devotions for our country's welfare. When I went to Church today, the house was crowded and I did not think I could get a seat - while hesitating near the door a gentleman came out and conducted me to a seat placing me on a bench with some ladies. I could not help feeling how delighted I would have been could it have been you by my side. Somehow I like the Episcopal Church in that all of a family takes the same pew.

Darling I often imagine how changed you all are now. In your letter Darling you said that you never expected to love life as well as you had done and never to be as happy as you had been. It is natural my Darling for you to feel Henry's loss very keenly. But My Love do not indulge too much in such feeling as these. We all have our duties to perform here and await patiently for God in his own good time to take us into himself. Let us not repine at his dispensations but try and bear them as coming from him. I know no one can ever fill Henry's place in the family, but still we should try and bear his loss. I want to write to comfort you my Darling but God help me I know not what to write. God alone must be our help in such troubles.

The weather has been clear for a day or two - but it is rainy and cloudy this evening. I hope it will not continue. We had a review yesterday of all the artillery here by Genl Bragg's Chief of Artillery. Genl. Bragg has not been relieved from command here and will not be although I expect he will go to Richmond before many weeks.

Every thing is so still and quiet that it seems like Sunday. I will try Darling and write to Mr. Cotton - I am very glad he was in Eufaula at the time he was. He has such a warm and sympathizing heart. I must write to Ada tomorrow or next day. I believe I am a poor correspondent to any one except you. I try to write you tolerably regularly. Give my love to all the family. I wonder when I will be able to see you all. Write me Darling as often as you can. I sometimes feel very lonely and I get more so when I do not receive letters from you or some of the family. I have no one here with whom I can talk freely and as I feel who can understand my feelings. Kiss little Eddie for his absent PaPa and tell him he must be a good boy and Darling we must try and make him love his cousin Henry [Henry Young, Jr., the small son of Henry and Maria Young] and be very kind to him you know I think a great deal of him. Goodby, love and kisses from your own. Hubert

Hubert's next letter to Anna reflects the extent to which the Confederate camps have settled down into inactivity. But he relays a joke making the point that Gen. Rosecrans is also showing no interest in stirring. With the encouragement of Gen. Withers and Gen. Deas, Hubert has decided not to go into the new Reserve Battalion with Robertson, although he thinks one of his lieutenants, Bruton, may go. Stockton is his other lieutenant.

"Camp Near Shelbyville, Tenn.
April 5th, 1863

"My Dearest Wife
It is a lovely sabbath afternoon. Every thing is quiet and still. The noisy wagons and the busy hum of every day life in camp has hushed. I have eaten my dinner and concluded I would spend an hour in writing to my Darling wife.

I went to church this morning. Carried Stockton and Bruton with me. Went by for Robertson and took him along also. I heard an ordinary sermon. The house was crowded. Robertson came out to Camp with us for dinner. He has left and all the other officers are endeavoring to pass away the afternoon by sleeping.

To-day looks as if Spring had commenced in reality. If Rosenkranz is waiting for fine weather he need wait no longer. A Yankee prisoner captured a few days ago got off a joke upon his General. When asked what news was stirring about his Camp when he left he said it was reported that old Rosy would advance in June. We have been here already longer than at any out place since I left Pensacola. When I say we I mean the battery and in fact we (the Battery) have been here longer than at any one place since we have been in the service. And the indications are that we will remain here sometime longer.

251

Robertson is still floating round waiting for his commission and uncertain when it will come. I will not go with him in the reserve Battalion. My General officers are very much opposed to my leaving the command, particularly Genl Withers and Genl Deas. Genl Deas says he had rather lose any regiment in his command than my Battery. I think that very likely McTyers Battery will go with Robertson. I do not know how they will like it. I expect Bruton will go with Robertson so I will have two vacancies in the company and I will not have very good material for getting officers from.

I heard this morning that Morgan was driven back from Liberty near Lebanon day before yesterday. He was attacked by a large force of Infantry and cavalry. Every where else every thing is quiet.

I have written you now My Darling all the news up this way. I am in very good health and hope to remain so. I felt a little uneasy a week or so ago when I was threatened with dyspepsia but I think now it was only a temporary thing and that I am entirely over it. I will write to Mr. Cotton tomorrow unless something interferes to prevent and I must write to Ma or Mr. Young or both soon.

Oh! Darling how I could enjoy your society this evening. It seems to me that this evening I have an especial longing for home and home faces. I believe you once thought that I would become so fond of military life that I would love home less. Oh! Darling what a mistake you made. The longer I am from home the more I love it [blotted with mud] more anxiously I desire to get back to it. I think I am especially a home man. I sometimes think that there are very few who love home as well as I do. In this perhaps I am wrong. But I feel that I love it too well ever to desire to be a public man when this war is ended if God spares my life all I desire is [to] live quietly at home. Pursue my profession, make a competence for my Darling and our boy and pass down the stream of time quietly with them. Darling do not indulge the idea that you are not going to live long. I want you with me. Without you how joyless would life be. Oh! Father in Heaven I pray Thee, end this war and reunite husbands and wives. Parents and children Brothers and Sisters. Nevertheless help us to say from our hearts. Thy will not ours be done.

I wonder how you are all employed this afternoon? I expect my Darling is thinking of her Dear Am I not right? All of you are perhaps thinking of him who is gone from among us. God help us all to live so as to meet him in that better land. Twelve months ago I was with the Battery in line of battle near the enemys camp at Shiloh. Little thinking that I was going through the bloody scenes of the next two days. I wonder how many more anniversaries of it I will live to see and whether as an old man I shall live "to fight my battles o'er again" by the domestic hearth. God in his goodness has spared me thus far and I am thankful.

Give my love to Ma Mr. Young and all the family. Is Mollie waiting for a letter from me or will she write. I do not remember which of us wrote the last letter. Tell her not _____ write me. I shall write to her soon _____ Darling I will now lay this aside [until] tomorrow morning. I am going to

_____ is reading our Bible this evening _____ specially like I will enjoy reading it _____ love and many kisses for you and our [boy] Goodby till tomorrow morning.

My Darling the beautiful weather of yesterday is gone. It is cloudy and raining this morning, not cold however. For I have nothing new this morning to write. Twelve months ago this morning I was listening to rattle of the musketry at Shiloh. Every body lately now seems to think it will be some time before we hear anything of that sort between the armies of Bragg and Rosenkranz. How changeable we are. Not [long] ago it was the common impression that we would [win] soon and some seemed to [expect] it almost [immediately]. Surely a [few] weeks or months will develop something. I must wait patiently for whatever is to happen.

Darling I hope I will get a letter from you to-day. I am never satisfied unless I am receiving them. You have written to me frequently that I had spoiled you. I expect you think now somebody else is spoiled. How are your Columbus friends? You have not mentioned them in some time. Give my love to all the family and tell them I am always glad to hear from any of them. Write me Darling as often as you can. I never tire of reading your letters. [Cross] them and fill them up as you please. Kiss Eddie for me and tell him I am very anxious to see him and hear him talk. I wonder [if] the little thing would know me now. Much love and many kisses for you both Darling from [your own] Dear -- Hubert

In his next letter, Hubert refers to the Yankee naval attack on Charleston. This was the same attack we have discussed earlier, which resulted in Alfred and George Young of Croft's Columbus Artillery being quickly sent from Savannah to reinforce the Charleston defenses, only to find that the attack had been repulsed before Croft's Battery arrived. Hubert seeks Anna's approval of his spending a pleasant afternoon with an attractive young lady. He continues to struggle with Henry's death.

"Camp near Shelbyville
April 8th, 1863

"My Darling Nannie
…Things are moving on here pretty much as usual. There were some rumors of an advance of the enemy on the Murfreesboro road yesterday. But I heard nothing more of it to-day. In fact everyone is taken up with the news from Charleston. News came this morning that the fight had commenced there yesterday and continued up to 6 o'clock PM when the enemy drew off. This evening later news came reporting that the fight had been renewed to-day and that one of the Yankee iron clads had been sunk and that our Forts and Batteries had sustained no damage. God grant that we may be successful there. I think if we can succeed in holding the enemy in check there that it will do a great deal towards bringing about peace. While I have a great deal of confidence in our men and works there I can not help feeling anxious – of

course it could not be expected that they would reduce the place in a few hours. I shall feel anxious until we hear more of the result of the fight and that the fight is over.

I expect you are all very much excited in Eufaula over the news, more so perhaps than we are here. Somehow the army has learned to take these things with more "sang froid" than those at home.

Well Darling I am going to tell you how I spent the afternoon. Robertson sent me word this morning (he is still in Shelbyville) to come out and dine with him at one o'clock. Accordingly I went out at the appointed time. But Robertson was nowhere to be found. I learned that he had gone out riding with a Lady. So I concluded I would hunt up a dinner somewhere else. So I went and dined with a part of Genl Withers staff viz Maj Ross, Capt Lanier, Surgeon Terry, and asst Surgn Jones. After dinner Dr. Jones rode out in the country with me a short distance. I went out to see a gentleman to see if I could get pasturage for my horses. The gentleman I went to see was not at home. So I rode on with Dr. Jones and made a call on a Young Lady, a Miss Owen, formerly of Montgomery Ala. I spent an hour there pleasantly and then came back to camp. I think it made me feel better. I have had the blues or something lately and have been feeling very badly and I thought some pleasant acquaintances would make me feel better. I found the young Lady fresh from school and a pleasant agreeable <u>little</u> woman. I get so lonely sometimes in Camp that I do not know what to do with myself when such feelings come on me. Oh! how ardently I long to be at home with my Darling wife and my friends. Do you think I did wrong Darling to go? Do you know that all the time I was sitting in the parlor I was thinking of you and wondering what you would say to me had you seen me there. Write me Darling fully and freely what you feel about it. The Young Lady invited me to come again.

I go out on picket next week again and will be gone until the following Monday. But Dearest you need not feel any uneasiness for every thing here is quiet. There are a good many rumors of troops concentrating at Knoxville for the purpose of going into Ky and a gentleman just from Tullahoma to-day said that Genl Breckenridge's Division were under marching orders and it was thought Ky was their destination. There seems to be a good deal of doubt about where Burnside's corps has gone to. It is reported that it has gone into Ky. Some however seem to think that it is a ruse of the Yankees to get troops from Genl Lee and then try another "on to Richmond".

I have been reading to-day some extracts from the speech of Ben Wood of New York. It is decidedly the most favorable for peace of any I have read from northern men. He speaks out boldly and talks plainly. The trouble is however that Lincoln is independent of Congress for nearly twelve months, as long as his money will last. Southern victories are the only thing that will end the war. I have hopes that if we can be successful this spring and summer that the war will end this year, at least come to such a stand still that it will end early next.

Well Darling I have written enough about matters of general interest I hope I will receive a letter from you tomorrow I want to hear constantly how you are all getting along. I want to hear from you and Eddie and Ma and Mr. Young and all the rest of the family. Since Henry's death I find myself constantly imagining that some thing has gone wrong when I do not hear regularly.

April is passing away. The nights however keep quite cool and we have frost every night. It is cloudy tonight and a little warmer and we may have rain before morning. I dread rainy weather for I am very badly provided against [it]. It seems [impossible] to get a tent.

All the officers have gone in town to a party tonight. They are quite common. From what I have heard of the Ladies here I think there are very few whose society I would like even were I in the best sort of mood for enjoying such things.

I stopped just here Darling and got to thinking of you and all at home. Oh! what would I not give to be able to clasp my Darling in my arms and print affectionate kisses on her sweet lips. I love you better and better every day my own Darling wife and I think I have the best and sweetest of wives. Before I was married Darling I had no idea how happy I could be. The thought that you are <u>mine</u> and that you love me. Oh! Dearest it gives me so much pleasure. Give my love to all the family and tell them I think of them all <u>very very</u> often. I have written to Mr. Cotten. I hope he will answer my letter and I will try and keep up a correspondence with him. Kiss Eddie for me Darling and with <u>much much</u> love to you and him and many kisses I close. As ever your own devoted and dear husband Hubert

In his next letter, Hubert has heard rumors that Grant is evacuating Mississippi and that he will reinforce Rosecrans in Tennessee, thereby allowing Confederate General Pemberton to leave the defense of Vicksburg and reinforce Bragg in Tennessee. None of this was correct. To the contrary, Grant was beginning his maneuvers around Vicksburg which would ultimately lead to its surrender on July 4th. Hubert agrees to Anna's purchasing a household servant if she has the money in her account. The Confederate paymaster has no funds with which to pay Hubert and the troops, and when he does draw pay, virtually all of it is consumed in providing sustenance for himself and his horse. Fortunately, Anna's father is financially able to provide for Anna in Hubert's absence. Hubert is anxious for Felix Robertson's promotion to major to come through. This will clear the way for Hubert to be promoted to Captain, thereby increasing his salary from $100 per month to $140.

"On Picket Eagleville Pike
7 Miles from Shelbyville Tenn
April 13th, 1863

My own Darling
Although I wrote you yesterday I feel like writing again tonight.

The company came out on picket this morning. I remained behind to examine a man who had been elected a 2nd Lt. in a battery and came out in the middle of the day. The sun was hot and when I got into camp I had a severe headache. It has all passed off now and I feel as well as ever.

I wrote you in pencil in my last that I had received yours of the 1st and 6th inst. Baker I expect had the one of the 1st and he came near wearing it out in his pocket. It reached me however at last. I will write to Mr. Young some day this week and to Mollie also if I can.

Now I have commenced writing I hardly know what to write. The army here is a good deal excited over the news that the Yankees are evacuating the Miss and the impression prevails that Grant will unite with Rosecrans and try and drive Genl Bragg from Tenn. We may be reinforced by Pemberton but I am afraid the confrontation will not hold out. What I mean by that is this that Pemberton's army away from his Forts and breast works will not be as much of a reinforcement for Genl Bragg as Grants army will be for Rosecrans. Well it is our fortune to contend with superior numbers and we must do our best and trust in God for the rest.

Genl Bragg and Johnston (I beg Johnston's pardon I should have named him first) were expected in Shelbyville this evening and a "big review" was expected to come off on Wednesday. We are digging ditches and building batteries somewhere in this country and the impression prevails that we must fight here or near here. I think the idea of even falling back as far as Tullahoma without a fight has been abandoned unless "Old Rosey" endeavors to get on our flank and cut off our communications with Chattanooga [which is exactly what Old Rosey later did. Hubert foresaw this move, but not Gen. Bragg. Ed.].

I am getting like George [Hubert's brother] who says he is tired of doing nothing and if they are going to fight it out he wants them to commence. Poor boy he gets to feeling right badly sometimes and when he talks of home you can see his countenance change. He is a great Mother's child and loves his sisters and little brother [Warren] very much and it is right sad to hear him talk of them. He writes regularly but as the enemy has the whole of the Potomac picketed in Southern Maryland, I doubt whether many of his letters reach home. I have not delivered him your message yet. I ought to have done it before but I will call him up and tell him now. Well I have just told him and he promises to write this week if he can. He sends his love to you and Eddie.

Speaking of Eddie I hope he has got well. I can't imagine what can be the matter with him. I can't help feeling some uneasiness about him. Write me Darling regularly how he is getting on. The little fellow has wound himself into my heart and I often find myself speculating upon how much happiness he is to bring us both. I know he must be great company to you at times. How I would enjoy watching his growth and improvement and seeing his little intellect expand. I hope the dear little fellow has entirely recovered.

Oh! Darling about your purchasing the girl. You know I have wished you to have one for sometime and from what you say of her I think she would suit you and I would be glad for you to purchase her. So if you have <u>money</u> enough buy her. I have not drawn any pay since January. The paymasters have no money—as soon as I can draw some I will send you some. But it makes a big hole in a hundred dollars to feed myself and have my horse taken care of.

My horse has not got well yet or rather his foot has not. If his foot was well I could sell him for about four hundred dollars but I do not care to part from him even at that price. Horses are very high. I am riding another one now and I may get him. If I do I will sell him as soon as "Charley" (my horse) gets well.

I wish Robertson would make haste and get his commission. I want to begin to draw one hundred and forty dollars a month. It will help me out.

I have found out that Fern Wood has been reinstated as Quarter Master of the 29th Ala. He had resigned but fearing the enrolling officer would conscript him he asked to withdraw it. But his letter did not reach Richmond in time so after his resignation was accepted he got himself reinstated. Clayton is not very well pleased at his course. I saw Baker (Henry) for a few minutes but he did not give me any news. I understand that McTyer has resigned. I am sorry for him. Bill is a good fellow.

I have just heard a musket fire, and I must find out what it is about. We may have an alarm tonight so Darling good by till morning. Love to all. Your own devoted – Hubert

Well Darling it is now Tuesday morning. Nothing occurred during the night except that it commenced to rain and is raining some this morning. The wind is blowing very hard and it is quite cold. Winter seems loath to depart.

Henry's obituary is indeed very good and as you say Darling true. I will return it in a letter soon for fear I might lose it.

I am afraid you will find some difficulty in reading this letter as I wrote the most of it last night on my lap by the light of a very inferior tallow candle. Give my love to all and write me about Eddie. I hope he is well. My love to Maria and a kiss for her babies. I have taken some cold and have a slight cough but I will soon be better. Again my love to all and much love and many kisses for you Darling and our boy. Good by. Your own devoted – Hubert

The next surviving letter from Hubert is torn and soiled, so that only portions of it are legible. Its date is missing, but it is with an envelope postmarked April 25, Shelbyville, Tennessee. In it, Hubert describes his efforts to purchase black fabric in Shelbyville for Anna's use in making mourning clothes in observance of Henry's death. Hubert also describes a reorganization of the artillery that Gen. Bragg has ordered.

"I am going to write you a short letter tonight, not usual with me so you must excuse me this time. I received yours and the Youngs letters by Dr. Bryan.

The first thing I did this morning was to go <u>down town</u> "shopping" (all the artillery are camped together now and we are three miles from town). I could find no black silk except some at 25 cts a skein which being no cheaper than in Eufaula I thought it useless to purchase. Flax thread can be bought at 50 cts a skein or hank. I will send you some as soon as I have an opportunity. I bought a dozen skeins of colored silk mostly brown which I will send in letters. I do not know that you will use it but I felt like I wanted to send you something. I paid 15 cts a skein for it. I could not find a single piece of mourning goods any where. I priced some calico colored and found it $3.50-$4.00 per yard. All the goods…[part of page torn]

[Part of page torn]…a half dozen little shops here with each about a good shoulder turn of goods in them. That is all there is in Shelbyville.

Of course my own Darling you were right to go in mourning. I expected it. I wish I could procure for you such things you need. I wish I could send you some money but unfortunately just now I am unable to do so. I have money owed me that that I could very well send you if I had it—about a hundred and sixty dollars. Well when I do send I must only make it the larger sum. You must draw on <u>your deposits</u> for the present. I will replace it in a little while. When I get to be Capt. I will have a little more.

This is the third letter I have written tonight – both the others however were on official business. The artillery organization of which I have written has commenced but is not perfected yet. When that is perfected I will not belong to any Brigade. We are however all camped together – moved out yesterday on the Lewisburg Pike.

I have the best camp I have ever had. Tolerably convenient to both wood and water and a beautiful grassy place. If there is any thing that I can procure for you Darling do not hesitate a moment to call on me. I <u>hope</u> you would not and not only yourself but any of the family. Excuse the brevity of this letter. I will write a longer one next time. Give my love to…[remainder of page torn]

In his next letter, Hubert's Maryland sister, Lydia, has lost a child. Hubert has first declined, then accepted an invitation for a "pic nic party," and teases Anna about "a young lady" who has sent him a flower. He realizes his reference to "home" is confusing, because he has two "homes." Despite his loyalty to Gen. Bragg, Hubert is not sympathetic with Bragg's criticisms of Breckenridge and other generals in the aftermath of Murfreesboro.

Camp near Shelbyville Tenn
May 1st, 1863

My own Darling

This is the 1st of May and a lovely day it is—clear warm and bright. Some of the officers of the artillery have gone to a pic nic near our camp. The Ladies up here indulge in such things occasionally. Although invited I did not feel like going and have remained in camp all day.

As one of the Brigades of our division has been ordered out here near our camp I expect I will go out on picket again on Monday. I thought when I was last there that I would not go again but now I feel differently and I do not know how much longer we will remain here.

I received today a long or rather several letters from home [Hubert is referring to his old home in Charles County Maryland]. They were written on the 18th and 22nd of April. They had only received one letter from us this year. Our letters are unfortunate in not reaching them.

Sister [Lydia S. Dent] has lost her eldest Child, Georgia, you will remember her. I expect her death grieved them all very much. Sister wrote me about it. She was only sick five days, was very patient and resigned, poor little thing, she is gone to a happier world – where her mother hopes to meet her. Sister's letter was quite sad – all the rest of the family were well. All of them are very anxious for the war to end and to have George home with them. Mollie especially seems to miss him so much. [This "Mollie" is not Anna's sister, Mary E. C. Young, but Hubert's younger sister, Mary S. Dent.]

An officer has just come by and pressed me so hard to go to the pic nic that I have partially consented. I may go directly. I wonder what you all are doing at home today. Well I am better off than most people. Here I am writing of two places and calling them home when they are a thousand miles apart almost. Well you understand me don't you Darling?

Somehow Darling I have not been feeling well lately. I have very little appetite. I have not tasted a piece of meat for two days and considering how little else we have except bread & meat. It is a little singular. I feel better however than I did and I think my fasting has done me good. You know it is a favorite remedy of mine. Well Darling I believe I will ride down to the pic nic party and see what they are doing so goodby. I will finish this tonight. Your own devoted & dear – Hubert

Well Darling I went to the pic nic, remained about an hour and left. I was only introduced to two Ladies, one married & one single. There were plenty of Gentlemen and not caring to push in I keep out and pretty quick.

A Young Lady however sent me a flower. One who saw me there and whom I would not know if I were to meet her. Don't you feel a little jealous. I expect I will call on her—but to tell the truth I feel very little like it. I can not say much of the beauty of the Ladies I saw there. In fact I did not see more than two or three that I considered good looking and they were nothing to boast of. Well enough of this.

I rode out yesterday evening in a direction I had never been before and I was struck with the appearance of the country. The scenery in some places was remarkably fine. The fields were covered with a green verdure and every thing looked so fresh and pleasing. I felt like I would like very much to go out in the woods with a pleasant party and spend a quiet day. And in fact as I passed a splendid beech grove I felt as if I could throw myself under its shade and indulge all alone in giving way to my own thoughts. I am afraid sometimes that I am a dreamer notwithstanding my apparent practical worldly manners. The rough & tumble life (pardon the expression) which one leads in the army is very well calculated to cure what the world calls romance – nevertheless I believe I still have some left. But enough of this.

There are many rumors of moves, changes &c&c, but we still remain in camp. How soon we may be called on to move I cannot tell but I expect pretty soon.

Our artillery organization is not complete yet. I do not like things at all as they now are. I hope they will improve. There will be I think a good deal of feeling about the promotions or rather the appointment of Field officers.

I want to send you some money the first safe opportunity. I do not care to risk the mail if I can do better.

Well Darling it is now Saturday morning. I was suddenly and unexpectedly interrupted last night and had to lay aside your letter. It is a lovely morning, the birds are singing, the dew drops are sparkling and all is bright and peaceful – "only man is vile." I want to go to church tomorrow. I have promised to go by for the officers of McTyers Battery.

Well Darling I must hurry up if I would mail this today. Give my love to all the family. Tell Eddie PaPa thinks often of him and is very anxious to see him. Bless his little heart. I hope I will be able to get home this summer but think it doubtful. I expect to be on the move.

I have read the official report of Genl Bragg of the battle of Murfreesboro. I think it well written. His tribute to the private Soldier is very fine and well deserved. Of his criticisms of the Generals, I have nothing to say. From what my officers say I think Genl Bragg is mistaken about Anderson's Brigade checking the advance of the enemy after Breckinridges repulse. The enemy were checked when he arrived.

Well my Darling I must close. Again my love to all. Write me as often as you can. I will write again on Sunday night or Monday morning. I wish you could be up here with me now, you would enjoy the scenery and I could take long rides with you which would be very pleasant. But I do not know how soon I must move. An army is a despotism. I despise it. With much love & many kisses for you and our boy goodby. Your own devoted Hubert

Hubert's promotion to captain finally came through. At the time Hubert wrote his third anniversary letter to Anna, he had been promoted to captain, but the orders had not reached him and he did not yet know it. He is promising to send her more money "if I ever get my commission as captain". He was officially commissioned captain on June 1, 1863.[582] Hubert and his battery have accompanied a reconnaissance force to investigate reports that Rosecrans was withdrawing from Murfreesboro, and found the reports to be incorrect.

260

Near Shelbyville Tenn
June 5, 1863

My own Darling Wife

I expect you will be getting anxious to get a letter before you receive this. I did intend writing to Mr. Young next but I could not feel satisfied to let the anniversary of our marriage pass without writing to you my Sweet Darling wife.

I received orders last Tuesday to be ready to march at 5:30 AM next morning with two days cooked rations and left accordingly going out on the Wiouville and Trinne pike. Two Brigades of Withers' Division, Anderson's and Deas, went out. We went on the pike as far as Rover and then turned off towards Versailles and Salem. We camped Wednesday night Twenty-one miles from our Shelbyville camp, went three miles farther next morning, and within about eleven miles of Murfreesboro. Our cavalry went three or four miles nearer to Mo and found a considerable force of the enemy just beyond Salem, too strong for us to attack, when we retraced our steps. I arrived in Camp just about Sunset having marched Twenty-seven miles. I left the Infantry behind. They could not keep up with me. It had been rumored for several days that the enemy were evacuating Murfreesboro and this advance was made in order to ascertain if the report was true – advances were made on the other roads at the same time. The enemy have drawn in their lines a long distance but are still occupying M. in force.

When I got up on Wednesday morning to leave I found it raining very fast and it continued until late in the morning and it commenced raining just as I reached camp yesterday evening. It ceased in a short time but commenced again in the night and looks as if it might pour down any moment this morning.

The news from Miss. is pretty good but we always want things better than they are. I have heard that Genl Gardner had repulsed Banks at Port Hudson. I hope it is true. Then let Bragg be re-enforced so we can push Rosecrans back and invade Kentucky again. If Genl Johnston could dispose of Grant's army so effectually that he could start a column of men towards Memphis it would force Rosecrans to fall back and perhaps we might get Nashville and go up as far as Bowling Green and bring the war to an end during this fall. Oh! How I wish my hopes may be realized.

Well Darling another anniversary of our marriage – the third. May we live to see many more – happy and beloved – well Dearest after three years of married life are you happy or not? Place you back where you were four years or five ago and could you look through the future to this point, what say you? Would you have taken me for better or for worse? Would you have entrusted me with your happiness and given me your young and loving heart? I can frankly answer my Darling such questions as these. I have been too happy with you Dearest and feel too happy in the thought that you are mine to have a single regret. I do love you dearly or so dearly Darling and I trust that this war will soon end so I can be with you and show you how fondly and truly I do love you. Oh! I would give so much Darling to be able to take you in my arms this morning and imprint kisses on your sweet lips. I was dreaming of you last night Love and my dreams, though I do not remember them, left an unpleasant impression. It is most always the case when I do not write to you regularly. I know that you will be looking for letters from me and I do not love for you to be disappointed and besides I love to write to you Darling. It is the nearest approach to talking with you which I love to do so well.

Darling your letter of 1st has just been handed me. I was very glad to get it and glad to hear that Harry had reached Eufaula safe with my letter and the money I sent. I have sent you now three hundred dollars since I came back. I promised you fifty dollars a month and I will try and save it and send it to you and if I ever get any commission as captain I will try and make it more.

My horse is a great deal better and if I had not rode him on this last march we made I think he would have been well. I have made application to buy one from the Battery if I can get him. I will keep him to ride until my horse gets entirely well and then try and send him home to you to sell. Horses must be high there. If Ed [Anna's younger brother] can get six hundred dollars for Morgan and Mr. Young has no use for him I think it would be well to sell him. It must cost a good deal to keep him.

It has commenced raining a short time ago and is now raining quite fast with every prospect for a rainy day. I intend sending this letter to the office this evening if I can so it will go tomorrow morning.

I see by the papers this morning that Grant has been heavily reinforced and has renewed the attack on Vicksburg. I don't like the complexion of affairs at all and what is singular I see also that Genl Breckenridge's Division has been sent back here. I hope Genl Johnston has not been deceived.

Yes Dearest I do hope this war will soon end. I am so anxious to get back and be with you. I am sometimes almost afraid that if I stay away from you much longer you will not love me as well as you have and the thought of such a thing troubles me very much. What is it my Darling that you wish to tell me – can't you write it? I think it would be safe – that is it would not reach any one except myself. Oh! me I wish I could see you if it was only for a few days. I am afraid you will forget half these interesting little secrets that you want to tell me before I can see you. I hope my Darling that your dream about my being a prisoner will never be realized. I have no fancy for northern prisons and there might be some retaliation going on about that time and I might be the unlucky individual.

The citizens have reported that the Yankees were leaving Murfreesboro and that old Rosecrans had his Hd Qrs in Nashville, and the contraction of the enemy's lines gave some color to the report. Something has been going on up there but what it is no one knows accurately.

I shall certainly write to Mr. Young tomorrow unless something important prevents me. And so Eddie is fond of horses – well he would not take after me if he was not. I have only about two things here in the company to love is George and the other my horse. I have had my horse so long and he has carried me safely through dangers and over so many miles that I have affection for him and he knows me so well. I turn him loose sometimes in camp and it is very seldom he will let any one catch him except myself – horses are frequently stolen in the army – well I am never afraid of any one getting my horse when he is loose for he will not be caught away from camp.

I shall look for a long letter from you soon Darling. Give my love to all the family. I hope Ma made her visit to Columbus. I think with you that it would do her good. Goodby Darling. <u>Much much</u> love and many kisses for you and Eddie from your own dear   Hubert

Hubert writes Anna of hearing reports that Rosecrans was finally moving, but moving slowly and cautiously. This too was incorrect, but it would only be a matter of weeks before the Yankees did begin their serious advance against Bragg. Hubert's concerns for Vicksburg are well founded, and others shared his view that Gen. Joseph E. Johnston with a force near Jackson should be quickly moving to the relief of Vicksburg, although Hubert overstates the size of Johnston's force. He continues to tease Anna about ending his "campaign among the ladies."

Camp Near Shelbyville Tenn
June 9th, 1863

My own Darling Nannie
I have just received your letter written the 5th inst. and oh! Darling I felt so happy when I read it. But I feel almost like accusing you of flattery but it is such sweet flattery that I can't consent to do it. I felt when I had finished reading it over the second time that I must get right down and commence writing to my Darling wife whom I love so well.

I did not expect yesterday Darling to be here in camp this morning. Genl Cheathim's Division has gone out to the front and ours was ordered out but the order was countermanded yesterday evening. It is currently reported that "Old Rosey" is advancing cautiously. I expected when I wrote my last letter that we would have been gone before this time but "large ladies move slowly" and old Rosey's army seems to be verifying this old adage. Well when he does come I expect Genl Bragg will give him the best fight he can. I can't pretend to predict the result.

I do not like the long silence from Miss and La. I am afraid the Yankees will burrow Pemberton out of Vicksburg and if they get that Port Hudson will go too. I can't imagine what Genl Johnston is about – he ought to have from thirty-five to forty-thousand men under him and ought to be able to commence operations on Grant's rear. I think a great deal is at stake on the result at Vicksburg. I believe I would rather give up more of Tenn if that would save it. I await the result with great anxiety. Now is the time for every body to be on the field.

Oh! Darling. There is a lady visiting Mrs. Fields (Henry) (the widow) named McLaughlin (pronounced <u>McLocklin</u>) who has a son in my company. I would be pleased if you would call on her. She must be quite an elderly Lady. Her son Duncan McLaughlin is nearly forty years old and one of the best soldiers I ever saw. He is one of my gunners and a favorite man with me. He told me about his Mother's visit to Mrs. Fields and I know he would be pleased to have you call and see her. She will not be there a great while. Tell her her son is well and very much liked by his officers and that I hope he will go back to her safe for such a good soldier must be a good son and that she may well be proud of him.

And so Darling you are afraid you will never keep house for me at least not for a long time. Well I hope Dearest that you will for I am very anxious to have you keep house for me. I know I would be so contented and happy. I am afraid you would spoil me by making me love home so well that I would never want to leave for any thing and that would not be right would it? I was getting anxious to go to housekeeping before I went into the service but I expect I will be more anxious than ever when I go to back. I wish I was at home to watch your housekeeping now and listen to your conversations with Eddie. I wonder if the little fellow has any idea of me and what sort of an idea he does have. I am sorry to hear that he is getting bad. You will have all the whipping to do on him I expect. Make him a good boy Darling if you do have to whip him.

I would like to see your Young Lady acquaintances from Miss. but tell them they had better look out how they give advice to married folks to play single and that if ever I get near them I intend having my revenge out of them certain.

Well Darling I think my <u>campaign</u> among the Ladies is definitely closed since I had to make Mrs. Owens mad. I have altogether retired to private life and do not expect to appear in public (among the Ladies) any more while the war lasts.

Richardson has returned and having bought himself a uniform I intend keeping all the cloth I have and having me a full suit – coat pants & vest, made in regular artillery style. I have some idea of keeping them here to be made but am not certain yet what I will do. It is right nice cloth and will make me a finer suit than the one McKenna made for me which is showing the effects of the sew already. I think I will get the trimmings here but do not know what they will cost.

Spurlock has not returned yet.

Yes Dearest I do love you with all my heart and I feel so happy that I have such a sweet Darling wife and I am proud of you Darling, proud that you took me for your husband and that you love me as only a true devoted wife can love a husband. Yes Dearest I too loved you when we married but not with the intense earnest deep-seated love I now feel for you. God bless you my own Dear wife and guard and protect you and bring us together again happily on earth and finally in heaven.

I hope I may be able to visit home before September but to be candid I fear I will not. I look if not for activity certain for vigilance during this summer. I think a great deal is at stake and I feel that I must do my part the best I am able. I wish I could get some horses for my battery. I need them very much and in fact the battery is hardly efficient without them.

You write to me asking if "I had not given you trouble looking up things." You see I have quoted your letter – why Darling! Don't you know it pleases me oh! so much to do any thing for you and you know it you sweet Darling you. If I had been there when you wrote that I would have scolded you and then kissed you and I expect there would have been more kisses than scolds. I look forward anxiously to the times when I may see you again and spend a short time at least with you. I will never become accustomed to being away from you Darling and sometimes it seems strange there ever was a time when you were not as dear to me as you are now and yet you are still my young bride. It does not seem that you are any older and were it not for our boy I could scarcely realize that you are not still a young bride. I do not suppose you are growing older in looks very fast after the advice of the Miss. Ladies. I think sometimes I am. I imagine occasionally that there must be some traces of crow's feet on my face. But I so seldom get a chance to look at myself tht I am not certain. Write me Darling and long letters I love to read them. They are never too long and rarely ever long enough to satisfy me not that I am complaining Darling for I am not. But I do love to get long letters from you.

I hope Ma and Ada will have a pleasant visit in Columbus and I hope Ma will return benefitted by the trip. Give my love to all the family and remember me to all friends. Tell Eddie he must be a better boy and not annoy MaMa so much and if he is not a better boy PaPa will not love him so well.

Well Darling I must close. Let us hope for the best and that this war will soon end and that we may [be] together again happier than ever. Truly we are in God's hands. With much love and many kisses for our boy and my own sweet Darling wife I close. Goodby your own devoted & loving – Hubert

Whether he really believes it or not, Hubert now writes Anna in a short letter that he doesn't believe there will be an immediate fight.

"Camp near Shelbyville Tenn
June 11, 1863

My own Darling
I intended writing you a long letter today but have been busy receiving ordnance stores and never got through until dark. I am tired, but as Mr. Spurlock is here and leaves in the morning I must send you a few lines. I am

265

very well – no news. I believe the idea of an immediate fight is all blown over.

I send by Mr. Spurlock my coat & vest. I will keep my cloth here and have it made up and will then have as many clothes as I can carry. We are having plenty of rain. I have a man very sick and am afraid he is going to die. He is from Barbour his name is Jones.

I was up late last night and it is getting late so Dearest I hope you will excuse this short letter. I will write you a long one soon. Give my love to all the family. I believe this will be the shortest letter I have ever written you. Kiss Eddie for me and with much love and many kisses for Eddie and my Darling I close. Your own devoted & dear husband Hubert

Hubert's letters continue to reflect the general concern over how long the starving defenders of Vicksburg under Gen. Pemberton will be able to withstand Grant's siege. The war department continues to take soldiers from Bragg's army to send to Mississippi, but Gen. Johnston seems slow to move to the relief of Vicksburg. Hubert continues to downplay the possibility of a fight in Tennessee soon. He pays a visit to Gen. Joseph Wheeler, whose official praise Hubert earned defending the bridge in the withdrawal from Corinth after Shiloh. Gen. Wheeler remembers Hubert's eager efforts in Pensacola to get leave after Eddie was born.

Camp near Shelbyville Tenn
June 13th, 1863

My own Darling
Yours of the 9th came to hand today and so you were beginning to think you would receive no more letters from me. You ask me what I would think if you were to cease writing to me. Well what you think if I were to cease writing to you? I would keep up a <u>great thinking</u> I expect if you were to stop.

We are having delightful weather now. This is certainly a fine climate. We have had very few, in fact I can't remember one oppressively warm day so for. One year ago we were sweltering under a Miss. sun and suffocating with Miss. dust. It is very different here now. Time is passing fast with me now. June is nearly have gone. I have been busy – quite busy the last few days which has made the time pass faster.

I have considerable curiosity Darling to know what that present can be you have for me and I think you might let me know. You remember the promise I made you last winter about a present to you for the anniversary of our marriage. Well Darling I had not forgotten it. An officer went to Charleston from here this winter or rather the last of March and I sent by him for one but he could not find such as I wished and said they were very scarce and very high. Well you shall have one as soon as I can find one that will suit you.

Yes Dearest you are right about the anniversary of our marriage being the day more perhaps than any other when you occupy the largest share by far of my thoughts. My own birthday may come and go and I hardly think of it but I always think of our marriage. I wish I had some handsome present for you but I am sorry to say I have none. It is awkward to be saying this and I know my Darling knows that I <u>never forget her</u> but think of her and love her always. Are you going to tell me what the present is? If you do not I believe I will write to Ma and ask her or have you all conspired to keep it a secret.

And so Darling you think our boy very interesting. I wish I could see him and hear him talking to his MaMa. When I get home I do not expect I will let you love him as well as you do now – if you do I might be jealous. What are you going to do when you get that Two dangers around you?

Well Dearest I will write something of army news now. Every thing has quieted down here to the same old thing. Genl Bragg has concluded I think that old Rosey is not ready to pay him a visit yet and another Brigade from this army has gone to Miss. (Genl Preston Smith's). They keep taking troops from Genl Bragg. I do hope that Johnston will succeed in doing something great and telling in Miss. He must be collecting a fine army and it seems is taking his time about moving. We have no late news from Vicksburg or Port Hudson. The wires were not working yesterday and I have heard nothing today. I think I will ride in Town this evening and see what I can hear.

I expect both armies in Tenn are watching with great anxiety the results of the operations on the Miss. It was reported in the newspapers a few days ago that Genl Kirby Smith had Millikens bend about Twenty-five miles above Vicksburg and had Grant's supplies cut off. I can't well see how he can cut off Grant's supplies without heavy batteries and then not effectively. It has been some time since Grant made his first attempt on Vicksburg and it seems now that he has commenced digging ditches and preparing to take the place by regular siege approaches. Unless Genl Johnston can compel him to raise the siege, the provision question might become an alarming one. A great deal I think depends on Vicksburg. I hope and pray we shall be successful there.

The newspapers in Virginia throw out mysterious hints of what Lee is doing but I pay very little attention to such nods and winks. I have long since found out that they amount to nothing.

I wish Darling I could visit home this summer. I know you would enjoy it as much as I and it would be so very pleasant but I have very little expectation of being able to get off. But of course if I see a good chance of going home I shall go. In the mean time I hope the end of the war is approaching where we can be together once more as we were before it commenced. I am so tired, so <u>very</u> tired, of this war.

Well Darling I believe I will get ready and go down town and call on Genl Wheeler this evening and finish this tonight. I may have some news to write then – so for the present Darling goodby. I will go to church tomorrow

I expect. Genl Bragg has been confirmed in the Episcopal Church. Goodby – your Hubert

Well Darling I have returned from Town – no news from any quarter. I went to call on Genl Wheeler, he was out of town about three or four miles on the Fairfield pike. I however rode out to see him – found him pleasantly situated at a good farm house –Talked with him a short time and rode back in a hurry as there was every appearance of a thunder storm. We however had no rain.

I rode my horse this evening for the first time in some time. He has recovered and is I think entirely well. I am very glad of it. He is a very valuable horse.

Well Darling I think all idea of an immediate fight is over in this quarter – and every thing has resumed the same old routine. The only change I have heard is that Genl Withers moves out of Town nearer our trenches. I suppose this is done to place him nearer his Division.

Genl Wheeler reminded me this evening of the time I was so anxious to get home to see my boy from Pensacola and asked after you and the boy. He is a very pleasant agreeable gentleman and the sort of man I think you would like – modest and retiring especially before Ladies and a gentleman in the old acceptation of that term. He does not look as well as he formerly did. He is a small man and not good looking but I like him very much.

I wish I could be with you tonight – every now and then I have a peculiar sort of home sickness or a great longing to be at home. I think of the pleasant hours I have spent and wish so much that I could enjoy some of them again. I hope I will Darling for I hope this war will end some time soon. Give my love to all the family and tell them I would be glad to hear from them at any time and any of them.

What is Will doing now and how is his health? [Hubert is referring to Anna's oldest brother, who at this time is in Eufaula and Columbus working on ironclad gunboats for the Confederate naval department.]

Since Genl Withers has moved it would not surprise me if we were to move out nearer the trenches ourselves. I hope not for I have a very pleasant camp and would dislike to give it up. We have been around Shelbyville a long time and I feel sometimes like I would like to change. I wonder if we will get back to Murfreesboro this summer. Well I must close. Goodby Darling – much love and many kisses for your and our boy – as ever your own devoted and loving husband – Hubert

31
The Road to Chickamauga: Bridgeport, Alabama

" If the Yankees seem disposed to let us remain here I would be glad for you
to come."

Hubert Dent to Anna

Finally, the period of passivity came to an end. Prodded by Grant and Halleck, Rosecrans started moving from Murphreesboro on June 24, 1863.

Unfortunately, over the next ninety days, Rosecrans would quickly carry out a series of skillful flanking maneuvers that compelled Bragg to give up first, Middle Tennessee, then the prize of Chattanooga and finally, all of Tennessee. These crucial positions were given up without a battle, and almost without firing a shot except in preliminary skirmishes. While Bragg's lack of élan and imagination was a major reason for these Confederate losses, it should also be borne in mind that Rosecrans' force was now 70,000 men, while the Army of Tennessee at this time had about 44,000 effectives. But when the Confederate army did finally stand and fight, the result was an overwhelming victory, in fact, the greatest Confederate victory of the entire war in the western theater: Chickamauga.

Leaving Murfreesboro, Rosecrans first made a demonstration against the Confederate left, held by Gen. Polk at Shelbyville. Rosecrans' main force swept around Bragg's right and reached Manchester, 12 miles behind Bragg's right. When Bragg realized his predicament, i. e., the enemy was in his rear, he hurried to concentrate his forces at Tullahoma, as though in preparation for giving battle there. But instead of fighting, he decided to fall back further to a position behind the Elk River. Rosecrans also then stopped, showing no inclination to advance further. Bragg took this opportunity to retreat further - across Sewanee Mountain, through Stevenson and Bridgeport, Alabama, and on to Chattanooga, thereby surrendering Middle Tennessee without a fight.

Bragg fully recognized that the abandonment of Middle Tennessee was a major blow. In fact, this was a disastrous week throughout the Confederacy. On July 3, Sheridan's Division occupied Bragg's former camp at Tullahoma in Middle Tennessee. On the same day, Pickett's charge at Gettysburg failed and the Confederates were thrown back. The next day, July 4, Gen. Pemberton surrendered Vicksburg to Grant, and Lee retreated from Gettysburg.

Hubert, acknowledging the abundance of Confederate setbacks, attempts to affect an optimistic attitude for Anna. He even writes of a possible visit from her, concluding that conditions in Chattanooga are not conducive to a visit at this time. Trying to reminisce about happier times, Hubert continues to think of Henry Young. Circumstances have led Hubert to write a despondent, brooding letter.

Camp near Chattanooga Tenn
July 11th, 1863

My own Darling:

I should have written to you yesterday but was busy all day riding around to see if I could find a place for you to stay when you come up here and I am sorry to say I could find some. Col Clayton and myself rode around town and in the country in the morning and in the evening I went up on Lookout. Every place was full. There are a great many refugees here and the public boarding houses are full. I suppose you might be able to stop at the Hotel but it is not a suitable place for a Lady to stay & I had rather you were at home than here and compelled to remain at the Spencer House – more especially as I could not be with you constantly.

I am quite unusually well. Since I came here I have taken a severe cold and I have been lying down nearly all day. I feel better this evening and I hope it will soon wear off. For the present Darling I think you had best remain at home. If I succeed in getting a place for you I can write or telegraph you.

I received yesterday your letters of the 1st & 5th July and was very glad to get them. I expect you all have the blues over the military news. I am getting accustomed to it – and do not feel dispirited either. I only think the war is certain to last a long time yet and that of itself makes me feel badly.

I do not know what this army will do – wait here I suppose until Rosecrans develops his plans and then try and protect Georgia. Gen.l Hardee's corps is going to Tyners Station where we were last summer. Some rumors of troops going to Miss. but I here nothing definite. Grant seems to be pushing on after Johnston and Miss is pretty much at the mercy of Yankees. North Alabama is in the same condition. I expect Gen.l Lee will wind up his aggressive campaign [into Pennsylvania] in Richmond pretty soon and things resume the old style only a little worse.

Well I do not know what a few months may bring forth. Fifteen months ago affairs were as gloomy as they are now and we redeemed them. We may do it again. Let us hope for the best. Darling I am very sorry that you can't come to see me and I know it is a great disappointment. I do not know when I will see unless you can come up here before we leave here. I do not know either for we may go further South – to Mobile or somewhere down that way. I will keep a lookout and if I can find a place will engage it for you. Tell Sissie if she is still with you that I hope Henry went through the recent battles safely. There seems to have been some very heavy fighting. I hope the results are better for us than the recent rumors indicate.

The weather is still cloudy and rainy. I never saw such weather in June & July. I would like to see a few clear days. I am tired of so much cloudy weather & mud. When I was up on Lookout yesterday evening I visited the point and Rock City. I thought of our visit there three years ago and of the many changes that had taken place. I thought of him who has left us and who was then so cheerful and lively. Poor Henry whenever I think of him I can't help feeling so sad. It is hard for me even now to realize that I will never see him again on this earth. But I will change the subject. I am suffering some from headache this evening so for the present I will close and finish in the morning so goodby – my love to all – your own husband – Hubert

Well Darling it is now Sunday morning and cloudy and foggy. I feel much better this morning and I hope soon to be well. I am tired of Chattanooga already and wish I was some where else. Plenty of whiskey about here and plenty of drunkenness. I think sometimes the country is ruined any way whether the Yankees get it or not. This army must be badly demoralized and three months of inactivity will only make it worse.

Well I must close. Give my love to all the family and <u>our</u> relations if they are still with you. I do not know when I can see you unless I can get a place for you some where up here. What is the political news down there? Is there much excitement? It looks foolish to be making a noise over such things at such a time as this. Well Darling I must close. Much love and many kisses for my Darling and our boy. From your own dear husband – Hubert

As he withdrew toward Chattanooga, Bragg burned the bridge across the Tennessee River at Bridgeport, Alabama, in an effort to forestall pursuit by that route. He now felt that the Federal army was barred from the Confederates in Chattanooga by the Tennessee River and by several ranges of rugged, precipitous mountains, passable only through a few gaps. But Bragg's sense of security from these obstacles was misplaced.

In addition to burning the bridge at Bridgeport, Bragg for a while took the prudent step of stationing a force at Bridgeport to guard the Tennessee River against a possible Federal crossing there. Hubert Dent's battery was a part of this force. Under orders dated July 12, Bragg directed Lt. Gen. Polk to send a brigade "to guard the river from Bridgeport to Shellmound." In compliance with this order, Polk on the same day ordered his division commander, Gen. Withers, to send Anderson's brigade, and further ordered that Dent's Battery, which many were still calling Robertson's Battery, be detached from Deas Brigade and sent with Anderson for this guard duty. [583] Dent and his battery would remain in the vicinity of Taylor's Store and Lumper near Bridgeport for at least a month.

During the month in which Hubert and his battery were stationed at Bridgeport, a somewhat unusual incident occurred. On the opposite side of the Tennessee River were Federal forces under Gen. Lytle. During this time, a group of ladies who had been visiting friends wished to cross the river to return to their homes in the Federally occupied area. Their request for permission to pass through the lines of both armies was granted, and a flag of truce was arranged. Capt. Dent and another Confederate officer, Capt. Barth, served as staff officers to meet the Federal party on the island in the middle of the river at Bridgeport to make the exchange. The Federals were represented by a tall captain from Illinois, "a very large fine looking man with a heavy full beard". While waiting for the ladies to come up, the two groups were "good naturedly chaffing each other about incidents of the war". The Federal captain pointed out a small Frenchman in his party, whom he called "Pierre", as the man who killed Gen. McCullough in the battle of Elkhorn. In the same vein, Hubert replied that he could have brought along the man who killed Gen. Rosecrans' Chief of Staff at Murphreesboro, knowing

271

that this had been done by men of Robertson's Battery. Hubert's companion, Capt. Barth, was less cordial to the Yankees, and commented to the Federal captain that it was "very unhealthy for Yankees in Dixie,"and that he "might not return home".[584] The party then completed their business and separated, but Hubert would have cause in the near future to recall Barth's ominous comment to the Federal captain.

Bridgeport was a small town in the extreme northeastern corner of Alabama, where the states of Alabama, Georgia, and Tennessee join together, about 26 miles west of Chattanooga across intervening mountains. It occurred to Hubert that this relatively quiet period of detached service on the banks of the Tennessee, secluded from the roistering camps of soldiers and the whiskey dens of Chattanooga, was a good place and time for a long-anticipated visit from Anna. In good spirits, Hubert wrote Anna from Bridgeport to propose arrangements for a two-week visit, if the Yankees let them stay there. Hubert tells her that there are a lot of Yankees on the opposite side of the river, but he does not think they would try to cross the river and reach Chattanooga from this point. As will see, Gen. Bragg apparently shared this view, and later events would prove them both badly mistaken, but not until after Anna's visit. Hubert reminds Anna that she will have to bring money for the trip, because the Confederate paymaster is still sporadic in meeting the army payroll. In Eufaula, Anna and her father are considering selling the house that Edward had bought for the couple, probably because Anna prefers to live with her large family at Fendall Hall, instead of alone, during Hubert's absence. Hubert still resents Henry Shorter's apparent retirement from military service after the Eufaula Rifles returned from Fort Barrancas and disbanded. Actually, Shorter did eventually reenter the army as an aide to Gen. Cullen Battle in Virginia; but either that had not yet occurred, or Hubert was unaware of it at the time of this letter. After the war, Hubert and Henry Shorter would become firm political allies.

Camp near Bridgeport Ala
August 1st, 1863

My own Darling Wife
I have just read your letter of the 27th and when I finished I concluded I would sit right down and write you. Your letter did me a great deal of good and made me feel much better after reading it.

There has been a good deal of excitement down here for the last two or three days. The Yankees are as thick as black berries on the other side of the river and are quite impudent. They have a high bluff and two good earth works and some eight or ten pieces of artillery – some of them heavy pieces and I can't say how many men. In position they have a decided advantage over us and if they attempt it can make this side of the river very uncomfortable & they may even be able to cross the river. I have no idea what they intend to do but I hardly think they will cross the river and try to reach Chattanooga from this point.

Day before yesterday in the evening Genl Anderson came to me and told me to go down to the river and select positions for two guns and open on the enemy at day light next morning. Accordingly I went down, selected the

272

positions, and took two guns down that night. About 11 o'clock I received orders not to fire without there was some pressing necessity. My guns are still there but no prospect of firing them soon.

The Yankees come down to the river bank and shout across to our men and ask them a great many questions. One of our men told them in reply to "what was the news from Charleston" that "Genl Gilmore was killed". Is that so, said the Yankee. Certainly, said our man. They offered to give coffee for Tobacco &c &c. They seem to be planting some heavy guns on the heights on the other side of the river. But enough of the Yankees. A few weeks will tell what they intend doing.

I went again yesterday Darling to see Mrs. Harris about getting a room for you. She will not consent to take you under two weeks. But if you can get off about the 10th or 12th of this month and the Yankees seem disposed to let us remain here I would be glad for you to come. I think it will be a right pleasant place to stay at. It is quiet and retired away from soldiers. I think the old man is a Preacher – at least every body calls him Preacher Harris. I do not think I can get more than one room in fact they do not care to take in any one and it is only as a matter of accommodation they do it at all. The best vehicle I can offer you to ride in will be a wagon. If you come prepared we can ride horse back as often as you wish. I have a bay horse here that will take you along very well. I am sorry it is so difficult to procure room here for I know it will disappoint Mollie as well as yourself for her not to come with you. Write me at once Darling what you think of it and whether you can come. Do not place much stress upon it for I am by no means certain we will remain here long enough for you to make the visit. You have been disappointed so often that you had better be prepared for another one. I can write you again several times before you will leave and will try and meet you in Chattanooga when you come if you do come.

I am no better off in the money line than when I wrote from Shelbyville so bring money enough with you to pay a month's board and your traveling expenses. The pay master is not here and I do not know when he will be – consequently I have no money. I do not expect I will draw any before the last of this month. I expect you can get some one to come with you as far as Chattanooga – about Eddie I will leave him entirely with yourself Darling. If you think he would be troublesome do not bring him. In case you do come and should be compelled to leave in a hurry he might be troublesome. So I will leave that matter entirely in your hands. But I do not think it necessary to write more about this just now. You will be about one and a half or two miles from my camp and with an old gentleman a Lady and their family. I do not expect they will be able to feed you very well for that was one of their objections to taking you. That provisions especially flour was very scarce.

In relation to selling our house and lot ("you see I talk big") I do not remember what Mr. Young gave for it but there is so much depreciation in Confederate money now that six thousand dollars is not as much as Two thousand was three years ago – at least it so in this country or in other words you could buy three years ago with one dollar more than you can buy now with three. These are simply my views. Mr. Young is right there and can judge much better than I – but whatever you do of course Darling will please me.

While on the subject of houses and lots – has Cato ever paid you the office rent for last year. Seventy-five dollars is too little for it now the way every thing is selling and I believe if he will not give more than that for it that I will lock it up next year. Why that will not more than buy me a pair of boots. It ought to be worth at least one hundred and Twenty-five dollars.

Have you read Genl [D. H.] Hill's address to his corps. He gives it to the exempts. Calls them "worthless creatures" and "poltroons" who have skulked from the field under the provisions of the exemption law. I intend cutting out one of them and forwarding it to Henry R. Shorter and if he gets fighting mad to invite him to meet me on the field under Yankee fire and then if he feels like fighting it out to tell him to pitch in on the Yankees and to give them fits.

Well my Darling it is now after dinner. Every thing has been remarkably quiet all day and it is the laziest weather or as lazy as any weather I ever felt. But my evening naps have been disturbed so much the past three days that I do not feel sleepy this evening and will finish this letter.

Your picture of yourself and Eddie talking about me in bed affected me a good deal. Poor little fellow. I wonder if he understands what it is to want to see his PaPa and if he would know me if he were to see me. I expect my letters have been rather gloomy lately but I am over that feeling now.

Every thing goes on in the company pretty much as usual. I have had eight men to desert since we left Shelbyville and I expect others will do the same thing. But that does not trouble me at all now. My company is getting gradually smaller and unless more men are given to me I will be compelled to give up two guns and make mine a four gun Battery like every other Battery in this army except one or perhaps two.

Bruton [one of the battery lieutenants] has been talking of taking the step he has for some time and he does it now because he is second in command. He was nearly crazy when I got to Shelbyville last winter and says he would not undergo the same thing again for any thing. I am glad of it for I never could have felt easy to have left the Battery in his charge. Richardson will be my second now and with all his careless ways and loose talk he will do better than Bruton. Stockton too is a good officer and I do not know who will fill the vacancy – probably Southwick will fill one and Sergt. Ziegler the other if ever I am promoted.

George is very well. He is now the third corporal in rank and if there should be three vacancies among the sergeants he will be one, which is no mean position. He is now at the river being gunner at one of Stockton's guns.

Well Darling I have written you a long letter but I expect you like myself do not object to them. Give my love to all the family. My next letter will be to Mr. Young. I must now bid you goodby. I hope we will see each other soon. But I have not such faith in it as would remove mountains – much love and <u>many many</u> kisses for my Darling & our boy who wants to see his PaPa. Your own devoted & anxious – Hubert

Although Hubert had given Anna good and sufficient reasons to decline the suggested visit, she did not turn down this invitation. She probably made the trip without Eddie, who was only two. One of the circumstances that made a the visit feasible was the availability of a railroad connection to Bridgeport. From Eufaula, Anna could take a boat or stage upriver to Westpoint, Georgia to board the Western and Atlantic Railroad, which took her all the way to Chattanooga, where Hubert could meet her, as his letter indicates, or where she could have connected with the Memphis and Charleston Railroad to ride the 26 miles to Bridgeport. The visit was apparently very satisfactory for both of them. As Hubert had feared in his letter, however, federal movements probably intervened and caused Hubert to suggest that she leave earlier than planned. Anna later wrote him that, "Although it is a great trial to leave you, still in that as in everything else, if you think best, just so I want to do."

On August 16, while Anna was visiting Hubert, Rosecrans started his initial maneuvering. He planned to make a feint, as though approaching Chattanooga from the northern route, but his actual intentions were to put his army across the Tennessee River at Bridgeport, southwest of Chattanooga. For this reason, the Federals were closely watching the activities of the Confederate brigade at Bridgeport, fearing that the rebels might be increasing their force or constructing works there at night. Among the Union correspondence, we find a note from Federal Gen. Lytle to Gen. Sheridan, dated August 16, 1863, probably while Anna and Hubert were happily riding horseback around the Bridgeport countryside, reporting that,

> "With a glass last night, we were all of the opinion that the rebels had a strong working party at the point named. A deserter, however, just swam across from the island (the color-bearer of the Seventh Mississippi) who says positively that they are not erecting works, and that they have *nothing but Robertson's Battery*...The deserter says the men last night were probably cooking rations.[emphasis supplied]." [585]

The Official Records reflect this report being transmitted by Sheridan up the line to Rosecrans' new chief of staff, Brig. Gen. James A. Garfield, (the future president of the United States, destined to be assassinated), with the assessment that the Confederates were "moving off".

Unfortunately, Gen. Sheridan's "moving off" assessment was entirely correct. Bragg, perhaps in the expectation of an attack on Chattanooga by a northern rout, pulled Anderson's Brigade and Robertson-Dent's Battery out of guard duty at Bridgeport. Anna may have been still been with Hubert when this order came, and if so, this development would have caused Hubert to promptly place her on the train back to Eufaula.

With no Confederate force guarding the crossing, the way was clear for Rosecrans to catch Bragg completely off guard by carrying out his real plan. Instead of proceeding toward Chattanooga from the north, he swung down southwest of Chattanooga, to Bridgeport and Stevenson, Alabama, the very area that Dent's Battery had been guarding until pulled out. Starting on August 29, Rosecrans now rebuilt the bridge across the Tennessee and began moving his Army across the Tennessee: by bridge at Bridgeport, by ferry at Stevenson, and by pontoons, boats and rafts all along the area. By September 4, Rosecrans had gotten his entire army across the river, thereby outflanking Bragg's army in Chattanooga. Rosecrans then continued over the mountains into the northwestern corner of Georgia.

In an effort to confuse Bragg, (which was entirely unnecessary), Rosecrans as he advanced spread his army over a very wide area, a tactic that would have been dangerous before an alert opponent. But Bragg was only vaguely aware of what was occurring, and seemed to have no particular plan to deal with it.

The strategic implications of his position gradually sunk in on Bragg. A superior army was now on Bragg's side of the Tennessee River (the southeastern side), and in his left rear. Rosecrans now had the option of by-passing Chattanooga and moving across north Georgia toward Atlanta, cutting off Bragg's line of supply from Atlanta and trapping his army in Chattanooga. Bragg concluded that his best opportunity lay in withdrawing south, to fight Rosecrans as his army came through the mountain passes, and this is what he did. He evacuated Chattanooga on September 8, and the Federals occupied it on September 9. Chattanooga was a prize of great value, and its surrender without firing a shot caused a huge outcry against Bragg. But given the position he had gotten into, and given that his objective was the enemy army, not specific geography, there was little else he could rationally do in the circumstances.

In Anna's next surviving letter to Hubert, apparently her first since returning from her visit to Bridgeport, she expressed how difficult it had been to leave Hubert at the end of her visit. Even Anna is alarmed that Chattanooga and all of Tennessee have now been yielded to the Federals without a fight. We also learn that her father, although a strong Methodist, does not always take seriously his preacher's admonitions against chewing tobacco:

"Eufaula, Ala
Sept 14, 1863

"My Dear Hubert -
    I haven't had a letter from you in three or four days. I ought not to feel worried for everything is in such confusion that I know that I can not hear regularly but I am always troubled when I don't hear from you often.
    Oh! Dearest how much I would give to have a long talk with you this morning. I miss you so much since I left you. Now don't let this keep you from sending for me when every thing is quiet. Although it is a great trial to leave you, still in that as in everything else, if you think best, just so I want to do.

Yes, Dearest and for the world I would not do anything that I thought you would not approve or that would wound you in the least, I think that I know your views on almost any subject (am I right!) And I try to do in everything as I think you would wish. I believe you feel the same way. I don't think that you would do or say anything that you think would give me pain.

I have been feeling anxious about you ever since I left. I thought long before this a dreadful battle would have taken place. It is the opinion of a good many that there will be no fight there ever. Won't it be dreadful if Rosecrans should just fortify himself at Chattanooga, they have the whole of Tenn…and got it…with very little trouble or very little fighting. I do hope that Gen. Bragg will drive him away. I feel uneasy about their getting so much of our country, we must have some place to raise provisions. I don't feel despondent or gloomy, but it would be gratifying to hear that the Yankees in Tenn were dreadfully whipped.

Maria is in town with her children. She has survived, but the Baby is quite sick. There is a good deal of sickness in the place but we have had very few deaths. Mrs. Zadoc Daniels died in Griffin a few days ago. She was brought here and buried this morning. I don't know any one who would be so little missed, she never went much in society.

Oh Honey you ought to have heard the sermon Mr. Cottrell preached yesterday, he gave it to tobacco chewers and smokers, and the use of tobacco generally. I agreed with him fully and I think you would too. I don't believe there is one of his male members who does not chew - there sat Pa chewing all the while as he usually does, but he seemed very much amused.

The Baby has brought a seat and put it near me and asked me to put him on it - he's very much interested in seeing me write and says that he is going to be a smart boy and write to Papa - he says Papa is good. He wants to be just like him. I feel more and more the importance for those who have children to set them good examples - they Generally think that whatever their parents do is right - I feel that what one of Mr. Chambers little boys said yesterday was what almost every child feels - Mr. Cottrell was talking to the children in Sunday School about their using tobacco and a good many promised never to use it. Hen C did not, he says that "whatever his papa does is right and he wants to do just like him." That is just the way our boy will be. Just ask him now why he did anything, he will say "Mama does it" - he don't know anything of his Papa yet but it will be the same way when he is with you. He is a very interesting child and I do want to raise him right, to be a comfort to us. There are many of his little sayings that I would like to write you but I haven't time this morning.

[Postscript across the top of front page] He sends a kiss to Papa. Honey you ought to have heard him [recently] - I was feeling miserably sad…he came up to me and said "Mama you got the blues." I told him that I was feeling bad about you, I was afraid that the Yankees were trying to kill you. He said "I go get my gun and kill old Yankees"- and he said his prayers that night and asked God "not to let the Yankees kill Papa but bring him home to me and Mama"...I must stop...I don't think that you will be able to read this letter - Good Bye my own love, many kisses and much love from the Baby and

Your Own Nannie

[A further postscript] Ada wanted me to ask you to inquire if there is a man on Gen. Hindman's staff named George Triplett. She knows his son John Triplett and wants to know where he is now. N."

As the Federals were approaching, Bragg badly needed reinforcements. For some weeks a drastic idea had been under discussion: detaching Gen. Longstreet's Corps from Robert E. Lee's Army of Northern Virginia and sending it south to strengthen the Army of Tennessee. Gen. Longstreet himself was in favor of the idea. With Lee's army idle on the Rapidan at this time, and with the danger in the west so great, Lee and President Davis approved. Lee, well aware of past failures of the Army of Tennessee to capitalize on its successes, expressly conditioned his approval upon an assurance that "vigorous pursuit" would follow any success. Longstreet's Corps, consisting of Hood's and McLaws' Divisions, departed Virginia for Georgia on September 9.

To his credit, after withdrawing from Chattanooga, Bragg skillfully used propaganda and carefully planted "deserters," to successfully convince Rosecrans he was in full retreat toward Rome or Dalton, so that Rosecrans was lulled into leaving his forces scattered in the mountain passes southeast of Chattanooga. Bragg's plan was to fight the Federals piecemeal while their forces were scattered and as they emerged from the mountain passes. This plan was sound, but unfortunately it was not effectively executed. In the ensuing maneuvers over the next several days, Bragg had opportunities to trap and destroy major portions of Rosecrans' separated army, including a golden opportunity at McLemore's Cove, but these chances were bungled, and the Federals escaped. Bragg's officers were becoming convinced that Bragg often did not know what he was doing.

By September 13, Rosecrans had finally realized that Bragg was not in retreat but was gathered for battle, and Rosecrans began hurriedly bringing his separated forces together. By the night of September 17, the two armies were confronting each other across Chickamauga Creek, Georgia, ten miles southeast of Chattanooga, and the stage was set for the greatest Confederate victory of the western theater.

32
Dent's Battery At Chickamauga

"...the battery for a moment or two was in great danger. But the gunners served their pieces like veterans, and their gallant captain [Dent] set an example worthy of emulation."

Brig. Gen. Arthur M. Manigault, war memoirs

With Hubert Dent's promotion to captain, and his formally assuming complete command of the battery, it had now became officially known as "Dent's Alabama Battery." His officers were 1st Lieutenant W. T. Stockton, 2nd Lieutenant D. L. Southwick, and 2nd Lieutenant G. B. Ziegler. Hubert's brother, George Hatch Dent, had now been promoted to First Sergeant, the highest-ranking non-commissioned officer in the battery.

Dent's Battery was equipped with its usual six Napoleon 12-pounders. In Hubert's August 1 letter to Anna from Bridgeport, quoted above, Hubert notes that if the manpower of his battery continued to diminish, he may have to reduce his six gun battery to a four gun battery, *"like every other battery in this army except one, or perhaps two."* This comment calls our attention to an interesting sidelight about the size of Hubert's battery. At the beginning of the war, there had been no standard number of guns in an artillery battery, and the number ranged from three to seven. When Felix Robertson and Hubert organized the battery at Pensacola in November and December of 1861, it had four 12-pounder Napoleon guns,[586] and the company fought the battle of Shiloh with these four guns.[587] After Shiloh, Gen. Beauregard adopted new organizational guidelines for the artillery, and ordered that all six gun batteries be reduced to four, and any excess lieutenants be reassigned.[588] Notwithstanding this order, by the end of the foray into Kentucky in November 1862, Robertson's Battery had six Napoleon 12-pounders, and in December it fought the Battle of Murfreesboro with six guns.[589] The explanation undoubtedly relates to the relationship between Captain Robertson and Gen. Bragg, the commander of the Army of Tennessee. Felix Robertson was known to be a close favorite of Bragg's. Indeed, in January 1863, Gen. Bragg published an order which reaffirmed Gen. Beauregard's four gun limitation for *other* units in his army, but which officially recognized an exception for Robertson's Battery (and one other battery) which allowed it to have six guns. General Orders No. 7, dated at Tullahoma, January 17, 1863, provided in part as follows:[590]

"The previous order in regard to the assignment of artillery to brigades will be rigidly adhered to as follows: One battery of four guns to each brigade of infantry....*Robertson's battery of six guns and Slocomb's of six guns, one in each corps, to be exceptions*. Semple's battery of five guns will be reduced to four. The extra gun will be turned in to the proper department...No change from this arrangement, either in number or kind of guns, will be allowed, without orders from these headquarters."

So when Hubert told Anna in his letter of August 1, 1863 that his is one of only one or two artillery batteries in the Army of Tennessee with six guns, he is accurately reflecting official policy, and is benefiting from Felix Robertson's special relationship with Bragg.

As Hubert prepared for the impending clash on Chickamauga Creek, he was acutely aware that his performance during his first battle as battery commander would be closely watched by his men, and perhaps others. He was anxious to earn the respect of his men and a good reputation for the battery. Before the battle, Hubert entrusted George with certain personal articles to give to Anna and others, with messages, in the event he should not survive the battle. This prompted George to ask,

"Why are you sending messages by me? As a commissioned officer, you won't run as much risk as I will!"

"Yes, I will in this battle," Hubert replied, explaining that he had resolved that the men would see him occupying more exposed positions of danger than anyone else in the company, to remove any perception that the battery might not participate in as much bloody fighting under the new captain as it had under Capt. Robertson.[591] Hubert's objectives in this respect would be fully achieved.

Because the right flank of the Confederate line overextended the Federal left, the main feature of Bragg's battle plan was to make a concentrated attack on the Federal left, go around its left flank, get between the Federals and Chattanooga, and force Rosecrans' army to the southwest into McLemore's Cove, a deadend valley from which escape would be difficult. The afternoon and night of Friday, September 18 were spent by Bragg's army fighting to get across Chickamauga Creek and into the planned positions.

Because of the poor railroad network remaining to the Confederacy, Hood's Division, the first of Lee's Virginia troops sent to reinforce Bragg, barely arrived in time. About four in the afternoon of Friday, September 18, Hood's Division arrived from Virginia, immediately joined the battle line, and pushed the Yankees back six or seven miles. Throughout the night, Bragg continued moving his men across Chickamauga Creek, until by morning, most were across. However, Rosecrans had become worried that his left flank was overlapped by the Confederate right, and during the night had transferred troops from his left to his right, so that now, the left end of his line considerably overextended the Confederate right. But Bragg did not know this, and he expected to open the battle by turning Rosecrans' left.

The fighting on the first day, Saturday, September 19, was a ferocious, seesaw battle resulting in much bloodshed, but not much advantage to either side. Deas' Brigade and Dent's Battery were not brought up in time to participate. During the fighting on the nineteenth, there was never a general advance of the Confederate line, but piecemeal fighting that spread from right to left. The fighting stopped only when there was not enough light to distinguish friend from foe. The Federals had 45,000 men on the field on the nineteenth, while Bragg had about 30,000. Nevertheless, the ferocity of the Confederate fighting led Gen. Rosecrans to overestimate Confederate strength and conclude that he was badly outnumbered.

On Saturday night, Gen. Longstreet arrived with the rest of his Corps from Virginia. Bragg was awakened, and during a conference at midnight, he reorganized his army into two wings—Longstreet commanding the Left and Polk the Right. He ordered the attack to begin at daylight, with the fatherest right division to begin and the others to attack in turn successively from right to left. The plan and objective were the same: to turn Rosecrans' left and force him into McLemore's Cove.

Dent's Battery was attached to Gen. Deas' Brigade, a part of Hindman's Division. Although Deas' Brigade and Dent's Battery had not been in the fighting on Saturday, they would see important action all day on Sunday, the 20th. In the midnight reorganization after Longstreet arrived from Virginia, Hindman's Division, and thus Deas' Brigade and Dent's Battery, were placed under the command of Gen. Longstreet in the Confederate left wing.

On the morning of Sunday, September 20, Gen. D. H. Hill, the fatherest right division, was late in commencing the attack, which resulted in late attacks by each successive division attacking in turn down the line. However, when it began, the attack on the Federal left was so strong that the Federal line was threatened with collapse. Gen. Thomas, commander of the Federal left, called for more reinforcements. The Confederate attack on the Federal left was thrown back, but in heavily reinforcing Thomas on the left, Rosecrans had to weaken his right by shifting troops from his right, and this proved to be his undoing.

At this point, Lady Fortune smiled upon the Southern Cause. In the confused shifting of Federal troops from their right, Federal Gen. Woods, acting on ambiguous orders, pulled his division out of the battle line in order to move to another point believed to need support. Not only did Woods' withdrawal create a large hole in the Federal line, but it occurred at the very moment that the Confederate left wing under Longstreet was commencing its assault, which was commencing later than planned due to Hill's late start. Seeing the opening in the Federal line, Hood immediately sent eight brigades formed into three lines charging into the gap. These brigades attacked through the Federal line, then turned and attacked the Federals from the side and rear, throwing the Yankees into panic-stricken disorder. The jubilant Confederate soldiers, recognizing their opportunity, began an irresistible rush that stormed over the running Yankees and everything else in the way. The stampede continued until it captured the headquarters of Gen. Rosecrans, who was running with the rest toward McFarland's Gap and the road back to Chattanooga. [592]

Meanwhile, somewhat to the left of this initial breakthrough, Hindman's Division, including Dent's Battery, charged into the Federal divisions of Generals Sheridan and Davis, routing them and quickly completing the collapse of the Federal right. From his position southeast of the Brotherton house, Captain Dent led his battery forward with the General advance, firing at the retreating Yankees.[593] As Dent's Battery moved forward, unleashing volleys of canister into the Yankees, Hubert was unaware that he was operating on the right of another Alabama contingent, the Fifteenth Alabama Infantry Regiment. This Regiment was commanded by Hubert's friend from their period of association with the Eufaula law firm of Pugh & Bullock: Colonel William C. Oates. Oates would later lose an arm near

Petersburg, Virginia; and serve as a post-war congressman and then governor of Alabama. One of Oates' recollections of this stage of the Chickamauga victory, which he described in his memoirs, was this:

"And just here I wish to mention that one of our batteries which kept just off on our right and did such splendid firing, as many of the Fifteenth Alabama men will remember, was the battery of that superb soldier from Eufaula, Ala, Capt. S. H. Dent, but we did not know what battery is was until after the close of the battle." [594]

Among the Union troops on Hubert's front was Lytle's Brigade, the Federal force that had been stationed across the Tennessee River when Dent's Battery was at Bridgeport, Alabama. As Hubert followed the retreating Federals, he happened to notice a lifeless body on the ground. He was momentarily shocked to recognize it as the body of the Federal captain with whom he had had the friendly talk at Bridgeport, eight weeks earlier. Hubert instantly remembered his friend Barth's prophetic comment that it was "very unhealthy for Yankees in Dixie," and that the Federal captain "might never return from Dixie."[595]

As the last of the fleeing Federal infantry before him disappeared from his field of view, Hubert heard heavy firing to the northeast. Without awaiting orders he limbered up and galloped toward the fighting. Through a gap near the Vittetoe house Hubert could see a column of Yankee artillery and wagon trains speeding away toward Chattanooga as fast as possible on the Crawfish Springs Road. He quickly unlimbered and started bombarding the retreating vehicles and troops. Under the heavy shower of exploding case shot and grape, the Yankee drivers abandoned their disabled guns and wagons in the road, blocking the road to more oncoming vehicles, throwing the retreating column into confusion, and resulting in the capture of many guns, wagons, caissons, and equipment. [596]

In descriptive language rarely found in military documents, Confederate Gen. Bushrod Johnson, in his after-action report, described the battlefield as he saw it at this triumphant point in the battle:

"The scene now presented was unspeakably grand. The resolute and impetuous charge, the rush of our heavy columns sweeping out from the shadow and gloom of the forest into the open fields flooded with sunlight, the glitter of arms, the onward dash of artillery and mounted men, the retreat of the foe, the shouts of the hosts of our army, the dust, the smoke, the noise of fire-arms—of whistling balls and grape-shot and of bursting shell—made up a battle scene of unsurpassed grandeur." [597]

These Confederate opportunities had resulted only in part from good fortune. Longstreet, his front-line Confederate officers, and the soldiers in the ranks all had the presence and the instinct to abandon old orders and reposition to exploit the openings to the fullest. Lincoln's Assistant Secretary of War, Charles A. Dana, who was with Rosecrans that day, later observed that, "Bull Run had nothing more terrible than the rout and flight of these veteran soldiers."[598]

But there was still difficult work ahead before the Confederates could rest. By early afternoon, the only high-ranking Federal officer remaining on the field was the commander of the Federal left wing, Gen. George H. Thomas. To slow the Confederate pursuit and save the Federal Army from complete destruction, he quickly patched together a strong force and improvised a defense along the crest of a "spur" of Missionary Ridge called Horseshoe Ridge, or sometimes called Snodgrass Hill. Snodgrass Hill was actually a series of hills, separated by steep ravines and gorges. Overgrown and wooded, it provided good defensive cover for the Yankees. It was difficult terrain for artillery, but Dent's Battery was about to learn to operate in it.

As Confederate Gen. Bushrod Johnson and his division continued to advance, he came to Snodgrass Hill, and learned of Thomas' strong defensive position there. Another Confederate force led by Kershaw had unsuccessfully attempted dislodge him by scaling a different face of the ridge. Gen. Johnson recognized the importance of the position and resolved to take it, but he needed reinforcements, and he needed artillery. His staff officer had earlier encountered Dent's Battery in the field and commandeered it for Johnson's Division,[599] so for the remainder of the day, Captain Dent served under the orders of Gen. Bushrod Johnson. Gen. Hindman also agreed to place at Johnson's disposal the Brigades of Anderson, Deas, and Manigault. In addition to Dent's Battery, artillery support would also be provided by Everett's Georgia Battery.

Johnson's force crossed the Vittetoe Road and started up the steep slope of the first hill, struggling through brambles and woods. At the top of the first hill, the infantry stopped to wait for Dent's and Everett's batteries to reach the top. It is difficult to visualize how these heavy guns, limbers, caissons and horses were dragged up the sharp and rugged hills encountered that afternoon, but often they were propelled in part by hand--by solders pushing and by grasping the wheel spokes and turning the wheels. Gen. Johnson carefully positioned the troops for the attack. Two sections of Dent's Battery, consisting of four Napoleons, were wheeled into place in front of Fulton's Brigade of Tennesseeans. The three howitzers of Everett's Georgia Battery were placed beside Dent. The remaining two-gun section of Dent's Battery was placed in front of Sugg's brigade. The objective was the next hill, the ridge west of "Hill Three," which required the infantry to rush down the slope of the hill they were on, into the gorge, and up the other side to reach the Yankees on the crest of the ridge.[600]

At 1:45, the artillery commenced fire into the woods before them, and at 2:00 the infantry began the assault. Dent's right section blasted the crest of the hill to protect the advancing infantry. Not many of the defending Ohioans were hit in this initial barrage, but the shells ignited brushfires, which soon blanketed the front with smoke. The Confederates fought their way up the slope to within a few yards of the crest, but the firepower of the Ohioans' repeating Colt rifles drove them back down the slope. Gen. Johnson now reformed his lines for another assault, incorporating newly arrived Southern troops. He detailed ten infantrymen to help in maneuvering Dent's guns. The two-gun section previously detached from Dent's

Battery was moved into the hollow on the right, ready to be rolled by hand up the hill as soon as the ridge was carried. Johnson gave the order for the renewed assault to begin, and in his words, "A most obstinate struggle now commenced for the possession of this spur of Missionary Ridge, the last stronghold of the enemy on the battle-field of Chickamauga."[601]

Dent and Everett commenced a deadly barrage of canister and case shot all along the crest of the opposite ridge, while the determined Confederate line pressed upward, keeping up incessant small arms fire. The Yankees were beginning to weaken from the blistering attack. However, about the time the Confederate's first assault had begun at 2:00 o'clock, Federal Gen. Granger had arrived at Thomas' headquarters with reinforcements, which Thomas placed under the command of Gen. Steedman and immediately directed to the ridge west of Hill Three. Steedman's men now rushed up the back slope of the ridge, over the crest, and burst upon the Confederates advancing up the other side, sending them reeling in retreat. Steedman's men pursued the Confederates headlong down the slope toward the hollow. At this point there was the real danger that the Confederate line would break and run under the momentum of this reinvigorated Union counterattack. As Gen. Johnson delicately expressed it, "The retreat on this hill was precipitate, and called for all the exertions I could command to prevent many of the troops from abandoning it."[602]

But the panic was quelled, and rout was prevented, when Hubert Dent and his gunners coolly stood their ground and started blasting away into the oncoming rush of blue jackets. Joined by Everett's howitzers, the artillery sprayed volleys of canister on Steedman's troops with deadly effect, killing the standard-bearer and stopping the charge. Almost 100 men of the 22nd Michigan were killed in the first two minutes of the first real combat that unit had ever seen. Hubert himself received a slight wound on the right leg below the knee, but he remained in command of his guns. The Confederate infantrymen rallied behind Dent's and Everett's guns, regained their composure, reloaded, and drove back Steedman's onslaught. Gen. Johnson was so pleased with the performance of his artillery that, even at the height of battle, he took the time to compliment Hubert on the performance of his battery.[603]

> "…Our batteries were promptly opened and gallantly served amid a shower of the enemy's bullets, and, together with the best and bravest of our infantry, who promptly rallied on our artillery, poured such a volume of fire upon the advancing foe that his onward progress was effectually stayed.
>
> I cannot here speak too highly of the gallantry of the men and officers of Dent's and Everett's batteries on this occasion. It elicited my highest admiration, and I at once endeavored involuntarily to express personally to the commanders my high appreciation of the work they had so nobly done."

Brig. Gen. Arthur M. Manigault later recalled the scene in his war memoirs:

> "Our men at the word of command, at three o'clock, went boldly forward, descending a hill into the gorge and advancing up the one opposite, Dent's Battery, 6 Napoleon guns, opening behind and above us on the enemy. A steady and rapid fire assailed us as we advanced, both artillery and infantry.

After an unavailing effort we were driven back, the enemy in turn charged us, and the battery for a moment or two was in great danger. But the gunners served their pieces like veterans, and their gallant captain set an example worthy of emulation."

After thus repelling the Union counterattack, Southern units then attacked up the slope again, but were stopped near the crest. This sort of seesaw battling back and forth became the pattern for the afternoon. Suggs' Tennesseeans slowly worked their way up the slope, while "a heavy fire from the Rebel batteries of Dent and Everett was turning the ridge into a living hell."[604] Casualties were huge. The 96th Ohio lost 100 men in twenty minutes.

After two hours of seesaw battle, fatigue began to show on the Confederates, who had been fighting continuously all day; portions of Deas' and Manigault's Brigades withdrew from the hill into a ravine to rest and be resupplied with ammunition. As these men withdrew, Dent and Everett raked the ridge with canister to prevent any possible Federal pursuit. But Gen. Johnson resolved not to abandon the fight for this position. "Repeatedly our men advanced," he later reported, "and were in turn forced to yield a portion of the ground they had gained. I directed our men to advance as far as possible, then hold their position and never retreat. We thus gradually approached the crest of the ridge."

By 4:30, Gen. Steedman's Federal units were disorganized and demoralized. Although portions of Gen. Johnson's force were still out of action due to exhaustion, he continued to press the attack with the troops he had, slowly inching closer to the crest. "It was finally nearly sunset," he reported, "when a simultaneous advance swept along our whole lines, and with a shout we drove the enemy from the ridge and pursued them far down the northern slope to the bottom of the deep hollow beyond." During this advance, Dent ordered two of his guns to be quickly wheeled by hand up to the crest of the ridge, from which they fired down the northern slope into the fleeing Yankees. These were the closing shots of the fight for Snodgrass Hill. Steedman retreated in disorder to the northeast.[605]

After seeing the abandoned federal position, a Confederate soldier later recalled, "I could have walked 200 yards and not stepped eighteen inches without stepping on a dead Yankee."[606]

Although during the fight for Snodgrass Hill Dent's Battery was detached from its assigned division, that of Major General Thomas C. Hindman, nevertheless Gen. Hindman felt it appropriate to comment in his official report on the value of Dent's Battery to his own operations that afternoon:

"Dent's Battery, of Deas' Brigade, was engaged throughout the struggle. Notwithstanding the repulses of our infantry, the officers and men of this battery stood to their guns undaunted and continued firing, inflicting severe loss on the enemy and contributing largely to the success of my operations." [607]

285

Hubert's Brigade Commander, Brig. Gen. Zach. C. Deas, (from whom Dent was also detached that afternoon), pointed out in his official report that Dent's Battery closely followed the brigade in the advance during the morning attack, and that "in the afternoon rendered signal service, fighting at the time with other commands on my right…the officers deserve special mention for their conduct."[608]

Certain interesting statistics reflect the intense level of activity of Dent's Battery and bear out the validity of four generals' singling out this company-level unit for praise. Maj. Gen. Hindman's division had five companies of artillery, consisting of eighteen guns, which fired a total of 508 rounds of artillery ammunition during the two-day battle. Of this total, 317 of the rounds, or 62%, were fired by the six guns of Dent's Battery, even though it was not involved in the first day of the battle.[609]

Three days after the battle, Hubert rendered his own "official report" to Anna:

"Chickamauga Station
Sept. 23rd 1863

"My Own Darling,
        I will now try and give you a connected account of the last great battle. I wrote you a short note yesterday in great haste expecting then to be called on to leave - and I was. We left there in great haste and marched just this side (North) of Chickamauga Station - I hear this morning that our cavalry are in Chattanooga and that the Yankees yesterday burned up about fifteen acres of wagons to prevent them falling into our hands. I wish we had plenty of supplies so we could push right after them. But enough of this I will tell you something of the fight.
        In the fight of Saturday I think the Yankees rather got the best of it. I wrote you about getting on the field and seeing Kolb's battery running like clever fellows. This was about all I saw of the fight on Saturday.
        Sunday the fight commenced about 10 AM on our right. Soon after, our Division advanced. Genl Deas Brigade on the right - Manigault's on the left - Anderson's as a support in rear of the center of the other two. Deas made a splendid charge. Manigault did not do so well. Anderson supported finely. I followed in rear of my Brigade. The Yankees had breast works of logs and timbers - our gallant fellows charged right over them - a great many Yankees remained behind the logs until our fellows jumped over them - when they started in full run for our rear - they passed me running at full speed asking "which way is rear."
        The bullets were whistling thick and fast around us all the time. It was quite amusing [to see] the blue jackets "streaking" it for the rear [portion of letter deteriorated. Ed.] Genl Hood having been wounded - Genl Johnston (Bushrod) took command of that part of the line.
        I will first mention that our division was under Longstreet's part of the line (the left) at this stage of the fight. My Battery was the only one near the

line, it seemed that the others did not follow up their Brigades like did mine - and Genl Johnston wanting a Battery in position, he took mine as the only one he could find. I went to the right and did not fight immediately with my Brigade any more during the battle. I put one half of my Battery in position under Stockton on a hill and took the other three and went ---- to the front and a little to the left. Pretty soon the Yankees came rushing back and made desperate effort to retake the hill on which my last mentioned guns were located. I fought there from about 1 or 2 o'clock until dark - bringing up another gun - and sending Stockton with two guns to my right as support. I behaved gallantly and was slightly wounded in the right leg just below the knee.

The Yankees made about six or eight different desperate efforts to take the hill - our Infantry would fall back to my guns - where they would make a stand and pretty soon my heavy guns would send them back - then our line would advance to recoil again. This as I have said occurred six or eight times - not rapidly but we would advance slowly and recoil slowly - a great many infantry ran entirely past my guns and reported in the rear that my Battery was certainly captured. [portion of letter deteriorated] My men but with few [exceptions] fought well and I felt very proud of [them] and I believe I can say to you that [they] are proud of their Captain. I lost ----------- men killed and wounded - Five killed dead - fourteen wounded, some of whom I am afraid will die - among the wounded is Lt. Stockton - a staff officer was assisting [portion of letter deteriorated. Ed.] Johnston's staff when he was shot in the face. He was a gallant man.

My horse was wounded in two places - seriously in the shoulder and in the left fore leg. The shot in the shoulder did not miss me more than an inch - it will be some time before he is fit for service. The blankets on behind my saddle were shot with a minnie ball and cut up like rats had been eating them. I have the ball that lodged in my blankets, also one cut out of my horse. I believe I will send them to Ed [Anna's fourteen-year old brother] as trophies of the battle.

Darling I can't tell you all the good things that have been said to me and about my Battery. But enough to make me vain. I don't think Dent's Battery is one whit behind Robertson's in reputation as far as the army is concerned - whether the news papers will blow about it I can't say - but hardly think they will as army correspondents are scarce and they do not write of these things like they did when the war was first commenced - but I do not care. [portion of letter deteriorated]

The last troops we fought from our position on Sunday evening were his [Rosecrans'] reserve troops and soldiers from the convalescent camp (Granger's Corps) They fought well too.

The field was rather barren of plunder. The prisoners reported that their wagons had all been sent to the rear with all their baggage. I got about a peck of coffee - a cavalry pistol - a good looking glass - with a soap & razors out of a Yankee caisson. I was looking for friction primers for my battery at the time.

The men made me presents of things they captured I have two silver pencils with gold pens. I want to send you one - both were given me - one man gave me a handkerchief and another a pretty good scarf. I have two Yankee pictures with fine cases - they came out of the caisson too. I want to send you the cases to have some pictures taken in them. One is a large case the other medium size - both fine cases. The men some of them got a good deal. I filled up my chests with fine Yankee ammunition captured on the field.

Our Brigade lost very heavily - out of about seventeen hundred men the loss in killed wounded & missing was Eight hundred & twelve, out of this number one hundred & forty-seven were missing - one half of these will in all likelihood turn up as stragglers. The balance may be either killed or wounded. The loss in officers in one Regt. was very heavy. The 22nd Ala - Lt. Col Weedon whom you remember I mentioned to you as a great favorite of mine was killed - a gallant man and true. The color bearer of the Regt. was shot down when Col Weedon seized colors and planted them ----- just in advance of his Regt. A Yankee color bearer at the same time planted his colors right opposite Col. Weedon and about fifty or sixty yards distant - Col W. shot at him with his Pistol and just as he did so a ball struck him and killed him. The Yankee color bearer ran and the Regt. (22nd) pressed on.

I know more of your acquaintances who were killed, the wounded you will hear of. I hear that Genl Clayton & Macon got through safely. M. had a horse killed so I hear. I could mention many instances of individual gallantry but you know more of the parties. Capt. May of Genl Anderson's staff (The Frenchman) was seriously wounded - he behaved with great gallantry. I myself led a charge of Infantry at one time and made myself so hoarse that I can scarcely talk - shouting and hurrahing so much.

I do not know what we are going to do next but I suppose we will try to regain middle Tenn.

Well Darling I have passed safely through another great battle and I thank God that I am safely through it. Dr. Thomason is at a Hospital - he sent me word yesterday that he had sent you a dispatch announcing my safety. I was glad to hear it and I hope you received the telegram.

Tell Mollie Lt. D went through all right. I know very little of the loss of officers. I hear we lost three Brigadiers besides the wound of Maj. Genl Hood - some reports say he is mortally wounded.

If I can get hold of a copy of the official report of Genl Johnston I want to see what he says about the Battery. He complimented us highly in the fight. Well Darling I have written you a long letter and now I do not know how or when I will send it. I am very much obliged [illegible] them the first opportunity.

The weather has been quite cold lately - overcoats in great demand - one of the blue shirts you sent me has been cut up to make lining for my coat. My tailor (Spaes) was killed I do not know how I will get my coat finished. I suppose you may direct to Chattanooga otherwise as before. I am tired - last night was the first good nights rest I have had in several nights. I have no idea how long we will remain here - but not long I think. Richardson [one of the battery's lieutenants] is still at the Hospital - and a good many more besides.

Love to all Darling - I hope you did not suffer uneasiness long. Tell my friends I am all right and ready to pitch in to the Yankees once more. I should like to crowd them now right out of Tenn - with much love & many kisses for my Darling & my boy I must say goodby - Your own devoted. Hubert"

Two days later, Hubert wrote again with more detail:

"Camp ---- Chickamauga Station
Sept. 25th 1863

"My Own Darling,

I sent a letter to you yesterday giving you some little account of the part performed by us in the late great battle. Our Brigade as I wrote you left the battle field on Monday evening and came to this point were we are guarding a pass leading from Harrison's landing out towards the railroad. I have just heard that they are advancing and we may have a small brush with them. Our Brigade is the only one here - we have a few cavalry in our front - the remainder of the army has advanced on Chattanooga and my guard tell me this morning that they heard very heavy cannonading in that direction last night. We have not a word of news as to what is going on.

You have already heard more news from the late battle than I know as I have not seen a newspaper since the fight - our loss I expect was very heavy - heavier I think than either Murfreesboro or Shiloh. I am satisfied that I was under longer continued hot fire than at Shiloh. I have very little idea---how many prisoners we took or guns or anything of that kind. I hear that we had--- fifty-four pieces of Artillery and more than fifteen thousand small arms and from six to eight thousand prisoners.

The only Brig. Genl we killed for the Yankees as far as I know was Genl Lytell or Little. He was at Bridgeport when we were there. Genl Hood, Preston Smith, Helm and Deshler on our side are certainly killed - but I do not report it as fact. I forgot another who also is certainly dead - Genl Adams.

We are following them very slowly it seems to me – Rosecrans' army was certainly very badly whipped and if Chattanooga was not such a strong natural position we might have nearly if not entirely destroyed his whole army. I suppose Genl Bragg knows best - at any rate I will trust him a while longer. I think when the whole truth comes out about this battle that it will be one of the severest and most decided of the whole war.

Darling I hope you received the dispatch Thomason sent you - for I know you suffered very greatly. Darling when you don't hear from me always think I am safe. Bad news travels faster than good. I am in warm places and under heavy fire - but thanks to a kind providence I came through safely.

I never felt in the least that I would be [hurt]. Stockton being the only experienced officer I had present I had a great deal to do and did not have time to notice the whistling of the balls. The company seem to be very proud of their Captain and of course that pleases me very much. This you know is the first fight in which I have led them as commander and I think they have plenty of confidence in me now if they did not before. I have been complimented highly by some Genl officers and I think my Battery will be favorably mentioned in the official reports of the battle.

Our troops did not capture much plunder in this fight. The Yankees had sent all their baggage to the rear and cheated us. I captured a quantity of coffee - one cavalry pistol and a good looking glass - something you remember we needed very much - an officer sent me a paper of darning needles - Lt. Meade. You did not see him. I will send you a pencil & pen given me by one of my men. I also got a small portfolio on which I am now writing paper & all - my company is in fine spirit and so is the whole army.

If old Rosey don't get out of our way "somebody might get hurt". I am short in officers & --- in men - Genl Deas has sent me twenty ----- try to help me out and says he is determined ------ up my Battery as soon as the army ------ and we are quiet for a few days.

Southwick and Ziegler are my two new Lts. [George] made 1st Sergeant or rather Sergeant Major ------. Lt. Mitchell of the 39th Ala was [killed]. He is a brother-in-law of Sissie Mitchell - I think Mollie knew him. I have not heard a word from Maj Cook. I hope he got through safely. I saw Julian McK[enzie] day before yesterday just getting back to his Co. Officers in that Battery get home very often. You will hear of the casualties in the company sooner than I. I was sorry to hear that Mrs. Barnett's son was so seriously injured.

I have a couple of balls one cut out of my horse and one out of my blankets which I want to send home as slight mementos from my Yankee friends. I hear that some troops have gone to Mobile - suppose Banks must be moving against the place. Do you know whether George Young was here or not?

Give my love to all the family Darling. Tell them the Yankees have not got me yet. A Regt & some cavalry have gone to the front. Perhaps we may have a small skirmish this evening. We have a fine position. Goodby Dearest God bless you and Eddie and may we all meet soon. Love & kisses to both from your own devoted and loving husband. Hubert

[In pencil across the side of the last page]: "A bottle of ink was turned over on my letter after it was sealed & directed. I have not time just now to write another."

[Across the top of the letter is this postscript]: "The darning needles are from ----- Meade. The other large ones from myself. I will send some Yankee pictures next time. I have just had a letter from Md. dated Sept 5th - all well - write to

Mollie[referring to Hubert's younger sister, Mary] Darling - direct to her at "Newport Charles Co Md" and enclose to 'John L. Lancaster' Richmond, Va. 'to be forwarded.'"

As Hubert was writing this letter of the 25th, on the same day, Anna was writing to him from Eufaula to express her intense relief on learning that he was unhurt. This is the best of the few extant letters from Anna. She portrays the suspense and anxiety prevailing at the home front after a battle, as the town waits for the news of who lived and who died. This family had already lost one son. Edward's walking into the front door of Fendall Hall and down the marble-tiled hallway holding the "dispatch" that Hubert is alive is a poignant scene of relief and joy in the Young family. To Anna, frantic with fear for Hubert, the fact that the South had won a great victory was unimportant until she learned whether Hubert was alive.

"Eufaula, Ala
Sept. 25th 1863

"Oh: My Dearest how thankful I am that you have passed through this battle safely. God has been merciful and kind to us, I have been perfectly wretched the early part of this week - In fact ever since I left you, I have been troubled and anxious, and I never prayed for you my Darling as I have the last few weeks. When we heard Tuesday morning that a terrible battle was raging in Northern Georgia - well I can never describe my feelings - and a thousand times did I think something terrible might befall you, Tuesday, Wednesday, and until noon yesterday, were days of agony to me, and night brought no rest.

"I can't account for it, although I have always been anxious about you when I knew that you were in battle, yet never have I felt as I did this time, and often in imagination did I see Pa coming up, bringing some dreadful news - but thank God this terrible blow has not come upon me.

My great anxiety for you, kept me from being much elated with the news of our great victory. I do hope that we have destroyed a good part of their army, but it makes me feel sad to think of the many noble lives sacrificed on that terrible battle field. Several prominent men from Columbus are killed - not a word has been heard from any one in the Eufaula Artillery. I think this is very strange as most of them have friends here. Mr. Sylvester is expected home this evening slightly wounded.

I have heard a good many say that they do not object to their friends receiving slight wounds, so they can have them home with them, but my Dearest I was oh so glad when I heard that you were unhurt. You must thank Dr. Thomason for me in sending the dispatch, I am glad to know that he is safe. I supposed that George had escaped unhurt too as he would have mentioned him. I shall look anxiously for a letter from you.

Annie [probably Annie Hewlett Young, the wife of Anna Young Dent's older brother, Will Young] had a real fit of hysteria when the dispatch came. All of us were frightened – Mamie [another family name for Mollie] saw Pa coming some time before our dinner hour and she went seeing after Ma who was in the back part of the house just as pale as she could be. Ma came up the passage just as Pa got in the front door, then I saw him for the first time. When I looked up he was holding both of his hands up and saying that he had a dispatch, my first thought was that you were killed and I said, Tell me what it is - Pa said Good news - Oh! My dearest I was so relieved, Annie commenced laughing and crying together, and I think most of us joined her in crying before a great while - I never had such a thankful feeling in my life - How I would like to sit down by you today and tell you all my feelings and hear you talk.

I had two letters from you Tuesday…

Uncle William [William Young of Columbus] hasn't heard from Willie [his son, William H. Young, Jr., a trooper with Wheeler's Cavalry Corps] since the 17th - he had been in two fights then, but was not hurt - if they are anywhere near you enquire for Willie - he is in the 3rd Georgia Cavalry, but I do not know his Captain's name.

Write me soon Dearest, tell me all bout the battle - I hope that all our friends escaped - I wish that we could hear something more from the Army, up to Tuesday is the latest news. Some of the papers say that Rosecrans has crossed the river, others think that is not so - I must say Good bye now - All your friends felt anxious about you here and rejoiced with me when I got the dispatch - much much love from Your devoted wife.   Nannie

33
Disaster At Chattanooga

"It was an awful day for us, Darling. 'Running' is something I have never tried before and I hope I may never have to try again. We lost nearly everything..."

Hubert Dent to Anna

During the Chickamauga battle, at 3:00 P. M. on Sept 20, when the federal right wing was in total collapse and full retreat, Gen. Longstreet had proposed to Bragg that a portion of the Confederate right wing join Longstreet's left wing to pursue and destroy the fleeing Federals. Bragg flatly refused, and walked away. The amazed Longstreet later wrote that Bragg thought the battle was lost because it had not gone the way Bragg had planned. Bragg was thereafter out of touch and had little or no part in the direction of the battle. In late afternoon, after the Confederates had completely swept the federals from the field, Gen. Polk went to Bragg's tent to report. Bragg had gone to bed but got up while Polk reported that the enemy was routed and could be totally destroyed by prompt pursuit, before he had time to reorganize and throw up defenses at Chattanooga. Polk later wrote, "General Bragg could not be induced to look at it in that light, and refused to believe that we had won a victory".[610] Bragg made no effort to claim the ultimate fruits of his soldiers' hard-won victory.

In Chattanooga, Rosecrans was making plans for further retreat when he realized that Bragg was not pursuing. He then gave up thoughts of retreat and started fortifying the city to hold it. Within two days, the Federals had converted the trenches originally dug by Bragg's men into "formidable earthworks".

Having now lost the chance to occupy Chattanooga as a part of the Chickamauga victory, Bragg still refused to attack, and could think of nothing more original than to try to starve the Federals out. He placed the city under semi-siege by spreading his army in a six-mile semicircle around part of the city. His left was at the base of Lookout Mountain, cutting off Rosecrans' railroad communication with his base at Nashville. Later he put artillery atop Lookout Mountain to shell the federals, but the range was too long to be effective. Bragg's right extended along Missionary Ridge to the Tennessee River.

On September 26, Generals Longstreet, Hill and Polk held a conference to discuss Bragg's "palpable weakness and mismanagement". Longstreet wrote Gen. Robert E. Lee, while Polk and Hill wrote President Davis, to point out Bragg's incompetence. Longstreet also wrote Secretary of War Seddon "...nothing but the hand of God can save us or help us as long as we have our present commander". On October 4, an extraordinary meeting was held attended by all of Bragg's top-ranking officers, who drafted and sent to President Davis a "round robin" petition reciting in detail Bragg's failures. These Confederate officers lamented:

> "Two weeks ago, this army, elated by a great victory which promised to prove the most fruitful of the war, was in readiness to pursue its defeated enemy. That enemy, driven in confusion from the field was fleeing in disorder

and panic-stricken across the Tennessee River. Today, after having been twelve days in line of battle on that enemy's front, within cannon range of his position, the Army of Tennessee has seen a new Sebastopol rise steadily before its view…it is certain that the fruits of victory of the Chickamauga have now escaped our grasp…. The Army of Tennessee, stricken with a complete paralysis, will in a few days' time be thrown strictly on the defensive, and may deem itself fortunate if it escapes from its present position without disaster."

Sadly, the prediction of the last sentence would soon be fully borne out.

Typically, Bragg sought to blame others for his own ineffectiveness after Chickamauga, identifying Generals Polk, Hill, and Hindman as being at fault. President Davis personally went to Bragg's headquarters on October 9 to investigate. Following a series of turbulent but inconclusive meetings, Davis returned to Richmond without resolving anything and, incredibly, leaving Bragg in command. Thereafter, Bragg slowly but systematically removed from his command every general who had criticized him.

Meanwhile, Lincoln, understanding the importance of Chattanooga and the seriousness of the threat, took prompt action. Rosecrans was removed and replaced with the highly able General Thomas, who had become known as "the Rock of Chickamauga" for his stand on Snodgrass Hill. Grant was made overall commander of the Department, and moved his headquarters to Chattanooga to assume active charge of operations there. Due to bungling by Bragg, the Federals seized control of a point on the Tennessee River that allowed them to reestablish direct communication with its supply base, ending the threat of starvation. Federal reinforcements poured into Chattanooga.

The opposing Confederate and Federal lines were so close that each could hear the band music of the other. Grant could watch Bragg and test him without extending his supply lines. Grant was waiting only for the arrival of Gen. Sherman and his troops, who arrived on November 14.

We see from Hubert's next letter to Anna that the Confederates, oblivious to the disaster which is about to befall them, are not girding for an imminent battle. They are occupying themselves with building shelters, trying to get warm, and seeking some comfort during a cold and uneventful siege. A sincere and devout Christian, Hubert turns to the Scriptures on Sundays. He explains to Anna why a leave at this time would be imprudent for him, and discusses his officers' capabilities.

"Camp on Missionary Ridge
November 16th, 1863

"My own Darling
    I wrote Mr. Young yesterday and in it said I would write you today. I have brought my table in my tent and have a comfortable fire and if nothing interrupts me I am going to write you a long letter.

It is cloudy and cold and looks like it might snow. I have been busy for three days past working to put up a shelter for my horses, and I am afraid now that it will snow or rain before I finish it. I am a little nervous from cutting wood and can scarcely write.

I spent a very quiet day yesterday. Every officer left camp except myself. I shut up my tent – made a good fire – took a thorough wash, put on clean clothes & spent the balance of the morning in looking <u>at you</u> and reading my bible. It seemed more like the sabbath than any I have passed in the army in a long time. After dinner I read my bible again and Thompson came in and I read several chapters aloud. I felt really better when night came. I wish I could spend all my Sundays in that manner.

I was sitting by my fire last night thinking of home, wondering how you were all engaged and wondering when I could have the privilege of sitting with you, but alas even if I am allowed to go home I will only enjoy the pleasure for a short time. But let me not repine. This war <u>must</u> end some day and then --- oh! well I will leave your imagination to fill the blank.

The picture you drew in your last letter (the 7th) of the happiness of your cousin is certainly a fine one. I am glad to hear it – sincerely glad that she is so happily married and so happily situated. I am satisfied that she is worthy of it all. No Darling I do not repine at such pictures. If I can't enjoy these things myself I am glad that there are some who can and especially when they are so worthy. Besides I hope some day to enjoy them, if not with the same amount of wealth at least with enough to content me, which is after all the best and greatest wealth.

I hope you arrived safely at home and from what you wrote I expect Ma is going to pay them a visit. If she does I hope she will be at home should I get a chance to go – but leaves of absence just now are not granted as liberally as they were a short time back and there is some talk of reorganizing those men who reenlisted at Pensacola. If anything of that kind is going to be done I will be compelled to remain here & look after it as I might go home and come back and find myself without a company. I feel satisfied that I can stay and keep the company together or enough to make a company. I received one recruit this morning under Genl Bragg's order giving a furlough for every recruit. I think I will get one or two more soon. I will take them just to keep my company full. I have nearly as many men now as some of the Infantry regiments. Most of the new men who have been transferred here seem to be very well pleased and if I could get rid of about a half dozen of the old crowd I would have a well behaved company and I do not know that I ought to complain for I have had no trouble since the fuss Richardson had when you were up here and that could have been avoided if he had not been so hasty. Just between us I wish I could get Richardson out of the company. Stockton would make a much safer second in command and he will have to learn a good deal about papers. But here I am filling up this letter with matters in which you are not at all interested. I will write of something else. But before I close I will ask one question. Suppose I could get a leave and do not do it because the reorganization goes on: would you prefer for me to remain and try and keep my position or go home and risk losing it?

Affairs here are going on pretty much as heretofore occasional shelling from batteries on both sides. Our Troops have built sheds and shanties until nearly all of them are comfortable. Very few have tents – but as long as they remain here they are independent of them. One can see every variety of style & structure by riding along our lines – "necessity is truly the parent of invention."

The assignment of Genl Hardee to this corps gives great satisfaction in our Division. Now if Genl Anderson could only get the Division – but I am afraid he will not. I very often go over and see him when he has nothing to do and find him very agreeable and entertaining. He has lived in nearly every state in the old union – that is extravagant but he has lived in several and knows a great many persons. I go over and play chess with Capt. Barth occasionally at night – and generally beat him too. In fact I am victor so far over all my competitors in the chess line – not that I can play so well either for there are plenty of men who can beat me.

It commenced sleeting a few moments ago but has stopped now. I look for it tonight – old winter is about to commence his reign in earnest.

Darling tell Mr. Young that I have written to express agent at Dalton about my box and have not heard from him yet – expect to hear tomorrow. I send to Chickamauga every morning and hope I will get it soon. I wrote to him about it yesterday.

I have bought me a silver watch lately – found I could not get on well without one. I am ashamed to tell you what I gave for it.

Well Darling I will not finish this letter this evening.

Stockton will return in two weeks and then I will see what I will do about going home or rather what Genl B. will do about it.

Our rations are improving some very much to my gratification. I hope congress will do some thing for officers. Our month's expenses for this month including the box Mr. Young sends me will be about one hundred dollars for each man – pretty heavy on 2nd Lts who get only ninety, and ordinarily it will run up to sixty or seventy.

Well Darling I close for tonight. Goodby. Your own Hubert.

Well Darling I will now finish my letter. I was aroused this morning about day light by a heavy artillery fire on our left which created some excitement. I jumped up myself and was about to dress when I happened to think that I heard yesterday that Robertson was going to take a Battery up on the left and open fire on a Yankee camp. So I laid still again. The firing soon ceased. Robertson either could do them very little damage or they soon got out of the way. Nothing else new. I expect to hear the result of the firing today sometime.

It did not rain or snow last night but it is still cloudy this morning. I wish I had my stables covered but it will take me a week to get the boards out. Write me a long letter Darling when you get this. It has been nearly a week since I received one. Give my love to all the family. I will write to Ada either tomorrow or next day. Breakfast is ready so I must close.

I expect I will send Richardson to Atlanta after ordnance stores but I do not intend to let him remain as long as he did before – ten days this time. Good by Darling, much love and many kisses from your own – Hubert

Grant attacked on November 23, first taking a Confederate outpost at Orchard Knob. On the 24th, he had Gen. Hooker attack the lightly–held Confederate positions on Lookout Mountain, and took possession of the mountain on the morning of the twenty fifth. This is sometimes romantically referred to as the "Battle Above the Clouds." Actually there were no "clouds," only early morning fog; and there was no significant battle—the small Confederate force offered token resistance and then withdrew according to plan. This force joined the main Confederate position in the Confederate right along Missionary Ridge, where the principal battle would now begin.

At daylight on November 25, Sherman launched an attack with his entire force against the Confederate right at the end of Missionary Ridge, defended by the Confederate division of Gen. Pat Cleburne. The Yankee assault was repulsed over and over by Cleburne's stubborn men. When the federals made contact at the top of the ridge, they were repelled by hand-to-hand bayonet fighting as savage as any in the war. When Sherman gained a foothold partway up the ridge, the Confederates charged downhill and forced their retreat, removing Sherman from this day's battle. Cleburne's valorous defense had wrecked Grant's objective of turning the Confederate right.

At about 3:30 P. M., Grant ordered Gen. Thomas to attack the center of the Confederate line, with the clear instruction to take only the first line of advanced rifle pits at the bottom of the ridge, and then to stop for further orders.

Bragg had arranged three descending lines of rifle pits: one at the base of Missionary Ridge, another line halfway to the top, and a third at the crest. At this point the crest was a steep 200 feet high and broken by ravines. The upper line of infantry was poorly placed at the natural crest (rather than the "military" crest), which meant that attackers could get close to the top before being exposed to fire from the defenders. The main battle had been expected on the Confederate right, and the center was thinly manned. It was so spread out that that the men could not touch each other with outstretched arms.

Dent's Battery was assigned to operate in support of Manigault's Brigade, in the center of the Confederate line. Dent's Battery was divided in two: one section of two guns was placed on the left or southern end of Manigault's brigade, near where it joined Tucker's Brigade on the left. This section was commanded by Lieutenant D. L. Southwick. Dent's two other sections, totaling four guns, were placed approximately 250 yards away, toward the right or northern end of Manigault's brigade, near where it joined Deas' Brigade on the right. These guns were directly commanded by Lt Ziegler and First Sergeant George H. Dent. As was his custom, Captain Dent stayed with the four-gun group.

In their initial rush, the Federals overran the Confederate skirmishers in the first line of rifle pits, and stopped only momentarily as ordered. But, exposed to a hail of fire from above, the Yankee soldiers could not remain stationary, so without orders they surged forward and upward.

Watching from below, Gen. Grant angrily asked Generals Thomas and Granger who ordered the men to start up the ridge. Granger replied that they started without orders. "When those fellows get started," he said, "all hell can't stop them." Grant was unmollified. "Well somebody will suffer if they don't stay there," he threatened. As it turned out, it would be the Confederates who "suffered."

The attackers swarmed up the ridge, taking advantage of the cover of the ravines, assisted by the Confederates' inability to see them until they were close to the top, and further assisted by the defenders' difficulty in firing downhill for fear of killing their own men. An hour after the attack began, the thin Confederate line at the crest began to falter.

When the battle in the Confederate center began, Brig. Gen. Manigault had felt some confidence that the Union attack would be repulsed. He first noticed Federals approaching the crest of the ridge a quarter mile to his right, in front of Gen. Deas's brigade. Concluding that Gen. Deas probably could not see them, he ordered Captain Dent to turn the cannons of his right section against this mass of Yankees, which Dent did. This seemed to scatter the Yankees, but actually they had merely taken cover in a ravine. Manigault had then gone to confer with Gen. Deas when an aide galloped up to report major breakthroughs by federal Gen. Willich on the left of Manigault's Brigade. Incredulous, Gen. Manigault returned to his brigade, and pulling up on a knoll beside Dent's left section, saw that the Confederate brigade to his left, Tucker's, had been routed by the Yankees under Gen. Willich. Tucker's men were escaping down the back slope of the ridge and the Confederate guns of Garrity's Battery of artillery were abandoned.

With his left flank now "in the air," Manigault realized that the position of his brigade was "critical in the extreme." He attempted to "change front", that is, to reposition his left regiment, the 28th Alabama, to front south, facing Willich's Yankees now in the abandoned positions of Tucker. He also directed Lieutenant D. L. Southwick, commanding Dent's left section of guns, to turn his guns to the left and open fire on the Yankees.

However, using the captured Confederate guns of Garrity, the Yankees simultaneously began shelling Manigault's center, which now began to falter. Bombarded from their left with Garrity's guns, and fearing that the regiment on their left, i. e. the 28th Alabama, would give way, the men in Manigault's center began melting away, first in one's and two's and then in larger groups. Furious, Manigault ordered his provost marshal to shoot any man heading for the rear that wasn't wounded. But it was too late. As his center snapped, Manigault turned his attention to attempting to save the four guns of Dent's Battery on his right, near the Blythe tenant house, where Manigault's two right regiments and Deas left regiment were still holding against pounding by federal Gen. Turchin.

With the collapse of his center, Manigault's left regiment, the 28th Alabama, became isolated and had little chance to survive. Federal Gen. Beatty's brigade (to Manigault's front) charged into the empty breastworks left by the fleeing center regiment, and swarmed into the right flank and rear of the 28th Alabama, so that it was now being hit from the front, rear, and both sides.

As Willich's Yankees pressed forward against the hurriedly-repositioned 28th, Lt. Southwick's section of two guns made a desperate effort to protect their fellow Alabamians by firing over their heads into the charging Yankees. Tragically, in their haste to stop the oncoming rush, Southwick's gunners lowered a cannon too much, and a round of canister went into the backs of their comrades, killing several. Soon thereafter, the federals gunned down Lieutenant Southwick, along with half of his men and most of his horses.

There was now nothing to stop Willich's and Beatty's jubilant Federals from overrunning Southwick's cannon position and seizing the two Napoleons. An Indiana unit then turned the Confederate cannons to the north and started firing down the line into Hubert Dent's two remaining sections of guns. In his aptly named, *The Shipwreck of their Hopes,*[611] historian Peter Cozzens describes the ensuing debacle:

> "The aim of the Hoosier infantrymen was atrocious. As their shot flew wide of their mark, one of Dent's cannoneers shouted defiantly, 'The old guns know whom they are shooting at and do not hurt us.'
>
> It was small consolation. Southward as far as Dent could see, the ridge was alive with Yankees 'sweeping over our position in pursuit.' And in front of his four remaining cannon, the Tenth and Nineteenth South Carolina was beginning to leak men rearward as the soldiers of Turchin's brigade, inspired by the success of Beatty on their flank, steeled themselves for a final push at the crest. North of Dent, Deas's left regiment also began to buckle under the weight of Turchin's resuscitated attack.
>
> Dent took the only rational course left to him: he tried to escape with his cannon and caissons via the Shallow Ford road. Dent ran one gun past the gauntlet of Yankees, onto the road and down the eastern slope. But before the second and third pieces reached the road, the Tenth and Nineteenth South Carolina collapsed, as did Deas's left. Terrified infantrymen blocked the path of Dent's caissons. As Dent tried to force a way through the throng, Beatty's and Willich's Yankees picked off nearly all his horses and toppled several of his crew. Those artillerymen not shot either surrendered to the Yankees, who came whooping down on them, or ran down the ridge with the infantry. One angry young cannoneer, a mere boy, threw rocks at the bluecoats until they gunned him down. The two cannon disappeared in a swirl of blue.
>
> With the road closed to him, Dent tried to take his last gun straight down the steep slope to his rear. Limber, cannon, and caisson bounced off the crest and slid down the slope. The caisson smashed into a tall tree stump, snaring an axle. Dent and his men worked feverishly to free it. General Manigault scraped together some seventy infantrymen to form a line to screen

the cannoneers while they worked. As they strained to lift the caisson over the stump, one of the gunners yelled: 'Look out, Captain." Glancing over his shoulder, Dent saw a Yankee color-bearer waving his flag only fifty yards away. On either side of him soldiers were falling in and capping their muskets. Dent warned Manigault, 'Leave the gun, General, and save yourself! The Yankees are on you!' Manigault saw them too—soldiers of Turchin's Eleventh, Thirty first, and Thirty sixth Ohio regiments pouring over his vacant breastworks. Before Manigault or Dent could react, the Federals let go a volley. 'To this day I do not understand why nearly all of us were not killed,' remembered Dent. But enough bullets found their mark. A man next to Dent was shot through the jugular vein. Several fell near Manigault, around whom 'the bullets whistled like a swarm of bees.'

Enough was enough. Manigault yelled at his inspector General to ride for it. "I thought my chance of escape doubtful in the extreme, but determined not to be taken if I could possibly help it." Manigault and the staff officer parted company. "Putting spurs to our horses, we dashed down the rough and rugged slope at nearly full speed, and at imminent risks of our necks, the ball pattering against the trees and rocks around me like hailstones."

Meanwhile, a section of Dent's Battery remained defiant to the last, isolated on the crest, firing double charges of canister at point-blank range into the faces of the oncoming Yankees.[612] But there was no time to reload, and many of the artillerists were shot or forced to surrender.

Convinced that further sacrifice of his men or himself would achieve nothing, Hubert decided that it was time to follow Gen. Manigault's example. Preceded by his brother, First Sergeant George H. Dent, and by Lt. Zeigler, Hubert galloped down the rear slope, to fight another day. As these three overtook a group of fleeing foot soldiers, Hubert dismounted and, with the help of his pistol, required the soldiers to form a defensive line against possible local pursuit. Thus organized, this group thereafter carried out an orderly retreat toward Chickamauga Creek. But Dent's Battery had been virtually wiped out. Its losses included five of its six Napoleons, two caissons, twenty-eight men, and thirty-five horses.[613]

Gen. Bragg ordered the Army to retreat to Dalton, Georgia, twenty-five miles southeast of Chattanooga on the Atlantic on Western Railroad, and assigned to the effective Pat Cleburne the job of blocking Federal pursuit. Federal Gen. Hooker followed, but was stopped by Cleburne in fierce fighting at Ringgold, Georgia, about halfway to Dalton. After receiving word from Bragg that the main Confederate army and its baggage had concentrated at Dalton, Cleburne also withdrew and joined the main army at Dalton. Hooker gave up the pursuit and returned to Chattanooga.

On the morning of November 29, Hubert wrote a short note to Anna from Resaca, not far from the main army camp at Dalton, Georgia, reporting the results of the battle, but later the same day wrote a second, more detailed letter. These letters reflect Hubert's deep mortification over being involved in a rout. Hubert was a proud and conscientious officer, concerned about his position in history. Being forced to run was something neither he nor his battery had ever experienced before. He expressed privately to Anna his disgust with the performance of the infantry. While he makes an effort to express encouragement and optimism for the benefit of the home front, his humiliation over losing his battery is overwhelming.

"Camp Near Resaca, Ga
Nov. 29th 1863

"My Darling -
I arrived here last night with the "Debris" of my Battery. The Yankees got 5 of my guns - only brought off one gun, 4 Caissons and 2 Limbers. Lieut. Southwick with his section was captured while firing - a good many men got away - but Southwick, with a good many others were taken. All others from about Eufaula are safe, Geo. and I are both out safe and were among the very last to leave the Hill. I do not know how many men I have lost. I saw four dead with that part of the Battery that was with me, besides several wounded. I can't tell anything of how many were killed with Southwick, but fear that several were. My killed, wounded and missing will run up to about 25 or 30 - very few were wounded that escaped.

I had no opportunity of writing or sending a dispatch. It was an awful day for us, Darling. "Running" is something I have never tried before and I hope I may never have to try again. We lost nearly everything from the center to our extreme left, and I do not know that I can add, like Francis I, "Save Honor" for our men ran most shamefully. I mean the Infantry, for as far as I can hear our Artillery did well. My Division saved only 4 guns out of 16 engaged, each Battery saved one. Breckenridge, I hear, lost all in his command except two. Robertson's reserve Artillery lost six. In fact I feel confident that we lost as many guns as we captured at Chickamauga, and they were generally better guns. I do not think our loss in men was very heavy. It can't be as great or anything like as great, as at Chickamauga. I think the loss of the Enemy in killed and wounded, must be much greater than ours. But we lost too much for the fighting we did.

Our line gave way first, of the part I could see, right in front of Southwick's Section - - it was defended by Genl Anderson's brigade. I have had a rough time on the retreat - my one gun is in rear of Lieut Zeigler helping to protect it.

General Cleburne's Division fought well and captured a good many prisoners - they are also in our rear. Major Courtney is behind with the 6 guns left in the Division, and I am now here in command of this part of the [artillery] Battalion, (a few caissons, wagons & men).

It has been raining a good deal lately and is very cold this morning. I will write you a long letter and give you something of a connected account of the fight but it may be several days before I write.

I do not know where we intend making another stand. I do not think our soldiers are disheartened, all that I hear talk of seem ashamed of running and anxious to give them another trial, and I believe that when we do fight again that we will whip them badly. Altho I have lost my Battery, I do not feel discouraged. If they give me another, I am ready to fight them again, and if they do not give me a Battery, I am willing to do anything to fight the Yankees. Old Bragg has been whipped for once, but better luck next time.

Well I must close. I am not certain that I can mail this, but will try - my love to all, Darling, and much love and many kisses for my Darling and my Boy from, Your own devoted Hubert."

Later the same day, Hubert wrote a longer, more detailed account of the defeat:

Camp near Resaca, Ga
Nov 29th 1863

My own Darling:

I wrote you a few lines hurriedly this morning and have sent them to the office. Believing that I will remain here all day, I have concluded to write you some account of what I saw of the fight.

As I wrote you before, on Tuesday the Enemy advanced their line and drove in our pickets. On Wednesday morning a line of Yankee skirmishers advanced and drove in our pickets still farther. Then we shelled them a little. All day Wednesday, we, from the top of Missionary Ridge, could see the Enemy massing their troops in our front. Lookout Mountain had been abandoned by us and the Enemy seemed to be moving troops from that point to our center and right.

Hindman's Division occupied about the center of our line, and Breckenridge on our left with his Corps, Cleburne's Division and perhaps other troops on our right. About 4 O.C. in the afternoon the whole Yankee line began to advance. My Battery was posted as follows, 4 guns under command of Lt. Zeigler and Sergt. Dent were posted just in rear of Gen. Manigold's Brigade. Two guns under command of Lt. Southwick were posted to the left of the other 4, distant about 250 yards and just in rear of Gen. Anderson's old Brigade. I remained habitually with the 4 guns.

As soon as the Yankee line came in proper distance, our Artillery opened on them and kept up a heavy fire, but it seemed to have no effect on their advance. Our troops under orders withdrew from the line of works at the foot of Missionary Ridge, and made the fight from a new line, constructed just below the crest of the Ridge. The withdrawal was made as soon as the Enemy advanced. This I have no doubt encouraged the Enemy.

On they came, now they are in our lower works and have commenced climbing the Hill. Shell, Spherical Case, Solid Shot and Canister, fall among them. Still they come. Our Infantry soon commence firing and the Artillery no longer able to fire effectively in front, commence an enfilading fire on their lines. But the Yankees lines do not falter. Now they are within a few steps of our works. Will our line hold them in check or give way? This suspense is short. Our line is broken immediately in front of Southwick's section, and the Yankee colors are planted between the guns. All that part of the line soon gives way. I ordered to open fire on the enemy who captured the guns but before the order can be executed, the line in front of me breaks and the Yankee colors are planted within a few steps of the Battery. I ordered the guns limbered up and succeeded in starting down the Hill, but the Enemy follow us up.

One of my guns lodges against a stump, I succeeded in getting it out; but before I could start down the Yankee line is in 20 steps of me and a volley is fired. Down go one of my drivers and several horses, the remaining horses excited start down the hill. The gun is overturned and abandoned. Two others just in advance of me are lost in the same manner. The bullets are flying around us thick and fast and the infantry are running ahead "SUAVE QUI PEUT" and away we go.

After running about 100 yards, I commenced to try to rally the infantry with whom I had then caught up, being mounted. It was slow work but we succeeded in getting a line formed. The Yankees did not pursue. We then withdrew slowly over Chickamauga Creek to the Station.

I lost 5 guns, 2 Caissons, excepting the limbers, and about 30 horses and have 28 men killed, wounded and missing (including Lt. Southwick). I think he was captured unhurt. I saw four dead men who were with me, and know of two others seriously if not mortally wounded, and in the Enemy's hands. Of the remainder I know nothing except that they are gone.

I could have escaped with very little loss by abandoning my guns at first, but I did not feel like doing that and succeeded in bringing off one. Yes Darling, the Old Battery is gone. I stayed by it and fought it as long as there was the slightest chance, and stayed and tried to bring it off, until staying longer would have sacrificed men and myself and accomplished nothing.

The truth is our Infantry behaved badly. I think they were frightened at the vast multitude of Yankees that were hurled against them. They could see every line as it formed and came up and, seeing that they were vastly outnumbered, they lost confidence in their ability to hold their position. We whipped them on the right and captured some prisoners, but the reminder of our line gave way shamefully.

I do not think our loss is very heavy, tho I have not heard anything on the subject. It seems to be that my Battery lost heavier than the Infantry by 200% and even greater than that. I think we lost in the neighborhood of 50 guns. Twelve out of 16 engaged in our Division were lost - we have six left.

Gen. Cleburne whipt the Yankees back who were pursuing us, and captured 1300 prisoners.

A great many of my men have lost all their clothes and blankets. I wonder if I could get any around Eufaula - I mean blankets, or something equivalent to them. If I thought I could I would ask for leave to go after them. Write me on the subject. I can't tell yet where our Army will stop. At present it is at Dalton 10 or 12 miles above here. I expect you had better address me there until I write again and let you know more about it.

I hope I will get another Battery. How it would please me to recapture my old guns - I hope to do it if the Yankees bring them down in Georgia. This victory will inflate the Yankees so much that it will prolong the war almost indefinitely I am afraid. I still feel confident of the final result - "Nil Desperandum" must be our motto. Individually, I believe I lost nothing except some money I loaned to some men who are gone.

I got just a little nearer the Yankees this time than ever before. When I left the hill side, the Enemy were in front of me just a little on my right. Lt. Zeigler's horse was shot. He, George Dent and myself were all mounted and left nearly together - - I believe I was behind. I tell you, Darling, I never felt so mean in all my life as when I was running - and as soon as I came up with the greater portion of the Infantry, I pulled out my pistol and commenced halting them and whenever I presented it they halted. It was the best argument and the most conclusive one I could use. It never failed. I do not know how I looked, but I feel "shoot"! And would have done it. I feel sometimes like I would like to have a Regiment of Infantry - my men did not leave until I ordered them. I wonder if I could not get a regiment to do the same way.

Well, Darling, tell our people they must not feel discouraged. The past is gone, we must use the present and be prepared for the future. The tide of war is slowly drifting into the heart of the Country. We will need all our fortitude, all our endurance and all our courage. Congress must repeal the Exemption law and the law allowing substitutes and bring every man in the Army who is able to fire a musket - we will need them.

Well, Darling, the sun is out but the wind is still blowing quite cold. Before the sun came out everything was freezing. I hope I will get letters from you soon.

Lt. Davidson has just left me. He says I am deeply sympathized with by all the Army who know me, and says further that Gen. Anderson wishes me to act as Inspector General on his Staff, until my Battery is refitted. I expect I will go as I think a good deal of him. The Army is still at Dalton, Davidson was sent down there to hurry back the wagons.

Well, Darling, this letter is filled with nothing but our defeat, and I expect you all do not talk of must else. Be of good cheer, Darling, all things will yet work out well for us. I saved my box and it is a great "save" I tell you. This defeat is awful, but it might have been worse. I believe I wrote that all from about Eufaula save Southwick are safe. I look for Richardson and Stockton tomorrow or the next day.

I intended trying to get a leave, but do not feel like asking for one now. A whipped man must not expect favors. I feel anxious to hear from the outside world, have not seen a newspaper in several days. Give my love to all the family.

No one can say Gen. Bragg made them retreat this time. He gave them a chance to fight, but Gen. Grant made them retreat.

Well I must close. Again my love to all. I would have dispatched but could not. I have been afraid you would hear of the loss of my Battery and think very naturally that I was gone with it - - But good bye - much love, from, Your Own, Hubert

Hubert continues to defend Bragg, and makes a valid point in observing that, this time, it wasn't Bragg that made the Confederates retreat, but General Grant. Nevertheless, the Southern public as well as the Confederate Cabinet had had enough of Bragg. Missionary Ridge was his last battle as commander. In Dalton on the night of November 28, Bragg sent his routine telegram report to Richmond, concluding with a request that he be relieved of command. Without further ado, within 48 hours he received notification that President Davis had "acceded to his request."

Despite Hubert's disappointment with the infantry, it is fair to point out that the Confederate Army on Missionary Ridge numbered 37,000, while Grant had almost 80,000 effectives.[614] And in this single battle, the hapless Bragg was opposed by all four of the North's most successful generals: Grant, Sherman, Thomas, and Sheridan. In killed wounded and missing, Braggs casualties were 6600, while Grant's were 5800.

Finding the right successor to command the Army of Tennessee was not easy. Gen. Hardee, the next in command, made it known that he did not feel competent for the position. Robert E. Lee recommended Gen. Beauregard. President Davis declined Lee's suggestion but offered the position to Lee himself, who begged off. General-Bishop Polk recommended Joseph E. Johnston, whom Davis did not like, but the support of Davis' old personal friend Polk carried weight. Davis and others in the cabinet were concerned over Johnston's "tendencies to defensive strategy." It was eventually concluded that he was the best available choice, and Davis appointed him, but with "doubt and misgiving." Gen. Polk took over Johnston's position as commander of the Department of Mississippi. To the chagrin of Bragg's critics, Davis gave him the position of military advisor to the President.

34
Winter At Dalton, Georgia

"Honey, your visit to me this winter did me a great deal of good. I am a better man than I was."

Hubert Dent to Anna

The enlisted men loved "Old Joe," as they quickly began referring to Johnston. They began to see him as a "military genius", and accorded him veneration similar to that accorded Lee by his men in Virginia. He kept their trust and confidence throughout his term as commander. Soon after arriving at Dalton, Johnston began measures to improve the men's lot. He sought to improve the commissary department to make food supplies less irregular, and to acquire sufficient clothing, blankets, shoes, and rifles. As the winter at Dalton progressed, it was said that thousands of soldiers who had "continued the flight from Missionary Ridge to their homes" returned. He declared an amnesty which brought back to the ranks many who had gone home in disgust. Morale rose. During the winter encampment, Gen. Pat Cleburne conducted classes for brigade commanders in the art of war, and they in turn instructed their regimental commanders. Gen. Joseph Wheeler gave his men rigorous training in cavalry tactics. In late March, there was a heavy snowfall, a delightful novelty to the boys from the deep South states. An impromptu snowball fight developed into a formal inter-divisional snowball battle involving 5000 men and a "battle line" a mile long, with generals, colonels, and other officers directing tactics.

During this winter interlude, Hubert's morale was greatly lifted by another visit from Anna, this time accompanied by little Eddie, who was now over two and a half years old. Hubert's letters home all reflect close interest in "the boy" and in his development, behavior, and discipline. The difficulties of traveling in wartime with a two year old were more than offset by Hubert's desire to spend time with his son in company with Anna. Dalton was located on the same rail line that had made feasible Anna's visit to Bridgeport. Again, she would have traveled by steamboat and/or stagecoach to West Point, Georgia, just north of Columbus; then via the Atlanta and West Point Railroad to Atlanta; then via the Atlantic and Western Railroad directly to Dalton in northeast Georgia. Even with these connections, it would have been a long, grueling trip. Anna and Eddie were likely accompanied by a servant or a family member, or both. After the visit, Hubert would write that it "did me a great deal of good," and that because of it he believes he is "a better man than I was." As an adult, "Eddie" would write of his visit to the Confederate army's winter quarters at Dalton, at age two, as though he actually remembered it, and perhaps he did.

The principal difficulty for the Army of Tennessee was its numerical inferiority to the Northern army. A number of plans were urged upon Johnston under which he would be reinforced from other commands long enough to carry out offensive operations against the federals. Johnston's usual response was to agree to accept the reinforcements, but decline going on the offensive. His basic approach was to wait for the enemy to attack, and "be ready, if we defeat them to press on into Tennessee."

As spring arrived, with the odors and flies which accompany artillery horses, Hubert wrote Anna of camp life:

Camp near Dalton, GA
May 1st, 1864

My Darling

Yours of the 27th was received this morning and the perusal of it gave me much pleasure. I also received a letter from Mr. Young and two newspapers the "Spirit" and the "Advocate."

Well Darling May is upon us but this morning did not look much like it had arrived. Instead of a bright clear pleasant day we had wind and rain enough to make it cool and a fire decidedly comfortable. It had been so warm that we had knocked out a great deal of the chinking and taken off a good many of the boards of our cabin. So last night and this morning we are blessed with plenty of air. I can't say however that it is very wholesome for we have too many old camps around us.

Maj. Courtney is talking of moving our camp and Beckham says if we move that he will put the entire regiment nearer together. While I would have not much objection to moving I am not anxious to get into a camp with so many horses. The flies are innumerable here and the greater the number of horses the greater the number of flies.

I am glad my box has arrived safely. I expect to need the articles again next winter.

About sending my horse home or rather sending a mule in his place the suggestion may be a very good one—but the difficulty would be in getting the mule—none worth any thing can be procured here for love or money. I can send home a very good mare and colt in his place if that would do any better, by waiting some weeks yet. You can speak to Mr. Young about it and see what he thinks. But I was thinking that as Morgan [the Youngs' horse] was taken, he would need a horse and that he had better keep the bay at least until there is another impressment.

I did intend going to church today but the rain prevented me. I have not been to church since I have been in Dalton and I ought to feel ashamed of such neglect – but I never did enjoy going to church in a strange place and among entire strangers.

The excitement about an advance of the enemy has all quieted down but many are under the impression that we cannot remain quiet much longer.

Well Darling I have had dinner. The good things of our boxes are all gone and we are coming down to plain meat and bread again. Well we can get along on it as well as the remainder of the army. We hope to get some coffee soon and then we will be all right for the campaign. We have received no money yet and what is worse we don't know when we will. The soldiers are needing money now about as badly as they ever have since they had been in the service. I have no money at all. I had to borrow to send the two glasses I sent by express a few days ago. So you see you are not the only one who is suffering from exhaustion of the pocket. Well I have a good many postage stamps and a small quantity of paper so I will not need much money.

And so Darling you think I am not writing you long letters now. Why Honey I think I write nearly as much on a half a sheet of this size as most persons do on a whole sheet and it saves paper. Honey your last letter was so kind and affectionate. It does my heart good to receive such letters from you. I wish as much that I could see you. If I were only by your side this evening how happy I should feel. Yes Darling you are the idol of my heart and I am so anxious to make you just such a husband as you desire I should be. I hope my love that you are feeling more cheerful now. Write me Darling all your feelings and thoughts. They always interest me and I want to know them. You know you have been accustomed to write these things to me and I expect to hear them. Let there be full and entire confidence between us Darling. We will be all the happier for it.

It is a cloudy dreary evening—nothing at all like the first of May. A year ago we were at Shelbyville having pleasant weather and parties and pic nics were numerous and largely attended. I hope we will regain that country before this year passes away.

Genl Johnston is receiving reinforcements and many think he will take the offensive if the enemy does not very soon.

Has Mollie made her visit to Macon yet? Tell her I hope she will have a pleasant visit.

I see by the "Spirit" that horses were given to two of Clayton's staff. The letter of thanks is badly expressed I think. It appears at the first part of it that the Editor of the paper had given the horses. I could not understand it at first. I thought Jim Buford or whoever was the Editor had become very liberal all at once. I understood it when I reached the bottom and saw to whom it was directed. I expect Junius' conscience is not entirely easy. I do not think it ought to be.

Oh there is a small piece of army news that I will write. Lt. Col. Bondurant of our Regt has been ordered to Mobile. That creates a vacancy in the Regt and as Maj Courtney is the senior major he may be promoted and then possibly the senior Capt may be made a major when all this done. When all this is done I would be second Capt in the Battalion.

Capt Kolb has been trying very hard to get Napoleon guns but has not succeeded yet. He threatened to resign a day or two ago unless heavier guns were given him. He has four howitzers.

I hear nothing more about transfers from my company. Genl Johnston was my friend and disapproved all the applications. He calls mine a Confederate Battery. To all appearances the men are contented.

I wish Southwick [Hubert's lieutenant who was captured at Missionary Ridge] could be exchanged. I expect Zeigler [another of his lieutenants] will be sent to the rear with the Baggage of all the artillery of Hood's Corps. This is contemplated when we move. I shall then have only two officers and will miss Southwick very much.

Richardson [another of his lieutenants, with whom Hubert is often dissatisfied] is doing very well now. But he is the same old Richardson. He carried the jeans Mr. Young sent him to Atlanta and I do not know but some things make me suspect that he sold it. I do not know that I would think so were it any one else besides him. I may however be all wrong.

Troops are coming up here from Savannah. At least such is the report. I have not seen any of them and it is reported that Genl [Stephen D.] Lee commanding the cavalry in Miss. is on his way here. All this looks very much like our generals expected this to be the scene of active operations. Genl Beauregard was at Wilmington a week ago and the capture of Plymouth is attributed to his presence. There were very few troops in Charleston when Thompson was there. All had left for other fields. I read today a long Yankee account of the fight west of the Miss.

[portion of letter missing]

...now for I feel that I am not ambitious. Look at Napoleon who sacrificed Josephine, whom he tenderly loved, to his ambition. That may be an extreme case but it is a type of what all ambitious men are and would do. If honor comes to me in the discharge of my duty let it come – but if it does not I do not think I could court its favors. Love to all Darling and much much love for you and Eddie from your own Hubert.

Hubert's assertion that he is not "ambitious" may be true, if the word is understood to mean an overvaulting craving for high station. But Hubert's letters as well as the course his life show a clear desire to serve and to provide leadership in support of the important causes which he valued.

As Hubert expected, the winter interlude at Dalton was about to end, but with an offensive by the enemy, not by Gen. Johnston. On March 3, 1864, Lincoln had placed General Ulysses S. Grant in supreme command of all the federal armies in the field, with the rank of Lieutenant General. Grant immediately designed an overall plan for coordinated attacks on the Confederates in Virginia and Georgia, with other supporting movements. Sherman was placed in command at Chattanooga with 100,000 federal troops at his disposal. Grant ordered him to start moving against the Confederates at Dalton, and on May 4, Sherman moved. Word of impending action reached Dalton immediately, and Hubert writes Anna of having received orders to be ready to march on short notice:

Camp near Dalton, GA
May 4th, 1864

We have just received orders to be ready to march at any moment and as I promised yesterday to write you today I want to do so although I am suffering so severely from sick headache that I can scarcely hold my head up.

I sent my horses out to graze yesterday and they were turned loose near the rail road. A train came along, stampeded Capt. Garrity's horses that were nearer the track than mine. His horses ran through mine and the whole were stampeded. I have lost five permanently I fear. I have been riding all morning looking for them and it is the effect of the sun that has affected my head. It is a serious loss. Garrity loss six. I have some men out still but I have but little hope of finding them. Darling my head is too painful to continue to write. I will try again after awhile.

Well Darling my head feels a little better and I want to try and finish this letter. When I received your letter of the 29th yesterday I read the enclosure from Mr. Young first and when he mentioned the accident to Eddie you may imagine how startled I was. I hope the bone of his finger was not injured. If it is it will be apt to be deformed. Darling write me which hand and which finger it was. I hope it will get well very soon. Poor little fellow, it must have been a most painful injury. Tell him he must be PaPa's little man and not cry about it.

I can't imagine what the order to be ready for action on short notice means. I have not heard a gun today or yesterday and as far as I knew every thing was quiet. But the two armies are so near together that a few hours any time can bring on an engagement.

Since I have commenced writing the last time I have heard of four of my horses and if I get them I will be pretty well satisfied although I dislike very much to lose a single one. They are so scarce and hard to get.

I have not heard any thing more from W.[illiam] H. Woods [of the Eufaula Light Artillery, the son of Edward Young's banking partner, Clayton R. Woods] about his sending his horse home. I will enclose a short note to Mr. Young about the horses.

The weather is moderating and the sun has been very warm today. Still the nights are cool. It is getting time we were having some summer weather now and it ought to have commenced with you some time ago.

Nearly everyone thinks that the collision so much talked of here cannot be postponed a great deal longer. I cannot think that the enemy will attack us in the front. They may attempt to pass one of our flanks and if they do I think Genl Johnson would attack them. Be cheerful Darling about the result. I think Genl J. will be victorious when he fights and I trust the same kind providence who has hitherto protected me will continue to do so.

I feel Honey that your visit to me this winter did me a great deal of good. I believe I am a better man than I was and Darling to you I owe it all under Heaven. I am reading 2nd Kings also. I will read tomorrow morning beginning at the 21st chap. I do all my reading in the morning as I am unable to purchase any candles now. You know commissaries are not allowed to sell anything to officers now – and I have never been able to draught any. Very often when I am reading I wonder where my Darling is and what she is doing because we have always been accustomed to read the Bible together.

George is absent after horses. I have not told him yet of Eddie's prayer but I intend doing it. I see George reading his bible regularly more and I do not think he did it before he went on furlough.

We will be annoyed now constantly with orders to be ready to move until this fight is over. I do not feel at all like moving this evening but if I am right well in the morning and I hope I will be I don't care how soon we move out.

I wrote to Ada yesterday and so Darling you think I am beginning to write a little oftener. Why Honey I have been writing every other day or nearly so and that is as often as I have ever written to you.

Well Darling it is now Thursday morning. I feel much better but my head is very sore.

I hear this morning that the enemy have retired from our front and a good many think the order to be ready to move means that Genl Johnston intends advancing. If this news be true I think we will be moving in less than three days. All our cavalry are coming up from our rear. I saw a good deal moving yesterday. I have recovered all my horses but one. I am very sorry to lose him. He was a fine horse that I had just drawn.

I expect a letter from you today or tomorrow. Well Darling I must hurry up and close. The mail man is waiting. It is bright and pleasant this morning. Give my love to all the family. Write as often as you can Darling. I am always so glad to hear from you. I look for active movements here soon. Give my love and a kiss to Eddie and tell him to be a brave little man with his hurt finger. Well goodby Darling. Much love and many kisses from your own loving husband – Hubert

By May 7, Sherman's army was lined up north of Dalton before Rocky Face Ridge, facing Johnston's army in a strong defensive position on the Ridge. Sherman had 100,000 men to Johnston's 45,000.

There was some skirmishing around Rocky Face Ridge, in which Dent's Battery took part.[615] But Hubert's comment in his last letter to Anna that, "I cannot think that the enemy will attack us in the front. They may attempt to pass one of our flanks..." correctly predicted exactly what happened. Despite outnumbering Johnston's Confederates by 2-to-1, Sherman was deterred by Johnston's strong defensive position. He first attempted to send a small contingent of cavalry raiders around Johnson's left flank to destroy the railroad bridge at Resaca, fifteen miles south of Dalton, which would have cut Johnston off from his Atlanta base, but this raid was defeated and driven off. Still reluctant to attack head-on, Sherman then decided to send his entire army around Johnston's left flank and quickly take a position behind him across his lines of supply. But Wheeler's cavalry discovered what Sherman was up to and the wily Johnston was ready. When Sherman reached Resaca, Johnston was already there behind breastworks, with not only his entire army, but an army reinforced by Gen. Polk and 14,000 troops just arrived from Mississippi.

Among these life-saving reinforcements from Mississippi was Croft's Battery, of Columbus, Georgia, commanded by Captain Edward Croft, his second-in-command, Lt. Alfred Young, and Lt. George B. Young. For help against Sherman's much larger force, Johnston had appealed to Richmond, and President Davis had directed General Leonidas Polk, then commander of the Department of Mississippi, to personally bring as much of his command as could be spared from Mississippi and reinforce Gen. Johnston against Sherman near Dalton. Among the troops brought from Mississippi by Gen. Polk was the cavalry division of Gen. W. H. "Red" Jackson, which included the Second Cavalry Brigade of Gen. Ross, to which Croft's Battery and the Young boys were now attached.

We last saw the Young boys and Croft's Battery a year earlier, in May 1863, as they were ordered from the Savannah defenses to Mississippi to aid in the relief of besieged Vicksburg. We will here digress and briefly trace their activities during the year since then.

32
Horse Artillery:
The *Young* Boys in Mississippi

"...The officers and men of Croft's...Battery deserve great praise for their promptness in the execution of orders, and gallant behavior in the presence of the enemy."

Brig. Gen. William H. "Red" Jackson

By May 19, 1863, the Confederates defending Vicksburg under Gen. Pemberton had been driven into the Vicksburg defenses and were under siege by Gen. Grant. The civilian population and the Confederate soldiers would endure the siege for over six weeks, with inadequate food, ammunition, or other supplies. In the vicinity of Jackson, Mississippi, Gen. Joseph E. Johnston had been given the assignment of attempting to raise enough Confederate troops to go to Pemberton's relief, and this was the impetus for Croft's Battery being sent from the Savannah defenses to Mississippi.

Croft's Battery had arrived at Canton, Mississippi, twenty five miles north of Jackson, on May 30, 1863, and was assigned to Gen. Loring's command. In early June, Gen. Johnston's Reserve Artillery Battalion was modified to include a quick-response artillery battery, known as "horse artillery." Captain Croft requested reassignment to this reserve and was authorized to convert his unit to "horse artillery." The principal difference in such a battery and other artillery units was in the number of horses assigned. A "horse artillery" unit had enough horses to permit all the members to ride, so it could accompany and support cavalry.[616] Although the Columbus battery would henceforth act as "horse artillery" in support of cavalry, there were times when its complement of horses fell below the number necessary for such a battery, and it was then sometimes referred to as a "flying battery."

From June 8 through June 18, Captain Croft was away on battery business, and Lt. Alfred Young was on leave, so that Lt. Richard Young was placed in command of the battery as it made preparations to go to the relief of Vicksburg. On June 29, the battery received its additional horses, now totaling 130 including officers' mounts, and eight mules. All cannoneers were now mounted and ready to march toward Vicksburg. [617]

Gen. Johnson had been able to raise an army of 15,000, about one third of Grant's strength. Communications with Pemberton in the besieged city to coordinate a plan of attack were difficult, with Grant's army between Pemberton and Johnston. After much delay, Johnston's force finally started moving toward Vicksburg on June 29. On July 4 he was near Vicksburg reconnoitering for a point of attack, when he found that he had arrived too late. After six weeks in the surrounded town, Pemberton's starving men had withstood the siege as long as they could. Vicksburg was surrendered on July 4, 1863. This was a devastating blow to the Confederacy, resulting in the surrender of 31,000 men and 172 cannon, and more importantly, loss of control of the Mississippi River.

Croft's Battery and the Young boys would remain in the Department of Mississippi for almost a year, monitoring the Federals in Vicksburg, opposing their sorties from that town, and carrying out various assignments. On September 1, 1863, Captain Croft, now 48 years old and in poor health, took a leave of absence to Columbus to recuperate, leaving Lieutenant Alfred Young in command. Not until October 11 did Captain Croft's health allow him to return to duty. Before leaving Columbus, he ran this notice in the Columbus *Daily Sun*:[618]

"CONTRIBUTIONS FOR YOUR HUSBANDS AND SONS IN THE ARMY

Any one who may desire to send a blanket or comforter to their relatives in my command, now at Canton, Miss., can have an opportunity of doing so by leaving them at the store of Gunby, Croft, & Co. during the next two days. Contributions thankfully received from any one.
EDWARD CROFT CAPT.
Columbus Light Art."

When Croft reached his camp in Mississippi, he found a critical shortage of winter clothing and blankets for the men. It was agreed that Alfred Young would go immediately to Columbus to obtain overcoats for the men from his father's factory, and remain there until the coats were made. Alfred left on November 11; because of a delay in manufacturing 100 of the overcoats, Alfred's detail was extended, but he was back in camp in Mississippi by Christmas, 1863.

As we have previously seen, in November 1863, Gen. Joseph E. Johnston had been transferred to command the Army of Tennessee at Dalton. To replace him as Confederate commander of the Department of Mississippi, Alabama and Eastern Louisiana, General Polk had been transferred from the Army of Tennessee.

In February 1864, Gen. Grant, as part of his offensive against Johnston at Dalton, ordered the Federal commander at Vicksburg, then Gen. Sherman, to launch an offensive against Jackson and Meridian, Mississippi, to keep the Confederates there occupied and perhaps release Yankee troops for use in northeast Georgia. Croft's Battery was involved in heavy and constant fighting as Sherman sallied forth from his Vicksburg stronghold and pushed the Confederates back from the Big Black River toward Jackson. On February 5, in a performance later reported to be "excellent"[619] Croft's Battery and another artillery unit were instrumental in stopping a Federal force attacking a Confederate cavalry brigade. However, on February 6, the Federals took Jackson. Croft's Battery had one killed, one wounded, 14 taken prisoner, and lost one artillery piece.

Croft's Battery continued to see heavy fighting as Polk's outnumbered Confederates were pushed back toward Meridian. On February 14, 1864 the Federals entered Meridian, and set about destroying the railroad and all Confederate installations. As the Confederates withdrew towards Demopolis, Alabama, Croft's Battery and the Young boys formed a part of the delaying force screening the withdrawal.

On February 20, 1864, Gen. Sherman stopped his eastward advance, departed Meridian, and began a return to Vicksburg. A Confederate cavalry brigade under Gen. Starke, supported by Croft's Battery, was sent to attack Sherman's rear and harass his withdrawal back to Vicksburg. In a successful action at Sharon, Mississippi, the Confederates captured a number of horses, mules, and wagons. Later Gen. Jackson, the Confederate cavalry division commander, reported that:

> "…The officers and men of Croft's and King's Batteries deserve great praise for their promptness in the execution of orders, and gallant behavior in the presence of the enemy."

It was the advance section of Croft's Battery, led by Lieutenant Alfred Young, that earned Gen. Jackson's praise at Sharon. Captain Croft was still in the Demopolis-Meridian area. [620]

In the spring of 1864, Gen. Grant reassigned Sherman out of Mississippi, placed him in command of 100,000 troops at Chattanooga, and ordered him to move against the Confederate Army of Tennessee under Gen. Joseph E. Johnson camped near Dalton, Georgia This caused the Mississippi career of the Youngs boys and Croft's Battery to come to an end. In response to the reinforcement of the federals in Chattanooga, the Confederate War Department ordered Gen. Polk to personally take heavy reinforcements from Mississippi to the Army of Tennessee at Dalton, and Croft's Battery was among the troops sent to aid the outnumbered Confederates. They would arrive at a highly opportune time.

36

Youngs and Dents Maneuver Toward Atlanta

"...I fear that Atlanta will be given up. If Johnston can be flanked out of every position from Dalton here I do not see why he cannot be flanked out of Atlanta."

Hubert Dent to Anna

Gen. Polk turned over temporary command of his Department of Mississippi to the head of his cavalry, Gen. Stephen D. Lee, and then assembled his designated troops in Columbus, Mississippi for the long march to Georgia. The expedition left Columbus, Mississippi on April 15, 1864 and two weeks later reached Eutaw, Alabama.

Records reflect that while on the march, Lt. Alfred Young rode to the rear to find the Chief Pay Quartermaster for the Cavalry Command, and on April 20 received his pay of $100 for the month of February.[621] From Eutaw, the column proceeded through Centreville, Montevallo, Columbiana, finally arriving in Rome, Georgia.

In dramatic fashion, Polk's reinforcements arrived just in time to assist in repulsing Sherman at Resaca and in foiling Sherman's effort to go around Johnston's flank.   As part of Sherman's flanking strategy, Federal troops were sent around the left of Johnston's army toward Rome, about 25 miles southeast of Resaca. It happened that Croft's Battery of horse artillery and the Young boys were at this time completing their long march from Mississippi, arriving at Rome with "Red" Jackson's cavalry, just in time to meet this Federal threat. On May 15, the Federal force was met outside Rome by Ross' cavalry brigade and Croft's Battery, and repulsed. It was later reported that "a few shots from [Croft's] Battery send them back," and the Yankees were driven away from Rome by Ross' Brigade.[622]

The Atlanta Campaign

This was the first time that the Dent brothers, Hubert and George, and Anna's cousins, the Young brothers, Alfred and George, were all in the Army of Tennessee operating within fairly close proximity of each other, as they would for the remainder of the war. Dent's Battery, because it was assigned to an infantry corps, would usually be found in the center of the main battles, providing close support to the infantry. Because it had become "horse artillery," attached to the cavalry, Croft's Battery would usually be found ranging out around the main army, scouting and protecting the army's flanks and rear. This duty by no means kept Croft's Battery from being involved in dangerous action, as we will soon see.

On May 13, 1864, Johnston's Confederate army had fallen back from Dalton to Resaca, 15 miles south, and was lined up west of Resaca, facing west, with Polk on the left, Hardee in the center, and Hood on the right. There was heavy skirmishing on May 13. In late afternoon on May 14, Hood attacked the federal left and pushed it back, while Polk was attacked by McPherson with little effect. Dent's Battery encountered difficulties, described by Daniel:[623]

"S. H. Dent's battery was on a ridge to the left of the Dalton Road, about a hundred yards from the Hardee-Hood obtuse angle. The guns were positioned so as to deliver a direct frontal fire. John Rowan's Georgia Battery constructed its works at a right angle to Dent to cover the Dalton Road. The men were strengthening their position when the skirmish line was quickly driven in. Dent's Battery suddenly came under blazing fire and 'the men were shot down as fast as they took position beside their guns.'" [v]

Johnston merely maintained his position on the 14th, and a clash on the 15th was indecisive. After dark on May 15, Johnston learned that the Federals were again attempting to outflank him by crossing a river several miles to his left and rear, near Calhoun. This made a general engagement unfeasible, requiring Johnston to withdraw toward Calhoun, five miles south.

Sherman's "flanking" movements, which forced Johnson to abandon his strong defensive position south of Dalton and again at Resaca, established the pattern which would prevail through the summer of 1864, and which would result in Johnston's being relentlessly pushed much of the way toward Atlanta without a pitched battle. When an attacker starts moving around a defender's flank, or side, the defender must get in front of him and fight, perhaps upon disadvantageous ground. Alternatively, if the defender feels he is too heavily outnumbered to risk a fight, he must fall back to keep the attacker from getting behind him, and hope for favorable developments, such as a blunder by the attacker. Called "Fabian" policy after the Roman General, a retreat to avoid battle with a larger army in the hope of better opportunities is a valid and respected strategy, but it infuriated the Confederate Government and public. General Johnston rationally concluded that, being outnumbered 2-to1 (a fact which editors and officials often failed to recognize), he would adopt the defensive, "to spare the blood of our soldiers by fighting from cover habitually," and to attack "only when bad position or division of the enemy's forces" provided advantageous conditions. Johnston's reluctance to clearly communicate these considerations to his superiors contributed to his difficulties.

Johnston continued his withdrawal from Dalton, to Resaca and on down the Western and Atlantic Railroad to Cassville, twenty miles south of Calhoun. Cassville was not actually on the railroad line but a few miles east of it. This confused Sherman who had assumed that Johnston would encamp at Kingston, on the railroad line. Sherman had hurried to Kingston

---

[v] Among the other units fighting at Resaca was the 28th Tennessee Regiment of infantry. Its commander, Col Stanton, was killed on May 13, and his second in command was promoted to regimental commander: Col. David Crockett Crook, of Sparta, Tennessee.

prepared to do battle, but Johnston was not there. This placed the Confederates on Sherman's left flank, and Johnston was about to attack Sherman's flank when a fragment of Hooker's Corps which was lost blundered into the Confederate army, and convinced Johnston that Sherman was advancing. The cautious Johnston abandoned plans to attack and withdrew to south of Cassville. Dissatisfied with his defensive position there, he then moved further south to a strong defensive line at Allatoona, 15 miles southeast of Cassville.

Sherman was familiar with the mountainous area of Allatoona, and had no interest in attempting an attack on Johnston there. Therefore, he changed his objective from Johnston's army to Atlanta itself, which was now only 50 miles southeast of Sherman's camp. After resting his men for a few days at Kingston, Sherman struck out across country, heading directly for Atlanta and attempting to bypass Johnston's army on its left. But again, Joe Wheeler's cavalry was watching Sherman and quickly reported this "end run" to Gen. Johnston. This time, "Old Joe" did not withdraw to the south; instead he did a quick slide of his whole army to the left, placing himself between Sherman and Atlanta.

On May 24, when Sherman arrived in the vicinity of New Hope Church, (25 miles from Atlanta), he found Johnston's army established in a defensive line extending from New Hope Church on the right to Dallas, 3 miles to the left. The Confederate left was defended by Gen. Hardee, the center by Gen. Polk, and the right by Gen. Hood.

Skirmishing around New Hope Church began on the morning of the 25th, and that afternoon Sherman sent Hooker against the middle of the Confederate right wing under Hood. The brunt of the attack fell on Stewart's Division (previously commanded by Hindman), to which Dent's Battery was attached. Repeated assaults by federal brigades were blown to pieces by massed Confederate artillery. This battle was conducted in a blinding rain during a spectacular thunderstorm. The roar of Hubert Dent's Napoleons competed with the booming peals of thunder cracking overhead, and the fire from his cannons' mouths blended with the brilliant flashes of chain lightening which periodically illuminated the darkened late afternoon sky. After three hours of violent fighting, Hooker was repulsed with heavy losses, which he placed at 1665 dead, but which the Confederates felt were actually much larger. [624]

There was skirmishing on May 26. Throughout the operations around New Hope Church, Jackson's Cavalry with Croft's horse artillery and the Young boys ranged around Johnston's left wing, guarding against Sherman's constant probes looking for a flanking opportunity.[625] Finding no opening on the left, on the 27th, Sherman made a concerted effort to turn the Confederate right but was again repulsed with the loss of 1500 men dead. On the 28th it was Johnston's turn to sustain heavy losses in an attack on the Federal right. The fighting ended when Sherman began a gradual shift of his army to the east toward the railroad line, with Johnston following so as to constantly remain on his front. The four days of fighting around New Hope Church, which the Yankee soldiers would call the "Hell Hole," was fierce and bloody. Each side lost about 3000 men.

During this campaign, both armies came to fully appreciate the value of constructing breastworks of dirt and logs before trenches. The Confederates were so good at it the Federal soldiers claimed the Rebels carried their breastworks with them, while the Confederates said Sherman's men marched with a rifle in one hand and a spade in the other.[626]

On May 30, 1864, Croft's Battery enlisted still another member of the Young family. As the war got closer to Columbus, Alf and George's younger brother, Richard T. Young, now 17, arrived at the company and was enrolled as a private.

As Sherman shifted his army eastward toward the railroad, Johnston did the same, and on June fourth, still in the rain, Johnston placed his right across the railroad north of Kennesaw Mountain, his left at Lost Mountain, and a center salient on Pine Mountain. From this position, Hubert wrote Anna. He mentions that he had been looking for her cousins, Alf and George. Having not found their battery among the infantry units, with whom Hubert has regular contact, he correctly concludes that they must be attached to the cavalry:

"Dent's Battery Johnston's Army
June 7th, 1864

"My Darling
I received your letter of the 1st just yesterday – was very sorry to learn that you had been sick – hope Darling that you are entirely well before this. I know that you must have suffered a great deal with your ear. Such things are so painful.
I wrote you a letter on the 5th Darling. We are in the same position. I do not believe our lines were formed when I wrote to you. Genl Hardee occupies the right - Hood the center and Polk the left - Our left rests at the foot of Lost Mountain. The right extends towards the rail roads. We are about seven miles from Marietta. The enemy are following us up very slowly. Our right occupies nearly the same position it did at New Hope. The left fell back at Lost Mountain.
We had more rain yesterday and the roads must be very muddy.
I was interrupted here Darling to ride out in front of our works to see the country to know how to use my guns. I went as far as our picket lines. It is reported that the enemy are moving to our right towards the rail roads. I am afraid we will [miss] them here. I have a very fine position and anxious to fight them just where I am.
I heard a rumor this morning that we had captured one of Sherman's couriers with dispatches for Washington stating that he had driven Johnston as far by flanking him as we could and that to get him further back he would be compelled to fight him. I think probably the conclusion is correct but I do not believe the report about the capture of the courier.
The weather is very warm. I have not felt summer until the last few days. Today the sun shines but very powerfully and the only shade we have is artificial.
I have not seen or heard directly from the relief committee. [Probably a group from Eufaula bringing supplies. Ed.] I heard a rumor that they were in

Marietta – but I have not seen any one that has seen them. I would like very much to see them but I hardly think they will venture out so far in the mud and I cannot go down there.

I am afraid our people will use up a great deal before the battle actually takes place and perhaps not be so well prepared as they are now. In my own opinion this campaign will continue all summer a good deal in the same manner that it has been carried on for the last thirty two or three days. Sherman is evidently very cautious and I have very little idea that he will attack us in our works. I expect some morning to get the order to move forward and fight the Yankees in their position as they do not seem disposed to fight us in ours.

Darling it is a real hot lazy day and this is the laziest work I think I've ever done.

Every thing seems to be going on well in Virginia although Grant has reached nearly the same position McClellan held two years ago. No one seems to be frightened. I think however that a great many are moving out. Mrs. Courtney has left there. She came as far as Columbia So. Ca. Maj. C has sent for her to come to Atlanta or Marietta. I feel very sorry for persons whose homes are in the hands of the enemy. I have seen some very distressed sights on this campaign. I hope I will get a newspaper today. I want to see if any thing is going on.

By the way the Black Republican Convention meets in Baltimore today and from the common newspaper statements there will be very much such another scene as there was there four years ago when we were there. Honey it seems a very long time since we made that trip – four years – what important events have been crowded together in these four years. How many homes have been made desolate? How many hearts saddened? I pray our Father in Heaven that the scene may be nearly over. Let us unite in returning thanks my Darling that we are as well off as we are. I pray God to make us sufficiently grateful. I feel Darling that he has been good to us. May his protecting hand continue to be over us.

You must have a sick family now. You sick. Ma unwell. Mr. Young complaining. Eddy's fingers sore. Quite a list of ailments. How are Ada and Helen getting on now. I suppose they have recovered both their health and spirits since they got back home.

I have not seen or heard any thing of any of your cousins lately. Is the Battery that Alf & Geo are with serving with infantry or cavalry. I have made several inquiries after it but have never found any one that knows where it was and so I came to the conclusion that it must be serving with cavalry.

I would like very well to see Mr. Cottrell [the Methodist minister from Eufaula, perhaps a member of the "Relief Committee"] Been trying look for him. Cleburne's Division is on our right and he may get there to see his step son and then come see me but I do not feel much like I would see him.

Remember me to all friends. My love to all the family. Write as often as you can Darling. I am always glad to hear from you but will be more so

than ever now. A kiss for Eddie. Much love & kisses for my Darling from
your own – Hubert

Although Hubert had not yet found them, Alf, George and Dick Young were nearby, helping to protect the flank of the "very fine position" in which Hubert had placed his battery. Soon after the date of Hubert's letter, Croft's Battery was fighting at the foot of Lost Mountain attempting to keep Sherman's inevitable probe from finding a way to turn the corner around the Confederate left. On June 17, a heavy column of Sherman's infantry charged the front of Gen. Ross' Brigade, into shot and canister fired by the guns of Croft's Battery. Although Croft's Battery and Ross' troopers "stood most gallantly and damaged the enemy seriously," the larger Yankee force got around Ross' left, forcing him to withdraw south to Anderson's Steam Mill. There Ross again attempted to stop the Yankees' end run, with heavy small arms fire and artillery from his dismounted troopers and Croft's Battery. Again the Yankee flankers were too strong; Ross and Croft were forced further south. By this point, Sherman's men had succeeded in turning the Confederate left, and their way was open to Marietta. [627]

Under this pressure, Gen. Johnston fell back to a strong defensive position based upon Kennesaw Mountain. Although this further retreat placed the Confederates less than twenty miles from Atlanta, the army continued to have complete faith that "Old Joe" knew what he was doing, and that at the right time, he would turn and whip Sherman. Kennesaw Mountain, 4 miles northeast of Marietta, is two and a half miles long and rises seven hundred feet high, giving Johnston good observation of Sherman's movements. The railroad goes through a pass between Kennesaw and Brush Mountain on the east. The Confederates strongly fortified it with massive breastworks. It was impregnable to direct assault. The Confederate center on the mountain itself was defended by Polk's old corps, now commanded by Gen. Loring. Hood was at first on the right across the railroad, at the base of Brush mountain, but was later shifted to strengthen the left. Hardee's Corps, to which Dent's Battery was attached, held the Confederate left, in a line which curved back across the road from Marietta to Lost Mountain.

From this position, Hubert wrote Anna on June 21. He has found the 'relief committee" from home.

"June 21ˢᵗ, 1864

My Darling
        You would have been amused to have seen me a few moments ago darning my socks. You know I do not like to wear socks with holes and as the pair I had was in that condition I got out a small gourd used for carrying powder and regularly darned my socks.
        We moved again on yesterday evening Darling and passed through Marietta and are bivouacked I expect about west from that place – going towards our left. We are on the Powder Springs road. It is reported that the enemy are in force about four miles from us. Gen.l Stevenson's Division is passing now. I expect we will move as soon as that passes.

Darling I hope you are all well at home now. It seems to me that nearly every letter I receive says something about some one being sick – good health is a great boon. I hope all the family are enjoying it now. Do not grow too sad and desponding my Darling. Sorrow and affliction will come Honey – but let us meet it in the right spirit and it will be for our good eventually. Remember that God is ever good and merciful and doeth all things well.

I spoke to Maj. Courtney of your kind offer and he desired me to thank you very heartily for your kindness and attention but that Mrs. C. had effected arrangements in Columbia SC and expected for the present to make that her home, but that if in any way that arrangement should be broken up she might then avail herself of your offer. Maj. C. tried yesterday to get a Twenty-four hours leave to visit her but it has not returned and I expect this move will defeat him.

We are having a cloudy drizzly morning – have had some rain and a good prospect for plenty more. This is an extraordinary spell of weather.

I stopped as I passed through Marietta yesterday evening and took supper with the relief committee and they gave me a piece of soap which I needed very much as some one stole the last piece I had a few days ago. I do not know when they will leave.

I have no idea Darling what is going on. In fact I never know certainly what is going on until I see the newspapers and when I see them I know how to make allowances for what I see stated as actually occurring and then guess at the truth. It amuses one who knows all about these things to see the highly wrought and highly colored pictures which are presented in our newspapers.

It is raining faster and I think we will have another rainy day. It is worse than it was on the retreat out of middle Tenn last summer, and that was very bad. Write me Darling as often as you can. Give my love to all the family and especially to Ma and tell her I hope if she is not already, that she soon will be well. Tell the girls that I may owe them letters but that I am not situated to write much and that I hope they will not wait for me. With much love and many kisses for my Darling & our boy I must say goodby. Your own devoted husband – Hubert

37
The Atlanta Campaign; The Columbus Youngs Encounter Death

"When we reflect that it was in the power of Mr. Young to have shielded all of his boys by exemptions, his devotion to the country and cause, as well as theirs, is made apparent."

The Columbus *Times*

Ellen and William Young of Columbus now had four sons in the Confederate Army. Three of these sons, i. e. Alfred, George, and Richard, were members of Croft/Young's Battery of artillery. Their third son, William H. Young, Jr. ("Willie") was a trooper in Major General Joseph Wheeler's cavalry corps. We have previously described some of the many ways in which Ellen and William supported the Confederate war effort. They were now subjected to a parent's ultimate sacrifice, the death of Willie.

As Sherman moved closer to Atlanta, to assist in the management of the heavy casualties Ellen and William had organized and equipped a volunteer ambulance unit, known as the Douglas Ambulance Corps. The June 4, 1864 edition of the *Columbus Times* describes a trip to the front made by William with the Ambulance Corps:[628]

"A PATRIOTIC FAMILY

"Mr. William H. Young, who is now at the front with the Douglas Ambulance Corps, has four sons in the Confederate Army, the last one, Dick Young, only seventeen years of age, having left for General Johnston's army last Monday [May 30]. Three of these sons have been participants in many of the most active scenes of this war and have proven their courage and patriotism in many hours of danger. Fortunately, up to this time, none of them have been injured. When we reflect that it was in the power of Mr. Young to have shielded all of his boys by exemptions, his devotion to the country and cause, as well as theirs, is made apparent. Knowing that he and his posterity had a personal interest in this great struggle, Mr. Young has acted throughout the war as a patriot and Christian and his example is worthy of imitation."

On June 11, only one week after this uplifting article exulting in the Young boys' safety, the sickening news arrived that Willy had been seriously wounded. As his cavalry unit was operating in the vicinity of Marietta, it encountered a force of federals, and in the ensuing skirmish, Willie was shot, although not immediately killed. He was taken to a hospital in Atlanta, but to no avail. Three days later, he died.

Anna wrote Hubert the details of her first cousin's death while sending Hubert a box of badly needed supplies, which he acknowledged in his letter of June 22:

"Dent's Battery Johnston's Army
June 22nd, 1864

My Darling

I received yesterday the boots and letters together with the Testament and book you very kindly sent me by Mr. Starnes. One of the Eufaula artillery passed my camp late yesterday evening and told me they were in Marietta. I immediately went up after them. Darling I am very glad you sent me the Testament. I shall carry it with me and try and read it regularly. I shall get a long ways behind in my Bible reading with you. The book sent I have glanced at and I think I will find it very interesting.

I was very glad to get the boots. One of my feet had been nearly on the ground. Yesterday morning however before I knew the new ones had come I got my shoemaker and went to my cooking wagon and sat down and waited until he mended them. They will last probably a month longer. As long as it is so muddy I shall wear the old ones.

I read with great interest Darling the account of the wounding and death of Willie Y. I had heard some of the particulars of his being wounded but nothing of the way in which he died. I am glad to hear that he died a triumphant death. Oh! "let me die the death of the righteous and let my last end be like his." May we all so live that we may meet him in that happy land where parting and death are no more. I am glad to hear that your Uncle W. is getting better. But I do not like the idea of keeping Willie's death from him. I suppose however that those around him are the best judges about informing him. I will try and see the other boys the very first opportunity. I have not been near... Division yet that I am aware of.

We are having more sunshine today than we have had in some time. I hope the sun will continue out all day. Genls Johnston and Hood have just passed going towards our front. I think we will be very apt to move today. We do not often remain in bivouac longer than two days and rarely as long as that. I can hear skirmishing going on now. Kolb is in position and had three men wounded yesterday. I do not think he has been on our front lines until recently. He has four Napoleon guns now and I expect is very proud of them.

The Eufaula Artillery is just below me on this same road. I saw Genl Baker yesterday. He was visiting the relief committee. Between us he stands very low as a Brig. Genl.

I have no other army news that I now think of Darling. I heard yesterday of the death of Robt Chambers. Your letter mentioned his illness. This war has laid low many a promising young man. God grant that it may end soon.

The news from Va. continues encouraging. I trust that Lee and his Lieuts will be able to defeat all the enemys attempts to take Richmond.

Things here indicate that Johnston does not intend to fall back any further but the chances of war are very uncertain. I think a week's clear weather will bring about a collision.

Keep up a cheerful feeling my Darling and whenever you do not hear from me regularly think every thing is going on right. Darling when I read your letters yesterday evening and saw what you had sent me you do not know my love how my heart yearned towards – how anxious I felt to take my own dear wife in my arms and imprint kisses on your sweet lips. Darling I think you are just the best dearest and sweetest of wives. I wish I could see you if it was only for a short time. I have a great many questions to ask and a great deal to talk about. I do not think I was ever more anxious to see you than I am now – but as long as these active operations continue there will be no chance to see you.

I will write a piece of news that I have just heard – a rumor that Forrest is here. I hope he will get in Sherman's rear.

Darling I wrote you what Maj. C. said of the offer you made his wife. I expect you will receive that but for fear it may not reach you I will repeat it. He thanked you very much for the offer but said that his wife had made arrangements for a home in Columbia for the present – but if that arrangement should fail in any way she might avail herself of yours & Ma's kindness. If she accepts I will let you know as soon as I can.

Well Darling I must hurry up Maj. C. has gone to the front to look out for position. I expect to move shortly. I hope Ma is getting better. She must suffer a good deal. Write me frequently my Darling. I am always so glad to hear from home. Tell Carrie I will try and write to her before a great while. Tell Eddie PaPa thinks a great deal about him and wants to see him very much, that he must be a good boy and love Mama and obey what she says. Darling impress it on him only the importance of always telling the truth. I know nothing more despicable than telling untruths.

Honey I will send you the letters about Willie. I have not yet shown them to George. He was back at the wagons this morning and has just returned. He was Twenty one years old yesterday. Time flies so rapidly. It seems to me only a short time since he was quite a small white haired boy. He inquires after you all every time I receive letters. Tell Eddie his Uncle George has not forgotten. By the way his and Eddie's birthdays as well as your own are in June. Eddie will be three years old before this reaches you. His birthday is the 25th is it not? Really I have seen so little of my own child that I scarcely know his birthday & Darling on your last birthday I was retreating out of middle Tennessee. I wonder what we'll be doing tomorrow or a week. I wish I could walk in your room that morning before you were up. What a surprise I would give you.

I trust this year will see the end of war, and let me go home Darling. Surely if we can defeat them here and in Virginia they will be willing then to let us alone.

Give my love to all the family Darling. Tell them I often think of them all and am over anxious to get back home with them. All have treated me with so much kindness that I love them all very dearly. My life before our marriage seems more like a dream than a reality. I must close. Goodby Darling much love & many kisses for you & Eddie from your own devoted and affectionate – Hubert

In a decision for which he would later be criticized, Sherman decided not to rely solely on his "flanking" efforts but instead to make a frontal assault on Johnston's line resting across Kennesaw Mountain. He was convinced that surprise and his superiority of numbers would carry the day. On the morning of June 27, 1864, the Battle of Kennesaw Mountain began with an assault by the Federals against the Confederates' entrenched positions. The Union soldiers charged bravely and fought with great courage, but could not withstand the terrific fire from the Confederates behind their parapets. The main attack was by Gen. Thomas, against the right of Confederate Gen. Hardee's position. The bloodiest fighting occurred at a sharp angle in the line where Tennessee regiments were defending, and the slaughter was so great the Yankees named it the "Dead Angle." Here the Federal flag was momentarily placed on the crest, but the Yankees were repeatedly driven back. Despite being systematically mowed down, they kept coming. Literally piles of Federal dead accumulated outside the Confederate trenches. But their valor was in vain. By 11:30 A. M., the attack was over and the battle ended. Sherman lost 3000 men to the Confederates' 630. Sherman's critics, then and now, say that this was an utterly useless slaughter, because Kennesaw could have been taken without a battle, which is exactly what occurred a few days later.

While the main battle for Kennesaw Mountain was going against Sherman, he still had troops out to the southwest attempting to circle Johnston's left flank. The Yankee flankers attacked the left of Ross' Brigade at daylight on June 27, near "Shaw's House." For five hours, Ross' troopers and Croft's Battery fought to hold the Yankees, until forced to withdraw to new positions a half mile south. [629] Confederate communications with Atlanta were again seriously threatened.

The next day, Alfred Young wrote to the *Columbus Sun* to report the names of the battery losses in the fighting around Shaw's House:[630]

> "Headqr's Croft's Battery, in the field, June 28, 1864.
> Ed *Sun*: please publish for the information of friends the following list of casualties suffered in the battery on the the the 26th and 27th:
> June 26—Corporal C. Whitehead, from Dale County, Ala., wounded through the hip; Private W. F. Pate, from Tallapoosa County, Ala., mortally wounded, since dead.
> June 27—Corporal F. A. Parker, from Tallapoosa County, Ala., killed; Private J. M. Wilson, from Randolph County, Ala., severely wounded in arm.
> A number of others were slightly wounded, but not enough so as to unfit them for duty. These men were at their posts, discharging their duty with spirit and cheerfulness, and bore the reputation of being among the best and bravest soldiers of the command. We mourn their loss and feel that a grateful country will hold in sacred remembrance those on the list whose strong arms and stout hearts will never battle more, and administer to the comfort to the manly forms mangled and torn in their country's defense.
> A. I. Young
> Lieut., Croft's Battery"

Sherman was now 120 miles from his Chattanooga base, with an army of 100,000 and 23,000 horses to feed. He could not stand still. Returning to his "flanking" strategy, on July 2 Sherman started around Johnston's left flank. Expecting this, Johnston knew he would have to abandon the mountain and Marietta, and his engineers had already fortified two fall-back positions for this event. On July 3, Johnston's army was moving into position on a ridge behind Nickajack Creek, 6 miles south of Marietta. But as Sherman advanced along the line of the railroad, Johnston fell back to his second prepared position, a five mile long line of entrenchments on the north bank of the Chattahoochee River, where he planned to make his final stand north of the Chattahoochee. Sherman was almost within sight of Atlanta, eight miles away. But, impressed with the strength of Johnston's new defensive position, Sherman paused to consider his options, while continuing to pour a heavy artillery barrage on the entrenched Confederates.

During this pause, but under heavy bombardment, Hubert wrote Anna. He is lamenting his heavy losses: only 40 of the 90 men who originally enlisted in the battery at Pensacola are left. His Barbour County friend, lawyer Henry D. Clayton, has been made a Major General and is commanding a division.

"July 7th, 1864

"My Darling
It is a dark and foggy morning. The air is very damp and last night was quite cool.

We are in position about half a mile north of the Chattahoochee, have a very good position. We never went in position until yesterday evening. We were subject to a very heavy artillery fire yesterday morning. While building my works I had one man killed and another wounded who went to the Hospital. Besides a third slightly wounded. The man killed was named Dixon and from Florida. The wounded man is the Cousin of Capt Parramore of conscript notoriety. He was not seriously wounded. I heard yesterday of the death of another man who went off wounded at New Hope Church. His name is Redman. He lived in the neighborhood of Taylor's Store. The campaign is telling on the effective strength of my company. Dixon was one of the original members of the company. Out of ninety men who enlisted at Pensacola two and half years ago we have less than forty men left. And some of them are disabled by wounds. A man came back to the Battery a few days ago who was wounded at Chickamauga. In fact two came back. Neither of them fit for duty. Their wounds not yet well.

Well Darling I will stop now and get my breakfast. The sun is coming out very bright and I expect a warm day. I received your letter of the 1st Inst night before last you would have been amused Honey had you seen me reading it over a very sorry fire.

I expect the Yankee Batteries will open again today. Sherman seems inclined to make this fight with artillery.

Well Darling I have had my breakfast. The Yankees have commenced shelling again this morning but not so furiously as they did yesterday. I can hear some artillery down to our left and across the river. Stevenson's Div. is across the river and Garrity's Battery of our Battalion. We are pretty near the river. Stewarts Div. is between us and the river. Most of our wagons and ordinance trains are across the river.

I hear nothing of any special interest. Did I write you that Richardson had returned. He got back on the 4th July. No other wounded have returned.

I was very glad Darling to get your long and affectionate letter of the 1st Inst. Such letters from you Darling always cheer me. Yes my Darling I do feel that you love me. If I did not I would feel very unhappy Darling. I wrote you Honey something about my dreams. I cannot write all about them. They are too long. But if I see you before I forget them I will tell you all about them Honey I think you are right in a great measure about your views about our separation and the troubles of this war. All such things are not unmixed evils and if properly improved will work to our advantage. But Darling I am so tired of this war and of separation from my Dearest wife that if it pleases our Heavenly Father I would rejoice so much to see peace. God grant that it come speedily. Notwithstanding our prospects just now do not look very bright I cannot help believing that there is a good prospect for peace by the end of this year. I do not think I have ever before believed so strongly that peace was so near. It may be that the wish in this case is so strong that my belief is the result of it. But still I believe it. If Providence spares me in the dangers of the future as he has protected me in the past. How happy I will be to return to my Darling Nannie. Darling you remember you wrote in your last letter that you intended to make me as good a wife as you could and make me think so too. Well Darling I am pleased that you feel that way. I have always thought that you were a good wife Darling but it pleases me for you to feel that way because then I think you love and respect your husband and are anxious to make him a good wife and make him happy. But Dearest in thinking so much about having a good wife I must not forget to try and be a good husband. I desire to be a good husband to you Darling to love cherish and protect you as a husband should and I pray Heaven Darling that I may never forget or neglect any thing that may increase our mutual love and happiness. Honey I do fear sometimes that I love you too well. It wells up from my heart and I cannot help it. I wish I could get home for about ten days. I <u>have</u> so much that I want to talk t you about that I care not to write. But this pleasure I do not expect. Well Darling we will only have the more to talk about when we do meet.

Have you heard that Clayton was a Maj Genl? Well he is and takes command of Stewarts Division. Stewart goes to Polks Corps. Clayton has risen rapidly and I think he will make a good Major General. Brown was strongly recommended. But Clayton got ahead of him. Hindman who had hurt one of his eyes and gone to the Hospital has returned and Brown has been sent back to his old Div. Some Alabamian will be made a Brig. To take Clayton's Brigade. Holtzclaw I expect.

328

There is one piece of news that I must write. The man who was taking care of the mare & colt back at the wagons has been missing since our last fall back and some fear he has deserted and taken the horse off with him. I will not think he has yet. But I cannot help wondering what has become of him.

Well Darling I will wait until this evening to see if any thing of importance takes place. Till then goodby – Hubert

Well Darling it is now past 5 o'clock PM. The enemy shelling again quite furiously. This is their usual custom every evening.

I was quite interested with your account of your visits to and acquaintances at the Hospital. That is right my Darling. Show the soldiers all the kindness you can without however becoming <u>familiar</u> with any. You understand Darling what I mean by this. But I have no fears of any thing of that kind for I know you and Ma are both remarkably prudent.

Give my love to all the family. Write often and tell me all your thoughts. George inquires after you all very frequently. Tell Eddie PaPa thinks of him very frequently and wants to see him very much. Goodby Darling much love and many kisses from your devoted Hubert

Hubert's approval of Anna's visits to "the hospital" refers to the old tavern building on the bluff above the Chattahoochee River, which Eufaulians had converted into a military hospital for sick and wounded Confederate soldiers brought to Eufaula for treatment. Its staff included Confederate Surgeons Dr. D. P. Baker and Dr. John S. Merriweather. As casualties from the Atlanta campaign increased, the women of Eufaula helped at the hospital, and some families with space at home took in ambulatory patients to make room for more serious cases at the hospital. Fendall Hall was one of the homes that took in and treated the wounded. Within a few weeks after Hubert's approval of Anna's visits to the hospital, the War Department assigned to the hospital medical staff another Confederate officer-surgeon, Dr. Hamilton M. Weedon. This attractive young officer would catch the eye of another of the Young girls, and would quickly become an important participant in the story of the Young family. But we're getting ahead of our story.

Sherman now resumed his successful flanking movements. While continuing a ceaseless bombardment of Johnston's entrenchments by Gen. Thomas and McPherson, Sherman on July 8 sent Gen. Schofield up the Chattahoochee, to Johnston's right. The Federal force crossed the Chattahoochee 10 miles upstream from the Confederate position, at the point where Soap Creek runs into the Chattahoochee. On July 9, Johnston awoke to learn that he had been outflanked on his right, and that the Federals were on the south side of the Chattahoochee with nothing between them and Atlanta He immediately gave orders to prepare to cross to the south side of the Chattahoochee that night.

Hubert was writing Anna when he learned that he would be making the night move across the Chattahoochee. He is now critical of Johnston and has little hope that he will defend Atlanta. Hubert has received from home a box of food that in transit became a mess, but puts a good face on it. Hubert and the army are is still under heavy artillery barrage, but can't return the fire due to ammunition shortage.

329

'July 9th, 1864

My Dear Darling – I received yours and Carries [Anna's little nine year old sister] of the 4 Inst on the night of the 7th, also one from Mr. Young of same date.

Gov Shorter wrote on one of the envelopes that the committee [presumably, the "Relief Committee" from Eufaula] would locate yesterday at Clayton's Division Hospital.

I also Darling received the box of vegetables. Every thing came very well. Unfortunately the stopper came out of the bottle of pure vinegar and it was lost. The pepper vinegar is very good. The beans potatoes and corn all of which we have tried we have found very good. The cucumbers did not appear very fresh but they tasted first rate. We keep our wagons across the river and have our cooking done there. And as we have to trust to others altogether, I had the catsup and Jam put by until such time as we could enjoy them better. I will write Charlie [Anna's nephew; Will and Annie Young's eight year old son] a little note thanking him for his vegetables.

We have been under a very severe artillery fire ever since we occupied our present position. A fragment of a shell entered one of my embrasures yesterday striking the face of the piece, injuring it slightly, and slightly wounding six men. I had to send the gun to the rear to be repaired. It was marvelous that it only slightly wounded six and seriously hurt no one. Three of them are from about Eufaula. It was a chance shot. And I hope they will not repeat it.

We are not allowed to fire at the Yankee Batteries. Ammunition too scarce but about sun-set on the 7th we opened on all the Batteries and kept a heavy fire for a few minutes. The enemy replied with all their guns and the uproar was almost deafning. Their fire has not been so steady and constant since. But they still keep up a heavy fire. About every two or three minutes a shell comes screeching over. We have been quite fortunate lately in getting quiet positions. But we have one uncomfortable enough now to make up for all past favors.

The weather is very warm – sultry – and the only shade we have is a brush arbor in our ditches. Very little air can reach us. But still the company is quite healthy.

One section of my Battery has been moved about three hundred yards further to the right. I sent Richardson [one of the company's lieutenants]. You never saw such a change as there is in him. Since he returned he has had very little to say and seems to take very little interest in any thing. I think he must have been "<u>cut</u>" by some of his friends down in Georgia. As he abuses that portion of the state I expect he presumed too much on short acquaintance.

The enemy are demonstrating on our left and trying to cross the river. It is thought that we will finally cross the river. Stevenson's and Cheathims [Confederate] Divisions are already across. And perhaps others that I know not of. I have no idea what will be the result. But I fear that Atlanta will be given up. If Johnston can be flanked out of every position from Dalton here I do not see why he cannot be flanked out of Atlanta. But I hope not. Every thing of a permanent character is being moved from there. We however have not. I think this whole army will be pretty well tanned in this campaign.

I will write to Mr. Young in a day or two. The man who had the mare & colt has turned up. He lost our train and was a long time finding it.

I doubt whether I will see any of the Committee soon. I hardly think they will come to my part of the front and I doubt whether I can get off to see them.

Tell Carrie her letter was received I will answer it after awhile.

The artillery fire has ceased here. But the pickets keep popping away. I hear an occasional piece of Artillery on our right. It is so very hot that I must postpone this until later this evening.

Darling I have just finished my dinner. Had a pretty good one. I will try now and finish this letter.

The enemy are still firing. And a little more briskly It will be apt to increase as the evening comes on.

I wish the Quarter masters Dept would get some money. I have not drawn any pay since I returned from home They owe me for four months and at the end of this month will owe me for five months which will be seven Hundred Dollars.

I hope Mr. Young can send for the horses. I do not know when I can send them home.

We have not heard from Maryland in a long time now. I am very anxious to hear from there since they have passed the act freeing the Negroes.

Give my love to all the family. Tell Carrie George says he will write to her but that he cannot write while we are moving around so actively. I wish I could be at home with you all for a short time. Could enjoy a rest now very well. And I need it. I wonder when this campaign will end. Write often my Darling. I will write to Mr. Young tomorrow or next day. Good by. Much love & many kisses for you & Eddie from your own devoted and loving Hubert

PS – we cross the Chattahoochee tonight. I will be on the Ga side of the river before morning I think. Your own H.

After Johnston's army reached the south side of the river, it sat still for the next eight days while Sherman with the rest of his army followed, unopposed. With Sherman approaching Atlanta from the north and east, Johnston now fell back to a line of trenches south of Peachtree Creek, 6 miles from the Atlanta city limits, and did nothing but wait. Davis and the Confederate government were outraged. Their view of Johnston was the same as that expressed by Hubert Dent on the banks of the Chattahoochee when he observed, "If Johnston can be flanked out of every position from Dalton here I do not see why he cannot be flanked out of Atlanta." No one believed that Johnston could or would make a fight for Atlanta.

On the morning of July 17, Johnston was sent a telegram stating that "..as you have failed to arrest the advance of the enemy to the vicinity of Atlanta, far in the interior of Georgia, and express no confidence that you can defeat or repel him, you are hereby relieved from the command of the Army and Department of Tennessee, which you will immediately turn over to General Hood."

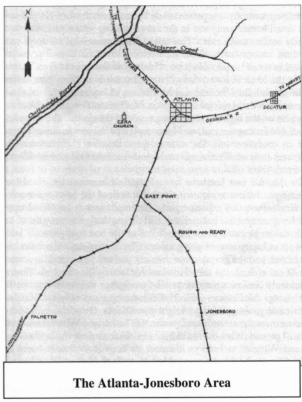

The Atlanta-Jonesboro Area

The sacking of Johnston was heavily favored within the government, but was disappointing to the soldiers, who still loved him. The appointment of Hood as his successor was controversial, especially within the military hierarchy, some of whom regarded him as a bold fighter but unqualified for responsibility for the entire army. Hood had established his reputation in Lee's army as commander of "Hood's Texas Brigade." He later commanded a division at Gettysburg, where he lost the use of his left arm. He came to Chickamauga with Longstreet and lost a leg while commanding the successful Confederate advance on the federal right wing. Although unable to sit a horse without being strapped to the saddle, he was still only 32 years old, highly active, and dedicated to offensive strategy. After recuperating in Richmond from the loss of his leg, he returned to duty under Johnston at Dalton. He quickly proposed to Johnston an aggressive campaign, stating that Lee favored it, but Johnston declined it, as he did all proposals to assume the offensive. Now it was Hood's turn to put his aggressive ideas into practice, which is what Jefferson Davis appointed him to do.

Despite all that was going on, the officers of Croft's Battery arranged to receive some of their back pay. The records reflect that on July 19, the cavalry's pay Quartermaster issued checks to Lieutenant Alfred Young for $100 for March 1864, and to Lieutenant George Young for $100 for November 1863.[631] It is interesting to note the differences between Hubert Dent and the Young boys in their approaches to pay. Hubert accepts the paymaster's lack of funds as one of the necessary sacrifices of his job. The Youngs search out a paymaster with funds and extract their pay.

In his first four days as commanding General, Hood would carry out two bold and well-conceived operations: the Battle of Peachtree Creek on July 20, and the engagement referred to as the Battle of Atlanta on July 22. However, while resulting in large Confederate losses, circumstances prevented these offensives from realizing their full potential for damaging Sherman.

Johnston had left the army in a good position on the south side of Peachtree Creek, which Sherman had to cross in order to reach Atlanta. Sherman's army was approaching the creek in two widely separated columns. On the July19, Hood learned that Gen. Thomas, with his Federal army of 50,000, was in the process of crossing Peachtree Creek, with parts of his army on both sides. That night Hood's plan was carefully explained to all his commanders. Hardee and Stewart were to fall on Thomas' divided force at 1 P. M. on July 20 and crush him, while Cheatham held off the other Federal column lead by Schofield and McPherson. After Thomas' army was neutralized, all three Confederate Corps were to attack and defeat Schofield and McPherson. But unforeseen circumstances would arise.

At one o'clock, when the attack on Thomas was scheduled to begin, it was learned that the federal force under McPherson was moving faster than expected, straight for Atlanta, opposed only by Wheeler's Cavalry, which was in danger of being outflanked. This required an emergency redeployment, which delayed Hardee's attack on Thomas until 4:00. This gave Thomas the time he needed to get all his troops over Peachtree Creek and at least partially in position, but a wide gap had been left on his front. On the order, the Confederates under Stewart and Hardee came surging out of their lines in a "furious sally", hurtling part of Thomas' men out of their breastworks. The Confederates then poured into the gap in the line and attacked the Yankees left and rear, but were repelled when Thomas brought up his reserve brigades. The Confederates reformed and charged again but were blasted by Thomas' reserve artillery, with great loss. Gen. Hardee was about to send Pat Cleburne's fresh troops in for a renewed effort, when he received orders from Hood to send a division to the right wing where McPherson was pressing hard against the Confederates. Nightfall ended the battle.

Hood's losses in this battle on Peachtree Creek, including prisoners, are estimated at 5000, the Federals about half that. In his disappointment, Hood severely criticized Hardee's execution of the plan, but this is probably unjustified. Hood was hereafter prone to unjustly blame Hardee whenever there were disappointing results, and bad relations between them grew.

Hood did not make extensive use of his artillery at Peachtree Creek. From Hubert's letter to Anna written at the next day, July 21, it is apparent that his battery, now attached to Cheatham's Corps (the old Hindman's Corps), was not in the action on the left against Thomas, but spent its day digging in on the right and then being moved to dig in somewhere else. Hubert recognizes Hood as a fighter, but worries that his aggressiveness may be "dangerous", and hopes he will not be destroyed as were his predecessors:

"In the Field"
July 21st, 1864

My Dear Nannie
    We have been expecting all the morning that a fight would take place. But excepting some skirmishing which has taken place on our right, have been nothing like fighting.

Stewarts corps with a portion of Hardee's drove the enemy on our left yesterday and from all I have been able to gather had quite a severe fight with them.

Yesterday was quite a busy day with our immediate command. We moved into position about day light yesterday, went to work to fortify about 12 o'clock, left and went to the left, remained there about an hour or more, were then ordered back to our first position. Before we got there however, were ordered on further to the right, and finally went into position and fortified. Finished our work early this morning and have been awaiting for the fight which was expected to take place today, the anniversary of the battle of Manassas. But it is now after 12 o'clock and no fight yet.

Hood seems disposed to fight. The Yankees are getting all around us and it is getting time we were doing something.

I expect the Columbus people were greatly excited when the Yankee raiders tore up the track on the Opelika and Columbus road. They seemed disposed to destroy every thing through the country and it seems impossible to prevent such things. The Yankees have possession of the Augusta road and consequently no communication in that direction.

I do not think it will be long before the fight comes off. Hood is treading in a dangerous path. This army has killed A[lbert] S[idney] Johnston, laid Beauregard and Bragg aside, and now Johnston (Old Joe) – so you see he is the fifth commander this army has had. I hope Hood will use his opportunities better than any of the others.

The Yankees are at their old game of shelling, But not as continuously as they did when we were on the other side of the Chattahoochee.

The weather continues very warm – not had much rain lately. We have however a very pleasant breeze today.

The Yankees have been throwing shells into Atlanta. But as far as I have heard did no harm.

I am looking for a letter from you today my Darling and I hope I will not be disappointed. It has been several days since I heard from you. Oh! me. I am so anxious Darling to see you and have a long talk with you. I have been a little home sick lately which is something unusual with me although I am always wishing I could get home. I often wonder Darling whether I shall live through this war and get back home to enjoy its blessings and pleasure But that is a subject upon which I do not care to dwell – so I put my trust in providence and will not anticipate evil. Honey you have had very little pleasure since you married. Are you sorry you did not postpone it until the war was over & you might then have captivated some unscathed hero – but I ought not to write this way ought I Darling? Well I will do better.

Genl Cheathim commands our corps and Brown our Division. I have been expecting that Hindman would return so as to get command of the corps, being the Senior Major Genl in it. But he has not returned and Cheathim has been sent here from Hardee's corps to command us.

334

Brig. Genl Stevens of Walker's Division was killed yesterday, also Major Preston who commanded a Battalion of Artillery in Walthall's Division. He was formerly chief of Artillery for Genl Johnston, afterwards Inspector of Artillery. I expect you heard me mention him while you were in Dalton last winter. I heard of no other casualties and in fact have not heard any other particulars of the fight.

Just now every thing is remarkably quiet. I cannot even hear a stray picket fire.

I saw Capt. Macon [Hubert's old First Sergeant and assistant adjutant at Ft. Barrancas] yesterday. He returned a few days ago. He is still with the Brigade. Clayton will make an effort to get him with him as soon as he can.

As soon as this fight is over I am going to try and get a week or ten days furlough. I could spend several days at home by getting ten days leave. Give my love to all the family Darling. Tell them I am very anxious to see them all. Kiss Eddie for his PaPa. Well Darling goodby. Much love and many kisses from your own Hubert.

July 22nd – Well Darling we fell back last night inside the works immediately around Atlanta. I suppose it may be formally announced that the siege of Atlanta commenced. I am already in position. Goodby – your own Hubert

The limited results of Peachtree Creek did not deter General Hood's aggressiveness in the least; he immediately devised a new plan to exploit another opportunity presented by the federal position. Hubert's postscript to Anna on the morning of July 22, reporting that the previous night his unit had been ordered to fall back "into the works immediately around Atlanta," was not, as he surmised, the beginning of a siege. It was an initial step in Hood's new offensive resulting later that day in the engagement known as the "Battle of Atlanta".

Gen. McPherson's Corps of Sherman's army was now positioned on the eastern side of Atlanta, in a line running north-to-south, about three miles east of Atlanta and five miles west of Decatur. On the night of July 20th, Hood learned that the southern end, or left flank, of McPherson's line southeast of the city was exposed and unprotected, a dangerous weak point for any army. In an excellent plan, similar in concept to Stonewall Jackson's historic flank attack at Chancellorsville, Hood started maneuvering to attack this federal weak spot, which realistically could result in spectacular success similar to that of Lee and Jackson at Chancellorsville.

On the 21st, Hood's engineers constructed a new line of inner defenses along the northern and eastern sides of the city, and Hood had his entire army withdraw toward these defenses. This confused Sherman, who thought it was the beginning of a retreat, but this was far from the case.

Visualizing Atlanta as a rough square, on the northern side, the Confederates of Stewart's Corps entered the trenches facing federal Gen. Thomas, while on the eastern side, Gen. Cheatham's Confederates, including Dent's Battery, took positions facing the Union line, consisting of Union General Schofield in the northern, or upper part of the Union line, and Union Gen. McPherson in the southern portion.

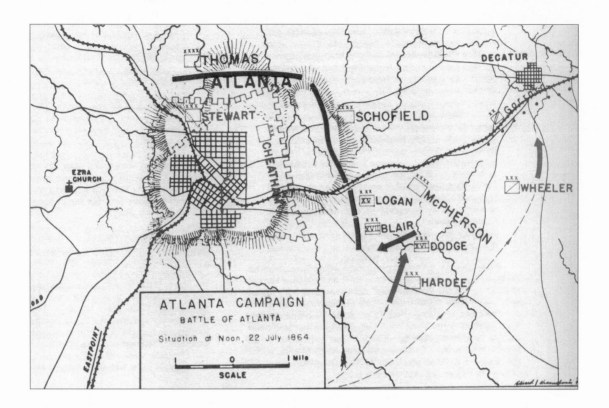

Hood gave Gen. Hardee the key assignment of attacking McPherson's unprotected left flank. At nightfall on July 21, Hardee was to proceed south out of the city, then swing wide to the east, far enough to get in position at daybreak to attack McPherson's flank, either at right angles to McPherson's line, or to its rear. His objective was to effect a classic "roll-up" of the entire Yankee line. His flank attack would be supported by Wheeler's cavalry, with simultaneous attacks by Cheatum against Schofield and McPherson all along the line on the eastern side of the city, while Stewart held Thomas on the northern side to prevent his going to the aid of Schofield and McPherson.

It almost worked. Due to delays including the usual problems of moving many troops along unfamiliar roads in total darkness, Hardee's attack did not begin until about midday on the 22nd, instead of at dawn as planned. Nevertheless, the attack came as a complete surprise to Sherman and his commanders, who were not only unaware of Hardee's presence there, but thought the Confederate army was in retreat. However, by the time of the attack, the situation at McPherson's left flank had changed. During the night of the 21st, the federal corps holding this end of the line, under federal Gen. Blair, repositioned itself, so as to "refuse" and entrench the line's end—that is, the end of the line was curled back on itself and placed in trenches, with the angle resting on a hill—resulting in a much stronger defensive position. But the even more serious problem was that, during the night, another federal division under Gen.

Grenville Dodge had been ordered to march to the end of the line to extend Blair's line even further. Dodge's men were fortuitously waiting, under arms, behind Blair at the time of Hardee's surprise attack. Instead of hitting the rear of the Union entrenchments, Hardee's attack encountered fresh federal troops with weapons in their hands and ready to defend. The Confederates attacked again and again, and despite bitter resistance, drove the federals back several hundred yards.

Gen. McPherson, rushing from Sherman's headquarters to assume personal command of his troops, was surrounded by Confederates behind his lines and ordered to surrender. Refusing, he attempted to fight his way out and was killed. Ironically, this attractive young General was a close friend of Hood's from their years at Westpoint together, and his death inspired grief on both sides.

The main participation of Dent's battery began with the commencement of the supporting attack of Cheatum's Corps against Schofield and McPherson along the eastern side of the city, which was designed to reduce pressure on Hardee as he attacked McPherson's left flank. Unfortunately, this attack did not get fully underway until the main thrust of Hardee's charge was almost over. At the order, Hindman's division climbed from their trenches and charged the Federal lines, accompanied by the two artillery units of Dent's Battery and Douglas' Texas Battery in close support. Captain Douglas describes the assault in a letter to his wife:

> "On yesterday, about four o'clock, Hindman's Division advanced from our works and attacked the enemy. My battery and Dent's advanced with the attacking column. We swept across the field and through the woods for three-fourths of a mile driving their advance line from their works and pressing upon their main line of works. Here the battle grew grand…Dent and myself got into position 400 yards from their works and opened with vigor on the enemy… while our batteries in our main line of works opened on the enemy at long range."[632]

The force of the Confederate assault knocked an opening through the federal line which resulted in the capture of a federal artillery battery. But Sherman's massed artillery fire on the Confederates forced their return to their original line with heavy casualties.

As Hubert was hurrying his men and horses back to safety from the rain of shrapnel from Sherman's massed artillery, he felt a sharp bolt of excruciating pain in his shoulder. Hit by Yankee fire, Dent would later refer to the wound as "painful," while others would call it "severe,"[633] but it did not cause him to leave the field. He continued in command of his battery until nightfall ended the battle. Although neither commander estimated casualties in the Battle of Atlanta, Confederate losses have been placed at 10,000 (of which 2500 were killed) to the Federals' loss of 3500.[w]

---

[w] The Confederate casualties on July 22 also included the commander of the 28th Tennessee Infantry Regiment, Colonel David Crockett Crook, who received a wound thought to be mortal. Taken to a private residence for treatment, Colonel Crook made a personal vow that if he were allowed to live, he would enter the Christian

After the war, Federal Gen. Blair wrote that Hoods' plan at Atlanta had been bold, brilliant, and "very near successful"; that its success was prevented by the "position taken up accidentally" by Grenville Dodge's federal Corps, and that if Blair's command had been forced back as was Dodge's, "there must have been a general rout of all the troops" of McPherson's army.[634]

It was now clear to all that the Confederate army under Hood was operating with a new philosophy: attack! The citizens of Atlanta were now being continuously bombarded night and day. As soon as Sherman's army had come within range, in a foretaste of his "total war" tactics to come, Sherman began lobbing hundreds of shells over the heads of the Confederate defenders into the homes and businesses of the civilians. Although there was enormous destruction of property, the citizenry took refuge in underground shelters, and there was rarely a word of dissatisfaction or surrender.

Having repulsed Hood east of Atlanta on July 22, 1864, Sherman decided to send part of his army to the western side of the city to cut the railroads to the west and otherwise isolate Atlanta from the Confederacy. For this purpose, Sherman moved McPherson's army, now commanded by Gen. O. O. Howard, around the northern side of the city and down the western side. Seeing this movement, Hood countered by ordering Gen. Stephen D. Lee (now commanding Hood's old corps) to move through Atlanta and out toward the west to intercept the Yankee movement, with the intention of then sending Stewart's Corps to attempt to flank the federal line. However on July 28, before a flank attack became feasible, the forces of Howard and Lee clashed at Ezra Church, several miles west of town, and despite repeated assaults during savage fighting, the Confederates were unable to dislodge the Federals from their dug-in positions.

In his memoirs, Hood ungraciously attempted to explain his lack of success at Ezra Church by suggesting that the Confederate soldiers had grown reluctant to attack breastworks, a false accusation disproved repeatedly in the remaining months of the war. Perhaps, after three bloody and unsuccessful offensives, some were beginning to question the wisdom of the change from Joseph Johnston's defensive tactics to Hood's "attack!" philosophy, but the soldiers' old saying was still true, that the Army of Tennessee would *charge hell with a cornstalk*.[635]

---

ministry. Following a long and difficult convalescence which permanently removed him from the war, he survived. Making good his pledge, Crook became a Methodist minister of the Alabama Conference, where he was assigned to churches including Enon, in Bullock County, near Union Springs, Alabama. He preached for many years and died in 1891 at the age of 53. In 1931, 66 years after Dent and Crook were wounded at the Battle of Atlanta, Dent's granddaughter, Joy McDowell, married Crook's grandson, John Allen Crook, Jr., in Eufaula.

38
Young's Battery;
Heroism At Lovejoy's Station

"Lieut. George B. Young, of Croft's battery,... continued to serve his howitzer when completely surrounded by the enemy within a few paces of him and refused to abandon it until ordered away by his brigade commander."

Brig. Gen. William H. ("Red") Jackson

Sherman became obsessed with destroying railroads, and while besieging Atlanta, he decided to send cavalry raiding parties behind the Confederate lines to the south of Atlanta to wreak havoc and destroy railroads. During the maneuvering leading to the battle at Ezra Church, he sent out two raiding parties: one under Gen. McCook to go around the west side of Atlanta, the other under Gen. Stoneman to go around the eastern side, each with the objective of getting in the rear of the Confederates and destroying the railroad at Macon, 25 miles south of Atlanta. McCook's party was about to have an unpleasant meeting with the Young boys.

Federal Gen. McCook, with 5000 men, was ordered to go down the west side of the Chattahoochee until he got behind the Confederates, then recross the river and head for Macon and its railroad. Unfortunately for McCook, however, Croft's Battery of Artillery and Ross' Cavalry Brigade were patrolling this area in the left rear of Johnston's Army, as a part of the Cavalry Division of Brigadier General William H. "Red" Jackson. After McCook's force recrossed the Chattahoochee, he was spotted by Ross' force. Because of the poor health of Captain Croft, Croft's Battery was at this time under the command of Lt. Alfred Young, with his brother Lt. George Young as second in command. Less than two months before, Alf and George's 17-year old brother, Dick, had also joined the battery.

After spotting McCook recrossing the Chattahoochee, Ross' cavalry and Croft's Battery began a pursuit of McCook's force which turned into a three-day running fight, in which McCook was the loser. He was chased eastward through Fayetteville and on to Macon. McCook was able to tear up about a mile and half of track, (which was later repaired), but in a fierce fight on July 29 the Confederates stopped his raid and drove him back along the route he had come. As McCook was chased to the north, he arrived at Newnan, which he found occupied by Confederates. Caught between cavalry units to his front and rear, including Croft's Battery of horse artillery, McCook was badly mauled. He managed to escape to safety across the river, but left behind 950 of his men as prisoners, and much plunder, badly-needed by the Confederates. In *"Haulin' Brass,"* Forbes reports that,

> "Ross and his artillery had so distinguished themselves in defeating McCook that General Jackson presented them the enemy cannon taken at Newnan…So it was then on July 30, at Newnan, that Lieutenant Alfred Young mustered the battery, to congratulate them on their part in McCook's rout and to assess the effects of this latest combat on his men, horses, and equipment."[636]

339

As we will later see, Croft's Battery, soon to be Young's Battery, was not yet finished with Sherman's railroad raiding parties.

Simultaneously with sending McCook around Atlanta to the west, Sherman had sent Federal Gen. Stoneman around the eastern side of Atlanta, with the objectives of not only destroying railroads, but also freeing Federal prisoners in military prison camps at Macon and Andersonville. Stoneman reached Macon, but the raid ended ignominiously when Stoneman was captured, and along with 500 of his men, was himself imprisoned in the Macon prison. [x]

Hood, noting the success of "Red" Jackson's Confederate cavalry against the Yankee cavalry, decided to send out a raiding party of his own. He sent Wheeler's Cavalry behind Sherman's lines into north Georgia to attack and disrupt Sherman's lines of supply and communication, with the hope of forcing a retreat, or at least reducing pressure on Atlanta. In early August, Wheeler with 4500 men destroyed 35 miles of track and burned bridges near Marietta, Dalton, and Resaca. He threatened Chattanooga and then rode into Tennessee, getting within a few miles of Nashville.

At this time, Dent's Battery was in the defensive lines of Cheatham's Corps guarding the eastern side of Atlanta. However, because of the death in action of the commander of the Eufaula Light Artillery, Lt. Oliver, a rumor reached Eufaula that Hubert Dent had been killed. Hubert hastened to write Anna to squelch and explain the rumor. In his letter, Hubert also confidentially tells Anna of the inadequacy of the prominent Eufaula lawyer, Alpheus Baker, as a brigadier general. It will be recalled that Baker had been the first captain of the Eufaula Rifles at Ft. Barrancas, when Hubert was his second in command. Hubert tells Anna of Wheeler's cavalry raid, and discusses opportunities for possible promotion through his friend, another Eufaula lawyer, Major General Henry D. Clayton, now a division commander. It will be recalled that at Fort Barrancas, then Colonel Clayton had made Hubert his regimental adjutant in the First Alabama Infantry Regiment. There was also talk of Macon's becoming a Lt. Colonel. Neither promotion materialized.

In The Field
August 11th, 1864

My Dear Nannie
The siege of Atlanta is dragging its weary lengths and thus far I can see but little change in the situation. It will soon be a month since Genl Hood took command of the army. It has already been a month since we crossed the Chattahoochee. We have done much fighting in that time and I do not think the enemy have gained much.

---

[x] It is an interesting coincidence that Maj. Gen. Stoneman was later exchanged for 45 Confederate privates held by the federals, one of whom was Pvt. Charles S. McDowell, Sr, who would in later years suggest that this gave him the rank of 1/45 of a major general, and whose son, Charlie, Jr. would marry Hubert Dent's daughter, Carrie, in Fendall Hall in 1902.

The enemy shelled Atlanta very severely yesterday and from the sound of cannon kept up after night I think. I do not know what damage they committed.

It is now reported that the enemy are moving back to our right. They however are still in our front over here on the left. I had one man painfully but not seriously wounded on the 9th and another severely wounded yesterday both by minnie balls. Genl Bate was wounded nearly a mile in rear of our line yesterday by minnie ball. I do not know how seriously. I hear nothing else of interest.

I received your letter of the 5th Darling and am sorry that such a report ever reached Eufaula. It was current in the army and I think it arose out of the fact that Capt Oliver was killed. Nearly all who know me know that I am from Eufaula, and Oliver being Captain of the Eufaula Battery, somehow the idea got out that I was the man killed. I did see Mr. Doughtie on his way from Oliver's burial but I was not present at the burial. He ought to have known that the report was untrue.

Oh! Honey I have another piece of news. I heard the 9th that Baker's Brigade was going to be broken up. It has been behaving so badly that Genl Hood determined to break it up and put the regiments in the other Brigades of the Division. Courtney told me the order had been issued. You need not mention it until you hear it as a fact as he (Baker) may even yet bring influences to bear to put a stop to it yet. But the Brigade has a poor reputation and of course it reflects on the Brigade commander. His wife better keep quiet about her husbands talents &c or some one may tell her unpleasant facts. If she does not mind, the last of the Eufaula Bar will be as good as out of the service.

Well Darling now I will tell you something about myself. About ten days ago I saw Macon and told him to tell Clayton that if he would promise to do something better for me when he could that I thought I would accept the position he offered me. He promised to let me hear further from it. Clayton when he spoke to me told me that he would give me higher rank if he could. I have only seen Clayton for a few moments since and then there was fighting going on and I was in a hurry to get a Section of my Battery in position and had no time to talk with him. The change could hardly be effected while the campaign is so active any way.

If Macon is Lt Col I know nothing of it. He will be however as soon as Clayton can get him with him. But all these things have to done at Richmond now and are slow coming out.

A Lieut Dickson from Fla came to see me yesterday. He was in the Hospital at Eufaula and saw you very frequently. Lt Banks in the same company he says [found] your acquaintance and probably visited the House. He seemed to be a very clever gentleman. Banks sprained his ankle getting away from the Yankees a few days ago and can't walk. I may go and see them today as they are near me. I am very well Honey but poor. You would be amused if you could see my "bunk" with logs put up at the head to keep off

341

[minnie] balls. But discretion in this instance is the better part of valor. I have another gun in the place of my disabled one so I have four guns again. The weather continues cloudy with some rain. I have seen no paper lately. Am uneasy about Mobile. The surrender of Fort Gaines seems to have been a disgraceful affair. Anderson must have sold out. I will write Mr. Young tomorrow if nothing prevents – show him what I said about accepting Clayton's offer. Write as often Darling as you can. My love to all. Much love & many kisses from your own devoted – Hubert

[Postscript] Yours & Mr. Y's of the 8th received. Will write again tomorrow. It is tolerably quiet just now. No news. Wheeler is reported to have gone to Sherman's rear –but nothing from him -- Hubert

With the failure of his two earlier "railroad raids" south of Atlanta by McCook and Stoneman, Sherman was beginning to suspect that cavalry alone could not accomplish the level of destruction he desired, and that infantry would be necessary. However, becoming aware that half of Hood's cavalry was off in Tennessee with Wheeler, Sherman decided to try another cavalry raid on the Macon Railroad south of Atlanta. This time the raid was led by Gen. Kilpatrick. Like McCook's and Stoneman's, Kilpatrick's raid would also be unsuccessful and result in heavy Yankee casualties, due in part, as we will see, to the heroic efforts of Young's Battery.

In early August, Captain Edward Croft's physical condition had compelled him to finally give up the attempt to remain with Croft's Battery. Approaching 50 years of age and in poor health after many hard marches, battles, and the "fever," he had for some time been able to lead the battery only sporadically. Alf Young had borne most of the responsibility for the unit. Accepting the fact that he could no longer actively command the battery, Captain Croft departed for Columbus, never to return. He was accompanied by his "body servant", Joe, who drove a two-mule wagon with Croft's horse tied behind.[637] On September 13, 1864, Lieutenant Alfred Young would be promoted to captain, the rank commensurate with the responsibility he was already bearing, and he would command the battery until the end of the war.[638] It's name became Young's Battery, although for a time, it was sometime still referred to as Croft's Battery.

Starting on August 18, Gen. Kilpatrick's raid, similar to McCook's, took him down the west side of the Chattahoochee, this time as far as West Point, on the Alabama line, where he recrossed to the eastern side. He then destroyed six miles of track of the West Point Railroad and headed northeast toward Jonesboro to strike the railroad there. Like McCook, he was spotted by scouts of Gen. "Red" Jackson's cavalry division, which was still operating in the area. Pending reinforcements from Hood, Gen. Jackson assigned Ross' brigade of cavalry to harass and delay Kilpatrick's progress toward Jonesboro. Assigned to assist Ross' delaying effort was one section of Young's Battery of horse artillery, consisting of a single 12 pounder howitzer and crew, commanded by Lt. George B. Young. George's howitzer was a somewhat lighter, shorter gun than the Napoleons used by Hubert Dent, but it was a more mobile weapon, particularly suitable for supporting fast-moving cavalry, and it could be particularly deadly firing canister into charging men and horses at short range.

Kilpatrick pressed the Confederate delaying force back to the east toward Jonesboro, until reaching the bridge across the Flint River just west of Jonesboro on the afternoon of August 19. George unlimbered his howitzer on the eastern end of the bridge, and began blazing away at the approaching Yankees. However, Kilpatrick's Yankees had greater artillery firepower; George and his crew were hit by a devastating barrage, resulting in the instant death of his corporal, A. F. Knight, who was literally "blown to pieces".[639] The outmanned Confederates were forced to withdraw, first into Jonesboro, and then through the town. George aided the Confederates' withdrawal by periodically unlimbering and shelling the pursuing Yankees until forced by their stronger artillery to move on. In bitter fighting, four privates of Young's Battery were wounded and five captured. Private Allen P. McDaniel was driving one of the gun mule teams when he was shot in the arm and side. As McDaniel fell to the ground, a Yankee lieutenant whacked him across the skull with his saber and left him for dead. Happily, McDaniel survived both gunshot and saber, and returned to his farm in Clay County, Alabama, where he died an old man in 1905.[640]

The Confederates retired outside of town beyond the range of the Yankee guns, which did not pursue. George sent a message reporting his heavy casualties to his brother Alfred, who had been ordered to remain "in reserve" back with Ross' supply train. Gen. "Red" Jackson was determined not to allow Kilpatrick's raiders enough time in Jonesboro to do significant damage to the railroad. As night fell, he rallied and regrouped his scattered units, and at 11:00 P.M., the Confederates counterattacked. Whooping and hollering, they stormed back into Jonesboro, driving the Yankees out of town to the east toward Lee's Mill. At daybreak on August 20, the Confederates were dogging the retreating Yankees near Lee's Mill on the road south toward Lovejoy's Station. Joined by reinforcements during the morning, the Confederates overtook Kilpatrick and surrounded him four miles from Lovejoy's Station.[641]

Preparing to assault the stalled and surrounded Yankees, Gen. Ross dismounted his cavalry troopers and deployed them in a line across a small road or lane. He placed his section of Young's Battery, i. e. the howitzer crew led by George Young, on a slight elevation beside the lane. Seeing these preparations, Kilpatrick realized the peril of his position and determined to make a desperate effort to break out of the encircling Confederate force.

Deployed in three successive columns, Kilpatrick achieved numerical superiority at the point where he needed it. Firing and wielding sabers, his concentrated force charged at full gallop down the lane covered by George Young's howitzer. It became apparent that the charge had the momentum to brush over the line of dismounted Confederate cavalry and make good the break-out, and perhaps run over the howitzer unit in the process.

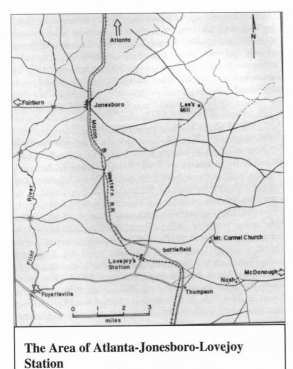

The Area of Atlanta-Jonesboro-Lovejoy Station

But George Young had different ideas. He resolved that if the Yankees were to escape, he would stand firm and inflict the greatest possible amount of damage on the fleeing Federals. As the on-rushing horde thundered toward him, George and his crew set up a murderous barrage from the howitzer. George's rapid-fire of double loaded shots of canister ripped into the enemy ranks with lethal effect. Positioned close to the route of the swarming mass of men and horses, the gun crew time and again repelled Yankee efforts to overcome and silence the death-dealing howitzer. George turned a deaf ear to those urging him to abandon the gun and save the lives of himself and his men, inspiring Confederate troopers to go to the aid of the embattled artillerists.

Sometimes surrounded by the masses of enemy cavalry, and seeing blue uniforms everywhere, the frenzied cannoneers fired everywhere - to the left, to the front, to the right, to the rear - in every direction where a patch of blue appeared, cutting down clusters of Yankee invaders with every blast.

Only when about to be overwhelmed by the sheer size of the blue deluge, when his ammunition was gone and Gen. Ross himself had ordered the abandonment of the gun, did George and his crew relinquish the position. The jubilantly fleeing Yankees then seized the howitzer and hauled it off as they departed at full speed toward Decatur and the safety of Sherman's lines, amid heavy Confederate pursuit.

But the Yankees had bought George Young's howitzer at great cost. In the wake of their running fight they left abandoned wagons, horses, ambulances, supplies, small arms, two pieces of artillery, four stands of colors, and 500 men killed, wounded or captured. They had succeeded in burning only a stationhouse and tearing up some track, which was quickly repaired. It was the end of Sherman's "railroad raids." Sherman later wrote that when on August 23 he saw Confederate supply trains arriving in Atlanta from the South, he "became more than ever convinced that cavalry could not or would not work hard enough to damage a railroad properly..."[642] He thus overlooked pesky details like George Young, his determined cannoneers, and many others like them who wouldn't stop fighting until the ammunition was gone.

In his official report, Gen. Jackson expressed considerable satisfaction with his Division's exploits against Kilpatrick, and singled out Lt. George B. Young for special praise:[643]

GENERAL ORDERS No. 23.

HDQRS. JACKSON'S CAVALRY
DIVISION, *Near Atlanta, Ga., August* 24, 1864.

The brigadier-General commanding desires to congratulate the officers and men of his command as also General Reynolds' brigade on their successful expulsion of the large and well-appointed raiding party under Kilpatrick, boasting "to destroy our rear communications and compel the Army of Tennessee to retire from Atlanta," and to tender his thanks for their energy and good fighting. He takes pleasure in noticing the part performed by General Ross and his gallant Texans in resisting with the most determined courage the entire force of the enemy, not less than 4,000 hurled upon his brigade as a *dernier resort,* to cut their way through, continuing to fire upon them till the last one had passed, inflicting heavy loss upon them and capturing one piece of artillery and four stand of colors, reflecting the highest credit upon himself and brigade; as also General Armstrong and brigade for the very vigorous pursuit, causing the enemy to abandon wagons, horses, and ambulances. He takes this occasion to make special mention of Lieut. George B. Young, of Croft's battery, who alone continued to serve his howitzer when completely surrounded by the enemy within a few paces of him and refused to abandon it until ordered away by his brigade commander. Soldiers, in meeting and repelling this the largest raiding party ever sent to your rear, you have won the lasting gratitude of your commanders and countrymen, and have reflected fresh glory upon the proud appellation of the Confederate Army. We inflicted upon the enemy a loss of 500 killed and wounded and prisoners, captured 2 pieces of artillery and 4 stand of colors, a number of horses, equipments, and small-arms, besides wagons and ambulances, with small loss to ourselves. He returns thanks to Generals Armstrong, Ross, and Reynolds for prompt action, hearty co-operation, and skillful handling of their respective commands.
By command of Brig. Gen. W. H. Jackson:

E. T. SYKES,
Assistant Adjutant-General.

As commander of the battery, it was the duty of Alfred Young to write the July-August muster roll records, and he duly recorded his brother's bravery:[644]

"Since the date of the last muster [30 July], the company has frequently engaged the enemy. The most important of which in its results to the company was the action of 20 August 1864 with Kilpatrick during his raid in rear of General Hood's army at Atlanta. First Lieutenant George B. Young accompanied General Ross' Cavalry Brigade with one 12-pounder howitzer to intercept the raid. The Brigade was run over in a charge made by the enemy with their whole force . Lieutenant Young with his gallant detachment remained firm in their position within 30 feet of the charging columns of the enemy firing in every direction upon them and preventing numerous charges upon his piece from being successful by rapid firing of double charges of canister inflicting great loss on the enemy. The howitzer was finally abandoned by order of General Ross but not until it was almost completely surrounded and every round of ammunition expended. For his gallantry, Brigadier General W. H. Jackson, Commanding Division of Cavalry, made special mention in Special Orders of Lieutenant G. B. Young. Too much praise can not be bestowed on the cannoneers and drivers composing the detachment. I take pleasure in naming them on this roll: [list follows]."

It was inevitable that a story as dramatic as George's would find its way into the hometown newspapers. The August 24 edition of Columbus' *Daily Sun* carried an account originating in a Griffin paper. It is a correct account, containing only modest amounts of overstatement; excusable hyperbole about a popular local boy:

"ROSS' BRIGADE AT LOVEJOY'S, THE GALLANTRY OF LIEUTENANT YOUNG

"A correspondent of the Griffin [Georgia] *Rebel* thus describes a fight of Ross' Brigade at Lovejoy's on the Macon and Western Railroad and the gallantry of Lieutenant George B. Young, son of Mr. William H. Young of Columbus.

The enemy charged in columns of regiments and it is strange that they did not kill or capture every man of [Ross'] Brigade. The horse-holders, seeing the charge, ran off and Ross' men fought both for their lives and their horses. They formed behind fences and as the enemy would pass them, they gave them the contents of their guns and six-shooters. It was in this charge that the old belching 12-pounder under Lieutenant George B. Young from Columbus, Ga, did noble and effective work. As a column would charge down on him, he would open so wide a break in it that it would pass him without running over his gun. He fired rapidly, turning his gun in three or four directions. The enemy made desperate attempts to take it, and twice General Ross sent word to Lieutenant Young that he had better leave his gun and try and save his men. His reply was, "Not while I have a shot left!" Then General Ross took thirty men and went up to the piece and said, "Well, Young, if you are determined to stay with your gun, we will stay with you." And, they did stay there 'till they had fired every round of ammunition he had. Next to the last round, a double charge of grape, cracked the gun but it did not frighten them from firing the last shot. General Ross says, "Lieutenant Young is one of the coolest and bravest men I ever saw under fire. Every one of his men stood by the piece. He lost one killed and five wounded. I regret I have not their names as men who fell acting so bravely should not be forgotten." At one time General Ross thought his whole brigade would be captured or killed, but as the cloud blew over, his men began to make their appearance and the horse-holders with the horses began to emerge from the bushes. The enemy halted long enough to carry off Lieutenant Young's gun and then took the direction to McDonough..."

39
The Fall Of Atlanta

"If we had been successful at Jonesboro we would have held Atlanta now and there is no reason why we should not have been successful. The men did not fight..."

Hubert Dent to Anna

On August 26, Sherman's men besieging Atlanta on the western side were seen by Hood's observers to be leaving their trenches and breastworks. Hood, aware that Wheeler's Cavalry had been operating in Sherman's rear, cutting railroads and disrupting supplies and communication, jumped to the conclusion that Sherman was falling back – retreating. This was severely wishful thinking by Hood. In fact, Sherman had decided to bypass Atlanta and the Confederates defending it. In a major advance, he was moving most of his army around the west side of Atlanta, to get south of Atlanta behind Hood's defensive lines. For several days, while Sherman's army marched around Hood's army, vulnerable to attack, Hood clung to the view that Sherman was not advancing in force. However, when Hood learned of Federal parties cutting railroads south of town (Sherman's favorite occupation), he began to take precautions. He moved surplus stores to his rear; and he sent five brigades to Jonesboro, twenty five miles south of Atlanta, to be in front of the Federals if they turned up there in force.

On August 30, it became obvious that Jonesboro was indeed Sherman's objective. To intercept him, Hood sent Hardee's Corps and Stephan D. Lee's Corps to Jonesboro, with Hardee in overall command and Cleburne commanding Hardee's Corps. Hood himself remained in Atlanta.

Hubert Dent, now attached to Stephen D. Lee's Corps, hurried Dent's Battery along over the twenty five miles south to the showdown in Jonesboro.

Hardee was instructed to launch an attack on Sherman at Jonesboro with his entire force on the morning of August 31, and drive Sherman back to the west and into the Flint River. Due to the late arrival of part of Hardee's force, during which the Federals had time to dig in, Hardee's attack did not begin until two in the afternoon. Confederate General Cleburne had some success on the left and captured some artillery, but on the right, Stephen D. Lee's Corps failed to penetrate the Federal line and fell back "demoralized". Hubert Dent, looking around at the conduct of the infantry during this unsuccessful assault, had the sickening feeling that this Confederate army had lost its vitality and its famous fighting spirit. He would later write that Jonesboro could have been won if the men had been willing to fight with their usual élan. As Gen. Hardee later replied to similar criticism from Hood, these men for two months had been bravely hurled against breastworks, outnumbered, day after day, in a series of costly repulses or fruitless victories. Hubert Dent, rarely critical of the Confederate soldier, knew all this, but nevertheless, in the privacy of his letters to Anna, later used severely critical terms in describing this battle.

During the night of August 31, Hood, who still had not fully grasped the fact that most of Sherman's army was proceeding south, ordered Hardee to send Stephen D. Lee's Corps *back* to Atlanta. And so on the morning of September 1, Hubert Dent, having marched his battery the twenty five miles from Atlanta the previous day and fought a hard battle, now limbered up to retrace the same twenty five miles.

As Hubert and the rest of Lee's Corps returned to Atlanta, Hood ordered Hardee to stay in Jonesboro and do his best to prevent Sherman's advancing to Macon. Sherman's army however, was moving to envelope Jonesboro, with Schofield's Corps from the east, Thomas from the north, and Howard from the west. On the afternoon of Sept 1, they all attacked Hardee's lone corps defending Jonesboro. Heavily outnumbered, Hardee's left was enveloped, and an entire brigade was captured with its artillery. But although Hardee was outmanned by almost 6-to-1, the rest of his line held, and by nightfall, he was able to withdraw six miles south to Lovejoy's Station (the site of George B. Young's valorous stand eleven days earlier)

Hood now woke up to the fact that Sherman's army had bypassed Atlanta and was proceeding south, which led Hood to the decision that he needed to concentrate his scattered army in front of Sherman. This meant abandoning the defense of Atlanta. It also required the destruction of tons of supplies and six trainloads of ammunition and ordnance, to avoid leaving it for the Yankees. Stephen D. Lee's Corps, which was returning to Atlanta, was stopped just before it reached the city. Lee was ordered to stand guard while the defensive trenches were stripped of men to send south, and then his corps was to also head south again to join Hardee at Lovejoy's. Hubert once again limbered up his battery to wrestle it back over the same twenty five miles for the third time in three days.

On the morning of September 2, the elements of Sherman's army which had remained north of Atlanta, marched into the now-undefended city and accepted its formal surrender from the mayor.

As Atlanta was being surrendered, Hood's army had concentrated at Lovejoy's Station, 30 miles south, where it was entrenched and girding for battle with Sherman's army gathered nearby. On September 3, Hood telegraphed President Davis a desperate appeal for reinforcements against his much-stronger opponent, but Davis had no troops to send. And then, to the astonishment of everyone, Sherman turned and walked away. Having received the report that Atlanta was in his hands, Sherman lost all immediate interest in Hood, and on September 6, marched his entire army back to Atlanta. Needless to say, the surprised Confederates were entirely happy to see him leave.

Writing the next day from his camp near Lovejoy's, Hubert Dent's view of Sherman's withdrawal to Atlanta is consistent with that of President Lincoln and others then and now; that it was a mistake and a missed opportunity for the North. It gave the exhausted Confederates badly needed breathing time to regroup and recruit. But Hubert was deeply depressed about the army. The loss of Atlanta was a devastating blow which dimmed even Hubert's boundless optimism about the ultimate success of the Confederate cause. In the privacy of his letters to Anne, he engages in uncharacteristic but strongly felt criticism of the soldiers' performance on this occasion. His dark mood leads him to speculate that, even if Lincoln were defeated by the Democrats in the coming November elections, the weary South might accept peace terms and reenter the Union, a result Hubert always strongly opposed on any terms:

Sept. 7th, 1864

My Dear Nannie

Yesterday morning it was discovered that the enemy had left our front again. Rumor says they have gone towards Atlanta and are destroying the rail road as they go. We have not yet moved.

My Battery on the evening of the 5th relieved Douglas' Battery on picket and we are still in the same position. We had a good deal of rain yesterday and it is cloudy and threatening rain this morning.

Genl [Stephen D.] Lee yesterday had each Division of his corps assembled and made a little speech to Clayton's (I expect) and Stevenson's. Just as he was about to address our Division the rain bust upon us and he had to postpone it.

He is trying to get up a better feeling in his corps. He told them of the poor fighting they did at Jonesboro on the 31st and talked to them very plainly about what they ought to do and how they ought to fight. I heard nearly all he said to Stevenson's Division and I presume he would have said the same thing to our Division.

The spirit of our troops is very bad and unless they do better I do not see what is to prevent Sherman from going any where he pleases. If we had been successful at Jonesboro we would have held Atlanta now and there is no reason why we should not have been successful. The men did not fight and Hood ought not to be blamed for that. I feel badly over the result of that fight. It is a new thing for our men to refuse to fight, or what is the same thing, to fight with no spirit. Our cause here is not in a good condition and I am sorry to see it.

I am in hopes Darling I will get a letter from you today or tomorrow. I sent to Griffin day before yesterday. But the army PO was destroyed at Atlanta with the mails and no arrangements had been made then for distributing the army mail. I shall send down again today. It has been two weeks since I had a letter from you.

Well Darling what do the people about Eufaula say about the nominees of the Chicago convention [the Democratic Convention]. I can't say that I hope for much unless we can check the enemy, and even if we succeed in doing that and they [the Democrats] are elected, we will have another thing to fear, and that is the disposition of our people to accept peace on any terms. I do not want to see the Confederacy go back into the Union on any terms. We are separated from them and I want to remain separated. If McClellan is elected and refuses to recognize our independence I believe he and his party would be worse enemies to our cause than Lincoln himself.

The army is a good deal faded and needs rest and severe discipline. It was very much disorganized in our last retreat. If the enemy have returned to Atlanta we may have a few days of rest. I think Sherman made a great mistake in not following us up vigorously. We could have made but a poor resistance.

Sherman from Atlanta can threaten Montgomery Augusta and Macon. Three important points. It was reported yesterday that a prisoner said they were going back to Atlanta and move out on the Augusta road. I do not think however that Sherman will move the bulk of his army far on that road.

I saw Capt Garrity yesterday just from Mobile. He says the people there are tolerably quiet but that we have very few troops there and he thinks a land force could take the city as the force now stands. Baker's Brigade and a few battalions being the only forces we have there besides the militia. And I tell you Baker's Brigade would not fight up here I hope it will do better at Mobile.

Lt Bond of Garrity's Battery who was wounded at Jonesboro was killed by a collision on the rail road. He is the third officer that Battery has lost since the campaign commenced.

I am getting along very well. My company is pretty full and healthy.

Richardson was tried but I have not seen the sentence. It will not be very severe I do not expect, as the principal charge was stricken out in consequence of its coming under an amnesty order of Genl Johnston's.

Who told you Darling that Macon was a Lt Col? Clayton has recommended him but if the President adheres to his previously expressed opinion he will not promote him as he has declined to make any promotions under the new staff bill. Macon deserves promotion too as much as a great many others and more than some who get it.

How does the mare & colt come on? Mr. Young wrote me that she did not improve much. I do not think she will as long as the colt runs with her. It will make the colt better but the mare will be longer improving.

It is a cloudy gloomy day. I wish I was at home with you all. How I could enjoy a day with the family now. It seems to me a very long time since I saw you all and from the way we are doing in this army it may be a long time yet before we have peace. I did intend writing to Mr. Young yesterday. But was too busy. I will write my next letter to him.

Ask Ed how he will trade his pony for my bay horse. I am tired of riding him, he does not suit me. I intend getting another the first good opportunity I have. But to make a good trade I must not be in a hurry.

We are just beginning to get newspapers again. Well Darling the mail man is waiting for this letter so I must hurry up. Give my love to all the family. Tell Eddie PaPa thinks of him very often and is very anxious to see him. For the present goodby. Much love & kisses from your own devoted husband – Hubert"

While Hubert's men and horses were enjoying a much-needed rest in pleasant and sunny weather, he wrote Anna again, three days later. He is still despondent about the fighting spirit of the army as reflected at Jonesboro, and is now also questioning the quality of the Generalship, which is unusual for Hubert. He questions Hardee's method of initiating his attack on the superior Federal force in the August 31 action at Jonesboro; but recognizes that Hardee's later losses on September 1 were the result of the Federally-initiated action, after Lee's Corps (which included Dent's Battery) had left to return to Atlanta, leaving Hardee heavily outnumbered, with one corps against most of Sherman's army. Although a visit from Anna is not feasible at this time, Hubert suggests that her 15 year old brother, Ed (Edward Billups Young) pay him a visit, because this may be the best chance he will have to see the Confederate army.

"Camp near Lovejoy's Station
Sept. 10th, 1864

My Darling
    The sun is not yet visible above the horizon but as I intend to start a man to Griffin quite early this morning I want to finish a letter to you before he leaves. You know we have had no mail for ten days or more and I am not certain of getting any today, but as I am very anxious to get letters I will send again today and also on Monday. I hope Darling you are receiving letters from me more regularly than I am from you. The last letter I had from you was the one brought by Col Ott. I expect a letter for me was destroyed with the mail at Atlanta when we evacuated. So I hope to get two or three today.
    There is some talk here of troops going to Virginia but it may be all talk. It is expected that Sherman will send troops to Grant and if he does I suppose Hood will send some of his to Genl Lee.
    What do you all think of the fall of Atlanta and our fighting at Jonesboro? For my own part I cannot think of it without shame and mortification. I will further say as I am writing to you Darling that I think there was very little Generalship shown either by Hood in sending the force there as he did or in Hardee making the attack as he did. It seems to me that if Hood felt strong enough to attack them at all that he ought to have attacked them in their rear instead of in front and Hardee instead of making a General assault with weak lines all along their works ought to have massed them on some good point and taken that and then pushed the enemy out on the right and left. But it is all over and I must hope it happened for the best and that we will do better next time.
    Hardee lost eight guns there. Just the number he captured from the Yankees on the 22nd of July. This loss however occurred on the 1st Sept. after our corps had left and the enemy making the attack. It is said they suffered very severely but succeeded in breaking our lines and carrying the works.
    Hardee's corps is about Jonesboro now. Stewarts & [S. D.] Lee's are just below Lovejoy's station on either side of the rail-road. All the troops are

resting and we may rest for several days. My horses needed rest very [much] and they are looking better already.

We have very heavy dews now. The sun shines out clear & warm during the day. The company is Generally in very good health – my own is very good. Capt. Garrity has returned to his company. Since he left on the 28th May he has lost every one of his Lieuts. Lyon and Hassell killed and Bond wounded and killed by a rail-road collision on his way home. I have seen nothing of it in the news papers but from what many persons tell me it must have been a very serious collision. About thirty-three were killed outright – besides a good many wounded.

I was in hopes I would have been able to get off home for a short time but no chance – no leave of absence to be forwarded except on Surgeon's certificate. If there was a place for you to remain any where near me I would ask you to come up but there is no place nearer than Griffin and that is fifteen miles off and I could only see you once or twice a week.

I do not feel as sanguine about peace now as I did a month ago or less. The fall of Atlanta will cause great rejoycing in the north and Lincoln to give greater effect to it reducing the draft to one hundred thousand men. I expect he apprehended some trouble in enforcing the draft for the full number called for and therefore reduced it to one hundred thousand. He plays his cards very adroitly and he had better, for the campaign will soon end and I do not regard his election as altogether certain. The truth is Darling I cannot see the end of this thing. If Lincoln is reelected the war will go on. If Fremont is elected the war I think will go on. If McClellan is elected there is no certainty that we will have peace, and the Yankees will be so much inspirited by the fall of Atlanta that they will take new interest in the war.

If I did not believe that there was a providence in all these things I would be entirely disheartened. But I cannot believe that our Father in Heaven intends that we shall be subjugated by such a race of people as the Yankees. But suppose Lincoln should overrun the country, what else could he do. Our Southern people would not stand and see their lands go into the hands of enemies tamely and making no resistance. No one supposes that life or property would be safe and the horrors of Mexico would be repeated. I cannot believe that our land will be given over to such punishment. God grant it may not be.

There is a good deal of complaint against Genl Hood but that is natural. Some are wishing for Joe Johnston, others for Bragg. Some men have lost all hope, others take the fall of Atlanta and the retreat of the army as matters of course. For my own part I do not mind the fall of Atlanta half as much as the way our troops fought. If they had fought well I would not have cared half so much, but to think we lost it by the timidly way – almost cowardice of our own troops.

I heard from Genl Anderson a few days ago. He was doing very well but could not talk yet. His lower face was fractured.

I never was more anxious to hear from home in the whole campaign than I am now. I wonder how many letters I will receive today or if I will receive any. I wish so much Darling that I could see you and have a long talk with you. I could enjoy it so much. Oh! this war – this cruel war! When will it end? I hope to be able to see you Darling before a great while. In the meantime Honey write frequently. Your letters are always so anxiously looked for and gladly received.

Give my love to all the family. Tell Ma I am very sorry to hear that she is not entirely well. She must suffer a great deal. Tell Ed he had better come up & see me now. It will be the best chance he will have to see the army. Tell the girls if I owe any of them letters that they must pardon me for I have been so busy lately that I can scarcely remember any thing of that kind.

Well Honey I have eaten breakfast and the mail man will soon be ready so I must hurry up. The sun is shining brightly and promises a warm day.

Have you read "Macaria?" It seems to be another pedantic exhibition from Miss Evans. I have however only read a small portion of it.

Tell Eddie his PaPa is very anxious to see him and he must grow fast so he can come and see me. Well Darling goodby. Much much love and many kisses from your own devoted affectionate husband – Hubert"

In his third and last letter from Lovejoy's Station, we see Hubert's normal optimism and good spirits beginning to return. He is reverting to his practice of encouraging the folks at home not to be disheartened by temporary setbacks. A visit from Anna is still not feasible, but Hubert is hatching a time-honored soldier's scheme: to exploit an alleged repair of equipment so as to inveigle a trip home out of it. Hubert's improved outlook lets him enjoy responding in kind to Anna's teasing about addressing her letters to the "Army of Tennessee," when the army is nowhere near Tennessee. Hubert does not realize that his light-hearted response predicted exactly what was about to actually happen.

"Near Lovejoy's Station
Sept. 13th, 1864

My Darling,

I went to call on Genl Clayton yesterday, found him very well, but feeling pretty blue over the condition of our affairs. He is very anxious to get off home for a few days. But his application was refused. He gave me a note to an acquaintance of his to see if I could not get board for you but the house was full and it was refused. I went to other places but all had excuses. I have no tent or you might come up my way for a few days. The principal objection is the want of something to eat. We are only drawing beef now. Very poor at that. Get no bacon and have no grease. We have flour but can't use it.

I am going in a few minutes to army Hd Qrs on business and while there I intend to see if there is no possible chance for me to get home. One of my guns needs a new vent piece and if it is sent to Macon I intend to try and go with it and if I get off will go home. But this is very uncertain.

The nights are becoming much cooler and I caught a severe cold last night which effects my head a good deal.

I thought the relief committee had gone home. But Clayton told me yesterday that they were in Griffin.

I did not see Macon. He was out and I left before his return. His promotion has been refused by the President. He still adheres to his original course to make no promotions or appointments under this new staff bill.

Clayton is pretty nearly whipped. I dislike to see such feelings among our people. While I regard the fall of Atlanta as a great and serious blow to us I do not think it renders our cause hopeless.

Well Darling I will ride and let you know the result on my return.

Well Darling no chance to get home unless I can be sent to Macon with one of my guns to be repaired. We have a review of our artillery tomorrow evening. I heard that Genl [Stephen D.] Lee reviewed his corps today. The Infantry part of it. I am very well fixed up now and my Battery is in very good Condition.

I am only writing you a short letter this time. Honey, I have often told you not to be uneasy about me when you did not hear from me for as a general rule when you do not hear I am all right. Bad news travels fast and should I be killed or wounded in any fight you would hear it very quickly.

My cold is troublesome.

Have you all gotten over the fall of Atlanta yet? I regret it. But stand that about as well as most people.

Mrs. Courtney is still in Griffin. She can't get any nearer. She was expected up on the cars yesterday but could not get passports and failed to come. I have not seen her since she last came. I wish I could get a pleasant place for you and bring you up here.

Well Darling beef & bread are ready. Goodby till morning.

It is now Wednesday the 14th Darling. Quite cool last night. But the sun will be warm today.

Jim B must be a fractious fellow to get into so many difficulties. I expect he feels rather soreheaded any way at his position at home.

And so Darling you think army of Tenn is ridiculous. Well Honey I suppose our people hope to get back into Tenn is the reason why it is not changed. However if you do not wish to add that just say Hood's army and it will answer as well.

I wonder if I will get a letter from you today. I hope so. Give my love to all the family. I am very sorry to hear of Ma's continued ill health. She must suffer a good deal. How does Eddie come on. I am very anxious to see him. There must be some of your letters behind yet. I hope they will come up today. We will have a fine day for our review. Well Darling goodby much love and many kisses from your own devoted Hubert"

One of the officer's of Ross' cavalry brigade wrote during this period that his brigade, which was accompanied by Croft-Young's Battery, "had participated in no less than 9 battles and 81 skirmishes within the 110 days" since it joined the Army of Tennessee in Rome on May 15.[645]

40
Return To Tennessee

"I think Lincoln will certainly be re-elected and four years more of war for us ...I have almost made up my mind to the fall of Richmond and a good many other disasters - but I feel more than ever confident of the result..."
                                          Hubert Dent to sister-in-law, Mollie Young

The cost of the Hood's Atlanta campaign in casualties to the Army of Tennessee is not agreed, but has been estimated at about 9000 men. Sherman's losses for a comparable period have been placed at 24,000. While Hood had not stopped Sherman, he had inflicted damage on him, slowed his aggression, and compelled caution. Sherman complained that he could not get his men to move 100 yards against Hood's Confederates without stopping to entrench.[646] But the serious problem for the South was that, while Sherman's losses could be replaced fairly easily, the Confederates' could not. Its continuing losses in men were irreplaceable. The reduced size of the Army of Tennessee was permanent.

While considering the best use of his small army, Hood wrote President Davis from Lovejoy's to suggest moving the Federal prisoners away from the military prison camp at Andersonville (about 150 miles south of Lovejoy's) so that Hood could maneuver freely without the need to protect the prison. Hood's army was simply not large enough to stop Sherman's further advance, and he suggested that the best use of his army now might be to move against Sherman's communications, that is, on his rear. President Davis agreed. Hood decided to move his camp from Lovejoy's Station on the Macon railroad, over to an area about ten miles away on the West Point-Montgomery Railroad, around the Georgia town of Palmetto, still only about 25 miles southwest of Atlanta.

Hubert writes while enroute to the new assembly area, reporting that his unit will be camping at Fairburn, which is also on the West Point-Montgomery railroad but closer to Atlanta. He has seen Bob Gunby, another of Anna's Columbus first cousins who is now a courier for Gen. Johnston. (Bob is the son of Anna's aunt, Jane Louise Beall, and her husband, Robert M. Gunby. We last saw Mr. and Mrs. Gunby during the Young family trip to the New York World's Fair in 1853, the year before Hubert moved to Eufaula. The elder Gunby is now President of William's Eagle Manufacturing Co., and is also the business partner of Edward Croft in Gunby and Croft's Store.) Hubert writes in a pique over the lack of mail from home, which is always extremely important to him:

"Near Fayetteville
Sept. 18th, 1864

We are on the march – have been all day and will start at 4 o'clock in the morning

I sent to the office today and the usual reply "no letter." I intend to send again tomorrow and hope we get one then. If I fail I do not know when I will get one as it will be the last opportunity I will have for some time.

I do not know where we are going to in the end. But tomorrow we are to march eighteen miles to Fairburn on the Westpoint Rail Road. Where next I do not know - our corps [Stephen D. Lee's] and theirs [Stewart's] are both moving in the same direction. I have not heard whether Hardee's is moving or not.

I am very well physically but feel very much annoyed at not receiving letters and a great deal of anxiety to hear from home. But I will not think any thing has happened until I can hear.

I have not time Darling to write much. It is now eight o'clock and I am writing by a short piece of borrowed candle.

I saw Bob Gunby today. He is very well – is a courier for Gen.l Johnston. We are reporting to him again and marching with the Division. There are rumors that we are going to Blue Mountain [near Anniston, Alabama] And various other rumors. Goodby Darling. Love to all. Much love from your anxious and perplexed husband. Hubert"

Hubert's reference to reporting to Gen. Johnston again is inaccurate and confusing, and is probably the result of a false report distorting a possible reorganization that was in fact being discussed. Concern over Hood's "high-casualty" type of warfare led President Davis to consider alternatives to Hood, but not Gen. Johnston again. Ultimately, he decided to keep Hood as Commander, but to place him under the general authority of Gen. Beauregard, who would be recalled from the minor position he was holding under Gen. Robert E. Lee, to command a new "Military Division of the West," consisting of the two departments of Gen. Hood and Gen. Richard Taylor. It was an awkward arrangement, but Hood did not object to it. Beauregard shared the views of Hood and Davis that the best use of Hood's army now was against Sherman's lines of communications and supply.

In Atlanta, Sherman was implementing the first of the cruel and inhumane policies which would later cause the Twentieth Century to regard him as the inventor of "Total War". He decreed the expulsion of all civilians from the city, so as to "make Atlanta a pure military garrison or depot, with no civil population to influence military measures." To the outraged protests that arose, he replied in substance that he just couldn't be bothered with the petty concerns of noncombatants. [647] He informed Hood that the civilians being ejected from their homes would be transported to the Confederate lines south of the city to be delivered to Hood's army under a flag of truce. Hood had no alternative but to cooperate and help the refugees the best he could, but he wrote further to Sherman,

"Permit me to say that the unprecedented measure you propose transcends in studied and ingenious cruelty all acts ever before brought to my attention in the dark history of war. In the name of God and humanity, I protest."[648]

With Sherman settled in Atlanta, Hood's army used the respite for refitting and repairing. President Davis visited the camp at Palmetto with other statesmen, made speeches, and reviewed the troops.

In late September, Hubert carried out the plan he had conceived weeks earlier of taking a trip to Eufaula in connection with equipment repair. He had earlier mentioned that he needed a "vent piece" for a gun. Now he took the entire gun to Columbus, undoubtedly to the Columbus Arsenal, which was one of the Confederacy's most important producers of cannon. Leaving the gun to be worked on, he then proceeded to Eufaula for a visit of probably several days.

Returning from Eufaula to retrieve his gun, Hubert was annoyed to find that it was not yet ready, and that he could have stayed another day at home. He used the time however to visit with William and Ellen Young at Beallwood, who as usual showered him with hospitality and gifts. George Young was home on leave, the family undoubtedly still basking in the glory of his famous stand at Lovejoy's Station only one month earlier. While Hubert is on this trip, Hood begins his move toward Sherman's rear, leading Hubert to comment to Anne that he may have trouble finding his company when he returns. He also finds time to have his photograph made:

"Columbus, GA
Oct. 6, 1864

My Dear Darling,
    "I am still in Columbus, will leave tomorrow morning. I could have remained twenty-four hours longer in Eufaula, and I feel very much annoyed that I did not know it.
    I find all well in Beallwood. George is still here and will not leave before next week.
    I shall go to West Point I think. My gun will be ready this evening. I could not have succeeded in procuring my photograph except by staying here as I have done. I get them this evening and will enclose the best looking one to you. I found that the features were very indistinct in a standing picture so I changed mine into the position you see. I have succeeded in getting a very nice hat - at a very nice price. George has given me a red cap and so I will be very fancy when I get that on.
    You never saw any one as anxious to do for another as Mr. Young and Aunt Ellen are for me. They were making some leggins for George Alf & Dick and insisted on my taking a pair, and when I said I did not need them they just made them for me any way.
    I am a little afraid that I will have some trouble about finding the company but will find out when I get to West Point.
    I am not writing you much of a letter Darling but as soon as I get back and get rested I will write you a long letter full & free. Just Direct your letters as usual except not to any place but to Hood's army.
    Tell Ma that Aunt Ellen and Mr. Young say they will be down when George gets off. Little Mollie is sick. I expect to go to Mrs. Echols probably tonight. I staid in Beallwood last night. I was unable to procure any cloth for my officers. Cousin Anna Thomas said she had a bundle for you which she

wished Will to take down but that he left sooner than she expected [referring to Anna Dent's brother, who is commuting weekly from Eufaula to work on gunboats at the Columbus Naval Iron Works]. Tell Eddie PaPa wishes that he had staid with him until last night. I may add more before I send this off. For the present Darling goodby. Love to all – Hubert

My Darling I am waiting now to go to … with (Mrs. Echols). George Miller is going out with me. I will leave early tomorrow morning. Every thing is ready.

I feel annoyed that I did not remain twenty four hours longer with you. Mr. Young would take no pay for the cloth. I never saw such a man did you?

I will write you Darling as soon as I get where I can. Much love Darling to all the family. I send two pictures, take your choice. I have a third one and you can keep these until I hear whether the first sent gets there safely or not. I do not believe they will send for me. Goodby Darling. Much much love for you & Eddie. From your own devoted – Hubert

After a period of rest and repair at Palmetto, Hood's army had started moving north of the Chattahoochee. By October 2, he was threatening the railroad in Sherman's rear near Marietta. On October 4 he captured garrisons and tore up 15 miles of track. With an army of 65,000, Sherman left now-depopulated Atlanta to pursue Hood, but he had difficulty predicting where Hood was going. On October 10, Hood crossed the Coosa River west of Rome, and Sherman started toward Rome. Hood threatened Resaca, tore up twenty miles of track and moved on to Dalton, where the Federal garrison of one thousand men surrendered to him. Following Hood, Sherman found himself back where he was in May, with still no clue as to Hood's objective.

Hood, who had not himself been entirely sure what he would do, made the decision to continue back into Tennessee, with the hope of luring Sherman out of Georgia after him. On October 17, he marched to Gadsden, Alabama, where Beauregard met with him and approved his Tennessee plan.

As Hood's army crossed into Alabama its rear had been guarded by Ross' brigade of cavalry and by Young's Battery of artillery. Enroute, while Young's Battery had camped briefly at Cave Springs, Georgia, Lieutenant George Young returned from a quick "shopping trip" to Columbus, where he had had uniforms made for the battery brigade officers, undoubtedly at his father's Eagle Mills.[649]

The soldiers were excited with renewed spirit to return to Tennessee, and gave a rousing Rebel Yell at the news. On Oct 22, the Army reached Guntersville, Alabama. Because of unexpected difficulties in finding an advantageous place to cross the swollen Tennessee River, Hood continued west along the river across north Alabama to Tuscumbia, with a view toward crossing there and continuing to Nashville.

Sherman's army had followed Hood out of Georgia nearly to Gadsden when he stopped, and after a few days, made a decision. He would not take the "bait." He decided not be lured into following Hood with his entire army back into Tennessee. Sherman's army was big enough to both defend middle Tennessee and to also pursue another plan that Sherman had been eagerly devising: a march from Atlanta to Savannah. Dividing his army, Sherman now sent Gen. Thomas' Corps to watch Hood and defend Nashville, while the rest of his army returned directly to Atlanta to prepare for his scheme.

After first burning Atlanta, unnecessarily and for no military gain, Sherman then began his infamous March to the Sea, a movement then unparalleled in its vindictive and wanton mistreatment of civilians. With no Confederate army to oppose them, Sherman and his men bravely looted, stole, pillaged and burned a swath of destruction sixty miles wide as he proceeded to Savannah, unimpeded by anything other than the load of stolen property carried off by his men.

At Tuscumbia, Alabama, heavy rains and waiting for Forrest's Cavalry stalled Hood's progress into Tennessee. A makeshift pontoon bridge was built across the Tennessee River, and a portion of Stephen D. Lee's Corps, including Dent's Battery, crossed over to Florence and went into camp there. But the pontoon bridge became partially submerged and the crossing had to be suspended.

Despite the rain and cold, Hubert writes a lighthearted letter to Anna's sister, Mollie, in which he teases Mollie unmercifully about her new beau. During the summer, the War Department had assigned to the military hospital in Eufaula an attractive Confederate medical officer, Dr. Hamilton M. Weedon. Hamilton had become friends with the Young family, and his older brother had become a private in Dent's Battery. Hubert is aware that Hamilton and Mollie are courting, and this prompts some heavy-handed but good natured joking at them all. Hubert cautions against expecting too much from the venture back into Tennessee.

Camp Near Florence Ala
Nov 7th 1864

Dear Mollie
    I do not know when I will have another chance of writing to you - especially if we leave here as soon as I expect. I have written to Nannie and given her all the army news so that I can't promise you an interesting letter. I have just seen Capt. Brannan who sends his kindest regards to the family and spoke of the time when he & Mrs. B took tea with you.
    Florence is a small town on the North bank of the Tenn river. It contained I suppose about one thousand inhabitants before the war. Has a fine building formerly used as a male school. I understand there are a great many young Ladies here and the –[letter torn] since the occupation of our army.
    You must all be having plenty of beaux just now. I do not know how I can put that brother in the forefront of the battle. I have tried to get him in several times and found it very difficult. He is certainly the greatest coward I ever saw and I think the only way to dispose of him is to have him shot for cowardice. I wish you could see him. He is quite a character. I heard three or

four days ago that...Dr. W was quite devoted to you and very constant in his attentions. That you rode out together every evening. How say you guilty or not guilty? I wish I could see him again I would talk to him about his brother and see how he talked. I asked Pvt. W one day how come there's such a difference between him and his brother. He said he was the oldest and that his Father kept him at home [letter torn] work while the others were sent to school. [torn] much truth there in the [torn] I can't say. Some of the men told me that Pvt. W written to his brother to make him a nurse in the Hospital there but his brother had declined and told him to stay in the front where he was. But enough on that subject.

The Presidential election comes off tomorrow. I think Lincoln will certainly be re-elected and four years more of war for us to go through with. I have almost made up my mind to the fall of Richmond and a good many other disasters - but I feel more than ever confident of the result and it may be that we may escape better than I anticipated. But I can see no sign of peace yet.

I should like to know where Sherman is and what he is doing. Hood remains here much longer than any one expected. I suppose he is getting [torn] clothing and supplies [torn] will then take up his position and [torn] for [torn] Tenn and perhaps Kentucky. I hope Hood will do well but you all must not expect too much from our movement.

Stockton & Zeigler [two of Hubert's Lieutenants] have gone to town, but I hardly think they will bring any news.

Tell Ada my next outside of Nannie will be to her and I may not write until I get into Tenn. I am afraid I will not see you all this Christmas. The chances are evidently rather bad. I do not know how about your visit to the army this winter. But if we remain long enough I will build a hut and prepare for a visit from Nannie and whosoever she may bring with her.

Well I must close goodby love to all write me soon and all the news. Has Mr. Cottrell [the Eufaula Methodist minister] left yet, if not remember me to him. Again goodby Your brother Hubert

Ten days after this letter, on November 17, Young's Battery arrived at Tuscumbia with Ross' Cavalry brigade. The next day it "was ordered across the [Tennessee] River at Florence, and moving at once to the front of the army, took position with the other cavalry commands at Shoal Creek," near Florence.

The men of Ross' Brigade and Young's Battery were informed on November 19 that they were "now in Forrest's Cavalry." Gen. Nathan Bedford Forrest, the legendary "wizard of the saddle," had arrived from west Tennessee and had been given command "of the entire cavalry then with the Army of Tennessee." To his two under-strength divisions of cavalry was now added Gen. "Red" Jackson's Division of two brigades, including Ross' Brigade, to which Young's Battery of horse artillery was attached.[650]

With Forrest's cavalry now across the Tennessee, Hood was finally able to get his entire army across. With a force of 30,000 men plus Forrest's Cavalry of 8000, he proceeded north in sleet, snow, rain and freezing cold. As the cavalry marched out of its camps on Shoal Creek, Ross' troopers and Young's cannoneers passed in review before Gen. Forrest.

Hood's ultimate objective was Nashville, now defended by a large force under Gen. Thomas. But Hood's intermediate goal was Columbia, Tennessee, about fifty miles southwest of Nashville. There he hoped to intercept and defeat a force of 23,000 under Federal Gen. Schofield coming from Pulaski to reinforce Thomas at Nashville. Jackson's division of cavalry was sent to Pulaski to attack Schofield as he left there.

When Ross' Brigade, then in the lead, approached Pulaski, it encountered a "large force of cavalry…Young's Battery was hurried up from the rear, placed in position…and commenced shelling the enemy lines." Ross reported that he "watched with interest the effect of the shelling." Alfred Young's artillerymen quickly drove the Yankees from the field, leaving prisoners and plunder in the hands of the Confederates.[651]

However, on November 24, Schofield reached Columbia ahead of Hood's main army and dug in to block Hood's advance.

When Hood arrived at Columbia, he decided to attempt his favorite tactic, to outflank the Federals and attack from the rear. First, on the night of November 28, Hood allowed Schofield to cross the Duck River unmolested and set up his defensive line facing Hood's army on the south side of the river. At dawn the next morning, Stephen D. Lee with two divisions and all of his artillery launched what looked and sounded like the beginning of a major cross-river frontal attack. Dent's Battery and the other artillery units set up a loud and mighty barrage, creating an uproarious din. Throughout the day on November 29, Dent and the other batteries pounded the Federal positions across the river. The barrage was effective in inflicting damage, but it was a feint. Under the cover of this diversion, the main force of Confederates led by Hood marched upstream from Columbia and crossed the river at a ford, with the objective of circling around to Springfield, a road junction in Schofield's rear, thereby blocking his escape to Nashville and trapping him. Ross' cavalry and Young's Battery crossed the Duck River with the main force.

All was proceeding well. It took most of the day for the encircling troops to maneuver toward Springfield. Exactly what went wrong is not clear, but as the sun went down, in a series of blunders and misunderstandings, the Confederates went into bivouac for the night without seizing or blocking the Columbia to Nashville road, which was Schofield's only escape route. Late in the day, Schofield had received information from his cavalry which alerted him that something was afoot, and he immediately started his army to withdrawing up the Springfield road toward Nashville. After nightfall, Schofield was able to march his entire army out of the trap, passing within sight of the nearby Confederate campfires. If the Confederates had earlier thrown even a modest force across the road, which apparently could have been done, the resulting trap would have fulfilled Hood's dream of a Stonewall Jackson-like debacle for the Federals.

Columbia is the most controversial of the "might-have-been," lost opportunities of the western theatre. The principal commanders give sharply contradictory accounts of the events, and despite extensive analysis by historians, it seems impossible to now sort out the reasons for the Confederates' disappointing near-miss.

The morning after Schofield's escape, Hood, disappointed and furious, resolved to overtake and rout him, and to drive him into the Harpeth River at Franklin, thirty miles further along the road toward Nashville. The stage was being set for what Hubert Dent later termed, "the bloodiest battle of the war for the duration of battle and numbers engaged."[652] It was also to be the beginning of the end of the Army of Tennessee.

41
Squandered Blood: The Battle of Franklin

"It was the most desperate fighting I ever witnessed"

Hubert Dent to Anna

At dawn the next morning, November 30, Hood had his army on the road to Franklin in close pursuit of Schofield. Arriving on the outskirts of Franklin in midafternoon, Hood and his officers viewed the situation: The site did not lend itself to a frontal attack. Franklin is on an elevation in the bend of the Harpeth River, with the River enclosing the northeastern side of the town. The southeastern side of town, from which direction the Confederate attack would have to be made, faced open fields. This open side of the town was fortified with well-constructed breastworks built by the Federals the last time they were here. Schofield's men were now occupying these works, after having first strengthened them even more. Federal cannon were well-placed all along the fortified line There was no cover in the open field in front of the fortifications; the ground gently sloped into unobstructed, unfenced pastureland.

But Hood was no longer in the mood for subtle maneuver. Despite misgivings expressed by his officers, Hood announced that they would attack Schofield in his trenches. Not only was he determined to attack, he was set on attacking immediately, even before all of his troops and artillery had arrived. Cheatham's and Stewart's Corps was present, but of Stephen D. Lee's Corps, only Johnson's Division participated. Although the initial main assault took place with only two artillery batteries in place, Courtney's Artillery Battalion, consisting of Dent's, Garrity's and Douglas' Batteries (attached to Stephen D. Lee's Corps) arrived by nightfall in time to support the infantry during the nighttime fighting.) [653]

Cheatham's Corps was placed on the left and Stewart's on the right. At four in the afternoon of November 30, as quickly as the troops could be lined up, the order to attack was given. Presented there was a rare scene of drama and courage: eighteen brigades of infantry with their supporting cavalry, led by officers with sabers drawn, the sabers and bayonets catching the glint of the waning winter sun, all proceeding deliberately across the huge open field in full view of the enemy waiting behind breastworks to let fly the first volley of death.

The attackers first encountered the Federals advance line, which violated its orders to fall back, and attempted to resist instead, until it was thrown back in panic to the main line of defense. The center of the Confederate charge overran the Federal breastworks, captured a Federal battery, and seemed to have a foothold, until Federal reserves were brought up for a counterattack, pushing the obstinate Confederates slowly back. Despite initial success along the line, the Confederates could not break the strong Federal position. The Confederates reformed and made attack after attack, in hand to hand fighting around the breastworks as bloody and savage as any of the war. Casualties on both sides mounted rapidly.

Toward nightfall, (which occurs about 5:15 on the last day of November in Franklin[654]), more artillery arrived from Columbia,[655] and Dent's battery became active in the battle for the first time. At seven o'clock, Johnston's Division, which had been held in reserve, was brought up and thrown into the bitter struggle, one of the few nighttime attacks made during the Civil War. The new troops desperately charged the Federal breastworks, stumbling and falling in the dark over the mounds of bodies of both comrades and enemy. Hubert later wrote that, "I never saw dead men piled up as I saw them there."

Hubert's brother, George H. Dent, the first sergeant of the Battery, was shot, but by a miracle, he escaped death or serious injury. Hit in the chest by a Yankee minie ball, he was saved by the thick company roll book and a sheaf of papers in the breast pocket of his uniform jacket.[656] In "the late evening hours,"[657] another of Hubert's men, Cpl. Henry Harmier (or Harmeyer) was seriously wounded in the left eye. Hubert thought he would lose the use of one or both eyes.[658] (Happily, Harmier, a German emigrant, lived to become a naturalized citizen and an alderman of New Orleans. Below is a photograph of him with Capt. Dent, Sgt. Dent, and three other survivors of Dent's Battery at the 1903 reunion of Confederate veterans in New Orleans. The bullet was not removed, and he wore a glass eye. Headaches compelled him to undergo an operation, resulting in an infection and his death on February 15, 1912, over 47 years after receiving the wound.[659])

The fighting continued until 9 o'clock p. m. Of the four-hour battle, one hour had been fought in daylight, and three had been in darkness.[660] The Confederates had not been able to take the Federal position, but at 11 p. m. Schofield pulled his troops out of the trenches and proceeded as rapidly as possible toward Nashville to join Gen. Thomas, leaving his dead, wounded, and the field to the Confederates. The battle was a draw; it was also a pointless battle that resolved nothing for either side.

Observing that "Pickett's charge at Gettysburg" has come to be synonymous with unflinching courage in the raw, historian Stanley Horn observes that, "The slaughter-pen at Franklin even more deserves the gory honor."[661] He points out that Pickett at Gettysburg had 1353 casualties, while the Army of Tennessee at Franklin had 6000 dead or wounded. Pickett's charge was preceded by two hours of heavy artillery barrage, while Hood attacked with no bombardment. Pickett's men crossed one mile of open field, and retired after one repulse. The Army of Tennessee had to cover two miles of open field, and renewed the attack again and again.

The Confederates had crippling losses of General officers: six were killed, including the highly effective Pat Cleburne; five more Generals were wounded, and one captured.

After Franklin, there was every reason for Hood to fall back. He had lost a major part of his army and officers; Nashville was well fortified and defended by an overwhelming force. But the aggressive Hood would not consider retreat. On the afternoon after the battle of Franklin, he had his army on the road north to Nashville, and by December 3 it was lined up in the hills near the city.

From this position outside Nashville, Hubert wrote Anna, adopting the optimistic but unrealistic view that the campaign thus far had been "decidedly successful." Hubert charitably makes excuses for Gen. Hood's decision to attack at Franklin, suggesting that Hood must not have known how strong the Yankees' breastworks were. He reports a raft of favorable but false rumors about other fronts.

"Near Nashville, Tenn
December 4th, 1864

My Darling

Since writing to you we have fought a fierce battle and are now within sight of the tall steeples and glittering spires of the city of Nashville. The fight occurred at Franklin on the 30th Nov. We lost very heavy in officers. Our loss in men was quite severe, among the killed was Genl. Cleburne, Brig. Genl. Strahl, Granbury, Adams, and I think some others although I cannot remember them. It was the most desperate fighting I ever witnessed. The enemy was strongly posted behind works. I think the losses on each side nearly the same. We may have lost a few more than the enemy but we captured more prisoners. But when we remember the genl officers killed our loss was much the more serious. Genl Cleburn's loss is very hard to repair.

We had some skirmishing at Columbia in which we damaged the enemy a good deal and pressed him very closely on his retreat from Columbia to Franklin. I think Genl Hood did not think the enemy's works were as strong as they were or he would not have rushed upon them as he did. They only reached Franklin a few hours before us, but their works were already built. Johnston's Division of our corps was all the troops [Gen. Stephen D.] Lee had in the fight. It fought very finely and was highly complimented.

The loss in the Division was not very heavy. My own loss was one man seriously wounded. He will lose one if not both of his eyes. His name is Harmier [Harmeyer] from New Orleans. George [H. Dent, his brother] was struck just over the region of the heart but he had a book and several other things in the side pocket of his coat and it saved him from a serious if not a mortal wound.

We have a good many rumors as usual, among others that Breckinridge has whipped Burbridge very badly and is on his way to unite with Hood. We have a rumor also that Sherman had been whipped out in Georgia and was on his way to Nashville. I hope he has been whipped. I heard just now that Forrest crossed the Cumberland last night and had captured a transport with 160 mules on it.

Our lines were advanced yesterday evening about 2/6 of a mile and I hear are to advance again this evening. I am ready harnessed to advance if needed. I regret that Col Beckham, our chief of artillery, was mortally wounded at Columbia. We regret his loss very much. Maj. Courtney is still absent. Richardson's [one of Hubert's lieutenants, who had been a source of difficulty] resignation has been accepted and he is no longer an officer of Dent's Battery. He talks of going to the Trans Miss Dept.

I expect heavy work before Nashville falls, if it falls at all, and unless Hood is going to take it, or try, I do not know what he plans. The weather continues very fine, which favors us. It is cold, but not too much as to interfere with our operations. I would like very much to hear from you but do not know when I shall be thus favored.

I hope we will soon be in Nashville. Our campaign thus far has been decidedly successful. But the great feat remains to be accomplished. The Yankees are decidedly afraid of us. They say they never saw such fighting in all their lives. And I do not believe such fighting was ever done before by any troops in the world. I wish I could give you a full account of the fight, but I cannot now.

I am writing this but do not know when I can send it off. But I will try and send it from army Hd Qrs. Write me Darling when you can and I may get it some time and I am very anxious to hear from you all. I am standing the campaign well and in fine health. I hope we will soon have regular communications with our friends at home.

I have just heard that Sherman was at Milledgeville. I think it reasonable that he may be. I hope he will not get down in your neighborhood. We are fighting part of Sherman's army up here. He cannot have a very large force with him.

Write Honey. Goodby my love to all the family. I do not expect to get home this winter. Much love and many kisses for my Darling & our boy from your own devoted – Hubert"

Reproduced nearby is a portion of Hubert's December 4, 1864 letter from "near Nashville," showing how the shortage of writing paper in the field required him to write both perpendicularly and horizontally across the page. [662]

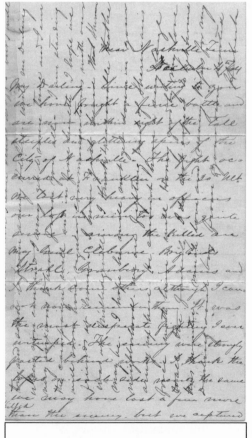

Hubert Dent's Letter of December 4, 1864 to Anna, with cross-writing due to lack of paper.

Capt. S. Hubert Dent (seated left) ; his brother and First Sergeant, George H. Dent (seated right); and other surviving members of Dent's Battery at the 1903 reunion of United Confederate Veterans in New Orleans.   Standing left is Cpl. Harmeyer [Harmier] who was wounded in the left eye during the Battle of Franklin. He thereafter wore a glass eye, and died on February 15, 1912 from an infection following an operation to remove the bullet 47 years after receiving the wound.

42
The Battle of Nashville:
The Valiant End of the Army of Tennessee

"We are still in front *of Nashville fortifying and shelling - disagreeable business. The worst part of the campaign is to come. We may look for severe winter weather soon and there will be no fun staying in the trenches."*

Hubert Dent to Anna

Although Hood had been unwilling to fall back after Franklin, and had insisted on advancing on Nashville, even he realized that his battered little army could not frontally attack the vastly larger Federal army of Thomas behind the fortifications of Nashville, which the Federals had been constructing for over two years. Nor did Hood have the manpower for anything like a siege of the city. So he chose a highly impractical middle course. He entrenched his army near the city to wait for Thomas to attack him, with the unrealistic objective of defeating Thomas' attack and then pursuing him into the city and capturing it.

During the pleasant weather of the first week of December, the Confederates hurried to dig entrenchments outside the city. The Federals had 20 miles of extensive breastworks around the city, including six strong, elevated forts. Against this, the Confederates hastily threw up four miles of trenches.

Hubert writes Anna from amid flying artillery shells, while she is visiting the Columbus Youngs. He tells her about the preparations before Nashville, expressing a very hopeful outlook and underestimating the Federal strength in Nashville. He discusses further the terrible carnage at Franklin. Hubert's report of 5000 Yankees "cut off" at Murfreesboro is correct; as we will presently see, this Federal force is being held with important help from Young's Battery.

"Near Nashville, Tenn
Dec 6th 1864

My Darling
Yours of the 16th ult. Reached me last night and I was very glad to hear from you and from all at home. I hope you had a pleasant visit in Columbus. You may be there yet, but before this reaches home I expect you will be there. I wrote day before yesterday, but as I have another opportunity of sending a letter I write again.
We are still in front of Nashville fortifying and shelling - disagreeable business. The worst part of the campaign is to come. We may look for severe winter weather soon and there will be no fun staying in the trenches.
You will hear the news of the battle of Franklin. It was a very severe fight - never saw or heard such desperate fighting. We took the first line very easily, but some portions of our troops failed to carry the second line, and the

others had to stop. Our men were on one side of the yankee works and the yankees on the other. I never saw dead men piled up as I saw them there. But I think the loss about the same on each side. We saw yankees dead for over a mile this side of Franklin.

We have five thousand yankees cut off at Murfreesboro which we hope to capture.

Chattanooga and the railroad up to Murfreesboro has been evacuated by the enemy. We expect to get the railroad from Decatur up in running order soon. We have five engines to put on the road.

The yankees have a force of twenty-five thousand men in Nashville and can't get any more except raw recruits. I do not know of course what General Hood will do, but I do not think he will storm the works around Nashville. For the present all we will do will be to cut off communications and await results. We have accomplished a good deal even if we do not capture Nashville. The fall of Nashville would benefit us more than the capture of Washington and as it is of so much importance, we may expect it to be well fortified and held as long as possible.

Darling I have written to you as often as I could and I wish you to write frequently to me - our communications will soon be pretty regular.

You did not say a word about Sherman. Where is he? And what is he doing? We hear that he is at Allen threatening Augusta and Savannah and that he has burned up Milledgeville. I hope he will not be able to reach Savannah. If he can be kept out of Savannah he ought to be captured. We hear from yankee papers that Breckenridge has utterly routed Burbridge in East Tenn. I hope he will march in this direction. Sick and wounded men are coming from the rear and I expect the Army is fully as strong as when we left Florence.

I wrote you that Richardson's resignation had been accepted. He has left. He has reported to the conscript officer and got on some kind of duty. He expects or rather talks of going to the Trans-Mississippi if he get a chance.

I heard from home, Maryland, about a month ago the 5th of November. All well there.

Well darling shells are flying around and I am sitting in the trenches writing on my knee so you must not expect a nicely written letter or as well as I sometimes do write. The weather is cloudy and threatens rain, but I hope it will not come soon. Give my love to all the family and write often darling. Tell Eddie not to forget me. Goodby. Much love and kisses for my darling and boy from you own devoted, Hubert"

Hubert's predictions of a return of severe winter weather were quickly borne out. On December 8, a winter storm hit, with snow, sleet, freezing temperatures, and ice. In a series of urgent communications, Grant ordered Thomas to attack Hood immediately. But Thomas was waiting until his arrangements and the weather were exactly as he wanted. After all, Hood was obliging him by sitting outside the city waiting to be attacked at Thomas' convenience.

Among the questionable decisions made by Hood at Nashville was his depriving himself of Forrest's Cavalry. He ordered Forrest to leave the main force and move to Murphreesboro, 25 miles west of Franklin, to operate against its railroad, menace the 8000 Federals stationed there, and "cut them off" as Hubert related to Anna in his last letter. As a unit of Forrest's "horse artillery," Young's Battery was a part of this operation.

On the same day that Hubert was writing Anna, December 6, in what is sometimes called the "little Battle of Murphreesboro," the Federals marched boldly out from Murfreesboro to engage Forrest and his horse artillery. At a crucial point in this fight, a portion of the Confederate line of infantry weakened and gave way. A member of Young's Battery, Private William A. Calloway, later wrote that he was standing a few feet from Gen. Forrest when a panicked Confederate color-bearer started running for the rear. Forrest shouted to the soldier three times to "Halt with those colors!" and when the soldier didn't stop, Forrest pulled his pistol, fired, and broke the arm of the fleeing soldier. Forrest seized the colors and galloped up and down the line, rallying the troops. "Red" Jackson's cavalry and Young's Battery then charged the advancing enemy, and were instrumental in stopping the Yankee surge. Private Callaway wrote further that:[663]

> "[Young's] artillery was getting in deadly work...Captain Young was also present urging the boys to 'shoot to kill.' Strange, not a member of my battery was hit..."

The Yankees were driven back into Murfreesboro and bottled up there. These Federal troops were thus unavailable to Thomas in Nashville, but this made it necessary for Forrest to remain in the area, so he was likewise unavailable to Hood during the main battle of Nashville on December 15 and 16.

During this time, Gen. Forrest assigned Ross' Brigade, including Young's Battery, to guard the southern approaches to Murfreesboro. On December 15, the same day as the first day's battle at Nashville, a Yankee train came up from Stevenson, Alabama, heavily laden with supplies for the Federal garrison at Murfreesboro. Ross' men stopped the train and a spirited fight ensued. Young's Battery was brought up, and an artillery barrage, followed by an infantry charge, resulted in capturing the train, 146 Federal soldiers, a lieutenant colonel, and 14 boxcars loaded with rations and supplies. The voluble Private Calloway (whose version agrees with that of Gen. Ross') later gave this description of the capture:[664]

> "We had to fight hard to take it, as it was guarded by about 200 men, and they were protected in a railroad cut. Young's Battery did efficient work in exploding shells over their heads. We finally drove them out, but they took refuge in a blockhouse. Our men were half starved, as usual, and ignored the proximity of the guard, who were still firing on us. It took General Ross several minutes to get enough men together to charge them, but he finally succeeded and drove them out. It was a sight worth while to see the boys going for those good thing to eat - sugar, coffee, bacon, hardtack, clothing, etc.-not to mention other things to drink. I loaded my old mare with all she could carry,

and the consequence was that I had to walk and lead her for a day or two. We set fire to what we could not carry away, and when the train was burning well we left in double-quick, just reaching the pike from Murfreesboro in time to keep from being cut off and captured by a brigade of cavalry sent out [from Murfreesboro] for that purpose. Let me tell you that eating and drinking (coffee, of course) was fine."

At Nashville, Gen. Thomas continued to receive orders from Grant to immediately attack Hood. Finally, on the morning of December 15, as the frustrated Grant started to Nashville himself to take the command away from Thomas, the attack was launched.

The Confederate line consisted of Stewart's Corps on the left; Stephen D. Lee's Corps, which included Dent's Battery, in the center; and Cheatham's Corps on the right. As already noted, Hood had reduced his already-depleted army even further by sending a division of infantry and two divisions of cavalry, including Young's Battery of horse artillery, on the expedition against Murphreesboro. It is estimated that Hood had 23,000 men at Nashville including cavalry, but others say only 15,000 were actually under arms. Thomas had 70,000, of which 55,000 were actively in the battle.[665]

The first day of the battle began with an attack by the Federals, using mostly black troops, on the Confederate right against Cheatham. This was actually a diversion, designed to keep Cheatham too busy to relieve the Confederate left, which is where the Yankees' real blow was struck. The Confederate left was based in part on four detached redoubts which had been hastily and inadequately built, one of which was occupied by Lumsden's Alabama Battery and a small detachment of infantry, with orders to hold the position "at all hazards." But the thin Confederate line on the left was no match for the overwhelming Federal force thrown against it, including 12,000 well-mounted cavalry of Wilson. Against all odds, based on sheer grit, the Confederates held back the tidal wave for over two hours. The men of Lumsden's Battery stayed at their guns until the Yankees were only yards away, when Captain Lumsden gave the order for every man to try to save himself. As the Confederate line crumbled, the Federals started a well-executed wheeling movement to their left, in an effort to break up the rest of the Confederate line. Hood attempted to reinforce the left by moving parts of Gen. Edward Johnson's Division from the center. But it was too late to stop the federal onslaught. As its left collapsed, the Confederate center had to fall back and reposition in order to avoid being enveloped by the Federal wheeling movement. This was accomplished in good order. From this new position, Johnson's artillery, including Dent's Battery, had an opportunity to actively participate for the first time that day, firing into the wheeling Federals[666] and helping to slow the advance. As night fell, the federal turning movement was stopped and the day's fighting ended.

Gen. Thomas, assuming the Confederates were beaten and the battle was over, returned to his headquarters in downtown Nashville. However, Gen. Schofield, who had known Hood at West Point, warned Thomas of Hood's bulldog determination, and predicted he was not retreating.

373

Schofield was right. During the night Hood fell back, but reassembled his army in a new position two miles south of his former line, in hastily-built shallow trenches. It is difficult to understand why Hood was willing to subject his men to still another near-hopeless assault by the huge federal force, but as the next day dawned, the tenacious Confederate soldiers were lined up as ordered, ready to do battle again. The arrangements were different today: Cheatham's Corps was moved to the left; Stewart's Corps defended the center; and Stephen D. Lee's Corps, which included Johnston's Division and Dent's Battery, was on the right.

In its position on the right, Lee's Corps was astride the Franklin Pike, the road south to Franklin. Hood ordered Lee, in the event the battle went against the Confederates, to hold the Franklin Pike as long as possible to provide an escape route for the army; and holding this escape route would indeed become important before the day ended.

At 9:00 A. M. on December 16, Thomas renewed the attack, beginning again with an assault on the Confederate right, now defended by S. D. Lee's Corps. This time it was not a diversion; the Yankees were making a concerted effort to capture the Franklin Pike, the Confederates' potential line of retreat to the south. Time after time, Lee's Corps--and Dent's Battery-- repelled waves of white and black troops, and held firm. It was said that the Yankee dead were so thick that the slopes of Peach Orchard Hill looked blue.[667]

On the left, however, the Yankee onslaught could not be held. As the Union force went around the Confederate left flank, Cheatham bent his left end around like a fishhook in a effort to face and repel the swarming enemy. Finally the Confederates were overwhelmed; the troops had no alternative but to flee south. With the left gone, the center was also forced to fall back. S. D. Lee's Corps on the right now stood alone to carry out its assignment of holding firm until the rest of the army could effect an escape south on the Franklin Pike. This was done valiantly. When Gen. S. D. Lee saw the left collapse, the center break, and his own troops begin to falter, he grabbed the Confederate Flag and rallied his troops long enough for Eufaulian Gen. Henry D. Clayton's Division to establish a new line and continue to hold.

Johnson's Division held part of the right line being defended by Lee's Corps. Courtney's Artillery Battalion of twelve guns, including Dent's Battery, was massed in the center of Johnson's line.[668] Confederates fleeing from the left and center streamed into the Franklin Pike behind this line. Throughout the day the Yankees had continued a heavy and effective artillery barrage against the massed but overpowered Confederate batteries. Presumably because of an ammunition shortage, Hubert and the other Confederate battery commanders were under orders to fire only on "lines of battle or well-defined bodies of men".[669] Hubert's gun crews continued to serve their guns, firing whenever permitted by their orders, in an effort to hold the Yankee hordes at bay long enough for the Confederate army to escape.

Gen. Edward Johnson, the division commander whom Dent's Battery was supporting, sent for Capt. Dent for a short conference. In response to this summons, Hubert found Gen.

Johnson about a half mile up the Confederate line to the left of Dent's Battery. While standing and conferring with Gen. Johnson, Hubert was hit in the calf of his right leg by a Yankee shell fragment.[670] Fortunately the wound did not require his leaving the field.

A few moments later, as Gen. Johnson and Hubert watched, the Confederate line began to give way. It had withstood the Federal tidal wave as long as it could. Gen. Johnson quickly ordered Hubert back to his unit. Hubert limped back, slowed somewhat by the pain in his right leg. Upon reaching his battery, Captain Dent found that most of the Confederate line had disappeared, and that his battery alone was continuing to fire away at the oncoming blue juggernaut.[671] Hubert immediately ordered his men to limber up and try to save the guns.

A steady rain had made the ground soft, increasing the difficulty of quickly moving tons of horses and guns,[672] but Hubert soon had much worse problems. As the battery emerged from a clump of woods in which it had been partially sheltered, the "terrible Yankee artillery fire" began hitting the gun horses, which fell in the traces and made quick retreat impossible. Further, the Federal infantry was now circling in the rear of the battery and would soon close off the only escape route. It became obvious that the sacrifice of his men and himself could not salvage his guns or serve any good purpose. Hubert ordered his men to abandon the four Napoleons and save themselves. Only then did the men of the Dent's Battery flee, some on foot and some on gun horses.[673]

But waiting until the last possible moment to quit the field can lead to desperate measures. Running alongside Hubert's horse, on foot, was Lieutenant Colonel C. J. Walker of the Tenth South Carolina Infantry Regiment. Dent reached down and pulled Walker up behind him on the horse. Hubert then overtook two of his own fleeing men and brought them aboard his strong warhorse, one on each side of the horse, each with a foot in a stirrup and clinging for life to the stirrup leathers.[674] This strange cavalcade then proceeded as fast as the heavily-burdened animal could travel, through the rapidly-closing gap in the encircling Yankees; then south toward the Franklin Pike and safety.

Gen. Edward Johnson, with whom Hubert had been talking only minutes before, was not so fortunate; he was overrun and captured by Yankee infantry.[675]

It was a mass of exhausted men, worn-out horses, guns and wagons that crowded onto the Franklin Pike and retreated south. Hood soon had his army in organized order, however, and the Federal pursuit was effectively opposed. The Confederates crossed the Harpeth River at Franklin, burned the bridge, and continued south. Below Franklin, Lee's Corps made a rearguard stand and defeated the pursuers. In the melee Gen. S. D. Lee was wounded, but he bought valuable hours for the escaping army. On December 19, Forrest's cavalry returned from Murphreesboro and assumed responsibility for the rearguard.

The main Confederate force retreated across the Tennessee River on December 25 and 26, and Forrest crossed on the 28th. Hood continued south to Tuscumbia, through Iuka to Corinth, and then to Tupelo, where he camped on January 10, 1865.

Deeply embarrassed by the debacle, Hood on January 13 telegraphed Secretary of War Seddon his request to be relieved of command. This request was immediately granted. Gen. Beauregard arrived two days later to assess what was left of Hood's army. In the Tennessee campaign it had lost sixteen Generals, thousands of soldiers, and half of its ordnance. Many of the army's best artillery units had been virtually wiped out as fighting units, including Dent's Alabama, Douglas' Texas, Tarrant's Alabama, Stanford's Mississippi, Lumsden's Alabama, the Eufaula (Alabama) Light Artillery, and Fenner's Louisiana.[676] Most of the higher ranking artillery officers were gone; only seven artillery field officers (that is, major and above) remained. Beauregard concluded that "… it was no longer an army".[677]

The men were enduring terrifically cold weather without adequate food, clothing, blankets or tents. An undated fragment of a letter from Hubert to Anna survives, which was probably written from Mississippi during this period. Hubert discusses reports from other fronts; his estimate of Kirby Smith's force is overstated. He holds out the usual hope of a visit from Anna, but dismisses it as unfeasible because of severe conditions and because the army is on the move.

"…that we are going to Geo but still nothing here indicates it. Sherman seems to be having every thing his own way in Georgia and unless we can keep open our communications with Richmond, Lee will be compelled to evacuate. We ought to bring some men over from the Trans Miss Dept. Kirby Smith has sixty-five thousand men over there doing nothing, as many if not more troops than Lee & Hood have both together.

Darling if you have not received my letter of Dec. 27t[h] let me know. Bob Gunby [Anna Dent's first cousin from Columbus] told me that he heard that Bob Lockhart [another Columbus first cousin of Anna's] had been killed but I have heard nothing more about it. I hope it is not true.

If I thought we would remain here any time I would try and get some place for you to stay and get you to come up & see me but Genl Elzey says we are only here temporarily. The men need clothing very badly and are so exposed to all weather having no shelter.

Genl (S. D.) Lee is here, wounded slightly in the foot. He is to be married in a short time to a Lady here. I think Dr. Neely is here and if he is I intend calling on him.

Darling if you have an opportunity, send me my uniform pants and a pair or two of socks and one shirt. I need nothing else.

Well Honey I must say good by. Unless you have a good opportunity do not send me any thing as I can make out without them. Give my love to all. Tell Eddie I send him a kiss. Much love Darling. Many kisses from your own devoted – Hubert"

43
The Twilight of the Confederacy;
Defending Mobile

"We are about a half mile from the Bay ...We are to have muskets and charge of a Battery of heavy guns ...We can see the Yankee ships from the Bay. Five were in sight yesterday."

Hubert Dent to Anna

At this point the story of Dent's Battery and Young's Battery diverges from that of the other remnants of the Army of Tennessee.

The commander of the Department of Mississippi and Alabama was Gen. Richard Taylor, (the son of Zachary Taylor, and brother of President Davis' deceased first wife). On Jan 23, Gen. Taylor was also given command of the remnants of the Army of Tennessee. It is not clear how many men were actually left, but the official returns for January 20, 1865 reflect an "effective total" of 17,000 infantry and artillery.[678] These men would not remain long under Gen. Taylor's command. Most of them would be ordered to North Carolina to become part of a force being assembled under the command of General Joseph E. Johnston to resist Sherman's army as it headed north after destroying Savannah. However, 4000 of the men did not make the trip to North Carolina, but were instead ordered to Mobile to assist in the defense of that city. This latter group would include Dent's Battery and Young's battery.

Gen. Hood had previously ordered many of the artillery "companies" with depleted ranks and equipment, including Dent's and Young's batteries, to assemble in Columbus, Mississippi to be "refitted." However, unlike the disaster after Missionary Ridge, there were now no reserve supplies of guns and horses to draw on. There was no longer any bronze available and the ordnance foundries had long since closed down.[679] So at Columbus, the scant supply of available guns, men, horses, supplies and equipment were simply rearranged, so as to reconstitute as many complete batteries as possible. Those batteries whose men, horses, or equipment were so depleted that it was not feasible to reconstitute them with available supplies, were stripped of their remaining equipment, which was used in re-fitting other batteries. The reconstituted batteries were sent to the Carolinas to fight Sherman. The units that did not get re-fitted and reconstituted were used for another purpose; they were "ordered to Mobile to man heavy guns temporarily and to be refitted there." [680]

As we have seen, Dent's Battery had lost all of its guns at Nashville. Whatever ordnance and horses Young's Battery had remaining after Nashville were used to reconstitute other batteries. These were now artillery units in name only, and both Dent's Battery and Young's Battery were among those ordered to proceed to Mobile to assist in the defense of Mobile[681] They did not have guns or horses, but they had experienced cannoneers who could be put to good use with the heavy guns defending Mobile's western perimeter.

On February 1, Hubert writes Anna while his unit is still camped near Columbus, Mississippi, awaiting transportation to Mobile. He is understandably depressed. He feels helpless with no cannon, and knowing of the severe shortage of ordnance, Hubert is skeptical of the report that he will be resupplied with guns in the spring. There is such a shortage of artillery officers that Captain Garrity, a battery commander, is now commanding the artillery battalion in place of Major Courtney, who has been sent to Georgia.

"Near Columbus [Mississippi]
Feb. 1ˢᵗ, 1865

My Darling – We are still in Columbus. Expecting to leave every day but no boat has arrived to take us off yet. It is now said that we will leave tomorrow. The river is falling very rapidly and I think boats will soon find navigation difficult unless we have more rain. The weather has been mild and pleasant for the past two days and there is every indication that the winter is gone.

I have not been to town since Sunday. Expect to go in this evening and will probably see your cousin. George [Dent, Hubert's brother] went in with me last Sunday evening and we remained to tea.

It is very singular that more of your letters reach me now since I last wrote. Darling write your next to Mobile, Ala, Dent's Battery, nothing more, and I think I will get them.

Dr. McFerrin told me that Dr. Elliott had he thought put Mr. Rice in charge of the school at Tuskegee when he first bought it. I expect he will make a fine school of it.

Is there much talk of peace about Eufaula? I was astonished to hear so much said about it up here. For my own part I have very little confidence in the ability of our commissioners to make peace. So if it comes I will only be the more rejoiced because it will be totally unexpected.

I do not know what we are to do in Mobile but the rumor now is that we will be fitted up for field service again in the spring. This I think doubtful for I do not think we can procure the stock necessary to fit out so many batteries.

I am suffering with a rising in my left ear. It pains me a good deal this evening. I have them frequently of late and am afraid it will injure my hearing.

I have no news here at all. I have not seen a newspaper for more than a week and am entirely behind in current events.

Maj. Courtney left us a few days ago for Macon, Geo where he was ordered to take command of Hotchkiss' Battalion. There is not a single major here to go Mobile with us. Capt Douglas has left for Texas on a ninety days furlough. Garrity is now commanding the Battalion. We have two other companies attached to our Battalion now, Barry's and Tarrant's Batteries. We have five companies in all.

Zeigler [one of the battery lieutenants] has just returned from Columbus. Says there is no boat yet but one is expected every hour. I am afraid the river will get so low that we will be compelled to march some distance to meet the boat. Nothing else new. I am about to start for Columbus myself and therefore must hurry up this letter so I can mail it.

Oh yes! Zeigler did bring another piece of news, which was that the US government had appointed commissioners to confer with ours and that Ex Pres. Pierce was among the number. This looks like something might be done.

I expect to get off in a month or less and hope to be at home with you in a month from today or in a very few days thereafter.

**Back in Eufaula: "Eddie"
(Edward Young Dent) at age 4 in
1865**

Well Darling, I do not think I would know what to do with myself if peace should be made but I do not look for it and I am afraid these negotiations will do us much harm. Every one will be looking to them for great results when I am afraid nothing will be done. I hope Mr. Davis is not whipped. I have heard some such expressions but I do not believe them.

Tell Eddie I am very anxious to see him and that he must be a good boy – not cry and do whatever his mama tells him. My photograph went to Md. safely. I received a letter from home of Dec. 18th – all well. They are anxious for one of you and also of Eddie. Give my love to all the family. I will write again if we remain here much longer but here of late I have become an irregular correspondent but it is because I cannot get letters from home. Well Honey goodby much love from your own devoted Hubert"

Six months earlier, in August 1864, the Federal fleet commanded by Admiral Farragut had forced its way into Mobile Bay. Farragut had overcome the Confederate guns of Fort Morgan at the mouth of the Bay, sunk the Confederate ironclad *Tennessee*, and shouting, "Damn the torpedoes!" had sailed through floating mines and assumed control of the Bay. By holding Mobile Bay, as well as Forts Gaines and Morgan at the mouth of the Bay, the Federals had choked off all blockade running activity. But the city of Mobile itself had remained in the hands of the Confederates. The capture of Mobile was a major objective of the Union, but its strong defenses and the need for troops elsewhere had delayed any effort to take possession of it. For six months, Mobilians had been going about their daily lives while nervously eyeing the fleet of Yankee ships anchored close by in the Bay.

In January, 1865, the Federals made the decision to move against Mobile, but it would be spring before Gen. Grant made troops available to actually begin operations.

Mobile is nestled against the northwestern side of Mobile Bay, at the upper end of the Bay, where the Mobile River flows into the Bay. The eastern defenses consisted of fortifications at Spanish Fort, on the eastern shore of the upper bay, and at Blakely, three miles northeast of Spanish Fort. On the western, or "landward" side of Mobile, the principal line of defense consisted of a string of breastworks and redoubts known as "Sheliha's Line of Works," after the Chief Engineer for the Gulf District who designed them, containing a large number of heavy cannon. It was in these western redoubts that Dent's Battery and Young's Battery were placed.

By February 10, Hubert was in position in his redoubt, and he wrote Anna of the arrangements. He has a low opinion of the discipline and morale of the city of Mobile, and is dismayed by what he regards as excessive use of alcohol. (In fact, throughout his life, Hubert would be generally opposed to the use of alcohol). He continues to be skeptical (correctly), that his company will ever be reequipped with horses and guns. As usual when his company is not on the move, he starts talking of a visit from Anna, or a furlough home.

"Mobile, Alabama
Feb. 10, 1865

I am about to get settled at last. Garrity's Battery and mine have been assigned to Battery 'M' and a redoubt near it. We are about a half mile from the Bay and about two miles from the central part of the city. We succeeded in moving at last, but after a long struggle. The weather continues cold but it has not rained for two days which is a decided improvement.

We are to have muskets and charge of a Battery of heavy guns – drill about four times a day and work the remainder of the time. We will be pretty busy but I am glad of it. We are promised that as soon as horses and artillery equipments can be obtained that we will be sent back in the field at Light City. This promise I expect is made as a sort of inducement to do well now and not murmur at the duties inforced now.

There seems to be a good deal of discipline here on paper and very little elsewhere. I do not wonder at the success of the Yankees in taking our cities if the defenses of all others were like those about Mobile. Gov Watts has closed up the liquor shops here but plenty of whiskey is still afloat in the city.

Maj Genl Gardner is being tried by Court Martial for drunkenness' when the Yankees made their raid on the Mobile and Ohio Rail Road some time ago. From what I hear I expect he will be acquitted and yet I am pretty sure he was drunk. He is a fine officer but no man in the habit of getting drunk is fit for any position of responsibility. Our cause has suffered a great deal already from this cause. Genl Gardner promised Genl Bragg when he recommended him for Brigadiership that he would not drink and I believe he kept that promise so long as he was in Bragg's army. But I suppose the temptations around here were stronger than his resolutions.

I am here without my horses and consequently will not go about much. I am invited out to dine on Sunday at Mr. Robert Smith's, one of the nicest gentleman in Mobile. If I can I shall attend church and then go there. I have met with a good many acquaintances since I arrived here, most of whom are located around here.

We can see the Yankee ships from the bay. Five were in sight yesterday. If the expedition now in preparation at New Orleans is coming to

Mobile we will have something to do here before long, but if as reported it is going to Galveston we will have a lazy time of it.

I want to see if <u>we</u> cant go to housekeeping while I am down here but we will talk this over when I get home, which I hope to do by the first of March or very soon thereafter.

Capt. Fenner is commanding our Regt now in the absence of Lt. Col Hoxton who remained in Columbus to stand up with Genl [S. D.] Lee who was to be married last night.

I am about to send this off to the city and I hope to get letters by the mail. Give my love Darling to all the family. Write soon and long letters. Tell Eddie his PaPa wants to see him very much and ask him how he would like to come down and stay with me. Well Darling goodby. Much love to all the family and much love & many kisses from your own devoted Hubert

The Mobile defenses were under the direction of Major General Dabney H. Maury, a West Point graduate, who was Commander of the District of the Gulf. Gen. Maury assigned the defense of the left wing of the Sheliha Line of Works to Colonel Charles Fuller. The organizational order[682] for March 10, 1865 reflects that Fuller's left wing included, among other artillery units: Dents Battery, commanded by Captain Stouten H. Dent; Young's Battery, commanded by Captain Alfred I. Young; and the Eufaula Battery, now commanded, since Captain Oliver's death at Atlanta, by Lieutenant William H. Woods (the son of Edward Young's banking partner, Clayton R. Woods, in the firm of "Young, Woods and Gardner").

Fuller's Left Wing extended for two miles around the western edge of the city, from Redan No. 6 on Government street (near Redoubt "H" on Virginia Street) to Redoubt "N" at the end of Bayou Street,[683] thus including Redoubt "M," where Dent's Battery was assigned.

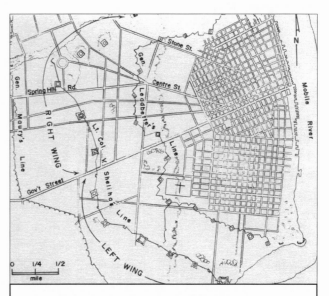

The defenses of the western (landward) perimeter of Mobile, 1865

For the first time, Dent's Battery and Young's Battery were positioned together behind breastworks within less than two miles of each other. We cannot confirm that Hubert made contact with Alf, George, or Dick Young during these weeks in the Mobile trenches, but it is reasonable to expect that their paths crossed.

During this unusually harsh winter, Dick Young, the youngest of the three Young brothers in Young's Battery, had suffered from chronic illness, and on March 2, 1865 he was admitted to Ross Hospital in Mobile for treatment. When he failed to improve, he was evacuated to the army's general hospital at Greenville, Alabama, 130 miles northeast of Mobile. For the past year this nineteen year old soldier had more than proven his courage in some of the worst fighting of the western theater; now his constitution had simply broken down under conditions of prolonged cold and hardship.[684] He was not able to return to duty before the war ended.

In late March, the Federal movement against Mobile began. Apparently the Federals did not relish facing the strong chain of redoubts and heavy artillery protecting the western approaches to town. Instead, The Union strategy was to attack from the eastern side, at Spanish Fort and Blakely. Consequently, the western breastworks occupied by Dent's and Young's Batteries, and the heavy guns which they were manning, would see only limited action when the fight came.

The overall Union commander was Gen. E. R. S. Canby, who began a two-pronged approach. He landed a force on the eastern shore near the mouth of Mobile Bay. This force advanced along the eastern shore toward Spanish Fort, with a fleet of shallow-draft iron-clads accompanying it offshore as the force proceeded north. Canby had 32,000 troops to oppose the Spanish Fort Garrison of 3500.

The Federal's second prong consisted of a force of 13,000 troops under Gen. Steele, who landed at Pensacola and, as a feint, marched north into Alabama, as though heading for Montgomery. But just across the Alabama line, at Pollard, Steele turned left and started marching southeast toward Blakely.

Canby's column and naval force arrived near Spanish Fort on March 17 and began a 13-day siege. On April 8, the Yankees breached the Confederate line and took the fort, as the Confederate troops retreated into Mobile with losses of about 250.

On April 1, the second Federal column proceeding from Pensacola under Steele arrived at Fort Blakely, four miles northwest of Spanish Fort, and preliminary skirmishing began. After Spanish Fort had fallen on April 8, Canby moved on to Blakely to support Steele. On April 9, at 5:30 in the afternoon, a combined force of 16,000 Federals attacked Fort Blakely from three sides. The 4000 Confederates now defending the fort were soon overpowered, with 250 killed and 3500 taken prisoner.

Earlier this same day, April 9, General Robert E. Lee, was "…compelled to yield to overwhelming numbers and resources…," and surrendered to Ulysses Grant at Appomattox. Because the surrender of the Fort Blakely garrison came at 5:30 P. M., the Battle of Blakely would later be sometimes referred to as "the last major battle of the Civil War." But as we will soon see, the war was not over and the agony was not yet ended.

In what General Grant would later call an unnecessary battle, on April 10 and 11 General Canby launched his final movement against the city of Mobile itself.

Having failed to stop the Yankees at Spanish Fort and Blakely, General Maury concluded that for his 10,000 Confederates to attempt to further defend Mobile against Canby's 45,000 Federals would be futile. On April 11, Maury ordered the evacuation of the city. Dent's, Young's and the other artillery batteries abandoned their heavy guns. Leaving much of its materiel, the entire Mobile garrison was evacuated north, with the intention of refitting in Meridian, Mississippi and then rejoining the remnants of the Army of Tennessee in North Carolina to continue the fight there under Gen. Joseph E. Johnston.

On the night of April 14, the deranged John Wilkes Booth shot Abraham Lincoln, an event which would have grievous consequences for the post-war South.

Part of the Mobile garrison proceeded to Meridian overland by way of Citronelle, Alabama. However, Col. Fuller's command of 2600 men who had manned the Left Wing at Mobile, including Dent's Battery and Young's Battery, went by boat up the Mobile and Tombigbee Rivers to the long-time Confederate base at Demopolis, Alabama, there to embark on trains for the 55 mile trip east to Meridian.[685] On April 15, Gen. Richard Taylor had ordered Col. Fuller "to move all troops, infantry and artillery of General Maury's command, as well as those at Demopolis…to…take trains for Meridian," in order to be outfitted as infantry.[686]

Hubert's and Alfred's batteries would have arrived in Meridian on April 16, and it was here that they received definite confirmation of Lee's surrender eight days earlier.[687] But preparations to proceed to North Carolina continued. Gen. Taylor ordered Gen. Maury to take command of the cannon-less "artillery batteries" arriving in Meridian, reorganize them into companies, battalions, and regiments, and issue them muskets; thereby effectively converting them into infantry. Ironically, in these circumstances Hubert had come full circle. He had joined the Confederate Army on February 9, 1861 as an infantryman in the Eufaula Rifles and had served almost a year in that role. After an eventful 3-year career as an artilleryman, he was now ready to serve once again as an infantryman.

On April 20, 1865 General Taylor reported to Confederate Secretary of War John C. Breckenridge that he had "completed equipment of the Mobile garrison for the field." However, the preparations to continue the fight in North Carolina were soon dashed. On April 26, General Johnston met with Gen. Sherman to arrange an armistice and negotiate terms of surrender for his army and all forces in the Carolinas, Georgia, and Florida.

In light of this development, Gen. Richard Taylor on April 27 contacted Gen. Canby about armistice terms. Following a meeting held near Mobile, Taylor announced on April 29 from his headquarters at Meridian that an armistice had been agreed upon. Over the next several days, the terms of surrender were worked out, and on May 4, 1865, Gen. Taylor traveled the 40 miles to Citronelle, Alabama to sign the formal document of surrender. By this action, the last Confederate forces east of the Mississippi River became prisoners of war.

During the following week the administrative details were carried out in Meridian for disarming and paroling thousands of Confederate soldiers and releasing them to begin new lives.

By May 9, 1865 the officers and men of Dent's Alabama Battery of artillery had taken the required oath not to fight again against the United States, had complied with their other administrative requirements and were ready to start home. Although gladdened by the prospect of home, to those who had fought so long and so diligently, it was a sad and pathos-laden moment. Defeat was a particularly bitter pill for one so thoroughly dedicated to the cause of Confederate independence as Hubert Dent. But Hubert's strong sense of responsibility also told him that the future had to be manfully faced with the correct spirit and attitude. With an acute sense of history, Hubert assembled Dent's Battery for its final muster, and expressed these sentiments:

> "Men, we are about to separate. In the fortunes of war our country has gone down in defeat, and yielding to the inevitable, our leaders have surrendered. It only remains for us to go to our homes, obey the laws, and be as good citizens as we have been true and gallant soldiers. The same devotion and courage you have shown as soldiers will bring you success in civil life. Now, wishing you abundant success, so that your old age may be spent in peace and content, I now give you my last command: 'Fare you well, break ranks, march.'"[688]

As Hubert's military career comes to a conclusion, it is appropriate to look at the assessment of his performance as a commander of artillery made by others in a position to judge. In *A Carolinian Goes to War*,[689] Brig. Gen. Arthur M. Manigault of Charleston set out his memoirs of the war years. As a commander of a Confederate infantry brigade supported by artillery, Gen. Manigault concluded that, as a general rule, the Yankees better understood the uses of artillery and employed their artillery more effectively than the Confederates. But Gen. Manigault saw notable exceptions:

> "In justice however, to some, I must state that there was a very respectable number of [Confederate] batteries that were fully equal to the best in the Yankee army, and on all occasions when not too heavily overmatched, proved too much for their opponents, forcing them to withdraw from the conflict, frequently leaving a piece or two behind, or driving the men from their pieces. Amongst this class, were the batteries of Dent, Robinson, and Garrity, of whom I saw a good deal, and never saw them yield or give way, unless fully authorized by the condition of affairs to do so."

With this important chapter of his life now honorably ended, Hubert Dent started making his way overland toward Eufaula, Alabama, exactly four years and three months after leaving for war.

44
The War Reaches Columbus and Eufaula

"Mr. [William] Young, who was in a little party that was contesting the incoming of the soldiers, was shot down on the corner where now stands the store of Messrs. Pon Bros."

Columbus Daily Enquirer-Sun

As Hubert and the Young boys make their separate ways toward Eufaula and Columbus, we will look at the recent experiences of their families at home during the last days of the war.

For four years, the Young families and other citizens of Columbus and Eufaula had made serious sacrifices to support the Confederacy. But it was only in the closing days of the war, while Dent's Battery, Young's Battery, and the Mobile garrison were retreating to Meridian, that the Columbus homefront saw actual military action, and that Eufaula saw the Yankee invaders "up close and in person." In the case of Columbus, it was a bloody and destructive encounter, with serious consequences for William Young and his family. Eufaula was relatively more fortunate.

Columbus, an important industrial center, was the first of the two communities to receive its baptism of fire. In mid-March, 1865, as part of the overall campaign that led to the assault on Mobile, Gen. Grant sent Gen. James H. Wilson and a strong force of cavalry on a raid deep into Alabama and Georgia. This operation was intended to not only divert attention from the planned movement against Mobile, but also to destroy the Confederacy's remaining manufacturing capabilities.

Wilson crossed the Tennessee River with 13,500 cavalrymen on March 22, 1865. One of his brigades soon captured Elyton (which later became "Birmingham") and destroyed the iron furnaces in Shades Valley. Another brigade under Gen. Croxton was sent to Tuscaloosa to burn the University of Alabama. Wilson then moved on Selma, where he faced Gen. Nathan Bedford Forrest's cavalry. But Forrest's renowned cavalry force had now become so diminished that, in his first defeat, he was overwhelmed by Wilson on April 2. Wilson then burned the Selma Arsenal, the Confederate Naval Ordnance Works, the Confederate Nitre Works, the Selma Iron Works, and other factories and foundries that had so well helped sustain the Confederacy's fighting ability.

Wilson then proceeded toward Montgomery. Governor Watts and the state government quickly gathered up government documents, gold and other public valuables and departed for Union Springs, with the intention of proceeding to Eufaula and establishing a new capital there.[690] On April 12, Wilson arrived at Montgomery and systematically burned factories, foundries, rolling mills, niter works, riverboats and railroad cars.

The Union raiders then continued to Columbus, Georgia, arriving there on April 16. This was the same day that Alfred and Richard Young were arriving at Meridian with Young's Battery to be refitted for service in North Carolina. On this day their hometown would be destroyed and their father, William Young, would be wounded, as well as financially devastated.

About 2:00 P. M. on April 16th, Wilson was spotted approaching Girard (now Phenix City), Alabama, on the west bank of the Chattahoochee River opposite Columbus on the east bank. Refugees from Montgomery had been streaming into Columbus for two days and the city was in a panic. The local militia worked feverishly to complete rifle pits defending the bridges on the Alabama side. The defense force consisted mostly of men too young or too old to be conscripted. Wilson's cavalry first planned to enter Columbus across the Dillingham Street Bridge, but Captain McGhee of the Confederate Naval Iron Works burned this bridge. Wilson then decided to attack by way of the Fourteenth Street Bridge, but he waited until dark to move. At 8:00 P. M. the Yankee Cavalry dismounted and attacked. The thin line of defenders in rifle pits before the bridge gave a spirited resistance which, together with artillery fire, repulsed the Federals' first assault. Wilson's dismounted troopers charged again. In the melee on a dark night, a contingent of Wilson's force, either by infiltration or by going around a flank, succeeded in reaching the bridge behind the defenders, and seized control of its entrance. The Confederate line had been holding, but when it was realized that the Yankees were in their rear, the inexperienced militiamen broke and ran for the bridge. In a crowded rush in the dark, both attackers and defenders streamed across the bridge in a confused mass, and Wilson's force soon had control of the city.[691] Wilson reported twenty-five casualties, and the Confederates eight or nine. The Columbus newspapers would later call this clash the "last battle" of the war. (It was eight days after the battle at Blakely.)

William Young was wounded during the Wilson raid, but there are differing accounts of how it happened. The most plausible report, and perhaps the most reliable, appeared in the *Columbus Daily Enquirer-Sun* dated May 8, 1894 on the occasion of William's death:

> "Mr. Young, who was in a little party that was contesting the incoming of the soldiers, was shot down on the corner where now stands the store of Messrs. Pon Bros."

A different report relates that, after Wilson's troops had entered the city, a body of troopers were approaching the edge of town when they come upon William Young riding his horse at a "jog-trot" up Hamilton Avenue on his way home. They shouted for him to stop, and when he didn't, they fired. He continued at the same pace and more shots were fired, but he continued to ignore the troopers, finally reaching his home in a wounded condition.[692]

Gen. Wilson reported that he had captured "the last great manufacturing place and storehouse of the Confederacy," along with over one thousand prisoners. He placed Col. Winslow in command of the city, with orders to "destroy every thing within reach that could be made useful for the further continuance of the Rebellion." Col. Winslow carried out these orders thoroughly. Within twenty-four houses the entire city was going up in flames.

All of the buildings of William Young's Eagle Mills, as well as its cotton supply, were burnt to the ground, at a loss later estimated in the one million dollar range.[693]

The city reverberated with explosions as the torch was put to the Confederate Naval Iron Works, the Confederate Arsenal, the Quartermaster Depot, and a large quantity of cannon, small arms, ordinance and commissary stores. Even though this was eight days after Lee had surrendered, Wilson burned six warehouses, a paper mill, two privately-owned iron works, four cotton factories, a flour mill, a pistol factory, three newspaper presses, 70,000 bales of cotton, fifteen locomotives, 200 railroad cars, and the two remaining bridges into Columbus.

The ironclad gunboat, *Jackson*, which Will Young at his Eufaula Foundry had put so much work and effort into, was blown up and sunk. This innovative fighting vessel had never seen action.

Eufaula, Alabama, fifty miles downriver from Columbus, feared similar treatment by the raiders, but it had no industrial facilities to interest Gen. Wilson; after destroying Columbus, he headed for Macon, Georgia. The Eufaula Youngs, however, would soon find themselves in the path of another force of invading Yankee cavalry, from a different direction: the mounted troopers of Gen. Grierson, sweeping up from Mobile after the capture of that city.

After the Federal occupation of Mobile, a portion of that force had been ordered to march north to take Montgomery. On the right flank of this force were 4000 cavalry under Major General Benjamin H. Grierson, who had fought at Blakely. By April 22, Grierson had reached Greenville, Alabama, where he learned that Wilson had already captured Montgomery and Columbus, and was moving to Macon. Grierson changed his plans and decided to head cross-country for Macon to join Wilson and assist him in taking Macon and Augusta. This change placed Eufaula in Grierson's line of march. Sending one brigade by a route through Union springs, Grierson and his other brigade went through Troy, arriving at Clayton, twenty miles west of Eufaula, on April 28.

In Clayton, Gen. Grierson learned of the April 26 meeting in North Carolina between Sherman and Johnston, and that hostilities had ceased. Nevertheless, he continued toward Eufaula, and instructed his other brigade to do the same.

The news of Grierson's approach had quickly spread throughout Eufaula and Barbour County, and the people were terrified. Frantic efforts were made to bury silver and hide valuables. It had been less than two weeks since they had heard horrible accounts of Wilson's destruction of Columbus, even after Lee had surrendered his army. The townspeople of Eufaula knew that the war was over, but they weren't sure whether General Grierson was aware of the situation. The Provost Marshal at Eufaula, Captain A. F. Pagnier, and other local leaders, decided to send a delegation to ride ahead and assure that Gen. Grierson was informed that the war had ended.[694]

This delegation consisted of the youngest son of Edward and Ann Young, i.e., "Ed" (Edward Billups) Young, now sixteen years old; another teenager, Edward Stern; and Captain James M. Hobdy, of Louisville.[695] This group went out carrying a flag of truce; it first returned without finding Grierson's force, but was then sent back again. The messengers spent that night at "Mr. Cunningham's on the Clayton Road." They started again the next morning, and this time met Gen. Grierson "at six mile branch," delivered their message that the war had ended, and returned.[696]

We know now that Gen. Grierson was already informed as to the status of the armistice negotiations, but in the confused rush of events of April 1865, the town leaders cannot be faulted for taking no chances. With knowledge of Sherman's recent wanton destruction of rural Georgia, as well as Wilson's burning of Columbus after Lee's surrender, some Eufaula inhabitants were fully convinced, correctly or incorrectly, that the mission of Ed Young and the truce team contributed to saving Eufaula from destruction.[697]

On April 29, 1865, the same day that Hubert Dent's commander, Gen. Richard Taylor, announced an armistice in Meridian, Grierson's cavalry arrived in Eufaula. The road from Clayton at that time entered Eufaula from the west over "College Hill," so that the thousands of men and horses of the Yankee force marched down College Hill in front of the Union Female College and within sight of Fendall Hall on Barbour Street. Gen. Grierson was hospitably received and entertained by Dr. and Mrs. J. C. Pope; some of the ladies pronounced him "a gentleman," and reported that his men "deported themselves without committing any depredation." His troopers were marched through the city and across the bridge over the Chattahoochee, to camp near Georgetown, Georgia. Learning that Wilson had ended hostile operations in Georgia, Grierson and his troops returned to Montgomery on May 1.

On May 10, troopers from Wilson's cavalry headquartered at Macon captured Jefferson Davis and some members of his cabinet at Irwinsville, Georgia, closing the last chapter of the Confederate States of America.

45
The Romance of Mollie Young and Hamilton Weedon

I think, as a whole, I have come out of the Rebellion a better fellow than I expected I would....It will require courage in you, dear Mollie, to leave your father's fine house to follow the fortunes of one so poor, but I believe that with the stimulation of your love, I can succeed..."

Hamilton to Mollie, September 1865

In the spring and summer of 1865, Eufaula and the Young family were attempting to cope with abject defeat at the hands of an overwhelming federal army, and general economic collapse as well. Dreams of an independent nation had gone up in smoke and a thriving agricultural economy was destroyed. Previously a center of one of the wealthiest and most prosperous sections of the country, Eufaula was now on its knees, struggling to subsist. The flower of its youth were in unknown graves. Edward and Ann Young's favored son, Henry - the latter half of "E. B. Young & Son"- would never return.

Despite these depressing circumstances, the occupants of Fendall Hall had reasons not to succumb to despair. One of these was the spirited Mollie Young, who would soon provide occasion for happiness. Certain of life's natural processes continue regardless of the circumstances. Although the Youngs' world had been turned upside down, these dark days received a burst of sunshine from the courtship and marriage of Mollie Young and Dr. Hamilton Weedon. Fortunately for us, the war and its aftermath required this attractive couple to conduct a part of their courtship by correspondence, thereby preserving it for us to follow today.

We have already noted the coincidence by which this family's path had indirectly touched that of two-year old Hamilton Weedon in Florida twenty-nine years earlier. It will be recalled that in 1836, Ann Fendall Beall Young's older brother, Robert Beall, Jr., the mayor of Macon, had joined a Macon militia unit which accompanied a force under Gen. Winfield Scott into central Florida in pursuit of the renegade Seminole chief, Osceola. We saw that the expedition was unsuccessful in finding Osceola, and that during this time in the Florida swamps, Robert Beall had contracted a disease from which he died soon after returning home. The following year, however, in 1837, Osceola was captured. He would soon die of disease in captivity, and during his last illness he was treated by the army surgeon, Dr. Frederick Weedon, who was Hamilton's father.

Hamilton Moore Weedon was born in Tallahassee, Florida on May 15, 1835 to Frederick and his wife, Mary Wells Thompson, but six weeks later the family moved to St Augustine. When Hamilton, the youngest of their ten children, was eighteen years old, he decided to follow his father's example. Hamilton entered the Medical College of New York, receiving the degree of Doctor of Medicine in 1855, and thereafter serving two years as resident surgeon of the City Hospital.[698]

In 1857, Hamilton's father was living on the islands off the tip of Florida known as the Dry Tortugas, where he died that year. Also living there were Hamilton's sister, Mrs. Henrietta Whitehurst and her husband, Dr. D. W. Whitehurst, the surgeon of Fort Jefferson, the military post there. After concluding his New York residency in 1857, Hamilton was spending a period in the Dry Tortugas with his family for health reasons when he learned that an epidemic of yellow fever was sweeping nearby Key West. He immediately went there and offered his services to help in treating the stricken population. He remained to develop a successful medical practice there, and was later appointed Port Physician for Key West.[699]

With the outbreak of war, Hamilton resigned his position, left his practice, and enlisted as a private in a Florida artillery battery. However, he soon became regimental surgeon for the Fourth Florida Infantry. Like Hubert Dent, he served during the major campaigns of the western theater. He became Chief Surgeon for Gen. Preston's brigade just before the battle of Murfreesboro; soon after Chickamauga, he became Chief Surgeon for Breckenridge's Division. Just before the fall of Atlanta, Hamilton was relieved of field duty and assigned to "post duty" at the army hospital in Eufaula, Alabama, and this is where he enters the story of the Young family.[700]

As casualties from Sherman's Atlanta campaign continued to mount, communities in the lower South had established hospitals to take in the wounded and provide treatment. The citizens of Eufaula had converted the old river tavern into a military hospital, and the Confederate government assigned army doctors to administer it, the first being Dr. Merriweather. As the huge casualties resulting in part from Hood's aggressive tactics around Atlanta poured into Eufaula in the summer of 1864, the hospital was overwhelmed. Dr. Hamilton Moore Weedon and Dr. Baker were ordered to Eufaula to augment the medical staff. To relieve the strain on the overcrowded hospital, members of the Eufaula community opened their homes and took in the more stable, ambulatory patients. Fendall Hall was one of the homes that took in and cared for Confederate wounded.[701]

From the November 6, 1864 letter from her brother-in-law, Hubert Dent, to Mollie, written from Florence, Alabama after Hubert crossed the Tennessee River enroute to Franklin and Nashville, we learned that Hubert had "heard three or four days ago that…Dr. W. was quite devoted to you and very constant in his attentions. That you rode out together every evening," and that Hamilton's older brother was now a private in Hubert's artillery company.

What Hubert did not know was that, by November 1864, little more than ninety days after his arrival in Eufaula, Hamilton Weedon was "head over heels" in love with Mollie. As we will see, he was a hopeless case, besotted with a deep infatuation with this mischievous, sometimes sharp-tongued young woman. Further, he had officially and formally declared his love to her, in writing. We know this because, shortly after Hubert's letter teasing Mollie about her new beau, and while Mollie was out of town, (perhaps visiting in Columbus), Hamilton wrote this sentimental letter[702] ("Miss Addie" is Mollie's close friend and confidante, Adriana Keitt Treadwell, who lived near Fendall Hall in the home originally built by John Gill Shorter):

"Nov. 9, 1864
Eufaula

"Dear Mollie,

It is a miserable, dark, rainy Saturday night, and I am alone, thank gracious. The good people of Eufaula must have retired, for I have not heard a footfall on the sidewalk for over an hour. Silence reigns supreme save the occasional popping of the fire, and the monotonous dripping of the water in the gutter. I like the stillness because it serves my purpose.

I have said I was alone, but beg pardon - not quite alone. I have two companions, my cigar - not a pipe this time - and a little blue-grayed person (imagining). For the last hour or two I have been puffing my cigar and talking to the little person as though she were present, trying to tell her how much I love her, though I know it can't be told. I took the little Hymn book, hallowed by her touch, looked a long time at the name on it, then at the little dried geranium leaf, wondering who gave it, and read several hymns. I intend to read it quite regularly here after, and probably by your return will have read it through. It may cause the confession of a sinner. Who knows.

I called on Miss Addie last night and stayed till ten o'clock, talking of you most of the time. She is a dear, good person, and a great friend of ours. She expects a letter from you Tuesday. I hope she will not be disappointed, because I expect you to send me some message. She and Miss Ada [Mollie's sister] rode horseback yesterday evening and I knew nothing of it till tonight, when I became exceedingly mouthy and said several words that somebody might have considered "bad." Miss Addie said she would write to you that I was very much smitten with a Miss Pain from Macon. You won't believe it, will you? When you hear that a pain has smote me, take it for granted that it is the rhumatism of nostalgia.

It is very late, and my dim tallow candle is burning very low, but before I tell you good night, promise if you find anything objectionable in this letter to burn it and let me know. I will not ask you to answer it, because I know if you think anything of me, or if you have not promised your parents not to, you will write to me.

> Good night, I love you dearly,
> With much devotion,
> H. M. Weedon

I hope you will say a little prayer for me tomorrow. Don't you want me to say one for you? H.M.W."

In March, after residing in Eufaula for only eight months, Hamilton was reassigned to Auburn, Alabama. We now know that, while Hamilton was still assigned to Eufaula, Mollie had given him some general indication that he interpreted as a commitment that, at some future, more settled time, she would marry him. Apparently, however, this was not a public engagement, and Mollie did necessessarily behave as an engaged woman.

Mary ("Molly") Elizabeth Cristina Young, soon to marry Dr. Hamilton M. Weedon

Under these circumstances, it is understandable that Hamilton did not like his new orders at all. He didn't want to leave Eufaula and Mollie; and he was disdainful of the town of Auburn, which he described as "a miserable little place."

He writes to Mollie, greeting her in French as "Friend of My Heart." They were both addicted to puns, and the reference in the body of his letter to "mine heart" is probably to a tedious fellow stagecoach passenger with a name like "Meinhardt." Glenville is the stagecoach stop north of Eufaula. "Roseland," where he sent the poem to Mollie, is the plantation near Glenville, owned by Colonel Washington Toney, the father of Mollie's other closest friend, Janie Toney. It would be interesting to know what the "orders" from Mollie were, that Hamilton is attempting to obey. She might have prohibited him from pressing her for a specific marriage date.

Auburn, Ala.
March 26, 1865

Ami De Mon Coeur,

I arrived here Friday morning, about worn out, and found a miserable little place almost in ruins. I am not at all satisfied with the change. Would much rather have been ordered to Camp Watts where I could be retired. There are seven hospitals here, and more doctors than I can get acquainted with in six months.

I found the Post Surgeon a very gentlemanly person. He offered to send me where I wanted to go so I chose the "Frank Ramsey" Hospital because I know the surgeon who has charge of it.

I arrived at Glenville about two o'clock on the day I left you, and remained there until the next morning. Silence seemed to have taken possession of that place. For half an hour at a time, I did not see a solitary individual in the streets. I did not even hear the ring of a blacksmith anvil, nor the voice of children at play.

"Mine heart" stuck to me with the utmost tenacity, propounding questions as fast as I could answer them. Questions of the most abstruse political nature, all of which I answered with a readiness and confidence, as well as plausibility which, in my opinion, gave mine heart a high opinion of my knowledge and political foresight. He continued on, however, that he had no poetry or romance in his nature, for when my attention was called from his political harangues to the sweet plaintive note of a dove in the distance, I also called his attention to it, and what do you think he said. Just what do you think. Why, he remarked in the most careless manner "The thing makes a right pretty racket." I felt like massacring, scalping, decapitating and sticking his head upon a pole for that horrible desecration, but was deterred by fear of the consequences.

I am terribly lonesome here, and don't believe I will ever get over it. I went to Camp Watts [army training camp near Notasulga, Alabama. Ed.] yesterday and saw Dr. Merriwether. That is but one little hospital with three medical officers there. I wish I were there. I think often of commencement at Tuskegee. I will make application to go to Florida or Texas.

Miss Ellen Pope [a lady of Eufaula] was the first person I met on my arrival. She had come down here to a concert given by the ladies for a benefit for the poor in So. Carolina.

All the medical men I have met here, with one or two exceptions are married; and many of them have their wives here. The Surgeon in charge of this hospital has his aunt and cousin with him. They are refugees from New Orleans. His cousin is quite pretty, and splendidly educated. Her name is Miss Ada [Legare], pronounced Lagree. They have a little cabin with two rooms for their accommodations. She also has a friend and is said to be an accomplished musician.

Thus ends the first lesson. If I write anymore, I will surely disobey orders, which I flatter myself I have stuck to right well.

Please send my kindest to your family.

If you answer this I will write again.

> Yours &c
> H. M. Weedon

I sent you a poem. You told me you had never read it.

Roseland
March 20, 1865

To: Mollie E. Young
              (top torn off)

Thou art my light of life, without thee, bliss
Even the bliss of angels, were but pain;
But with thee, earth hath not a wilderness.
So dark, but t'would be blessed paradise."

"Speak some light - some cheering word,
        My heart is sad tonight.

And my sick fancy fondly broods, o'er
    Coming hours of blight
And let me clasp again thy hand, and
    feel that here thy art.
To-morrow - Oh! to-morrow, love, I
    know though must depart."

Hamilton's duty in Auburn did not last long. As the Confederacy began to collapse, he was soon ordered to join the army being assembled in North Carolina under Gen. Joseph E. Johnston, as Hubert Dent and the Mobile garrison were preparing to do in Meridian. However, like Dent and the Mobile garrison, he never reached North Carolina. While enroute, Gen. Johnston surrendered on April 26. Hamilton was taken into custody and then paroled by the Federals in Macon, Georgia.

At this point, Hamilton Weedon, age 30, was engaged to be married and anxious to proceed with it, but like most paroled Confederate soldiers, he was penniless. He couldn't support a wife if he had one. He realized that he must first become financially responsible before he could expect Mollie to set a date, or for Edward Young to consent to it. Accordingly, he decided to immediately return to Key West, the scene of his pre-war successful practice, resume the practice of medicine, and earn the "wherewithal" with which to enter into marriage.[703]

We don't know whether he stopped at Eufaula for a visit, but later correspondence indicates he may not have discussed his plans with Mollie personally. He went down the Chattahoochee to Apalachicola in the steamer, *Uchee*, and took another steamer to New Orleans. In Apalachicola, he sent the short note below. "Miss Janie" is Eliza Jane Toney, another of Mollie's close friends who appears throughout the correspondence, the daughter of Colonel Washington Toney, who lived with his family in the elaborate Roseland Plantation north of Eufaula.

"Apalachicola
May

"Dear Mollie,
    I have just been informed that the *Uchee* would return at two o'clock. It is now half past one, and I have time only to tell you I arrived here safely last night and will take a steamer for New Orleans tomorrow at three P.M.
    There are others who have been waiting for six weeks. Ain't I lucky. Yellow fever is prevailing in Key West but I must go.
    Write to me at K. W. as soon as the mail route is open.
    My love to all at home, also to Misses Janie and Addie.
    God bless you.

       I love you dearly,
       H.M. Weedon

Excuse the pencil note. I am writing on an old side-board. I sent this by your <u>Beau</u> <u>Ideal,</u> Jas Griffin."

On June 3, Hamilton writes from New Orleans that he left Apalachicola on the steamer "Sophia," May 29, had a difficult five-day voyage on a crowded ship including a large party of children, and that most of the passengers, himself included, got seasick. He finds New Orleans "a much finer city than I expected to see," but allows that he "would like it more if there were not so many hateful yankees here. Confederate soldiers are not allowed to keep on their buttons." He plans to try to take a boat to Havana before going on to Key West.

Soon after arriving in Key West, Hamilton writes Mollie of his difficulties getting there, and his situation. He speaks of his sister, who resides in Key West with her husband, Dr. Whitehurst ("Dr. W"). He did not make the trip to Havana. As a paroled Confederate officer, Hamilton was prohibited from sailing to that foreign port. He also mentions that he cannot hold public office. Under President Johnson's reconstruction policy, this was denied to those who had resigned from federal service (in Hamilton's case, the Navy position of Port Physician of Key West) to become Confederate officers. Hamilton reveals to his sister the "secret" of his engagement, which she does not at first believe. Carrie, Ada, and Helen, are, of course, Mollie's sisters. "Game chickens" are fighting roosters, still a popular sport in the rural south.

"Key West
June 20, 1865

"Darling Mollie,
        I write this hoping I might be able to send this sometime this week. A vessel sailed for Apalachicola three days ago, but I did not know anything of it until she had left. I was really vexed when I was informed of it.
        I arrived here a week ago today, in the steam transport "Constitution" from New Orleans. I was to have gone to Havana in a Schooner but after I was all ready, I was informed by the provost marshall that I would not be allowed to sail for a foreign port, so I returned to my hotel almost in despair. That was one of the things that happened for the best, however, for I was notified by the quarter-master the next day that the "Constitution" had just arrived from New York and would return via Key West in a day or two, so on the 9th, I think it was, I left N. O. and arrived here on the morning of the 13th. The steamer did not come nearer than Sand Key, a little island nine miles from here, and I came up in a pilot boat.
        We had a delightful passage. The weather was fine, and sea so smooth that no one was sick. Among the passengers was ex-Gov. Moore of Alabama on his way to Fort Pulaski and Maj. Genl. Murray, family and staff in route for Baltimore.

I took all by surprise when in a half hour after my arrival the sitting room was filled with my old friends. Dr. W.[hitehurst, Hamilton's brother-in-law] was informed while visiting a patient that a number of people had gone into his house in a hurry, so he rushed home with visions of fits, fire, etc. before him. I found them all well but very unhappy in consequence of our national misfortune. Sister has fallen away very much since I last saw her.

I have gone regularly into practice to repair damages. I had two patients in less than two hours of my arrival. I found two Yankee doctors, both married to Key West girls, diving deep into my old business. But I have waked this gentleman up already. Though my rebellious proclamation makes me ineligible to any public office, I am satisfied I will get two-thirds of the private practice.

I wrote you a hurried note from Apalachicola by Steamer Uchee. Also, one from New Orleans. I hope you received them. I heard in the former place that Yellow fever was here but it was not so, the town has been perfectly free from it this year. I did not find my business in as good a fix as I expected, but I believe I can soon get things straight again.

This place has changed very much since I left it, socially and otherwise. Many of the best families have gone North to live, and their places sublet by yankees of the meanest stamp, but I intend to shut my eyes to all that. The place must give me another start and then I will seek another home, in the selection of which, you must also be suited.

I have dreamed up the following little plan which is respectfully submitted for your approval. I think it is just the thing. I have submitted it to Dr. Whitehurst and sister, who are both pleased with it. This is the plan - I will be in Eufaula toward the last of Oct. or first of Nov. and as soon after we are married, as you can depart, we will come here and spend the winter. Next spring we will go elsewhere to settle permanently - say Columbus, Eufaula, or any other place that may seem better. Of course, your Mother must come with us. I believe a winter in this climate would go a great way toward her rhumatism, and I am sure you will enjoy it.

When I told my secret to sister she did not believe it - thought it exceedingly improbable - but her skepticism is now dislodged, and she loves you because I love you. She desires me to present her love and inform your mother and yourself that it will do her great pleasure to have you spend the winter with her. I have already accepted the invitation.

Do answer this letter as soon as possible, and state the exact time for me to be on hand. If you can find any one going to New York, it will be a good change. Charleston, Savannah, Richmond, or any of these places will do to mail letters to this place. Let them mail your letters in for this place. They are somewhat uncertain, though, and in view of that, you must not wait for an answer before you write again. I intend to write every chance. You must do the same.

All the beauty of the island is in the room below me this afternoon. They have congregated to make clothes for this "ragged Rebel" as all was pleased to call me. They are all talking at once, as usual, and I am fully satisfied, are doing a good deal more play than work. I went down just now to call them to order but I was shamefully maltreated and driven from that paradise of curls, crinolin, and cologne water. Miss Ida Sara shook her curls and said, "girls, I expect we are making these things now for Dr. W. to go off and get married in. "Many a shaft at random sent, whose aim the archer little meant."

Miss Lizzie Brown, whom you have heard me speak of, is among them. She is as pretty as ever. She was telling me a very funny circumstance that occurred the other night. I had sent her word that I was coming to see her that night, and while she was in the parlour waiting my arrival, she heard a quick step on the porch, which she thought was mine. She hurried out and took the person's hand in both of hers, shaking it with such energy as almost to dislodge the gentleman's spectacles from his nose, saying at the same time "Doctor, I am so glad to see you." The Doctor for her turned out to be a little yankee Naval surgeon, of a stature somewhat between that of Dr. Villaret And Tom Thumb, was completely appalled by the warmth of the reception, and I, of course, appalled at being taken for such a man.

Give a great deal of love at home for me, also to the Toney and McKenzie families. Kiss Janie, Carrie, Addie, Ada, and Helen for me, at the same time let them understand that I would rather do my kissing by proximity than by proxy.

Say to Dr. Baker that I have not forgotten the game chickens. If I can't get a good chance to send them, I will bring them when I came. The stores here are filled with nice fruit. How much I wish I could send you some. I never see it but I think of you.

I send you some Photographs and sea-moss. This moss is by some persons arranged in a highly artistic manner representing landscapes, animals & etc. I will try to procure some such representation for you.

Don't forget to write soon.

I love you dearly,

H.

Thus far, we have only seen Hamilton's side of this correspondence. We will later see that Mollie also writes sprightly, amusing, sometimes acerbic letters. But the letter Hamilton now receives in response to his proposed schedule for getting married is not amusing to him. We have only a fragment of Mollie's letter, but she rejects out of hand every part of his "little plan" for an October or November wedding followed by a long winter residence with his family. She purports to be surprised that he is in Key West, rather than Quincy or Mariana (Hamilton's brother is a doctor in Quincy, Florida), although he had written her at least two letters in which he said he was going to Key West. She couldn't leave Eufaula any earlier than December or January. Besides, her friend Janie Toney "is not willing" for her to leave before spring, and Mollie suggests that he stay in Key West until spring, closing with a terse "goodbye." Looks like storm clouds on the horizon.

(Letter Fragment, Mollie to Hamilton)

Last Friday night there was a party at Mr. McKenzie's. I did not go as I was not feeling very well, and we were expecting a cousin of mine that night. I believe I have given you all the Eufaula news.

Ma is still suffering from rhumatism. She has been a great deal worse since you left. Dr. Baker has been to see her, and is trying cold water, and different medicines from any that she has used, but nothing seems to do her good. Dr. Alkin, one of my cousins in Yankeedom, says that he will send her something that will benefit her. I hope he will do so soon.

I was surprised to hear that you had gone in business in Key West. I expected you were either in Quincy or Mariana by this time.

Give my love to your sister, and many thanks to her from ma and myself to spend the winter with her, but I have no idea that Ma can leave the house by that time, as she is not able to walk across the room now, and to my leaving them for the whole winter - they will not hear of it. Nor would I like to leave Ma for so long a time unless she is much better. What do you say to my not going until the last of December or first of January? Janie says she is not willing to have me leave her, even to go with you - much as she loves you - until spring. Write me what you think about December or January. I, of course, wish you to remain in Key West until spring, if it is to your interest to do so, but under all circumstances I think it best for me to do as I have written you.

The family all sends their kind regards to you. Helen sends love, and says don't forget the things you promised her.

Good-bye,

Yours, etc. Mary"

From these letters we hear more of the onset of the arthritic condition in Mollie's mother, then referred to as "rheumatism," or sometimes, "inflammatory rheumatism." First attacked in April 1863, this condition would bedevil Ann Young for the rest of her life. It would limit her mobility and quickly grow steadily worse, until by October of 1864 she was no longer able to walk and was confined to a chair.

A depressed Hamilton writes on July 15, taking a low-key approach and not pressing the issue most on his mind. After gentle chiding, he writes an interesting letter, perhaps containing veiled object lessons for Mollie:

"Key West
July 15th 1865

"My sweet Mollie (you don't deserve to be called so)
Another vessel in today from Apalachicola, and no letter for me. Why have you not written? I am blue, very blue indeed. Afraid you are at your old

398

tricks. If I were not cognizant of your having, at one period of your life, written to others, I would be tempted to believe you spoke truly when you said you did not know how to write. I might have expected this when you were defending yourself before you committed the crime. You remember you used to tell me, "How can you expect letters when we have no mail arrangements?" Now, I judge this to be a case of malice purpose and sentence you to write one long letter at least once a week, and send it to McKenzie or Atkins & Durham to be forwarded whenever vessels leave. Numerous vessels have arrived here from Apalachicola within the last month and not one word for me. Please don't let it be so again. The steamer *"Linda"* will leave there for here in about five days, and if she wont bring me something from you I will "give up."

I arrived here one month and two days ago yesterday. It has been a long time to me, but so much is gone. Only two months and a half now, ain't it? Say yes, or I will call Ada.

Let me tell you how I spend the time. Well, I get up about seven o'clock, and if I have no very sick patients to visit, I play with the children or go to the stable and pet my horse until breakfast time, which is eight o'clock. I then visit my patients which takes me usually until 12 o'clock. From that time until noon I smoke a cigar (I am death on cigars, though I have not smoked a pipe since I promised you I would not), read the paper, or talk with sister. After dinner, I go to my room, keep cool and read, write, or take a nap if the notion strikes me. At five p.m. I again visit my sick patients, and if I have time, go to the bath-house on the beach and plunge in. After tea, I sit in the piazza with Dr. W. & sister entertaining our friends or I go visiting.

My favorite place to visit is at the home of the Honorable Probate Judge, Winer Bithil. He lives near us and his family is very pleasant. I call him "Big Bithil" for he is a man of enormous bodily proportions, and he supposes, profound wisdom. The light of Winer's cigar has been seen for years in exactly the same spot from eight to half past eleven P.M. Call when you will, Winer's found closely wedged in a tremendous willow rocking chair, behind that cigar, descanting upon the most abstruse legal and political questions.

He had two very pretty, curly-haired daughters, Mellie and Ida. Mellie is very much in love with a friend of mine, who was in the Confederate Navy, but I don't think he likes her quite well enough to marry her. I have known her a long time and have her confidence. She showed me a letter from him which she received yesterday, and says she will answer it today - so profit by the example. He did not commit on love very strong. Called himself her friend, etc. Long absence probably has caused the gentleman to grow cold.

She was sick a few days ago, and sent for me. I found her weeping bitterly. Her mother and maiden aunt went into long explanations and suggested many causes of her sickness, but I knew more of the true cause than they. Consequently, I prescribed a trip to the north this summer, where her beau is now and intends to spend the summer. Some old fogies, if they knew this, would denounce me for swaying from the orthodox practice of pills, powders & etc. but I would tell those Gentlemen that physicians should not search the body and mind for the cause of disease, but they must also put their ears to the heart. Also, that the heavens above and earth beneath and the waters under the earth do not alone contain all the remedies for the cure of diseases, but that every passion and emotion of humanity can be made to serve our purpose. Please, Mary, do not say anything of the above circumstances to anyone. Nor show my letters to anybody but your mother.

Good night
I love you dearly,
H.

In Mollie's next letter, she is still aloof, describing her busy social life, giving Eufaula news, and launching thinly veiled darts at Hamilton and his family. There is little evidence here of an impending marriage. Hamilton is assured that Mollie's behavior is "splendid," in the unbiased view of her friend Janie Toney. We learn that the Yankee troops are still occupying Eufaula, as they would for years to come. The Youngs' friend, Julian McKenzie, former officer of the Eufaula Light Artillery, now operates the steamer *Shamrock* between Eufaula and Apalachicola, and he will be a frequent carrier of correspondence between the two. Mollie reports that Hubert Dent and Will Young have made a trip to Apalachicola.

" Eufaula, Ala.
 July 18, 1865

I expect, Dr. Weedon, you have concluded ere this that I do not intend writing to you. Mr. Dent and brother Will returned from Apalachicola. I wrote you a week ago, but have not had an opportunity of sending it yet, and thinking you would not thank me for an old letter, I write again this morning to go by Julian McKenzie who leaves on the "Shamrock" tomorrow for Apalachicola. I am so very lazy about writing, that I never do so unless I am certain my letters can go after they are written.

I received your note from Apalachicola, your letter from New Orleans, and two from Key West.

Many thinks to you for the sea-weed and photographs, especially those of your sister and yourself. Who were you mad at when you had yours taken? We all think it splendid if you do look a little angry. Your sister is very much like you, only much better looking. I know I shall love her very much if she is at all like her photographer.

I saw Dr. Alexander after he returned from New Orleans. He told me about being with you, and complimented you very highly to some other ladies, but I know if I write you what he said your patients will suffer for several days to come, as it will take you some time to get over it.

The yankees are still here, but as they are not allowed to enter private houses without a special invitation. We are not troubled with them, though they have been invited to two or three houses to dine and take tea. You can well imagine who would ask them to see them. I wish they could feel it their duty to return home, as I am sure none of us would very sad at their departure. But enough of them.

The last of June, as usual, Mr. Van (Houten), and his scholars gave a concert. I attended it, went with Mr. McDuffies, a young soldier of this place, and enjoyed myself very much. The next night there was a party at the College Chapel, and those who went said it was very pleasant indeed. Mr. Van, three Kentucky soldiers, Miss Addie [Treadwell] and Miss Laura Castleberry spent the next evening at our house. Mr. Van enquired very particularly after you and regretted that you were not here to attend his concert.

By the way, one of those Kentucky soldiers is an acquaintance of yours, Dr. Mann. I believe he was surgeon of a Kentucky Brigade. He is quite a handsome, fascinating gentleman. The young ladies are all charmed with him. I took a horseback ride, went to church with him, and last Friday morning, he, Ada, and I went out to Col. Toney's. Don't imagine I am in love with him also. By writing this I am only obeying orders. You remember you ordered me to write you every thing I did while you were gone. I heard that D. Mann thought of making this his home, as he cannot return to Kentucky now.

We went out to the country church last Sunday, and Ada and I spent the day with Janie and Carrie. Janie sends much love, and says I am "behaving splendidly."

I wish you to write me why your sister thought it improbable that you were going to be married. Did she think that you would be very choice in your selections, or that you were so bad nobody would have you. I hope the first so. The real reason, though I am inclined to believe that it is the last.

Be sure to write me, Mollie

Mollie writes again only two days later. It is a somewhat warmer letter, with a clever pun, but she brings in her mother to help oppose the suggestion that Mollie go to Key West:

"Eufaula, Alabama
July 20th, 1865

I wrote you a long letter, Dr. Weedon, six pages, day before yesterday to go by Apalachicola but as brother Will leaves to-night for New Orleans, I will write a short note by him. I am afraid to write two long letters, or too long letters, or too often, for fear that you will get tired of reading them.

Now that I have commenced this, I scarcely know what to write, as I answered all questions, and gave you all the news in my letter the other day, and it has been so long since I have written letters that I have almost forgotten how.

I want you, some time very soon, to write Addie. She told me a few days ago, that she did not believe you were as good a friend of hers as you pretended to be. Although you have sent her messages in every letter, I have not delivered but one. She does not know that I receive letters from you. So be careful not to say anything about it when you write to her.

Last Sunday while I was at Col. Toney's, Sterling had St. George brought out for me to look at. He is a perfect beauty. I don't think you would recognize him as your horse. This is the first time I have seen him since you left.

I must tell you something funny that happened the other day. Dr. Mann and Lieut. Nuckolls called, and I went down with my hair perfectly plain, and as I thought looking hideous, and "old as the hills." As soon as I got in the parlour, Dr. Mann said, "Miss Mollie, I thank you for coming to see me with your hair fixed so; it is the most becoming way I ever saw you wear it." So now what is to be done?

Did I write you that Dr. Thomason passed through here a few days after you left? He stopped only a few minutes down town. I did not see him. He said he would be back in two months, and would make us a short visit, so I will not be surprised to see him anytime now.

I have company now so you will have to be contented with this. Whenever I can write anything of interest to you I will try and do so.

Helen sends love, and says she had much rather you do your own kissing then have me do it for you. Ada has just come in from Addie's, and sends love also.

I wrote you in my last letter what I thought about going to Key West, and sent a message to your sister from Ma and myself. Ma says as soon as she is able to do so, she wishes to write you a note, and let you know what she thinks about my going.

Good-bye
Yours, Mary

With logic which is unfathomable to those who have read this correspondence, Mollie in her next letter reprimands Hamilton for "quarrelling so." With that blame settled, she seems to now accept him back in her good graces, more or less, although there is still no hint that a marriage is being planned. Her strong Methodist rearing emerges as she needles him about not going to church and for smoking. She reminisces about the previous summer (1864) when the wounded soldiers were at Fendall Hall, and Drs. Weedon and Baker were there. She mentions a trip involving "Mr. Martin, Addie, and Ada." Addie may have been chaperoning the early stages of a romance; four years later, Mollie's sister Ada married James H. G. Martin:

"Eufaula, Ala.   (Received at night Aug. 12, 1865)
August 1st. 1865

I received your letter, Dr. Weedon, dated July 15th. Last Saturday, and will write to go by the "Shamrock."

I hope you have received my letters before this, and recovered from the "blues". You might have known that I had written. Did I not promise to do so. You don't deserve an answer this soon for quarreling so, but I suppose I must forgive you this time if you will promise to do better in the future. As to my writing to you once a week, how do you expect me to do so, when you don't set me the example? There are but two boats running regularly between here & Apalachicola, and very often I do not know when they are here, but brother Will has gone to New Orleans to buy a boat, and then I can probably write oftener. How is it that I have not heard anything of the Methodist Church in Key West? I am afraid you have forgotten how regularly you attended it here. The first letter you write after receiving this I wish to hear that you have been there, and to be able to tell me something about it. I see that you will bear watching about that.

Writing about that young lady in Key West, and her beau, you said (after admitting that he did not like her well enough to marry her) "long absence has probably caused the gentleman to grow cold." I want to know if that is the effect absence generally has upon gentlemen. This question must certainly be answered. Julian McKenzie returned from Apalachicola last Sunday. Says he met a gentleman there, an acquaintance of yours from Key West, who inquired after you. I believe he said he was a Lieut. in the Confederate Navy, possibly this might be the gentleman all those tears were shed for.

I have had two very pressing invitations lately to go to New York, but I have no idea of accepting them. Eufaula has changed since you were here. A great many of the stores have been opened, and are now filled with goods.

I don't think I will recognize you when we meet, if you smoke as much as you wrote me you did. I thought you promised never to touch a pipe, and only smoke a cigar occasionally. I am afraid you don't wish to remember part of your promise.

Edward has been quite sick for the last two of three days, with fever, but is able to be up today. Sunday Dr. Baker went sent for, and they came back with the news that he was in the country, and Dr. Thornton could not be found, so it was late in the evening before we could get a physician, and, of course, we were feeling very anxious about Bud as he had a very high fever. We all wished that day, and Ma especially, that you had settled here so that we could have a doctor when we wished to, as we thought you might possibly be kept in place.

We have a quantity of ripe grapes now. They remind me of last summer when we had the wounded soldiers here, and you and Dr. Baker. By the way I understood you to say that Dr. B. gave me that name last summer, and he says you did it. I will leave this open until to-morrow, and write more if I do not go in the country. Janie, I hear, is in town, and I am expecting her here every moment. I have not seen her in over a week, a long time for us to be without seeing each other, ain't it?

Don't fail to write Addie. You will have plenty of time while smoking. She expects to leave Saturday for Forsyth, Ga. to visit her brother and sister-in-law - will be absent about two or three weeks. Mr. Martin, Addie, and Ada spent last week over at Mrs. Castleberry's - had a delightful visit, of course.

Pa has just told me that they expect the "Shamrock" to leave at daylight to-morrow, so my letter will go one day earlier than I expected, as we did not think the boat would go until the day after.

One piece of advice before I close - don't be having the <u>blues</u> so much - and quit <u>smoking</u> so often - and I think you will feel better. Don't you wish I would stop talking so. Well, I will stop for this time. <u>All</u> send <u>love</u>.

Yours etc. Mary

In his next letter, the ever-patient Hamilton is grateful just to hear from Mollie. He grumbles about her putting off the wedding date, and anxiously seeks her approval to his being in Eufaula around the first of December.

"Key West
August 20, 1865

"Dear Mollie,

The steamer *Linda*, which I have been so anxiously looking for, arrived about ten days ago, but she brought no letter for me, so I gave up the hope of ever hearing from you. I felt wretchedly. I could forgive you when you were at Columbus and when I was at Auburn, but under the present circumstances, I could not have forgiven you. Night before last I dreamed that I received two letters. One had a yellow envelope, and the other a white, and when I was telling my dream at the breakfast table, these letters were handed to me, one white and the other yellow. I recognized yours as the white one dreamed of.

It is unnecessary to say that it did not improve my appetite and I immediately retired to some quiet place to read it. I thank you, dear Mollie, with all my heart for it. It made me feel so happy to know you had not forgotten me or thought too little of me to write. If you were at all sentimental in your nature, I would tell you I pressed it, but I wont tell you as now.

It was very good, considering it was your <u>first</u> <u>effort</u>. Yes, and I might say with truth, that it was <u>splendid</u>. "All went Merry as a Marriage Bell" until the conduct of that man Mann made me feel many morbid misgivings. What manner of man can he be, that so many fair ones should be willing to charm themselves for his sake. And who is McDuffy? Another ghost to haunt me in my dreams? I don't feel like playing MacBeth with him in this contest "or any other Mann."

You must continue to tell me all about your little fun. I won't be jealous. I know what you will say when you come to this - it will be "<u>I</u> <u>don't</u> <u>care</u> <u>if</u> <u>you</u> <u>do</u>." Please write often, because I can't help measuring your feeling by the number and tone of your letters. Sometimes I think you don't think as much of me as I would like you to, and such reflections don't contribute much to my happiness.

There is one very disagreeable feature in your letters, and that is you have put me off two months longer. Now that is wretchedly mean of you. And just to think that sweet Janie Toney is a *particess criminis*. Tell her that I intend to convene a court of inquiry at Roseland [the Toney plantation] next Dec., to investigate this <u>highest</u> <u>crime</u> <u>known</u> <u>to</u> <u>the</u> <u>code</u> <u>of</u> <u>Cupid</u>, and woe unto her if she is found guilty.

I have been waiting anxiously for the exodus of this miserable hot month of Aug., but it seems to creep out at a snails pace. My intention was to have been in Eufaula about the middle of Oct., but I suppose you have good reasons for putting me off. So acting upon your suggestion I will be there about the first of Dec. What say you to that? Write me fully. I desire you to see Key West. You may like it much. I think it is a great deal better than Quincy, Marianna or any other place in Florida. It is a fine business place, to say the least of it. You astonish me when you say that you expected I was either in Quincy or Marianna. It would not be adroit of me to leave a large place for a smaller one or one with plenty of money for one with none. The main reason for my staying here now is the people on the mainland are all poor, all their wealth is in cotton, and a very small quantity of that. Bob Ferguson and a few others are the only ones who have it and they hold it as tight as Bob holds that spectacle case. Greenbacks are the only things peculiar to the Yankees that I don't despise.

Whenever I leave this place it will be for a city. That is, if I don't stop in Eufaula. I believe that Columbus will, in time, be a large manufacturing town. If so, that will be the town for me.

I have fun having my buggy repaired to ride you around the island in the evening, but I expect it will be so long before you come that all the new fixings will be worn off when you get here.

I send this by steamer "Union" which supplies the naval stations on the coast between this place and Pensacola. She will return by the same route, so if you will write as soon as you get this, and send it to McKenzie, she will bring it to me on her return. Via New York is the quickest way to get letters to me. I expect the mail route is complete between Eufaula and New York now, and if not there is always someone going. We have a regular mail between here and there.

I don't like you to say you are a lazy correspondent. The inference is that you have but little interest in those to whom you write. With proper feeling, writing is no task at all, or rather it is a very pleasant one. I know, however, you frequently say things you do mean, and I will consider that one of them. You should have, by all means sent me the letter you had written before. No matter how old it was, it would have been interesting to me. I will read with the greatest interest anything you write.

Do not depend upon the Apalachicola route to sent letter to me. Vessels do not come as frequently now as formerly. Send your letters to New York.

Please send my kindest regards to all at home. To your mother, make my sincere condolences. I hope your cousin's prescription will benefit her, but my advice is that a climate will do more for her than medicines. My love to Ada and Helen. Tell Helen I will bring the things, but really, in all my excitement and anxiety, I have forgotten what they are. You must tell me what they are. How is it that Addie sent me no message? Can she be mad with me? I hope not. Give her my love. I send you a little bouquet sent me from New York by Martha - you should prize it very highly.

You guessed rightly - the last reason you gave for sister not believing what I told her is that. She sends love to you.

Don't forget to remember me most kindly to the Toney family.	Please write frequently, Yours, with much love, H.

In his next letter, Hamilton is again relieved and grateful just to hear from Mollie, but still apprehensive about what is on her mother's mind. Is Ann Young discouraging the possibility of Mollie's moving to Key West, or does she have even more serious concerns? He is still trying to get a firm commitment from Mollie that he can "be on hand" in Eufaula by the first of December to marry her, and he obliquely makes his case. With an eye out for her mother's possible concerns, he assures Mollie he will not "locate" anywhere that does not suit her, and that he is in Key West only to get a "start." Never oblivious to the importance of material considerations, Hamilton makes it a point to mention, (perhaps for the benefit of Mollie's father), that he has accumulated $3000, is doing "remarkable well" in his practice, and expects to continue to do so:

"Key West
Sept. 3, 1865

"My Sweet Darling Mollie,
I have just received another letter from you, mailed by your brother in New Orleans. You don't know how dearly I love you, when you indicate to me in that way, that you have not grown cold toward me. That letter rather surprises me because I was not looking for one from you just then. I thought you would wait for an answer to the one you wrote two days before. I am glad you did not do so, because that letter has added a great deal to the love I already had for you.
The last part of the letter frightened me. You say your mother intends writing a note in relation to your coming to Key West with me. Now what on the face of the earth can that mean? I wonder. You know I kept scared until I heard that talk she had for me when I returned from Auburn. I wish you had hinted what that note would contain, because I will feel quite nervous until I receive it. She must not feel afraid to trust you with me, for I am sure that there is not a person alive who would take better care of you than I would.
Addie is mistaken when she supposes that I am not as friendly with her as I pretended. I like her very much - fully as much as I ever indicated. I will

do as you advise and write her very soon. I also intend writing to Janie. Give her and Carrie [Mollie's 10-year old sister] plenty of love from me.

You pleased me very much when you mentioned St. George. I am so glad to know that he is looking well. He is a noble horse, and I value him highly for the good service he has done me. I wish, if possible, to take him home - when I get one - and care for him in his old age. I am afraid that he is not worked enough. I desire that he should make his cornbread by the sweat of his brown.

Now about that <u>hair</u> business. You ask what is to be done. I answer that Special Order no. 1 is hereby announced, and you may arrange it to suit yourself, if you will promise to braid it when I come. All this provided you do not fall into the "waterfall" <u>this</u> <u>fall</u>.

So, Dr. T. was in town and expected to be back in two months, was he? I suppose he is there by this time then, having a jolly, good time. Now, I know all this is after my letter, sweetheart, and nothing else. I wonder how he will want his hair fixed. Oh, for a steel trap at that front gate to catch the rascals by the feet. The result will be, I am afraid, that you will be so vain there will be no doing anything with you when I return.

You say that you are afraid to write two long letters or write too often for fear that I may get tried of reading them. I am thankful for your kind consideration, but please don't express it any more in this quarter. I read your letters over again. The only fault I find is that they are too few and too short. I never get tired of anything you touch. You should not have written so short a letter by your brother. You must have known several days before that he was going, consequently, you had plenty of time. And another thing I wish to call you attention to, which is down right swindling. You begin your letters half way down the page and end the same way. Now what is that but cheating me.

Moreover, you never mention Miss Jennie Crawford's name, my "sweetheart", as you want to call her. Do she and Miss McLeroy ride as much as ever? Who is stowing sheep's eyes on Miss Helen Bachus? Tell me how she treats the Yankees. Who are the beaux of Miss Addie? You know she usually has several at the same time. Did it not amuse you to see her try to look sad when Maj. - I forget his name - was killed in So. Ca. Dear me, what uphill business it was for her to look sorrowful. Mind, keep this secret.

Mr. Locke told me, when last we met, that he proposes going to New York. Has he gone? Please ask Dr. Baker if he has heard from Drs. Wilkinson and Merriwether. Try to get Merriwether's address. I should like to write to him. I know no man, of my army acquaintance, that I have formed a greater attachment for than for him.

I met Capt. Paniet in New Orleans. He is looking exceedingly seedy. I am satisfied that he was never so well off as when he wore a Capt.'s uniform. What has become of Byrne & Brady? I expect that Brady will make Eufaula his future home.

407

It is expected that the steamer *"Linda"* will run regularly between New York and Apalachicola via. this place. If so, what a nice thing it will be. I can then write to you regularly, and receive letters from you also - if <u>you</u> <u>will</u> <u>write</u>.

The weather has been exceedingly hot, but no Yellow fever has made its appearance. I have nearly all the practice in town, and done remarkably well. I think, as a whole, I have come out of the Rebellion a better fellow than I expected I would. All my little worldly goods, gathered together, might amount to probably three thousand dollars. A small fortune to be sure, but thank God for that. It will require courage in you, dear Mollie, to leave your father's fine house to follow the fortunes of one so poor, but I believe that with the stimulation of your love, I can succeed to an extent, <u>at</u> <u>least</u>, common among men of my profession.

I will be able to determine by next Dec., when I see you, where I will "locate," as your Doctors say. Be assured that I will not require you to stay in any place that would be objectionable to you. My only reason for staying here at present, is, as I have before said, that I can do well in the way of making another start. However, we will arrange all these things when we meet. What do you say to my being on hand by the first of December? Will you be ready by that time? I hope you will not put me off longer than that. I am all ready now, just waiting for you, or rather unjustly waiting for you.

My love to all at home. Tell Helen that I will take her advice and do my own kissing in the future - but it is so unbecoming in a Doctor to make a cupping-gloss by his mouth.

Your last letter was sent from New Orleans via. New York. If the postal arrangement is complete from Eufaula to New York that will be the way to write. Write to me often. Good by - God bless you is the prayer of

Yours most truly   H

Sister sends love to you. Remember me most kindly to Col. and Mrs. Toney & Miss Boss. Tell Sterling I thank him much for taking such good care of my horse. [Sterling Toney is Janie's brother, who will become a Eufaula lawyer, and will later move to Louisville, Kentucky with Gen. Alpheus Baker and establish a successful law practice with him there.]

Mollie wrote the next day (before receiving his foregoing letter, of course) and somewhat breezily gives the long-awaited confirmation that she will allow him to come to Eufaula and marry her "some time the first of December," conditioned upon his promise to "be right good and mind every word I say." Mollie and the Youngs have been visited by her Columbus kin: her mother's sisters, Aunt Mary Lockhart and Aunt Ellen Young; and her cousin by marriage, Clara Wildman, the wife of Ellen's son Alfred, former captain of Young's Battery. We learn that Mollie's close friend, Addie [Adriana Treadwell. Ed.], is planning to marry in January. She married Henry Russell Shorter. [brother of Gov. John Gill and Col Eli. Ed.] Mollie's brother, Will Young, the former steamboat captain and engineer, has bought a vessel, apparently a steamboat, in New Orleans and is bringing it up the Chattahoochee.

"Eufaula, Ala.
September 4th 1865

It is well for you, Dr. Weedon, that I received your letter of Aug. 20th yesterday, for I had determined not to write (no matter how much I wished to do so) until I heard from you again, and you don't deserve an answer this soon. But the "Shamrock" leaves in the morning and as the river is so very low the boats cannot run regularly. It may be a long time before I have another opportunity of writing.

I have not heard from you before in five weeks, and had begun to think that you had fallen in love with some Key West Lady or Martha & had forgotten to write.

Since I wrote last, my aunts, Mrs. Lockhart, Mrs. Wm Young, and Mrs. Wildman of Columbus have been down to see us, and of course, we all enjoyed their visit very much, and Dr. Thomason too has been here. He arrived Thursday night, came up Friday and spent the day with us, was here Friday night and Saturday evening, left on the cars Sunday morning for Nashville, from where I believe he intends going to New Orleans. Don't expect we will see him again very soon if ever. Dr. Mann left for Kentucky week before last. He had not decided whether he would return here or not. I have written you three letters before this, and can't imagine why you have not received them. I hope you have received the last one I wrote, as there is something in it I wish attended to especially.

I spent the day with Addie to-day, and she told me if I wrote to you, which she thought I ought to do, to give her love to you, and tell you if you wished to see her single to come this Winter, as she promised to marry in January (2). You may possibly be here before then.

Did I write you, you could come the first of Dec. If I remember right I said the last of Dec. or the first of January, but if you will promise to be right good, and mind every word I say, I will let you come some time the first of December. We have had one wedding here since you left. The gentleman is about 64 years old and the lady 56, the gayest couple I have seen in a long time.

Brother William succeeded in getting a boat in New Orleans, the "Glide", and come within a hundred and twenty miles of home, and had to stop on account of the low river - been there over a week.

Not one word have I heard from the Methodist Church. I am afraid you are not behaving as well as you might, and what to do about that.

Ma is still suffering with Rhumatism. She sent to Hamilton, Georgia to a physician there, for some medicine which cured a lady worse than Ma and I do hope it may have the same good effect upon her.

You should appreciate this letter very highly, I am so sleepy I can scarcely hold my eyes open long enough to write.

I saw Janie yesterday, but could not deliver your message as it was at the Church door that I saw her, and too many were standing around. All send their regards. My love to your sister.

I will write by the first one I hear going to New York, and answer all questions.

I prize Martha's bouquet very highly, I know it grieved you dreadfully to part with it.

Good night - Yours & etc.
Mary

I enclose a note from Ada, and brother William's wife [Annie Hewlett]. Helen sends love. The last part of that note signed H. was written by Ada, hoping you would think it was me that needed the banisters to the steps.
M."

The "enclosed note" does not survive.

Writing ten days later, apparently without having yet received Mollie's foregoing letter, Hamilton complains, inaccurately, of having received only two letters from her since arriving in Key West. This is an understatement, perhaps resulting from the anxiety of unrequited love. In fact, there are five extant letters from Mollie, although he has not yet received the last one. Hamilton repeats his usual entreaty that he be "on hand" in Eufaula to marry Mollie on December first, not yet aware of her acquiescence in this persistent request in her last letter.

"Key West
Sept 13th 1865

"My Sweet Mollie,
I sent you a long letter by way of New York, but hearing that a steamer leaves tomorrow for St. Marks I thought I would talk a letter with you before going to bed. I do not know how this will reach you after it gets to Tallahassee but I will risk a short note anyway. Today is three months since my arrival here, and I have received only two letters from you. Just think of it. Do, dear Mollie, write to me oftener. Think how many letters I have written to you, and how seldom you have written to me.

A steamer arrived from Apalachicola yesterday, and if you had done as I often told you - that is send letters to McKenzie - I would have received them by now. I have one hope left. The *"Linda"* is yet to come, and if she brings me nothing look out for a scolding. I send Addie a letter today by New York also. I want you to both answer them by the same route. What do you think of my coming on late in Nov. so as to be on hand for the first of Dec. I am getting very impatient, and if I have to wait until the last of Dec., it will be terrible. Never has time passed so slowly with me before. I just know that

Oct. will be about three months long. I expect Drs. T. & M. have been interesting you so much that you have thought seldom of me, but I think of you all the time, dear Mollie. Remember me to all at home. Also to the Toney family. Give the girls plenty of love from me. Tell Janie that if she lets anyone take away my sweetheart I will hold her personally responsible.

Good night. God bless you.

I love you with all my heart.

H."

The indefatigable Hamilton Weedon now sends letters by every available artery of communication, this time warning Mollie that he will be "marching up" College Hill in early November and she had better be ready for him. He's still worried about what is on her mother's mind:

Key West
Sept. 21st 1865

Dearest Mary,

Here I am again. Are you not most tired of getting letters from me? I wrote you a very long letter by way of New York, and one by way of Ft. Marks near Tallahassee, and expect you will get them, but a steamer goes tomorrow to New Orleans, and will probably touch at Apalachicola, so I thought I would write you today and set you a good example. I told you in my last letter that another Steamer would leave Apalachicola about the 1st. of Oct. so you must not fail to have a letter there for me. Send them by McKenzie or Mr. Scott and they will be forwarded to me. I have received but three letters from you. You said you had written four. How is that? Where did you send the others? I received two from Apalachicola and one from New Orleans. I can't afford to lose your letters - they are too scarce.

You will see me marching up that hill early in November next, so you must be prepared to meet me...

I see you are pleading "low water" now as an excuse. You must send at least three letters a month or be held personally responsible.

Make my kindest regards to all at home. Tell your mother to be sure and send that note by the first chance. I turn pale whenever I think of it.

Sister sends love to you.

Goodbye - Yours entirely,

H.

At long last, Hamilton is overjoyed to finally receive Mollie's letter of September 4, containing the long-sought authorization that he be "on hand" in Eufaula in early December. In fact, so there will be no confusion, (or perhaps in an effort to make the agreement airtight), Hamilton recites his understanding of what the letter told him he could do. Irrepressible, he

411

immediately exceeds his authority by planning to depart in early November, and starts negotiating for an earlier wedding date:

"Sept. 26, 1865

"Dear Mollie,

The *"Linda"* arrived last evening from Apalachicola. I stood on the wharf waiting for her arrival hoping, yet doubting. Three letters were sent ashore - none for me. Oh, how I scolded you. I had been looking for her arrival so long. I never felt more disappointed in my life. In about an hour afterwards a gentleman called and left a letter saying that it was enclosed in one to him by a Mr. Scott of Apalachicola.

I thank you dear M. for it. It was a sweet little letter and it told me I could come so as to be there early in Dec. You may be sure I will be there in good time. I expect to start from here in early Nov. and maybe you will agree to be a very good girl and not even wait for the 1st of Dec. Now will you do it if I am extraordinarily good? Tell Addie she must hurry up that lucky man, and we will all go to glory together. I don't thank you for saying you thought I had fallen in love with some Kentucky girl, a northerner. You knew that was not so. But wait - I will have revenge.

Tell Ada that my buggy has a high back - very high - no probability of falling out - Let not her heart be troubled, but I want some good carpenter to go immediately to work on the church steps. It grieves me to think that my very good friend, one I thought so very pious, and one upon whom purity sat so well, should fall. How did she slide? back or sidewise? Give her plenty of love from me. Tell her not to despair. To get up and try it again. The stepping stones to grace are always slipping. Tell her she will find greater consolation in the Pilgrim's Progress.

The *"Linda"* will be in Apalachicola again in about twelve days. Be sure to have a half doz. letters there for me.

Remember me most kindly to all
A great deal of love
Yours   H.

Sister sends love to you.
I hope your mother is better

This is the last surviving letter of the series. Hamilton did not succeed in having the wedding held earlier than December. It was on December 19, 1865, that the Rev. William Shapard pronounced them man and wife.[704] The ceremony was performed at Fendall Hall,[705] and the festive celebration which undoubtedly followed provided the family and Eufaula with a happy and welcome diversion from the gloom and depression of defeat constantly hanging over the community.

If Mollie and Hamilton went to Key West, they did not remain long. They soon made their home in Eufaula, as Mollie and her mother had intended all along.

Edward Young had begun the practice of carving out lots from the land upon which Fendall Hall was located, to provide homes for his children as they married. Hubert and Anna lived in such a house near Fendall Hall, and now Edward provided a lot for Mollie and Hamilton, which became the site of their first marital home. [706]

In July 1868, Hamilton went into the pharmacy business with George Hatch Dent,[707] Hubert Dent's younger brother. As we will later discuss, George moved to Eufaula from Maryland, and would marry Helen Young, the sister of Mollie and Anna. Their drugstore, located on Broad Street, was known as "Weedon and Dent," and would continue in successful operation for many years.

After several years of living in a "vine covered cottage" near Fendall Hall, in the 1870's, Hamilton and Mollie built a larger two story home on Barbour Street. Now known as the "Pappas-Jones-Wilbourne House," it still stands today, minus part of its second story, which burned and was not replaced. Here they would rear six children, (two others died in infancy), as follows:

Anna Young Weedon, born in 1867, and married John Robert Barr, a Eufaula shoe merchant, in 1887;

Mary Norma Weedon, who was called "Noonie" by her family, born in 1868, married James LeGrand Ross, a hardware merchant of Eufaula, in 1888, and died in 1933;

Hamilton Moore Weedon, Jr., born 1869, followed the example of his father and grandfather by becoming a physician. He graduated from medical school in Mobile, and studied further at the Polyclinic, in New York. In 1889, he married Julia Henderson of Troy Alabama, where they settled and where he practiced medicine. He died about 1910;

Edward Beall Weedon, born in 1871, was employed in the Weedon and Dent pharmacy and took over the operation of the store in 1897. He married Mary Garland in 1891, and died in 1953;

Walter Roy Weedon; born in 1874, and died around 1920;

Frederick Weedon, born 1875, and died in infancy;

William Weedon, born 1877, and died in infancy;

Herbert G. Weedon, born 1879.

Despite the somewhat temperamental letters we have seen from Mollie, the evidence suggests that she and Hamilton settled into a happy and loving marriage. Among their papers is found the following note, dated December 19, 1879, addressed to "Dr. Hamilton M. Weedon, At Home:"

"To the one I love Best"
"On this the 14th anniversary of our marriage, added to the dressing
case I give the pen rack, paper cutter, and gold pen. The pen I wish you to keep

in your pocket, and write with all the time, and every time you use it think of one who loves you dearly. Yours affectionately, Mollie"

As we have seen from his early letters to Mollie, Hamilton Weedon was a personable man of some erudition. His writing reflects wit and polish. In person he was an entertaining companion who "was a delight to associate with." As a physician, he inspired confidence. Urbane and competent, he has been described as "a Chesterfield."[708] Over the years, Hamilton, like all of Edward Young's sons-in-law, took an active role in community affairs. In the 1880's, we find him serving as a member of the Board of trustees of the city school system and the city council. Later, he served on the board of directors of the Eufaula Library Society. [709]

Mollie was not to enjoy a long life. After 26 years of marriage, she died in 1891 at the age of 49. Hamilton was then 57.

In 1895, at the age of 61, Hamilton married Bessie Fannin. Originally from Raleigh, North Carolina, Bessie was teaching art at Alabama Brenau College, the Eufaula successor to the Union Female College. The couple moved to Spartanburg, South Carolina, and had one child, Fannin Weedon. [710]

Hamilton's second wife had died and he had moved back to Eufaula at the time of his death in 1908 at the age of 74. In death, he would return to his original love. He is buried beside Mollie in the Young family plot at Fairview Cemetery in Eufaula. Like all Confederate veterans, his headstone carries the name of his military unit: "H.M. Weedon, 4 Fla. Inf. CSA."

Dr. Hamilton Moore Weedon, husband of Molly Young

Barbour Street home of Molly and Hamilton Weedon as it appears today. Built in the early 1870's, it had a second storey which burned after their deaths and was not replaced. Its parlors had wall murals by L. F. Liefrank, as did the nearby homes of Molly's' sisters, Helen (Mrs. George H.) Dent and Anna (Mrs. Hubert) Dent at Fendall Hall.

Part IV

Reconstruction and Redemption

46
The Ineligible Mayor,
Or,
Starting Anew Under Radical Reconstruction

"To the Mayor of Eufaula, Alabama [Stouten H. Dent]: An election was held in your city on the 28th of March [1867], being in violation of General orders...is null and void..."

Maj. Gen. Roger Swayne, Military Governor, District of Alabama and
Director, Alabama Freedmen's Bureau

The terms of surrender agreed to at Meridian between Gen. Taylor for the Confederates and Gen. Canby for the Union, allowed the paroled Confederate officers to keep their privately-owned horses. This would turn out to be an important provision for former artillery Captain Hubert Dent, who owned two horses. Leaving Meridian after taking the required oath on May 9, 1865, Hubert traveled with his two horses across the devastated South for nine days, having no idea what he would find upon reaching Eufaula. He arrived there on May 18 to a joyous homecoming. After a happy reunion with Anna and Eddie, and with all his Young "in-laws," Hubert looked around to assess the situation of himself, his family, and community.

Eufaula had escaped the physical destruction and burning suffered at the hands of Wilson and Sherman by so much of the lower South, including nearby Columbus, Montgomery, Selma, and most of central Georgia. But the business and agricultural economy of Eufaula was completely destroyed. There was no civil government in effect, there was no legal or court system in operation, and there was little or no legally negotiable currency in circulation. The flower of its youth were in unknown graves. The ragged remnants of glamorous military units which had been sent off with so much optimism and hope four years earlier, were now slowly drifting home, a few at a time, hungry, dispirited, and of course penniless. They were finding the homefront not much better off.

Edward Young's financial standing was undoubtedly damaged severely by the defeat of the Confederacy. The Union blockade had brought to a close his cotton factoring, financing, and warehousing businesses, as well as his mercantile commission business and store. His banking firm of Young, Woods and Garner was based principally upon Confederate currency and Confederate securities, now worthless. However, although Edward suffered financially from the defeat, he was not rendered destitute. He still retained assets. The family still occupied Fendall Hall. One of his assets that we know of was 3200 acres of fertile farmland well-located near the Union Pacific Railroad in the Platte River valley of Nebraska. Purchased during the war, probably upon favorable terms, its value would only rise as a result of the war's end and Nebraska's approaching statehood two years later. This and other assets, together with Edward's native entrepreneurial acumen, would see the family through these difficult days and would contribute to his business recovery. In the meantime, he had a large, personable family, most of whom enjoyed good health, whom he continued to support comfortably in Fendall Hall. Let us briefly review the Young family at the close of the Civil War:

Edward was 63 and in good health. He would live for many years to come and be active in business and banking until he died. Ann was 55 years old, but suffered from a debilitating arthritic condition. In April of 1863, Ann was stricken with what was described as "rheumatism," and by October of 1864, its intensity had progressed to the point that she "had lost the power to walk." Thereafter, "she became as helpless as a child" till her death [in 1876]. She spent over thirteen years of pain and intense agony.[711]

Will, the oldest son, was 32, and still operated his foundry, the Eufaula Iron Works, though that business would never be as profitable as it had been with its wartime contracts with the Columbus Naval Iron Works. Will and his wife, Annie Maria Hewlett, had one son, Charlie, now 9 years old.

Henry, the second son, had been killed two years before, on February 19, 1863 at Chunkey Bridge, Mississippi, leaving his wife, Maria Marshall McRae, a son, Henry Augustus, Jr., now four, and a daughter, Julia, now 3.

Anna, the oldest daughter, was now 25 and grateful for the safe return of her Hubert, 31, who, incredibly, had survived four years of being at the very epicenter of the most deadly fights of the Civil War. Their son Eddie was now four.

Mollie, the second daughter, age 23, married Dr. Hamilton Weedon in December, 1865, and they set up housekeeping near Fendall hall.

None of the remaining five Young children was yet married. They were:
Ada, the third daughter, 19;
Helen, sometimes called "Ollie," 18;
Ed, the youngest son, 16; and
Carrie, the youngest child, 10.

Hubert Dent's first priority upon arriving at home was to find a way to support Anna and his son. We have seen that, as a Confederate soldier at the battlefront, he could accept his affluent father-in-law's financial assistance to Anna. But now it was time for him to resume his duty as breadwinner, and if that required manual labor, then that's what he would do. Returning soldiers in Barbour County and throughout the South, finding themselves in far worse poverty than that of Hubert Dent, were resorting to the most menial work to eke out a living for their families.

Hubert had been a lawyer and had left a successful practice to fight for the Confederacy, but that profession could not put food on his table now. There was no court system or any legal system in operation. Indeed, there was no government. The only property Hubert owned was his two horses, and they became the means of his livelihood. He began the operation of a drayage service. With his two horses and a dray, or wagon, he would haul for pay bales of cotton, lumber, merchandise, or any other heavy load a customer might need moved. In this way former Captain Dent earned his first post-war dollar, and provided sustenance for his wife and child.[712]

Conditions of devastation and economic collapse across the former Confederacy cried out for farsighted national statesmanship, for programs of economic and social recovery, for a reduction of sectional hate, and a forbearance of maneuvering for sectional economic and political advantage. Such an enlightened policy was foreshadowed by Abraham Lincoln in his second inaugural address on March 4, 1865: "With malice toward none; with charity toward all; with firmness in the right…let us strive to finish the work we are in; to bind up the nation's wounds…to do all which may achieve and cherish a just and lasting peace among ourselves…"

Lincoln's conciliatory policy was based upon his constitutional view that, because secession had been illegal and void, the Southern states were still states of the union. In Lincoln's view, although the majority of Southerners had committed treason, they should be allowed to start anew - to participate in forming new state governments - if they were willing to take the prescribed oath of allegiance, thereby earning a presidential pardon and creating a "loyal electorate." This "loyal electorate" could then establish a new state government in the usual three-step way: the election of a constitutional convention, the adoption of the proposed constitution, and the election of state and Federal officers under the new state constitution. As early as December 1863, Lincoln had already begun carrying out this liberal policy by proclamation in Southern states then under control of the federal army: Tennessee, Louisiana, and Arkansas. Lincoln had pardoned all former Confederates (except certain limited classes) upon their taking the oath to be loyal in the future and to accept the new laws regarding slavery. Lincoln was moving toward an even more generous policy when the war closed.

But Lincoln's magnanimous approach was opposed by a wing of his Republican Party, "the Radicals," who felt that the authority to "reconstruct" the states should reside in Congress and not the President. The Radicals were led in the House of Representatives by Thaddeus Stevens of Pennsylvania, and in the Senate by Charles Sumner of Massachusetts. They advocated immediate political and social equality between whites and recently-freed slaves in the South (a policy which had the effect of maintaining the Radicals in political power for years to come). They also pressed (although unsuccessfully) for confiscation of the property of Confederate supporters, in order to provide "40 acres and a mule" and other benefits to the freed slaves. The Radicals felt that the South could be dealt with as conquered provinces and that Southern whites were no longer protected by United States constitution.

If Lincoln had lived, perhaps his political skills, prestige, and wisdom would have carried the day, and his far-sighted reconstruction policies might have been implemented. But John Wilkes Booth's bullet eliminated that outcome. Lincoln's successor, Andrew Johnson, attempted with loyalty and determination to carry out Lincoln's statesman-like plan, but he simply did not have the stature or political ability to successfully oppose the vindictive and strong-willed Radicals.

Ironically, with the death of Lincoln, the Republican Radicals found themselves opposed by a president who was both a Southerner and a Democrat. Andrew Johnson was a tailor who became wealthy and owned slaves, but had been a strongly pro-Union senator from Tennessee. He was a resident of Greeneville, in the mountains of East Tennessee, a section that had few slaves and was intensely anti-secession in its politics.[y] In the election of 1864, Lincoln had chosen Johnson as his vice-presidential running mate, to add a bipartisan coalition flavor to his campaign to be reelected for a second term. Now Johnson was in the White House.

Eufaulians and other Alabamians soon found themselves whipsawed in the struggle between the competing views of President Johnson and the Congressional Radicals over reconstruction policy. Soon after his accession, Johnson issued his Proclamation of Amnesty and Reconstruction, which substantially adopted Lincoln's plan. Alabama and the other Southern states proceeded to act to comply with this proclamation.

On June 21, 1865, a month after Hubert Dent arrived home after surrendering in Meridian, President Johnson appointed then-moderate Lewis Parsons as provisional governor of Alabama. Military officers toured the state, administering the oath to "support, protect and defend, the constitution of the United States," thereby creating a "loyal electorate," as Lincoln had contemplated. On August 31, these Alabamians elected delegates to a constitutional convention, which thereafter adopted a constitution which met all the requirements of Johnson's reconstruction proclamation. In November, elections for governor, legislature, and county officials were held. Robert M. Patton, another moderate, was elected governor, and was approved to take office by President Johnson on December 20. As required by the president, the legislature ratified the Thirteenth Amendment, formally prohibiting slavery.

In Eufaula, as some degree of stability returned to the legal system, Hubert Dent was able to give up his drayage service, hang out his "shingle", and begin to build a law practice, from which he supported Anna and Eddie. He was soon to have a new mouth to feed. On April 8, 1867, Anna delivered their second child, a daughter, named Anna Beall Dent (who came to be called "Nannie," the pet name given her mother by her father). She was baptized on June 30, 1867 by the Rev. William Shapard (who had married Mollie and Hamilton Weedon a year and a half earlier). We will here anticipate events and list the six children that Anna and Hubert will have:

---

[y] Across from Andrew Johnson's home on Main Street in Greeneville lived his friends, James and Elizabeth McDowell, and their two sons, James, Jr. and Charles. The wedding suit worn by James, Sr when he and Elizabeth were married was made by Andrew Johnson, the tailor, before he became a political leader. When the secession crisis came, James McDowell joined with his friends in the "Greeneville Convention" to try to head off secession. But when secession occurred, the McDowells broke with their friends and strongly supported the South. James' sons, James Jr. and Charles fought for the Confederacy. After the defeat, the McDowells migrated south, ultimately settling in Eufaula, Alabama around 1870. James called on President Johnson at the White House while Johnson was still in control of reconstruction, and was given a pardon. The President picked up a crystal paperweight on his desk and gave it to James as a memento of their old friendship, which remains in the McDowell family today. In Eufaula, the McDowells became a part of the story of the Youngs when, in 1901, Edward Young's granddaughter (Hubert and Anna's daughter), Caroline Dent, married James McDowell's grandson, Charlie, Jr.

Edward Young Dent, born 1861, married Annie McCormick 1889, died, 1946;

Anna Beall Dent, born 1867, married Jackson Edward Long, 1887; married William W. Mangum, 1904, died 1963;

Hubert Warren Dent (who later changed his name to Stanley Hubert Dent), born 1869, married Etta Tinsley, 1897, died 1938;

Henry Augustus Dent, born 1872, married Etta Copeland McCormick, 1931, died, 1971;

Kate Louise Dent, born 1875, married George N. Hurt 1895, died, 1959.

Caroline ("Carrie") Dent, born 1879, married Charles S. McDowell, Jr, 1902, died, 1966.

The current mayor of Eufaula, C. J. Pope, had taken office in March 1865, and the federal troops under Gen. Grierson had entered the town the following month. Now, in March of 1867, Eufaula proceeded to hold its first postwar municipal election of a mayor and city council. By this time, Hubert Dent was building a busy law practice. As one of many returning war heroes, he was being thrust into positions of community leadership in the new and difficult circumstances. Hubert was now asked to stand for mayor, and on March 16, 1867, he was elected as Eufaula's first postwar mayor, along with eight city council members.[713]

At the City Council meeting of March 18, Hubert came forward and took the oath of office while the old council retired and the new council began transacting business. Unfortunately, Hubert and most of his new city council would not be allowed to serve their terms. The Radical-controlled Congress passed far-reaching new legislation, which would have disastrous consequences for the recovery of the prostrate South.

On March 2, 1867, two weeks before Eufaula conducted its municipal elections under President Johnson's conciliatory policy, the Radical-controlled Congress passed the "Military Reconstruction Act," followed by three other Reconstruction Acts.[z] These Acts voided the state governments that had been set up under the Lincoln-Johnson proclamations and declared them illegal. The South was to be administered for an indefinite time by military occupation governors. Military rule was supreme. The question of whether to permit any civil government at all was discretionary with the military governors, and any civil government permitted was subordinate to the military governors. For this purpose, the South was divided into five military districts. Major General John Pope took command of the Third Military

---

[z] In March 1866, over Johnson's veto, Congress had passed the Civil Rights Act, which sought to confer the vote on blacks, and had enacted the Freedmen's Bureau Act, also over Johnson's veto. A Joint Committee on Reconstruction concluded that Southerners could offer "no evidence whatever of repentance for their crime." In the 1866 congressional elections (from which the Southern states were excluded) the Radicals obtained a "veto-proof" majority, which enabled them to eventually exclude President Johnson from the reconstruction process entirely.

District, consisting of Florida, Georgia, and Alabama. Maj. Gen. Wager Swayne was military governor of the District of Alabama and head of the Alabama Freedmen's Bureau.

The new acts set out stringent conditions which each former Confederate state must meet before it could be considered for the restoration of its representation in Congress. These included the adoption of a new constitution meeting certain requirements. But perhaps the most drastic and self-serving feature of the Radical measure was in who was excluded from public life.

The acts provided that no one could be allowed to vote, either on the new constitution or in any other election, and could not hold state or federal office, if he had voluntarily participated in the civil war against the United States. To vote or hold office, every man had to be able to take the "iron clad test oath" that he had not so participated. Because the Radicals claimed the former Confederate soldiers might lie about their service, the military registrars were given the discretion to inquire behind the oaths, and refuse to register those who were in the military registrar's opinion disqualified for having participated in rebellion.

The old "loyal electorate" registration lists compiled under President Johnson's reconstruction plan, requiring only an oath of future allegiance, were thrown out, and the military governors were given the duty of conducting a new registration process, to include all freedmen over 21 years, and such whites as could swear to the new "iron clad test oath" of having never voluntarily participated in the civil war.

When Eufaula held its municipal elections and elected Hubert Dent mayor on March 16, 1867, the military authorities had not yet carried out the new registration process, and Eufaula had undoubtedly used voting rolls established under the terms of President Johnson's reconstruction orders. In compliance with military orders, the results of this election were duly reported to the federal military authorities. Thereafter, at the city council meeting of May 28, Mayor Hubert Dent reported receipt of the following letter from Alabama's military governor:[714]

> "Headquarters, District of Alabama
> Montgomery, Alabama
>
> May 16, 1867
> To The Mayor of Eufaula, Alabama
>
> Sir:
> An election was held in your city on the 28th March for municipal officers, being in violation of General orders.
> The election is null and void but those persons now acting who can subscribe to the enclosed oath will be probably retained in their positions.
> You will therefore call on each municipal officer to subscribe thereto and forward the oath of those who can do so to these headquarters.

Very Respectfully,
Your Obedient Servant

Roger Swayne
Major General"

Dent and his council continued to meet and transact the city's business during June and part of July. However, yielding to the inevitable, at the July 16,1867 meeting, Dent made this announcement:

"His Honor [Mayor Hubert Dent] stated that an order had been received from the Military Headquarters of the District appointing Alderman G. M. McGinty mayor *vice* S. H. Dent; and Messrs. C. Rhodes, Henry Bernstein, and J. J. Carter alderman in lieu of himself [Dent], Aldermen Daniel and Collins, who were disqualified in consequence of being unable to take the necessary oath. Alderman McGinty came forward and took the oath of office and assumed the duties of Mayor. [The newly-appointed aldermen] then came forward and were duly installed…On motion, all standing committees were declared dissolved…"

The oath referred to by Maj. Gen. Swayne's correspondence is not today available in the records of the council minutes, and one Eufaula historian has guessed, incorrectly, that Dent and the aldermen were unwilling to pledge to support the Constitution and the laws of Congress. If that were all that was required, there would have been no problem at all. Like most Confederate soldiers, Hubert had accepted the results of the war and had already taken that oath at the time of his parole in Meridian in May 1865. But to take the new, "iron clad test oath" requiring him to swear that he had never voluntarily borne arms against the United States, would have been perjury, which Dent was unwilling to commit.

Using this requirement and their almost unlimited discretion under the new Radical reconstruction acts, the military governors began wholesale removals of white Southerners from offices throughout the South. They removed thousands of elective officers, from county clerks to governors. They suppressed newspapers, jailed editors for criticizing reconstruction, prohibited public meetings, stopped court proceedings, dismissed juries, and required all jurors to take the ironclad test oath which excluded former Confederates. In some instances they enacted laws, levied taxes, and made appropriations from the public treasuries. Using the new registration rolls, each seceding state was required to adopt a new constitution, which must contain these same suffrage requirements and exclusions, and to ratify the Fourteenth Amendment, following which Congress would decide whether the state's representation in Congress would be restored.

The new registration system assured that the Republicans would win all the elections in the Southern states. In October 1867, when General Pope finished the process of registering the blacks and deciding which whites were eligible under the iron clad test oath, the Alabama voting rolls contained 61,295 whites and 104,418 blacks.[715] This, even though the next census showed that whites outnumbered blacks 520,000 to 475,000.

In Barbour County, Alabama, Gen. Pope's soldiers registered only 773 white men out of the 2,867 white men in the county. Radical control of the county was assured.[716]

Many of the vacancies created by the removal of white Southerners were filled by "carpetbaggers" and "scalawags." Carpetbaggers were Northerners who had come south after the war owning nothing but the clothes in their carpetbags. While some were perhaps sincerely seeking to help blacks, most were regarded by the Southern whites as self-seeking adventurers who were out to pick the bones of the defeated South for whatever profit might be available. "Scalawags" were native white Southerners who cooperated with the carpetbaggers to carry out Radical rule. While perhaps some were conscientious in their support of the Radicals, most scalawags were regarded as traitors to the South who were taking advantage of an opportunity to share in the plunder and power of Radical rule.

The Radicals' needed the votes of the Southern states to keep them in control of Congress, as well as to elect a president, in the upcoming 1868 elections. Alabama ultimately complied with the entire Radicals' requirements; its Constitution of 1868 was declared accepted; and its representation in Congress was restored. Its new congressional delegation, all Republicans, was seated in July 1868.

One of Alabama's new senators, George E. Spencer, was a New Yorker who had lived for a time in Iowa and then served in the Union Army. He remained in Alabama after the surrender in 1865 to see what opportunities he might take advantage of. He found plenty. Even the most sympathetic modern historians describe Spencer as "the champion of chicanery."[717] We will presently see how he fully justified this title in matters directly affecting Barbour County and Hubert Dent.

The other Alabama senator, an Ohioan, was also a former Union soldier who had come to Alabama in 1867, only months before being made Alabama's Senator. Of the six-man house delegation, five had arrived in the state since the war, five were Republicans, and four were recent agents of the Freedmen's Bureau. Under any definition of the newly coined term, Alabama's Senators and Congressmen were "carpetbaggers." The new governor, William Hugh Smith, was an Alabamian who had opposed secession, had "entered Confederate Service and then deserted," and had eventually crossed over into federal lines until the war was over. He met the definition of a "scalawag."

Under this system, Alabama would remain under military occupation for eleven years, and the Republican Party would be continually perpetuated in power until 1874.

The effect of the defeat and reconstruction on Edward Young's plantation-owning friends and business customers is illustrated by the experience of Edward's longtime friend, John Horry Dent (who, it will be recalled, is not related to Edward's son-in-law, Hubert Dent.) John Horry had been one of Barbour County's wealthy and successful plantation owners. He was loyal to the Confederacy, although he had realistic doubts about whether it could succeed. His two sons had served in the Confederate army, one of whom, Horry, had died. Dent had reluctantly served two years as a member of the unpopular local Confederate conscription bureau; he had invested $44,000 in Confederate and state bonds. It is estimated that the defeat cost John Horry Dent at least three fourths of his net worth, but even at that, he was still well off at war's end. Following the surrender in April 1865, Dent's slaves did not immediately leave his plantation, Bleak House, but stayed to gather the 1865 crop. By Christmas, all of his slaves had quit, and he was required to enter into employment contracts with them. He devised arrangements which appear to be a forerunner of "sharecropping." A third of the crop was paid to the hands, divided according to the amount of labor contributed by each. He provided housing and provisions, charging the cost thereof to each hand's share. Dent found the new arrangements to be wholly unsatisfactory. He could not hire enough labor to work his acreage, and those he hired would not work with the diligence he expected and was accustomed to. In disgust, he made the decision to abandon large-scale planting entirely. In 1866, he precipitously sold his 1280 acre plantation and departed from Barbour County, leaving his friends of thirty years, the Youngs, Catos, McNabs, Pughs, Shorters, Bullocks and others. He immediately bought a smaller "farm" of 400 acres in Cave Springs, Georgia, near Rome, which he named "Cottage Home."[718] But as we will see, Edward Young would stay in touch with his old friend and business customer.

Hubert's younger brother, George Hatch Dent, the First Sergeant of Dent's Battery, had been paroled in Meridian, Mississippi at the same time as Hubert, on May 9, 1865. He had then made his way back to Charles County Maryland, where his father, his stepmother, his brother Warren, and his sisters still resided. After spending a period of time with his family there, however, he decided to follow Hubert's example and seek opportunities in Eufaula, Alabama.

George moved to Eufaula in about 1868, when he was 25 years old. At this time, Mollie and Hamilton Weedon had recently established their household there and Hamilton was practicing medicine. George and Hamilton became acquainted, undoubtedly through the family connection with Hubert. The two men apparently found themselves congenial, because they soon decided to form a partnership to go into the pharmacy business together.

In July 1868, the two future brothers-in-law opened a drugstore under the name of Weedon and Dent. It was located at 179 Broad Street, adjacent to Edward Young's banking and business offices, and consisted of a three-story building, 28 by 85 feet in size. Dr. Weedon continued practicing medicine for a time, but soon retired from that profession to devote his energies to the pharmacy business. This business, which we will discuss more later, would operate successfully for over fifty years, into succeeding generations.

For the general elections of November 1868, the Radical Republicans nominated Ulysses Grant for president, who strongly supported the Radicals' reconstruction policy. The Democrats nominated Horatio Seymour, war governor of New York, who ran on a platform which scathingly denounced the Radical reconstruction policies. Throughout Alabama, "Democratic and Conservative Clubs" (the official name of the Democratic Party during this era) were formed to support the Democratic ticket and platform. Such a club was formed in Eufaula, and its membership included Edward Young, as well as his son and sons-in-law. They all signed the public resolutions denouncing the Radicals in the most scathing terms:

> "Whereas, in the present political situation of the Southern States, we see the wicked workings of a depraved and corrupt party destroying the freedom of the press and the liberty of the person; agitating the public peace and quiet, paralyzing the business enterprise of the people… inflicting upon a brave and chivalrous people, who in war, were worthy to be the enemies of the most warlike race on earth, the most infamous, degrading, and tyrannical legislation for their humiliation and government; and…
>
> Whereas…wincing under the injustice and tyranny of the Radical party, now ruling the country, and believing it our bounded duty to oppose with unbroken ranks an administration which has already well nigh driven us to despair, be it
>
> Resolved, 1st, That we, the Democratic and Conservative Club of the city of Eufaula, in view of the danger to the constitutional rights of all the States being overturned by the intrigues of a party, seeking nothing but power, place, and spoils, and after calm and anxious consideration, Do Determine To Give Our Firm, United, and Enthusiastic Support to the Platform and To the Nominee of the National Democratic Party which assembled in New York on the 4th Inst…" [719]

Among the many Eufaulians signing this call to action were "E. B. Young, Sr."; his son, Edward Billups Young (usually called E. B. Young, Jr., or "Ed"); his son-in-law, Hubert Dent; and his son-in-law Dr. Hamilton Weedon. Ironically, Ed was the only one of these four who could take the ironclad test oath required of a voter, and at age 19, he was not old enough to vote. Also signing the resolution were Noah W. Roberts, who in a few years would marry Caroline Young, and J.G.L. Martin, Ada Young's future father-in-law. Despite this strong support by Southerners, the Democrats were defeated, and Ulysses Grant became president.

In these post-war years, in addition to his banking business, Edward Young resumed dealing in cotton to some extent, although cotton factoring did not become his main business activity as in the decades before the war. Surviving business papers during this period reflect his continued commercial activity. We see receipts for business taxes paid to the City of Eufaula on January 30, 1867 in the amount of $249, and income taxes paid to the United States Internal Revenue on April 15, 1867. In 1868, we find Edward paying Federal excise taxes on a carriage, a sure indicator of prosperity.

On April 3, 1867, Edward conveyed complete ownership of Fendall Hall to his wife, Ann, together with the ten acres upon which it was located. The deed recites that Edward was "not…indebted to any person," and that he wished "to place her in a situation that she may always have a home, so as to protect and sustain her." And here began a tradition of female ownership of Fendall Hall. Although not planned, it happened that Fendall Hall was owned by

Ann or a female descendant of Ann's in each of five generations for over 100 years. To briefly look ahead in our story, the successive owners after Ann and Edward were:

Ann's daughter, Anna Beall Young Dent;
Anna's daughter, Louise Dent Hurt; and
Louise's daughter, Mary Maude McCullohs, who, with her sons, conveyed the property to the Alabama Historical Commission in 1972.

When the time came for Ann and Edward's youngest son, Edward Billups, to pursue his higher education, he elected to attend the University of Georgia. Edward was undoubtedly looking forward to having another son join him in the business, and Ed knew there was a place for him in his father's bank. When Ed was a college junior, after three years at the University of Georgia, he returned home and started out as a "runner" in his father's banking business.[720] Ed was back in Eufaula by 1869, when he was 20 years old.

During this period, Edward was making sales from his Nebraska lands. In 1862, the U. S. Congress had passed the Homestead Act, which made 160 acres of public land available free to settlers who would occupy it for five years. This act probably temporarily dampened to some extent the potential profit available in private land transactions, but it greatly stimulated the settlement of Nebraska. In 1862, Congress had also enacted the Union Pacific Railroad Act, which resulted in the arrival of the railroad in Nebraska in 1867, and in that year the Territory achieved Statehood. These circumstances all contributed to a rush of settlers into the area, which could only improve the value of the 3200 well-located acres which Edward had purchased from Eli Shorter under wartime conditions, probably at a favorable price.

Although Eli had sold 3200 acres of his Nebraska lands to Edward Young in 1861, Shorter still retained for himself ownership of substantial amounts of land there. In October of 1869, Eli Shorter made a trip to Nebraska to see his land and assess the prospects for Nebraska. Writing from Fremont in the Platte Valley, the same area where Edward's lands were also located, Shorter reported to the readers of the *Bluff City Times* of October 28, 1869:

"The land [of the Platte River Valley] is all rich and produces corn, wheat, oats, and potatoes in great luxuriance. Not many years will pass before the Platte Valley will be filled with people…Lands in the Valley, as far as Columbus and some miles beyond are held from $8 to $15 per acre according to the proximity of the railroad."

By comparison, with the advent of emancipation, property values in the plantation districts of the South plummeted. When John Horry Dent sold his Barbour County "Bleak House" plantation in 1866, he received only $8 per acre, and within a year, with the onset of Radical Reconstruction policies, its value had further declined to less than $2 per acre. [721]

In 1869, Edward contracted to sell 1000 acres of his Nebraska lands to one J. L. Dunhams of Columbus, Georgia. Dunhams had previously had business matters with

Edward's brother, William, in Columbus. Dunhams paid Edward for the land, in large part, by giving him an interest-bearing note secured by a mortgage on the Nebraska land. It was apparently contemplated that, as the property or portions of it were re-sold by a real estate agent in Fremont, Dunhams' debt to Edward would be paid from the proceeds of these sales. But Edward protected his own position by requiring that Dunhams' obligation to pay interest to Edward commence immediately, and continued regardless of when or whether Dunhams was able to resell the property. In the following letter,[722] Dunhams is complaining about this interest burden. Also, we see that he is anxious to keep lawyers for his creditors from learning of this transaction. (Some things never change.) The letter also reflects that Ed was beginning to assume responsibilities in his father's business affairs, and that Edward was also placing reliance on his lawyer son-in-law, "Captain Dent," [by which title Hubert would be known for the rest of his life]:

"Columbus [Georgia], June 11, 1869

"E. B. Young, Esq.
Eufaula, Ala.

"Sir,

I have your 10th and note the instructions left with Capt. D. and Ed, which are satisfactory, but I am very anxious to know those sent to your agent at Fremont, so far as my interest is concerned, so I may then better determine at what time he will likely sell, and I may know when this abominable interest I am paying will stop.

Please caution Capt. D. and Ed. not to admit I have any interest in these lands, but if interrogated by anyone, to treat the matter as if the trade had been closed out long ago and settlement made. Your Bro. [William Young] and myself have kept my affairs very confidential here, and I trust you and your agents will do likewise in Eufaula, as the least clue to the facts would give me trouble with lawyers here, which by the same prudence and management on the part of your agents would prevent. Let them read the above and all will be well.

I note you have sold your cotton and know your mind is relieved and I am glad of it.

Many thanks for card and much happiness to the young couple. I am too old to appreciate such events now. I suppose you will be quite busy until you get away.

Yours truly
J. L. Dunhams"

Mr. Dunhams' wishes for "happiness to the young couple" refer to another wedding which was about to take place one week later in Fendall Hall. George Dent's moving to Eufaula was not the only way in which he followed the example of his older brother. He

427

began courting Hubert's sister-in-law, Anna's younger sister, Helen, age 22. His suit was successful, and within a year of his arrival in Eufaula, George and Helen were married. The wedding was held at Fendall Hall on June 17, 1869, and the service was performed by the Rev. A. J. Briggs.[723] Like Anna and Hubert, and Mollie and Hamilton, they began married life in a house built on a lot carved out of the Fendall Hall grounds and given to them by Ann and Edward Young.[724]

As the two Beall sisters, Ann and Ellen, had married the two Young brothers, Edward and William, we now have two Young girls, Anna and Helen, married to the two Dent brothers, Hubert and George. The children of these two doubly related Dent couples called themselves "double first cousins." To again anticipate events, the five children that George and Helen will have are:

Warren Young Dent, born 1870, married Elizabeth Rhodes 1894, died 1927
Nellie Beall Dent, born 1872, married William Humphrey Foy 1892
George H. Dent, Jr., born 1874, married Mary Harralson 1894, died 1943
Helen Augusta Dent, born 1886, married Wesley Clark Williams, 1906, died 1972
Louie Dent, born 1874, married Genevieve Lockwood, 1896

Hamilton Weedon had once written to Mollie that, "Greenbacks are the only things peculiar to the Yankees that I don't despise." The business of Weedon & Dent was now beginning to earn copious amounts of greenbacks. The two brothers-in-law were believers in the power of advertising, and each issue of the *Bluff City Times* contained extensive descriptions of the diverse products carried by their well-stocked drugstore. In the *Times* of June 3, 1869, the editor calls attention to their store, still referring to it as "new," although it had opened the year before.

> "New drug store. Messrs. Weedon and Dent call attention to their large selection of fresh and pure drugs, which they offer at such reduced prices as will challenge comparison with the markets of Savannah and Charleston. Dr. Weedon is a regular practicing physician, and of course, thoroughly understands his business both of buying and compounding, and both he and Mr. Dent, as well as their clerks, will always be found attentive and obliging. Selling exclusively for cash, they give their customers the advantage of the interest of their money. ..."

In their ad of June 17, 1869 (the day upon which George and Helen were married) the firm gave the virtues of shopping at home:

> "Weedon and Dent
> Wholesale and Retail Druggists
> (Next door to Young and Woods Bank)
> Eufaula Alabama

"They have a complete and fresh stock of everything usually kept by druggists, and can and will sell at Savanna and Charleston prices. You will save nothing by purchasing in Columbus, Macon, or Atlanta. They buy and sell exclusively for cash, and their customers get the benefit of cash transactions. Give a call and be satisfied."

George and Hamilton's aggressive merchandising did not limit itself to the traditional sundries of a drugstore, as indicated by this advertisement in the *Times* of November 4, 1869: "Weedon & Dent, Solvable Pacific Guano. 80 tons of this most reliable standard manure just received at our depot in Eufaula, and 300 tons more to arrive shortly." This ad was run periodically over the next several years.

By 1869, Colin Gardner was no longer a member of Edward's banking firm, and it was called "Young and Woods Bank." In that year, Clayton R. Woods also withdrew from the partnership. Among Edward's papers we find a power of attorney dated October 15, 1869 given by Clayton R. Woods to his son, William Henry Woods, authorizing Henry to act for his father in dissolving the partnership. (We last saw William three years earlier, commanding the Eufaula Light Artillery alongside Dent's Battery in the Mobile breastworks in March 1865). Clayton Wood's age, as well as Edward's desire to enter into business with his youngest son, Ed, may have been among the factors precipitating this change. The business was thereafter known as "E. B. Young & Son Bankers."[725]

Edward's oldest son, Will [James William Young], was still aggressively conducting his foundry business, and was a frequent advertiser in the "*Bluff City Times*." In the issue of April 29, 1869, the *Times* editor mentions Will's business, and calls attention to his ad:

> "The Eufaula Iron Works, of which Captain J. W. Young is proprietor, are as good as any in the state. If you want any thing, from a four penny nail to a forty horse power steam engine, call the Captain—you'll find him a Generous upright clever gentleman, and everything of his manufacture of superior quality—see his advertisement."

In the postwar South, prominent citizens were often given military titles for the slightest excuse, or as a courtesy without any excuse at all. Will Young had never served in the military, but in the 1850's had been a steamboat captain for two years, which is presumably the origin of his title of "Captain." Will's newspaper advertisement gave a lengthy list of every possible metal product that he stood ready to manufacture:

> "Eufaula Ironworks, Manufacturer
> Steam Engines
> Boilers
> Circulars
> Saw Mills
> Sugar Mills
> Gin Gearings

Railing
Wing Gudgeons
Ovens, Spiders
Extra Lids
Sash Weights
Grate Bars
Ventilators, mill gearings, water wheels, whistles, hitching posts, columns, brackets, kettle, fire dogs, babbit metal
Tallow boxes.

"Iron and brass castings of every description made to order. Old cast iron bought or exchanged. All work at the risk of the purchaser when delivered to drays or boats. TERMS POSITIVELY CASH. For information apply to J. W. Young, Eufaula Alabama."

Will sometimes varied his ads: many issues of the *Times* during 1869 simply had single sentences scattered throughout the paper at the ends of articles, some of which were: "If you want railing go to the Eufaula Ironworks." "If you want a steam engine go to the Eufaula Ironworks." "If you want a sugar mill go to the Eufaula Ironworks," etc.

In this era, advertisements in the form of simple statements of professional services offered were customary among lawyers. Thus, Hubert Dent joined his brothers-in-law in the pages of the *Bluff City Times* to announce his availability as a lawyer. The issue of April 29, 1869, and each issue for several years, contained this "card":

"S. H. Dent
Attorney at Law
Eufaula, Alabama
"Will practice in all the counties of the Eighth Judicial Circuit and in the Supreme Court of Alabama. Is also prepared to represent petitioners in bankruptcy."

Hubert's "shingle" from this period is reproduced below:

Six months after George and Helen married, still another of Edward and Ann's daughters was married: Ada Louise, age 23. On December 23, 1869, two days before Christmas, the Rev. Briggs performed his second wedding of the year in Fendall Hall when he joined Ada and James ("Jim") H. G. Martin in matrimony.[726] The Martins were old friends of the Youngs. James' father, J. G. L. Martin was a Frenchman who had also settled in Eufaula in the 1830's and had prospered in business. He and his partner had started with a store called "Martin and Couric." He later constructed the Chewalla House hotel, and engaged in insurance and other businesses. He had served as a middle-aged "minute man" with Edward Young in the Home Reserves during the Civil War. Before he became disqualified, J. G. L. Martin was serving as Treasurer of the City of Eufaula during the hard times immediately after the war, when it was difficult to find funds for city services. His son, James, at the age of 19 had enlisted as a real soldier in the Eufaula Rifles with Hubert Dent in 1861, and when the Rifles disbanded in 1862, James had reenlisted as sergeant of the Eufaula Light Artillery, along with Ada's brother, Henry Young. Ada and James would have only one child, who died in infancy. He was buried in the Young plot at Fairview Cemetery with the simple inscription, "Our Little Jimmie." James entered business as a real estate broker and cotton dealer, but later read law and was admitted to the bar. As we will later relate, he became active in the Democratic Party, and during the administration of Grover Cleveland, the first Democratic president elected after the Civil War, formed a law firm in Washington, D. C., Shelly and Martin. Later, he and Ada returned to live in Eufaula.

During the post-war years, there was a frantic rush to build railroads. One of the ways of raising the large amounts of capital needed for such ventures was to induce the state legislature to buy or guarantee bonds issued for the purpose, or to induce city or county governments, as well as private individuals, to invest directly in the projects. Some of the

431

worst scandals of Alabama's Reconstruction legislatures related to railroad grants or bond guarantees obtained by bribing the members of the legislature, with the proceeds being squandered through mismanagement, or simply stolen by friends of the carpetbag legislators.

Some of the railroad projects were honest and sound, however, and had the potential of bringing business and prosperity to the localities they served. Edward Young was very conscious of the commercial potential of increasing the railroads serving Eufaula. He had taken the lead in raising $300,000 in public and private subscriptions to bring the Southwestern Railroad from Georgia into Eufaula, and he continued on a selective basis to provide support to those railroad projects he felt were sound and beneficial to the community. On November 9, 1869, Edward attended a public meeting at town hall with other businessmen to hear a proposal by Col. Crenshaw of Greenville, Alabama to consider building a railroad from Eufaula to Greenville. Edward decided to support the project, and pursuant to resolutions proposed by John McNab, agreed to serve on a committee to raise subscriptions of $40,000 as Barbour County's share of the needed investment. Other business leaders on the subscription committee included Eli S. Shorter, John McNab, J. G. L. Martin, Reuben Kolb, Captain Tullis, J. T. Kendall, and G. A. Roberts (father of Noah, Carrie Young's future husband).[727]

Early in 1870, Hubert made a change in his law practice, and went into partnership with the respected James McClure Buford, under the firm name, "Buford and Dent." Buford was the younger brother of Eufaula lawyer and state senator, Major Jefferson Buford. His rank dated from wars with the Creek Indians in 1835-1836. It will be recalled that, in the decade of the 1850's, Jefferson Buford had been a member of the pro-secession group known as the Eufaula Regency, and in 1856 had left his Eufaula practice to lead a group of pro-Southern settlers to Kansas, at his own expense, to influence the slave vs. free state vote there. Returning to Barbour County, Jefferson had died in 1862. His younger brother, James McClure Buford, had graduated from college at Columbia, S. C. in 1850 and attended law school in New Orleans. He was admitted to the Alabama bar in 1852, and while practicing law in Eufaula also served as editor of the Eufaula Regency newspaper organ, *Spirit of the South*, which later became *The Eufaula News*.[728]

Commenting on the new law partnership, the editor of the *Times,* in the issue of January 27, 1870, said:

> "New law firm. As will be seen from their card, Messrs. J. M. Buford and S. H. Dent have formed a co-partnership for the practice of their profession. If they have been forced to this because their individual practice is more than any one man can do, it is certainly not more than they deserve. They may be unable to 'get blood out of a turnip' but they can get money for their clients from pockets where none is generally supposed to have been."

The new advertisement simply announced: "Buford and Dent. Office on the south side of Broad Street, over E. W. Bostick & Company, Eufaula, Alabama." This same ad would run in the *Times* for several years

An inveterate traveler, after the war Edward Young resumed his periodic trips to New York, both for business and to visit his family there. His railroad route north took him near Rome, Georgia. In the "farm journal" which John Horry Dent meticulously continued to maintain at "Cottage Home," his new farm at Cave Spring, near Rome, he reported that on September 10, 1870, "Mr. E. B. Young reached here this morning by 2:00 train, called by to see me on his way from New York." Despite the inconvenient time of Edward's early morning arrival, Dent seemed very glad to see his old friend. Edward remained for a three-day visit, leaving on September 13 on the 8:00 A. M. train for Eufaula.[729] This would not be Edward's last visit to "Cottage Home."

Business was not the only interest of the Young families. Most of them devoted serious attention to growing various varieties of fruit and vegetables in their gardens. We find Edward bragging on Will's peaches to J. M. Macon, Editor of the *Times*, in the issue of July 7, 1870:

"Fine Peaches. Mr. E. B. Young showed us, a few days since, a luscious, soft peach grown on the premises of his son, J. W. Young, Esq., of this city. It was almost as large as a man's fist, perfectly ripe and juicy, being altogether almost as fine a specimen as we ever saw. This was one of about a dozen of the first year's crop of young trees, and considering the early season, was certainly very fine. Who can beat it?"

The following summer, Will's brother-in-law tried to "beat" him, and to get a business plug besides. The *Times*, in its June 15, 1871 issue, was playfully skeptical:

"Large Cabbage.
"A 12-pound cabbage, of the early flat Dutch variety, was exhibited on the streets on Tuesday. Its history is as follows:
The seed of this variety was sold by Weedon & Dent, in bags printed at this office. Dr. Weedon, who is 'pretty much' of a horticulturist, planted some of them in the early spring, and is now boasting of his great skill in having raised a hundred about as big as this. If he had sent us the specimen, its history would have been complete, and we would the more rapidly have 'swallowed' the balance of the story."

During 1871 and 1872, the *Eufaula Times* first begins mentioning "match games" of "base ball" between teams in Eufaula and Georgetown, and interest in the new game grew quickly.

Eufaula's Hart Hall was the scene of traveling theater productions which Eufaulians enjoyed. In December 1870, the famous actress, Laura Keene, was in Eufaula to perform in a series of three plays. One of the plays was "Our American Cousin," which will be recognized as the play which Miss Keene was performing in Washington at Ford's Theater, on the night five years earlier when Booth assassinated Abraham Lincoln.

Reuben Kolb, whom we first met as a private in the Eufaula Rifles and later as commander of "Kolb's Battery" of artillery, concluded that Eufaula could support another opera house. With his partners, the firm of "Kolb, Couric, and Hayes," he opened a fine new opera house on Broad Street. Unfortunately, the venture did not succeed, and Kolb encountered financial difficulties. In the *Times* of April 17, 1872, we find Buford and Dent, as attorneys for the mortgage holder, advertising a public auction of the property for the purpose of foreclosing on the mortgage.

In addition to his family and his law practice, Hubert Dent had two other overriding interests. One was the political fight to oust the Radical Republican regime in Barbour County and in Alabama, which we will later discuss. Hubert's other principal interest was the Methodist Church. He was a devout Christian and Methodist from his youth in Maryland. This inclination was only bolstered by his marriage to Anna Young and by his wartime experiences. Her parents, Ann and Edward, had been pillars of the Methodist Church since the first such church was built in Irwinton in the mid 1830's. Anna and her siblings had been reared as devout Methodists, and this was consistent with Herbert's rearing. The *Times* of July 15, 1869 reports Hubert's participation in the Eufaula churches' sponsorship of the Eufaula Bible Society, whose mission was to provide Bibles to those who could not otherwise afford them in the counties of Barbour, Henry, and Dale. Hubert was the lay representative of the Eufaula Methodist Church; Rev. Briggs was the minister representative. In 1874, he helped organize Eufaula's first Young Men's Christian Association, and its 75 members elected him as president.[730] Soon, Hubert would join his father-in-law, Edward Young, as a member of the Board of Stewards, the governing body of the Methodist Church, and we will find him taking a leadership role in the affairs of that Church.

Dent also continued his interest and membership in his old military unit, the Eufaula Rifles. Originally formed in the late 1850's as a unit of the Alabama Militia, the company had been incorporated into the Confederate Army at Fort Barrancas in 1861. After the one-year enlistments of its members had expired in 1862, the company had disbanded, as its officers and men found positions in other units. After the war, the unit had been revived, under its old name of Eufaula Rifles, again as a part of the state militia organization, a forerunner of today's National Guard. On August 21, 1872, Hubert Dent was elected to serve as its Captain in command. This historic unit would continue in existence in Eufaula into the twentieth century.

The new law firm of Buford and Dent was winning cases and prospering. The Circuit Court Docket of August 1871 reflected the trials of three cases involving clients represented by Hubert and his firm.[731] In one case, Buford and Dent represented Meyer in a suit against Stewart & Company for money owed to Hubert's client under a contract. Stewart & Company was strongly defended by the firm of "Shorter and Brother" (now consisting of Eli S. Shorter and his younger brother, Henry R Shorter) and by Judge John Cochran, three able and well-known lawyers. Despite this heavy opposition, Hubert won the case, the jury returning a verdict for Meyer. Further, the judge overruled the defendant's motion for a new trial. In the case of *White vs. Armstrong*, Hubert defended Armstrong against White's claims under an alleged contract. White was represented by Henry Shorter. Again, the jury returned a verdict for Hubert's client. But in a third case, Hubert fought unsuccessfully on behalf of one Browder to eject Bates from property allegedly owned by Browder. The jury decided for Bates. However, winning two out of three jury verdicts in one term of court could only draw favorable attention to this rising law firm.

Hubert also continued to be involved in politics. On Aug 24, 1871, Hubert, along with Jere Williams, Michael Cody, D. F. Hart, W. J. Bray, and others gave notice in the *Times* of their calling a convention of the Democratic and Conservative Party of Barbour County, to be held in Clayton on September 23 to nominate candidates for county offices in the upcoming elections, requesting all beats to send delegates, and requesting all candidates to be present. At this time, party primaries to select the parties' nominees had not yet been adopted. All selections of party nominees to run in the November General elections were made in conventions, at each level of government: beat, county, state, and national. Conventions at the local level, although composed of delegates, were actually open to whoever was interested enough to attend and vote. We will hereafter see this process at work in Barbour County during the 1872 elections.

Among the numerous railroad proposals which continued to arise was a project to construct a railroad south to Abbeville, and eventually to the Gulf of Mexico, with a branch from Abbeville to a point in Dale County such as Ozark. Edward Young agreed to support this project and to be an incorporator of the company, to be called the "Eufaula, Abbeville, and Gulf Railroad." A meeting of the incorporators was held in Eufaula on September 11, 1871, with Edward serving as president of the meeting and Hubert Dent acting as secretary. The group resolved to open the books to public subscribers and that subscription books be placed at the offices of E. B. Young & Son, J. G. L. Martin and Son, John McNab's offices, and others. Hubert Dent was appointed to a committee of incorporators to serve as delegates to a meeting to be held in Ozark. Other delegates were Alpheus Baker, Mayor G. A. Roberts, Henry R. Shorter, and others.[732]

The Eufaula, Abbeville, and Gulf Railroad proposal received strong editorial backing from the *Bluff City Times*. It endorsed the approach of immediately raising enough money to permit "surveying the whole line at once," so as to "strike while the iron is hot." There was some debate as to whether the route should closely follow the Chattahoochee River, so as to pass through Columbia and Gordon, or swing in a more westerly direction. The paper took no position on the exact route, but urged that, "What the people want is a road to get to market. This road will not confine them to Eufaula. If our merchants can't offer them the inducement of other markets they will have better facilities for going elsewhere. If they do, then the people will stop here, and hence the road will be as beneficial to the sections below us, as it will be to Eufaula. Let us all unite, in the best interests, of all, to build the road. Then the trade will take care of itself."[733]

It was later announced that, 10% of the capital stock having been subscribed to, a meeting was called for November 16 to elect officers and directors of the company. E. B. Young served as presiding officer of the special meeting. Col A. J. Lane was elected president of the company and J. G. L. Martin was elected Secretary. Elected to the company's Board of Directors were E. B. Young, W. J. Bray, Mayor G A. Roberts (future father-in-law of Carrie Young), H. Bernstein, Col. Lane, J. G. L. Martin (Ada Young's father-in-law), and others. The new board adopted resolutions proposing to the City of Eufaula that it subscribe to $75,000 of the capital stock of the Eufaula, Abbeville, and Gulf Railroad, to be paid for with bonds of the City of Eufaula payable in 20 years with coupons attached for interest at 8% payable semiannually. It was further proposed to Henry County that it subscribe for $150,000 of the stock, to be paid for by the issuance of Henry County bonds upon the same terms. E. B. Young and the other members of the Board pledged themselves to construct the road to the Florida line as expeditiously as possible.[734]

The *Times* enthusiastically endorsed the efforts of Col. Lane, president of the Eufaula, Abbeville and Gulf Railroad, in encouraging the people of Dale County to support the proposal for a branch of this road to Dale, instead of a competing proposal for a road from Dale County to Troy to Montgomery. The *Times* makes the point that the trade of Dale coming to the Eufaula market is "exceedingly valuable and fully appreciated by our people," and that "Eufaula is the legitimate market for the people of Dale," etc. [735]

On October 12, 1871, Ann and Edward's youngest son, Ed, married Mamie Jennings, the daughter of J. B. and Flora Jennings. When the Civil War began, the Jennings family was residing in St Joseph, Missouri, and were pro-Southern in their sympathies. During the war, probably because much of Missouri came under the control of the Federal army, the Jennings family emigrated to Eufaula. At the conclusion of the war, the family had moved to New Orleans for a time, but upon the death of Mr. Jennings, the family returned to Eufaula again. In reporting the wedding, the *Times* quoted from an account of the wedding which had appeared in the St. Joseph *Morning Herald*, which observed that the bride, Mamie, "is the daughter of our old fellow townsman the late Joseph B. Jennings. Not one of the old settlers of St. Joseph will fail to remember Mr. Jennings. His name ever stood first in all the earlier enterprises which have contributed to the prosperity of our city…" [736]

As we have seen, Ed was employed in "E. B. Young & Son Bankers," and in the successor national bank later organized, and would continue to carry on the family traditions of business and public service. Ed and Mamie would rear six children, (in addition to a son who died in infancy July 16-17, 1872), as follows:

Anna Young, born 1873, married Charles C. Holt in 1894, and died in 1943;
Maybelle Young, born 1876, and died in 1961;
Edward Billups Young, Jr., born 1878, married Meta Valentine Baldwin in 1899, died 1927;
William Hubert Young, born 1881, married Arabella Dean Virgin in 1904, and died in 1924;

Flora Young, born 1884, married John Charles Wheeler in 1910, and died in 1966;

Ada Young (II), born in 1887, and lived to the age of 103, dying in 1990.

After Ed's marriage to Mamie, Ann and Edward had only one unmarried child left at home: little Carrie. She studied piano under Professor Van Houten, who had taught music in Eufaula for many years. The *Times* of June 28, 1872 reports the annual concert at the Opera House by his pupils. Carrie Young, now 17, performed with her friends the overture from *La Grand Duchess*, arranged for four pianos. The *Times'* critique of the performance allowed that all of Professor Van Houten's programs were excellent, in that "they are not monotonous in the least..."

In 1873, Edward Young and Hubert Dent participated in an effort to resolve a controversy involving one of the railroad construction projects affecting Eufaula and Barbour County. The Vicksburg and Brunswick Railroad had planned to construct a line from Albany, Georgia westward to Cuthbert, Georgia to Eufaula to Clayton and beyond. Col. Eli S. Shorter of Eufaula was president of this railroad, and it had received financial support from Barbour County and its citizens. The line had reached Cuthbert, and work had been done on grading the route westward into Eufaula, when financial difficulties intervened. There began to be talk that the road would not be completed into Barbour County, and that it might change its route to instead proceed north from Cuthbert, through Lumpkin to Columbus, bypassing Barbour County. This created a furore among investors and taxpayers in Barbour County. The *Times* warned, "Columbus is working with all her vim to get the road extended in that direction...It behooves the people of Eufaula therefore to put forth their energies and prevent if possible the diversion of the road at Cuthbert from its old and direct route to this city..."[737]

Edward Young served as president of a meeting held at J. G. Guice's Store to discuss the matter. Edward and Eli Shorter were, of course, old acquaintances and had had business dealings over the years. Edward diplomatically described the purpose of the meeting as an effort to "reconcile the different interests of the Vicksburg and Brunswick Railroad, and to endeavor to agree upon some plan satisfactory to all parties by which the road may be extended." The meeting adopted resolutions calling for a larger public meeting of all those favoring the extension, to be held at Hart's Hall, to which would be invited Col. Eli Shorter, as well as the presidents of other railroads seeking to serve Eufaula.[738] The *Times* urged a large attendance at the meeting, which it said was "...pregnant with the interests of Eufaula..." And later, "...the road as it now stands does not give satisfaction to the taxpayers of the county nor does it meet their expectations when subscribing money for its construction and its affairs are unsatisfactory to many of its stockholders..."[739] At the meeting, Eli Shorter apparently attempted to give assurances that the extension would be completed, but the audience remained dissatisfied. At the urging of Gen. Henry D. Clayton and others, resolutions were adopted appointing Hubert Dent and other business leaders to conduct an investigation. Dent, along with R. A. Solomon, J. T. Kendall, J. W. Mabry, and others were to "inquire into the prospect if any of an immediate or ultimate extension of said road..." and to inquire into "the facts and causes resulting in a discontinuance of the work on said road and what has caused the failure to build the same as was originally contemplated..."[740] The next day, the *Times* was respectful of Shorter, but skeptical: "The writer was glad to hear Col. Shorter say that the controlling interests in the road and the directors were in favor of the extension, and since Col. Shorter said it we will not doubt it and will expect early work in that direction. It all depends on how much they desire it...In the meantime let the committee appointed last night go on with their work under the resolutions." As it turned out, the work of the committee may have become of little relevance when the Georgia legislature turned down proposals to provide an infusion of financial support to save the struggling railroad.[741]

In addition to his law practice, Hubert Dent sometimes became involved in other business ventures. In 1873, he became associated with an insurance company, Mobile Life Insurance Company. This association was probably at the behest of J. G. L. Martin, (the father of Hubert's brother-in-law, James H. G. Martin), a successful insurance dealer who was agent for many companies, including Mobile Life. Consistent with a common marketing practice of the time, Mobile Life would appoint company officers and directors in the markets where it wished to do business. Thus, for "president" of the Eufaula area it appointed Hubert Dent; and its local board of directors included family connections and associates, such as J. M. Buford (Hubert's law partner), Hamilton Weedon (Hubert's brother-in-law), family friends J. C. McKenzie, John O. Martin, J. G. L. Martin, and others.[742]

47
The Elections of 1872,
Hubert Dent and The Dual Legislatures of Alabama

"...these desperate men may attempt to carry out their program by force of arms, and backed by federal bayonets may usurp power which is not legally theirs, and have matters their way..."

The Eufaula Times

Although Gen. Pope had used his authority to veto Hubert's election as mayor of Eufaula, Hubert remained politically active. Barred from voting or holding office by the Radical reconstruction acts, Hubert could not be deterred from exercising his freedom to point out the effects of the Radicals' abusive policies and to speak out against the continued military occupation. An expression of his view of the Radicals in approximately 1871 appeared in a letter to the editor of the *Bluff City News*:

> "We do not think any set of rules and law-makers in any country ever afforded more complete evidence of ignorance and...incompetence...They have had control of the government for nearly three years, during which time not a hostile gun has been fired, not a single case of resistance to the United States has occurred, and what is the condition of the people and the country? The people are borne down with oppression and heavy burdens in the shape of taxes. Ten of the States that formed a portion of the Confederacy are governed almost exclusively by military power...
>
> In the South, misery, despondency and starvation...during the brief period, they have done more towards the ruin of the country than they were able to accomplish by four years of continual and active hostilities with their immense armies and powerful navies... Legislators are still tinkering away at Reconstruction in their own way...the country, as badly as it needs reconstruction, needs something else. It needs peace and order...[743]

In 1872, Hubert would have an opportunity to "make a difference." It was an important election year and would be a hotly fought election throughout Alabama, for a number of reasons. President Grant was seeking a second term, but was faced with a revolt by the liberal wing of his party, which was opposed to the Radicals' Reconstruction policy, as well as the rampant corruption. This wing decided to organize its own political party, which was called the "Liberal Republicans." In May 1872, in advance of the regular Republican convention, the Liberal Republicans held their own party convention in Cincinnati, and adopted a platform denouncing the Radical's Reconstruction policy, corruption, and the spoils system. The liberals nominated Horace Greeley, the editor of the New York Tribune, for president, and Missouri governor B. Gratz Brown for vice president. These candidates advocated repeal of the disenfranchisement of former Confederates, and withdrawal of troops from the South. The platform of this party was music to the ears of Southern Democrats, and there began to be talk of endorsing the Liberal Republican ticket and platform.

The outcome of the 1872 elections in Alabama would also be particularly important to Alabama's Radical Republican United States Senator, George E. Spencer. Spencer was the Yankee officer from New York and Iowa who stayed in Alabama after the surrender to become Alabama's first post-war senator, and he was nearing the end of his six-year senatorial term. He had achieved control of Federal patronage in Alabama and wielded enormous power. Supported by the Grant forces, Spencer desperately wanted the election of a Radical-controlled legislature so that he could remain in the Senate. Hubert Dent would be in the forefront of the political and legal battle to wrest control of the Alabama Legislature from Spencer and the Radicals.

As a result of the census, Congress had earlier allocated an additional congressional seat to Alabama. Because the Alabama legislature had not yet "redistricted" the state, the additional congressman was to be elected from the state at large in 1872. The names of M. B. Wellborn and Alpheus Baker, both of Eufaula, had been mentioned as worthy candidates for this seat. In the May 8, 1872 issue of the *Times*, a letter under the pseudonym "Barbour" (a common practice at the time), offered this suggestion:

"Mr. Editor,
The names of two of our prominent citizens have been suggested as suitable candidates for congress for the state at large in next fall's election.
"...[W]e beg to suggest a third. We detract nothing from the merit or claims of either of those already mentioned, but we think the claims of a gentleman whose name we are about to suggest are secondary to those of no other person. Indeed, we consider them, if not superior, at least equal to those of anyone else. If unsurpassed gallantry on unnumbered battlefields in defense of the south; if unspotted integrity in all the relations of life; if fine ability, rare prudence, and undoubted moral courage, can lend anything to the claims of anyone for that position, then his do not pale in comparison with those of either of the distinguished Gentlemen whose names have already been brought forward. We allude to Captain S. H. Dent, the junior partner of the well-known and able law firm of Messrs. Buford and Dent.
"We write this without any knowledge, information, suggestion, or even suspicion on his part of such a thing! And if he can be prevailed on to allow his name to be placed before a nominating convention, none more worthy of consideration can be found in this section of the state."

In publishing this letter, the *Times* editor, J. M. Macon, added his editorial endorsement:

"For Congress: We publish with pleasure the communication of "Barbour" suggesting Capt. S. H. Dent as a suitable candidate for election to Congress from the state at large. All the writer says of him we can heartily endorse and more, as from our personal association with him at home and in the army we think we know him as well, or better, than anyone else.

We have already endorsed the suggestion of Col. M. B. Wellborn for the same position, but as the choice of candidates rests with a convention with which we will have no connection and as we can endorse the suggestion of both, without disparagement to either, we feel that there is no inconsistency in so doing."

Editor Macon did in fact know Hubert "in the army." He is the "Macon" frequently mentioned in Hubert's wartime correspondence, starting at Fort Barrancas when Hubert was the regimental adjutant, and Macon was his first sergeant and assistant adjutant. It will be recalled that Hubert assisted in getting Macon commissioned as an officer. Macon later served as adjutant to Major General Henry D. Clayton, and was promoted to captain. After the war, Captain Macon commenced the publication of the *Bluff City Weekly Times*, which will later become a daily and change its name to the *Eufaula Daily Times*.

Hubert did not allow the suggestion of his candidacy for Congress to proceed any further, and the state Democratic convention later nominated Alpheus Baker, Hubert's old commander in the Eufaula Rifles. However, as we will see presently, Hubert would render important political service to the Democrats in other dramatic ways. In the high-stakes fight for control of the Alabama Legislature, Hubert Dent would ultimately consent to be a Democratic candidate for the legislature from Barbour County. But this would come only after a spring and summer of intense political activity, as the Southerners groped for a political strategy which might stand a chance of ridding themselves of Radical domination.

In late May 1872, on the recommendation of Gen. Grant, the Radical-controlled Congress finally repealed the exclusion of former Confederate soldiers from voting and holding office, and allowed all but a small category of Confederates to participate. For five years, those who had voluntarily served in the Confederate army had been prohibited from voting or holding office. Some of the South's most able leaders had thus been effectively excluded from public life. The Radicals' unexpected decision to enact the amnesty law was a result of several pressures. Many people in the north were growing tired of the southern question, and were leaning to the view that the South should be allowed the ability to deal with its own problems. The corruption and incompetence of the Carpetbag governments was a factor in this feeling. Southerners felt the Radicals had granted amnesty in an effort to combat the arguments of the Liberal Republican candidates and platform. *The Eufaula Times* observed that, "[The amnesty act's] unexpected passage can only be accounted for in the nomination of Horace Greeley…thus far has the Cincinnati Convention has resulted in good for us."[744] The amnesty act fueled the movement among Southern Democrats to endorse the Liberal Republican candidates and platform.

On June 4, a meeting of the citizens of the Eufaula beat (or precinct) was held to elect delegates to the Barbour County Democratic convention to be held two days later in Clayton. Presided over by Hubert's law partner, J. M. Buford, this meeting elected Hubert as a delegate, along with Eli Shorter, M. B. Wellborn, J. M. McKleroy, James H. G. Martin

(Hubert's brother-in-law, Ada Young's husband) George C. McCormack, Alpheus Baker, Henry Shorter, G. A. Roberts, and others. At the urging of Eli Shorter, the meeting also unanimously adopted resolutions urging the Democratic Party, scheduled to meet later in Baltimore, to cooperate with the Liberal Republican party in the election of Greeley and Brown.[745]

The Barbour County convention of the "Democratic and Conservative Party" assembled in Clayton two days later on June 6. Hubert Dent was elected the permanent President of the convention. Hubert appointed a nominating committee of two delegates from each beat, chaired by Henry D. Clayton, to meet and submit nominations for delegates to the Alabama state Democratic convention to be held in Montgomery on June 19. While this committee was meeting, the convention heard "well-timed and eloquent" speeches by Col. M. B. Wellborn and General Alpheus Baker. The committee later returned and submitted its report, which was adopted unanimously, naming Barbour County's delegates to the state convention, which included Hubert Dent, Michael Cody, Henry D. Clayton, Henry Shorter, Dr. J. M. Barr, James L Pugh, Alpheus Baker, Alto V. Lee, Herbert Dent (living in Clayton, the son of John Horry Dent, unrelated to Hubert) and a long list of other Eufaula and Barbour County leaders.[746] Although official delegates were designated, these political conventions at all levels were entirely "open," in that the president was authorized to certify as a delegate any citizen of the county in sympathy with the views of the meeting who wished to participate in the convention.

Gen. Henry D. Clayton offered a resolution to the effect that, because it is important to inform the Baltimore convention of the views of the people it represents, it is resolved that, "the removal from place and power of the corrupt and extravagant dominant party, is the paramount object of patriotic desire," and "the Baltimore Convention should ratify the nomination made by the Cincinnati Convention." The resolution was adopted by a vote of 54 to 2.

It was apparently felt that it would be premature for this convention to select its nominees for county offices, i. e. state senator, state representatives, and county solicitor, until after the state and national conventions had determined the direction of the party as a whole, so Hubert adjourned the county convention temporarily, to meet again in Clayton on July 24, which date was later postponed to August 8.

Meanwhile, in early June, the Radical wing of the Republican Party held its convention in Philadelphia, and, as expected, renominated Grant and adopted a platform which continued all its old policies in effect. The *Times* commented that, while "...pretending to be honest and economical, they have kept in power for years a gang of the most corrupt men, thieves and profligates that ever disgraced a nation."[747]

In July, Hubert Dent and the other delegates assembled in Montgomery for the state convention of the "Democrat and Conservative" party. The convention's nominees included Thomas H. Herndon for governor, and Alpheus Baker for one of the two congressman-at-large seats. It also recommended that the Baltimore Convention of the national Democratic

Party endorse Greeley and Brown, the Liberal Republican nominees, and adopt their platform. The state convention also elected Alabama's delegates to the Baltimore Convention; the delegates selected to represent the second congressional district included Hubert Dent as alternate delegate.[748]

In Baltimore, the Democrats from the northern states were lukewarm toward the movement to accept the Liberal Republican candidates, Greeley and Brown, as the Democratic nominees. In the past Greeley had violently opposed the Democratic Party and most of its principles. He had been a high tariff man, an abolitionist, and a Radical during and immediately after the war. But the southern Democrats saw the editor of the powerful New York Tribune as a man who had posted bail for Jefferson Davis when he was being held prisoner for treason, and a man who, by 1872, had become a strong and sincere opponent of Radical Reconstruction and "Grantism" in General. It seemed that an alliance of Democrats and Liberal Republicans stood a chance of defeating Grant, which the Southerners would do almost anything to accomplish. As observed by the *Bluff City Times*: "Horace Greeley has been a lifelong enemy of the Democratic Party, and has done much and said much against the South, but the first object of patriotic desire is to get rid, not only of Grant, but of Grant Republicanism characterized by usurpation, misrule, theft, and demonism."[749] The northern delegates reluctantly acquiesced; Greeley and Brown became the Democratic nominees.

Back at home, Hubert Dent lost no time in beginning to work for the ticket. He led Barbour County Democrats in organizing "Greeley and Brown Clubs." Hubert served as vice-president of one such club, and was a featured speaker at many of their meetings.[750] Because Greeley had been a well-known abolitionist and Republican, the Democrats hoped to persuade Barbour County blacks to support him, and sought to work with other Barbour County "Liberal Republicans" in support of the joint ticket. A kickoff barbecue was held on July 27, to which the Democrats had invited all voters, both black and white, to attend. Some blacks did attend. There was also a large turnout of ladies. Hubert Dent, the first speaker, explained the objects and goals of the campaign, followed by speeches by Eli Shorter, James L. Pugh, John Cochran, and others. [751]

Hubert reconvened the Barbour County convention of the Democratic and Conservative Party on August 8. The Democrats were still attempting to work out cooperative arrangements with the Liberal Republicans, and probably for that reason, the convention further postponed making its nominations for county offices. However, the convention elected a new Democratic Executive Committee, and authorized the president of the convention (Hubert Dent) and the Executive Committee to reconvene the convention later, or to simply take such action as they deemed advisable. The Executive Committee consisted of John Cochran as chairman, Hubert Dent, Dr. J. M. Barr, Michael Cody, Henry D. Clayton, J. M. Macon, G. A. Roberts, J. M. Hobdy, Whit Clark, and J. C. McRae.[752]

The Liberal Republicans of Barbour County held their county convention in Clayton on the morning of August 21, and selected nominees for county offices. Later the same day, Hubert and the other members of the county Democratic Executive Committee met to determine its next move. Although these Democrats were campaigning hard for the Liberal

Republican candidates for President, the Democrats concluded they could not support that party's nominees for local offices. The Executive Committee considered the idea of proposing a new, joint county convention between Democrats and Liberal Republicans to cooperate and nominate a joint ticket, but this idea was rejected. Finally, a committee was appointed to have a conference with the Liberal Republicans "to negotiate Generally on the subject of the campaign." Further maneuvering was to occur.

Hubert Dent reconvened the county Democratic Convention in Clayton for its third meeting on September 11, and this time it actually made nominations. For state senator from Barbour, the convention renominated the incumbent, J. W. Mabry, a staunch Democrat. For Barbour's three state representatives, the nominees were: Michael Cody, also a staunch Democrat; A. Graves, a black; and D. C. Bennett. Adding the latter two may have been a compromise effort to achieve a ticket which would attract blacks and other Liberal Republicans. The unusual step of nominating a black was consistent with the Democrats' strategy of cooperating with these groups to try to defeat Grant and the Radicals at all levels. In any event, for unknown reasons it did not work, and this particular ticket fell apart. John Cochran, as Chairman, called another meeting of the Democratic Executive Committee, and invited the Liberal Republicans to meet with them. After this meeting on September 25, Graves and Bennet were off the ticket as nominees for the legislature, and were replaced by Hubert Dent and Major Jere N. Williams, two strong Democrats. Alto V. Lee was nominated for county solicitor.

The *Times* was very happy with this change; it was now a solid, conservative, Democratic slate. Perhaps it had the support of the Liberal Republicans; the *Times* portrayed it as an amicable agreement among what the *Times* called "the Liberal and Conservative Committee:"

"Our Ticket"

"At a Meeting of the Liberal and Conservative Committee of Barbour County, held in this city yesterday, the following Gentlemen were nominated for the Senate and House of Representatives: For Senator, J. W. Mabry; for Representatives, Major J. N. Williams, Capt. S. H. Dent, and M. Cody, Esq.

Messrs. Bennett and Graves, who were previously nominated, having positively declined to run, this nomination was made and we are satisfied it will give entire satisfaction.

We have a ticket now and feel it can be elected if our citizens will but do their duty. They are all good men and true, and if sent to Montgomery Old Barbour will again occupy the proud position in the councils of the state she held in days of yore.

These candidates…are determined to canvas the county thoroughly, assisted by other good speakers. Now let every true lover of his country put his shoulder to the wheel, and victory will perch on our standard, and radicalism, carpetbagism, scalawagism, with all their attendant evils, will be driven from our midst.

We repeat it, let every man do his duty and our glorious old county will be redeemed from the grasp of the ignorant, unprincipled men who have so long dishonored her in the eyes of the world.

We call on all good men, white and colored, whatever their past party affiliation may have been, to come to the help of the country in her hour of need."[753]

During 1872, the Young family was saddened by a decision made by the oldest son, Will, and his wife, Anna Maria Hewlit. It will be recalled that Will had brought Annie as his bride from her home in Newark, New Jersey in 1854, over twenty years earlier. Will's childhood friend, Tom Jackson, reports that Will and Annie had "led a happy and contented life for many years" in their home on College Hill in Eufaula.[754] But eventually, Annie came to greatly miss her home and family, and earnestly begged Will to take her back to the home of her childhood. "Like the good husband that he was, he gratified her whims and took her to her old home." Leaving his large family in Eufaula, where he enjoyed a position of some standing in the community, was consistent with the independent, self-sufficient element in Will's character. Back in Newark, Will, Annie, and their 16 year old son, Charlie, lived in the modest home where Will had boarded with Annie's family during his apprenticeship many years earlier. In Newark, Will entered into business as an engineer, machinist, and commission merchant dealing in machinery of all kinds, including railroads, steamboats, and sawmills. To let his Barbour County friends know of his new and relocated business, his ran an ad (reproduced nearby) on August 21 and for several times thereafter in the *Eufaula Times*.

To briefly look ahead in our narrative, Will Young died suddenly on January 15, 1889, at the age of 55. That Will's death and burial were in the North seems fitting, because he had been born there, during a visit by Ann and Edward to New York while they were residing in Marion, Georgia, the year after their marriage. And as a teenager, Will had returned to New Jersey and New York to pursue a mechanical engineering apprenticeship, and had selected his wife there. Writing in 1896, Tom Jackson reported that Will's widow, Annie, then 65, was

J. W. YOUNG,
Engineer and Machinist
(FORMERLY OF EUFAULA, ALA.)
General Machinist Commission
MERCHANT,
NO. 377, HIGH STREET,
NEWARK, N. J.

Will buy on Commission all kinds of Machinery, Brass Goods, Iron, Pipe, Oils, etc, In fact, everything connected with Railroadso Steamboats, Saw Mills, etc.
☞ All orders addressed as above will receive prompt and personal attention.
july23–d1w3m

Ad in *Eufaula Times* of August 21, 1872, reporting Will and Annie's move to Newark

still living in the cottage in Newark; and that her son Charlie had a good position with, fittingly, a bank in Newark.[755] Charlie maintained contact with Eufaula, returning in later years to visit at Fendall Hall.[756] If he left any descendants, however, contact with them has been lost.

The efforts of the Barbour County Democrats of 1872 to attract black voters to the Greeley-Brown ticket appear to have been enjoying some success. The *Times* tells us that, "The Greeley and Brown Club meeting on Thursday night last was very well attended by both whites and blacks, and very able and eloquent speeches were delivered by Mr. John L.

McKleroy and Capt. S. H. Dent." And later, "The citizens of Richards' beat met...Speeches were made by Major Jere Williams and Alto V. Lee...after which a Greeley and Brown Club was formed...The colored men present all joined the Club, and are going to cast their votes for the Liberal Ticket."[757]

However, this success created a new problem. As several black leaders publicly made known their support of Greeley and Brown, they were subjected to intimidation and threats from other blacks loyal to the Radicals. One incident that became a *cause celebre* involved a black man named Milledge Holt. Holt had published statements that he was supporting the Greeley-Brown ticket, and was thereafter intimidated by a crowd of blacks who came to his house at 2 a. m. and threatened his life. To discourage such intimidation, the law firm of Buford and Dent devised an innovative legal action, in which Congressional acts which had been passed to protect the Radicals were used against the Radicals. In 1870 and 1871, in response to allegations of Ku Klux activities in the South, Congress had enacted a series of three statutes called the "Force Acts," or sometimes called the "Enforcement Acts." These statutes imposed heavy penalties on persons convicted of using threats, force, bribery, or other means to interfere with citizens voting, and authorized the president to use federal troops to enforce these laws. Southerners regarded the laws as a means of perpetuating Radicals in office, but in 1872 Barbour Democrats made effective use of them for different purposes. [758]

With the firm of Buford and Dent as special counsel for the prosecution, charges were brought against the black leaders of the crowd that had gone to Milledge Holt's house. John Cochran later joined the prosecution team. Since this was a federal prosecution, a preliminary hearing was held before a United States Commissioner, to determine whether the accused would be released or would be held under bond for action by the next federal Grand Jury. The blacks were able to retain able counsel; Col. M. B. Wellborn and Sterling B. Toney were strong conservative Democrats, but they were also lawyers, and agreed to defend the accused blacks. During the three-day hearing, which took on the character of a full-scale trial, Capt Dent interrogated witnesses for both sides, establishing that a crowd of Radical blacks, including Austin Geary and Dick Hart, were demonstrating in the streets in the early morning hours to celebrate a Republican victory in North Carolina; that at 2 a. m. the crowd went to the home of Milledge Holt and his wife and started singing and yelling, "Hurrah for the Greeley Negroes! Hurrah for Milledge Holt, he's a d----d Democratic nigger!" that some of the crowd said that if Holt resisted, they would "shoot his d----d head off;" that Milledge returned the threat but then said he was going to town for protection; and that he then went for the police.[759]

In closing argument for the prosecution, Major Buford first reflected upon "the enormity of the Enforcement Act, the hellish passion in which it originated and the infernal purpose for which it was devised." He said, "There should be no complaint now on the part of its originators and abettors, that this political sword had been found to possess two edges rather than one." Was it the crowd's object to "have fun?" "Why did this crowd go armed, if they were on a peaceable parade? Why had they, by their own confessions, pistols in their pockets, with which they threatened to shoot off Holt's head? He discussed in detail the evidence establishing these facts. In closing arguments for the defense, Col. Wellborn first stated that he agreed with Major Buford's opinion of the Enforcement Act, which Wellborn said was "born in political passion and prejudice, and was one of the most obnoxious laws to the South ever passed by Congress." Compelled by the evidence to admit that Dick Hart and Austin Geary were in the crowd, Wellborn contended that they merely violated a city ordinance against being disorderly. "...Their noise awakened [Holt], it is true, but they did him no violence...My understanding of Ku-Kluxism is where a party of men disguise themselves and go out on strictly unlawful purposes. There were no disguises in this crowd." "The crowd made no threats to injure Holt if he voted for Greeley and Brown; it is true that someone one in the crowd may have called him a d----d Democratic Negro...There are no Ku-Kluxes in this county; not even our opponent will say there are...[The crowd] was more afraid of [Holt] than he of them."

John Cochran closed the case on behalf of the prosecution, observing: "I don't believe that the votes of the colored people are any more free now than their services were in the time of slavery. I believe that their votes are controlled by terrorism. I solemnly believe that they think they can't abandon their party thralldom without endangering their lives, and it is for the purpose of doing away with this state of things that I appear on behalf of the United States [i. e., for the prosecution]."[760]

The law and facts were so clear that even the United States Commissioner, probably a Radical appointee, had to find for the prosecution. Geary and Hart were held over on bonds of $500 each for action by the next term of the federal Grand Jury. The next Grand Jury would not be until after the election. It is likely that the case never went to trial, and was quietly dismissed (as is often the case with politically-inspired criminal prosecutions). But the prosecution had achieved its purpose. The *Times* exulted over this rare victory in federal court: "The result of this trial will, we hope, put a stop to the disgraceful and shameful treatment which some of the Greeley colored men of this city have borne from their colored opponents. What is sauce for the Greeley gander should be sauce for the Grant goose." [761]

The Democrats campaigned intensely throughout the county, appealing for both white and black votes. The Radicals campaigned with similar vigor. The *Times* published with approval a letter under the pseudonym, "Piney Woods," praising the effective efforts of the Democratic candidates:[762]

"Our County Ticket"
"The canvass is being conducted with great ability and effect by our county ticket. Messrs. [J. W.] Mabry, [Michael] Cody, [Jere N.] Williams and [Alto V.] Lee [candidate for county solicitor] have been actively and earnestly at work during the past week, in the southern and southwestern portion of the county, and it is said that the people are responding with hearty and earnest approval of the sentiments of patriotism and words of wisdom uttered by the candidates...
"Mr. Dent, in the eastern portion of the county is also striking heavy blows. His great personal popularity throughout the county; his

acknowledged ability, and incorruptible fidelity to every trust, adds much to our hopes of success.

"Who can be laggard in such a race? Our country, family, honor—aye our lives are at issue…Let us redeem our county from the hand of the Goths and Vandals. We can, we must, we will do it.

"People of Barbour County, "awake! arise! Or be forever fallen!""

In these tense times, the possibility of physical clashes at the polls on Election Day often loomed in the background. As Election Day approached, Jacob Black, the black Chairman of the Republican Executive Committee, wrote John Cochran, the Democratic Chairman, suggesting that they work together to have peace on Election Day. Cochran responded, readily pledging his cooperation toward this end, although he expressed regret that the Radicals had only recently come to this position. Cochran soon wrote Black again to report that A. E. Williams, one of the Radical candidates for the legislature, was advising his black supporters to go to the polls carrying guns. When A. E. Williams issued his denial of this quote, the Times published the correspondence, along with a statement by Hubert Dent, one of A. E. Williams' Democratic opponents:[763]

"In order to give the public an opportunity of judging what amount of credit is due to [A. E. Williams'] vindication, we [the *Times*] publish the following:

'A. E. Williams said in his public speech at Reynoldsville on Friday the 29th inst [of October] that he was sorry he could not endorse the advice of Mr.. Black (which was to go to the election unarmed) but that he advised them all to carry arms to Eufaula on the day of the election and if they did not carry them to the polling place to have them in Eufaula where they could lay their hands on them at the shortest notice!!!

'This language was uttered to a crowd of colored men in the presence of C. F. Massey, George Bouyer, and others; and afterwards in my presence and of the parties named, he repeated it and admitted that he did use the language as above.

S. H. Dent'"

As it turned out, on November 5, "the election went off in a most quiet manner, considering the great number" of people who were in Eufaula for the event.[764] The election results were less happy. At the national level, the Democratic strategy of combining with the Liberal Republicans was disastrous. Grant was reelected over Greeley by a large margin, and the Radicals' majority in the U. S. House was increased from 35 to 105. Grant carried all the northern states and all the "reconstructed states" except the three that had overthrown Radical control: Tennessee, Georgia, and Texas. The humiliated Greeley said that he was "the worst beaten man who ever ran for high office," and died 30 days later. The same result was reflected in the Alabama statewide races. The Radical candidate for governor, David P. Lewis, and the entire Radical slate, were elected.

But the important issue of control of the Alabama legislature was different. The results showed that the Democrats had won control of both houses by a small margin, which included victories by Hubert Dent and the other Barbour County Democrats! However, the forces of Sen. Spencer were swinging into action, and trouble was brewing.

The defeated Radical candidates for the legislature in both Barbour and Marengo Counties were disputing the election of the Democratic victors. It was apparent that, because the results of statewide legislative races were so evenly divided, control of the state legislature would depend upon the outcome of disputed results in the seats in Barbour and Marengo Counties. To retain their control, the Radicals launched a bitter, dirty and protracted fight, which would result for a time in two bodies meeting simultaneously, each claiming to be the lawful legislature of the state.

Hubert Dent and the other Barbour County Democratic legislators, and Alto Lee, county solicitor, filed suit in the Barbour County circuit court at Clayton, alleging that Box No. 1 of the Eufaula Beat had been illegally handled, that the ballots voted in it were invalid, and asking for an injunction prohibiting the counting of these votes in determining the winners of the county races. Chancellor (Judge) B. B. McCraw, who heard the case, is said to have been a scalawag, [765] but he ruled for Hubert and the Democrats, at least initially. On November 11, Chancellor McCraw issued an injunction directed to the Probate Judge, the Sheriff, and the circuit Clerk, enjoining and prohibiting them from opening, comparing, or counting the ballots cast in the said box so far as the election of state senator, representative, or county solicitor is concerned, and prohibiting them from giving any certificate of election to any person predicated on the votes in the said box, until further order of the court. The enjoined officers, acting as the Board of Supervisors of the county, complied with the injunction, and on November 12, certified the votes cast for each candidate, reflecting Hubert Dent and the other Democrats as the winning candidates. [766]

Next, Hubert and the other Democratic candidates for the House and Senate applied for Certificates of Election from Secretary of State Jabez Parker. Parker was a Democrat who had been elected in 1870. Although he had been defeated for reelection, he was still legally in office until the incoming administration was sworn in. The Radical candidates from Barbour who were also claiming victory, i.e., A. E. Williams, Thomas J. Clark, and Samuel Fantroy, for the House, and Jacob Black, for the Senate, also filed competing applications with Parker, with their supporting evidence. Looking for help, Secretary of State Parker submitted the conflicting evidence to the state Attorney General, John W. A. Sanford, for a legal opinion. Sanford was said to be a man of conviction and independence, but here he took the spineless course of advising Parker to simply issue *no* Certificates of Election in the contested races.[767]

The stakes were high, and the pressure on Secretary of State Parker was great. Perplexed as to what to do, he selected a body of three well-regarded lawyers from among the leaders of the state Bar to advise him. They were Samuel Rice, a Liberal Republican; William G. Jones, a Democrat; and Thomas J. Judge, a Democrat. On November 14, In a well-reasoned opinion supported by ample legal authority, this body of advisors unanimously advised Parker that he should lawfully issue certificates of election to Hubert Dent and the other Democratic Barbour County contenders, which he did.[768] Parker also issued certificates of election to the Democratic candidates for the disputed Marengo County legislative seats. The Barbour and Marengo seats would give the Democrats a majority of one in the state Senate, and of "several" in the House.

On November 16, the *Eufaula Times* (now sometimes referring to the Democrats as the "liberal" candidates) reported:

> "The Democratic candidates for the legislature and county solicitor for Barbour have been declared elected, and Col. J. W. Mabry for the Senate, J. N. Williams, S. H. Dent, and M. Cody for Representatives, have certificates of election, and will take their seats next Monday. A. V. Lee has already entered on the duties of his office as solicitor.
> …We suppose that the radicals will contest, and at the opening of the session they will try hard to oust the above-named Gentlemen, which we have no fear of their doing, if none but legal votes are allowed. And that two, at least, of the boxes in the county were foul and consequently illegal, there is not a shadow of doubt in the mind of any honest man. We suppose that the Legislature will ventilate the whole matter thoroughly, and will be governed by the evidence as it will be fully brought out before it, which will, if we have been correctly informed satisfy the most prejudiced that the liberal candidates above named were fairly elected and ought to be seated. If so old Barbour can boast of as able a representation as any county in the state."

Maneuvering in the background of all this was one of the real parties in interest to this dispute, the carpetbag United States Senator George E. Spencer. Spencer had early seized control all federal patronage in Alabama.[769] Closely tied to the national machinery controlling the Grant campaign, Spencer was said to derive large amounts of funds from the internal revenue officers, the Mobile Custom house, and the postmaster at Mobile.[770] If the certificates of election of Hubert Dent and his Barbour colleagues should stand, Spencer's empire would be headed toward an abrupt end. Further, if he was to be returned to the U. S. Senate within the time provided by law, he did not have time for leisurely litigation, and he now undertook maneuvers which fully justified the title given him by historians: "the champion of chicanery."

By law, the new legislature was to meet on November 18 in Montgomery and organize itself for business. The Radicals undertook a bold, two-pronged scheme, designed first, to prevent the Democratic majority from organizing the regular legislature by denying it of the necessary quorum, and second, to *create* their own, competing legislature that would do their bidding.

To deny the legislature a quorum (which consists of one more than half the total members), the Radical legislators absented themselves from the capitol on November 18. They assembled instead in the federal courthouse in Montgomery, to set up a rump legislature. But since they were only a minority, this alone could not deny a quorum to the regular legislature meeting in the Capitol. To achieve this, the Radicals had earlier caused federal warrants to be issued for the arrest of the Marengo and Barbour County delegations whose elections were being disputed. Accordingly, the previous day, the Marengo delegation, while enroute to Montgomery, had been arrested by federal officers in Faunsdale, Dallas County, and taken to Mobile to appear before the federal court there.[771]

The warrants for Hubert Dent and his collegues were apparently not timely executed. When the regular legislature was called to order at midday at the Capitol in November 18, the attending Democratic members included Hubert Dent and his colleagues from Barbour, and all were duly sworn in and seated.[772] Further business could not be transacted, however, because the absence of the Marengo delegation and all of the Radicals deprived it of a quorum.

At 2:00 p. m. Hubert and the other Barbour county legislators were notified that federal warrants for their arrest had been issued. They immediately went to the federal magistrate in Montgomery, posted the required bond of $1000, and were released.[773] Thus, this simplistic ploy had gained nothing for the Radicals.

By November 21, the Marengo delegation had made bond in Mobile and been released, had traveled to Montgomery, and had been seated in the regular legislature meeting in the capitol, giving the Democrats a quorum in each house, so that this ploy also benefited the radicals but little.[774] By prevailing law at the time, the Alabama House of Representatives was to be comprised of 100 members, and the Senate, 33. Thus the "capitol legislature" was now organized with 54 house members and 19 senators, all bearing proper certificates of election and each house having more than a quorum, thereby permitting it to lawfully legislate.

On the other hand, the rump meeting of Radicals at the courthouse (the "courthouse legislature" as it came to be called) had only 14 senators and 45 or 46 representatives who had certificates of election, obviously not a quorum. Undeterred by this detail, Radicals simply proceeded to *create* a quorum. The rump senate and house each brought in five Radicals, who had run for the legislature but who had admittedly not been elected, and swore them in as members.[775] Based on this pretext, the "courthouse legislature" organized and set itself up for business, purporting to be the legislature of Alabama. The *Eufaula Times* was dismayed by these events, and forecast the appearance of "federal bayonets:"

"Radical Doings in Montgomery"
"It seems that the radical party managers and members of the legislature are doing their utmost to mold a senate and house to suit their own purposes and frustrate the will of the people. Their performances there are simply outrageous and revolutionary and in keeping with their antecedents since the close of the war. 'Rule or ruin' is their motto. Backed as they are by the powers of the general government, they have come to believe that, however illegal their acts, they will be sustained and upheld in

them, and they are determined to override justice, law, and order to obtain control of the state, that they may plunder the people with impunity. The trick played to keep the members from Marengo from taking their seats as published in our issue yesterday has been frustrated and these Gentlemen are now in their places. The members from this county were next arrested, but they gave bond and are seated. Up to last account a quorum of both houses will be obtained and the legislature will proceed with regular business in spite of the continued absence of Radical members, who are endeavoring to run a separate concern at the United States courtroom. How it will terminate we cannot well see. Should the strict letter of the law be followed of course the legislature will be conservative on joint ballots but these desperate men may attempt to carry out their program by force of arms, and backed by federal bayonets may usurp power which is not legally theirs, and have matters their way."[776]

The *Times'* prediction that federal bayonets would soon be seen was completely accurate. The outgoing governor, Lindsay, had recognized the regular, "Capitol legislature" as the lawful body. After the Democrats of the Capitol legislature organized, as required by law they dutifully tallied the votes for the state officers, and proclaimed the Radical candidate, David P. Lewis, to be elected governor. They also declared the election of the Radical candidates, Alexander McKinstry, as Lieutenant governor; Patrick Ragland, as Secretary of State; as well as the other state offices won by the Radicals.

Gov. Lewis apparently accepted the validity of the Capitol legislature, at least for the limited purpose of declaring him elected, because he forthwith took the oath as governor.[777] But he then immediately repudiated that legislature. He asserted that the certificates of election issued to Hubert Dent and the other Barbour County representatives were based on only "partial returns," and that complete returns showed that these candidates, as well as the Marengo County Democratic candidates, had actually been defeated. On this basis, Lewis declared the "courthouse" rump to be the lawful legislature and telegraphed the nearest Federal troops, in Opelika, to come to the capital. Further, the newly sworn in Radical Secretary of State, Ragland, promptly issued certificates of election to Hubert Dent's opponent and the other Radical contenders in Barbour and Marengo Counties.

When the Federal troops arrived, Gov. Lewis had them stationed near or on the Capitol grounds.[778] He then called upon the Democrats to accept the entire courthouse body and to expel enough Democrats to make it the minority party. When the Democrats refused this demand accompanied by an implied threat, the courthouse rump began enacting legislation.

Thus, for four months, from November 1872 through March 1873, Alabama had two competing legislatures.[779] The rump segment met at the courthouse and purported to enact laws and transact state business; while the regular, certified legislature met in the capitol and did the same, the two sometimes acting in direct contradiction of each other.

During this time, we find Hubert under the strain of frequently traveling back and forth between Eufaula and Montgomery, performing his legislative duties and carrying on the fight in Montgomery while also trying to attend to his law practice at home. The *Times* reports on November 3, that, "Capt. S. H. Dent, Representative Elect from this county was in the city on Sunday and yesterday [Monday], but if he had not left by the 4 a. m. train yesterday he would have been scarce in these parts during the day."

As the sordid saga continued, the champion of chicanery was becoming increasingly nervous about his reelection to the U. S. Senate. Said to have "a full purse," Spencer was dispensing money freely to ensure the loyalty of his crowd at the courthouse.[780] Large numbers of this group later received appointments to federal jobs.[781] His agents even offered bribes, unsuccessfully, to some in the capitol legislature to induce them to change sides.

Unwilling to risk waiting for a settlement of the standoff, Sen. Spencer on December 3, 1872 had the courthouse rump proceed to reelect him to the U. S. Senate.[782] However, soon thereafter, Hubert Dent and his fellow members of the regular legislature assembled at the Capitol and elected Francis W. Sykes of Lawrence County as successor to Spencer as U. S. Senator.[783]

Spencer and the Radicals now appealed to his friend, President Ulysses Grant, to come to their aid, which he did. The courthouse legislature sent a committee to meet with President Grant to explain the situation to him. The regular legislature at the capitol also selected a committee, chosen from the "front rank" of the Alabama Bar, to present their case to the president. Grant met with both groups and heard their presentations. However, rather than entering this political thicket himself, Grant acted through his Attorney General, George Henry Williams, by referring the matter to him. Upon considering the matter, Attorney General Williams, a stalwart Republican, did not render an opinion on the rights of the parties arising from the circumstances. Instead, he proposed a plan of "compromise." Not surprisingly, under the "compromise," Hubert Dent and his Barbour colleagues would be out, and the Radicals would control the legislature.

In effect, the Attorney General's "plan" provided as follows:[784]

In the House, on a designated day, all House members holding certificates of election from Secretary of State Parker would take their seats in the house chamber, *except* that:
   a.   The Democratic representatives from Barbour County, i. e. Hubert Dent, Jere Williams, and Michael Cody, would be excluded. In their places, the Radical candidates holding certificates of election from the newly-sworn in Secretary of State Ragland would be seated.
   b.   Regarding the Marengo House contests, neither set of claimants would have a vote until the House had examined the poll lists of Marengo county, recounted the votes, and declared the result.
2. In the Senate, on the designated day, all senators holding certificates of election from Parker would be seated, *except* that:

a. The Democrat from Barbour, J. W. Mabry, would not be seated. In his place, the radical candidate, Jacob Black, holding a certificate of election from Ragland, would be seated.

b. In a contest regarding the senator for the senatorial district consisting of Butler and Conecuh counties between the Democrat, E. W. Martin and the Radical, William Miller, Jr., neither claimant would have a vote until the Senate examined the poll lists of those counties, counted the votes, and declared the winner.

Although elaborately stated, the plan simply "compromised" Hubert Dent and the other members of the Barbour Democratic contingent out of their seats in the house and senate. This gave the Radicals sufficient votes to decide the Marengo house contests in their own favor and end up controlling the house. The only arguable benefit to the Democrats was that, in the evenly-divided Senate, there was the bare possibility that if the Butler-Conecuh contest were decided in favor of the Democrat Martin instead of the Radical Jones, the Democrats could have a one vote majority in the Senate. (But, as we will see presently, the Radicals devised an underhanded way around this potential impediment.)

While Hubert and his fellow Democrats were absorbing this one-sided proposal, Hubert returned to Eufaula for a few days. The *Times* reports on December 17, the week before Christmas, that "Capt. S. H. Dent and Hon. M. Cody returned from Montgomery on Saturday last. Capt. Dent is still in the city, and will remain at home until his case is passed upon by the Legislature, or until a telegram may summon him to Montgomery." One of the reasons that Hubert came home at this time is probably because the Alabama Conference of the Methodist Church was holding its Annual Conference in Eufaula. The Conference had convened on December 10. This was a major event in the life of the church, and as an active Methodist, Hubert would have wanted to be present at some point. Perhaps he had some advance notice of an unusual recognition that would be accorded him. On December 18, the Annual Conference elected him as a member of the Board of Trustees of the Southern University. [aa]

SOUTHERN UNIVERSITY

The next session of this Institution will commence on the first *Wednesday in October*. It is one of the cheapest and most thorough Colleges in this country. The instruction is of the highest character in all the Schools of its Collegiate, Medical and Law Departments. Board is from $10 to $16 per moth. For particulars and catalogue, address Dr. A. S. Andrews, or Prof. O. F. Casey.

A. S. ANDREWS, President.
Greensboro, Ala., Aug. 13.   d2tow w1m

Ad for Southern University, of which Hubert Dent Served as a trustee. It later merged to become a part Birmingham Southern University.

The Southern University was a college for men at Greensboro, Alabama operated by the Alabama Conference of the Methodist Church. After years of preparation, Southern had begun instruction in 1859, with assets of $200,000 and a bright future. The Civil War had swept away its faculty, its students, and its financial endowment,

---

[aa] The ministerial assignments of this Annual Conference reported the assignment of the Rev. David Crockett Crook to Troy and Brundidge, in the Union Springs District. We last encountered him as Col. Crook, commander of the 28th Tennessee Infantry Regiment, with near-mortal wounds sustained at the Battle of Atlanta, the same occasion on which S. H. Dent received a less serious wound. By the time Col. Crook recovered, the War was over. He carried out his *in extremis* commitment to become a minister, entered the Methodist ministry in Tennessee, and later transferred to the Alabama Conference. In 1931 his grandson, John Allen Crook, would marry Hubert Dent's granddaughter, Joy McDowell.

leaving nothing but the main building and grounds upon which it stood. At the time Hubert was appointed to the Board, Southern had recently reestablished departments of Theology, Law, and Medicine, and was fighting to survive. "During the trying times of Reconstruction the trustees struggled heroically, maintaining the life of the institution against difficulties well-nigh insurmountable."[785] One of the measures taken to increase enrollment was to advertise the college's offering in local newspapers. The ad reproduced nearby appeared in the Eufaula Times on August 13, 1872, and numerous other times.

Over time the Southern University not only survived, it prospered and became a quality institution of higher learning. All three of Hubert's own sons, other Young grandsons, and young men from throughout South Alabama and beyond, would graduate with degrees from the Southern University. When the North Alabama Conference of the Methodist Church later came into existence, it also sponsored another such institution, Birmingham College, which was also successful. In 1918, the year after Hubert Dent's death, the two Conferences of the Church voted to merge the two colleges into one. Thus was born Birmingham-Southern University, the high quality institution which operates in Birmingham, Alabama today.

In December of 1872, perhaps the Democrats concluded that it was in the public interest to have an early end to the absurd spectacle of competing legislatures, and to achieve a recognized government. Perhaps they were influenced by the consideration that, with federal troops on the capitol lawn and the resources of the Federal government arrayed against them, they had little chance of prevailing in this contest. Or they may have felt that the days of the Radical regime would soon be over anyway. For whatever reasons, the Democrats, joined by the Barbour Democrats Dent, Williams, Cody, and Mabry, reluctantly decided to acquiesce in the Attorney General's cynical "compromise" of the "dual legislatures."

The *Montgomery Advertiser* had high praise for Hubert Dent and his colleagues for their conduct in this matter. The *Times* reprinted the editorial:

> "The Barbour Delegation"
> "We [the *Eufaula Times*] are exceedingly gratified to be able to lay before our readers the following just and dutiful tribute to the members of the General Assembly from this county which we find in that sterling paper, the *Montgomery Advertiser*. We feel assured that nothing could be more acceptable to the better portion of our citizens than to see the men they had delighted to honor, so highly commended by a journalist whose praise is never bestowed when it is not rigidly merited:
> '...In consenting to yield their strict legal rights, under the peculiar circumstances of the case, the able and patriotic Representatives from Barbour, who, for the past thirty days have so bravely defended the honor of their county, the rights of their constituents, the dignity and privileges of the General Assembly of Alabama, and the integrity of the Constitution and laws, deserve the thanks of every conservative in the legislature and in the state. It was believed by the conservative members of the General Assembly upon consultation, that a wise expediency demanded

acquiescence in the plan of adjustment proposed by the Attorney General of the United States! But that acquiescence could never have been indicated, if the senator and members from Barbour upon whom the hardest conditions were imposed and the largest demands made, had not voluntarily consented to submit to the necessary sacrifice! Instead, therefore, of remaining in the legislature on their legally impregnable *prima facie* title, they have consented to allow their Radical opponents the advantage secured for them in the Attorney General's plan, and will, themselves, contest the seats, which are theirs according to all parliamentary rules.

'It was proper, as the Barbour Representatives thought, to aid their friends in the General Assembly in carrying out the policy of acceptance of the scheme of legislative organization proposed by the Washington cabinet, and they have not hesitated a moment as to their course! There is nothing mean or selfish about such men, and they will yet have their reward.'"

Commenting favorably upon each member of the Barbour delegation, the *Advertiser* made these observations about Hubert Dent:

"Capt. Dent, one of Barbour's conservative representatives, stands among the most promising young men of this state. He is cool, well informed, and the structure of his intellect is eminently logical. He is a rising lawyer, and yet destined to be a conspicuous figure, as we predict, in the politics of the state. He commanded what was known as Dent's Battery during the war and was recognized as a courageous and competent officer and thorough patriot!"[786]

Despite this settlement, Spencer had reason to continue to worry about his seat in the U. S. Senate. He still had to gain control of the Alabama Senate, and this is perhaps the most reprehensible part of the swindle. A senate committee worked through the Christmas holidays reviewing evidence in the Martin-Jones contest, and thereafter the divided committee rendered two reports, one favoring the election of the Democrat Martin, and the other, the Radical Miller. Sen. Edwards, a Democratic member of the committee, wished to have some time at home in Blount County, but did not wish to be absent when the Martin-Miller contest might be called up for a vote. Hearing of this, Sen. Glass, a Republican from Macon County, agreed to enter into a "pair" with Edwards. This is a time-honored legislative device, legally binding, used when two members on opposites sides of an issue wish to be absent on the day the issue is voted on. Each agrees with the other not to vote, thereby producing the same result as if they had both been present and voted. Under Edwards' and Glass' pair agreement, entered in the presence of other senators as witnesses, each pledged "as senators and Freemasons" that for a period of fifteen days, neither would vote on the Martin-Miller contest.

Comfortable with his "pair" agreement, the Democrat, Edwards then left for his home in Blount County, thinking that Glass was on his way to Macon County. However, Glass surreptitiously returned to Montgomery the same day, and waited in his room at the Madison

456

House hotel. The next day, by prearrangement, the Radical Lt. Gov. McKinstry called up the Martin-Miller contest for action, whereupon a Democratic senator moved to adopt the committee report declaring the Democrat Martin the winner. A Radical senator offered a substitute motion accepting the report certifying the Radical Miller as the winner. Also by prearrangement, as the roll was being called, Glass entered the senate chamber and violated his pair agreement by casting his vote, the deciding vote, in favor of the substitute motion.[787] Pandemonium broke out as Democratic senators clamored for the floor, objecting to this illegal and unethical action.

In the rulings which he now made, Lt. Gov. McKinstry justified the contempt which the *Eufaula Times* had expressed for him months earlier, when it referred to him as an "unprincipled old braggart," who demonstrates "what a dearth of material there is in the radical Party when they have no one better than he is to place in nomination for such an office..."[788] Steadfastly ignoring all objections, McKinstry allowed Glass to vote, ruled the substitute motion adopted, refused to allow further voting, reconsideration, or motions of any kind, and in violation of all parliamentary procedures, ruled the Radical candidate Miller to be the duly elected senator.[789] This gave the Spencer Radicals a majority of one, and precluded the election of any competing candidate for the U. S. Senate.

No reelection of Spencer other than that of the courthouse rump ever took place. Nevertheless, the Radical-dominated United States Senate seated Spencer, and denied the contest of Sykes, who had been elected by the regular legislature.[790]

The legislative "compromise" which gave the radicals the Barbour County seats did permit the Barbour Democrats to continue their contests for the disputed seats in court and/or by parliamentary means, which they did. But as a practical matter, this was expected to become academic, and it did become academic, after the Radicals succeeding in gaining control of the temporary organization of the legislature. In any event, months later, to no one's surprise, the Republican-dominated Alabama Supreme Court sustained the position of the Republicans in the Barbour County races.[791] Commenting on a related decision by that Court, the Eufaula Times called the Court a "corrupt judiciary," and its judgment an "unutterable lie," in holding that

> "...a fraction of the Legislature, which never for one instant contained a quorum of lawfully elected members, was the legal and constitutional General Assembly of the State of Alabama, and that its acts are therefore valid law of the commonwealth. In other words, the Supreme Court of Alabama, composed of Republicans, has declared an unmitigated and brazen falsehood...Truly have the people of this land fallen into a den of official thieves. Honor and truth are banished from high places. Men cease to be surprised at the most hideous moral enormities..."[792]

By these means, the New York adventurer Spencer was able to oust men like Hubert Dent and his Barbour colleagues from the Alabama legislature, and to perpetuate himself in office for another six years, until March 1879. A recent (1994) work of revisionist Alabama history written by Rogers, Ward, Atkins and Flynt, seeks to justify and defend Radical reconstruction based on alleged benefits to blacks. The factual record compels the authors to make admissions such as these:

> "Spencer was reelected, but his black followers were the losers. They were exploited, manipulated, and routinely betrayed—less by the Democrats than by the only party that promised them help and support" [i.e. the Republicans].[793]

Hubert Dent returned to Eufaula to resume his law practice, with the feeling that he had done his duty and that the days of the corrupt Radical regime were numbered.

48
The Address of the Fifty

"...there is no unprejudiced *man of any party, who dares deny, that [Judge Kiels' Court] has long since become an admitted burlesque, and a public mockery."*

The Address of the Fifty

Political events in Eufaula during this era often involved participation of one or more members of the extended Young family. In the Eufaula municipal elections of 1873, Hubert Dent assisted in getting his brother-in-law, Dr. Hamilton Weedon, involved in city politics. A city convention was held at the Opera House to nominate candidates for mayor, city clerk, and marshal. The *Times* of February 18, 1873 reported that it was attended by "the largest crowd we have ever seen in the Opera House." Chairman John Cochran appointed a committee of nine, consisting of two from each ward, to draft resolutions governing the convention. Hubert Dent was appointed to this committee, and among the resolutions reported was one providing that all in attendance would support the nominees resulting from the meeting, which was adopted. After the principal candidates were nominated, including Wells Bray for Mayor, Capt. Dent announced a request that the voters of the Third Ward meet that night at 7:30 at Guice's Cotton Office in Hart's Block to select candidates for alderman, or city councilman, from that ward. Similar meetings were scheduled for other wards. The *Times* reported the results of the Third Ward meeting:

> "At a meeting of the citizens of this ward, held last night in the office of J. T. Guice to nominate the aldermen, Dr. D. G. Stern was called to the chair...The meeting then proceeded to balloting, which resulted in the selection of Dr. H. M. Weedon and Mr. W. A. Hancock, as nominees for alderman from that ward, by a large majority, and on motion the nominations were made unanimous."

The city election on February 24 "passed off quietly and peaceably but not without great interest and hard work on both sides." For mayor, Wells Bray defeated the Radical nominee, J. H. Locke (who had also been the Radical candidate opposing Alto Lee for county solicitor the previous year, the contest of which was still in the courts.) Hamilton Weedon was elected to the city council without dispute. The other Democrats were also elected, but one or two had to withstand election disputes by their Radical opponents, which were not successful.

The leader of the Radical Republicans in Barbour County was one Elias M. Kiels. Regarded by Eufaulians as the ultimate scalawag, he was the most hated symbol of Radical reconstruction at the local level. Kiels had lived obscurely in Barbour County for many years, engaging in a variety of occupations. In the 1840's he had operated a dry goods and grocery store on Broad Street.[794] From an 1853 entry in the farm journal of John Horry Dent, we see Kiels buying cotton from J. H. Dent.[795] Before the war, Kiels had secretly favored the Union, and he contrived to avoid service in the Confederate Army.

When the horde of Republican carpetbaggers, backed by the Federal troops, arrived to take over state government, Kiels saw his opportunity. He declared himself a Republican, allied himself with them, and became part of the Radical organization. He procured a job as "collector of revenue," perhaps with the help of the dispenser of patronage, U. S. Senator Spencer, and accumulated some means.[796]

Even with the Radical-controlled black vote, Kiels failed in his effort to get elected Mayor of Eufaula in 1870. He then successfully ran for judge of the City Court, a position which, despite its name, was elected by the voters of the entire county. Although he had no legal qualifications of any kind, Kiels' control of the black vote in the county achieved his election. Using the judgeship as his power base, for the next four years he conducted what was regarded as a dictatorship over the community. He was seen as an unscrupulous demagogue in the typical carpetbag-scalawag pattern of Sen. Spencer, manipulating the votes of the unsophisticated, recently-freed blacks for his own purposes and profit, the blacks themselves receiving little or no legitimate benefit.

In December 1873, while purporting to charge the grand jury, Kiels unleashed a barrage of criticism against the white community of Eufaula. Playing to his black constituents, Kiels lambasted the whites in general with accusations of all kinds of the most reprehensible conduct, hereafter discussed in more detail. His racial demagoguery left the populace seething.

Eufaula's feelings of outrage against Kiels reached the boiling point in connection with the city elections of February 23, 1874, two months later. During this period, Alabama Democrats were making plans for a major campaign push in the November General election to take control of the state away from the Radicals. In this February Eufaula city election, which might be regarded as a forerunner of events in November, the tension was heightened when Elias Kiels sought to consolidate his power by handpicking and placing on the ballot his black candidates for city marshal and for a vacancy on the city council.

In an effort to curb what was felt to be a common practice by blacks of multiple voting and voting by non-residents or other ineligibles, the Democratic Eufaula city council enacted a strong poll-watching ordinance. On election day, large numbers of blacks were milling around town, said to be aroused by the Radicals to a high pitch of belligerence against the whites.

As the voting proceeded, a Democratic poll watcher questioned the voting of a black person whom the Democrats contended was "well-known to be an idiot." A quarrel ensued, which other blacks and whites entered; fists started swinging; possibly a knife was drawn, and as the dispute escalated, 25 or 30 shots were fired. When the smoke cleared however, no one had been killed or even seriously hurt in the melee. But the Republicans lost the election.

Eufaulians were incensed when the Radical press of the state, calling the episode a "riot," attacked the white community as the responsible instigators of the trouble. Among the specific individuals included in the Radicals' finger pointing were Dick Solomon, one of the

Democratic candidates, and George H. Dent, who, it was claimed, were determined "to carry the election."[797] The town resolved to expose Kiels and set the record straight on what were regarded as irresponsible lies by Kiels and his allies in the Radical newspapers.

On March 28, in a mass meeting of Eufaulians, Edward B. Young, his son-in-law, Hubert Dent, and a total of fifty of the town's "most influential attorneys, bankers, public officials, businessmen, and ministers," were appointed to a committee to prepare and publish a comprehensive public statement of the true facts about Kiels and about the election-day troubles.[798] The resulting document, known as *The Address of the Fifty,"* was a sizable pamphlet, of which two thousand copies were printed and distributed. It was also reproduced in the *Montgomery Advertiser*.

The first signature appearing on the *Address* (after that of its chairman, John McNab) is Edward Young's, followed by that of J. G. L. Martin, (Ada Young's father-in-law), and soon followed by Hubert Dent's and the signatures of the other town leaders.

The statement effectively conveys the honest indignation of citizens who feel that their community and its affairs have too long been lied about and mishandled by self-seeking demagogues:

Eufaula, April 9, 1874

"To our Fellow Citizens:

"The undersigned Committee of Fifty, among the oldest citizens of this community,[bb] was appointed by the desire and unanimous vote of a large assembly, irrespective of party, at the City Hall of Eufaula, on the evening of the 28th ultimo.

"Anonymous correspondents…of the *State Journal* at Montgomery, [the Radical newspaper] have recently assailed our people as the enemies of peace and order and charged them with the authorship of the riot in the city on the 23rd of February last.

"At the opening of the last December term of the City Court of Eufaula, they were called upon to listen in silence to a tirade of mendacious and offensive accusations, uttered from the bench in the shape of a charge to the grand jury by a person occupying that high position, who prostituted it to the purposes of injustice, and availed himself of the unusual chance of a respectable audience to malign the community in which he lives and utter slanders upon it which could not there be replied to.

[bb] One of the fifty signatories, James Patton McDowell, had only arrived in Eufaula with his family in about 1870, and soon become a participant in community affairs. The McDowell family had emigrated after the war from Greeneville, East Tennessee, a pro-Union area, where they had been strong Southern supporters. James' son, Charles Samuel McDowell, Sr. later married Margaret (known as "Maggie"), the daughter of Col. Archibald S. McKay of Barbour County. The McDowells would enter the story of the Youngs and Dents in 1901, when Charlie and Maggie's oldest son, Charlie, Jr married Hubert Dent's youngest daughter, Caroline ("Carrie").

"It is remembered that speaking of the white people here generally, that he contrasted them unfavorably with those of other sections of the state, that he characterized us as a mob; stated that we proscribed and endeavored maliciously to injure those who differed with us in political opinion; denounced us as law breakers; charged that we were unfriendly to the interests of the colored man, and that with evil intentions we had introduced and formed the Order of Patrons of Husbandry, which he stigmatized as nothing less than a second edition of the Ku Klux; claimed that we sympathized with criminals and habitually strove to screen them from punishment; declared that some of the most prudent and respectable lawyers at his Bar deserved to be, and but for his mercy, would be stricken from the rolls for giving legal advice to parties who he desired to punish; foully aspersed the City Council of Eufaula by the assertion that they were enemies of public order, and the abettors and apologists of murder!"

The citizens went on to "pledge their honor and veracity for the accuracy" of the facts to be set forth, with a "respectful request for consideration by a candid public."

The statement asserted that the white population of the town had been slandered by the accusation that they were the authors of the municipal election "riot." These citizens had the right to seek to elect a qualified city council and marshal, in opposition to "a ticket with an incompetent black candidate for marshal, and a black pauper, who signs his name with a cross-mark, for alderman in one of the most important wards in the city." The latter ticket

"...was started by a few designing leaders, backed mainly by ignorant and irresponsible negroes, many of them the loungers and vagrants who infest the streets and most of them, even if correctly inclined, without the capacity to understand their own interests..." These colored people, influenced by this opposition, and with their prejudices aroused by the antagonism against the whites, appeared at the polls on the day of election, in a temper which manifested their desire to generate disturbances. The influence of mean whisky was plainly visible, and green hickory sticks freshly cut as if for the occasion were noticed in the hands of some of them not notorious as observers of the peace."

The statement went on to relate that despite these circumstances, the city authorities were able to maintain order for several hours, until an aggressive black person with a knife entered the voting enclosure in connection with voting by a black man "well-known to be an idiot." Others intervened, and a shot was fired by a black, which provoked firing in reply.

The *Address* charged that the riot did not occur by accident, "but as the natural result of causes which have long been at work in this community and which have lately developed themselves in a gradual increased bitterness of feeling on the part of the blacks toward the whites, and a greatly increased boldness and frequency of crime, committed by the former."

> "This unhappy state of affairs we are reluctantly forced to declare is mainly due to the wicked influence of one individual in our midst, Elias M. Kiels, judge of the City Court of Eufaula."

The statement points out that Kiels has no qualifications to be a judge; has never "made the slightest preparation for the discharge of his judicial duties;" that he obtained the seat through false pretenses; and that he clings to his seat despite calls for his resignation from his entire bar, with a single exception.

> "...there is no unprejudiced man of any party, who dares deny, that he has so administered the law in the court where he presides, that it has long since become an admitted burlesque, and a public mockery. He has lowered the dignity of his tribunal to that degree that no inhabitant who feels any pride in the county where he dwells and possesses intelligence sufficient to have an idea of what a court should be, can think if it without humiliation..."

The Address goes on to describe a magistrate with no instinct for justice or any sense of propriety. He places on the grand jury members of his party fresh from the penitentiary for theft, so that they can receive a juror's pay. He retains a felon as the doorkeeper of his courtroom. He virtually guarantees an acquittal to every offender who appeals to him from any judgment rendered in the Mayor's Court.

> "The thieves and violators of public decency, the prowlers and drunkards, and vagrants together with disorderly women were taught that in his court was a safe asylum to which they could fly with confidence of protection and acquittal."

The statement recited that the effect upon the community, upon the people of other parts of the county, who came to Eufaula to trade, was disastrous. They could only come in groups, in fear of being robbed in the suburbs. Property was stolen nightly. Men were tortured with apprehension if they left their homes.

The Address of the Fifty was the beginning of the end for Elias M. Kiels. Within less than a year, Radical rule in Barbour County and Alabama was overthrown, and Kiels was gone from the state forever.

49
"Redemption"

"The Negroes had come in columns, two together...noisy...turbulent, boisterous, cursing the whites. They were armed with clubs, ready to abuse, to browbeat, to threaten."
Testimony of Hubert Dent before Congressional Committee

For years, with almost religious fervor, the single-minded political objective of most white Alabamians had been to throw off the yoke of corrupt Radical Republican rule, or in the language of the day, to "redeem" the state. The Democrats' near-success in obtaining control of the Alabama legislature in 1872 had provided much encouragement that Radical rule could soon be defeated, and it was decided that 1874 would be the year of "redemption." For many reasons, there was growing opposition in the north to the Radical Republicans' reconstruction policy. Divisions had developed within the Alabama Republican party. North Alabama whites who had sometimes voted Republican were returning to the Democratic fold. While the bulk of the blacks remained loyal to the Republicans, some had become disillusioned with the broken promises of white carpetbaggers.

The Democrats were more united than ever. Shrewdly, the Democrats nominated for governor George S. Houston, a prominent north Alabama leader who before the war had been a "unionist," but not a very strong one, and had not opposed the Confederacy. He ran on a platform declaring that, for years the Radicals had inflamed the passions of the races, had administered the state with corruption and extravagance, and that it was time for the whites to unite in self-defense. A furious campaign was conducted throughout the state.

In Barbour County the Democrats also ran a strong ticket, including Gen. Alpheus Baker for City Judge, John McNab for circuit clerk, Gen. Henry D. Clayton for circuit judge. Kiels was running for reelection as City Judge, and he also waged an aggressive campaign throughout the county.

On Election Day, November 4, 1874, Alabama was "redeemed." The Radicals were swept out, and the Democrats won all state offices and control of both houses of the legislature. This was the permanent end of Republican power in Alabama. Not until the election of Gov. Guy Hunt in 1986 did a candidate bearing the label of "Republican" occupy the governor's office (and, except for its name, his party bore no similarity to the one rejected in 1874.)

The state's redemption was marred by tragic circumstances in Barbour County. Election day was extremely tense. As the Radical leader of the county, Elias Kiels had arranged for Federal troops to be posted in Eufaula, Clayton, and other precincts in the county. In response to Kiels' fears of trouble, Capt Daggett, the Federal commanding officer in Eufaula, had wired his commanding General in Atlanta, Gen. McDowell, for permission to place his troops a reasonable distance from the polls, but out of sight. Perhaps due in part to changing official attitudes about maintaining the Radicals is power, Gen. McDowell tersely replied, "You are stationed at Eufaula to aid United States Civil Officers to execute processes of United States Courts."

On the morning of November 4, large numbers of blacks streamed into Eufaula, 800 coming in from the north down Eufaula Street, and 500 from the south on Old Dale Road, marching in "military formation." Col. Eli Shorter saw many of them armed with clubs and pistols.[799] Whites were also out in large numbers. The air was laden with tension, mistrust, and antagonism. The situation was a powder keg, ready to explode at the slightest provocation. It exploded; blood and death in the streets were the results.

The trouble started in late morning, after most of the voting had been completed. The facts are in dispute, but the evidence indicates that the riot began when a black voter, attempting to vote the Democratic ticket, was assaulted by a black Republican named Milas Lawrence. A white Democrat, Charles Goodwin, sought to protect the black voter, and in the scuffle a shot was fired (by Milas Lawrence, according to Dorman) which set off firing by both sides from every direction.[800] The shooting lasted for only a few minutes. The casualties are not certain, but one eyewitness, newspaper editor John Black, reported that nine or ten blacks were killed, and 70 people were wounded, including eight whites.

But the violence was not over. At the rural community of Spring Hill, in northern Barbour County 18 miles from Eufaula, the voting place was in the country store of Michael Cody, who had been one of Hubert Dent's fellow Democratic candidates for the legislature in 1872. Elias Kiels was present at this polling place all day as an election supervisor, and had brought with him his 17-year old son, Willie. Gunshots were heard during the day. There were federal troops in the community, but pursuant to his orders, Captain Daggett had instructed the soldiers to stay away from the crowd. By five or six o'clock in the afternoon, the voting had been completed, the polls were closed, and the votes were about to be counted, when a group of armed white men entered the store and shot out the lights. Kiels and his son took cover behind the counter. According to Kiels' own testimony, his life was saved when he was protected by three of the men in the group, the Comer brothers, and one of them, J. W. Comer, was shot in the leg protecting Kiels.[801] However, one of the shots fired in the dark struck young Willie C. Kiels and killed him.

Proceedings for the impeachment of Kiels were later commenced in the Alabama legislature, but they were soon rendered unnecessary. In early December 1874, Elias Kiels fled from Barbour County, never to return, and took up residence in Washington, D. C. On December 16, he telegraphed Gov. Houston his resignation as City Court judge, and the governor appointed Gen. Alpheus Baker to the vacancy. Barbour County had also been "redeemed."

The election day events in Barbour County became a minor *cause celebre*, and Kiels became a national figure. Pursuant to a Congressional resolution, The Speaker of the House appointed a Select Committee of five congressmen to investigate Barbour County, consisting of three Republicans and two Democrats, called the Coburn Committee. The committee started taking testimony in Washington on December 24, the first witness being Kiels himself.

In January, after hearing brief testimony in Montgomery and Mobile, the committee interrogated numerous witnesses in Eufaula who had been in positions to observe the events, including Col. Eli Shorter, Captain Hubert Dent, Dr. Hamilton Weedon, John McNab, and others.

Dr. Hamilton Weedon testified that he had just been starting off to his drugstore to fill two prescriptions when he suddenly heard the wrangling about some man who had been intimidated and threatened to be mobbed by some Negroes because he had voted the Democratic ticket. [802]

Hubert Dent testified that he had witnessed the difficulty, and that after the initial shots were fired[803]

> "...the Negroes had fled indiscriminately...there were four or five hundred in a body massed in a block south of the voting place, in the middle of the street...the whites believed that they were going to renew the attack upon them and destroy the town. The Negroes had come in columns, two together...noisy...turbulent, boisterous, cursing the whites. They were armed with clubs, ready to abuse, to browbeat, to threaten."[cc]

When the Coburn Committee concluded its investigation on February 23, 1875, it rendered a majority and a minority report. To no one's surprise, the three Republicans concluded that the entire trouble was instigated by whites, who mercilessly mistreated and killed the "defenseless colored men." The two Democrats concluded that, despite threatening and offensive demonstrations by the blacks, the white citizens and peace officers through extraordinary diligence had preserved order until late morning, after most of the voting had been completed; that then a colored man who had voted Democratic was rushed by another black, provoking an affray in when the blacks commenced a general attack upon the whites; that the whites provoked no difficulty and only fought on the defensive and used weapons only in self-defense.[804]

The excitement eventually died down. The Youngs, Dents, Weedons, and other Eufaulians, finally free from the hated Radical regime, turned to the long-term tasks of resolving the numerous economic and social problems arising from defeat, and to establishing a mutually fair and trusting relationship with its black citizens in the new era.

Some Federal troops still remained, but they caused no trouble, and even this token presence ended two years later. In what has been called "the crowning crime," in 1876 the

---

[cc] Testimony by Col. Eli Shorter indicated that he, and perhaps others, had asked Captain Daggett to personally go and urge the blacks in the interests of peace not to march into town in "military organization" with weapons, and when Daggett declined, Shorter made the same request to the Deputy U. S. Marshall, W. J. Williford. (Walker, p. 270). Found among the miscellaneous business papers of Edward Young is a contemporaneous handwritten notation, apparently about this issue. Written in an unfamiliar hand on the back of a Sept 1874 tax receipt is this notation: "T. G. Crayon was policeman who went to notify Negroes not to bring in their guns. Also notified Col. (sic) Daggett and Williford" (Papers of E. B. Young in possession of his family).

Radicals literally stole the presidency from the Democratic candidate who had won it, Samuel Tilden, and awarded it to the Republican, Rutherford B. Hays. The South acquiesced in this final outrage based upon Hays' commitment to remove all Federal troops from the South, a commitment which he promptly carried out in full.

Part V

Renewal and Recovery

50
The Eufaula National Bank

"I am making arrangements here to establish a Nat'l Bank at Eufaula, Ala and I see prospects very good to get up $100,000 capital... I would like you to give me all the information required how to proceed and if necessary I would go to Washington."
Edward B. Young to Comptroller of the Currency

With the advent of stable and responsible government, Eufaulians were ready to move forward with renewed business and commercial activity. In 1875, a Eufaulian, J. A. B. Besson, published a short history of Eufaula. (Besson's sister, Eliza, was Mrs. J. G. L. Martin, Ada Young's mother-in-law.) From the text as well as the advertisements in the back of the book, we see the activities of some of the Youngs and their connections, as well as the optimistic air that now pervaded the community.

Hubert Dent's legal career had prospered, and he was now practicing in a prestigious partnership with his old friend, Col. William C. Oates, of neighboring Henry County. Oates had commanded the Fifteenth Alabama Infantry Regiment when it fought alongside Dent's Battery during Sunday morning at Chickamauga. Oates' loss of an arm later in the war was not detrimental to his post-war political career. He became a congressman and, in 1894, with Hubert Dent's enthusiastic support, Oates would defeat Eufaula Populist Reuben Kolb for governor, as we will later discuss. Oates and Dent would become close allies in a number of political battles, and would serve and vote together in the Alabama Constitutional Convention of 1901. But in 1875, they were, like other lawyers of the day, announcing the services of their law firm in Besson's *History*:[805]

W. C. OATES.   S. H. DENT.

OATES & DENT,
ATTORNEYS AT LAW,
EUFAULA, ALA.

CIRCUIT OF PRACTICE: HENRY, DALE, BARBOUR
AND BULLOCK COUNTIES IN ALABAMA,
UNITED STATES DISTRICT COURTS AND CIRCUIT
AT MONTGOMERY,
SUPREME COURT OF ALABAMA; ALSO, IN
SOUTHWESTERN GEORGIA.

☞ Smmonses executed twenty days before Court. Judgment first Term, if no defense. When claims are sent for collection, give full name of each owner of debt or member of partnership; and if an Account, the name of a witness to prove it.

469

Hubert's brother and brother-in-law, George Dent and Dr. Hamilton Weedon, were doing well in their pharmacy business, and their advertisement in Besson's *History* shows some of their wares:

THE PLANTERS
VEGETABLE LIVER PILLS.

THIS IS NO PATENT MEDICINE.— The Pills are carefully compounded in strict accordance with a recipe used by many of our oldest and best Southern Physicians. Those who practice medicine here are best acquainted with the various types and phases of disease in this latitude, and consequently know best what our sick people require. These Pills are used with the most splendid effect in all sorts of

FEVERS

where a safe and gentle laxative or purgative is required, and as a remedy in

Dyspepsia or Torpor of the Liver

they cannot be surpassed. They do not cause griping or piles, and will not leave you constipated, as most purgative medicines do.

Heartburn, Headache, Colic, Jaundice, Costiveness

ARE READILY CURED BY THESE PILLS.

Remember also that the FARMERS FEVER PILLS surpass all others for *Chills and Fevers*, and that

Sarsaparilla Bitters

IS THE MOST SATISFACTORY BLOOD-PURIFIER KNOWN

MANUFACTURED BY

WEEDON & DENT,

WHOLESALE & RETAIL DRUGGISTS,

EUFAULA, ALA.

In 1875, Weedon & Dent acquired an important new employee. Warren Fillmore Dent was the younger brother of Hubert and George. Born March 3, 1855, in Charles County, Maryland, he was the third son of Dr. S. W. and Emma Smoot Dent. We last encountered young Warren as a 10 year old Confederate agent, helping his father smuggle Confederate mail from Virginia into Maryland. Like his father and his two older brothers, Warren attended school at Charlotte Hall in St. Mary's County, Maryland, graduating from there in June 1872. Aware of the success of his two older brothers in Eufaula and the opportunities available there, he followed them and settled in Eufaula in 1875, at the age of 20. George and Hamilton immediately hired him to work for Weedon & Dent. It was not possible for Warren to further emulate his two brothers by also marrying a Young sister; the youngest, Carrie, had married Noah Roberts shortly after Warren arrived in town. Nevertheless, Warren chose well. He married a granddaughter of the Youngs' old friend, John Horry Dent. In 1880, Warren married Mary Elizabeth Wellborn, the daughter of "Minna" and Eufaula lawyer, Col. M. B. Wellborn, Sr.[dd] After working successfully for Weedon & Dent for ten years, Warren would start his own wholesale drug business in Montgomery, but we will hear more about Warren later.

Ada Young's husband, James H. G. Martin, had opened a grocery store, and also advertised in Besson's *History*:

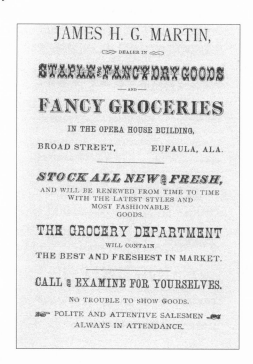

[dd] This adds an interesting but confusing coincidence to the relationships. The three Dent brothers from Maryland, i. e. Hubert, George, and Warren, were not related to John Horry Dent (who, it will be recalled, had migrated to Barbour County from Charleston, South Carolina, in about 1836.) In 1859, while John Horry Dent and his family were still living in Barbour County (i. e. before his post-war move to Cave Springs, near Rome, Georgia), his oldest daughter, Emma Julia, nicknamed "Minna," had married M. B. Wellborn of Eufaula. Their daughter, Mary Elizabeth, was thus a "Dent descendent," but it was a different Dent family; she was not related to Warren F. Dent, until she became his wife. The Confederate Veteran, Vol XXXIII, pg. 188; Hopkins (cited infra), p. 14, 113

Besson's extravagant descriptions of Eufaula reflect the relief and upbeat attitudes that came with the end of Reconstruction:

> "Her [Eufaula's] climate is salubrious, and does not require acclimatizing for Northern or Western people to live here comfortably and healthfully all the year around. No one ever visits her hospitable people who do not feel glad they have made them a visit and would be pleased to make it their home....
>
> The dire effects of the late civil war are fast fading away; public confidence is now rapidly being restored; better laws are being enacted; the laboring classes have gone to work with an energy and good will never before witnessed since the war and a general good feeling exists between labor and capital, and we may safely predict that it will not be long before this whole Southern land shall again "blossom as the rose."
>
> The curse of political corruption, that hung like a millstone around the neck of the people, fastened upon them by a set of unscrupulous and contemptible scalawags and carpet-baggers, has now been removed and hope encouragingly beckons onward. And, now, Eufaula presents advantages of illimitable extent, both in a commercial and financial point of view..."[806]

Edward Young shared this optimism, and in 1875, the first year after the ouster of the Radicals, he led the way to business revival by establishing a new national bank. Edward had opened the first bank in the town and county in 1839, the Irwinton Bridge Bank. It was an unregulated bank which flourished for at least six years before closing its doors. Edward had returned to banking in 1859 with the Young, Woods and Gardner banking partnership. After the war, he had continued his banking firm in partnership with Woods, and later in business with his son, Ed, under the name, "E. B. Young & Son Bankers." These were unregulated banking firms. At age 73, Edward now decided that the time was ripe for Eufaula to have a national banking association, which would be regulated by the Comptroller of the Currency under the federal banking laws. An application for a charter for such a bank must be reviewed and found to be sound and feasible by the Comptroller of the Currency, and thereafter its operations must be audited each year by Federal bank examiners. Among other advantages, this would put Edward ahead of his main competitor, John McNab, who had not converted his banking business into a national banking association.

We find Edward again in New York, probably to raise capital for his projected new bank, when he took the initial step toward organizing. He wrote the following letter to the New York Office of the Comptroller of the currency:[807]

"Hon. Jno. M. Broadhead   New York, Sept 3, 1875

"Dear Sir,

          I am making arrangements here to establish a Nat'l Bank at Eufaula, Ala and I see prospects very good to get up $100,000 capital. And would like to get a charter with the privilege to extend to $300,000. We have an old charter that was issued to some parties there some years ago, and they made no use of it and left it with us. I wish to know if we could act on that, but it does not embrace in it our name. Then we thought that there might be some alterations since that was granted. I would like you to give me all the information required how to proceed and if necessary I would go to Washington. As I wish to know this before we opened the books for subscriptions yet we know enough to warrant to make application for it. Your attention to this will confer a favor on us.

                                        Yours Truly
                                        Edw. B. Young

Address me
Care of Frisbee Roberts Jr
P. O. Box 3406
New York"

This letter is date-stamped into the New York office of the Comptroller on the next day, September 4, by L. B. Curtis, the "acting Comptroller," and thereafter "respectfully referred to the Comptroller of the Currency," by him.

These officials promptly provided the necessary forms. Under date of October 18, the group filed a "Certificate of Organization" and "Articles of Incorporation," reflecting that the name of the proposed Bank would be the Eufaula National Bank; that its Board of Directors would consist of seven stockholders; that its first Board meeting was held at the offices of E. B. Young and Son, Eufaula, Alabama on October 18, 1875; that its capital stock would consist of $58,000 divided into 580 shares of $100 each, but may be increased to a sum not exceeding $200,000. The list of subscribing stockholders was as follows:

Name	Residence	No. Of Shares
Edw. B. Young	Eufaula, Ala	100 shares
B. B. Fields	Eufaula, Ala	5 shares
H. Lampley	Eufaula, Ala	5 shares
R. H. McDonald	New York	100 shares
W. H. Foy	Eufaula, Ala	10 shares
S. H. Dent	Eufaula, Ala	50 shares

Geo. W. Dent	Eufaula, Ala.	50 shares
R. J. Woods	Eufaula, Ala	10 shares
H. M. Weedon	Eufaula, Ala.	50 shares
Henry E. Robinson	New York	200 shares
	Total	580

On September 28, 1875 a letter over Edward's signature, but actually written by his son, Ed, in his beautiful, polished hand, amended the application. Addressed to the Hon. Jno. Jay Knox, Comptroller, the letter was on behalf of a slightly different list of stockholders, and proposed capital of $100,000, with authority to increase to $250,000, and the privilege of commencing business after $50,000 was paid in.

This amended filing was accompanied by a letter signed by Congressman Jere N. Williams (although the letter itself written in Ed Young's flourishing hand.) It will be recalled that Jere Williams was one of the other state representatives who, along with Hubert Dent, lost their seats to the Radical candidates in 1872 during the time of the "dual legislatures." Elected to Congress in the 1874 Democratic sweep, Williams now urged Comptroller Knox to approve Edward Young's application:

> "I cheerfully recommend the application of Mr. Edw. B. Young and others for the establishment of a National Bank at Eufaula, Ala, in the Second Congressional District of Alabama.
> I understand that two applications of this character have been previously made and nothing was done under them. I am satisfied that the parties are in earnest in this application, and hope it will receive favorable attention at your hands."

One of the most important activities of Eufaula banks was financing the cotton crop, and the post-war return of large cotton production was one impetus for Edward's decision to expand into a nationally chartered bank. In addition to serving the financial needs of the large plantation owners, Edward saw an opportunity to profit from meeting the borrowing needs of the smaller cotton farmers. Writing over his own signature as "Cashier," Ed Young on November 13 transmitted additional documents and commented on one of the policies planned for the new bank:

> "We experience so much trouble here during the cotton season for want of small loans, we deem it advisable to finance ones as small as the [banking] act allows."

The application process was slowed by a typical bureaucratic maneuver: the Comptroller notified the applicants that his office had adopted new forms, and that all the documents would have to be resubmitted on the new forms. Ed Young wrote back that it would cause long delays to get new signatures from the New York investors, who were about to depart for California, and asking to be allowed to proceed with the old forms and file new ones later. It is not clear whether this was allowed or not.

On November 20, Ed transmitted what was apparently the final Certificate of the Officers and Directors. Not all stockholders were directors, of course. The two officers of the Bank were Edward B. Young, president; and "E. B. Young, Jr.," Cashier; with the following seven directors:

Name	Residence	No. Of Shares
Edw. B. Young	Eufaula, Ala	100 shares
W. H. Foy	Eufaula, Ala	10 shares
S. H. Dent	Eufaula, Ala	50 shares
Geo. W. Dent	Eufaula, Ala.	50 shares
R. J. Woods	Eufaula, Ala	10 shares
H. M. Weedon	Eufaula, Ala.	50 shares
Henry E. Robinson	New York	200 shares
	Total	470

The bank commenced business in January 1876, although part of its subscribed capital was paid in later installments, totaling $58,000 by May 1876.

The names of most of the directors and stockholders are familiar to us. S. H. Dent, G. H. Dent, and H. M. Weedon are, of course, three of Edward's sons-in-law. (James H. G. Martin, Ada's husband, is the only one missing.) R. J. Woods was the son of Edward's old banking partner, Clayton R. Woods; the son by now was a successful merchant in his own right. We lack information about the two New York investors, Henry E. Robinson, and R. H. McDonald. W. H. Foy was not yet a family connection (but in 1908, his descendant, another William Humphrey Foy, would marry Hamilton and Mollie Weedon's granddaughter, Mary Weedon Ross).

The first federal examination was conducted February 1, 1876, shortly after the Bank opened. It reflected deposits of $19,000 and total resources of $90,000. The examiner commented that the bank "...has a list of stockholders ambitious to make it a success and have hopes of it being realized." The examiner gave these assessments of the officers:

President: "E. B. Young, a merchant and Banker for many years. Successful in business and popular."

Cashier: "E. B. Young, Jr., son of the president, young man, good habits and business qualifications. The business of the Bank will be done almost entirely by him with no assistants."

Directors: "Seven in number. Have no indebtedness to bank and will be so situated to aid the Bank at all times."

Stockholders: "Ten persons compose the list and are regarded as representing the most wealth of any citizens of the city."

The examiner commented on the Bank offices: "Formerly occupied by Young & Son Bankers, is centrally located convenient and rented by the Bank [from E. B. Young] at $500 per annum."

The June 1877 report of examination showed deposits of $22,000, and total resources of $117,000. Edward caused the bank to pay a large "dividend", which the examiner recorded as "10%," presumably meaning a 10% rate of investment return to the stockholders based on their capital contribution. This was probably more than the bank had actually earned, so that the payment was probably a partial return of capital. This was undoubtedly a public relations gesture by Edward to portray a successful first year of operations. Thereafter, the bank settled down to paying its investors from earnings a yearly dividend providing a 5% annual return on their original capital contribution. [ee]

In 1878, after the bank had been in operation for two years, its loans were $20,000 and its total resources had increased to $131,000. It paid a 5% dividend. The examiner remarked in his report, "In good condition. Making money," and made these comments on the people involved:

> "President: E. B. Young: Experienced and competent, though between seventy-five and eighty years old. [He was seventy-six.]
> Cashier: E. B. Young, Jr.; Competent.
> Directors: Seven; all good business men; the directors own 465/580 of the stock
> Stockholders: only ten in number; (a close corporation, well managed.)"

In the January 1879 examination, deposits had increased to $98,000, and total resources had increased to $211,000. A 5% dividend was paid. The officers shown are Edward as president and Ed as Cashier, with these directors: S. H. Dent, R. J. Woods, G. H. Dent, and H. M. Weedon. The examiner made these comments:

> "The Bank is owned by the President Mr. Young, Sr., his son the Cashier, and his sons-in-law who are the directors and it is very well managed and does for so small an institution an immense business, mainly in cotton exchange of which it handles over a million dollars annually."

Although the stock ownership of the Bank would change slightly from time to time over the years, it was always a Young family bank. It was effectively controlled by the family, and it would flourish and provide employment for members of the family for over a quarter of a century.

[ee] All dividends discussed herein are calculated based on the investors' original capital contributions, not current market values of the stock. The stock rarely changed hands, so that determining a market value was difficult even then, and today no market information is available.

Edward and Ann's only remaining unmarried child was their youngest, Caroline, or "Carrie." On January 12, 1876, Fendall Hall celebrated its last wedding of this generation when Carrie, age 20, married Noah W. Roberts. We last encountered Noah in 1868, when he joined Edward, Hubert, and Hamilton in signing the public resolution in support of the Democratic ticket opposing Grant and the Radical Republicans. Noah's parents, Ann and George Albert Roberts, were friends of the Youngs and active in the affairs of the town. Edward had participated in business enterprises with Albert Roberts, who was also serving as mayor of Eufaula.

The first four of the Young girls, i.e. Anna, Mollie, Helen, and Ada, had been actually married in Fendall Hall. However, at the time of Noah and Carrie's wedding, a new Methodist Church building had just been completed. In fact, at the dedication ceremony later in the year, Edward, who had probably been a substantial financial contributor to the project, would make the presentation of the completed church to the Bishop for consecration.[808] In a break with family practice, Carrie and Noah were married in the new church rather than at Fendall Hall, and theirs was the first wedding in the new church. However, the church ceremony was undoubtedly followed by a large and festive celebration at Fendall Hall.

Noah would have a career in business and would later serve as an officer of the cotton mill backed by George and Hubert Dent, which became an important Eufaula industry. Carrie and Noah would not have children.

Although Ann and Edward Young were now the only residents of Fendall Hall, it is doubtful that that sizable home ever became an "empty nest." With all six of their surviving children living and rearing children in Eufaula, it is certain that Fendall Hall continued to rock with the sounds of children and grandchildren.

One of the grandchildren, Anna and Hubert's son, "Hu" at the age of six was already showing signs of the alertness that would later lead to a career in Congress. An extant letter dated May 3, 1875, is purportedly from Hu to his Maryland grandfather, Dr. S. W. Dent, but is actually written for him by Hubert, who explains that the idea for the letter, and the language in it, is entirely that of little Hu: "Dear Grandpa, When your horses lay little colts I want you to save me two to hitch up to my little wagon to haul wood with. Papa works his horses so hard they wont lay colts…Mama say you and Grandma must come to see us too, and bring aunt Emma and Aunt Ella…"[809]

We will now look in on the Columbus Youngs.

51
Rising from the Ashes;
The Eagle and Phoenix Mills

"[William Young] has...pretty much controlled things in Columbus, and very naturally for his energy and foresight has built up the manufacturing interests, without which Columbus would be a dead town."

Raphael Moses, political opponent of William Young

We left William and Ellen Young on the night of April 16, 1865 as William was wounded during the sack of Columbus by Gen. Wilson's Federal cavalry. On that terrible night the Eagle Mills, the largest cotton mill facility in the South, William Young's principal ambition since his earliest days in Georgia, was burned to the ground. The loss to the shareholders was estimated at $1,000,000.

The Confederate defeat also brought to an end to the old Bank of Columbus. William had been one of the principal founders of the bank, investing the fortune he had accumulated as a commission merchant in Apalachicola. He had also guided it through its successful early years as president. His interests at Eagle Mills had since caused him to give up the presidency of the bank, but its closing was a loss of a major investment.

Columbus business and industry was almost totally destroyed. Many of these businesses would never operate again; but that was not the case with William H. Young. In a relatively short time, his instinctive economic drive would lead to a phenomenal recovery. He and his shareholders would soon enjoy a level of success and wealth far beyond that of the pre-war period.

Almost as soon as William's wound inflicted by Gen. Wilson's trooper had healed, the stockholders of the Eagle Mills met and voted to appoint him to salvage anything that was left of the now-defunct company. He was authorized to sell its ruined properties, collect any other assets, pay its debts, and close out the affairs of the company. With his usual sure-footedness, William landed on his feet. He was able to liquidate the wreck of the company on such favorable terms that he returned to his shareholders an amount significantly larger than their original investment.[810] But this was just the first step.

In 1866, even while Federal troops of occupation were still in the area, William assembled a group of optimistic stockholders and formed a new textile corporation having initial paid-in capital of $463,000. He used the name of his old company, but to dramatize his expectation that the new venture would successfully emerge from the destruction of the old, he named it, "The Eagle and Phoenix Manufacturing Company," after the mythical Egyptian bird which rose from its own ashes. (Over time, the spelling more frequently became "Phenix," which will be used herein.) The new company literally rose from the ashes of the old, because when the real estate of the old company was sold at public auction, it was bid in by the new company. Construction of a new mill began in 1867. It became operational in 1868, with 3000 spindles.

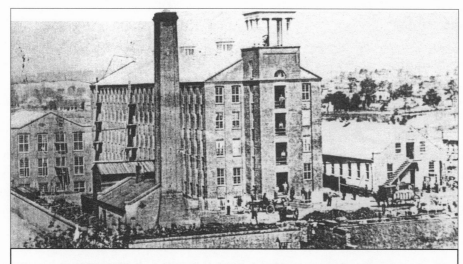

William Young's "Eagle & Phenix Mill No. 1," built in 1867

The new mill had scarcely become operational when William began planning for expansion. William's experience and acumen made him fully recognize the rare opportunities presented by a combination of an abundance of low-cost labor (both black and white) with few job opportunities, cheap water-powered energy from the Chattahoochee River, a plentiful near-by supply of cotton with little transportation cost, and a continued world-wide demand for cotton fabric. William knew this was the time to seize the moment and expand rapidly. In 1868 his stockholders authorized the construction of a second mill. Construction of Mill No. 2 began in 1869, and it became operational in 1871, with another 3000 spindles, thereby doubling the prior capacity.

To pay for the second mill, and perhaps with the feeling that this would not be the last, the stockholders voted to increase the capital stock to $1,250,000. Although the new issue almost tripled the prior capitalization, the new stock was promptly bought up by eager businessmen. William's brother, Edward, in Eufaula became a stockholder, and also his friend John Horry Dent, now located at his new farm, "Cottage Home," at Cave Springs, near Rome, Georgia. In his diary for Friday, January 31, 1870, J.H. Dent reports, "Have to go to Rome today to forward money to W. H. Young for shares in Eagle and Phoenix Manufacturing Company."[811]

Always an innovator, William experimented briefly with immigrant labor. In 1870, he imported 50 workers from England. The experiment was disastrous. William later described the English workers as "turbulent," and concluded that, "We get along very much better with our own people who have been raised about here." Company officers said the English "wanted ever so many things provided for them," and concluded that the imported labor "could not accomplish the work that our own hands could do."[812]

The first two mills were highly successful. With dividends flowing, in 1872 the stockholders authorized a third mill. This mill was planned to again double the company's existing capacity, but was to be built without any increase in the outstanding capital stock. While these plans would eventually be carried out, they were significantly delayed by a serious snag: the nationwide business panic of 1873.

The "panic," or what would today be called a depression or recession, began with the failure of Jay Cooke's New York financial house in September, and rapidly led to the reduction of business activity across the country. By November, the Eagle and Phenix was operating on a part-time schedule, as were other large Columbus industries. Nevertheless, Eagle and Phenix, the largest of Columbus' five cotton mills, survived the first year of the depression with a slight profit, as did Columbus Manufacturing Company, the second largest.

One of William's more unusual innovations turned out to be highly successful, particularly during this depression. In April of 1873, the company had established for the use of its employees a savings department, which eventually operated as a separate entity, the "Eagle & Phenix Savings Bank." William later recounted the episode that gave him the idea:

> "One of the [workers] had her dress caught in the machinery and the superintendent of the room took his knife and cut through $60 in greenbacks. He asked why she kept her money there and she said she had no place else to keep it, that if she kept it in her trunk somebody might take it. So she always carried it with her."[813]

Indeed, at the time it occurred, this incident was singular enough to reach the pages of the *Eufaula Times*, forty miles down the Chattahoochee River, which, on June 27, 1873, reported this story, which differs only slightly in detail from William's telling:

> "Almost a fatal accident. A young lady operative named Page, was caught in the belting at the Eagle and Phenix Mill yesterday, and was seriously, though it is thought not fatally, crushed. In cutting her out, $100 in greenbacks on her person was destroyed (quoting the Columbus Sun)"

When the 1873 depression hit Columbus, because of the scarcity of specie (gold) in circulation, merchants were being asked not to insist on specie payments, but to accept the notes of certain banks at face value. But the merchants were wary. Confidence in banks was low, and it became lower in March 1874, when the Bank of Columbus suspended redeeming its notes in specie.

In these circumstances, the Eagle and Phenix Savings Bank became the city's chief financial institution. It began paying its employees with its own certificates, or "scrip," backed by the Eagle and Phenix Company. In a remarkable show of confidence in William's organization, Columbus merchants agreed to accept the company scrip for merchandise. By October 1873, over forty Columbus merchants accepted Eagle and Phenix scrip in lieu of specie or banknotes. Indeed, this scrip soon became virtually the only circulating medium in the area. One New York merchant advertised that he would exchange his dry goods for $100,000 worth of Eagle and Phenix scrip.[814] Eagle and Phenix also sold its own goods at a five percent discount if paid for in its own certificates. The Eagle and Phenix Savings Bank operated successfully for many years, and eventually merged with the bank that became Columbus Bank and Trust Company.[815]

Downriver in Eufaula, which had no manufacturing industry to speak of, the local newspaper editors were constantly advocating the advantages of developing a cotton mill in Eufaula. Through Edward Young, Eufaulians were of course familiar with the success of the Eagle and Phenix. His brother William was a periodic visitor to Eufaula, and was known there. In October 1872, when Eufaula had held its Southeast Alabama and Southwest Georgia Agricultural and Mechanical Fair, the Eagle and Phenix Company had contributed a noteworthy exhibit. The *Times* held this company up as an example of what is possible in its issue of February 14, 1873:

> "Eagle and Phenix Manufacturing Company"
> "We have, through their agent at this point, Mr. E. B. Young, the last annual report to the stockholders of the Eagle and Phenix Manufacturing Company of Columbus, Georgia. It is a most lucid and satisfactory exhibit of the affairs of the company and their operations last year.
> "We have not the space to review it, but would say that all who fear to invest their money in a well conducted cotton factory, should read and study this report and they will learn something to their advantage."

The depression delayed but did not stop William's expansion plans. In 1874, a woolens department was established. In 1876, construction of Mill No. 3 began. Also, the first two mills were reconfigured to accommodate 10,000 spindles. Mill No. 3 became operational in 1879, resulting in a total of 46,000 spindles in the expanded complex. This expansion was accomplished without any new outside capital, but by reducing the dividend to "only" 6 percent and paying for the expansion from current and accumulated funds.[816]

In the eleven years following the opening of the first Eagle and Phenix mill, five years of which were during a severe depression, the company had quadrupled its size. It was now producing over 110 varieties of goods, and was the largest cotton and woolen mill in the South.[817]

As soon as technology was developed for indoor electric lighting, the Eagle and Phenix installed it. In 1880, only one year after it became available, John Hill, the original designer of Mill No. 3, equipped it with electric lights.[818]

Eagle and Phenix owned two blocks of houses in Columbus in which some of its "operatives" (workers) lived. But across the Chattahoochee in Girard, Alabama, where the majority of Columbus' mill workers lived, Eagle and Phenix owned over 80 homes, most of them consisting of two rooms, which it leased for two to three dollars a month. Edward King, writing for Scribner's Monthly in 1873 on Southern conditions, observed, "The little town of Girard, across the river, built by mill proprietors for their operatives, is charming;" the workers' "houses and gardens were models of neatness and comfort."[819] Eventually, "Girard" became the present-day "Phenix City," Alabama, taking its name from William Young's company, by which so many of its inhabitants were employed. [820]

One historian has concluded that, by the late 1870's, two groups of interlocking directorates had emerged in Columbus. One group was centered around and allied with William Young and the directors of Eagle and Phenix. Another group gravitated toward the management of the second largest mill, the Muscogee Manufacturing Co. Directors of these two mills served as directors of other businesses, i. e. banks, railroads, land companies, and industries. But Eagle and Phenix directors rarely served as directors of other businesses allied with Muscogee Manufacturing, and vice versa.

Of Columbus' five cotton mills, the Eagle and Phenix overshadowed them all. Its dominance sometimes caused it to become a political issue. A Columbus lawyer, Raphael J. Moses, had some quarrel with William Young at the end of the war concerning the failure of the Bank of Columbus. Thereafter, Moses became a dedicated political enemy of William's and never turned down an opportunity to fight William or oppose his influence. In 1877, Moses claimed that William and his attorneys had bought the *Enquirer-Sun* for its editor, John King, for the principal purpose of having a platform from which to oppose Moses and his allies.[821]

In the congressional race of 1878 for the fourth district, which encompassed Columbus, a debate arose about Eagle and Phenix's issuance of certificates during the 1873 panic. The issuance of these certificates had rendered the company liable for a federal tax on lending institutions, totaling $30,000. In 1878, the Democratic congressman from the fourth district, H. R. Harris, assisted the company by obtaining the passage of a bill relieving Eagle and Phenix of the $30,000 it owed for the lending tax, and the bill was signed into law by President Rutherford B. Hays. In response, Raphael Moses ran against Harris for congress based upon Harris' support of the tax exemption for Eagle and Phenix. Moses described the company as a "grasping" monopoly that needed no federal aid. Although Moses dropped out of the race, another candidate, Henry Persons, took up the same issue and used it to defeat the incumbent Harris. It is interesting to note that Harris, William Young's ally, received 63 percent of the vote in Columbus itself, but was defeated in other counties.[822]

By 1889, Eagle and Phenix was consuming 16,000 bales of cotton a year; employing 1800 operatives, who, with their families, numbered about 5500 to 6000 of Columbus' population; and was disbursing $5000 daily for labor, cotton, and other operating expenses.

Three of William and Ellen's five surviving boys were now employed in the family business. Alfred Irwinton Young, whom we knew as commander of Young's Battery, now 49 years old, was Secretary-Treasurer and Cashier of Eagle and Phenix. Richard T. Young, whom we also knew as a Confederate soldier, was "second superintendent" of the mills. Alec C. Young, at 39 the youngest son, was manager of sales for the company. George B Young, the hero of Lovejoy Station in August 1864, was now a farmer, as was his younger brother, James E. Young.

In 1889, the calculation was made that, from the inception of the Eagle and Phenix Manufacturing Co. through January 1, 1888, the company had paid out to its investors a total of $1,725,820. Stated differently, the investors had been repaid their capital of $1,250,000, and had received $475,820 in addition.[823] This represents an average annual return of 7 percent a year for a period of twenty years, five of which years were during a serious depression. In addition, the investors' still owned their interests in the company, which was holding accumulated profits of $650,000, physical plant and equipment worth millions, and all good prospects for continued success.

ANNUAL REPORT

TO THE

STOCKHOLDERS

OF THE

Eagle & Phenix Manufacturing Co.

OF

COLUMBUS, GEORGIA.

For the Year 1887.

COLUMBUS, GA.:

THOS. GILBERT, PRINTER, BOOK-BINDER, AND MANUFACTURER OF PAPER BOXES.

In the economic depression of the early 1890's, a group of Atlanta investors maneuvered their way into control of the company, advocating the need for changed management methods. In 1892, William Young, then 85, decided to relinquish responsibility for the company. Contemporary accounts report that William "was content to step down and let others take up his great life's work."[824] He died two years later on May 7, 1894.[825]

To conclude the story of Eagle and Phenix, the new management was soon involved in labor strife, and in 1896, the company was placed in receivership. Appointed as receiver was G. Gunby Jones, an ally and former employee of William's who had worked for the company in the 1870's.[826] Jones organized a group of investors who bought the company out of receivership and restored it to profitability. Through this and successor organizations, the mills constructed by William Young continued to operate into the twenty-first century, and did not close for the last time until June 2002, over 150 years after William started the fledgling industry. [827]

William Henry Young, in his later years

One enthusiastic thesis-writer has gushed that William Young had "a genius for organization little short of Napoleonic."[828] Hyperbole concerning William Young's place in commercial history is not new. In his lifetime, admirers called him the "Father of Cotton Manufacturing in the South." But William disclaimed this title, acknowledging that, at the time he founded his original Eagle Mills in the mid-1850's, two cotton mills had already commenced in Columbus the previous year. However, not to carry modesty too far, William pointed out that both of those two earlier mills soon failed without returning anything to their investors, and that he had bought out the assets of one of them. William admitted that he might be said to have been the "Father of *Successful* Cotton Manufacturing in the South." [829]

Ironically, it was William Young's dedicated political enemy, Raphael Moses, who most accurately and simply described William's towering importance to Columbus, Georgia during the postwar decades. In his autobiography, Moses wrote:

"…his [William Young's] factory influence is very great. He has with his friends pretty much controlled things in Columbus, and very naturally for his energy and foresight has built up the manufacturing interests, without which Columbus would be a dead town." [830]

52
The Pioneers Depart:
The Deaths of Ann and Edward Young

"Not Slothful in Business, Fervent in spirit, Serving the Lord."
Gravestone Inscription, Edward B. Young

In 1873, the Methodist minister who had served Eufaula for several years was the Rev. E. M. Bounds. Mr. Bounds was an excellent preacher and was unusually well-loved by Eufaula Methodists. During his tenure, he baptized seven of the grandchildren of Ann and Edward Young. When the ministerial appointments were announced at the end of the 1873 Annual Conference, the Eufaula congregation was surprised and disappointed to learn that the Bishop had transferred Mr. Bounds to the St. Louis Methodist Conference. It is a feature of Methodist Church governance that ministers are assigned and transferred among churches by the Bishop, based on his assessment of the needs of the overall Methodist Church. While the wishes of a local congregation will be taken into consideration, they are not necessarily decisive. In this case, Eufaula Methodists felt so strongly that they appointed Hubert Dent as their representative to go to see Bishop Marvin at his Selma office to discuss the matter. Hubert was successful in his mission, and the Bishop agreed to recall the transfer and send Mr. Bounds back to Eufaula.[831]

During Mr. Bounds' continued pastorate after Hubert's successful appeal, he inspired Eufaula Methodists to construct a new church building. The new structure was conceived and begun in 1874, while Edward Young and his son-in-law, Hubert, were serving on the four-member Board of Stewards (the local governing body of the church). Edward and Hubert were also on the four-member board of trustees, the group responsible for administering church property.

The cost of the new church, exclusive of the lot, was $13,000. It can be safely assumed that a significant part of that amount was contributed by Ann and Edward Young. At age 74, Edward was the oldest male member of the church. He and Ann had been among the active leaders and supporters of the congregation since the construction of the first Methodist Church of old Irwinton in the mid-1830's. The new church was built at the corner of Eufaula and Barbour streets (the site of the present 1918 church[ff]).

During the construction, a disagreement with the contractor arose over a disputed claim for extra work, which looked as if it might lead to litigation. Mr. Bounds appointed Hubert Dent and J. T. Kendall to attempt to resolve the matter. Hubert succeeded in persuading the contractor to reduce his claim to $150, which was paid. The construction was sufficiently complete to permit Carrie Young and Noah Roberts to be the first couple married in the new church on January 12, 1876.

[ff] Ann Young would have been pleased to know that, when the 1874 structure was replaced with a new building in 1918, the church building committee included her son-in-law, Noah W. Roberts, and her grandson, E. B. Weedon. (Flewellen, p. 238.)

The official dedication of the church however, was later, on April 4, 1876. For the Young family, this would be a memorable service, for several reasons, but mainly because it was the last attendance at church by their mother, Ann Young. For the past 13 years, beginning in April 1863 Ann Young had increasingly suffered from what was called "inflammatory rheumatism," an arthritic condition which quickly grew worse until by October 1864 she became immobile and was "helpless as a child till her death."[832] At the time of the dedication ceremony, the family arranged for her to be brought in her chair to this occasion which meant so much to her. She contributed the silver communion service, which is still used by the church today. Her daughter, Anna Dent, contributed the "pulpit Bible." Her husband, Edward, was given the "happy privilege" of formally presenting the church to the Bishop for consecration.[833] Ann's pleasure in this spiritual event was increased by the large number of her numerous children and grandchildren who were doubtless present for the occasion. One month later, on June 5, 1876, (the birthday and wedding anniversary of her daughter, Anna Dent,) Ann Fendall Beall Young died at the age of 66. It was considered quite fitting that this woman of strong faith was the first person to be buried from the new church.

Ann Fendall Beall and Edward Brown Young in their later years.

Ann was buried in the family plot at Fairview Cemetery that Edward had provided years earlier. Up to now it had only held three graves: her son, Henry, the Confederate soldier; his comrade in arms, Charles Kliffmuller; and her sister Ellen's infant son, Edward Beall Young, who had died in 1838. On Ann's gravestone, her children had carved the appropriate inscription, "Blessed are the pure in heart for they shall see God."

Ann had been a lady of considerable courage and a sunny disposition. Her old friend, Tom Jackson, whom she had taken into her family as a homeless orphan boy, observed, "The last ten years of her life were years of intense agony, for no physical torture can exceed that of inflammatory rheumatism. She suffered patiently, submissively…"[834] Forty years previously, with two small sons she had accompanied her husband into an unsettled wilderness, arriving in the wake of an uprising of infuriated Creek Indians whose lands had only recently been taken from them. While her husband wrestled commercial prosperity from the new land, she bore nine children. In a rough frontier, she instilled in her family the solid Methodist faith and values by which she herself had been reared in Warren County, Georgia. Having joined the Methodist Church in 1830, she was an "ardent and true" supporter of that church. Her minister, Rev. Bounds, observed that, "She impressed her children, and every one else, that she was raising them to be Methodists…her children never dreamed of joining…any other church." Edward's family had originally been Presbyterian, but although reared "with inclinations to another communion," he "paid a willing tribute to her piety by uniting with her in lifelong service to the Methodist Church." [835] Ann was soon provided by her husband with a comfortable and affluent position in the growing community, to which she brought civilizing refinement. She managed a big household, presiding with grace and light-hearted good humor over the elegant Fendall Hall which Edward built for her. Rev. Bounds later wrote that, "Living in a beautiful home, itself the creation and growth of her taste and care, she dispensed its generous hospitalities and illustrated the wifely and motherly graces."[836] As a middle-aged matron, she did not hesitate to undertake the rigors of Civil War travel to journey to the distant army camp at Pensacola to bring home her pregnant daughter, Anna, at a time when fighting seemed eminent. As a young wife, Ann lost an infant daughter, and she later experienced the wartime loss of a favored son, Henry. Otherwise she was rewarded by seeing all of her children grow into productive citizens. Ann endured with stoic grace a painful decline in health, but she lived to see all eight of her children enter into good marriages, settle in nearby homes, and begin families. She had the joy of knowing and helping to rear seventeen[837] of her grandchildren who had been born at the time of her death.

At age 74, Edward undoubtedly had difficulty adjusting to life without Ann. She had been "the mainspring" of their large family.[838] Exercising "taste and tact," she had provided a stable and predictable domestic background for his intense activity in the business world. It is likely that this very intensity helped him through the necessary adjustment. He was immersed in making the new Eufaula National Bank a success. Working with his son, Ed, in the new enterprise provided Edward with purpose and pleasure. The old house still rocked with noise and activity from the steady stream of Edward's twelve sons, daughters, and spouses, as well as the seventeen grandchildren coursing through the house at various times.

Edward continued his travels, including his trips to New York. At the time of Ann's death he had immediately written the unwelcome news to their old friends, Mr. and Mrs. John Horry Dent, at "Cottage Home," in Cave Springs, near Rome, Georgia, in a letter which Dent received on June 10, 1876. Little more than two months later, Edward went to New York. John Horry's journal reflects that, in August, "Mr. E. B. Young of Eufaula, my old friend reached here this afternoon by 5:02 p.m. to make us a visit."[839]

At Christmastime, 1877, John Horry Dent reports having "received from my friend E. B. Young two bottles French brandy as a Christmas gift."[840]

Although now a widower, Edward Young's remaining years were nevertheless busy and satisfying. There has been preserved a priceless letter which he wrote to his seventeen-year old grandson and namesake, Edward Young Dent, (the "Eddie" of Hubert's wartime letters) who was off at college. In this letter, Edward also sends messages to his other seventeen-year old grandson, Henry Augustus Young, Jr., (only son of Henry Young, Sr., who was killed in the wartime railroad accident at Chunkey Bridge, Mississippi.). These two first cousins, born within two months of each other, were both attending the Southern University, the Methodist-sponsored college at Greensboro, Alabama, of which Eddie's father, Hubert, was a trustee.

Written at age 76, the year before his death, this rare letter reveals much about Edward Young in his last years. Whimsically writing in multicolored ink, he exhibits the "jovial proclivities" that young Tom Jackson observed in him in the 1840's. He remains in active direction of the Eufaula National Bank, relating details of its operations and alert to the activities of his competitors. In apparent good health, he still relishes business, and begrudges time away from his office for minor sickness. Edward's daughters are at Fendall Hall regularly, visiting or caring for his health needs, or he is in their homes for meals. He is aware of details of the health, business and expenditures of his children and their spouses. He keeps up with local gossip, as well as with news events of the day, and marvels at the miraculous inventions of "that man Edison." He is involved with his grandchildren and, despite having "a good many letters to write every day," he enjoys taking the time to write a long, multicolored letter to Eddie and Henry. The following transcription of his letter uses the same colors in which the original is written:

"Eufaula, April 3rd, 1878

My Grand Son
        Your letter of 31 received on yesterday and was glad to hear from you and to know that you received the powders for making the inks. You can regulate them by adding water if they get to thick. I would have sent you more but I had to divide with Jim and sent you half of mine but they will last a long time.
        I know Doct Mitchell well. He staid with me during the Conference here and I saw him in Montgomery last Dec. [Ed. Note: The Annual Conference of the Methodist Church was held in Eufaula in 1872, and possibly again later.]
        I dined with your Father and Mother [Hubert and Anna] last Sunday. They had green peas. So had Hellen. Your Mother picked Saturday & several quarts of strawberries. All things are quite forward. It now looks like we are going to have a great fruit year, as the Peaches are full.
        [He then describes in clinical detail the treatment of a "large carbuncal," i. e. carbuncle, or painful rising similar to a boil, under his left shoulder] …it had to be poulticed three times a day yet I did not

loose an hour from the office as we had so much to do…Ada …came and dressed [it] all the time.

I find it hard to get up enough to fill up a letter these times, as news is scarce about just now. Your Pa [Hubert] had a head ache Monday but was about on yesterday. Your Mother [Anna] and all the children well. So is all the rest of them. Your Aunt Hellens baby grows fast and as fat as he can be. [This would be Louie Dent]. They weighed him sometime ago. He then weighed 18 lbs. I think that he will go now to 20 lbs. Your Aunt Carrie is here at this time.

They say Clarence Glenn and Mattie Cottan marries the 18th. Perhaps I'm mistaken in the name. It's the youngest. The oldest is married….

I have one of the new silver dollars. It has not been out the mint three weeks. It's a pretty piece of money. Only the eagle is not well proportioned. The work is verry fine. It's a pretty piece of engraving.

Did you read that account in the "Sun" of that man Edison machine to take off words spoken and can be preserved for years and then spoken in the same voice a hundred years hence. If he brings it to perfection it will be wonderful. Doct Weedon [his son-in-law, Hamilton Weedon, Mollie's husband] says that there will be no such thing as a blind man. By electricity they will be able to see colors and distinguish one person from another. And further they will make tubs and so fasten them together and lay a rail road on the bottom of the ocean and connect America and Europe. There is no knowing what will be done. Yet if they go on the way that they have done--if a man had said years before what telegraphs would do they would have said that he was crazy to send a message to NY and back in two hours.

I suppose that you and Henry is getting along in your studies trying to learn fast.

I have given you a fancy letter to show you how the different inks can be used. You can put a ¼ pint to each powder and have enough to last you twelve months and you and Henry can use it. I think the red the prettiest that I ever saw. It is now used by all the Banks, that and the green mostly.

Doct Weedon is taken up a good deal with his plantation. He has 200 acres in Corn and now planting Cotton. He is going to put in 400 acres. Mother [Anna] has got her carriage fixed up and looks like a new one. Ed [Edward's youngest son] has bought a one horse barouch-- quite a pretty one.

I have scraped up all but to tell you about business is quite dull at this time as the farmers is busy planting out. There is a good demand for money. We have more applications that we want and have to refuse a good many. We cannot supply all of them and it appears like the People or McNab [his competitor banks] is not doing anything in that way.

489

I showed your letter to your father and mother and all your Uncles and Aunts is glad to hear from you and send love to you and Henry. Tell him that his mother [Maria McRae, widow of Henry, Sr.], Julia [Henry's 16 year-old sister], and the rest [are] well. When you feel like writing I would be glad to hear from you. I have a good many letters to write every day.

Edw B. Young

George [H. Dent, his daughter Helen's husband] is putting a new room to his house."

Edward died a year later, on May 22, 1879, only three years after Ann, at the age of seventy-seven. (Edward's brother, William Henry Young, would die in Columbus five years later in 1884.) Edward was buried beside Ann in the family plot in Fairview Cemetery. His children placed there a graceful obelisk rising fifteen feet from the center of the plot. Edward had been intensely loyal to his adopted Southern home, but had also carefully maintained his ties to home and family in New York. Thus the inscription on his gravestone proudly announces that he was "Born in New York City," but states with equal pride that he "Died in Eufaula, Alabama." In composing his further epitaph, his children perceptively caught their father's character, acknowledging his combining of the material and the spiritual:

"Not slothful in business,
Fervent in spirit,
Serving the Lord."

Edward had written his will on June 14, 1869, and had added codicils (amendments) in 1870 and 1871. As executors, he designated his oldest son James W. (Will) Young, and his lawyer son-in-law, Hubert Dent. His appointment of Will is interesting. It suggests that Will had earned his father's confidence despite having chosen not to enter his father's business, and having generally pursued a somewhat independent course. And too, Will was Edward's only adult son; Ed was only 20, not yet a legal adult. By the time of Edward's death, however, Will had moved to Newark and could not serve. It was a competently drawn will, probably composed with assistance from Hubert. However, the entire four-page document was handwritten in the clear, legible hand of Edward himself. Edward's signature is accompanied by his seal, in the form of a red wafer attached to the paper and also embossed into the paper. It is witnessed by W. B. Brannon; Jno. W. Tullis, a Eufaula businessman; and P. D. Woolhopter, a Eufaula accountant. The latter two also witnessed the later codicils.

Edward left one third of his estate to "my beloved wife, Ann F. Young." Because she died first, this provision became inoperative. It will be recalled that in 1867, he had deeded Fendall Hall to her outright. Upon her death, it reverted back to him. Thus, Fendall Hall and Edward's entire estate was now divided equally among his living children, with a share for Henry's two children.

The will reflects that while he lived, Edward had been open handed and generous in making gifts to his children. But because he wanted to treat all of them exactly the same, he had kept strict records of his gifts so that they could be equalized upon his death. This is accomplished through provisions such as these:

> "I wish to make all my children equal with each other and so intend it and to share and share alike...as I have no favorites among them..."

> "I having given my son James W. [Will] Young landed property with money to the amount of about $4000 this to be deducted from his part."

> "To my son Henry A. Young, now deceased, having advanced to him and his heirs the sum of $5500 besides given his children a lot of land of two acres for which I have given a Deed for the same, to the value of about $1000, after deducting this from his portion, I then give to his son Henry A and his daughter Julia McRae Young an equal portion..."

> "I have given to my Daughter Anna B. Dent the wife of S. H. Dent property to the amount of $3100, this to be deducted from her portion..."

> I have given to my Daughter Mary E. C. Weedon [Mollie], $3000. After deducting this amount she is to have her equal share.

> "I have given my son Edward B. $1000, this to be deducted from his share of the estate.

Edward had not yet made gifts to some of his daughters, which he made clear. Carrie, his youngest, was then only 14, and had not even completed her education, which he is careful to provide for:

> "I have not given my daughters Ada, Hellen, and Carrie any portion of my Estate up to this time and therefore they come in equal, as all have finished their education except Carrie and she is to have her education the same as the others and this is not to be deducted from her portion but is to share equal with the others after this provision is paid out of the estate."

The disposition of Edward's 13 shares of his brother William's company is not disclosed in the will. He simply directs that it be handled as noted on the certificate:

> "...I have made an entry on the 13 shares of Eagle and Phenix Manf. Co, and wish that to be carried out as I directed..."

In this era, the old customs against wives and other women holding ownership of property in their own names had come to an end. However, it was still not unusual for fathers to vest title to their daughters' property in the names of their husbands. Edward would have none of this, although he tactfully expressed confidence in his sons-in-law:

> "…I wish it understood that my Daughters are to have all the control of the proceeds of my Estate that falls to them in their own right. As to those that are married, I have full confidence in their husbands, yet this can be used by them for the benefit of both."

While having no favorites and treating his children equally, Edward could not resist a small special remembrance for his first grandchild and namesake, "Eddie:"

> "I also give and bequeath to my grandchild Edward Y. Dent my watch as a free gift to him."

Edward wanted to avoid any controversy and litigation over his estate, and discouraged it in this way:

> "…I further insert that if any of my heirs should be dissatisfied and go to Law (which I hope they will not) as I wish them to keep out of all Law, that such party shall loose out of his or her share all the expenses that may accrue by law suits, they shall not only pay their own, but the expenses of such suit as my executors would have to pay for defending the same, as I wish them to avoid all law. I make this provision and give my Executors full power to carry this out fully."

A year after executing his will, Edward became worried about possible issues under the will. On August 1, 1870, he executed a codicil, probably without consulting his lawyer, to reflect his practice of giving each child a lot for a house carved out of the property upon which Fendall Hall was located. Actually he had already given a lot to Mollie and Hamilton at the time his original will was signed, but it now occurred to him to be sure the same benefit was conferred on the others. There is a technical legal question about this bequest, because since 1869, Fendall Hall had not been owned by Edward, but by Ann, to whom he had deeded it, and who was still alive at the time of this codicil. But this was a harmless issue, and the codicil emphasized Edward's intention of equal treatment. Also by this amendment, although it was already covered, Edward made explicit the authority of his executors to handle his Nebraska lands however they deemed appropriate. He also reaffirmed his desire for harmony among his children:

> "…I have given to my daughter Mary [Mollie Weedon] a lot of land on Block No. 40 and I now bequeath to my daughters Ada, Hellen, and Carrie and also to my son Edward each a lot of equal value as they may select out of the lots adjoining or what I may hold as to the value of the same and I also give my Executors rights to sell my lands in

Nebraska or to dispose of the same as they may think best or if any heirs should agree to divide the same among themselves, they are at liberty to do so. I have tried to form this will in such a manner as to make each of my children equal and therefore hope that they will so live in harmony and good will to each other, as they should do."

A year later, on July 5, 1871, Edward made his third and last codicil, to allow for gifts he had now made to Ada, Helen, and Carrie. He probably also composed this codicil without seeking Hubert's help. The provision about Carrie's gold watch is not entirely clear to us, but is probably apparent to those who knew the circumstances. He continued to emphasize his desire for harmony among his children:

"I have given my daughter Ada $4000 and to my daughter Hellen the same amount in her right. Also to my son Edward $1000 more, and to my daughter Carrie a Gold Watch. This I made on a share of Eagle and Phenix stock for her. Therefore she is not to claim that. And whatever I may give hereafter to them, or any of them, they will account for to the other of the heirs as I want each one to be equal as near as can be made with all by children and not to have any one dissatisfied, and to live in peace and harmony with each other."

We note that the gifts Edward made to his children prior to his death totaled over $25,000. It is difficult to judge the purchasing power of nineteenth century dollars when compared with inflated twenty-first century American currency. But we know that after Edward's death, Anna and Hubert Dent bought the interests of her seven siblings in Fendall Hall for $4000, suggesting a total market value of about $4600 for this sizable, elegant, and expensively built house with several acres of grounds. So the value of Edward's gifts in the years prior to his death could be said to approximate the value of five Fendall Halls. It is reasonable to assume that these lifetime gifts constituted the smaller portion of his net worth.

Edward's wish for family harmony after he was gone was rewarded. It was a complicated estate, with a number of diverse business interests to work through and conclude; Hubert and Ed would work together administering it for many years. There is no evidence of any family dissatisfaction or controversy. Further, this harmony among the Eufaula Youngs prevailed even against the background of sensitive decisions which had to be made in the aftermath of Edward's death.

First was the question of ownership of Fendall Hall, an elegant and desirable residence, to which all of Edward's children undoubtedly felt sentimental attachment. Hubert's successful law practice, together with Anna's share of her father's estate, clearly rendered them financially able to purchase the home. The success of the Weedon and Dent pharmacy in the decade since its inception in 1868 also rendered both of those families financially able to make the acquisition, but earlier in the 1870's, Hamilton and Mollie had already built a comfortable two-story home on Barbour Street, (the first story of which survives today as the Pappas-Jones-Wilbourne house). George and Helen had also acquired a fine home on Barbour Street, (hereafter discussed), which they were decorating elegantly. George is said to have asked Helen if she would like for them to acquire her father's old home, but she preferred the convenience of living closer to town. [841] The relative youth of Ed and Mamie Young, the Martins and the Robertses may have made them less interested in assuming the financial obligations of owning Fendall Hall at this time. Will, of course, was living in Newark. In any event, the family agreeably concluded that Anna, their oldest sister, would become the owner of Fendall Hall. For a price of $4000, Hubert and Anna purchased her siblings' seven/eighths interest, which, as previously noted, reflects a total market value of about $4600 for the entire property. Just as Edward had placed ownership in Ann's name during her lifetime, Hubert and Anna now placed title to the property in Anna's sole name. Many years later, in sad circumstances, this legal arrangement turned out to be important.

An even more important question related to the presidency of the Eufaula National Bank. Ed had worked closely with his father in E. B. Young & Son Bankers since returning from the University of Georgia ten years earlier. Ed had been closely involved in the process of organizing the Eufaula National Bank from the beginning. The bank had had only two officers and employees: Edward and Ed. At the time of it's opening in 1876, the Federal examiner reported that the new bank's plan of operation was that "the business of the bank will be done almost entirely by him [Ed, the Cashier] with no assistants." While there is no historic indication of it, it is not unreasonable to speculate that at age thirty, Ed may have had some thought that leadership of the bank might devolve upon him.

The decision, of course, was up to the board of directors. These included Hubert, owner of 100 shares; his brother, George, owner of 50 shares; and George's business partner, Hamilton Weedon, with 50 shares. With 200 shares, the New York director-investor, Henry E. Robinson, was the largest single stockholder-director. Ed had not been a director or stockholder prior to his father's death.

After a process that probably involved consultations among the directors, stockholders and family members, it was decided that the momentum of the bank's success thus far could best be sustained by appointing a new president having the community standing of Hubert Dent. The logic of the decision is not difficult to follow. Since his marriage to Anna, Hubert had always been accepted and well regarded within the Young family. The confidence which Edward had placed in him over the years was well known. As a returning war hero, Captain Dent, (the title by which he would be known for the rest of his life), had been an active political leader during Reconstruction. He had been elected as Eufaula's first post-war mayor, and was later elected as a member of what became the "dual legislature," although in both instances the Radicals had blocked his taking office. During twenty years of law practice, Hubert had built a high reputation at the Bar. At age 46, it was felt that Hubert had the maturity and credentials to inspire community confidence in the continued success of the Eufaula National Bank.

To Ed's credit, if he felt any disappointment over this decision, it never surfaced or interfered with his close relationship with Hubert. Hubert had been like a big brother to him, sending him Yankee artillery shells from the war, and inviting him to visit the army's winter

494

encampment. Ed's feelings about his older brother-in-law are best reflected in Ed's naming his second son, born in 1881, William Hubert Young. Their closeness continued as they worked together over the years in administering Edward's estate and in the Eufaula National Bank. For his part, Hubert was careful to see that Ed's interests were protected. Ed was immediately made a director of the bank, and within a few years, he was made Vice-President and Cashier of the bank, with a salary equal to Hubert's.

When the new President of the Eufaula National Bank and his family moved into Fendall Hall, which probably did not occur until after the New Year of 1880, Anna and Hubert's family had reached its full size of six children. We will briefly report the status and preview the futures of these important players in the Young story as we begin the decade of the 1880's.

Edward Young Dent, the "Eddie" of Hubert's wartime letters, was now 19, and still a student at Southern University in Greensboro, Alabama. However, he would soon return to Eufaula and become an officer in the Eufaula National Bank. This branch of the Dents was a family that loved nicknames, perhaps instigated by Hubert himself, who had turned the name of his wife, Anna, into "Nannie." Because Eddie was the big brother of the other five children, he became known in the family as "Biggie."

Anna Beall Dent, now 13, was called "Nannie." As the oldest daughter, her "coming-out" may have provided part of the impetus for the lavish refurbishing of Fendall Hall, a period of its history which has today been impressively restored by the Alabama Historical Commission. Nan's would be the first wedding of the new Generation to be celebrated at Fendall Hall.

Stanley Hubert Dent, age 11, was known within his family as "Hugh," or "Hu." He had been christened "Hubert Warren Dent," after his father and grandfather, and that name was duly recorded in the Young Bible in 1869 in Edward Young's own clear hand. For reasons unknown, as a young man Hugh changed his name to "Stanley Hubert Dent," which inevitably led to his being incorrectly referred to as "S. H. Dent, Jr." Hugh had an outstanding political career, ultimately serving as Chairman of the U. S. House of Representatives Committee on the Armed Forces during World War I, as we will later discuss.

Henry Augustus Dent, age 8, was named after his uncle who had died during the Civil War at Chunkey Bridge, Mississippi. He became a more reserved personality that the others, and was just called "Henry." He would have a long career as a naval officer in the Navy Paymaster Corps. As we will later discuss, Henry Dent was in the Spanish-American War, and later accompanied the "Great White Fleet" on a portion of its trip around the world ordered by President Theodore Roosevelt, retiring at the rank of captain.

Kate Louise Dent, five years old at this time, was nicknamed "Weesie." During Hubert's last years as a widower, Weesie and her family would live with her father in Fendall Hall. Weesie became the owner of the family home, and gave it the name of Fendall Hall.

Weesy's daughter, Mary Maude McCullohs and her family would reside in the house until conveying it to the Eufaula Heritage Association/Alabama Historical Commission in 1972.

Caroline ("Carrie") Dent had just been born when the family moved into Fendall Hall. When Edward Young died in May 1879, his daughter, Anna, was expecting her last child, who was born four months later in September. Carrie became an active leader in the civic, religious, and literary affairs of Eufaula and of the State of Alabama. As we will hereafter discuss, she would provide the perfect complement to the legal and political career of her husband, Lt. Gov. Charles S. McDowell, Jr., a progressive force in Alabama politics during the 1920's.

53
Relaxed and Prosperous 'Eighties;
The *E. B. Young Fire Company Number 3*

"Several hundred people gathered at the intersection of Broad and Eufaula Streets last afternoon to witness the trial of the new Silsby engine recently purchased by E. B. Young Fire Company, No. 3. The verandahs and sheds and sidewalks were crowded with anxious sightseers ...The beautiful engine ...glittered prettily in the sunlight..."

Eufaula Times

For the extended Young family and as well as other Eufaulians, the decade of the 1880's was a period of prosperity and relaxed good times. As a regional trade center, Eufaula was growing and "booming." Edward and Ann Young's sons and sons-in-law conducted businesses which were successful and rewarding. Of Edward and Ann's eight children, six were living and rearing families in Eufaula. Their oldest, Will (James William) had moved to Newark, N. J., with his wife Annie Hewlett, in 1872, (although he still made periodic visits to Eufaula, as we will relate.) The second oldest, Henry, had been killed during the War, but his widow, Maria McRae Young, still resided in Eufaula with their children, Henry, Jr and Julia. The families of the six remaining Young children, referred to in this narrative as the "Young families," consisted of:

Anna Young and her husband, S. Hubert Dent;
Mollie Young and her husband, Dr. Hamilton M. Weedon;
Ada Young and her husband, James H. G. Martin;
Helen Young and her husband, George H. Dent;
Ed Young, Jr., and his wife, Mamie Jennings; and
Carrie Young and her husband, Noah Roberts.

During the 1880's, we see these families' diligence and innovation rewarded with a lifestyle marked by material comfort, lighthearted and quaint social activities, vacations and leisurely travel, hunting, fishing, civic involvement, church participation, and political leadership. Political activity was still important, but it was at a less intense level than before. The bitter and destructive turmoil of almost two decades of political confrontation, bloody civil war, defeat, military occupation, and humiliating reconstruction were in the past. These events were by no means forgotten, but they were over, and the present was something to be taken advantage of and enjoyed.

The years of this decade were ushered in with the quaint old custom of "New Year's calling." As carried out in Eufaula, it proceeded according to a definite and understood ritual. The Eufaula ladies, both young and not young, both married and single, would band together into separate groups. Each group would announce that it would receive gentleman callers on New Year's night at the home of one of the members of the group. The gentlemen of the community, young and old, married and single, would likewise form small groups which would be also publicly announced, and which would then travel around town together calling on the ladies on New Year's night. The calls were to begin no later that 7:30 p. m. In order to start then, the Gentlemen were expected to assemble in their groups by 7:00, and the ladies were to be ready to receive them a half hour later. The *Eufaula Daily Times* assumed the function of publishing the names of the respective groups, and generally coordinating the festivities.[842]

There were nine groups of ladies "receiving" on January 1, 1882, as listed in the *Times*, which asserted that "Our list of ladies was corrected to a late hour last night and is correct." One of the listed groups was receiving at the Barbour Street residence of George and Helen Dent, and included the following ladies: Mrs. George H. Dent; Mrs. C. E. Guice; Mrs. Noah W. Roberts (Carrie Young); Mrs. L. J. Richardson; Mrs. E. B. Young (Ed's wife, Mamie); Mrs. R. J. Woods; Miss Julia Young (the college-age daughter of Henry Young, deceased), Annie and Mary ("Noonie") Weedon (daughters of Hamilton and Mollie); Nannie Dent (oldest daughter of Hubert and Anna); Willie Mitchell; Nellie Beall Dent (George and Helen's daughter); Mrs. W. A. Juhan (Mrs. Guice's mother and frequent visitor from Macon, Ga); and Mrs. Viola Rogers, of Macon.

In its list of the groups of gentlemen callers, the *Times* mentioned that "Messrs. George H. Dent, C. Wood Guice, Lucius J. Richardson, and Edward B. Young (Jr.) will constitute a 'quartet of boys' who will enjoy the evening to the utmost." Another group of younger gentlemen was composed of Robert Martin, Sumpter McTyre, Ed Dent (Hubert and Anna's oldest) and Eugene Martin. One or two older gentlemen announced their plan to go calling by themselves.

The following year, in its January 8, 1883 issue, the *Times & News* reports that, "Despite bad weather, a large number of gentlemen engaged in the delightful old custom of 'New Year calling.'" Editor Jelks[gg] observed that, "We are pained to note that in many of our large sister cities the custom is growing into disrepute, but in Eufaula the very old but ever delightful occupation promises to be indulged in more generally as the years go by." Jelks described the homes where he called, mentioning the residence of J. T. Kendall as "one of the most brilliant assemblies of the evening." Mrs. J. T. Kendall (Mary Jane, a sister of Maria McRae Young, Henry Young's widow), wore black silk; while Mrs. E. B. Young wore cream satin; Mrs. M.(aria) M.(cRae) Young, silk and grenadine; and Miss Julia McRae (another sister of Maria), white organdy.

One of the important social institutions of the time, which also had a deadly serious purpose, was the volunteer fire company. Like most communities, Eufaula had no

---

[gg] William Dorsey Jelks was reared and educated in Union Springs, AL., 45 miles east of Eufaula. After graduating from the University of Alabama, he acquired an interest in the *Union Springs Herald*. He soon left the *Herald* and bought the *Eufaula Daily Times*; also publishing the *"Weekly Times & News."* The *Times*, which Jelks published for 19 years, is said to have achieved the largest circulation of any newspaper in the state, and was probably the most often quoted. In 1883, Jelks married Alice, daughter of Henry R. and Addie Keitt Shorter. In 1898, he was elected to the state senate from Barbour County. He became president of the senate, succeeded to the governorship upon the death of Gov. Samford, and was then reelected governor for a full term. Upon leaving the governor's office in 1907, he founded Protective Life Insurance Co. of Birmingham, which is today a flourishing, publicly-held company there (Owen, Dictionary, p. 899).

professional fire service, and its citizen fire companies provided important protection against the ever-present threat of fire. In an era of mainly wooden construction, or at best, wood and brick, when all heating was by coal or wood burning stoves or open fireplaces, and all lighting was by open flame from candles, kerosene lamps, and later gas, fire was a far more frequent and common danger than today. For instance, on the morning of December 28, 1882, a fire in a grate heated the brick wall between the Eufaula National Bank and Bray's Hardware Store, setting fire to the woodwork in the store. This could have resulted in a serious loss to Hubert Dent and Ed Young, but the fire was fortunately discovered and quickly extinguished before much damage was done.[843] The *Times and News* of March 25, 1884 described a more frightening narrow escape at George and Helen Dent's house:

> "The alarm of fire went out from Mr. G. H. Dent's residence on Barbour Street about 9 Monday night and the department responded immediately. But their efforts were fortunately dispensed with in the timely suppression of the flame that at one time seriously threatened the destruction of Mr. Dent's handsome residence and costly furniture. Mr. Dent says the alarm was caused by the upsetting of a kerosene lamp which had been placed on a bureau in the children's room where they were romping and playing at the time. The bureau, which was out from the wall, has a swinging mirror and one of the children getting behind it shoved it forward and against the lamp, which overturned on the floor and scattered oil all over the room. The screams of the children brought their father and Rev. Dr. Andrews, who with his family was present, to the rescue, and the fire was quickly put out, although the blaze was several feet high when they discovered it. All parties are to be congratulated over their escape from danger and financial loss."

Fire victims were not always so fortunate. During the decade of the 1880's the downtown business section of Eufaula was swept by several large and destructive fires, which would have spread to even more catastrophic proportions except for the heroic efforts of the town's volunteer fire companies.

But in addition to its serious duties, the citizen fire company also had a lighter side. It was the center of much social and sporting activity. The companies frequently held socials, dinners, bazaars, fund-raising events, and parades in which the entire town participated. But most exciting were the contests and tournaments, in which the uniformed firemen competed to test their prowess and speed in performing their fire-fighting functions. Intramural contests were held among the city's firefighting teams, in which the citizens rooted for their favorite team; and tournaments were held among the companies of surrounding towns, in which the entire town rooted for and bet on its home team. The enthusiasm with which the public followed the competitive fortunes of these fire companies was fully as intense as that accorded today's professional baseball and football teams. The local newspapers gave as much coverage to the activities of its favored fire companies as it did to state and national events.

In the early 1880's, Eufaula had two fire companies, the Phoenix, and the Cleburne. In 1881, the Cleburne Fire Company, which had been operating since 1867, had concluded that its hand pumps were no longer adequate; its existing engine could not throw water to the height of three and four story buildings. It requested a committee of citizens, which included Hubert Dent, to canvass the city for private subscriptions to purchase a new steam powered pumping engine. The following year, it purchased for $3000 a new, state of the art, steam fire engine from the LaFrance Company of Elmira, New York, of which it was very proud. It named its new engine the "*Islay Reeves*," and it was "ornamented with that young lady's picture." Islay was the teenage daughter of Major M. N. Reeves, a popular Eufaula businessman, Baptist minister and son-in-law of John McNab. Islay attended Vassar College, and later married Harmon Lampley. By 1883, the Phoenix Fire Company, which was then also operating with hand pumps, felt it was time for it to also upgrade to a steam-powered pump, and it entered into a contract with the La France Company, subject to city council approval, to purchase a new steam engine for $3250. The Phoenix petitioned the Eufaula city council, proposing that the Phoenix would pay the first $1000 of the cost, if the city would assume the balance of the payments, and would also give the Phoenix 1000 feet of hose and the proceeds of disposing of its present hand engine.[844] The plans of the Phoenix were shattered, however, when a competing petition was unexpectedly filed with the council.

Ed Young, Jr. was now 34, and was one of the popular young businessmen of the town. Ed and his wife, Mamie, were among the leaders of a young, upscale social set. In 1881, Ed had been appointed City Treasurer by the city council, a position he would discharge for the coming decade. Under the leadership of Ed and his brother-in-law, Hubert, the Eufaula National Bank was thriving, and they had other business interests besides. Under the old business name earlier used by his father, "E. B. Young & Co," Ed Young, Hubert, and Ed Dent operated an insurance agency which carried a good portion of Eufaula's fire insurance coverage. As a large fire insurer, Ed Young had a pecuniary interest in first-class fire protection. Motivated in part by that consideration, but probably also for the sheer fun of it, Ed joined with a group of young Eufaula leaders who chose this time to found a new fire company. This group met on the night of Saturday, May 12, 1883, and elected Ed Young as its president. In addition to Eli S. Shorter Jr., as vice president, the officers included Ed's nephew, Ed Dent, as treasurer. The event was covered by the *Eufaula Times*:

"New Fire Company
Saturday morning there appeared in this paper a statement to the effect that certain young men would meet on Saturday night with a view to organizing another fire company. The meeting was held by some 35 young men at Simpson and Johnston Warehouse, and a company was organized with the following officers: E.B. Young, President, E.S. Shorter, Vice President, W. A. Davis, Secretary, E.Y. Dent, Treasurer, E.T. Martin Foreman, W.W. Flewellen, Assistant Foreman, W.D. Wellborn, Foreman of Hose; C.T. Roberts Assistant Foreman of Hose.
A committee was appointed to wait on the City Council in regard to purchasing an engine, and the meeting adjourned to meet on Thursday night

500

next, at which time the company will probably be named and the work of organization be completed in all particulars.

The new company is made up from the ranks of the most prominent young men of the city, both socially and in a business way. For instance, the two head officials are among the largest property holders in Eufaula, and four of the officers are fire insurance agents; hence it is but reasonable to suppose, after taking all the facts into consideration, the company will prove to be one of the livest and most thorough in all that goes to make a fire company efficient, to be found in two states. It will be an honor to the city, and with our other two companies will make the Eufaula Fire Department one of the best to be found. It is presumed there will be no trouble about the company's getting a steamer."[845]

The next day, a committee of the new company, which had not yet chosen its complete name, filed its petition with the Eufaula City council, as follows:

"Fire Company's Petition, Eufaula May 15, 1883.
 To The Honorable City Council of Eufaula:
Believing that the necessity exists for another fire company in our city, the undersigned have formed an organization to be known as _____ Fire Company Number 3, and has elected officers [listing them].

This organization we propose to make permanent, provided the city will assume payment of the remainder of the cost of a steam power engine after the company shall have raised the sum of $1,000. Messrs. E. B. Young, E.S. Shorter, E.T. Martin, M.S. Roberts, and W.D. Wellborn are a committee to lay this petition before you. Pledging a faithful discharge of our duties as firemen at all times, we hope that your honorable body may find it proper to grant our request."

Signed: [by all of the members]: E.T. Martin, W. A. Davis, M.S. Roberts, W.D. Wellborn, E.B. Young, C. S. Rhodes, J.M. Kendall, J.E. Sapp, M. D. Wellborn, Jr., T.G. Berry, W.W. Flewellen, J.P. Buford, T. H. Appling, L. Clisby, O.H. Peacock, W.M. Bray, E.B. Freeman, S.B. McTyre, J.W. Chastain, E.S. Shorter, [E.] Y. Dent, J.L. Ross, C.T. Roberts, W.F. Lock, W.T. Flournoy, J.T. Kendall, Jr. and others."

Two days later, the new group had already raised $600 in subscriptions.

The council at its regular meeting postponed consideration until the next regular meeting, which resulted in the petitions of the Phoenix and the "No. 3" being considered at the same time. It was fairly clear that the council would not authorize the purchase of two new fire engines at the same time, so that only one of the petitions was expected to be granted. As originally presented, the financial burden on the city resulting from the Young group's proposal was about the same as that of the Phoenix. The new group decided to use its combined financial clout to substantially "sweeten" their proposal and make it more attractive to the city. They agreed to assume the entire cost of the new engine, except for the sum of $1250, to be borne by the city, which the new company would lend to the city at 6% interest if the city wished, and the company would be given two old hand engines. The city council delayed action again. The *Times* editorialized in favor of the Young group:

"Number 3.

"Members of Fire Engine Company Number 3 are willing to bet that the council will at its next meeting accept the very fair proposition which they made to it. Should the council agree to the petition of Number 3, the city will be out the value of the two hand engines, about $300, and $1,250 in cash. Number 3 is composed of our monied men, and they can very well afford to loan the city the $1,250, should the city want it, at 6%, until such time as the city will be able to repay the amount, and they propose to do that. We believe the committee of the company have not yet decided the make of the steamer they shall purchase, but it is believed they lean toward the Silsby. The committee consisting of E.B. Young, Willie M. Davis, and E.S. Shorter, are doing all the necessary work and are daily flooded with engine circulars from every part of the United States.

"Enough is known or suspected of the council committee's intentions to almost insure a favorable report on the petition of the company at the next council confrontation."[846]

Although "street talk" and editorial comment assumed that the Young group would be the easy winner, hot and heavy politics apparently intervened, and the outcome was a tie which had to be broken by the Mayor Pro Tem:

"The Council Yesterday.

"The council yesterday evening decided to grant the petition of Fire Company Number 3. In granting the petition the council gives Number 3 $1,000 and the proceeds of the two hand engines now owned by the city. The petition of the Phoenix Company was not granted. The vote stood 3 against 3. Mayor Pro Tem Glenn voting for the petition of Number 3."[847]

Not only did the new group win by only a whisker, they had to agree to reduce the city subsidy from the proposed $1250 down to $1000, but this seemed to cause no problem. The next evening, the members of the new fire company met to celebrate their success and to confer a name on their new organization, which the *Times* of May 31 presented in this manner:

"E.B. Young, Number 3

"The new fire company had a meeting Tuesday night. It was a very jubilant gathering. The entire membership was much elated at the action of the council the evening before. No business was transacted except the naming of the engine. Mr. E. S. Shorter in a neat little speech suggested the name that heads this article. Upon the suggestion there was much enthusiasm and the name was adopted unanimously. This is a very deserving tribute to the worthy president of the company, and we know it was as gratifying as it was unexpected."

The "E. B. Youngs," as they came to be called, lost no time in equipping the new company. By June 1, they had purchased a new Silsby Number 5 steam fire engine manufactured by the Silsby Company of Seneca Falls, New York, paying "spot cash," probably in the $3500-$4000 range. On July 17, the machine was shipped by water and rail from New York via Savannah, and its progress toward Eufaula was a topic of daily interest in the town. The *Times* of July 31, predicting that it would arrive in Eufaula "next week," disclosed that "The boys have been sighing for their new engine…We may expect a lively trial and blow-out next week, followed up by much practice. The members of the company are quite enthusiastic in their opinions as to the merits of the Silsby engine and probably there will be some contest between the Youngs and the Cleburnes." On August 2, the *Times* was reporting that, "The new engine of the E.B. Young Fire Company reached Savannah Tuesday morning in the charge of J. P. Fuller, engineer. It will probably reach Eufaula today." The engine finally arrived on August 4, amid high local interest. The *Times* of the 5th reported that "The engine is very pretty and staunch looking…For the present the engine is in the vacant room next door east of McNab's Bank on Broad Street, and there it was visited by scores of curious minded during the day."

Two days later, much of Eufaula turned out for the first public demonstration of what the new Silsby could do. The *Times* of August 7 reported the event:

NUMBER "3"
Trial Test of New Fire Engine

Several hundred people gathered at the intersection of Broad and Eufaula streets last afternoon to witness the trial of the new Silsby engine recently purchased by E. B. Young Fire Company, No. 3. The verandahs and sheds and sidewalks were crowded with anxious sightseers and the whole scene presented an animated appearance. The beautiful engine was drawn up Broad street from McNab's corner, and it glittered prettily in the sunlight. Many exclamations of admiration were heard on all sides as people impatiently waited for the trial test to begin. The engine is undoubtedly very pretty, and the Young boys appeared very proud of it, and it seemed well that they should.

Fire was put in the engine's furnace and it warmed up in a twinkling, just 6 minutes and 11 ½ seconds elapsing between fire and water. A splendid stream was thrown through the 100 feet of hose, with 1 1/8 nozzle a distance of 235 feet, and that against a strong breeze which must have cut off twenty feet.

Two streams were thrown through 500 feet of hose with 7/8 inch nozzle a distance of 200 feet.

Three streams were thrown through a ¾ inch nozzle a distance of 179 ½ feet.

One stream was thrown through two lengths of 50 feet of hose a distance of 265 feet.

This is indeed a splendid record, and the Silsby shows remarkable powers. The engine is a Silsby No. 5, and is a model in every respect, being very powerful and very beautiful. Last afternoon's trial test was eminently satisfactory to the company and to all interested.

The engine was in charge of engineer Teller of the Silsby Fire Engine Co, Seneca Falls, New York.

In the test the judges of time were Capt. J. M. McKleroy, Mr. G. C. McCormick, and Mr. T. J. Everitt.

Judges of Distance: Capt. Jno. O. Martin, Col P. McKay, and Mr. S. Lewy

Time Keepers: Maj. W. C. Dawson and Mr. C. C. Skillman

The next day, the E. B. Youngs published a resolution of thanks to the judges and timekeepers, to the Cleburne Fire Company for the use of their hose and hose reel, to the members of the Cleburne and Phoenix who helped, and to Mr. J. C. Guice for the use of his horses. On August 10, the city council accepted the new engine and voted to buy 1000 feet of hose for the company, costing $1000, to be paid in four installments of $250. The *Times* of September 8 reported that No. 3 would use the building next to McNab's Bank on Broad Street for its engine room, and the rear room would be the company's hall, the rent to be paid by the city council.

Edward Billups Young

Mamie Jennings Young

In the wake of all the hoopla, Ed Young's mischievous brothers-in-law decided it was time for them to "honor" Ed for the popularity and success of his namesake fire company. Reflecting their waggish wit, Hamilton and George unveiled and marketed at Weedon & Dent a new, highly acclaimed cigar, named the "E. B. Young Number 3 Cigar." It was promoted in an ad campaign which ran many weeks in the local newspapers:

504

"The E. B. Young Number 3 cigar, sold by Weedon & Dent, is a magnificent weed. The lovers of tobacco will find in it comfort for much that is sorrowful in their every day experience. Smoke away the blues and your troubles with "Young Number 3.""[848]

In a special supplement on the occasion of the East Alabama Fair, the *Times* of November 16 was still advertising, "Call on Weedon & Dent for the E. B. Young cigar. The best in the market." Ed was undoubtedly the first member of the Young family to have a cigar named after him, and probably the first Eufaulian so "honored." It is probable that he received much ribbing from his buddies.

Through diligent practice, the E. B. Youngs would become highly competent, but on the occasion of one of its first fire calls, the company had not yet perfected all of its procedures, and its performance gave the Cleburnes a good laugh. The story was reported by the *Times* of September 12:

"An Amusing Incident
"Monday morning while the little fire on the bluff was in progress, about a half dozen members of Number 3 arrived at their engine room after the engine had been removed by the Company. The door had been locked and these fellows had no knowledge of the removal of the engine or even that there had been other members on hand before them, and an industrious one of the belated ones begun to note the absentees with a view of fining them when the company should again meet. Much indignation was expressed at the supposed tardiness of the rest of the company and the engineer. After threatening to break down the door and uttering maledictions upon their plight, they were told by a member of the Cleburne Company that their engine and company might then by found down the street a short way returning from the fire. They were much crestfallen. Assistant foreman Flewellen in this connection was the father of a *bon mot*. As if they had not been sufficiently punished before, he told the tardy members that they should the next time "find" the engine before they undertook to "fine" any of the members."

The most active Eufaula social group at this time was the "Euterpians." It was dedicated to having fun, and it was usually seen holding some unusual kind of party or innovative social event. For instance, one standing on Broad Street on a Spring day in April 1884 would have seen a strange and festive procession passing. There were six gaily decorated wagons, pulled by equally gaily decorated animals, with about 8 to 10 young people in each wagon. In one of the wagons was an "Italian Band" which gave out inspiring music as the happy party proceeded to Eufaula Street on the way to Tony's Mill Pond, the scene of the main festivities. The *Times* reported, "The wagons and the animals were decked in a gorgeous array of colors and the fair ladies were clad in the captivating arrangements befitting the season. The style of the Euterpians in attending a picnic is to be commended for its economy and practicality. We can think of no better way for a gathering of this character for a day in the woods or by a stream on a fishing excursion than good roomy wagons."

Although mainly dedicated to pleasure, the Euterpians were not above enjoying themselves by helping a popular worthwhile cause. The E. B. Young Fire Company had incurred heavy expenses in getting organized, and in the winter of 1883, the Euterpians decided to give a "grand masquerade and domino ball" for the benefit of the E. B. Young Fire Company, to be held on December 27, 1883. The *Times* promoted the event heavily, claiming credit for itself for designing and printing the invitations, which the paper claimed were "the neatest thing ever turned out in Eufaula." "You can shake your gory locks at us," it claimed, "We did it." Tickets were on sale at Weedon & Dent and William A. Barnett's. Costumes for the event were ordered from New Orleans. It was said that "The fancy dress domino ball is the talk of the day." Later, "Undoubtedly the Euterpians will make it the grandest of all previous entertainments." Still later, "The prospect now is for the very biggest thing the Euterpians have ever gotten up." As might be expected, with "hype" of this kind, the Ball was indeed a large, enjoyable success, with a good turnout and a good purse for the E. B. Young Fire Company.

Like many Eufaulians, Dr. Hamilton Weedon, Mollie Young's husband, was a social sportsman. During 1883, he invited the Eufaula Gun Club to hunt on his plantation south of town for a series of dove shoots in March and April. By April 11, it was reported that club members had bagged over 2000 birds, an astonishing number by today's standards. The hunters gave a good sample of the birds to the Weedon family. There was one potentially serious accident during the hunt on March 31. Rev. J. E. Chambliss, the Baptist minister, was shot by a gun in the hands of young Willie McKleroy, the teenage son of Eufaula lawyer, John McKleroy, (who had been a popular candidate for governor of Alabama in the 1882 elections.) In an incident not unlike those still occurring today, the teenager fired without realizing that Rev. Chambliss was within range. "Only one shot, a number 8 bird shot, entered just on the inner edge of the left eye against the nose…." Fortunately, it was later reported that an Atlanta oculist, although he could not locate the shot, concluded that it would not trouble him much and would soon be well.

Steamboat parties down the Chattahoochee to various points were a popular Eufaula pastime, and fishing excursions of all kinds were frequent. In May 1883, we next find Hamilton Weedon on a "fishing frolic" in Florida with a friend, Joe Haley, sending word back that they were "in good health and having an immense time." The most popular destination for Eufaula excursion parties was referred to by *Times* Editor Jelks as, "Eufaula's Seaport, ancient Apalachicola." Apalachicola Bay, usually just called "the Bay," was further characterized by Editor Jelks as "Eufaula's Coney Island." A typical excursion of young people is described in the *Times & News* of April 7, 1885:

"A Merry Bay Crowd"
"Saturday evening a merry crowd of young people with several older heads took passage on the *Thronateeska* [a popular steamboat] for Apalachicola, Florida. They will crowd about as much pleasure as possible in

the coming six days. The party will be chaperoned by Mesdames E. B. Tullis, E. C. Martin and P. P. Watson, and will consist of Dr. H. M. Weedon and two sons (probably Hamilton, Jr., age 16 and Edward Beall, age 14); Misses Julia Young (Henry Young's daughter, 23), Lillie Drewry, Annie and Mary ("Noonie") Weedon, (Hamilton's daughters, 18 and 17), Florrie Jennings, and Queen Martin. Messrs W. H. Foy, W. T. Simpson, Jr., J. L. Ross, and C. P. Roberts are going along to load the rifles, bait hooks, and make themselves otherwise useful."

While the adults were enjoying a full and enjoyable social life, they made sure that their children not only received good educations, but also were properly introduced to the social aspects of life in Eufaula. The Eufaula High School was a private, "most excellent school for boys" conducted by Professor T. A. Craven. On July 4, 1882, "the Shorter Opera House had a crowded audience to hear the speeches for prizes on the part of the boys of Eufaula High School." Three prizes were awarded and Third Prize went to "Master Hugh Dent." Hugh (more properly, "Hu," for Hubert) was Anna and Hubert's second son, age 13, and more will be heard of his speaking and political abilities.

The Eufaula children had their own social group, the "Thalians," which held periodic parties and outings, sometimes at Fendall Hall. The *Times & News* of July 18, 1884 reports that "The Thalian Frolic Thursday night…was a charming occasion for the little folks and was enjoyed as well by a number of older lads and lassies. The reverie was continued to a witching hour and the young folks carried home with them a charming picture which will adorn memory's art gallery for many years…Capt. and Mrs. S. H. Dent did whatever could be done to make it an event to be remembered, and succeeded most admirably." A month later, the Thalians were entertained at a "moonlight picnic" at the R. J. Woods home. In July 1881, Helen and George Dent gave a party for the ninth birthday of their second child, Nellie Beall Dent, which was "largely attended and enjoyed by the friends of the little miss."

While their fathers were participating in the social activities of the volunteer fire companies, Eufaula's teenage boys were members of the "Eufaula Boys' Hose Company." In June 1885, a large crowd attended the exhibition of the Boys' Hose Company in the Opera house. The "exhibition" had nothing to do with firefighting, and it included girls. The *Times & News* of June 7 described the event: "It was a young American demonstration, no grown person being upon the stage to direct or prompt. Master Hugh Dent in a very dignified, graceful, and patriotic little speech introduced the reader of the Declaration of Independence, William T. Comer.…Master Dent also introduced Master Harry Shorter, who delivered a brief, eloquent, and patriotic little speech on the subject of American independence and closed with a salute to the stars and stripes…He was followed by Misses Lizzie Rhodes and Laura Long, who sang a duet, "Bye Bye Baby," and brought the house down." ("Miss Lizzie Rhodes" was 13 when she brought the house down; nine years later, she "brought down" George H. Dent, Jr, [George and Helen Dent's oldest son], by marrying him, in 1894).

The following week, the Boys' Hose Company elected its officers, including H. R. Shorter, president; "Hu" Dent, secretary; and others.

In 1881, Anna and Hubert's oldest child, Edward Young Dent (who came to be routinely called, "Ed Dent," to distinguish him from his uncle, Ed Young, Jr.) graduated from Southern University in Greensboro, along with his first cousin, Henry A. Young, Jr. (whose father had been killed during the War). Ed immediately went to work in the Eufaula National Bank as assistant cashier. His duties including working in the E. B. Young & Company insurance agency, and he would later become a member of the bank's Board of Directors.

In January 1883, Will Young, who had moved to Newark in 1872, made one of his trips back to Eufaula to visit his brother, sisters, and their families, residing mainly with his younger brother, Ed, while there. Will had been a steamboat captain in his youth, and during this visit, he gave consideration to acquiring a new steamship to operate on the Chattahoochee. Steamship traffic on the Chattahoochee in the post-War period was very heavy. Although Columbus was a railroad hub, the river was still its only means of commercial transportation to and from the southern Chattahoochee Valley. A number of ships were busily plying that river, including the *Thronateeska*, the *Caddo Belle*, and the *Everingham*. There was valid reason for Will to think there might be an opportunity there. The *Eufaula Daily Times* of January 3, 1883 reported that, "We are informed by Mr. J. W. Young that up to yesterday morning he had been promised about $10,000 for his proposed steamboat to run on the Chattahoochee in the interests of Eufaula. Such a boat would do Eufaula great good and we hope that Mr. Young will succeed in getting it up at once. Eufaula doesn't pay enough attention to her river trade. Columbus works hard for it." On January 10, he was interviewed further by the paper:

"The Eufaula Steamboat

I have been over to Georgetown [the town opposite Eufaula on the Georgia side of the Chattahoochee] today in the interest of my proposed Chattahoochee steamboat to run for the benefit of Eufaula," observed Mr. J. W. Young yesterday afternoon.

What success?

"Oh, I received the best encouragement and the Georgetown people are alive to the importance of the undertaking. Taking population into consideration, those people gave me more encouragement than the people of Eufaula."

Will you succeed in getting the enterprise on foot?

"Yes, I am very confident. I have been promised about $15,000 and I haven't been all around by a good deal. I want $20,000 to put the boat in motion. And I know what I am about, too. I have been master of four Chattahoochee steamers in past years. I ran the first line to Bainbridge [Georgia town on the Flint River which flows into the Chattahoochee south of Eufaula], and if I succeed in getting this boat, I will make Bainbridge going down and coming up. I propose to have a boat that will accommodate all travelers. A man will pay for what he gets and no more. I want a light draught boat to carry about 800 bales, and to have separate cabins for white and colored passengers."

508

Then you are hopeful of success?
"Yes, very hopeful."

Despite his confidence, Will apparently encountered obstacles to his plans. The steam boating business was now conducted somewhat differently than before the War. Instead of individually-owned vessels, the profits were being made by steamboat lines operating several ships, and there was cutthroat competition among these companies.[849] The boats on the Chattahoochee were operated by the People's Line and the Central Line. Even while Will was considering acquiring a boat, a third company, the Merchants and Planters, was entering the market. As Chattahoochee historian Lynne Willoughby observed,"…[B]reaking into the Chattahoochee trade was never easy. The Central and People's Lines formed a pool in the hopes of destroying their common enemy." Further, promoters were maneuvering toward consolidating all three lines into one large company, which would have little difficulty staving off smaller competition, and this in fact eventually occurred.[850] It is not surprising that, upon further investigation, Will and his modest investors decided against plunging into this fight.

In 1882, the Board of Trustees of the Union Female Academy were advocating that Eufaula should implement a city system of public schools. Prodded by this overture, a meeting was held at Milton's store in the summer of 1882 among Capt. S. H. Dent, James Milton, John W. Tullis, and John C. Thomas. As a result of this meeting, a city board of education was formed, trustees were elected, and preparations for a city public school system were begun.[851] By 1886, the city was still struggling with the need for better city public education facilities. In December of that year, the Eufaula city council revised the terms of school board members from one year to two, and appointed Dr. Hamilton Weedon to the new, longer-term board.[852]

Hubert also served several terms as Barbour County Superintendent of Education. In November 1883 we find him giving official notice in that capacity, joined by P. A. Craven, then secretary of the county board of education, calling a convention of all Barbour County teachers at the Eufaula City Hall.

Eloise Buford was the daughter of Hubert Dent's old law partner from the early 1870's, James M. Buford. After having studied voice at the Musical Institute of Boston, Eloise visited Alabama in 1883. She was quite a talented singer, but it was perhaps Hubert's friendship with her father that motivated him to take the lead in honoring her in Eufaula. A public notice in the *Times* graciously proposed a performance for Eloise's benefit at the Shorter Opera House on a date to be selected by her. The invitation was signed by Hubert, joined by the old friends of James Buford, (and friends of his deceased older brother, Major Jefferson Buford, of "Eufaula Regency" days): Henry R. Shorter, Reuben Kolb, Eli Shorter, John Tullis, and others. Eloise accepted the invitation, and her performance before a large audience on January 23 received "rave" reviews. She continued to give well-attended concerts in Alabama and Georgia. Later that year, James Buford and his wife moved to Atlanta, where they were visited by Eloise in March 1885. The *Atlanta Constitution* observed that, while in Boston Eloise had "acquired the merited title, 'Songbird of the South,'" and further reported that she was embarking for Europe to continue her musical education.

Although Hubert had retired from the practice of law when he became president of the Eufaula National Bank in 1879, he continued to regard himself as a lawyer, and sometimes acted in a legal capacity. When Circuit Judge Henry D. Clayton found it necessary to recuse himself, Hubert was appointed special judge to act in his place. In May 1883, one Harry Seals had been released on a bail bond, conditioned upon his appearing to answer any indictment that might be found "at the following term of circuit court." However, the "following term of court" was adjourned by Judge Clayton because of the illness of his sister, so the grand jury went home with no indictments. Seals was later indicted during a later term of court, but failed to appear. The state sued his bondsman, contending the condition of the bond had been violated. Presiding in Clayton, Judge Dent ruled for the bondsman, holding that the condition that Seals appear at "the following term of court" had not been violated, because it did not cover a failure to appear at a *future* term of court.

In the city ward meetings of April 1884, Hubert Dent and R. J. Woods were nominated by acclamation for city councilman (alderman) from Eufaula Ward Three, and in the ensuing elections in May, they were elected to those positions. When the council was organized, Hubert received good committee assignments: he was appointed to the important Finance Committee and to the Police Committee. He was also elected Mayor Pro Tem, a position he would hold under Mayor G. L. Comer, and Mayor M. N. Reeves. In the weekly reports of the city council meetings, we frequently find Hubert presiding, due to the absence or disability of the mayor. The *Times & News* of December 9, 1884 reports Capt. Dent presiding as mayor pro tem while the rules were suspended at the request of James H. G. Martin (Hubert's brother-in-law) to permit consideration of a measure backed by the Eufaula Cotton Exchange. An ill-considered ordinance made it unlawful for cotton bales to remain in the street over 24 hours, and the Cotton Exchange sought its repeal, which the council granted. With Hubert presiding in the absence of Mayor Comer on May 19, 1885, the city council postponed action on a request by Fire Chief E. P. Martin that the charter of the Cleburne Fire Company be forfeited due to certain controversial actions the company had taken. The council eventually declared the charter forfeited; the company's hall, its equipment, and the *Islay Reeves* were turned over to a new volunteer company. In June 1885, Capt. Dent was appointed to a committee of the council to investigate the city tax books maintained by City Clerk E. L. Catteville, who had recently committed suicide. Later, Committeemen Dent and Glenn reported that Catteville's books had a deficit "so far" of $2300. (Dent and Glenn had been assisted in examining the books by Noah Roberts, Hubert's brother-in-law, as special accountant, who was paid $70 for his special work.) In August, the council voted to settle its claims with Catteville's widow and bonding company by accepting $1000, thus closing the matter. Noah Roberts was a contender to be appointed successor city clerk, but the council selected Lloyd Guice. At the council meeting in the week of June 23, 1885, Mayor Reeves turned the chair over to Alderman Dent while Reeves took the floor to advocate a measure requiring the erection of suitable covers over the public wells at the intersections of Broad and Randolph Streets, and Broad and Eufaula Streets.

While all the "Young" families were loyal Methodists, none were as active in their support of the church as Hubert and George. Most Methodist activities involved one or both of these Dent brothers or their wives. The *Times & News* of March 31, 1881 reported that, "Tonight at the residence of S. H. Dent will be given a musical by the Ladies' Donation Society of the Methodist Church. Enough is said of the character of the program when it is known that Professor Van Houten will be the musical director." Anna's sister, Helen, sponsored a similar event in April: "The Methodist Church sociable held at Mr. George H. Dent's Tuesday evening was largely attended and is represented as having been a most delightful affair. $50 was realized." In May, Helen held another "sociable" which also netted $50.

On October 20, 1881, "In conformity to a call from the International Sunday School Convention, the Methodist school of this city held a mass meeting on Monday evening last, when interesting addresses were made by Dr Rivers (the Methodist minister), Professor Craven (a popular schoolteacher), and Capt. S. H. Dent."

Hubert served as secretary of the District Conference of the Church, and he and George attended its meeting in Columbia that summer, when Hubert was elected to serve as a delegate to the upcoming Annual Conference (i. e., the "state convention"). In May 1882, Dent was a lay delegate from Alabama to southern Methodism's "national convention," the General Conference in Nashville, which was held only at three or four year intervals. Hubert would ultimately have the unusual distinction of serving as an Alabama delegate to three of these General Conferences of the Church. In 1883, he and George were again Eufaula delegates to the Methodist District meeting in Clayton, along with James T. Kendall, John C. McRae, and others. And again in 1884 Hubert was a delegate to the Eufaula District, which again elected him a delegate to the 1884 Annual Conference.

Hubert wrote extensively about Methodist history. In 1884, the *Christian Advocate*, the newspaper of the Methodist Church then published in St. Louis, featured a paper by Hubert on "The Centenary of Methodism." He later wrote a comprehensive history of the Eufaula Methodist Church (which is still in possession of his family).

Edward Brown Young had been a frequent traveler, usually for business reasons, or to visit his New York family. His children and their families in the 1880's also had the means to travel extensively. They continued his practice, sometimes for business reasons but more often for pleasure. These trips often appeared long and leisurely. In the week of July 11, 1882, we find Ed Young, Jr. traveling on a "northern tour," accompanied by his wife, Mamie, and by their niece, Julia Young (daughter of Ed's deceased brother, Henry.) In the same week, George and Helen Dent, together with all the children, left for Maryland, undoubtedly for a visit with his family there, to be gone for two months and returning in September. By August 8, Ed Young had returned from his trip, and Hubert Dent then departed for "the east," joining George and his family for the Maryland visit. Ed Young and Hubert apparently alternated in their travels so that one remained in the bank in the absence of the other. The *Times* of July 31 reprinted an article from the *Independent*, of Port Tobacco, Maryland, about Hubert's visit; Hubert is given a courtesy promotion in military rank:

"Col. S. Hubert Dent, son of Dr. Stouten W. Dent, is on a visit to this county. Col. Dent has quite retired from his lucrative practice in Eufaula, Alabama, and has now engaged in the banking business in his adopted state. He is President of the National Bank of Eufaula. The Colonel is a frequent visitor to his native county, and takes a deep interest in the land of this birth. Though his father the doctor, has been ailing of late, he has now so far recovered as to be able to ride around in a buggy with him, 'to visit the fairy haunts of childhood hours.'"

The younger generation also joined in the traveling. In the week of July 8, 1883, Hubert's bachelor son, Ed Dent, left "for the north," in a party including his buddies, "Sumpt" McTyer, Eli Shorter, Jr., Ralph Jordan, and J. M. Thornton, Jr. It was a long excursion; Ed and Sumpt were gone for over a month. Also in July 1883, Ed and Mamie Young, together with other Eufaula couples, vacationed at Blue Ridge Springs, Virginia. Ed and the other men returned in late July, leaving their families for a longer visit.

The late summer of 1883 found three of the "Young" families visiting in New York, together with other Eufaulians. Hamilton Weedon took his two oldest daughters, Annie (now sixteen), and "Noonie," (Mary Norma, now fifteen) to New York by way of Savannah, with plans to "visit various points in the east." At the same time, Anna and Hubert Dent, and her sister, Ada and James H. G. Martin were also in New York. Other Eufaulians visiting there at the time were Mrs. E. C. Martin, Harmon Lampley, Mr. and Mrs. Eli Shorter, and others. In October, Ed Young, Jr. attended the bankers' convention in Louisville, Kentucky.

The wives and husbands did not always travel together. In July 1884, Ada's husband, James, traveled with E. C. Martin to the "east, to spend some weeks." Before James returned to Eufaula, Ada departed to accompany friends to "the springs of North Carolina and Virginia." By August 12 however, James joined Ada and other Eufaula relatives at Allegheny Springs, Virginia. At the same time, Ada's sister, Carrie Roberts, traveled "to Atlanta to spend a few weeks," in the company of her mother-in-law, Mrs. G. A. Roberts; her sister-in-law, Mrs. W. H. Pruett, and her husband's nephew, Master Ed Roberts. Carrie's husband, Noah, however, left for New York in August, probably on a business trip for the store which he and W. H. Pruett operated together, not returning until September 1. Atlanta and north Georgia were also the destinations for Ed Dent during his three-week vacation that August. His fifteen-year-old brother, Hugh, was also visiting in Atlanta.

In late 1884, the Eufaula Dent brothers received sad news. The *Times* of October 2, reported that, "Private letters bring information of the alarming illness of Dr. S. W. Dent of Charles County, Maryland. Dr. Dent is the father of Capt. S. H. Dent, Mr. George H. Dent, and Mr. Warren Dent of Eufaula and is now nearly 78 years old. In common with many Eufaulians we regret to learn of his illness." A week later, the news had not improved: "...the venerable father of Messrs. Dent of Eufaula continues dangerously ill at his Maryland home." The end came on the seventh, reported by the *Times* on October 10, 1883:

"Death of Dr. Dent

Dr. S. W. Dent died at his home in Charles County, Maryland last Sunday afternoon in the 78th year of his age. Dr. Dent was the father of Capt. S. H. Dent, Mr. George H. Dent, and Mr. Warren F. Dent of Eufaula, and his wife, three sons and five daughters survive him. He was born in Charles County in 1806, and his whole life was spent near his birth place. Some years ago he visited his sons in Eufaula and many of our people remember him as a hale, hearty, genial old gentleman of many laudable and admirable traits. During the late war Dr. Dent was an earnest and enthusiastic supporter of the cause of the South for which two of his sons gallantly fought. His sympathy for the South was so marked that it drew the attention of federal authorities and more than once he was made to suffer.

Dr. Dent lived out a long life usefully, honorably, and successfully, and now that he is gone he is entitled to that proudest epithet—he was a good man."

The *Times* of the 17th reprinted an article from the *Independent*, of Port Tobacco, Maryland:

"The Late Dr. Dent

"We are pained to announce the death of Dr. Stouten W. Dent who died at his residence near Centerville, Sunday, October 7, 1883, aged about 79 years. Dr. Dent has been in failing health for some time past, but his indomitable energy and will sustained him until Sunday when he was forced to succumb. There is no man who ever lived among us better known and more highly respected for his high tone principle than was Dr. Dent. He began life very poor but by strict integrity, industry and unrelenting energy he accumulated a sufficient competence to provide for himself and his family and to give his children a classical education. He was much loved by his section of the county, by the poor especially whom he never failed to attend in sickness when called upon whether paid or not and his loss will be deeply felt. He leaves a widow and eight children, five daughters and three sons surviving him. Three of the daughters are married and two single. The three sons are in the South, two of whom are engaged in the apothecary business, and the third practicing law and managing he National Bank of Eufaula, Alabama. Our sincere sympathy is extended to his sorrowing family."

The following spring, in March 1885, George and Helen Dent took one of their most memorable trips. In the general elections of November 1884, the Democrats had swept Alabama and the nation, and Grover Cleveland had defeated Blaine to become the first Democrat elected president since the Civil War. Eufaula businessman R. J. Woods received a telegram from his New York brother, William H. Woods, stating, "Am just from headquarters and can say that Cleveland is certainly elected, and will not be counted out." Particularly for Southerners, this was a major historic turning point. It set off celebrations and public meetings at the opera house in Eufaula. (The *Times* reported that some blacks believed that they would be placed back into slavery.) George H. Dent had been in the forefront of the struggle to elect Democrats in Alabama and nationally ever since he migrated to Alabama in 1868. Savoring the momentous victory, George decided to take part of his family and go to Washington to be present for Cleveland's inauguration on March 4. The *Eufaula Times & News* published a special edition on the inauguration, including for the first time, steel or woodcut prints depicting Washington scenes, a map of Washington, the inaugural parade, the capitol, the White House, etc. While in the Washington area, Helen and George also stopped in Charles County Maryland, to visit his mother and sisters there. The Dents returned to Eufaula on March 17. The *Times & News* of April 7 again quoted the Maryland newspaper about George and Helen's visit:

> "The *Independent*, published in Charleston, Maryland, makes most pleasant and complimentary mention of the presence in that county recently, of Mr. and Mrs. George H. Dent and their little son, Louie. It was a visit Mr. Dent was paying his mother, Mrs. Dr. S. W. Dent. It says 'There are not many now in Charles County who would recognize in the handsome dignified and very pleasant Mr. G. H. Dent, the little freckly faced boy that once rode around the county on his father's errands. As it was Mrs. Dent's first visit north in the winter season she and her son greatly enjoyed the snow."

A grand Exposition was held in New Orleans in 1885, which many Eufaulians attended. Editor Jelks commented that those returning from the event talked like "newly married men...The excursionists say the show is the greatest and best the world ever saw." In February, Ed Young, Jr. traveled to New Orleans with his friend R. J. Woods and Mrs. Woods, to attend the New Orleans Exposition. It is not clear whether Ed's wife, Mamie, made this trip or not. In April, Hamilton Weedon went to the Exposition, taking one of his four sons. Although George and Helen Dent had just returned from a lengthy trip to President Cleveland's inauguration a few weeks previously, they nevertheless accompanied Hamilton to the New Orleans Exposition, taking three of the four children they had at that time, (perhaps giving an excursion to the children who had not made the Washington trip).

Noah W. Roberts, husband of Caroline Young

Three years later, in August of 1888, Hubert Dent also took part of his family to Washington, where they called upon President Cleveland at the White House. Among the family who met the President was Henry Augustus Dent, (Hubert and Anna's third son), who was then fifteen years old. Capt. Dent had just been introduced to the president when Henry, not intending to be left out, said, "Haven't been presented to the President." With this, President Cleveland turned to Henry and said, "Yes, I must shake hands with the young man, for he might be noted one day." As it turned out, in 1894, during his second administration, President Cleveland appointed Henry as a naval officer and assistant paymaster in the Navy Paymaster's Corps, in which Henry served for twenty five years.[853]

Noah Roberts, Carrie Young's husband, became a merchant. In August of 1881, Noah went into partnership with W. H. Pruett to operate a grocery store. The *Times* announced this new enterprise:

> "Messrs. W. H. Pruett and N. W. Roberts have associated themselves together for the purpose of carrying on a wholesale and retail staple and fancy grocery business. This firm has laid in recently a large and fresh stock of everything necessary to feed the hungry, and invite the public to call and examine before purchasing."

Noah ran a big ad in the *Times* of September 1, a column wide, from the top of the page to the bottom, listing their "staple and fancy groceries" and other wares, opening at Number 2 Hart's Block. Noah's partner, W. H. Pruett, was also his brother-in-law, Pruett having married Noah's sister, Anna Roberts. In later years, Pruett would be elected Probate Judge of Barbour County.

Simultaneously with the commencement of this new business venture, Noah and Carrie broke ground for the construction of a new residence at the corner of Randolph and Shorter Streets. As we will later discuss, five of the six Eufaula "Young" families were acquiring, building, or improving homes during 1881-1884.

Although Hubert had retired from the practice of law when he became bank president, in the mid 1890's we find him joining with Eufaula attorney, A. H. Merrill, in advising the city council as to their rights against William D. Chaffin, a defaulting contactor who had undertaken to furnish an adequate public water supply for the city.[854]

The E. B. Young Fire Company No 3 continued to provide Eufaula with enjoyable social and competitive events, but far more important were its effective efforts in fire control. Examples of its heroic services appeared almost weekly. The *Times and News* of September 2, 1884 recounts "a disastrous conflagration," which resulted in the loss of the Eufaula Mills. This important industry was a flourmill owned by Ed Young's friend, R. J. Woods, which employed many Eufaulians:

> "The E. B. Young No. 3 took up her position at the cistern at the intersection of Broad and Orange Streets, so the Cleburne engine was ordered to the town branch. After 10 or 15 minutes of playing from that point the temporary dam gave way, and as the fire was very hot under the boiler it soon exhausted the water in the boiler so as to burn and injure the [Cleburne's] boiler and render it useless.
> Meanwhile the E. B. Young was throwing a double stream through 1000 feet of hose, and while it was doing good work at such a great disadvantage, yet it was powerless to contend with so great a fire under full

headway, and it could only beat back the flames from the flour, meal, and grain that had been removed from the mill, and partially subdue the intense heat that threatened to fire the Barbour Machine Works just across the street on the east."

The loss to the Eufaula Mills was over $100,000; its insurance was limited to $58,000, of which E. B. Young & Co. carried $35,000. Warren F. Dent, who at that time was Foreman of the E. B. Youngs, made a public statement thanking members of the Cleburne Company for their assistance to the Youngs at important times during this fire.

On September 30, 1884, the *Times & News* reported a "fire of burning cotton bales which had been thrown off the train and were lying on the platform and probably were fired from a spark thrown out by the engine. The E.B. Young Company promptly responded to the alarm . . . the steamer was stationed at the upper cistern and a line of hose was run from the engine directly down Eufaula Street to where the burning cotton was, a distance of about 250 yards, and a double stream was played upon the fire for near one hour before it could be subdued." The editor's praise for the Youngs' efforts even credited them with lowering insurance rates:

"The city now has a better water supply in case of fire than at any time before, and that the E. B. Young Fire Company Number 3 with its recent arduous experience is in better condition for fighting fire than ever before. But for its splendid fight on the day the compress burned there is no telling what would have been the result as a strong east wind was bearing the heat and flames directly toward the heart of the city. We firmly believe the engine of this company on that day saved property and value of which would buy 100 such engines. It certainly saved the old Howard House, where if that large frame building had burned a half of the town would have gone with it at that time and in that high wind.

We might state also that on that day an agent of the Southeast Tariff Association was in the city, and seeing what the E. B. Young Fire Company could do and knowing that there was still another fire steamer and spirited fire company in the city he, in readjusting the insurance rates, lowered them when it was his purpose in visiting the city to raise them. So that with the *Islay Reeves* and *E. B. Young* both in working order and an ample supply of water at command we do not see how it would be possible for another very destructive fire to occur in the city."

The editor's optimistic prediction of no more destructive fires was dashed two months later, when Long's Hotel, operated by G. T. Long, was destroyed during the week of November 18. "The Cleburne Fire Engine played from the cistern at the intersection of Broad and Eufaula while the E. B. Young played from the cistern in front of the opera house." The intense competition between adherents of the two fire companies gave rise to a minor controversy, which the *Times & News* sought to dampen:

516

"It has been stated that Cleburne Company threw water on the fire 25 minutes before the E. B. Young Company. This is a grave mistake. There was not more than 2 minutes difference, if that, in the time of the playing of the two engines. The first to throw water being the Cleburne."

This series of fires gave rise to speculation that Eufaula was "cursed by the presence of one or more of the most dangerous incendiaries," but no evidence of that ever developed and periodic fires continued to bedevil the city. In the week of February 17, 1885, the Grange Warehouse burned, destroying 1400 bales of cotton. It was the oldest and largest in the city, owned by H. M. Comer of Savannah. "The Cleburne had a stream of water on the fire and ten minutes later the E. B. Youngs got to work. By the time the engines got to work the warehouse was hopelessly lost, and they turned their attention to the saving of Hart's Block, the finest and largest block of stores in the city. The wind changed and Hart's Block was saved by a steady stream of water. But for the steamers the block would have burned anyhow. In that hour's work alone they saved ten times their value in property." However, the loss to the owner of the warehouse was $110,000, part of which was insured through E. B. Young & Company with the Underwriter's Agency of New York.

Interspersed among this serious work, the Eufaula fire companies were involved in constant drills, tournaments, and contests at home and in neighboring towns which, although partly social in nature, also honed their firefighting skills. On March 26, 1884, the Eufaula Fire Department held its annual parade, inspection, and drill. The companies assembled on Broad Street in front of the opera house, with Cleburne No 1 on the left, E. B. Youngs in the center, and the Hook and Ladder Company on the right. After inspection by the mayor and city council, there was an elaborate drill in all of the maneuvers and movements required in fighting an actual fire. A large crowd of Eufaulians turned out for the event.

But the biggest local event of the decade was yet to come. In April 1885 the E. B. Youngs announced a "Grand Fireman's Tournament" to be held May 20, to celebrate the Youngs' second anniversary as a fire company. The company planned a gala parade, contest, banquet, and ball, to be attended by fire companies from throughout the area. The *Times & News* quickly picked up the theme and began stirring up local support. The paper noted the favorable economic aspects, the pure fun of it, and as Editor Jelks often noticed, the pretty women that would be present:

"It will draw to the city a large number of visitors from abroad who will spend considerable money in our midst, and it will tend to advertise the city and greatly to promote that social and friendly intercourse with our neighbors that is always productive of good. It will impart a little life and interest to the city for the time and furnish a theme to talk about for a week. Beside, it will grace our balconies and windows with galaxies of female beauty and loveliness, and half a dozen happy unions of hearts and lives may be the result."

The public was urged to make contributions to defray the costs of prizes, entertainment of guests, and other expenses. The E. B. Youngs soon sent out "handsomely engraved invitations" to all neighboring cities requesting the pleasure of their attendance at the Grand Tournament. Committees were appointed to raise money for prizes and to handle other arrangements The E. B. Youngs' local colleagues/competitors, the Cleburnes, churlishly declined the invitation to participate in the anniversary celebration, but no one believed they would be able to adhere to this tasteless rejection.

The *Times & News* gave almost daily reports on developments: "The Firemen now practice daily for the Tournament of the 20th…and it insures its proficiency and reliability in the hour of danger." "The Citizens' Fire Co. of Union Springs will take part." "The Cleburne No. 2 will doubtless take part."

As the preparations proceeded, and as the track was laid out, an article in the *Times & News* of May 12 called on Warren Dent, the E. B. Youngs' foreman, to change the route of the parade and contest. It urged that the tournament be conducted "on Broad Street so that on either side verandas and balconies can be used to watch the start and close of the running squads and the entire exercises… It is pointed out that as the track now lies [on Randolph Street], the large crowd present can't see the entire contest because there are no verandas or balconies on either side of Randolph Street opposite the starting point," closing with, "What does Foreman Warren Dent have to say?" It was first reported that Warren stated that if anyone would raise $50 for the purpose a new track would be laid as suggested. However, it was later reported that "Since every man doing business on Broad Street, particularly the saloon keepers, want the new track in front of his door, Foreman Dent and the Company decided to leave it where it is and build a flight of seats in the shade which will afford ladies and others a full view of the track and the exercises."

A ladies cooperative committee had been appointed to assist in the supper and ball on the evening of the twentieth, and to decorate the hall, ballroom, engines, and reels taking part in the parade. The supper committee included Mrs. J. G. L. Martin (Ada's mother-in-law), Helen (Mrs. George H) Dent, and many others. The decorations committee included Anna (Mrs. S. H.) Dent, Mrs. Warren F. Dent, Mrs. C. S. McDowell, Sr., Mrs. Maria Young, Ada Young Martin, and many others.

Finally, the big day arrived, and was a resounding success. The flavor and suspense can be conveyed only by the description of Editor Jelks himself, using the arcane jargon of the sport, preceded by banner headlines and concluding by noting the many beautiful women:

TOURNAMENT !
GALA DAY FOR EUFAULA
A Spirited and Exciting Contest.
THE RESULT!
The Fireman's Ball and Banquet

"Yesterday will long be remembered by Eufaulians and those from neighboring cities and towns and the surrounding country. The occasion was the celebration of the second anniversary of the E. B. Young Fire Co. No 3, a company composing the flower of the city's young manhood, and already distinguished for its gallantry and efficiency in the hour of danger...

The 4 o'clock morning train on the Southwestern Railroad brought the Mechanics Fire Co., No 2, of Americus, Ga., and also a good delegation from Watchful Fire Co, of Cuthbert, both organizations being accompanied by a number of friends and citizens from those places. The 9 o'clock train brought the Winn Fire Co., of Clayton, about 22 in number and quite a delegation of ladies and Gentlemen, and the regular passenger train from Montgomery brought in the Citizens Fire Co, of Union Springs, some 20 odd strong, together with a number of ladies and Gentlemen from that city and from all along the line. The reception committee of the E. B. Youngs...met the visiting companies with the Montgomery Brass Band at the depot...

During the forenoon people from the country came flocking in from all around and by noon the city and sidewalk were full of people. For an hour before the parade, Brannon, the auctioneer...sold pools from the Judges' stand, and it was still a matter of doubt as to which company, if any, was the favorite...the field selling well in every pool...

When the Mechanics No. 2 of Americus appeared on the track, they were greeted with the most enthusiastic cheering. A finer specimen of young manhood never entered any contest. In white pants, red stockings, cream shirts and jockey caps they went first to the scratch, and had their own steamer at the cistern. They were considered the dangerous boys for others in the contest. They made a fine run to the plug, 14 seconds, but hopelessly busted in the coupling and retired without a record.

The Citizens Company of Union Springs then took position at the sandbag, amid great cheering, as the personnel of the running squad was very fine, and in their dark blue uniforms looked like they were here for business. At the drop of the bag away they went, but at a distance of some thirty steps from it, Mr. Joe M. Ellis who was on the drag and nearest the reel, was tripped in some way and fell, and the reel passed over his chest. By the fall and being dragged some thirty feet he was quite painfully and badly bruised up. He had a rib broken beside. The squad ran on, however, and got to the plug in 15 1/8 seconds and made a record of 22 ½ points.

Then Cleburne No 1 of Eufaula next appeared, their running squad appearing in red pants and stockings, buff shirts and with caps. They made a beautiful run to the plug in 12 ¾, but the cut-loose got hold of the wrong end of the hose and lost six or eight seconds in fumbling and all hope of winning was lost. Time 33 5/8.

The E. B. Youngs then come to the scratch full of hope and confidence, and amid great cheering. They made the run to the plug in 12 ½ seconds and competed terms of contest in 28 ½ seconds.

The Winns of Clayton, a fine company and with a crack running squad, then entered, and much was expected of them, and right gallantly did they respond. They made the run to the plug in 14 5/8 seconds and time in 30…

The judges then awarded the prizes as follows: To E. B. Young No 3 of Eufaula, $50 in gold as first prize, and $10 in gold as first to the plug. The Winns of Clayton were awarded the second prize of $25 in gold…

After this time Capt S. H. Dent, in a few witty and will-timed remarks, presented the prizes, sympathizing with the vanquished and congratulating the victors. And so ended the second anniversary…which was witnessed by a crowd of not less than 3000 persons, a portion of whom were as bright-eyed and beautiful women as ever smiled destruction upon brave hearts."[855]

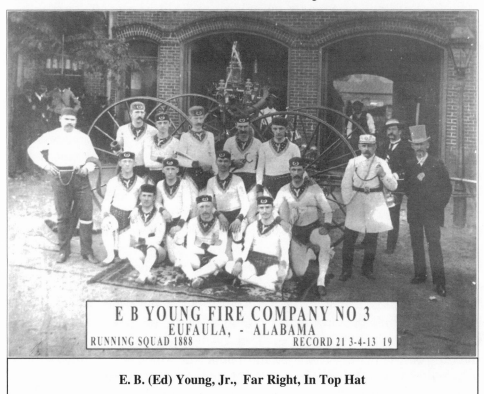

E. B. (Ed) Young, Jr., Far Right, In Top Hat

A few weeks later the E. B. Youngs held their annual elections. Ed Young was reelected president, and Ed Dent was elected assistant engineer. To everyone's surprise, Warren Dent resigned as foreman and declined reelection. The selection of his successor was postponed and he agreed to serve until then. The *Times & News* of June 9, 1885 commented that Warren "would have been reelected by acclamation. He made the most active, spirited, and efficient foreman and his resignation was such a dumbfounder to the company that they called for time in which to consider the matter as to who should be his successor." The reason Warren declined to continue this responsibility soon appeared. On August 11, 1885, the paper announced that Warren was leaving to begin his own drug business in Montgomery, (about which more later). Later, the E. B. Youngs elected W. W. Flewellen to succeed Warren as Foreman.

Another exciting day in Eufaula during the 80's was the 1886 visit of Jefferson Davis. The State of Alabama was constructing a monument to the Confederate war dead adjacent to the state capitol in Montgomery, near the spot where Jefferson Davis was inaugurated as President of the Confederacy. In his seventies, Jefferson Davis was in retirement at Beauvoir, on the Mississippi Gulf coast, and had declined invitations to come to Montgomery to lay the cornerstone of the new monument. However, he yielded to entreaties that he make the trip so that his beloved daughter, Winnie, could see the veneration in which he was held by Southerners. Davis' trip became a triumphal tour through Montgomery, Atlanta, Savannah, and other points in Alabama and Georgia.

The citizens of Eufaula were thrilled to learn that their former chieftain would stop in that city for an evening. No community had supported the cause of secession and the Confederacy more solidly than Eufaula. Anticipating the historic visit, Editor Jelks of the *Eufaula Times and News* described the Confederacy's only president as "the living embodiment of a grand and glorious past." Continuing, Jelks said that it was in Eufaula

> "...that the South found some of its ablest and most eloquent defenders. The Shorters, the Bullocks, the Pughs, the Cochrans, the Bakers and Dents splendidly led this people, both in field and forum, and Eufaula shed as pure and precious blood as ever flowed from mortal veins."[856]

In May 1886, President Davis, Winnie and party made the overnight stop in Eufaula, arriving at 10:00 p. m. amid tumultuous welcoming ceremonies. Davis spoke briefly from the balcony of the St. Julien Hotel, and later at a reception at the home of Dr. and Mrs. W. M. Reeves. Captain Dent was undoubtedly involved in the welcoming festivities, but the family member who later had the most vivid recollection of the event was his youngest daughter, Carrie. Only six years old, she may not have then fully understood the history, but she knew it was important. Carrie's oldest brother, Ed Dent (whom she called "Biggy," now 25 years old) lifted his little sister onto his shoulders, high over the crowd, so that she could see and hear Jefferson Davis speak. Carrie never forgot the scene. Years later, as an adult, Carrie Dent McDowell was one of the most capable and loyal officers of the United Daughters of the Confederacy, at both the state and national levels, for over half a century. At meetings and conventions of that dedicated organization, into the 1960's, Carrie basked in the pleasure of being presented as a "real daughter" who had personally seen and heard Jefferson Davis speak, thanks to "Biggy's" broad shoulders.[857]

54
New Leadership; Flush Times At The Eufaula National Bank

"There is no safer or more flourishing banking house in the state than the Eufaula National Bank. There is none of its stock that can be bought at any price, and the bank is constantly growing."

The Eufaula Times

During Eufaula's good economic times of the 1880's, the Eufaula National Bank, under the leadership of Hubert Dent and Ed Young, Jr. continued to grow with as much vigor as it had under Edward Brown Young himself in the 1870's. In the Examiner's Report of February 1880, the first examination after Hubert and Ed took over, the bank showed deposits of $106,000 and total resources of $226,000. The bank paid a dividend providing a 5% return to the investors. Under "General Remarks," Examiner L. B. Curtis stated that, "It is hard to get up any 'remarks' in regard to this bank, it is in splendid condition." At this time, the directors and their stockholdings were: S. H. Dent, president, 50 shares; E. B. Young, Jr., cashier, 10 shares; H. M. Weedon, 50 shares; George H. Dent, 50 shares, and R. H. McDonald (one of the New York investors), 100 shares.

The following year, deposits were up to $174,000, and total resources were up to $306,000. Examiner Curtis' remarks reflect the nature of the bank's business: "Loan and discounts are mostly to planters, the collateral is all good, being a lien on everything belonging to the planter in the shape of personal property...Dues and loans are to cotton buyers, secured by warehouse receipts for cotton, well insured and insurance policies assigned to the bank...The bank is well officered and making money." It again paid its investors a dividend of 5% on their original investments.

The examination of March 1882 shows that deposits had increased to $183,000 and total resources to $338,000. Examiner L. B. Curtis notes that most of the bank's loans are made to planters to "make a crop" and that the bank has taken a chattel mortgage on everything the planter has "except his wife and children." "Their paper is first class and they anticipate no loss on any of it...Their business is increasing and they are making money." The bank's dividend to its investors in 1882 was increased to an amount equal to a 6% return on their investments.

The annual visits of L. B. Curtis to Eufaula to examine the bank on behalf of the Comptroller of the Currency had made him a familiar figure in the town, to the extent that the *Times* sometimes reported his arrival, as on April 1, 1883: "National Bank Examiner L. B. Curtis is in the city, and examined into the condition of the Eufaula National Bank last night." Curtis' report reflected that the bank continued to pay a 6% dividend 1883.

That spring, the Bank was repainted, prompting the *Times* of May 13 to observe, "The National Bank has donned a spring dress of paint." The next month, the publication of the bank's financial statement (as required by law), lead to this editorial comment in the *Times* of June 27, 1883:

"Eufaula National Bank.

"The report of the condition of the Eufaula National Bank, as published in these columns yesterday morning, makes a fine showing for that solid institution. The deposits for instance, are at present $50,000 in excess of what they were at this time one year ago. Individual deposits now amount to within a few hundred of $160,000. This is indeed a fine showing for the dull summer.

"There is no safer or more flourishing banking house in the state than the Eufaula National Bank. There is none of its stock that can be bought at any price, and the bank is constantly growing. Such institutions managed by such officers deserve the fullest confidence of the business public."

The bank declared a 6% dividend again in January of 1884. With stable returns of this kind, Hubert and Ed were able to procure additional investors in the bank. This was desirable because the size and total amount of loans that a bank can lawfully make are restricted by the size of its paid-in capital; the more its capital, the larger the loans it may lawfully make. Eufaula National was authorized by its charter to issue capital stock of up to $250,000, but the bank had been authorized by the Comptroller of the Currency to commence business when it received paid-in capital of $50,000. The bank had commenced business with actual paid-in capital of $58,000 in 1876. In the week of February 26, 1884 Capt. S. H. Dent took a business trip to New York. Stopping in Washington enroute, Hubert happened to encounter Lucien Walker of the *Times & News* staff, who later reported in a letter to the *Montgomery Advertiser* that, "Capt. S. H. Dent of Eufaula, the able and popular president of the Eufaula National Bank was in Washington enroute to New York...Capt. Dent has few equals as an able financier and sterling Christian gentleman deservedly popular throughout southeast Alabama and wherever he is known." New York is where Hubert's father-in-law had raised part of the capital to begin the bank in 1875. In all probability, Hubert was in New York on this occasion to arrange for additional investment capital for the bank, because soon thereafter, in June, Ed Young filed with the Comptroller of the Currency a certification that the bank had received additional paid-in capital of $42,000. Its total capital was now $100,000. This certificate makes no mention of who contributed this additional capital, but later stockholder lists identify Roswell A. Roberts of Yonkers, N. Y. as owning 400 shares, and Isabella Brownson, also of Yonkers, as owning 50 shares. With each share having a stated par value of $100, they are probably the sources of the additional $42,000. We lack information about these stockholders, but point out that, when Edward B. Young, Sr. went to New York in 1875 to raise investment capital for the bank, and while there made application to the Comptroller of the Currency, he wrote that he could be addressed "Care of Frisbee Roberts, P. O. Box 3406, New York," who may have been connected with Roswell A. Roberts.

Ed Young was not slow in publicizing this large increase in capital. The *Times & News* of June 10 carried this editorial:

"We notice from a circular letter recently issued by Mr. E. B. Young, Cashier, that this Bank's capital has been increased to $100,000 or doubled. The surplus profits are $35,000. We are glad to note the evidence of prosperity which the increased capital gives and congratulate the institution on its past magnificent management. The gentlemen who are respectively president and cashier, as well as each member of the Board of Directors, are financiers of experience and wisdom and its present highly congratulatory condition is the natural result of a conservative and wise policy. May it grow in power and usefulness."

The Examination Report of November 1884 reflects that in July, soon after the new investors had come on board, the bank paid a second dividend which resulted in an annual return of 5% on the new total paid-in capital.

The following year, 1885, the Report of Examination reflected a change in the bank's board of directors: George Dent and Hamilton Weedon are now off the board, being replaced by R. J. Woods, another successful Eufaula businessman (and a son of Edward Young's old banking partner, Clayton R. Woods); and Hubert's oldest son, Ed Dent, now working in the bank. George and Hamilton were probably pleased to make their seats available to Hubert's boy and to a businessman who was undoubtedly a large depositor. Examiner Curtis remarked that "This Bank is well managed and in a sound and flourishing condition." It paid a 5% dividend that year.

The Comptroller sent a new examiner, C. J. Campbell, for the report filed June 1886, and the tenor of his report was very similar to those of Mr. Curtis. Mr. Campbell remarked that, "This Bank is now and always has been well managed." It continued to pay a dividend of 5% of invested capital.

Examiner Campbell's report of March 1887 reflects loans of $188,000, total resources at a new high of $382,000, and the remark that, "This Bank has always been under capable and excellent management." It paid its usual dividend of 5% on invested capital.

This 1887 report disclosed significant changes in the board of directors and in their holdings of stock. The board now consisted of: S. H. Dent (president), 196 shares; E. B. Young, Jr. (cashier), 214 shares; Ed Dent (assistant cashier and teller), 10 shares; M. S. Roberts (bookkeeper), 10 shares; and R. A. Roberts, 400 shares. We see that Ed Young has acquired more bank stock, greatly increasing his ownership interest, which is now slightly more than Hubert's. A new employee and director, M. S. Roberts, is the brother of Carrie Young's husband, Noah Roberts. It is not surprising that R. A. Roberts of Yonkers, who three years before had bought 400 shares and become the largest stockholder, would now be added to the board; in fact, this would normally have been expected to occur when he first made the investment. Whether he had any family relation with the Eufaula Robertses is not known, but considering that he is based in Yonkers, New York, there may be no connection with Noah Roberts' family, which had been in Barbour County for many years. [hh]

[hh] Roswell A. Roberts and Isabella K. Brownson of Yonkers were first identified as stockholders in an 1895 filing with the Comptroller of the Currency made for the purpose of extending the corporate existence of the bank for another 20 years. R. A. Roberts' location is made somewhat confusing by the fact that a few of the examination reports in the 1890's, in listing the directors, show his address as Eufaula, while others show it as

In his report of December 1888, Mr. Campbell made note of the annual salaries of the officers. We find Hubert Dent and Ed Young both drawing salaries of $3000. Hubert's son, Ed Dent, was paid $1200.

As an auxiliary to their banking business, Hubert, Ed Young, and Ed Dent also owned an insurance agency under the name, "E. B. Young & Company," which operated out of the bank offices. Ed Dent had the main responsibility for conducting this business. This insurance agency was apparently quite successful. Whenever there were fires in town which made the papers, it was the quaint custom to publish the names of the insurance agencies and companies which insured the damaged properties. Reporting those damaged by a big fire in January 1881, the *Times* stated that the Alabama Warehouse was insured by E. B. Young & Company for $1500, that the cotton was protected by E. B. Young & Company for $5000, and that the building of Weedon & Dent was insured by that firm for $3000. The city council minutes disclose that the insurance on the city-owned bridge across the Chattahoochee was carried by E. B. Young & Company, which is not surprising, since he was the city treasurer. The *Times* of November 28, 1882 carries the agency's ad: "Insure with E. B. Young & Company, General insurance agents. Life, fire, accident, and bond. Gin houses, contents a specialty. Eufaula. Alabama." In July 1883, the burning of the residence of Thomas E. Johnston on the southwest corner of Barbour and Randolph was reported; its furnishings were insured for $1500, of which $1200 was with E. B. Young & Co. When a series of fires led to speculation that an arsonist was at work, the agency received this attention-getting coverage on October 14, 1883:

E. B. Young & Company, General Agents

In this issue of the *Weekly Times & News* our city and country friends will find the advertisement of E. B. Young & Company Insurance Agents. It will not be for lack of information as to where they may seek protection if any of the readers of this journal should find that in an hour when they knew not, the destroying fiend should burn down in the night-time their dwelling, their barn, or their gin without having had the wisdom and foresight to place upon their property a liberal policy...E. B Young & Company represent some of the best companies on earth and a prudent man will not sleep well until a policy has been placed at least upon his own shelter."

Yonkers. This may be clerical error, resulting from the fact that most of the stockholders were in Eufaula. His occupation is listed as "capitalist," or sometimes, "retired capitalist."

55
The Weedon & Dent Pharmacy

The firm of Weedon and Dent, founded by Hamilton Weedon and George H. Dent in 1868, continued to innovate and grow in the 1880's. It carried a large and diversified inventory, which usually had a value in the range of $15,000 and consisted of drugs, chemicals, paint, oils, varnishes, perfumes, soaps and toilet articles, combs and a variety of other sundries. It advertised a "delightful and lasting perfume," made on the premises, which "would last until your handkerchief came back from the wash."

The firm suffered a temporary setback in January 1881, when one of the devastating fires which swept through Eufaula's business distinct during the '80's severely damaged the store. The firm temporarily moved out of its damaged quarters in order to carry out a major repair and renovation of the premises. By August 1881, it was back in its "handsome new quarters," ready for fall business. In October 1883, we find Weedon & Dent constructing a modern concrete sidewalk in front of their store, at a cost of $225.

To assist them in serving their customers, soon after the new drugstore opened in 1868, George and Hamilton had hired Edward C. Bullock, Jr., the son of the much-loved Eufaula lawyer and civic leader, E. C. Bullock, who had died of typhoid fever during the first year of the war. Bullock faithfully served Weedon and Dent in all capacities, but by 1877, he wished to start his own drug business.[858] Bullock opened the drug house of E. C. Bullock & Company, with Dent and Weedon assisting by investing in and retaining an ownership in the new company. The business succeeded, and in December 1882, Bullock bought out the interests of Weedon and Dent, dissolved Bullock & Company, and continued the business under his sole name.

An important part of Weedon & Dent's business was supplying farmers with seed, fertilizer, and other supplies. Among the kinds of fertilizer that it advertised were: soluble Pacific guano, low Georgia formula, acid phosphates and chemicals, "dissolved bones," and something with the unlikely name of "mastodon guano." It developed new farm products, such as seed for a new strain of corn called "Golden Dent Corn." Many of the firm's sales to farmers were on credit. In this era, General stores and other suppliers willing to advance goods and money until the crops came in were extremely important to small farmers who had difficulty obtaining bank credit. In selling fertilizer, for instance, the firm said, "We buy for spot cash and sell low. We will lend you the money to buy for cash, thereby giving you the advantage." Commenting on the strength of the area's economy, the *Times* of September 22, 1883 quoted Weedon & Dent as saying that "their collections on advancements of money to farmers so far this season are greatly in excess of last season."

In the summer of 1883, there had been much talk about the "cotton caterpillar," and how much damage it might inflict on the crops. The *Times* of July 22 turned to George Dent for an authoritative report: "Mr. George H. Dent of the firm of Weedon and Dent, a house perhaps more largely interested in the cotton crop than any other in Eufaula, yesterday forenoon made inquiries of some 20 odd farmers living in a radius of 15 miles of Eufaula regarding the cotton caterpillar. Not one of them asked said that he had the caterpillar in his cotton."

Hamilton Weedon was an experimenter in horticulture. He owned a farm (at that time still referred to as a "plantation") four miles south of Eufaula of at least four hundred acres, where he grew cotton, corn, and other crops. He also experimented on the premises of his Barbour Street home. He probably developed the strain of seed for "Golden Dent Corn" sold at the store. His horticultural views were sometimes sought out. In a June 1, 1883 interview with the *Times*, Hamilton advocated wheat and oats as suitable crops for the area: "Dr. Weedon has on his place in town, about a quarter of an acre of wheat, from which he will gather a big yield. The Doctor thinks this is very fine wheat and oat country. The only difficulty at all about it is the want of seed that are rust proof. He does not think it at all impossible to get them. High authorities, however, were divided as to the cause of rust…There is no doubt, continued the Doctor, that we have under proper seasons the finest wheat and oats country to be found anywhere."

Weedon & Dent did a brisk business in gifts, especially at Christmas. It advertised an assortment of the popular gift items of the day: "The very best stock of dressing cases…celluloid, pressed rubber…ever brought to Eufaula. A complete stock of card cases, cigar cases, reticules, razor cases…The most elegant holiday presents at the lowest imaginable prices are to be had from Weedon & Dent."

A significant part of the business of Weedon & Dent was its wholesale commerce with other stores in southern Alabama and Georgia. One of its most popular items in the wholesale trade was "Weedon and Dent's Farmer's Pills," a medication compounded and patented by Dr. Weedon himself which attained renown in two states as an effective remedy.[859] The company was now manufacturing and selling "immense quantities," "thousands" of these pills, receiving wholesale orders from as far away as Savannah. The success of the wholesale side of the business was based on sending out "drummers," or traveling salesmen to call on stores in other towns to sell them Weedon & Dent products.

One of their most effective drummers was George's younger brother, Warren F. Dent. Warren had become an employee in 1875, when he joined his two older brothers in migrating from Charles County, Maryland to Eufaula. In 1880, Warren had married Mary Elizabeth Wellborn, the granddaughter of the Youngs' old friend, John Horry Dent, and the daughter of "Minna" and Eufaula lawyer, Col. M. B. Wellborn, Sr.

Sadly, in August 1881, Warren and Mary Elizabeth lost an infant child, the *Times & News* of the 18th noting that, "These parents have the sympathy of the community in their affliction." However, on December 30, 1882, they became the parents of a healthy little girl, named Minna, after Mary Elizabeth's mother, Emma ("Minna") Julia Dent.

Warren had become a popular member of the community. At the city ward meetings of May 23, 1882, he was nominated as candidate for alderman from Eufaula's Ward One, although he was edged out in the city election the following week.

In 1884, we find Mary Elizabeth taking baby Minna to visit Mary Elizabeth's grandfather, John Horry Dent, at Cave Springs, Ga. The *Times & News* of July 15 reports that, "Mrs. Warren F. Dent and Miss Minna Dent, the latter the sweetest of Alabama babies, left yesterday to spend several weeks at Cave Springs, Georgia on a visit to Major John H.[orry] Dent. ["Major" is a courtesy title; he was never in the military, but served on the Confederate Conscription Bureau.] Warren refuses to be comforted and has taken the road for Weedon & Dent's celebrated remedies and will not return, perhaps before his family does. He goes this week to southwest Georgia."

Warren was a valued salesman to Weedon & Dent in south Alabama and south Georgia. For instance, the *Times* of July 24, 1883 reports that "Mr. Warren Dent left yesterday on a trip through southwest Georgia in the interests of the large and popular drug house of Weedon & Dent." On August 3, it is reported that, "Our genial and clever Mr. Warren F. Dent has returned from a drumming trip in the interests of Weedon & Dent, the druggists. We are glad to know that he was quite successful."

When Warren was not on the road, he helped run the store. We find a lighthearted interview with him in the *Times* of August 8, 1882, which provides interesting insight into the kinds of products that were big sellers in this era. Its also reveals the nineteenth century's "dirty little secret" about narcotics, which were legal and unregulated:

"A Talk With A Druggist
"Mr. Warren F. Dent, of the big drug house of Weedon & Dent, was found in the early hours of Saturday morning sitting in the doorway quietly chewing the cud of reflection—or chewing gum, we failed to note which.
"Good deal of kerosene burned hereabouts," began Mr. Dent, looking at a pile of empty barrels in front of the store. "We sell from fifty to one hundred and twenty-five barrels a month, ourselves. Much of it is shipped to neighboring towns. Well, say we sell 1000 barrels a year; that is about 40,000 gallons, quite enough to make a good size lake."
Snuff is one of our most important articles," continued the druggist. "Our snuff trade amounts to about 10,000 pounds a year, over $6000 worth. So you see there are a great many dippers of the sneeze-creating substance. Think of the number of dips in 10,000 pounds! We have a customer, a young married man, who buys it for himself and wife, a good jar at a time."
"And the morphine and opium trade is astonishing. Since January we have sold 150 ounces of morphine; and the demand for it is growing all the time. But I'd much rather sell Farmers' pills, manufactured by yours truly, Weedon & Dent."
"How about quinine?" [a common malaria remedy] we asked.
"Quinine is not used as much as formerly, though we sell large amounts. You see there are substitutes for quinine, which appear to be coming into general use. For instance, Farmers' Pills are better for chills."
"Just so. You appear to have it on those pills."

528

"Exactly. Good thing. There was a man in here the other day from away over in South Alabama, who carried a box of the pills in his pocket. He said they kept off the chills."

"Merely carried them in his pocket?"

"Yes!"

"Good morning."

When the E. B. Young Fire Company held their annual elections in June 1885, to everyone's surprise, Warren Dent resigned as foreman and declined reelection. The *Times & News* of June 9, 1885 commented that Warren "would have been reelected by acclamation. He made the most active, spirited, and efficient foreman and his resignation was such a dumbfounder to the company that they called for time in which to consider the matter as to who should be his successor." The reason Warren declined to continue this responsibility soon appeared. The *Times & News* of August 4 reported that "The *Advertiser* of the 31st says that Mr. Warren F. Dent, one of the most successful young businessmen in Eufaula, spent yesterday in Montgomery." And then on August 11, 1885, this article:

"To Leave Us

Mr. Warren Dent has made arrangements to go into the drug business in Montgomery. Mr. A. R. Harvey, of Union Springs, a most excellent young man, will be associated with him. The firm will be Dent & Harvey, and they will do a wholesale drug business. Warren's friends will be pained to lose him from Eufaula though he leaves us to embark in business for himself and under flattering auspices. The young men will succeed from the first, the *Times* feels perfectly confident in saying, and they will deserve it all too."

George and Hamilton's revenues from their store had reached the point that permitted, or required, new areas of investment, and they decided to diversify by investing in good rental property in the Eufaula's booming business district. A major fire in early 1883 had destroyed some buildings on Eufaula Street. In March, George and Hamilton purchased two lots which had been made vacant by the fire from Mrs. Mary Perkins and Mayor G. L. Comer, for $1950 each. They later announced, in the *Times* of March 17, their plans to build two single story storehouses. "The buildings will have high parapet walls, a neat and handsome appearance, and will be so constructed that they can be turned into one large store room on short notice." The brick walls would be sufficiently thick to permit the addition of another story if desired in the future. In fact, during construction, the plans were changed to add a second story to both buildings. In April, Weedon and Dent also purchased the "Brannon lot" next to the *Times* offices, for $2000, and began construction of another building there. The walls of the first two Eufaula street buildings had been completed by June, and the brothers-in-law announced that they had rented both floors of one of the stores to "a large furniture firm which will open here next fall." By July 10 the woodwork was being put in "Weedon & Dent's new block on Eufaula Street." By July 21 the *Times* reported brick laying had begun on their Brannon lot building, adding that "Weedon & Dent are live men, and they are successful." Soon they were advertising the availability for rental of "a store and one room upstairs" in one of the new buildings.

Weedon & Dent was a frequent advertiser in the pages of the *Eufaula Times*. Hamilton and George had an easy relationship with Editor Jelks, and they were often the targets of good-natured ribbing in the *Times*. On one occasion the *Times* suggested, "Ask Mr. George Dent the difference between German carp and catfish. He has been bragging on having carp for his table the past week; it turned out to be only catfish." Later the *Times* reported, "Considerable amusement was created in front of Weedon & Dent's Drug Store Saturday afternoon over the efforts of a multitude to catch a wild rooster." The best jibe was after the fire that destroyed the Grange Warehouse, where Weedon & Dent had stored sacks of guano. The *Times* reported that Weedon & Dent were resacking the guano and claiming that "it is just as good, if not a little better than it was before, as it is now nicely cooked, while all the balance is raw and unpalatable...If anybody wants some good cooked guano they know where to get it."

| **George Hatch Dent** | **Helen Augusta Young Dent** |

56
The Renovation of Fendall Hall

"The large and beautiful residence of Capt. S. H. Dent, has been thoroughly overhauled by carpenters and painters, but the most important and convenient improvement made, is the introduction of a complete and admirable working system of water works..."

The Eufaula Weekly Bulletin

**Anna and Hubert Dent
In their Middle Years**

During the period 1881-1884, as their businesses prospered, five of the six Eufaula "Young" families were busily acquiring, building, or improving their homes. We have seen that in August 1881, Noah and Carrie Young Roberts had broken ground for construction of their new residence at the corner of Randolph and Shorter Streets. Four of the Young families would locate on Barbour Street.

The first of the renovations were by the new occupants of Fendall Hall. After Edward Young's death in 1879, Anna, Hubert, and their six children had moved into the house, probably in 1880. By 1881, renovations had begun which would extend over several years. Architectural changes were made, which included removing a back staircase, and included installing a partition with double doors and frosted glass which shielded the rear portion of the lengthy, black-and-white marbled entry hall. The most dramatic change at Fendall Hall was the installation of an indoor plumbing system. Such a system was unheard of in Eufaula at the time, most of the citizens using "chamber pots" and outdoor "privies." Fendall Hall's new plumbing system, which included hot water for baths, as well as sewerage disposal, was revolutionary enough to generate a news article in the *Eufaula Weekly Bulletin* of March 26, 1881:

"Residence Water-Works
"The large and beautiful residence of Capt. S. H. Dent, at the head of Barbour street, as we stated some weeks ago has been thoroughly overhauled by carpenters and painters, but the most important and convenient improvement made, is the introduction of a complete and admirable working system of water works, by the Folsom Brothers of this city. In a well in the back yard, they have inserted what is known as a "deep well pump," by means of which water is raised from the well, and forced though a lead pipe to an eight hundred gallon tank in the top of the house just under the observatory. From this tank lead pipes lead to all the rooms in the house, furnishing an ample supply of water for drinking and ablution, and also supplies two or three

bath tubs in different apartments, both for adults and children. It also supplies the water for a beautiful fountain in the front yard, and the elevation of the tank is sufficient to throw a jet of water twenty feet high from the nozzle of the fountain. Then, again, there is a hot water tank in the kitchen, connected by pipes with the cooking stove, by which hot water is supplied to every apartment and bathroom in the house, thus furnishing a supply of both cold and hot water, as either or both are wanted. From the bath tubs and washstands pipes are connected so as to turn water off after being used, into a sewer under the house, which conveys it entirely away. It is altogether the most admirable and convenient arrangement, in the way of furnishing a water supply, that any residence in all this section boasts of, and we believe that when its advantages and practicability are tested and established in the instance, a number of other fine family residences in the city will be similarly supplied with this new system of water works."

The writer's prediction about others wanting similar systems was correct; within months, Anna's sisters, Helen and Mollie were installing indoor plumbing in their homes. Describing the activities of the Folsom Brothers, plumbers, the *Weekly Bulletin* of Sept 17, 1881 reported that "They are now putting water fixtures in the private residences of Mr. George H. Dent and Dr. H. M. Weedon…"

It is not certain what powered the force pumps[ii] that conducted water to the cisterns beneath the "observatory" of Fendall Hall, but there can be no doubt that the system worked, and indeed it saved the house from destruction by fire, according to the March 6, 1883 *Times*:

"Almost Destroyed
    "The handsome two story residence of Capt. S. H. Dent on upper Barbour Street narrowly escaped destruction by fire Sunday afternoon. It appears that some Negroes on an adjoining lot discovered the south side of the roof of the building to be on fire about 2:30 o'clock and sounded the alarm. Capt. Dent has private water works in his house and at the top of the roof he has two tanks holding about 600 gallons of water. The top of the house is crowned with a cupola admitting of easy egress to the roof. The water being within 10 feet of the fire busy hands with buckets soon extinguished the flames, not, however, until a hole 8 by 10 feet had been burned through the roof. The close proximity to the fire of an abundant supply of water is all that saved the building. It is supposed that the fire was caused by a spark from a chimney nearby.
    "Capt. Dent's residence is by many regarded as the handsomest in the city and its loss would have been not only a misfortune to him but to all of

---

[ii] It has been suggested that the force pump may have been powered by windmill, but there is not yet evidence of that. The *Times* of Sept. 17, 1881 reports there being two water windmills in Eufaula at that time, at the homes of R. J. Woods and J. C. Stevens. And the *Weekly Bulletin* article quoted above makes no mention of a windmill. The pump was probably manually operated by household servants (who were available at moderate wages) to periodically fill the tanks.

Eufaula. Considerable excitement was caused by the alarm of the fire, but the residence is too far up town to be reached by the firemen in time to save it should it catch on fire with no water on hand."

George and Helen Dent had acquired the attractive home on Barbour Street once occupied by the villainous scalawag, Judge Elias Kiels, whom George and other Democrats had vigorously sought to oust from office. The exterior front of the house had a double set of gracefully curving exterior stairs from the ground up to the second story, in what Alabamians know as the "Gorgas" style (after the Gorgas Home on the University of Alabama campus). While the Hubert Dents were making Fendall Hall a showplace, George and Helen were doing the same with their elegant home. If Hubert set the example for his brother, George, in indoor plumbing, it was George who set the example for Hubert in interior beautification. The artist who painted the rich murals for which Fendall Hall is best known today was apparently first discovered and utilized by George and Helen Dent. The *Times* of May 24, 1883 reports as follows:

"Liefrank & Slade
"Mr. Leifrank of the firm of Liefrank & Slade left yesterday for Columbus, Georgia. The firm of which Mr. Liefrank is the energetic head has been doing some magnificent work in Eufaula toward adorning and beautifying our already handsome houses and he comes highly recommended from other places. He refers with pride to Messrs. R. J. Woods and G. H. Dent of this city as to the character of his decorations."

During 1883, the Columbus firm of Liefrank and Slade opened a branch office in Eufaula on the corner of Randolph and Broad Streets, and for several days in late May and June, advertised their wares and services in the *Times*, including pure ready-mixed paint; oils and varnishes, glass, wall paper, art goods, artist material, oil paintings, window shades, and other items. By June 22, Leifrank had apparently finished his wall paintings in George and Helen's house, leading the *Times* of June 22 to report the results:

"Handsome Parlors
"Probably the most beautiful suite of private parlors in Alabama are those of Mr. George H. Dent, at his handsome Barbour street residence in this city. These parlors are simply magnificent since they passed through the skillful hands of Mr. Leifrank of the firm of Leifrank & Slade, frescoers and house decorators. The frescoe work is simply perfect in design and the most beautiful in finish. Birds and flowers and vines and cherubs and the most delicate tracery, as wrought by the hand of a master, which together with the most skillfully executed mosaic make Mr. Dent's parlors as beautiful as art can

533

make them. Indeed the walls, panels, doors and ceilings look like so many paintings of rare artistic finish, and the parlors in all their appointments constitute a study even for an artist. Mr. Leifrank is certainly master of his work, and so perfectly and beautifully is it shown in Mr. Dent's parlors that we can give no just idea of the artist's great skill. The work is after the latest European models which combine with Mr. Liefrank's originality in making the parlors superb, magnificently beautiful."

By July 4, the publicity accorded its interior artistic painting apparently prompted Liefrank & Slade to slightly change its *Times* ad to emphasize "Careful attention given to Decorating Houses," by its "Branch office in Eufaula, Ala."

In 1883, Mrs. Martha Jane Cato, the widow of secessionist leader and lawyer, Lewis Lewellen Cato, died, and their historic old home on Barbour Street on College Hill next door to Fendall Hall went on the market. A center of secessionist activity, the Cato House had been the scene of jubilant celebrations the night Alabama adopted the ordinance of Secession from the Union. Ed Young, Jr., who was now participating in the prosperity of the Eufaula National Bank and its related insurance business, decided that it was time for him to provide Mamie and his growing family with a fine home. The *Times* of July 28, 1883 reported that Ed bought the Cato House for $3600. Ed and Mamie's family at this time consisted of four children, two girls and two boys: Annie, age 10; May Belle, age 7; Edward Billups, Jr., age 5; and William Hubert, age 3. (Another son had died shortly after birth in 1872.) Ed, Mamie and the four children completed the move into their new home in November 1883. Two more children would be born after moving into the new house: Flora, born in 1884, seven months after the move; and Ada, born in 1887. Ed Young and his family would occupy this beautiful residence until his death in 1910 (at which time it would be repurchased by one of Lewis L. Cato's sons, Dr. J. C. Cato). There were now four "Young" families in comfortable homes on Barbour Street.

The following year, Hamilton and Mollie Weedon followed the example of her sister, Helen, and also engaged the services of D. F. Liefrank to decorate the interiors of their Barbour Street home. The *Times & News* of May 27, 1884 reported that "Mr. Liefrank, whom our people will remember for some excellent work he did here a year ago, is now in Eufaula engaged in beautifying Dr. Weedon's parlors."

Liefrank returned to Eufaula later in 1884. The *Times & News* of November 11 reported that, "Mr. D. F. Liefrank, well known to our people...will be in the city some weeks in pursuit of the calling in which he is a master. Mr. Liefrank refers with pride to a number of the handsomest finished homes in this city as the work of his hands. His services can be secured at very reasonable compensation."

Liefrank & Slade's ads, and newspaper references to the firm, cease after 1884, so it was probably during Liefrank's visit in late 1884 that Anna and Hubert Young decided to join her sisters, Helen and Mollie, and have D. F. Liefrank decorate the interiors of Fendall Hall also. There is a family tradition that Liefrank resided in Fendall Hall while he worked, and that he was "temperamental." Although three of the four "Young" homes on Barbour Street had interiors decorated by Liefrank, his Fendall Hall paintings are the only ones presently known to survive, in Eufaula or elsewhere. They have been carefully restored by the Alabama Historical Commission, whose "Docent Notes" offer this commentary on his work at Fendall Hall, (erroneously spelling his name, "LeFranc"):

> "The murals [in the entry hall] are painted on the original plaster walls...
>
> "He painted some of the murals freehand but used stencils on the repeating patterns. Apparently he had no stencil brush. The stenciled patterns appear to have been done with an ordinary paintbrush. These murals have been called frescos, but they are not. Frescoes are painted on wet, damp plaster and the paint sinks into the plaster surface...The murals were papered over early in the [20th] century. Five layers of paper were removed in the early [1970's] so the murals could be preserved...
>
> [In the company parlor] LeFranc's murals are more impressive here than in the hall. Each violin shaped enclosure on the ceiling contains flower arrangements. LeFranc picked them on early morning walks. He brought them back, arranged them, and painted them into the ceiling design. The murals are also influenced by designs excavated at Pompeii. Over the hall door is a copy of an illustration from a child's book, *In Fairyland*, William Allingham, 1875. We think that the children may have asked that it be placed there...
>
> [In the second parlor] the murals continue into this room with some changes. The 'temperamental Monsieur LeFranc' became intrigued by Mrs. Dent's silver pattern and the color of her china. He used some of both in decorating this room. We believe that the lavender in the cornice was a color from her china. The dragon design on the ceiling repeats the design of the stair runners in the hall."

We have noted some of the business trips that Hubert made to New York, as well as those that he and Anna made there together, in the mid-1880's. During this period, Fendall Hall was entirely refurbished with fine furnishings, carpeting, draperies and fixtures, acquired, according to family tradition, in New York.

Family tradition suggests that part of the Dents' motivation for the 1881-1885 refurbishing may have been to provide a setting for a fashionable "coming out" party for their oldest daughter, "Nannie" (Anna Beall Dent). It is equally likely that, having recently moved into a twenty year old home, Anna simply wanted to update it to reflect current fashions and her own tastes. In any event, by 1883, Nannie, now 17, was attending the Nashville Female College (sometime referred to as the "Nashville College for Young Ladies.") The *Times* of October 19, 1883 reports that, "Capt. S. H. Dent left last afternoon for Nashville. He took with him his charming daughter Miss Nannie Dent who will be left at school at Nashville." Nannie was fortunate to have two of her Eufaula first cousins attending the same college with her. These were Mollie and Hamilton Weedon's two oldest: Annie Weedon, age 16, and "Noonie" (Mary Norma) Weedon, age 15. The girls' families made periodic trips to Nashville to visit them. On April 14, 1884 it is reported that, "Mrs. S. H. Dent and little daughter (either Kate Louise, age 9, or Carrie, age 5) left yesterday afternoon on a visit to her daughter at school in Nashville." In June the girls were all in Eufaula for summer vacation. Nannie sometimes brought college friends home to visit at Fendall Hall.

It happened that Nannie's graduation from the Nashville Female College in June 1885, fell on her parents' Silver wedding anniversary. The *Times* of June 9 reported that, "The Captain had been to Nashville to witness the graduation of his daughter, Miss Nannie, and only returned on the noon train. The celebration of his 25th wedding awaited him. Numerous presents from the family and friends were showered upon them. The *Times* joins their army of friends and admirers wishing them both happiness, prosperity, and many returns of the anniversary occasion."

Miss Nannie Dent did not remain a "Miss" very long. Two years after returning from college, on October 26, 1885, she was married to Jackson Edward Long.[jj] The wedding festivities undoubtedly took place at the refurbished Fendall Hall. Nannie and Jackson Long[kk] soon had a succession of three children: first came Hubert Dent ("Bud") Long in 1888, then Martha Jane Long (McGhee) in 1890. But then tragedy struck: Jackson Long died in April 1891 at the young age of 26. At the time of his death, Nannie was expecting their third child, who was born five months later in September 1891. A daughter, she was named in part for her deceased father: Jackson Eddy Beall Long (Willingham), and throughout her life was called "Jack." Nannie, now a twenty-four year old widow with three infant children, moved back into Fendall Hall to live with her parents. Also still living at Fendall Hall at this time were Nannie's three brothers, Ed (Biggy), Hubert (Hugh) and Henry, and her two sisters, Louise ("Weesie") and Carrie. Although Fendall Hall was a spacious home, it could not have comfortably accommodated these additional residents. Accordingly, Hubert and Anna added a bedroom and bath to the east side of the first floor, to create something of a separate apartment for Nannie and her children.[ll] Nannie reared her children in Fendall Hall for thirteen years. In 1904, she remarried William W. Mangum, and later settled with him and the three children in Rome, Georgia, in which vicinity a large family of her descendants resides today.

[jj] Jackson Long was the son of N. W. E. Long, and the grandson of Nimrod Washington Long of Uchee and Hurtsboro in adjacent Russell County. Nimrod Washington Long (Jackson's grandfather) had earlier settled in Twiggs County, Georgia in the 1820's, where he had become a substantial landowner. Edward and William Young were merchants in Twiggs County at the same time and must have been acquaintances. In fact, Nimrod migrated to Uchee in Russell County, Alabama in the 1830's about the same time Edward and Ann Young were moving to Irwinton. But while Edward was an entrepreneur, Nimrod became a planter, and was one of the largest slaveholders of the area. In the 1860 census, he reported 178 slaves, and at the end of the war, signed in to the Freedmen's Bureau 250 slaves. He was able to rebuild his pre-war fortunes based upon earlier investments in land and railroads.

[kk] The two families became connected again years later: N. W. E. Long's brother was George Washington Long. The latter's great-grandson, John Allen Crook, Jr. married Hubert Dent's granddaughter, Joy McDowell, in 1933.

[ll] When the Alabama Historical Commission acquired Fendall Hall in 1972, the prevailing doctrine was to return the house to its original configuration when first completed in 1859. Thus, Nannie's apartment was torn away, as was a kitchen that had also been added to replace the original detached kitchen destroyed by tornado in 1919.

Two years after Nannie's first marriage, her oldest brother, Ed ("Biggy"), married Annie Stuart McCormick, on February 7, 1889. Ed had graduated in 1881 from the Southern University in Greensboro, Alabama, and had gone to work at the Eufaula National Bank with his father and his Uncle Ed Young. Ed and Annie provided Hubert and Anna with five more grandchildren: George McCormick Dent, 1890; Anna Beall ("Nana") Dent (McGough), 1891; Catherine Allan ("Tank") Dent, 1893; Edward Young Dent, II, 1895; and Stuart Hubert Dent, 1899.

Six years after Ed married, his younger sister, "Weesie" (Kate Louise), married George N. Hurt on Jan 23, 1895. Weesie and George provided Anna and Hubert with three grandchildren who survived infancy: Ada Louise, 1896; Mary Maud, 1899, and Nan Dent, 1901. One of these, Mary Maud Hurt McCullohs, would with her family become the last descendants of Ann and Edward Young to occupy Fendall Hall. After five Generations, Mary Maud and her sons, Harry Lee ("Mack") McCullohs and Hubert Dent McCullohs, would convey the historic old home to the Eufaula Heritage Association in 1972, which transferred it the following year to its present owner, the Alabama Historical Association.

Painted white when completed by the Youngs circa 1859, Fendall Hall is now presented by the Alabama Historical Commission in the colors selected by the Dents during the 1880's renovation. Paint tests revealed this brown polychrome fashionable at the time.

View of the entrance hall, showing the marble tiles originally installed by the Youngs in 1859, the Dents' "crown of thorns" chandelier, and the D.F. Liefrank wall murals commissioned by the Dents in about 1884.

View of the first of Fendall Hall's "double parlors," showing the marble mantel and fireplace installed by the Youngs, and the mirrors, chandelier, and Liefrank wall paintings later added by the Dents.

Ann and Edward Young installed these pocket doors, with Bohemian etched glass panels, to divide the "double parlors." The Dents later adapted the second parlor for use as a formal dining room, and had D.F. Liefrank decorate the medallions on the lower part of the doors.

Ceiling of the front parlor, with Dent chandelier and D.F. Liefrank murals.

Enlarged detail from a Liefrank mural shows Cupid's lily pad being pulled by dragonflies.

57
The Quest For Railroads and Industry

"[The proposed railroad is] a movement ... to give [Eufaula's] trade...easy access to market, and to secure it beyond the power of rival cites to draw away...to gain a market by rail and enjoy all the benefits of a quick and ample outlet into the world."

S. H Dent, Citizens Committee

The railroad building rage of the 1870's had cooled, but the business leaders of Eufaula during the 1880's were very aware that adequate railroad service was crucial to the community's continued prosperity. There were constant efforts to work with promoters and organizers of railroads to have additional tracks come through Eufaula or Barbour County; Hubert and George Dent were often in the forefront of these efforts. One past railroad issue that remained pending was the old Vicksburg and Brunswick Railroad, which we last discussed in 1873. It had planned a road from Albany, Georgia, to Cuthbert, to Eufaula, to Clayton, and beyond. Based on this plan, Barbour Countians has invested substantially in it. However, when there began to be talk of diverting the road from Cuthbert to Columbus, Edward B. Young, Sr. presided over a public meeting to protest. When we left the subject in 1873, S. H. Dent and others had been appointed to a committee to conduct an investigation. Despite financial difficulties, the line from Eufaula to Clayton had been completed, which was very important to the county. But the company had gone into bankruptcy, and the section east from Cuthbert to Alabama had never been built. The Eufaula-to-Clayton segment was taken over and operated for a time as a branch of the Southwestern Railroad. In 1883, a further reorganization created a separate company for this segment, which was named the Eufaula and Clayton Railroad. The *Times* of April 4 and 8, 1883 reported that a telegram had been received from company president, W. G. Raoul, announcing that George H. Dent and G. L. Comer had been elected to the board of directors of the new company.

Hubert Dent led an effort to revive another railroad project which had been originally proposed, but abandoned, years before. The proposal was to construct a railroad from Eufaula south and southwest to Abbeville, Headland, and Ozark. The front page of the *Times* of August 11, 1885 carried *"An Address To The Citizens Of Barbour, Henry, And Dale Counties,"* signed by John D. Roquemore and S. H. Dent as a "Committee for the Corporators and Citizens Committee." In this appeal, Dent and Roquemore stated that this was "a movement on the part of Eufaula to give to the trade which is hers by position and preference, easy access to market, and to secure it beyond the power of rival cites to draw away, and an effort on the part or the communities to be reached by it, to gain a market by rail and enjoy all the benefits of a quick and ample outlet into the world." The company, named the Eufaula Southern Railway Co., was to open its books to subscriptions on August 17, and the corporators were asking citizens of Eufaula and vicinity to subscribe to $75,000, Henry County, $50,000, and Dale County, $25,000. The *Address* emphasized that "We are building the road for ourselves...there is no scheme on foot to entrap the investors into a project which has nothing in view but profits to the originators. Home people alone will be looked to for subscriptions..."

This idea was one that Hubert Dent and Edward B. Young, Sr. had supported fourteen years earlier. The Eufaula, Gulf, and Abbeville Railroad had been chartered in 1871 to construct a road south from Eufaula into Henry and Dale Counties' and beyond. Col A. J. Lane was president and J. G. L. Martin (Ada Young's father-in-law) was Secretary. Its Board of Directors included E. B. Young, W. J. Bray, Mayor G A. Roberts (future father-in-law of Carrie Young), H. Bernstein, Col. Lane, J. G. L. Martin and others. When the idea was revived in 1885 by Dent and others, one old businessman interviewed by the *Times* of May 29 remembered the earlier effort by Edward Young and others, commenting that, "The preliminary survey was made...The stock was made up...The stockholders, however were never called upon for any subscription, the project being abandoned before that step was taken...It is the only road I want to see built...I believe it is the only road that can go out of Eufaula that would not harm the city. But if it goes to the Gulf, not terminating this side of the water, it would be a big thing to Eufaula and no mistake. I wish [the backers] success in the undertaking."

In a lengthy editorial on the same date as the *"Address,"* Editor Jelks of the *Times* reported on a mass meeting that had been held about the project, which he enthusiastically supported:

"Good Meeting
In the Interests Of The Eufaula Southern Railroad
"Several hundred business men met in Shorter Opera House, Monday night, 3rd, in pursuance to a call issued by the Board of Corporators of the Eufaula Southern Railroad. Capt. S. H. Dent was made Chairman, and W. D. Jelks, Secretary.

Capt Dent...discussed the value of the proposed road to Eufaula. He believed that when it reached Headland it would bring at least 15,000 bales of cotton to Eufaula that we do not now get...He thought the road would be of vast advantage to us, and was an absolute necessity, not only to reclaim the cotton, the past few years going elsewhere, but as well to hold the territory already our own, but which waits the coming of a road from any direction.

He believed it could be built...not...by 'talk or gush' but by cash...It required the hearty cooperation of all our people. Every interest was at sake and the clerk and the merchant prince must do each his share toward building it...Capt. Dent was heartily cheered throughout the address.

He was followed too by John Roquemore in much the same strain...

Major W. N. Reeves and Mayor Comer made brief addresses...Mr. George McCormick said when called upon he would do his share of the work but somebody else had to do his share of the talking. Mr. Edmondson... believed the road would be of vast advantage to the city, and he for one would give as much money toward its construction as any man, his means being considered. Mr. C. S. McDowell [Sr., then a 'drummer' for Richardson and McCormack Grocery] gave a humorous sketch of his business trips in Henry and Dale and then spoke glowingly of the enterprise....

The meeting after a two hours session adjourned in a beautiful humor and indeed in the midst of great enthusiasm…The *Times* believes the road will be built."

A committee was appointed to canvass the town and county for subscriptions, including, in addition to the corporators: George H. Dent, H. Lampley, S. Lewy, W. D. Jelks, Dr. J. M.Barr, L. Y. Dean, J. C. Guice, J. H. Reeves, W. H. Bray, and others.

The *Times* of August 18 reported that, "The subscriptions to the Eufaula & Southern are still gradually crawling up, and the outlook is still cheering and hopeful. Let every property owner, businessman, capitalist, and permanent citizen of Eufaula bear distinctly in mind, that if the road is ever built, it must be largely by Eufaula capital, pluck, and enterprise." On August 25, the paper carried a front-page letter from John McNab, owner of the "other" Eufaula bank and one of the city's influential businessmen. Writing from Saratoga, New York, where he was spending several months, he voiced strong support for the proposed railroad, and urged its success. The same paper reported that Dent and Edmondson had returned from a solicitation trip through Dale and Henry Counties. Ozark subscribed $20,000. Headland guaranteed $15,000, which, added to earlier amounts, totaled only $25,000, or one-half the amount hoped for. Unfortunately, despite the widespread optimism, the necessary capital never became available, and Barbour would have to wait until the 20th century for the proposed line to the south.

Eufaula's leadership continued to pursue opportunities to attract additional railroads to the area. In 1901, A group of promoters led by a Col. Machem was sponsoring a railroad link from Brunswick, Georgia to Birmingham, Alabama as part of a plan to connect the Atlantic to the Pacific by way of a route through the southern states. Towns along Alabama's eastern border were excited by this prospect, and each competed to persuade Col. Machem that a route through it was best. During the week of May 16, 1901, a public meeting had been held in Eufaula, chaired by Capt. S. H. Dent, to discuss the Brunswick & Birmingham railroad. Businessmen had subscribed to bonds totaling $56,000. The Eufaula meeting was now urged to make those promises good by subscribing to a fund to acquire right of way to offer to the proposed road, free of charge. An editorial pointed out that there was already a partially completed roadbed from Albany to Cuthbert and that this was a natural route for the road. "If Eufaula can have the good luck to influence the B&B road to pass through the city, than the old Brunswick & Albany road bed is decidedly the best route from Albany to Eufaula." It will be recalled that Hubert Dent had been appointed to investigate the failure of this road to reach Eufaula in 1873.

During the week of May 21, 1901, Eufaula's Railroad Committee, consisting of Mayor George Dent, Capt McKenzie, and John T. Foy, met again in Sycamore, Alabama with representatives of Col. Machem, later reporting, "The Committee feels that Eufaula and Barbour County have offered all that any place along the route can do." The Committee feels that…"if the road is ever built…the southern [Eufaula] route will be chosen, although Mr. Brobsen was as close in his remarks as the proverbial oyster…" This competition continued to make news during 1901 and 1902.

Led by *Eufaula Times* editor, William Jelks, Eufaula's leaders had long recognized the need to attract industry, particularly a cotton mill, to provide jobs and economic stimulus. As early as 1872, the *Times* held up William Young's Eagle and Phenix as an example of what is possible in its issue of February 14, 1873: "...all who fear to invest their money in a well conducted cotton factory, should read and study [the Eagle and Phenix financial] report and they will learn something to their advantage."

In the town's eagerness to commence a cotton mill, there were some false starts. In its April 16, 1881 issue, the *Eufaula Weekly Bulletin* announced that a group of local investors were incorporating "The Magnolia Mills" to manufacture cotton. The investors were the brothers-in-law George H. Dent and Hamilton W. Weedon, as well as John M. McKleroy, W. H. Bray, A. H. Merrill, and others. Giving strong editorial support to the movement, the *Bulletin* urged, "The capital stock of the company, $50,000, should be taken up at once...The mill ...will consume about ten bales of cotton in twenty four hours, and the night run with electricity can easily be made. The product of this ten bales of cotton would be worth at present prices about $875,000. This would leave a good margin for profits and expense---all of which Eufaula would get the benefit of." Still looking to William Young's company as an exemplar, the editorialist pointed out, "The Eagle & Phenix Mills at Columbus made a 20.5% dividend last year. One fifth of the capital stock is in water power, and they run only in the daylight. From this we might safely expect a factory here to pay at least twenty-five percent..." Despite this optimism, the proposed factory did not materialize.

The following year, in April of 1882, the *Times & News* again announced that the dream was about to become a reality. A new company had been organized to construct and operate a cotton mill, with $75,000 capital, with aggressive businessman, R. J. Woods as its president. The directors included Hubert Dent, George Dent, Ed Young, Jr., John W. Tullis, A. H. Merrill, and others. The property had been selected and acquired, and Editor Jelks felt that "henceforth, our history will be onward and upward." Unfortunately, the time had still not yet come. Eufaula would get its cotton mill, and the Dents would be players, but it would be later in the decade before this occurred. For now, the cotton factory was postponed "until next spring," and then indefinitely, and the property was transferred to R. J. Woods for other purposes.

Six years later in 1888, the long-desired cotton mill finally became a reality. Prominent Eufaulians bought stock in the venture, called "Eufaula Cotton Mills." Its Board of Directors consisted of S. H. Dent, Noah Roberts (Carrie Young Roberts' husband), J. W. Tullis, W. N. Reeves, A. H. Merrill, G. L. Comer, A. J. Martin, and others. Tullis was elected president, and Noah Roberts secretary-treasurer. In June, it was reported that machinery for 120 looms and 3744 spindles had been ordered. The mill was being constructed on 20 acres along south Eufaula Street, behind George Dent's Barbour Street residence. In early July, the *Times & News* reported that "the first brick of the Eufaula Cotton Mills was laid yesterday by Miss Nellie Bell [should be 'Beall'] Dent, assisted by charming little Helen Dent." Nellie Beall was the sixteen year-old daughter of George and Helen, and "little Helen" was their infant daughter, born only a few weeks previously. The mill would become an important factor in Eufaula's economy. It initially employed 100 people, with a weekly payroll of $500. Vacant houses on Dale road were leased for mill workers. In "a little brick house on George Dent's property," a school or reading room for the benefit of the workers was formally opened with a program including Eufaula ministers, and songs by the Presbyterian choir. Nine months after it began operations, the Eufaula Mills paid its stockholders a dividend of "one percent a month from the time it has been running."[860]

By 1901, the Eufaula Cotton Mills, which had begun operations in 1888, had become Chewalla Mills, and in March of that year a major reorganization was reported. George H. Dent was elected to the Board and was also made vice-president of the company. Hubert Dent continued on the board, along with B. B. McKenzie (president), George L. Comer, Eli S. Shorter, Jr, T. J. Ramser, and others. The *Times & News* of March 28 reported that the company had "made many improvements since it passed under new management, almost doubling the output...it is now one of the model mills of the south...The officers deserve much credit for their work in placing it in the good and paying condition it is now in." This mill and its successors would contribute to Eufaula's economy for over 100 years.

58
Henry Young, Jr., Anniston Banker

Henry Augustus Young, Jr. was only two years old when his father, a Confederate private assigned to administrative duties on the staff of Gen. Kirby Smith, was killed in a train wreck in 1863 at Chunkey Bridge, Mississippi, while traveling to join Gen. Smith in Smith's new assignment as commander of the Trans-Mississippi Confederate Army. Little Henry's younger sister, Julia, was only three months old when her father was killed. The two children were reared in Eufaula by their mother, Marie McRae Young, (whose wedding to Henry, Sr. had been the occasion for the first wedding reception held in Fendall Hall after its completion.) When their grandfather, Edward Young, died in 1879, Henry, Jr. and Julia received their father's share of Edward's estate.

Henry, Jr. attended college at Southern University, the Methodist-sponsored academy in Greensboro, Alabama (and one of he predecessor institutions of the present-day Birmingham-Southern College in Birmingham.) Henry's first cousin, Edward Young Dent, attended Southern at the same time. The boys did well in their collegiate studies and graduated in 1881. The Eufaula *Times & News* of July 14, 1881, recounted part of the graduation exercises:

> "Speaking of our young townsmen, Mr. H. A. Young, who stood deservedly high at Greensboro, one of the city papers has this to say: 'The next speaker was Mr. H. A. Young of Eufaula. His theme was not given in the program, owing to the fact as he explained in his introductory remarks that he had been sick and unable to prepare a regular speech for the occasion. But taking as his text a line from Byron, he made a very interesting address abounding in happy thoughts, expressed in chaste and elegant language. His address gave very decided indications of oratorical ability, and was received with marked evidences of approval."

At the same time, Henry's younger sister, Julia M. Young, was doing equally well at the Columbus Female College in Georgia. The *Times & News* of May 12, 1881 reported, "Miss Julia M. Young has received the First Honor at the Columbus Female College. Eufaula has just cause to be proud of its representatives in the schools abroad. We congratulate her relatives and friends in the city at this will deserved award." Julia would later marry Albert Barnett and reside in Eufaula until her death without children.

After Ed Dent and Henry Young graduated from Southern University, Ed immediately went to work in the Eufaula National Bank as assistant cashier. But his cousin Henry did not have such an opening awaiting him, and Henry took a while to find his niche. For a time, Henry read law in the offices of the Eufaula lawyer, Col. M. B. Wellborn.[861] However, he soon concluded that his quiet temperament did not suit him for this profession.[862] In August 1881, it was reported that the trustees of the Abbeville Male & Female Institute [about twenty miles south of Eufaula] had elected J. M. Spurlock and Henry Young, both of Eufaula, as "co-principals" of the school. It was said that "Messrs Spurlock and Young are young men, highly recommended, graduates of the Southern University of Greensboro, Alabama…They have the character, capacity, and energy to command the confidence and support of the public…" The joint position of two "co-principals" seems an unusual arrangement, and apparently there were second thoughts about it. In September it was reported that "James Spurlock, Jr. left last week to take charge of the Abbeville School. He will be the sole principal." But Henry soon had a good job. On January 5, 1882, it was reported that "Mr. Henry A. Young leaves this afternoon for Mobile, where he has a position as Professor in the Barton Academy." Henry continued to make periodic visits back to Eufaula. He was there the following summer. The next year, in June 1883, the *Times & News*, now regarding him as a Mobilian, reported that "Mr. Henry A. Young, of Mobile, is in town."

However, as the bearer of the genes of his father and grandfather, Henry was soon drawn to commercial and banking pursuits. Henry first exhibited his grandfather Edward's business acumen with an investment in the mid-1880's. The new town of Birmingham was booming, and real estate values were rising. Henry went to Birmingham with $3000 and bought a 100-foot lot at the corner of 25th Street and Second Avenue for a purchase price of $9000, paying only one third, $3000, in cash. Twelve days later, he sold the property for $12,000. [863] Henry reported that the same lot later re-sold for $22,000.

Aroused by this success, Henry wrote his friend and fellow Eufaulian, Max Wellborn, Jr. about the fertile business opportunities in Birmingham. Henry and Max had been schoolmates in Eufaula, and it was in the law offices of Max's father, Col. Maximilian Bethune Wellborn, Sr., that Henry had read law.[mm] Max was at that time keeping books for a Vicksburg bank, and Henry's letter excited him. The two friends soon made plans to enter into real estate ventures together in Birmingham. However, when they arrived in Birmingham in late 1886, they found that land prices had skyrocketed to such a high level that there was nothing within their reach, and that the land boom did not now have its earlier appeal. [864]

Disappointed, Henry and Max had decided to return to Eufaula when, the night before they were to leave, someone knocked on the door of their hotel room at 1 A. M. It turned out to be Captain John M. McKleroy, a friend and prominent Eufaula lawyer. The previous year, he had narrowly lost the Democratic nomination for Governor to Thomas Seay, and had now moved to Montgomery where he was practicing law. The hotel was full, McKleroy needed a place to spend the night, and he had been directed to this room occupied by two Eufaula men in the hope of sharing their lodging. In the ensuing conversation about their business plans, McKleroy urged the young men to go to Anniston, Alabama, which was enjoying a healthy boom of its own. He had recently prepared a contract for investors planning to invest several million in new industries there, the news was out, and the real estate market was buzzing. Based on these coincidental circumstances, Henry and Max made the decision to seek their

---

[mm] In 1859, M. B. Wellborn, Sr. had married a daughter of John Horry Dent, Emma Julia ("Minna"). It will be recalled that in 1880, their daughter, Mary Elizabeth, married Warren Dent, who was not related to John Horry but was the youngest brother of Stouten Hubert Dent and George Hatch Dent. Thus Max Wellborn, Jr. and Warren Dent were brothers-in-law.

fortunes in Anniston. At daylight the next morning they packed their bags and departed for Anniston, 60 miles to the east.[865]

Henry Young arrived in Anniston on January 6, 1887 at the age of 26 to begin his business career. Anniston had originated as a privately owned town around the Woodstock Iron Company, owned by Sam Noble and Gen. Daniel Tyler. In 1883 the town was opened to public investment. Soon after their arrival, Henry and Max Wellborn, with $3000 cash between them, formed a partnership and entered the business of real estate and insurance. Their first major investment was the purchase of a lot on the corner of Noble and Eleventh, for $5000, which they bought with their $3000 cash and a $2000 loan from the First National Bank of Anniston. They were able to sell the lot for $7500 three months later.[866] Sam Noble soon began the publication of a newspaper, named "*The Hot Blast,*" in which Henry and Max invested some of their early profits.

Although the initial frenzy of commercial activity began to cool, Anniston's population continued to increase. Henry and Max saw in the resulting housing shortage the need and opportunity for a building and loan association. They were able to sell subscriptions to 600 shares of stock, still short of the 1000 share minimum required by law, when a friend arranged a meeting with Anniston's founder, Sam Noble. With Noble at the meeting was A. L. Tyler, the president of Woodstock Iron. These businessmen were impressed with Henry and Max's plans and both subscribed for stock; Noble also bought stock for his children and sister-in-law. With the backing of these investors, Henry and Max had no difficulty filling the required stock subscription list. The building and loan association was created and began business with Max as president and Henry as secretary-treasurer. They profitably operated the firm for seven years. [867]

Amid his busy entrepreneurial activity, Henry found time to marry Flora Frye of Monroe County, and on October 24, 1887, their daughter, Mary Graeme, was born.

In early 1888, Henry accompanied Max to Cave Springs, Ga. for a visit with Max's grandfather, John Horry Dent, where Henry renewed his acquaintance with the former Eufaula planter who had been a close friend (and business customer) of Henry's father and grandfather. [868] Henry also often made visits to his old home town of Eufaula.[869]

By 1888, the Anniston real estate boom was maturing, the firm of Wellborn and Young was feeling the effects, and Henry decided to leave the firm to accept a job as bookkeeper for the newspaper, the *Hot Blast* (the predecessor of the *Anniston Star*). Although they were no longer business partners, Henry and Max would remain close friends the rest of their lives. In later years, Max would become active in banking and would be appointed as the first chairman of the board of governors of the Federal Reserve Bank of Atlanta.

After a period of working with the newspaper, Henry also entered the banking field and began a career with the First National Bank of Anniston which lasted for many years, and which culminated in his serving for a decade as president of that bank and assistant chairman of its board. [870]

In 1905, Henry's daughter, Mary Graeme, married Charles G. Dobbins in Anniston, and they had one son, Peter Young Dobbins, born in 1910. Charles Dobbins was a journalist with a variety of interests. A native of Greensboro, Alabama, he graduated from Samford University and received a master's degree from Columbia University and doctorates from Jamestown College and the College of St. Francis. During the course of a rich career, Dobbins would serve as president of the Alabama Press Association, executive secretary of the American Council on Education, Alabama Director of the Office of Price Stabilization, trustee of Auburn University, and many other positions of responsibility. Before World War II, Henry's son-in-law was publisher and editor of the *Anniston Times*. After naval service in China during World War II, he became editor of the *Montgomery Advertiser*.

When Charles Dobbins moved to Montgomery with Mary Graeme to assume the editorship of the *Advertiser*, Henry, then in his eighties and suffering from cancer, reluctantly moved with them. On May 10, 1946 at the age of 85, Henry Young died in his daughter's home in Montgomery, following a fifty-seven year career as a civic and business leader of Anniston.[871] The occasion prompted his admiring son-in-law to make Henry the subject of his lead editorial in the *Montgomery Advertiser* on May 12, 1946, entitled, "Death of An Old Southerner:"

> "At our house here in Montgomery last week a man died. He was Henry Augustus Young, a native of Eufaula, a citizen of Anniston for more than 57 useful years and of late a resident of Montgomery...Everybody who knew H. A. Young is sad. In a way, his is the death of more than just one man, for he was a symbol of his time.
> "Born March 19, 1861, in Eufaula, just as the Civil War was starting, he knew well the meaning of Reconstruction. His father was killed as a Confederate soldier....[H]e managed to get an education at Southern University in Greensboro. He tried a little law at Eufaula, but being modest and quiet of nature, a kinsman told him he would starve to death as a lawyer and had better try something else. He taught school for a while in Mobile, but decided starvation would be more pleasant in some other pursuit."

Dobbins described the serendipitous circumstances of Henry's migration to Anniston with his friend M. B. Wellborn, his employment at the *Hot Blast,* his long career with the First National Bank, and then continued:

> "A man of superb restraint, he said little but it was to the point. By some secret technique, he told people exactly what he believed about them, yet retained their affection. He loved humor...He hated pretense and show. His wife, Flora...used to say, "If Mr. Young has a darned place at the knee of his trousers, he always crosses that knee UP!' Once at a resort, when the ladies were bragging on their ancestry with considerable spirit, one turned to him and asked, 'And who were your ancestors, Mr. Young?' He removed his pipe from his mouth only long enough to answer, 'Brigham!'

"...Old Southerner that he was, he never forgave the Yankees as a whole. Fiercely he would say, "After the War they put their feet on our necks, and they've never taken them off!' But when thousands of those Yankee boys came to Fort McClellan [in Anniston] during World Wars I and II, he took them into his home and came to love many of them as individuals.

"...Eternal pessimist, he was astonished to have lived so long. With every birthday he would confidently predict that this was the last...He had amazing strength and appetite until, during the war, cancer struck. He fought it hard, determined to look after this editor's family until he could return from the war.

"When the family was re-united, and the decision made to move to Montgomery, 'Pa' Young finally agreed to come along. One does not easily leave the home and friends of 57 years. But he was the good sport an Old Southerner would have to be.

"And he liked it here....[H]e even gave grudging approval to newspaper work, though his opinion of newspapers was often expressed to Editor Harry Ayers in these words: 'If I see it in the *Anniston Star* I know its either a week old or a damn lie.'

"...The nurses at St. Margaret's [Hospital] came to love him for his whimsical uncomplaining spirit and treated him well, but he divided his time between predicting he'd never get out and tactfully letting us know that he wanted out....

"His gentle kindness never failed...Now that he's under the Anniston sod he loved so much we keep remembering things about him and wonder how our present generation can measure up to men like him. ...[N]obody seems to know the formula for producing men with the sweetness of the Old Southerner we lost at our house last week."[872]

59
Democratic Committee Chairman James H. G. Martin

"...attention is directed to the able and eloquent letter of Capt. J. H. G. Martin in today's paper,...Capt. Martin comes to the point with characteristic force...We invite a careful perusal of the excellent document. It tells its own story very forcibly..."

The Eufaula Daily Times

In the mid-1870's, Ada Young's husband, James H. G. (Jim) Martin, had started his business career as a merchant, operating a store selling groceries as well as staple and fancy dry goods. By the 1880's, he was dealing in real estate and also brokering cotton. In the *Times* of November 30, 1882, James advertised a number of up-scale real estate listings, including residential homes; a plantation of 2040 acres on the Chattahoochee; a plantation with 1000 acres; and a cotton gin and grist mill on 100 acres.

But James' most important business activity during this time was buying and selling cotton. Cotton production had resumed its importance as the dominant occupation of the area, and commercial activity surrounding the production and sale of cotton was a principal factor in the economy of Eufaula and Barbour County. In 1879, to promote the general interests of the cotton industry, James Martin had joined with a group of other businessmen to establish the Eufaula Cotton Exchange. He served as a member of its first Board of Directors. [873] James' cotton interests grew rapidly, and he traveled extensively, sometimes taking Ada with him on long cotton-buying trips. In March, 1883 we find him in Montgomery, but he is more frequently in Georgia. The *Times* of March 20 reports that:

> "One Eufaula cotton man has bought over 40,000 bales of cotton this season, paying for the same about $2,000,000. Capt. J. H. G. Martin is the man and his purchases have embraced 8 towns in Georgia. Capt. Martin is one of the livest cotton men in two states."

On June 30 it is reported that, "Capt. James H. Martin is over in southwest Georgia looking after his large cotton interests." One of James' principal markets was in Americus, Georgia. On September 25, "Capt. J. H. G. Martin and Mrs. Martin are in Americus. Capt. Martin is spending the better part of his time there buying cotton."

Consistent with the common practice of the time, James, (who is often called "Jim,") was given the courtesy title of "Captain." He was a 16 year old private in the Eufaula Rifles when it marched off to Fort Barrancas in 1861 with his future brother-in-law, Lt. S. H. Dent, as second-in-command. When the Rifles disbanded after 12 months, James reenlisted as a 17 year old sergeant in its successor, the Eufaula Light Artillery. This was more than enough to make him a "captain" by the 1880's.

Like the other "Youngs," James had a cotton farm in addition to his other business interests. It was located south of town and for a time was operated by his overseer, Punch Doughtie. (Doughtie moved around, and is sometimes found managing farmland for other landowners. At one point, he managed the "McKay-McDowell" plantation in Henry County.)

As a well-liked member of the community, James H. G. Martin gradually became involved in Democratic party politics, eventually being mentioned as a candidate for congress himself. As we will see, he lost no time in declining this overture. In the general elections of November, 1880, the Republican candidate for president was James A. Garfield,[nn] with Chester Arthur for vice President. The Democrats' Presidential nominee ws Winfield Scott Hancock of Pennsylvania, (who had fought against Pickett's charge at Gettysburg), and William H. English for Vice President. Of particular interest to Eufaulians, Col. William C. Oates of adjacent Henry County, Hubert Dent's old friend and law partner, was the Democratic candidate for congress from the Third District, encompassing Eufaula and Barbour County. James H. G. Martin, as chairman of the Eufaula Beat (precinct) Executive Committee, published a schedule of Col Oates' speaking engagements in the area, and also issued a call for Eufaula Democrats to meet and rally to the Democratic cause. The Eufaula *Times & News* carried this notice on October 28, 1880:

"Beat Meeting.
"The Democratic and Conservative voters of Eufaula Beat are requested to meet at the courthouse on Saturday evening 30th instant at 7:00. This meeting is of great importance and is called at night for the purpose of giving an opportunity to a large number of voters who could not be present in day time. It is earnestly hoped that those of our citizens residing in the city limits will make it convenient to come.
By order. Beat Executive Committee, J. H. G. Martin, Chairman."

In November, the Republicans Garfield and Arthur were elected. However, Democrat William C. Oates was elected to congress from Alabama's Third District. The defeated Republican candidate conducted a drawn-out election contest, which was eventually dismissed.

By the time of the 1882 elections, James Martin, now 36, had been elected Chairman of the Barbour County Democratic Executive Committee. Barbour Countians would be particularly active in this election year for two reasons: Alabama was electing a governor, and Eufaula lawyer John McKleroy was seeking the Democratic nomination for that office. Also,

---

[nn] As a coincidental sidelight, James A. Garfield had been made Chief of Staff to Union General Rosecrans a few months before the Battle of Chickamauga. It will be recalled that Garfield was a recipient of the report forwarded by Gen. Sheridan in April 1863 that Robertson's Battery (then commanded by Hubert Dent) was among the Confederate forces guarding the Tennessee River crossing at Bridgeport, Alabama. Anna was visiting Hubert at his camp in Bridgeport at the time this report was forwarded to Garfield.

Congressman Oates was seeking reelection. In April 1882, Oates had married a Eufaula girl, Sarah ("Sallie") A. Toney, youngest daughter of the late Col. Washington Toney. The wedding was at Roseland, the Toney residence five miles north of Eufaula. (Sallie was the younger sister of Janie Toney, who, it will be recalled, was Mollie Young Weedon's friend and co-conspirator during Mollie's flirtatious courtship with Hamilton Weedon. Sallie's younger brother, Sterling Toney, had taken care of Hamilton's horse, "St. George," when Hamilton was transferred to another duty station late in the War. Sterling became a successful lawyer in Eufaula and later in Louisville, Kentucky.)

Oates had strong political support in Eufaula. He had studied law there under Pugh and Bullock; he had once had a law partnership with S. H. Dent; and his new wife was a Eufaulian. However, there were other Eufaulians potentially interested in running for congress, including John Roquefort, a well-regarded lawyer. On April 11, 1882, James gave notice of a meeting in his office of a meeting of the County Executive Committee to plan for the County Democratic convention. The editor of the *Times and News* encouraged the members to "…respond to Mr. Martin's call and that will open the political battle in Barbour," but cryptically added, "We forebear comment until the committee decides on plans for the fight."

Much to James' surprise, an article soon appeared in the *Eufaula Bulletin*, advocating *him* for congress, followed up by a letter in the *Times and News* of April 18, supporting the suggestion. It is interesting to find here the anti-lawyer feeling which has prevailed to some extent in all Generations:

Editor, *Times and News*;
   Myself and many others whom I have heard express themselves endorse the article in Sunday's *Bulletin* advocating J. H. G. Martin for Congress. From what I can learn he might object to announcing himself as a candidate, but that should not be necessary. It would, in my opinion, be a welcome novelty to the public to see one man nominated for an office who has not button-holed and bored to death every man in the country with his personal importunity. To nominate a man for office whose every breath in public life had not been with an eye to his own advancement would indeed be a rarity, but I believe it can be done, and I hereby call upon the friends of J. H. G. Martin to organize, and work, and present his name to the Democratic Convention when it assembles, and I believe it will meet with success. It would be a great tribute to the young men of the country, who have redeemed us from Republican rule and of whom he is a fair representative and among whom he has always been an able and tireless worker, these young men have done all for this country and are entitled to some recognition.
   Since the Indians left, and this congressional district was first organized, it has never been represented in Congress except by a professional lawyer. Let us change it this one time and thereby demonstrate that as a people, we acknowledge patriotism and intelligence in other walks of life, and that

long faithfulness and unselfish devotion to one's party will occasionally be recognized even when the subject is not the owner of a law license.

An Old Comrade"

In a graceful and flowery letter, James promptly declined this suggestion, expressing strong support for the one-armed Oates, and also taking the opportunity to advocate McKleroy for governor. His letter is published as a main article in the *Times and News* of April 25. These extracts reflect the bitterness from the war and reconstruction that was still strong:

"Our Oates

The Silver-Tongued Martin's Forcible Document

"Mr. Editor:

Permit me through your valued paper, to thank the quite partial friends who have recently, in your columns made me the object of most flattering notice. While I have at present no ambition beyond that of an humble toiler in the ranks of the great [Democratic] party of the country, I am not entirely free from the weaknesses and vanities of the world, and find it none the less pleasant and agreeable to be the subject of such complimentary attention. I beg to assure you and these friends, that I am deeply grateful for the warm manifestations. I cannot be a candidate for Congress, chiefly for the reason that such a course would be in conflict with my honest conviction. I have ever made it the political study of my life that these convictions should be unselfish. I have ever held, that when a man only views the political machinery of the country from a personal standpoint, and only watches the changes of the times and the disposition of the parties with a sole view to his own advancement, and who in the absence of any general uprising in his favor seek, by constant letter writing and persistent supplication to thrust himself upon a convention of his people, and wraps himself in the garb of low demagoguery and brazen cupidity, I could not, Mr. Editor, be such a candidate.

In the next place, I am greatly impressed with the fact that our present gallant incumbent, the Hon. Wm. C. Oates, of Henry, is entirely competent to serve us; that he is politically worthy in all respects, and beyond this, that the highest end, the public good, will be greatly subserved by his return to Congress....[B]y his distinguished service, both in war and in peace, he has illustrated those high accomplishments which should endear him to all liberty loving people. He may have had his faults, who has not? If he has, and you put them in the balance to weigh, will not his shed blood, his buried arm, and his four best years of a glorious young manhood, spent in renowned and brilliant service for his country balance aught? Or was this war of which we so seldom hear in these latter days, except in the insults of our foes...a mere idle sentiment? A foolish experiment which should be buried in the past and remembered no more? Was Stonewall Jackson a red handed murderer, and Robert E. Lee a traitor? Are our people preparing to endorse the declaration made by a Republican Congressman on the floor of the House last week, "that

551

the only right acquired by rebels in the late war was to have their property confiscated and themselves hung…?"

It was but a few years back when a fluent tongue would recount the heroic deeds of our gallant soldiery to a public ear, and tell of their unfaltering devotion to a country's cause; how poor and mangled creatures would calmly die in lonely fields, unadministered by woman, uncomforted by love; how for long agonizing years, in weariness of body but in strength of soul, half clad, half fed, they, barefooted, trod by night the icy mountains of Virginia and Tennessee,…and in terribly uneven combats, to grapple with death at the cannon's mouth…

But to return to my subject…Col Oates is the most prominent man in [the wiregrass section, the counties in the southeastern corner of Alabama]…The wire-grass has never gone back on one of our candidates…This section has ever been bound to us not only by political, but the very closest commercial ties;…even should Col. Oates be objectionable (which he is not)…when the citizens of the wire grass come to us and ask us to join them in returning him to Congress…it would ill become the people of Barbour to decline. It has pretty generally developed into custom everywhere, to return each incumbent for a second term…unless he shall have done something to forfeit the confidence and respect of his constituents….Let us return him again, and…by a majority so abundant and overwhelming …that his constituents may…have the benefit of his great talent and tireless industry.

Those of us who actively mingle in politics have near us a subject well calculated to enlist all our energy. Our close neighbor and distinguished friend, Hon. J. M. McKleroy, is a candidate for Governor….He is eminently worthy and specially fitted to brightly adorn the high office to which aspires….[B]y virtue of his close and intimate comradeship with every young man in this section who touched elbows in the struggle with Kiels and his vandals, he has a right to expect their entire devotion to his interest in the coming struggle. Let us render him a faithful and industrious service, and …work with an eye single to the accomplishment of Mr. McKleroy's nomination.

J. H. G. Martin
Eufaula, Ala., April 21, 1882"

On his editorial page, Editor Jelks said this about James' letter:

"Col. Oates' attention is directed to the able and eloquent letter of Capt. J. H. G. Martin in today's paper, respecting the congressional race. Capt. Martin comes to the point with characteristic force and his remarks will receive that consideration that his utterances are always entitled to. We invite a careful perusal of the excellent document. It tells its own story very forcibly and needs no explanation. Next week we will have more to say on the subject."

The following week, Jelks simply observed that, "Last week, J. H. G. Martin, a gentleman of sterling worth who needs no introduction at our hands, eloquently and forcibly presented the claims of Col. Oates in our columns. In declining himself to oppose Oates, Capt. Martin paid him a tribute that is met with a most hardy reception wherever it has been read— all over the district."

On May 2, James published notice as Chairman announcing that the County Democratic convention would be held in Clayton on May 31, to select delegates to the state convention, and calling on the beat chairmen to have their meetings on Monday May 29 to select delegates to the county convention in Clayton.

Apparently sensing that he could not displace Oates, John D. Roquemore announced on May 16 that he had been a candidate for congress on the assumption that Col. Oates would not be renominated, but that circumstances had now changed, and he felt that it would be only right to renominate Oates for a second term. Accordingly, Roquemore withdrew his candidacy, for which he was praised by the *Times and News* of that date.

Hailing James Martin as "the justly popular and thoroughly wide-awake chairman of our Executive Committee," the *Times and News* of May 23 called for "a rousing Barbour County Convention and all will be well." Nominees for congress were to be selected by a separate convention of delegates from the counties comprising the third congressional district. James Martin also served as the chairman of the Executive Committee for the third congressional district, and he called a meeting of that committee to be held during the state Democratic Convention.

In preparation for the upcoming County Convention, the Eufaula Beat No. 5 held its meeting at the courthouse on May 29 and elected its delegates, consisting of James H. G. Martin, George H. Dent, S. H. Dent, C. S. McDowell, Sr., Judge Henry D. Clayton, R. J. Woods, J. T. Kendall, Reuben F. Kolb, George C. McCormick, and others.

James called the Barbour County Convention to order on May 31, 1882. On the motion of C. S. McDowell, Sr., Judge Henry D. Clayton was elected permanent chairman. In addition to nominating candidates for the House and Senate from Barbour, the Convention endorsed Eufaula lawyer John McKleroy for governor; elected 26 delegates including J. H. G. Martin and his brother-in-law, Hubert Dent to the Third District Congressional Convention; and elected delegates to the state Democratic Convention, which also included Martin and Dent. The Convention also reelected James Martin for another two year term as Chairman of the County Executive Committee.

The talk of nominating James for congress had not died out. In its column called "County Convention Chat," the *Times & News* of May 30 reported, "They do say that Capt. Jim Martin begins to look like a congressman. He is a 'full team.'" Despite this head-turning praise, James never let the suggestion be seriously pursued.

At the state Democratic Convention in early June 1882, there was a hot contest for the nomination for governor, with Eufaulian John McKleroy and Edward O'Neal of Lauderdale County among the leading candidates. The Convention observed the "two-thirds rule," which governed the Democratic party (at both the state and national conventions) for many years, requiring a vote of two thirds of the delegates to obtain the nomination. After 23 ballots, O'Neal defeated McKleroy. Thereafter, McKleroy was elected Chairman of the State Democratic Executive Committee, and James Martin was elected one of the three state committeemen from his congressional district.

Following the convention, it was reported on June 20 that, "Capt Jim Martin has returned from a trip to Columbus and other points. Like all our delegates, he has recovered from the effects of the State Convention." This trip to Georgia was undoubtedly a necessary business trip, needed to attend to James' busy cotton brokerage business, which had probably been neglected to some extent during weeks of political activity. However, he and Ada soon went on a genuine vacation and took an extensive trip to the North. The *Times & News* of July 4 reports that, "Capt. J. H. G. Martin and wife are in Waukesha, Wisconsin. They will go to Canada, then Niagara, Saratoga, and other fashionable points before returning home."

They were gone for over a month. James and Ada arrived back in Alabama in September, in time for him to attend the Third Congressional District convention on September 12. His brother-in-law, Hubert Dent, was elected permanent president of that convention. All opposition to Col. Oates had faded. Col. Richard Holmes Powell, a legislator and newspaper editor of Union Springs, nominated Oates. There were no other nominations and Oates was selected by acclamation. Reuben Kolb was made chairman of the congressional executive committee for the next two years.

In the general elections, all Alabama Democratic candidates were elected and Col. Oates was returned to congress. As United States senator, the Alabama Legislature appointed Hubert Dent's old law mentor and fellow soldier of the Eufaula Rifles, James L. Pugh. John T. Morgan was also appointed U. S. senator.

Jim Martin's reelection as county chairman, as well as his election to the state executive committee, placed him in the forefront of Democratic party activities during the state and national elections of 1884. President Garfield had been shot on July 2, 1881, only four months into his term. He died in September and was succeeded by his vice-president, Chester A. Arthur. Eufaula received "inside information" about Arthur from one of its former citizens, William Henry Woods. A son of Edward Young's old banking partner in "Young, Woods, and Gardner," and brother of Eufaula businessman, R. J. Woods, William had migrated to New York and achieved financial success there.[oo] As Garfield lay dying from Giteau's shot, The *Times and News* of September 1, 1881 reported that former Eufaulian William Woods "has had business dealings with Chester A. Arthur and considers him a grand

---

[oo]In fact, an earlier (February 10) quote from a New York correspondent of the *Philadelphia Times* had called him "one of the millionaires of New York." We previously saw William in the Mobile defenses, commanding the Eufaula Light Artillery alongside Dent's Battery, and later, he acted under his father's power of attorney in dissolving the Young & Woods partnership.

man. He thought the South would have less to fear from his administration than the present one." Notwithstanding William Woods' favorable view of Arthur, in 1884 the Republicans declined to renominate him, and turned to James G. Blaine of Maine as their presidential nominee. The Democrats nominated Grover Cleveland, thus setting the stage for the first Democratic president since the Civil War.

James H. G. Martin's period as county party chairman required him to preside over a period of evolution and change in Alabama's electoral system. It will be recalled that, in the 1870's, the beat and county Democratic conventions were open to practically whoever wished to participate. Even though there were officially selected delegates, there was no limit on their numbers, and any supporter of the party who wished could be certified as a delegate by the chairman. At that time, the overriding objective was to defeat the Radical Republicans in the general election, and party unity was considered paramount. Democrats were willing to rally behind the candidate with the best chance of winning, and intra-party fights were frowned upon. By the 1880's however, the Democratic party was firmly in control; its nominees were likely to be elected to office; and competition for the nomination was sometimes keen. Accordingly, in 1882 and 1884, we find James Martin and his executive committee setting specific numbers of delegates to be elected by the beats to attend the county conventions, and by the counties to attend the state and congressional district conventions, and we find more formal procedures for electing these delegates. The method of allocating delegates among the beats, based upon votes cast in the last election, became a sensitive matter, subject to controversy and editorial comment in the papers.

Further, despite these improvements, a strong feeling was developing that the convention system of selecting Democratic party nominees should be abandoned entirely, in favor of a direct primary election system. Surprisingly, we find this view supported by Editor Jelks in the *Times & News* of April 29, 1884. Commenting on the upcoming county convention, he opines that "...almost half the white voters of Barbour County will refuse to participate and will refuse to abide by its actions," because they oppose nominations by convention. "This is a just grievance against the convention system, and it is not well or wise to ignore it." Jelks then proposed his plan for determining whether nominees are to be selected by convention or direct primary. But James Martin and his executive committee were not ready for this change. Over the signatures of James H. G. Martin as chairman, Reuben F. Kolb, George L. Comer, and others, the committee expressed its judgment that "it is in the best interest of the people to nominate in convention candidates for all county offices to be filled at the August election." The committee called for the county convention to assemble in Clayton on May 28 to select delegates to the state convention and other business; directed that each beat shall send to the county convention one delegate for each 25 votes cast for the Democratic candidate for governor in the 1882 elections; and provided that this convention would not select delegates to attend the congressional district convention, which would be selected later.

In the Eufaula beat meeting on May 27 to elect its delegates, on the motion of Reuben Kolb, James H. G. Martin was made permanent chairman. He appointed E. B. Young, Jr. (his brother-in-law) and John O. Martin to serve as tellers to receive the votes. More widespread participation in this delegate selection was encouraged by allowing Democrats to come in and vote whenever they wished throughout the morning of the appointed day, until 1:30 p. m. The elected delegates included George H. Dent, J. H. G. Martin, R. J. Woods, and others.

The county convention of 1884 was duly called to order in Clayton the following day by Chairman Martin. General Clayton was again elected presiding officer and served "for 10 hours without dinner or supper." After making all necessary nominations, which included G. T. Long for Sheriff, the convention selected delegates to the state convention, which included J. M. McKleroy, Henry D. Clayton, Reuben Kolb, James H. G. Martin, Alto V. Lee, and others. In electing a new executive committee, the convention respected the wishes of James Martin, who, after four years as chairman, "begged that he be excused from further service." "Thanks were returned to J. H. G. Martin for valuable and patriotic party services as chairman of the county executive committee."

The state Democratic Convention was held in early June and nominated Gov. Emmet O'Neal for a second term, to run on a Democratic ticket headed by Grover Cleveland for president.

Later, in a meeting of the new Barbour County Executive Committee, that body unanimously adopted resolutions offered by its new chairman, Judge Henry D. Clayton, extending "our thanks and the thanks of the party in the county for the able, efficient, and impartial manner in which [James H. G. Martin] discharged his official duties during his administration." Actually, James' political services were not quite concluded, and he would be called upon again.

The Third Congressional District Democratic Convention was scheduled to meet in late August, to select the Democratic candidate for congress. Col. William C. Oates was seeking the nomination for another term. Other Eufaulians interested in running were John D. Roquemore and Major Jere N. Williams, the latter having previously served in Congress. Reuben Kolb, the popular farmer-businessman, was opposed to Oates. Kolb would later become the leader of a populist movement challenging the conservative leadership of the Democratic Party (the "Bourbons"), and Oates was a "Bourbon" to the core. Kolb realized that Oates would be renominated by the convention, so as a member of the congressional democratic executive committee, Kolb submitted a "minority report," advocating abandoning the convention and having a direct primary election to select the Democratic nominee for congress. This even though, as a member of the county committee, Kolb had rejected a primary to select Barbour County candidates.

In advocating his position, Kolb became embroiled in an exchange of published letters with an Oates supporter, Gen. A. C. Gordon of Abbeville. Gen. Gordon took offense at Kolb's strong language and called him to account. The days of dueling were long over, but one of its more civilized procedures was still used to settle personal disputes: peacemaking through representatives of the parties. Hubert Dent and his brother-in-law James Martin were now called upon to serve this function. In an article entitled "A Satisfactory Settlement Through Mutual Friends", the *Times & News* of July 8, 1884 explained the situation: "We are gratified at being able to lay before our readers the following settlement of an unpleasantness between Gen. A. C. Gordon of Abbeville, Ala and Capt. R. F. Kolb, of this city. Our readers will remember that we printed in our last weekly an article by Capt. Kolb, in reply to a letter of some length from Gen. Gordon. To this article of Capt. Kolb's Gen. Gordon took offence and printed in the *Abbeville Times* of last week a severe reply. Capts. S. H. Dent and J. H. G. Martin being mutual friends, undertook to settle the difficulty, and succeeded happily, as will be seen from the letters below:"

"Eufaula, Ala., July 7, 1884
"All matters connected with a personal difference which has occurred between Gen. A. C. Gordon and Capt. R. F. Kolb, through recent newspaper publications by these Gentlemen, having been referred to us by a party of mutual friends of the 'disputants' for investigation (and with a hope of adjustment) we have after full and proper inquiry agreed upon and recommended as satisfactory and just publishing the below letters, signed by each of them. This result we trust will be accepted by the friends of both the parties as fair and honorable, and in keeping with the dignity and high character of the principals. It concludes the points of difference between them in a friendly spirit and we hope that all interested will endorse it likewise, and forget that ought unpleasantness occurred.

S. H. Dent
J. H. G. Martin"

In his agreed letter, Kolb stated that he had been "misunderstood;" that he wished to "disclaim any purpose either direct or remote of casting any reflection whatever upon the character of Gen. Gordon, or of his friend Col. William C. Oates, and I herewith cheerfully withdraw everything contained in my letter that could be possibly construed as a personal reflection on either of these Gentlemen. I make this disclaimer with pleasure and in the interest of good order and the peace of our party, recognizing that we are all good Democrats…" Gordon's agreed letter responded that since Kolb had "seen proper to disclaim any purpose of reflecting on my friend Col. W. C. Oates or myself…I hereby cheerfully withdraw my card…and regret that I should have been made to feel the necessity of printing such a communication."

James Martin himself now jumped into the fray over a congressional primary. With this personal dispute settled, and free from any constraints of impartiality as committee chairman, James now acted as Congressman Oates' spokesman in calling Kolb's hand and *agreeing* to a direct primary election. In a lengthy letter (he wrote no other kind) to the *Times & News* of July 8, these extracts appear:

To Capt. R. F. Kolb, Owner and Proprietor of Minority Report, So-Called, of Executive Committee of 3rd Congressional District:
My Dear Sir: This Congressional District having been thoroughly supplied with documents from yourself and others, showing the crooked ways and devious paths that both sides have sought to take with reference to our

approaching Congressional Convention, I am led greatly against my personal inclination to say few words. Heretofore I have been an active and warm supporter of the Hon. Wm. C. Oates for congress and failing to see anything in his course in the council of the nation to justify me opposing him I should again be pleased to see him the nominee of the district…I now propose to you and those whom you represent, (and…I do so with the full sanction and consent of the Hon. W. C. Oates) and doubt not but that I can obtain the endorsement of my proposition by the Congressional Executive Committee of the dist. that we…shall ignore and wipe out all that has passed in reference to the selection of delegates to a congressional convention for this district, and shall order a primary election be held at any reasonable date in each beat in this congressional district, said election to be covered with all the safeguards that honesty and propriety would demand, and that the person receiving the highest number of votes in said primary election when aggregated shall be declare the nominee of our party….[W]ith full authority, I challenge the opponents of Wm. C. Oates to meet us in a primary election, and let the result settle it…You have made many and specious pleas in support of your points. I now defy you come to the polls…Oates and his friends stand ready to burn all the bridges behind them, having already carried nearly a majority of the voting power in this district, and they are ready to surrender this advantage and begin over again the battle with their opponents…I take it upon my self with authority to dare you to this issue, and to brand your backers as political cowards and plotters if they decline this test.

Yours truly, J. H. G. Martin

Of course, Kolb could not decline such an aggressive challenge. In the *Times & News* of July 15, he stated that he had permission of Major J. N. Williams and John D. Roquemore

James ("Jim") H. G. Martin, husband of Ada Young Martin

to fully accept Martin's proposition "as fully as Martin claims to speak for Col. Oates." "Let the mutual friends of Major Williams and Mr. Roquemore decide which of them will take the field against Col. Oates in a primary election and the one receiving the largest white Democratic vote be declared the nominee of the Party."

All of this turned out to be hot air. Despite the tall talking by James Martin and Reuben Kolb, no primary election was held in the third congressional district in 1884. The *Times & News* of September 2 reported that the congressional convention went off as "reasonably harmonious," and that Oates was unanimously nominated, which "gives the gentleman two more years in congress." Although primary elections began to be sporadically used in local situations, it would be 1902 before the Alabama Democratic Party first required them for statewide offices, and in that year, Editor Jelks would be elected governor of Alabama in the first statewide gubernatorial primary election. From then on, in a phrase which would become a stock newspaper observation, winning the Democratic primary was "tantamount to election" in Alabama. The Republican Party was no longer a factor, and the November general election became a mere formality.

In the national general elections of November 1884, Grover Cleveland was elected as the first Democratic president since the Civil War, which led to rejoicing throughout the south and in Barbour County. Perhaps as a result of this development, Jim Martin was soon led into a new career, which required him and Ada to move to Washington, D. C. After reading law and being admitted to the bar, Jim began a law partnership in Washington with a C. M. Shelley, under the firm name, "Shelley & Martin." The firm held itself out as practicing "in U. S. Courts and in the Executive Departments of the Government."[874] Undoubtedly, James made use of his political skills and his Democratic Party ties to represent clients in the Democratic administration of President Cleveland. Family members visiting Washington during this period reported that he appeared to have significant influence in the administration.[875] After some years in Washington, Jim and Ada would return to make their home in Eufaula.

60
Political Upheaval in the 1890's

"...Chairman Dent on an occasion like this has a soothing way with him... Most any chairman in the world would have provoked and assisted a bolt, but his wise and temperate words, delivered in a low tone with much feeling quieted the waters as if by magic."

Eufaula Times & News

In the Fall of 1891, Eufaula's first telephone exchange began operating. The *Eufaula Times* of August 6 marveled at the miracle, reporting that "the business of the town can be done without anybody having to leave his office," and quoting the *Macon Telegraph* as authority that telephone messages "can be sent hundreds of miles. It has been done here, and men in Macon have talked with men in Selma, Alabama."

In addition to technological change, Eufaula and Alabama were also about to experience political change. Since its "redemption" from the Radical Republicans in 1874, Alabama's politics had generally been in the hands of the conservative Democrats who had provided leadership during the War Between the States. This "rule of the generals" and former Confederate officers (later sometimes called "Bourbons" by their detractors) was, with rare exceptions, competent, economical, and honest. But the farmers and laborers of the state had not experienced the relative good times of the 1880's enjoyed by the merchants, professionals and others in the urban areas. This circumstance, combined with the wave of populism gathering momentum across the country, resulted in a political revolt against the traditional Democratic Party organization of Alabama.

It had become common for Eufaula and Barbour County to contribute leadership in important state issues, and in the 1890's, Eufaula men of stature were on both sides of the great controversies. The "farmers' revolt" was centered on its principal leader, Eufaulian Reuben Kolb, whom we have previously encountered in a number of different contexts. In the War, Kolb had initially served as a private in the Eufaula Rifles under First Lieutenant Hubert Dent. Like Hubert, Kolb later became captain in command of an artillery company, Kolb's Battery. It will be recalled that some of Hubert's wartime letters to Anna mentioned Kolb's Battery, not always in flattering terms. A cotton planter and merchant after the war, Kolb bankrupted in the 1870's and then became an agri-businessman, shipping his special breed of watermelon, "Kolb's Gem," throughout the country. Appointed state Agriculture Commissioner in 1881 and again in 1888, Kolb became a vigorous advocate for the farmers' cause. He helped found the Farmers' Alliance; in 1887 he was elected president of the Farmers National Congress at its Chicago convention.[876] Reuben Kolb's genial manner and genuine concern for the farmers' problems made him extremely popular throughout the state with farmers and other discontented groups of voters. In 1890, at the national convention of farmers in St. Louis, Kolb embraced that group's radical populist platform then gaining momentum across the nation: abolition of national banks, free and unlimited coinage of silver, a fairer tax system, anti-corporate legislation, and public ownership of all transportation and communication facilities. On this platform, Kolb entered the 1890 race for governor of Alabama.

In this era, the Democratic Party was seen as the principal vehicle for preventing Republicans and blacks from seizing political control of the state, as during Reconstruction. Candidates using tactics which weakened the Party's cohesiveness, or promoted a split or a third party, were strongly disfavored by the voters. In the 1890 election, the regular Democrats portrayed Kolb as having virtually left the Democratic Party by adopting positions greatly at variance with its traditional principles. The Republican Party, still quite active, sought to profit from this intraparty strife. Hubert Dent, the quintessential conservative ("Bourbon") Democrat, was among the leaders of the fight for "organized democracy," (the term then used to denote the regular Democratic Party machinery), and against Kolb in Barbour County.[877] At this time, there was still no statewide primary for the Democratic nomination, so that the battle was fought at the local level in the town beats and county conventions for delegates to the state convention in Montgomery. After a vigorous and bitter fight across the state for delegates, the state Democratic convention in a close vote rejected Kolb and selected Thomas Goode Jones as the Democratic nominee for governor in 1890. Although some of Kolb's followers claimed he had been "cheated" by the party "machine," Kolb accepted the convention results and endorsed Democratic nominee Jones, who went on to defeat the Republicans and win the general election. But Kolb was not yet finished, and Hubert Dent would become an even more active adversary.

Two years later, in 1892, when Gov. Jones' ran for renomination, Kolb entered the race again, seeking to portray himself as still loyal to the Democratic Party by calling himself and his followers "Jeffersonian Democrats." The race for county delegates, fought out in county conventions across the state, was even more divisive and bitter than in 1890. Kolb's supporters often alleged fraud, particularly in the manipulation of the votes of blacks, and often walked out of the county conventions (or "bolted" in the language of the day), to send their own slates of delegates to the state convention to contest the seating of the delegates credentialed by the regular county party.

In the 1890 state Democratic nominating convention, Eufaulian Reuben Kolb had barely carried the delegation of his home county of Barbour, through a disputed settlement of the vote at the Spring Hill beat.[878] Now, in early 1892, much media attention was given to the upcoming Barbour County convention to see whether Kolb could clearly carry his own home county. The conservative Democratic Party organ, the *Montgomery Advertiser*, on January 2nd quoted the *Eufaula Times*: "We know of but three supporters Kolb has in Eufaula," and on January 16 observed, "The report is common that he can't carry his own county..." On February 2, the *Advertiser* reported that the *Eufaula Daily Mail* was "enthusiastic against its fellow townsman, Captain Kolb.... Like other Eufaula people it knows him and to know him is sufficient to put one down against him."

The Barbour Democratic Executive Committee issued a call for the various beats to hold meetings on April 4 and select delegates to the county convention to be held April 6. On March 31, both Gov. Jones and Capt. Kolb appeared at a Eufaula political rally and spoke to a crowd of 3000 to 4000 voters. The assemblage was called to order by Hubert Dent, who stated its object to be "a discussion of the issues between the candidates for governor," saying

561

there would be "no personalities" but they were "to have good natured politics."[879] Although Hubert was a strong political adversary of Kolb, apparently they maintained cordial personal relations. It will be recalled that in 1884, a public dispute between Kolb and A.C. Gordon had been resolved through the efforts of Hubert and his brother-in-law, Jim Martin, in their roles of "mutual friends" of the disputants. Kolb was a borrower from Hubert's Eufaula National Bank. (In 1900, it would become necessary for that bank to foreclose its mortgage on Kolb's residence.)[880]

The Eufaula city beat met as scheduled on April 4 and elected Hubert Dent as its chairman. Hubert's son "Hugh" had by now graduated from University of Virginia law school and had begun practicing in Eufaula. Future congressman Hugh Dent was elected secretary of the beat meeting over which his father was presiding.[881] Eufaula's delegates to the county convention included Hubert; his son, Hugh; his brother, George H. Dent; and C. S. McDowell (probably the senior). (Hugh was elected as a delegate to the "judicial convention," which was to select the Democratic candidates for judgeships.) In the beat elections for the county convention, a large majority of delegates supporting the renomination of Gov. Jones was elected.

The County convention convened in Clayton on April 8 amid much tension between the Jones delegates and those of Kolb. It was later reported that the Kolb delegates had met the night before and were planning to seek a pretext for "bolting" the convention.[882] Hubert Dent was unanimously elected permanent Chairman of the county convention. The trouble began when the leader of the Kolb delegates insisted that the allocation of delegates be based upon the number of white voters in each beat rather than the total registered voters as directed by the county committee, threatening that the convention must be "fair" to the Kolb faction or they would leave. While some of the more hotheaded Jones delegates started calling "goodbye!" Chairman Dent took another approach, described by the *Eufaula Times & News* in this manner:

> "But Chairman Dent on an occasion like this has a soothing way with him. He made a speech in a low voice that could be distinctly heard to the furthest end of the room, so great was the stillness. He was cool and wise. He told them that of course it was their privilege to bolt the convention if they wanted to do so, but that decency would suggest that they do it in order and quietly. He begged them, however, not to go but remain in their fathers' house, under the shadow of the great Democratic roof.
> Most any chairman in the world would have provoked and assisted a bolt, but his wise and temperate words, delivered in a low tone with much feeling quieted the waters as if by magic."[883]

Some of the Kolb delegates went into a corner to organize a walkout, but soon returned to the floor and continued to participate in the convention until its conclusion. The convention ultimately adopted a resolution affirming its loyalty to the Democratic Party, endorsing the administration of Gov. Jones, and instructing Barbour's 17 delegates to the state convention in Montgomery to vote as a unit for the renomination of Gov. Thomas G. Jones.

Among the 17 delegates elected to represent Barbour were Hubert Dent and his brother, George H. Dent.[884] Exultant over this Jones victory, the *Montgomery Advertiser* gloated that "Kolb's small minority [was] unable even to bolt in Barbour."[885] The *Birmingham Age-Herald* was inspired to editorialize extravagantly: "Barbour, a great old County, has been prolific of service to…Alabama. In peace, war and reconstruction she has done her duty. She has given to the State brave captains, learned statesmen, working patriots, great orators…. In the councils of the party and the State, her virtues are splendid as of old, her name a tower, her voice a bugle call…"[886]

Before adjourning, the Barbour County Democratic convention took another action, one relating to Hubert Dent. Earlier, in its March 4, 1892 issue, the *Montgomery Advertiser* had quoted the *Eufaula Times* to the effect that "Many friends of Captain Dent have been urging him for use of his name in the race for circuit judge. The *Times* has been aware of this movement for some time but the Captain until yesterday had never agreed to serve if nominated and elected." In a report that may have been inaccurate, the *Times* then quoted Captain Dent as saying that, while he was not seeking the position, "he would serve if the district wants him." The *Times* concluded, "All of the people of Barbour will rally with pleasure to him."[887] Now, at the County Democratic convention on April 8, the following resolution was presented and adopted:

> "Whereas, Hon. S. H. Dent has signified his willingness to accept the office of Judge of the 3rd Judicial District of Alabama, and whereas the people of this County recognize in him a man of the highest purity and integrity, and fully capacitated to discharge the many duties of said office, therefore be it
> Resolved, that the Democrats of Barbour county in convention assembled do hereby present the name of Hon. S. H. Dent to the Judicial Convention of said 3rd Judicial Circuit of Alabama for said office as Judge of said Circuit court, and that the delegates from this County … are hereby instructed to use all honorable means to secure his nomination."

However, after this resolution was adopted "amidst great applause," Hubert spoke of his "great appreciation of the compliment conferred," but said that he would not be a candidate for the office and that his mind had been for some time made up. "He thanked his friends heartily."[888] After Hubert's candidacy for the Legislature during Reconstruction in 1872 (resulting in the infamous "dual Legislatures"), he never again sought or served in elected public office, other than his years of service on the Eufaula City Council. He would also remain an active force for many years in the Democratic Party at the county and state levels.

Reuben Kolb did not take his Barbour County defeat graciously. The *Birmingham News* quoted Kolb as claiming that Jones won the Barbour County delegates with "negro and Republican votes,"[889] although Kolb later denied having made the assertion. The alleged statement was particularly ironic in light of the fact that it was Kolb who was actually seeking the support of black and Republican voters. To get to the bottom of the matter, the *Birmingham News* on April 9 sent its reporter to interview the convention chairman, Capt. S.

H. Dent. In a detailed analysis of the various beats, Dent showed the falsity of the charge, concluding, "I am in a position to say that Jones did not carry a single beat by Negro or Republican votes." Refuting Kolb's claim that he actually carried the popular vote in Barbour County, Dent said, "Jones had about two votes to Kolb's one in the county." The *Birmingham News* reporter concluded that "Capt. Dent is a fair man and what he says can be absolutely relied on."[890]

The 1892 Alabama Democratic Convention assembled on June 8 in the chambers the House of Representatives in Montgomery. It was preceded by numerous credentials disputes between competing Jones and Kolb county delegations, and the "air was thick with rumors" of a planned bolt by the Kolb delegates. Many viewed it as "the most intensely interesting and largely attended party gathering since the war." The *Montgomery Advertiser* noted "a sort of undercurrent of feeling" that the convention's actions would "have a powerful bearing for the future of the party..." and would "settle for all time to come the status of the white race in Alabama."[891] The Barbour County delegation included Hubert and George Dent, Gen. Henry D. Clayton, J. G. Guice, Henry Shorter, and others.

To set the tone for this weighty gathering, the party leadership selected Hubert Dent to serve as its temporary Chairman. After being unanimously elected and introduced by the state committee chairman, Hubert Dent spoke to the delegates of the need for party harmony and unity, recalling the difficult days of Reconstruction when state government was dominated by self-seeking Republicans and recently-freed slaves considered unprepared for political power, and the successful overthrow of that corrupt regime by the Democratic Party:

> "I thank you most sincerely for the compliment of calling me to the position of your temporary Chairman. I do not take it, however, as a compliment to me personally, but to the section from which I came and to my people, and for them and in their name I thank you.
>
> A convention of representative Democrats is always important, for upon its actions largely depend the peace, good government, and prosperity of the people of our beloved State.
>
> No convention of the Democratic Party of Alabama for the past quarter of a century has had duties more important and more delicate than these which confront you. But when I look into your upturned faces an see before me such a body of intelligent men, of whom any state might well be proud, and when I consider that you have left your homes and your business, your firesides and your family, not in the interest of any one man or any body of men but that you are here as patriotic citizens to work for the success of the Democratic Party and thereby secure honest government, peace and happiness to all our people. I am satisfied that while making no sacrifice of principle your action will be characterized by such wisdom, moderation and fairness that no good Democrat will have any JUST cause of complaint.
>
> This much I can say for any true Democrat that, however great may be his personal disappointment for himself or his friends at your action: he may even feel that in the heat and zeal of personal rivalry and competition many

things may have been said and done not ex tly in accordance with the law of brotherly love and charity, yet for all that he accepts the result. He not only accepts it, but when the battle is joined with our foes, he is found not like Achilles sulking in his tent over some fancied or even real wrong, but in the forefront of the contest doing his devoir for Democracy, for good government and for the best interests of Alabama.

Another thing I can say for the true Democrat, he believes in his party, and when it acts through the regular and legally constituted channels, he always seeks to make that action history by having it ratified at the polls

Again I can say for the true Democrat that he believes his party has principles and he believes in those principles.

And if I were called on to give an epitome of the principles of the Democratic Party, I would state negatively that they are opposition to the centralization of power, opposition to the consolidation of capital, opposition to class legislation and the building up of monopolies, and affirmative in favor of the enactment of just laws, so that both the blessings and the burdens of government like the dews of Heaven may fall impartially upon all.

But there is another mission of the Democratic party of the South, aye, of the solid South, if you please, that solidity which is the admiration of our friends and the envy of our foes. That solidity which those in the regions beyond look upon something like we do upon the Pension Bureau, that they are not in it and they can't dissolve it.

I know you have already anticipated me when I say that mission is to preserve the purity of the Caucasian blood and the supremacy of the Anglo-Saxon race.

I say this in no spirit of hostility to the negro, for I verily believe that we "who are native here and to the manner born," are really better friends of the negro and have more true sympathy with him than those who with no special love for the negro, but for political purposes seek through him to ruin and degrade us. I am satisfied that I speak to many Gentlemen here personally familiar with the history of Alabama from 1868 to 1875, when she presented a spectacle that was enough to excite the commiseration of her bitterest foes, who is there who wishes to see that history repeated or even run the risk of having it repeated: who is there who wishes to see re-enacted the scenes which disgraced your Legislative halls, where ignorance ruled and corruption held high carnival?

Should it come to pass by our divisions that the State of Alabama is again turned over to that hungry and ignorant horde, who can tell how many decades the march of Alabama's progress will be turned backward! Instead of progress and prosperity we will have stagnation and despair. In a word, we might properly write all over Alabama "Ichabod. Ichabod. The glory has departed. The glory has departed." [pp]

If there is any Democrat who for personal gain or through personal ambition would dare have Alabama run that risk, I am satisfied that the

---

[pp] From I Samuel 4, referring to Israel's defeat by the Philistines and its loss of the Ark of the Covenant

patriotic sons of Alabama will bury him politically so deep that the hand of resurrection will never reach him. Wherein has the Democratic Party of Alabama failed in her pledges or her promises to her people insofar as it was in her power to grant them?

If you complain of federal legislation, why hold the Democratic Party responsible when she has not had full control of the government in more than thirty years? Does not every reasonable man know that Democratic division means Republican success, and the history of Alabama from 1868 to 1875 shows you what Republican success means. Why any patriotic man should seek to do this is past my comprehension. When the future of the Democratic Party is the brightest and the most hopeful of any that it has had in more than twenty-five years. It is in the power of the Democratic Party by wise action and united effort to secure the next President of the United States and to retain control of the next House of Representatives, and I further believe that by the some wise and prudent course before another political quadrennium will pass, we will secure control of that last entrenched citadel of Republican power, the Senate of the United States.

When the flag of Democracy shall float in triumph over every department of the National Government, if that great party shall prove faithless to the pledges and recreant to her high trusts, then will be the time to seek through other organizations and other means that relief which the people demand. But until she is thus weighed in the balance and found wanting let us be true in our fealty to her flag and do all in our power to give her that measure of power and success, by which, I believe we alone can hope to secure the relief so much needed by all of our people." [892]

The Democratic media of the state approved Hubert's handling of the opening of the convention. The Birmingham *Age-Herold* said, "Captain S. H. Dent of Barbour, the temporary chairman of the Democratic State Convention, is one of the best men in Alabama. In private and public life, he is a model citizen. The State has no worthier son."[893]

This convention ultimately renominated Gov. Jones over Reuben Kolb by a large majority, 372 to 68. The Kolb supporters did not accept Hubert Dent's appeal for party unity, and refused to accept the results of the convention. Contending that Kolb had been a "swindled out of" delegates to which he was rightfully entitled, Kolb and his supporters, on the night after Gov. Jones' renomination, bolted the regular Democratic convention, held their own convention, and nominated Kolb for governor. Continuing the effort to avoid the charge of having created a new party separate from the Democratic Party (which it now clearly had done), the Kolb faction adopted the name, "Jeffersonian Democrats," and launched a third party campaign to defeat the regular Democrats in the general election scheduled for August 1. As the Democrats had expected, Kolb now openly made a strong bid for black voters, demanding "a free vote and an honest count." Republicans also supported the "Jeffersonian Democrats." A populist movement had now been organized under the name "People's Party," and it also rallied behind Kolb. On the stump and in the press throughout the state, each side rained denunciations, accusations and recriminations upon the other. In the election, 250,000 votes were cast, and Gov. Jones was declared the winner with an 11,425-vote majority. Kolb claimed that he had been cheated out of the election by ballot-box stuffing and crooked vote-counting in the Black Belt, that votes had been cast by "dead Negroes and faithful hound dogs," and that he had actually carried the state by 40,000 votes. Some historians have accepted the view that the election results were indeed fraudulent and that Kolb was "counted out" in the Black Belt.[894] But there was no legal procedure for contesting the election, and Gov. Jones' victory stood. However, the rupture in the Democratic Party deepened even further in the congressional and presidential elections scheduled three months later in November. Kolb's Jeffersonian Democrats and the Populists held their own convention and nominated "fusion" candidates for congress in every district, which candidates were also accepted by the Republican Party. In addition, the Jeffersonian-Populist fusion fielded candidates for electors supporting the Populist candidate for president and vice president in opposition to the Democratic nominees, Grover Cleveland and Adlai Stevenson. The fusion candidates were defeated, and Cleveland won the presidency.

The fighting between the two wings of the Democratic Party continued in the 1894 Governor's race. In 1893, the Jeffersonian Democrats' executive committee had proposed to the regular Democratic Executive Committee, of which Hubert Dent was now a member, a compromise for bringing the party back together. The *Montgomery Advertiser* complained that the proposed plan "…lets in every third partyite…who bolted the party nominations for president and congressmen last November. It proposes to invite every enemy of the party into the party citadel…"[895] In a conciliatory response, Hubert Dent and the other members of the Democratic Executive Committee declined the proposal; they could forgive all except the Kolbites votes for Republican and Populist candidates in the November elections. In fact, the executive committee imposed a test for participation in Democratic primaries and conventions during 1894: one must have voted for "Cleve and Steve" in the November 1892 elections.[896]

In a joint convention, the Jeffersonian Democrats and Populists in 1894 nominated a "fusion" slate, with Eufaulian Reuben Kolb as its candidate for governor. Kolb's stature among his followers had now reach near-mythic proportions. He was loved as a political martyr and savior of the downtrodden, and was expected to win the governor's race and proceed to national office in 1896. The regular Democrats, or "True Blues" as they called themselves, nominated the old friend and one-time law partner of Hubert Dent, Congressman William C. Oates, "the one-armed hero of Henry County." A conservative party regular who profited politically from his loss of an arm in the Civil War, Oats had been elected to Congress in 1880 and thereafter reelected, with strong support in Barbour County from Hubert Dent and Hubert's brother-in-law, County Democratic Chairman Jim Martin. The race between Kolb and Oates has been characterized as "the most memorable campaign in the State's history." The business community and those unwilling under any circumstances to desert the Democratic Party fought diligently for Oates. Farmers and labor, suffering acutely from the hard times of the "panic of 1893," fiercely supported Kolb. Kolb sought and received votes and money from the Republicans, who wanted to break the "solid South" and were happy to throw their support to Kolb. His supporters wore corncobs while Kolb himself traveled in a cob-covered wagon, and Oates' adherents wore oats in their lapels and hatbands. Furious campaigning occurred in every part of the state, Kolb and Oates clubs were formed, school children became involved, homes and churches were divided, charges and counter-charges were hurled, abuse was heaped on Kolb, Oates was attacked for "social improprieties" (i.e. illegitimate children), and each side alleged the other was planning election fraud. When the dust cleared on August 6, Oates was declared the winner with a 27,000-vote majority, while the Kolb forces indignantly charged vote-counting fraud of historic proportions in the Black Belt counties, which were said to have held back their totals until after the white counties had reported.[897] But there was still no election contest law permitting a challenge of the results. After Oates was sworn into office amid talk of armed insurrection, Kolb and a crowd of his supporters held their own "inauguration" from the back of a wagon on Dexter Avenue in front of the capitol, and Kolb sent messages to the Legislature demanding recognition as the lawful governor. All this was ignored, and the political career of Reuben Kolb, the charismatic exponent of change, came to a close. [898]

61
State Chairman of the "Sound Money" Democrats

"This seems to be an age of adulteration...the   crowd that got hold of the Democracy recently has adulterated it so much that if you were to take off its label and our oldest and best citizens were to meet it in the road, they would not recognize it."

Hubert Dent, State Chairman, Sound Money Democrats.

Although the Jeffersonian-Populist candidate had been defeated in 1894, populism itself had not been stopped, and the movement continued to gain momentum across Alabama and the nation. Ironically, the Alabama Democratic Party and its national counterpart would ultimately adopt some of the populists' most important objectives. But this shift would occur only over the determined opposition of the conservative wing of the party, and in 1896, Hubert Dent would take a leadership role in this opposition. Even more ironically, Dent and his fellow conservatives in 1896 would find themselves committing the very act they had severely criticized and punished the Kolbites for: "bolting" the Democratic Party.

To understand the unexpected and drastic political position taken by Hubert Dent and his conservative colleagues in 1896, it is important to review the most controversial of the measures sought by the Populists and adopted by the Democrats: the unlimited or "free coinage of silver." Based upon certain treatises in vogue at the time, farmers and labor leaders became convinced that the reason for their poverty during the periods of depression in the 1890's was because there was not enough money in circulation. U. S. currency was backed by gold, which was in short supply, thereby limiting the amount of currency in circulation. Large silver strikes in the western states provided a plentiful supply of silver, however. Egged on by the silver mine owners, the farmer and labor leaders were convinced that if the government would accept and mint into coins this entire silver output, this would bring economic prosperity. Further, the free silver advocates demanded that under this "bi-metallist" standard, the value of the silver coins be set by law at the ratio of "16-to-1," that is, 16 ounces of silver would be decreed to have the value of 1 ounce of gold. One of the main problems with the proposal was that, although this had been the prevailing ratio in the market at an earlier time in history, the new Western silver strikes had by 1896 caused the market value of silver to decline vis-à-vis gold, to perhaps 20-to-1 and even 30-to-1.

The free silver coinage issue had great appeal to Democrats in the West and South, including Alabama. However, many businessmen, bankers, and other conservative Democrats, including Hubert Dent, saw the measure as invalid and insidious. These Democrats, called "Sound Money Democrats," or "Gold Democrats," saw that the unlimited coinage of silver at the 16-to1 ratio would debase the currency and lead to inflation, hurting business and commerce as well as farmers and wage earners. The *Montgomery Advertiser*, the leading organ of Alabama's Sound Money Democrats, called it a scheme for the Treasury to issue "fiat money."[899] Attacking the policy as well as the mine owners who were behind it, the *Advertiser* scathingly observed, "When the 371 ¼ grains of silver that go to make a big dollar were worth more than a hundred cents the mine owners sold their products to Europe. Now that 371 ¼ grains are worth about 63 cents they insist that the government shall stamp it into a dollar and shall open the mints to all the silver in the world at this ratio of 16-to1."[900] As a banker, S. H. Dent was acutely aware of the windfall that the free-silver proposal would provide to debtors who had borrowed "full-value" gold-backed dollars but who could then pay off their loans with artificially over-valued silver dollars of lesser value than those borrowed. The sound money men realized that even though inflation might lead to higher wages or farm receipts, prices and expenses would rise correspondingly and leave the farmer-laborer no better off than before. The gold dollars would actually be driven out of circulation as gold holders hoarded rather than spent that less-inflated and more intrinsically valuable medium, thus worsening rather than improving the "money famine" about which the free silver enthusiasts were complaining.

However, by the time of the regular Alabama State Democratic convention the Spring of 1896, the delegates were influenced by the collapse of wages and farm prices, the severe plight of farmers and workers resulting from the "panic of '93," the widespread demands for economic relief, and the emphatic claims that the free coinage of silver would bring prosperity. Despite the opposition of the Sound Money Democrats, including Hubert Dent, the convention adopted a platform endorsing the free coinage of silver, and nominated a free silver Democrat for governor, Capt. Joseph F. Johnston of Birmingham. Alabama's Populists and Republicans joined in nominating Capt. A. T. Goodwyn as a "fusion candidate,[qq] who was also supported by the remaining Jeffersonians. Although Hubert Dent and the Sound Money Democrats were unhappy with the regular organization's acceptance of a free silver candidate and platform, they had no intention of separating from the state Democratic Party on this issue. To them, it was far more important to maintain party unity and defeat the Jeffersonians-Populists-Republicans at the state level. The *Advertiser* rejected Populist predictions of a "bolt" by the Alabama Gold Democrats: "the Sound Money Democrats of Alabama are of the most stalwart, loyal, honest, patriotic type, and they don't want to see Goodwyn, the Republican candidate, here succeed and thereby turn the state over to the...Kolbs."[901]

But Alabama politics in 1896 was complicated by the fact that, not only was the state electing a governor and other state officers in August, but a national presidential election would also be held three months later in November. At the Chicago Democratic Convention in July, the national party was caught up in the free silver movement. It adopted the populist platform of free coinage of silver at the 16-to1 ratio, supported an income tax, opposed government intervention to stop strikes, and refused to endorse the record of the party's own sitting president, Grover Cleveland, a conservative Gold Democrat. Passing over Cleveland, the convention nominated a previously unknown thirty-six year old Nebraska congressman, on the basis of his electrifying speech ending with the impassioned peroration, "...we will answer their demands for a gold standard by saying to them: You shall not press down upon the brow of labor this crown of thorns, you shall not crucify mankind upon a cross of gold!" It was said that, if the Democrats had not nominated William Jennings Bryan, he would have

---

[qq] Active at the 1896 Populist convention was its temporary secretary, one Warren S. Reese of Montgomery, a former Democratic officeholder who had abandoned the Democrats in 1895 to become a Republican, and in 1896 became a Populist-Republican. *Montgomery Advertiser,* April 29, 30, 1896; *Eufaula Times*, Nov. 28, 1895. Reese's son would later play a negative role in the story of the Youngs and Dents.

been the nominee of the Populist Party, and in fact that party soon adopted him as their nominee. The Republicans nominated William McKinley on a strong gold standard platform.

Gold Democrats across the country were appalled by the actions of their national party, which in their view had "made a Populist platform, put a bolting Populist agitator on it as reward for his speech of the wildest Populist character, repudiated the Democratic administration, insulted the sound money contingent in the convention..."[902] There was immediately talk of holding a separate convention and nominating a Gold Democratic slate to oppose both Bryan and McKinley. In Alabama, the Gold Democrats were equally upset, but they bided their time. The presidential election was not until November. Their first priority was to defeat the Jeffersonians-Populists-Republicans in the state elections on August 4, and secure Alabama for the regular Democratic Party. The *Montgomery Advertiser* counseled: "...keep cool and go slow. There is enough time to determine what's best to be done, and in the meantime, Democrats of Alabama should put aside national matters to concentrate on the state election only a few weeks off so as to beat Goodwyn (the Jeffersonian-Populist-Republican candidate) and his gang without a row about the national ticket. Let us put aside all dissension until the August election is over."[903]

On August 4 the Democrat, Capt Johnston, was elected governor by a comfortable margin, along with the Democratic slate. With the state firmly in the hands of the regular Democrats, the Gold Democrats were now free to act on the national issues. On Election Day itself, even before the totals were in, an assemblage of Gold Democrats from across the state convened in the Montgomery city council chambers. Attending from Barbour County were S. H. Dent, J. L. Pitts, J. G. Guice, and F. B. Field. The *Advertiser* noted, "The character and standing of the gentlemen present from different portions of the State evidences the strong hold the movement has upon the people...a sound money ticket will receive a large vote." Reviewing some of the delegates, the editorialist observed, "Messrs. Dent, Guice and Pitts of Eufaula, are names familiar to the Party of the whole State as among the strongest Democratic leaders there for years.[904] Historian A. B. Moore reports that participants in the convention included "such prominent Democrats" as Congressmen G. P. Harrison and R. H. Clarke, future governor Charles Henderson, Eufaula banker-lawyer S. H. Dent, F. P. Glass, J. H. Fitts, and E. L. Russell.[905] Former governor Thomas Goode Jones would also become a principal leader in the movement.

On the motion of Capt. J. M. Falkner, Capt. S. H. Dent was called to serve as chairman of the assembly. The *Advertiser* praised this choice: "Capt. Dent, the Chairman of the conference and of the State Committee, is one of the leading citizens of Eufaula in every respect, and one who has always taken the part of a patriot in the work of the Party."[906] Upon being introduced by Capt. Falkner, Hubert opened the meeting with crowd-pleasing remarks:

> "I consider it a compliment, a very high compliment, to be called upon
> to preside over this meeting, for I believe I see before me Gentlemen who
> stand for true, unadulterated Democracy (Applause).
>   This seems to be an age of adulteration. A great many of the articles of
> food in daily use are adulterated...but done so skillfully that the article

preserves the appearance and a great deal of the flavor of the original article. But I will tell you that the crowd that got hold of the Democracy recently has adulterated it so much that if you were to take off its label and our oldest and best citizens were to meet it in the road, they would not recognize it. (Prolonged applause)

We have done our duty, I have no doubt, to our State ticket, and we are called upon here now to do something to preserve for ourselves and our children those true principles of Democracy which have had such a glorious record in the past. We do not want to see these principles die. We want them to survive, and small though this meeting may be, I an sure that there are many honest and true hearts all over Alabama today beating in sympathy with the action which we shall take toward the preservation of those grand principles for which Democracy has been so signally distinguished.

But I will not detain you, Gentlemen, with a speech.... As I said before, we have done our best in the interests of the State ticket, and we are now going to do something for what we consider the true Democracy, and we are now ready to complete the organization. (Applause)."[907]

Hubert appointed a Committee on Permanent Organization, which met while further speeches were being made. It soon reported, recommending that a national committeeman be named to attend the provisional national committee meeting in Indianapolis which had been called for August 7 by Sound Money Democrats in the East; and that a provisional Alabama state executive committee of five be created. On the motion of Mr. Tillman of Jefferson, this proposal was unanimously adopted, with the amendment that the chairman of the present conference, Hubert Dent, be made state chairman, and that he appoint the remaining four members of the state executive committee. Although Hubert accepted, the proposal caused him to engage in some "thinking aloud" from the podium about his mixed emotions in breaking with his Party, whether he could afford the time away from the bank, and whether he was the right man for such a job:

"Gentlemen, I certainly am interested in this movement, and feel it very deeply, and...there is a feeling of sadness connected with it. But I feel that it is the duty of every patriotic, sound money Democrat to take part in these proceedings, and do what he can to make this effort successful. (Applause). And I promise that so far as in me lies, I will give you the best effort that is within my power. I would have preferred—I do not know that I shall be able to give the time that is necessary to that committee. As my neighbors know, I have been absent from home necessarily for nearly two months, and have but recently returned and therefore business is pressing on me just now, and I think...that perhaps some other gentleman could be found who is equally willing and more able, and perhaps has more time at his disposition than I. As I said, my heart is in this matter. My feelings are in it. When I look at that platform which has been referred to here, when I read it and scan it, the thought occurs to me that the promises which are there are idle promises. They catch the ear of a great many people, but when we can, by an Act of the

Legislature, put sense in the head of a fool, and by Act put honesty in the heart of a knave and contentment in every home in Alabama, then there might be some chance to accomplish some of the things that are promised in the Chicago Platform. (Applause) But until these wonderful things can be accomplished, I propose to adhere to the old principles which have distinguished the Democratic Party for so long…"[908]

The next day, the Montgomery *Advertiser*, in reponse to criticism that it and the Sound Money Democrats had "bolted" the Party, replied that "…it is the free silver, pro-Populist element that has bolted the Party, and there is abundant evidence that the reckless abandonment of the time-honored principles and precedents of the Party in the demagogic rush for success is a poor investment."[909]

On August 7, the national executive committee of the Sound Money Democrats, consisting of Alabama's committeeman J. M. Falkner and those from thirty-two other states, met in Indianapolis and issued a call for a national convention to be held there on September 2. The *Advertiser* urged its readers to support this as the "true" Democratic Convention,[910] and reported a speech in Birmingham by former Gov. Thomas Goode Jones supporting the Sound Money Democrats. The editor characterized Jones' speech as "the effort of his life," concluding that that "his arraignment of the Chicago Platform was severe and unanswerable; his defense of Democratic doctrine and principles was superb; and his defiance of the threats of silver men to bar all so-called bolters forever from political preferment was patriotic and manly."[911]

Calling themselves the "National Democratic Party," the convention of conservative gold Democrats assembled in Indianapolis as scheduled on September 4 and 5. On the first morning the Alabama delegation organized, electing Hubert Dent as its chairman, George W. Jones its secretary, Capt J. M. Falkner, national committeeman. Former Gov. Thomas Goode Jones was appointed to the Committee on Permanent Organization, as well as the Platform Committee. The keynote address of the convention was given by New York Governor Flowers, who was escorted to the chair by Gov. Jones. The party platform which Gov. Jones helped to write was said to be "the most superb declaration of Democratic principles that has been enunciated in years…. There is no attempt to dodge or straddle on any issue…it is not adulterated with any of the paternalism of the Republican and Populist parties…"[912] The convention nominated Illinois Senator John M. Palmer for president and Kentuckian, Gen. Simon Bolivar Buckner for vice president. Palmer had been a Union general, and Buckner a Confederate general, both serving in the Battle of Chickamauga where Dent's Battery had distinguished itself. In the balloting for presidential nominee, the Alabama delegation initially split, voting 16 for Palmer and 6 for Edward S. Bragg, a former Union general from Wisconsin. The *Advertiser* explained, "This division was more artificial than real. Chairman Dent, Governor Jones, Captain Falkner, and some others, thought that General Bragg should be complimented, but it was the intention of the delegation to go solid for Palmer at the earliest possible moment, and the vote was changed at once after the roll call was over. The *Advertiser* correspondent felt that the Alabama delegation "was unquestionably largely instrumental in making the ticket and the platform."[913]

It was a convivial convention, one its highlights being the brass band brought from Birmingham by the Alabama delegation. The band's most popular piece was an original composition by the bandmaster entitled, the "Falkner March," honoring Alabama's national committeeman. In a demonstration of sectional reconciliation, at the conclusion of the convention the Alabama delegation and its band escorted the Massachusetts delegation to the train depot, then the New York delegation, and then those of Ohio and other northern states were honored in this way. There were warm responses, and an Indianapolis crowd of several thousand gathered, "manifesting its admiration of…the spectacle of Southerners and Northerners showing so much kindness to each other, refreshing…to the Northern assemblage."[914]

In the fall, a spirited campaign among the presidential contenders took place, during which Palmer and Buckner journeyed to Alabama and spoke at Birmingham, Montgomery, and smaller towns in South Alabama. On Election Day, Alabama went overwhelmingly for Bryan, but McKinley was elected president by a large margin. The Gold Democrats could take some satisfaction in having taken votes away from Bryan and contributing to his defeat. Alabama's conservative Gold Democrats, while none would ever admit to favoring a Republican, were undoubtedly comfortable with McKinley and his conservative platform rather than the Populist-Democrat Bryan. Hubert Dent's Barbour County colleague, J. G. Guice, expressed it best at the Montgomery Sound Money conference, when he said that he did not propose to vote for McKinley, but that if a halter were put around his neck and he were forced to vote for McKinley or Bryan, he would vote for McKinley.[915]

Dent and Alabama's Gold Democrats have been accused of acting hypocritically in opposing the presidential nominee of the regular Party, after having earlier castigated and punished the Kolbites for similar actions. However, there were differences. Kolb and his Populist-Republican allies in 1894 had sought in a state election to overthrow the regular state Democratic organization, thus jeopardizing the principal means by which Republican-black political domination (then the pole-star of Alabama politics) had been avoided. But in 1896, the Gold Democrats were careful to fully support the regular state Party in the state election, even when they were not happy over its platform and gubernatorial candidate. These conservatives opposed the regular Party only in the national election, based on issues like free silver that were not significantly affected by the state government anyway. In any event, despite pre-election threats, the regular Democrats made no attempt to punish or exclude the gold Democrats because of their 1896 opposition to Bryan. New gold discoveries in the Klondike and other places thereafter reduced the importance of free silver question. With the Democrats' adoption of some of its main issues, and other circumstances, the Populist Party faded from the state and national scene.

PART VI

The Twentieth Century

62
Hubert Dent and the Alabama Constitution of 1901

"I feel that it is my *duty to put myself on record as being opposed to [the "grandfather clause"]...It is my conviction that it is in conflict with the Constitution of the United States..."*

Delegate Hubert Dent, speaking to the 1901 Convention.

After a great deal of public debate, the Alabama Legislature authorized the holding of an election on April 25, 1901, to determine whether a convention would be convened to write a new constitution to replace the 1875 document. In the same election, delegates would be elected who would serve in the event the voters approved the holding of the convention. However, the actual selection of delegates would occur in the Democratic primary to be held on March 9, when that party would nominate its candidates for delegates. In Barbour County, the voters were to nominate two delegates from Barbour County as a whole, one candidate from its senatorial district, and two from its congressional district. In January 1901, the Eufaula *Times & News* published the following letter:

"Mr. Editor: As the time is approaching for the people to begin to look around for suitable men to represent them in the Constitutional Convention, which meets next spring, and as that convention is of vital importance to all the citizens of the state, it behooves us to select the best, wisest, and most learned person to go to that convention, and in looking over the number of competent persons who would ably fill the place in our county, I can see no one more suitable, better qualified ... than our highly respected citizen, Capt. S. H. Dent. He is sound and conservative in principle, learned in the law, and being in close touch with people, fully understands their wants and wishes. We could not select a better representative to go to the Constitutional Convention and hope that he will gratify his numerous friends by suffering his name to be announced as a candidate for the position. Voter."

The editor of the *Times & News* [π] joined in the recommendation:

"We join heartily with Mr. Voter in his suggesting the name of Capt. S. H. Dent, who is a man of the people and for the people. He is much interested in farming and other interests of the county, and no one could be sent from Barbour County who has the good of the people at heart more than he has. He is conservative, and his opinions will go a long ways with other members over the state. We need such a man at this time and the voters of Barbour would do well in selecting Capt. S. H. Dent as delegate to the convention."

[π] W. D. Jelks had been succeeded as owner-editor of the newspaper by A.L. Muir. Jelks had become the president of the Alabama Senate, and had succeeded to the governorship upon the death of Samford. Jelks would be elected governor in his own right in 1902.

Hubert allowed his name to be placed in nomination, and in the primary, there were three candidates for the two delegate positions from Barbour: Hubert Dent; Dr. L. L. Winn, and lawyer George Legare Comer. Comer was the only candidate who advertised his candidacy in the newspaper.

On the day of the March 9 Democratic primary, there was a low turnout due to rain and the fact that all three candidates were well-liked. Dent and Winn were elected. The narrow vote difference between Winn and Comer prompted Comer to contest the result in the Democratic Party Convention, but his contest failed. The delegate elected from the third congressional district was former congressmen (and Hubert's old running mate from 1872), Jere Williams. A. H. Merrill was elected without opposition as the delegate from Barbour's senatorial district.

The Fifteenth Amendment, adopted in the aftermath of the Civil War, prohibited denial of the vote to any citizen because of his race, color, or previous condition of servitude. Blacks had been voting in Alabama since that time, but most white Alabamians of that era did not believe that African Americans of the time were ready for the responsibilities of voting. They viewed black voters as unknowledgeable and largely illiterate, whose vote was being routinely manipulated by white politicians for their own purposes, to the detriment of both races. They pointed to ballot box fraud involving the black vote which had become notorious. The *Birmingham News* of July 30, 1902 said that, "From cheating Republicans and Populists," the Democrats had turned to cheating themselves. "Every election was begrimed with the filth of fraud." The principal purpose of the proposed Convention was to implement what was regarded in that time as "reform."

Prior to the April 25, 1901 election, the *Times and News* editorially urged Eufaulians to go out and vote on the issue of whether or not to hold a constitutional convention. The editor stated that, "This is the most important election that you have been called to decide since 1875, and it is a duty incumbent on every voter to cast his ballot. It will be left to you to decide whether we will have a reform constitution or go on doing business under the old one." In the election, the convening of the constitutional convention received overwhelming statewide approval.

The 155 elected delegates convened in Montgomery on May 21, 1901. When Convention President, John B. Knox of Anniston announced the standing committees, Hubert Dent was appointed to the Suffrage Committee, which would have principal responsibility for the most important issue to come before the convention, i. e., voting and elections. Hubert would take unexpected positions on these key issues.

As it began its work, the Suffrage Committee recognized that blacks could not be disenfranchised because of their race, but reasoned that voting restrictions could be imposed which were not based on race, such as literacy requirements. Thus, the majority report of the Suffrage Committee proposed restrictions which, among others, included the requirement that voters be able to "…read and write any article of the Constitution of the United States in the

English language..." [916] Most black people of that time could not comply with this requirement.

However, the proposed restrictions presented the Suffrage Committee with a difficulty, in that they would probably also operate to disfranchise a number of poor whites. The Democratic Party platform which had advocated the holding of the convention, and upon which most of the delegates had been elected as delegates, had provided that no voting restriction would be adopted which took the vote away from any white. The Committee majority solved this by introducing the "grandfather clause." It proposed a temporary, one year registration period during which voters could be registered without regard to the new restrictions, if they were "lawful descendants of persons who had honorably served in...the American Revolution, or in the War of 1812, or in the war with Mexico, or in any war with the Indians, or in the Civil War between the States, or in the land or naval forces of the Confederate States, or of the State of Alabama in the war between the States..." No meaningful number of blacks could comply with this qualification.

The "grandfather" proposal met stiff opposition from Hubert Dent. Three other members of the Suffrage Committee joined Hubert in filing a minority report advocating the deletion of this provision, upon the ground that it violated the fifteenth amendment, and other constitutional prohibitions. Speaking on the floor of the convention, Hubert argued as follows:

"MR. DENT: ...Under ordinary conditions, Mr. President and Gentlemen of the Convention, I should hesitate very much to set up my judgment against the judgment of the large number of gentlemen on this floor who differ with me on the proposition, but representing...my own people and...my own judgment and my own conscience, I feel that it is my duty to put myself on record as being opposed to [the 'grandfather clause']...It is my conviction that it is in conflict with the Constitution of the United States...

'The rule is general with reference to the enactments of all legislative bodies...that the motives of the legislators...will always be presumed to accomplish that which follows as the natural and reasonable effects of their enactments...'

Now I ask what is the natural and reasonable effect that will follow [the grandfather clause] if adopted? By way of illustration...say we had a clause in this provision which said that the descendants of the settlers of this country...who came from European countries should be voters in the State of Alabama. I ask any candid gentleman on this floor if the effect of that would not be practically to limit suffrage to white people in the State of Alabama. Now if there was no provision in the Constitution of the United States which forbade such a rule, it could be done..., but I do not see how it can be made plain not to be in conflict with the Constitution of the United States. They lay down three rules. They say that you must not discriminate against a Negro on account of his race, second, on account of his color, and third, on account of his previous condition of servitude. Now you take the practical application of this [grandfather clause]. What chance could the Negro have to come in under this article when he was in a condition of servitude and could not become a soldier in the wars to which reference is made here. You are reasonable men, you are thinking men...

But there are other objections to this amendment. For myself I believe it is in contravention to the spirit that has animated the people of this country from the Declaration of Independence down to this time...[Look at Section 30 of] the report of the Committee on Preamble and Declaration of Rights...We have just adopted this section: "Section 30. That no...hereditary distinction, privileges, honor, or emolument shall ever be granted or conferred in this State..." Now I ask the gentlemen of this Convention, does not this section under consideration [the grandfather clause] grant an hereditary right or privilege to the sons of those who were soldiers in the wars referred to. If that is not its meaning, I must confess that I do not understand the force and effect of the English language...For these reasons, Mr. Chairman, I advocate striking out [the grandfather clause] of the report of the Committee on Suffrage."[917]

In defense of the grandfather provision, a number of convention delegates argued that it was a necessary provision in order for the convention to comply with the pledge of the Democratic party that no white man would be disfranchised by the new constitution. Hubert Dent gave this argument short shrift, retorting as follows:

"MR DENT: ...I have heard a great deal said in reference to party pledges, and the pledges contained in the platform. I do not propose to violate what I consider the spirit of the pledges of the Democratic Party, but...I propose to present my views of those pledges for what they are worth to this Convention. We are pledged here not to disfranchise any white man. I take it that that means that we are not to do it if we can avoid it and ...make a Constitution that will be beneficial and acceptable to the people of Alabama. But Mr. Chairman,...Whatever Constitution we make will be submitted back to the people for their ratification or their rejection. Now let me illustrate my view of the principle involved. We represent the people of Alabama as their agents. Now, a principal sends out his agent to make a contract for him and he limits him..., stating that he is to make the contract in a particular way. The agent goes and finds it is impracticable to make such a contract as his principal has prescribed, but he in the exercise of his discretion, makes a contract upon the condition that it shall be ratified by his principal...He submits it back to his principal and says: "...I made a contract as near to [the one you prescribed] as I could and which I think will be beneficial to you, and you have the right now to say whether you will stand by that contract or reject it." If he does that, I want to know who is hurt?

If we make a Constitution here, doing the very best we can, for what would be to the very best interests of the people of Alabama, suppose we do violate in letter some of the pledges made by the Democratic party in its platform; if we refer it back to the people, and they accept it, who is hurt by it?"[918]

In more formal language, the Minority Report[919] submitted by Dent and his three colleagues gave detailed reasons for their opposition to the grandfather provision:

> "We are of the opinion that the...clause, on its face, violates the Federal Constitution, which we have taken an oath to support. It undertakes by indirect means, to deny or abridge the right to vote to citizens of the United States on account of race, color or previous condition of servitude, which is forbidden by the Fifteenth amendment to that instrument. This is done by conferring the right to vote upon a class, viz, descendants of soldiers, this class including practically all of the white and excluding practically all of the Negro race."

With incisive reasoning which sounds very much like a modern U. S. Supreme Court opinion, the dissenters point out the arbitrariness of the provision:

> "It does not prescribe a qualification bearing any proper relation to the capacity of the voter to understand and discharge the responsibilities of the elective franchise, but fixes an arbitrary status, depending solely upon his descent from an ancestry over which he had and has no control, and which is impossible of attainment by any exertion on his part. The test required is not a rule or condition to which all citizens similarly situated may conform. This, we understand from the decisions of the United States Supreme Court, is necessary to make it valid."

Dent and the three other signers of the Minority Report then proceeded to list other important grounds for their opposition, some of which were these:

> "It establishes a permanent, hereditary, governing class, which is undemocratic, unrepublican and un-American."
>
> It is not in keeping with the dignity of a progressive, just, and enlightened State...
>
> It is impractical of administration, owing to the impossibility of establishing, with any certainty, descent from remote ancestors. The field of speculation into which we are carried opens wide the doors of frauds and perjury.
>
> It is not necessary. The ballot can be secured to the honest and capable without resorting to this subterfuge.
>
> Out of respect for the opinion of thoughtful and fair minded men everywhere, we ought not to incorporate in our fundamental law this unwise and questionable scheme. It will retard the investment of capital, and check the flow of immigration to our State. Alabama should take no backward step.
>
> The adoption of a fair and honest suffrage plan would secure the sympathy and confidence of our fellow citizens in every section of the Union.

By accepting this novel device we are launching the ship of state upon uncharted seas. We had better pursue the course our fathers traveled…

We adhere firmly to the Jacksonian Democratic doctrine of equal rights to all, special privileges to none."

Two thousand copies of this Minority Report were ordered printed, and it became the center of convention debate. These were unusual positions for a conservative, "Bourbon" Democrat of 1901 to be taking. Hubert was in the company of well-known public figures of Alabama. The other three signers of the Minority Report were: Hubert's friend and ally, former governor William C. Oates; Frank S. White, later elected United States Senator from Alabama; and U. S. Congressman (and future World War I General) George P. Harrison. These committee members were joined in opposing the clause by delegates ex-Governor Thomas Goode Jones and Senator John Tyler Morgan. In their 1994 work, *Alabama, the History of a Deep South State*, historians Rogers, Ward, Atkins, and Flynt discussed this minority report:

"S[touten] H. Dent of Eufaula, a paragon of conservative but strongly held ethical principles, placed his name on it…The opponents favored a literate electorate and strict requirements to vote. Yet they strongly objected to the duplicity inherent in the effort to disfranchise the black man. They charged that despite the Fifteenth Amendment the majority report had deliberately erected a system that would operate unequally on whites and blacks…[The dissenters] were paternalistic and full of the white man's burden to help the inferior. Still, in 1901, these few voices pleading for requirements that bore equally on whites and blacks were in sharp contrast to men such as Tom Heflin who raged about the coming race war."[920]

Although Hubert was espousing a position at variance with the views of many Alabamians, his standing remained high; he and his allies were not criticized, but respected. The July 4, 1901 issue of the *Eufaula Times & News* discussed the actions of the on-going constitutional convention:

"The much talked of and long sought Suffrage Committee's report has at last been filed with the Convention. It did not come alone but was accompanied by a minority report. The report is full and concise and is evidence of much time and attention in working out a reform for the purity of the ballot in this state. The grandfather clause in the report is the only section that met with opposition to the committee, which will be fought out in the convention. The minority has given good reasons for opposing this section and have taken safe grounds in their exceptions, which will appeal to the conservative members of the convention. The minority report is supported by some of the brainiest and conservative men of the state who possess the courage and ability to stand up for what they think is right in this matter."

Historian Andrew B. Moore has written that, although the grandfather clause was opposed by "prominent men like ex-Governors Jones and Oates, F. S. White, [S.H.] Dent, George P. Harrison, and Senator Morgan,...the arguments of the giants availed nothing."[921] The Convention rejected the Minority Report by a resounding vote of 109 to 23. Hubert Dent later cast his vote against the entire suffrage article, but it was overwhelmingly adopted by the Convention.

An ancillary debate about the side issue of what constituted "honorable service" for eligibility under the grandfather clause prompted an interesting reminiscence by Hubert Dent about the character of the Confederate soldiers he had served with forty years earlier:

"MR DENT: ...I know something, Mr. President, of the sacrifices, the endurance and the courage of Confederate soldiers. I hope I will not be considered as egotistic in saying that I derive that knowledge not from hearsay, not from history, but from four years and three months actual service in the State of Alabama and in the Confederate service...Many a private in the ranks would compare favorably with many gentlemen in the convention as to their intelligence and ability. They understood the situation of the Confederacy, and however it may have been in other fields, and in other armies, I know that after the battle of Chickamauga where the southern general failed to secure the fruits of his victory, there were plenty of men in the Confederate service who recognized right then and there that we were engaging in a hopeless struggle. When they charged with an enthusiasm and courage that never was excelled on any battle field, I do not care when or where it was fought--while they stayed by their colors and fought after that time--it was without hope of success, and I tell you it required the highest sort of patriotism and the highest sort of courage to remain true, under the circumstances, and I honor them the more because they did remain true under those conditions and circumstances.

I want to state an incident that happened in my own command....When we crossed the Tennessee River, when Bragg fell back from Shelbyville, Tenn., and reached Chattanooga, I had a man in my command, a good soldier, a faithful soldier, always at his post and always ready for duty, who came to me and stated that he had received information that his wife and children has been plundered and robbed by Federal troops, and that they were suffering and on the point of starvation. He procured some money from me to send to his family. A day or two later he received a letter ...from his wife [which] explained the conditions and her surroundings, how she had been treated, and she appealed to him to come home and make some provision for her and the children. I was so interested in it myself that I made an application for a furlough for ten days, and did not send it through the regular channels, but went in person with the application to see if I could not procure a furlough for him. I did not succeed. When I came back and told him, I could see the effect which it had upon him. I think it was the very next morning we were ordered from Chattanooga down towards Bridgeport, to a little place called Taylor's store, to act with the brigade of General Patton Anderson. This man came to me and called me off and I had a long talk with him. I could see that he was disturbed and had something on his mind. He referred repeatedly to the condition of his family and how much he felt for them and how anxious he was, not knowing exactly how they had fared since he had received the letter. While we were talking he handed me back the amount which he had gotten from me a day or two before. Where he got the money I do not know. When we parted we had been talking a long time, and I told him that we had better get some rest as we had to move the next day. He grasped me by the hand and said, Captain, I will never forget you, you have been wonderfully kind to me. Next morning at roll call that man was gone. Now I tell you Gentlemen, you may look upon that at a desertion, technically it was, but who of us would have better stood the test?

      I want to tell you the further history of that man. I had to report him as a deserter. I made inquiry to find out what became of him and I was told that he went back and arranged about his family, saw them cared for and then afraid to come back to join his command, he joined John Rody's Cavalry and fought with that command through the remainder of the war. What would you do in a case like that? [922]

After discussion among the delegates about how that soldier would be treated under the grandfather clause, Hubert continued:

      "MR. DENT: I know of some other cases. At the battle of Missionary Ridge a large part of my command was captured. One, by some means or other, I never understood how, was exchanged and got back to his command just before the surrender. He told me of his treatment in prison at Camp Douglas, somewhere upon the lakes. He said he could not have suffered worse, to use his own language, if he had been in hell itself; that they tortured and punished prisoners to force them to enlist in the Union service, not to fight us, but the Indians. He told me that a member of my command had succumbed under that treatment and thinking it was a matter of life and death, to save his life he took the oath of allegiance, stipulating that he was not to come South but to fight against the Indians in the Northwest. What would you do in a case like that?[923]

After discussion, the delegates decided not to attempt to define further the term "honorable service."

   Hubert Dent's civic rectitude emerged in connection with another sensitive issue that came before the Convention. By 1901, the idea had become prevalent among some segments, that if a crime were heinous or violent enough, and if the assailant's identity were known, it was permissible to execute the presumed assailant without bothering with the delays of a legal trial, particularly if the presumed criminal were black. This sometimes occurred with the acquiescence of the county sheriff. The Convention had preliminarily approved a provision giving the governor authority to suspend county sheriffs, even before any charges were brought, if the governor felt that a sheriff had been derelict in his duty. A movement arose in the Convention to reconsider and delete this provision, based upon the argument, ironically, that such a summary suspension before a trial was unfair to sheriffs. Speaking forcefully in support of giving the governor this authority, Hubert candidly laid out the real issues behind this provision:

> "MR. DENT: ...[T]he trouble about mob law, fellow delegates, is that...it is growing. Mobs execute vengeance upon criminals, for different offenses. The newspapers are full of them, and the people understand that this spirit is growing. Surely something ought to be done to suppress that growing spirit of mob violence, and insubordination to law. Now the sheriff is the most important executive officer in a county, and the fact stands glaring to the delegates to this Convention that mobs and mob violence has not been suppressed in Alabama, and no sheriff or officer has ever been punished so far as it has come to my knowledge."[924]

Dent pointed out the protections available to accused sheriffs under the proposed provision, and then returned to the importance of suppressing mob action:

> "Let us look at what has happened in Alabama. It is common history. Didn't the Governor of Alabama telegraph a Sheriff of a county in this State to know the circumstances under which a prisoner was mobbed, and what was the reply? "It is none of your business." What could the governor do? What power had he? I am told upon authority which is to be relied upon that, in a county of the State, where the Governor was actually present, when a prisoner was in the custody of the Sheriff, and when there were threats to mob him, the Governor went to the Sheriff and told him he would tender him the services of the military to protect his prisoner, and he declined to ask for them. What could the governor do? And in that very instance the Governor took the responsibility of ordering the military to that point, and the sheriff and his friends and the friends of the mob were on their guard and were notified that the military would arrive, and the mob, led by the son of the Sheriff, went into the jail and executed the prisoner....I say that the Governor ought to have some power in this matter when he is charged with the duty of executing the law. I do not believe this goes too far...[T]here ought to be some expression of opinion by this Convention that will have a tendency to repress it."[925]

As the Convention worked throughout the spring and summer of 1901, the business and social life of Eufaula continued apace. Caroline Dent, the youngest of Hubert and Anna's three beautiful daughters, was now 22 years old. Usually called "Carrie," or "Bab," she was bright and talented. Carrie had graduated from the Union Female College with gold medals in most of her subjects, and she had studied voice in Washington, D. C. Back in Eufaula, Carrie was active in the affairs of Eufaula's young set. On April 25, it was reported that a dozen young women were enjoying "an indoor picnic," at the home of Captain and Mrs. D. B. McKenzie. Chaperoned by Mrs. Ed H. Roberts, it included Misses Caroline Dent, Katie

McDowell, Martha Graves, Caro Copeland, Lizzie Merrill, Ethel Bray, Annie Belle McKay, Stella Foy, and others. It was reported that, "They gathered together early this morning and have had fun untold. An immense box of fine candies bearing Dr. A. P. Brown's card and compliments was presented to them during the morning." Dr. Brown, a young dentist, may have addressed the candy to all the girls, but his real target was Katie McDowell, whom he later married. Also, Katie had a handsome older brother, a successful young lawyer in the community, Charles Samuel McDowell, Jr., who had his eyes on Carrie Dent. Charlie was an officer in the "Eufaula Rifles," which was still active as a local militia unit, and he presented a dashing appearance in his uniform and sword. Carrie seemed to return his interest, but she was pursued by many of the young men. In fact, the men of the "Rifles" elected Carrie the "sponsor" of the company.

The festivities of Eufaula's annual Confederate Memorial Day were reported by the *Times & News* of April 18, and May 9. The "Marshals" for the day included C. S. McDowell, Jr; Ed Young; Warren Dent (although he had lived in Montgomery since 1885); J. C. Cato; Henry Shorter, E. P. Long, L. Y. Dean, Jr., and others. The event was opened with "a few happy and fitting remarks" by George H. Dent, who, the year before, in 1900, had been elected to a two year term as Mayor of Eufaula. Mayor Dent introduced the orator for the occasion, Mr. Lee J. Clayton.

In August 1902, Alabama held its first statewide Democratic Primary. William D. Jelks, the owner-editor of the *Eufaula Times & News* and good friend of the Youngs and Dents, had been serving the unexpired term of deceased Gov. William Samford. Jelks now received the Democratic nomination and was thereafter elected governor in his own right.

In Montgomery, the proceedings of the constitutional convention were wearing to a close. The *Times & News* of August 22 reported that "Capt. S. H. Dent returned to Montgomery this morning. He stated to the *Times* reporter that the active work of the convention would perhaps end Wednesday when the convention would take a short recess preparatory to a real finish. This is good news. As all are patiently waiting for the document as a whole." The convention adopted a constitution and adjourned in early September; Gov. Jelks set the ratification election for November 11. Oscar W. Underwood led the State Democratic Campaign Committee supporting ratification, while the Barbour County Executive Committee held meetings and adopted resolutions supporting ratification. In the week of Oct. 10, convention delegates Hubert Dent and J. J. Winn, joined by Congressman Henry D. Clayton, Jr., made speeches in Eufaula in favor of ratification. On Oct 19, Hubert Dent and Alto V. Lee spoke in Clayton for ratification.

In the November election, the new constitution would receive statewide approval by a comfortable margin, but soon after Hubert's October speeches, he would suffer one of the major tragedies of his life.

63
The Closing of The Eufaula National Bank

"The losses have been occasioned by misfortune rather than mismanagement..."
U. S. Comptroller of the Currency

At seven minutes after noon on Monday, October 21, 1901, a short telegram was transmitted from the Eufaula National Bank to the Comptroller of the Currency in Washington bearing the simple message, "We are forced to suspend." With these words the financial institution founded by Edward Young a quarter century earlier came to an end. Within hours of this telegram, Mr. George R. DeSaussure of the Comptroller's Atlanta office had been ordered to go to Eufaula the same evening to take over the affairs and liquidation of the bank. When the news became public, the citizens of Eufaula, as well as businessmen across the state, were stunned. They had come to regard this conservative bank as a Rock of Gibraltar. What had happened to bring it to this end?

In an earlier chapter, through the Comptroller's Reports of Examination, we followed the successes of the bank under Hubert and Ed's leadership throughout the 1880's. The bank survived the panic of '93 and continued to succeed through the 1890's, until it was finally overtaken by economic events which affected the entire nation and particularly the rural South. We will take a detailed look at the circumstances leading to this calamity.

The 1890 examination report reflected deposits of $225,000, total assets at an all-time high of $411,000, and $4,000 in dividends paid, resulting in a return to the investors of 4% on their paid in capital. Examiner C. J. Campbell described the bank's loans as "a very clean portfolio of first class business paper," concluding that, "This bank has always been carefully and very successfully managed."

The 1891 report was down somewhat, reflecting deposits of $145,000, and total assets of $340,000, but a 4% dividend was paid and management was found to be "First class in every respect, and pay close attention to the business of the bank."

The bank's deposits in November 1892 were $150,000, its total assets were back up to $399,000, and it again paid a 4% dividend. Examiner Campbell found "loans well distributed and the bank has a good line of city and county paper well secured. Collateral loans are secured by notes and cotton—good margin."

Despite the economic depression resulting from the "panic of '93," which severely affected the farm economy, the 1893 report was similar: "Loans well distributed. All first class business paper. Only loan near limits is Eufaula Gas Co., $9446 with good endorsers." The banks management is "capable, prudent and good reputation. Management efficient and successful." The bank paid a dividend of 4%, plus the same salaries which had been set in the prosperous 1880's: Hubert, as president, $3000; Ed Young, as Vice President and Cashier, $3000; Ed Dent, assistant cashier, $1500, and M. S. Roberts (brother of Carrie's husband, Noah), as bookkeeper, $1200.

Deposits in May 1894 were $131,000, total assets were $342,000, and a new examiner, J. K. McDonald, found "General character of loans good. Securities consist of mortgages on crops and live stock, cotton, notes...considered good for loans against which held. Well distributed...Officers prudent and capable..."etc. However, in this year of depression following the panic of '93, the dividend was reduced to 3%, and most salaries were lowered: Hubert and Ed Young were reduced from $3000 to $2400, and Ed Dent was reduced from $1500 to $1200.

In 1895, the twenty-year charter granted to Edward Young and his co-incorporators in 1875 would expire. Accordingly, Ed Young on behalf of the bank filed a petition on September 23, 1895 to extend the bank's charter for another twenty years, until 1915. With this petition pending, a new examiner, Mr. William H. Burgwyn, conducted the 1895 examination. He found deposits of $189,000, total assets of $386,000, and a dividend paid of 3%. He analyzed the bank's loans as, "General character of loans and discounts very good. Current notes 8%. Accommodations well distributed. Collateral of good quality..." He agreed with earlier examiners that management is "capable, prudent, of good reputation, and their management has been efficient and successful." After reviewing statistics of the banks' performance since its inception, Mr. Burgwyn concluded, "I see no reason why the Bank's charter should not be extended, and respectfully recommend the same." Accordingly, the Comptroller extended the charter until November 27, 1915.

As the agricultural depression continued into 1896, the banks deposits were down to $80,000, and total assets were $341,000, but "General character of loans good," and "collateral of good quality." Examiner Burgwyn found, "This enterprise is active operation--credit good--business not so prosperous as in former years owing to price of goods [i.e. cotton]." Hubert took another cut in salary from $2400 to $2100, but left his brother-in-law Ed Young still drawing $2400, and the others also unchanged. A dividend of 3% was paid, which turned out to be the last dividend the bank would ever pay. But the examiner found that, "bank's condition is sound." In this year, Hubert and Ed began a separate business called the "Eufaula Savings Bank," which operated from the premises of the Eufaula National. This "Savings Bank" paid a small amount of interest to its depositors, unlike the Eufaula National, which paid no interest. The Savings Bank never attracted a large number of depositors.

The economy's failure to recover was beginning to take its toll. The January 1897 examination, while satisfactory, exposed clouds on the horizon. Deposits were $136,000, and total assets, $313,000. "General character of loans and discounts is good...well distributed...collateral of good quality." However, its reserves were found to be insufficient and the bank skipped its dividend for the first time since its founding by Edward Young in 1875. Examiner Burgwyn made these mixed findings: "Bank is considerable borrower by way of C/D and rediscounts, but its condition is sound and its business is prosperous. Management is conservative. It passed its January dividend out of abundant caution. Its loans, like all the banks doing this kind of business--advances to farmers--are mostly 8 and 9 month paper, maturing in October and November." In addition to skipping a dividend, Hubert accepted a third salary cut from $2100 to $1800, but still leaving Ed Young's salary at $2400 and the others unchanged. Also in this report we find a new employee: Ed Young's son, Edward Billups Young, Jr., now 19, is shown as a "collector," at $300 per year.

Cotton prices continued to fall and in 1898, fell from 12 ½ cents to 8 cents per pound, resulting in an increase in defaulting loans. In his 1898 examination, Mr. Burgwyn began finding significant problems with the bank, which he summarized as follows:

> "Condition of bank sound, but not satisfactory. Bank is a large borrower both by way of rediscount and bills payable and by issue of certificates of deposit for $15,000…These amounts, with the $10,000 due the First Nat'l Bank of Anniston, Ala., make an aggregate of $77,615. Its past due paper is large and much of its active paper is made so by renewal. Bank is a frequent borrower and it would appear that, but for this ability to borrow, it would be greatly embarrassed. It is impossible to tell what losses there may be in those loans with real estate at the back of them, that is loans on mortgage notes…There also may be losses in the stocks and securities account, in the Martin and Fondon claims, but until the sale of the assets (accounts, stock, notes) this loss cannot be estimated."

The bank's basic problem was beginning to show. Falling cotton prices and a depressed economy not only resulted in more defaulting loans, but also reduced the values of assets taken as security for loans (such as cropland, merchandise, shares of stock). The bank could not convert these assets into enough cash to satisfy the underlying defaulting loans, thereby causing the bank to be short of cash. This made it necessessary for the bank to borrow money to meet depositors' demands and other obligations. This situation could not continue indefinitely. Needless to say, the bank paid no dividend in 1898.

The July 1899 report was conducted by a new examiner, W. R. Henry, who found multiple serious problems, and who was far less gentlemanly than Mr. Burgwyn in his assessment of management. Mr. Henry found, "General character of loans and discounts, not good. Accommodations not well distributed." He found "Paper in bad condition, unsecured except so far as land notes are secured by land which is still held by bank." He identified a lengthy list of assets, past due loans, and bad loans which would result in probable losses to the bank of $27,000. He criticized some bank administrative practices. He pointed out that the bank was not declaring a dividend because "losses too heavy." He concluded, "Bank in poor condition," but then conceded, "Business fairly good." Not content to point out deficiencies, Mr. Henry felt it appropriate to criticize the competence of the officers: "Officers of limited ability—good reputation—and the condition of the bank shows a want of proper caution…"

Because of the Bank's developing difficulties, Mr. Henry conducted another examination in May 1900. He cited essentially the same deficiencies he mentioned in 1899, again identifying $27,000 in loans and assets which should be written off as losses. He again criticized the competence of the officers, (although he is sometimes inconsistent in his comments): "Officers capable and of good reputation. Such a mass of old paper and heavy losses, that I cannot say that officers are either prudent or management successful." "This bank is in bad condition, and its business is small. Directors do not give it the attention they should. Estimates of values of land…are taken from President and Cashier of the bank. They state that they fear no losses on these items, but Examiner is of the opinion that they will [have] some loss and the Directors could not better employ their time, than by giving them a thorough examination…The President and Cashier concede a loss of $15,000 on the paper, past due and old debts renewed. This bank shows no improvement in any respect since Office Letter of August 5th, 1899."

In light of the deteriorating condition of the bank, Mr. Henry's harsh comments about management's competence, prudence, and attention are understandable. However, we will see that a more comprehensive and thoughtful analysis by one of his colleagues later took an entirely different view of the causes of the banks' difficulties.

The death knell of the bank was sounded in July 1902, although it was able to keep its doors open for three more months until October. In the summer, U. S. Comptroller of the Currency Charles G. Dawes[ss] ordered a special examination of the bank, which was rendered by Examiner W. A. Mason on July 16, 1902. Mr. Mason devalued or disallowed a lengthy list of assets totaling $65,000, and recommended that the stockholders be assessed that amount to make up the deficiency. Mr. Mason doubted (correctly) that they would be able to raise the additional capital, and foresaw the bank's liquidation, but nevertheless recommended that the bank be allowed until the fall, when crops were in, before taking further action. Mr. Mason's report to the Comptroller provided a thorough and thoughtful analysis of the reasons why the bank was in a failing condition. The report also incidentally provides interesting insight into the workings of the cotton economy in rural Alabama 35 years after the Civil War.

"Eufaula, Ala
July 16, 1901

"Hon. Charles G. Dawes
Comptroller of the Currency
Washington, D. C.

"Dear Sir:
After a careful examination into the condition of this Bank I am of the opinion that the capital stock is impaired to the extent of $63,665.21. The losses have been occasioned by misfortune rather than mismanagement, and I am further convinced – notwithstanding irregularities in cash items, there has been no criminal malfeasance on the part of the management. An assessment of 65% on the authorized capital of $100,000 will be necessary to restore the capital of this Institution…

[ss] Future World War I General and Vice President under Calvin Coolidge.

<u>Effect of such an Assessment:</u>

Knowing local conditions as I do I cannot but think the effect of the necessary 65% assessment will be to eventually place this Institution in liquidation. As explained elsewhere, this particular field in Alabama is not a promising one for banking at the best. The little business done in Eufaula is divided among three Banks. Local bank stock, under these conditions, does not appeal to one as a good investment. ...[T]he entire holdings of stock in this Bank is confined to the Dent family and their immediate relatives. Young, Roberts, Fields and Brunson are related either directly or indirectly to Dent. All are endowed with an abundant characteristic Southern honor and pride, but with only a war remnant of what was once vast fortunes and estates. I surmise they will exercise their every energy to save the Bank, and I am equally certain they have not the means, and I doubt if they can command the necessary money to restore its capital...

Whatever may, on the part of the Comptroller, be required of this Institution I am of the opinion they are entitled to some consideration in the manner and time of paying any assessment that may be imposed upon them. As is generally understood the money market is exceedingly close in the South at this period of the year. The medium of circulation is set loose by the Fall marketing of the cotton crop, and notwithstanding their willingness and other manifestations of good intent, the stockholders have not and positively cannot obtain the necessary money to pay such assessments before the Fall marking of cotton begins...

<u>Status of Bank:</u>

As may be inferred from the list of stockholders, this Institution is and has been since its inception a family affair. It is a one man's Bank run by two men. President Dent and Cashier Young assume unquestioned the entire responsibility. The Board of Directors is farcical and scheduled on paper only to meet the requirements of the law. Both Dent and Young are, I believe, honorable Gentlemen, and have no intent or disposition to take advantage of the relatives who are...the immediate stockholders of this Bank. That their management has not been successful can be attributed to misfortune rather than loose methods or mismanagement. When the bottom dropped out of the Eufaula boom a few years ago, the bottom of this bank almost dropped out with it. Again, the heavy slump in the price of cotton in the Fall of 1898 from 12 ½ to 8 cents, brought additional hardships and losses throughout this whole section of the country. These reverses were unforeseen and came unforetold, and cannot, with any degree of fairness, be charged to the management. These misfortunes, however, were no less disastrous, and to them can be charged the responsibility for all losses and also the possession of so large a line of unproductive assets. Real estate has constantly been acquired as the only alternative to protect the interest of the Bank in debts previously contracted, and when such real estate once acquired it has been almost impossible to dispose of it....

The future of this Bank, with its capital restored, does not appear promising. The field is crowded. Eufaula has three banks whereas one would suffice and two would be a plenty. Messrs. Young and Dent are wideawake, progressive, and no doubt get their share of the patronage, but business is simply not at hand to support three Banks in a prosperous manner…

The management recognized and admit the serious of this condition of affairs, and explained to me they contemplate either absorbing or selling to one of the other Banking Institutions….

Overdrafts:

Overdrafts appear to be epidemic in the South and this Bank is no exception. Throughout Alabama at this time of the year and up to the time of marketing the cotton crop, usually in September, money is very scarce and planters, as well as merchants, avail themselves of the privilege of overdrawing. The overdrafts found with this Bank are in most part good, providing there is a good cotton crop, and it appears to me the practice is particularly hazardous under these circumstances….

Loans and Discounts:

The character of loans and discounts in this Bank is far from good. It must be admitted, of course, that conditions in the South are different, and Banking especially in this section of Alabama is far short of the standard of Northern Institutions, and I might add fully 90% of the loans in this Bank would be considered doubtful and bad debts in a Northern Bank. For example, a plantation Negro possessing 10 acres of clay knobs, a mule and energy enough to buy or steal his cotton seed, is expected to grow 3 bale of cotton, therefore he is entitled to a loan of $60 or $75, which he gets and must have to feed [himself] and his family from one crop to another. The security given is a crop lien note. The 3 bale of cotton is considered far more valuable than the land, and if the crop fails the Bank waits until next season, puts in a little more money and takes a new lien. The colored denizen pays from 15 to 40% [of the debt due] and the Bank carries the rest.

The immediate prospects are that the cotton crop this year in Barbour and adjoining Counties will be short, and conditions financially not likely to be much improved.

Another class of paper found in this Bank, and equally or more hazardous than the other, is direct loans to cotton buyers and speculators. They are, as a rule, irresponsible and at the earliest indication of loss usually succeed in shouldering the loss onto the Bank. The greater part of the losses in this Bank have come from such business and there seems to be but little help for it, for it must be said out of justice to the management it is the principal business that comes to the Banks of Eufaula….

Real Estate:

The real estate holdings of the bank are not desirable property, but rather comprise plantations and residence properties acquired as the only alternative for debts previously contracted. Their values cannot be determined by any standard of demand or sales of like property because there is no demand and like properties are not selling. This condition can be better understood in conjunction with the history of the City of Eufaula. Eighteen years ago this little city was a trade center that supplied planters throughout the whole of Southern Alabama and Western Georgia. Real estate brought fancy prices and was in good demand. The reaction set in when the newly built Georgia Central Railway cut off the entire country, 60 miles to the North, and another line soon following had the same effect 40 miles to the South of Eufaula. The boom over, the reaction has become worse and worse each year. Great brick storerooms that formerly rented for $200 per month now bring but $5.00 and many in the heart of the town are empty and boarded up and used for Negro quarters and storage of cotton.

Much of this bank's real estate was acquired as far back as 1895, and these conditions explain why it was never disposed of and under these conditions this real estate not a good asset...."

During the latter part of the summer of 1901, while Hubert was attending sessions of the Constitutional Convention in Montgomery, he and Ed were undoubtedly also searching for a solution to the bank's problems. As they had indicated to Examiner Mason, their goal was probably to negotiate a merger or sale of the bank to another Eufaula bank. These efforts were obviously unfruitful. Eufaula National opened as usual on Monday, October 21. Apparently it was a busy morning, with a number of depositors making withdrawals. By noon, the bank was out of cash with which to meet requests for withdrawals, and it was forced to close its doors, resulting in the telegram to the Comptroller's Office notifying him of the suspension of business. Eufaulians learned of the news from the *Eufaula Times* of Monday afternoon, and the story was reprinted in the weekly *Times & News* of October 24:

"One of the greatest shocks that has struck the business world of our little city was that the Eufaula National Bank had closed its doors. The only reason assigned was `that there was an unaccountable run made on the bank this morning and it had to close up business.'

The closing up of the bank caused much distress to the businessmen who were seemingly paralyzed at the above announcement, as it was considered one of the stable institution of the state....

There was a great amount of funds tied up in real estate and outstanding loans. The collections have been slow is one of the probable causes for the scarcity of cash. Many persons who are not able now to have their money tied up in the bank will make it possible to have a little tightening of the lines in business circles. The citizens all feel sorry that this dire calamity should come at this time, but do not censure the officials of the bank, but rather sympathize with them. The Eufaula National is one of the oldest banking institutions in the city and the utmost confidence was placed in the men who had control of it and it is considered a calamity that has fallen on the city.

A statement as to the condition has not been given and who will look after the business has not been made known as the bank examiner has not been here.

There is everything to hope for, that it will pay out in the regular course, but time will have to intervene before the business can be satisfactorily arranged. The people were standing about in little knots discussing their losses in a rational manner and taking their tie up in a rational way though it struck many a hard blow."

By the next day, Tuesday, the 22nd, control of the bank's affairs had been taken over by National Banking Examiner George R. DeSaussure, as reported by the *Times and News* of the 24th:

"Bank examiner G. R. DeSaussure of Atlanta, examiner for state of Georgia came last night and is today in consultation with the Eufaula National Bank officials. Nothing has been given out as to what he will do in the case. The government is expected to wind up the business of the concern in most expeditious manner and looking to the interests of all concerned. Perhaps the government may turn the whole affair over to a receiver to close up the business as it will require time to make the collections and dispose of the real estate."

Adding to the embarrassment which Hubert Dent must have felt during this ordeal was a dispute that arose with his old friend, one-time law partner, and political ally, former Gov. William C. Oates. Some years before, Oates had delivered approximately $40,000 of bonds to the bank, which now became a subject of controversy. The bank had credited him with the deposit and then treated the bonds as any other deposit, liquidating them and using the proceeds for general bank purposes. Gov. Oates contended that he authorized the liquidation of some of the bonds, but not others. These circumstances were painful to both men. Not only had Oates and Dent practiced law together in the 1870's, but only two years before the bank closed, Hubert's son, Hugh, had also practiced law with Gov. Oates in Montgomery. Further, Hubert had been working throughout the summer with Oates in the constitutional convention, in their efforts to defeat the proposed "grandfather clause." Gov. Oates' loss immediately gained media attention. His discomfort and mixed feelings over the circumstances are apparent in a *Times & News* interview on the 31st:

"Ex-Governor William Oates came in Friday night to look after his financial interests. It has been rumored and was published in the Montgomery paper that Mr. Oates has $50,000 in Alabama bonds in the bank here.

In a talk with this reporter, the ex-Governor was asked if the report was true and he intimated that it was, although he did not say so plainly. He seemed much broken up, and looked very blue over the affair.

When asked by a citizen about the new constitution, he said he took no sides; he neither endorsed it nor opposed it; it made no difference to him whether it was voted up or down. He did not intend to speak for it or against it...Mr. Oates left for Montgomery Saturday morning."

In another article in the same issue, Gov. Oates was quoted by the *Montgomery Advertiser* to this effect:

"I calculate my loss at something over $40,000.
"Nine of the bonds I consented for them to use in 1893 when the bank was threatened with trouble but the use of none of the others was authorized except to collect the coupons and to put them up to my credit, which was done as far as I know."

Evidence that Oates' losses arising from the bank failure did not diminish his friendship and respect for Hubert Dent is found in Oates' war memoirs. Published in 1905, four years after the bank closed, Oates described the actions of the Fifteenth Alabama Infantry Regiment, which he commanded, on September 20, 1863, at Chickamauga. Describing the Confederates' break through the Federal line on the second day, Col. Oates recalled:

"And just here I want to mention that one of our batteries which kept just off on our right and did such splendid firing, as many of the Fifteenth Alabama men will remember, was the battery of that superb soldier from Eufaula, Ala., Capt S. H. Dent, but we did not know what battery it was until after the close of the battle."[926]

The *Times & News* of October 31 continues to indicate that, although Eufaulians were concerned and upset, they did not blame Hubert Dent and Ed Young for what had happened to the bank:

"...[b]oth Gentlemen have the best of reputations and are well and favorably known over the state. The citizens here sympathize with them in the failure and know that it was not caused by any lack of interest or improper management..."

Some Eufaulians were able to see a light side to the difficult situation. The *Times & News* reported:

"Money in the Bank?"
"A man went into a store this morning and wanted a suit of clothes and said he would pay for them when he got his money out of the Eufaula National. It transpired that he had no money there, never had, nor did he ever have a cent in any bank. He did not get the clothes.
"There are more people about town who claim to have money in the bank than were ever known in Eufaula. Ask a man for that little bill he owes

594

and he says, 'Oh, I can't pay, money is all in the bank. Can't pay until the bank settles up.' In some instances this is true, but as a rule it is a joke and intended for a joke. Of course, the boys must have their fun, no difference who pays the freight."

New York lawyers were in Eufaula and Montgomery on behalf of creditor New York banks. Although the Special Examination into the affairs of the bank had unequivocally concluded that "the losses have been occasioned by misfortune rather than mismanagement," and that "there has been no criminal malfeasance on the part of the management," newspaper reports indicated that United States Attorney Warren S. Reese, Jr. in Montgomery was nevertheless conducting a Grand Jury investigation into the bank's affairs. He brought Examiner George DeSaussure and others to Montgomery to testify before the Grand Jury. The federal district judge at this time was former Gov. Thomas G. Jones, who, although a Democrat, had been appointed to the bench by President Theodore Roosevelt. Judge Jones cautioned the jurymen and court officials to carefully protect the confidentiality of the grand jury proceedings. Finally, on December 5, 1901, the Grand Jury rendered an indictment against Ed Young. Although the indictment consisted of 97 pages and 46 counts, most of this bulk related to several cash items of $2000-$4000 repetitiously alleged, as well as a number of charges relating to former Gov. Oates' account with the bank. Bail bond in the amount of $7500 was posted on Ed's behalf by his brothers-in-law, Eufaula Mayor George H. Dent and W. F. Jennings.

Ed and the family would have to endure over two years of waiting before the case was disposed of. The length and prolixity of the indictment indicates that, in drafting his indictment against Ed, U. S. Attorney Warren Reese had had difficulty in alleging facts (1) which he could prove, and (2) which also constituted a criminal offense. This is not surprising in light of the Comptroller's earlier finding that there was no criminal misconduct. Reese's difficulty was not lost on Ed's defense counsel. Ed was represented by Harmon, Dent, and Weil, (the Montgomery law firm of his nephew, Hugh Dent) and by A. A. Wiley, (later elected to Congress). These lawyers made a series of well-founded attacks on the legal sufficiency of indictment. When required by the court to elect which counts it was proceeding on, the government selected its best 12 counts and dismissed the other 34 counts. These remaining 12 counts charged Ed, as cashier or teller of the bank, with making "false entries," when he made book entries of "cash items," or checks received by the bank, which, according to the complaint, he knew had no value. The problem with these charges was that, even though Ed may have indeed entered check deposits based on checks which had no value, this was not criminal conduct; he was *required* by statute to make the entries. Judge Jones, following clear precedent, rejected the government's position, holding that, if the bank had in fact received the checks "in any actual transaction with the cashier," then the statute commands him to report it, whether the check turns out to have value or not, and regardless of whether he knew its value. Judge Jones held quite logically that, "Obedience to that command, truly making the entry,…cannot make him a transgressor against this provision."[927] With this ruling on February 18, 1904, the last charge was thrown out, and Warren Reese's case for the government fell apart.

These difficult circumstances undoubtedly took their toll on the entire family, but on none more than Hubert's wife, Anna. While awaiting her brother's trial, her frail health failed. She was taken to a Montgomery hospital for treatment, but the following day, February 27, 1902, Anna Beall Young Dent died in Montgomery at the age of 62.[928]

The *Times & News* of March 6, 1902 carried this report:

"In Memoriam

Mrs. Anna Beall Dent, a short notice of whose death at Montgomery appeared in yesterday's *Times*, was the eldest daughter of Edward B. Young and Ann Fendall Beall, who married … and moved to Eufaula some 65 years ago.

Mrs. Dent was born in Eufaula in June 1840 and spent practically all of her lifetime here. She was married June 5, 1860 to Capt. S. H. Dent. He and the six children of their marriage viz: Mr. Edward Y. Dent, Mrs. Nannie Dent Long, S. H. Dent, Jr., Esquire, Lt. Henry A. Dent, Mrs. Louise Hurt, and Miss Caroline Dent all survive her. Such is the brief outline of the life of this sainted woman; but to adequately record her virtues and good works would fill volumes. In all the relations of life, as wife, mother, sister, friend, she was devoted through a Generous spirit. A beauty of person and grace of manner fittingly bespoke the brightness of mind and sweetness of spirit. In the home where she so long reigned a gentle mistress, she will be missed as only such a wife and mother can be. From the wider circles of life, her death removes a member whose fidelity and usefulness will be held in an affectionate and lasting remembrance.

Mrs. Dent was a devout Christian. For many years she was a serious and active member of the Methodist Church. She exemplified its doctrines in her life and character, and gave freely of her labor and means to the promotion of its work and program. She was a conspicuous personage in the line of godly women, whose devotions and sacrifices have ever been the tenderest yet the strongest proof of the divine atonement.

The bereaved family received from the entire community a sympathy as deep and sincere as their appreciation of the excellence of her who is departed; while the writer finds a melancholy pleasure in recording this deficient tribute to her worth."

Another article, quoted from the daily edition, reported:

"The funeral of Mrs. Anna Beall Dent took place yesterday morning at 11:00 from the Methodist Church. The church was crowded to its utmost. The funeral was preached by Dr. Peterson, which was very touching and sympathetic. Dr. Mangum in conclusion paid a loving tribute to Mrs. Dent. The casket was almost covered with the most beautiful and rare flowers. The sweetest and most appropriate music for such an occasion was rendered by the choir. A large procession followed the remains to the cemetery to see the noble and Christian woman laid to rest."

The *Times & News* of March 13, 1902 carried an article and resolution in memory of Anna Beall Dent by her colleagues in the United Daughters of the Confederacy: "We have lost a friend whose noble qualities won the love and respect of each member of the Barbour County UDC as well as everyone who came within the influence of her sweet presence."

Ed Young's exoneration was not the end of the family's ordeal. The Bank's receiver (represented by attorney George L. Comer, whom Hubert had defeated the previous year for Barbour County Delegate to the constitutional convention) began to assert claims against Hubert for Hubert's pro rata share of the assessment against the bank's stockholders, for notes owed the bank, and for claims by the depositors of the "Savings Bank", and it became necessary for Hubert to declare personal bankruptcy. The filing of a voluntary bankruptcy petition on Hubert's behalf in federal court in Montgomery was reported in the *Times & News* of May 29, 1902. He was represented in the matter by his son, Hugh, and Hugh's firm of Harmon, Dent and Weil. The petition reflected assets of $33,992, and liabilities of $62,631. Henry R. Shorter was appointed the receiver to take over and liquidate Hubert's property. Shorter published notice on October 30 of a public auction for the sale of a long list of Hubert's farm lands and city properties. Fortunately, Fendall Hall itself was never at risk; upon Edward B. Young's death in 1879, it had been acquired by Anna in her name, and upon her death her estate had been bequeathed to her children.

Hubert did have extensive farmlands that went under the auctioneer's hammer. However, his children, who had some financial means, banded together and, acting through Ed Dent, bid in at auction several thousand acres of their father's former lands. These lands they returned to Hubert, and as a 69 year old cotton planter, he began to rebuild his fortunes. Portions of these Barbour County lands (the "Driggers Place" and the "Bush Place") are still owned by his great-grandchildren.

Ed Young took a position on Gov. Jelks' staff in Montgomery immediately after the bank's closure, and later was employed with Protective Life Insurance Co.,[929] the business founded by Gov. Jelks after the end of his term as governor (a company which still flourishes today.) Ed died in 1910 at the age of 61.

Hubert's son, Ed Dent, who had borne principal responsibility for operating the insurance business of "E. B. Young & Co.," continued to operate that insurance business on his own behalf after the bank's closure.[930] Ed Dent later renamed the agency the E. Y. Dent Insurance Co., expanded and improved its business, and enjoyed a successful career in insurance throughout his long life. He was appointed as State Superintendent of Insurance during the administration of Gov. William Brandon, 1922-1926. He died in 1946 at the age of 85.

There was at least one very bright spot for the Dent family in this otherwise sad year of 1902: the marriage of Anna and Hubert's youngest daughter, Caroline, to the personable young lawyer, Charles S. McDowell, Jr. The last of the six Dent children to be married (except for Henry, who didn't marry until middle age), Carrie's wedding on October 15 came only seven months after the funeral of her mother. In a later chapter, we will come to know Carrie Dent and Charlie McDowell better.

Earlier in the year, George H. Dent had been elected president of the school board. The *Times & News* of March 13 also carried a light-hearted account of a football game on College Hill in which the senior and junior girls of Union Female College opposed the freshman and sophomore girls. The senior-junior team, of which Miss Flora Young (Ed Young's daughter) was captain and quarterback, won 15 to 5. The sophomore-freshman team included Flora's sister, Miss Ada Young, at right tackle; Miss Jenny Kendall, at left guard, and others.

The annual Memorial Day exercises of 1903 were reported on April 17, and included a recital by Mrs. Hamilton M. Weedon, Jr. of *"The Battle of Chickamauga"*, an original poem by her father-in-law, Dr. Hamilton Weedon, Sr. A military salute was fired over the grave of Mrs. Roxana Wellborn, the originator and first president of the Memorial Association in Eufaula. The list of marshals for the day included Ed Young, George Dent, Sr., C. S. McDowell, J. D. Clayton, Lee Irby, Will Foy, and others.

From the 1880's onward, communities throughout the South had been building monuments honoring the Confederate war dead. Virtually every southern town installed a Confederate monument on its town square or in a central place of honor. By 1904, the Barbour County Chapter of the UDC had raised the necessary funds to construct a monument in Eufaula. It was dedicated on Thanksgiving Day, 1904, amid a celebration of parades, floats, and oratory. As the band played "The Bonnie Blue Flag'" the procession of honorees, led by the sons of veterans, made its way west from the Courthouse to the monument. Mayor George H. Dent and the city council rode in a fine carriage, behind which followed citizens and schoolchildren. After prayers, Captain Stouten Hubert Dent called the roll of the old Confederate veterans standing around the base of the monument, who answered to their names. While "Dixie" was played, the sculpture was unveiled: a base and shaft 35 feet high made of Georgia marble, and a soldier carved of Italian marble, facing east toward "new horizons." [931]

The Alabama Legislature in its 1892-1893 session had created the Alabama Girls' Technical Institute at Montevallo, Alabama, "for the education of white girls in Alabama."[932] In 1911, Hubert Dent was appointed as the trustee of that school from the third congressional district. Hubert enthusiastically served the board until his death in 1917 six years later. He was said to have never missed a regular meeting of the trustees, and only one special meeting. The resolution adopted by his fellow trustees upon his death lauded his "great mental acumen, wise judgment, and keen interest in education."[933] The name of the institution was later changed to "Montevallo College."

Capt. S. Hubert Dent at one of his gun positions during a visit to the Chickamauga Battlefield Park. Circa 1914

64
Another "Captain Dent"

"We steamed into [San Francisco] Bay on the morning of May 6 [1909]...The Secretary of the Navy reviewed the combined Fleets, which was the greatest gathering of war ships ever assembled under the American flag..."

Journal of Capt. Henry A. Dent, USN

Anna and Hubert's third and youngest son, Henry, did not plan on a naval career; it just happened. Born August 4, 1872 and named for his mother's brother who died at Chunkey Bridge, Mississippi during the Civil War, Henry Augustus Dent attended Southern University at Greensboro, Alabama, like his two older brothers, Ed and Hugh. He graduated in 1890 with a degree in engineering. He thereafter did graduate work in engineering at Rose Polytechnic Institute in Terra Haute, Indiana, and at Vanderbilt University. However, due to the "panic of 1893," which became an economic depression enduring through the 1890's, engineering positions were difficult to find.[934] At this time, Henry's uncle, James H. G. Martin (Ada Young's husband) was practicing law in Washington with the firm of "Shelly and Martin." As a former active leader of the Alabama Democratic party, Jim Martin was influential with the administration of Democrat President Cleveland. With Martin's assistance and that of Alabama's Sen. James L. Pugh, a Eufaula native and old friend of Hubert Dent,[935] President Cleveland on March 15, 1894 appointed Henry as a commissioned officer of the U. S. Navy Paymaster Corps. Henry would enjoy a successful and satisfying naval career for the next twenty five years, during which he would sail throughout the globe and attain the rank of captain (the equivalent of an army full colonel).

In 1895, only a few months after Henry Dent was commissioned, Cuban rebels began an insurrection against the Spanish rule of that island. Exaggerated accounts of Spanish brutalities by William Randolph Hearst's "yellow press" fueled American sympathy for the Cuban rebels and led to tension with Spain. The *Maine*, an American battleship, was ordered to Havana on an ostensibly "friendly" visit, but actually to protect American property and citizens. When the ship was blown up, the assumption was widespread (but probably incorrect) that the Spanish had perpetrated the act. Despite Spain's effort to yield virtually all the concessions demanded by the United States, short of Cuban independence, President McKinley asked Congress for a declaration of war, which Congress enacted on April 18, 1898.

When the war began, Henry was assigned to the *USS Marblehead*, one of a class of ships known as "protected cruisers." Although Henry was a staff officer rather than a "line officer," his assignment to the *Marblehead* resulted in his seeing extensive heavy action against the Spanish, including an engagement viewed by some as "one of the most remarkable events of the Spanish American War:"[936] the cutting of the cables at Cienfuegos.[937]

The *Marblehead* served with the North Atlantic Squadron, and when war was declared, Rear Admiral Sampson at Key West was ordered to blockade a stretch of Cuba on its northeastern coast from Cardenas to Bahia Honda. The *Marblehead*, commanded by

Captain McCalla, was put in charge of attacking Spanish boats in that sector. After the Cuban northern coast came under the control of the U. S. Navy, Admiral Sampson decided to expand the blockade to include Cuba's south coast, and accordingly, the *Marblehead* was ordered to Cienfuegos, a coastal town in the center of the island's southern coast. Enroute, on April 29 the *Marblehead* and two sister ships encountered the Spanish supply ship, *Argonauta*, heading for Cienfuegos with supplies, rifles, ammunition, and army units. The *Marblehead* and the others fought three Spanish gunboats seeking to protect the supply ship, but *Argonauta* was taken, and its army units made prisoners.

The cruiser, *USS Marblehead*, aboard which young Henry Dent served, 1898

On May 11, 1898, near the lighthouse at the entrance of Cienfuegos Harbor, the *Marblehead* located the underwater telegraph cables that were used by the Spanish for communication among Cienfuegos, Havana, and Spain. The young Paymaster Henry Dent was about to observe one of the most exciting and dangerous engagements of the war. Captain McCalla decided to cripple the Spanish communications by cutting the cables. He called for volunteers from the *Marblehead* and the *Nashville* to form a party to raise the cables with grappling hooks and sever them. The attack group was conveyed by sailing launches which were towed by a steam launch to a point near the cable house. The steam launch then took up a position 150 yards offshore to provide covering fire. About 75 yards from shore the grappling hooks were dropped. As they approached closer to shore however, the open boats were swept by a withering attack from Spanish troops hidden in gullies and ravines around the cable house. A hail of bullets showered death and injury on the attacking Americans. The *Marblehead's* guns bombarded the batteries lining the onshore rifle pits, where the Spanish were firing Mauser rifles directly into the Americans. The fury of the firefight totally destroyed the nearby lighthouse. But the attacking Americans "coolly" went about their business. One of the volunteers described the action:

> "The lifting of the cable was a very perilous and laborious task but the cutting crew went about their job coolly. Bullets were piercing the boat and the water was coming in. But coolly as ever we put a bullet in the hole and it helped keep the water out. Large shells dropped around us nearly lifting us out of the water. Shells from our own ship and the Spanish batteries passed overhead."[938]

The two main cables were successfully cut, but the intensity of the enemy fire forced the Americans to abandon an attempt to cut a smaller cable. Of the men in the attack party, 49 were later awarded the Congressional Medal of Honor, more than in any other single engagement in the Spanish War.[939]

601

After the action at Cienfuegos, the *Marblehead* was ordered to patrol off of Santiago, in whose harbor the main Spanish fleet under Admiral Cervera was now holed up. Because the blockade of Santiago was expected to be lengthy, in early June the *Marblehead* and two sister ships were sent down the coast several miles to the east to capture the excellent anchorage in Guantanamo Bay in order to secure a safe base for supplying and repairing American ships. On June 7, following a fierce fight with the Spanish ship *Sandoval*, the *Marblehead* and her accompanying ships swept away the Spanish mines, cut the underwater telegraph cables, and captured the lower part of Guantanamo Bay. On June 10, the *Marblehead* supported the landing of a battalion of United States Marines assigned to occupy the remainder of Guantanamo Bay. The marines met some resistance from the Spanish ship, *Sandoval* and a small detachment of Spanish troops. Six days later, the *Marblehead* and another ship bombarded the Spanish fort at Guantanamo and "reduced it to impotence in fifteen minutes." By June 25, the *Sandoval's* commander, being cornered, scuttled his own ship. The naval base acquired at Guantanamo Bay through the efforts of the *Marblehead* and the marines remains in American hands to this day. For the several engagements in which the *Marblehead* was involved during the war, young Henry Dent received the West Indian Campaign Medal, with a bar for each engagement.[940]

Meanwhile, during June 1898, the American Army under Gen. Shafter landed near Santiago, and under pressure from that army's operations, Admiral Cervera decided to take his fleet out and make a run for it. On July 3, the Spanish fleet steamed at full speed out of Santiago harbor, turning west in a daring effort to escape the blockading American ships. But they were no match for the Americans, who chased and picked them off one by one, destroying or beaching every Spanish vessel, with only one American death.

With its capture of the Philippines from Spain during this war, the United States had become a colonial power, and over the next decade, Henry Dent saw the American Navy expand rapidly. By 1907, American naval strength had become second only to Great Britain among the world powers. In that year, President Theodore Roosevelt decided to display American naval power by sending its Atlantic Fleet on an extended cruise to show the flag in major world ports. This turned into a cruise around the world, but the decision to circle the globe had not yet been finally announced when the cruise began, and came about incrementally. The Atlantic Fleet consisted of sixteen new battleships manned by 14,000 men and officers. All the ships were newly painted a gleaming white, except for gilded scrollwork on their bows, and it later came to be known as "The Great White Fleet."

Henry Dent, now 35 years old, had by now advanced in rank to the point that he was appointed Fleet Paymaster on the staff of Admiral Evans, the Fleet commander. As Fleet Paymaster, he accompanied the Great White Fleet on its flagship during the first phase of its famous cruise, from Hampton Roads, Virginia, down the west coast of South America, around the Horn of South America, (the Panama Canal, though under construction, had not been completed), and up the west coast to San Francisco. On this cruise, Paymaster Henry Dent bore principal responsibility for handling the necessary funds and disbursing periodic pay to the 14,000 sailors and officers of the fleet.

On December 16, 1907, the day of the Fleet's departure from Hampton Roads, President Roosevelt was aboard his yacht, the *Mayflower,* anchored at the "Tail of the Horseshoe" in lower Chesapeake Bay, and at 11:15 A. M., as the Fleet passed in review, each fired a 21 gun salute to the President.

Henry Dent kept a journal in a leather-bound notebook, where he recorded some of his experiences and observations during the cruise, which we will refer to as we follow his course:

"...The day set for departure from Hampton Roads, December 16, 1907, was an almost perfect day, - clear and cool. The President arrived on the Mayflower a little after 8:00. The Admirals and Captains went to pay their respects and say good-bye. The Admiral [Evans] asked the President what message he could give the Fleet as to our movements after we reached the Pacific coast. He said you can tell them that it is the present intention to have the Fleet return to the Atlantic coast by way of the Suez Canal. This was not said in the presence of witnesses, so of course, it can be changed. However it is probably the intention unless events happen to make a change desirable or necessary.

Led by the *Mayflower* the Fleet started the long cruise, following the *Mayflower* in columns. It made a very pretty sight."

Writing on February 18, 1908:

"The trip to Port-of-Spain was made without special incidents...One death occurred in the Fleet during the trip.... [During] the celebration of crossing the "line"...Neptune had many victims as there were few on board who had crossed before.[tt]

We made a slow passage and arrived at Rio de Janeiro January 12, one day behind our scheduled time. Some Brazilian ships met us outside and escorted us in. The shore at all available places was filled with people, and the harbor was full of boats of various kinds. Our welcome was very noisy. It seemed as if the whole city turned out to welcome us. A very elaborate program of entertainment had been prepared with all available time taken up. There were from two to three each day. On account of court-martial and other duty I escaped many, which pleased me just as well.

The chief event that I attended was a dinner given by the Minister of Foreign Affairs. It was a very large affair, and pleasant enough as such things go. Admiral Evans was still sick and unable to take part in any ceremonies. A return party on behalf of the fleet was given on board the *Minnesota.*

...On January 22nd, the President of Brazil reviewed the Fleet and paid a visit to the *Minnesota*, Admiral Thomas being the next in rank to Admiral Evans, who was too sick to receive him.

...After this function was over the Fleet sailed for Sandy Point – one day behind schedule. A mail was received on board a few hours before sailing.

[tt] Referring to the naval custom of hazing men who had never sailed across the Equator before.

This was practically our first mail...and we were glad to get it...The Argentines sent a squadron of four ships out to meet us when we were off their coast. They did not meet up with the main Fleet the day expected, having missed each other, but found us the next morning and exchanged salutes with us.

...We entered the Straits [of Magellan] about noon January 31st and anchored for the night a few hours later...We got underway on the morning of February 1st and reached Punta Arenas [Sandy Point, a Chilean city in the Straits of Magellan] a little after noon.

Writing on February 19th:

The Chileans had a man-of-war with several high officials to welcome us. There was entertaining here...Punta Arenas has grown very much since I was there – nearly nine years ago.

We got underway about 11:00 P. M. on the 7th and passed out of the Straits about eight the next night. We had fairly good weather ...The scenery is rather good most of the way and parts of it are very beautiful, especially in some of the narrower parts. The country, however, is rather desolate looking, what trees there are being rather dwarfed. The higher mountains were covered with [snow] and with an occasional glacier it makes a picturesque background....The Chilean man-of-war is accompanying us. We found good weather in the Pacific...The *Chicago*, enroute to the east coast, passed us not far from Valparaiso [Chile]. On the 14th we ran in close by Valparaiso by previous agreement. The shore was well-lined with people to see us pass. We exchanged salutes and then passed in review by a Chilean man-of-war on board of which was their President, saluting him as we passed. The next day we passed fairly close to Coquimbo [city on the coast of Chile], but did not go inside. The cruise is rapidly becoming more and more like a junketing trip. Going by the two ports named caused us to lose at least one and possibly two days, as we had to slow down so as not to reach Valparaiso too soon and again so as not to reach Callao at night. We have had remarkably pleasant weather and are still wearing blue. It is just about the temperature at which either can be worn. We expect to reach Callao tomorrow morning....

Written March 9, 1908:

We reached Callao [city on coast of Peru, serving as Lima's port] on February 20th and were noisily received. There appeared to be a good deal of spontaneity in our welcome. The Peruvians profess to have a friendship for us and there is no reason why they are not sincere, so far as I am aware of the relations between the two countries.

The President gave a dinner on the 22nd at the Exposition Grounds, Lima, which I attended. The arrangements were excellent. All guests were presented to the President and other officials. A definite seat was assigned to each guest with instructions as to where it was ... there was no confusion among about 700 present.

604

The President is a comparatively young man and has a very good face. He made a very good speech at the dinner – not too long. Admiral Thomas replied for the Fleet.

While there were plenty of functions, they were generally limited to one each day, so that there was not the surfeit as at Rio…

On the 23rd I went to Lima, [traveled] around the city a little, took a car ride to the seaside resort and afterward went to see a game of "Pelota" [a handball game]. I had never seen the game played before. While it must take a good deal of skill it did not appeal to me especially. There was a bullfight given for our benefit but I had no desire to attend. I had seen one in Madrid and that was enough to satisfy me.

In Peru, Henry was eager to make a railroad trip to the town of La Oroya, which is high in the summit of the Andes, about 125 miles from Lima. An "official" party from the Fleet was making the trip, but it was limited to 41 officers. This excursion was quickly filled, so Henry undertook to hire a special train and organize another party, which ended up with another 40 officers at $145 each. It departed on the same day as the official party, on January 26, 1908 at 6:45 A. M. Even the sometimes blasé Henry is awed by the spectacular scenery, and unexpected events would lead to high adventure and fun. Henry's journal describes the trip:

"The railroad follows the course of the Rimac River. It is almost impossible to describe the scenery. I have never taken a trip to equal it, and would not have missed it for anything. The road is very crooked and at places four or five tracks can be seen at one time. There are a number of switchbacks to lessen the steep grades. There are several high bridges and one where the road comes out of one tunnel, crosses a gorge by means of a bridge and enters another tunnel. We had a good train crew and they would stop at any picturesque point that we wished to give us a good view of the scenery. …It is certainly a remarkable piece of engineering.

We stopped at Mantucana [a town 63 miles from Callao] nearly 8000 feet above sea-level – for luncheon and had a very good one – very Spanish however. Rio Blanco – about 11,000 feet above sea-level – was the end of our trip, but we arranged to go on to Chicla – the old end of the road – by paying $25 additional – and about 1000 feet higher. We took two mining people with us from Rio Blanco. Chicla is 12,215 feet above sea-level, 88 miles from Callao. The highest point is 18 miles further and is 15,665 feet above sea-level. I should like to have gone there, but we saw the prettiest part of the scenery, so did not miss much in that respect. We were all willing to pay the price, but the RR people would not take us beyond Chicla. On our return we stopped for about half an hour at Rio Blanco, and the mining people gave us a light lunch. One member of the party was overcome by "soroche" [altitude sickness] here, due to going up the hill too fast, but he soon recovered. Several, possibly all, were slightly affected, but none of the others to any disagreeable extent. We gave the two mining people three cheers just as we were leaving, and which they returned....All who were in the party were pleased with the trip, and there were no complaints. It was unanimously considered a big success.

Writing on March 10th:

"When we had descended to about 9,000 feet, we were held up by a landslide. There was no possibility of clearing the obstruction inside of several hours, but we remained there about two hours in the hopes that a train would come up on the other side and we would transfer to it. It was difficult to find out anything definite. Finally we gave up any hope of getting through, and ran back to the first station above that had a hotel – Tamboraque, which is just under ten thousand feet above sea level. The hotel was rather small so that we overran it. We finally succeeded in getting something to eat, but it was somewhat of a make-shift. However all took it philosophically and set out to make the best of it. Someone suggested that we organize the "Llama Society, Landslide Chapter" with enthusiasm. I was elected president, and others to the different offices. In all we had a very enjoyable evening.

The official party arrived about 11:00. Two or three were very sick with *"soroche,"* and all more or less so. We had all the hotel so that they had to sleep in the train, except one or two of the very sick and about two of the higher officers of the party. There were eight of us in two small crowded rooms, yet we made out pretty well. We resumed our journey the next day about 6:00 A. M. We found about five landslides in all. In two cases we had to walk around and take a train on the other side. Our party was still in good spirits and looked very well while the official party as a rule looked fogged out and "in the dumps" – we came back together. We finally arrived back in Callao a little before 1:00 P. M. on the 29th.

Perhaps because his journal was partly for home consumption, and his parents and family were opposed to the use of alcohol, we find that Henry omitted details reflecting just how enjoyable the evening in Tamboraque was. But the story got out, and found its way into the American media. In a pocket of Henry's leather-bound journal are found two newspaper clippings from the *New York Herald,* dated February 28, 1908 and April 19, 1908. Both articles describe the landslide and the night at the hotel. The April 19 article has pictures of the *USS Connecticut* and the *USS Vermont*, but is headlined, "SIXTY NAVAL OFFICERS FORM A NEW ORDER AMONG ANDEAN CLOUDS." It reports the efforts of the "official party" to find lodging in a small hotel:

"…So when the train bumped down the incline to Tamboraque station half a dozen officers made their way to the little village, where a dim bunch of lights indicated the location of the Hotel of Perpetual Health. Lieutenant Castleman, of Rear Admiral Thomas' staff, opened the door of the Inn, thinking of the proper Spanish questions for the drowsy landlord he expected to encounter.

Instead he was received with a shout. Sixty officers were seated on chairs and tables in the low-ceilinged room of the hotel. At the table toward one side sat Fleet Paymaster Dent, wearing a noble crown consisting of an inverted waste basket and a feather duster.

He had just been installed as the President of the Society of the Llama…

With the assistance of the wine of the country the Society of the Llama was organized. Its official seal was prescribed to consist of a llama rampant upon a landslide. The business which came before the society kept it in session until a late hour, yet the spirit of the Andes had so thoroughly imbued the members that they were abroad early and ready to proceed when the train pulled out for the first landslide…."

Back in Callao, there was a dinner on board the *Connecticut* for the President of Peru, following which the President embarked on a Peruvian man-of-war and proceeded a short distance out where he reviewed the American Fleet as it steamed away.

The Fleet next stopped at Magdalena Bay on the southern tip of Baja California, Mexico, where it engaged in several days of target practice. The *Missouri* blew off the muzzle of one of her six inch guns. Here they "heard that the Fleet was to return to the East Coast by way of Australia, Manila and the Suez Canal, leaving San Francisco about July 1st. It was stated later that a stop would be made in Japan and China and also New Zealand…Admiral Evans asked to be relieved of command just after San Francisco is reached, and it was soon stated that Admiral Sperry would have command on the return trip." Upon reaching San Diego, Admiral Evans health had deteriorated to the point that he was put ashore, with plans to take a rest at some springs and rejoin the Fleet in San Francisco. Henry continues his account of the trip up the California coast; he has clearly had his fill of parties and parades:

Writing on December 31, 1908:

"…Our first home port was San Diego. The first thing practically was a parade on shore – the inevitable as a rule. We were anchored off Coronado…An automobile ride was given us – to a grove in the country where a picnic lunch awaited us. The ride lasted pretty well all day and was a very enjoyable one. The balls I did not attend, as I do not care for them and there were always enough who wanted to go.

Our next stop was Los Angeles – one division at each of the four so-called ports. The main event there was a dinner. The decorations were beautiful and the affair as pleasant as such things usually are. This was followed the next morning by an automobile ride through the City. We passed by the schools where the children were lined up to see us and they pelted us with flowers as we passed, so that by the end of the ride we had almost an automobile-full of flowers. There were a number of entertainments…the ship was over-run with visitors.

Santa Barbara was our next stop. Here we had something different and it was really very pretty. It was a flower parade and battle. The vehicles in the parade were all decorated with flowers and they made a most effective and pretty display. After passing by the reviewing stand once or twice they began

607

throwing flowers. The spectators would throw at those in the parade and they would throw back. In a little while it was very lively and it certainly made a very pretty and effective scene. It was so different from the usual run of entertainments and so novel and pretty that I think it the most enjoyable function of all we had. A flower dance was given at night. It was given by amateurs and was well-gotten up and compared most favorably with a professional show of the same kind. There were a number of children in it and it must have taken a great deal of time and patience to have drilled them so well.

The Fleet stopped for one day at Monterrey to pick up Admiral Evans ("looking some better") to take the fleet into San Francisco – Henry did not go ashore – and then went on the Santa Cruz. There Henry toured a grove of "big trees," which he found "interesting but somewhat disappointing…" And then the triumphal entrance into San Francisco Bay:

> "San Francisco was considered the end of the trip around and the culmination so to speak. We steamed into the Bay on the morning of May 6th and were joined just inside the entrance by the Pacific Fleet and proceeded up the Bay in one long line. It must have been a very pretty sight from shore. The Secretary of the Navy reviewed the combined Fleets, which was the greatest gathering of war ships ever assembled under the American flag, from the *Yorktown*…"
>
> Of course there was the inevitable parade on shore. It was not unduly long and it evoked much cheering from the on-lookers who evidently appreciated it. A banquet in honor of the Secretary and the high officers of the Fleet was one of the principal entertainments on shore. It was fairly pleasant. But, as usual, the speech-making was rather long drawn out. An automobile ride through the City and near suburbs was fairly pleasant. One day was given to Oakland. There was the usual parade which I managed to escape, taking a automobile ride instead…The ride was followed at night by a banquet…
>
> Admiral Evans left the Fleet a few days after San Francisco was reached and Admiral Thomas succeeded to the command. He had really borne the brunt of the work on the trip around, due to the illness of Admiral Evans. He remained in command only about a week, being relieved by Admiral Sperry just before the Fleet sailed from San Francisco for Puget Sound."

The Fleet left San Francisco on May 16th or 17th, and upon reaching Puget Sound divided among two or three places. Henry went with the flagship to Bellingham, Washington, where "the inevitable" parade took place, and then proceeded to Seattle, where he enjoyed an automobile ride to Snoqualmie Falls. From Seattle, most of the ships went to Tacoma, whence Henry and the First Squadron returned to San Francisco around June 1, 1908.

With the change in Fleet commanders, Henry's assignment as Paymaster for the Atlantic Fleet came to an end, as did his role in the "great white fleet's" world cruise. However, his adventures were not over. He was immediately reassigned as Fleet Paymaster of the Pacific Fleet, and he would continue to cruise with that Fleet in the Pacific Ocean for another year. He was scheduled to report to the Pacific Fleet in San Francisco on June 30, 1908, and since he was able to settle and close up his Atlantic accounts early ("my accounts being in such shape they did not require very much work to finish"), he decided to take some time off for a trip to Yosemite Park, using free tickets given by the Southern Pacific Railroad. He made the trip with three other Fleet officers:

"After a hot trip through the San Joaquin Valley we reached El Portal – the entrance to the Park – late in the afternoon, where we spent the night, leaving early the next morning by stage for the Sentinel Hotel in the middle of the Park...The Valley does not impress you so much at once, but the grandeur and beauty grows on you, I think, the more you see of it...The two most prominent features on the ride in are El Capitan Peak and "Bridal Veil" Falls. That afternoon we followed the river several miles fishing but had no luck. We tried a swim and found the water so cold that we could only remain a few minutes.

Early the next morning we went to Mirror Lake to see the sunrise and then took the trail for Glacier Point, passing Vernal and Nevada Falls. We reached the Point about noon. It is about 3,000 feet above the valley and gives a fine view of it. After luncheon we left for Wawona by stage arriving late in the afternoon. Early the next morning we left by stage to visit the "big trees." Their "bigness" grows on you rather than strikes you suddenly. This is accounted for in part probably by their being surrounded by what would ordinarily be considered large trees....We returned to Wawona for luncheon and left soon after for the Sentinel Hotel by stage. We had arranged to have horses meet us at Fort McMonroe, and from there followed the Pahono Trail to Glacier Point. This follows along the ridge and gives you a fine view of the valley at many points. From what I saw of the valley I consider it one of the best trips that can be taken. We did not reach Glacier Point until after dark, where we had arranged to have dinner. After dinner we walked down a short trail to the Sentinel Hotel. This looks down the steep side of the mountain and is narrow and very steep especially in some places. It was a very dark night and none of us had been over the trail...looking back on it was a somewhat risky undertaking – the people at the Point not wanting us to take the trip...After spending the night at El Portal we left the next morning for San Francisco, and after about an hour there, left for Tahoe....

We arrived at Lake Tahoe the next morning. It is quite a large lake about 6,000 feet above sea level, of very clear water and surrounded by mountains, many of which are snow-capped, and making a charming picture. I spent the day there, returning on the night train, reaching San Francisco the next morning. I would like to have remained longer for it seemed to be a delightful spot for a vacation...."

Henry reported to the flagship of the Pacific Fleet at the Mare Island Yard on June 30, 1908, and soon began a new cruise that took him to Samoa and Hawaii. At Honolulu, "we were given a big surprise by the receipt of orders to make a cruise down the west coast of South America as far as Chile, after completing target practice [at Magdalena Bay]." Returning to San Francisco, the Fleet headed south in late August, arriving at Magdalena Bay November 1st, and after a month of target practice proceeded south on December 1, 1908.

"We followed the coastline pretty closely on the way to Panama…We were anchored about five miles off at Panama – due to shoal water…There was one thing I wanted to see and that was the Canal – to make a trip over the work. In this I was disappointed. However I had to make a trip across to Colon [city at the Atlantic terminus of the Canal] for funds that had been brought down for me, and this gave me a fair idea of the Canal in general. The railroad follows fairly close to the Canal, crossing it two or three times, so that you can get a fair idea of the work by making the trip by train, although not so good as a trip made along the Canal itself would afford. As far as I heard and saw, and it seemed to be the general opinion, men who are building the Canal have no doubt but that it will be successfully completed and on time – not later than January 1, 1915. [uu]

We left Panama on December 22, 1908 and spent Xmas at sea. This is the first Xmas that I can recall that I actually spent at sea.

We arrived at Talcahuano, Chile January 3, 1909. We first heard of the earthquake in Italy on arrival…Talcahuano is a small place with nothing of special interest except that it it's the chief naval station of Chile. I had visited it about nine years previously but recalled very little about it.

We left January 14 and reached Valparaiso the next day. I was glad to stop at Valparaiso…as it was the only place of large size in South America that I had not visited. It had recovered almost completely from its earthquake, so far as being rebuilt is concerned. Our reception was apparently very cordial and a number of entertainments were given us. I made a hurried trip to Santiago…The trip is a fairly interesting one – the scenery being good…It is very much like any other Spanish-American City…there is a hill very near the center of the city, from which a fine view of the city and surrounding country can be obtained. I left late in the afternoon and arrived at Valparaiso that night."

The Pacific Fleet next visited Callao (the seaport for Lima, Peru), from which Henry had explored the Andes and been elected president of the Llama Society the year before. He wanted to make this excursion again. "On my trip up the Oroya Road in 1908 I did not go to the highest point," so he arranged for a special train that would go all the way. But this time Henry encountered far more dangerous circumstances, from which he was fortunate to escape alive. He left Callao the afternoon of February 7th, spent the night at Mantucana at 7,800 feet, and proceeded the next morning:

[uu] In fact, the Canal was completed early. Originally projected to take ten years, it was finished in seven, by August 1914.

"When we stopped for water, about 45 minutes later, another member of the party and myself got in the engine to ride for a while. A few minutes later we arrived at Chaupichica Bridge – 9,500 feet elevation, and saw that the road was blocked by a derrick on some cars – the road was being rebuilt – so we stopped just a few feet from the bridge to wait for the road to be cleared so we could pass. A few minutes later I saw an engine come out of a tunnel on the other side of the bridge…in a few minutes I realized that it was running at a great speed and that a collision [with the derrick cars] would occur…Just a short space of time after I realized there would be a collision, the [oncoming] engine struck the [derrick] cars, which were braked or otherwise secured, the derrick fell toward the engine and then a cloud of steam shot up in the air…Then a crash of timbers giving away and about the same time I saw the derrick car start toward us. The side of the engine I was on was next to the mountain which was almost perpendicular…When I saw the [derrick] car start I left the engine and climbed up the side of the mountain as fast as I could. Just as I was leaving I saw the engineer of [our] train reverse his engine. When I climbed as far as I could I turned around and saw our train was backing and then the [derrick] car coming along. It struck our engine after it had backed about fifteen feet but it was a light blow as the train was going in the same direction and the car had evidently run off the track from the way it slackened speed just before it struck our train. Some of our people had very narrow escapes. Our conductor was lying along side the track just beneath where I was, having evidently been knocked down by the car. He was bruised up but apparently not seriously hurt. [Our] engineer showed good presence of mind in backing…The engine that caused the trouble fell into the river with the old part of the bridge – about one third…There were about thirteen people killed – part of whom were at work on the bridge and the rest the crew of the engine. A few minutes after the accident a man who…lodged temporarily on the standing part of the bridge…and could not hold on any longer, fell, striking the crosspieces every few feet on his way down…it was horrible to witness. The bridge was, I would judge, 125 or 150 feet high….Of course we could not continue our trip, so, waiting a while and seeing that we could render no assistance, we returned….

The accident occurred very near where I was held up by a land-slide nearly a year before…I was glad to escape without injury…It was a more narrow escape than I care to have again."

Leaving Callao, the Fleet visited the Galapagos Islands. "The Flagship stopped at two, neither of which were inhabited so far as we saw." It was reported that these two volcanic islands were comparatively new, and "had not entirely cooled off. The fishing was very fine, and we laid in enough to last for quite awhile." From there the fleet returned to Panama, and was then divided, the Flagship and Henry proceeding to San Jose, Guatemala, where Henry visited Guatemala City. The next stop was Acajutla, Salvador, and then to Magdalena Bay again. After more target practice, the Flagship and the *Pennsylvania* on April 14 headed back to San Francisco, to be present there to welcome two Japanese ships expected on May 1. The two ships arrived as scheduled and a series of entertainments was given for the Japanese, many of which Henry was able to avoid, much to his relief. A change of command of the Fleet took place on May 17, Admiral Sebree taking command. This also ended Henry's assignment as Fleet Paymaster for the Pacific Fleet. However, he accompanied the flagship to Seattle and attended the "Exposition" then taking place there. He "closed up his accounts" as Pacific Fleet Paymaster on June 6, 1909.

During his first fifteen years in the Navy, Henry had spent about two thirds of his time on sea duty.[941] His last ten years of service, including the years of World War I, were spent assigned to shore duty in the United States. In 1916, he attained the rank of captain (equivalent to the army rank of full colonel). After twenty five years of working with paymaster accounts and bookkeeping records, Henry's eyesight had gradually become seriously impaired, and in 1919, at age 47, he was retired from active service for "physical disability incurred in line of duty."

The Children of Anna and Hubert Dent, circa 1930

Front: Henry, "Hugh," Edward. Rear: Nan, Louise, Carrie

Henry returned to his boyhood home following his retirement. Despite his flawed eyesight, Henry enjoyed otherwise robust health, and would live out a long life in Eufaula, where he participated in civic and church activities. On January 31, 1931, at age 60, Henry finally gave up his bachelorhood. He married Etta Fontaine Copeland McCormick, the 55 year-old widow of William L. McCormick.[vv] They resided in her home on Randolph Street, and Henry was heard to comment on the coincidence that the Randolph Street home had been originally built by James L. Pugh, who as a U. S. Senator in 1894, had assisted in arranging Henry's presidential appointment as an officer of the Navy Paymaster Corps. Henry later become owner of controlling interest in McCormick Grocery Co., and directed the affairs of that longtime Eufaula enterprise until changing trends in the grocery industry eliminated the role of smaller wholesalers and led to the company's dissolution in the early 1960's. Upon the death of Etta[ww] in 1956, Henry resided with his widowed sister, Carrie Dent McDowell, until her death in 1966. Henry was heard to comment during this time that he was "the oldest officer on the Navy's retired list."

[vv] The two families were already connected: Henry's older brother, Edward Young Dent, had married Annie Stuart McCormick, the sister of William L. McCormick (Thompson, p. 483).

[ww] One of William and Etta McCormick's grandsons, John Fontaine Andrews, resides today in Montgomery, Al, where he is one of the area's foremost bond lawyers, while his wife, Ellen Rainer Andrews, is a popular doctor of veterinary medicine.

He apparently expected to occupy that position indefinitely; in 1971 he pledged a contribution to the Eufaula Methodist Church payable over five years. This pledge was made good by his executor following Henry's death in June 1971, just short of his 99th birthday.

65

President Wilson's Adversary: Congressman Dent

"...S. H. Dent [Jr.] represented the end of the Southern tradition of the gentleman politician."
Historian, Robert David Ward

Anna and Hubert's second son was christened Hubert Warren Dent, but as a young man, he changed it to Stanley Hubert Dent. He was usually called "Hu" or "Hugh," and was routinely designated as "S. H. Dent, Jr.," (although his father's first name was not Stanley, but Stouten). Born August 16, 1869, Hugh, like his brothers, Ed and Henry, attended the Methodist-sponsored college, Southern University at Greensboro. There he studied law, but graduated with a Bachelor of Arts degree in June 1886. He continued his legal studies at the University of Virginia, studying under John Minor Wisdom, and graduated with a law degree in June 1889.[942] He was admitted to the bar and began the practice of law in Eufaula the same year.

Even as a boy, Hugh had shown a predisposition for politics, and as a young lawyer, he was active in the Democratic Party, speaking for local candidates and the Democratic ticket. In 1892, his father, Hubert, who had been serving as Barbour County Superintendent of Education, resigned from that position, and Hugh was appointed to fill the unexpired term. He was also active in the affairs of the Alabama Bar Association. On July 5, 1893, he presented before that body his scholarly treatise on "The Common Law System of Pleading."[943]

Although Hugh was a serious student of the law and a diligent lawyer, he also had a lighter side. He loved baseball, and was a creditable player. In July 1892, the E. B. Young Fire Company (named for Hugh's Uncle Ed Young, its president), had "an enthusiastic meeting...for the purpose of organizing a base ball club." The *Times* Editor, W. D. Jelks was elected club president, and Hugh's brother, Henry was made umpire. But Hugh himself became one of its star players at second base. The 23 year-old lawyer ultimately became the team manager, and the team came to be called "the Dent Nine." In a game in Albany, Georgia, the Eufaula boys were defeated 4 to 2, but the *Albany News* was very impressed with the visiting second baseman, observing:[944] "Second Baseman Dent, of the visiting team, plays ball just because he likes it. Although just of age, he is one of Eufaula's prominent attorneys and enjoys a practice of from $4000 to $5000 per year." Back home, the Eufaula fans claimed biased umpiring in Albany, but in a later game were defeated again. Again the *Albany News* praised Dent: "Every player was on his mettle and played ball like he meant it. The second base playing of Dent of the visitors was exceptionally fine. He made 8 put-outs, 4 unassisted, without an error." Soon after, Eufaula was able to convincingly defeat Ozark 8 to 1, with Dent as second baseman making 2 runs and 2 base hits for 4 at bats.

On June 23, 1897, Hugh married Etta Tinsley of Louisville, Kentucky. The following year Etta returned to Louisville to have their first child, Alice Lucile, on August 19, 1898. But little Alice lived only until May 19, 1899.

After practicing law in Eufaula for a decade, perhaps Hugh felt that he wanted a larger setting in which to test his considerable legal talents. For whatever reason, Hugh and Etta moved to Montgomery in 1899. Upon first arriving in Montgomery, Hugh went into partnership with his father's old friend and partner, former Gov. William C. Oates. Hubert Dent and Oates had "read law" together in Eufaula under James Pugh and E. C. Bullock in the mid-1850's. Later, with Oates in Abbeville and Hubert in Eufaula, they had practiced as a partnership under the name "Oates & Dent" in the mid-1870's. Oates was elected governor for the 1894-1898 term, with considerable support from Hubert Dent. Oates had begun a law practice in Montgomery, and in 1899, he took on Hubert's son as a partner.[945] After working with Oates in Montgomery for a year, Hugh entered into new arrangements with Montgomery lawyers Lee H. Weil and Robert Lee Harmon, and the firm of Harmon, Dent and Weil was formed.[xx]

Etta and Hugh had their second child (and only surviving child), William Tinsley Dent, in Montgomery on November 19, 1900.

Hugh Dent, 1902, Montgomery Bar

Hugh's speaking ability was recognized when he was asked to give the opening address at the annual convention of the Sons of Confederate Veterans meeting in Montgomery in 1902. The Montgomery Advertiser of November 13, 1902 called his effort a "splendid eulogy of the men who wore the gray." In the course of his oration, filled with classical allusions, Hugh made a very prescient point. He pointed out that while the south had fully accepted the results of the war in the extinction of slavery and the indissolubility of the Union, the "real issue" of the war remained unresolved. i. e., the question of whether the United States would have a centralized government or whether the individual states still had separate sovereignty. Dent observed:

"The Confederate soldier has always accepted in the most perfect good faith the terms of surrender agreed upon by Lee and Johnston…Nowhere in our Southland has Hamilcar sworn young Hannibal to hatred and vengeance, but everywhere to loyalty and to love—and this notwithstanding the hardships…of reconstruction…. But [the Confederate soldier] and his sons have recognized the settlement of only two great questions…the extinction of human slavery forever from American soil…and the indissolubility of the Union of States…. But the underlying principle which was the real cause of civil strife, that war never settled… The time will come when it will be a burning issue, not in war but in politics, with no sectional …division…. The true issue was a contest between a Federal or a Confederated form of government, and a centralized or consolidated government…. The Southron

---

[xx] Lee H. Weil became the father of Roman Weil, one of the early partners of the Montgomery firm of Rushton, Stakely and Johnston, which was organized soon after Word War II. By 1949, Lee himself was "Of Counsel" to that firm.

said when he surrendered, I admit the abolition of slavery. I admit the indissolubility of the Union as intended by those who framed and adopted its Constitution, but I deny that the conception of government for which I fought was wrong in principle and I still maintain a centralized government with all power lodged in one place or in one head would in the end be subversive of the great ideas of liberty and freedom inherited from our Revolutionary sires."

Less than ten days after Hugh expressed these principles, events occurred that changed the course of his career and ultimately placed him in a position to actually implement his espoused principles of government. On Nov. 22, 1902, Tennent Lomax, the Solicitor of Montgomery County (the same position known today as "District Attorney") died. Friends of various office-seekers immediately began to lobby Gov. Jelks for the appointment to fill Lomax' unexpired term. Jelks met with all interested delegations, but it soon became clear that Hugh Dent was the "frontrunner." The *Advertiser* of Nov. 26 reported:

> "It was semi-officially announced at the State Capital yesterday that S. H. Dent, Jr., would be appointed solicitor of the City Court of Montgomery. Dent's endorsements from the bar of Montgomery were said to be especially strong. He stands high in the esteem of his fellow members of the bar and several strong delegations of his friends saw the Governor yesterday and Monday in his interest. They found that the Governor had all ready considered the matter and that his opinion of Mr. Dent as a man and a lawyer was very high. The friends of Mr. Dent were gratified by the intimation of the Governor that he considered Mr. Dent a worthy successor to the eloquent Mr. Lomax. [Mr. Dent is] …possessed of a pleasing appearance and an excellent voice for public speaking…"

As a long-time friend of the Dent family during Gov. Jelks' years as owner-editor of the *Eufaula Times*, there was never any real doubt that Jelks would appoint his old friend to the vacancy. The official announcement confirmed this relationship:

> "The appointment of S. H. Dent, Jr.…was announced yesterday. Private Secretary J. Kirk Jackson, acting under instructions from Governor Jelks, made the formal and official announcement of the appointment yesterday afternoon. The appointment was in no wise unexpected. The opposing candidates and their close friends realized Monday evening that Governor Jelks intended to name Mr. Dent. The Governor had known him since boyhood. A close friendship existed between the two, and it was known that Governor Jelks entertained a high opinion of Mr. Dent's ability and legal attainments. The Governor, it is said, regarded him as an ideal man for the place." [946]

There were only two years left to serve in Lomax' six-year term, and at the end of the Lomax term in 1904, Hugh was elected without opposition to a full six-year term. Hugh compiled a creditable record. During 1904-1906, he had a conviction rate of 61% of the cases he tried.[947] During 1906-1908 there was a large increase in the number of cases handled, totaling 844, and his conviction rate was 85% of cases tried. Thirty-four of these were the most serious kind, i. e., murder cases, and he won convictions in twenty-one.[948] Hugh's success would enable him to make the solicitorship a stepping-stone for a further political career.

Alabama's Second Congressional District at this time consisted of the nine counties of Montgomery, Baldwin, Butler, Conecuh, Covington, Crenshaw, Escambia, Pike, and Wilcox, of which Montgomery was by far the most important and populous. In the Democratic primary of May 18, 1908, Hugh Dent was elected as one of the Second District's two delegates to the Democratic National Convention in Denver.

In the same primary, the nomination for congressman was won by the incumbent, A. A. Wiley, who died 30 days after his nomination. To fill the vacancy, a special election was called for September 12, 1908. Soon after Wiley's death, candidates began lining up: William H. Samford of Opelika, Charles R. Bricken of Luverne, A. C. Sanders, of Troy, and Robert Tyler Goodwyn of Montgomery, all announced their candidacies. S. H. Dent, Jr. and Thomas J. Hall were also reported to be considering running.

The prospect of having three congressional candidates from Montgomery County, with the risk of splitting Montgomery's vote, was not palatable to the county political leaders, who wanted a Montgomery Democrat as their congressman. The Montgomery *Journal* soon advocated that they "agree upon some plan by which only one of them will go into the district primary, and then Montgomery County may get the Congressman..."[949] Just such an arrangement was soon announced through a public letter:

> "The undersigned as mutual friends of Mr. Tyler Goodwyn and Mr. S. H. Dent, Jr., beg to state that after a conference undertaken for the good of the Democratic Party in the city and county and which was cheerfully assented to by both Gentlemen, we reached the conclusion that Mr. Goodwyn withdraw from the congressional race and Mr. Dent announce his candidacy at this time.... [N]o two men in the county possess so many mutual friends and this agreement was reached for the purpose of avoiding a bitter fight in Montgomery County which would probably ensue if Mr. Goodwyn and Mr. Dent are both candidates. We hope the people will commend the high motives which actuate Mr. Goodwyn...and ...will give Mr. Dent their ...support."[950]

Candidate Hall cynically expressed suspicion of "a cold blooded trade in this thing," and the Montgomery *Journal* asked, "What was the trade?" But Goodwyn never held public office thereafter, and there is no indication of what such a "deal" might have involved.

On the same day the letter was published, Dent announced his candidacy, and immediately departed for the Democratic Convention in Denver. There, his activity in party affairs earned favorable comments which were reported back in Montgomery:

"S. H. Dent of Montgomery, who was a member of the Committee on Permanent Organization, was requested by the chairman of the committee, Senator McCreary of Kentucky, to write the report of the committee, which he did. A number of senators, governors, delegates and Congressmen who know of the vacancy in the second district, expressed the opinion that if elected he would make his mark in Congress and take rank among the ablest men in that body. Senator McCreary was very complimentary in his remarks about Mr. Dent and his splendid work on the committee.[951]

Returning home, Hugh lost no time in jumping into the campaign that was already underway. In speeches he outlined a four-part platform: (1) he believed in the old fashioned principles of Jeffersonian Democracy: home rule, local self-government, a strict construction of the Constitution in favor of the states, and the largest amount of individual liberty consistent with the public good; (2) he opposed the immigration of undesirable aliens and favored strict legislation on this subject; (3) he adhered to the theory of regulation of public service corporations; and (4) he opposed the "antishipping" bills then pending in Congress, which would prohibit shipment of alcoholic beverages from a "wet" state into a "dry" state. (Alabama had been operating under a county option system, but statewide prohibition was to take effect in 1909). Dent would make "anti-shipping" prohibition the key issue in the campaign and use it to win the election.

Dent's strongest opponent was William H. Samford of Opelika, who in a bid for the vote of the Anti-Saloon League strongly supported the "antishipping" bill. On September 1, the Anti-Saloon League published a circular announcing that only Samford had stated his support for the anti-shipping bill, while S. H. Dent had expressed his unalterable opposition. The letter was signed by the League's "superintendent," one Reverend Brooks Lawrence. The stage was set for Hugh to use Reverend Brooks as a foil to turn the prohibition issue to his own advantage.

In a speech before a large crowd at LaPine, (in southern Montgomery County) Dent first outlined his reasons for opposing the bill, and challenged Samford's support of a measure to prohibit an individual from importing into his own home for his own private consumption whiskey in any form that he desires. Warming to his subject, Dent then he turned on the Anti-Saloon League's Rev. Lawrence, a man who "dictates to this people who shall be their congressman...from the private *sanctum sanctorum* of his office in Birmingham, a man who never prosecuted anyone in his life, a man who does not know anything...about the conviction of a violator of the law...":

"I want to ask you, who is Mr. Brooks Lawrence? ...[H]e has quit the Christian calling of a minister of the Gospel...and gone into politics in Alabama. Who is he and where did he come from? Born and raised in the State of Ohio, born and reared above Mason and Dixon's Line, he has not a single solitary drop of Southern blood coursing in his veins. His heart does not beat in unison and sympathy with the material interests of this people. He has no use for you except this: he has organized a league. He has secured to himself an

618

office and a home, doubtless in Birmingham…That league is drawing whatever money it can from the women and children in the land and putting it into its treasury, and he has his hand there…and he digs and digs…

I had thought that the reign of the carpetbagger had long since ceased in Alabama. I thought that the last one had been driven from Alabama soil…but it seems that after all these years of peace and repose…that his spirit is sought to be revived and his body resurrected in the person of Mr. Brooks Lawrence from the State of Ohio…

I propose from now on to the close of this campaign…to tell the people what I think of him…and his meddling in the political affairs of this district….What will be the next step that Brooks Lawrence will take? Give him a little authority and he will grasp for more until he will have it all…I suggest that we repeal all our election laws…and select Brooks Lawrence from the State of Ohio as the Supreme Director and Exalted Ruler of Alabama…"[952]

An accomplished lawyer, Hugh Dent was well capable of reasoned analysis of issues, but here he also showed a talent for a little well-placed demagoguery. And it worked. Even the most sophisticated voter could appreciate the effectiveness of Dent's sarcasm and ridicule. The *Advertiser* of September 8 reported, "…[T]he arraignment of Reverend Brooks Lawrence by candidate S. H. Dent was the chief topic of conversation." In the ensuing days, both Samford and the League officials attempted to answer the issue and deflect the attack, but with little success. With a well-organized and well-financed campaign, Dent won the day. Samford carried five counties and Dent carried only Montgomery County, but that was enough: Dent, 4104; Samford, 3681; Bricken, 2322; Hall, 623; Sanders, 414.

The *Advertiser* of September 23 concluded that "When the anti-shipping bill and Brooks Lawrence were introduced in the campaign, the other candidates were quickly eliminated…Mr. Dent's splendid vote in Montgomery as well as the fine vote he received in Pike County is held directly responsible for his nomination by the safe majority which he received."

At the age of 40, Hugh Dent entered the Congress, taking his seat on March 15, 1909. He immediately witnessed a sharp party fight over the organization of the House. Republican William Howard Taft had been elected President, along with a majority of Republicans in both houses of Congress. A group of western Republican "Insurgents" sought to ally with the Democrats to amend the House rules so as to curtail the power of the long-time dictatorial Republican Speaker, "Uncle Joe" Cannon. With help from some bolting Democrats, northern and southern, Cannon ultimately won and saved his power for the time being. Hugh Dent and the Alabama delegation all remained loyal to the Democratic leadership in opposing Cannon, but Cannon was able to attract some Southern Democrats' votes by promising them help in achieving a lower tariff, in which the Southerners had a strong interest. [953]

The principal reason for President Taft's calling the 61st Congress into session was to revise the tariff, presumably downward, and it was on this issue of vital importance to his constituents that freshman Congressman Dent chose to make his maiden speech to the House.

The traditional position of the Democrats, and particularly Southern Democrats, had been to oppose all tariffs except "for revenue only," and to oppose tariffs which protected northern industry. The long-festering tariff dispute had been a serious contributing cause of the Civil War. Southerners felt that imposing tariffs on imported goods literally took money from their pockets: It allowed northern industry to charge higher prices which the agricultural South would have to pay to purchase manufactured goods, and it prompted other countries to impose tariffs on the South's main export, cotton, and thus reduce foreign sales.

The Payne-Aldrich Tariff Act proposed by the Republicans actually lowered tariffs, as desired by President Taft, but it did not go far enough to satisfy Southern Democrats like Hugh Dent. On the day before the final vote, April 8, 1908, he rose to address the House for the first time. "I am utterly opposed to the principle of protection," he said. He viewed protection as a perversion of the power of government, allowing one man to be robbed for the benefit of another. Hugh wondered rhetorically how such a pernicious doctrine could be put over on the American people by the Republicans: "The people must be deceived, the people must be kept in doubt, or the difficulties…made so hard that the General public shall not be able to understand what such a bill means." "The great interest which I represent, said Dent, "is that of the cotton producer. The manner in which he has been ridden is a shame and a disgrace to all the principles of fairness in the administration of government." However, despite solid Democratic opposition, the bill was easily enacted in the House, and later, the Senate. [954]

Returning to Montgomery for a break after the vote, Dent continued to blast the Republicans in the newspapers. Pointing out that several Republican representatives were owners or part owners of factories making protected articles, he observed that, "The tariff-protected manufacturers of the North and East no longer send paid lobbyists to Washington to work on the outside for favorable tariff legislation. The have their paid political lobbyists elected to Congress so that they can work on the inside and vote as well…"[955]

In July, Dent supported a joint resolution proposing a constitutional amendment authorizing an income tax; it passed overwhelmingly, 318 to 14.

House committee assignments were announced on the last day of this session; Dent was placed on the Judiciary Committee, the Military Affairs Committee, and Public Lands. The first two of these were choice assignments, although in 1908, Military Affairs did not enjoy the importance and influence that it has today. Within a decade, however, World War I would thrust that committee into the forefront of Congressional activity, and as its chairman, the Eufaula native would find himself exercising responsibility over matters of grave national import.

After four months at home, Dent returned to Washington for the second session of the 61st Congress. In the organizational proceedings, Dent voted for a renewed resolution stripping Speaker Cannon of his dictatorial powers. This time it succeeded.

On May 10, 1910, Hugh spoke on the floor against a bill providing for the incorporation under federal law of companies engaged in interstate commerce. His states' rights instincts rebelled at such interference with the traditional state function of creating corporations: "This brings the law dangerously near to the regulation of the internal commerce of the state. The protection of the states in their reserved powers is an ancient doctrine...state lines must be maintained...if individual liberty is still prized as one of the greatest blessings of the human race."[956] A month later, Dent spoke against a proposal to authorize the creation of federal postal savings banks, on similar grounds of states rights and strict construction: "I cannot find any warrant in the constitution for this legislation. The power to establish post-offices certainly can not be distorted so as to grant authority to establish savings banks." [957]

In the 1910 elections Hugh Dent was returned to office with no opposition. The Democrats won a majority in the House (but not the Senate), and in accordance with the Democratic Platform, soon proposed a constitutional amendment requiring the direct election of senators by the people. The Republican senate adopted a rider authorizing federal supervision of such elections. Seeing this as similar to the old "force bills," the Southern Democrats vigorously fought it, but without success. On the final vote, Hugh Dent was the only one of Alabama's nine representatives who voted against the constitutional amendment, not because Dent was opposed to the direct election of senators (which was a very popular measure), but because he opposed the possibility of federal intrusion into elections.[958] This vote would come back to haunt Dent in later years.

True to his position expressed in his first election campaign, Dent in this session voted in favor of a bill requiring all immigrants to the United States to pass an educational test before being admitted.

To the dismay of Alabama citizens who had purchased land originally acquired from the Creek Indians, it was discovered that title to this land was actually still held by the federal government. As a careful lawyer and a native of a county created entirely from former Creek lands, Hugh Dent would have been particularly sensitive to this title defect. Dent helped Congressman Oscar W. Underwood obtain the passage of legislation curing the problem. Underwood later gave Dent the principal credit: "When the bill went to the Senate, it was not understood over there and never was understood...until my colleague, Mr. Dent, went into conference and finally persuaded them to adopt the House view of the matter."[959]

In the elections of 1912, Congressman Dent was opposed in the Democratic primary by O. C. Wiley, the brother of A. A. Wiley, whose death in 1908 had created the vacancy filled by Dent. Hugh's campaign opened with a torchlight parade and escort to the courthouse, where he gave his only major speech of the campaign. There was little excitement to the election. With overwhelming support from Montgomery County, Dent was reelected 8273 to 6698. In the November general elections, President Taft was defeated by Woodrow Wilson.

In 1914, Dent was re-elected without opposition. By 1916, Dent had become the second ranking majority member of the Military Affairs Committee, which resulted in his acting as lieutenant to the chairman, James Hay of Virginia. Dent's first major involvement with national military issues began with the debate over the National Defense Act of 1916. Europe had been embroiled in a bloody war for two years, and there was increasing agitation in America to enhance the country's military "preparedness." Originally a Republican issue, President Woodrow Wilson had adopted the view that the military establishment needed upgrading. The military advocated a large standing army raised by conscription, while the "little army" adherents preferred a smaller standing army augmented in time of war by volunteers. Wilson initially sided with his Secretary of War, Lindley K. Garrison, in supporting the army's proposals. However, when this approach was strongly opposed by Chairman Hay and Hugh Dent of the House Military Affairs Committee, Wilson vacillated and seemed to switch to the Committee view, causing Garrison to resign in February 1916.

In March, the House Military Affairs Committee reported its own bill, of which Hugh Dent was one of the principal authors. The military establishment had advocated an army of 281,000, with no reliance placed on the National Guard. The Committee saw that such an army could not be implemented without compulsory conscription, which it felt the country would not accept. Instead, the committee provided for an army of 141,000 and made the National Guard an additional important component of the military forces. Speaking on the floor of the House in support of this bill on March 17, Dent said the committee was convinced the country was not ready for a large standing army. The committee had therefore adopted a compromise which increased the regular army to provide a nucleus from which to build in time of war, and had enhanced the National Guard with additional training under prescribed discipline. Dent told the House that: "I believe the sentiment of this nation is in favor of building up a second line of defense from the citizen soldiery who mix and mingle daily in the business and social life of the people among whom they live."[960] Fighting off an amendment which would double the proposed army to 220,000, Dent again took the floor on March 20, arguing that an army of this size could not be raised without compulsory service or doubling its pay, and "This country is not yet ready…for either one of these things."[961] The amendment was defeated and Dent's bill passed the House with an overwhelming vote of 403 to 2. However, it still remained for the Senate to act.

In the elections of 1914, Dent had escaped opposition. Now, while dealing with perhaps the most important national issue of his congressional career to date, Hugh Dent also had to face his most difficult election campaign since 1908. The Democratic Primary was to be held on May 9, 1916, and two candidates had announced against him: A. C. Sanders of Troy and W. H. Screws of Montgomery. Dent faced a dilemma: He was needed in Washington because the Defense Act was still pending in the Senate. However, Hugh's concern over Screws' potential political strength made it essential that he return to Montgomery to campaign. Accordingly, House Majority Leader Claude Kitchin granted him special permission to return to Montgomery for the campaign.

By April 1, Dent was in Montgomery delivering his first speech of the campaign, in which he stressed the difficult times posed by the possibility of war, and the importance of not sending an inexperienced representative to Washington during such dangerous times. His speech was well received. In other speeches he explained his positions on the military bill and his opposition to a large standing army. However, he was not allowed to campaign long. On April 7, he received two telegrams. Military Affairs Committee Chairman Hay wired, "Several important events here I think necessitate your immediate return. You being the ranking member of the committee, we do not care to take action in your absence." [962]

Majority Leader Kitchin also wired:

> "...I trust you will be able to return at once. It is necessary for me to call upon you from time to time to keep a quorum in the House and to line up Democratic members on matters of vital importance. I may have imposed on you on many occasions, but you have proven so effective in keeping Democrats in line I am forced to call on you again." [963]

The Kitchin telegram has the look of having been arranged for public consumption to provide political cover for Hugh's leaving his campaign, but Chairman Hay was serious about "several important events" having occurred. What had happened was that the Senate had rejected Hay and Dent's military bill and enacted a widely divergent bill calling for an army of 175,000 and a weak National Guard. On April 2, a conference committee had been appointed to reconcile the two versions, with Hay and Dent as two of the three House conferees. Dent's participation in this conference committee was, indeed, crucial.

Dent issued a statement to his district that he hoped to return to the campaign, but that "...I consider it my first duty to remain on guard in Washington with other loyal Democrats in carrying out the program of the President."[964] The *Montgomery Journal* on April 8 was careful to emphasize the need for Hugh's return to Washington: "Mr. Dent will be an important figure in the final consideration of the preparedness bill..."

While Dent was away in Washington, Screws carried on a vigorous and aggressive campaign, accusing Hugh of being a "do nothing" congressman, attacking his positions on the military bill, and accusing him of being one of the major impediments to "preparedness."

Even though absent from the district during this crucial time, Dent successfully weathered his most dangerous challenge to date. In fact, he did better than in 1908; he was now elected by the whole district rather than just Montgomery County. He carried five of the nine counties: Montgomery, Baldwin, Butler, Crenshaw, and Covington. The totals were: Dent, 7366; W. H. Screws, 5674; and A.C. Sanders, 4807.

Meanwhile, in Washington, Hugh Dent was striving in the House-Senate conference committee to retain as much of the House-passed military bill as possible. On May 20, the committee reported a compromise of the issues: the House yielded to the 175,000-man army, and the Senate yielded to a strong National Guard which the president could call into service as a regular part of the army. Thus revised, the bill passed both houses and was signed into law by President Wilson on June 5, 1916.

Only months after winning reelection and concluding the legislative fight over the military bill, circumstances arose which placed Hugh Dent at the pinnacle of his congressional career. In September, Chairman James Hay was appointed to the federal bench, and on September 5, 1916, Dent was elected to succeed him as the new Chairman of the House Military Affairs Committee. Seven months later, the United States would be at war with Germany. During that interim, Dent would place himself at odds with President Wilson and become the center of a stormy policy debate over one of the most important issues arising in the early days of the war.

In the fall of 1916, as the war clouds were gathering, Army Chief of Staff, Gen. Hugh L. Scott made this report:

"The volunteer system in this country, in view of the highly organized, trained and disciplined armies that possible opponents possess, should be relegated to the past.... The only democratic method is for every man in his youth to become trained in order that he may render efficient service if called upon in war." [965]

Without consulting with any members of the Military Affairs Committees of Congress, the army quietly prepared a bill based on its desire for an army raised solely by conscription. On April 2, 1918, when Wilson appeared before Congress to recommend a declaration of war on Germany, he also called for "...an army of at least 500,000 men based on the principle of universal liability to service, and the authorization of additional increments of 500,000 each as they are needed or can be handled in training."

When Wilson's Secretary of War Newton D. Baker appeared to testify before the House Military Affairs Committee on April 6, the Southern Democrats on the committee, including Dent and six others, informed him that they "tentatively" opposed the conscription feature of the bill, indicating that they would yield if shown the necessity for a compulsory draft. Hugh Dent said, "I desire to cooperate with the War Department, even to the extent of yielding, if absolutely necessary, some of my convictions regarding conscription." Later generations who took compulsory conscription for granted might regard this position as eccentric. But in 1917, the nation's limited experience with the process did not immediately recommend it to all. In fact, both President Wilson and his Secretary of War, Newton D. Baker, had originally opposed conscription. Only after the U. S. broke diplomatic relations with Germany on Feb 3, 1917, did Baker and Wilson became convinced by the War Department of the necessity for a compulsory draft. But a majority of the Military Affairs Committee, as well as many House members, could not accept this proposition; they saw no reason not to use volunteers to the extent possible, and only then resort to conscription. The army and the administration were adamant in their view that the volunteer system could have no place in the program.

President Wilson summoned Dent to the White House on April 9, and told him that the safety of the nation rested on passing the draft bill. Dent replied that the feeling on his committee and throughout the house was in favor of a volunteer plan; that even if his committee reported a draft bill it was doubtful the House would pass it; and that it was felt that the required number of men could be raised from volunteers. Wilson did not agree with this view, and the meeting resulted only in more sharply defining the two men's differences.[966] Departing from the White House, Dent told the media, "There is no question on the part of anyone as to giving the President all the men and money needed to carry on the war. The only controversy is as to the means of doing it."[967]

On April 11, Wilson called Democratic Speaker Champ Clark and Majority Leader Claude Kitchin to the White House. Both confirmed the correctness of Dent's report of opposition in the House to conscription, but also told the president it could be passed if volunteering were used first.[968] President Wilson declined to budge.

On April 17, Dent requested another meeting at the White House, during which he again stressed the opposition in the House. He probably proposed to the President that a compromise be worked out, but received no reponse.

Wilson and his leaders now fully realized that they could not look to Hugh Dent to advocate or defend the administration's interests on the floor of the House in this matter. In fact, neither could they depend upon the Democratic Speaker Champ Clark or Democratic Majority Leader Claude Kitchin. The president was therefore forced to resort to an unusual measure. He turned to the ranking Republican on the Military Affairs Committee, Julius Kahn of California, to handle the Democratic administration's proposed military legislation. Kahn, taken into the confidence of the War Department and furnished with all necessary information, accepted the challenge. Further, President Wilson himself went to the capitol to personally assure key representatives and senators that there could be no compromise between volunteer and draft systems. But even while Wilson was in the capitol lobbying for his bill, Congressman Dent led the Military Affairs Committee in adopting an amendment to the administration bill, requiring that volunteering be tried first.[969]

On April 23, Hugh Dent introduced his bill and the report of the majority of the Military Affairs Committee which supported it. It authorized the president to call for 500,000 volunteers, apportioned among the states, and an additional 500,000 if necessary. It further provided that if the President should decide that these forces could not be effectually raised under the call for volunteers, the President could raise them by selective draft.

Kahn's minority report did not propose a bill, but simply attacked the volunteer plan, citing a letter to Chairman Dent from Secretary Baker: "The drafting system [is] a process by which the forces of the country can be called as they shall be needed, according to an equal and just system...." In a public letter, President Wilson explained that "The idea of the selective draft is that those should be chosen for service in the army who can be most readily spared from the prosecution of other activities which the nation must engage in and to which it must devote a great deal of its best energy and capacity...The volunteer system does not do this. When men choose themselves they sometimes choose without due regard to their other responsibilities...There is an universal obligation to serve...and a public authority should choose those who shall do the rest of the nation's work."[970]

Debate on the bill began in the House on April 23, with Dent speaking first. Pointing out that he had tried to reach a compromise with the President, Dent then pointed out the unfairness of the draft as proposed by the army: "Is it universal liability to service to take a selected class between the ages of nineteen and twenty-five and then to exempt certain members of that class? It is one of the most arbitrary systems of stating who shall go into the army...that could be conceived of."

The debate wore on for three days. During the second day, the president himself again visited Capitol Hill to "twist arms," which had its effect, as the volunteer supporters began to lose ground. However, on the third day of debate, Speaker Champ Clark came down from the rostrum to address the House, which had been apprehensively awaiting his statement of position. Without equivocating, Clark bluntly said that he was in favor of the volunteer section of the bill. Speaking in defense of its sponsors, he rhetorically asked, "Why should Chairman Dent and the majority of his committee be assailed with inhuman rancor because they stand for the American doctrine of giving an opportunity for the brave, the patriotic, to volunteer to fight for their country?" Speaker Clark closed by saying that only by using inappropriate language could he adequately answer those critics who falsely claimed that the volunteer supporters were delaying the raising of necessary troops for the war.

However, even the Speaker's support was not enough to overcome White House influence. Following the close of debate, Kahn offered an amendment deleting the volunteer provisions, and on a roll call vote, it passed by 313 to 109. Among those voting with Dent were both Speaker Clark and Majority Leader Kitchin, but many of his early supporters fell by the wayside. The *Mobile Register* took note of this: "Mr. Dent was 'bunkered' by his own side...considerable sympathy must be felt for Mr. Dent. He himself had a sincere belief in his program and he trusted that the other members were as sincere as himself." [971]

Having lost the policy issue of war-time volunteerism, Dent thereafter accepted this decision and threw himself enthusiastically into the job of obtaining final passage of the bill the president wanted. As a member of the House-Senate Conference committee and then on the House floor, he shepherded the bill though a tangle of delays and fights over side issues, always protecting the president's draft policy. He thereby earned Wilson's gratitude and good graces. In a letter to Hugh, President Wilson said, "I want to express to you my sincere appreciation of the service you and your colleagues have rendered in helping to bring the bill to a final consideration free from any feature which might embarrass the system of draft upon which it is based..." [972] The bill was finally signed into law on May 18, 1917.

The *Montgomery Advertiser,* although it had not favored the volunteer policy, observed this about Dent:

"Since the passage of the conscription bill Mr. Dent has become a recognized leader of the administration forces. His capacity and energy have given hope to both the administration and to the country at large. It would seem that Alabama...is now supplying the unofficial leader of the Democrats who are in sore need of just such a man." [973]

However, the more ardent conscription advocates of the Northeast were not so forgiving. Prior to the 1918 elections, the National Security League, a strongly pro-"preparedness" organization, undertook to "purge" Congress of "un-American" members and socialists; Hugh Dent was high on the purge list. The *Boston Transcript* of August 22, 1918 published a long and vituperative editorial entitled "Down With Dent," lambasting him for his military positions, some of which the paper badly misrepresented.[974] None of this had much effect in south Alabama. With war raging in Europe and Hugh as the well-known chairman of the Military Affairs Committee, no candidate wished to confront him at the ballot box, and he was again returned to his seat without opposition. Unfortunately, in November 1918, the Democrats lost control of the Congress by a narrow margin of two in the Senate and twenty-one in the House. As a result, Hugh reverted to being the ranking minority member of the committee rather than chairman. Soon after the general election, the war came to a close with the signing of the armistice on November 11, 1918.

In the spring of 1919, Hugh Dent was in London, along with Congressman W. J. Field of Kentucky. Still basking in the war's ending in an Allied victory, London was in an exuberant tumult, and so crowded that hotel accommodations were unavailable to anyone not in uniform, even American congressmen. Dent and Fields stopped two American officers in the street, introduced themselves, and explained their inability to find hotel rooms. The two officers gladly gave the congressmen their hotel rooms, later reporting that because uniformed American officers "were the object of much admiration and respect," they had no trouble obtaining other accommodations.[975] It is not known whether Dent, as the ranking Democratic member of the Armed Services Committee, was at this time possibly enroute to an appearance at the peace conference then underway at Versailles.

Even as the ranking committee member of the minority party, Dent was to have significant influence over the direction of post-war military policy. President Wilson and the army came out in support of a Republican measure which would retain a large army and universal compulsory service even in peacetime. Dent and his "little–army" allies strongly opposed the bill. Dent and Democratic Leader Kitchin called a House Democratic Party caucus for Feb 9, 1920, at which they effectively advocated that the party repudiate compulsory training. The caucus endorsed Dent's position by a large vote, thereby repudiating the president and killing the proposed bill.[976]

Of the six congressional elections since Hugh Dent entered Congress in 1908, his strong political standing had shielded him from opposition in three of them, the last contested election being in 1916. By 1920 however, Hugh Dent's political situation was more ambiguous. Not only was he now only the ranking member of the Military Affairs Committee instead of its chairman, but with the coming of peace and disarmament, his committee itself had receded into relative unimportance. On the qualifying date, two candidates entered the race against him for the May 12, 1920 Democratic Primary: L. H. Brassel, an Escambia native now practicing law in Montgomery; and John Russell Tyson, Chief Justice of the Alabama Supreme Court.

Much of the campaign mounted against Dent was scurrilous and unprincipled. In a speech on April 18, Brassel pointed out that Dent had voted against the amendment providing for direct election of U. S. senators, which was fair comment, but Brassel went on to charge that Dent had lost his position as chairman of Military Affairs in 1918 because he was incompetent for the job in wartime. This was absurd, of course; he lost it because the Democrats lost control of the House. But the tenor of the campaign grew worse. Capt. E. P. Smith, speaking for Tyson at Brewton, Alabama, charged Dent with being at fault for not protecting men in the ranks of the army from having black officers placed over them, and accused Dent of dereliction because sick white soldiers had to occupy beds near sick black soldiers. A rumor was circulated that Dent was responsible for the appointment of Emmet Scott, a Tuskegee black, as Third Assistant Secretary of War. [977]

The campaign as a whole did not appear to be arousing much interest. Dent apparently made no effort to refute these attacks, and stood on his record.[978] The lackluster campaign came to an end on May 12, and after several days of uncertainty, it became apparent that the low road had led to victory: Tyson was the winner, with 9,029 first and second choice votes against Dent's 7,729.

His congressional career closed, Hugh settled down with Etta and his son, Tinsley, in their comfortable two-story home at the corner of Norman Bridge Road and Felder Avenue in Montgomery (which still stands today), and returned to the practice of law. Tinsley, now 20, was attending his father's alma mater, the University of Virginia, from which he would soon graduate with honors as a member of Phi Beta Kappa. (Tinsley's later career as an executive with the Alabama Power Company would be cut short by his death of cancer June 2, 1952, at age 52, in Montgomery.)

It was thirteen years before Hugh again emerged into public life. In 1933, when Congress proposed the twenty-first amendment abolishing national prohibition, it specified that the amendment be submitted to the states for ratification, not by legislatures, but by state conventions called for that purpose. Hugh, who opposed prohibition, performed much of the necessary legal work connected with holding the Alabama convention. He further decided to offer himself as a candidate for state-at-large delegate to the ratification convention. In the election on July 18, Hugh was elected with 79,067 statewide votes, (a total equal to that received by future governor Frank W. Dixon). When the convention opened on August 8, 1933, Dent was unanimously elected as President of the body. In his acceptance speech, (which would be the last recorded public speech of his life), he criticized the Eighteenth Amendment authorizing prohibition: "…it is a misfit in our constitutional system. All other amendments operate upon the national or state government. This amendment for the first time applies directly to the individual citizen…"[979] The Alabama convention went on to ratify the proposed twenty-first amendment.

Perhaps this civic activity reawakened Hugh's interest in political battle. The following year, in 1934, Hugh entered the race for Judge of Montgomery County Circuit Court (place number 2, the first being held by Judge Walter B. Jones, the son of former Gov. Thomas Goode Jones). The other candidates were Thomas W. Martin and Eugene W. Carter. But Hugh Dent's political day was past. Carter was elected, with Dent coming in a distant third: Carter 6219, Martin, 5047, Dent, 2816.[980]

In his last public service, Dent's considerable legal scholarship was effectively utilized. During the administration of Gov. Bibb Graves, the Legislature voted to recodify (reorganize) Alabama's legislative acts or statutes, and Dent was appointed Code Commissioner to carry out this task. His work was ratified by the Legislature in 1940, after his death. The 1940 Code served as the basic statutory law of Alabama until 1958, when it was recompiled, still based largely upon Dent's work. [981]

On Wednesday, October 6, Gov. Graves appointed Hugh to serve as a Special Circuit Judge of Montgomery County during the illness of one of the regular judges. But early the following morning, October 7, 1938, Hugh Dent died of a heart attack at the age of 69. The *New York Times* carried an article describing his political career, while the *Montgomery Advertiser* contained a lengthy editorial of praise which concluded that, "Mr. Dent was a nobleman among Alabamians."[982] Historian, Robert David Ward found that "In many respects, S. H. Dent represented the end of the Southern tradition of the gentleman politician."[983] Writing in 1971, Ward also offered this summary of Dent's political outlook:

> "Stanley Hubert Dent was a most conservative man. The product of place and position, the beneficiary of favor and influence, he led no battles against the *status quo*, he sought no changes in American structure or process. If he eschewed the racial rantings of some of his Southern colleagues, he did so from the patrician's stance of patronage and tutelage to his inferiors. But in matters of military policy Dent often found himself in alliance with social crusaders, labor unions, and advanced progressives. The motives and ideologies that led these groups to common ground were diverse. Yet all shared a fear of military power either as a coercive agent of growing federal authority, or for its effect and influence on the individual...
>
> "For Dent and his colleagues the obligations of citizenship must be freely given if their vigor was to be maintained. When obligation was demanded it lost its vitality. If long pursued, coercion would destroy the free man and his free society, it would lead to the vicious duality of protecting freedom by the methods of dictatorship. The Southern conservative of 1917 might be appalled by most facets of our contemporary scene, but he would share the mounting apprehension of military power that marks our day." [984]

66
Carrie Dent and Charlie McDowell

"...under a runoff system, Charles S. McDowell would probably have been nominated by the Democrats and elected governor of Alabama in 1926."

J. Mills Thornton, the *Alabama Review*

"Charlie McDowell...always will be the standard of excellence by which they will measure men who seek public office."

Duard LeGrand, Editor, *Birmingham Post Herald*

"Mrs. Charles McDowell...a distinguished woman in her own right."

Atticus Mullins, Columnist, *Montgomery Advertiser*

Born September 23, 1879, she was Anna and Hubert Dent's last child, and was named simply, Caroline Dent, (after her mother's sister, Caroline Young Roberts). But few ever called her that. She was usually "Carrie," but as the "baby" of a family that loved nicknames, she was also "Babbie," or "Bab." She was about six months old when, in 1880, following the death the previous year of her grandfather, Edward Brown Young, she moved into Fendall Hall with her parents, her three brothers, and her two sisters.[yy] As a child of 6, Carrie saw and heard Jefferson Davis when he visited in Eufaula during his 1886 tour of the South. As she grew into a young woman, Carrie was known for her beauty. A Eufaula admirer wondered, *"Where is a more charming girl than Miss Caroline Dent? Brown tressed and hazel eyed, dimples playing hide and seek in her sweet oval face."*[985] Her long hair, when released, reached her knees (but it was always worn "up"). Another Eufaula native remembered her as "the youngest and prettiest of Captain S. H. Dent's daughters."[986]

Caroline Dent, circa 1898, age 19

Carrie received her elementary, high school, and college education at the Union Female College in Eufaula, (which her grandfather Young had helped to found), graduating in 1897 with an AB degree and a degree in music.[987] There she gave evidence of a quick and facile mind, winning the gold medal of excellence in most of her subjects. Musically talented, she studied voice for a season in Washington, D. C., residing there with her father's younger

---

[yy] Ed ("Biggie"), Anna Beall ("Nannie"), Hugh, Henry, and Louise ("Weesie")

unmarried sister, "Aunt Ella" Dent. Throughout her life Eufaulians would enjoy Carrie's singing; she was an accomplished pianist and organist as well. Following her graduation, Carrie taught school for three years, part of this as a member of the faculty of the "primary department" of Union Female Academy, and part in a one-room school in Peachburg (then called "Flora") in Bullock County near Union Springs. She spent an adventurous summer "keeping house" for her older brother Henry who was then a young officer of the Navy paymaster corps stationed at the naval base at Bremerton, Washington. Photographs from that summer show a winsome beauty on the porch of Lieutenant Dent's quarters surrounded by admiring, white-uniformed young naval officers.

Carrie had no shortage of suitors, but the young man most frequently seen ascending the front steps of Fendall Hall was a lawyer who had already distinguished himself in the law and politics of Barbour County, Charlie McDowell. Like Carrie herself, Charlie was bright and industrious, and she could not have failed to recognize in him the spark of a driving ambition.

Charlie was born in Eufaula October 17, 1871. After graduating from high school, the ambitious 17-year old entered the University of Alabama for the 1888-1889 year. As a uniformed cadet, he pledged Delta Kappa Epsilon fraternity, and resided on the "third stoop of Woods Hall."[988] His time at the University of Alabama made a deep impression upon Charlie, and in later years, his friends recalled, "he always referred to his 'cadet days' as the halcyon days of his young life."[989]

Cadet Charlie McDowell, 17, (4th from right) with the DKE chapter before the "Little Round House" at UA, 1888-1889

Charlie's financial resources did not permit him to continue his college education after that single year, and he returned to Barbour County to become a wholesale grocery "drummer." He was a very successful traveling salesman. There is an oft-told story that Charlie was once hurrying in his buggy to reach a rural store to make a large sale before a competing salesman got there and preempted the sale. Charlie's buggy got stuck in the mud, and the competitor's buggy trotted past on his way to beating Charlie and making the sale. Not to be defeated, Charlie unhitched his horse from the buggy traces, galloped bareback past the astonished competitor, arrived first, and won the lucrative order.

But the ambition of C. S. McDowell, Jr. was larger than this. In a scrapbook which he began keeping in September 1896, Charlie wrote:

"There was always the desire to practice law in my mind. Unable financially to obtain an education, I abandoned the hope; but interested in the law, while working as a traveling salesman as a grocer drummer, I carried a *Walking American Law* and *Blackstone's* in my grip, while on the road. I was offered the position of probate clerk at Clayton at a salary of $25 per month. I accepted, quit the mercantile life and read law, then was admitted to practice in 1896."

The newspaper in Clayton, the county seat some 20 miles from Eufaula, noted Charlie's promising future:

"We take the opportunity to whisper a modest compliment for our Memorial Day orator who was none other than our popular adopted son, Mr. Charles S. McDowell, Jr. He has recently been admitted to the Bar, and this was his maiden effort at a public speech. But if future victories are to be…so easily and gracefully won as his success on this day, we can safely predict that triumphs all along will make his pathway throughout life…"

Charlie's father, Charles Samuel McDowell, Sr., had been born and reared in Greeneville, East Tennessee.[zz] That part of Tennessee had been strongly pro-Union in the Civil War, while the McDowell family were strong Southern sympathizers. One night in January 1863, [990] seventeen year old Charles, Sr. climbed from the second story window of their home which still stands today on Greeneville's Main Street, made his way to the nearest Confederate recruiting sergeant, and enlisted as a private in Lynch's Battery of the Confederate Army. His older brother, William Patton, later enlisted also. Young Charles, Sr. was captured by the Yankees in August 1863, imprisoned for several weeks, and then released as part of an exchange of 45 Confederate privates for the federal cavalryman, Major General Stoneman. With the sense of humor characteristic of the McDowells, in later years Charles relished in saying that by that exchange, his Civil War rank was "1/45th of a major General." Following the defeat of the Confederacy, the McDowell family probably were not comfortable continuing to reside in the Greeneville area, and they migrated south. They settled first in Rome, Georgia for several years, and then in Eufaula. In Eufaula on December 8, 1870, Charles, Sr, married Margaret Starr McKay (pronounced "McCoy" in the Scottish way). Charles and Margaret would have five children, of which Charlie, Jr. was the oldest. [aaa]

Charlie, Jr. took his last order as a "drummer," and left the mercantile business on August 30, 1895.[991] He served as Probate Clerk in Clayton, Barbour's County seat, for two years in 1895-1897, (earning less than he had made as a "drummer)," while he "read law." During this interlude, although living in Clayton, he of course stayed in close contact with his Eufaula home 25 miles away. The *Eufaula Times* of November 19, 1895 reports that, "Mr.

[zz] Charles, Sr. was the son of James Patton McDowell and his wife, Elizabeth Burkhardt

[aaa] Charlie's three brothers were: Dr. William Patton ("Ditty"), a pioneer practitioner of pediatric medicine in Norfolk, Virginia; Archibald McKay ("Arch"), a Eufaula lawyer; and Edwin Kenneth ("Ed"), who had a career in government service in Washington, D. C. His sisters were: Janet Little ("Jan"), who married Barbour County Probate Judge Huey R. Lee; and Katherine ("Katie"), who married a dentist, Dr. Alfred P. Brown.

Charles S. McDowell, Jr., the polite and accommodating clerk in the probate office in Clayton, spent Sunday with his parents in this city." After being admitted to the Bar in 1896, it was not long before Charlie jumped into the political affairs of the county. The personable new lawyer was elected at the age of 26 to the Barbour County Board of Revenue (the county governing body) in 1897, on which he would serve for six years until 1903. Also in 1897 he became Barbour County's Superintendent of Education, a position he would hold until 1906. On the occasion of his fifth appointment to this position, a local newspaper observed, "Since [McDowell's] taking charge of this office, the term of public schools in Barbour has been increased from three to an average of seven months, and the system on which he conducts the office is recommended by the state superintendent as a model..."[992] Charlie also found time to serve as Chairman of the Barbour County Democratic Executive Committee; and during 1898-1899 he was additionally a member of the Alabama State Democratic Executive Committee. [993]

Although there was no military threat in sight, membership in the local militia was popular among the town's young men. Charlie enjoyed being a member of Eufaula's company, which still bore the name of Hubert Dent's old Civil War unit, the "Eufaula Rifles," now officially Company G, Second Infantry, Alabama National Guard. Charlie was elected as its captain and commissioned by Gov. Joseph F. Johnston on August 17, 1899, and served as its commander until 1903.[994]

Much of the Eufaula Rifles' activity was social. Perhaps because Carrie Dent was known to be Charlie's "sweetheart," but more probably because of her own popularity, the men of the Eufaula Rifles elected her their "sponsor." As her insignia of rank, she wore a miniature sword on a sash around her waist at military social functions. In the 1901 Memorial Day parade, Carrie Dent, as sponsor of the Eufaula Rifles, and her maid of honor, Miss Amma McRae[bbb], rode in the carriage of honor. During the ceremonies, the soldier winning the drill prize was recognized. The *Eufaula Times and News* reported: "The company's sponsor, Miss Caroline Dent, with a sweet smile and pleasant word, for the third time, presented to the young triumphant soldier, the public evidence of the honors he had won—the company's medal, which will adorn his coat for 30 days."

Captain Charlie McDowell, as commander of the Eufaula Rifles, circa 1901

Charlie McDowell also became a lieutenant colonel on the military staffs of Governors Samford (1900-1901) and Jelks (1901-1907), and a full colonel on the staff of Gov. Henderson (1915-1919).[995] These military staff positions were normally ceremonial only, but in January 1902, Eufaulian Gov. William D. Jelks designated Lt. Col. McDowell of his military staff to serve on an unusual and celebrated court-martial. Lt. Col. Osceola Kyle of Decatur, an officer in the 3rd Infantry, Alabama National Guard, was charged by his regimental commander, Col. E. L. Higdon of Birmingham, with "conduct unbecoming an officer and a gentleman," in that he wrote Col. Higdon a "sensational" letter. Although the incident was a tempest in a teapot, the

bbb Daughter of John McRae, the brother of Henry Young's widow, Maria McRae Young trial lasted for many days, escalated into extensive testimony about politics in the National Guard, and attracted intense interest and banner headlines every day. Lt. Col. McDowell and the board of four other officers (including Col. E. H. Graves of Eufaula), found Kyle guilty of "unbecoming conduct" in writing an insulting letter to his commander, and fined him $1.00. Gov. Jelks was degusted with the verdict and set it aside. He said if the defendant's letter were an offense the punishment was inadequate; if the letter were not an offense, he should be acquitted.[996] Jelks further relieved from duty all of the Alabama 3rd Infantry Regiment staff and field officers. Later, when feelings cooled, the officers were restored and the charges were quietly disposed of.

As time passed Charlie McDowell was seen more and more frequently with "Babbie," as he usually called Carrie Dent. But while she was responsive to him, she showed no eagerness to make commitments, and continued to have other suitors. On one occasion, Charlie assumed that he would escort her to a major upcoming social event, as he had many times before, but neglected to actually discuss the matter with her until shortly before the event. He was stunned to learn that she had already accepted an invitation to attend with another beau. Charlie was furious, and his brothers later observed him in the woodlot with an ax, chopping up his portrait of Babbie. But "stay tuned."

A flirtatious, dimpled Carrie Dent, circa 1901

Charlie's scrapbook contains the program of a "Grand Military Concert" at the opera house on June 6, 1901 for the benefit of the Eufaula Rifles, wherein practically every skit, song, or event features Miss Carrie Dent. Across the program Charlie has written, *"Gotten up by 'her.' She was the whole show."* When Carrie was teaching in the one-room schoolhouse in Peachburg, Charlie would sometimes leave his law office and take the train from Eufaula to Peachburg for the day, thereby distracting Miss Dent from her duties, much to the glee of her pupils.

Carrie and Charlie were married on October 15, 1902. Because Carrie's mother had died only seven months earlier, their wedding at Fendall Hall was subdued. But it was still an appealing event: an unusual "Lilliputian" wedding, in which all the participants were children of the couples' families. The *Times & News* of October 23, 1902 reported the miniature nuptials:

"Dent-McDowell Wedding
"The young Benedicts and matrons of Eufaula have two charming additions to their number in the persons of Col. C. S. McDowell, Jr., and his bride, nee Miss Caroline Dent, who were married on Wednesday evening last at the home of the bride's father, Capt. S. H. Dent, on College Hill.
"This fascinating couple is so well known in the social world, that it would be painting the lily, or gilding refined gold to attempt to picture their personal charms. Yet, for one who has known the lovely young wife from her

school girl days, it is impossible to refrain from speaking of the genial, sunny nature and the strength of character, which stamps her a peer among women. Her intellectual attainments make her a fit companion for her handsome distinguished husband whose future in his chosen profession of the law is already assured by his successes in the past.

Owing to the recent bereavement of Mrs. McDowell in the death of her mother the occasion was a more exclusive one than the multitude of friends of both parties would have otherwise desired. The guests were limited to the two families represented by the bride and groom and a few intimate friends…

Promptly at nine o'clock the strains of the wedding march from violin and piano broke upon the ear—both instruments under the skillful touch of artists of rare ability, Mrs. Louie Dent [Genevieve Lockwood, wife of Helen and George's son] and Miss Lucy Glenn [lifelong close friend of Carrie].

Then two little maidens, Jack Long [daughter of Carrie's sister, Nannie] and Catherine Dent [daughter of Carrie's brother, Ed Young Dent], entered trailing rolls of white ribbon and were met under the broad arch between the two rooms by Masters George Dent [grandson of George and Helen] and Hubert Long [son of Carrie's sister, Nannie], who also left each a trail of white ribbon as they advanced. Other Lilliputian attendants followed with all the dignity and grace of grown people: Nanna Dent [another daughter of Carrie's brother, Ed Dent], Janet McDowell [Charlie's youngest sister] and last, two day fairies, Mary Maude and Ada Louise Hurt [daughters of Carrie's sister "Weesie"], who bore the magic circlet which was to bind the happy pair together.

The entrance of Miss Martha Long, the little maid of honor [another daughter of Carrie's sister, Nannie] heralded the coming bride, who appeared on the arm of her father. She was attired in a soft white silk with a rich over dress of point lace, the chief charm of which lay, not in its costly beauty, but in the fact of its being the bridal veil of her beloved mother.

The groom, accompanied by his brother, Dr. William P. McDowell, approached from the opposite direction and received his bride from her father's arm…

Dr. Peterson, pastor of the Methodist church, officiated, assisted by Rev. E. L. Hill of the Presbyterian Church…"

There is abundant evidence that each worshiped the ground the other walked upon, and their love affair never ended.

After the wedding, Carrie and Charlie purchased and moved into a modest, single-story house at 415 West Broad Street at the foot of "College Hill." Built prior to 1894, the McDowells bought the house in 1902 from Levy W. Foy and his wife, Frances.[997] This would be the only house Carrie and Charlie ever lived in. Although later substantially rebuilt and enlarged, it would be their home until both of their deaths.

On November 15, 1903, their first daughter, Annie Dent McDowell, was born. She was the center of their universe, until her sudden death from an unexplained illness a year and a half later. Charlie and Carrie were devastated; the scar left by this child's death would last a lifetime. Despite their strong hopes for another child, it was eight years before they were blessed again. On November 17, 1911, another daughter was born, who brought such abundant joy they decided to call her "Joy"—Caroline Joy McDowell.

In 1908, at 37, Charlie fulfilled what he recalled as a boyhood ambition by being elected Mayor of Eufaula. He took office upon the expiration of three successive terms served by Carrie's Uncle George H. Dent, (from 1902-1908). At this time, the Eufaula Gas and Electric Light Company was offering to construct a new electric light plant. Charlie favored a city-owned plant, and criticized the service being provided by the old company: "It has reached the point where we know not the moment when all will be in darkness," he said, "...lamps and candles have become a household necessity...to use them for reading is ruinous to one's eyesight." In 1911, the council followed Mayor McDowell's recommendation and, after a citizens' vote approving the necessary bond issue, the City entered the electric business.[998] In a ceremony celebrating the completion of the new electric plant, the lights of Eufaula came on as the button was pressed by the Mayor's seven-month-old daughter, Joy McDowell.[999]

Alabama adopted statewide prohibition in 1909, (superceding a county option system under which Barbour was wet). Like his brother-in-law, Congressman Hugh Dent, Charlie McDowell did not favor the prohibition laws, but as Mayor he made a valiant effort to carry out his responsibility to enforce the laws on the books. In the face of rampant bootlegging, Mayor McDowell informed the council, "The prohibition laws...are being violated every day," and sought an appropriation of additional funds for enforcement. "...It is going to be stopped," he pledged. True to his commitment, 44 bootlegging and moonshine cases were tried during the next six months.

Charlie was reelected in 1910 for another two-year term. In his 1910 report to the council, he pointed out a projected budget deficit of $4,000, but warned against solving it by eliminating services. "...Put in the same business methods you would in your own business," he recommended, "and you will have solved the problem." Unfortunately, this advice did not quite solve the problem; the actual shortfall turned out to be $6,462. Mayor McDowell then warned that their new slogan needed to be, "a clean sheet and a red line...a fine campaign card for those who care to be reelected." [1000]

In 1911, Mayor McDowell also announced his "greatest regret of the year," the closing of Brenau College. This had originally been Carrie's old alma mater, the Union Female College, which because of financial difficulties and decreasing enrollment had been leased in 1904 to Brenau College Conservatory of Gainesville, Georgia.[1001] Professor Van Hoose, president of that college, along with Professor Pierce, had moved to Eufaula and taken over the old Female College, operating it as "Alabama Brenau."[1002] Despite an initial large enrollment necessitating an enlargement, "Alabama Brenau" closed in 1911, and the old college which Edward Young helped to found was gone forever. As McDowell left office in

1912, he warned of the need for enlarging the City's white school and the need for providing for the continued lease of the Colored school building. He also pointed out that the buildings of the old college were fast deteriorating, and advocated that state aid be sought to convert them into a state industrial school for girls. However, the following year the old college was "patched up" for use as a public school,[1003] and was not torn down until 1920.

The mayoral project in which Charlie took the most pride was his enlargement and beautification of Fairview Cemetery, and the construction of the entrance park which now adorns that end of Randolph Avenue. Charlie later described the park project in notes in his scrapbook: "To my mind, that old alley entrance was an eyesore, and the 'haunted house' lot (the present park) was a disgrace to the City of Eufaula. I was mayor of Eufaula. I tried to enthuse my Council to aiding me in my undertaking to obtain this lot. They were indifferent but willing for me to do anything I desired. Finally, after much worry, work and planning, I purchased for the City…the park property…I was happy over the purchase. The alley was abandoned; the trees, brushes, briars, and the old house were cleared away. … Personally I spent much time out there. I personally laid out the walks and drive – the new and present entrance – I planned the fountain…[City personnel] built it for me…hauled the gravel for the walks and drive…set out the oak trees and from the old Union Female College I moved the iron fence – and enclosed Fairview Park."[1004]

The Democratic National Convention of 1912 was held in Baltimore, Maryland. Mayor Charlie McDowell was elected as a delegate; he and Carrie were there for the opening of the convention on June 25. Alabama Sen. Oscar W. Underwood was a leading candidate for president. Other principal contenders were Speaker Champ Clark of Missouri, and Virginia-born Gov. Woodrow Wilson of New Jersey. Charlie and the Alabama delegation backed Underwood, as instructed by the Alabama Democratic Party. It took many ballots for a candidate to obtain the two-thirds vote required by Democratic rules. After forty-six ballots, Underwood and Clark finally withdrew, allowing Wilson to be nominated. Wilson went on to defeat the Republican, William Howard Taft, as well as Theodore Roosevelt's breakaway "Bullmoose Party."

The law firm of McDowell & McDowell was born in 1913. Charlie's younger brother, Archibald McKay McDowell ("Arch" or "Archie"), had graduated from high school in 1900, worked for ten years at the Commercial National Bank of Eufaula, and then enrolled in the University of Alabama Law School (with financial help from Charlie). In 1913, Arch graduated from law school, returned to Eufaula, and went into partnership with Charlie.[1005] The two brothers would practice law together under the name of McDowell & McDowell until their deaths, during which time Arch would be just as active in providing leadership to his town and county as his older brother.

Meeting in Birmingham on July 10, 1915, the Alabama Bar Association elected Charlie McDowell as its president for the 1915-1916 term, to succeed Ray Rushton of Montgomery. For a self-educated, small-town lawyer who had never attended law school, this recognition from his fellow lawyers of Alabama appears to have been particularly gratifying. Charlie sent Carrie in Eufaula a somewhat dramatic telegram: "I am bringing you home tonight the presidency of the Alabama Bar Association to which my brother lawyers unanimously elected me today."[1006] The following year at the 1916 convention of the Bar in Decatur, a principal topic was a recent change in the method of electing Alabama's appellate judges. Previously, they had run only in the November general elections, in what was tantamount to a non-partisan (non-party) election. The 1915 Legislature required them to run for nomination by a party in the spring party primaries. In an incisive indictment of a bad law, Bar President McDowell roundly criticized this change:

"If the unyielding and zealous advocates of the primary system for choosing judges are logical, they must go further than they have gone and declare, virtually, that they do not want men upon the courts…because of their legal attainments, but because of their political alignments. All men recognize a difference between a judicial and a political office, and we should recognize a corresponding difference between candidates for these offices.

…The judge does not make the law, and it is not therefore material what he thinks about current political issues. He is chosen to serve the people, not represent them; he does not translate their convictions into statutes nor shape the policy of the State. His office is simply to hold the scales of justice even as between man and man, and he should never be forced into a contest which must inevitably engender passion and prejudice which are fatal to judicial poise…"[1007]

Unfortunately, the partisan election of Alabama judges continues to the present day (2003), and is now even more detrimental to the system of justice than in 1916. Its evils have never been more effectively exposed then in McDowell's 1916 comments, which were recently reprinted in the January 2002 issue of "The Alabama Lawyer," the monthly publication of the Alabama Bar. [1008]

Back in Eufaula in 1915, Carrie and Joy returned from their regular summer visit with Carrie's older sister, Nannie Dent Jackson Mangum, and her family in Rome, Georgia. Having enjoyed the facilities of the Rome Country Club, on her return Carrie suggested to friends that Eufaula should have a similar facility. The idea caught on, and the Eufaula Country Club came into existence, with Dr. W. S. Britt as president and Charlie McDowell as vice president. It continues to thrive today.

Active in his church, during 1916-1917 Charlie served as Moderator of the Presbyterian Synod. In June 1917, two months after America's declaration of war on Germany, we find Charlie as one of the featured speakers at a rally to raise funds for the Red Cross in support of the war effort.[1009] During this war, Charlie served as Chairman of the Legal Advisory Board, an arm of the Selective Service System, which administered the draft laws,[1010] while Carrie worked with the Red Cross in organizing women to prepare surgical dressings.[1011]

The long and productive life of Carrie's father, Capt. Stouten Hubert Dent, came to a close on March 26, 1917, at the age of 84. Active, slender, and moderate in habit, Hubert had continued in good health, superintending the farming of his lands, until a few months before his death at Fendall Hall. Among the dispositions to be resolved as a result of his death was the matter of Fendall Hall. It had been owned by his wife, Anna Beall Young, and upon her death in 1902, she had willed it to her children equally. Of course, he continued to occupy it during the fifteen years by which he survived her. For a number of years prior to his death, Carrie's sister, "Weesie" (Louise), her husband, George Hurt, and their two children, had lived in the big house with Hubert to provide a household and care for Hubert as he grew older. In recognition of Weesie's doing this for their father, the other children had deeded the home to Weesie in 1912. When Capt. Dent died in 1917, Charlie McDowell hoped that he might have a chance to purchase the house for Carrie. As a successful lawyer, it was well within his means to do so, and he wanted to present to Carrie the elegant, locally-renowned old home in which she had been reared from the age of six months. Initial conversations with Weesie and George indicated this might be possible, but they ultimately decided to remain in the house. There they would rear their two daughters, Nan and Mary Maud, and live out their lives.

Charlie was disappointed, but he soon set to work making other arrangements. Carrie, Joy, and Charlie temporarily moved out of their modest house at the foot of College Hill while it was virtually rebuilt. It became a handsome, two-story house of Tudor design. The first story was brick, reached by marble steps opening onto a large roofed front porch with overhanging eaves. (When it was Charlie's turn to host the Commercial Club luncheon, Carrie would set up dining tables and serve the men on this spacious porch, to avoid her house becoming permeated with cigar smoke.) The second story was cream stucco and brown half-timbers in the Tudor manner. Inside was a capacious, well-appointed, and comfortable home, containing some of her mother's Victorian style furnishings which had adorned Fendall Hall. In the rear of the house were a garage, greenhouse, servants' facilities, other outbuildings, and a large garden centered on a fountain and lily pool (with the garden incorporating part of the rear lot of the adjacent house, which Charlie had also acquired). By March 1919, the family was comfortably settled back into the newly reconstituted home.[1012]

Having served in many leadership positions in Eufaula, Charlie's political horizons were about to be expanded. On November 17, 1917, an open letter to him appeared in a local paper, signed by dozens of voters from communities throughout Barbour County, asserting that "you can be of service to Barbour County in the next legislature," and "insisting" that "you announce as a candidate for the state senate." [1013] Whether this was an orchestrated beginning of his campaign or a spontaneous draft, Charlie accepted the invitation and jumped into the race. The local paper gave him strong backing, predicting that he would have little opposition. In the August 13, 1918 Democratic Primary, he was elected to the Alabama Senate from the 24th District (Barbour County) by a large vote, defeating two opponents: McDowell, 1,065; G. E. Jones, 518; and R. M. Lee, 184. Upon assuming his Senate seat, he was given excellent committee assignments: Finance and Taxation, perhaps the most important Senate Committee; Education, in which Charlie as a former superintendent of education would have had a special interest; and Judiciary, which affected his own profession.[1014] The state press applauded his election. The *Montgomery Journal,* which, unlike McDowell, supported national prohibition, made this comment on August 15, 1918:

"Charlie McDowell is a splendid fellow with an attractive personality. It is a pity he comes to the senate tied down with the promise to vote against the national prohibition amendment. But for that handicap he would have a very bright future in Alabama politics. Genial, brainy, polished, companionable, lovable in disposition, he has the faculty of drawing men to him."

In the regular legislative session of 1919, the Alabama Legislature rejected the proposed amendment to the United States constitution which would allow women to vote. In an unusual departure from his progressive attitudes, Sen. Charlie McDowell was one of the leaders of this rejection. Under date of Oct 17, 1920, he wrote this comment in his scrapbook:

"A bit of history. I was one of the 19 in the Senate that put though this resolution [of rejection]. A bitter fight it was. 35 states had ratified. But Alabama, true to her teachings, kept the faith of the people and held firm. In September 1920, Tennessee, the 36th state, ratified the provision for the registration of women."

Carrie had diplomatically taken the position that it didn't much matter to her whether women got the vote or not. In 1920, on the first Election Day after the passage of women's suffrage, Charlie and Carrie agreed to meet at the polling place at a certain time and vote together. Due to a change in her schedule, Carrie arrived first, voted, and left. Charlie 'kidded' her ever afterward, claiming she was so eager to vote she couldn't wait for him.[1015] Next to the scrapbook comment quoted above, Charlie carefully preserved "Bab's" first Registration Certificate, noting approvingly that she voted for Cox (the Democrat nominee for president) in 1920.

In 1921, Charlie was an organizing member and first president of the Eufaula Kiwanis Club, in which he would remain active for many years.

It is doubtful that Carrie McDowell was actually indifferent to the question of votes for women. While effectively supporting and complementing Charlie in his pursuit of law and politics, Carrie Dent McDowell also pursued her own many interests. She turned her fertile intellect and appealing personality toward the civic, literary, and religious affairs of her community and state. If she had lived in the present era, Carrie too would have had a professional career, or would have been a business executive or political leader. But in the early years of the twentieth century, those options were not open to her. Women of her abilities devoted their energies to good works. And in a time when domestic help was usually available, Carrie had the freedom to conduct her household while vigorously pursuing a variety of important interests outside the home.

Throughout her life, Carrie's first interest after her family was the Methodist Church. Her parents, the Dents, and her grandparents, the Youngs, had been active leaders in that church, and Carrie followed the example. Charlie was just as loyal to the Presbyterian church of his Scots-Irish forebears, and neither of them gave consideration to changing churches. Throughout their marriage, Carrie and Joy attended the Methodist Church, while Charlie attended the Presbyterian, an arrangement that worked very satisfactorily. For over 50 years,

Carrie taught an adult Sunday school class, which was ultimately named the McDowell Sunday School Class. In addition to her extensive local church activity, over the years Carrie held many of the positions of leadership open to women at the district and state (or conference) level. The principal women's arm of the highly-organized Methodist Church was the Women's Missionary Society, (or later, Women's Society of Christian Service). From 1916 to 1924, Carrie served as Superintendent of Young People of the Women's Society for the Alabama Conference. From 1933-1943, she served as Alabama Conference Vice-President of the Women's Society. She twice received the distinction of being named by the Alabama Conference as an honorary life member of WSCS. There were very few committees or projects of the Methodist Church at all levels that she did not at one time chair or actively serve.[1016]

Carrie was an active leader in the Alabama Federation of Women's Clubs. An accomplished musician in voice, piano and organ, she worked in the Alabama Federation of Music Clubs. An avid gardener, she held leadership roles in the Federation of Alabama Garden Clubs. She served the latter as Chairman of the Conservation Section, long before conservation activity became fashionable.[1017] She considered one of her most worthwhile activities to be her service of over 20 years on the Board of Trustees of the Eufaula Carnegie Library, during which she led the board as its chair for 10 years. [1018]

But, second only to her church, Carrie's most cherished interest was the United Daughters of the Confederacy, or "UDC." As the child of Captain Hubert Dent, who never missed a convention of the United Confederate Veterans, Carrie was reared on stories and memories of the War Between the States and of the Confederacy. Along with other women of her generation, she was imbued with the near-sacred duty of preserving and transmitting to the next generations the importance of honoring those who died or otherwise sacrificed for the Confederacy, and protecting the "truths" of Confederate history. They did not defend slavery, of course, but they defiantly defended the right of the states to secede. (Carrie herself believed that, if the Confederacy had won The War, the Southern states would have eventually rejoined the union, but "on their own terms.") She became a member of the UDC as a young woman, even before her 1902 marriage to Charlie, and when she died in 1966 at the age of 86, she had recently flown home from a national UDC convention. In the interim, she had served on or chaired virtually every committee or project of the UDC, and had held most offices at the local and state level, as well as serving in national capacities. Generations of Eufaulians were recruited by her for the UDC auxiliary, the "Children of the Confederacy." Others have memories of seeing "Miss Carrie" coming to the schoolhouse, which foretold that it was Confederate Memorial Day and they were about to hear a presentation on Gen. Lee, Gen. Jackson, or President Davis.

The deep emotional link with the events of 1861-1865 which Carrie and others of her time felt is typified by a speech she made while serving as President of the Alabama Division of the UDC (i. e. state president), to which she had been elected in the early 1920's. In her numerous activities, Carrie spoke frequently; she was an articulate, even eloquent, speaker. On this occasion she was giving a Memorial Day address in Florence, Alabama, sponsored by the Florence chapter of UDC. Many Confederate veterans were still living at this time, and Carrie's audience included a group of them. Excerpts are presented here:

"I count it a great honor to speak to you on this occasion, for this is indeed the South's "day of days." It has been called the "Sabbath of the South," and it could have no more fitting name, for it is a sacred day--sacred to the memory of the brave soldiers who are gone, and holding in sacred love those still with us.

"We owe a debt of gratitude to those women whose tender thoughts gave us this beautiful custom. [She then traces the beginnings of Confederate Memorial Day, from a group of Columbus ladies placing flowers on soldiers' graves immediately after the war.]

"…Upon the walls of childhood's memory, there always hang some pictures that stand out beyond all others. Among the earliest recollections of those days, I recall with special vividness the Memorial Days in my little hometown. In that period, some 20 years after the war, the Confederate soldiers were in the vigor and prime of their mature manhood. I can see them now, a long line of them, marching with erect shoulders and firm tread out to the cemetery, where we gathered among the trees at the Soldiers Square, where were buried those who had died in the days of the war, or had been killed in battle. I can see my gallant grey-clad father, riding at the head of the column, across his shoulders a wreath of roses and around his horse's neck a similar garland. And in the eyes of them all was the light of battle, and the glory that was theirs shown there. O veterans, with such a memory, is it any wonder that I love you, that I love to work for you, or that I shall treasure the honor of being the leader of the UDC of Alabama as the greatest heritage that I shall leave to my little daughter?

"…. 'All the world loves a soldier.' … But soldiers of the Confederacy—in the eyes of the Daughters of the Confederacy, they excel them all. We know the hardships you endured. We know your courage and your bravery through it all. We know that many times your bodies were weak from the lack of food. We know that many times you were cold from lack of clothes. We know your feet were sore and bruised from lack of shoes. But did you complain? No word of complaint passed your lips, but your unconquerable spirit remained bright and cheerful to the end. O veterans, we love you for your courage, and you shall be forever enshrined in our hearts…. 'The glory of those who wore the grey' shall live as long as there shall exist a chapter of the UDC…

"We shall tell the story of these valiant men to our children's children…. Unless we are true to the memory of our fathers, their fame will die. Unless we tell the truths of history, and right the many wrongs, it will not be done. Let me beg you to teach these things to your children, let them know that their forefathers were not rebels, but that they fought for principles, not which they *thought* were right, but which they *knew* were right. [She then discusses the history and legal basis for the doctrine of secession, a right which

642

had been generally recognized since the constitution was ratified by the states, and which she viewed as the 'real cause, the vital issue' in the war.]

"...I beg of you to see that the children use histories that give the true facts of that period in our country's history, in order that justice may be done to those concerned. And above all, let us preserve the sentiment in our children which we feel for the Confederacy. Sentiment is the soul of a nation.... How many unforgotten names live forever in our memories because of sentiment! Lee, the greatest name on the pages of history...Stonewall Jackson, the noble, the gentle though stern Christian soldier; Jefferson Davis, 'most maligned of men was he,' the true worth of his great character not recognized even by his own people.

"And those noble sons of our own Alabama: The Gallant Pelham, a mere youth, commended for his valor by the great Lee himself; 'Fighting Joe' Wheeler, so recently honored by his state in the placing of his statue in the Hall of Fame; Morgan; Pettus; Forrest; and the scores of others whose names are written upon the hearts of their people.

"...And as we teach our children to honor and love the Stars and Stripes, may we not forget at the same time to teach them to love that other flag, the Stars and Bars, our very own flag,

'For its fame on countless pages,
Sung by poets and by sages,
Shall go sounding down the ages,
For 'tis wreathed around with glory,
And twill live in song and story.'"

Lt. Gov. Charlie McDowell as President of the Alabama Senate, 1923

Membership in the UDC required descent from a Confederate veteran, but within the general membership there was an ever-dwindling "elite" of which Carrie was a part, consisting of "Real Daughters," i. e. first generation descendents of veterans. But she had an even greater distinction in having actually seen and heard Jefferson Davis himself during his 1889 tour of the South. For this distinction she was often introduced to meetings and conventions with some awe. Charlie fully shared Carrie's enthusiasm for honoring their Confederate heritage, and was himself a member and officer of the Sons of Confederate Veterans.

Sen. Charlie McDowell also shared Carrie's speaking skills. In the Senate, his "qualities of leadership, which included a polished eloquence and forcefulness in debate, soon won him statewide recognition."[1019] As he approached the end of his state Senate term for 1919-

1922, his popularity and effectiveness led to suggestions that he run for governor. He declined these suggestions, but decided to run for lieutenant governor. His ever-active ambition would have led him to think of the improved possibilities for 1926 if he were successful in 1922. One newspaper portrayed him as being "distinguished in the senate for an insistence upon economic administration of the state government and for his strong stand against excessive taxation."[1020] National prohibition having now been enacted, the *Montgomery Journal* strongly supported McDowell for lieutenant-governor: "The *Journal* …has known him for many years, and it can not readily recall ever having observed one in public life more conscientious and faithful. He is faithful in his friendships, in his duty and loyalty to principles in which he believes. All his career…from early manhood till this good day, he has fully sustained this estimate of his character…"[1021] The Democratic Primary was scheduled for August 8, 1922. Running for governor was Probate Judge William W. Brandon of Tuscaloosa. Then as now, candidates for governor and lieutenant governor in Alabama did not normally run jointly as an official "ticket." However, Charlie McDowell and Bill Brandon were friends and allies; in this race Charlie was seen as an unofficial "running-mate" of Brandon.[1022] Both men won handily in literal landslides: Brandon defeated Bibb Graves 163,000 against 44,000, while Charlie defeated Sen. Berrien Phillips of Lee County: 135,000 against 45,000.[1023] In the privacy of his scrapbook, Charlie modestly noted: "I carried every county in Alabama, including home county of my opponent, by large majority."

In October 1922, Lt. Gov-elect Charlie and Carrie held a celebration of their 20th wedding anniversary at their home on Broad Street. The local paper reported that troops of friends gathered to congratulate "this popular and well-beloved couple who are the toast of Eufaula at all times and on all occasions…The entire house was thrown open, with its old English connecting doors, practically making it one drawing room."

January 1923 saw Eufaulians celebrating the inauguration of their townsman as the new lieutenant governor of Alabama. A large contingent of Charlie's friends and supporters traveled to Montgomery for the event on a special train chartered by the Eufaula Commercial Club. Eufaula's Cowikee Mills Band played during the inaugural ceremonies. The Eufaula *Times and News* called Charlie "another in the list of Barbour County leaders in government…rugged, tried, and true."[1024]

Joy, 11, and Carrie McDowell at the State Inaugural, January 15, 1923

During his term, Lt. Gov. McDowell established a reputation for fairness and good humor as presiding officer of the Senate. One of his notable projects principally benefited his home county of Barbour: a new bridge across the Chattahoochee. The first bridge across that river at Eufaula had been built by the Irwinton Bridge Company, the firm sponsored and largely owned by Carrie's grandfather, Edward B. Young. That bridge had been replaced by a succession of wooden bridges. In 1921, the central span of the wooden covered bridge was discovered to be in a dangerous condition. A modern new bridge was needed, and Charlie undertook to help, but this turned out to be more easily said than done. Federal funds could be obtained to partially cover the $150,000 construction costs, but additional funding was necessary. Georgia was willing to provide part of the financing, but expected Alabama to do the same. However, because the Georgia border was the *west* bank of the river (i. e. the Eufaula side), the bridge would be located on Georgia territory, and Alabama law then forbade expending state funds beyond the state borders. Lt. Gov. C. S. McDowell, Jr. obtained passage of a

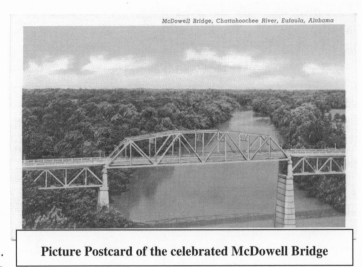

Picture Postcard of the celebrated McDowell Bridge

statute authorizing Alabama's participation in the cost of construction of interstate bridges.[1025] As a result, in July 1923, Alabama and Georgia signed a compact whereby 50% of the construction costs would be derived from federal funds otherwise allotted to the two states, in equal shares; and the remaining 50% of the costs would be state funds contributed equally by the two states. Lt. Gov. McDowell obtained the appropriation of the necessary Alabama funds, and spearheaded the effort to obtain the necessary federal approval and funding of

Joy McDowell, 14, christens the McDowell Bridge, 1925

these unusual arrangements. In recognition of Charlie's key role in the project, the new bridge was named the "McDowell Bridge." Built of modern reinforced steel and concrete construction, the McDowell Bridge had an 18-foot wide roadway and was 685 feet long, with its center span 85 feet above the riverbed. [1026]

The bridge was formally dedicated on December 15, 1925 in a gala celebration called "one of the biggest in the city's history," before a large crowd from surrounding areas using special excursion rates granted by the Central of Georgia Railroad.[1027] There was a noonday barbecue and music by a military band from Ft. Benning. In the afternoon, there was a football game between Enterprise and Thomasville, Ga. The ceremony included speeches by Charlie's friend, Gov. Bill Brandon, who openly declared that McDowell should be the next governor of Alabama. Other speakers included Gov. Clifford Walker of Georgia; Highway Department officials; and the President General of the United Daughters of the Confederacy. Charlie McDowell had been scheduled to have a central role in the proceedings, but was confined to his bed by a bad case of the flu. Instead, 14-year old Joy, with Carrie standing beside her, christened the bridge by breaking a bottle of Chattahoochee River water.[1028] The McDowell Bridge would serve for 37 years, until it was torn down (still in excellent condition) to make way for the rising waters of the newly-impounded Lake Eufaula in 1962, necessitating a new bridge and causeway.

645

In June 1924, Charlie, Carrie, and Joy were in New York City for the Democratic National Convention at Madison Square Garden. The presidential candidates included William G. McAdoo (Woodrow Wilson's son-in-law); Al Smith; and Alabama Sen. Oscar W. Underwood. Charlie of course supported Sen. Underwood. From June 24 to July 10, no candidate could obtain the necessary two-thirds vote. For over 100 roll call ballots, as Alabama's alphabetical position caused it to be called first, Gov. Bill Brandon's loud voice predictably boomed out (with no loudspeakers), *"Alabama casts 24 votes for Oscar W. Underwood!"* The convention ran so long that a provision of the Alabama constitution was triggered, providing that if the governor were absent from the state for over 20 days, the lieutenant governor would assume the governorship in the interim. Accordingly, Lt. Gov. McDowell and family hurried back to Alabama, where Charlie took over as governor, but his term was brief, July 10-11. The convention finally nominated New Yorker John W. Davis as a compromise, allowing Gov. Brandon to return to Alabama after a 21-day absence.

As early as 1915 and before, there had been voices urging Charlie to run for governor and advocating his candidacy, both in the Eufaula and in the state press. As his term as lieutenant governor drew to a close, the pressure to run intensified. In 1926, at the age of 55, he concluded that his time was ripe, and threw his hat into the ring. McDowell's chances looked excellent. Strongly supported by Gov. Brandon, the outgoing governor actively campaigned across the state for Charlie and placed the resources of his administration behind him (causing some to refer to Charlie as "the Crown Prince"). Charlie was supported by conservatives and the business interests, who regarded him as a "Moses," come to lead them from the wilderness. The Hanson newspaper chain, i. e. the Birmingham *News* and the Montgomery *Advertiser*, brought their complete editorial support to bear on his behalf.

This race has been described as a contest between the "conservative" and "progressive" wings of the Democratic Party. McDowell been given the "conservative" label, presumably because he was backed by the business interests, but his attitudes and platform were actually quite progressive for the time, certainly as progressive as his opponents'. He outlined these principal planks of his platform: [1029]

    1. Convicts to be removed from the mines and lease system ended.
    2. Present two-cent gasoline tax to be retained to the counties.
    3. A complete system of permanent good roads during your lifetime, without an increase in property taxes.
    4. Education to receive first consideration with the ideal of "An equal chance to every child," nine months school term, and increased pay for teachers.

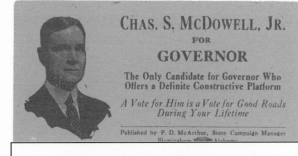

CHAS. S. McDOWELL, JR.
FOR
GOVERNOR
The Only Candidate for Governor Who Offers a Definite Constructive Platform
A Vote for Him is a Vote for Good Roads During Your Lifetime
Published by F. D. McArthur, State Campaign Manager Birmingham, Alabama

McDowell's 1926 Campaign Card

    McDowell's most dramatic proposal was for a $75,000,000 bond issue to "get Alabama out of the mud" and build a statewide network of paved roads.[1030] By the mid-1920's the automobile had come into its own, but the dirt roads of the state were still of the nineteenth century, which Charlie felt would continue to hold back progress in the state. Charlie's highway program, sometimes called "the Rogers Plan," was authored by Gov. Brandon's highway director, C. M. A. (Maxie) Rogers, who patterned it after North Carolina's successful highway-building experience.

Charlie McDowell announced his candidacy in a kickoff rally in his home courthouse in Eufaula. In the next morning's *Montgomery Advertiser,* Editor Grover Hall, Sr. in his florid, Bible-strewn style, gave a resounding editorial endorsement to McDowell and his platform, entitled "The Captain's Call To Battle": [1031]

"In the bulrushes of Barbour yesterday a full-grown leader was found. In the flags by the Chattahoochee's brink the daughters of Pharaoh came upon him, and rejoiced

At a time when some others were faltering and quibbling and backbiting, this son of Amram [i. e., Moses. Ed.] stepped boldly out, swept aside those who would offer the state's future as a hostage to fortune by proposing any old compromise for the sake of victory, and took command of the citizen army. He asserted his pre-eminent right, in the present circumstances, to lead the constructive, progressive forces of the commonwealth at this crucial hour in its history….

On every legitimate question now before the people, McDowell takes high ground, and speaks as a statesman and a leader. …[O]ne will look in vain for an undignified or unworthy sentence…for low appeals to class prejudice, the ungenerous thrusts or acrimonious epithets….

The outstanding feature of the address, of course, is Mr. McDowell's elaboration of his well-known views on the road question…Here he achieves genuine distinction and leaves no doubt in unbiased minds that while the others are out to build roads by piece meal, McDowell is out to build a system of highways and link up the scattered communities of a great state. …

McDowell thunders back the war-cry: 'There isn't but one way to do it! Authorize enough money to complete the highway system. Rush construction…It will take $75,000,000 to do it, and it is folly to talk of any thing less. Away with quibbling and temporizing! Away with petty politics!'

It is McDowell or Mud!

The gentleman from Barbour leaves little to be desired…on other vital questions. He promises unqualifiedly to end the convict lease system.

…He declares for an equal chance for every child, that is to say, for nine months school everywhere, for better equipment, and better teachers by means of higher salaries…"

Editor Hall's pithy "McDowell or Mud!" took hold and became the campaign slogan:

McDowell's campaign slogan, inspired by Grover Hall's editorial.

Charlie had three opponents, all categorized by historians as "progressives." A. H. Carmichael was supported by the "education" forces and prohibitionists. A. G. Paterson, president of the Public Service Commission, opposed a bond issue and advocated a "pay as you go" road program, while the other "progressives" supported only a $25,000,000 highway bond issue.[1032] The third "progressive" candidate, Col. Bibb Graves of Montgomery, appeared to have no support among the media or party leadership. However, his demagogic advocacy of heavy taxation of corporations and his avowed concern for "the common man" brought the support of the bloc vote that would win the race for him: the Ku Klux Klan. Graves was the Grand Cyclops of the Montgomery Klavern of the KKK.[1033]

Politically influential throughout the nation, in 1926 the Ku Klux Klan reached the height of its power in Alabama. Hugo Black, a Klan-endorsed candidate (and member) running for the U. S. Senate in the same primary, actually warned Charlie that he would lose because he had not sought Klan support.[1034] Black's prediction turned out to be correct. When the votes were counted on August 10, the Klan "had taken Graves, who had virtually no other organized support, and made him governor over McDowell, who had a superior organization and great financial resources."[1035] The Klan also elected the little-known Hugo Black to the U. S. Senate over three well-known candidates. (Black later went on to become a justice of the U. S. Supreme Court, noted for his defense of civil liberties.) Numerous other Klan-endorsed candidates were elected across the state in 1926. How was this accomplished?

In 1915, the Anti-Saloon League had achieved the passage of the "double-choice" primary law, which eliminated runoff primary elections by giving voters the option, after voting for their preferred candidate, to then mark a vote for their "second choice" candidate in that race. If no candidate received a majority of the first choice votes, the second choice votes were then counted and added to the first choice totals. The candidate who received the highest aggregated total of first and second choice votes was elected. It was a quirky system for several reasons; for instance, counting the second choice vote had the effect of *canceling* that voter's first choice vote, his real preference. It was sold as an economy measure, but "the AntiSaloon League hoped this complicated procedure would aid well-organized minority blocs, and indeed it did."[1036]

Grover Hall, Sr. in the *Advertiser* observed: "In Alabama it is hard to tell where the League ends and the Klan begins."[1037] These two similar "socio-economic" groups with similar political interests were well-organized, and knew how to use the complicated ballot procedure to their advantage. While the complexity of the ballot induced many voters not to bother with voting a second choice, the Klan and the League went to lengths to educate their members on how it was done. Further, if circumstances led a member to favor a candidate other than the Klan candidate, it was not difficult to persuade him to cast a "second choice" vote for the Klan candidate.[1038] During 1926, a Klan-sponsored sample ballot, already marked with the Klan's choices, was passed out by the Klan leaders "by the tens of thousands," and it was meticulously adhered to by many voters. [1039]

Historian J. Mills Thornton, writing in *The Alabama Review,* provides this analysis of the results of the August 10 primary: "In first choice votes, Graves, McDowell, Carmichael, and Patterson received approximately 61,000, 60,000, 54,000, and 47,000 votes respectively. In second-choice votes, however, Graves with his Klan endorsement polled 21,978. McDowell received only 7,943. Graves was declared the winner by almost 16,000 votes. About two-thirds of those who participated in the primary, 141,770 voters, did not bother, or were unable, to indicate a second choice, while 40,954 second-choice ballots were voided because they were cast either for Carmichael or for Patterson. It seems likely that a runoff would have resulted in a very different outcome. Graves may perhaps have fallen heir to some portion of Patterson's support, but the greater part of Carmichael's vote would have gone to McDowell."[1040] Thornton then reaches this conclusion:

> "Thus, under a runoff system, Charles S. McDowell would probably have been nominated by the Democrats and elected governor of Alabama in 1926."

"As it was," Thornton continues, "Graves was chosen on the basis of the Klan bloc— the one-third or more of the vote that the Klan and the League controlled 'in all weathers and under all circumstances.'"[1041]

Some time after the election, Archie Carmichael, the "education" candidate, apologetically acknowledged to Charlie that Carmichael's entry into the race had been a mistake; it had drawn votes away from McDowell which would have allowed the latter to win, and the education interests would have been better served if McDowell, also pro-education, had been elected. [1042] Ironically, although the Graves administration began with only a $25,000,000 road bond issue, it quickly became obvious, as McDowell had predicted, that this was not nearly enough. Within a few years, the legislature had authorized over $75,000,000 in road bonds.

Writing forty years later in 1966, Duard LeGrand, a Eufaula native who became editor of the *Birmingham Post-Herald,* recalled Charlie McDowell and the 1926 election:

> "…In a year when most candidates were careful to have their Klan dues paid and fearful to face the voters without Klan endorsement, Charlie McDowell stood splendidly alone, scornful of the Klan and of all who solicited votes in a Klan robe.
>
> He began his campaign in the upstairs courtroom of his hometown courthouse…. [LeGrand then relates a friendly conversation Charlie had with two local black men who attended the rally.]
>
> Alabama voters that year were not well disposed toward candidates who disdained the Klan or expressed a feeling of neighborliness toward Negroes.
>
> So they sent Bibb Graves to the state capitol and Hugo Black to the U. S. Senate.
>
> They sent Charlie McDowell home: home to his office above the shoe store on the corner of Broad and Randolph, home to Miss Carrie, his wife, the youngest and prettiest of Captain S. H. Dent's daughters.
>
> But he came home in honor, his integrity uncompromised.
>
> And to this day those who remember him are proud to have shared citizenship with a man who, in seeking office, was incapable of appealing to the base nature of the electorate and was prepared to stand alone if need be, for the right as he saw it.
>
> For them, Charlie McDowell, the man who lost, always will be the standard of excellence by which they will measure men who seek public office."[1043]

Back in Eufaula, Charlie resumed his comfortable life on Broad Street with Carrie and Joy, and continued his law practice with Arch at McDowell & McDowell. In October 1927, Charlie and Carrie observed their silver wedding anniversary with "…an elegant and brilliant affair in every detail, assembling several hundred friends of this city. The handsome home of old English type on Broad Street was aglow with the warmth of many lights…Receiving with Col. and Mrs. McDowell were their charming young sixteen year old daughter, Miss Joy and attendants at the wedding of 25 years ago…"[1044]

During this time, Charlie decided it was time for him to become a landowner. At this period, land, not stocks and bonds, was the most common form of investment. Particularly in the South, land ownership was a traditional sign of material security; and as a product of a financially-modest background, Charlie wanted to own land. Accordingly, in December, 1927, when Phenix Mutual Life Insurance Company foreclosed a mortgage it held on a 500-acre farm near Eufaula, Charlie bid it in for $10,000. (He paid $2000 cash down, with the balance secured by a mortgage and 5 notes payable over five years.) The farm, which Charlie named "Riverside," was located on the banks of the Chattahoochee River at the community of "Terese," 7 miles south of Eufaula on highway 431. It was a beautiful piece of land; flat and fertile. It was farmed by two or three black tenants who lived on the place and, using mule-powered plows, raised cotton and peanuts for cash, and had vegetable gardens for their own use. The timing of Charlie's Riverside mortgage debt turned out to have been less than ideal. Two years later, the stock market crash of 1929 ushered in the Great Depression. His difficulties are made clear by notes he later entered in a financial journal [the emphasis is his]:

> "Paid first two notes in advance and $500 on third.
> Depression caught me. Tenant died. <u>H—l was to pay.</u>
> Struggled on, paid interest in full to 1934. They renewed balance of $4300…
> This is a <u>fine place</u>. My wife should not sell for less than I gave for it. Should have $15,000 and time will bring it.
> It represents <u>hard earned savings</u>.
> Paid up in full. Mortgage cancelled, Book 118, pages 144-148, Clayton property book. 2/3/38."[ccc]

As a lawyer, Charlie was able to weather the Great Depression better than most. He had been appointed Division Counsel for the Central of Georgia Railroad, which served Eufaula. The railroads were among the biggest businesses of the era, and the most desirable legal clients. They customarily retained the most influential lawyer in the area, and in Barbour county and environs, that was Charles S. McDowell, Jr. He handled right-of-way transactions and disputes, defended claims from fires and injuries to people and livestock, and generally protected the legal and political interests of the Central of Georgia in his district. For this he probably received a substantial monthly retainer to assure his availability, plus fees for the individual matters handled. In addition, Charlie and Carrie received lifetime free passes to travel, not only on the Central of Georgia, but also with other affiliated railroads throughout the country. The railroad was a particularly significant client to have during the years of depression.[1045]

Satisfying though it may have been to quietly practice law and tend his new farm, Charlie's lifelong itch for political involvement soon reasserted itself. In 1930, he decided to again run for the state Senate, a decision intended at least in part to clearly demonstrate that the circumstances of his 1926 defeat had left no feelings of resentment.[1046] As usual, his fellow Barbour Countians accommodated him; and he was returned to the senate. There he was appointed chairman of the powerful Judiciary Committee.[1047]

Joy McDowell would have preferred to attend the University of Alabama, which was now coeducational. But her father, despite his lifelong attachment to the University, still did not consider it an appropriate choice for women. Accordingly, Joy enrolled for the 1927-1928

[ccc] Riverside's epilogue is that Charlie's hard-earned investment in farmland turned out far better than he could have imagined. In 1963, the U. S. Corps of Engineers bought from Carrie half of the acreage, i.e., about 250 acres, to make way for the rising waters of Lake Eufaula, thereby transforming the remaining 250 acres into lakefront recreational property far more valuable than the whole farm ever was. Today (2003), it is jointly owned and enjoyed by Charlie and Carrie's grandchildren and great-grandchildren.

school year in Methodist-sponsored Huntingdon College in Montgomery (then called Woman's College of Alabama). Graduating in June 1932, Joy, then 21 years old, began teaching in the elementary school of Union Springs, Alabama, 40 miles west of Eufaula on the Montgomery highway. One day in front of Jordan Drug Store, a Union Springs "hangout," she was introduced to John Allen Crook, Jr., a young officer of the First National Bank. She did not even finish out the school year. They were married in a large wedding at the Methodist Church of Eufaula on March 15, 1933, (which John Allen would remember as the "bank holiday," declared by President Roosevelt to stem the tide of depression-induced bank failures sweeping the country). The guests included Gov. B. M. Miller, Lt. Gov. Hugh D. Merrill, and many of Sen. McDowell's fellow legislators; and Joy's wedding gifts included a set of silver goblets from the Alabama Senate. Carrie and Charlie were soon presented with a succession of grandchildren: John Allen, III ("Sonny"), in 1934; Charles McDowell ("Charlie Mc"), in 1938; and Caroline Joy (Caroline), in 1943.

Although Charlie had attended the University of Alabama for only one year in 1888-1889, he was as firmly attached to his alma mater as if he had earned several graduate degrees there. He long harbored the ambition of serving on its board of trustees. In 1915, Gov. Emmett O'Neal had appointed him to the board of trustees of the Alabama Polytechnic Institute, now Auburn University. Although Charlie served faithfully on the Auburn board for over 12 years, he was actually biding his time for an opportunity to move to the board he really wanted. His chance finally came. The third congressional district seat on the University of Alabama board of trustees had been occupied by former Congressman, federal Judge Henry D. Clayton [Jr.], since 1920. On December 21, 1929, Clayton died. Soon thereafter, on May 30, 1930, the University of Alabama board of trustees (which enjoys the power to fill its own vacancies) elected Charlie as the third district trustee, and he was easily confirmed by the Alabama Senate. Reelected in 1939, he would exercise the position with relish for thirteen years until his death.[1048] His colleagues on the board recalled that the two things in Charlie McDowell's life that meant the most to him were the presidency of the Alabama Bar Association, and his trusteeship of the University of Alabama.[1049] Perhaps because of his activity on behalf of the University and his membership on its board of trustees, the UA chapter of Phi Beta Kappa elected him an honorary member. He proudly wore the distinctive key on his watch chain and would later dangle it before his small grandsons, with the admonition that they must earn a "real" one.[ddd]

[ddd] One of them – "Sonny" Crook – did just that.

His 1931-1935 senate term was Charlie's last elected public office, but McDowell & McDowell did not go unrepresented in the Alabama Senate. In 1935, Charlie's brother Arch succeeded him as the senator from Barbour, defeating J. L Houston, 1,951 to 1,343.[1050]

The enduring love affair between Charlie and Carrie is touchingly documented in notes which Charlie entered in a financial journal which he prepared in August 1933, entitled, "For Her Information and Convenience." If his investment advice sounds

Charlie (left) and Arch McDowell "in action" in Court at Eufaula late 1930's.

exceedingly quaint today, it should be recalled that he was writing during the very depths of the Great Depression, when many fortunes and businesses had been totally wiped out. Excerpts:

"To Babbie:
I can imagine now, your laughing at me, when you shall have seen this book, read these lines, and recalled my crazy way of doing things. I have never subscribed to the idea that a 'detail' man was a crank.... If details stamp me as a crank, I confess to being one, and I really think that I am. I certainly am about you. Here, in the section that I have lived, I have had the time to engage in details, and I have indulged in them in the practice of law. Perhaps, under other climes, where the rush of things took more time than I could spare, I might have been different. But be as it may, this book is prepared for you, for your information 'when I have crossed the bar,' so that you will know just exactly, in detail, how your worldly estate stands. One can show no more affection for his loved one, than to try to provide for them when he shall have passed away.
Since October 15, 1902 (a great day for me) my earnest endeavor has been to make provision for you when you shall need it. You have had lots of fun laughing at me for 'making reservations.' Well – I am still at it, and I hope they are ample. I trust the reservations herein made will be sufficient to keep you not only from need and want, but from worry. You are a good financier, but a poor bookkeeper. This book, which will show you everything that you have, is intended to present to you what you have when you have to face the world....
My long experience in the active practice of the law has furnished me with an opportunity to see so many estates dissipated, and those loved ones in

653

want, simply from bad management.... As I write these lines, my mind recalls the many good women who have to want for lack of discretion in handling their financial affairs. It is really appalling. ...

The estate that will come to your keeping will be a modest one, but sufficient to provide an easy living for you, if managed properly....

Be careful making loans. Fact of it is I have my doubts that in the long run one makes anything in loans, even at 8%. For a while it looks good, and loan interest is appealing, but one or two bad loans wipe out all profit. Security not less than '3 to 1' should be obtained. At this very time, even those here in Eufaula who have carefully demanded such security will have a hard time getting their money back. Don't invest in bank stock, it is dangerous; purchase no stock in companies. Sooner or later they fail. Sometimes I really think that the only safe place for a woman to put her insurance money is in United States Government Bonds. That is the safest place. The rate of interest is low but safety takes care of it...

But why should I give you advice and instructions. You have more sense and judgment than any person I ever knew. So forget the advice hereinabove set out...I should be glad to erase the advice part, but it is already written and cannot be stricken out.

Before many days I shall be 62 years of age. I expect to remain here a long time yet, but to 'set my house in order' has long been my intention. The sketch of the estate started, I will keep the book 'up to date.'...

To you Babbie, this book is dedicated. Were it not for you, there would be no estate. Every dollar made and saved was inspired by your own splendid self. I pray that Joy may be like you. You two have given me great joy, peace, and pride. I believe my devotion to you both is well-known.

Dad"

"Sonnie" Crook is included.

In addition to their frequent visits to Union Springs to visit Joy and her growing family, the 1930's saw Charlie and Carrie engaging in more extensive travel, including a visit to Quebec and other Canadian points.

On January 1, 1935, the University of Alabama played Stanford in the Rose Bowl, their first meeting since the 1927 Rose Bowl, which had ended in a 7-7 tie. Alabama Trustee Charlie McDowell and Carrie were there for Alabama's fourth Rose Bowl appearance since 1926. They attended a New Year's Eve party the night before, at which Hollywood celebrities were present, including Alabama football "great," Johnny Mack Brown, formerly of Dothan, later a Hollywood western actor. Carrie later recounted that at midnight when the kissing started, the only man near her was Joe E. Brown (a character actor of the day noted for his large mouth), and she had no interest in kissing him! The next day Charlie and Carrie saw Coach Frank Thomas lead the Crimson Tide to a 29-13 victory over Stanford. Playing at Alabama's left end was Don Hutson; at right end was one Paul "Bear" Bryant.

In June 1936, Charlie was elected from the third congressional district to his third and last Democratic National Convention, held in Philadelphia. Franklin Roosevelt was easily renominated.

A flattering portrayal of the McDowells' roles in Eufaula city life at this time was given by *Alabama* magazine, a popular journal of politics and business, in its issue of October 18, 1937. Beneath a triptych of photographs of Arch (left), Carrie (seated at the Methodist organ), and Charlie (right), the writer gave this admiring account: "Longtime Sparkplugs of Eufaula's political life and pace-setters of its civic and social activity have been the McDowells. State Senator Archie McDowell, younger of the two brothers has a reputation at home for quiet efficiency, in the legislature for fighting longest and hardest for governmental economy and abolition of the spoils system. Mrs. Charles McDowell is a talented pianist and singer, has headed local and state music clubs, garden clubs and other women's organizations, is a former Alabama president of the UDC, regent for the Confederate museum in Richmond, state director for the Jefferson Davis Highway. She and Col. McDowell have the distinction of both being listed in Who's Who. Sagacious

UA Trustee C. S McDowell, Jr. (left) at New York Polo Grounds for Alabama (7)-Fordham (6) game (with Montgomery Police Comm. Col. William Screws), October 1939

Colonel McDowell has...been lieutenant governor, twice Barbour's senator, is senior member of the McDowell firm which handles Barbour's legal affairs...Tales of the colonel's sly coups in capturing state and federal money for civic improvements abound in his home county..."

October 1939 saw UA Trustee Charlie McDowell and Carrie at the Polo Grounds in New York City for the Alabama-Fordham football game. Alabama won: 7 to 6. [1051] On this trip they also attended the New York World's Fair.

Charlie's health failed in 1943. After months of difficult illness, he died May 25, 1943, at the age of seventy-two.

Two years later, Carrie presented an oil painting of Charlie to the State of Alabama. The Senate held a ceremonial unveiling of the portrait on June 21, 1945. At this time, Eufaulian Chauncey Sparks was Governor of Alabama. Atticus Mullins, the longtime political columnist for the *Montgomery Advertiser* and close friend of Charlie's, gave this account of the proceedings: [1052]

> "...It was a semi-solemn occasion, not one that Lieut. Gov. Charles McDowell would have enjoyed had he been alive. He was always full of life as a Senator and as presiding officer of the Senate and his infectious smile always accompanied the most drastic of rulings, rulings that he always made in fairness and consideration and according to parliamentary usage.
>
> Mrs. Charles McDowell was present, a distinguished woman in her own right, as was Col. Archie McDowell, a brother, distinguished in his own right. And friends of Charley McDowell (I like to call him Charley because he was one of the most lovable and loyal friends I ever had) came from all parts of Alabama.
>
> Former Senator J. Miller Bonner, of Wilcox, a close personal friend of the man being honored made the presentation speech. I have heard Miller Bonner speak a thousand times, more or less, but he never made a more effective or simpler speech than he made yesterday. He had served several terms with Charley McDowell. They were great friends. It was one of the noblest, one of the finest, probably the greatest speech Miller Bonner ever made. He could make such a speech because he said what he felt in his heart.
>
> As for the writer, I could not keep back a tear. For many years, nearly thirty, I had known Charley McDowell as a friend and confidante...
>
> Those in the Senate chamber were asked to stand by the acting presiding officer, Senator Clayton of Barbour, as Gov. Sparks walked into the chamber. And other tears came to the eyes of friends of Charley McDowell as Gov. Sparks detailed his joy in accepting a portrait of a man who has honored Alabama. Gov. Sparks, a neighbor of the McDowells in Eufaula for years, detailed the history of the man being honored. It was stirring. Charley McDowell was a self-made man. He made his own way in life.
>
> ...The portrait was unveiled and it is an excellent likeness of that progressive man who changed the thought of Alabama in the middle 1920's."
> [eee]

During the twenty-one years by which Carrie survived Charlie, she continued living in the Tudor house on Broad Street, pursuing her many interests with undiminished enthusiasm; traveling, enjoying her grandchildren, and generally continuing the full and rich life that she

---

[eee] Undoubtedly at Carrie's prompting, a few days later the *Advertiser* carried a short addendum to cure the omission of the names of those who unveiled the portrait: John Allen Crook, Jr (then age 12) and Charles McDowell Crook (then age 7), and the presence at the event of Mr. and Mrs. J. A. Crook.

and Charlie had led. In 1953, at age 74, she and Charlie's sister, Jan McDowell Lee, took a European tour, which Carrie had long wished to do. The following summer, Carrie was accompanied by her two youngest grandchildren (Caroline and Charlie Mc) on a Pullman train trip to Washington, D. C. During a visit with third district Congressman George Andrews of Union Springs, Carrie learned of his proposed legislation to build a lock and dam at Ft. Gaines, impounding the waters of the Chattahoochee River for the future Lake Eufaula, which would place half the acreage of "Riverside" under water. Later, the group had lunch in the Senate dining room with former Eufaulian, Henrietta McCormick Hill,[fff] wife of U. S. Senator Lister Hill, who also stopped at the table to greet "Miss Carrie." Returning home, the travelers took the overnight boat from Washington down the Chesapeake Bay to Norfolk for a few days' visit with Charlie's younger brother, Dr. William P. McDowell ("Ditty"), who was still actively practicing pediatric medicine there.

In 1959, the UDC at its national convention in Detroit recognized Carrie's service by naming her an Honorary Life President of the General Organization.[1053] In a newspaper interview, she explained the work of the Randolph Relief Fund, of which she had served as national chair for ten years. It is a benevolent fund which "cares for the needy daughters of the Confederate soldiers. There are many of these daughters still living, but only one Confederate veteran left." She stated, "the UDC is emphasizing their educational program for the descendants of the Confederacy. The Alabama Division alone has an educational endowment of over $100,000 which is used for scholarships in the various colleges and universities in Alabama. These scholarships are much sought after and appreciated." [1054]

In 1965, Carrie became one of the original incorporators of the Eufaula Heritage Association, which was instrumental in acquiring and saving the Shorter Mansion as a Eufaula landmark, and which inspired an active program of preservation of Eufaula's many historic homes and buildings which still continues today. [1055]

"Miss Carrie" McDowell had become something of an institution in Eufaula, and Joel Smith, the publisher-editor of the *Eufaula Tribune,* often followed her activities in his columns. This affectionate sketch by Smith in the early 1960's portrays Carrie's approach to life in her eighth decade:[1056]

> "...[L]ike a stately oak in the middle of the forest she doesn't show her age. She has the stamina of a young matron and this little lady doesn't have time to think about getting old. She's too busy devoting her time to her beloved First Methodist Church, Carnegie Library and the Eufaula Historical Museum or the UDC and the Children of the Confederacy.
>
> Miss Carrie, dressed in tiny spiked heels and smart clothes, seldom misses a library board meeting, a service at her church or a get together of the Daughters...She joined the Methodist Church in 1888, a few years after her brother, Capt. Henry Dent, a real Southern gentleman who doesn't mind folks knowing he's 90. Kind and tolerant, Miss Carrie keeps things straight at her

---

[fff] In 1931, Henrietta's widowed mother, Etta Copeland McCormack, had entered into a late-in-life marriage with Carrie's long-time bachelor brother, Navy Captain Henry A. Dent.

church. Officially she's the historian and she believes in adhering to the discipline of the Methodist Church...Rev. Ellisor has remarked that Miss Carrie is a person who 'acts more than she reacts.' And I think that best describes this wonderful woman. She was church organist for years, teaches a class named in her honor, is an honorary steward, and she has held every office in the local, district, and conference WSCS. In fact, Miss Carrie has even preached on occasion...

Just a sure as Confederate Memorial Day or Robert E. Lee's birthday rolls around Miss Carrie...treks up to the school house to make one of her annual talks to the students. For she loves her Southland and to her the Confederacy still lives. She often attends state and national conventions held by the Daughters or the Children of the confederacy.

Miss Carrie...still entertains for brides-to-be or the UDC in her charming Old English home on Broad Street. As a guest at a dinner party in her home, I commented once on the magnificent chandelier that hangs in her dining room, observing that it must be quite a chore to keep it sparkling and shining. Miss Carrie informed me that she personally climbs up a ladder and carefully removes and cleans each tiny prism. ...[O]n a hot afternoon last summer someone spied her sitting [on her porch] in a rocking chair, her tiny heels propped up on a rail, as she fanned away like mad."

Carrie frequently had one or more of her three grandchildren visiting in Eufaula on weekends and in the summertime, or she often made the one-hour drive to Union Springs to visit them. She participated in their rearing and had a significant influence upon them. She reveled in becoming a great-grandmother and an octogenarian, and with her expansive vocabulary, said she looked forward to becoming a "nonagenarian." Although Carrie enjoyed robust health until her last day, she did not quite achieve the latter goal. On July 9, 1966, following a July Fourth visit with Joy, John Allen, the grandchildren and great-grandchildren, she died in Union Springs at the age of eighty-six. Of Anna and Hubert Dent's children, she was the last, but one, to die. Her older brother, Navy Captain Henry Dent, died in 1971, just short of his ninety-ninth birthday.

Joy McDowell Crook and Carrie Dent McDowell.
Easter 1956 in Union Springs

67
Epilogue:
The "Young Bicentennial," 2002

During June 7-9, 2002, the descendants of Ann and Edward Young gathered at Fendall Hall to celebrate the 200th anniversary of Edward's birth in New York in 1802 (which actually occurred on August 24, 1802). Two years of networking had produced the names and addresses of over 300 living descendants. These addresses reflected that the Youngs, first a New Jersey family, then a New York family, had "come full circle." It had become a Southern family, but only for a few generations. By the summer of 2002, the Youngs were a widely based *American* family. Since Edward's death in 1879, the progeny of his and Ann's eight children had scattered to at least 20 states, including:

New Jersey	Utah	Illinois	Alabama
North Carolina	California	Kentucky	Hawaii
Tennessee	Pennsylvania	Colorado	Ohio
Texas	Maryland	Montana	Missouri
Virginia	Indiana	Massachusetts	Minnesota

But the Young descendants were eager to preserve contact with their roots. From throughout the United States they enthusiastically came to celebrate their Eufaula heritage; some may have never before been in Eufaula. Total attendance at the "Young Bicentennial," as it was billed, was over 250 (including spouses). The Young heirs also demonstrated their enthusiasm in material ways. When it was announced that the Friends of Fendall Hall were undertaking to raise $100,000 to match an equal grant by the Alabama Historical Commission to establish an endowment for the improvement of the old home, the assembled heirs pledged contributions totaling $90,000.

Of Edward and Ann Young's eight children who survived to adulthood, two of them, Caroline Young Roberts, and Ada Young Martin had no children who survived infancy. Two of the Young children, James William Young and Henry Augustus Young, had children, but no descendants have yet been located. As for the remaining four, i.e. Anna Young Dent, Mollie Young Weedon, Helen Young Dent, and Edward Billups Young, most (but not all) of their living descendants were located, and many attended the 2002 gathering. The number of descendants (and spouses) of each of these children attending the 2002 "reunion" was as follows: Helen and George H. Dent, 46; Edward Billups and Mamie Young, 46; Mollie and Hamilton Weedon, 19; Anna and Hubert Dent, 135; William and Ellen Beall Young of Columbus, Georgia, 10.

One family of descendants attending the "Young Bicentennial," that of Walter Beh (a great-great-grandson of Anna and Hubert Dent), illustrates the Young peregrinations: Anna Beall Young Dent, her daughter "Nan," and Nan's daughter, Martha, were all born in Eufaula between 1840 and 1890. But Martha's daughter, Jane, was born in Rome, Ga, in 1918, while Jane's son, Walter, was born in New Jersey, in 1945, where the first American Young had settled in 1685. Continuing the migrations, Walter's children were born in Hawaii in the 1970's, where he has practiced law for over 30 years. Some of Walter's children may not have previously heard of the historic little town of Eufaula, Alabama, but they made the long pilgrimage there in June 2002 and now well understand its significance to their heritage.

The End

On June 7-9, 2002, over 200 descendants of Edward and Ann Young gathered at Fendall Hall in Eufaula, Alabama to celebrate the 200th anniversary of Edward's birth (which actually was August 24, 1802). The event was chaired by one of Edward and Ann's great-great-grandsons, Eufaula Businessman, Frank Garrison, Jr., and his wife Connie.

The most prolific of Edward and Ann Young's children were Anna and her husband, Hubert. Pictured above, their descendants outnumbered by far all the other Young branches at the 2002 gathering.

Walter Beh, lawyer of Kailua, Hawaii, and great-great-grandson of Anna and Hubert Dent, brought his family 4000 miles to the Young Bicentennial, their first visit to Eufaula. Above (left to right), Megan Beh Bartlett, Walter Beh, Eric Bartlett, Andrew beh, and Hazel Beh examine the original Confederate flag carried by Captain Dent's Battery of artillery during the Civil War. *(Eufaula Tribune Staff Photo)*

The Crook family at Fendall Hall, June 2002: Edith, McDowell and Charlie (rear); Caroline and Jim (front).

Acknowledgements

The most interesting facts in the Prologue about Robert Young's migration from Scotland, and about his progeny in New Jersey and New York, are the result of research by family member, John A. Leo III, of Fairfax, VA, although any inaccuracies in the narrative account are my own. Mr. Leo also provided valuable assistance by maintaining in computerized form the data about the descendants of Ann and Edward Young, and the listing of those descendants in the Appendix was prepared by him. I am most grateful for his patient help.

Approximately half of the original Civil War letters of Hubert Dent are in the possession of two of his great-granddaughters, Catherine Dent Brantley and Betsy Dent Miller of Jacksonville, Florida. Mrs. Brantley and Mrs. Miller carried out the laborious task of transcribing these handwritten letters into more readable form. I am grateful for their making these transcriptions available for this work, which is the first time these letters have been publicly available. The remaining letters were transcribed by the Collections staff of Auburn University, which makes copies of them available to the public. The originals of these are held by H. Dent McCullohs of Atlanta.

While compiling information about Hubert Dent's father, Dr. Stouten Warren Dent of Charles County, Maryland, I was provided with important help and guidance by Lieutenant Commander Leon Wilde, USN, of Arnold, MD, for which I am most appreciative.

The map of Pensacola Bay area in 1861 and the diagrams of the campaigns of Shiloh, Atlanta, and Jonesboro, are taken from Stanley F. Horn's 1941 seminal work, "The Army of Tennessee," and are used with the permission of the University of Oklahoma Press.

Maps of the Mobile Defenses, Lovejoy Station, and other maps-drawings, are used with the permission of Col. William Forbes, author of "Haulin' Brass," a 1993 detailed and scholarly account of "Croft's [later Young's] Flying Battery" of Columbus, GA, and of that book's publisher, Morningside House, Inc.

The map of the Apalachicola/Chattahoochee river Valley is used with permission of the University of Alabama Press.

Photographs of the Irwinton Bridge and certain other early Eufaula photographs are used with the kind permission of their owners and of Joel Smith, publisher of the *Eufaula Tribune*, [himself a collateral relative of Anne Fendall Beall, through the Beall family]. In 1999, the Tribune published these photographs in an excellent compilation, "A Eufaula Album, A Pictorial History of Eufaula, Alabama."

The color photographs depicting Fendall Hall after the Dent renovations first appeared in the Winter 1999 issue of *Alabama Heritage* magazine, and are used herein with the kind permission of Montgomery photographer, Jay Sailor, and the University of Alabama Press

Endnotes

[1] A. Van Doren Honeyman, Editor, Somerset Historical Quarterly, Vol. VI, 1917 Edition, published by Somerset County Historical Society; Plainfield, New Jersey: "There have also been Youngs in New Jersey of Scotch descent, from Robert Young, who settled in Newark; he was born about 1663 and died 1726." (Hereafter cited as "Somerset Historical").

[2] John E. Stillwell, M. D., *Historical and Gen.ealogical Miscellany, Early Settlers of New Jersey and Their Descendants* (New York, 1932) p. 502 et. seq., containing excepts from *Wodrow's History of the Sufferings of the Church of Scotland From the Restoration To the Revolution,* by Rev Robert Wodrow, Minister of the Gospel at Eastwood, Glasgow, 1830, Sect. XII p. 331 et. seq. (Hereafter referred to as Stillwell/Wodrow); See also *The Reform Presbyterian Church in America,* Perth Amboy, New Jersey (Library File: 285.5 G467, p. 228) as copied by Boyd C. McQuown and provided by him to Albert N. McQuown Sr. of Austin, Texas in 1962, found at website: vnla.com/vnl/Gen./mcq/Mcquown.htm

[3] Ibid.

[4] Ibid.

[5] Ibid

[6] Ibid.

[7] Orra Eugene Monnette, *First Settlers of Ye Plantations of Piscataway and Woodsridge* Olde East New Jersey 1664 to 1714. (Los Angeles, California, The Leroy Carman Press, 1932.) F144.P68M74, p. 119 (which includes excepts from *History of BerGen. and Passaic Counties, New Jersey*, by W. W. Clayton, 1882, p. 47) (Hereafter cited as "Monnette"); J. Montgomery Seaver, *Young Family Records* (2000 North Broad Street, Philadelphia, PA, American Historical-Gen.ealogical Society, 1929) p. 20 et seq (hereafter cited as "Seaver"); Somerset Historical Quarterly, supra

[8] David Lawrence Pierson, *Narratives of Newark in New Jersey, 1666-1916* (Pierson Publishing Company, 756 Broad St, Newark, 1915-1916), p.6-13 (Hereafter cited as "Pierson's Narratives".) These narratives were revised from a series of articles in the Newark Evening News, in anticipation of the 250th anniversary celebration of Newark.

[9] William Nelson, Editor, Documents Relating to the Colonial History of New Jersey, Vol VI, Extracts from American Newspapers Relating to New Jersey, Vol. VI. 1766-1767. Prepared at the request of the New Jersey Historical Society, 1903

[10] Monnette, p. 58. Only portions of the "quit rent rolls" are available today. This one relates to 1696

[11] Seaver, p. 20 et seq.

[12] Monnette, p. 119

[13] Charles Candee Baldwin, *The Baldwin Gen.ealogy 1500-1881* (Cleveland, OH Leader Printing , 1881) (hereafter, "Baldwin Gen.ealogy.")

[14] Pierson's Narratives, p. 137-138

[15] Pierson's Narratives, p. 85

[16] NJ Calendar of Wills, Volume I, page 382 from Liber 2 page 17; also Abner Morse, *Gen.ealogical Register of the Descendants of Several Ancient Puritans* (Boston, H.W. Dutton & Sons,1861)

[17] Some of which were: John Ward, October 31, 1694; John Ward, Jr. (son of the foregoing) May 2, 1695; and Samuel Roos, May 31, 1702. New Jersey Archives (East Jersey Deeds)

[18] New Jersey Calendar of Wills

[19] Baldwin Gen.ealogy, p. 483

[20] The Gen.ealogical Magazine of New Jersey, Vol I, p. 33- 40, *The Newark Minutemen* (Hereafter cited as N. J. Gen. Mag.)

[21] N. J. Gen. Mag.

[22] Narratives, p. 165 et. seq.

[23] Ibid.

[24] Pierson's Narratives, p. 165-168

[25] Pierson's Narratives, p. 168

[26] Pierson's Narratives, p.172

[27] N. J. Gen. Mag., p. 40

[28] N.J. Gen. Mag.

[29] Pierson's Narratives, p. 12

[30] Seaver; See also Edward Brown Young Family Bible, in possession of his descendant, Hubert Dent McCullohs of Atlanta, Ga., and other family members (Hereafter cited as "E. B. Young Bible").

[31] William S. Stryker, Adjutant General, Compiler, *Official Register of the Officers and Men of New Jersey in the Revolutionary War,* (originally published, Trenton, 1872; Reprinted by Gen.ealogical Publishing Co, Baltimore, 1967; Reprinted for Clearfield Company, Inc., Baltimore, MD, 1997), p. 330, (hereafter cited as "Stryker").

[32] N. J. Gen. Mag., p. 34-35

[33] N. J. Gen. Mag, p.40

[34] Ibid. p. 34-35

[35] Stryker, p 332-333

[36] Stryker, p. 332-333

[37] Stryker, p. 332-333

[38] N. J. Gen. Mag., p. 33

[39] Ibid.

[40] Ibid, p 35, 40

[41] Stryker, p. 830

[42] Stryker, p. 830; William H. Shaw, Compiler, *History of Essex and Hudson Counties, New Jersey,* (Philadelphia, Everts & Peck, 1884), Chapter XII, Essex County in the Revolutionary War, Enlisted Men from Essex County

[43] Stryker, p. 338

[44] Stryker, p. 338

[45] Jonas appears on tax rolls in Newark from 1789-1796.

[46] The evidence of where Jonas and Prudence were living when little James was born is conflicting. E. B. Young's family Bible (in handwriting appearing to be that of Edward Brown Young himself) says that his father James, was born in Burlington, N. J.., but there is no other indication they ever lived there. James' New York City death certificate says he was born in New York (but the person providing this information may have incorrectly assumed this simply because James had been living there for many years at the time of his death.) Because Jonas, his father and brothers all joined the Newark Minutemen in 1775, when James was three, this suggests that this may have been James' family home since his birth, which seems likely. For the death certificate to be correct, it would have to be assumed that Jonas and Prudence were in New York at the time of James birth in 1771 but then went back to Newark in 1775 for Jonas to join the Newark Minutemen.

[47] N.J. Gen. Mag. P. 40

[48] NJ Calendar of Wills Volume 7, page 262. Lib 30, page 336.

[49] Hamp Ewing, *Young Family Line*, (privately published, 1925)

[50] Young Bible

[51] Biographical Souvenir of Georgia and Florida; Biographical Sketches of Early Settled Families (Chicago: F. A. Batty & Company, 1889) p. 817 (Hereafter, "Biographical")

[52] Biographical Souvenir, p. 817

[53] E. B Young Bible.

[54] E. B. Young Bible

[55] Ethel Hall Bjerkoe, Cabinetmakers of America, Their Lives and Works, (Doubleday, 1957; revised, 1978, Schiffer Limited, Exton PA), p. 238, (hereafter cited as "Bjerkoe"); Biographical Souvenir, p. 817

[56] Richmond Huntley, " Stephen and Moses Young Also Worked in the Phyfe Manner", *American Collector, The Magazine for Antique Collectors and Dealers*, Vol VI, January 1938, Number 12 (hereafter cited as "Huntley"); Biographical Souvenir, p. 817

[57] Bjerkoe, p. 238

[58] Huntley

[59] Carl W. Drepperd, *A Dictionary of American Antiques,* (Boston, MA, Charles T. Branford Company, 1952), p. 396, (hereafter cited as "Drepperd.")

[60] Chicora Antiques, Inc., C. Lyman McCallum, Jr, Gallery, http://www.chicoraantiques.com; Bjerkoe, p.238

[61] Bjerkoe, p. 238

[62] Huntley

[63] E. B. Young Bible

[64] Biographical Souvenir, p. 817

[65] As of this writing (2002), this artifact is in the hands of Catherine (Mrs. Lewis) Brantley of Jacksonville, Fl., a fifth Generation descendant of Edward's.

[66] Biographical Souvenir, P. 817

[67] E. B. Young Bible

[68] Biographical Souvenir, p. 817

[69] Biographical Souvenir, p. 817

[70] Lynn Willoughby, *Fair to Middlin'; The Antebellum Cotton Trade of the Apalachicola/Chattahoochee River Valley* (Tuscaloosa; The University of Alabama Press 1993) p. 1-6. (Hereafter, "Willoughby")

[71] Willoughby p. 1-6

[72] Willoughby p. 1-6

[73] Willoughby p. 1-6

[74] Biographical, p. 817

[75] J.L.O. Faulk and B. W. Jones, comp. History of Twiggs County, Georgia (Columbus, Ga.; Press of Columbus Office Supply Co.) p. 51 (Hereafter, "Faulk")

[76] John C. Butler, Historical Record of Macon and Central Georgia (Macon, Georgia, 1958 and 1960) p. 115 (Hereafter, "Butler")

[77] J.L.O. Faulk and B. W. Jones, comp. History of Twiggs County, Georgia (Columbus, Ga.; Press of Columbus Office Supply Co.) p. 51 (Hereafter, "Faulk")

[78] E. B. Young Bible

[79] Henry A. Dent, A Sketch of One Branch of the Beall Family, Eufaula, Al., 1925, Revised 1927. p. B, Unpublished manuscript in possession of family. Hereafter, "Uncle Henry on Bealls".

[80] Biographical Souvenir, p.819

[81] Elizabeth R. Billups," A History of the Beall Family; A biography of my family," Alvarado, Texas, Aug.28, 1895. p.7. Unpublished manuscript by a sister of Ann Fendall Beall, in possession of family (Hereafter, "Billups").

[82] Billups, p.7

[83] Uncle Henry on Bealls

[84] Uncle Henry on Bealls, p. B

[85] Uncle Henry on Bealls, p. B

[86] Billups, P. 4,5

[87] Uncle Henry on Bealls, p. B

[88] Billups, P. 4,5

[89] Billups, p. 5

[90] Uncle Henry on Bealls, p. B

[91] E. Young Bible.

[92] E. B. Young Bible

[93] E. B. Young Bible

[94] E. B. Young Bible

[95] Faulk p. 51

[96] Biographical Souvenir, p. 818

[97] Butler, p.115, 131,132

[98] Butler, p. 132

[99] Billups, p. 5

[100] Butler, p. 133

[101] Ida Young, Julius Gholson, Clara N. Hargrove, History of Macon, Georgia (Macon Women's Club.) p. 87,88 (Hereafter," Ida Young"); See also, Butler, p. 133

[102] Ida Young, p. 88; Butler, p. 133

[103] Ida Young, p. 88

[104] Billups, p. 5

[105] Ida Young, p. 88,89

[106] Ida Young, 84,85

[107] Fretwell, p.247

[108] Ida Young, p. 85

[109] Ida Young. p. 86

[110] Ida Young. 86

[111] Ida Young. p.85

[112] Ida Young. p.85

[85] Ida Young. p.85

[86] Ida Young· p85

[114] Ida Young, p. 85

[115] Ida Young, p. 85

[116] Ida Young, p. 85

[117] Ida Young, p. 85; Butler, p. 141

[118] Ida Young, p. 86

[119] Billups, p. 5

[120] Butler, p. 141

[121] Ida Young, p. 87

[122] Chitwood, p. 257

[123] Fretwell, p247

[124] Memorial Record of Alabama, (Madison and Fuller, Madison, Wisconsin, 1893) p.468-469 (Hereafter, " Memorial, Alabama"), available Montgomery (Alabama) Public Library.

[125] Patricia R. Wickman, Osceola's Legacy, (Tuscaloosa and London, The University of Alabama Press, 1991), p.144 et seq.

[126] O. P. Chitwood, F. L. Owsley, and H. C. Nixon, The United States; from Colony to World Power 2nd Ed (New York: D. Van Nostrand Company, Inc., 1954) p. 215. (Hereafter, "Chitwood").

[127] W. W. Rogers, R. D. Ward, L. R. Atkins, W. Flynt, Alabama; the History of a Deep South State, (Tuscaloosa: The University of Alabama Press, 1994) p 53. (Hereafter," Rogers")

[128] Rogers, p54

[129] Rogers, p54

[130] Anne Kendrick Walker, Backtracking in Barbour County; A Narrative of the Last Alabama Frontier, (Richmond: The Dietz Press, 1941) p. 4 (Hereafter, "Walker").

[131] Rogers, p89

[132] Rogers, p90.

[133] Rogers, p90

[134] Mark E. Fretwell, This So Remote Frontier; the Chattahoochee Country of Alabama and Georgia, (Historic Chattahoochee Commission: 1980) pp. 232,233. (Hereafter, " Fretwell")

[135] Fretwell, p232-233; Rogers, p. 91

[136] Walker, pp. 8,9.

[137] Fretwell. 234; Rogers, p. 91

[138] Fretwell, p.234

[139] Fretwell, p. 235

[140] Fretwell, p.235

[141] Rogers, p. 91,92

[142] Fretwell, p. 239

[143] Fretwell, pp. 237-239

[144] Fretwell, p. 238

[145] Fretwell, p. 239,240

[146] Fretwell, 239, et. seq.

[147] Fretwell, p. 245

[148] Fretwell p. 246

[149] Rogers, p. 138

[150] Fretwell, p. 215, 258

[151] Young vs. McKenzie and Harrison, 3 Ga. 31; 1847 WL 1302 (S. C. of Ga., 1847

[152] Recital in Deed, Sheriff Hodges to Young, Barbour County Probate Records

[153] This contract is recorded at Book B, pp 611-612, in the office of the Judge of Probate of Barbour County, Al.

[154] Mattie Thomas Thompson, History of Barbour County Alabama (Eufaula, Al., 1939) p 37. (Hereafter, "Thompson") This somewhat eccentric history contains some known inaccuracies. Accordingly, its facts are accepted herein with care, and only when reasonably consistent with other sources.

[155] Fretwell, p. 258

[156] Rogers, et al, Alabama, Hist. Of a Deep South State, p. 111.

[157] Fretwell, p.215, 258

[158] Harrison vs. Young, 9 Ga 359, 1851 WL 1438 (Ga), (S. C of Ga, 1851)

[159] Thompson, p38

[160] Thompson, p38

[161] Lewy Dorman Papers; History of Barbour County. 1930's, unpublished manuscript, University of Alabama Special Collections and Eufaula Carnegie Library. (Hereafter, "Dorman, Hist. Of Barbour")

[162] Marie Bankhead Owen, The Story of Alabama (New York: Lewis Historical Publishing Co. 1949) p. 367 (hereafter, " M. B.Owen)

[163] Willoughby, p 69

[164] Willoughby, p. 89

[165] Walker, p. 140:Thompson, p. 70

[166] Willoughby, p. 20

[167] Willoughby, p. 20

[168] Walker, p. 140

[169] Willoughby, p. 26,27

[170] Willoughby, p. 21

[171] Willoughby, p. 103

[172] Walker, p.95

[173] Willoughby, p. 103

[174] Ray Mathis, Introduction to the John Horry Dent Journals (Hereafter, " Mathis, Introduction to Journals"), p. xii

[175] J. H. D., Vol I, p. 37

[176] Willoughby, p. 103

[177] J. H. D., Vol. I. p. 1

[178] J. H. D., Vol. I, p. 42

[179] J. H. D , Vol I, p. 65

[180] J. H. D., Vol. I, p. 98

[181] Young Bible

[182] Young Bible

[183] Barbour County Tract Book

[184] Records of Office of Judge of Probate, Barbour County, AL

[185] E. g., Elmer to Young, March 22, 1843; Morrison and Hanson to Young, June 6, 1845; Moore to Young, June 16, 1845; Records of the office of Judge of Probate, Barbour County, AL

[186] Biographical Souvenir, p. 818

[187] Biographical Souvenir, p. 818

[188] Willoughby, p. 5,6

[189] Willoughby, p. 5,6

[190] Willoughby, p. 6

[191] Willoughby, p. 18

[192] Willoughby, p. 18

[193] Willoughby, p. 6

[194] Willoughby, p. 107

[195] Gerke to Young, Probate Records

[196] Wellborn to Young, Probate Records

[197] J. H. D. Vol. I, p. 99

[198] J. H. D, Vol. I, p. 179-181

[199] Records of Office of Judge of Probate, Barbour county, AL

[200] Mathis, p.xii

[201] Young Bible, New York City death certificate

[202] New York City death certificate

[203] Young Bible

[204] J. A. B. Besson, History of Eufaula, Alabama, the Bluff City of the Chattahoochee, 1875 (reprinted, Spartanburg, South Carolina, 1976 The Reprint Company Publishers) p 18 (hereafter, "Besson").

[205] Besson, p. 18

[206] Records of Office of Judge of Probate, Barbour County, AL

[207] Willoughby, p.70

[208] Willoughby, p. 70

[209] Willoughby, p. 70

[210] Thomas J. Jackson, a resident of Eufaula during 1844-1854, wrote his reminiscences in a series of columns in the Columbus Enquirer-Sun during 1895-1896. In 1991, most of these columns were compiled by Thomas Joseph Peddy, in four volumes which do not disclose a publisher, but which are available in the reference department of the Bradley Library in Columbus, Ga., and the Carnegie Library of Eufaula. These articles will be cited herein as "Jackson", followed by the date of the issue of the Columbus Enquirer-Sun in which the particular article appears. Thus, this note references Jackson, Jan. 5, 1896. Peddy did not include in his compilation the columns containing Jackson's reminiscences of the 1853 New York World's Fair excursion.

[211] Jackson, Jan. 5, 1896.

[212] Jackson, Jan 5, 1896

[213] Jackson, Jan. 5, 1896

[214] Jackson, Jan. 5, 1896.

[215] Jackson, Jan. 19, 1896.

[216] Jackson Feb. 9, 1896.

[217] Jackson, Feb. 16, 1896

[218] Jackson, Feb. 23, 1896

[219] Jackson, March 1, 1896.

[220] Jackson, April 26, 1896

[221] Jackson, Jan. 12, 1896.

[222] Jackson, Jan. 12, 1986.

[223] Jackson, March 8, 1896

[224] Jackson, March 15, 1896

[225] Billups p. 5

[226] Research of John Leo, Fairfax, VA

[227] Uncle Henry on Bealls, p. C; Billups, p. 6

[228] Billups, p. 6

[229] U. S. Census, 1850, Barbour County

[230] Jackson, March 1, 1896

[231] Jackson March 8, 1896

[232] Billups, p.7

[233] Jackson, March 8, 1896

[234] Jackson, March 8, 1896

[235] Young vs. Harrison, et al, 3 Ga 31, 1847 WL 1302 (Ga) (S. C. of Georgia, 1847); 6 Ga 130, 1849 WL 1553 (Ga.), (S. C. of Georgia, 1849). Hereafter, "Georgia Reporter"

[236] Harrison vs. Young, 9 Ga 359, 1851 WL 1438 (Ga), (S. C of Ga, 1851)

[237] John H. Martin, Compiler. Columbus, Georgia, From Its Selection as a Trading Town in 1827 etc. Columbus Ga., 1874, p. 117 (Hereafter, "Martin")

[238] Martin, p. 117

[239] Thompson, p. 37

[240] Conversations with Mary Maude Hurt McCullohs (Young's great-granddaughter), during the 1960's

[241] Martin, p. 117

[242] Irwinton Bridge Co to Young, May 27, 1844, Probate Records

[243] Robert C. Dale to Young; Vincent Tammy to Young; William Ridgill to Young; John L. Hunter to Young, Deed Records Office of Judge of Probate, Barbour County, AL (hereafter, "Probate Records").

[244] Sheriff Hodges to Young, Probate Records.

[245] Young and Calhoun vs. Harrison, et al, 6 Ga 130; 1849 WL 1553 (Ga), (S. C. of Ga, 1849)

[246] Ibid.

[247] Young and Calhoun vs. Harrison, et al, 6 Ga 130; 1849 WL 1553 (Ga), (S. C. of Ga, 1849), at p. 4

[248] Minutes of Eufaula Town Council of May 10, 1847. (Hereafter, "council minutes")

[249] Ibid.

[250] Council Minutes, Jan 8, Nov. 12, 1849;April 23, 1855; June 9, 1855

[251] Georgia Reporter, supra

[252] Council Minutes of July 12, 1847

[253] Council Minutes, Aug. 14, 1848

[254] Young and Calhoun vs. Harrison, et al, 6 Ga 130; 1849 WL 1553 (Ga), (S. C. of Ga, 1849)

[255] Council Minutes Feb. 19, 1849

[256] Council Minutes, Feb. 16, 1850; Dec 29, 1851; Jan 12, 1852

[257] Council Minutes, Nov. 22, 1852

[258] Council Minutes, March 2, April 11, 1853

[259] Council Minutes, May 9, June 13, 1853; Feb 13, 1854; May 8, 20, 1854; March 19, 1855

[260] Council Minutes, May 4, 1855

[261] Council Minutes, Nov 16, 1855

[262] Council Minutes, Jan. 22, 1856

[263] Harrison v. Young, 9 Ga. 359, 1851WL 1438 (Ga), S C of Ga 1851; Young vs. Harrison, 17 Ga 30, 1855 WL 1644 (Ga), S. C. Ga 1855;Young v. Harrison, 21 Ga 584, 1857 WL 1970 (Ga), S. C of Ga. 1857.

[264] Council Minutes, March 18, June 5, 1857

[265] Ibid.

[266] Council Minutes June 5, 1857

[267] Council Minutes, Feb 3, 1854

[268] Jackson, March 15, 1896

[269] Jackson, March 15, 1896

[270] Jackson, July 19, 1896

[271] Jackson, July 12, 1896

[272] Jackson, March 15, 1896

[273] Jackson, March 15, 1896

[274] Dorman, Hist. Of Barbour, p. 326

[275] Fretwell, p. 213

[276] Fretwell, p. 213

[277] J. H. D. Vol. I, p.99

[278] Fretwell, p. 213

[279] Fretwell p. 213

[280] U. S. Census, 1830, Twiggs County, Ga.

[281] U. S. Census of 1840, Barbour County, Al.

[282] U. S. Census of 1860, Barbour County, Al.

[283] Records of the Office of Judge of Probate, reverse index, Barbour County, Al.

[284] JHD, Vol. III, p.220

[285] JHD, Vol. IV, p. 56

[286] Ray Mathis, John Horry Dent, South Carolina Aristocrat on the Alabama Frontier (University, Al, The Historic Chattahoochee Commission and the University of Alabama Press, 1979), p. 97,98 (hereafter, "Aristocrat")

[287] Henry Mayer, "'A Leaven of Disunion': The Growth of the Secessionist Faction in Alabama", The Alabama Historical Quarterly, April, 1969, Vol XXII, No. 2., p.104, 105. (Hereafter, "Mayer")

[288] Mayer, p. 106

[289] Thompson, p. 560

[290] Thompson, p. 335

[291] Thompson, p. 377

[292] Lewy Dorman, <u>Party Politics in Alabama From 1850 Through 1860</u> (Wetumpka, Al.,Wetumpka Printing Company, 1935) p. 47 (hereafter, "Dorman, Politics").

[293] Walker, sheet facing p. 165

[294] Dorman, Politics, p. 63,64, quoting from Spirit, Oct. 22, 1850

[295] Dorman, Politics, p.58

[296] Jackson, June 28, 1896

[297] Encyclopedia Britannica; Britannica Online, an Internet service (hereafter, "Britannica").

[298] Britannica

[299] Britannica

[300] Jackson, May 24, 1896

[301] Jackson, May 3, 1896

[302] Jackson, May 3, 1896

[303] Jackson, May 10, 1896

[304] Jackson, May 10, 1896.

[305] Jackson, May 24, 1896.

[306] Jackson, June 7, 1896.

[307] Jackson, June 14, 1896.

[308] Jackson, June 21, 1896.

[309] Jackson, June 21, 1896

[310] Jackson, July 5, 1896.

[311] Jackson, July 12, 1896.

[312] Jackson, July 19, 1896

[313] Jackson, August 2, 1896

[314] Jackson, August 16, 1896.

[315] Jackson, Sept. 30, 1896.

[316] Jackson, Sept. 13, 1896

[317] Jackson, Sept. 20, 1896

[318] Jackson, Sept 27, 1896

[319] Jackson, Oct, 11, 1896

[320] Jackson, Oct. 11, 1896.

[321] Jackson, Oct. 18, 1896

[322] Young Bible

[323] Records of Trinity Church, New York City

[324] Rogers, p 169

[325] Mathis, p. xv

[326] Mathis, p. xv

[327] Jackson, Sept. 27, 1896; Thompson, p. 562; Smartt, p. 43

[328] Young Bible

[329] Jackson, Sept. 27, 1896

[330] J. H. D. Vol II, pp. 43,44

[331] J. H. D., Vol. II, p.123

[332] J. H. D., Vol. III, p. 11

[333] J. H. D., Vol. III, p. xx

[334] J. H. D., Vol III, p. xv

[335] Henry A Dent, A Sketch of the Dent Family, Eufaula, Al., Nov. 1956. p.4, unpublished manuscript in possession of family. Hereafter, "Uncle Henry on Dents")

[336] Harry Wright Newman, <u>Charles County Gen.try</u>, (Washington, D. C., published by the Author, 1940), p.92

[337] Thomas McAdory Owen, <u>History of Alabama and Dictionary of Alabama Biography</u>, (Spartanburg, S. C., The Reprint Company, Reprinted 1978) p. 480 (Hereafter, " T. M. Owen")

[338] Jackson, March 22, 1896

[339] Jackson, March 22, 1896

[340] EuGen.ia Persons Smartt, <u>History of Eufaula (1933, reprinted, 1995), p.48</u>

[341] E. B. Young Bible

[342] E. B .Young Bible

[343] Smartt, p. 50, 51

[344] Walker, p141

[345] Walker, p141

[346] Smartt, p. 51

[347] Smartt, p. 150, 151

[348] Smartt, p. 50

[349] Jackson, March 15, 1896

[350] JHD, Vol. IV, p.21

[351] JHD, Vol. III, p. 250

[352] J. H. D. Vol. III.

[353] Young family tradition

[354] Recitals in later deed to Ann Young, April 25, 1867, in possession of family

[355] "Docent Notes", Alabama Historical Commission, for use at Fendall Hall. (Hereafter, "Docent Notes")

[356] Docent Notes

[357] JHD, Vol. III, p.220

[358] JHD, Vol. IV, p. 56

[359] Docent Notes

[360] Docent Notes

[361] Alabama Historical Commission, General Management Plan, Fendall Hall (hereafter, "Management Plan")

[362] Memorial Record of Alabama, p. 417-418 (Hereafter, "Memorial Record"); T. M. Owen, p 480

[363] Memorial Record, p.417-418; T. M. Owen, p. 480

[364] Walker, p. 161

[365] Marie Bankhead Owen, The Story of Alabama, (Lewis Historical Publishing Co., Inc., New York, 1949), p. 276, (hereafter, "M. B. Owen").

[366] Management Plan.

[367] Young Bible

[368] Thompson, p 473

[369] Jackson, March 1, 1896

[370] Jackson, May 17, 1896)

[371] Jackson, March 15, 1896

[372] Jackson March 15, 1896

[373] E. B. Young Bible

[374] Letter from Hubert to Anna, June 7, 1864, quoted infra

[375] Letter from Hubert to Anna, June 7, 1864, quoted infra

[376] Letter from Hubert to Anna, June 7, 1864, quoted infra

[377] Letter from Hubert to Anna, August 1st, 1863, quoted infra

[378] Willoughby, p. 87

[379] Willoughby, p. 99

[380] Willoughby, p. 89

[381] Willoughby, p 87; Walker, 158

[382] John Horry Dent Plantation Journals, Vol. A-I, p 1 (Hereafter, "J. H. D.")

[383] J. H. D., Vol IV, p. 73

[384] J.H.D., Vol. IV, p. 12

[385] Smartt, p. 45-46

[386] T. M. Owen, p. 1826

[387] Spirit of the South, Eufaula newspaper, Feb. 18, 1851 (Hereafter, "Spirit".)

[388] Thompson, p. 71; Smartt, p. 94 (some dates and certain other details given by these authorities are incorrect.)

[389] Willoughby, p. 29

[390] Dorman, Hist of Barbour, p. 326

[391] Smartt, p.59

[392] E. B. Young business papers in possession of his family

[393] Willoughby, p. 108

[394] Spirit, Nov. 12, 1850

[395] Willoughby, p. 116

[396] Willoughby, p. 122

[397] Willoughby, p. 124

[398] Willoughby, p. 129

[399] Willoughby, p. 130-131

[400] Willoughby, p. 135-136

[401] Souvenir, p. 818; Worsley, p.1, 260

[402] Willoughby, p. 107, 108

[403] Etta B. Worsley, *Columbus on the Chattahoochee*, (Columbus, Columbus Office Supply Co. 1951), p. 261, hereafter, "Worsley"

[404] Willoughby, p. 88

[405] Worsley, p. 260,261.

[406] Willoughby, p. 87,88

[407] Willoughby, p. 88

[408] Willoughby, p. 87

[409] Souvenir, p. 817

[410] Souvenir, p. 819

[411] F. Clason Kyle, Pictorial History of Columbus (Norfolk, Va., The Dunning Company, 1986).

[412] Souvenir, p. 819

[413] Martin, p. 118

[414] Souvenir, p. 819; Telfair, pp. 100, 125. The authorities conflict as to Eagle Mill's significant dates. Its founding is given as 1850 (Harris, p. 23;Lupold, p. 2), 1851 (McDonald thesis, 32, cited infra), and others. We have accepted 1855 as the date of William's move to Columbus from Apalachicola, and thus the earliest date he could have founded or acquired Eagle, which is the date given in Souvenir, p. 819, which seems based on an interview with William Young while he was alive, and forms the basis for the obituary upon his death, see Columbus Daily Enquirer-Sun, Tuesday, May 8, 1894. But Souvenir also contains inaccuracies. It gives 1867 as the date of consolidation with Howard and acquisition of the other waterfront lots. This appears to be a misprint. Martin, p. 118, quotes a news article from the April 10, 1860, Columbus Enquirer reporting and commenting on the acquisition of Howard. See also Telfair, p. 100, 125. The latter authorities seem more consistent with events. Souvenir may also be inaccurate in giving 1835 as the date William and Edward closed the Marion business and separated. Eufaula evidence suggests this was later, probably 1836, or possibly 1837.

[415] Roger Harris, Introduction to History of Columbus, Ga., (Columbus, Ga., Communicorp, Inc.,1992) p.23 (hereafter "Harris").

[416] Harris, p. 23

[417] Worsley, p. 261

[418] John S. Lupold, Columbus, Georgia, 1828-1978, (Columbus College, 1978), (hereafter, "Lupold")

[419] Worsley, p. 261

[420] Worsley, p. 261

[421] Worsley, p. 260

[422] J. H. D. Vol IV, p.54

[423] J. H. D. Vol IV, p. 57, 65

[424] J. H. D. Vol V, p. 205

[425] J. H. D. Vol V p. 206

[426] Rogers, P. 189

[427] Thompson, p. 228

[428] Malcolm C. McMillan, ed. The Alabama Confederate Reader, U of Al. Press, 1963 (hereafter, "McMillan") p. 55, 57

[429] McMillan, p. 57

[430] McMillan, p.57

[431] McMillan p. 57

[432] Rogers, p. 187

[433] Rogers, p. 187,188

[434] S. H. Dent papers in possession of his family.

[435] S. H. Dent papers in possession of his family.

[436] Young Bible

[437] Martin, p. 146

[438] Muster Roll, Co. B, 1st Infantry Regiment, Alabama Volunteers, National Archives

[439] Records of 1st Infantry Regiment, Alabama Volunteers, National Archives

[440] Young Bible

[441] Records of 1st Infantry Regiment, Alabama Volunteers, National Archives

[442] Arthur Middleton Manigault, Brig. Gen., C. S. A., A Carolinian goes to War (Columbia, S. C., U. of S. C. Press, 1983,2nd Printing, 1988, Paperback Edition, 1992), p.196 (hereafter, "Manigault")

[443] Green Beauchamp, "Reminiscences", unpublished manuscript, Eufaula folder, Alabama Department of Archives, Montgomery (hereafter, "Beauchamp")

[444] Faye Lind Jensen , Power and Progress in the Urban South: Columbus Georgia, 1850-1885, Doctoral Dissertation, Emory University, 1991, p 88 (hereafter, "Jensen"), Bradley Library, Columbus, Ga.

[445] Muster Roll, Eufaula Light Artillery (hereafter, "Muster Roll"), Ala. Dept. of Archives and History (ADAH)

[446] Eufaula Times and News, May 18, 1899, clipping in Eufaula Folder, ADAH

[447] Muster Roll

[448] Beauchamp

[449] Dorman, Hist. Barbour County

[450] Dorman, Hist. Barbour County

[451] Stephen E. Ambrose, Nothing Like it in the World, the Men who Built the Transcontinental Railroad 1863-1869 (New York, Simon & Schuster, 2000) p. 24 (Hereafter, "Ambrose").

[452] Ambrose, p. 40

[453] Ambrose, p. 89,90

[454] Maxine Turner, Navy Gray, Engineering the Confederate Navy on the Chattahoochee and Apalachicola Rivers, (Macon, Georgia, Mercer University Press. Reprint, 1999), p.53 (hereafter, "Turner')

[455] Turner, p. 156

[456] Telfair (Louise Jones DuBose), A History of Columbus, Ga, 1828-1928, (Columbus, The Historical Publishing Co., 1929), p. 101, (hereafter, "Telfair")

[457] Turner, p. 327, quoting the Clayton (Alabama) News Banner in 1859-60,on unspecified dates.

[458] Turner, p. 144

[459] Turner, p. 159

[460] Turner, p. 150

[461] Turner, p. 159

[462] Turner, p. 176

[463] Turner, p. 161

[464] Jackson March 15, 1896

[465] Turner, p. 162

[466] Turner p. 107

[467] Turner, p. 298

[468] Turner, p. 212

[469] Turner, p. 214

[470] Jensen, p. 88

[471] Jensen, p. 88,89

[472] Martin, p. 144

[473] Jensen, p. 103-104

[474] Jensen, p. 104

[475] Telfair, p. 100

[476] Telfair, p. 101

[477] Telfair, p. 101

[478] Telfair, p. 101; Jensen, p 91

[479] Jensen, p. 91

[480] Telfair, p. 100

[481] Lt. Col. Louis Bonnigal, Capt. Melvin J. Sowards, and Capt R. E. Mildner, <u>The Role of Private Industry in Columbus, Ga.</u>, p. 9-10, Monographs on the Battle of Columbus, Ga, Class in American History, University of Ga., Columbus Center, Spring, 1957 (hereafter, "Bonnigal"), Bradley Memorial Library, Columbus, Ga.

[482] Bonnigal, p. 9-10

[483] Bonnigal, p. 9-10

[484] Worsley, p. 287-288

[485] Worsley, p. 287-288

[486] William Forbes II, <u>Haulin' Brass, Capt. Croft's Flying Artillery Battery, Columbus, Georgia</u> (Dayton, O, Morningside Press, 1995), p. 24, et seq. (hereafter, " Forbes")

[487] Forbes, p. 35

[488] David Williams, <u>Rich Man's War</u>, (Athens. Ga., University of Ga. Press, 1998), p. 54 (hereafter, Williams)

[489] Forbes, p. 31

[490] Forbes, p. 34,35

[491] Forbes, p. xi

[492] Forbes, p. 42,43

[493] Forbes, p. 47

[494] Forbes, p. 66

[495] Forbes, p. 69

[496] Forbes, p. 73

[497] Forbes, p. 88-89

[498] Forbes, p. 90,93,96

[499] Forbes, p. 100; *The Daily Sun* (Columbus, GA) May 24, 1863

[500] Harry Wright Newman, *Charles County Gen.try,* p. 72 (Hereafter cited as "Newman's Gen.try").

[501] Harry Wright Newman, *The Maryland Dents*, (Richmond, Va,: The Dietz Press, Inc, 1963), p. 144 (hereafter cited as "Newman Dents").

[502] Newman Dents, p. 72

[503] *The Biographical Cyclopedia of Representative Men of Maryland and District of Columbia* (Baltimore: National Biographical Publishing Co., 1879), pp. 470-471. (Hereafter cited as "Cyclopedia of Maryland"). Because this work was published during Dr. Dent's lifetime, it is presumably based upon information provided or approved by him.

[504] Cyclopedia of Maryland, pp. 470-471.

[505] Cyclopedia of Maryland, pp. 470-471.

[506] Newman, p.92

[507] Cyclopedia of Maryland, pp. 470-471.

[508] Newman, p.92

[509] Cyclopedia of Maryland, pp. 470-471; Newman Dents, p.92

[510] Leonard Wilson, Ed. *Makers of America* (Washington, D. C., B. F. Johnson, Inc, 1917) p.442 (Hereafter, "Makers of America")

[511] Lawrence M. Denton, *A Southern Star For Maryland, Maryland and the Secession Crisis,* (Baltimore, MD, Publishing Concepts, 1995) p.30 (hereafter cited as "Denton").

[512] Cyclopedia of Maryland, pp. 470-471.

[513] Denton, p. 69-70

[514] Denton, p. 66, 67,69

[515] Letter of May 19, 1861, from Hubert Dent to, Anna, quoting May 9 letter from Dr. Dent to Hubert.

[516] Denton, p. 98, et seq.

[517] Denton, p.1 et seq.

[518] Denton, p. 176

[519] Letter of May 19, 1861, from Hubert Dent to, Anna, quoting May 9 letter from Dr. Dent to Hubert.

[520] Website of Co. H, 1st Maryland Infantry, C.S.A.

[521] Hubert to Anna, June 27, 1861, quoting letter from Maryland family to Hubert dated June 15, 1861.

[522] Company Muster Roll, National Archives

[523] Website of First Maryland Infantry Regiment

[524] Letter from Hubert Dent to Anna, Sept. 2, 1862, quoted *infra*.

[525] Dent family papers in possession of Hubert's descendants Catherine Brantley and Betsy Miller of Jacksonville Florida

[526] Thomas A. Jones, *J. Wilkes Booth* (Chicago: Laird & Lee, 1893; Facsimile Reprint, Bowie, MD.: Heritage Books, Inc., 1990) p. 24 (hereafter cited, "T. A. Jones")

[527] T. A. Jones, p.28-30

[528] T. A. Jones, p.30

[529] T. A. Jones, p. 72, 78-79

[530] T. A. Jones. p. 123

[531] *The Confederate Veteran*, Vol 19, 1911, p.344

[532] Stanley F. Horn, The Army of Tennessee, (Norman and London, University of Oklahoma Press, 1941,1952), p. vii, (Hereafter, "Horn")

[533] Larry J. Daniel, Cannoneers in Gray, The Field Artillery of the Army of Tennessee, 1861-1865 (Tuscaloosa, The University of Alabama Press, 1984, paperback, 1989) p.30 (Hereafter, "Daniel")

[534] Daniel, p.30

[535] Horn, p. 143

[536] Letter of April 25, 1909, Felix Robertson to S. H. Dent, among Dent's papers in possession of his family.(Hereafter, "Robertson Letter of 1909")

[537] Letter of April 21, 1928, Edward Young Dent (Hubert's oldest son) to Judge Felix D. Robertson (son of Captain Robertson), in possession of Dent's family.

[538] Letter of April 9, 1862, Hubert Dent to his wife, Anna, hereafter quoted in its entirety. Any differences in Robertson's 1909 account and Dent's are resolved in favor of Dent's account written three days after the battle.

[539] Robertson's letter of 1909

[540] Official Reports, Series I, Vol. X/1, No. 191, Report of Col. Daniel W. Adams, May 10, 1862. ("Hereafter, Col. Adam's Report") See also No 192, Report of Col. Z. C. Deas, Commanding First Brigade.

[541] Col. Adam's Report, Col. Deas' Report

[542] Robertson's Letter of 1909

[543] Robertson's Letter of 1909

[544] Daniel, p. 34

[545] Col. Adams Report

[546] Robertson's Letter of 1909

[547] Official Reports, Series I, Vol. X/1, No. 190, Report of Brig. Gen. Jones M. Withers, Commanding 2nd Division.

[548] Daniel, p. 38

[549] Daniel, p. 38

[550] Horn, p. 136

[551] Daniel, p. 43

[552] Undated and untitled clipping found among the wartime correspondence of S. H. Dent, together with a clipping from the Mobile Register and Advertiser dated April 24, 1862, in an envelope addressed to Dent's wife Anna in Eufaula, under date of 5/1/62.

[553] Horn, p. 147

[554] Horn, p. 148

[555] Notes in the papers of S. H. Dent, in possession of his family.

[556] Official Reports, Series I, Volume X/1, No. 52, Report of Brig. Gen. Patton Anderson

[557] Official Reports, Series I, Vol X/1, No. 84, Report of Col. Joseph Wheeler, Nineteenth Alabama Infantry, commanding Brigade, of operations May 28-29, 1862

[558] Horn, p. 152

[559] Daniels, p. 46 et seq.

[560] Robertson's letter of 1909

[561] Horn, p. 170

[562] Horn, p. 187

[563] Original in Dent's papers in possession of his family

[564] Young Bible

[565] Beauchamp

[566] Daniel, p 58

[567] Daniel, p.65

[568] Daniel, p. 66

[569] Daniel, 79

[570] Daniel, p. 80

[571] Daniel, p 65

[572] Daniel, p. 88

[573] Daniel, p.79

[574] Daniel, p. 79

[575] Letter of April 21, 1928, Edward Young Dent to Judge Felix D. Robertson, in possession of Dent's family.

[576] Muster Roll, June-July 1862, Eufaula Light Artillery, Alabama Department of Archives (Hereafter, "Muster Roll")

[577] Muster Roll, Eufaula Light Artillery

[578] Beauchamp

[579] Joseph H. Parks, General Edmund Kirby Smith C. S. A. (Baton Rouge and London, Louisiana State University Press, 1954, 1982), p. 252 (hereafter, "Parks").

[580] Jackson, March 25, 1896

[581] Daniel, p. 80

[582] Official Records, Series 1, Vol XXXII/3 [S#59].

[583] Official Reports, Series I, Vol XXIII/2 [S#35], Confederate Correspondence, etc. #12

[584] Notes in handwriting of S. H. Dent in possession of his family.

[585] Official Reports, Series I, Vol XXX/3 [S#52], Union Correspondence, etc. #3

[586] Daniel, P. 30

[587] Daniel, p. 34

[588] Daniel, p. 46

[589] Daniel, p. 56, 64

[590] Official Records, Series 1, Vol. XX/2 [S#30]; Daniels, p.87

[591] Interview with S. H. Dent, clipping from Montgomery Advertiser, undated but during the time Dent was on the Montevallo Board of Trustees.

[592] Horn, p. 264

[593] Tablet # 181, Chickamauga Battlefield National Park

[594] William C. Oates, The War between the Union and the Confederacy, (New York and Washington, The Neale Publishing Company, 1905) p. 258

[595] Notes in handwriting of S. H. Dent in possession of his family.

[596] Tablet # 181, Chickamauga Battlefield National Park. Today, one Battlefield marker reflects Dent's Battery as conducting this bombardment, and another reflects Everett's Battery as doing it. A handwritten draft of letter to the Battlefield authorities written by Hubert Dent, found among his papers, asserts that the Official Reports (see O.R. Series I, Vol. XXX/2 [S#51], No. 414, Report of Col. John S. Fulton), as well as the battlefield markers, reflecting that Everett's Battery bombarded this retreating artillery and wagons are in error. While expressing admiration for Everett's Battery, Dent states that survivors of his battery confirm his recollection of the episode, and neither Everett's Battery nor any artillery other than Dent's was in sight. He reports that he had six guns firing from about the position attributed to Everett on the marker.

[597] Official Reports, Series I-Vol XXX/2 [S#51], Aug 16 -Sept. 22, 1863, No. 412, Report of Brig. Gen. Bushrod R. Johnson (Hereafter, "Bushrod Johnson O. R.")

[598] Horn, p. 264

[599] Peter Cozzens, This Terrible Sound (Urbana and Chicago, Univ. of Ill. Press, 1992,1996), p. 433. (Hereafter, "Cozzens, Sound")

[600] Cozzens, Sound, p. 435

[601] Bushrod Johnson .O. R.

[602] Bushrod Johnson O. R.

[603] Bushrod Johnson O. R.

[604] Cozzens, Sound, p.449

605 Tablet #160, Chickamauga Battlefield National Park

606 Cozzens, Sound, p. 485

607 Official Reports, Series I, Vol XXX/2[S#51], No. 341, Report of Maj. Gen. Thomas C. Hindman

608 Official Reports, Series I, Vol XXX/2[S#51], No. 352, Report of Brig. Gen. Zach. C. Deas

609 Hindman's O. R.

610 Horn, p.272

611 Peter Cozzens, The Shipwreck of Their Hopes, (Urbana and Chicago, University of Illinois Press, 1994,1996), p.326 et seq. (hereafter, "Cozzens, Shipwreck")

612 Wiley Sword, Mountains Touched With Fire, (New York, St. Martin's Press, 1995), p. 291. (Hereafter, "Sword")

613 Daniel, p. 115

614 Horn, p301

615 Handwritten notes among the papers of S. H. Dent, in possession of his family.

616 Forbes p. 107

617 Forbes, p. 108-109

618 Forbes, p. 126

619 Forbes, p. 145

620 Forbes, p. 152

621 Forbes, p. 182,183

622 Forbes, p. 188

623 Daniel, p. 144

624 Horn, p. 330

625 Forbes, p. 190

626 Horn, p. 331

627 Forbes, pp.193,194

628 Forbes, p.192

629 Forbes, pp. 194,195

630 Forbes, p. 196

631 Forbes, p. 202

632 Daniels, p.159

633 Memorial Record, p. 419; Owen, Dict. Of Al Biog., p. 483

634 Horn, p. 357

635 Horn, p. 362

636 Forbes, p. 205

637 Forbes, p. 206

638 Forbes, p. 218

639 Forbes, p. 209

640 Forbes, p. 209

641 Forbes, p. 211

642 Horn, p. 363

643 O. R. Series I Vol. LII/2 [S#110]

644 Forbes, p. 213

645 Forbes, p. 218

646 Horn, p. 368

647 Horn, p. 369

648 Horn, p. 369

649 Forbes, p. 218

650 Forbes, p. 222

651 Forbes, p. 227

652 Handwritten notes among the papers of S. H. Dent, in possession of his family.

653 Interview with Historian-Docent Jamie Gillum, Carter House Visitor's Center, Franklin Battlefield Park, Nov. 30, 2003 (hereafter, "Gillum"); battle map prepared by Gillum.

654 Writer's observation

[655] Gillum.

[656] Letter of June 5, 1931 from Hubert's oldest son, Edward Young Dent (the "Eddie" of Hubert's letters to Anna), in possession of his family

[657] Gillum

[658] Letter of June 5, 1931 from Hubert's oldest son, Edward Young Dent (the "Eddie" of Hubert's letters to Anna), in possession of his family

[659] Correspondence with Harmier's descendant, W. F. W. Muller of New Orleans, Oct. 16, 1996; Conversation with Thomas Cartwright, Director of Carter House Visitor's Center at Franklin Battlefield Park, Sept. 29, 2003

[660] Gillum

[661] Horn, p. 403

[662] Original in possession of the writer

[663] Forbes, p. 232-233

[664] Forbes, p. 237-238

[665] Horn, p.417

[666] Official Reports, Series I, Vol. XLV/1 [S#93]Report of Lt. Col. Hoxton.

[667] Horn, p. 416

[668] Official Reports, Series I, Vol. XLV/1 [S#93]Report of Lt. Col. Hoxton.

[669] Official Reports, Series I, Vol. XLV/1 [S#93]Report of Lt. Col. Hoxton.

[670] Handwritten notes among the papers of S. H. Dent, in possession of his family.

[671] Handwritten notes among the papers of S. H. Dent, in possession of his family.

[672] Official Reports, Series I, Vol. XLV/1 [S#93]Report of Lt. Col. Hoxton.

[673] Handwritten notes among the papers of S. H. Dent, in possession of his family.

[674] Handwritten notes among the papers of S. H. Dent, in possession of his family.

[675] Horn, p. 417

[676] Daniels, p. 181

[677] Horn, p. 422

[678] Horn, P422

[679] Daniel, p. 182

[680] Forbes, p. 250-251

[681] Forbes, p. 250-251

[682] Official Reports, Series I, Vol XLIX/1 [S#103]

[683] Forbes, p. 255

[684] Forbes, p. 255

[685] Handwritten notes among the papers of S. H. Dent, in possession of his family; Also Horn, p. 257.

[686] Forbes, p. 257

[687] Forbes, p. 258

[688] Leonard Wilson, Ed., Makers of America, (Washington, D. C.,B. F. Johnson, Inc. Publisher, 1917), p 445 .(Hereafter, "Wilson")

[689] Manigault, p. 196

[690] Rogers, p. 221

[691] Martin, pp.178-180

[692] Telfair, p 137

[693] Souvenir, p. 820

[694] Dorman, Hist. Of Barbour; Walker, p.142, 204; Smartt, p. 79; Thompson, p. 231

[695] Dorman, Hist. Of Barbour; Smartt p.79; Thompson, p. 231

[696] Smartt, p. 79

[697] Thompson, p. 231

[698] Memorial, Alabama, p.468-469

[699] Memorial, Alabama, p.468-469

[700] Memorial, Alabama, p.468-469

[701] Molly Young to Dr. Hamilton Weedon, Aug 5, 1865, Special Collections, Auburn University

[702] All of the correspondence between Molly and Hamilton hereafter quoted is held in the Special Collections of Auburn University.

[703] Memorial, Alabama, p. 469

[704] Young Bible

[705] Helen Sylvester Foley, Compiler, <u>1860 Marriage Records, Barbour County, Alabama</u> (Miran Publishers, Fort Worth Texas), available in Alabama Department of Archives and History, Montgomery, Al. (Hereafter, "Foley").

[706] Walker, p. 141,142

[707] Thompson, p 557

[708] Thompson, p. 557

[709] Walker, p. 296-297

[710] Thompson, 558; also, Weedon family papers in possession of Emma Foy, Eufaula, Alabama

[711] "Sketch of Mrs. A. F. Young," by her long-time Methodist minister, Rev. E. M. Bounds, published in an undated newspaper clipping found in Dent family Bible in possession of writer.

[712] Wilson, p.446; Memorial Record, p. 419; Owen, Dict. of AL Biog., p. 483

[713] Council Minutes, March 18, 1867

[714] Council Minutes, May 28, 1867

[715] Rogers, p. 244

[716] Walker, p. 229

[717] Rogers, p.250

[718] Mathis, Introduction to Journals, p. xvi

[719] Walker, p. 237 et seq.

[720] Memorial, Alabama, p. 478

[721] Mathis, Introduction to Journals, p. xvii

[722] Edward B. Young's papers in possession of his family

[723] Young Bible; Helen Sylvester Foley, Compiler, <u>1860 Marriage Records, Barbour County, Alabama</u> (Miran Publishers, Fort Worth Texas), available in Alabama Department of Archives and History, Montgomery, Al. (Hereafter, "Foley").

[724] Walker, p. 141

[725] Records of the Comptroller of the Currency, 1876 report of examination, Eufaula National Bank

[726] Young Bible; Helen Sylvester Foley, Compiler, <u>1860 Marriage Records, Barbour County, Alabama</u> (Miran Publishers, Fort Worth Texas), available in Alabama Department of Archives and History, Montgomery, Al. (Hereafter, "Foley").

[727] Bluff City Times, Nov. 11, 1869 (Hereafter, "Times")

[728] Owen, Dictionary, p. 251-252

[729] J. H. D., p.430, 431

[730] Flewellen, p.163

[731] Times, Aug, 31, 1871

[732] Times, Sept. 14, 1871

[733] Times, Sept 21, 1871

[734] Times, Nov. 23, 1871

[735] Times, Dec. 14, 1871

[736] Times, Nov. 2, 1871

[737] Times, Feb. 8, 1873

[738] Times, Jan 31, 1873

[739] Times, Feb. 5, 11,1873

[740] Times, Feb, 12, 1873

[741] Times, Feb.8, 28, March 1, 1873

[742] Times, Feb 27,28, March 1, 1873

[743] Walker, p. 236

[744] Times, May 26. 1872

[745] Times, June 5, 1872

[746] Times, June 7, 1872

[747] Times, June 8, 1872

[748] Times, June 25, 1872

[749] Times, July 11, 1872

[750] Times, July 11,18, 1872; August 1, 1872

[751] Times, July 28, 1872.

[752] Times, August 6, 1872

[753] Times, Sept. 26, 1872

[754] Jackson, Sept. 27, 1896

[755] Jackson, Sept. 27, 1896

[756] Thompson, p. 563

[757] Times, Sept 12, Oct 4, 1872

[758] Times, Sept. 12, 13, 14, 1872

[759] Times, Sept. 12, 13, 14, 1872

[760] Times, Sept. 12, 13, 14, 1872

[761] Times, Sept. 14, 1872

[762] Times, Oct. 8, 1872

[763] Times, Oct 31, 1872

[764] Times, Nov. 5, 1872

[765] Dubose/Greer, p. 357

[766] Times, Dec 4, 1872

[767] Dubose/Greer, p. 357

[768] Dubose/Greer, p. 357; see entire opinion at Times, Dec 4, 1872

[769] Rogers, p.250

[770] Dubose/Greer, p. 352

[771] Times, Nov. 19, 1872

[772] Times, Nov. 19, 1872

[773] Times, Nov. 19, 1872

[774] Times, Nov. 20, 1872

[775] Fleming, p. 755-756;Times, Nov 20, 1872

[776] The Times, Nov. 21, 1872

[777] Dubose/Greer, p. 366

[778] Fleming, p. 756

[779] Rogers, p 252

[780] Fleming, p. 759; Dubose/Greer, p. 371 et seq.

[781] Fleming, p. 759

[782] Fleming, p. 756; Dubose/Greer, p. 373

[783] Dubose/Greer, p. 374; Fleming p. 756

[784] Dubose/Greer, p. 382 et seq.; Fleming, p. 757; The Times, Dec 15, 1872

[785] Owen, Dictionary, p.1259, 149

[786] The Times, Dec. 20, 1872

[787] The Times, Feb. 2, 1873

[788] The Times, Aug. 25, 1872

[789] Dubose/Greer, p. 397 et. seq.; Fleming, p. 759

[790] Fleming, p. 761

[791] The Times, March 1, 1872

[792] The Times, March 8, 1872

[793] Rogers, p. 252

[794] Jackson, Feb. 16, 1896

[795] J.H.D. Vol. II p.151

[796] U. S. Census, 1870

[797] Walker, p. 254,255

[798] Walker, p. 254 et seq.; Flewellen, p. 126, et seq.

[799] Walker, p. 270

[800] Flewellen, p. 130 et seq.; Walker, p. 275

[801] Flewellen, p. 134

[802] Walker, p. 273

[803] Walker, p. 272

[804] Walker, p.279 et seq.

[805] J.A.B. Besson, <u>History of Eufaula Alabama, the Bluff City of the Chattahoochee</u>, (1875 by J.A.B.Besson; Reprinted by The Reprint Company, Spartanburg, S. C., 1976), p. xviii (hereafter, "Besson")

[806] Besson, p. 23,25-26

[807] Records of the Comptroller of the Currency, Eufaula National Bank

[808] Smartt, p. 110

[809] copy of letter among papers of Stanley Hubert Dent, Alabama Department of Archives

[810] Souvenir, p. 820

[811] J.H.D., Vol. XII, p. 388

[812] Jensen, p. 170

[813] Article, Columbus Ledger/Enquirer, Jan. 10, 2000

[814] John S. Lupold, <u>Columbus, Georgia, 1828-1978</u> (Columbus Productions, Inc., 1978) p. 55(Hereafter, "Lupold")

[815] Jensen, p. 166; Article, Columbus Ledger/Enquirer, Jan. 10, 2000

[816] Souvenir, p. 820; Jensen, p. 166

[817] Lupold, p. 55; Souvenir, p. 820

[818] Lupold, p. 55

[819] Jensen, p. 173

[820] Article, Columbus Ledger/Enquirer, Jan. 10, 2000

[821] Jensen, 185, et seq.

[822] Jensen, p. 187,188

[823] Souvenir, p. 820

[824] Columbus *Enquirer-Sun,* May 8, 1894

[825] Columbus *Enquirer-Sun,* May 8, 1894

[826] Telfair, p. 199

[827] Columbus *Ledger-Enquirer*, June 23, 2002

[828] Cecil Ward McDonald, <u>Economic History of Columbus, Georgia To The Civil War</u>, Master's Thesis, Ala. Polytechnic Institute, 1940

[829] Souvenir, p. 817

[830] Jensen, p. 163, quoting Moses, "Autobiography," p. 54

[831] Smartt, p. 109

[832] "Sketch of Mrs. A. F. Young," by Rev. E. M. Bounds, published in undated newspaper clipping found in the Dent family Bible, in possession of writer.

[833] Smartt, p.109-110

[834] Jackson, March 8, 1896

[835] "Sketch of Mrs. A. F. Young," by Rev. E. M. Bounds, published in undated newspaper clipping found in the Dent family Bible, in possession of writer, (hereafter sometimes cited as "Rev. Bounds' Sketch."

[836] Rev. Bounds' sketch, cited supra.

[837] Rev. Bounds' sketch, cited supra.

[838] Rev. Bounds' sketch, cited supra.

[839] J. H. D., Vol XII, p. 96

[840] J. H. D., Vol XII, p. 284

[841] Conversations with their granddaughter, Genevieve Williams Wood Harris, June 2001

[842] The Daily Times, Dec 31, 1882

[843] The Daily Times, Dec 29, 1882

[844] The Daily Times, May 27, 1883

[845] The Daily Times, May 15, 1883

[846] The Daily Times, May 23, 1883

[847] The Daily Times, May 30, 1883

[848] The Daily Times, Oct. 20, 1883

[849] Lynn Willoughby, <u>Flowing Through Time</u>, (Tuscaloosa and London, The University of Ala Press, 1999) p. 105, 137,140

[850] Eufaula Times, February 20, 1883

[851] Thompson, p. 263

[852] Flewellen, p. 180

[853] Thompson, p.393

[854] Flewellen, p. 197

[855] Eufaula Times & New, May 26, 1885

[856] Flewellen, p. 189

[857] Thompson, 243; Flewellen, p.189; Interviews with Carrie Dent McDowell, 1950's.

[858] Thomas M. Owen, Dictionary of Alabama Biography, (Chicago, The S. J. Clarke Publishing Co., 1921), hereafter, ("Owen, Dictionary") p. 255.

[859] Thompson, p.81

[860] Flewellen, p. 185

[861] *Eufaula Tribune*, May 14, 1946

[862] *Montgomery Advertiser* editorial by his son-in-law, C. G. Dobbins, May 12, 1946

[863] Linton C. Hopkins, *Biography of Maximilian Bethune Wellborn*, (published by his children, lithographed by Darby Printing Co, 1960) p. 36 (hereafter cited as "Hopkins")

[864] Hopkins, p. 38

[865] Hopkins, p. 38-39; *Eufaula Tribune*, Nov 2, 1944

[866] Hopkins, p. 43-44

[867] Hopkins, p. 46

[868] Hopkins, p. 46

[869] *Eufaula Tribune*, May 14, 1946

[870] *Eufaula Tribune*, May 14, 1946

[871] *Eufaula Tribune*, May 14, 1946

[872] *Montgomery Advertiser*, May 12, 1946

[873] Flewellen, p. 156

[874] Stationery letterhead in possession of family

[875] Conversations with H. Dent McCullohs, 2003; Family tradition

[876] Eufaula *Daily Mail,* March 4, 1888

[877] *Memorial Record,* p. 420

[878] *Eufaula Times and News*, April 14, 1892

[879] *Eufaula Times and News,* April 3, 1892

[880] Special Report on the Eufaula National Bank by the Comptroller of the Currency, July 16, 1901

[881] *Eufaula Times and News*, April 7, 1892

[882] *Montgomery Advertiser*, April 14, 1892

[883] *Eufaula Times and News*, April 14, 1892

[884] *Eufaula Times and News,* April 14, 1892

[885] *Montgomery Advertiser*, April 8, 1892

[886] Quoted from the *Birmingham Age-Herald* by the *Eufaula Times and News,* April 14, 1892

[887] *Montgomery Advertiser,* March 4, 1892

[888] *Eufaula Times and News*, April 14, 1892

[889] Quoted in the *Eufaula Times and News*, April 14, 1892

[890] *Birmingham News* article quoted in the *Eufaula Times and News*, April 14, 1892

[891] *Montgomery Advertiser*, June 7, 1892

[892] *Montgomery Advertiser,* June 10, 1892

[893] *Birmingham Age-Herold*, quoted in *Eufaula Times*, June 16, 1892

[894] Moore, p. 624

[895] Quoted by Moore at p. 629

[896] Moore, p. 628-629

[897] Moore, 628; Rogers, *"Deep South,"* p. 314-315

[898] Moore, p. 623-640

[899] *Montgomery Advertiser*, July 10, 1896

[900] *Montgomery Advertiser*, July 9, 1896

[901] *Montgomery Advertiser*, July 14, 1896

[902] *Montgomery Advertiser*, July 11, 1896

[903] *Montgomery Advertiser*, July 14, 1896

[904] *Montgomery Advertiser*, Aug. 5, 1896

[905] Moore, p. 645

[906] *Montgomery Advertiser*, Aug. 5, 1896

[907] *Montgomery Advertiser*, Aug. 5, 1896

[908] *Montgomery Advertiser*, Aug. 5, 1896

[909] *Montgomery Advertiser*, Aug. 6, 1896

[910] *Montgomery Advertiser*, Aug. 8, 1896

[911] *Montgomery Advertiser*, Aug. 11, 1896

[912] *Montgomery Advertiser*, Sept. 4, 1896

[913] *Montgomery Advertiser*, Sept. 4, 1896

[914] *Montgomery Advertiser*, Sept. 4, 1896

[915] *Montgomery Advertiser*, Aug. 5, 1896

[916] Journal of the Constitutional Convention, (Montgomery, AL, Brown Printing Co., 1901), p. 537, (Hereafter, "Journal").

[917] Official Proceedings of the Constitutional Convention of the State of Alabama, May 21st, 1901 to September 3rd, 1901 (Wetumpka, AL, Wetumpka Printing Co., 1940) p. 2767-2771 (Hereafter, Constitutional Proceedings)

[918] Constitutional Proceedings, p. 2729-2730

[919] Journal, p. 537

[920] Rogers, p. p. 347

[921] Andrew B. Moore, History of Alabama (Tuscaloosa, AL, Alabama Book Store, 1951) p.655 (Hereafter, "Moore").

[922] Constitutional Proceedings, p. 3109-3111

[923] Constitutional Proceedings, p. 3111-3112

[924] Constitutional Proceedings, p. 4142

[925] Constitutional Proceedings, p. 4143.

[926] William C. Oates, The War Between the Union and the Confederacy (New York and Washington, The Neale Publishing Co., 1905) p. 258

927 Opinion of the Court, U. S. vs. E. B. Young, Middle District of Alabama, No. 3852, Records of National Archives

928 Undated newspaper clippings, Charlie McDowell's Scrapbook

929 Conversations with Ed Young's descendant, Elizabeth Wheeler Brown, 2001

930 Thompson, p. 70

931 Flewellen, p. 224; Smartt, p. 148

932 Owen, Dictionary, p. 656

933 Resolution of the Trustees, annual meeting of May 23, 1917

934 Conversations with Henry's sister, Carrie Dent McDowell, during 1950's.

935 Conversations with Henry's nephew, H. Dent McCullohs, 2001

936 William Furey and Patrick McSherry, The Cutting of the Cables at Cienfuegos, accessed on the internet at www.spanamwar.com (hereafter, "Furey")

[937] Joel C. Dubose, *Notable Men of Alabama* (Spartanburg, S. C. The Reprint Co., 1976) p. 65

[938] Private Herman Kuchmeister's Account, Furey, at www.spanamwar.com

[939] Jose Poncet, *The USS Marblehead*, accessed by internet at www.spanamwar.com

[940] Smartt, p. 255

[941] Smartt, p. 255

[942] Joel C. Dubose, *Notable Men of Alabama* (Spartanburg, S. C., The Reprint Company Publishers, 1976), p. 64, 65 (Hereafter, "Dubose")

[943] Robert David Ward, "The Political Career of Stanley Hubert Dent, Jr," Master's Degree Thesis, Alabama Polytechnic Institute, 1951, p. 6 (Hereafter cited as "Ward"), Citing *Proceedings, Alabama State Bar*

Association, 1893, 70-75. Although Mr. Ward's thesis is not published, he adapted and expanded portions of it for an article in the Alabama Historical Quarterly, Fall and Winter 1971, (hereafter quoted and cited). Most of the facts in this chapter are derived from these detailed and well-researched works of Mr. Ward, who is more recently co-author of the well-received book, *Alabama, the History of a Deep South State.*

[944] *Eufaula Times & News,* August 11, 1892; see also July 14, 28, Aug. 11, 1892

[945] Dubose, 64-65

[946] Ward, p. 8, quoting *Montgomery Advertiser,* Nov. 27, 1902

[947] Ward, p. 9

[948] Ward, p. 9, 10

[949] Ward, p. 14, quoting the *Montgomery Journal,* June 23, 1908

[950] Ward, p. 15, quoting the *Montgomery Journal,* July 2, 1908

[951] Ward, p. 18, quoting *Montgomery Journal,* July 9, 1908

[952] Ward, p. 23, quoting *Montgomery Advertiser,* September 7, 1908

[953] Ward, p. 35, et seq.

[954] Ward, p. 43 et seq.

[955] Ward, p. 46-47

[956] Ward, p. 50-51, citing *Congressional Record,* 61 Cong., 2 Sess. (May 5, 1910), 105

[957] Ward, p. 51-52 citing Congressional *Record,* 61 Cong., 2 Sess. (June 9, 1910), 7735

[958] Ward, p.54-57

[959] Ward, p.60

[960] Ward, p. 73, citing *Congressional Record,* 64 Cong., 1 Sess. (March 17, 1916), 4340

[961] Ward, p. 77, citing *Congressional Record,* 64 Cong., 1 Sess. (March 20, 1916), 4468

[962] Ward, p. 85, quoting *Montgomery Journal,* April 9, 1916

[963] Ward, p. 84, quoting *Montgomery Advertiser,* April 8, 1916

[964] Ward, p. 85, quoting *Montgomery Advertiser,* April 8, 1916

[965] Ward, p. 91, citing Palmer, *Baker,* I, 184

[966] Ward, p. 97, citing *The New York Times,* April 17, 1917

[967] Ward, p. 97, quoting *Birmingham Age-Herald,* April 10, 1917

[968] Ward, p. 98, quoting *Birmingham Age-Herald,* April 13, 1917

[969] Ward, p. 101, citing *Birmingham Age-Herald,* April 19, 1917

[970] Ward, p. 105, citing *Mobile Register,* April 20, 1917

[971] Ward, p. 123 quoting *Mobile Register,* May 1, 1917

[972] Ward, p. 127, quoting *Congressional Record,* 65th Cong., Special Session (May 1, 1917) 2215

[973] Ward, p. 131, quoting *Montgomery Advertiser,* May 19, 1917

[974] Ward, Robert David, "Stanley Hubert Dent and American Military Policy, 1916-1920." Alabama Historical Quarterly, Vol XXXIII, Fall and Winter 1971, Nos. 3 & 4., p. 186. (Hereafter cited as "Ward, Hist. Quart.")

[975] Harry L Smith, M. D, *Memoirs of An Ambulance Company Officer* (Rochester, Minn., the Doomsday Press, 1940). Chap. 11

[976] Ward, Hist Quart., p. 187-188

[977] Ward, p. 133-134, citing *Montgomery Journal,* April 18, 1920; *Mobile Register,* May 15, 1920.

[978] Ward, p. 134 et seq.

[979] Ward, p. 136 et seq, citing *Statistical Register* (1934); *Montgomery Advertiser,* August 8, 9, 1934

[980] Ward, p. 136, citing *Montgomery Journal*

[981] Ward, p. 138, citing *Montgomery Advertiser,* October 8, 1938

[982] Ward, p.139, citing *Montgomery Advertiser,* October 7, 1938; and *New York Times,* October 8, 1938

[983] Ward, p. 139

[984] Ward, Hist. Quart., p. 189

[985] Unidentified newspaper clipping, Charlie McDowell's Scrapbook

[986] Duard Legrand, Editor, writing in the Birmingham *Post Herald,* clipping from 1966 (otherwise undated).

[987] *Eufaula Tribune,* Nov. 17, 1959

[988] Conversations with Charlie's wife, Carrie Dent McDowell, and his daughter, Joy, during the 1950's

[989] Minutes of University of Alabama Board of Trustees, May 29, 1943, Memorial to C. S. McDowell, Jr., (hereafter, UA Memorial)

[990] Muster Roll of Lynch's Tennessee Light Artillery

[991] McDowell's Scrapbook

[992] McDowell's Scrapbook

[993] *The Story of Alabama, A History of the State* (New York, Lewis Historical Publishing Company, 1949), Vol. IV, p. 38, (hereafter cited as "Story of Alabama"); *Register of the Officers and Students of the University of Alabama, 1831-1901*, Thomas W. Palmer, comp, (Tuscaloosa, U. of Alabama, 1901), p. 330

[994] McDowell's Scrapbook

[995] *Montgomery Advertiser,* Nov. 14, 1926

[996] *Montgomery Advertiser,* Jan. 2, 3, 4, 5, 10,11,12, 30, 1902

[997] *Historic Eufaula, A Treasury of Southern Architecture, 1827-1910,* Eufaula Heritage Association, 1972, p. 90

[998] Flewellen, p. 218-219

[999] Smartt, p. 156; undated newspaper clipping in McDowell's Scrapbook

[1000] Flewellen, p. 229

[1001] Smartt, p. 150

[1002] Flewellen, p.223

[1003] Flewellen, P. 231-232

[1004] McDowell's Scrapbook

[1005] *The Story of Alabama,* Vol. IV, p. 322

[1006] McDowell's Scrapbook

[1007] Keith Norman, "Executive Editor's Report," *The Alabama Lawyer,* Vol 63, No. 1, January 2002, at p. 11.

[1008] Keith Norman, "Executive Editor's Report," *The Alabama Lawyer,* Vol 63, No. 1, January 2002, at p. 11.

[1009] Flewellen, p. 237,240

[1010] McDowell Scrapbook

[1011] The *Eufaula Tribune,* Nov. 17, 1959.

[1012] Conversations with Mary Maude McCullohs during 1970's, who recalled that the McDowells moved back into the renovated house prior to an infamous tornado which struck Eufaula in March 1919.

[1013] Undated clipping, McDowell Scrapbook

[1014] Marie Bankhead Owen, Compiler, *Alabama Official and Statistical Register, 1919,* (Montgomery, AL, Brown Printing Co., 1920), p. 395 (hereafter, "Official Register")

[1015] Conversations with Carrie Dent McDowell during 1950's

[1016] *The Eufaula Tribune*, Nov. 17, 1959

[1017] Henry S. and Marsha K. Marks, *Alabama Past Leaders*, (Huntsville, AL, Strode Publishers, 1982) p. 190

[1018] *Eufaula Tribune,* Dec. 15, 1964, Nov. 17, 1959

[1019] *Montgomery Advertiser*, undated clipping *circa* May 25, 1943

[1020] Unidentified clipping, McDowell's scrapbook

[1021] *Montgomery Journal,* May 15, 1921, McDowell Scrapbook

[1022] Moore, p. 767

[1023] Official Register, 1923, p. 365-366

[1024] Flewellen, p. 257

[1025] Smartt, p. 168

[1026] Smartt, p. 168-169

[1027] Smartt, p. 169

[1028] Flewellen, p. 264-265

[1029] McDowell campaign literature in writer's possession

[1030] Moore, p.769

[1031] *Montgomery Advertiser*, undated clipping from 1926

[1032] Moore, p.769-770

[1033] Wayne Flint in *Alabama Governors*, edited by Samuel L. Webb and Margaret E. Armbrester (Tuscaloosa, University of Alabama Press, 2001) p. 174

[1034] Conversations with Carrie Dent McDowell during 1950's and 1960's

[1035] J. Mills Thornton, III, "Alabama Politics, J. Thomas Heflin and the Expulsion Movement of 1929," *The Alabama Review*, April 1968, Vol XXI, No. 2, p.87 et seq, (hereafter, "Thornton")

[1036] Thornton, p. 89

[1037] Thornton, p.89, quoting *Montgomery Advertiser*, Nov. 13, 1929

[1038] Thornton, p. 89

[1039] Thornton, p 89, quoting the *Selma Times Journal*, Dec. 29, 1929

[1040] Thornton, p. 90

[1041] Thornton, p. 90, quoting *Montgomery Advertiser,* Nov. 12, 1929

[1042] Conversations with Carrie Dent McDowell during the 1950's

[1043] Duard LeGrand column, *Birmingham Post-Herald* clipping, unspecified date in 1966

[1044] Unidentified clipping, McDowell's Scrapbook

[1045] Conversations with Charlie McDowell's son-in-law, John Allen Crook, during the 1950's

[1046] Conversations with Carrie Dent McDowell during 1950's

[1047] Flewellen, p. 306

[1048] Minutes of UA board of trustees

[1049] UA Memorial

[1050] Official Register, 1935, p. 151 et seq.

[1051] *Birmingham Post*, Oct. 10, 1939

[1052] *Montgomery Advertiser,* June 22, 1945

[1053] Flewellen, p. 392; *Eufaula Tribune*, Nov. 17, 1959

[1054] *The Eufaula Tribune*, Nov. 17, 1959.

[1055] Flewellen, p. 411

[1056] *Eufaula Tribune*, undated clipping from early 1960's

Appendix

The Descendants of Edward & Ann (Beall) Young

Edward Brown Young, b. 1802 New York City, NY, d. 1879 Eufaula, Barbour Co., AL
+Ann Fendall Beall, b. 1810 Warren Co., GA, m. 1832 Warrenton, Warren Co., GA, d. 1876 Eufaula, Barbour Co., AL
  — James William Young, b. 1833 New York City, NY, d. 1889 Newark, Essex Co., NJ
    +Anna Marie Hewlett, b. 1831, m. 1854 Newark, Essex Co., NJ
      — Charles Augustus Young, b. 1856 Eufaula, Barbour Co., AL
  — Henry Augustus Young, b. 1835 Marion, Twiggs Co., GA, d. 1863 Chunky, Newton Co., MS
    +Maria Marshall McRae, b. 1840 Marlboro, Marlboro Co., SC, m. 1860 Eufaula, Barbour Co., AL, d. 1924 Eufaula, Barbour Co., AL
      — Henry Augustus Young Jr, b. 1861 Eufaula, Barbour Co., AL, d. 1946 Montgomery, Montgomery Co., AL
        +Flora G. (--?--), b. circa 1880 Alabama, m. circa 1901
          — John H. Young, b. circa 1903 Alabama
          — Henry Augustus Young III, b. circa 1905 Alabama
          — May Young, b. circa 1913 Alabama, d. 1973 Birmingham, Jefferson Co., AL
            +Charles G. Dobbins, b. say 1887, m. after 1930 Anniston, Calhoun Co., AL
              — Peter Young Dobbins, b. after 1930
      — Julia McRae Young, b. 1862 Eufaula, Barbour Co., AL, d. before 1889 Eufaula, Barbour Co., AL
        +Albert E. Barnett, b. 1861 Alabama, m. 1888 Eufaula, Barbour Co., AL
  — Ellen Louisa Young, b. 1838 Irwinton (now Eufaula), AL, d. 1839 Warrenton, Warren Co., GA
  — Anna Beall Young, b. 1840 Irwinton (now Eufaula), AL, d. 1902 Montgomery, Montgomery Co., AL
    +Stouten Hubert Dent, b. 1833 Charles Co., MD, m. 1860 Eufaula, Barbour Co., AL, d. 1917 Eufaula, Barbour Co., AL
      — Edward Young Dent, b. 1861 Eufaula, Barbour Co., AL, d. 1946 Eufaula, Barbour Co., AL
        +Annie Stuart McCormick, b. 1871, m. 1889 Eufaula, Barbour Co., AL, d. 1922
          — George McCormick Dent, b. 1890 Eufaula, Barbour Co., AL, d. 1940
            +Helen Mitman, b. 1893 Pennsylvania, m. 1919 Philadelphia, PA, d. 1963
              — Sarah Dent, b. 1920 Eufaula, Barbour Co., AL
                +Merritt Beall Davenport, b. 1918, m. 1944
              — Margaret Dent, b. 1921 Eufaula, Barbour Co., AL
                +Benjamin Franklin Garrison, b. 1918, m. say 1940, d. 1997 Eufaula, Barbour Co., AL
                  — Helen Mitman Garrison, b. 1941 Eufaula, Barbour Co., AL, d. 1995 Eufaula, Barbour Co., AL
                    +Robert Cochran Molette, b. 1934, m. 1962, d. 1970
                      — Robert Cochran Molette Jr, b. 1963
                        +Renee Kidd, b. 1963, m. 1993
                          — Lane Garrison Molette, b. 1997
                          — Lyndsey Helen Molette, b. 2000
                      — Page Garrison Molette, b. 1966
                      — Margaret Dent Molette, b. 1969
                        +John Mark Deakle, b. 1970, m. 1998
                          — Helen Sasaki Deakle, b. 2000 Daphne, Baldwin Co., AL
                  — Benjamin Franklin Garrison Jr, b. 1943 Eufaula, Barbour Co., AL
                    +Constance Martin, b. 1946, m. 1968
                      — Benjamin Franklin Garrison III, b. 1969
                        +Sarah Johnson, b. 1968, m. 1994
                          — Sarah Abney Garrison, b. 1996
                          — Benjamin Franklin Garrison IV, b. 1999
                      — Constance Elizabeth Garrison, b. 1971
                      +Mark Vincent, b. 1965, m. 1999
                        — William Augustus Vincent, b. 2001
                — Sarah Elizabeth Garrison, b. 1946 Eufaula, Barbour Co., AL
                +Robin Cordell Mangum, b. 1945, m. 1964
                  — Robin Cordell Mangum Jr, b. 1965
                    +Elizabeth Moring, b. 1965, m. circa 1990
                    — Leah Solita Mangum, b. 1992
                      — Ann Page Mangum, b. 1996
                  — Frank Garrison Mangum, b. 1967
                — Edward Dent Garrison, b. 1952 Eufaula, Barbour Co., AL
                +Mary McKenzie, b. 1953, m. say 1973
                  — Catherine Garrison, b. 1977
                  — Mary Helen Garrison, b. 1980
                — Susan Ruth Garrison, b. 1960 Eufaula, Barbour Co., AL
                +Norris Keith Smart, b. 1959, m. 1985
                  — Sarah Samantha Smart, b. 1986
                — Sadie Margaret Smart, b. 1990
                +Kevin Scott McCathran, m. 2000

Annie McCormick Dent, b. 1923 Eufaula, Barbour Co., AL, d. 1995
+John Roberts Covington, b. 1915, m. 1948, d. 1971
—— George Dent Covington, b. 1949
—— David Roberts Covington, b. 1950, d. 1970
—— Stuart Leland Covington, b. 1951
   +Elizabeth DeSomery Morse, b. 1957, m. 1995
—— Carol Margaret Covington, b. 1953
   +Frank Edel McGrath, b. 1953, m. 1993 Eufaula, Barbour Co., AL
—— Helen Covington, b. 1954
George McCormick Dent Jr, b. 1925 Eufaula, Barbour Co., AL, d. 1959 Townsville, Vance Co., NC
+Hilda Howard, b. 1929 Alexander City, Tallapoosa Co., AL, m. 1950 Alexander City, Tallapoosa Co., AL
—— Hilda Dent, b. 1954 Carmel, Monterey Co., CA
   +Horace Randall Williams, b. 1951 Lafayette, Chambers Co., AL, m. 1980 Atlanta, Fulton Co., GA
      —— Horace Dent Williams, b. 1988 Montgomery, Montgomery Co., AL
      —— George McCormick Dent Williams, b. 1992 Montgomery, Montgomery Co., AL
—— George McCormick Dent III, b. 1954 Jacksonville, Duval Co., FL
   +Nancy Hamilton McTague, b. 1952, m. 1985 Montgomery, Montgomery Co., AL
      —— Nathan McTague Dent, b. 1973
—— Laura Anna Dent, b. 1958 Jacksonville, Duval Co., FL
Anna Beall Dent, b. 1891 Eufaula, Barbour Co., AL, d. 1942
+George Edward McGough, b. 1890, m. 1914
—— George Edward McGough II, b. 1916 Eufaula, Barbour Co., AL, d. after 2000 Ft. Lauderdale, Broward Co, FL
   +Elizabeth Coleman Watkins, b. 1921 Glasgow, Barren Co., KY, m. say 1941, d. 1986 Louisville, Jefferson Co., KY
   —— George Edward McGough III, b. say 1942
   —— Mary Winn McGough, b. say 1943
      +David L. Wyatt, b. say 1943, m. 1976
         —— Rachel Wyatt Strohbeck, b. 1976 Louisville, Jefferson Co., KY
            +Daniel Hamilton, b. say 1976, m. 1995 Georgetown, Floyd Co., IN
               —— Cassidy Alexandra Hamilton, b. 1998 Corydon, Harrison Co., IN
      +William J. Strohbeck, b. say 1943, m. 1980 Louisville, Jefferson Co., KY
         —— Ryan J. Strohbeck, b. 1982 Louisville, Jefferson Co., KY
   —— Chester Watkins McGough, b. 1947
      +Marla Heim, b. 1954, m. 1978
         —— Claira Elizabeth McGough, b. 1988
—— Edward Dent McGough, b. 1919 Eufaula, Barbour Co., AL, d. 1976 St. Petersburg, Pinellas Co, FL
   +Ann Marie Green, b. 1917 Ogden, Weber Co., UT, m. 1946
      —— Edward Dent McGough Jr, b. 1946
         +Barbara Jean Beattie, b. 1947 Gainesville, Alachua Co., FL, m. 1968
            —— Evan Dent McGough, b. 1969 Panama City, Bay Co., FL, d. 2001 Ocala, Marion Co., FL
               +Cheri Gendron, b. 1968 Silver Spring, MD, m. 1993 St. Petersburg, Pinellas Co, FL
                  —— Morgan Elizabeth McGough, b. 2001 Ocala, Marion Co., FL
         +Kathleen Karen McGrayel, b. 1945 Denver, Denver Co., CO, m. 1981
            —— Melissa Ann McGough, b. 1983 Gainesville, Alachua Co., FL
            —— Matthew Richard McGough, b. 1985 Gainesville, Alachua Co., FL
Catherine Allan Dent, b. 1893 Eufaula, Barbour Co., AL, d. 1939
Edward Young Dent II, b. 1895 Eufaula, Barbour Co., AL, d. 1896 Gainesville, Forsyth Co., GA
Stuart Hubert Dent, b. 1899 Eufaula, Barbour Co., AL, d. 1979 Jacksonville, Duval Co., FL
+Attala Bibb Walker, b. 1909 Montgomery, Montgomery Co., AL, m. say 1934, d. 1981 Jacksonville, Duval Co., FL
—— Catherine Allan Dent, b. 1937 Jacksonville, Duval Co., FL
   +Lewis Braxton Brantley, b. 1937, m. 1969 Jacksonville, Duval Co., FL
      —— Richard Lewis Brantley, b. 1956 Jacksonville, Duval Co., FL
         +Dolores Gail Jolley, b. 1957 Jacksonville, Duval Co., FL, m. 1978 Jacksonville, Duval Co., FL
            —— Richard Bronson Brantley, b. 1978 Jacksonville, Duval Co., FL
         +Renee Joann Stolt, b. 1958 Spokane, Spokane Co., WA, m. say 1986
      —— Karen Sue Brantley, b. 1959 Jacksonville, Duval Co., FL
         +David Lawrence Akins III, b. 1952 Huntsville, Walker Co., TX, m. 1980 Jacksonville, Duval Co., FL
            —— Jessica Lauren Akins, b. 1986 Cartersville, Bartow Co., GA
            —— Benjamin Calloway Akins III, b. 1990 Jacksonville, Duval Co., FL
      —— Linda Gail Brantley, b. 1961 Jacksonville, Duval Co., FL
         +Sidney Lamar Chapman, b. 1944 Gulfport, Harrison Co., MS, m. 1984 Jacksonville, Duval Co., FL
            —— Tiffany Anne Chapman, b. 1981 Jacksonville, Duval Co., FL
            —— Steven Lawrence Chapman, b. 1987 Jacksonville, Duval Co., FL
            —— Michael Lewis Chapman, b. 1987 Jacksonville, Duval Co., FL
   +John Cummins Wulbern, b. 1936 Rye, Westchester Co., NY, m. 1959, d. circa 1968
      —— Robert Cummins Wulbern, b. 1961 Jacksonville, Duval Co., FL

688

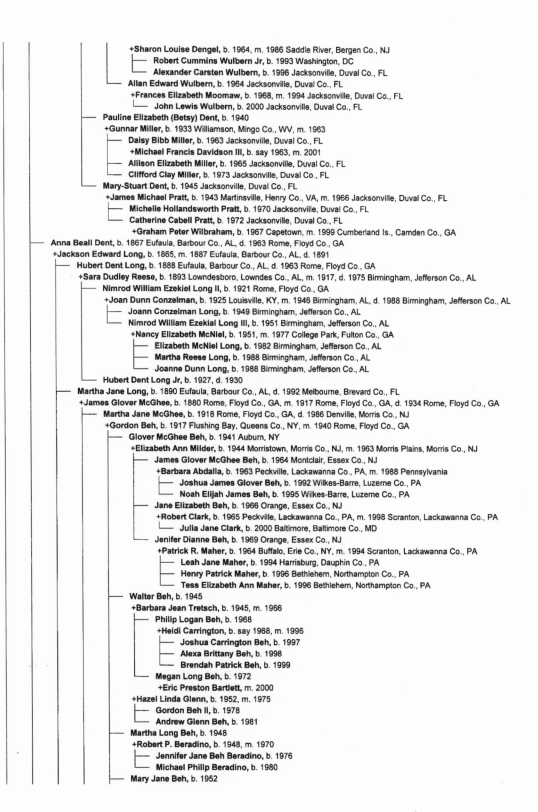

```
                        +Sharon Louise Dengel, b. 1964, m. 1986 Saddle River, Bergen Co., NJ
                         ├──  Robert Cummins Wulbern Jr, b. 1993 Washington, DC
                         └──  Alexander Carsten Wulbern, b. 1996 Jacksonville, Duval Co., FL
                     └── Allan Edward Wulbern, b. 1964 Jacksonville, Duval Co., FL
                         +Frances Elizabeth Moomaw, b. 1968, m. 1994 Jacksonville, Duval Co., FL
                         └──  John Lewis Wulbern, b. 2000 Jacksonville, Duval Co., FL
             ── Pauline Elizabeth (Betsy) Dent, b. 1940
                 +Gunnar Miller, b. 1933 Williamson, Mingo Co., WV, m. 1963
                 ├── Daisy Bibb Miller, b. 1963 Jacksonville, Duval Co., FL
                 │   +Michael Francis Davidson III, b. say 1963, m. 2001
                 ├── Allison Elizabeth Miller, b. 1965 Jacksonville, Duval Co., FL
                 └── Clifford Clay Miller, b. 1973 Jacksonville, Duval Co., FL
             ── Mary-Stuart Dent, b. 1945 Jacksonville, Duval Co., FL
                 +James Michael Pratt, b. 1943 Martinsville, Henry Co., VA, m. 1966 Jacksonville, Duval Co., FL
                 ├──  Michelle Hollandsworth Pratt, b. 1970 Jacksonville, Duval Co., FL
                 └──  Catherine Cabell Pratt, b. 1972 Jacksonville, Duval Co., FL
                      +Graham Peter Wilbraham, b. 1967 Capetown, m. 1999 Cumberland Is., Camden Co., GA
     ── Anna Beall Dent, b. 1867 Eufaula, Barbour Co., AL, d. 1963 Rome, Floyd Co., GA
         +Jackson Edward Long, b. 1865, m. 1887 Eufaula, Barbour Co., AL, d. 1891
         ── Hubert Dent Long, b. 1888 Eufaula, Barbour Co., AL, d. 1963 Rome, Floyd Co., GA
             +Sara Dudley Reese, b. 1893 Lowndesboro, Lowndes Co., AL, m. 1917, d. 1975 Birmingham, Jefferson Co., AL
             ── Nimrod William Ezekiel Long II, b. 1921 Rome, Floyd Co., GA
                 +Joan Dunn Conzelman, b. 1925 Louisville, KY, m. 1946 Birmingham, AL, d. 1988 Birmingham, Jefferson Co., AL
                 ── Joann Conzelman Long, b. 1949 Birmingham, Jefferson Co., AL
                 ── Nimrod William Ezekial Long III, b. 1951 Birmingham, Jefferson Co., AL
                     +Nancy Elizabeth McNiel, b. 1951, m. 1977 College Park, Fulton Co., GA
                     ├──  Elizabeth McNiel Long, b. 1982 Birmingham, Jefferson Co., AL
                     ├──  Martha Reese Long, b. 1988 Birmingham, Jefferson Co., AL
                     └──  Joanne Dunn Long, b. 1988 Birmingham, Jefferson Co., AL
             ── Hubert Dent Long Jr, b. 1927, d. 1930
     ── Martha Jane Long, b. 1890 Eufaula, Barbour Co., AL, d. 1992 Melbourne, Brevard Co., FL
         +James Glover McGhee, b. 1880 Rome, Floyd Co., GA, m. 1917 Rome, Floyd Co., GA, d. 1934 Rome, Floyd Co., GA
         ── Martha Jane McGhee, b. 1918 Rome, Floyd Co., GA, d. 1986 Denville, Morris Co., NJ
             +Gordon Beh, b. 1917 Flushing Bay, Queens Co., NY, m. 1940 Rome, Floyd Co., GA
             ── Glover McGhee Beh, b. 1941 Auburn, NY
                 +Elizabeth Ann Milder, b. 1944 Morristown, Morris Co., NJ, m. 1963 Morris Plains, Morris Co., NJ
                 ├── James Glover McGhee Beh, b. 1964 Montclair, Essex Co., NJ
                 │   +Barbara Abdalla, b. 1963 Peckville, Lackawanna Co., PA, m. 1988 Pennsylvania
                 │   ├──  Joshua James Glover Beh, b. 1992 Wilkes-Barre, Luzerne Co., PA
                 │   └──  Noah Elijah James Beh, b. 1995 Wilkes-Barre, Luzerne Co., PA
                 ├── Jane Elizabeth Beh, b. 1966 Orange, Essex Co., NJ
                 │   +Robert Clark, b. 1965 Peckville, Lackawanna Co., PA, m. 1998 Scranton, Lackawanna Co., PA
                 │   └──  Julia Jane Clark, b. 2000 Baltimore, Baltimore Co., MD
                 └── Jenifer Dianne Beh, b. 1969 Orange, Essex Co., NJ
                     +Patrick R. Maher, b. 1964 Buffalo, Erie Co., NY, m. 1994 Scranton, Lackawanna Co., PA
                     ├──  Leah Jane Maher, b. 1994 Harrisburg, Dauphin Co., PA
                     ├──  Henry Patrick Maher, b. 1996 Bethlehem, Northampton Co., PA
                     └──  Tess Elizabeth Ann Maher, b. 1996 Bethlehem, Northampton Co., PA
             ── Walter Beh, b. 1945
                 +Barbara Jean Tretsch, b. 1945, m. 1966
                 ├── Philip Logan Beh, b. 1968
                 │   +Heidi Carrington, b. say 1968, m. 1996
                 │   ├──  Joshua Carrington Beh, b. 1997
                 │   ├──  Alexa Brittany Beh, b. 1998
                 │   └──  Brendah Patrick Beh, b. 1999
                 └── Megan Long Beh, b. 1972
                     +Eric Preston Bartlett, m. 2000
                 +Hazel Linda Glenn, b. 1952, m. 1975
                 ├──  Gordon Beh II, b. 1978
                 └──  Andrew Glenn Beh, b. 1981
             ── Martha Long Beh, b. 1948
                 +Robert P. Beradino, b. 1948, m. 1970
                 ├──  Jennifer Jane Beh Beradino, b. 1976
                 └──  Michael Philip Beradino, b. 1980
             ── Mary Jane Beh, b. 1952
```

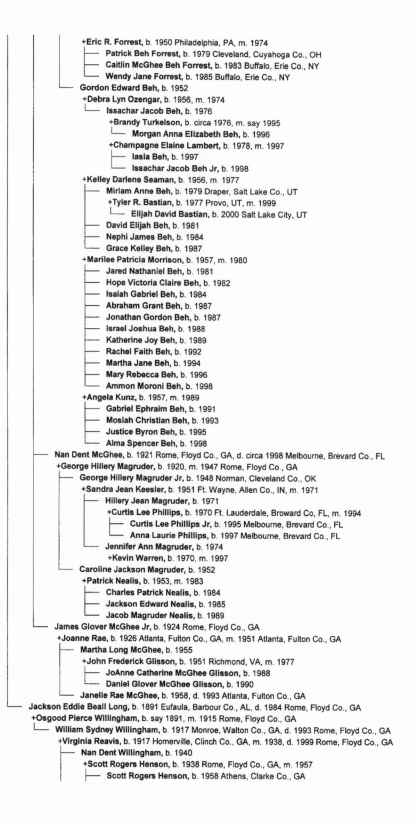

+Eric R. Forrest, b. 1950 Philadelphia, PA, m. 1974
├── Patrick Beh Forrest, b. 1979 Cleveland, Cuyahoga Co., OH
├── Caitlin McGhee Beh Forrest, b. 1983 Buffalo, Erie Co., NY
└── Wendy Jane Forrest, b. 1985 Buffalo, Erie Co., NY
Gordon Edward Beh, b. 1952
+Debra Lyn Ozengar, b. 1956, m. 1974
└── Issachar Jacob Beh, b. 1976
    +Brandy Turkelson, b. circa 1976, m. say 1995
    └── Morgan Anna Elizabeth Beh, b. 1996
    +Champagne Elaine Lambert, b. 1978, m. 1997
    ├── Iasia Beh, b. 1997
    └── Issachar Jacob Beh Jr, b. 1998
+Kelley Darlene Seaman, b. 1956, m. 1977
├── Miriam Anne Beh, b. 1979 Draper, Salt Lake Co., UT
│   +Tyler R. Bastian, b. 1977 Provo, UT, m. 1999
│   └── Elijah David Bastian, b. 2000 Salt Lake City, UT
├── David Elijah Beh, b. 1981
├── Nephi James Beh, b. 1984
└── Grace Kelley Beh, b. 1987
+Marilee Patricia Morrison, b. 1957, m. 1980
├── Jared Nathaniel Beh, b. 1981
├── Hope Victoria Claire Beh, b. 1982
├── Isaiah Gabriel Beh, b. 1984
├── Abraham Grant Beh, b. 1987
├── Jonathan Gordon Beh, b. 1987
├── Israel Joshua Beh, b. 1988
├── Katherine Joy Beh, b. 1989
├── Rachel Faith Beh, b. 1992
├── Martha Jane Beh, b. 1994
├── Mary Rebecca Beh, b. 1996
└── Ammon Moroni Beh, b. 1998
+Angela Kunz, b. 1957, m. 1989
├── Gabriel Ephraim Beh, b. 1991
├── Mosiah Christian Beh, b. 1993
├── Justice Byron Beh, b. 1995
└── Alma Spencer Beh, b. 1998
── Nan Dent McGhee, b. 1921 Rome, Floyd Co., GA, d. circa 1998 Melbourne, Brevard Co., FL
+George Hillery Magruder, b. 1920, m. 1947 Rome, Floyd Co., GA
├── George Hillery Magruder Jr, b. 1948 Norman, Cleveland Co., OK
│   +Sandra Jean Keesler, b. 1951 Ft. Wayne, Allen Co., IN, m. 1971
│   ├── Hillery Jean Magruder, b. 1971
│   │   +Curtis Lee Phillips, b. 1970 Ft. Lauderdale, Broward Co, FL, m. 1994
│   │   ├── Curtis Lee Phillips Jr, b. 1995 Melbourne, Brevard Co., FL
│   │   └── Anna Laurie Phillips, b. 1997 Melbourne, Brevard Co., FL
│   └── Jennifer Ann Magruder, b. 1974
│   +Kevin Warren, b. 1970, m. 1997
└── Caroline Jackson Magruder, b. 1952
    +Patrick Nealis, b. 1953, m. 1983
    ├── Charles Patrick Nealis, b. 1984
    ├── Jackson Edward Nealis, b. 1985
    └── Jacob Magruder Nealis, b. 1989
── James Glover McGhee Jr, b. 1924 Rome, Floyd Co., GA
+Joanne Rae, b. 1926 Atlanta, Fulton Co., GA, m. 1951 Atlanta, Fulton Co., GA
├── Martha Long McGhee, b. 1955
│   +John Frederick Glisson, b. 1951 Richmond, VA, m. 1977
│   ├── JoAnne Catherine McGhee Glisson, b. 1988
│   └── Daniel Glover McGhee Glisson, b. 1990
└── Janelle Rae McGhee, b. 1958, d. 1993 Atlanta, Fulton Co., GA
── Jackson Eddie Beall Long, b. 1891 Eufaula, Barbour Co., AL, d. 1984 Rome, Floyd Co., GA
+Osgood Pierce Willingham, b. say 1891, m. 1915 Rome, Floyd Co., GA
└── William Sydney Willingham, b. 1917 Monroe, Walton Co., GA, d. 1993 Rome, Floyd Co., GA
    +Virginia Reavis, b. 1917 Homerville, Clinch Co., GA, m. 1938, d. 1999 Rome, Floyd Co., GA
    ├── Nan Dent Willingham, b. 1940
    │   +Scott Rogers Henson, b. 1938 Rome, Floyd Co., GA, m. 1957
    │   ├── Scott Rogers Henson, b. 1958 Athens, Clarke Co., GA

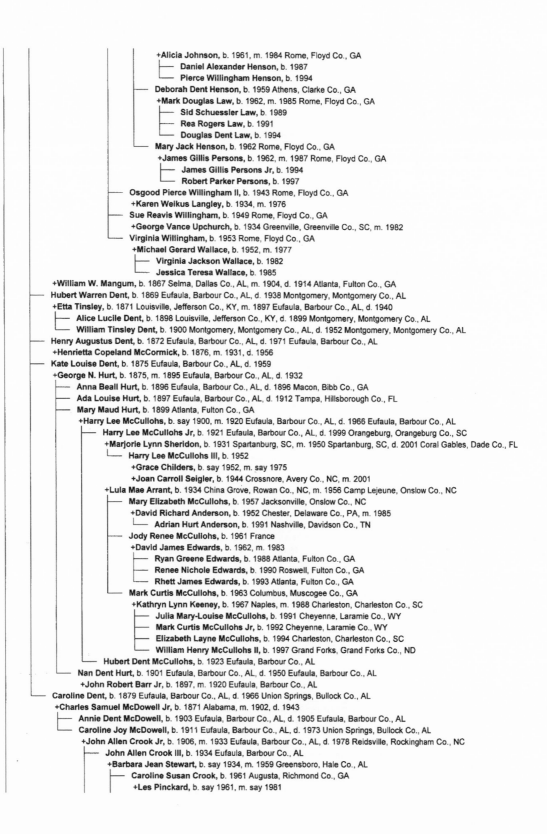

```
                              +Alicia Johnson, b. 1961, m. 1984 Rome, Floyd Co., GA
                              ├──    Daniel Alexander Henson, b. 1987
                              └──    Pierce Willingham Henson, b. 1994
                       ──  Deborah Dent Henson, b. 1959 Athens, Clarke Co., GA
                          +Mark Douglas Law, b. 1962, m. 1985 Rome, Floyd Co., GA
                              ├──    Sid Schuessler Law, b. 1989
                              ├──    Rea Rogers Law, b. 1991
                              └──    Douglas Dent Law, b. 1994
                       ──  Mary Jack Henson, b. 1962 Rome, Floyd Co., GA
                          +James Gillis Persons, b. 1962, m. 1987 Rome, Floyd Co., GA
                              ├──    James Gillis Persons Jr, b. 1994
                              └──    Robert Parker Persons, b. 1997
              ──  Osgood Pierce Willingham II, b. 1943 Rome, Floyd Co., GA
                 +Karen Weikus Langley, b. 1934, m. 1976
              ──  Sue Reavis Willingham, b. 1949 Rome, Floyd Co., GA
                 +George Vance Upchurch, b. 1934 Greenville, Greenville Co., SC, m. 1982
              ──  Virginia Willingham, b. 1953 Rome, Floyd Co., GA
                 +Michael Gerard Wallace, b. 1952, m. 1977
                     ├──    Virginia Jackson Wallace, b. 1982
                     └──    Jessica Teresa Wallace, b. 1985
       +William W. Mangum, b. 1867 Selma, Dallas Co., AL, m. 1904, d. 1914 Atlanta, Fulton Co., GA
 ──  Hubert Warren Dent, b. 1869 Eufaula, Barbour Co., AL, d. 1938 Montgomery, Montgomery Co., AL
    +Etta Tinsley, b. 1871 Louisville, Jefferson Co., KY, m. 1897 Eufaula, Barbour Co., AL, d. 1940
       ├──  Alice Lucile Dent, b. 1898 Louisville, Jefferson Co., KY, d. 1899 Montgomery, Montgomery Co., AL
       └──  William Tinsley Dent, b. 1900 Montgomery, Montgomery Co., AL, d. 1952 Montgomery, Montgomery Co., AL
 ──  Henry Augustus Dent, b. 1872 Eufaula, Barbour Co., AL, d. 1971 Eufaula, Barbour Co., AL
    +Henrietta Copeland McCormick, b. 1876, m. 1931, d. 1956
 ──  Kate Louise Dent, b. 1875 Eufaula, Barbour Co., AL, d. 1959
    +George N. Hurt, b. 1875, m. 1895 Eufaula, Barbour Co., AL, d. 1932
       ├──  Anna Beall Hurt, b. 1896 Eufaula, Barbour Co., AL, d. 1896 Macon, Bibb Co., GA
       ├──  Ada Louise Hurt, b. 1897 Eufaula, Barbour Co., AL, d. 1912 Tampa, Hillsborough Co., FL
       ├──  Mary Maud Hurt, b. 1899 Atlanta, Fulton Co., GA
       │    +Harry Lee McCullohs, b. say 1900, m. 1920 Eufaula, Barbour Co., AL, d. 1966 Eufaula, Barbour Co., AL
       │       ──  Harry Lee McCullohs Jr, b. 1921 Eufaula, Barbour Co., AL, d. 1999 Orangeburg, Orangeburg Co., SC
       │          +Marjorie Lynn Sheridon, b. 1931 Spartanburg, SC, m. 1950 Spartanburg, SC, d. 2001 Coral Gables, Dade Co., FL
       │          └──  Harry Lee McCullohs III, b. 1952
       │              +Grace Childers, b. say 1952, m. say 1975
       │              +Joan Carroll Seigler, b. 1944 Crossnore, Avery Co., NC, m. 2001
       │          +Lula Mae Arrant, b. 1934 China Grove, Rowan Co., NC, m. 1956 Camp Lejeune, Onslow Co., NC
       │             ──  Mary Elizabeth McCullohs, b. 1957 Jacksonville, Onslow Co., NC
       │                +David Richard Anderson, b. 1952 Chester, Delaware Co., PA, m. 1985
       │                └──  Adrian Hurt Anderson, b. 1991 Nashville, Davidson Co., TN
       │             ──  Jody Renee McCullohs, b. 1961 France
       │                +David James Edwards, b. 1962, m. 1983
       │                   ├──  Ryan Greene Edwards, b. 1988 Atlanta, Fulton Co., GA
       │                   ├──  Renee Nichole Edwards, b. 1990 Roswell, Fulton Co., GA
       │                   └──  Rhett James Edwards, b. 1993 Atlanta, Fulton Co., GA
       │             ──  Mark Curtis McCullohs, b. 1963 Columbus, Muscogee Co., GA
       │                +Kathryn Lynn Keeney, b. 1967 Naples, m. 1988 Charleston, Charleston Co., SC
       │                   ├──  Julia Mary-Louise McCullohs, b. 1991 Cheyenne, Laramie Co., WY
       │                   ├──  Mark Curtis McCullohs Jr, b. 1992 Cheyenne, Laramie Co., WY
       │                   ├──  Elizabeth Layne McCullohs, b. 1994 Charleston, Charleston Co., SC
       │                   └──  William Henry McCullohs II, b. 1997 Grand Forks, Grand Forks Co., ND
       │       ──  Hubert Dent McCullohs, b. 1923 Eufaula, Barbour Co., AL
       ──  Nan Dent Hurt, b. 1901 Eufaula, Barbour Co., AL, d. 1950 Eufaula, Barbour Co., AL
          +John Robert Barr Jr, b. 1897, m. 1920 Eufaula, Barbour Co., AL
 ──  Caroline Dent, b. 1879 Eufaula, Barbour Co., AL, d. 1966 Union Springs, Bullock Co., AL
    +Charles Samuel McDowell Jr, b. 1871 Alabama, m. 1902, d. 1943
       ├──  Annie Dent McDowell, b. 1903 Eufaula, Barbour Co., AL, d. 1905 Eufaula, Barbour Co., AL
       ──  Caroline Joy McDowell, b. 1911 Eufaula, Barbour Co., AL, d. 1973 Union Springs, Bullock Co., AL
          +John Allen Crook Jr, b. 1906, m. 1933 Eufaula, Barbour Co., AL, d. 1978 Reidsville, Rockingham Co., NC
             ──  John Allen Crook III, b. 1934 Eufaula, Barbour Co., AL
                +Barbara Jean Stewart, b. say 1934, m. 1959 Greensboro, Hale Co., AL
                   ──  Caroline Susan Crook, b. 1961 Augusta, Richmond Co., GA
                      +Les Pinckard, b. say 1961, m. say 1981
```

691

```
                          ┌──  McDowell Pinckard, b. say 1983
                          └──  Stewart Pinckard, b. say 1985
                  └──  John Allen Crook IV, b. 1964 Reidsville, Rockingham Co., NC
                      +Kate Hardenburgh Durham, b. say 1964, m. say 1984
                              ┌──  John Allen Crook V, b. 2000 Morristown, Morris Co., NJ
                              ├──  Georgia Grace Hardenberg Crook, b. 2002 Morristown, Morris Co., NJ
                              └──  Charles Durham Crook, b. 2003 Morristown, Morris Co., NJ
          ┌──  Charles McDowell Crook, b. 1938 Union Springs, Bullock Co., AL
          +Edith Rushton Johnston, b. 1947, m. 1970 Montgomery, Montgomery Co., AL
              ┌──  Charles McDowell Crook Jr, b. 1972 Montgomery, Montgomery Co., AL
              ├──  Caroline Johnston Crook, b. 1976 Montgomery, Montgomery Co., AL
              └──  James Watkins Crook, b. 1981 Montgomery, Montgomery Co., AL
          └──  Caroline Joy Crook, b. 1943 Union Springs, Bullock Co., AL
              +Gary Robert Gage, b. say 1942 Cleveland, Cuyahoga Co., OH, m. 1969 Union Springs, Bullock Co., AL
                  ┌──  John Crook Gage, b. 1975 Pensacola, Escambia Co., FL
                  │    +Alisa Faith Ellis, b. 1974 Gulfport, Harrison Co., MS, m. 2003 Gulfport, Harrison Co., MS
                  └──  Charles Ernest Gage, b. 1980 Pensacola, Escambia Co., FL
                       +Tara Marie Jones, b. 1981 Bradenton, Manatee Co., FL, m. 2003 Bradenton, Manatee Co., FL
──  Mary Elizabeth Christina Young, b. 1842 Irwinton (now Eufaula), AL, d. 1891 Eufaula, Barbour Co., AL
    +Hamilton Moore Weedon, b. 1834 Tallahassee, Leon Co., FL, m. 1865 Eufaula, Barbour Co., AL, d. 1908 Eufaula, Barbour Co., AL
        ┌──  Annie Young Weedon, b. 1867 Eufaula, Barbour Co., AL, d. 1947
        │    +John Robert Barr, b. 1865, m. 1887 Eufaula, Barbour Co., AL, d. 1921
        │        ┌──  James Hamilton Barr, b. 1888 Alabama, d. 1956
        │        │    +Julia Simpson, b. 1886, m. circa 1912, d. 1979
        │        ├──  Lucian E. Barr, b. 1889 Eufaula, Barbour Co., AL
        │        │    +Carolyn Coleman, b. circa 1893 Louisiana, m. circa 1915
        │        │        ┌──  Annie L. Barr, b. circa 1917 Texas
        │        │        ├──  Lucian E. Barr Jr, b. circa 1922 Alabama
        │        │        └──  Ida C. Barr, b. circa 1927 Texas
        │        ├──  James M. Barr, b. 1893, d. 1970
        │        │    +Daisy Oppenheimer, b. 1895, m. circa 1913, d. 1969
        │        │        └──  James William Barr, b. 1928, d. 1979
        │        │             +Gloria Martin, b. 1930, m. 1947
        │        │                 ┌──  Annie Barr, b. 1948
        │        │                 │    +Ronald A. Foster, b. 1943, m. say 1968
        │        │                 │        ┌──  Wendy Paige Foster, b. 1968
        │        │                 │        │    +Jason Clark, b. 1969, m. circa 1988
        │        │                 │        │    └──  Grace Anne Clark, b. 1999
        │        │                 │        └──  James Wesley Foster, b. 1972
        │        │                 │    +Thomas Hurst, b. 1949, m. after 1972
        │        │                 └──  Nancy Barr, b. 1950
        │        │                      +Michael Charles Dixon, b. 1941, m. 1976
        │        │                          ┌──  Michael Charles Dixon Jr, b. 1967
        │        │                          │    +Hope Cotton, b. 1969, m. 1998
        │        │                          │    └──  William Mack Dixon, b. 2000
        │        │                          ├──  Claudia Dixon, b. 1969
        │        │                          │    +Henry Lewis Balcom IV, b. 1970, m. 2000
        │        │                          ├──  Heather Barr Dixon, b. 1970
        │        │                          ├──  Marian Christine Dixon, b. 1977
        │        │                          └──  Rebecca Janie Mac Dixon, b. 1980
        │        ├──  John Robert Barr Jr, b. 1897
        │        │    +Nan Dent Hurt, b. 1901 Eufaula, Barbour Co., AL, m. 1920 Eufaula, Barbour Co., AL, d. 1950 Eufaula, Barbour Co., AL
        │        ├──  Walter Weedon Barr, b. 1899 Eufaula, Barbour Co., AL
        │        │    +Annie Talberg, b. circa 1901 Georgia, m. circa 1921
        │        └──  Ross Barr, b. 1901, d. 1922
        └──  Mary Norma Weedon, b. 1868 Eufaula, Barbour Co., AL, d. 1933
             +James LeGrand Ross, b. 1863, m. 1887 Eufaula, Barbour Co., AL, d. 1938
                 ┌──  Mary Weedon Ross, b. 1889 Eufaula, Barbour Co., AL, d. 1975
                 │    +William Humphrey Foy Jr, b. 1886 Eufaula, Barbour Co., AL, m. circa 1911 Eufaula, AL, d. 1956 Eufaula, Barbour Co., AL
                 │    ├──  Mary Norma Foy, b. circa 1913 Alabama
                 │    └──  Carrie M. Foy, b. circa 1915 Alabama
                 │         +Thomas Hinman Moorer, b. 1912 Mt. Willing, Lowndes Co., AL, m. say 1931
                 │             ┌──  Thomas Randolph Moorer, b. 1932
                 │             │    +Zoe Witt, b. 1940, m. say 1960
                 │             │    └──  Thomas Richard Moorer, b. say 1962
```

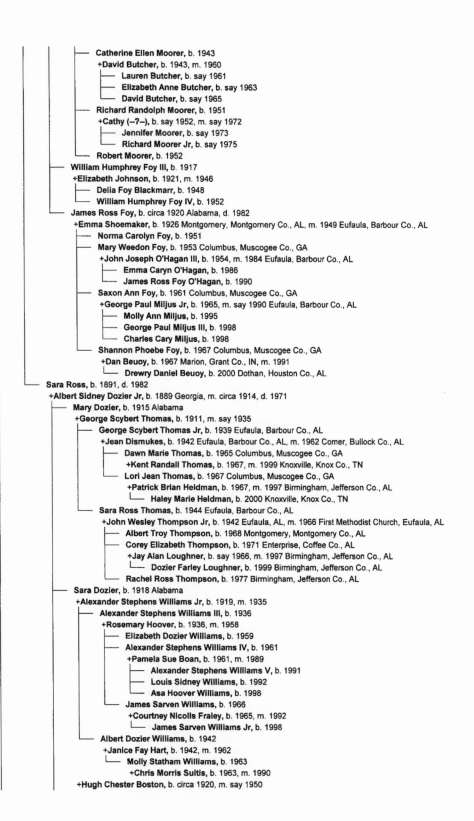

```
├─── Catherine Ellen Moorer, b. 1943
│   +David Butcher, b. 1943, m. 1960
│   ├─── Lauren Butcher, b. say 1961
│   ├─── Elizabeth Anne Butcher, b. say 1963
│   └─── David Butcher, b. say 1965
├─── Richard Randolph Moorer, b. 1951
│   +Cathy (--?--), b. say 1952, m. say 1972
│   ├─── Jennifer Moorer, b. say 1973
│   └─── Richard Moorer Jr, b. say 1975
└─── Robert Moorer, b. 1952
```

William Humphrey Foy III, b. 1917
+Elizabeth Johnson, b. 1921, m. 1946
- Delia Foy Blackmarr, b. 1948
- William Humphrey Foy IV, b. 1952

James Ross Foy, b. circa 1920 Alabama, d. 1982
+Emma Shoemaker, b. 1926 Montgomery, Montgomery Co., AL, m. 1949 Eufaula, Barbour Co., AL
- Norma Carolyn Foy, b. 1951
- Mary Weedon Foy, b. 1953 Columbus, Muscogee Co., GA
  +John Joseph O'Hagan III, b. 1954, m. 1984 Eufaula, Barbour Co., AL
  - Emma Caryn O'Hagan, b. 1986
  - James Ross Foy O'Hagan, b. 1990
- Saxon Ann Foy, b. 1961 Columbus, Muscogee Co., GA
  +George Paul Miljus Jr, b. 1965, m. say 1990 Eufaula, Barbour Co., AL
  - Molly Ann Miljus, b. 1995
  - George Paul Miljus III, b. 1998
  - Charles Cary Miljus, b. 1998
- Shannon Phoebe Foy, b. 1967 Columbus, Muscogee Co., GA
  +Dan Beuoy, b. 1967 Marion, Grant Co., IN, m. 1991
  - Drewry Daniel Beuoy, b. 2000 Dothan, Houston Co., AL

Sara Ross, b. 1891, d. 1982
+Albert Sidney Dozier Jr, b. 1889 Georgia, m. circa 1914, d. 1971
- Mary Dozier, b. 1915 Alabama
  +George Scybert Thomas, b. 1911, m. say 1935
  - George Scybert Thomas Jr, b. 1939 Eufaula, Barbour Co., AL
    +Jean Dismukes, b. 1942 Eufaula, Barbour Co., AL, m. 1962 Comer, Bullock Co., AL
    - Dawn Marie Thomas, b. 1965 Columbus, Muscogee Co., GA
      +Kent Randall Thomas, b. 1967, m. 1999 Knoxville, Knox Co., TN
    - Lori Jean Thomas, b. 1967 Columbus, Muscogee Co., GA
      +Patrick Brian Heldman, b. 1967, m. 1997 Birmingham, Jefferson Co., AL
      - Haley Marie Heldman, b. 2000 Knoxville, Knox Co., TN
  - Sara Ross Thomas, b. 1944 Eufaula, Barbour Co., AL
    +John Wesley Thompson Jr, b. 1942 Eufaula, AL, m. 1966 First Methodist Church, Eufaula, AL
    - Albert Troy Thompson, b. 1968 Montgomery, Montgomery Co., AL
    - Corey Elizabeth Thompson, b. 1971 Enterprise, Coffee Co., AL
      +Jay Alan Loughner, b. say 1966, m. 1997 Birmingham, Jefferson Co., AL
      - Dozier Farley Loughner, b. 1999 Birmingham, Jefferson Co., AL
    - Rachel Ross Thompson, b. 1977 Birmingham, Jefferson Co., AL
- Sara Dozier, b. 1918 Alabama
  +Alexander Stephens Williams Jr, b. 1919, m. 1935
  - Alexander Stephens Williams III, b. 1936
    +Rosemary Hoover, b. 1936, m. 1958
    - Elizabeth Dozier Williams, b. 1959
    - Alexander Stephens Williams IV, b. 1961
      +Pamela Sue Boan, b. 1961, m. 1989
      - Alexander Stephens Williams V, b. 1991
      - Louis Sidney Williams, b. 1992
      - Asa Hoover Williams, b. 1998
    - James Sarven Williams, b. 1966
      +Courtney Nicolls Fraley, b. 1965, m. 1992
      - James Sarven Williams Jr, b. 1998
  - Albert Dozier Williams, b. 1942
    +Janice Fay Hart, b. 1942, m. 1962
    - Molly Statham Williams, b. 1963
      +Chris Morris Sultis, b. 1963, m. 1990
+Hugh Chester Boston, b. circa 1920, m. say 1950

693

```
                              +Carl Espy Stewart, b. circa 1920, m. say 1960
                          Albert J. Dozier III, b. 1921, d. 1945
                              +Sara Brooks, b. circa 1922, m. circa 1941
            Hamilton Moore Weedon Jr, b. 1869 Eufaula, Barbour Co., AL, d. before 1930 Troy, Pike Co., AL
            +Julia Henderson, b. 1870 Alabama, m. circa 1896 Troy, Pike Co., AL
                Mildred Weedon, b. 1898 Alabama
                    +Robert S. Blount, b. circa 1895 Georgia, m. circa 1923
            Edward Beall Weedon, b. 1871 Eufaula, Barbour Co., AL, d. 1953
            +Mary Garland, b. 1879 Alabama, m. circa 1898 Eufaula, Barbour Co., AL, d. 1914
                John Garland Weedon, b. 1899 Alabama
                Edward Beall Weedon Jr, b. circa 1901 Alabama
                    +Virginia L. (--?--), b. circa 1902 Georgia, m. circa 1924
                        Mary R. Weedon, b. circa 1925 Alabama
                        Edward Beall Weedon III, b. circa 1927 Massachusetts
            Walter Roy Weedon, b. 1874 Eufaula, Barbour Co., AL, d. 1921
            Frederick Weedon, b. 1875 Eufaula, Barbour Co., AL
            William Weedon, b. circa 1876 Eufaula, Barbour Co., AL, d. 1877 Eufaula, Barbour Co., AL
            Herbert G. Weedon, b. 1879 Eufaula, Barbour Co., AL
            +Josephine B. Reed, b. circa 1890 Alabama, m. circa 1907
                Margaret Weedon, b. circa 1908 Tennessee
                Annalger Weedon, b. circa 1910 Alabama
                    +Elbat L. Whelden, b. circa 1907 Florida, m. circa 1928
    Ada Louise Young, b. 1846 Eufaula, Barbour Co., AL, d. 1932 Eufaula, Barbour Co., AL
    +James H. G. Martin, b. circa 1845 Alabama, m. 1869 Eufaula, Barbour Co., AL, d. 1913
        James G. L. Martin, b. 1873 Eufaula, Barbour Co., AL, d. 1873 Eufaula, Barbour Co., AL
    Helen Augusta Young, b. 1847 Eufaula, Barbour Co., AL, d. 1932 Eufaula, Barbour Co., AL
    +George Hatch Dent, b. 1843 Charles Co., MD, m. 1869 Eufaula, Barbour Co., AL, d. 1918 Eufaula, Barbour Co., AL
        Warren Young Dent, b. 1870 Eufaula, Barbour Co., AL, d. 1927 Eufaula, Barbour Co., AL
        +Elizabeth Rhodes, b. 1872, m. 1894 Alabama, d. 1930 Eufaula, Barbour Co., AL
            George Hatch Dent III, b. 1895 Eufaula, Barbour Co., AL, d. 1970 Eufaula, Barbour Co., AL
            +Mary Kathryn Hill, b. 1902, m. 1928 Fitzpatrick, Bullock Co., AL, d. 1995 Auburn, Lee Co., AL
                George Hatch Dent IV, b. 1932 Eufaula, Barbour Co., AL
                    +Annie Laurie Lanier, b. 1934 Langdale, Chambers Co., AL, m. 1952 Ft. Gaines, Clay Co., GA
                        George Henry Dent, b. 1955 Fayetteville, Cumberland, NC
                        +Jeanne Leigh Zimmerman, b. 1951 McCune, Crawford Co., KS, m. 1982 McCune, Crawford Co., KS
                            Amy Leigh Dent, b. 1985 Mbabane, Swaziland
                            Laura Anne Dent, b. 1986 San Bernardino, CA
                            Kathryn Jean Dent, b. 1992 Nairobi, Kenya
                        David Rhodes Dent, b. 1963 Kingstree, Williamsburg, SC
                        +Vanessa Ellen Harris, b. say 1963, m. 2002 Buford, Gwinnett Co., GA
                        Warren Lanier Dent, b. 1965 Kingstree, Williamsburg, SC
                        William Dudley Dent, b. 1968 North Carolina
                        +Mary Lynn Marple, b. say 1968, m. 1997 Auburn, Lee Co., AL
                            Emery Baxter Dent, b. 2002 Opelika, Lee Co., AL
        Chauncey Rhodes Dent, b. 1896 Eufaula, Barbour Co., AL, d. 1970 San Diego, San Diego Co., CA
        Nellie Beall Dent II, b. 1896 Eufaula, Barbour Co., AL
        +Ike Fagen Blue, b. circa 1902 Alabama, m. 1928 Eufaula, Barbour Co., AL
            Elizabeth R. Blue, b. circa 1929 Alabama
            +Asa Roundtree, b. say 1929, m. say 1950
                John Roundtree, b. say 1952
            Earnest F. Blue, b. after 1930 Alabama, d. 1950 Union Springs, Bullock Co., AL
    Nellie Beall Dent, b. 1872 Eufaula, Barbour Co., AL, d. before 1907
    +William H. Foy Jr, b. 1864 Alabama, m. 1892 Eufaula, Barbour Co., AL
        Levy Foy, b. 1893 Alabama
        Frederick Foy, b. 1896 Alabama
        +Bolin K. (--?--), b. circa 1903 Virginia, m. circa 1927
    George Hatch Dent Jr, b. 1874 Eufaula, Barbour Co., AL, d. 1943 Eufaula, Barbour Co., AL
    +Mary Harraison, b. 1874, m. 1894, d. before 1910
        Helen Dent, b. circa 1898 Alabama
        Elizabeth Dent, b. circa 1901 Eufaula, Barbour Co., AL
        +George A. Wilson, b. say 1896, m. say 1921
    Louie Dent, b. circa 1878 Eufaula, Barbour Co., AL
    +Genieve Lockwood, b. circa 1882 Crystal Springs, Copiah Co., MS, m. circa 1902
    Helen Augusta Dent, b. 1886 Eufaula, Barbour Co., AL, d. 1972 Birmingham, Jefferson Co., AL
    +Wesley Clark Williams, b. 1870 Cherokee, Colbert Co., AL, m. 1906 Eufaula, Barbour Co., AL, d. 1952 Birmingham, AL
```

694

George Dent Williams, b. 1907 Eufaula, Barbour Co., AL, d. 1966 Russell Co., AL
+Daisy Christina Dudley, b. 1911 Seale, Russell Co., AL, m. 1938 Kentucky
    George Dent Williams Jr, b. 1941 Columbus, Muscogee Co., GA
    +Fay Ferrell, b. say 1942, m. 1963
        George Dent Williams III, b. 1963 Columbus, Muscogee Co., GA
        +Jodi Alene Stoner, b. say 1964, m. 1986 Helena, Lewis and Clark Co., MT
            Nathaniel Archer Williams, b. 1988 Eugene, Lane Co., OR
            Taylor Austin Williams, b. 1990 Eugene, Lane Co., OR
    Clark Dudley Williams, b. 1943 Columbus, Muscogee Co., GA
    +Virginia Pitts, b. 1944 Columbus, Muscogee Co., GA, m. say 1962
        Wesley Clark Williams II, b. 1963 Columbus, Muscogee Co., GA
        +Darla Wagner, b. 1961 Wood River, Madison Co., IL, m. 1994 Columbus, Muscogee Co., GA
            Christina Leigh Williams, b. 2000 Bay Minette, Baldwin Co., AL
        Catherine Elizabeth Williams, b. 1965 Columbus, Muscogee Co., GA
        +John Holmes, b. say 1965, m. say 1995
    +Suzanne McKinley, b. 1943 Columbus, Franklin Co., OH, m. 1969 Opelika, Lee Co., AL
Augusta Williams, b. 1908 Eufaula, Barbour Co., AL, d. 1931
Nell Williams, b. 1912 Eufaula, Barbour Co., AL, d. 1993 Echo Lake, Jefferson Co., AL
+Louie Reese Jr, b. 1910 Birmingham, Jefferson Co., AL, m. 1933, d. 1993 Echo Lake, Jefferson Co., AL
    Louie Reese III, b. 1937 Birmingham, Jefferson Co., AL
    +Alice Lindsay Nathan, b. 1938 Binghamton, Broome Co., NY, m. 1962
        Alice Wiley Reese, b. 1962 Birmingham, Jefferson Co., AL
        +Richard Francis Klimpt, b. 1957 Joplin, Jasper Co., MO, m. 1987 Birmingham, Jefferson Co., AL
        Lynn McCarty Reese, b. 1964 Birmingham, Jefferson Co., AL
        +William Edward Anderson Jr, b. 1964 Atlanta, Fulton Co., GA, m. 1992 Birmingham, Jefferson Co., AL
            William Edward Anderson III, b. 1995 Marietta, Cobb Co., GA
            Sarah Lindsay Anderson, b. 1998 Marietta, Cobb Co., GA
        Louie Reese IV, b. 1968 Birmingham, Jefferson Co., AL
    Lynnell Williams Reese, b. 1940 Birmingham, Jefferson Co., AL
    +Robert Charles Benson, b. 1931 Germantown, Phila. Co., PA, m. 1973
    Julene Reese, b. 1943 Birmingham, Jefferson Co., AL
    +Douglas G. Eisele, b. 1936 Huntington, Huntington Co., IN, m. 1965
        Matthew Douglas Eisele, b. 1968 Statesville, Iredell Co., NC
        Anna Kindler Eisele, b. 1969 Statesville, Iredell Co., NC
        +Royce Gordon Shingleton Jr, b. 1965, m. 1997 Seaside, Walton Co., FL
            Royce Gordon Shingleton III, b. 1999 Birmingham, Jefferson Co., AL
            McCarty Kindler Shingleton, b. 2001 Birmingham, Jefferson Co., AL
            Hannah Vick Shingleton, b. 2001 Birmingham, Jefferson Co., AL
        Emily Williams Eisele, b. 1970 Statesville, Iredell Co., NC
        +Christopher Garrison Lewis, b. 1969 Washington, DC
        Rebecca Lynn Eisele, b. 1974 Statesville, Iredell Co., NC
        +Justin Thomas Shingleton, b. 1971 Atlanta, Fulton Co., GA, m. 2000 Maggie Valley, Haywood Co., NC
    +Michael Hollingsworth Roberts, b. 1946 Greenville, GA, m. 1977, d. 1997 Hiawassee, Towns Co., GA
        Victor Louis Roberts, b. 1979 Augusta, Richmond Co., GA
        Nell Hollingsworth Roberts, b. 1980 Albany, Dougherty Co., GA
    Wesley Reese, b. 1948 Birmingham, Jefferson Co., AL
Genevieve Williams, b. 1917 Birmingham, Jefferson Co., AL
+John Hancock Wood, b. 1912 Albany, Albany Co., NY, m. 1941, d. 1960 Decatur, Morgan Co., AL
    Helen Wood, b. 1943 Birmingham, Jefferson Co., AL
    +George Cantrell, b. 1943 Huntsville, Madison Co., AL, m. 1968 Norfolk, VA
        Mark Wood Cantrell, b. 1972 Cincinnati, Hamilton Co., OH
        +Brenna Godbey, b. say 1976, m. 1996 Chicago, Cook Co., IL
        Margaret Dent Cantrell, b. 1974 Ft. Thomas, Campbell Co., KY
    Elizabeth Hancock Wood, b. 1947 Decatur, Morgan Co., AL
    +Neal Presley Conner, b. 1946 Birmingham, Jefferson Co., AL, m. 1969 Decatur, Morgan Co., AL
        Clark Elyard Conner, b. 1970 Aberdeen, Harford Co., MD
        Wesley Hancock Conner, b. 1976 Decatur, Morgan Co., AL
    Genevieve Williams Wood, b. 1948 Decatur, Morgan Co., AL
    +Richard Dominick Mackiewitz, b. 1948, m. 1969 Decatur, Morgan Co., AL
        Kimberly Cottingham Mackiewitz, b. 1970 Opelika, Lee Co., AL
        +William Joseph Morgan Jr, b. 1974, m. 2000 Brandon, Hillsborough Co., FL
            Kathryn Lynn Morgan, b. 2000 Brandon, Hillsborough Co., FL
        Richard Dominick Mackiewitz Jr, b. 1976 Sarasota, Sarasota Co., FL
        +Angela Jean Bullock, b. 1973, m. 2000 Jacksonville, Duval Co., FL
+Julian Harris, b. 1904 Decatur, Morgan Co., AL, m. 1967, d. 1994 Decatur, Morgan Co., AL

Edward Billups Young, b. 1849 Eufaula, Barbour Co., AL, d. 1910 Montgomery, Montgomery Co., AL
+Mary Bell Jennings, b. 1850 Aberdeen, Monroe Co., MS, m. 1871 Eufaula, Barbour Co., AL, d. 1912 Macon, Bibb Co., GA
— son Young, b. 1872 Eufaula, Barbour Co., AL, d. 1872 Eufaula, Barbour Co., AL
— Annie Young, b. 1873 Eufaula, Barbour Co., AL, d. 1943 Murfreesboro, Rutherfd. Co, TN
+Charles Couch Holt, b. 1865 Monroe Co., GA, m. 1894 Eufaula, Barbour Co., AL, d. 1920 Macon, Bibb Co., GA
— Edward Young Holt, b. 1895 Macon, Bibb Co., GA, d. 1959 Dallas, Dallas Co., TX
+Margaret Alice Sheppard Skillman, b. 1903 Sulphur Springs, Hopkins Co., TX, m. 1923 Dallas, TX, d. 1972 Dallas, TX
— Edward Young Holt Jr, b. 1926 Dallas, Dallas Co., TX
+Verna Charlene Stavely, b. 1928, m. 1951 Naval Hospital Chapel, San Diego, CA
+Erline Perry, b. 1934 Jamesville, Martin Co., NC, m. 1962 Naval Observatory Chapel, Bethesda, MD
— Perri Michele Holt, b. 1963 Oceanside, San Diego Co., CA
+John McLean Bayer, b. 1965 Redstone Arsenal, Huntsville, AL, m. 1995 Washington, DC
— Bailee Michele Bayer, b. 1996 Portsmouth, VA
— Noah McLean Bayer, b. 1999 Bethesda, Montgomery Co., MD
— Edward Young Holt III, b. 1966 Bethesda, Montgomery Co., MD
+Kimberly Renee Patterson, b. 1968 Norfolk, VA, m. 1995 Chesapeake, VA
— Ryan Edward Holt, b. 1997 Chesapeake, VA
— Conner Young Holt, b. 2000 Chesapeake, VA
— Andrew Skillman Holt, b. 1967 Bethesda Naval Hospital, Bethesda, MD
+Donna Marie Bocchichio, b. 1970 West Islip, Suffolk Co., NY, m. 1993 Ft. Lauderdale, Broward Co, FL
— Ashley Nicole Holt, b. 2000 Fairfax Co., VA
— Heather Madison Holt, b. 2000 Fairfax Co., VA
— Margaret Alice Sheppard Skillman Holt, b. 1931 Dallas, Dallas Co., TX
+Grayson Douglas Gill, b. 1928 Dallas, Dallas Co., TX, m. 1955 Dallas, Dallas Co., TX
— Emily Sheppard Gill, b. 1957 Dallas, Dallas Co., TX
+Robert Linwood Mills, b. 1953 Williamsburg, VA, m. 1982 Dallas, Dallas Co., TX
— Edward Douglas Mills, b. 1984 Virginia Beach, VA
— Valerie Holt Mills, b. 1987 Virginia Beach, VA
— Virginia Woodward Gill, b. 1959 Dallas, Dallas Co., TX
+Steven Riggs Smith, b. 1956 Beaumont, Jefferson Co., TX, m. 1983 Laguna Beach, Orange Co., TX
— Daniel Douglas Smith, b. 1985 Laguna Niguel, Orange Co., CA
— Margaret Skillman Smith, b. 1987 Laguna Niguel, Orange Co., CA
— Grayson Douglas Gill Jr, b. 1963 Dallas, Dallas Co., TX
+Elizabeth Herron Bryant, b. 1962 Jackson, Hinds Co., MS, m. 1988 Jackson, Hinds Co., MS
— May Belle Young, b. 1876 Eufaula, Barbour Co., AL, d. 1961 Murfreesboro, Rutherfd. Co, TN
— Edward Billups Young Jr, b. 1878 Eufaula, Barbour Co., AL, d. 1927 Albany, Dougherty Co., GA
+Meta Valentine Baldwin, b. 1881 Dawson, Terrell Co., GA, m. 1899 Eufaula, Barbour Co., AL, d. 1967 Albany, Dougherty Co., GA
— William Baldwin Young, b. 1901 Eufaula, Barbour Co., AL, d. 1958 Albany, Dougherty Co., GA
+Patty Eppes, b. say 1901, m. 1923 Albany, Dougherty Co., GA
— Meta Baldwin Young, b. 1924 Albany, Dougherty Co., GA
+William Dyer Shackleford, b. say 1920, m. 1947 Albany, Dougherty Co., GA
+Mary (--?--), b. circa 1901, m. 1942
— William Hubert Young, b. 1881 Eufaula, Barbour Co., AL, d. 1924 Birmingham, Jefferson Co., AL
+Arabella Dean Virgin, b. 1885 Macon, Bibb Co., GA, m. 1904 Macon, Bibb Co., GA, d. 1958 Knoxville, Knox Co., TN
— Annie Holt Young, b. 1905 Macon, Bibb Co., GA, d. 2001 Gainesville, Alachua Co., FL
+William Harris Rollen, b. 1902 Grandview, TX, m. 1927 Frisco City, AL, d. 1997 Oak Ridge, Anderson Co., TN
— William Harris Rollen Jr, b. 1931 Macon, Bibb Co., GA
+Delores Marie Correia, b. 1936 New Bedford, Bristol Co., MA, m. 1953 New Bedford, Bristol Co., MA
— Linda Marie Rollen, b. 1954 New Bedford, Bristol Co., MA
+Albert Ricardo D'Aguiar, b. 1955 New Bedford, Bristol Co., MA, m. 1973
— Craig Michael D'Aguiar, b. 1974 New Bedford, Bristol Co., MA
+Wendy Marie Doepel, b. say 1974, m. 1994? Ocala, Marion Co., FL
— Thomas Michael D'Aguiar, b. 1994
— Jacob Ryan D'Aguiar, b. 1997
+Raymond L. Jordan Jr, b. 1942 New Bedford, Bristol Co., MA, m. 1980 New Bedford, Bristol Co., MA
— Nathan L. Jordan, b. 1981 New Bedford, Bristol Co., MA
— William Harris Rollen III, b. 1956 Lake Worth, Palm Beach Co., FL, d. 1997 Lantana, Palm Beach Co., FL
+Jennifer Hammack, b. say 1956, m. say 1976
+Nervana Joyce Braden, b. 1936, m. 1959
— Donna Lynne Rollen, b. 1961 Knoxville, Knox Co., TN
+Eric Lewis Beeco, b. 1962 Winston Salem, Forsyth Co., NC, m. 1985 Claxton, Knox Co., TN
— Erika Lynne Beeco, b. 1993 Oak Ridge, Anderson Co., TN
— Melissa Joyce Rollen, b. 1963 Knoxville, Knox Co., TN
+Frank Hughes, m. say 1984 Claxton, Knox Co., TN
— Hubert Young Rollen, b. 1933 Perry, Houston Co., GA

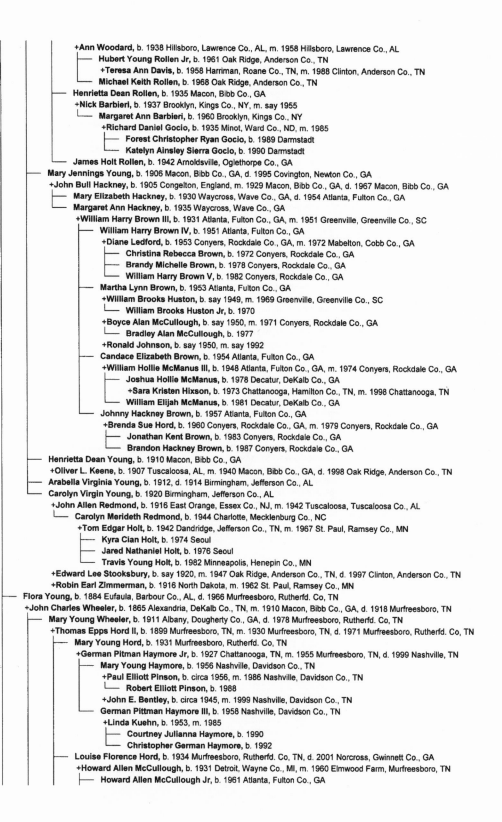

+Ann Woodard, b. 1938 Hillsboro, Lawrence Co., AL, m. 1958 Hillsboro, Lawrence Co., AL

    Hubert Young Rollen Jr, b. 1961 Oak Ridge, Anderson Co., TN

    +Teresa Ann Davis, b. 1958 Harriman, Roane Co., TN, m. 1988 Clinton, Anderson Co., TN

    Michael Keith Rollen, b. 1968 Oak Ridge, Anderson Co., TN

Henrietta Dean Rollen, b. 1935 Macon, Bibb Co., GA

+Nick Barbieri, b. 1937 Brooklyn, Kings Co., NY, m. say 1955

    Margaret Ann Barbieri, b. 1960 Brooklyn, Kings Co., NY

        +Richard Daniel Gocio, b. 1935 Minot, Ward Co., ND, m. 1985

            Forest Christopher Ryan Gocio, b. 1989 Darmstadt

            Katelyn Ainsley Sierra Gocio, b. 1990 Darmstadt

James Holt Rollen, b. 1942 Arnoldsville, Oglethorpe Co., GA

Mary Jennings Young, b. 1906 Macon, Bibb Co., GA, d. 1995 Covington, Newton Co., GA

+John Bull Hackney, b. 1905 Congelton, England, m. 1929 Macon, Bibb Co., GA, d. 1967 Macon, Bibb Co., GA

    Mary Elizabeth Hackney, b. 1930 Waycross, Wave Co., GA, d. 1954 Atlanta, Fulton Co., GA

    Margaret Ann Hackney, b. 1935 Waycross, Wave Co., GA

        +William Harry Brown III, b. 1931 Atlanta, Fulton Co., GA, m. 1951 Greenville, Greenville Co., SC

            William Harry Brown IV, b. 1951 Atlanta, Fulton Co., GA

            +Diane Ledford, b. 1953 Conyers, Rockdale Co., GA, m. 1972 Mabelton, Cobb Co., GA

                Christina Rebecca Brown, b. 1972 Conyers, Rockdale Co., GA

                Brandy Michelle Brown, b. 1978 Conyers, Rockdale Co., GA

                William Harry Brown V, b. 1982 Conyers, Rockdale Co., GA

            Martha Lynn Brown, b. 1953 Atlanta, Fulton Co., GA

            +William Brooks Huston, b. say 1949, m. 1969 Greenville, Greenville Co., SC

                William Brooks Huston Jr, b. 1970

            +Boyce Alan McCullough, b. say 1950, m. 1971 Conyers, Rockdale Co., GA

                Bradley Alan McCullough, b. 1977

            +Ronald Johnson, b. say 1950, m. say 1992

            Candace Elizabeth Brown, b. 1954 Atlanta, Fulton Co., GA

            +William Hollie McManus III, b. 1948 Atlanta, Fulton Co., GA, m. 1974 Conyers, Rockdale Co., GA

                Joshua Hollie McManus, b. 1978 Decatur, DeKalb Co., GA

                +Sara Kristen Hixson, b. 1973 Chattanooga, Hamilton Co., TN, m. 1998 Chattanooga, TN

                William Elijah McManus, b. 1981 Decatur, DeKalb Co., GA

            Johnny Hackney Brown, b. 1957 Atlanta, Fulton Co., GA

            +Brenda Sue Hord, b. 1960 Conyers, Rockdale Co., GA, m. 1979 Conyers, Rockdale Co., GA

                Jonathan Kent Brown, b. 1983 Conyers, Rockdale Co., GA

                Brandon Hackney Brown, b. 1987 Conyers, Rockdale Co., GA

Henrietta Dean Young, b. 1910 Macon, Bibb Co., GA

+Oliver L. Keene, b. 1907 Tuscaloosa, AL, m. 1940 Macon, Bibb Co., GA, d. 1998 Oak Ridge, Anderson Co., TN

Arabella Virginia Young, b. 1912, d. 1914 Birmingham, Jefferson Co., AL

Carolyn Virgin Young, b. 1920 Birmingham, Jefferson Co., AL

+John Allen Redmond, b. 1916 East Orange, Essex Co., NJ, m. 1942 Tuscaloosa, Tuscaloosa Co., AL

    Carolyn Merideth Redmond, b. 1944 Charlotte, Mecklenburg Co., NC

        +Tom Edgar Holt, b. 1942 Dandridge, Jefferson Co., TN, m. 1967 St. Paul, Ramsey Co., MN

            Kyra Cian Holt, b. 1974 Seoul

            Jared Nathaniel Holt, b. 1976 Seoul

            Travis Young Holt, b. 1982 Minneapolis, Henepin Co., MN

+Edward Lee Stooksbury, b. say 1920, m. 1947 Oak Ridge, Anderson Co., TN, d. 1997 Clinton, Anderson Co., TN

+Robin Earl Zimmerman, b. 1916 North Dakota, m. 1962 St. Paul, Ramsey Co., MN

Flora Young, b. 1884 Eufaula, Barbour Co., AL, d. 1966 Murfreesboro, Rutherfd. Co, TN

+John Charles Wheeler, b. 1865 Alexandria, DeKalb Co., TN, m. 1910 Macon, Bibb Co., GA, d. 1918 Murfreesboro, TN

    Mary Young Wheeler, b. 1911 Albany, Dougherty Co., GA, d. 1978 Murfreesboro, Rutherfd. Co, TN

    +Thomas Epps Hord II, b. 1899 Murfreesboro, TN, m. 1930 Murfreesboro, TN, d. 1971 Murfreesboro, Rutherfd. Co, TN

        Mary Young Hord, b. 1931 Murfreesboro, Rutherfd. Co, TN

        +German Pitman Haymore Jr, b. 1927 Chattanooga, TN, m. 1955 Murfreesboro, TN, d. 1999 Nashville, TN

            Mary Young Haymore, b. 1956 Nashville, Davidson Co., TN

            +Paul Elliott Pinson, b. circa 1956, m. 1986 Nashville, Davidson Co., TN

                Robert Elliott Pinson, b. 1988

            +John E. Bentley, b. circa 1945, m. 1999 Nashville, Davidson Co., TN

            German Pittman Haymore III, b. 1958 Nashville, Davidson Co., TN

            +Linda Kuehn, b. 1953, m. 1985

                Courtney Julianna Haymore, b. 1990

                Christopher German Haymore, b. 1992

        Louise Florence Hord, b. 1934 Murfreesboro, Rutherfd. Co, TN, d. 2001 Norcross, Gwinnett Co., GA

        +Howard Allen McCullough, b. 1931 Detroit, Wayne Co., MI, m. 1960 Elmwood Farm, Murfreesboro, TN

            Howard Allen McCullough Jr, b. 1961 Atlanta, Fulton Co., GA

+Jaime Marvine Wood, b. 1964 Decatur, DeKalb Co., GA, m. 1997 Big Canoe, Pickens Co., GA
└── Ryan Wheeler McCullough, b. 1999 Atlanta, Fulton Co., GA
── Scott Henry McCullough, b. 1963 Atlanta, Fulton Co., GA
+Katrina Lee Gray, b. 1960 Tallahassee, Leon Co., FL, m. 1991 Pensacola, Escambia Co., FL
├── William Scott McCullough, b. 1992 Greenville, Greenville Co., SC
├── Mallory Cameron McCullough, b. 1995 Kansas City, MO
└── Charles Gray McCullough, b. 1998 Nashville, Davidson Co., TN
── Thomas Hord McCullough, b. 1967 Atlanta, Fulton Co., GA
── David Carter McCullough, b. 1969 Atlanta, Fulton Co., GA
+Elizabeth Paige Larrabee, b. 1972 Philadelphia, PA, m. 1996 Atlanta, Fulton Co., GA
├── Bain Leonhardt McCullough, b. 1999 Atlanta, Fulton Co., GA
└── Carter Young McCullough, b. 2002 Atlanta, Fulton Co., GA
── Thomas Epps Hord III, b. 1936 Murfreesboro, Rutherfd. Co, TN
+Eliabeth Farrar Emanuel, b. 1945 Shelbyville, Bedford Co., TN, m. 1973 Shelbyville, Bedford Co., TN
└── Elizabeth Giles Hord, b. 1982 Nashville, Davidson Co., TN
── Charles Wheeler Hord, b. 1940 Murfreesboro, Rutherfd. Co, TN
+Joy Lou Pratt, b. 1944, m. 1967 Huntingdon, Carroll Co., TN
├── Joy Marchbanks Hord, b. 1970 Murfreesboro, Rutherfd. Co, TN
│   +Neal Cook, b. say 1970, m. 2001 Murfreesboro, Rutherfd. Co, TN
│   └── Alexander Richard Cook, b. 2002 Charlotte, Mecklenburg Co., NC
├── Mary Elizabeth Hord, b. 1972 Murfreesboro, Rutherfd. Co, TN
├── Charles Wheeler Hord Jr, b. 1973 Murfreesboro, Rutherfd. Co, TN
└── Benjamin Epps Hord, b. 1978 Murfreesboro, Rutherfd. Co, TN
── John Charles Wheeler Jr, b. 1914 Murfreesboro, Rutherfd. Co, TN, d. 2001 Nashville, Davidson Co., TN
+Verna Mae Ellis, b. 1914, m. 1939 Nashville, Davidson Co., TN, d. 1943 Murfreesboro, Rutherfd. Co, TN
+Elizabeth Anne Noreen, b. 1922 Dearborn, Wayne Co., MI, m. 1944 Martha & Mary Chapel, Dearborn, MI
├── Elizabeth Anne Wheeler, b. 1945 Nashville, Davidson Co., TN
│   +Jerry Elijah Brown, b. 1945 Alabama, m. 1969 St. Paul's Methodist Church, Nashville, TN
│   ├── Elizabeth Brooks Brown, b. 1972 Nashville, Davidson Co., TN
│   └── Lindsay Young Brown, b. 1975 Hanover, Grafton Co., NH
├── Claudia Young Wheeler, b. 1946 Nashville, Davidson Co., TN
│   +John Alexander Leo III, b. 1943 Cooper Hospital, Camden, NJ, m. 1967 St. Paul's Methodist Church, Nashville, TN
│   ├── Laura Ashley Leo, b. 1971 Bethesda Naval Hospital, Bethesda, MD
│   │   +Michael Ivan Williams, b. 1958 Burlington, Alamance Co., NC, m. 1997 Linville Falls Church, Burke Co., NC
│   │   ├── Ryan Michael Williams, b. 1999 Alamance Regional Med. Ctr., Burlington, NC
│   │   └── Kaitlyn Ashley Williams, b. 2001 Alamance Regional Med. Ctr., Burlington, NC
│   └── Matthew Wheeler Leo, b. 1974 Fairfax Co., VA
└── Joan Charlene Wheeler, b. 1952 Nashville, Davidson Co., TN
    +Jeffrey Gene Knutson, b. 1965 Vincent, Crittenden Co, Iowa, m. 1995 Loretto Chapel, Santa Fe, NM
── Ada Young, b. 1887 Eufaula, Barbour Co., AL, d. 1990 Hermitage, Davidson Co., TN
── Caroline Young, b. 1855 Eufaula, Barbour Co., AL, d. 1934 Eufaula, Barbour Co., AL
+Noah W. Roberts, b. circa 1851 Alabama, m. 1876 Eufaula, Barbour Co., AL, d. before 1920

698

Index

Buford, ---, Maj.; 446-447
Buford, Eloise; 509
Buford, J. P.; 501
Buford, James McClure; 101, 308, 432, 438, 441, 509
Buford, Jefferson, Maj.; 65, 98, 101-102, 432, 509
Buggy House; 85
Building & Loan Association; 545
Bull Run, VA, Battle; 283
Bullfight; 605
Bullmoose Party; 637
Bullock County, AL; 65
Bullock, Edward C., Jr.; 526
Bullock, Edward Courtney, Sen. (AL).; 58, 65, 80, 82, 89-90, 104, 110, 120, 133, 150, 153, 158-160, 526, 615
Burbridge, ---, Gen.; 367, 371
Burgwyn, William H.; 587
Burkhardt, Elizabeth; 632
Burnett's Company; 151
Burning Train; 373
Burnly, ---; 142-143
Burnside's Corps; 254
Burr, Aaron; 74
Bush Place, Barbour County, AL; 597
Business Recovery; 416
Business; 416
Butler County, AL; 454, 617
Butler, Benjamin, Brig.Gen.; 187-188
Butt, Joe; 129, 133
Butt, Susan B.; 25
Buttermilk Whitewash; 85
Byrne, ---; 407

Cabinetmaker; 20
Caddo Belle (steamship); 508
Caissons; 195-196, 300
Calhoun, GA; 317
Calhoun, John A.54-56
Calhoun, John C.; 54, 56, 64-65
California; 64, 607
Callao, Peru; 604, 606-607, 610-611
Calloway, William A., Pvt.; 372
Camp Alabama, FL; 128-129
Camp Bullock, Knoxville, TN; 160, 243
Camp Chase, MD; 249
Camp Douglas Prison; 583
Camp Mercer, GA; 181-182
Camp Watts, AL; 167, 392-393
Campbell, C. J.; 524-525, 586
Campbell, M.; 169
Campbell, William; 203, 208
Canal Street, New York City, NY; 21
Canby, E. R. S., Gen.; 382-383, 416
Cannon; 111, 196-197, 204, 299, 339
Cannon, "Uncle Joe," Speaker of the House; 619-620
Cannoneers in Gray (pub.); 201, 234, 238
Cannoneers; 197
Canton, MS; 313-314
Capitol Legislature; 452
Cargile, Billy; 145, 158
Cargile, Thomas; 58
Carmichael, A. H.; 648-649

Carnegie Library; 657
Caroline (Negro child); 63
Carpetbag Government; 46, 65, 441
Carpetbaggers; 423, 460, 464, 619
Carriage House; 85
Carter, Eugene W.; 629
Carter, J. J.; 422
Carthage, TN; 224
Cary, ---; 101
Cassville, GA; 317-318
Castle Garden at the Battery, Manhattan, NY; 71
Castleberry, ---, Mrs.; 403
Castleberry, Laura; 401
Castleman, ---, Lt.; 606
Casualties;
    Atlanta Campaign; 337, 357, 390
    Chickamauga, GA; 285, 287-288, 300-301, 303
    Dent's Battery; 327
    Fort Blakely, AL; 382
    Franklin, TN; 365-367
    Hartsville, TN; 231
    Jackson, MS; 314
    Kennesaw Mountain, GA; 326
    Lovejoy's Station, GA; 344-345
    Missionary Ridge, TN; 284, 305
    Murfreesboro, TN; 234-237
    New Hope Church, GA; 318
    Peachtree Creek, GA; 333
    Shiloh, TN; 204, 237
    Spanish Fort, AL; 382
    Tennessee Campaign; 376
    Young's Battery; 343
Cataclysm; 97
Cato, ---; 274
Cato, J. C., Dr.; 534, 585
Cato, L. L., Mrs.; 157
Cato, Lewis Lewellen, Sen. (AL); 58, 65-66, 98, 102-103, 118
Cato, Martha Jane, Mrs.; 534
Cato, Sterling G.; 66, 98
Catteville, E. L.; 510
Causten's Bluff, GA; 181
Cavalry;
    Exercise; 248
    Tactics; 306
Cave Springs, GA; 360, 424
Central Georgia Insurance Company; 90
Central House (Hotel), Eufaula, AL; 47
Central of Georgia Railroad; 91, 645, 651
Central Park, NY; 74
Central Steamboat Line; 509
Certificate of Organization; 473
Certificate of the Officers & Directors; 475
Certificates of Deposit; 38
Certificates of Election; 449-450, 453
Cervera, ---, Admiral; 602
Chaffin, William D.; 515
Chais, M., Mr.; 129
Chambers, ---; 101, 105, 135
Chambers, ---, Col.; 120
Chambers, ---, Mrs.; 219

Chambers, Hen; 277
Chambers, Robert; 324
Chambliss, J. E., Rev.; 506
Chancellorsville, VA; 335
Charles County, MD; 81, 183-184, 187, 189, 191-192, 217, 259, 424, 512-514
Charleston Arsenal; 176
Charleston Harbor, SC; 182
Charleston, SC; 37, 40, 71, 109, 114, 150-151, 165, 182, 253, 266, 273, 309, 384
Charlotte (Negro woman); 62-63
Charlotte Hall Academy; 81, 183-185, 190, 471
Chastain, J. W.; 501
Chattahoochee (Conf. steamer); 166, 168-171
  (model, ill.); 174
Chattahoochee Entrepreneurs; 23
Chattahoochee River; 7, 31, 34-35, 52, 59-60, 90-91, 93, 95, 161, 165, 168-169, 174-175, 327, 329, 331, 334, 339-340, 342, 386, 388, 435, 506, 508-509, 657
Chattahoochee River Valley; 8, 10, 12, 24, 26, 43, 61, 89
Chattahoochee, FL; 169-170
Chattahoochee-Apalachicola River System (ill.); 41
Chattahoochee-Apalachicola River System; 40, 91-92
Chattahoochee-Apalachicola River Valley; 7, 40-41, 44, 60, 161, 165, 169
Chattanooga, TN; 193, 218, 220-224, 230, 233, 236, 250, 269, 271-273, 276-278, 280, 282, 286, 288-289, 293-294, 300, 309, 315, 327, 340, 371
Chattel Mortgage; 62-63
Cheatham, B. F., Gen.; 225, 231, 233, 333-336, 373-374
Cheatham's Corps; 333, 337, 340, 365, 373-374
Cheatham's Division; 263, 330
Chesapeake Bay; 188, 603
Chess; 296
Cheves' Landing, GA; 181
Chewalla (steamer); 87, 159
Chewalla Creek, AL; 70, 80, 88
Chewalla Hotel, Eufaula, AL; 69, 431
Chewalla Mills; 542
Chicago (US ship); 604
Chicago Democratic Convention; 570
Chicago World's Fair; 73
Chicago, IL; 350
Chickamauga Battlefield Park (ill.); 599
Chickamauga Creek, GA; 278, 280, 300, 303
Chickamauga Station, GA; 286, 289, 303
Chickamauga, GA; 269, 279, 296, 327, 332
Chickamauga, GA, Battle; 193, 282, 284, 293-294, 301, 549, 573, 582, 594
  Casualties; 285, 287-288, 300-301, 303
  Losses; 289, 300-301, 303
  Troops Strength; 280
Chicla, Peru; 605
Chief of the Piece; 197
Child Discipline; 241
Children of the Confederacy; 641, 657-658
Chile, President of; 604
Christian Advocate (pub.); 511
Christian Principles; 98-99
Christie's Minstrels; 72
Chunkey Bridge, MS; 244, 417, 543, 600

Chunkey River; 244
Church of England; 10
Cienfuegos, Cuba; 600-602
Cigars; 399, 403, 504
Cincinnati Convention; 441
Cincinnati, OH; 223, 249
Citizens Fire Company, Union Springs, AL; 518-519
Citronelle, AL; 383
City Guards; 135, 157-158
City of Eufaula (steamboat) (ill.); 60
Civil Rights Act; 420
Civil Unrest; 463
Civil War; 7, 29, 46, 72, 77, 88-89, 116, 578
  First Shots Fired; 114
Civilians
  Mistreatment; 358, 361
Clais, M., Mr.; 130
Clark, ---, Mr. & Mrs.; 115
Clark, Champ; 625-626, 637
Clark, John W., Capt.; 129, 131, 137, 159, 208
Clark, Thomas J.; 449
Clark, Whit; 117, 443
Clark's Company; 209
Clarke, R. H.; 571
Clay County, AL; 343
Clay, Henry; 46, 64
Clayton Generals; 112
Clayton Guards; 150, 156
Clayton, ---; 257
Clayton, ---, Mrs.; 236
Clayton, AL; 46, 99-101, 159, 387, 449, 511, 553, 555, 562, 632
Clayton, Henry D., Gen.; 66, 98, 119, 121, 124, 127, 134, 137, 139, 221-222, 231, 270, 288, 308, 327-328, 335, 340-342, 351, 354-355, 374, 437, 441-443, 464, 510, 553, 556, 564
Clayton, Henry D., Jr.; 585, 652
Clayton, J. D.; 598
Clayton, Joe; 236, 241
Clayton, Lee J.; 585
Clayton's Division Hospital; 330
Clayton's Division; 350
Clayton's Regiment; 219
Cleburne Fire Company; 500, 503-505, 510, 515, 517-519
Cleburne, Pat, Gen.; 202, 238, 297, 300, 303, 306, 333, 348, 366, 367
Cleburne's Division; 301-302, 320
Clemens, Jere, Maj.Gen.; 110, 242
Cleveland, Grover, Pres.; 431, 513-514, 555-556, 559, 567, 570, 600
Cleveland's Inauguration; 514
Clisby, L.; 501
Clothing; 303, 306, 314
Cobb, Hamner, Bishop; 220
Cobb, Howell; 107
Cobb, Tom; 120
Coburn Committee Investigation; 465-466
Cochran, John; 65-67, 86, 103-105, 120, 133, 146, 152-153, 215, 434, 443-444, 446-448, 459
Cock Fighting (game chickens); 395, 397
Code Commissioner; 629

704

Cumberland River; 194-195, 224, 230, 367
Cunningham, ---, Mr.; 142, 388
Cupola; 84-85, 95
Curiosities (spent shells as ornaments); 147
Currency; 416
Curtis, L. B.; 473, 522

Daggett, ---, Capt.; 464-466
Daguerreotype; 84
Daily Sun, Columbus, GA (np.); 180, 314, 346
Dale County, AL; 45, 326, 434
Dallas, GA; 318
Dalton, GA; 222, 278, 296, 300, 304-307, 309, 311-312, 314-315, 317, 331-332, 335, 340, 360
Dana, Charles A., Asst. Sec. of War; 282
Daniel, ---, Alderman; 422
Daniel, J. W. L.; 103
Daniel, James; 48
Daniel, Larry J.; 201, 234, 238-239, 247, 317
Daniel, Z. J.; 46
Daniels, Zadoc, Mrs.; 277
Dannelly, ---, Pvt.; 28
Davidson, ---, Lt.; 304
Davis, Jefferson, Conf. Pres.; 64, 104-107, 189, 194, 216, 231, 233, 238, 243, 278, 293-294, 305, 312, 331-332, 349, 357-358, 377, 379, 388, 443, 521, 630
Davis, John W.; 646
Davis, R. M., Esq.; 177
Davis, W. A.; 500-501
Davis, Willie M.; 502
Davis, Winnie; 521
Davis' Cabinet; 388
Davis' Division (Union); 281
Dawes, Charles G.; 589
Dawson, ---, Capt.; 134, 143
Dawson, W. C., Maj.; 504
Day of Fasting, Humiliation & Prayer; 249
Dead Angle, Kennesaw Mountain, GA; 326
Dean, L. Y.; 540
Dean, L. Y., Jr.; 585
Deas, Zach. C., Gen.; 251-252, 286, 290
Deas' Brigade; 261, 271, 280-281, 283, 285, 297-298
Deas' Regiment; 299
Debt Collections; 101-102
Decatur, GA; 335, 344, 371
Declaration of Independence; 19
Declaration of War; 624
Deep South; 22, 186
Defense of Washington, DC; 187
Delaney, Charles; 46
Delegation; 387-388
Delta Kappa Epsilon, University of Alabama (ill.); 631
Democratic & Conservative Clubs; 424-425
Democratic & Conservative Party; 435, 442
Democratic Convention; 88, 350, 550, 577, 617
Democratic Executive Committee; 443-444, 448, 567, 633
Democratic National Convention; 637, 646, 655
Democratic Party; 99, 104, 186, 425, 431, 442, 549, 561-562, 564-566, 573, 578-579, 614, 646
Democratic Primary Election; 577, 622

Democrats; 223, 350, 445, 447, 449-450, 452, 454-455, 459, 464, 466-467, 477, 514, 548, 555, 560, 569-570, 574, 577, 621, 623, 627
Demopolis, AL; 314, 383
Demoralized; 271, 285
Dent & Harvey (wholesale drugs); 529
Dent Brothers; 25, 512
Dent Family; 83, 185, 590
Dent Nine (baseball team); 614
Dent, ---; 221
Dent, Alice Lucile; 614
Dent, Anna (ill.); 122, 531
Dent, Anna Beall Young See also: Young, Anna Beall
Dent, Anna Beall Young (Mrs. Stouten Hubert Dent, aka Anne, Annie, Nan, Nannie, Sissy); 7, 37, 88, 99-101, 104-106, 108-114, 116-123, 129-131, 134, 136, 138, 140, 142, 144, 148, 150, 152, 168, 183, 185, 198, 200, 204, 208, 213-214, 216, 219-221, 223-224, 226, 228-229, 231, 235, 239-241, 244-245, 247, 249, 251, 253, 255, 257-258, 260, 262-263, 265, 268-269, 272, 275-276, 278-280, 286, 291-294, 300, 306-307, 309, 311, 316, 319, 323, 327-330, 333, 340, 348, 350, 352, 354, 357, 359-362, 365-366, 370, 372, 376-377, 380, 413-414, 416-417, 419, 426-428, 434, 477, 486-489, 491, 493-495, 497, 508, 511-512, 518, 534-537, 549, 584, 596-597, 600, 612, 614, 630, 658-659
Dent, Anna Beall (Nan, Nana, Nannie, child of Hubert & Anna Dent); 419-420, 495, 535-537, 630
Dent, Annie Stuart McCormick; 420, 537, 612
Dent, Caroline (Carrie, Bab, Babbie) See also: McDowell, Caroline
Dent, Caroline (Carrie, Bab, Babbie); 340, 419-420, 461, 496, 521, 536, 584-585, 596-598, 630, 633-634
Dent, Caroline (Carrie) (ill.); 612, 630, 634
Dent, Catherine (daughter of Ed Young Dent); 635
Dent, Catherine Allan (Tank); 537
Dent, Edward Young (Ed, Eddie, Biggie); 131, 143, 153, 231, 240-242, 249, 251, 253, 255-257, 260, 263-266, 273-275, 290, 306, 309-311, 320-321, 325, 329, 331, 335, 351, 354-355, 360, 371, 376, 379, 381, 416-417, 419-420, 488, 492, 495, 498, 500-501, 508, 512, 521, 524-525, 536-537, 543, 586, 596-597, 600, 612, 614, 630, 635
Dent, Edward Young (Eddie) (ill.); 379
Dent, Edward Young II; 537
Dent, Elizabeth; 183
Dent, Ella; 184, 186, 477, 631
Dent, Emma Catherine; 184, 477
Dent, Emma Julia (Minna); 471, 527, 528
Dent, Emma Smoot; 184, 471
Dent, Etta; 628
Dent, Etta Fontaine Copeland McCormick; 612-613, 657
Dent, Etta Tinsley; 614-615
Dent, Frederick Levi; 184
Dent, George H., Jr.; 428, 507
Dent, George H., Mrs. (Helen); 498, 518
Dent, George Hatch; 88, 116, 119-120, 132-133, 137, 144-145, 184-188, 190, 193, 218, 224-226, 228, 231-232, 256, 259, 263, 274, 279-280, 290-291, 297, 300-302, 304, 311, 316, 325, 329, 331, 366, 367, 378, 413, 424, 427-428, 431, 461, 470, 471, 476-477, 490, 493-494, 497-

716

724

Rolling Machine; 172
Rome Country Club; 638
Rome, GA; 220, 278, 316, 356, 360, 433, 536, 638
Roosevelt, Franklin; 655
Roosevelt, Theodore, Pres.; 595, 602-603, 637, 652
Roquefort, John; 550
Roquemore, John D.; 538-539, 553, 556, 558
Rose Bowl; 654
Rose Polytechnic Institute; 600
Rosecrans, ---, Gen.; 234-236, 247-251, 253, 255-256, 260-263, 267, 269, 270-271, 275-278, 281-282, 287, 290, 292-294, 549
Rosecrans' Army; 280, 289
Rosecrans' Headquarters; 281
Roseland Plantation, AL; 393-394, 405
Ross Hospital, Mobile, AL; 381
Ross, ---, Gen.; 312, 343-346, 372
Ross, ---, Maj.; 254
Ross, James LeGrand; 413, 501, 507
Ross, Mary Weedon; 475
Ross' Brigade; 312, 316, 321, 326, 339, 342, 345-346, 360, 362-363, 372
Rothschild, ---; 176
Rotten Row, Eufaula, AL; 46
Rough & Ready Pioneers; 109
Rousseau, L., Commodore; 157
Rover, TN; 261
Rowan, John; 317
Rowan's Georgia Battery; 317
Ruggles, Daniel, Brig.Gen.; 137, 198, 203, 211
Ruses & Disinformation; 211
Rushton, Ray; 637
Rushton, Stakely & Johnston Law Firm; 615
Russell County, AL; 179
Russell, E. L.; 571
Russia; 80

Saffold, GA; 168
Sailor, Jay; 662
Saint; See: St.
Salary Cuts; 587
Salem, TN; 261
Salt; 158
Samford University; 546
Samford, William, Gov. (AL); 498, 576, 585, 617-619, 633
Samoa; 610
Sampson, ---, Rear Admiral; 600-601
San Diego, CA; 607
San Francisco Bay; 600
San Francisco, CA; 602, 608-609, 612
San Jacinto; 27
San Joaquin Valley; 609
San Jose, Guatemala; 611
Sand Key, FL; 395
Sanders, A. C.; 617, 619, 623
Sandoval (Spanish ship); 602
Sandy Point (Punta Arenas), Chile; 603-604
Sanford, John W. A., Atty. Gen.; 449
Santa Anna, ---; 27
Santa Barbara, CA; 607
Santa Cruz, CA; 608

Santa Rosa Island, FL; 109, 125, 140, 142-143, 146, 158
Santiago, Chile; 602, 610
Sapp, J. E.; 501
Sappington, ---; 175-176
Sara, Ida, Miss; 397
Sarpy County, NE; 163
Saulsbury, Joe; 47
Savannah General Hospital; 182
Savannah, GA; 40-41, 61, 71, 78, 80, 91-92, 96, 161, 173, 177, 181-182, 253, 309, 312-313, 361, 371, 377
Savings Banks; 597, 621
Sawmill; 39
Scalawags; 423, 449, 459
Scales, Thomas P. C.; 43, 48
Scapegoats; 238
Schofield, ---, Gen.; 329, 333, 336-337, 349, 363-366, 373-374
Scot, George; 11
Scot, Robert; 11
Scotland; 10-11, 661
Scott, ---, Capt.; 201
Scott, ---, Mr.; 411-412
Scott, D. C.; 47
Scott, Dred; 99
Scott, Emmet; 628
Scott, Hugh L., Gen.; 624
Scott, William; 173
Scott, Winfield, Gen.; 28-29, 389
Scouts; 198
Screws, W. H.; 622-623
Screws, William, Col. (ill.); 655
Scribner's Monthly (pub.); 482
Scrip; 480-482
Sea Duty; 612
Seals, Harry; 510
Searcy, James T., Dr.; 220
Searcy, Stella; 220
Seasickness; 71
Seattle, WA; 608
Seay, Thomas; 544
Sebree, ---, Adm.; 612
Secession; 54, 64, 66, 86, 98, 100-104, 115, 151, 156-157, 175, 186, 188
    Illegal; 418
    Movement of 1850; 62
Second Congressional District (AL); 617
Secret Confederate Agent; 191
Secretary of the Navy; 600, 608
Seddon, ---, Conf. Sec. of War; 293, 376
Seigler, ---, Lt.; 362
Selective Service System; 638
Selling the House; 272-273
Selma Arsenal; 176, 385
Selma Iron Works; 385
Selma, AL; 150, 169, 385, 416
Seminole Campaign; 29
Seminole Indians; 28
Seminole War; 26, 28-29, 163
Semple's Battery; 279
Senate Chambers, Washington, DC; 78
Senate Education Committee; 639

South America; 602
South Carolina; 65, 87, 101-102, 175
South Carolina Troops;
    10th Inf. Regt.; 299, 375
    19th Inf. Regt.; 299
Southeast Alabama & Southwest Georgia Agricultural &
    Mechanical Fair; 481
Southeast Tariff Association; 516
Southern Confederacy; 101-102
Southern Cooking; 76-77
Southern Democrats; 439, 441
Southern Guard, Columbus, GA; 175
Southern Pacific Railroad; 609
Southern Prosperity; 66
Southern Rights; 54, 64-65, 100
Southern Shield (np.); 45-46, 48, 69
Southern Sympathizers; 183, 186, 191-192, 217, 250
Southern Telegraph Company; 114
Southern University; 454-455, 488, 495, 508, 537, 543, 544,
    600, 614
Southern University Advertisement (ill.); 454
Southwestern Railroad; 91-92, 432, 519, 538
Southwick, D. L., Lt.; 274, 279, 290, 297-299, 301-303, 308-
    309
Spaes, ---, (tailor); 288
Spain; 31, 211, 600-602
Spanish American War; 211, 495, 600-601
Spanish Explorations; 31
Spanish Fleet; 602
Spanish Fort, AL; 379, 382-383
Spanish Gunboats; 601
Sparks, Chauncey, Gov. (AL); 656
Sparks, L. A.; 81
Sparta, TN; 224, 317
Spartanburg, SC; 414
Special Orders; 346
Specie (gold & silver coin); 176-178
Spencer, George E., Sen. (AL); 423, 440, 449-450, 453, 456-
    458, 460
Sperry, ---, Adm.; 607-608
Spies; 190
Spirit (np.); 307-308
Spirit of the South (np.); 65-66, 91, 156, 163, 432
Sporting Activities; 499-500
Spring Hill, AL; 465
Spurlock, ---; 264-266
Spurlock, J. M. (Jr.); 543-544
St. Augustine, FL; 29
St. George (H. Weedon's horse); 402, 407, 550
St. Johns River; 28
St. Joseph, MO; 436
St. Julien Hotel, Eufaula, AL; 521
St. Louis Methodist Conference; 485
St. Luke Methodist Church, Columbus, GA; 71
St. Margaret's Hospital, Montgomery, AL; 547
St. Mary's County, MD; 183, 190, 192
St. Paul, ---, Capt.; 137
Stagecoaches; 47, 70
Stamp Act of 1875; 15
Stampede; 310
Stanford University; 654

Stanford's Mississippi Battery; 376
Stanton, ---, Col.; 317
Starke, ---, Gen.; 315
Starnes, ---, Mr.; 324
Starr, John W.; 39
Starvation; 33, 582
State Elections; 576
State Government; 418, 420
State Journal, Montgomery, AL (np.); 461
State Militia (AL); 33
State Superintendent of Insurance; 597
State-Federal Conflict; 32
States Rights; 29, 621
Stationery; 73
Steam Engines; ; 166, 168, 501
Steamboat Accident; 59-60
Steamboat Lines; 509
Steamboat Parties; 506
Steamboats; 59, 60-61, 70-71, 78
Steam-powered Pumping Engines; 500
Steamships; 508
Steedman, ---, Gen.; 139, 284-285
Steele, ---, Gen.; 382
Steele, A. B., Prof.; 81
Stephen & Moses Young's Cabinet & Chair Ware-House; 20,
    21
Stephens, Alexander, Conf. V.P.; 107
Stepney's Ginger-Pop Shop, Eufaula, AL; 48
Stern, D. G., Dr.; 459
Stern, Edward; 388
Stevens, ---, Brig.Gen.; 335
Stevens, Thaddeus, Rep.; 418
Stevenson, Adlai; 567
Stevenson, AL; 220, 269, 276, 372
Stevenson's Brigade; 160
Stevenson's Division; 321, 328, 330, 350
Stewart & Company; 434
Stewart County, GA; 45
Stewart, ---, Gen.; 333, 336
Stewart's Corps; 334-335, 338, 352, 358, 365, 373-374
Stewart's Division; 318, 328
Stock Dividends; 476
Stock Market Crash of 1929; 651
Stock; 35, 523, 545, 588, 654
Stockholders; 53, 89, 94, 473-476, 478-480, 524, 589-590
    Report, 1887 (ill.); 483
Stockton, W. T., 1st Lt.; 251, 274, 279, 287, 290, 296, 304,
    362
Stockwell, Dick; 46
Stoneman, ---, Gen.; 339-340, 342, 632
Stones River; 234
Stores, General Merchandise; 37
Stow, L. F.; 46, 69
Stow, Lafayette; 58
Stowe, Harriett Beecher; 77
Strahl, ---, Gen.; 367
Straits of Magellan; 604
Strategy; 317
Strawberries; 117
Stuart, James (Duke of York); 10
Stuart, Jeb; 193